MORAL ISSUES IN BUSINESS

First Canadian Edition

William H. Shaw
San Jose State University

Vincent Barry
Bakersfield College

Spiro Panagiotou
McMaster University

NELSON / EDUCATION

NELSON / EDUCATION

Moral Issues in Business, First Canadian Edition
by William H. Shaw, Vincent Barry, and Spiro Panagiotou

Associate Vice President, Editorial Director:
Evelyn Veitch

Editor-in-Chief, Higher Education:
Anne Williams

Publisher:
Cara Yarzab

Marketing Manager:
Amanda Henry

Developmental Editor:
Jenny O'Reilly

Permissions Coordinator:
Marian Evans

Production Service:
Macmillan Publishing Solutions

Copy Editor:
Rodney Rawlings

Proofreader:
Dianne Fowlie

Indexer:
Maura Brown

Senior Production Coordinator:
Ferial Suleman

Design Director:
Ken Phipps

Managing Designer:
Franca Amore

Interior Design:
Olena Sullivan

Cover Design:
Olena Sullivan

Cover Image:
Jack Hollingsworth/Asia Images/Getty Images

Compositor:
Macmillan Publishing Solutions

Printer:
Edwards Brothers

Library and Archives Canada Cataloguing in Publication Data

Shaw, William H., 1948–
    Moral issues in business / William H. Shaw, Vincent Barry, Spiro Panagiotou.—1st Canadian ed.

Includes bibliographical references and index.
ISBN: 978-0-17-644130-2

    1. Business ethics—Textbooks. I. Barry, Vincent E. II. Panagiotou, Spiro III. Title.

HF5387.S473 2009   174'.4   C2009-900080-6

ISBN-13: 978-0-17-644130-2
ISBN-10: 0-17-644130-1

Brief Contents

Contents

Preface to the First Canadian Edition

The present volume is an adaptation to the Canadian context of the tenth edition of William H. Shaw and Vincent Barry's *Moral Issues in Business*, which was written with the American student in mind. The structure and organization of the original remain the same. The content, however, wherever context-sensitive, has been revised or (occasionally) completely rewritten to reflect the Canadian context.

As *Moral Issues in Business* enters its first Canadian edition, business ethics is now a well-established academic subject. Most colleges and universities offer courses in it, and scholarly interest in the field continues to grow. This is all to the good: it is difficult to imagine an area of study that has greater importance to society or greater relevance to students.

Yet some people may still scoff at the idea of business ethics, jesting that the very concept is an oxymoron. To be sure, recent years have seen the newspapers filled with lurid stories of corporate misconduct throughout the globe. And many suspect that what the newspapers report represents only the tip of the proverbial iceberg. Yet these reports should push the reflective person, not to make fun of business ethics, but rather to think more deeply about the nature and purpose of business in human society and about the moral quality of the choices individuals must inevitably make in their business and professional lives.

Business ethics has an interdisciplinary and practical character. Questions of economic policy and business practice intertwine with issues in politics, sociology, and organizational theory. Business ethics is practical, in the sense of being ultimately concerned with action, though it is anchored in philosophy, an area of study thought to be particularly abstract. But even philosophy can be (and in the view of many, should be) practical, as abstract questions in epistemology, normative ethics, and political philosophy mingle with analysis of practical problems and concrete moral dilemmas. Furthermore, business ethics is not just an academic study, but also an invitation to reflect on our own values and on our own responses to the difficult moral choices that the world of business can pose. In this sense, business ethics may be a study in self-knowledge. Accordingly, this Canadian edition of the book maintains the same principal objectives as the previous (American) editions: to expose students to the important moral issues that arise in various business contexts; to provide students with an understanding of the moral, social, and economic environments within which those problems occur; to introduce students to the ethical concepts relevant for resolving those moral problems; and to assist students in developing the necessary reasoning and analytical skills for doing so. Although the book's primary emphasis is on business, its scope extends to related moral issues in other organizational and professional contexts.

Moral Issues in Business has four parts. Part One, "Moral Philosophy and Business," discusses the nature of morality and presents the main theories of normative ethics and the leading approaches to questions of economic justice. Part Two, "Capitalist Business and Its Basis," examines the institutional foundations of business, focusing on capitalism as an economic system and the nature and role of corporations in our society. Part Three, "The Organization and the People in It," identifies a variety of ethical issues and moral challenges that arise out of the interplay of employers and employees within an organization, including the problem of discrimination. Part Four, "Business and Society," concerns moral problems involving business, consumers, and the natural environment.

Finally, although they are not collected together under a separate chapter, the moral challenges facing business in today's global economy are well represented in *Moral Issues in Business*. Chapter 1 discusses ethical relativism, Chapter 4 (very briefly) outsourcing and globalization, and Chapter 8 bribery of foreign officials. The essays by Paine et al. (on company codes), Maitland (on international sweatshops), and De George (on the obligations of multinational corporations) deal explicitly with moral issues arising in today's global economic system, as do Cases 1.1, 5.2, 8.3, 10.2, and 11.1. International themes and comparisons are touched on throughout the book, as in Schumacher's essay on Buddhist economics.

CHANGES IN THIS EDITION

This edition too remains committed to providing students with a textbook that they will find clear, understandable, and engaging. It gives expanded treatment to the many ethical issues facing real people in the world of work: civil liberties on the job, personnel policies and procedures, union issues, drug testing, job satisfaction, downsizing, AIDS in the workplace, conflicts of interest, worker participation, day care and maternity leave, the "mommy track," and employee health and safety, among other topics.

This edition has reduced the number of case studies from fifty to thirty-two. Eight of them are new, and many others have been revised or adapted to fit the Canadian context. The cases vary in kind and in length, but they are designed to enable instructors and students to pursue further some of the issues discussed in the text and to analyze them in more specific contexts. They should provide a lively springboard for classroom discussion and the application of ethical concepts.

This edition also contains fewer supplementary readings, thirty instead of thirty-two, four of them being new. The readings address both theoretical topics and applied issues such as drug testing, sexual harassment, animal rights, downsizing, whistleblowing, advertising, discrimination, living-wage laws, consumerism, the ethics of sales, and much more. These readings are intended to augment the text by permitting selected topics to be studied in more detail and by exposing students to alternative perspectives and analysis. In selecting and editing the readings, we have sought to provide philosophically interesting essays that will engage students and lend themselves well to class discussion.

WAYS OF USING THE BOOK

A course in business ethics can be taught in a variety of ways. Instructors have different approaches to the subject, different intellectual and pedagogical goals, and different classroom styles. They emphasize different themes and start at different places. Nevertheless, because of the range of topics covered, because of the three types of material in the book—text, case studies, and readings—and because of the amount of material we have provided, teachers have great flexibility in how they use *Moral Issues in Business* and how they organize their courses.

Naturally, the book can be taught cover to cover as is, but in a semester course this will require a brisk pace. Many instructors will wish to linger on certain topics, touch briefly on others, and skip some altogether. Assigning all the cases and extra readings as well as the text of a chapter obviously provides for the greatest depth of coverage, but the text can easily be taught by itself or with only some of the cases or readings. The book readily permits topics to be dealt with briefly by assigning only selections from the case studies, the readings, or the text itself, instead of the chapter as a whole.

The chapters themselves are relatively self-contained, allowing them to be taught in various orders without loss of coherence. Instructors eager to get to the more specific moral issues discussed in later chapters might skip Parts One and Two (perhaps assigning only Solomon's "It's Good Business") and begin with the topics that interest them. Other instructors may choose to start with the analysis of capitalism in Chapter 4 or with the discussion of corporate responsibility in Chapter 5, then spend the bulk of the term on the chapters devoted to particular moral topics in business, returning later to some of the issues of Part One. Still other teachers may wish to devote much of a semester to the foundational concerns of Parts One and Two and deal more briefly and selectively with later matters.

ACKNOWLEDGMENTS FOR THE FIRST CANADIAN EDITION

Our intellectual debt to others is nowhere more evident than in the writing of textbooks, whose authors can rarely claim that the ideas being synthesized, organized, and presented are theirs alone. This is of course especially true in the case of this edition, since it owes its very existence, structure, and organization and most of its content to Shaw and Barry's tenth edition. I owe a great debt of gratitude to Shaw and Barry, and to all those reviewers whose constructive criticism has contributed to the success of the several editions of the original work. I must also thank the following reviewers, and some others who chose to remain anonymous, for their thoughtful criticisms and helpful suggestions in connection with this edition: Greg Daneke, University of Calgary; Diane Huberman-Arnold, Carleton University; Chris MacDonald, Saint Mary's University; Brian Orend, University of Waterloo; and David Weitzner, York University. Finally, many thanks to Laurie Panagiotou, B.Sc.N., RN(EC) for being understanding and for writing up the case study "The Tainted Blood Scandal."

Spiro Panagiotou

Part One

Moral Philosophy and Business

1

The Nature of Morality

Sometimes the rich and mighty fall. Ask Kenneth Lay, chairman and CEO of Enron until that once-mighty company nosedived and crashed. Founded in the 1980s, Enron soon became a dominant player in the field of energy trading, growing rapidly to become America's seventh-biggest company. Wall Street loves growth, and Enron was its darling, admired as dynamic, innovative, and—of course—profitable. The fact that nobody could quite understand exactly how the company made its money didn't hurt, either. In 1998 the value of Enron stock increased 40 percent. The next year it shot up 58 percent, and in 2000 it went up an unbelievable 89 percent.

After *Fortune* magazine voted it "the most innovative company of the year" in 2000, Enron proudly took to calling itself not just "the world's leading energy company" but also "the world's leading company." But when Enron was forced to declare bankruptcy in December 2001—at the time the largest Chapter 11 filing in U.S. history—the world learned that its legendary financial prowess was illusory and the company's success built on the sands of hype. And the hype continued to the end. Even with the company's financial demise fast approaching, Kenneth Lay was still recommending the company's stock to its employees—at the same time that he and other executives were cashing in their shares and bailing out.

Enron's crash cost the retirement accounts of its employees more than a billion dollars as the company's stock fell from the stratosphere to only a few pennies a share. Outside investors lost even more. The reason Enron's collapse caught investors by surprise—the company's market value was $28 billion just two months before its bankruptcy—was that Enron had always made its financial records and accounts as opaque as possible. It did this by creating a Byzantine financial structure of off-balance-sheet special-purpose entities—reportedly as many as 9,000—that were supposed to be separate and independent from the main company. Enron's board of directors condoned these and other dubious accounting practices and voted twice to permit executives to pursue personal interests that ran contrary to those of the company. When

Enron was obliged to redo its financial statements for 1997–2000, its profits dropped $600 million and its debts increased $630 million.

Still, Enron's financial auditors should have spotted these and other problems. After all, the shell game Enron was playing is an old one, and months before the company ran aground, Enron vice-president Sherron Watkins had warned Lay that the company could soon "implode in a wave of accounting scandals." Yet both Arthur Andersen, Enron's longtime outside auditing firm, and Vinson & Elkins, the company's law firm, had routinely put together and signed off on various dubious financial deals, and in doing so made large profits for themselves. Arthur Andersen, in particular, was supposed to make sure that the company's public records reflected financial reality, but Andersen was more worried about its auditing and consulting fees than its fiduciary responsibilities. Even worse, when the scandal began to break, a partner at Andersen organized the shredding of incriminating Enron documents before investigators could lay their hands on them. As a result, the eighty-nine-year-old accounting firm was convicted of obstructing justice. In 2005 the U.S. Supreme Court overturned that verdict on a technicality, but by then Arthur Andersen had already been driven out of business. (The year before Enron went under, by the way, the U.S. Securities and Exchange Commission fined Andersen $7 million for approving misleading accounts at Waste Management, and it also had to pay $110 million to settle a lawsuit for auditing work it did for Sunbeam before it, too, filed for bankruptcy. And when massive accounting fraud was later uncovered at WorldCom, it came out that the company's auditor was—you guessed it—Arthur Andersen.)

Enron's fall also revealed the conflicts of interest that threaten the credibility of Wall Street's analysts—analysts who are compensated according to their ability to bring in and support investment banking deals. Enron was known in the industry as the "deal machine" because it generated so much investment banking business—limited partnerships, loans, and derivatives. That may explain why, only days before Enron filed bankruptcy, just two of the sixteen Wall

Street analysts who covered the company recommended that clients sell the stock. But the rot doesn't stop there. Enron and Andersen enjoyed extensive political connections, which had helped over the years to ensure the passage of a series of deregulatory measures favourable to the energy company. Of the 248 members of the U.S. Congress sitting on the eleven House and Senate committees charged with investigating Enron's collapse, 212 had received money from Enron or its accounting firm.[1]

Stories of business corruption and of greed and wrongdoing in high places have always fascinated the popular press, and media interest in business ethics has never been higher. But one should not be misled by the headlines and news reports. Not all moral issues in business involve giant corporations and their well-heeled executives, and few cases of business ethics are widely publicized. The vast majority of them involve the mundane, uncelebrated moral challenges that working men and women meet daily.

Although the financial shenanigans at Enron were technically complicated, once their basic outline is sketched, the moral wrongdoing is pretty easy to see: deception, dishonesty, fraud, disregarding one's professional responsibilities, and unfairly injuring others for one's own gain. But many of the moral issues that arise in business activities are complex and difficult to answer. The topic of business ethics includes not just the question of the moral or immoral motivations of businesspeople, but also a whole range of problems that arise in the context of business. Those issues are too numerous to compile, but consider these typical questions:

- Is passing a personality or honesty test a justifiable pre-employment condition? Are drug tests? What rights do employees have on the job? How should business respond to employees who have AIDS? What, if anything, must it do to improve work conditions?

- Should manufacturers reveal all product defects? At what point does acceptable exaggeration become lying about a product or a service? When does aggressive marketing become consumer manipulation?

- What are businesses' environmental responsibilities? Is a corporation obliged to help combat social problems such as poverty, pollution, and urban decay? Must business fight sexism and racism? How far must it go to ensure equality of opportunity? How should organizations respond to the problem of sexual harassment?

- May employees ever use their positions inside an organization to advance their own interests? Is insider trading or the use of privileged information immoral? How much loyalty do workers owe their companies? What say should a business have over the off-the-job activities of its employees?

- What obligations does a worker have to outside parties, such as customers, competitors, or society generally? When, if ever, is an employee morally required to blow the whistle?

Such questions imbue business issues with moral significance. The answers we give to them are determined largely by our moral standards, principles, and values. What these standards and principles are, where they come from, and how they can be assessed are some of the concerns of this opening chapter. In particular, you will encounter the following topics:

1. The nature, scope, and purpose of business ethics

2. The distinguishing features of morality and how it differs from etiquette, law, and professional codes of conduct

3. The relationship between morality and religion

4. The doctrine of ethical relativism and its difficulties

5. What it means to have moral principles, the nature of conscience, and the relationship between morality and self-interest

6. The place of values and ideals in a person's life

7. The social and psychological factors that sometimes jeopardize an individual's integrity

8. The characteristics of sound moral reasoning

ETHICS

Ethics (or moral philosophy) is a broad field of inquiry that addresses a fundamental query that all of us, at least from time to time, inevitably think about, namely, How should I live my life? That question, of course, leads to others, such as, What sort of person should I strive to be? What goals should I pursue? What standards or principles should I live by? Exploring these issues immerses one in the study of right and wrong. Among other things, moral philosophers and others who think seriously about ethics want to understand the nature of morality, the meaning of its basic concepts, the characteristics of good moral reasoning, how we can justify our moral judgments, and, of course, the principles or properties that distinguish right actions from wrong actions. Thus, ethics deals with individual character and the moral rules that govern and limit our conduct. It investigates questions of right and wrong, fairness and unfairness, good and bad, duty and obligation, and justice and injustice, as well as moral responsibility and the values that should guide us.

You sometimes hear it said that there's a difference between a person's ethics and his or her morals. This can be confusing, because what some people mean by saying that something is a matter of ethics (as opposed to morals) is often what other people mean by saying that it is a matter of morals (and not ethics). In fact, however, most people (and most philosophers) see no real distinction between a person's "morals" and a person's "ethics." And almost everyone uses "ethical" and "moral" interchangeably to describe people we consider good and actions we consider right, and "unethical" and "immoral" to designate bad people and wrong actions. This book follows that common usage.

Business and Organizational Ethics

The primary focus of this book is ethics as it applies to business. *Business ethics* is the study of what constitutes right and wrong, or good and bad, human conduct in a business context. For example, would it be right for a store manager to break a promise to a customer and sell some hard-to-find merchandise to someone else, whose need for it is greater? What, if anything, should a moral employee do when his or her superiors refuse to look into apparent wrongdoing in a branch office? If you innocently came across secret information about a competitor, would it be morally permissible for you to use it for your own advantage?

Recent business scandals have renewed the interest of business leaders, academics, and society at large in ethics. In 2003, for example, the Association to Advance Collegiate Schools of Business, which comprises all the top business schools internationally, introduced new rules on including ethics in their curricula, and in 2005 the Business Roundtable (U.S.A) unveiled an initiative to train American CEOs in the finer points of ethics. But an appreciation of the importance of ethics for a healthy society and a concern, in particular, for what constitutes ethical conduct in business go back to ancient times. The Roman philosopher Cicero, for instance, discussed the contested example of an honest merchant from Alexandria, who brings a large stock of wheat to Rhodes, where there is a food shortage. On his way there, he has seen other traders sailing from Alexandria to Rhodes with substantial cargos of grain. Should he tell the people of Rhodes, or say nothing and sell at the best price he can? Some ancient ethicists argued that although the merchant must declare defects in his wares as required by law, as a vendor he is free—provided he tells no untruths—to sell his goods as profitably as he can. Others, including Cicero, argued to the contrary that all the facts must be revealed and that buyers must be as fully informed as sellers.[2]

"Business" and "businessperson" are broad terms. "Business" may denote a corner hot-dog stand or a multinational corporation that does business in several countries. A "businessperson" may be a gardener engaged in a one-person operation or a company president responsible for thousands of workers and enormous corporate investments. Accordingly, the word *business* will be used here simply to mean any organization whose objective is to provide goods or services for profit. *Businesspeople* are those who participate in planning, organizing, or directing the work of business.

This book, however, takes a broader view as well. It is concerned with moral issues that arise anywhere that employers and employees come together. That is, it is as much about organizational ethics as about business ethics. An *organization* is a group of people working together to achieve a common purpose. The purpose may be to offer a product or a service primarily for profit, as in business. But the purpose may also be to provide a not-for-profit service such as health care, as in medical organizations, or public safety and order, as in law-enforcement organizations, or education, as in academic organizations, and so on.

The cases and illustrations presented in this book deal with moral issues and dilemmas in both business and non-business organizational settings.

People occasionally poke fun at the idea of business ethics, declaring that the term is a contradiction or that business has no ethics. Such people take themselves to be worldly and realistic. They think they have a down-to-earth idea of how things really work. In fact, despite its pretence of sophistication, that attitude is embarrassingly naive. People who express it have little grasp of the nature of ethics and only a superficial understanding of the real world of business. After you have read this book, you will perhaps see the truth of this judgment.

MORAL VERSUS NON-MORAL STANDARDS

Moral questions differ from other kinds of questions. Whether your office computer can download a copyrighted album from the Web is a factual question, not a moral question. On the other hand, whether you should download the album is a moral question. When we answer a moral question or make a moral judgment, we appeal to moral standards. These standards differ from other kinds of standards.

Wearing shorts to a formal dinner party is boorish behaviour. Murdering the King's English with double negatives violates the basic conventions of proper language usage. Photographing the finish of a horse race with low-speed film is poor photographic technique. In each case a standard is violated—fashion, grammatical, technical—but the violation does not pose a serious threat to human well-being.

Moral standards are different because they concern behaviour that is of serious consequence to human welfare, that can profoundly injure or benefit people.[3] The conventional moral norms against lying, stealing, and murdering deal with actions that can hurt people. The moral principle that human beings should be treated with dignity and respect uplifts the human personality. Whether products are healthful or harmful, work conditions safe or dangerous, personnel procedures biased or fair, privacy respected or invaded are also matters that seriously affect human well-being. The standards that govern our conduct in these matters are moral standards.

A second characteristic follows from the first. Moral standards take priority over other standards, including self-interest. Something that morality condemns—for instance, the burglary of your neighbour's home—cannot be justified on the non-moral grounds that it would be a good training exercise for more adventurous burglaries in the future, or that it would be a thrill to do it or that it would pay off handsomely. We take moral standards to be more important than other considerations in guiding our actions.

A third characteristic of moral standards is that their soundness depends on the adequacy of the reasons that support or justify them. For the most part, fashion standards are set by clothing designers, merchandisers, and consumers; grammatical standards by grammarians and students of language; technical standards by practitioners and experts in the field. Legislators make laws, boards of directors make organizational policy, and licensing boards establish standards for professionals. In all these cases, some authoritative body is the ultimate validating source of the standards and thus can change the standards if it wishes. By contrast, moral standards are not made by such bodies, although they are often endorsed or rejected by them. More precisely, the validity of moral standards depends not on authoritative fiat but rather on the quality of the arguments or the reasoning that supports them. Exactly what constitutes adequate grounds or justification for a moral standard is a debated question, which, as we shall see in the next chapter, underlies disagreement among philosophers over which specific moral principles are best.

Although these three characteristics set moral standards apart from others, it is useful to discuss more specifically how morality differs from three things with which it is sometimes confused: etiquette, law, and professional codes of ethics.

Morality and Etiquette

Etiquette refers to the norms of correct conduct in polite society or, more generally, to any special code of social behaviour or courtesy. In our society, for example, it is considered bad etiquette to chew with your mouth open or to pick your nose when talking to someone; it is considered good etiquette to say "please" when requesting and "thank you" when receiving and to hold a door open for someone entering immediately behind you. Good business etiquette typically calls for writing follow-up letters after meetings, returning phone calls, and dressing appropriately. It is commonplace to judge people's manners as "good" or "bad" and the conduct that reflects them as "right" or "wrong." "Good," "bad," "right," and "wrong" here simply mean socially appropriate or socially inappropriate. In these contexts, such words express judgments about manners, not ethics.

So-called rules of etiquette that you might learn in an etiquette book are prescriptions for socially acceptable behaviour. If you want to fit in, get along with others, and be thought well of by them, you should observe common rules of etiquette. If you violate the rules, then you're rightly considered ill-mannered, impolite, or even uncivilized, but not necessarily immoral.

Rules of etiquette are generally non-moral in character: "Say 'congratulations' to the groom but 'best wishes' to the bride"; "Push your chair back into place upon leaving a dinner table." But violations of etiquette can have moral implications. The male boss who refers to female subordinates as "honey" or "doll" shows bad manners. If such epithets diminish the worth of female employees or perpetuate sexism, then they also raise moral issues concerning equal treatment and denial of dignity to human beings.

Scrupulous observance of rules of etiquette does not make one moral. In fact, it can camouflage moral issues. A few decades ago in some parts of the United States, it was considered bad manners for blacks and whites to eat together. Those who obeyed the convention and were thus judged well-mannered certainly had no grounds for feeling moral. The only way to dramatize the injustice underlying this practice was to violate the rule and be judged ill-mannered. For those in the civil rights movement of the 1960s, being considered boorish was a small price to pay for exposing the unequal treatment and human degradation that underlay this rule of etiquette.

Morality and Law

Before distinguishing between morality and law, one should understand the term *law*. Basically, there are four kinds of law: statutes, regulations, common law, and constitutional law.

Statutes are laws enacted by legislative bodies. The law that defines and prohibits theft is a statute. The federal parliament, the provincial and territorial legislative assemblies in Canada, or the Congress and state legislatures in the U.S. enact statutes. (Laws enacted by local governing bodies such as city councils usually are termed *ordinances*.) Statutes make up a large part of the law and are what many of us mean when we speak of laws.

Limited in their knowledge, legislatures often set up boards or agencies whose functions include issuing detailed regulations of certain kinds of conduct— *administrative regulations*. For example, provincial (or state) legislatures establish licensing boards to formulate regulations for the licensing of physicians and nurses. As long as these regulations do not exceed the board's statutory powers and do not conflict with other kinds of law, they are legally binding.

Common law refers to laws applied in the English-speaking world when there were few statutes. Courts frequently wrote opinions explaining the bases of their decisions in specific cases, including the legal principles they deemed appropriate. Each of these opinions became a precedent for later decisions in similar cases. The massive body of legal principles that accumulated over the years is collectively referred to as common law. Like administrative regulations, common law is valid if it harmonizes with statutory law and with still another kind, constitutional law.

Constitutional law refers to court rulings on the requirements of the Constitution and the constitutionality of legislation. For example, Canada's *Constitution Act* (1982), just like the U.S. Constitution, empowers the courts to decide whether laws are compatible with the Constitution. Although the courts cannot make laws, they have far-reaching powers to rule on the constitutionality of laws and to declare them invalid. Our Supreme Court has the greatest judiciary power and rules on an array of cases, some of which bear directly on the study of business ethics.

Although people sometimes confuse the two, legality and morality are different things. On one hand, breaking the law is not always or necessarily immoral. On the other hand, the legality of an action does not guarantee that it is morally right. Let's consider these points further.

1. *An action can be illegal but morally right.* For example, helping a Jewish family to hide from the Nazis was against German law in 1939, but it would have been a morally admirable thing to do. Of course, the Nazi regime was vicious and evil. By contrast, in a democratic society with a basically just legal order, the fact that something is illegal provides a moral consideration against doing it. For example, one moral reason for not burning trash in your backyard is that it violates an ordinance that your community has voted in favour of. Some philosophers believe that sometimes the illegality of an action can make it morally wrong, even if the action would otherwise have been morally acceptable. But even if they are right about that, the fact that something is illegal does not trump all other moral considerations. Nonconformity to law is not always immoral, even in a democratic society. There can be circumstances where, all things considered, violating the law is morally permissible, perhaps even morally required.

Probably no one in the modern era has expressed this point more eloquently than one of the leaders of the African-American Civil Rights Movement, the famous Dr. Martin Luther King, Jr. Confined in a city jail in Alabama on charges of parading without a permit, King penned his now famous "Letter from Birmingham Jail" to eight of his fellow clergymen who had published a statement attacking King's unauthorized protest of racial segregation as unwise and untimely. King wrote:

> All segregation statutes are unjust because segregation distorts the soul and damages the personality. It gives the segregator a false sense of superiority and the segregated a false sense of inferiority. Segregation, to use the terminology of the Jewish philosopher Martin Buber, substitutes an "I–it" relationship for an "I–thou" relationship and ends up relegating persons to the status of things. Hence segregation is not only politically, economically, and sociologically unsound, it is morally wrong and sinful. . . . Thus it is that I can urge men to obey the 1954 decision of the Supreme Court,* for it is morally right; and I can urge them to disobey segregation ordinances, for they are morally wrong.[4]

2. *An action that is legal can be morally wrong.* For example, it may have been perfectly legal for the chairman of a profitable company to lay off 125 workers and use three-quarters of the money saved to boost his pay and that of the company's other top manager,[5] but the morality of his doing so is open to debate.

Or, to take another example, suppose that you're driving to work one day and see an accident victim sitting on the side of the road, clearly in shock and needing medical assistance. Because you know first aid and are in no great hurry to get to your destination, you could easily stop and assist the person. Legally speaking, though, you are not obligated to stop and render aid. Under common law, the prudent thing would be to drive on, because by stopping you would bind yourself to use reasonable care and thus incur legal liability if you fail to do so and the victim thereby suffers injury. Many provinces in Canada, as well as many states in the U.S., have enacted so-called Good Samaritan laws to provide immunity from damages to those rendering aid (except for gross negligence or serious misconduct). But in all Canadian (with the exception of Quebec) and in many American jurisdictions the law does not oblige people to give such aid or even to call an ambulance. Moral theorists would agree, however, that if you sped away without rendering aid or even calling for help, your action might be perfectly legal but would be morally suspect. Regardless of the law, such conduct would almost certainly be wrong.

What then may we say about the relationship between law and morality? To a significant extent, law codifies a society's customs, ideals, norms, and moral values. For changes in law tend to reflect changes in what a society takes to be right and wrong, though sometimes changes in the law can alter people's ideas about the rightness or wrongness of conduct. However, even if a society's laws are sensible and morally sound, it is a mistake to see them as sufficient to establish the moral standards that should guide us. The law cannot cover the wide variety of possible individual and group conduct, and in many situations it is too blunt an instrument to provide adequate moral guidance. The law generally prohibits egregious affronts to a society's moral standards and it is in that sense the "floor" of moral conduct, but breaches of moral conduct can slip through cracks in that floor.

Professional Codes

Somewhere between etiquette and law lie *professional codes of ethics*. These are the rules that are supposed to govern the conduct of members of a given profession. Generally speaking, the members of a profession are understood to have agreed to abide by those rules as a condition of their engaging in that profession. Violation of the professional code may result in disapproval by one's professional peers and, in serious cases, loss of one's licence to practise that profession. Sometimes these codes are unwritten and are part of the common understanding of the members of the profession—for example, that professors should not date their students. In other instances,

---

*In *Brown v. Board of Education of Topeka* (1954), the U.S. Supreme Court struck down the half-century-old "separate but equal doctrine," which permitted racially segregated schools as long as comparable quality was maintained.

the code may, in part or in whole, be written down by an authoritative body so that it may be better taught or more efficiently enforced.

The rules in written codes are sometimes so vague and general as to be of little value, and often they amount to little more than self-promotion by the professional organization. This is often the case when industries or corporations publish statements of their ethical standards. In other cases—for example, with attorneys—professional codes can be very specific and detailed. It is difficult to generalize about the content of professional codes of ethics, however, because they frequently involve a mix of purely moral rules (for example, client confidentiality), of professional etiquette (for example, the billing of services to other professionals), and of restrictions intended to benefit the group's economic interests (for example, limitations on price competition).

Given their nature, professional codes of ethics are neither a complete nor a completely reliable guide to one's moral obligations. First, not all the rules of a professional code are purely moral in character; and even when they are, the fact that a rule is officially enshrined as part of the code of a profession does not guarantee that it is a sound moral principle. As a professional, you must take seriously the injunctions of your profession, but you still have the responsibility to critically assess those rules for yourself.

Regarding those parts of the code that concern etiquette or financial matters, bear in mind that by joining a profession you are probably agreeing, explicitly or implicitly, to abide by those standards. Assuming that those rules don't require morally impermissible conduct, then consenting to them gives you some moral obligation to follow them. In addition, for many, living up to the standards of one's chosen profession is an important source of personal satisfaction. Still, you must be alert to situations in which professional standards or customary professional practice conflicts with the ordinary demands of morality. Adherence to a professional code does not exempt your conduct from scrutiny from the broader perspective of morality.

Where Do Moral Standards Come From?

So far you have seen how moral standards are different from various non-moral standards, but you probably wonder about the source of those moral standards. Most, if not all, people have certain moral principles or a moral code that they explicitly or implicitly accept. Because the moral principles of different people in the same society overlap, at least in part, we can also talk about the moral code of a society, meaning the moral standards shared in common by its members. How do we come to have certain moral principles and not others? Obviously, many things influence us in the moral principles we accept: our early upbringing, the behaviour of those around us, the explicit and implicit standards of our culture, our own experiences, and our critical reflections on those experiences.

For philosophers, though, the important question is not how in fact we came to have the particular principles we have. The philosophical issue is whether the principles we have can be justified. Do we simply take for granted the values of those around us? Or, like Martin Luther King, Jr., are we able to think independently about moral matters? By analogy, we pick up our non-moral beliefs from all sorts of sources: books, conversations with friends, movies, various experiences we've had. The philosopher's concern is not so much with how we actually got the beliefs we have, but whether or to what extent those beliefs—for example, that women are more emotional than men or that telekinesis is possible—can withstand critical scrutiny. Likewise, ethical theories attempt to justify moral standards and ethical beliefs. The next chapter examines some of the major theories of normative ethics. That is, it looks at what some of the major thinkers in human history have argued are the best-justified standards of right and wrong.

But first we need to consider the relationship between morality and religion on the one hand and that between morality and society on the other. Some people maintain that morality just boils down to religion. Others have argued for the doctrine of *ethical relativism*, which says that right and wrong are only a function of what a particular society takes to be right and wrong. Both those views are mistaken.

RELIGION AND MORALITY

Any religion provides its believers with a worldview, part of which involves certain moral instructions, values, and commitments. The Jewish and Christian traditions, to name just two, offer a view of humans as unique products of a divine intervention that has endowed them with consciousness and an ability to love. Both these traditions posit creatures that stand midway between nature and spirit. On one hand, we are finite and bound to earth, not only capable of wrongdoing, but also born morally flawed (original sin). On the other, we can transcend nature and realize infinite possibilities.

Primarily because of the influence of Western religion, many North Americans and others view themselves as beings with a supernatural destiny, as possessing a life after death, as being immortal. One's purpose in life is found in serving and loving God. For the Christian, the way to serve and love God is by emulating the life of Jesus of Nazareth. In the life of Jesus, Christians find an expression of the highest virtue—love. They love when they perform selfless acts, develop a keen social conscience, and realize that human beings are creatures of God and therefore intrinsically worthwhile. For the Jew, one serves and loves God chiefly through expressions of justice and righteousness. Jews also develop a sense of honour derived from a commitment to truth, humility, fidelity, and kindness. This commitment hones their sense of responsibility to family and community.

Religion, then, involves not only a formal system of worship but also prescriptions for social relationships. One example is the mandate "Do unto others as you would have them do unto you." Termed the "Golden Rule," this injunction represents one of humankind's highest moral ideals and can be found in essence in all the great religions of the world:

> Good people proceed while considering that what is best for others is best for themselves. (*Hitopadesa*, Hinduism)

> Thou shalt love thy neighbour as thyself. (*Leviticus* 19:18, Judaism)

> Therefore all things whatsoever ye would that men should do to you, do ye even so to them. (*Matthew* 7:12, Christianity)

> Hurt not others with that which pains yourself. (*Udanavarga* 5:18, Buddhism)

> What you do not want done to yourself, do not do to others. (*Analects* 15:23, Confucianism)

> No one of you is a believer until he loves for his brother what he loves for himself. (*Traditions*, Islam)

Although inspiring, such religious ideals are very general and can be difficult to translate into precise policy injunctions. Religious bodies, nevertheless, occasionally articulate positions on more specific political, educational, economic, and medical issues, which help mold public opinion on matters as diverse as abortion, euthanasia, nuclear weapons, and national defence. Roman Catholicism has a rich history of formally applying its core values to the moral aspects of industrial relations and economic life. The following for example stand in that tradition: Pope John Paul II's encyclical *Centesimus Annus*, many of the Pastoral Letters by the Canadian Conference of Catholic Bishops (not to mention a plethora of statements by the U.S. National Conference of Catholic Bishops), and the 1997 report by the Pontifical Council for Social Communication on advertising as well as its 2002 report on ethics and the Internet.

Morality Needn't Rest on Religion

Many people believe that morality must be based on religion, either in the sense that without religion people would have no incentive to be moral or in the sense that only religion can provide moral guidance. Others contend that morality is based on the commands of God. None of these claims is very plausible.

First, although a desire to avoid hell and to go to heaven may prompt some of us to act morally, this is not the only reason or even the most common reason that people behave morally. Often we act morally out of habit or simply because that is the kind of person we are. It would just not occur to most of us to swipe an elderly lady's purse, and if the idea did occur to us, we wouldn't do it because such an act simply doesn't fit with our personal standards or with our concept of ourselves. We are often motivated to do what is morally right out of concern for others or just because it is right. In addition, the approval of our peers, the need to appease our conscience, and the desire to avoid earthly punishment may all motivate us to act morally. Furthermore, atheists generally live lives as moral and upright as those of believers.

Second, the moral instructions of the world's great religions are general and imprecise: They do not relieve us of the necessity to engage in moral reasoning ourselves. For example, the Bible says, "Thou shall not kill." Yet Christians disagree among themselves over the morality of fighting in wars, of capital punishment, of killing in self-defence, of slaughtering animals, of abortion and euthanasia, and of allowing foreigners to die from famine because we have not provided them with as much food as we might have. The Bible does not provide unambiguous solutions to these moral problems; so even believers must engage in moral philosophy if they are to have intelligent answers. On the other hand, there are lots of reasons for believing that, say, a cold-blooded murder motivated by greed is immoral; one need not believe in a religion to figure that out.

Third, although some theologians have advocated the *divine command theory*—that if something is wrong (like killing an innocent person for fun), then the only reason it is wrong is that God commands us not to do it—many theologians and certainly most philosophers would reject this view. They would contend that if God commands human beings not to do something, such as commit rape, it is because God sees that rape is wrong, but it is not God's forbidding rape that makes it wrong. The fact that rape is wrong is independent of God's decrees.

Most believers think not only that God gives us moral instructions or rules but also that God has moral reasons for giving them to us. According to the divine command theory, this would make no sense. In this view, there is no reason that something is right or wrong, other than the fact that it is God's will. All believers, of course, believe that God is good and that He commands us to do what is right and forbids us to do what is wrong. But this doesn't mean, say critics of the divine command theory, that God's saying so makes a thing wrong, any more than your mother's telling you not to steal makes it wrong to steal.

All this is simply to argue that morality is not necessarily based on religion in any of these three senses. That religion influences the moral standards and values of most of us is beyond doubt. But given that religions differ in their moral principles and that even members of the same faith often disagree on moral matters, you cannot justify a moral principle simply by appealing to religion—for that will only persuade those who already agree with your particular interpretation of your particular religion. Besides, most religions hold that human reason is capable of understanding what is right and wrong; so it is human reason to which you will have to appeal in order to support your ethical principle.

ETHICAL RELATIVISM

Some people do not believe that morality boils down to religion but rather that it is just a function of what a particular society happens to believe. This view is called *ethical relativism*, the theory that what is right is determined by what a culture or society says is right. What is right in one place may be wrong in another, because the only criterion for distinguishing right from wrong—and so the only ethical standard for judging an action—is the moral system of the society in which the act occurs.

Abortion, for example, is condemned as immoral in Catholic Ireland but is practised as a morally neutral form of birth control in Japan. According to the ethical relativist, then, abortion is wrong in Ireland but morally permissible in Japan. The relativist is not saying merely that the Irish believe abortion is abominable and the Japanese do not; that is acknowledged by everyone. Rather, the ethical relativist contends that abortion is immoral in Ireland because the Irish believe it to be immoral and that it is morally permissible in Japan because the Japanese believe it to be so. Thus, for the ethical relativist there is no absolute ethical standard independent of cultural context, no criterion of right and wrong by which to judge other than that of particular societies. In short, what morality requires is relative to society.

Those who endorse ethical relativism point to the apparent diversity of human values and the great variety of existing moral codes to support their case. From our own cultural perspective, some seemingly immoral moralities have been adopted. For example, polygamy, pedophilia, stealing, slavery, infanticide, and cannibalism have all been tolerated or even encouraged by the moral system of one society or another. In light of this fact, the ethical relativist believes that there can be no non-ethnocentric standard by which to judge actions.

On the other hand, some thinkers believe that the moral differences between societies are smaller and less significant than they appear. They contend that variations in moral standards reflect differing factual beliefs and differing circumstances rather than fundamental differences in values. But suppose they are wrong about this matter. The relativist's conclusion still does not follow. A difference of opinion among societies about right and wrong no more proves that none of the conflicting beliefs is true or superior to the others than the diversity of viewpoints expressed in a college seminar establishes that there is no truth. In short, disagreement in ethical matters does not imply that all opinions are equally correct.

Moreover, ethical relativism has some unpleasant implications. First, it undermines any moral criticism of the practices of other societies as long as their actions conform to their own standards. We cannot say that slavery in a slave society like that of the American South 150 years ago was immoral and unjust as long as that society held it to be morally permissible.

Second, and closely related, is the fact that for the relativist there is no such thing as ethical progress. Although moralities may change, they cannot get better or worse. Thus, we cannot say that our moral standards today are any more enlightened than they were in the Middle Ages.

Third, it makes no sense from the relativist's point of view for people to criticize principles or practices accepted by their own society. People can be censured for not living up to their society's moral code, but that is all. The moral code itself cannot be criticized, because whatever a society takes to be right really is right for it. Reformers who identify injustices in their society and campaign against them are only encouraging people to be immoral—that is, to depart from the moral standards of their society—unless or until the majority of the society agrees with the reformers. The minority can never be right in moral matters; to be right it must become the majority.

The ethical relativist is correct to emphasize that in viewing other cultures we should keep an open mind and not simply dismiss alien social practices on the basis of our own cultural prejudices. But the relativist's theory of morality doesn't hold up. The more carefully we examine it, the less plausible it becomes. There is no good reason for saying that the majority view on moral issues is automatically right, and the belief that it is automatically right has unacceptable consequences.

Relativism and the "Game" of Business

In his well-known and influential essay "Is Business Bluffing Ethical?," Albert Carr argues that business, as practised by individuals as well as by corporations, has the impersonal character of a game—a game that demands both special strategy and an understanding of its special ethical standards.[6] Business has its own norms and rules that differ from those of the rest of society. Thus, according to Carr, a number of things that we normally think of as wrong are really permissible in a business context. His examples include conscious misstatement and concealment of pertinent facts in negotiation, lying about one's age on a résumé, deceptive packaging, automobile companies' neglect of car safety, and utility companies' manipulation of regulators and overcharging of electricity users. He draws an analogy with poker:

> Poker's own brand of ethics is different from the ethical ideals of civilized human relationships. The game calls for distrust of the other fellow. It ignores the claim of friendship. Cunning deception and concealment of one's strength and intentions, not kindness and openheartedness, are vital in poker. No one thinks any the worse of poker on that account. And no one should think any the worse of the game of business because its standards of right and wrong differ from the prevailing traditions of morality in our society.[7]

What Carr is defending here is a kind of ethical relativism: business has its own moral standards, and business actions should be evaluated only by those standards.

One can argue whether Carr has accurately identified the implicit rules of the business world (for example, is misrepresentation on one's résumé really a permissible move in the business game?), but let's put that issue aside. The basic question is whether business is a separate world to which ordinary moral standards don't apply. Carr's thesis implies that any special activity following its own rules is exempt from external moral evaluation, but as a general proposition this is unacceptable. The Mafia, for example, has an elaborate code of conduct, accepted by the members of the rival "families." For them, gunning down a competitor or terrorizing a local shopkeeper may be strategic moves in a competitive environment. Yet we rightly refuse to say that gangsters cannot be criticized for following their own standards. Normal business activity is a world away from gangsterism, but the point still holds. Any specialized activity or practice will have its own distinctive rules and procedures, but the morality of those rules and procedures can still be evaluated.

Moreover, Carr's poker analogy is itself weak. For one thing, business activity can affect others—such as consumers—who have not consciously and freely chosen to play the "game." Business is indeed an activity involving distinctive rules and customary ways of doing things, but it is not really a game. It is the economic basis of our society, and we all have an interest in the goals of business (in productivity and consumer satisfaction, for instance) and in the rules business follows. Why should these be exempt from public evaluation and assessment? Later chapters return to the question of what these goals and rules should be. But to take one simple point, note that a business/economic system that permits, encourages, or tolerates deception will be less efficient (that is, work less well) than one in which the participants have fuller knowledge of the goods and services being exchanged.

In sum, by divorcing business from morality, Carr misrepresents both. He incorrectly treats the standards and rules of everyday business activity as if they had nothing to do with the standards and rules of ordinary morality, and he treats morality as something that we give lip service to on Sundays but that otherwise has no influence on our lives.

HAVING MORAL PRINCIPLES

Most people at some time in their lives pause to reflect on what moral principles they have or should have and on what moral standards are the best justified. (Moral philosophers themselves have defended different moral standards; Chapter 2 discusses these various theories.) When a person accepts a moral principle, when that principle is part of his or her personal moral code, then naturally the person believes the principle is important and well justified. But there is more to moral principles than that, as the philosopher Richard Brandt emphasized. When a principle is part of a person's moral code, that person is strongly motivated toward the conduct required by the principle, and against behaviour that conflicts with that

principle. The person will tend to feel guilty when his or her own conduct violates that principle and to disapprove of others whose behaviour conflicts with it. Likewise, the person will tend to hold in esteem those whose conduct shows an abundance of the motivation required by the principle.[8]

Other philosophers have, in different ways, reinforced Brandt's point. To accept a moral principle is not a purely intellectual act like accepting a scientific hypothesis or a mathematical theorem. Rather, it also involves a desire to follow that principle for its own sake, the likelihood of feeling guilty about not doing so, and a tendency to evaluate the conduct of others according to the principle in question. We would find it very strange, for example, if Sally claimed to be morally opposed to cruelty to animals yet abused her own pets and felt no inclination to protest when some ruffians down the street set a cat on fire.

Conscience

People can, and unfortunately sometimes do, go against their moral principles, but we would doubt that they sincerely held the principle in question if violating it did not bother their conscience. We have all felt the pangs of conscience, but what exactly is conscience and how reliable a guide is it? Our conscience, of course, is not literally a little voice inside of us. To oversimplify a complex piece of developmental psychology, our conscience evolved as we internalized the moral instructions of the parents or other authority figures that raised us as children.

When you were very young, you were probably told to tell the truth and to return something you filched to its proper owner. If you were caught lying or being dishonest, you were probably punished—scolded, spanked, sent to bed without dinner, denied a privilege. On the other hand, truth telling and kindness to your siblings were probably rewarded—with approval, praise, maybe even hugs or candy. Seeking reward and avoiding punishment motivate small children to do what is expected of them. Gradually, children come to internalize those parental commands. Thus, they feel vaguely that their parents know what they are doing even when the parents are not around. When children do something forbidden, they experience the same feelings as when scolded by their parents—the first stirrings of guilt. By the same token, even in the absence of explicit parental reward, children feel a sense of self-approval about having done what they were supposed to have done.

As we grow older, of course, our motivations are not so simple and our self-understanding is greater. We are able to reflect on and understand the moral lessons we were taught, as well as to refine and modify those principles. As adults we are morally independent agents. Yet however much our conscience has evolved and however much our adult moral code differs from the moral perspective of our childhood, those pangs of guilt we occasionally feel still stem from that early internalization of parental demands.

The Limits of Conscience

How reliable a guide is conscience? People often say, "Follow your conscience" or "You should never go against your conscience," but not only is such advice not very helpful, it may sometimes be bad advice. First, when we are genuinely perplexed over what we ought to do, we are trying to figure out what our conscience ought to be saying to us. When it is not possible to do both, should we keep our promise to a colleague or come to the aid of an old friend? To be told that we should follow our conscience is no help at all.

Second, it may not always be good for us to follow our conscience. It all depends on what our conscience says. On the one hand, sometimes people's consciences do not bother them when they should—perhaps because they didn't think through the implications of what they were doing or perhaps because they failed to internalize strongly enough the appropriate moral principles. On the other hand, a person's conscience might disturb the person about something that is perfectly all right.

Consider an episode in Chapter 16 of Mark Twain's *The Adventures of Huckleberry Finn*. Huck has taken off down the Mississippi on a raft with his friend, the runaway slave Jim, but as they get nearer to the place where Jim will become legally free, Huck starts feeling guilty about helping him run away:

> It hadn't ever come home to me before, what this thing was that I was doing. But now it did; and it stayed with me, and scorched me more and more. I tried to make out to myself that *I* warn't to blame, because *I* didn't run Jim off from his rightful owner; but it warn't no use, conscience up and says, every time: "But you knowed he was running for his freedom, and you could a paddled ashore and told somebody." That was so—I couldn't get around that, no way. That was where it pinched. Conscience says to me: "What had poor Miss Watson done to you, that you could see her nigger go off right under your eyes and never say one single word? What did that poor old woman do to you, that you could treat her so mean? . . . " I got to feeling so mean and miserable I most wished I was dead.

Here Huck is feeling guilty about doing what we would all agree is the morally right thing to do. But Huck is only a boy, and his pangs of conscience reflect the principles that he has picked up uncritically from the slave-owning society around him. Unable to think independently about matters of right and wrong, Huck in the end decides to disregard his conscience. He follows his instincts and sticks by his friend Jim.

The point here is not that you should ignore your conscience but that the voice of conscience is itself something that can be critically examined. A pang of conscience is like a warning. When you feel one, you should definitely stop and reflect on the rightness of what you are doing. On the other hand, you cannot justify your actions simply by saying you were following your conscience. Terrible crimes have occasionally been committed in the name of conscience.

Moral Principles and Self-Interest

Sometimes doing what you believe would be morally right and doing what would best satisfy your own interests may be two different things. Imagine that you are in your car hurrying home along a quiet road, trying hard to get there in time to see the kickoff of an important football game. You pass an acquaintance who is having car trouble. He doesn't recognize you. As a dedicated fan, you would much prefer to keep on going than to stop and help him, thus missing at least part of the game. You might rationalize that someone else will eventually come along and help him if you don't, but deep down you know that you really ought to stop. On the other hand, self-interest seems to say, "Keep going."

Consider another example. You have applied for a new job, and if you land it, it will be an enormous break for you: it is exactly the kind of position you want and have been trying to get for some time. It pays well and will settle you into a desirable career for the rest of your life. The competition has come down to just you and one other person, and you believe correctly that she has a slight edge on you. Now imagine that you could spread a nasty rumour about her that would guarantee that she wouldn't get the job, and that you could do this in a way that wouldn't come back to you. Presumably, circulating this lie would violate your moral code; on the other hand, doing it would clearly be to your benefit.

Some people argue that moral action and self-interest can never really conflict, and some philosophers have gone to great lengths to try to prove this, but they are almost certainly mistaken. They maintain that if you do the wrong thing, then you will be caught, your conscience will bother you, or in some way "what goes around comes around," so that your misdeed will come back to haunt you. This is often correct. But unfortunate as it may be, sometimes—viewed just in terms of personal self-interest—it may pay off for you to do what you know to be wrong. People sometimes get away with their wrongdoings, and if their conscience bothers them at all, it may not bother them very much. To believe otherwise not only is wishful thinking but also shows a lack of understanding of morality.

Morality serves to restrain our purely self-interested desires so we can all live together. The moral standards of a society provide the basic guidelines for cooperative social existence and allow conflicts to be resolved by appeal to shared principles of justification. If our interests never came into conflict—that is, if it were never advantageous for one person to deceive or cheat another—then there would be little need for morality. We would already be in heaven. Both a system of law that punishes people for hurting others and a system of morality that encourages people to refrain from pursuing their self-interest at great expense to others help to make social existence possible.

Usually, following our moral principles is in our best interest. This idea is particularly worth noting in the business context. Several recent writers have argued persuasively not only that moral behaviour is consistent with profitability but also that the most morally responsible companies are among the most profitable.[9] Apparently, respecting the rights of employees, treating suppliers fairly, and being straightforward with customers pay off.

But notice one thing. If you do the right thing only because you think it will pay off, you are not really motivated by moral concerns. Having a moral principle involves having a desire to follow the principle for its own sake—just because it is the right thing to do. If you do the right thing only because you believe it will pay off, you might just as easily not do it if it looks as if it is not going to pay off.

In addition, there is no guarantee that moral behaviour will always pay off in strictly selfish terms. As argued earlier, there will be exceptions. From the moral point of view, you ought to stop and help your acquaintance, and you shouldn't lie about competitors. From the selfish point of view, you should do exactly the opposite. Should you follow your self-interest or your moral principles? There's no final answer to this question. From the moral point of view, you should, of course, follow your moral principles. But from the selfish point of view, you should look out solely for "number one."

Which option you choose will depend on the strength of your self-interested or self-regarding desires in comparison with the strength of your other-regarding desires (that is, your moral motivations and your concern for others). In other words, your choice will depend on the kind of person you are, which depends in large part on how you were raised. A person who is basically selfish will pass by the acquaintance in distress and will spread the rumour, whereas a person who has a stronger concern for others, or a stronger desire to do what is right just because it is right, will not.

Although it may be impossible to prove to selfish persons that they should not do the thing that best advances their self-interest (because, if they are selfish, then that is all they care about), there are considerations that suggest it is not in a person's overall self-interest to be a selfish person. People who are exclusively concerned with their own interests tend to have less happy and less satisfying lives than those whose desires extend beyond themselves. This might be dubbed the "paradox of hedonism" or the "paradox of selfishness." Individuals who care only about their own happiness will generally be less happy than those who care about others. Moreover, people often find greater satisfaction in a life lived according to moral principle, and in being the kind of person such life entails, than in a life devoted solely to immediate self-interest. Thus, or so many philosophers have argued, people have self-interested reasons not to be so self-interested. How do selfish people make themselves less so? Not overnight, obviously, but by involving themselves in the concerns and cares of others, they can in time come to care sincerely about those persons.

MORALITY AND PERSONAL VALUES

Some philosophers distinguish between morality in a narrow sense and morality in a broad sense. In a narrow sense, morality is the moral code of an individual or a society (insofar as the moral codes of the individuals making up that society overlap). Although the principles that make up our code may not be explicitly formulated, as laws are, they do guide us in our conduct. They function as internal monitors of our own behaviour and as a basis for assessing the actions of others. Morality in the narrow sense concerns the principles that do or should regulate people's conduct and relations with others. These principles can be debated, however. (Take, for example, John Stuart Mill's contention that society ought not to interfere with people's liberty when their actions affect only themselves.) And a large part of moral philosophy involves assessing rival moral principles. This discussion is part of the ongoing development in our moral culture. What is at stake are the basic standards that ought to govern our behaviour—that is, the basic framework or ground rules that make coexistence possible. If there were not already fairly widespread agreement about these principles, our social order would not be possible.

But in addition we can talk about our morality in a broader sense, meaning not just the principles of conduct that we embrace but also the values, ideals, and aspirations that shape our lives. Many different ways of living our lives would meet our basic moral obligations. The type of life each of us seeks to live reflects our individual values—whether following a profession, devoting ourselves to community service, raising a family, seeking solitude, pursuing scientific truth, striving for athletic excellence, amassing political power, cultivating glamorous people as friends, or some combination of these and many other possible ways of living. The life that each of us forges and the way we understand that life are part of our morality in the broad sense of the term.

It is important to bear this in mind throughout your study of business ethics. Although the usual concern is with the principles that ought to govern conduct in certain situations—for example, whether a hiring officer may take an applicant's race into account, whether employees may be forced to take an AIDS test, or whether corporate bribery is permissible in countries where people turn a blind eye to it—your choices in the business world will also reflect your other values and ideals or, in other words, the kind of person you are striving to be. What sort of ideal do you have of yourself as a businessperson? How much weight do you put on profitability, for instance, as against the quality of your product or the socially beneficial character of your service?

The decisions you make in your career and much of the way you shape your working life will depend not just on your moral code but also on the understanding you have of yourself in certain roles and relationships. Your morality—in the sense of your ideals, values, and aspirations—involves, among other things, your understanding of human nature, tradition, and society; of one's proper relationship to the natural environment; and of an individual's place in the cosmos. Professionals in various fields, for example, will invariably be guided not just by rules but also by their understanding of what being a professional involves, and a businessperson's conception of the ideal or model relationship to have with clients will greatly influence his or her day-to-day conduct.

There is more to living a morally good life, of course, than being a good businessperson or being good at your job, as Aristotle (384–322 BCE) argued long ago. He underscored the necessity of our trying to achieve virtue or excellence, not just in some particular field of endeavour, but also as human beings. Aristotle thought that things have functions. The function of a piano, for instance, is to make certain sounds, and a piano that performs this function well is a good or excellent piano. Likewise, we have an idea of what it is for a person to be an excellent athlete, an excellent manager, or an excellent professor—it is to do well the types of things that athletes, managers, or professors are supposed to do.

But Aristotle also thought that, just as there is an ideal of excellence for any particular craft or occupation, similarly there must be an excellence that we can achieve simply as human beings. That is, he thought that we could live our lives as a whole in such a way that they can be judged not just as excellent in this respect or in that occupation, but as excellent, period. Aristotle thought that only when we develop our truly human capacities sufficiently to achieve this human excellence would we have lives blessed with happiness. Philosophers since Aristotle's time have been skeptical of his apparent belief that this human excellence would come in just one form, but many would underscore the importance of developing our various potential capacities and striving to achieve a kind of excellence in our lives. How we understand this excellence is a function of our values, ideals, and worldview—our morality in a broad sense.

INDIVIDUAL INTEGRITY AND RESPONSIBILITY

Previous sections discussed what it is for a person to have a moral code, as well as the sometimes-conflicting pulls of moral conscience and self-interest. In addition, we have seen that people have values and ideals above and beyond their moral principles, narrowly understood, that also influence the lives they lead. And we have seen the importance of reflecting critically on both moral principles and moral ideals and values as we seek to live morally good and worthwhile lives. None of us, however, lives in a vacuum, and social pressures of various sorts always affect us. Sometimes these pressures make it difficult to stick with our principles and to be the kind of person we wish to be. Corporations are a particularly relevant example of an environment that can potentially damage individual integrity and responsibility.

Organizational Norms

One of the major characteristics of an organization, indeed of any group, is the shared acceptance of organizational rules by its members. Acceptance can take different

forms; it can be conscious or unconscious, overt or subtle, but it is almost always present, because an organization can survive only if it holds its members together. Group cohesiveness requires that individual members "commit" themselves—that is, relinquish some of their personal freedom in order to further organizational goals. One's degree of commitment—the extent to which one accepts group norms and subordinates self to organizational goals—is a measure of one's loyalty to the "team."

The corporation's goal is profit. To achieve this goal, top management sets goals for sales, market share, return on equity, and so forth. For the most part the norms or rules that govern corporate existence are derived from these goals. But clearly there's nothing in either the norms or the goals that necessarily encourages moral behaviour; indeed, they may discourage it.

Mounting evidence suggests that most managers experience role conflicts between what is expected of them as efficient, profit-minded members of an organization and what is expected of them as ethical persons. In a series of in-depth interviews with recent graduates of the Harvard MBA program, researchers Joseph L. Badaracco, Jr., and Allen P. Webb found that these young managers frequently received explicit instructions or felt strong organizational pressure to do things they believed to be sleazy, unethical, or even illegal.[10] Another survey found that managers at all levels experience role conflicts because of "pressure from the top" to meet corporate goals and comply with corporate norms. Of the managers interviewed, 50 percent of top managers, 65 percent of middle managers, and 84 percent of lower managers agreed that "managers today feel under pressure to compromise personal standards to achieve company goals."[11]

The young managers interviewed by Badaracco and Webb identified four powerful organizational "commandments" as responsible for the pressure they felt to compromise their integrity:

First, performance is what really counts, so make your numbers. Second, be loyal and show us that you're a team player. Third, don't break the law. Fourth, don't over-invest in ethical behavior.[12]

Although most corporate goals and norms are not objectionable when viewed by themselves, they frequently put the people who must implement them into a moral pressure cooker. The need to meet corporate objectives, to be a team player, and to conform to organizational norms can lead otherwise honourable individuals to engage in unethical conduct.

Conformity

It is no secret that organizations exert pressure on their members to conform to norms and goals. What might not be so widely known is how easily individuals can be induced to behave as those around them do. A dramatic example is provided in the early conformity studies by social psychologist Solomon Asch.[13]

In a classic experiment, Asch asked groups of seven to nine college students to say which of three lines on a card (right, below) matched the length of a standard line on a second card (left, below):

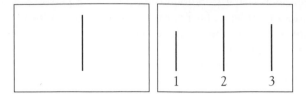

Only one of the subjects in each group was "naive," or unaware of the nature of the experiment. The others were shills or stooges of the experimenter, who had instructed them to make incorrect judgments in about two-thirds of the cases and in this way to pressure the naive subjects to alter their correct judgments.

The results were revealing. When the subjects were not exposed to pressure, they invariably judged correctly, but when the stooges gave false answers, the subjects changed their responses to conform to the unanimous majority judgments. When one shill differed from the majority and gave the correct answer, naive subjects maintained their position three-fourths of the time. However, when the honest shill switched to the majority view in later trials, the errors made by naive subjects rose to about the same level as that of subjects who stood alone against a unanimous majority.

Why did they yield? Some respondents said they didn't want to seem different, even though they continued to believe their judgments were correct. Others said that although their perceptions seemed correct, the majority couldn't be wrong. Still other subjects didn't even seem aware that they had caved in to group pressure. Even those who held their ground tended to be profoundly disturbed by being out of step with the majority and confessed to being sorely tempted to alter their judgments. Indeed, a subsequent study found that students who stood firm in their judgments suffered more anxiety than those who switched. One student with the strength of his correct convictions was literally dripping with perspiration by the end of the experiment.

In these experiments, which cumulatively included several hundred students, the subjects were not exposed to the authority symbols that people inside an organization face: bosses, boards, presidents, professional peers, established policy, and so on. Nor would their responses entail the serious long-range impact that bucking the system can carry for members of an organization: being transferred, dismissed, frozen in a position, or made an organizational pariah. And, of course, the students did not bring to these experiments the financial and personal investments that individuals bring to their jobs. Men and women within an organization are under greater pressure to conform than were the students in Asch's studies.

Groupthink   Almost all groups require some conformity from their members, but in extreme cases the demand for conformity can lead to what social psychologists call "groupthink." Groupthink happens when pressure for unanimity within a highly cohesive group overwhelms its members' desire or ability to appraise the situation realistically and consider alternative courses of action. Members of the group close their eyes to negative information, ignore warnings that the group may be mistaken, and discount outside ideas that might contradict the thinking or the decisions of the group. For example, when the U.S. Senate Intelligence Committee investigated the U.S. intelligence community's false presumption that Saddam Hussein possessed weapons of mass destruction that posed a grave threat to American security interests, the committee's July 2004 report specifically identified groupthink as the problem.

When under the sway of groupthink, group members may have the illusion that the group is invulnerable or that because the group is good or right, whatever it does is permissible. Individuals in the group tend to self-censor thoughts that go against the group's ideas and rationalize away conflicting evidence, and the group as a whole may implicitly or explicitly pressure potential dissenters to conform. Groupthink thus leads to irrational, sometimes disastrous decisions, and it has enormous potential for doing moral damage.

Diffusion of Responsibility

Pressure to conform to the group and to adhere to its norms and beliefs can lead to the surrender of individual moral autonomy. This tendency is enhanced by the fact that group actions frequently involve the participation of many people. As a result, responsibility for what an organization does can become fragmented or diffused throughout the group, with no single individual seeing himself or herself as responsible for what happens. Indeed, it may be difficult to say exactly who should be held accountable. This diffusion of responsibility inside an organization leads individuals to have a diluted or diminished sense of their own personal moral responsibilities. They tend to see themselves simply as small players in a process or as cogs in a machine, over which they have no control and for which they are unaccountable. They rationalize to themselves contributing to actions, policies, or events that they would refuse to perform or to authorize if they thought the decision were entirely up to them. "It's not my fault," they think. "This would happen anyway, with or without me." Diffusion of responsibility encourages the moral myopia of thinking, "I'm just doing my job," instead of taking a 20/20 look at the bigger picture.

This sense of diminished individual moral responsibility for an outcome that many people bring about or allow to happen is something that social psychologists began studying more closely as a result of the sad case of Kitty Genovese, a young woman in New York City who was stabbed to death in 1964. Although the murder was not in itself so unusual, it made headlines and editorial pages across the United States because thirty-eight of her neighbours apparently witnessed her brutal slaying. In answer to her pitiful screams of terror at 3 a.m., they came to their windows and remained there for the thirty or more minutes it took her assailant to brutalize her. (He evidently left for a while and then returned to finish the job). Of the thirty-eight, not one attempted to intervene in any way; no one even phoned the police.

Why didn't Kitty Genovese's neighbours help her? Most social psychologists believe that an individual's sense of personal responsibility is inversely proportional to the number of people witnessing or involved in the episode. Thus, the greater the number of people observing an event, the less likely any of them will feel obliged to do anything. In emergencies, we seem naturally to let the behaviour of those around us dictate our response—a phenomenon often called *bystander apathy*. But the point is more general. In any large group or organization, diffusion of responsibility for its actions can lead individuals to feel anonymous and not accountable for what happens. Submerged in the group, the individual may not even question the morality of his or her actions.[14]

Pressure to conform to organizational norms and a diminished sense of personal responsibility for group behaviour undermine individual integrity and moral autonomy. Business corporations are not necessarily worse than many other groups in this respect, but certainly the pressure in business to help the company make a profit or achieve its other goals, to do what is expected of you, and generally to be a loyal and cooperative team player can foster, or at least do nothing to inhibit, these group propensities. Beyond that, many corporations fail to institutionalize ethics. They don't articulate or communicate ethical standards to their members; they don't actively enforce them; and they retain structures and policies that thwart individual integrity.

Although what is expected of members of a corporation sometimes clashes with their own moral values, they are rarely encouraged to deal with the conflict in an open, mature way. In fact, the more willing one is to suppress individual moral urges in the cause of organizational interests, the more "mature," "committed," and "loyal" one is considered to be; conversely, the less willing he or she is, the less "mature" and more "suspect." For example, when an employee of the American company Beech-Nut expressed concerns about the fact that the concentrate the company was producing for its "100% pure" apple juice contained nothing more than sugar water and chemicals, his annual performance review described his judgment as "colored by naïveté and impractical ideals."[15] Or consider the reports of Wall Street analysts pressured by their firms to recommend to clients stocks or bonds the analysts knew to be "junk" or "dogs."[16] Employees frequently have to fight hard to maintain their moral integrity in a showdown with organizational priorities.

Often, however, the problem facing us is not that of doing what we know to be right, but rather of deciding what is the right thing to do. We need to answer many difficult and puzzling moral questions in our business and organizational contexts. How do we go about doing that?

Is there some reliable procedure or method for answering moral questions? In science, the scientific method tells us what steps to take if we seek to answer a scientific question, but there is no comparable "moral method" for engaging moral questions. There is, however, general agreement about what constitutes good moral reasoning.

MORAL REASONING

It is useful to view moral reasoning at first in the context of *argument*. An argument is a group of statements, one of which (called the *conclusion*) is claimed to follow from the others (called the *premises*). Here's an example of an argument:

Argument 1

If a person is a mother, the person is a female.

Fran is a mother.

Therefore, Fran is a female.

The first two statements (the premises) of this argument happen to entail the third (the conclusion), which means that if I accept the first two as true, then I must accept also the third as true. Not to accept the conclusion while accepting the premises would result in a contradiction— holding two beliefs that cannot both be true at the same time. In other words, if I believe that all mothers are females and Fran is a mother (the premises), then I cannot deny that Fran is a female (the conclusion) without contradicting myself. An argument like this one, whose premises logically entail its conclusion, is termed *valid*.

An *invalid* argument is one whose premises do not entail its conclusion. In an invalid argument, I can accept the premises as true and reject the conclusion without any contradiction. Thus:

Argument 2

If a person is a mother, the person is a female.

Fran is a female.

Therefore, Fran is a mother.

The conclusion of this argument does not necessarily follow from the true premises. I can believe that every mother is a female and that Fran is a female and deny that Fran is a mother without contradicting myself.

One way to show this is by means of a *counterexample*, an example consistent with the premises but inconsistent with the conclusion. Let's suppose Fran is a two-year-old, a premise perfectly consistent with the two stated premises. If she is, she can't possibly be a mother. Or let's suppose Fran is an adult female who happens to be childless, another premise perfectly consistent with the stated premises but obviously at odds with the conclusion. If an argument is valid (such as Argument 1), then no counterexamples are possible.

A valid argument can have untrue premises, as in the following:

Argument 3

If a person is a female, she must be a mother.

Fran is a female.

Therefore, Fran must be a mother.

Like Argument 1, this one is valid. If I accept its premises as true, I must accept its conclusion as true; otherwise I will contradict myself. Although valid, this argument is unsound because one of its premises is false—namely, "If a person is a female, she must be a mother." Realizing the patent absurdity of one of its premises, no sensible person would accept this argument's conclusion. But notice why the argument is unsound—not because the reasoning procedure is invalid but because one of the premises is false. *Sound arguments*, such as Argument 1, have true premises and valid reasoning. *Unsound arguments* have at least one false premise, as in Argument 3, or invalid reasoning, as in Argument 2.

Now let's consider some *moral arguments*, which can be defined simply as arguments whose conclusions are moral judgments, assertions about the moral worth of a person, action, activity, policy, or organization. Here are some examples that deal with affirmative action for women and minorities in the workplace:

Argument 4

If an action violates the law, it is morally wrong.

Affirmative action on behalf of women and minorities in personnel matters violates the law.

Therefore, affirmative action on behalf of women and minorities in personnel matters is morally wrong.

Argument 5

If an action violates the will of the majority, it is morally wrong.

Affirmative action on behalf of women and minorities in personnel matters violates the will of the majority.

Therefore, affirmative action on behalf of women and minorities in personnel matters is morally wrong.

Argument 6

If an action redresses past injuries that have disadvantaged a group, it is morally permissible.

Affirmative action on behalf of women and minorities in personnel matters redresses injuries that have disadvantaged these groups.

Therefore, affirmative action on behalf of women and minorities in personnel matters is morally permissible.

Argument 7

If an action is the only practical way to remedy a social problem, then it is morally permissible.

Affirmative action on behalf of women and minorities in personnel matters is the only practical way to remedy the social problem of unequal employment opportunity.

Therefore, affirmative action on behalf of women and minorities in personnel matters is morally permissible.

The first premise in each of these arguments is a moral standard, the second an alleged fact, and the conclusion a moral judgment. *Moral reasoning* or argument typically moves from a moral standard, through one or more factual judgments about some person, action, or policy related to that standard, to a moral judgment about that person, action, or policy. Good moral reasoning will frequently be more complicated than these examples; often it will involve an appeal to more than one standard as well as to various appropriate factual claims. Still, these examples illustrate its most basic form.

Defensible Moral Judgments

If a moral judgment or conclusion is defensible, then it must be supportable by a defensible moral standard, together with relevant facts. A moral standard supports a moral judgment if (1) the standard, taken together with the relevant facts, logically entails the moral judgment, and (2) the standard itself is a sound standard. If someone argues that affirmative action for minorities and women is right (or wrong) but cannot produce a supporting principle when asked, then the person's position is considerably weakened. And if the person does not see any need to support the judgment by appeal to a moral standard, then he or she simply does not understand how moral concepts are used or is using moral words like "right" or "wrong" differently from the way they are commonly used.

Keeping this in mind—that moral judgments must be supportable by moral standards and facts—will aid your understanding of moral discourse, which can be highly complex and sophisticated. It will also sharpen your own critical faculties and improve your moral reasoning and ability to formulate relevant moral arguments.

Patterns of Defense and Challenge

In assessing arguments, one must be careful to clarify the meanings of their key terms and phrases. Often premises can be understood in more than one way, and this ambiguity may lead people to accept (or reject) arguments that they shouldn't. For example, "affirmative action" seems to mean different things to different people (see Chapter 9 on job discrimination). Before we can profitably assess Arguments 4 through 7, we have to agree on how we understand "affirmative action." Again, Argument 5 relies on the idea of "violating the will of the majority," but this notion has to be clarified before we can evaluate either the moral principle that it is wrong to violate the will of the majority or the factual claim that affirmative action does violate the majority's will.

Assuming that the arguments are logically valid in their form (as Arguments 4 through 7 are) and that their terms have been clarified and possible ambiguities eliminated, then we must turn our attention to assessing the premises of the arguments. Should we accept or reject their premises? Remember that if an argument is valid and you accept the premises, you must also accept the conclusion.

Let's look at some further aspects of this assessment process:

1. *Evaluating the factual claims.* If the parties to an ethical discussion are willing to accept the moral standard (or standards) in question, then they can concentrate on the factual claims. Thus, for example, in Argument 4 they will focus on whether affirmative action on behalf of women and minorities is in fact illegal. In Argument 7 they will need to determine whether affirmative action is really the only practical way to remedy the social problem of unequal employment opportunity. Analogous questions can be asked about the factual claims of Arguments 5 and 6. Answering them in the affirmative would require considerable supporting data.

2. *Challenging the moral standard.* Moral arguments generally involve more than factual disputes. The moral standards they appeal to might be controversial. One party might challenge the moral standard on which the argument relies, contending that it is not a plausible one and hence not acceptable. The critic might do this in several different ways—for example, by showing that there are exceptions to the standard, that the standard leads to unacceptable consequences, or that it is inconsistent with the arguer's other moral beliefs.

In the following dialogue, for example, Lynn is attacking Sam's advocacy of the standard "If an action redresses past injuries that have disadvantaged a group, it is morally permissible."

Lynn: What would you think of affirmative action for Jews in the workplace?
Sam: I'd be against it.
Lynn: What about Catholics?
Sam: No.
Lynn: People of Irish extraction?
Sam: They should be treated the same as anybody else.
Lynn: But each of these groups and more I could mention were victimized in the past by unfair discrimination and probably in some cases continue to be.
Sam: So?
Lynn: So the standard you're defending leads to a judgment you reject: namely, that Jews, Catholics, and Irish should be compensated by affirmative action for having been disadvantaged. How do you account for this inconsistency?

At this point Sam, or any rational person in a similar position, has three alternatives: abandon or modify the standard, alter his moral judgment, or show how women and minorities fit the original principle even though the other groups do not.

3. *Defending the moral standard.* When the standard is criticized, then its advocate must defend it. Often this requires invoking an even more general principle. A defender of Argument 6, for example, might defend the redress principle by appealing to some more general conception of social justice. Or defenders might try to show how the standard in question entails other moral judgments that both the critic and the defender accept, thereby enhancing the plausibility of the standard. In the following exchange, Lynn is defending the standard of Argument 5: "If an action violates the will of the majority, it is morally wrong":

Lynn: Okay, do you think the government should impose a national religion on all Canadians?
Sam: Of course not.
Lynn: What about requiring people to register their handguns?
Sam: I'm all for it.
Lynn: And using kids in pornography?
Sam: There rightly are laws against it.
Lynn: But the principle you're objecting to—that an action violating the will of the majority is wrong—leads to these judgments that you accept.

Of course, Lynn's argument is by no means a conclusive defence for her moral standard. Other moral standards could just as easily entail the judgments she cites, as Sam is quick to point out:

Sam: Now wait a minute. I oppose a state religion on constitutional grounds, not because it violates majority will. As for gun control, I'm for it because I think it will reduce violent crimes. And using kids in pornography is wrong because it exploits and endangers children.

Although Lynn's strategy for defending the standard about majority rule proved inconclusive, it does illustrate a common and often persuasive way of arguing for a moral principle.

4. *Revising and modifying the argument.* Arguments 4 through 7 are only illustrations, and all the moral principles they mention are very simple—too simple to accept without qualification. (The principle that it is immoral to break the law in all circumstances, for example, is implausible. Nazi Germany furnishes an obvious counterexample to it.) But once the standard has been effectively challenged, the defender of the argument, rather than abandon it altogether, might try to reformulate it. For instance, the defender might replace the original, contested premise with a better and more plausible one that still supports the conclusion. Premise 1 of Argument 4 might be replaced by "If an action violates a law that is both democratically decided and not morally unjust, then

the action is immoral." Or the defender might revise the conclusion of his or her argument, perhaps by restricting its scope. A more modest, less sweeping conclusion will often be easier to defend.

In this way, the discussion continues, the arguments on both sides of an issue improve, and we make progress in the analysis and resolution of ethical issues. In general, in philosophy we study logic and criticize arguments not to be able to score quick debating points but rather to be able to think better and more deeply about moral and other problems. Our goal as moral philosophers is not to "win" arguments but to arrive at the truth—or, put less grandly, to find the most reasonable answer to an ethical question.

Requirements for Moral Judgments

Moral discussion and the analysis of ethical issues can take various, often complicated, paths. Nevertheless, the preceding discussion implies certain minimum adequacy requirements for moral judgments. Although there is no complete list of adequacy criteria, moral judgments should be (1) logical, (2) based on facts, and (3) based on sound or defensible moral principles. A moral judgment that is weak on any of these grounds is open to criticism.

Moral Judgments Should Be Logical To say that moral judgments should be logical implies several things. First, as indicated in the discussion of moral reasoning, our moral judgments should follow logically from their premises. The connection between (1) the standard, (2) the conduct or policy, and (3) the moral judgment should be such that (1) and (2) logically entail (3). Our goal is to be able to support our moral judgments with reasons and evidence, rather than basing them solely on emotion, sentiment, or social or personal preference.

Second, our moral judgments should be logically compatible with our other moral and non-moral beliefs. We must avoid inconsistency. Almost all philosophers agree that if we make a moral judgment—for example, that it was wrong of Smith to alter the figures she gave to the outside auditors—then we must be willing to make the same judgment in any similar set of circumstances—that is, if our friend Brown, our spouse, or our father had altered the figures. In particular, we cannot make an exception for ourselves, judging something permissible for us to do while condemning others for doing the very same thing.

Moral Judgments Should Be Based on Facts
Adequate moral judgments cannot be made in a vacuum. We must gather as much relevant information as possible before making them. For example, an intelligent assessment of the morality of insider trading would require an understanding of, among other things, the different circumstances in which it can occur and the effects it has on the market and on other traders. The information supporting a moral judgment, the facts, should be relevant—that is, the information should actually relate to the judgment; it should be complete, or inclusive of all significant data; and it should be accurate or true.

Moral Judgments Should Be Based on Acceptable Moral Principles We know that moral judgments are based on moral standards. At the highest level of moral reasoning, these standards embody and express very general moral principles. Reliable moral judgments must be based on sound moral principles—principles that are unambiguous and can withstand critical scrutiny and rational criticism. What, precisely, makes a moral principle sound or acceptable is one of the most difficult questions that the study of ethics raises and is beyond the scope of this book. But one criterion is worth mentioning, what philosophers call our "considered moral beliefs."

These beliefs contrast with our gut responses, with beliefs based on ignorance or prejudice, and with beliefs we just happen to hold without having thought them through. As philosophy professor Tom Regan explains, our considered beliefs are those moral beliefs "we hold *after* we have made a conscientious effort . . . to think about our beliefs coolly, rationally, impartially, with conceptual clarity, and with as much relevant information as we can reasonably acquire."[17] We have grounds to doubt a moral principle when it clashes with such beliefs. Conversely, conformity with our considered moral judgments is good reason for regarding it as provisionally established.

This does not mean that conformity with our considered beliefs is the sole or even basic test of a moral principle, any more than conformity with well-established beliefs is the exclusive or even fundamental test of a scientific hypothesis. (Copernicus's heliocentric hypothesis, for example, did not conform to what passed in the medieval world as a well-considered belief, the Ptolemaic view that the earth was the centre of the universe.) But conformity with our considered beliefs seemingly must play some part in evaluating the many alternative moral principles that are explored in the next chapter.

SUMMARY

1. Ethics deals with individual character and the moral rules that govern and limit our conduct. It investigates questions of right and wrong, duty and obligation, and moral responsibility.
2. Business ethics is the study of what constitutes right and wrong (or good and bad) human conduct in a business context. Closely related moral questions arise in other organizational contexts.
3. Moral standards concern behaviour that has serious consequences for human well-being, and they take priority over other standards, including self-interest. Their soundness depends on the adequacy of the reasons that support or justify them.
4. Morality must be distinguished from etiquette (rules for well-mannered behaviour), from law (statutes, regulations, common law, and constitutional law),

and from professional codes of ethics (the special rules governing the members of a profession).

5. Morality is not necessarily based on religion. Although we draw our moral beliefs from many sources, for philosophers the issue is whether those beliefs can be justified.

6. Ethical relativism is the theory that right and wrong are determined by what one's society says is right and wrong. There are many problems with this theory. Also dubious is the theory that business has its own morality, divorced from ordinary ideas of right and wrong.

7. Accepting a moral principle involves a motivation to conform one's conduct to that principle. Violating the principle will bother one's conscience, but conscience is not a perfectly reliable guide to right and wrong.

8. Part of the point of morality is to make social existence possible by restraining self-interested behaviour. Sometimes doing what is morally right can conflict with one's personal interests. In general, though, following your moral principles will enable you to live a more satisfying life.

9. Morality as a code of conduct can be distinguished from morality in the broader sense of the values, ideals, and aspirations that shape a person's life.

10. Several aspects of corporate structure and function work to undermine individual moral responsibility.

Organizational norms, group commitment, and pressure to conform (sometimes leading to bystander apathy or groupthink) can all make the exercise of individual integrity difficult.

11. Moral reasoning consists of forming moral judgments, assessments of the moral worth of persons, actions, activities, policies, or organizations. Moral reasoning and argument typically appeal both to moral standards and to relevant facts. Moral judgments should be entailed by the relevant moral standards and the facts, and they should not contradict our other beliefs. Both standards and facts must be assessed when moral arguments are being evaluated.

12. Philosophical discussion generally involves the revision and modification of arguments; in this way progress is made in the analysis and resolution of moral and other issues.

13. Conformity with our considered moral beliefs is an important consideration in evaluating moral principles. A considered moral belief is one held only after we have made a conscientious effort to be conceptually clear, to acquire all relevant information, and to think rationally, impartially, and dispassionately about the belief and its implications. We should doubt any moral principle that clashes with many of our considered beliefs.

CASE 1.1

Made in Usacan—Dumped Elsewhere[18]

When it comes to the safety of young children, fire is a parent's nightmare. Just the thought of their young ones trapped in their cribs and beds by a raging nocturnal blaze is enough to make most mothers and fathers take every precaution to ensure their children's safety. Little wonder that when fire-retardant children's pajamas first hit the market, they proved an overnight success. Within a few short years more than 200 million pairs were sold, and the sales of millions more were all but guaranteed. For their manufacturers, the future could not have been brighter. Then, like a bolt from the blue, came word that the pajamas were killers. The Usacan Consumer Protection Directorate (UCPD) moved quickly to ban their sale and recall millions of pairs. Reason: The pajamas contained the flame-retardant chemical Tris (2,3-dibromoprophyl), which had been found to cause kidney cancer in children.

Because of its toxicity, the sleepwear couldn't even be thrown away, let alone sold. Indeed, the UCPD left no doubt about how the pajamas were to be disposed of—buried or burned or used as industrial wiping cloths. Whereas just months earlier the manufacturers of the Tris-impregnated pajamas couldn't fill orders fast enough, suddenly they were worrying about how to get rid of the millions of pairs now sitting in warehouses.

Soon, however, ads began appearing in the classified pages of a number of Usacan publications: "Tris-Tris-Tris . . . We will buy any fabric containing Tris," read one. Another said, "Tris—we will purchase any large quantities of garments containing Tris." The ads had been placed by exporters, who began buying up the pajamas, usually at 10 to 30 percent of the normal wholesale price. Their intent was clear: to dump the carcinogenic pajamas on overseas markets.

Tris is not the only example of dumping on the part of Usacan business. There is the case of the 450,000 baby pacifiers, of the type known to have caused choking deaths, that were exported for sale to a Third World country; and of the synthetic male hormone that was made available to another Third World country as an appetite stimulant for children, after it was found to stunt the growth of Usacan children; of the weed killer Gallant dumped in . . . you guessed it, yet another Third World country. The list goes on and on . . .

Manufacturers that dump products abroad clearly are motivated by profit, or at least by the hope of avoiding financial losses resulting from having to withdraw a product from their domestic market. For government and health agencies that cooperate in the exporting of dangerous products, sometimes the motives are more complex. For example, when Usacan researchers documented the dangers of the Perfor Ultra intrauterine device—among the adverse reactions were pelvic inflammation, blood poisoning, tubal pregnancies, and uterine perforations—its manufacturer

started losing its domestic market. As a result, the company worked out a deal with the Office of Population within the Usacan Directorate for International Assistance, whereby DIA bought thousands of the devices at a reduced price for use in population-control programs in forty-two underdeveloped countries.

Why do governmental and population-control agencies approve for sale and use overseas a birth control device proved dangerous in Usacan? They say their motives are humanitarian. Because the rate of dying in childbirth is high in Third World countries, almost any birth control device is preferable to none. Analogous arguments are used to defend the export of pesticides and other products judged too dangerous for use in Usacan: foreign countries should be free to decide for themselves whether the benefits of those products are worth their risks. In line with this, some Third World government officials insist that denying their countries access to these products is tantamount to violating their countries' national sovereignty.

This reasoning has found a sympathetic ear in Usacan, for it turns up in the "notification" system that regulates the export of banned or dangerous products overseas. Based on the principles of national sovereignty, self-determination, and free trade, the notification system requires that foreign governments be notified whenever a product is banned, deregulated, suspended, or cancelled by a Usacan regulatory agency. The Usacan Foreign Office, which implements the system, has a policy statement on the subject that reads in part: "No country should establish itself as the arbiter of others' health and safety standards. Individual governments are generally in the best position to establish standards of public health and safety."

Critics of the system claim that notifying foreign health officials is virtually useless. For one thing, other governments can rarely establish health standards or even control imports into their countries. Indeed, most of the Third World countries where banned or dangerous products are dumped lack regulatory agencies, adequate testing facilities, or well-staffed customs departments.

Then there's the problem of getting the word out about hazardous products. In theory, when regulatory government agencies in Usacan find a product hazardous, they are supposed to inform the Foreign Office, which is to notify local health officials. But agencies often fail to inform the Foreign Office of the product they have banned or found harmful, and when it is notified, its communiqués typically go no further than Usacan embassies abroad. When foreign officials are notified by Usacan embassies, they sometimes find the communiqués vague or ambiguous or too technical to understand.

But even if communication procedures were improved or the export of dangerous products forbidden, there are ways that companies can circumvent these threats to their profits—for example, by simply changing the name of the product or by exporting the individual ingredients of a product to a plant in a foreign country. Once there, the ingredients can be reassembled and the product dumped. Usacan does prohibit its pharmaceutical companies from exporting drugs banned within its jurisdiction, but sidestepping the law is not difficult. "Unless the package bursts open on the dock," one drug company executive observes, "you have no chance of being caught."

Ironically and unfortunately, the effects of overseas dumping may come home to Usacan. Some of the most toxic or dangerous pesticides (dieldrin, DDT, 2,4,5-T, etc.) are banned in Usacan. However, no law prohibits the sale of these banned pesticides overseas, where thanks to corporate dumping they are routinely used in agriculture. In one three-month period, for example, Usacan chemical companies exported four million pounds of banned and withdrawn pesticides. It is now estimated, through spot checks, that 10 percent of the food imported into Usacan is contaminated with residues of banned pesticides. With the doubling of imports of food stuffs from overseas, the problem of pesticide-laced food will only grow worse for Usacan consumers.

Discussion Questions

1. Complete the following statements by filling in the blanks with either "moral" or "non-moral" (for example, factual, scientific, legal):

   a. Whether dumping should be permitted is a _____ question.

   b. "Are dangerous products of any use in the Third World?" is a _____ question.

   c. "Is it proper for the Usacan government to sponsor the export of dangerous products overseas?" Is a _____ question.

   d. Whether the notification system works as its supporters claim it works is a _____ question.

   e. "Is it legal to dump this product overseas?" is a _____ question.

2. Explain what dumping is, giving some examples. Does dumping raise any moral issues? What are they? What would an ethical relativist say about dumping?

3. Speculate on why dumpers dump. Do you think they believe that what they are doing is morally permissible? How would you look at the situation if you were one of the manufacturers of Tris-impregnated pajamas?

4. If no law is broken, is there anything wrong with dumping? If so, when is it wrong and why? Do any moral considerations support dumping products overseas when this violates domestic law?

5. What moral difference, if any, does it make who is dumping, why they are doing it, where they are doing it, or what the product is?

6. Putting aside the question of legality, what moral arguments can be given *for* and *against* dumping? What is your position on dumping, and what principles and values do you base it on?

CASE 1.2

The Debate on Genetically Modified Crops and Food[19]

The rebuke of the Europe-wide ban on bioengineered crops and food by the World Trade Organization has sent anti-biotech advocacy groups scrambling. The United States, Argentina, and Canada had argued that the moratorium had more to do with protectionism than precaution, and the WTO agreed. Well-funded activists are now flooding the Internet with hysteria-grams trying to recast this stunning victory for common sense and careful science into a morality play: nefarious corporations aligned with bully nations (Canada?) force feeding "Frankenfoods" to helpless consumers.

Even before the lengthy and complex decision was handed down, Greenpeace blasted the WTO as "unqualified to deal with complex scientific and environmental issues." Friends of the Earth Europe scowled that "European safeguards" were being "sacrificed to benefit biotech corporations." The U.S.-based Consumers Union lambasted what it called a "preemptive effort to chill the development of new policies for regulating GM crops."

Let's separate the chaff from the wheat. If this decision is upheld by WTO members, Europe will not be forced to alter its regulations or labeling requirements or "force" consumers to "buy and eat food that they do not want," as Europe's leading consumer organization, BEUC, claims. It will demand the EU observe its own regulatory process—using sound science to evaluate new products. That's not been happening. Although the EU officially lifted its legal ban on GM crops and foods in 2004, squabbling among member states have left the moratorium in place, with 16 products bottled up in committees.

Some European countries have been exploiting the controversy to protect their farmers and keep prices high, international agreements and public policy be damned. Even with this ruling, political realities suggest this subterfuge may not end soon. Just last Monday, the Greek agricultural minister announced Greece would defy EU regulations and broaden its unauthorized ban on GM-modified maize seeds.

Greenpeace and Co. has been on the attack since the first generation of biotech crops—soybeans, wheat, cotton, and canola that generate natural insecticides, making them more resistant to pests and drought—were introduced more than a decade ago. Why? Because they were brought to market by corporations and aimed mostly at commodity crop farmers, biotech farming has generated enormous economic and environmental benefits, dramatically reducing reliance on environmentally harmful pesticides by supercharging the natural defenses of a crop using genetic material already in place or by introducing genes from other plants or animals.

We're now entering the second phase of the biotech revolution—addressing malnutrition and aiding smaller farmers. Scientists are developing nutrition-enhanced crops and foods such as "golden rice" that could help tens of millions of malnourished children who go blind or die each year from vitamin A deficiency. On the horizon are futuristic "farmaceuticals"—medicines made by melding basic methods of agriculture with advanced biotechnology, such as potatoes transformed into edible vaccines against diarrhea, a leading cause of death in the developing world.

Yet, in a dark, parallel universe of the privileged, anti-biotechnology groups contend we should abandon even these revolutionary lifesaving uses of crop biotechnology. Egged on by socially responsible investors and funded by the organic and natural product industries, which thrive on GM food scares, professional protestors are quick to cite the lowest common denominator in fabricated scientific disputes: the so-called "precautionary principle"—the controversial notion, rejected by mainstream science, that innovation should be shelved unless all risks can be avoided. They assert that "Trojan Horse" genes not subject to built-in checks and balances in nature could unleash a "genetic Godzilla," causing environmental havoc. Slogans like "better safe than sorry" may have a nice ring of moderation, but they are scientifically simplistic. There have been no documented health problems linked to GM crops and absolutely no evidence that genetic modification poses greater risks than crossbreeding and gene-splicing, which have given us such products as the tangelo and seedless grapes. The U.N.'s Food and Agriculture Organization has endorsed the safety and health benefits of biotech crops, urging their extension to the developing world.

The hypothetical risk of biotechnology has to be balanced against the lives being lost as new products remain trapped in a regulatory maze. In 2002, Zambia and Zimbabwe, wary of offending their major trading partners in the EU, cited the "precautionary principle" in rejecting donations of bioengineered grain that could have helped feed ten million undernourished people, thousands of whom ultimately died.

Today in the Philippines, where 42 percent of the diet comes from white rice, a recent study by UN food experts estimates that Golden Rice could avert 879 deaths, 1,925 corneal ulcers, and 15,398 cases of night blindness every year. A Philippines-based anti-biotechnology group with ties to Greenpeace has aggressively lobbied against Golden Rice on the grounds that the benefits from beta-carotene are minimal—claims rejected by scientists.

We should also be skeptical of opinion polls cited by biotech opponents suggesting that consumers, particularly in Europe, are dead set against these new products. "If you really want to understand whether European shoppers will buy genetically modified foods given the opportunity, ignore the agents provocateurs, the media, and the panicked reactions of the big supermarket chains, and look instead at the behavior of ordinary consumers," notes David Bowe, a member of the European parliament's Committee on Environment, Public Health and Consumer Policy. "When Safeway and Sainsbury's put GM tomato puree side by side with their non-GM counterpart in 1999 the proof was definitely in the puree. The GM product was seen to offer real added value. It was less expensive and in numerous blind tastings consumers seemed to prefer the flavor. It sold as well as the non-GM product."

While not a silver bullet, GM technology offers unique tools to address international food needs. Biotech crops are grown mostly in major farming nations like the U.S., Argentina, and Canada, but farmers in developing countries such as Brazil, China, India, and in Eastern Europe, with hungry stomachs to feed, are vigorously embracing the technology. Last year, 8.5 million farmers in 21 countries grew biotech crops on 222 million acres, an 11-percent year-to-year increase.

There are valid concerns about biotechnology, including the degree to which corporations should be allowed to patent beneficial seeds, keeping in mind that Monsanto, Bayer, Novartis, and other firms need to recoup their development costs, which have multiplied exponentially because of the country-by-country Rube Goldberg-like approval process.

But years of demagoguery and misinformation have taken an enormous toll—polluting public opinion, profoundly altering the trajectory of biotechnology applications, and damaging the financial wherewithal of corporations and university research projects. The biggest losers are the children, frozen out of the benefits of the green revolution that many of us take for granted.

Discussion Questions

1. What's the author's principal argument for the use of GM crops and foods?

2. How does he respond to fears of the hypothetical risks posed by GM foods? Do you think his response is (a) adequate and (b) fair to the opposition?

3. Consider the occurrence of "emotive" or value-laden terms used by the author and discuss the manner in which you think it affects the effectiveness of his appeal for the use of GM crops and foods.

4. Do you think that the author's position is presented from a "moral" point of view? Explain and defend your answer.

Notes to Chapter 1

1. For more on the Enron scandal, see Bethany McLean and Peter Elkind, *The Smartest Guys in the Room: The Amazing Rise and Scandalous Fall of Enron* (New York: Penguin, 2003), which is the basis of the fine 2005 documentary film *Enron: The Smartest Guys in the Room*. See also Kurt Eichenwald, *Conspiracy of Fools: A True Story* (New York: Broadway, 2005).

2. Cicero, *Selected Works* (London: Penguin, 1971), 177–180.

3. On characteristics of moral standards, see Manuel G. Velasquez, *Business Ethics*, 6th ed. (Upper Saddle River, NJ: Prentice Hall, 2006), 9–10.

4. Martin Luther King, Jr., "Letter from Birmingham Jail," in *Why We Can't Wait* (New York: Harper & Row, 1963), 85.

5. *Newsweek*, May 26, 1997, 54.

6. Albert Z. Carr, "Is Business Bluffing Ethical?," *Harvard Business Review* 46 (January/February 1968).

7. Ibid., 145.

8. Richard B. Brandt, *A Theory of the Good and the Right* (New York: Oxford University Press, 1979), 165–170.

9. James E. Post, Anne T. Lawrence, and James Weber, *Business and Society: Corporate Strategy, Public Policy, and Ethics*, 10th ed. (New York: McGraw-Hill, 2002), 104–105; "Shares of Corporate Nice Guys Can Finish First," *New York Times*, April 27, 2005 (online); Marjorie Kelly, "Holy Grail Found," *Business Ethics*, Winter 2004; and Thomas Donaldson, "Defining the Value of Doing Good Business," *Financial Times* (supplement on "Mastering Corporate Governance"), June 3, 2005, 2.

10. Joseph L. Badaracco, Jr., and Allen P. Webb, "Business Ethics: A View from the Trenches," *California Management Review* 37 (Winter 1995): 8.

11. See Milton Snoeyenbos, Robert Almeder, and James Humber, eds., *Business Ethics*, 3rd ed. (Buffalo, NY: Prometheus Books, 2001), 136.

12. Badaracco and Webb, "Business Ethics," 10.

13. See Solomon E. Asch, "Opinion and Social Pressure," *Scientific American*, November 1955, 31–35.

14. See Malcolm Gladwell, *The Tipping Point* (Boston: Little, Brown, 2000), 27–28, and John M. Doris, *Lack of Character* (Cambridge: Cambridge University Press, 2002), 28–29, 32–33.

15. Lynn Sharp Paine, "Managing for Organizational Integrity," *Harvard Business Review* 72 (March/April 1994): 108.

16. Barton G. Malkiel, "The Great Wall Street?," *Wall Street Journal*, October 14, 2002, A16.

17. Tom Regan, *Defending Animal Rights* (Urbana: University of Illinois Press, 2001), 45.

18. The basic facts outlined in this case are true. The names of countries and agencies are of course fictional.

19. Source: Jon Entine, "Let Them Eat Precaution: Beyond the WTO Decision on GMOs," *National Review Online*, February 08, 2006, at www.nationalreview.com/comment/entine200602080747.asp.

IT'S GOOD BUSINESS

ROBERT C. SOLOMON

Robert C. Solomon argues for the immediate, practical relevance of ethics for our business lives. He debunks the idea that business is fundamentally amoral or immoral. Business is not a blind scramble for profits and survival but rather an established practice with firmly fixed rules and expectations, and people in business are professionals. Although unethical business, like crime, sometimes pays, there is no conflict between ethical business behaviour and success. Solomon concludes with eight crucial rules for ethical thinking in business.

WHY ETHICS?

Seminars in business ethics . . . almost always begin with and are periodically brought back around to such practical questions as "What does this have to do with my job?" or "Will understanding ethics help me do my job better?"

Such questions deserve and demand three immediate, practical answers.

1. *Ethical errors end careers more quickly and more definitively than any other mistake in judgment or accounting.* To err is human, perhaps, but to be caught lying, cheating, stealing, or reneging on contracts is not easily forgotten or forgiven in the business world. And for good reason: Such actions undermine the ethical foundation on which the business world thrives. Almost everyone can have compassion for someone caught in an ethical dilemma. No one can excuse immorality.

For every glaring case of known unethical conduct that goes unpunished, a dozen once-promising careers silently hit a dead end or quietly go down the tubes. On relatively rare occasions, an unhappy executive or employee is singled out and forced to pay public penance for conduct that everyone knows—he or she and the attorney will loudly protest—"goes on all the time." But much more often, unethical behavior, though unearthed, will go unannounced; indeed, the executive or employee in question will keep his or her job and may not even find out that he or she has been found out—may never even realize the unethical nature of his or her behavior. A career will just go nowhere. Responsibilities will remain routine, promotions elusive.

What makes such career calamities so pathetic is that they are not the product of greed or immorality or wickedness. They are the result of ethical naiveté.

They happen because an employee unthinkingly "did what he was told to do"—and became the scapegoat as well.

They happen because a casual public comment was ill-considered and had clearly unethical implications—though nothing of the kind may have been intended.

They happen because a middle manager, pressed from above for results, tragically believed the adolescent clichés that pervade the mid-regions of the business world, such as "In business, you do whatever you have to do to survive."

(It is both revealing and instructive that although we often hear such sentiments expressed in seminars for middle managers, we virtually never hear them in similar seminars for upper-level executives.)

They happen because upper management wasn't clear about standards, priorities, and limits, or wasn't reasonable in its expectations, or wasn't available for appeal at the critical moment.

They happen because an anonymous employee or middle manager hidden in the complexity of a large organization foolishly believed that such safe anonymity would continue, whatever his or her behavior.

They happen, most of all, because a person in business is typically trained and pressured to "think business," without regard for the larger context in which business decisions are made and legitimized.

Unethical thinking isn't just "bad business"; it is an invitation to disaster in business, however rarely (it might sometimes seem) unethical behavior is actually found out and punished. . . .

2. *Ethics provides the broader framework within which business life must be understood.* There may be a few people for whom business is all of life, for whom family and friendship are irrelevant, for whom money means only more investment potential and has nothing to do with respect or status or enjoying the good life. But most successful executives understand that *business is part of life.* Corporations are part of a society that consists of something more than a market. Executives and employees do not disappear into their jobs as if into a well, only to reappear in "real life" at the end of the business day.

Successful managers, we now all know, stay close to their subordinates—and not just as subordinates. The best corporations in their "search for excellence" begin and remain close to their customers, and not just in their narrowest role as consumers. Money may be a scorecard, a measure of status and accomplishment, but it is not the ultimate end. Business success, like happiness, often comes most readily to those who do not aim at it directly.

Executives are most effective and successful when they retain their "real life" view of themselves, their position, and the human world outside as well as inside the corporation. Business ethics, ultimately, is just business in its larger human context. . . .

3. *Nothing is more dangerous to a business—or to business in general—than a tarnished public image.* A few years ago, *Business and Society Review* reported the results of a Harris Poll—one among many—that showed that public confidence in the executives running major corporations had declined "drastically" . . . ; 87% of the respondents in a parallel poll agreed that most businessmen were more interested in profits than in the public interest. Whether or not such suspicions seriously affect sales, they indisputably hurt the bottom line in a dozen other hurtful ways—not least among them the pressure for government regulation. The fact is that a tarnished image has direct consequences, for sales, for profits, for morale, for the day-to-day running of the business. Distrust of an industry ("big oil," "the insurance racket") can hurt every company, and distrust of an individual company can quickly drive it to bankruptcy. . . .

THE MYTH OF AMORAL BUSINESS

Business people have not always been their own best friends. John D. Rockefeller once boasted that he was quite willing to pay a man an annual salary of a million dollars, if the man had certain qualities:

> [He] must know how to glide over every moral restraint with almost childlike disregard . . . [and have], besides other positive qualities, no scruples whatsoever, and [be] ready to kill off thousands of victims—without a murmur.
> —Robert Warshow, *Jay Gould* (1928)

Such talk is unusually ruthless, but it exemplifies horribly a myth that has often clouded business thinking—what University of Kansas business ethicist Richard De George calls the "myth of amoral business." According to the myth, business and ethics don't mix. People in business are concerned with profits, with producing goods and services, with buying and selling. They may not be immoral, but they are amoral—that is, not concerned with morals. Moralizing is out of place in business. Indeed, even good acts are to be praised not in moral terms but only in the cost/benefit language of "good business."

The myth of amoral business has a macho, mock-heroic corollary that makes ethical paralysis almost inevitable. It is the dog-eat-dog rhetoric of the Darwinian jungle—"survival of the fittest." In fact, almost everybody and most companies manage to survive without being the "fittest." The anxiety of switching jobs, of not getting promotions, of losing an investment, or of going bankrupt, however upsetting, is rarely a "matter of life and death." In *The Right Stuff,* Tom Wolfe sympathetically quotes the wife of one of the Air Force test pilots. She mentions a friend's complaint about her husband's dog-eat-dog existence on Madison Avenue and reflects, "What if her husband went into a meeting with a one-in-four chance of survival?"

If the myth of amoral business and its Darwinian corollary were nothing but a way of talking on the way to the office, it would not be worth attention or criticism. But the fact is that it does enter into business thinking, and often at exactly the critical moment when an ethical decision is to be made. Worse, the amoral rhetoric of business quickly feeds public suspicion of business and easily becomes part of the condemnation of business. A handful of scandals and accidents that might otherwise be viewed as the unfortunate byproducts of any enterprise become "proof" of what the businessmen themselves have been saying all along—that there is no interest in ethics in business, only the pursuit of profits. . . .

Business people who do not talk about ethics often complain a great deal about "regulation" without realizing that the two are intimately connected. Legal regulation is the natural response of both society and government to the practice of amorality, however nobly that practice is couched in the rhetoric of "free enterprise." If a business scandal or tragedy is quickly and convincingly chastised by business people, there is neither time nor pressure for regulation. But when scandal and tragedy are at the same time surrounded by ethical neglect or silence or, worse, yet another appeal to "the market" as the long-term corrective, government regulation becomes inevitable. In case anyone still wants to ask why ethics should be relevant to the bottom line, one might simply reply that regulation is the price business pays for bad ethical strategy. . . .

THE THREE Cs OF BUSINESS ETHICS

. . . Business ethics is not an attack on business but rather its first line of defense. Adam Smith knew this well enough: Business has prospered because business has dramatically improved the quality of life for all of us. Moreover, the emphasis on freedom and individuality in a business society has done more than any conceivable socialist revolution to break down traditional inequities in power and wealth, even if it inevitably creates some inequities of its own. Business ethics begins with consumer demand and productivity, with the freedom to engage in business as one wishes, and with the hope—inconceivable in most parts of the world— that one can better one's life considerably through one's own hard work and intelligence. These are the values of business ethics, and the whole point of business ethics is to define and defend the basic goals of prosperity, freedom, fairness, and individual dignity.

Many critics of business are trained in the rhetoric of ethics, but most business people are not. Those in business naturally prefer to stick with what they know and sidestep the ethical issues—which is ruinous. It is one thing to know that product Z costs $0.14 to make and retails for $1.59, that raising the price to $1.79 would increase profits and not dampen demand, that cheaper materials or foreign labor could lower the cost of manufacturing to $0.09, although sales would eventually diminish as consumer expectations went unsatisfied. But it is something more to think about the quality of product Z, the contribution it makes to American life (even if only by way of amusement or novelty). Not incidentally, these ethical virtues may be essential to the bottom line as well.

Business ethics is nothing less than the full awareness of what one is doing, its consequences and complications. Thinking about ethics in business is no more than acknowledging that one has taken these into account and is willing to be responsible for them. It is being aware of

1. the need for *compliance* with the rules, including the laws of the land, the principles of morality, the customs and expectations of the community, the policies of the company, and such general concerns as fairness;

2. the *contributions* business can make to society, through the value and quality of one's products or services, by way of the jobs one provides for workers and managers, through the prosperity and usefulness of one's activities to the surrounding community;

3. the *consequences of* business activity, both inside and outside the company, both intended and unintended, including the reputation of one's own company and industry. . . .

Part of the problem for business ethics is the image of business as "big" business, as a world of impersonal corporations in which the individual is submerged and ethics is inevitably sacrificed to bureaucratic objectives. To set the image straight, therefore, let us remind ourselves of a single vital statistic: Half of American business is family business; 50% of the GNP; 50% of the employees. Some of these family businesses are among the Fortune 500. Others are Mom and Pop groceries and Sally and Lou's Restaurant. But it is essential to remember that however much our focus may be on corporations and corporate life, business in America is not a monolithic, inhuman enterprise. As the great French philosopher Rousseau once said of society, we might say of American business life that its origins are in the family, that its "natural" model *is* the family. Business is ultimately about relationships between people—our compliance with the rules we all form together, our contributions to the well-being of others as well as to our own, the consequences of our activities, for good and otherwise. There is nothing amoral or unethical about it. . . .

BUSINESS SCUM

The most powerful argument for ethics in business is success. Ethical businesses are successful businesses; excellence is also ethical. But ethics is no guarantee of success. To say so on our part would be—unethical. The fact is that there are, as we all know, business scum—those shifty, snatch-a-buck operations that give business a bad name. And some of them, ethics be damned, are profitable.

Brake Breakers, Inc., is a small franchise in the Midwest that specializes in brake, suspension, and wheel repairs. Company policy includes hiring men with little education and working them long hours at a single semiskilled job. Wages are accordingly minimal, and employee turnover is more often a matter of burnout than of leaving for another job. (This saves a lot on fringe benefits and pensions; no one has ever collected on them.)

Foremost among the employees' skills, however, is the delivery of a prepackaged sermon designed to convince all but the most cautious customer that the $149.25 brake-rebuilding special is far preferable to the mere replacement of the brake shoes, which is all that is usually required (and often all that is actually done).

Managers are rewarded on the basis of the success of these little speeches by their employees. Their job is first and foremost to make sure that the minimum is never enough—not hard given the level of mechanical know-how of most of the customers. But even with the $149.25 special, extra costs are almost always included, sometimes for some other (unnecessary) part but more often than not because of the "unexpected difficulty" of this particular repair. When a customer insists on the minimum repair, it is up to the manager to see to it that more absolutely necessary work is "discovered" in the middle of the job. (This is called the "step method.") Few customers are in a position to do more than complain and curse for the moment, but no one ever expects them to come back anyway.

Managers are expected to keep actual costs down. Used parts are sold in place of new parts. (Sometimes, the car's original part is cleaned or polished and simply reinstalled.) A few miles down the road, who can tell?

Within the company, employees are reminded daily, "There are fifty people waiting for your job." Everyone is hired with the promise "Within three years, you can work up to a managerial position." In fact, managers are always hired from outside—typically friends of the boss. (It is understood that they will supplement their salaries by skimming within the shop.) Managerial turnover, accordingly, is low. Brake Breakers is not the sort of company that can afford to have a disgruntled manager quit in disgust, although any charges he might bring against the company could dependably be turned against him as well.

Brake Breakers, Inc., is everyone's stereotypical image of unethical business in action. Its people sell a shoddy product to customers who don't need it, and they don't always sell what they say they are selling. Employees are treated like serfs, and accounting procedures at every level of the company are, to put it politely, suspect. The customer is virtually never satisfied, but it is the nature of the business that people who need brake repairs need them fast and do not know what has to be done or how much it should cost. They are ripe for the taking, and they are taken. The price is still low enough and the job near enough adequate that no one sues. The "lifetime guarantee" isn't worth the paper it's printed on, but it is a fact about brake jobs that there is only so much that can go wrong, and a disgruntled customer usually doesn't bother coming back anyway. It's a perfect setup. At least half of the profits, even on a modest system of objective ethical accounting, are obtained by cheating the customer and the employees.

How does Brake Breakers, Inc., stack up according to our three Cs of business ethics? Not very well.

Compliance: Minimal; just enough to avoid legal penalties and major lawsuits but far below the level of concern for ethics that we all expect of every business.

Contributions: Well, they do fix brakes, even if some of them aren't broken. But a dozen more dependable businesses—both national franchises and local service stations—would do a better job with less flimflam. To provide a service is not in itself a contribution. We also want to know if it is a service that would otherwise be performed as well and as cheaply by other firms.

Consequences: Disgruntled customers, hesitation among motorists to have their brakes checked when they ought to, occasional accidents, a notoriously bad reputation for car-repair shops in general (hurting those that do good, honest work), and an exemplary case of unethical business to turn consumers and congressional investigators against business in general.

It is too often supposed that the business of business ethics is to prove to the management of such unethical enterprises as Brake Breakers, Inc., that crime does not pay. That is too much to ask for.

- Show them, perhaps, that they are setting themselves up for lawsuits.

  In fact, it just hasn't happened.

- Show them, then, that they are losing customers.

  In fact, it is a business with a regular supply of customers, no repeat customers in any case and little dependence on word of mouth. (In fact, they depend on the absence of word of mouth, since people are often too ashamed at having been "taken" to tell their friends about it.)

- Show them how well Midas and Meineke [another well-known U.S. company in the automobile service industry] have been doing because of their reputation for dependability.

  But, the manager at Brake Breakers tells us with a laugh, "We ain't Midas."

- Argue, then, that unethical business practices cannot possibly pay off in the long run.

  "In the long run," the amused manager tells us, unknowingly echoing the economist John Maynard Keynes, "we're all dead."

The fact—sad, perhaps—is that unethical business, like crime, sometimes pays. In any system based on trust, a few deceivers will prosper. There is no guarantee that ethics is good for the bottom line. There is no guarantee that those who do wrong will get caught or feel guilty. There is no guarantee—in business or elsewhere—that the wicked will suffer and the virtuous will be rewarded (at least, not in this life). But, that said, we can nonetheless insist without apology that good ethics is good business. Where immorality is so easily identified, we can be sure that morality is the general rule, not merely an accessory or an exception. The *point* of doing business is to do well by providing the best service or product at a reasonable cost. Those businesses that exploit the *possibility* of getting away with less are merely parasitic on the overwhelming number of businesses that are doing what they are supposed to.

PRACTICES MAKE PERFECT: A BETTER WAY TO LOOK AT BUSINESS

A practice is any association of definitely patterned human behavior wherein the description and meaning of kinds of behavior involved and the kinds of expectations involved are dependent upon those rules which define the practice.
—John Rawls
(professor of philosophy, Harvard University)

Business is not a scramble for profits and survival. It is a way of life, an established and proven *practice* whose prosperity and survival depend on the participation of its practitioners. Business ethics is not ethics applied to business. It is the foundation of business. Business life thrives on competition, but it survives on the basis of its ethics.

Business is first of all a cooperative enterprise with firmly fixed rules and expectations. A view from a visitors' gallery down to the floor of the New York Stock Exchange may not look very much like a cooperative enterprise with fixed rules and expectations, but beneath the apparent chaos is a carefully orchestrated set of agreements and rituals without which the Exchange could not operate at all. There can be no bogus orders, and bid ranges are carefully controlled. The use of information is restricted, but traders trade information as well as securities. The rules of the Exchange, contrary to superficial appearances, are uncompromising. Break them and you're off the floor for good. Right there at the busy heart of capitalism, there is no question that *business is a practice*, and people in business are *professionals*.

In business ethics, it is often profitable to compare business with a game. Games are also practices. Baseball, for instance, is a practice. It has its own language, its own gestures with their own meanings, its own way of giving significance to activities that, apart from the game, might very well mean nothing at all. (Imagine a person who suddenly runs and slides into a canvas bag filled with sand on the sidewalk, declaring himself "safe" as he does so.) The practice is defined by certain sorts of behavior—"pitching" the ball in a certain way (if, that is, the practice designates you as the "pitcher"), trying to hit the ball with a certain well-defined implement (the "bat"), running a certain sequence of "bases" in a certain order subject to certain complex restrictions (one of which is that one not be "tagged" by another person holding the ball). Anyone who has tried to explain what is happening in a baseball game to a visitor from another country with a different "national pastime" can attest to the complexity of these rules and definitions, though most Americans feel quite familiar with them and can focus their attention—as players or as spectators—on such simple-sounding concerns as "Who's up?" and "Who's on first?"

Business is like baseball in that it is a practice. A day at the stock exchange makes it quite clear just how many rituals, rules, and restrictions are involved in every buy-and-sell transaction. . . . The business world is far more open to extra "players" and to alternative courses of action than is baseball, but within the institutions that make up the practice of business, roles and alternatives are clearly specified—as "jobs" and "positions," as obligations and options. Strategic ethics begins by emphasizing business as a practice with strict rules and expectations that acceptable players honor implicitly—or they are out of the game. To throw out players who cheat is as important to a healthy enterprise as is the inevitable exit of players who can't play well. Bad business is much more damaging to business than are badly run businesses.

Business, like baseball, is defined by its rules. Some of these have to do with the nature of contracts. Many have to do with fairness in dealing with employees, customers, and government agents (hence the existence of such policing bodies as the Internal Revenue Service, the Securities and Exchange Commission, the Food and Drug Administration, etc.). Indeed, the notion of fairness in exchanges is more central to business than to any other practice—whether in terms of work and salary, price and product, or public services and subsidies. Without fairness as the central expectation, there are few people who would enter into the market at all. (Consider the chill on the market following dramatic "insider trading" cases.) Without the recognition of fair play, the phrase "free enterprise" would be something of a joke. The rules of business, accordingly, have mainly to do with fairness. Some of these rules ensure that the market will remain open to everyone. Some of the rules protect those who are not players in the practice but whose health, jobs, or careers are affected by it. Some of the rules have to do with serving the needs or wishes of the community (the law of supply and demand can be interpreted not only as an economic mechanism but as an ethical imperative). Some have to do with "impact"—the effects of a business on its surrounding communities and environment. If business had no effects on the surrounding community but was rather a self-enclosed game, there would be no more public cry for business ethics than for "hopscotch ethics" (which is not to say that there is no ethics to hopscotch).

It is within this description of a practice that we can also define the terms "virtue" and "vice" in business ethics. Some virtues and vices go far beyond the bounds of business, of course; they are matters of morality (honesty, for instance). But in business ethics there are virtues and vices that are particular to business and to certain business roles. Close accounting and "watching every penny" are virtues in a shipping clerk but not in someone who is entertaining a client. Keeping a polite distance is a virtue in a stockholder but not in a general manager. Tenaciousness may be a virtue in a salesman but not in a consultant. Outspokenness may be a virtue in a board member but not in the assistant to the president. Being tough-minded is a virtue in some managerial roles but not in others.

In general, we can say this: A virtue sustains and improves a practice. A virtue in business is an ethical trait that makes business in general possible, and this necessarily includes such virtues as respect for contracts as well as concern for product quality, consumer satisfaction, and the bottom line. A vice, on the other hand, degrades and undermines the practice. Shady dealing and reneging on contracts are vices and unethical not because of an absolute moral law but because they undermine the very practice that makes doing business possible.

Thinking about business as a practice and business people as professionals gives us a set of persuasive responses to the Brake Breakers case:

1. Business in general depends on the acceptance of rules and expectations, on mutual trust and a sense of fairness, even if—as in any such practice—a few unscrupulous participants can take advantage of that trust and betray that concern for fairness.

2. Brake Breakers, Inc., can continue to prosper in their scummy ways only so long as they remain relatively insignificant, with a small enough market share not to bring down the wrath of major competitors and sufficiently little publicity not to inspire a class-action suit. Unethical behavior may bring profits, but only limited profits.

3. It is clearly in the interest of business in general and other firms in that particular industry to warn consumers about Brake Breakers, even to put them out of business. The success and strength of a profession and its independence from externally imposed regulations depends on the internal "policing" of unethical behavior. Doctors have never doubted this; lawyers are learning. But so long as business thinks of itself as unregulated competition where "anything goes" rather than as a profession to be protected from abuse, this vital policing for survival will go unattended, or it will be attended to by the government.

4. The practice of business is a small world. Fly-by-Night Enterprises Ltd. and Brake Breakers, Inc., may succeed for a while, but, in general, people catch on—fast. Irate customers tell their friends—and their lawyers. They also get even. They sue, for triple damages. They write the newspapers, or "60 Minutes." They drop a note to the IRS, or they call the Better Business Bureau. The banker's kid who was cheated on the job complains to his father the month before the lease has to be renewed. Or the victim happens to be a litigious lawyer with time on his hands. But the effects of unethical business practices are not always so obvious as a dip in the bottom line or a subpoena waiting at the office. They are often slow and insidious, the bottom of a career eaten out from under, or a company that is doing "OK" but could and should be doing much better. There are no guarantees that unethical behavior will be punished, but the odds are pretty impressive.

5. In any profession, it's hard to get clean again. Suppliers tighten their terms; priority status disappears. The hardheaded businessman is supposed to say "Who cares?" But if so, there are few hardheaded businessmen, only a small number of bottom-line-minded sociopaths. Character is who you are, the thing you are trying to prove by making money in the first place. One of the classic movie lines is "My money's as good as anyone else's." Perhaps. But are *you* as good? That isn't just a matter of money.

Why should Brake Breakers, Inc., get ethical? Let's ask another question: How would you feel about yourself if you spent your working days as a manager of Brake Breakers? What would you tell your kids? . . .

THINKING ETHICS: THE RULES OF THE GAME

Ethics is, first of all, a way of thinking. Being ethical is also—of course—*doing* the right thing, but what one does is hardly separable from how one thinks. Most people in business who do wrong do so not because they are wicked but because they think they are trapped and do not even consider the ethical significance or implications of their actions.

What is thinking ethically? It is thinking in terms of *compliance* with the rules, implicit as well as explicit, thinking in terms of the *contributions* one can make as well as one's own possible gains, thinking in terms of avoiding harmful *consequences* to others as well as to oneself. Accordingly, [here are] eight crucial rules for ethical thinking in business.

Rule No. 1: *Consider other people's well-being, including the well-being of non-participants.* In virtually every major religion this is the golden rule: "Do unto others as you would have them do unto you"; or, negatively, "Do not do unto others as you would not have them do unto you." Ideally, this might mean that one should try to maximize everyone's interests, but this is unreasonable. First of all, no one really expects that a businessman (or anyone else) would or should sacrifice his own interests for everyone else's. Second, it is impossible to take everyone into account; indeed, for any major transaction, the number of people who will be affected—some unpredictably—may run into the tens or hundreds of thousands. But we can readily accept a minimum version of this rule, which is to make a *contribution* where it is reasonable to do so and to avoid *consequences* that are harmful to others. There is nothing in the golden rule that demands that one deny one's own interests or make sacrifices to the public good. It says only that one must take into account human effects beyond one's own bottom line and weigh one's own gain against the losses of others.

Rule No. 2: *Think as a member of the business community and not as an isolated individual.* Business has its own rules of propriety and fairness. These are not just matters of courtesy and protocol; they are the conditions that make business possible. Respect for contracts, paying one's debts, and selling decent products at a reasonable price are not only to one's own advantage; they are necessary for the very existence of the business community.

Rule No. 3: *Obey, but do not depend solely on, the law.* It goes without saying, as a matter of prudence if not of morality, that businesses and business people ought to obey the law—the most obvious meaning of *compliance*. But what needs to be added is that ethical thinking is not limited to legal obedience. There is much unethical behavior that is not illegal, and the question of what is right is not always defined by the law. The fact is that many things that are not immoral or illegal are repulsive, disgusting, unfair, and unethical—belching aloud in elevators, throwing a disappointing dish at one's host at dinner, paying debts only after the "final notice" and the threat of a lawsuit arrives, fleecing the feebleminded, taking advantage of trust and good faith, selling faulty if not dangerous merchandise under the rubric "Buyer beware." Check the law—but don't stop there.

Rule No. 4: Think of yourself—and your company—as part of society. Business people and businesses are citizens in society. They share the fabric of feelings that make up society and, in fact, contribute much of that feeling themselves. Business is not a closed community. It exists and thrives because it serves and does not harm society. It is sometimes suggested that business has its own ethical rules and that they are decidedly different from those of the larger society. Several years ago business writer Albert Carr raised a major storm in the *Harvard Business Review* by arguing that business, like poker, had its own rules and that these were not to be confused with the moral rules of the larger society. The comparison with poker has its own problems, but, leaving those aside for now, we can see how such a view not only invites but *demands* the most rigorous regulation of business. Business is subject to the same ethical rules as everyone else because businessmen do *not* think of themselves as separate from society. A few years ago, the then chairman of the Ford Foundation put it bluntly: "Either we have a social fabric that embraces us all, or we're in real trouble." So too with ethics.

Rule No. 5: Obey moral rules. This is the most obvious and unavoidable rule of ethical thinking and the most important single sense of *compliance*. There may be room for debate about whether a moral rule applies. There may be questions of interpretation. But there can be no excuse of ignorance ("Oh, I didn't know that one isn't supposed to lie and cheat"), and there can be no unexcused exceptions ("Well, it would be all right to steal in *this* case"). The German philosopher Immanuel Kant called moral rules "categorical imperatives," meaning that they are absolute and unqualified commands for everyone, in every walk of life, without exception, not even for harried executives. This is, perhaps, too extreme to be practical, but moral rules are the heart of ethics, and there can be no ethics—and no business—without them.

Rule No. 6: Think objectively. Ethics is not a science, but it does have one feature in common with science: The rules apply equally to everyone, and being able to be "disinterested"—that is, to think for a moment from other people's perspectives—is essential. Whether an action is *right* is a matter quite distinct from whether or not it is in *your* interest. For that matter, it is quite independent of your personal opinions as well.

Rule No. 7: Ask the question "What sort of person would do such a thing?" Our word "ethics" comes from the Greek word *ethos*, meaning "character." Accordingly, ethics is not just obedience to rules so much as it is the concern for your personal (and company) character—your reputation and "good name"—and, more important, how you feel about yourself. Peter Drucker summarizes the whole of business ethics as "being able to look at your face in the mirror in the morning."

Rule No. 8: Respect the customs of others, but not at the expense of your own ethics. The most difficult kind of ethical thinking that people in business have to do concerns not a conflict between ethics and profits but rather the conflict between two ethical systems. In general, it is an apt rule of thumb that one should follow the customs and ethics of the community. But suppose there is a conflict not only of mores but of morals, as in the apartheid policies of South Africa. Then the rule to obey (and support) one's own moral principles takes priority. What is even more difficult is what one should do when the moral issue is not clear and moral categories vary from culture to culture. A much debated example is the question of giving money to expedite a transaction in many third-world countries. It is "bribery" in our system, "supporting public servants" in theirs. Bribery is illegal and unethical here because it contradicts our notion of a free and open market. But does the same apply in the third world, where business (and social life) have very different presuppositions?

Ethical thinking is ultimately no more than considering oneself and one's company as citizens of the business community and of the larger society, with some concern for the well-being of others and—the mirror image of this—respect for one-self and one's character. Nothing in ethics excludes financially sound thinking, and there is nothing about ethics that requires sacrificing the bottom line. In both the long and the short run, ethical thinking is essential to strategic planning. There is nothing unethical about making money, but money is not the currency of ethical thinking in business.

Review and Discussion Questions

1. Solomon describes the view that business and ethics don't mix as the "myth of amoral business." Why does he think it is a myth? Do you agree?

2. Do most businesspeople respect the "Three Cs"? In your experience, how much unethical behaviour is there in business today? What happens to companies like Brake Breakers? Can they be successful?

3. Does the existence of "business scum" undermine Solomon's claim that businesspeople are professionals and that business is a practice with definite rules?

4. What are the "rules of the game" in business today? Should those rules be changed in any way?

5. Assess Solomon's claim that "there is nothing about ethics that requires sacrificing the bottom line" (p. 29). Is it compatible with his statement "There is no guarantee that ethics is good for the bottom line" (p. 26)?

MORAL RESPONSIBILITY IN THE AGE OF BUREAUCRACY

DAVID LUBAN, ALAN STRUDLER, AND DAVID WASSERMAN

Large bureaucratic organizations frequently dilute an individual's sense of moral responsibility, and members of such organizations are all too likely to acquiesce in organizational misconduct. One reason for this is that inside the organization knowledge can be so fragmented that an individual may be partially or wholly ignorant of what the organization is doing. David Luban, Alan Strudler, and David Wasserman examine this problem. Whereas most moral theories presuppose that the moral agent knows that a decision must be made and what choices are available, these authors explore the moral responsibilities of individuals in organizational situations in which they lack this knowledge.

BACKGROUND OF THE PROBLEM

The bureaucratic fragmentation of knowledge and dilution of responsibility are pervasive phenomena in modern society. To set the stage for our analysis, we first describe the scope of the problem and briefly review some of the research, commentary, and debate it has provoked. We conclude this background section by discussing the research most relevant to our own concerns, the Milgram studies of destructive obedience to authority.

The Collectivization of the Workplace

Most work in modern society is done by organizations: corporations, governments, hospitals, foundations, universities, accounting firms, armies. Even such supposedly independent professionals as physicians and lawyers practice in large organizations to an ever-increasing extent. The HMO [Health Maintenance Organization] has replaced the family physician, and the new graduates of today's law schools join firms, of which the largest now employ over a thousand lawyers, rather than hanging out a shingle. The problems of professional and business ethics have thus become the problems of supervisors and subordinates in organizational settings. Indeed, in a culture such as ours, where our first question to each other is often not "How do you do?" but "What do you do?", the ethics of the workplace has enormous impact on how we think of morality in general. To a great extent, ethics in the organizational setting has come to define ethics as a whole. We speak of team players and loose cannons, leaders and followers, as categories of moral judgment and not simply of social description.

Reprinted from MICHIGAN LAW REVIEW, August 1992, Vol. 90, No. 8. Copyright 1992 by The Michigan Law Review Association.

The Organization Man and the Other-Directed Society

The transformation of the workplace appears to have wrought a transformation in values, replacing individual responsibility and internal norms with group identification and external norms. As the postwar American economy assumed its contemporary form, several leading social scientists and commentators explored the psychology of "The Organization Man," in the famous title of William H. Whyte's book. Whyte used this term to describe "the ones of our middle class who have left home, spiritually as well as physically, to take the vows of organization life."[1] He ascribed to them the "Social Ethic," which includes "a belief in the group as the source of creativity" as well as "a belief in 'belongingness' as the ultimate need of the individual."[2]

David Riesman described middle-class Americans as a "Lonely Crowd," and elaborated a famous typology of characters. In Riesman's scheme, people of premodern societies were *tradition-directed*, and the sanction for deviation was *shame*; in early modern societies people were *inner-directed*, guided by an internal moral compass, acquired in childhood, which induces *guilt* when one deviates. In contemporary society, however, we have become *other-directed*: our "contemporaries are the source of direction for the individual. . . . [T]he process of paying close attention to the signals from others . . . remain[s] unaltered throughout life."[3] For other-directed individuals, the sanction for deviance has changed: "As against guilt-and-shame controls, though of course these survive, one prime psychological lever of the other-directed person is a diffuse *anxiety*."[4] Sociologist Robert Jackall conducted interviews with 143 managers in several contemporary American corporations. In the anxiety-ridden world of middle management, "[m]anagers have a myriad of aphorisms that refer to how the power of CEOs, magnified through the zealous efforts of subordinates, affects them. . . . [One such maxim is] 'When he sneezes, we all catch colds'. . . ."[5] Jackall comments:

> As a result, independent morally evaluative judgments get subordinated to the social intricacies of the bureaucratic workplace. Notions of morality that one might hold and indeed practice outside the workplace . . . become irrelevant. . . . Under certain conditions, such notions may even become dangerous. For the most part, then, they remain unarticulated lest one risk damaging crucial relationships with significant individuals or groups.[6]

Historical Perspective

The collectivization of the workplace and the threat it poses to traditional moral values are hardly new phenomena; they have been recognized, and lamented, for the past 150 years. The erosion of individual responsibility and the evils of bureaucracy have engaged conservative writers since the advent of the industrial revolution. Over a century ago, Karl Marx likewise criticized what he called "the real mindlessness of the state." "The bureaucracy is a circle from which no one can escape," Marx contended. "The highest point entrusts the understanding of particulars to the lower echelons, whereas these, on the other hand, credit the highest with an understanding in regard to the universal; and thus they deceive one another."[7] In 1932, Reinhold Niebuhr wrote his classic treatise *Moral Man and Immoral Society*, in which he argued that

> [i]ndividual men may be moral. . . . They are endowed by nature with a measure of sympathy and consideration for their kind, the breadth of which may be extended by an astute social pedagogy. . . . But all these achievements are more difficult, if not impossible, for human societies and social groups. In every human group there is less reason to guide and to check impulse, less capacity for self-transcendence, less ability to comprehend the needs of others and therefore more unrestrained egoism than the individuals, who compose the group, reveal in their personal relationships.[8]

Niebuhr's argument recognizes that the increasing organization of society will be accompanied by a dilution of morality.

. . . [T]he problems Marx and Niebuhr discussed in a theoretical vein came to life in the most horrible way possible during World War II, where ostensibly civilized human beings tortured and slaughtered twelve million men, women, and children in extermination camps. The names of the camps—Auschwitz, Treblinka, Majdanek—have become synonymous with the incomprehensible willingness of ordinary human beings to do anything, no matter how atrocious, when ordered to do so by those in authority. Here, again, an explanation may be offered in terms of the division of responsibility within groups. Consider a historian's description of the euthanasia program Hitler ordered to eliminate mentally retarded, handicapped, or genetically ill Germans (individuals Hitler called "useless eaters"):

> The euthanasia program . . . demonstrated how, through fragmentation of authority and tasks, it was possible to fashion a murder machine. Hitler had enunciated an off-hand, extra-legal decree, and had not wanted to be bothered about it again. Brandt had ordered the "scientific" implementation of the program and, like Hitler, wished to hear no complaints. The directors and personnel of institutions rationalized that matters were out of their hands and that they were just filling out questionnaires . . . , though in reality each form was the equivalent of a death warrant. . . . The personnel at the end of the line excused themselves on the basis that they were under compulsion, had no power of decision, and were merely performing a function. Thousands of people were involved, but each considered himself nothing but a cog in the machine and reasoned that it was the machine, not he, that was responsible.[9]

The horrors of Nazism are without parallel, but the bureaucratic pattern of organization that fragments the knowledge required for moral decision-making is common to large institutions throughout contemporary society. Jackall describes the typical corporate structure in terms not unlike those Marx used to characterize "the real mindlessness of the state":

> Power is concentrated at the top in the person of the chief executive officer (CEO) and is simultaneously decentralized; that is, responsibility for decisions and profits is pushed as far down the organizational line as possible.

> . . . [P]ushing details down protects the privilege of authority to declare that a mistake has been made. . . . Moreover, pushing down details relieves superiors of the burden of too much knowledge, particularly guilty knowledge.
> . . . [Middle managers] become the "point men" of a given strategy and the potential "fall guys" when things go wrong.[10]

Hannah Arendt described the bureaucratic phenomenon as a novel form of governance appearing alongside the classical distinction among rule by one (monarchy), rule by "the best" (aristocracy), rule by the few (oligarchy), and rule by the many (democracy). She wrote of

> the latest and perhaps most formidable form of . . . dominion: bureaucracy or the rule of an intricate system of bureaus in which no men, neither one nor the best, neither the few nor the many, can be held responsible, and which could be properly called rule by Nobody. (If, in accord with traditional political thought, we identify tyranny as government that is not held to give account of itself, rule by Nobody is clearly the most tyrannical of all, since there is no one left who could even be asked to answer for what is being done. It is . . . impossible to localize responsibility and to identify the enemy. . . .)[11]

Such rumors of the demise of responsibility may be exaggerated; yet Arendt's description has the ring of familiarity. A graphic contemporary analogue appeared in litigation surrounding the Dalkon Shield. In his opinion, Federal Judge Frank Theis angrily noted:

> The project manager for Dalkon Shield explains that a particular question should have gone to the medical department, the medical department representative explains that the question was really the bailiwick of the quality control department, and the quality control department representative explains that the project manager was the one with the authority to make a decision on that question. . . . [I]t is not at all unusual for the hard questions posed in Dalkon Shield cases to be unanswerable by anyone from Robins [the manufacturer].[12]

One must not be naive, of course: often the defense of fragmented knowledge will be entered falsely and cynically, as a form of liability screening. Executives in the hot seat should be treated with the same skepticism that greeted German officials who "didn't know." Despite this healthy skepticism, however, we remain convinced that fragmented knowledge is a genuine phenomenon that we cannot simply dismiss as a lame excuse.

The Psychology of Destructive Obedience

Social scientists have labored to understand the Holocaust and to answer the all-important question whether it could occur in other settings. Stanley Milgram conducted perhaps the most significant—and certainly the most famous—experimental studies to address this issue. Milgram's experiments underscore our thesis because they illustrate the ways in which social and institutional pressures to obey reinforce, and are reinforced by, the fragmentation of knowledge in modern bureaucracies and other large organizations.

In Milgram's experiments, volunteers in a Yale University experiment were ordered by the experimenter to administer gradually increasing electric shocks to another "subject" (actually a confederate of the experimenter), ostensibly to study the effect of punishment on learning. As the "shocks" increased in intensity, the confederate displayed increasing discomfort, demanded that the experiment stop, screamed with pain, complained of a heart condition, and finally fell silent as if he were unconscious.[13] In this original experiment, sixty-five percent of the subjects went all the way, administering the highest possible, potentially lethal, level of shock. Those subjects who administered the maximum shock expressed great discomfort at the cruel task they were assigned; many of them berated the experimenter, protested, or insisted that they would not proceed with the experiment—all the while continuing to flip the switches.

Milgram conducted a number of important variations on the original experiment, several of which suggest the role that incomplete and fragmented knowledge may play in facilitating destructive obedience and the abdication of individual responsibility. In one version, the experiment was removed from the anxiety-relieving auspices of Yale to a seedy-looking storefront operation in nearby Bridgeport. Less able to reassure themselves that the experimenters knew what they were doing, fifty-three percent of the subjects refused to go all the way. This suggests that compliant subordinates often believe that their qualms are merely the result of incomplete understanding, and assume that those in charge have good reasons for what they are doing.

The rate of compliance also declined when the subject could see the victim, and declined even further when the subject was actually required to hold the victim's hand on the contact-plate. In this latter version of the experiment, seventy percent of the subjects stopped before administering the maximum level of shock. . . .

Another form of ignorance that appears to have played a significant role in Milgram's experiments was the absence of a clear-cut moment of decision. Few subjects would have hesitated to give a mild, tingling shock; most probably would have refused to give an initial shock of maximum voltage. The gradual escalation of voltage was insidious because it deprived subjects of an obvious stopping point, encouraging them to defer resistance until they saw themselves as committed, or as compromised. This kind of slippery slope may characterize many of the decisions made in contemporary organizations.

Another variant of the Milgram experiments, however, provides some encouragement that resistance and reform may be possible in organizational settings. In this study, the subject was assigned to a team administering the shocks, while the other team members were really confederates of the experimenter. Milgram discovered that compliance was extraordinarily sensitive to peer pressure. When the other team members refused to proceed with the experiment, only ten percent of the subjects remained obedient to the experimenter and "went all the way." Conversely, when a teammate rather than the subject took charge of physically administering the shock, 92.5% of the subjects went along with the experiment up to the maximum shock. . . .

The Milgram studies, then, suggest the role of imperfect and fragmented knowledge in organizational misconduct. The less individuals appreciate the consequences of their acts, the need to decide, and the available alternatives, the easier it will be for them to engage in destructive obedience. Milgram's experiments suggest that the fragmentation of knowledge promotes organizational wrongdoing by blunting the edge of moral conflict.

Although Milgram's research focused on subordinates, parallel problems arise for supervisors. As we have seen, bureaucratic structures serve to deny supervisors knowledge of operational details, blunt their awareness of harsh consequences, and help them rationalize what they cannot ignore. The result is the deep paradox of the "rule by Nobody": when neither superiors nor subordinates may be held responsible, we face an uncanny situation in which responsibility has seemingly been conjured out of existence.

The Inadequacy of Ethical Tradition and Philosophical Theory

. . . We believe that the specter of fragmented knowledge, divided responsibility, ambiguous orders, and unknown consequences is inadequately addressed in the moral discourse of Western societies. Virtually every approach to normative ethics, from the Ten Commandments to the latest wrinkles in philosophy journals, focuses primary attention on moral problems in which four *knowledge conditions* are satisfied—knowledge conditions that are frequently absent in individual decision-making and almost never found in organizational settings.

First, the decision-maker recognizes that he or she has come to a fork in the road: The decision-maker knows *that* a decision must be made. Do I or don't I cheat on the examination? Do I or don't I protest when I hear an acquaintance tell an anti-Semitic joke? Situations such as these are readily identifiable as moral decisions. Typically, when we face one of these questions, we know that we face it.

Second, the decision-maker recognizes that he or she must make the choice in a fairly short, distinct period of time: The decision-maker knows *when* a decision must be made, or at least *by* when it must be made. The examination is tomorrow; I must confront the acquaintance about his anti-Semitic joke now or never.

Third, the decision-maker confronts a small number of well-defined options: The decision-maker knows *what choices* are available. For example, a lawyer, learning that her client is using her services to perpetrate a fraud, can quickly catalogue her options: do what the client asks, try to talk the client out of the plan, blow the whistle on the client, or resign.

Fourth, the decision-maker has the information needed to make the decision: The decision-maker knows *what is needed* to make the choice. Even in situations of radically incomplete information, theories of rational decision-making under uncertainty allow us to assign probability-estimates to these various outcomes in order to generate a recommendation, though that recommendation may be merely to flip a coin.

These, then, are the four knowledge conditions of moral decision-making: we know *that* a decision must be made, *when* a decision must be made, *what choices* are available, and *what is needed* to make the choice. From the Biblical "Thou shalt not steal" and the Golden Rule, to Kant's cat-egorical imperative and the utilitarian injunction to achieve the greatest good for the greatest number, the core precepts of the major systems of ethical thought are directed to agents who satisfy the knowledge conditions. If the condi-tions are not satisfied, ethical systems generally respond with mitigation or even immunity: forgiving those who "know not what they do" is basic to Western understand-ings of moral responsibility.

Ignorance can, of course, be culpable; but most philoso-phers and legal theorists who acknowledge the phenomenon of culpable ignorance have implicitly confined it to a small range of exceptional cases: conspirators who attempt to pre-serve their deniability, or drunks who have willfully stupe-fied themselves. The possibility that the modern workplace may place millions of ordinary individuals in a state of culp-able ignorance throughout their careers has never, to our knowledge, been explicitly addressed in moral theory.

In an organizational setting, one or more of the four knowledge conditions typically fails at a critical juncture. As the Milgram experiments illustrated, individuals in bureaucratic settings may not fully appreciate that a deci-sion must be made, understand when it should be made, realize what choices are open to them, and comprehend what the consequences of different choices will be. A law firm associate asked to research a small point of law or a junior architect asked to design a detail may have no idea that the project as a whole raises deep questions of profes-sional ethics. Even if they have their suspicions, it is often impossible to pinpoint a moment of truth when the deci-sion must be made. No clear list of options, or even clear understanding of who to speak with, may exist, and the subordinate may never believe she has sufficient informa-tion to fashion a solution.

The failure of these knowledge conditions is created or maintained by organizational structure. Typically, super-visors parcel out subtasks to a number of subordinate employees. None of the subordinates may have more than the most general idea of what the entire project is about, while the supervisor may know nothing about the details of each subordinate's subtasks. No member of the organization might recognize a moral problem, because the problem arises not from what any *one* member of the team is doing, but rather from all their actions put together. The fact that each is merely a member of a team lulls them into a sense of security, so that they feel no pressing need to find out more about what is going on. . . .

This, then, is the central philosophical question that the problem of fragmented knowledge raises: *Is it possible to formulate satisfactory principles of individual responsibility when any or all of the four knowledge conditions presupposed by standard moral theories fail?*

RESPONSIBILITY WITHOUT KNOWLEDGE

. . . At bottom, four approaches exist to the problem of "deeds without doers." First, we can simply accept as a tragic fact of modern existence that organizational wrongs may be committed for which no one—neither individuals nor the organization—can rightly be held responsible. More optimistically, we can either hold the organization itself morally responsible for the wrongdoing or hold all the individuals affiliated with the organization strictly liable. Finally, we can extend standard principles of culp-able ignorance to explain why individuals in organizations may be held responsible for their actions even though the knowledge conditions fail. This is the approach we will defend. . . .

Extending Individual Responsibility

The simplest way of extending the concept of culpable ignorance to situations in which the knowledge conditions fail is to invoke an analogy to drunk driving. By the time a driver has had six drinks, he may no longer have the reflexes or judgment to avoid an accident, and thus in one sense he is not responsible for what he does behind the wheel. Obviously, though, we *do* hold him responsible. Why? The answer seems simple enough: although we agree that once he became drunk he lost effective control of his actions, we blame him for becoming drunk in the first place. Though he was not fully responsible at the time of the accident, it was his own fault that he was not responsible. In Aristotle's words, "when one has once let go of a stone, it is too late to get it back—but the agent was responsible for throwing it, because the origin of the action was in himself."[14]

Analogously, we may agree that individuals in organiza-tional settings often do not know enough to be held respon-sible for organizational wrongdoings and yet we insist that they should have known. They were willfully blind. Thus, for example, if an SS officer claimed that he did not know about the SS's murderous activities, we may wish to insist that his ignorance is blameworthy. He should have known what he was joining.

The drunk driving analogy suggests that we can hold people responsible for getting into the very predicament that at first glance seems to relieve them of responsibility. If we focus on the act of drinking, this suggests that an employee is responsible for the predicament he gets into by joining an organization that fragments relevant knowledge. Except in the case of outlaw groups like the SS, however, we do not want to treat the act of joining an organization, like the act of heavy drinking, as suspect or presumptively wrong.

We would do better to focus on the driving aspect of the drunk driving analogy. Driving is a valuable activity, and our licensing procedures are designed to make it widely available. Because of the lethal potential of the automobile, however, the privilege of driving hinges on an exercise of alertness, caution, and self-restraint that we do not require of pedestrians or passengers. We allow pedestrians and passengers to impair their reflexes and judgment with alcohol, but we treat it as a legal and moral offense for a driver or prospective driver to do so.

Analogously, because of the great potential for harm arising from the division of labor and fragmentation of knowledge in a corporate or bureaucratic organization, employees may acquire duties far more demanding than doing no evil. They must look and listen for evil and attempt to thwart it if they discover it. These duties, however, are not as limited and well defined as those imposed on the driver. We expect prospective drivers to "just say no," but we cannot expect organizational employees to know everything about the operation in which they are involved. While drinking is a gratuitous impediment to driving, fragmented knowledge inheres in the structure of the organization itself. We are left with a question that does not arise in the context of drunk driving: What and how much precaution do we require of the individual employee?

We cannot answer this question definitively, but we can begin by suggesting several obligations that arise from the specific risk of organizational enterprise: the risk that an individual will do or contribute to great harm without knowing it.

1. *Obligations of investigation.* The first, most obvious, possibility is to hold individuals in organizational settings morally responsible for discerning the nature of their own projects and for discovering what other employees are doing with their work products. The idea is obvious because it remedies the absence of knowledge in the most straightforward way: by demanding that individuals do their best to acquire the knowledge they lack.

2. *Obligations of communication.* A second possibility is to hold individuals who possess troublesome knowledge morally responsible for communicating it to others in the organization. Obviously, communication may be a risky course of action: supervisors treasure their "deniability," and shooting the messenger is often their knee-jerk response. Yet riskiness does not distinguish this from other moral responsibilities: we often believe that people have moral obligations to act against their self-interest.

3. *Obligations of protection.* The previous suggestions imply that supervisors may have moral obligations to protect their subordinates from adverse consequences of investigation and communication. For example, they may be morally responsible for protecting whistleblowers from retaliation.

4. *Obligations of prevention.* Those in management positions may have moral obligations to forestall wrongdoing by setting up structures that avoid the problems we have been examining. Such preventive mechanisms might include ombudsmen, incentive structures that reward

moral action, channels for anonymous information about problems, and so on. . . .

5. *Obligations of precaution.* In some cases, we may be able to analogize the act of joining an organization to the act of heavy drinking: the individual knows or should know that once she becomes involved, her discretion and knowledge will be so constricted that she cannot be held responsible for wrongdoing that, in broad outline, she can reasonably anticipate. The fatal misstep is involving herself in the first place. More often than not, would-be employees of organizations have some prior sense of the organization's values and culture. We may therefore hold individuals responsible for joining the organization in the first place, as we might hold an individual German responsible for joining the SS.

That individuals in an organization have obligations like these, and that their breach provides a basis for assigning the individuals responsibility for wrongs done in ignorance, seems plausible. But this approach to extending individual responsibility for organizational wrongdoing raises two critical questions. First, how demanding are these obligations? . . . Second, how much vigilance is enough? . . .

As we have described them, the moral obligations of the individual employee seem to fall somewhere between *perfect* duties like not killing, with fairly precise boundaries, and *imperfect* duties like charity or self-improvement, that require only some indeterminate effort. If we attempt to make these duties perfect, through more precise formulation, we risk defining them too narrowly; if we attempt to make them imperfect, by demanding a "reasonable" effort, we risk making them too vague. . . .

What is an individual responsible for in failing to fulfill these *preemptive duties*, as we shall call the obligations of investigation, communication, protection, prevention, and precaution? Should we blame her only for the breach of the preemptive duty, or should we blame her for the resulting offense as if she had known all the relevant facts (and thus hold her immune from censure if no harm results)? Is the employee responsible just for failing to investigate (at the time she fails to do so), or does she lose her excuse of ignorance with respect to any facts the investigation would have yielded?

Neither approach seems fully satisfactory. In limiting responsibility to the breach of preemptive duties, we impose the same blame or punishment regardless of what wrongs result; in withholding the excuse of ignorance for the offense, we treat a negligent employee as if she were responsible for intentional wrongdoing. And if we assign responsibility *only* when a wrong is actually done, we fail to censure those lucky enough to ignore their special obligations without adverse effect. . . .

The critical inquiry is whether, in acting in a way that creates an excuse, the individual is at fault for the offense excused. . . . Applied to organizational wrongdoing, [this] approach . . . would ground the employee's responsibility for the harm in her preemptive duties to investigate, prevent, and so forth. By breaching these duties, the employee has played a role in causing or contributing to the commission of the offense. The key question would not be whether the employee deliberately, recklessly, or negligently breached her duty but whether, by failing to perform it, she intentionally, recklessly, or negligently facilitated the wrongdoing.[15]

Thus, if an employee should have known that by investigating a new project before it commenced, she could ascertain whether it involved exporting toxic substances, and there was some reason to suspect that it might, she would be responsible for negligently exporting those substances, even if, by the time she exported them, the most diligent inquiry would not have revealed their toxic character. Had she actually known that an investigation could have revealed that information, but failed to investigate, she would be responsible for recklessly exporting toxic substances, even if, by the time she exported them, she was no longer able to ascertain their toxic character.

In some cases, this approach may lead us to hold employees who act in ignorance responsible for intentional wrongdoing. If the employee deliberately insulated herself from knowledge about the exports, intending to export toxic substances without being told that specific exports were toxic, she would be responsible for their intentional export despite her ignorance at the time she exported them. But if she deliberately insulated herself from such knowledge only because she hated confrontations, she would be responsible for no more than reckless export, since she did not know the character of the substances or intend or hope that they might be toxic. This approach, then, avoids the harshness of denying an employee an excuse for organizational wrongdoing if she has any fault for creating the excuse. It treats her as responsible for wrongdoing only to the extent that she is at fault for excusing or justifying its commission. . . .

CONCLUSION

The preemptive obligations we are proposing have in recent years become widely accepted in both public and private bureaucracies. Governmental agencies typically have ombudsmen, and state and federal governments have enacted protections for whistleblowers. In the wake of several incidents, the Exxon Corporation has enacted regulations requiring employees who notice possible misconduct or dangerous situations to notify their superiors in writing; the superiors, in turn, are required to respond in writing, and if no written response is forthcoming, the employee must jump the chain of command and inform higher-level executives.

Regarded as public policy proposals, our preemptive obligations are already found in corporate manuals and memoranda. We are not offering a proposal for regulations whose time has come, however, but an account of individual moral responsibility. That is, we argue not only that bureaucratic organizations should institute policies along the lines we have suggested, but also that individual executives within the organizations are morally blameworthy for failing to implement such policies and that individual employees and executives are morally blameworthy for violating preemptive obligations *even in the absence of policies implementing them.*

Notes

1. William H. Whyte, Jr., *The Organization Man* 3 (1956).

2. *Id.* at 7.

3. David Riesman, *The Lonely Crowd* 22 (1950) (emphasis omitted).

4. *Id.* at 26.

5. Robert Jackall, *Moral Mazes: The World of Corporate Managers* 22 (1988).

6. *Id.* at 105.

7. Karl Marx, *Critique of Hegel's "Philosophy of Right"* 46–47 (Joseph O'Malley, ed., 1970).

8. Reinhold Niebuhr, *Moral Man and Immoral Society* xi–xii (rev. ed. 1960).

9. Robert E. Conot, *Justice at Nuremberg* 210–211 (1983).

10. Jackall, *supra* note 5, at 17, 20–21.

11. Hannah Arendt, *On Violence* 38–39 (1970).

12. *In re* A. H. Robins Co. "Dalkon Shield" IUD Prods. Liab. Litig., 575 F. Supp. 718, 724 (D. Kan. 1983).

13. See Stanley Milgram, *Obedience to Authority: An Experimental View* 3–4 (1974).

14. Aristotle, *Nichomachean Ethics* bk. III, ch. V, 1114a, at 124 (J.A.K. Thomson trans., rev. ed. 1976). . . .

15. Similarly, if a person negligently provoked another to use deadly force, he would not lose his right to kill in self-defense. If he exercised that right, however, he would be guilty of negligent homicide for creating the need for self-defense. If he provoked another in order to give himself a legal justification for killing that person, he would be guilty of intentional homicide.

    To bear any responsibility for the ultimate offense, the agent must be at fault for creating the specific excusing or justifying condition he relies on. If he negligently provoked someone without reason to expect that she would resort to deadly force, he would not be guilty of homicide in creating the need for self-defense. He would be responsible at most for negligent provocation and the use of no deadly defensive force.

Review and Discussion Questions

1. In the modern world, most individuals work in organizations. Describe how this can affect people's sense of responsibility and the morality of their conduct.

2. Describe Stanley Milgram's famous experiment. What are its most significant implications?

3. What four knowledge conditions are presupposed by the standard theories of moral decision making? Are the authors correct to assert that "in an organizational setting, one or more of the four knowledge conditions typically fails at a critical juncture"?

4. What do the authors mean by the problem of "deeds without doers"? What general approach to this problem do they take, and what are the three rival approaches that they put aside?

5. According to the authors, what five obligations do individuals inside an organization have? Do you agree? Do you think that the authors demand too much of the individual? Suppose an individual neglects to fulfill one of these duties. To what extent are we justified in blaming the person for any subsequent organizational misconduct?

Up to Code: Does Your Company's Conduct Meet World-Class Standards?

Lynn Paine, Rohit Deshpande,
Joshua D. Margolis,
and Kim Eric Bettcher

Codes of conduct are legally required for any publicly traded company with a presence in the United States. But the issue goes well beyond the United States. Disturbed by the corruption and excesses in corporate activities, corporations themselves, governments, investors, employees and consumers all over the globe have proposed codes and guidelines to govern corporate behaviour. These initiatives reflect an increasingly global debate on the nature of corporate legitimacy. Given the legal and business considerations, it is unlikely that any company would want to be without a code in the future. But what should it say? In search of some reference points for managers, the authors undertook a systematic analysis of a select group of codes. In this article, they present their findings in the form of a "codex," a reference source on code content. The Global Business Standards Codex contains a set of overarching principles as well as a set of conduct standards for putting those principles into practice. It is meant to provide companies wishing to create their own code with a starting point grounded in ethical fundamentals and aligned with an emerging global consensus on basic standards of corporate behaviour. The provisions of the codex may well have to be customized to a company's specific business and situation.

Codes of conduct have long been a feature of corporate life. Today, they are arguably a legal necessity—at least for public companies with a presence in the United States. As of 2004, both the New York Stock Exchange and the Nasdaq require listed companies to adopt and disclose a code of conduct. And under the Sarbanes-Oxley Act, public issuers of securities must disclose whether they have adopted a code for their senior executives (and if not, why not). Similarly, federal guidelines direct judges to take into account the adoption of a code when determining whether a company convicted of a crime had an effective ethics and compliance program in place—and thus when setting a fine. The legal case for a code is further bolstered by various requirements and enforcement policies in specific areas of the law. The EPA, for example, considers a company's compliance efforts when it assesses penalties for environmental infractions. Moreover, the courts of Delaware, legal home to more than half of all U.S. publicly traded companies and 58% of the Fortune 500, have held that boards are responsible for ensuring that management implements a compliance and reporting system informed by the federal sentencing guidelines.

Reprinted by permission from "Up to Code: Does Your Company's Conduct Meet World-Class Standards?," *Harvard Business Review*, December 2005.

The matter goes beyond U.S. legal and regulatory requirements, however. Calls for defined standards of corporate conduct have issued from many corners of the globe. Sparked by corruption and excess of various types—from garden-variety deception and bribery to labor abuses and elaborate schemes of market manipulation—dozens of industry, government, investor, and multisector groups worldwide have proposed codes and guidelines to govern corporate behavior. Examples include the United Nations Global Compact and the Consumer Charter for Global Business. Meanwhile, the European Commission has endorsed conduct codes as a tool for promoting corporate responsibility and urged companies to embrace, at a minimum, the Fundamental ILO Conventions and the OECD Guidelines for Multinational Enterprises. And in other regions, bodies as varied as Hong Kong's Independent Commission Against Corruption, South Africa's King Committee on Corporate Governance, the Brazilian Institute of Corporate Governance, and the Japanese prime minister's 2002 advisory panel on the quality of life have advised companies to develop codes.

While they do not have the force of law—at least, not yet—these initiatives reflect an increasingly global debate on the nature of corporate legitimacy. They are slowly defining the terms and conditions of companies' license to operate—or what is sometimes called the corporate social contract—around the world. By adopting its own code, a company can clarify for all parties, internal and external, the standards that govern its conduct and can thereby convey its commitment to responsible practice wherever it operates.

Company codes serve myriad other practical purposes. A code can help employees from diverse backgrounds work more effectively across geographic and cultural boundaries. It can also serve as a reference point for decision making, enabling companies to operate with fewer layers of supervision and to respond quickly and cohesively in times of crisis. It can even aid in recruitment, helping attract individuals who want to work for a business that embraces world-class standards. Of course, a code can also help a company manage risk by reducing the likelihood of damaging misconduct. And as part of managing their own brands, some companies examine the codes of their potential suppliers and partners. India's Tata Group, for example, requires any company that wants to use the Tata name to adhere to the group's code of ethics.

Given all the legal, organizational, reputational, and strategic considerations, few companies will want to be without a code. But what should it say? Apart from a handful of essentials spelled out in Sarbanes-Oxley regulations and NYSE rules, authoritative guidance is sorely lacking. The codes and guidelines promulgated by business, government, and civic groups in recent years contain a lengthy and confusing menu of possibilities.

In search of some reference points for managers, we undertook a systematic analysis of a select group of codes. After distilling and comparing their content, we sought to identify the motivating principles behind them. We were surprised to find that, despite the codes' seeming variety, they share many similarities in the standards of conduct they put forth and the ethical principles to which they give expression. We also found that differences among the codes are in many cases complementary rather than conflicting, although the codes do differ on some crucial points that are not easily reconciled.

In this article, we present our findings in the form of a "codex" a reference source on code content. It contains a set of overarching principles and a set of conduct standards for putting those principles into practice. Standards and principles are the bricks and mortar for formulating a code. Standards capture how companies and their personnel should treat their major constituencies, while principles give the standards their legitimacy. Although rarely expressed explicitly, principles answer the question, "Why do we accept these standards as guidelines for our conduct?"

Our Global Business Standards Codex is intended not as a "model code" that companies should adopt as is, but as a benchmark for those wishing to create their own world-class code. It represents our attempt to gain a comprehensive, but simplified, picture of the conduct expected of today's corporations.

The provisions of the codex must be customized to a company's specific business and situation, and individual companies' codes will include their own distinctive elements as well. What the codex provides is a starting point grounded in ethical fundamentals and aligned with an emerging global consensus on basic standards of corporate behavior.

Of course, a world-class code is no guarantee of world-class conduct. A code of ethics can no more ensure ethical conduct than a code of laws can ensure legal conduct. A code is only a tool, and like any tool, it can be used well or poorly—or left on the shelf to be admired or to rust. But the better it is made, the greater the chance it will fulfill its intended purpose.

COLLECTING THE DATA

We began by reviewing five widely recognized sets of conduct guidelines for multinational companies: The Caux Round Table Principles for Business (CRT Principles), the OECD Guidelines for Multinational Enterprises (OECD Guidelines), the UN Global Compact, the Interfaith Center on Corporate Responsibility's Principles for Global Corporate Responsibility (ICCR Principles), and the Global Reporting Initiative (GRI). We focused on guidelines for first-order conduct, largely ignoring those for implementation and oversight. We refer to these five sources as "codes" even though only the first four appear in a traditional code format. We tried to infer the governing precepts for conduct behind the GRI's proposed performance indicators.

We chose these codes for several reasons. First, they are meant for companies in general, not for a single company or a specific sector, such as apparel or extractive industries, for which specialized codes have recently been developed. Second, they relate to a broad spectrum of corporate activity

rather than a single issue (such as corruption), function (procurement), or constituency (employees). Third, they speak to companies worldwide. Fourth, they are multinational in origin. Finally, each was developed through a multiparty process involving many individual and organizational participants. To date, more than 2,200 companies, including 98 of Fortune's Global 500, have joined the UN Global Compact, and 39 governments have endorsed the OECD Guidelines. Taken together, the multiparty codes reflect a range of views from different sectors of society: business, government, and nonprofit (which includes civic, religious, and environmental organizations).

We also examined the codes of 14 of the world's largest companies, including the top ten in the BusinessWeek Global 1000 for 2003 (all from the United States or the United Kingdom) and the top two companies from continental Europe and Asia as shown on the Financial Times 2003 list of the World's Most Respected Companies. Since we looked only at companies' codes, however, and not at other documents these companies have issued on specific topics such as conflicts of interest, we do not claim to have a complete picture of the companies' policies.

For U.S. legal and regulatory requirements on code content, we reviewed the Sarbanes-Oxley Act, along with the SEC's implementing regulations and the NYSE and Nasdaq corporate governance rules. We distilled the precepts for corporate conduct found in the 23 sources (the five multiparty codes, the 14 individual company codes, and the four legal and regulatory sources) and categorized them by the constituencies whose interests were principally at stake. (Go to gbscodexresearch.hbr.org to see our background analysis of the combined codes.) As a check on our research, we reviewed numerous other code-of-conduct studies by academics as well as organizations such as the Conference Board and the OECD. And to protect against cultural blind spots, we compared the codes of nine companies from five emerging markets: Brazil, China, India, Nigeria, and Russia.

THE COMMON GROUND

Viewed together, the source codes contain provisions relating to the six traditional corporate stakeholders: customers, employees, investors, competitors, suppliers/partners, and the public. Although the stances toward these constituencies vary—companies are urged to "create value for," "deal fairly with," or "fulfill obligations to" their constituencies—the codes uniformly recognize that companies have responsibilities to several groups.

A number of general provisions, applying to all activities and all parties, appeared in many documents. Nearly all the codes enjoin companies to observe the law, protect the environment, avoid bribery, and conduct business in a truthful manner. Other recurring provisions include disclosing relevant information in a timely fashion, keeping accurate records, honoring agreements, respecting human dignity and human rights, protecting health and safety, and contributing to society through innovation.

Among the guidelines that apply to specific constituencies, we found those concerning customers to be the most similar. Companies are consistently called upon to meet the quality requirements of customers, protect their health and safety, and treat them fairly. Environmentally safe products and services are also frequently called for, and provisions relating to truthfulness and transparency in customer dealings are among the most common. Privacy and the protection of confidential customer data also receive a moderate level of attention.

Regarding employees, the codes consistently mandate that companies protect workers from injury and illness in the workplace, avoid discrimination, provide equal employment opportunity, and respect their dignity and human rights. Provisions forbidding retaliation against employees who report misconduct are also widespread. Various codes mention open communication, responsiveness to suggestions and complaints, fair and reasonable compensation, and assistance in developing skills.

Similarities in provisions relating to investors, suppliers/partners, competitors, and the public are less numerous and less pronounced. Those that do occur are often specific applications of the general provisions. The standards covering suppliers, for example, pick up the fair-dealing, environmental protection, antibribery, and human rights themes introduced earlier.

THE DIFFERENCES

We unearthed a fault line between codes written by people who represent business and those written by groups that represent multiple sectors of society. The business sector codes—those created by the Caux Round Table and by individual companies for their own use—are much more attentive to the economic health of the enterprise and to employees' responsibilities to the corporate entity. By contrast, the four multisector codes (OECD Guidelines, UN Global Compact, ICCR Principles, and GRI) are largely silent on such matters as diligence in carrying out the company's business, prudence in using company resources, and care in protecting company assets. Infrequently mentioned in the multiparty codes are provisions concerning conflicts of interest and self-dealing, issues that were central to the corporate scandals of 2001 and 2002 and that appear prominently in the company codes and the regulators' guidelines. Indeed, conflict of interest has historically been among the most frequently covered topics in company codes.

Not surprisingly, the business sector codes place more emphasis on responsibilities to investors. Only one of the multisector codes (GRI) addresses financial returns to investors, and none mentions insider trading, whose prohibition is required by regulatory guidelines and which is in fact prohibited by the majority of company codes. Investor and financial concerns are not wholly neglected in the multisector codes. Two codes call on companies to provide investors with accurate and timely information, and one requires them not to obstruct share owners' legal rights. Moreover, the multisector codes include general precepts on financial disclosure, accounting, audits, and financial reporting. But the specific requirements of economic trusteeship—insofar as it involves the creation of economic value- receive little attention.

The multisector codes also have comparatively little to say about business-to-business conduct, especially between competitors. While the multisector codes issue broad guidelines such as "adhere to competition laws" and "cooperate with competition authorities," the business sector codes call explicitly for free and fair competition, respect for rivals' property rights, and appropriate gathering of competitive information. In the supplier/partner domain, the multisector codes focus on labor and environmental standards, while the business codes address a wider set of issues.

Compared with the business sector codes, the multisector codes are more oriented toward employees and the general public. For example, all the multisector codes call on companies to recognize employees' right to free association and collective bargaining, whereas only four of the business sector codes do (and three of those are from non-U.S. companies). Similarly, all the multisector codes include restrictions on using forced and child labor; only five company codes do. While topics such as employment safeguards and reasonable notice of major employment changes receive attention from multisector groups, the NYSE governance rules explicitly state that codes may preserve at-will employment arrangements. That is, under the NYSE's rules, companies may follow the longstanding and unique-to-the-U.S. legal principle that, in the absence of an employment contract of specific duration, an employee may be dismissed at any time—with or without notice.

The themes of stakeholder responsiveness and engagement are much more prominent in the multisector codes. For example, the GRI and the ICCR Principles call for worker participation in certain decisions and activities, and the OECD Guidelines call for cooperation with government authorities and community officials. The ICCR document even proposes that companies go beyond dialogue and actually abide by the recommendations put forth by some stakeholders, though it is the only code that makes such a recommendation.

The two groups of codes also reflect different postures toward public policy concerns. The multisector codes ask companies to actively address such issues as corruption, labor practices, human rights, and environmental protection. Apart from the CRT Principles, few of the business codes take an activist stance on these issues. The business codes typically condemn bribery, labor abuses, and environmental degradation in companies' own operations; but the multisector codes go further, advocating that companies reach out to persuade others—in their value chain, in their community, in the society at large—to address these issues as well.

The appropriate scope of corporate activism is up for debate. Many of the codes—especially the multiparty codes—ask companies to collaborate on, contribute to, or otherwise support causes that are of broad public significance. Under the UN Global Compact, companies are even charged with providing health, education, and housing for employees in certain circumstances. The CRT Principles say that companies should promote free trade, open markets, and democratic institutions. But such activity is arguably an incursion into the powers of the state. By the dictates of classical liberalism, such matters should be handled by public officials following democratic ideals of participation and due process. To be sure, the multiparty codes enjoin companies to recognize the government's jurisdiction over society at large, to avoid improper involvement in politics, and to pay their taxes in a timely manner. And the individual companies' codes seem to concur—at least with the first two provisions. (Company codes rarely discuss tax obligations.)

Yet the proper division of labor among companies, governments, and civic actors is far from settled. Differences may well reflect disparate underlying assumptions about democracy and due process. In democratic societies that have accountable governments, corporate activism may seem unnecessary or unjustified, whereas the absence of a legitimate and well-functioning government may make corporate activism seem essential.

To the extent that individual companies do adopt an activist position, it is likely to be issue specific—focused, for example, on the environment, bribery, or human rights. Companies also seem less reluctant to use their influence to shape the practices of their suppliers and partners than to embrace general public advocacy. Indeed, more than half the company codes require suppliers and partners to refrain from bribery, and a similar number say preference should be given to those who observe applicable environmental standards. Overall, though, while the multisector codes are more activist than the business codes, individual companies can be found on all points of the activism spectrum.

Not all differences among the codes track the divide between business and nonbusiness perspectives, and some follow no obvious pattern. One example is the treatment of compensation, a topic addressed explicitly by the CRT Principles, two multisector codes, and four company codes. While the CRT Principles call for "compensation that improve[s] workers' living conditions," the company codes favor pay that is "fair" or "competitive." Depending on market conditions and how these terms are interpreted, the required pay levels could be quite similar—or they could be radically different.

GOVERNING PRINCIPLES

Despite such differences in emphasis and content, we found that most of the roughly 130 precepts we identified in the 23 source documents could be seen as practical applications of just eight basic principles, most of which echo longstanding themes in ethical and legal thought. Without insisting on a rigid system of classification, we found that the standards cluster loosely around the following principles:

The Fiduciary Principle By law, the officers and directors of a corporation are fiduciaries for the company and its shareholders. However, all employees stand in a fidu-

ciary relationship to the corporate entity in that they are entrusted to protect its resources and act on its behalf in carrying out their job-related responsibilities. Traditionally, trusteeship has included duties of diligence, candor, and loyalty to the beneficiary over the self. Thus, disclosing conflicts of interest and prohibitions on unauthorized self-dealing have been traditional guidelines for trustees. The same logic dictates that fiduciaries may not benefit themselves at the expense of the entity they serve—by, for example, pursuing for their own personal benefit business opportunities that belong to the corporation. At the core of the fiduciary principle, however, is the notion of diligence, prudence, and energetic effort applied in the service of another. Negligence, carelessness, and halfhearted effort are clear, if less frequently discussed, violations of this principle. Although fiduciary concepts are not covered in the multisector codes, they are central to the functioning of the economy and should, under recent regulations on code content, be included in any company's code.

The Property Principle Whether justified by arguments from the standpoint of human dignity and liberty or from that of wealth maximization and economic development, the property principle is today regarded as central to individual and societal well-being, the ultimate test of any ethical system. Theft and embezzlement of tangible property are the classic violations of this principle, and injunctions against these behaviors are found across the ages. As intangible property has grown in importance, definitions of theft have expanded to include misappropriation of intellectual property and other types of proprietary information. Respect for property continues to mean safeguarding the property in one's rightful possession, avoiding waste, and not infringing on the property rights of others. The codes we examined make relatively few explicit references to these mandates—perhaps because they are so ingrained as to be assumed—but a few provisions specifically enjoin the protection and maintenance of property and forbid theft and other forms of misappropriation.

The Reliability Principle Several directives invoke the principle of reliability, or fidelity to commitments. To cope with uncertainty, most societies have developed ethical norms around keeping promises, fulfilling contracts, and even carrying out one's stated intentions-especially if meant to induce reliance by others. Complex schemes of cooperation would not be possible without these ways of forming binding commitments, as they allow different parties to coordinate their activities into an unknown future. They bring an element of predictability to an otherwise unpredictable flow of events. The law of contract is an elaboration of this basic idea. As legal scholar Charles Fried has observed, "By promising we transform a choice that was morally neutral into one that is morally compelled." Classic violations of the reliability principle include breach of promise, breach of contract, and other less formal types of betrayal or going back on one's word. More generally, the reliability principle implies care in making commitments—not promising more than one can deliver—and in following through on agreements and other obligations that are voluntarily incurred.

The Transparency Principle A number of directives are concerned with accuracy, truth, and disclosure of information—or what has come to be called "transparency." Although this term does not signify total openness, its core ideas of honesty and respect for truth have been treated as fundamental ethical imperatives from time immemorial. Injunctions against fraud and deceit—the characteristic violations of this precept—are found in many ethical traditions and virtually all legal systems. Transparency also implies taking care to present information accurately and not to mislead. And it may mean correcting misinformation or offering information that is material to the recipient in important ways—affecting personal or financial well-being, for instance. Justifications for such transparency requirements include promoting dignity and freedom, enabling wise decision making, advancing knowledge, enabling cooperation, promoting society's ability to function, ensuring economic efficiency, preventing corruption, and, simply, upholding the intrinsic value of truth.

The Dignity Principle Although corporate officials and employees have fiduciary obligations to protect and promote the company's interests, they are nonetheless expected to do so in a way that respects other people—whether those people are other employees, customers, supply chain workers, or members of the general public. Indeed, respect for the person is perhaps the starting point for all ethical thought. It leads directly to protections for health, safety, expression, and privacy, and to proscriptions on humiliation, coercion, and offenses against basic human rights. It also implies affirmative efforts to develop human potential, and it often means special concern for those who are incapacitated or otherwise particularly vulnerable. All of the codes include at least some provisions that ensure respect for the person.

The Fairness Principle The concept of fairness has been central to ethical thought throughout the ages. Its importance rests on its role in facilitating cooperation, securing legitimacy, and ensuring group survival. Four types of fairness have received particular attention: reciprocal fairness, or fairness in exchange; distributive fairness, or equity in allocating benefits and burdens among members of a group; fair competition, which concerns conduct among rivals; and procedural fairness, which entails due process.

Fairness has many interpretations, but treating like cases alike is a core aspect. Unfairness almost always involves differential treatment—favorable or unfavorable—among parties that are similarly situated. Although some forms of differential treatment are quite legitimate, the vast majority of the codes we reviewed forbid discrimination among employees on the basis of non-work-related characteristics, and equal pay for equal work is a recurrent idea. Many of the codes also call more generally for fair treatment, as well as fair competition and fair dealing.

The Citizenship Principle The various codes differ considerably on the degree to which companies should be activists on public and societal issues, but they agree on several basic issues of citizenship. Perhaps the most fundamental civic duty is respect for law, and all the codes call for observation of relevant laws and regulations. In addition, citizens are generally thought to bear some responsibility for maintaining the "commons"—such shared and indivisible goods as the natural environment, public spaces, or legitimate government. Just as individuals should clean up after themselves, companies, too, should repair any damage to the commons resulting from their activities. Beyond this baseline, citizenship implies a willingness to deal with public authorities in good faith and may even imply some additional contribution by way of charity, civic support, or help in addressing broad societal problems.

The codes include several directives pertaining to the duties of citizenship and their classic violations, such as breaking the law, freeloading, and bribing public officials. At the same time, the codes make clear that the corporation is no ordinary citizen. Rather than being full participants in the political and public policy-making processes, companies are directed to avoid "improper" involvement in political activities and to recognize the government's obligation and jurisdiction concerning society at large.

The Responsiveness Principle Unlike the previously discussed principles, this one may have its origins in the modern corporate context as a corrective to the indifference that often characterizes bureaucratic systems. It implies a readiness to engage with other parties that may be affected by a company's activities or may have a justifiable claim (even if not an entitlement) to attention. Although the multisector codes typically call for greater responsiveness than the business codes, the CRT Principles strike something of a middle ground, with precepts on engaging with suppliers and responding to complaints and suggestions from customers, employees, and investors.

Some of the provisions found in our source codes—avoid fraud, for instance, and ensure a safe working environment—arise from only one main principle. Others, like guidelines on gifts and entertainment, have links to several. For example, much of what passes for business entertainment may be more aptly described as personal entertainment at corporate expense. Such diversions of corporate property to personal use are not only breaches of fiduciary obligation, but they are also a form of waste that violates the property principle. And in some cases, excessive gifts are simply a means to secure an unfair competitive advantage.

Although the principles have ancient roots, the precepts found in the codes are tailored to the modern business context and recognize the corporate entity as an actor in its own right. In these respects, the codes reveal their contemporary origins, for the modern corporation is a relatively recent invention, and the idea that businesses should observe a set of ethical standards is even more recent. In early-twentieth-century legal circles, the corporation's capacity for moral judgment and responsibility was hotly contested. The idea continues to be debated by a few theorists, though by now it is widely accepted-as evidenced by the sheer number of corporate codes of ethics.

By emphasizing the common threads running through these codes and connecting them to enduring themes in ethical and legal thought, we do not mean to deny important differences in how the precepts are understood and applied around the world. Nor do we suggest that they are consistently observed. But we do see an emerging core of global standards of conduct.

The core precepts articulated in these codes reflect ethical principles that have arisen to address problems and concerns in virtually all societies—problems of trust, cooperation, fairness, safety, security, and so on. Given the central role of business in society today, it is not surprising that these same principles should be applied to corporate behavior. We urge business leaders to heed the rising chorus and to take steps now to ensure that their companies' practices are, in fact, up to code.

CREATING THE CODEX

The Global Business Standards Codex reflects our findings on standards of conduct as well as our conclusions about the ethical principles informing them. At its core is the body of standards around which we found wide agreement. This group includes not only regulatory requirements and items that appeared with some consistency across the various codes but also ones that occurred with high frequency in either business sector or multisector codes. For example, we included provisions on conflicts of interest, the use of company resources, and employee privacy—topics that appear in half or more of the company codes but in few of the multisector codes. By the same reasoning, we included provisions on forced and child labor and employees' right to flee association, both listed in all the multisector codes but in only a handful of the business sector codes.

In a few instances, we included provisions that we judged to be important and required by the underlying principles of the codex even though they appeared infrequently. Fair treatment of minority share owners and responsiveness to share owners' concerns, for example, were mentioned in only one company code and absent from most of the multisector codes.

We organized the codex by principle to reveal the ethical basis of the various standards. To facilitate implementation, the codex also displays the main constituency affected by each provision. Although further research will be required to determine the extent to which companies actually adhere to these standards, the codex may be taken as a first approximation of global best practice.

As we said at the beginning, we offer the codex not as a minimum code but as a reference that companies can use to assess their current code or to craft a new one. Some may adopt a minimalist approach, avoiding violations of the principles and standards articulated here. Others may focus on achieving excellence, enacting these principles in their

most robust form. Many will want to take a position on issues outside the consensus area or include their own distinctive values and commitments alongside the basics found in the codex. But all will want to consider where they stand relative to this set of widely recognized standards of conduct for global business.

If our hypothesis is correct, companies will ultimately be judged—and their very license to operate may in some cases depend—on their responsiveness to this emerging global consensus.

THE GBS CODEX

For companies that want to assess their code of conduct or craft a new one, we offer the Global Business Standards Codex, a roundup of widely endorsed conduct guidelines for companies around the world. We arranged the standards according to eight underlying ethical principles [outlined above]. Although many standards are informed by more than one principle, we have listed each standard only once. We also included several supplementary provisions (shown in italics) that are worthy of managers' consideration even though they did not meet our criteria for inclusion in the core group. For clarity, we have indicated which constituency (customers, employees, investors, suppliers/partners, competitors, the public, or even the company itself) is most affected by each. Grounded in ethical fundamentals, this codex can be taken as a first approximation of global best practices for companies and their directors, officers, and employees.

I. FIDUCIARY PRINCIPLE: Act as a fiduciary for the company and its investors. Carry out the company's business in a diligent and loyal manner, with the degree of candor expected of a trustee.

Key Concept: Diligence

Constituency: Company

Standard:
Promote the company's legitimate interests in a diligent and professional manner.
Maintain the company's economic health.
Safeguard the company's resources and ensure their prudent and effective use.
Refrain from giving excessive gifts and entertainment.

Constituency: Investors

Standard:
Provide a fair and competitive (or better) return on investment.

Key Concept: Loyalty

Constituency: Company

Standard:
Use position and company resources only for company purposes (not for personal gain).
Disclose potential conflicts between personal and company interests.
Refrain from activities involving actual conflicts of interest, such as self-dealing and competing with the company.

Key Concept: Loyalty

Constituency: Company

Standard:

Refrain from receiving excessive gifts and entertainment. Refrain from pursuing for personal benefit opportunities discovered through position or company resources.

Constituency: Investors

Standard:

Refrain from trading in the company's securities on the basis of confidential company information.

II. PROPERTY PRINCIPLE: Respect property and the rights of those who own it. Refrain from theft and misappropriation, avoid waste, and safeguard the property entrusted to you.

Key Concept: Protection

Constituency: Company

Standard:

Protect company assets, including confidential and proprietary information, funds, and equipment.

Key Concept: Theft

Constituency: Company

Standard:

Do not misappropriate company resources through theft, embezzlement, or other means.

Constituency: Competitors

Standard:

Respect rivals' property rights, including those regarding intellectual property.

III. RELIABILITY PRINCIPLE: Honor commitments. Be faithful to your word and follow through on promises agreements, and other voluntary undertakings, whether or not embodied in legally enforceable contracts.

Key Concept: Contracts

Constituency: Suppliers/Partners

Standard:

Pay suppliers and partners on time and in accordance with agreed-on terms.

Key Concept: Promises

Constituency: All

Standard:

Honor promises and agreements.

Key Concept: Commitments

Constituency: All

Standard:

Fulfill implicit and explicit obligations to all constituencies.

IV. TRANSPARENCY PRINCIPLE: Conduct business in a truthful and open manner. Refrain from deceptive acts and practices, keep accurate records, and make timely disclosures of material information while respecting obligations of confidentiality and privacy.

Key Concept: Truthfulness

Constituency: All

Standard:

Be honest and respect truth in all activities. Record transactions in a fair and accurate manner.

Constituency: Suppliers/Partners

Standard:

Deal with suppliers and partners honestly.

Key Concept: Deception

Constituency: Customers

Standard:

Avoid deceptive and misleading statements and omissions in customer-related activities, such as marketing, sales, and research.

Constituency: Competitors

Standard:

Do not acquire commercial information by dishonest or unethical means.

Key Concept: Disclosure

Constituency: All

Standard:

Make timely disclosures of relevant financial and nonfinancial information.
Engage in transparent accounting and financial reporting.

Constituency: Investors

Standard:

Provide investors with relevant, accurate, and timely information.

Constituency: Customers

Standard:

Give customers adequate health and safety information, warnings, and labels.
Provide accurate information about the content, use, and maintenance of products.

Constituency: Employees

Standard:

Give reasonable notice of operational changes likely to have a major effect on employees' livelihood.

Key Concept: Candor

Constituency: Employees

Standard:

Communicate in an open and honest manner, subject to legal and competitive constraints.

Constituency: Public

Standard:

Communicate and consult with communities affected by environmental, health, and safety impacts of the enterprise.

Key Concept: Objectivity

Constituency: All

Standard:

Adhere to independent auditing and financial-reporting standards.

V. DIGNITY PRINCIPLE: Respect the dignity of all people. Protect the health, safety, privacy, and human rights* of others; refrain from coercion; and adopt practices that enhance human development in the workplace, the marketplace, and the community.

Key Concept: Respect for the Individual

Constituency: All

Standard:
Respect the dignity and human rights of others.

Constituency: Employees

Standard:
Adopt work practices that respect employees' dignity and human rights.
Prevent harassment in the workplace.

Constituency: Suppliers/Partners

Standard:
Prefer suppliers and partners whose employment practices respect dignity and human rights.

Constituency: Public

Standard:
Support and protect human rights within the company's sphere of influence.

Key Concept: Health & Safety

Constituency: All

Standard:
Protect human health and safety.

Constituency: Customers

Standard:
Ensure that products and services sustain or enhance customer health and safety.

Constituency: Employees

Standard:
Protect employees from avoidable injury and illness in the workplace.
Provide a work environment that is free from substance abuse.

Constituency: Suppliers/Partners

Standard:
Prefer suppliers and partners whose work practices respect international labor standards on health and safety.

Key Concept: Privacy & Confidentiality

Constituency: Customers

Standard:
Respect customers' privacy.
Protect confidential customer information.

Constituency: Employees

Standard:
Respect employee privacy.
Protect confidential employee information.

Key Concept: Use of Force

Constituency: Employees

Standard:
Abstain from directly or indirectly using forced or child labor.

Constituency: Public

Standard:
Ensure that security personnel respect international standards on the use of force.
Contribute to the elimination of forced labor and abusive labor practices,

Key Concept: Association & Expression

Constituency: Employees

Standard:
Recognize employees' right to free association and collective bargaining.

Constituency: Suppliers/Partner

Standard:
Prefer suppliers and partners whose work practices respect international labor standards on free association and collective bargaining.

Constituency: Customers

Standard:
Respect customers' cultures.

Constituency: Public

Standard:
Respect local cultures.

Key Concept: Learning & Development

Constituency: Employees

Standard:
Assist employees in developing skills and knowledge.
Create employment opportunities that enhance human development.

Key Concept: Employment Security

Constituency: Employees

Standard:
Safeguard employment and employability.

VI. FAIRNESS PRINCIPLE: Engage in free and fair competition, deal with all parties fairly and equitably, and practice nondiscrimination in employment and contracting.

Key Concept: Fair Dealing

Constituency: All

Standard:
Deal fairly with all parties.

Constituency: Investors

Standard:
Deal fairly with minority share owners.

Constituency: Customers

Standard:
Treat customers fairly in all aspects of transactions.

---

*In corporate codes, the term "human rights" typically refers to the issues of nondiscrimination, health and safety, and rights to free association. The term "international labor standards" generally refers to this set of issues as well.

Set prices that are reasonable and commensurate with quality.

Constituency: Employees

Standard:

Offer fair and reasonable compensation.

Constituency: Suppliers/Partners

Standard:

Deal fairly in all activities, including pricing, licensing, and rights to sell.

Key Concept: Fair Treatment

Constituency: Employees

Standard:

Practice nondiscrimination and provide equal employment opportunity.

Constituency: Suppliers/Partners

Standard:

Provide equal opportunity to suppliers owned by minorities and women.

Key Concept: Fair Treatment

Constituency: Suppliers/Partners

Standard:

Prefer suppliers and partners whose employment practices respect international labor standards on nondiscrimination.

Key Concept: Fair Competition

Constituency: Competitors

Standard:

Engage in free and fair competition.

Refrain from colluding with competitors on prices, bids, output, or market allocations.

Refrain from seeking or participating in questionable payments or favors to secure competitive advantage.

Constituency: Suppliers/Partners

Standard:

Require suppliers and partners to refrain from bribery and improper payments.

Key Concept: Fair Process

Constituency: Employees

Standard:

Do not retaliate against employees who report violations of law or company standards.

VII. CITIZENSHIP PRINCIPLE: Act as responsible citizens of the community. Respect the law, protect public goods, cooperate with public authorities, avoid improper involvement in politics and government, and contribute to community betterment.

Key Concept: Law & Regulation

Constituency: All

Standard:

Obey applicable laws and regulations.

Do not participate in money laundering or other illegal activities that support terrorism, drug traffic, or other organized crime.

Constituency: Investors

Standard:

Do not obstruct legal rights of share owners.

Constituency: Competitors

Standard:

Adhere to competition laws.

Constituency: Public

Standard:

Adhere to environmental laws and standards domestically and internationally.

Adhere to the letter and spirit of tax laws and make timely payments of tax liabilities.

Key Concept: Public Goods

Constituency: All

Standard:

Do not condone or participate in bribery or other forms of corruption.

Protect and, where possible, improve the natural environment.

Promote sustainable development.

Constituency: Customers

Standard:

Ensure that products and services sustain or enhance the natural environment.

Constituency: Suppliers/Partners

Standard:

Prefer suppliers and partners who observe applicable environmental standards.

Constituency: Public

Standard:

Do not use lack of scientific certainty as a reason to postpone cost-effective measures to address threats of serious damage to the environment.

Key Concept: Cooperation with Authorities

Constituency: Customers

Standard:

Cooperate with public authorities to address threats to public health and safety from the company's products and services.

Constituency: Employees

Standard:

Cooperate with employee groups, government, and others to address employment dislocations created by business decisions.

Key Concept: Political Noninvolvement

Constituency: Public

Standard:

Recognize government's obligation and jurisdiction concerning society at large.

Avoid improper involvement in political activities and campaigns.

Key Concept: Civic Contribution

Constituency: All

Standard:

Contribute to the economic and social development of local communities and the world.

Develop innovations in technology, products, processes, and practices.

Constituency: Public

Standard:

Contribute to charitable causes.

Support employee involvement in civic affairs.

Take a leading role in preserving and enhancing the physical environment.

VIII. RESPONSIVENESS PRINCIPLE:

Engage with parties who may have legitimate claims and concerns relating to the company's activities, and be responsive to public needs while recognizing the government's role and jurisdiction in protecting the public interest.

Key Concept: Addressing Concerns

Constituency: Investors

Standard:

Respect share owners' requests, suggestions, complaints, and formal resolutions.

Constituency: Customers

Standard:

Offer products and services whose quality meets or exceeds customers' requirements.

Provide timely service and remedies for customer complaints.

Constituency: Employees

Standard:

Engage in good-faith negotiation in cases of conflict.

Respond to employees' suggestions, requests, and complaints.

Key Concept: Public Involvement

Constituency: Public

Standard:

Collaborate with community groups, and support public policies that promote economic and social development.

Cooperate in efforts to eliminate bribery and corruption.

Support and protect democratic institutions.

Support diversity and social integration.

Review and Discussion Questions

1. Present a business situation where you think that the authors' Fiduciary Principle and Dignity Principle come into conflict with one another. Do you think that this conflict is inherent in an agent's discharging both fiduciary and respect-for-others duties or merely an upshot of how the authors determine the range of one's duty to respect others? Explain and elaborate.

2. Suppose that you are assigned the task of creating a Code, based on the authors' GBS Codex, for a corporation that is involved, like Maple Leaf Food Canada, in the processing of food products. Present here that part of your code which deals with the provisions relevant to the company's *clients* (consumers) and *suppliers*.

3. What, if anything, does the authors' research reveal about the claims of "ethical" and "cultural" relativism in the business domain? Explain.

Further Reading for Chapter 1

Ethics

David Callahan, *The Cheating Culture* (Orlando, FL: Harcourt, 2004) argues that cheating is on the increase throughout American society.

James Rachels, *The Elements of Moral Philosophy*, 4th ed. (New York: McGraw-Hill, 2003) is an excellent, clear introduction.

George Sher, ed., *Moral Philosophy*, 2nd ed. (San Diego: Harcourt Brace Jovanovich, 1998) and **Louis P. Pojman**, ed., *Ethical Theory*, 4th ed. (Belmont, CA: Wadsworth, 2002) offer more advanced readings on various topics in moral philosophy.

Moral Reasoning

Patrick Hurley, *A Concise Introduction to Logic*, 9th ed. (Belmont, CA: Wadsworth, 2006) is a good introduction to all the main areas of logic.

Joel Rudinow and **Vincent Barry**, *Invitation to Critical Thinking*, 5th ed. (Belmont, CA: Wadsworth, 2004) provides a guide to argument assessment.

Business and Morality

Both **Richard T. De George**, *Business Ethics*, 6th ed. (New York: Macmillan, 2006) and **Manuel G. Velasquez**, *Business Ethics*, 6th ed. (Upper Saddle River, NJ: Prentice Hall, 2006) contain useful introductions to moral philosophy in relation to business. A valuable reference work is *The Blackwell Encyclopedia of Management, vol 2: Business Ethics*, 2nd ed., ed. **Patricia Werhane** and **R. Edward Freeman** (Malden, Mass.: Blackwell, 2005). **Robert E. Frederick**, ed., *A Companion to Business Ethics* (Malden, MA.: Blackwell, 1999) is a collection of essays by different authors on all aspects of business ethics. Two pertinent discussions of moral conduct in business are **Glenn Martin**, "Once Again: Why Should Business Be Ethical?" *Business and Professional Ethics Journal* 17 (Winter 1998) and **Kevin Gibson**, "Excuses, Excuses: Moral Slippage in the Workplace," *Business Horizons* 43 (November–December 2000). **William H. Shaw**, ed., *Ethics at Work: Basic Readings in Business Ethics* (New York: Oxford University Press, 2003) contains essays on various moral issues that arise in business.

Three good sources of advanced work in business ethics are the *Business and Professional Ethics Journal*, the *Business Ethics Quarterly*, and the *Journal of Business Ethics*.

2

Normative Theories of Ethics

In an award-winning television drama, police captain Frank Furillo firmly believes that the two toughs just brought in by his officers are guilty of the rape-murder of a nun earlier that morning inside the parish church. But the evidence is only circumstantial. As word of the crime spreads, the community is aghast and angry. From all sides—the press, local citizens, city hall, the police commissioner—pressure mounts on Furillo and his department for a speedy resolution of the matter. On the street outside Furillo's office, a mob is growing frenzied, hoping to get their hands on the two young men and administer "street justice" to them. Someone in the crowd has even taken a shot at the suspects inside the police station!

The police, however, have only enough evidence to arraign the suspects on the relatively minor charge of being in possession of goods stolen from the church. Furillo and his colleagues could demand a high bail, thus keeping the defendants in custody while the police try to turn up evidence that will convict the men of murder. But in a surprise move at the arraignment, the district attorney, acting in conjunction with Furillo, declines to ask the judge for bail. The men are free to go, but they and their outraged public defender, Joyce Davenport, know that their lives will be worthless once they hit the streets: community members have sworn to avenge the much-loved sister if the police are unable to do their job. If they wish to remain in police custody, and thus safe, their only choice is to confess to murder. So the two men confess.

Davenport argues passionately but unsuccessfully against what she considers to be a police-state tactic. Anyone in that circumstance, guilty or innocent, would confess. It is an affront to the very idea of the rule of law, she contends: police coercion by way of mob pressure. No system of justice can permit such conduct from its public officials. Yet the confession allows the police to locate the murder weapon, thus bringing independent confirmation of the culprits' guilt. Furillo's tactic, nevertheless, does not rest easily with his own conscience, and the screenplay closes with him entering the church confessional later that night: "Forgive me, Father, for I have sinned . . ."

Furillo is understandably worried about whether he did the morally right thing. His action was successful, and it was for a good cause. But does the end always justify the means? Did the police and district attorney behave in a way that accords with due process and the rights of defendants? Should community pressure influence one's professional decisions? Did Furillo act in accordance with some principle that he could defend publicly? In a tough and controversial situation like this, the issue does not concern the moral sincerity of either Furillo or Davenport. Both can be assumed to want to do what is right, but what exactly is the morally justified thing to do? How are we to judge Furillo's tactics?

Chapter 1 noted that a defensible moral judgment must be supportable by a sound moral principle. That is because when we judge something as wrong, we are not judging simply that it is wrong but also that it is wrong for some reason or by virtue of some general characteristic.[1] Moral principles thus provide the confirmatory standard for moral judgments. The use of these principles, however, is not a mechanical process in which one cranks in data and out pops an automatic moral judgment. Rather, the principles provide a conceptual framework that guides us in making moral decisions. Careful thought and open-minded reflection are always necessary to work from one's moral principles to a considered moral judgment.

But what are the appropriate principles to rely on when making moral judgments? The truth is that there is no consensus among people who have studied ethics and reflected on these matters. Different theories exist as to the proper standard of right and wrong. As the British philosopher Bernard Williams put it, we are heirs to a rich and complex ethical tradition, in which a variety of different moral principles and ethical considerations intertwine and sometimes compete.[2]

This chapter discusses the different normative perspectives and rival ethical principles that are our heritage. After distinguishing between what are called consequentialist and nonconsequentialist normative theories, it looks in detail at several ethical approaches, discussing their pros and cons and their relevance to moral decision making in an organizational context:

1. Egoism, both as an ethical theory and as a psychological theory

2. Utilitarianism, the theory that the morally right action is the one that achieves the greatest total amount of happiness for everyone concerned

3. Kant's ethics, with his categorical imperative and his emphasis on moral motivation and respect for persons

4. Other nonconsequentialist normative themes: duties, moral rights, and prima facie principles

The chapter concludes with an attempt to tie together the major concerns of the different normative theories and suggests a general way of approaching moral decision making.

CONSEQUENTIALIST AND NONCONSEQUENTIALIST THEORIES

In ethics, *normative theories* propose—some thinkers might say "prescribe"—some principle or principles for distinguishing right actions from wrong actions. These theories can, for convenience, be divided into two kinds: consequentialist and nonconsequentialist.

Many philosophers have argued that the moral rightness of an action is determined solely by its results. If its consequences are good, then the act is right; if they are bad, the act is wrong. Moral theorists who adopt this approach are therefore called *consequentialists*. They determine what is right by weighing the ratio of good to bad that an action will produce. The right act is the one that produces (or will probably produce) at least as great a ratio of good to evil as any other course of action.

Of course, the question arises immediately, Consequences for whom? Should one consider the consequences only for one's self? Or the consequences for everyone affected? The two most important consequentialist theories, *egoism* and *utilitarianism*, are distinguished by their different answers to this question. Egoism advocates individual self-interest as its guiding principle, whereas utilitarianism holds that one must take into account everyone affected by the action. But both theories agree that rightness and wrongness are solely a function of an action's results.

By contrast, *nonconsequentialist* (or *deontological*) theories contend that right and wrong are determined by more than the likely consequences of an action. Nonconsequentialists do not necessarily deny that consequences are morally significant, but they believe that other factors are also relevant to the moral assessment of an action. For example, a nonconsequentialist would hold that for Kevin to break his promise to Cindy is wrong not simply because it has bad results (Cindy's hurt feelings, Kevin's damaged reputation, and so on) but because of the inherent character of the act itself. Even if more good than bad were to come from Kevin's breaking the promise, a nonconsequentialist might still view it as wrong. What matters is the nature of the act in question, not just its results. This concept will become clearer later in the chapter as we examine some specific nonconsequentialist principles and theories.

EGOISM

In the late summer of 2000, a dismayed American public learned that the Firestone tires on Ford Explorers, one of America's most popular vehicles, were dangerously prone to split apart on the road, causing the SUVs to roll over and crash. When officials began demanding a recall, the controversy was reminiscent of an earlier one involving Firestone's "500" steel-belted radials, which a subcommittee of the U.S. House of Representatives had implicated in at least fifteen deaths. When Firestone announced that it was discontinuing the controversial "500," American newspapers at the time interpreted this to mean that Firestone would immediately remove the tires from the market. In fact, Firestone intended only a "rolling phaseout" and continued to manufacture the tire. Asked later why the company had not corrected the media's misinterpretation of its intent, a spokesperson said it was Firestone policy to ask for corrections only when it was beneficial to the company to do so—in other words, only when it was in the company's self-interest.

The view that equates morality with self-interest is referred to as *egoism*. Egoism contends that an act is morally right if and only if it best promotes the agent's own long-term interests. (Here an "agent" can be a single person or, as in the Firestone example, an organization.) Egoists use their best long-term advantage as the standard for measuring an action's rightness. If an action produces or will probably produce for the agent, in the long run, a greater ratio of good to evil than any other alternative action, then that action is the right one to perform, and the agent should take that course to be moral.

Moral philosophers distinguish between two kinds of egoism: personal and impersonal. Personal egoists claim they should pursue their own best long-term interests, but they do not say what others should do. Impersonal egoists claim that everyone should follow his or her best long-term interests.

Misconceptions about Egoism

Several misconceptions haunt both versions of egoism. One is that egoists do only what they like, that they believe in "Eat, drink, and be merry." Not so. Undergoing unpleasant, even painful, experience would be consistent with egoism, provided that such temporary sacrifice is necessary for the advancement of one's long-term interests.

Another misconception is that all egoists endorse *hedonism*, the view that pleasure (or happiness) is the only thing that is good in itself, that it is the ultimate good, the one thing in life worth pursuing for its own sake. Although some egoists are hedonistic—as was the ancient Greek philosopher Epicurus (341–270 BCE)—other egoists have a broader view of what constitutes self-interest. They identify the good with knowledge, power, or what some modern psychologists call self-actualization. Egoists may, in fact, hold any theory as to what is good.

A final but very important misconception is that egoists cannot act honestly, be gracious and helpful, or otherwise promote other people's interests. Egoism, however, requires us to do whatever will best further our own interests, and this may sometimes require us to act in ways which advance the interests of others. In particular, egoism tells us to benefit others, if we expect that our doing so will be reciprocated, or that the act will bring us pleasure, or that it will promote our own good in some way. For example, egoism might discourage a shopkeeper from trying to cheat customers because it is likely to hurt business in the long run. Or egoism might recommend to the chair of the board that she hire as a vice-president her nephew, who is not the best candidate for the job but of whom she is very fond. Hiring the nephew might bring her more satisfaction than any other course of action, even if the nephew doesn't perform his job as well as someone else might.

Psychological Egoism

So egoism does not preach that we should never assist others but rather that we have no basic moral duty to do so. The only moral obligation we have is to ourselves. Although you and I are not required to act in the interests of others, we should so act if that is the best way to promote our own self-interest. In short: Always look out for "number one."

Proponents of the ethical theory of egoism generally attempt to derive their basic moral principle from the alleged fact that human beings are by nature selfish creatures. According to this doctrine, termed *psychological egoism*, people are, as a matter of fact, so constructed that they must behave selfishly. Psychological egoism asserts that all actions are in fact selfishly motivated and that truly unselfish actions are therefore impossible. Even such apparently self-sacrificial acts as giving up one's own life to save the lives of one's children or blowing the whistle on one's organization's misdeeds at great personal expense are, according to psychological egoism, done to satisfy the person's own self-interested desires. For example, the parent may seek to perpetuate the family line or to avoid guilt, and the worker may be after fame or revenge.

Problems with Egoism

Although egoism as an ethical doctrine has always had its adherents, the theory is open to very strong objections. It is safe to say that few, if any, philosophers today would advocate it as either a personal or an organizational morality. Consider these objections:

1. *Psychological egoism is not a sound theory.* Of course, self-interest motivates all of us to some extent, and we all know of situations in which someone pretended to be acting altruistically or morally but was really only motivated by self-interest. The theory of psychological egoism contends, however, that self-interest is the only thing that ever motivates anyone.

Now this claim seems open to many counterexamples. Take the actual case of a man who, while driving a company truck, spotted smoke coming from inside a parked car and a child trying to escape from the vehicle. The man quickly made a U-turn, drove up to the burning vehicle, and found a little girl trapped in the back seat, restrained by a seat belt. Flames raged in the front seat as heavy smoke billowed from the car. Disregarding his own safety, the man entered the car and removed the infant, who authorities said would have otherwise died from the poisonous fumes and the flames.

Or take a more mundane example. It's Saturday, and you feel like having a beer with a couple of pals and watching the ball game. On the other hand, you believe you ought to take your two children to the zoo, as you had earlier suggested to them you might. Going to the zoo would bring them a lot of pleasure—and besides, you haven't done much with them recently. Of course, you love your children and it will bring you some pleasure to go to the zoo with them, but—let's face it—they've been rather cranky lately and you'd prefer to watch the ball game. Nonetheless, you feel an obligation and so you go to the zoo.

These appear to be cases in which people are acting for reasons that are not self-interested. Of course, the reasons that lead you to take your children to the zoo—a sense of obligation, a desire to promote their happiness—are your reasons, but that by itself does not make them self-interested reasons. Still less does it show that you are selfish. Anything that you do is a result of your desires, but that fact doesn't establish what the believer in psychological egoism claims—namely, that the only desires you have, or the only desires that ultimately move you, are self-interested desires.

Psychological egoists (that is, advocates of the theory of psychological egoism) will claim that deep down both the heroic man who saved the girl and the non-heroic parent who took the children to the zoo were really motivated by self-interest in some way or another. Maybe the hero was hoping to win praise or the parent to advance his or her own pleasure by enhancing the children's affection for the parent. Or maybe some other self-interested consideration motivated them. Psychological egoists can always claim that some yet-to-be-identified subconscious egoistic motivation is the main impulse behind any action.

At this point, though, the psychological egoists' claims sound a little farfetched, and we may suspect them of trying to make their theory true by definition. Whatever example we come up with, they will simply claim that the person is really motivated by self-interest. One may well wonder how scientific this theory is, or how much content it has, when the hero and the coward, the parent who goes to the zoo and the parent who stays home, are equally selfish in their motivations.

A defender of egoism as an ethical doctrine might concede that people are not fully egoistic by nature and yet continue to insist that people ought morally to pursue only their own interests. Yet, without the doctrine of psychological egoism, ethical egoism loses much of the force or attractiveness it might have. Other types of ethical principles are possible. Admittedly, we all care about ourselves, but how much sense does it make to see self-interest as the basis of right and wrong? Do we really want to claim that someone acting altruistically is behaving immorally?

2. *Ethical egoism is not really a moral theory at all.* Many critics of egoism as an ethical standard contend that it misunderstands the nature and point of morality. As Chapter 1 explained, morality serves to restrain our purely self-interested desires so we can all live together. If our interests never came into conflict—that is, if it were never advantageous for one person to deceive or cheat another—then we would have no need for morality. The moral standards of a society provide the basic guidelines for cooperative social existence and allow us to resolve conflicts by appeal to shared principles of justification.

It is difficult to see how ethical egoism could perform this function. In a society of egoists, people might well agree publicly to follow certain rules so their lives would run more smoothly. But it would be a very unstable world, because people—being egoists—would not hesitate to break the rules if they thought they could get away with it and benefit personally by it. Nor can egoism provide a means for settling conflicts and disputes, because it simply enjoins on each party to do whatever is necessary to promote effectively their own interests.

Many moral theorists maintain that moral principles apply equally to the conduct of all persons and that their application requires us to be objective and impartial. Moral agents are seen as agents who, despite their own involvement in an issue, can be reasonably disinterested and objective; that is, who try to see all sides of an issue without being committed to the interests of a particular individual or group, including themselves. If we accept this attitude of detachment and impartiality as at least part of what it means to take a moral point of view, then we must look for it in any proposed moral principle.

Those who make egoism their moral standard are anything but objective, for they seek to guide themselves by their own best interests, regardless of the issue or circumstances. They do not even attempt to be impartial, except insofar as impartiality furthers their own interests. And, according to their theory, any third party offering advice should simply represent his or her own interest.

3. *Ethical egoism ignores blatant wrongs.* The most common objection to egoism as an ethical doctrine is that by reducing everything to the standard of best long-term self-interest, egoism takes no stand against such seemingly immoral acts as theft, murder, racial and sexual discrimination, deliberately false advertising, and wanton pollution. All such actions are morally neutral until the test of self-interest is applied.

Of course, the defender of egoism might argue that this objection begs the question by assuming that such acts are immoral and then repudiating egoism on this basis when, in fact, their morality is the very issue that moral principles such as egoism are meant to resolve. Still, egoism must respond to the widely observed human desire to be fair or just, a desire that at least sometimes seems stronger than competing selfish desires. A moral principle that allows the possibility of murder in the cause of self-interest offends our basic intuitions about right and wrong; it clashes with many of our considered moral beliefs.

UTILITARIANISM

Utilitarianism is the moral doctrine that we should always act to produce the greatest possible balance of good over bad for everyone affected by our actions. By "good," utilitarians understand happiness or pleasure. Thus, the greatest happiness of all constitutes the standard that determines whether an action is right or wrong. Although the basic theme of utilitarianism is present in the writings of many earlier thinkers, Jeremy Bentham (1748–1832) and John Stuart Mill (1806–1873) were the first to develop the theory explicitly and in detail. Both Bentham and Mill were philosophers with a strong interest in legal and social reform. They used the utilitarian standard to evaluate and criticize the social and political institutions of their day—for example, the prison system. As a result, utilitarianism has long been associated with social improvement.

Bentham viewed a community as no more than the individual persons who compose it. The interests of the community are simply the sum of the interests of its members. An action promotes the interests of an individual when it adds to the individual's pleasure or diminishes the person's pain. Correspondingly, an action augments the happiness of a community only insofar as it increases the total amount of individual happiness. In this way, Bentham argued for the utilitarian principle that actions are right if they promote the greatest human welfare, wrong if they do not.

For Bentham, pleasure and pain are merely types of sensations. He offered a "hedonic calculus" of six criteria for evaluating pleasure and pain exclusively by their quantitative differences—in particular, by their intensity and duration. This calculus, he believed, makes possible an objective determination of the morality of anyone's conduct, individual or collective, on any occasion.

Bentham rejected any distinctions based on the type of pleasure except insofar as they might indicate differences in quantity. Thus, whenever equal amounts of pleasure are involved, throwing darts is as good as writing poetry and baking a cake as good as composing a symphony; reading Stephen King is of no less value than reading Shakespeare. Although he himself was an intelligent, cultivated man, Bentham maintained that there is nothing intrinsically better about cultivated and intellectual pleasures than about crude and prosaic ones. The only issue is which yields the greater amount of enjoyment.

John Stuart Mill thought Bentham's concept of pleasure was too simple. He viewed human beings as having elevated faculties that allow them to pursue various higher kinds of pleasure. The pleasures of the intellect and imagination, in particular, have a higher value than those of mere physical sensation. Thus, for Mill the utility principle allows consideration of the relative quality of pleasure and pain, not just their intensity and duration.

Although Bentham and Mill had different conceptions of pleasure, both men equated pleasure and happiness and considered pleasure the ultimate value. In this sense they are hedonists: pleasure, in their view, is the one thing that is intrinsically good or worthwhile. Anything good is good only because it brings about pleasure (or happiness), directly or indirectly. Take education, for example. The learning process itself might be pleasurable to us; reflecting on or working with what we have learned might bring us satisfaction at some later time; or by making possible a career and life that we could not have had otherwise, education might bring us happiness indirectly. In contrast, critics of Bentham and Mill contend that things other than happiness are also inherently good—for example, knowledge, friendship, and aesthetic satisfaction. The implication is that these things are valuable even if they do not lead to happiness.

Some moral theorists have modified utilitarianism so that it aims at other consequences in addition to happiness. Other utilitarians, wary of trying to compare one person's happiness with another's, have interpreted their theory as requiring us not to maximize happiness but rather to maximize the satisfaction of people's desires or preferences. The focus here will be utilitarianism in its standard form, in which the good to be aimed at is human happiness or welfare, but what will be said about standard or classical utilitarianism applies, with the appropriate modifications, to other versions as well.

Although this chapter will also consider another form of utilitarianism, known as *rule utilitarianism*, utilitarianism in its most basic version, often called *act utilitarianism*, states that we must ask ourselves what the consequences of a particular act in a particular situation will be for all those affected. If its consequences bring more total good than those of any alternative course of action, then this action is the right one and the one we should perform. Thus a utilitarian could defend Frank Furillo's decision not to request bail, thereby coercing a confession from the suspects.

Six Points about Utilitarianism

Before evaluating utilitarianism, one should understand some points that might lead to confusion and misapplication. First, when deciding which action will produce the greatest happiness, we must consider unhappiness or pain as well as happiness. Suppose, for example, that an action produces eight units of happiness and four units of unhappiness. Its net worth is four units of happiness. Suppose also that an opposed action produces ten units of happiness and seven units of unhappiness; its net worth is three units. In this case we should choose the first action over the second. In the event that both lead not to happiness but to unhappiness, and there is no third option, we should choose the one that brings fewer units of unhappiness.

Second, actions affect different people to different degrees. Your playing your radio loudly might enhance two persons' pleasure a little, cause significant discomfort to two others, and leave a fifth person indifferent. The utilitarian theory is not that each person votes on the basis of his or her pleasure or pain, with the majority ruling, but rather that we add up the various pleasures and pains, however large or small, and go with the action that brings about the greatest net amount of happiness.

Third, because utilitarians evaluate actions according to their consequences, and actions produce different results in different circumstances, almost anything might, in principle, be morally right in some particular circumstance. For example, whereas breaking a promise generally produces unhappiness, there can be circumstances in which, on balance, more happiness would be produced by breaking a promise than by keeping it. In those circumstances, utilitarianism would require us to break the promise.

Fourth, utilitarians wish to maximize happiness not simply immediately but in the long run as well. All the indirect ramifications of an act have to be taken into account. Lying might seem a good way out of a tough situation, but if and when the people we deceive find out, not only will they be unhappy, but also our reputations and our relationships with them will be damaged. This is a serious risk that a utilitarian cannot ignore.

Fifth, utilitarians acknowledge that we often do not know with certainty what the future consequences of our actions will be. Accordingly, we must act so that the expected or likely happiness is as great as possible. If I take my friend's money, unbeknownst to him, and buy lottery tickets with it, there is a chance that we will end up millionaires and that my action will have maximized happiness all around. But the odds are definitely against it; the most likely result is loss of money (and probably of a friendship, too). Therefore, no utilitarian could justify gambling with purloined funds on the grounds that it might maximize happiness.

Sometimes it is difficult to determine the likely results of alternative actions, and no modern utilitarian really believes that we can assign precise units of happiness and unhappiness to people. But as Mill reminds us, we really do have quite a lot of experience as to what typically makes people happy or unhappy. In any case, as utilitarians our duty is to strive to maximize total happiness, even when it may seem difficult to know what action is likely to promote the good effectively.

Finally, when choosing among possible actions, utilitarianism does not require us to disregard our own pleasure. Nor should we give it added weight. Rather, our own pleasure and pain enter into the calculus equally with the pleasures and pains of others. Even if we are sincere in our utilitarianism, we must guard against the possibility of being biased in our calculations when our own interests are at stake. For this reason, and because it would be time-consuming to do a utilitarian calculation before every action, utilitarians encourage us to rely on rules of thumb in ordinary moral circumstances. We can make it a rule of thumb, for example, to tell the truth and keep our promises, rather than to calculate possible pleasures and pains in every routine case, because we know that in general telling the truth and keeping promises result in more happiness than do lying and breaking promises.

Utilitarianism in an Organizational Context

Several features about utilitarianism make it appealing as a standard for moral decisions in business and non-business organizations.

First, utilitarianism provides a clear and straightforward basis for formulating and testing policies. By utilitarian standards, an organizational policy, decision, or action is good if it promotes the general welfare more than any other alternative. A policy is considered wrong (or in need of modification) if it does not promote total utility as well as some alternative would. Utilitarians do not ask us to accept rules, policies, or principles blindly. Rather, they require us to test their worth against the standard of utility.

Second, utilitarianism provides an objective and attractive way of resolving conflicts of self-interest. This feature of utilitarianism dramatically contrasts with egoism, which seems incapable of resolving such conflicts. By proposing a standard outside self-interest, utilitarianism greatly minimizes and may actually eliminate such disputes. Thus, individuals within organizations make moral decisions and evaluate their actions by appealing to a uniform standard: the general good.

Third, utilitarianism provides a flexible, result-oriented approach to moral decision making. By recognizing no actions of a general kind as inherently right or wrong, utilitarianism encourages organizations to focus on the results of their actions and policies, and it allows them to tailor their decisions to suit the complexities of their situations. This facet of utilitarianism enables organizations to make realistic and workable moral decisions.

Critical Inquiries of Utilitarianism

1. *Is utilitarianism really workable?* Utilitarianism instructs us to maximize happiness, but in difficult cases we may be very uncertain about the likely results of the alternative courses of action open to us. Furthermore, comparing your level of happiness or unhappiness with mine is at best tricky, at worst impossible—and when many people are involved, the matter may get hopelessly complex. Even if we assume that it is possible to make comparisons and to calculate the various possible results of each course of action that a person might take (and the odds of each happening), is it realistic to expect people to take the time to make those calculations and, if they do, to make them accurately? Some critics of act utilitarianism have contended that teaching people to follow the

basic utilitarian principle would not in fact promote happiness because of the difficulties in applying utilitarianism accurately.

2. *Are some actions wrong, even if they produce good?* Like egoism, utilitarianism focuses on the results of an action, not on the character of the action itself. For utilitarians, no action is in itself objectionable. It is objectionable only when it leads to a lesser amount of total good than could otherwise have been brought about. Critics of utilitarianism, by contrast, contend that some actions can be immoral and thus actions we must not do, even if doing them would maximize happiness.

Suppose a dying woman has asked you to promise to send the $25,000 under her bed to her nephew in another part of the country. She dies without anyone else's knowing of the money or of the promise that you made. Now suppose, too, that you know the nephew is a spendthrift and a drunkard and, were the money delivered to him, it would be wasted in a week of outrageous partying. On the other hand, a very fine orphanage in your town needs such a sum to improve and expand its recreational facilities, something that would provide happiness to many children for years to come. It seems clear that on utilitarian grounds you should give the money to the orphanage, because this action would result in more total happiness.

Many people would balk at this conclusion, contending that it would be wrong to break your promise, even if doing so would bring about more good than keeping it. Having made a promise, you have an obligation to keep it, and a deathbed promise is particularly serious. Furthermore, the deceased woman had a right to do with her money as she wished; it is not for you to decide how to spend it. Likewise, having been bequeathed the money, the nephew has a right to it, regardless of how wisely or foolishly he might spend it. Defenders of utilitarianism, however, would insist that promoting happiness is all that really matters and warn you not to be blinded by moral prejudice.

Critics of utilitarianism, on the other hand, maintain that utilitarianism is morally blind in not just permitting, but also requiring, immoral actions in order to maximize happiness. Philosopher Richard Brandt states the case against act utilitarianism this way:

> Act-utilitarianism . . . implies that if you have employed a boy to mow your lawn and he has finished the job and asks for his pay, you should pay him what you promised only if you cannot find a better use for your money. . . . It implies that if your father is ill and has no prospect of good in his life, and maintaining him is a drain on the energy and enjoyments of others, then, if you can end his life without provoking any public scandal or setting a bad example, it is your positive duty to take matters into your own hands and bring his life to a close.[3]

In the same vein, ethicist A. C. Ewing concludes that "[act] utilitarian principles, logically carried out, would result in far more cheating, lying and unfair action than any good man would tolerate."[4]

Defenders of act utilitarianism would reply that these charges are exaggerated. Although it is theoretically possible, for example, that not paying the boy for his work might maximize happiness, this is extremely unlikely. Utilitarians contend that only in very unusual circumstances will pursuit of the good conflict with our ordinary ideas of right and wrong, and in those cases—like the deathbed promise—we should put aside those ordinary ideas. The anti-utilitarian replies that the theoretical possibility that utilitarianism may require immoral conduct shows it to be an unsatisfactory moral theory.

3. *Is utilitarianism unjust?* Utilitarianism concerns itself with the sum total of happiness produced, not with how that happiness is distributed. If policy X brings two units of happiness to each of five people and policy Y brings nine units of happiness to one person, one unit each to two others, and none to the remaining two, then Y is to be preferred (eleven units of happiness versus ten), even though it distributes that happiness very unequally.

Worse still from the critic's point of view, utilitarianism may even require that some people's happiness be sacrificed in order to achieve the greatest overall amount of happiness. Sometimes the general utility may be served only at the expense of a single individual or group. Under the right of "expropriation" ("eminent domain" in the U.S.), for example, the federal or provincial government may appropriate private property for public use, usually with compensation to the owner (such compensation is not guaranteed by the Canadian Constitution, though it is covered under statutory law). Thus, the government may legally purchase your house from you to widen a highway—even if you don't want to sell the house or want more money than the government is willing to pay. The public interest is served at your private expense. Is this just?

Or consider the Dan River experiment in the United States, part of the long-running controversy over the cause of "brown lung disease" (byssinosis). Claiming that the disease is caused by the inhalation of microscopic fibres in cotton dust, textile unions fought for years for tough regulations to protect their workers. The U.S. Occupational Safety and Health Administration (OSHA) responded by proposing cotton dust standards, which would require many firms to install expensive new equipment. A few months before the deadline for installing the equipment, officials at Dan River textile plants in Virginia asked the state to waive the requirements for a time so the company could conduct an experiment to determine the precise cause of brown lung disease. Both the state and the federal Department of Labor allowed the extension. In response, the textile workers union contended, "It is simply unconscionable to allow hundreds of cotton mill workers to continue to face a high risk of developing brown lung disease."[5]

Suppose that the Dan River project did expose workers to a "high risk" of contracting lung disease. If so, then a small group of individuals—633 textile workers at ten locations in Danville, Virginia—were being compelled to carry the burden of isolating the cause of brown lung disease. Is that just?

Although their critics would say no, utilitarians would respond that it is, if the experiment maximizes the total good of society. Does it? In fact, the results of the experiment were inconclusive, but if the project had succeeded in identifying the exact cause of the disease, then thousands of textile workers across the country would have benefited. Researchers might also have discovered a more economical way to ensure worker safety than by installing expensive new equipment, which in turn would have profited both consumers and the textile industry. Certainly, utilitarians would consider the potentially negative impact on workers, but only as one factor among others. At the time of the decision, after the interests of all affected parties have been weighed, if extending the deadline is likely to yield the greatest net benefit or utility, then doing so is just—even though workers might be injured.

The Interplay Between Self-Interest and Utility

Both self-interest and utility play important roles in organizational decisions, and the views of many businesspeople blend these two theories. To the extent that each business pursues its own interests and each businessperson tries to maximize personal success, business practice can be called egoistic. But business practice is also utilitarian in that pursuing self-interest is thought to maximize the total good, and, so long as it conducts itself by the established rules of the competitive game, may be seen as advancing the good of society as a whole. The classical capitalist economist Adam Smith (1723–1790) held such a view. He argued that if business is left to pursue its self-interest, the good of society will also be served. Indeed, Smith believed that only through egoistic pursuits could the greatest economic good for the whole society be produced. The essence of Smith's position can be seen in the following passage from his *The Wealth of Nations* (1776), in which he underscores the interplay between self-interest and the social good and between egoism and utilitarianism:

> Every individual is continually exerting himself to find out the most advantageous employment for whatever capital he can command. It is his own advantage, indeed, and not that of the society, which he has in view. But the study of his own advantage, naturally, or rather necessarily, leads him to prefer that employment which is most advantageous to the society. . . .
>
> As every individual, therefore, endeavours as much as he can . . . to employ his capital . . . [so] that its produce may be of the greatest value, every individual necessarily labors to render the annual revenue of the society as great as he can. He generally, indeed, neither intends to promote the public interest, nor knows how much he is promoting it. . . . He intends only his own security; and by directing that industry in such a manner as its product

may be of the greatest value, he intends only his own gain, and he is in this, as in many other cases, led by an invisible hand to promote an end which was no part of his intention. Nor is it always the worse for the society that it was no part of it. By pursuing his own interest he frequently promotes that of the society more effectually than when he really intends to promote it. I have never known much good done by those who affected to trade for the public good. It is an affectation, indeed, not very common among merchants, and very few words need be employed in dissuading them from it.[6]

Many today would agree with Smith,* conceding that business is part of a social system, that cooperation is necessary, and that certain competitive ground rules are needed and should be followed. At the same time, they would argue that the social system is best served by the active pursuit of self-interest within the context of established rules. Thus, the position these individuals recommend has been dubbed the ethics of "restrained egoism." It is egoistic because it recommends the pursuit of self-interest; it is restrained because it permits pursuit of self-interest only within the rules of business practice.[7]

KANT'S ETHICS

Most of us find the ideal of promoting human happiness and well-being an attractive one and, as a result, admire greatly people like Mother Teresa (1910–1997), who devoted her life to working with the poor. Despite the attractiveness of this ideal, many moral philosophers are critical of utilitarianism—particularly because, like egoism, it reduces all morality to a concern with consequences. Although nonconsequentialist normative theories vary significantly, adopting different approaches and stressing different themes, the writings of the preeminent German philosopher Immanuel Kant (1724–1804) provide an excellent example of a thoroughly nonconsequentialist approach to ethics. Perhaps few thinkers today would endorse Kant's theory on every point, but his work has greatly influenced subsequent philosophers and has helped shape our general moral culture.

Kant sought moral principles that do not rest on contingencies and that define actions as inherently right or wrong apart from any particular circumstances. He believed that moral rules can, in principle, be known as a result of reason alone and are not based on observation (as are, for example, scientific judgments). In contrast to utilitarianism and other consequentialist doctrines, Kant's ethical theory holds that we do not have to know anything about the likely results of, say, my telling a lie to my boss in order to know that it is immoral. "The basis of obligation," Kant wrote, "must not be sought in human nature, [nor] in the circumstances of the world." Rather it is *a priori*, by which he meant that moral reasoning is not based on factual knowledge and that reason by itself can reveal the basic principles of morality.

---

*Chapter 4 examines Smith's position in more detail.

Good Will

Chapter 1 mentioned Good Samaritan laws, which shield from lawsuits those rendering emergency aid. Such laws, in effect, give legal protection to the humanitarian impulse behind emergency interventions. They formally recognize that the interventionist's heart was in the right place, that the person's intention was irreproachable. And because the person acted from right intention, he or she should not be held liable for any inadvertent harm except in cases of extreme negligence. The widely observable human tendency to introduce a person's intentions in assigning blame or praise is a good springboard for engaging Kant's ethics.

Nothing, said Kant, is good in itself except a good will. This does not mean that intelligence, courage, self-control, health, happiness, and other things are not good and desirable. But Kant believed that their goodness depends on the will that makes use of them. Intelligence, for instance, is not good when used by an evil person.

By *will* Kant meant the uniquely human capacity to act from principle. Contained in the notion of good will is the concept of duty: Only when we act from duty does our action have moral worth. When we act only out of feeling, inclination, or self-interest, our actions—although they may be otherwise identical with ones that spring from the sense of duty—have no true moral worth.

Suppose that you're a clerk in a small convenience store. Late one night a customer pays for his five-dollar purchase with a twenty-dollar bill, which you mistake for a ten. It's only after the customer leaves that you realize you shortchanged him. You race out the front door and find him lingering by a vending machine. You give him the ten dollars with your apologies, and he thanks you profusely.

Can we say with certainty that you acted from a good will? Not necessarily. You may have acted from a desire to promote business or to avoid legal entanglement. If so, you would have acted in accordance with, but not from, duty. Your apparently virtuous gesture just happened to coincide with duty. According to Kant, if you do not will the action from a sense of your duty to be fair and honest, your action lacks moral worth. Actions have true moral worth only when they spring from a recognition of duty and a choice to discharge it.

But then what determines our duty? How do we know what morality requires of us? Kant answered these questions by formulating what he called the "categorical imperative." This extraordinarily significant moral concept is the linchpin of Kant's ethics.

The Categorical Imperative

We have seen that egoists and utilitarians allow factual circumstances or empirical data to determine moral judgments. In contrast, Kant believed that reason alone can yield a moral law. We need not rely on empirical evidence relating to consequences and to similar situations. Just as we know, seemingly through reason alone, such abstract truths as "Every change must have a cause," so we can arrive at absolute moral truth through non-empirical reasoning, and thereby discover our duty.

For Kant, an absolute moral truth must be logically consistent, free from internal contradiction. For example, it is a contradiction to say that an effect does not have a cause. Kant aimed to ensure that his absolute moral law would avoid such contradictions. If he could formulate such a rule, he maintained, everyone would be obliged to follow it without exception.

Kant believed that there is just one command (imperative) that is categorical—that is necessarily binding on all rational agents, regardless of any other considerations. From this one categorical imperative, this universal command, we can derive all commands of duty. Kant's *categorical imperative* says that we should always act in such a way that we can will the maxim of our action to become a universal law. So Kant's answer to the question "What determines whether an act is right?" is that an act is morally right if and only if we can will it to become a universal law of conduct.

The obvious and crucial question that arises here is, "When are we justified in saying that the maxim of our action can become a universal law of conduct?"

By *maxim*, Kant meant the subjective principle of an action, the principle (or rule) that people in effect formulate in determining their conduct. For example, suppose building contractor Martin promises to install a sprinkler system in a project but is willing to break that promise to suit his purposes. His maxim can be expressed this way: "I'll make promises that I'll break whenever keeping them no longer suits my purposes." This is the subjective principle, the maxim, that directs his action.

Kant insisted that the morality of any maxim depends on whether we can logically will it to become a universal law. Could Martin's maxim be universally acted on? That depends on whether the maxim as law would involve a contradiction. The maxim "I'll make promises that I'll break whenever keeping them no longer suits my purposes" could not be universally acted on, because it involves a contradiction of will. On the one hand, Martin is willing that it be possible to make promises and have them honoured. On the other, if everyone intended to break promises when they so desired, then promises would not be honoured in the first place, because it is in the nature of promises that they be believed. A law that allowed promise breaking would contradict the very nature of a promise. Similarly, a law that allowed lying would contradict the very nature of serious communication, for the activity of serious communication (as opposed to joking) requires that participants intend to speak the truth. I cannot, without contradiction, will both serious conversation and lying. By contrast, there is no problem, Kant thinks, in willing promise keeping or truth telling to be universal laws.

Consider, as another example, Kant's account of a man who, in despair after suffering a series of major setbacks, contemplates suicide. While still rational, the man asks whether it would be contrary to his duty to take his own life. Could the maxim of his action become a universal law of nature? Kant thinks not:

> His maxim is this: From self-love I make it my principle to shorten my life when its continued duration threatens more evil than it promises satisfaction. There only remains the question whether this principle of self-love can become a universal law of nature. One sees at once a contradiction in a system of nature whose law would destroy life by means of the very same feeling that acts so as to stimulate the furtherance of life. . . . Therefore, such a maxim cannot possibly hold as a universal law of nature and is, consequently, wholly inconsistent with the supreme principle of all duty.[8]

When Kant insists that a moral rule be consistently universalizable, he is saying that moral rules prescribe categorically, not hypothetically. A hypothetical prescription tells us what to do if we desire a particular outcome. Thus, "If I want people to like me, I should be nice to them" and "If you want to go to medical school, you must take biology" are hypothetical imperatives. They tell us what we must do on the assumption that we have some particular goal. If that is what we want, then this is what we must do. On the other hand, if we don't want to go to medical school, then the command to take biology does not apply to us. In contrast, Kant's imperative is categorical—it commands unconditionally. That is, it is necessarily binding on everyone, regardless of his or her specific goals or desires, regardless of consequences. A categorical imperative takes the form of "Do this" or "Don't do that"—no ifs, ands, or buts.

Universal Acceptability There is another way of looking at the categorical imperative. Every person, through his or her own acts of will, legislates the moral law. The moral rules that we obey are not imposed on us from the outside. They are self-imposed and self-recognized, fully internalized principles. The sense of duty that we obey comes from within; it is an expression of our own higher selves.

Thus, moral beings give themselves the moral law and accept its demands on themselves. But that is not to say we can prescribe anything we want, for we are bound by reason and its demands. Because reason is the same for all rational beings, we all give ourselves the same moral law. In other words, when you answer the question "What should I do?" you must consider what all rational beings should do. If the moral law is valid for you, it must be valid for all other rational beings.

To see whether a rule or principle is a moral law, we can thus ask if what the rule commands would be acceptable to all rational beings. In considering lying, theft, or murder, for example, you must consider the act not only from your own viewpoint but also from the perspective of the person lied to, robbed, or murdered. Presumably, rational beings do not want to be lied to, robbed, or murdered. The test of the morality of a rule, then, is not whether people in fact accept it but whether all rational beings thinking impartially and rationally would accept it regardless of whether they are the doers or the receivers of the actions. This is an important moral insight, and most philosophers see it as implicit in Kant's discussion of the categorical imperative, even though Kant (whose writings are difficult to understand) did not make the point in this form.

The principle of universal acceptability has important applications. Suppose a man advocates a hiring policy that discriminates against women. For this rule to be universally acceptable, the man would have to be willing to accept it if he were a woman, something he would presumably be unwilling to do. Or suppose the manufacturer of a product decides to market it even though the manufacturer knows that the product is unsafe when used in a certain common way and that consumers are ignorant of this fact. Applying the universal acceptability principle, the company's decision makers would have to be willing to advocate marketing the product even if they were themselves in the position of uninformed consumers. Presumably they would be unwilling to do this. So the rule that would allow the product to be marketed would fail the test of universal acceptability.

Humanity as an End, Never as Merely a Means In addition to the principle of universal acceptability, Kant explicitly offered another, very famous way of formulating the core idea of his categorical imperative. According to this formulation, rational creatures should always treat other rational creatures as ends in themselves and never as only means to ends. This formulation underscores Kant's belief that every human being has an inherent worth resulting from the sheer possession of rationality. We must always act in a way that respects this humanity in others and in ourselves.

As rational beings, humans would act inconsistently if they did not treat everyone else the way they themselves would want to be treated. Here we see shades of the Golden Rule. Indeed, Kant's moral philosophy can be viewed as a profound reconsideration of this basic nonconsequentialist principle. Because rational beings recognize their own inner worth, they would never wish to be used as entities possessing worth only as means to an end.

Thus, when investment brokers at Toronto, Montreal, or Vancouver encourage unnecessary buying and selling of stocks in order to reap a commission (a practice called "churning"), they are treating their clients simply as a means and not respecting them as persons, as ends in themselves. Likewise, Kant would object to using patients as subjects in medical experiments without their consent. Even though great social benefit might result from such experiments, the researchers would intentionally be using the patients solely as a means to the researchers' own goals and thus would be failing to respect the patients' basic humanity.

Kant maintained, as explained above, that an action is morally right if and only if we can will it to be a universal law. We now have two ways of reformulating his categorical imperative which may be easier to grasp and apply:

First reformulation: An action is right only if the agent would be willing to be so treated were the positions of the parties reversed.

Second reformulation: One must always act so as to treat other people as ends in themselves.

Kant in an Organizational Context

Like utilitarianism, Kant's moral theory has application for organizations.

First, the categorical imperative gives us firm rules to follow in moral decision making, rules that do not depend on circumstances or results and that do not permit individual exceptions. No matter what the consequences may be or who does it, some actions are always wrong. Lying is an example: no matter how much good may come from misrepresenting a product, such deliberate misrepresentation is always wrong. Similarly, it would be wrong to expose workers to some occupational health risk on the grounds that, for example, it advances medical knowledge.

Second, Kant introduces an important humanistic dimension into business decisions. One of the principal objections to egoism and utilitarianism is that they permit us to treat humans as means to ends. Kant's principles clearly forbid this. Many would say that respect for the inherent worth and dignity of human beings is much needed today in business, a field of human endeavour in which encroaching technology and computerization tend to dehumanize people under the guise of efficiency. Kant's theory puts the emphasis of organizational decision making where it belongs: on individuals. Organizations, after all, involve human beings working in concert to provide goods and services for other human beings. The primacy Kant gives to the individual person reflects this essential aspect of business.

Third, Kant stresses the importance of motivation and of acting on principle. According to him, it is not enough just to do the right thing; an action has moral worth only if it is done from a sense of duty—that is, from a desire to do the right thing for its own sake. The importance of this point is too often forgotten. Sometimes when individuals and organizations believe that an action promotes the interests of everyone, they are actually rationalizing—doing what is best for themselves and only imagining that somehow it will also benefit others. Worse still, they may defend their actions as morally praiseworthy, when they are in fact only behaving egoistically. They wouldn't do the morally justifiable thing if they didn't think it would pay off for them. By stressing the importance of motivation, a Kantian approach serves as a corrective to this. Even an action that helps others has moral value for Kant only if the person doing it is morally motivated—that is, acting on principle or out of moral conviction.

Critical Inquiries of Kant's Ethics

1. *What has moral worth?* According to Kant, the clerk who returns the ten dollars to the customer is doing the right thing. But if his action is motivated by self-interest (perhaps he wants to get a reputation for honesty), then it does not have moral worth. That seems plausible. But Kant also held that if the clerk does the right thing out of instinct, habit, or sympathy for the other person, then the act still does not have moral worth. Only if it is done out of a sense of duty does the clerk's action have moral value. Many moral theorists have felt that Kant was too severe on this point. Do we really want to say that giving money to famine relief efforts has no moral worth if one is emotionally moved to do so by pictures of starving children rather than by a sense of duty? We might, to the contrary, find a person with strong human sympathies no less worthy or admirable than the person who gives solely out of an abstract sense of duty.

2. *Is the categorical imperative an adequate test of right?* Kant said that a moral rule must function without exception. Critics wonder why the prohibition against such actions as lying, promise breaking, suicide, and so on must be exceptionless. They say that Kant failed to distinguish between saying that a person should not except himself or herself from a rule and that the rule itself has no exceptions.

If stealing is wrong, it's wrong for me as well as for you. "Stealing is wrong, except if I do it" is not universalizable, for then stealing would be right for all to do, which contradicts the assertion that stealing is wrong. But just because no one may make of oneself an exception to a rule, it does not follow that the rule itself has no exceptions.

Suppose, for example, that we decide that stealing is sometimes right, perhaps in the case of a person who is starving. Thus, the rule becomes "Never steal except when starving." This rule seems just as universalizable as "Never steal." The phrase "except . . ." can be viewed not as justifying a violation of the rule but as building a qualification into it. Critics in effect are asking why a qualified rule is not just as good as an unqualified one. If it is, then we no longer need to state rules in the simple, direct, unqualified manner that Kant did.

In fairness to Kant, it might be argued that his universalization formula can be interpreted flexibly enough to meet commonsense objections. For example, perhaps we could universalize the principle that individuals should steal rather than starve to death or that it is permissible to take one's own life to extinguish unspeakable pain. And yet to qualify the rules against stealing, lying, and taking one's life seems to invite a non-Kantian analysis to justify the exceptions. One could, it seems, universalize more than one moral rule in a given situation: "Do not lie unless a life is at stake" versus "Lying is wrong unless necessary to avoid the suffering of innocent people." If so, then the categorical imperative would supply at best a necessary, but not a sufficient, test of right. But once we start choosing among various alternative rules, then we are adopting an approach to ethics that Kant would have rejected.

3. *What does it mean to treat people as means?* Kant's mandate that individuals must always be considered as ends in themselves and never merely as means expresses our sense of the intrinsic value of the human spirit and has profound moral appeal. Yet it is not always clear when people are being treated as ends and when merely as means. For example, Kant believed that prostitution is immoral because, by selling their sexual services, prostitutes allow themselves to be treated as means. Prostitutes, however, are not the only ones to sell their services. Anyone who works for a wage does so. Does that mean that we are all being treated immorally, because our employers are presumably hiring us as a means to advance their own ends? Presumably not, because, we may retort, we freely agree to do the work. But then, the prostitute might have freely chosen that line of work, too.

OTHER NONCONSEQUENTIALIST PERSPECTIVES

For Kant, the categorical imperative provided the basic test of right and wrong, and he was resolutely nonconsequentialist in his application of it. You know now what he would say about the case of the deathbed promise: that the maxim permitting you to break your promise cannot be universalized, and hence it would be immoral of you to give the money to the orphanage, despite the happiness that doing so would bring. But nonconsequentialists are not necessarily Kantians, and several different nonutilitarian moral concerns emerged in the discussion of the deathbed promise example.

Critics of act utilitarianism believe that it is faulty for maintaining that we have one and only one moral duty. A utilitarian might follow various principles as rules of thumb, but they are only calculation substitutes. All that matters morally to utilitarians is the maximization of happiness. Yet this idea, many philosophers think, fails to do justice to the richness and complexity of our moral lives.

Prima Facie Obligations

One influential philosopher who argued this way was the British scholar W. D. Ross (1877–1971).[9] Ross rejected utilitarianism as too simple and as untrue to the way we ordinarily think about morality and about our moral obligations. We see ourselves, Ross and like-minded thinkers contend, as being under various moral duties that cannot be reduced to the single obligation to maximize happiness. Often these obligations grow out of special relationships into which we enter or out of determinate roles that we undertake. Our lives are intertwined with other people's in particular ways, and we have, as a result, certain specific moral obligations.

For example, as a professor, Rodriguez is obligated to assist her students in the learning process and to evaluate their work in a fair and educationally productive way— obligations to the specific people in her classroom that she does not have to other people. As a spouse, Rodriguez must maintain a certain emotional and sexual fidelity to her partner. As a parent, she must provide for the individual human beings who are her children. As a friend to Smith, she may have a moral responsibility to help him out in a time of crisis. Having borrowed money from

Chang, Rodriguez is morally obligated to pay it back. Thus, different relationships and different circumstances generate a variety of specific moral obligations.

In addition, we have moral duties that do not arise from our unique interactions and relationships with other people. For example, we ought to treat all people fairly, do what we can to remedy injustices, and make an effort to promote human welfare generally. The latter obligation is important, but for a nonconsequentialist like Ross it is only one among various obligations that people have.

At any given time, we are likely to be under more than one obligation, and sometimes these obligations can conflict. That is, we may have an obligation to do A and an obligation to do B, where it is not possible for us to do both A and B. For example, I promise to meet a friend on an urgent matter, and now, as I am hurrying there, I pass an injured person who is obviously in need of assistance. Stopping to aid the person will make it impossible for me to fulfill my promise. What should I do? For moral philosophers like Ross, there is no single answer for all cases. What I ought to do will depend on the circumstances and relative importance of the conflicting obligations. I have an obligation to keep my promise, and I have an obligation to assist people in distress. What I must decide is which of these obligations is, in the given circumstance, the more important. I must weigh the moral significance of the promise against the comparative moral urgency of assisting the injured person.

Ross and many contemporary philosophers believe that all (or at least most) of our moral obligations are prima facie ones. A *prima facie obligation* is one that can be overridden by a more important obligation. For instance, we take the keeping of promises seriously, but almost everyone would agree that in some circumstances—for example, when a life is at stake—it would be not only morally permissible, but morally required, to break a promise. Our obligation to keep a promise is a real one, and if there is no conflicting obligation, then we must keep the promise. But that obligation is not absolute or categorical; it could in principle be outweighed by a more stringent moral obligation. The idea that our obligations are prima facie is foreign to Kant's way of looking at things.

Consider an example that Kant himself discussed.[10] Imagine that a murderer comes to your door, wanting to know where your friend is so that he can kill her. Your friend is in fact hiding in your bedroom closet. Most people would probably agree that your obligation to your friend overrides your general obligation to tell the truth and that the right thing to do would be to lie to the murderer to throw him off your friend's trail. Although you have a genuine obligation to tell the truth, it is a prima facie obligation, one that other moral considerations can outweigh. Kant disagreed. He maintained that you must always tell the truth—that is, in all circumstances and without exception. For him, telling the truth is an absolute or categorical obligation, not a prima facie one.

Ross thought that our various prima facie obligations could be divided into seven basic types: duties of fidelity (that is, to respect explicit and implicit promises), duties of reparation (for previous wrongful acts), duties of gratitude, duties of justice, duties of beneficence (that is, to make the condition of others better), duties of self-improvement, and duties not to injure others.[11] Unlike utilitarianism, Ross's ethical perspective is pluralistic in recognizing a variety of genuine obligations. But contrary to Kant, Ross does not see these obligations as absolute and exceptionless. On both points, Ross contended that his view of morality more closely fits with our actual moral experience and the way we view our moral obligations.

Ross also saw himself as siding with commonsense morality in maintaining that our prima facie obligations are obvious. He believed that the basic principles of duty are as self-evident as the simplest rules of arithmetic and that any person who has reached the age of reason can discern that it is wrong to lie, to break promises, and to injure people needlessly. However, what we should do, all things considered, when two or more prima facie obligations conflict is often difficult to judge. In deciding what to do in any concrete situation, Ross thought, we are always "taking a moral risk."[12] Even after the fullest reflection, judgments about which of these self-evident rules should govern our conduct are only "more or less probable opinions which are not logically justified conclusions from the general principles that are recognized as self-evident."[13]

Assisting Others

Nonconsequentialists believe that utilitarianism presents too simple a picture of our moral world. In addition, they worry that utilitarianism risks making us all slaves to the maximization of total happiness. Stop and think about it: Isn't there something that you could be doing—for instance, volunteering at the local hospital or orphanage, collecting money for Third World development, helping the homeless—that would do more for the general good than what you are doing now or are planning to do tonight or tomorrow? Sure, working with the homeless might not bring you quite as much pleasure as what you would otherwise be doing, but if it would nonetheless maximize total happiness, then you are morally required to do it. However, by following this reasoning, you could end up working around the clock, sacrificing yourself for the greater good. This notion seems mistaken.

Most non-utilitarian philosophers, like Ross, believe that we have some obligation to promote the general welfare, but they typically view this obligation as less stringent than, for example, the obligation not to injure people. They see us as having a much stronger obligation to refrain from violating people's rights than to promote their happiness or well being.

From this perspective, a manufacturing company's obligation not to violate, say, the Ontario Ministry of Labour regulations and thereby endanger the safety of its employees is stronger than its obligation to open up day-care facilities for their children, even though the cost of the two is the same. The company, in other words, has a stronger duty to respect its contractual and legal employment-related obligations than to promote its employees' happiness in other ways. Likewise, for a company to violate people's rights by despoiling the environment through the discharge of pollutants would be morally worse than for it to decide not to expand a job training program in the inner city, even if expanding the program would bring about more total good.

Different non-utilitarian philosophers may weight these particular obligations differently, depending on their particular moral theory. But they typically believe that we have a stronger duty not to violate people's rights or in some other way injure them than we do to assist people or otherwise promote their well being. A utilitarian, concerned solely with what will maximize happiness, is less inclined to draw such a distinction.

Many moral philosophers draw a related distinction between actions that are morally required and charitable or *supererogatory* actions—that is, actions that it would be good to do but not immoral not to do. Act utilitarianism does not make this distinction. While we admire Mother Teresa and Albert Schweitzer for devoting their lives to doing good works among the poor, we see them as acting above and beyond the call of duty; we do not expect so much from ordinary people. Yet people who are not moral heroes or who fall short of sainthood may nonetheless be living morally satisfactory lives.

Non-utilitarian theorists see the distinction between morally obligatory actions and supererogatory actions not so much as a realistic concession to human weakness but as a necessary demarcation if we are to avoid becoming enslaved to the maximization of the general welfare. The idea here is that each of us should have a sphere in which to pursue our own plans and goals, to carve out a distinctive life plan. These plans and goals are limited by various moral obligations, in particular by other people's rights, but the demands of morality are not all-encompassing.

Moral Rights

What, then, are rights, and what rights do people have? Broadly defined, a *right* is an entitlement to act or have others act in a certain way. The connection between rights and duties is that, generally speaking, if you have a right to do something, then someone else has a correlative duty to act in a certain way. For example, if you claim a "right" to drive, you mean that you are entitled to drive and that others should—that is, have a duty to—permit you to drive. The particular right to drive under certain conditions is derived from our legal system and is thus considered a *legal right*.

In addition to rights that are derived from some specific legal system, we also have *moral rights*. Some of these moral rights derive from special relationships, roles, or circumstances in which we happen to be. For example, if Tom has an obligation to return Bob's car to him on Saturday morning, then Bob has a right to have Tom return his car. If I have agreed to water your plants while you are on vacation, you have a right to expect me to look after them in your absence. As a student, you have a right to be graded fairly, and so on.

Even more important are rights that do not rest on special relationships, roles, or situations. For example, the rights to life, free speech, and unhampered religious affiliation are widely accepted, not just as the entitlements of some specific political or legal system but also as fundamental moral rights. More controversial, but often championed as moral rights, are the rights to medical care, decent housing, education, and work. Moral rights that are not the result of particular roles, special relationships, or specific circumstances are called *human rights*. Such rights have several important characteristics.

First, human rights are universal. For instance, if the right to life is a human right, as most of us believe it is, then everyone, everywhere, and at all times, has that right. By contrast, there is nothing universal about your right that I keep my promise to help you move or about my right to drive 65 miles per hour on certain roads.

Second, and closely related, human rights are equal rights. If the right to free speech is a human right, then everyone has this right equally, to the same extent. No one has a greater right to free speech than anyone else. In contrast, your daughter has a greater right than do the daughters of other people to your emotional and financial support.

Third, human rights are not transferable, nor can they be relinquished. If we have a fundamental human right, we cannot give, lend, or sell it to someone else. We cannot waive it, and no one can take it from us (though this does not mean that the State may not, under very special conditions, suspend such rights). By comparison, legal rights can be renounced or transferred, as when one party sells another a house or a business.

Fourth, human rights are natural rights, not in the sense that they can be derived from a study of human nature, but in the sense that they do not depend on human institutions the way legal rights do. If people have human rights, they have these rights simply because they are human beings. They do not have them because they live under a certain legal system. Human rights rest on the assumption that people have certain basic moral entitlements merely on the basis of their humanity. No authoritative body assigns them human rights. The law may attempt to protect human rights, to make them explicit and safe through codification, but the law is not their source.

Rights, and in particular human rights, can be divided into two broad categories: negative rights and positive rights. *Negative rights* reflect the vital interests that human beings have in being free from outside interference. The rights guaranteed in the *Canadian Charter of Rights and Freedoms* (or in the U.S. *Bill of Rights*)—freedom of speech, assembly, religion, and so on—fall within this category, as do the rights to freedom from injury and to privacy. Correlating with these are duties that we all have not to interfere with others' pursuit of these interests and activities. *Positive rights* reflect the vital interests that human beings have in receiving certain benefits. They are rights to have others provide us with certain goods, services, or opportunities. Today, positive rights often are taken to include the rights to education, medical care, a decent neighbourhood, equal job opportunity, comparable pay, and so on. Correlating with these rights, there are positive duties for appropriate parties to assist individuals in their pursuit of these interests.

Thus a child's (positive) right to education implies not just that no one should interfere with the child's education but also that the necessary resources for that education ought to be provided. However, in the case of some positive rights—for example, the right to a decent standard of living, as proclaimed by the United Nations' 1948 *Human Rights Charter*—it is unclear who exactly has the duty to provide the goods and services required to fulfill these rights. In addition, interpreting a right as negative or positive is sometimes controversial. For example, is my right to liberty simply the right not to be interfered with as I live my own life, or does it also imply a duty on the part of others to provide me with the means to make the exercise of that liberty meaningful?

The significance of positing moral rights is that they provide grounds for making moral judgments that differ radically from utilitarianism's grounds. Once moral rights are asserted, the locus of moral judgment becomes the individual, not society. For example, if every potential human research subject has a moral right to be fully informed about the nature of a medical experiment and the moral right to decide freely for himself or herself whether to participate, then it is wrong to violate these rights—even if, by so doing, the common good would be served. Again, if workers have a right to compensation equal to what others receive for doing comparable work, then they cannot be paid less on the grounds that this will maximize total well-being. And if everyone has a right to equal consideration for a job regardless of colour or sex, then sex and colour cannot be introduced merely because so doing will result in greater net utility.

Utilitarianism, in effect, treats all such entitlements as subordinate to the general welfare. Thus, individuals are entitled to act in a certain way and entitled to have others allow or aid them to so act only insofar as acknowledging this right or entitlement achieves the greatest good. The assertion of moral rights, therefore, decisively sets nonconsequentialists apart from utilitarians.

Nonconsequentialism in an Organizational Context

We have already looked at Kant's ethics in an organizational context, but the themes of the other nonconsequentialist approaches also have important implications for moral decision making in business and non-business organizations.

First, in its non-Kantian forms nonconsequentialism stresses that moral decision making involves the weighing of different moral factors and considerations. Unlike utilitarianism, nonconsequentialism does not reduce morality solely to the calculation of consequences; rather, it recognizes that an organization must usually take into account other equally important moral concerns. Theorists like Ross emphasize, contrary to Kant, that there can often be rival and even conflicting obligations on an organization. For example, obligations to employees, stockholders, and consumers may pull the corporation in different directions, and determining the organization's proper moral course may not be easy.

Second, nonconsequentialism acknowledges that the organization has its own legitimate goals to pursue. There are limits to the demands of morality, and an organization that fulfills its moral obligations and respects the relevant rights of individuals is morally free to advance whatever (morally permissible) ends it has—public service, profit, government administration, and so on. Contrary to utilitarianism, organizations and the people in them need not see themselves as under an overarching obligation to seek continually to enhance the general welfare.

Third, nonconsequentialism stresses the importance of moral rights. Moral rights, and in particular human rights, are a crucial factor in most moral deliberations, including those of organizations. Before it acts, any morally responsible business or non-business organization must consider carefully how its actions will impinge on the rights of individuals—not just the rights of its members, such as stockholders and employees, but also the rights of others, such as consumers. Moral rights place distinct and firm constraints on what sorts of things an organization may do in order to fulfill its own ends.

Critical Inquiries of Nonconsequentialism

1. *How well justified are these nonconsequentialist principles and moral rights?* Ross maintained that we have immediate intuitive knowledge of the basic prima facie moral principles, and indeed it would seem absurd to try to deny that it is wrong to cause needless suffering or that making a promise imposes some obligation to keep it. Only someone who is the moral equivalent of colour-blind could fail to see the truth of these statements; to reject them would seem as preposterous as denying some obvious fact of arithmetic—for example, that $12 + 4 = 16$. Likewise, it appears obvious—indeed, as Thomas Jefferson wrote in the American Declaration of Independence, "self-evident"—that human beings have certain basic and inalienable rights, unconditional rights that do not depend on the decrees of any particular government.

Yet we must be careful. What seems obvious, even self-evident, to one culture or at one time in human history may turn out to be not merely not self-evident but actually false. That the earth is flat and that heavier objects fall faster than lighter ones were once "obvious truths." Likewise, the inferiority of women and of various non-white races was long taken for granted; this supposed fact was so obvious that it was hardly even commented on. The idea that people have a right to practise a religion that the majority "knows" to be false—or, indeed, to practise no religion whatsoever—would have seemed morally scandalous to many of our forebears and is still not embraced in all countries today. Today, many vegetarians eschew meat eating on moral grounds and contend that future generations will consider our treatment of animals, factory farming in particular, to be as morally benighted as slavery. So what seems obvious, self-evident, or simple common sense may not be the most reliable guide to morally sound principles.

2. *Can nonconsequentialists satisfactorily handle conflicting rights and principles?* People today disagree among themselves about the correctness of certain moral principles. Claims of right, as we have seen, are often controversial. For example, do employees have a moral right to their jobs—an entitlement to be fired only with just cause? To some of us, it may seem obvious that they do; to others, perhaps not. And how are we to settle various conflicting claims of right? Jones, for instance, claims a right to her property, which she has acquired honestly through her labours; that is, she claims a right to do with it as she wishes. Smith is ill and claims adequate medical care as a human right. Because he cannot afford the care himself, acknowledging his right will probably involve taxing people like Jones and thus limiting their property rights.

To sum up these two points: first, even the deliverances of moral common sense have to be examined critically; and second, nonconsequentialists should not rest content until they find a way of resolving disputes among conflicting prima facie principles or rights. This is not to suggest that nonconsequentialists cannot find deeper and theoretically more satisfactory ways of grounding moral claims and of handling disputes between them. The point to be underscored here is simply the necessity of doing so.

UTILITARIANISM ONCE MORE

Until now, the discussion of utilitarianism has focused on its most classic and straightforward form, act utilitarianism. According to act utilitarianism, we have one and only one moral obligation, the maximization of happiness for everyone concerned, and every action is to be judged according to how well it lives up to this standard. But a different utilitarian approach, rule utilitarianism, is relevant to the discussion of the moral concerns characteristic of nonconsequentialism—in particular, relevant to the nonconsequentialist's criticisms of act utilitarianism. The rule utilitarian would, in fact, agree with many of these criticisms. (Rule utilitarianism has been formulated in different ways, but this discussion follows the version defended by Richard Brandt.)

Rule utilitarianism maintains that the utilitarian standard should be applied not to individual actions but to moral codes as a whole. The rule utilitarian asks what moral code (that is, what set of moral rules) a society should adopt to maximize happiness. The principles that make up that code would then be the basis for distinguishing right actions from wrong actions. As Brandt explains:

A rule-utilitarian thinks that right actions are the kind permitted by the moral code optimal for the society of which the agent is a member. An optimal code is one designed to maximize welfare or what is good (thus,

utility). This leaves open the possibility that a particular right act by itself may not maximize benefit. . . . On the rule-utilitarian view, then, to find what is morally right or wrong we need to find which actions would be permitted by a moral system that is "optimal" for the agent's society.[14]

The "optimal" moral code does not refer to the set of rules that would do the most good if everyone conformed to them all the time. The meaning is more complex. The optimal moral code must take into account what rules can reasonably be taught and obeyed, as well as the costs of inculcating those rules in people. Recall from Chapter 1 that if a principle or rule is part of a person's moral code, then it will influence the person's behaviour. The person will tend to follow that principle, to feel guilty when he or she does not follow it, and to disapprove of others who fail to conform to it. Rule utilitarians must consider not just the benefits of having people motivated to act in certain ways but also the costs of instilling those motivations in them. As Brandt writes:

The more intense and widespread an aversion to a certain sort of behavior, the less frequent the behavior is apt to be. But the more intense and widespread, the greater the cost of teaching the rule and keeping it alive, the greater the burden on the individual, and so on.[15]

Thus, the "optimality" of a moral code encompasses both the benefits of reduced objectionable behaviour and the long-term costs. Perfect compliance is not a realistic goal. "Like the law," Brandt continues, "the optimal moral code normally will not produce 100 percent compliance with all its rules; that would be too costly."[16]

Some utilitarian thinkers in earlier centuries adopted or came close to adopting rule utilitarianism (although they did not use that term). For example, the nineteenth-century legal theorist John Austin wrote: "Utility [should] be the test of our conduct, ultimately, but not immediately. . . . Our rules [should] be fashioned on utility; our conduct, on our rules."[17] This accords well with the rule-utilitarian idea that we should apply the utilitarian standard only to the assessment of alternative moral codes; we should not try to apply it to individual actions. That is, we should seek to determine the specific set of principles that would in fact best promote total happiness for society. Those are the rules we should promulgate, instill in ourselves, and teach to the next generation.

What Will the Optimal Code Look Like?

Rule utilitarians, such as Brandt, argue strenuously that the ideal or optimal moral code for a society will not be the single act-utilitarian command to maximize happiness. They contend that teaching people that their only obligation is to maximize happiness would not in fact maximize happiness.

First, people will make mistakes if they always try to promote total happiness. Second, if all of us were act utilitarians, such practices as keeping promises and telling the truth would be rather shaky, because we would expect others to keep promises or tell the truth only when they believed that doing so would maximize happiness. Third, the act-utilitarian principle is too demanding, because it seems to imply that each person should continually be striving to promote total well-being.

For these reasons, rule utilitarians believe that more happiness will come from instilling in people a pluralistic moral code, one with a number of different principles. By analogy, imagine a traffic system with just one rule: Drive your car in a way that maximizes happiness. Such a system would be counterproductive; we do much better in terms of total human well-being to have a variety of traffic regulations—for example, obey stop signs, yield to the right, and pass only on the left. In such a pluralistic system we cannot justify cruising through a red light with the argument that doing so maximizes total happiness by getting us home more quickly.

The principles of the optimal code would presumably be prima facie in Ross's sense—that is, capable of being overridden by other principles. Different principles would also have different moral weights. It would make sense, for example, to instill in people an aversion to killing that is stronger than the aversion to telling white lies. In addition, the ideal code would acknowledge moral rights. Teaching people to respect moral rights maximizes human welfare in the long run.

The rules of the optimal code provide the sole basis for determining right and wrong. An action is not necessarily wrong if it fails to maximize happiness; it is wrong only if it conflicts with the ideal moral code. Rule utilitarianism thus gets around many of the problems that plague act utilitarianism. At the same time, it provides a plausible basis for deciding which moral principles and rights we should acknowledge and how much weight we should attach to them. We try to determine those principles and rights that, generally adhered to, would best promote human happiness.

Still, rule utilitarianism has its critics. There are two common objections. First, act utilitarians maintain that a utilitarian who cares about happiness should be willing to violate rules in order to maximize happiness. Why make a fetish out of the rules?

Second, nonconsequentialists, while presumably viewing rule utilitarianism more favourably than act utilitarianism, still balk at seeing moral principles determined by their consequences. They contend, in particular, that rule utilitarians ultimately subordinate rights to utilitarian calculation and therefore fail to treat rights as fundamental and independent moral factors.

MORAL DECISION MAKING: TOWARD A SYNTHESIS

Theoretical controversies permeate the subject of ethics, and as we have seen, philosophers have proposed rival ways of understanding right and wrong. These philosophical differences of perspective, emphasis, and theory are significant and can have profound practical consequences. This chapter has surveyed some of these issues, but obviously it cannot settle all of the questions that divide moral philosophers. Fortunately, however, many problems of business and organizational ethics can be intelligently discussed and even resolved by people whose fundamental moral theories differ (or who have not yet worked out their own moral ideas in some systematic way). This section discusses some important points to keep in mind when analyzing and discussing business ethics and offers, as a kind of model, one possible procedure for making moral decisions.

In the abstract, it might seem impossible for people to reach agreement on controversial ethical issues, given that ethical theories differ so much and that people themselves place moral value on different things. Yet in practice moral problems are rarely so intractable that open-minded and thoughtful people cannot, by discussing matters calmly, rationally, and thoroughly, make significant progress toward resolving them. Chapter 1 stressed that moral judgments should be logical, should be based on facts, and should appeal to sound moral principles. Bearing this in mind can often help, especially when various people are discussing an issue and proposing rival answers.

First, in any moral discussion, make sure participants agree about the relevant facts. Often moral disputes hinge not on matters of moral principle but on differing assessments of what the facts of the situation are, what alternatives are open, and what the probable results of different courses of action will be. For instance, the directors of an international firm might acrimoniously dispute the moral permissibility of a new overseas investment. The conflict might appear to involve some fundamental clash of moral principles and perspectives and yet, in fact, be the result of some underlying disagreement about what effects the proposed investment will have on the lives of the local population. Until this factual disagreement is acknowledged and dealt with, little is likely to be resolved.

Second, once there is general agreement on factual matters, try to spell out the moral principles which different participants are, often implicitly, appealing to. Seeking to determine these principles will often help people clarify their own thinking enough to reach a solution. Sometimes they will agree on what moral principles are relevant and yet disagree over how to balance them; identifying this discrepancy can itself be useful. Bear in mind, too, that skepticism is in order when someone's moral stance on an issue appears to rest simply on a hunch or an intuition and cannot be related to some more general moral principle. As moral decision makers, we are seeking not merely an answer to a moral issue but an answer which can be publicly defended, and the public defense of a moral judgment usually requires an appeal to some general principle. By analogy, judges do not hand down judgments based simply on what strikes them as fair in a particular case. They must relate their decisions to general legal principles or statutes.

A reluctance to defend our moral decisions in public is almost always a warning sign. If we are unwilling to account for our actions publicly, chances are that we are doing something we cannot really justify morally. In addition, Kant's point that we must be willing to universalize our moral judgments is relevant here. We cannot sincerely endorse a principle if we are not willing to see it applied generally. Unfortunately, we occasionally do make judgments—for example, that Alfred's being late to work is a satisfactory reason for firing him—which rest on a principle we would be unwilling to apply to our own situations; hence, the moral relevance of the familiar question: "How would you like it if . . . ?" Looking at an issue from the other person's point of view can cure moral myopia.

Obligations, Ideals, Effects

As a practical basis for discussing moral issues in organizations, it is useful to try to approach those issues in a way that is acceptable to individuals of diverse moral viewpoints. We want to avoid as much as possible presupposing the truth of one particular theoretical perspective. By emphasizing factors that are relevant to various theories, both consequentialist and nonconsequentialist, we can find some common ground on which moral decision making can proceed. Moral dialogue can thus take place in an objective and analytical way, even if the participants do not fully agree on all philosophical issues.

What concerns, then, seem common to most ethical systems? Following Professor V. R. Ruggiero, three common concerns suggest themselves.[18] A first concern is with *obligations*. Every significant human action—personal and professional—arises in the context of human relationships. These relationships can be the source of specific duties and rights. In addition, we are obligated to respect people's human rights. Obligations bind us. In their presence, morality requires us, at least prima facie, to do certain things and to avoid doing others.

A second concern common to most ethical systems is the impact of our actions on important *ideals*. An ideal is some morally important goal, virtue, or notion of excellence worth striving for. Clearly, different cultures embrace different ideals and, equally important, different ways of pursuing them. Our culture respects virtues such as tolerance, compassion, and loyalty, as well as more abstract ideals such as peace, justice, fairness, and respect for persons. In addition to these moral ideals, there are institutional or organizational ideals: efficiency, productivity, quality, customer service, and so forth. Does a particular organizational activity serve or violate these ideals? Both consequentialists and nonconsequentialists can agree that this is an important concern in determining the moral quality of actions.

A third common consideration regards the *effects* of actions. When reflecting on a possible course of action, one needs to take into account its likely results. Although nonconsequentialists maintain that things other than consequences or results can affect the rightness or wrongness of actions, few if any of them would ignore consequences entirely. Almost all nonconsequentialist theories place some moral weight on the results of our actions. Practically speaking, this means that in making a moral decision, we must identify all the interested parties and how they would be affected by the different courses of action open to us.

Ruggiero isolated, then, three concerns common to almost all ethical systems: obligations, ideals, and effects. In so doing he provided a kind of practical synthesis of consequentialist and nonconsequentialist conceptions that seems appropriate for our purposes. A useful approach to moral questions in an organizational context will therefore reflect these considerations: the obligations that derive from organizational relationships or are affected by organizational conduct, the ideals at stake, and the effects or consequences of alternative courses of action. Any action that honours obligations while respecting ideals and benefiting people can be presumed to be moral. An action that does not pass scrutiny in these respects will be morally suspect.

This view leads to what is essentially a two-step procedure for evaluating actions and choices. The first step is to identify the important considerations involved: obligations, ideals, and effects. Accordingly, we should ask if any basic obligations are involved. If so, what are they and who has them? What ideals does the action respect or promote? What ideals does it neglect or thwart? Who is affected by the action and how? How do these effects compare with those of the alternatives open to us? The second step is to decide which of these considerations deserves emphasis. Sometimes the issue may be largely a matter of obligations; other times, some ideal may predominate; still other times, consideration of effects may be the overriding concern.

Keep the following rough guidelines in mind when handling cases of conflicting obligations, ideals, and effects:

1. When two or more moral obligations conflict, choose the stronger one.

2. When two or more ideals conflict, or when ideals conflict with obligations, honour the more important one.

3. When rival actions will have different results, choose the action that produces the greater good or the lesser harm.

These guidelines imply that we know (1) which one of the conflicting obligations is greater, (2) which of the competing ideals is higher, and (3) which of the actions will achieve the greater good or the lesser harm. They also suggest that we have some definite way of balancing obligations, ideals, and effects when these considerations pull in different directions.

The fact is that we have no sure procedure for making such comparative determinations, which involve assessing worth and assigning relative priorities to our assessments. In large part, the chapters that follow attempt to sort out the values and principles embedded in the tangled web of frequently subtle, ill-defined problems we meet in business and organizational life. It is hoped that examining these issues will help you (1) identify the obligations, ideals, and effects involved in specific moral issues and (2) decide where the emphasis should lie among the competing considerations.

SUMMARY

1. Consequentialist moral theories see the moral rightness or wrongness of actions as a function of their results. If the consequences are good, the action is right; if they are bad, the action is wrong. Nonconsequentialist theories see other factors as also relevant to the determination of right and wrong.

2. Egoism is the consequentialist theory that an action is right when it promotes the individual's best interests. Proponents of this theory base their view on the alleged fact that human beings are, by nature, selfish (the doctrine of psychological egoism). Critics of egoism argue that (a) psychological egoism is implausible, (b) egoism is not really a moral principle, and (c) egoism ignores blatant wrongs.

3. Utilitarianism, another consequentialist theory, maintains that the morally right action is the one that provides the greatest happiness for all those affected. In an organizational context, utilitarianism provides an objective way to resolve conflicts of self-interest and encourages a realistic and result-oriented approach to moral decision making. But critics contend that (a) utilitarianism is not really workable, (b) some actions are wrong even if they produce good results, and (c) utilitarianism incorrectly overlooks considerations of justice and the distribution of happiness.

4. Kant's theory is an important example of a purely nonconsequentialist approach to ethics. Kant held that only when we act from duty does our action have moral worth. Good will is the only thing that is good in itself.

5. Kant's categorical imperative states that an action is morally right if and only if we can will that the maxim (or principle) represented by the action be a universal law. For example, a person making a promise with no intention of keeping it cannot universalize the maxim governing his action, because if everyone followed this principle, promising would make no sense. Kant believed that the categorical imperative is binding on all rational creatures, regardless of their specific goals or desires and regardless of the consequences.

6. There are two alternative formulations of the categorical imperative. The first is that an act is right only if the actor would be willing to be so treated if the positions of the parties were reversed. The second is that one must always act so as to treat other people as ends, never merely as means.

7. Kant's ethics gives us firm standards that do not depend on results; it injects a humanistic element into moral decision making and stresses the importance of acting on principle and from a sense of duty. Critics, however, worry that (a) Kant's view of moral worth is too restrictive, (b) the categorical imperative is not a sufficient test of right and wrong, and (c) distinguishing between treating people as means and respecting them as ends in themselves may be difficult in practice.

8. Other nonconsequentialist theories stress other moral themes. Philosophers such as Ross argue, against both Kant and consequentialists, that we are under a variety of distinct moral obligations. These are prima facie, meaning that any one of them may be outweighed in some circumstances by other, more important moral considerations. Nonconsequentialists believe that a duty to assist others and to promote total happiness is only one of a number of duties incumbent on us.

9. Nonconsequentialists typically emphasize moral rights—entitlements to act in a certain way or to have others act in a certain way. These rights can rest on special relationships and roles, or they can be general human rights. Rights can be negative, protecting us from outside interference, or they can be positive, requiring others to provide us with certain benefits or opportunities.

10. In an organizational context, nonconsequentialism (in its non-Kantian forms) stresses the plurality of moral considerations to be weighed. While emphasizing the importance of respecting moral rights, it acknowledges that morality has limits and that organizations have legitimate goals to pursue. Critics question whether (a) nonconsequentialist principles are adequately justified and whether (b) nonconsequentialism can satisfactorily handle conflicting rights and principles.

11. Rule utilitarianism is a hybrid theory. It maintains that the proper principles of right and wrong are those that would maximize happiness if society adopted them. Thus, the utilitarian standard does not apply directly to individual actions but rather to the adoption of the moral principles that guide individual action. Rule utilitarianism avoids many of the standard criticisms of act utilitarianism.

12. Despite disagreements on controversial theoretical issues, people can make significant progress in resolving practical moral problems through open-minded and reflective discussion. One useful approach is to identify the (possibly conflicting) obligations, ideals, and effects in a given situation and then to identify where the emphasis should lie among these different considerations.

CASE 2.1

The Ford Pinto[19]

By the late 1960s, the importation of subcompact cars made in Japan and Germany began to worry the North American car manufacturers, as the imports were eating up more and more of the subcompact auto market. Never one to take a back seat to the competition, the Ford Motor Company decided to meet the threat from abroad head on. In 1968, Ford executives decided to produce the Pinto. The Pinto, known inside the company as "Lee's car" after the president of Ford in the U.S., Lee Iacocca, was to weigh no more than 2,000 pounds (about 907 kilograms) and cost no more than $2,000.

Eager to have its subcompact ready for the 1971 model year, Ford decided to compress the normal drafting-board-to-showroom time of about three-and-a-half years into two. The compressed schedule meant that any design changes typically made before production-line tooling would have to be made during it.

Before producing the Pinto, Ford crash-tested various prototypes, in part to learn whether they met a safety standard proposed by the U.S. National Highway Traffic Safety Administration (NHTSA) aimed at reducing fires from traffic collisions. This standard would have required that by 1972 all new autos be able to withstand a rear-end impact of 20 mph (about 32.18688 km/h) without fuel loss, and that by 1973 they be able to withstand an impact of 30 mph. The prototypes all failed the 20-mph test. In 1970 Ford crash-tested the Pinto itself, and the result was the same: ruptured gas tanks and dangerous leaks. The only Pintos to pass the test had been modified in some way—for example, with a rubber bladder in the gas tank or a piece of steel between the tank and the rear bumper.

Thus, Ford knew that the Pinto represented a serious fire hazard when struck from the rear, even in low-speed collisions. Ford officials faced a decision. Should they go ahead with the existing design, thereby meeting the production timetable but possibly jeopardizing consumer safety? Or should they delay production of the Pinto by redesigning the gas tank to make it safer and thus concede another year of subcompact dominance to foreign companies? Ford not only pushed ahead with the original design but also stuck to it for the next six years.

What explains Ford's decision? The evidence suggests that Ford relied, at least in part, on cost-benefit reasoning, which is an analysis in monetary terms of the expected costs and benefits of doing something. There were various ways of making the Pinto's gas tank safer. Although the estimated price of these safety improvements ranged from only $5 to $8 per vehicle, Ford evidently reasoned that the increased cost outweighed the benefits of a new tank design.

How exactly did Ford reach that conclusion? We don't know for sure, but an internal report, "Fatalities Associated with Crash-Induced Fuel Leakage and Fires," reveals the cost-benefit reasoning that the company used in cases like this. This report was not written with the Pinto in mind; rather, it concerns fuel leakage in rollover accidents (not rear-end collisions), and its computations applied to all Ford vehicles, not just the Pinto. Nevertheless, it illustrates the type of reasoning that was probably used in the Pinto case.

In the "Fatalities" report, Ford engineers estimated the cost of technical improvements that would prevent gas tanks from leaking in rollover accidents to be $11 per vehicle. The authors go on to discuss various estimates of the number of people killed by fires from car rollovers before settling on the relatively low figure of 180 deaths per year. But given that number, how can the value of those individuals' lives be gauged? Can a dollars-and-cents figure be assigned to a human being? NHTSA thought so. In 1972, it estimated that society loses $200,725 every time a person is killed in an auto accident (adjusted for inflation, today's figure would, of course, be considerably higher). It broke down the costs as follows:

Future Productivity Losses	
Direct	$132,000
Indirect	41,300
Medical costs:	
Hospital	700
Other	425
Property damage	1,500
Insurance administration	4,700
Legal and court expenses	3,000
Employer losses	1,000
Victim's pain and suffering	10,000
Funeral	900
Assets (lost consumption)	5,000
Miscellaneous accident costs	200
Total per fatality	$200,725

Putting the NHTSA figures together with other statistical studies, the Ford report arrives at the following overall assessment of costs and benefits:

Benefits

Savings	180 burn deaths, 180 serious burn injuries, 2,100 burned vehicles
Unit cost	$200,000 per death, $67,000 per injury, $700 per vehicle
Total benefit	(180 × $200,000) + (180 × $67,000) + (2,100 × $700) = $49.5 million

Costs

Sales	11 million cars, 1.5 million light trucks
Unit cost	$11 per car, $11 per truck
Total cost	12.5 million × $11 = $137.5 million

Thus, the costs of the suggested safety improvements outweigh their benefits, and the "Fatalities" report accordingly recommends against any improvements—a recommendation that Ford followed.

Likewise in the Pinto case, Ford's management, whatever its exact reasoning, decided to stick with the original design and not upgrade the Pinto's fuel tank, despite the test results reported by its engineers. Here is the aftermath of Ford's decision:

- Between 1971 and 1978, the Pinto was responsible for a number of fire-related deaths. Ford puts the figure at 23; others place the number at 54—including an off-duty RCMP officer in Windsor, ON; critics of the company say the figure is closer to 500, partly on the grounds that for some years crash-scene investigators did not know what to look for. According to the sworn testimony of Ford engineers, 95 percent of the fatalities would have survived if Ford had located the fuel tank over the axle (as it had done on its Capri automobiles).

- NHTSA finally adopted a 30-mph collision standard in 1976. The Pinto then acquired a rupture-proof fuel tank. In 1978 Ford was obliged to recall all 1971–1976 Pintos for fuel-tank modifications.

- Between 1971 and 1978, approximately fifty lawsuits were brought against Ford in connection with rear-end accidents in the Pinto. In the Richard Grimshaw case, in addition to awarding over $3 million in compensatory damages to the victims of a Pinto crash, the jury awarded a landmark $125 million in punitive damages against Ford. The judge reduced punitive damages to $3.5 million.

- On August 10, 1978, eighteen-year-old Judy Ulrich, her sixteen-year-old sister Lynn, and their eighteen-year-old cousin Donna, in their 1973 Ford Pinto, were struck from the rear by a van near Elkhart, Indiana. The gas tank of the Pinto exploded on impact. In the fire that resulted, the three teenagers were burned to death. Ford was charged with criminal homicide. The judge in the case advised jurors that Ford should be convicted if it had clearly disregarded the harm that might result from its actions, and that disregard represented a substantial deviation from acceptable standards of conduct. On March 13, 1980, the jury found Ford not guilty of criminal homicide.

For its part, Ford has always denied that the Pinto is unsafe compared with other cars of its type and era. The company also points out that in every model year the Pinto met or surpassed the government's own standards. But what the company doesn't say is that successful lobbying by it and its industry associates was responsible for delaying for seven years the adoption of any NHTSA crash standard. Furthermore, Ford's critics claim that there were more than forty European and Japanese models in the Pinto price and weight range with safer gas-tank position. "Ford made an extremely irresponsible decision," concludes auto safety expert Byron Bloch, "when they placed such a weak tank in such a ridiculous location in such a soft rear end."

Has the automobile industry learned a lesson from Ford's experience with the Pinto? Some observers thought not, when twenty years later an Atlanta jury held the General Motors Corporation responsible for the death of a Georgia teenager in the fiery crash of one of its pickup trucks. Finding that the company had known that its "side-saddle" gas tanks, which are mounted outside the rails of the truck's frame, are dangerously prone to rupture, the jury awarded $4.2 million in actual damages and $101 million in punitive damages to the parents of the seventeen-year-old victim, Shannon Moseley.

After the verdict, General Motors said that it still stood behind the safety of its trucks and contended "that a full examination by the National Highway Traffic Safety Administration of the technical issues in this matter will bear out our contention that the . . . pickup trucks do not have a safety related defect." Subsequently, however, the Department of Transportation determined that GM pickups of the style Shannon Moseley drove do pose a fire hazard and that they are more prone than competitors' pickups to catch fire when struck from the side. Still, GM rejected requests to recall the pickups and repair them, and later the Georgia Court of Appeals threw out the jury's verdict on a legal technicality—despite ruling that the evidence submitted in the case showed that GM was aware that the gas tanks were hazardous but, to save the expense involved, did not try to make them safer.

Expense seems to be the issue, too, when it comes to SUV rollovers. After nearly three hundred rollover deaths in Ford Explorers equipped with Firestone tires in the late 1990s, the U.S. Congress mandated NHTSA to conduct rollover road tests on all SUVs. (Previously, the agency had relied on mathematical formulas based on accident statistics to evaluate rollover resistance, rather than doing real-world tests.) In August 2004 NHTSA released its results, and they weren't pretty—at least not for several of Detroit's most popular models. The Chevrolet Tahoe and the Ford Explorer, in particular, have a 26 to 29 percent chance of rolling over in a single-vehicle crash, almost twice that of models from Honda, Nissan, and Chrysler. The Saturn Vue couldn't even finish the test, because its left-rear suspension broke, leading General Motors to recall all 250,000 Vues.

Ford and General Motors have the anti-rollover technology necessary to make their SUVs safer. The problem is that rollover sensors and electronic stability systems add about $800 to the price of a vehicle, so the companies have offered them only as options. The same is true of side-curtain airbags to protect occupants when a vehicle rolls over. They cost about $500. Improved design—wider wheel tracks, lower centre of gravity, and reinforced roofs to protect passengers in a rollover—would also help. Embarrassed by the test results, the companies promised to make more safety features standard equipment on new SUVs. Lawsuits by rollover victims are also prodding the companies to enhance their commitment to safety. Two months before NHTSA released its results, Ford had to pay $369 million in damages—one of the largest personal-injury awards ever against an automaker—to a San Diego couple whose Explorer flipped over four-and-a-half times when they swerved to avoid a metal object on the highway.

Discussion Questions

1. What moral issues does the Pinto case raise?

2. Suppose Ford officials were asked to justify their decision. What moral principles do you think they would invoke? Assess Ford's handling of the Pinto from the perspective of each of the moral theories discussed in this chapter.

3. Utilitarians would say that jeopardizing motorists does not by itself make Ford's action morally objectionable. The only morally relevant matter is whether Ford gave equal consideration to the interests of each affected party. Do you think Ford did this?

4. Is cost-benefit analysis a legitimate tool? What role, if any, should it play in moral deliberation? Critically assess the example of cost-benefit analysis given in the case study. Is there anything unsatisfactory about it? Could it have been improved upon in some way?

5. Speculate about Kant's response to the idea of putting a monetary value on a human life. Is doing so ever morally legitimate?

6. What responsibilities to its customers do you think Ford had? What are the most important moral rights, if any, operating in the Pinto case?

7. Was GM responsible for Shannon Moseley's death? Compare that case with the case of Ford and the Pinto.

8. Assess Ford's and GM's actions with respect to SUV rollovers. Have they met their moral obligation to consumers, or have they acted wrongly by not doing more to increase SUV safety? Should they be held either morally or legally responsible for deaths from rollovers that would not have occurred in other vehicles? What should automakers do to increase SUV safety?

CASE 2.2

The Confused Network Administrator

Tom Parsons graduated from the Computer Science Program of a polytechnic university two years ago and he was fortunate enough to find a job as a network administrator at the head office of the Toronto Financial Group, a multinational banking and investment firm employing over five hundred people at its head office. A year ago Tom was married to Tanya and they are presently expecting their first child.

During his two years at TF Group Tom has done extremely well and he appears to be in line for a promotion in the foreseeable future. His happy settling in at TF Group has been in part due to the help given him by Tim Horne, a fellow-employee in the Accounting Department, and whom Tom is gradually coming to consider as a very close friend. Tim's wife, Tina, also works for TF Group as the deputy executive assistant to a senior manager. Tom and Tanya have been to the Hornes' for dinner only once, but they were treated like old friends. Still, Tom thought that Tina liked her wine a bit too much, while Tanya got the impression that Tina's eyes were a bit too flirty with Tom.

Tom's duties at work include his monitoring the corporation's emails in order that he may allow through any emails to staff that might have been blocked by the spam filters. It is the firm's strict policy that though the network administrator may open emails marked as "spam," he or she cannot divulge to anyone the contents of emails sent to staff.

One day Tom gets a helpdesk request asking that a certain email be "unblocked" and sent on to its intended recipient. Recognizing the name of his friend on it, Tom attends to the request right away. He opens the email to make sure that it is not "spam" before he sends it on. He opens it and realizes that it is addressed not to Tim but to Tina Horne. It is not spam but a love letter to her from someone who obviously has been having an affair with her. Since it is not spam, Tom releases it.

Later over dinner, a distressed and confused Tom tells Tanya all about Tina's email and they have a discussion as to what Tom should do. Tanya suggests that Tom should tell Tim. "You owe it to your friend to tell him that his wife is cheating on him. I always thought Tina was a slut and this proves it. Who is next on her list, eh?" Tom is reluctant to do so in view of the firm's strict policy that the network administrator is not to divulge email information to third parties. "I know Tim is a good friend, but what if I am found out? I could lose my job. We cannot afford to have that happen, especially now that there is a baby on the way." The discussion goes back and forth till late when Tom says, "I'll sleep on it and decide what to do in a few days."

Discussion Questions

1. Was Tom right to tell his wife about Tina's email? Whatever your view, explain your reasons for it. (Bear in mind that an action may be obligatory to do, obligatory to refrain from doing, or permissible.)

2. Do we have special duties to our friends? If so, (a) do they override duties we might have to others by virtue of their being human being (even though they are not our friends) and (b) do such duties override

duties we have in our capacity of holding a certain office at work? Whatever your answers, explain and defend your position.

3. Consider the dilemma Tom is facing from a *utilitarian* standpoint and write out the rationale for your decision.

4. Consider the dilemma Tom is facing from a deontological standpoint and write out the rationale for your decision.

5. Consider the dilemma Tom is facing from a prima-facie-obligations point of view (the view of W. D. Ross) and write out the rationale for your decision.

Notes to Chapter 2

1. T. M. Scanlon, *What We Owe to Each Other* (Cambridge, MA: Harvard University Press, 1998), 197–8.

2. Bernard Williams, *Ethics and the Limits of Philosophy* (Cambridge, MA: Harvard University Press, 1985), 16.

3. Richard B. Brandt, "Toward a Credible Form of Utilitarianism," in Hector-Neri Castañeda and George Nakhnikian, eds., *Morality and the Language of Conduct* (Detroit: Wayne State University Press, 1963), 109–110.

4. A. C. Ewing, *Ethics* (New York: Free Press, 1965), 40.

5. Molly Moore, "Did the Experts Really Approve the 'Brown Lung' Experiment?," *Washington Post*, National Weekly Edition, June 4, 1984, 31.

6. Adam Smith, *The Wealth of Nations* (New York: Modern Library, 1985), 223–225.

7. Tom L. Beauchamp and Norman E. Bowie, eds., *Ethical Theory and Business*, 6th ed. (Upper Saddle River, NJ: Prentice Hall, 2001), 16.

8. Immanuel Kant, *Grounding for the Metaphysics of Morals* (Indianapolis: Hackett, 1988), 30–31 (translation modified).

9. See, in particular, W. D. Ross, *The Right and the Good* (London: Oxford University Press, 1930).

10. Immanuel Kant, *Practical Philosophy*, ed. M. J. Gregor (Cambridge: Cambridge University Press, 1996), 611–615.

11. Ross, *The Right and the Good*, 21.

12. Ibid., 30.

13. Ibid., 31.

14. Richard B. Brandt, "The Real and Alleged Problems of Utilitarianism," *Hastings Center Report*, April 1983, 38.

15. Ibid., 42.

16. Ibid., 42.

17. John Austin, *The Province of Jurisprudence Determined*, ed. W. E. Rumble (Cambridge: Cambridge University Press, 1995), 49.

18. Vincent Ryan Ruggiero, *The Moral Imperative* (Port Washington, NY: Alfred Publishers, 1973).

19. This case study is based on Douglas Birsch and John H. Fielder, eds., *The Ford Pinto Case* (Albany, NY: SUNY Press, 1994). Some details are from the CBC Radio Archives, archives.cbc.ca/IDC-1-69-1754-12095/life_society/road_safety/clip6. For a recent discussion, see John R. Danley, "Polishing Up the Pinto: Legal Liability, Moral Blame, and Risk," *Business Ethics Quarterly* 15, no. 2 (April 2005): 205–236. On SUV safety, see "Ford to Pay $369 Million in Rollover Accident," *New York Times*, June 4, 2004 (online); "Safety Data Give SUVs Poor Grade in Rollover Tests," *Wall Street Journal*, August 10, 2004, A1; and "Stability Shouldn't Be Optional," *Business Week*, August 30, 2004, 50.

ONE PHILOSOPHER'S APPROACH TO BUSINESS ETHICS

R. M. HARE

R. M. Hare, professor of philosophy at Oxford University and later the University of Florida, was one of the most distinguished moral philosophers of our times. In this essay, after discussing the nature of philosophy and explaining his particular approach to ethics, he distinguishes two levels of moral thinking. He goes on to argue that the market rests on ethics but that it can be undermined by a phenomenon known as the "prisoners' dilemma." He then discusses three responses to the dilemma—morality (or custom), self-regulation, and legislation. He concludes with a brief discussion of the relationship between morality and the law. Although Professor Hare wrote a number of books and countless essays, his Moral Thinking: Its Levels, Method, and Point *(1981) is perhaps the most helpful guide to his moral philosophy.*

From Christopher Cowton and Roger Crisp, eds., *Business Ethics: Perspectives on the Practice of Theory* (1998). Reprinted by permission of Oxford University Press.

I must start by explaining . . . my title. I say "*one philosopher's approach*" because not all philosophers agree. There are a great many different ethical theories, nearly all of which have something to be said for them. One has to look at them all and see what truths they bring out, and also what mistakes they make, and try to find a theory which preserves the truths and avoids the mistakes; and that is what I have done. There has to be a theoretical basis for the rational discussion of moral problems in business, just as of anything else, and no one should think that we can do without it. That would leave us at the mercy of whatever prejudices we started with. My own theory is in the main a combination of the insights I find in Kant and in the utilitarians—two sorts of philosophy that are thought to be quite irreconcilable but which actually fit together very well if we understand what is going on in them. . . .

So what is philosophy, and what good does it do? When I am asked this question, the answer I always give is that it is the study of *arguments* to find a way of telling good from bad ones. In short, philosophy, broadly speaking, is *Logic*. By "Logic" I mean . . . any study that casts light on what are good reasons for holding opinions that we hold, or what would be good reasons for abandoning them. If there are good reasons, then we ought to be able to defend them in argument; and that is what philosophy is about.

Obviously, in order to study arguments, we have to ask what implies what or what follows from what. And this takes us straight into the study of *language*. For what follows from what somebody says depends on what his words mean. Their meaning is intimately bound up with what they imply; if they implied something different they would mean something different. So you cannot study arguments without studying the meanings of words, and the logic that that meaning generates. . . .

My own particular interest . . . is moral philosophy. I have therefore devoted most of my working life to elucidating the meanings of the words we use when we ask and try to answer moral questions. Such words are "ought," "right," "wrong," and also "good," as they are used in moral discussion. I think that the understanding of the logic of these words casts a flood of light on moral arguments. It often enables one to spot false steps in them, such as suppressed premises which have not themselves been argued for, ambiguities or equivocations, and so on. It is also helpful in revealing what the structure of a good argument on a certain question would have to be like. . . .

The best way I can illustrate for you what philosophy is and how it can help is by taking some problems in business ethics and talking about them in a philosophical way. I said just now that I shall be applying a particular ethical theory which I think is well supported, being, as I said, a combination of the true insights in the utilitarians and Kant. It is also consistent with the Golden Rule, the foundation of Christian morality and other moralities too: that we should do to others as we wish they should do to us if we were in their situations. In effect this will lead us, as Kant said, to treat their ends as our ends, or, as the utilitarians say, to do the best we can for them, treating them all impartially.

I have got this theory by selecting the best bits from other people's theories. My own contribution, if there was one, was to put the theory on a firmer logical basis. I think, unlike some other moral philosophers nowadays, that there is a logical structure for moral reasoning implicit in the very meaning, and thus in the logical properties, of the words or concepts we are using when we ask moral questions. So long as we go on asking the same questions, we are stuck with those concepts and with that logic; if we altered the concepts and the logic, we would be asking different questions. But this is not an appropriate place to argue that issue. I will merely say that if we want to be rational in our moral thinking, we must have something to control the thinking, that is, a logic, and that this can only be determined by the meanings of the words we are using.

TWO LEVELS OF MORAL THINKING

All the theories that I am drawing on face a well-known difficulty which their opponents try to exploit. But it is not hard to avoid this difficulty if one understands what is going on in our moral thinking. The difficulty is that all these theories seem to have counter-intuitive consequences. Many of these concern special duties that we think we have to those close to us in various ways: our family, our patients if we are doctors, our firm if we are in business. Taken strictly, both the Kantian prescription to treat all humans as ends, and the Christian command to do to all of them as we wish should be done to us, and the utilitarian principle of furthering the interests of all impartially, would, it is said, lead mothers to pay equal regard to the welfare of all children without favouring their own children; lawyers to try to do as well for their clients' opponents as for their clients; doctors to pay no attention to the fact that their patients are *their* patients; and employees or managers to give no more weight to the interests of their own firms and their shareholders than to the interests of their competitors. And it is held that this is absurd.

However, this is not a real difficulty. . . . The solution is to recognize that moral thinking takes place at two levels at least. There is, first of all, the intuitive level at which we do, and should do, most of our moral thinking for most of the time. At this level we apply fairly simple and general principles which have proved best on the whole in our experience and in that of our forebears. These are the principles that one follows if one has the common virtues of honesty, for example, and truthfulness, and fairness, and kindness, and courage, and determination, and so on.

Loyalty is one of these virtues, and so are other kinds of partiality such as I listed just now. So, *at this level*, we do expect mothers to give their own children's interests priority over those of other children, and lawyers to seek the advantage of their own clients to the possible detriment of other people's clients. But the principles which we employ, or the virtues that we commend, at this level need some justification. How do we know, when we are bringing up our children, whether the virtues that are now commended are the ones we ought to cultivate in them? Perhaps more vigorous aggressive devil-take-the-hindmost principles would be better for them to have.

In any case the principles I have mentioned will certainly come into conflict with one another in difficult cases. No business person will need reminding of this, for these conflicts are obvious in business. The duties of honesty and truthfulness and fairness and public responsibility can certainly, and often do, conflict with the duty of loyalty to one's firm. There has to be some way of resolving these conflicts of duties; that is what business ethics is all about.

The task of resolving the conflicts, and of justifying the principles in the first place, belongs to a higher level of thinking which I am going to call critical thinking. The expression is used in a number of related senses; but what I mean by it is the thinking which criticizes and assesses the principles which are appealed to, and the decisions which are made, at the lower intuitive level. In order to decide whether ruthlessness, for example, is a virtue in business, we have to ask whether it is a good thing to cultivate it. Or would we do better to cultivate other gentler virtues? The answer to this question will depend on what we are after when we are educating our children, or for that matter students in business.

It is at this higher critical level that the theories I mentioned earlier—Kantianism, utilitarianism, and Christian *agape*—come into their own. It is perfectly consistent to say that *at the intuitive level* there are virtues and principles which we ought to follow, often without much thought, like the principle that we ought not to tell lies, or that we ought to look after our firm's interests, or alternatively that of the public; but to go on to say that when we examine these principles in the light of critical thinking we are not appealing to those principles themselves—that would be arguing in a circle. So, for example, it might be the case that it was good to have, at the intuitive level, principles requiring partiality to one's children or clients or firm; but that in justifying such principles we can appeal to impartial principles.

Let me illustrate how this could be done. We might say that it is a very good thing that employees think in general that they ought to serve the interests of their own firms. This is a good thing, not just for the firms themselves, but also for the public in general. If firms are to operate efficiently and successfully they have to be able to rely on loyalty; and if they do not operate efficiently and successfully, the interests of all—not just the firms' shareholders, but also their customers and the public in general—will suffer. That is a feature of the economic system by which we operate in capitalist economies, and I believe myself that it is the best way, in the general interest, of organizing things. That other types of economic system do not do so well for people in general has, I think, been amply shown by what went on in the Soviet Union and Eastern Europe during the Cold War era, and in other parts of the world. So the typical business virtues *are* a good thing. And they include the virtue of loyalty.

So this *partial* virtue can be justified by critical thinking, which appeals to the *impartial* principle of doing the best for people in general. An impartial critical thinker will recommend the cultivation of these partial virtues. We can see how in this way the difficulty I mentioned earlier can be got over. We should indeed cultivate the virtues and principles to which the opponents of Kantianism and utilitarianism appeal; in our ordinary dealings we should, for example, be partial and loyal to our firms and our clients and our patients and our children; but the reason is that the cultivation of these partial virtues is justified by an *impartial* appeal to the good of all, of which these theories are expressions.

The same can be said about the other virtues. The reason why honesty is rightly called a virtue is this: its cultivation by all, which leads to the firm acceptance of it, so that people feel awful if they have been dishonest, conduces on the whole to the good of all treated impartially. One can say the same about truthfulness, consideration for others, and all the rest.

So the objection that Kantianism and utilitarianism and Christian morality yield absurd results is easy to get over. The results seem absurd only because we are mixing up the two levels of moral thinking. The apparent difficulty is created by appealing to our common intuitions or moral convictions, and claiming that the theory yields results inconsistent with them. But these common convictions are implanted in us for use at the everyday intuitive level. At that level we ought to follow them; and the reason is that, as the theory itself shows, critical thinking would recommend the implanting of these convictions, as being for the best. So, for example, Christian *agape*, founded on universal love, would bid us teach to business students the virtue of

loyalty to their own firms (which is far from universal—that is, it requires us on occasion to fight against the interests of rival firms); but the reason for this is that the cultivation of this virtue by all will lead, in a properly functioning market, to the maximal furtherance of the interests of all.

ETHICS AND THE MARKET

Mention of the market brings me to my main illustration of what I have been saying. It is sometimes claimed that the market is a substitute for ethics. It would be, in a way, nice for business people if it were so. By operating in the market, and doing the utmost to secure their own advantage (which may mean damaging other people), they would be doing all that a good business person can be expected to do. They would not have to bother about moral considerations, and that would be a weight off their minds. The most important thing I have to say in this paper is that this is a simple mistake. . . .

The point is that the market is no substitute for ethics, because the market will not function without ethics. I could give examples from modern business life; but history provides us with a simpler one. The same thing has happened in all civilized economies, but I will take my example from China, because that is more picturesque. In front of the main audience chamber in the Forbidden City, the Imperial Palace in Beijing, there are two pillars. The one on the right as one faces the palace supports a sundial. I do not know whether this symbolizes the constancy of the heavenly motions, or the virtue of punctuality, or what. The other contains the standard set of weights and measures. This was put in that prominent position, many centuries ago, to symbolize the truth that honesty in trade is the foundation of prosperity. What does this teach us about business ethics? It teaches us that there could be no efficient market unless people could trust one another. Suppose, for example, any trader could sell what he called pound loaves of bread, but which actually weighed a fraction less, so that he would make an immediate gain. But then, if he got away with it, everybody would start doing the same.

The result would be that nobody would know how much bread they were getting for their money, and the market would function far less efficiently, if at all. However oriental the bargaining, it would be no use going from stall to stall seeking the best price, because you simply would not know what price you were getting *per pound;* indeed, the very word "pound" would have become meaningless. The same applies with even greater force to the currency; if people start making counterfeit coins and notes and get away with it, the time will soon come when we don't know what "dollar" means either.

That is what is meant by saying that the market is not a substitute for ethics, but depends on it . . . I could have used modern examples like market-rigging, insider dealing, misleading advertising and packaging, and the like. But . . . the point is perfectly well illustrated by my simple model from Beijing. To generalize: unless certain minimum standards of honesty, truthfulness, fair dealing, and so on are observed in the market, the market will not function efficiently, or even at all, and the good that the market is supposed to bring about will not be achieved. I shall come in a moment to the question of *how* people are to be got to observe these standards.

The standards are for use at what I called earlier the intuitive level. Their inculcation can be amply justified by thinking at the critical level, as is shown by what I have just been saying. If they were not inculcated, the whole fabric of society, including business society, would collapse. We have here an example of the phenomenon known as the "prisoners' dilemma." Here too, I need not go into the technicalities. Because the phenomenon is a commonplace of game theory, I am sure that it will be familiar. . . .

The essence of these dilemmas is that, of two or more parties, each knows that whatever the others do, it will be to his (or her) individual advantage to take a certain course; but if all take that course, they will collectively do worse than they would if they had all taken some other course. Our present example illustrates this very well. It is to the individual trader's advantage to file a bit off his "pound" weight, provided that he can get away with it; and this will be so whatever the others do. If they remain honest, he will get more money for less bread; but if they do the same as he has, he will still get more money for less bread than if he had not filed down his "pound" weight. If everybody does it, or even just a few people, the market will start operating inefficiently and all will suffer. But all the same, the dishonest will suffer less than the honest.

RESPONSES TO THE PRISONERS' DILEMMA

How then are we to set about avoiding this decline of the market? There are three ways that are canvassed. They are not mutually exclusive, and various mixtures of them are possible. They can also be used concurrently to prevent different malpractices, or even the same malpractice. But for simplicity I will consider just the three. I am going to call these three ways "custom," "self-regulation," and "legislation."

I can explain these words in terms of my simple example. It might be the case that merchants just did not file down their pound weights—it was simply "not done." Morality might come into it: they might have been brought up as children to be honest, and taught that it was dishonest to tamper with one's weights. So they might be using this principle in their intuitive thinking, and they might have been so well taught that they simply could not live with themselves if they did any such thing.

They might even, if they were more articulate, have done some critical thinking, in which they would have seen the results that would follow if people tampered with weights. They might have concluded from this that they could not will weight-tampering as a universal law for others to follow as well as themselves; and they therefore might have been unwilling to subscribe to a universal principle permitting this, and so they might have become sure that it was wrong to do it. But however they had come to have this principle, it might work very well if everybody had it. . . .

However, we must not think that, if morality by itself, unsupported by self-regulation or legislation, cannot keep enough people straight to make the market work, it is no use at all. This is obvious in my simple example from Beijing, and also in more modern examples. It will be much easier to keep people straight if *most* of them want to keep straight anyway. Then if you have self-regulation or legislation, the authorities, whoever they are, will have a much easier time enforcing the rules or the laws. They will only have to keep their eyes open to catch the delinquents, who in such a fundamentally moral community will be few. If they had to keep tabs on everybody, there would have to be much more paperwork, many more inspectors, many more court cases and lawyers to manage them, and so on. So the market would be, again, less efficient than it could be, and the costs would be huge. . . .

So it is certainly a help if people are moral, but not enough. The first step towards regulation, if regulation is needed, is usually called self-regulation. What happens is that various professional bodies are set up with the job of making rules and securing compliance with them. They usually have powers of inspection or at least power to investigate complaints. In the weakest case—the nearest to unaided morality—these bodies have no real teeth except publicity. For example, we have in Britain a body called the Press Council. This can hear complaints against newspapers which, it is alleged, have reported unfairly or untruly and so damaged individuals or companies. There are many cases when a complaint is upheld, although there is no *legal* redress because, for example, the law of libel does not cover the offence committed. This body has no teeth; all it can do is to blacken the name of the offending newspaper in its reports. But even this may do some good. . . .

The next step, obviously, if needed, is to give such bodies teeth. This can only be done—short of bringing in the law—by having professional associations whose members are bound by the regulations made by their ruling bodies. If they break the rules, they can in the last resort be slung out, as lawyers and doctors can be if they commit recognized malpractices. This is obviously a more powerful engine for securing good conduct. It is preferred by many practitioners to statutory regulation, because they like to be governed by their own peers and not by the legislature. . . .

However, the system has one obvious disadvantage. . . . The objection is that these bodies, because they are not directly responsible to the public, do not sufficiently protect the public interest, whatever they may do for the interests of their own constituents. For example, suppose we have an Advertising Standards Authority to enforce a code of practice among advertisers, and suppose that this body is elected by, and responsible to, the members of that group (let us say the advertising agencies or their clients). Then the body may ban practices which are detrimental to its constituents . . . but may do nothing about practices which are to the advantage of advertisers themselves but harm the public in general. . . .

For these reasons a call will arise for the legislature or the government to step in itself and *appoint* regulatory bodies enforcing, not their own rules, but laws laid down from above in what is thought to be the public interest. The disadvantage of doing this is often said to be that the legislators, not being members of the profession in question, do not always have the knowledge to make the best rules; and that therefore the system, besides becoming cumbrous and unworkable and even easy to circumvent, may fail to achieve the desired objects in the public interest. I would say that this is especially likely to be true in the financial area.

In most financial centres and other walks of life where regulation is attempted, we can see examples of all these methods, and indeed there are many different variants of them. . . . As I said, they can be used concurrently. What are we doing when we are deciding between them in a particular field? Reverting to my distinction between intuitive and critical thinking: just as, there, the best intuitions are the ones whose inculcation does the best on the whole for everybody treated impartially, so here the best rules and regulatory systems are the ones which do the best for those affected. Those affected in the first instance are the members of the profession in question or the participants in the market. In some areas they are the main people affected. Some financial malpractices, for example, may do enormous harm to individual people or firms, but not harm the public much except by damaging the operation of the market. In such cases self-regulation is perhaps all right; the main interests are protected.

But in other cases malpractices may harm a wider public (for example by precipitating a stock market crash). When that is the situation, the public through its representatives in the legislature will rightly call for legislation to take the matter out of the hands of cosy professional bodies and subject it to the law of the land, in the public interest. But, as I said, the legislators may get it wrong.

The best advice I can give is that everybody in a particular walk of life, be they doctors or lawyers or business people, would be sensible if, first of all, they cultivated sound *moral* principles, so as to avoid even self-regulation and the bureaucracy that it brings with it; and that if recourse has to be had to self-regulation, the bodies that do it should conduct themselves in such a way that the public does not think that the professionals are feathering their own nests, but have the interests of the public primarily at heart. In this way we shall avoid legislation, and get an efficient market with the minimum of regulation. But I know that I am asking for a lot.

MORALITY AND THE LAW

I will end with another example of a question that often troubles business people. What difference to the *morality* of an act does it make that it would be against the *law*? Cases like this are familiar. The actual case I am thinking of concerned a firm called the Beech-Nut Company. . . . An executive of this company ordered a product from its inventory to be kept on the market; the product claimed to be apple juice, but was in fact mostly sugared water. The company had innocently bought this from fraudulent suppliers and had an enormous stock of the stuff. Let us suppose that the executive knew that to sell the product was illegal. The executive, however, thought he was *morally* obliged to sell the product and try to get away with it, because of the loyalty he owed to his company and its shareholders, who

would lose a lot of money if the company went out of business. He thought the public would not come to any harm by drinking sugared water.

I will answer this question as briefly as I can. There are two ways in which the unlawfulness of an act affects its morality. The first way is this: it may be that the legal consequences of the act are such that people (for example the shareholders) will be harmed. In the present case, if the firm were sentenced to a large fine, the shareholders would suffer, and this would be a consequence, or probable consequence, of the illegality of the act. That is why wise firms employ attorneys. It is simply an example of the truth that the consequences of acts are relevant to their morality.

. . . Our acts are what we do, and what we do is the difference that we make to the course of events, that is to say the consequences that we bring about. So if this executive gets his shareholders into legal trouble, we shall say he has harmed their interests; that is one of the things he did. In this sense consequences are part of the act, and may be a morally relevant part.

That then is the consequentialist reason for keeping on the right side of the law. It may tell against other consequentialist reasons for *breaking* the law. If the executive thought that the probable balance of advantage for his shareholders lay with breaking the law, then, so far as this reason goes (namely the reason of loyalty to shareholders, which, as I have said is *one* moral reason) he morally ought to break it.

This first reason for keeping the law may sound cynical, but it is a moral reason all the same, to be appealed to in appropriate cases at the intuitive level. But there is another reason which may be thought less cynical. I said that there were these two levels of moral thinking, and that at the intuitive level what we do is stick to the sound moral principles in which we have been raised. Loyalty to one's company is one of these principles, but only one. Since we are here operating at the intuitive level, and there are other principles (honesty to the public in this case), we may, and do, have a conflict between these principles. But the relevant thing here is that one of the principles that may come into conflict is the principle that we ought to keep the law. This is an intuitive moral principle in which most of us have been raised, and it is a good thing that we have. Things would go worse not only for others but for us if we had not been raised in this way.

But what we have here is a possible conflict between this principle and the principle of loyalty. I said earlier that there would be these conflicts of principles, and that in such cases it was the function of critical thinking to resolve the conflict so as to get the best outcome, morally speaking, in the particular case. So, faced with such a conflict, we shall give a great deal of weight to our duty to keep the law, and shall break this principle only with repugnance, if we have been well brought up. But in some cases we may think that, all things considered, we ought to break the law, because to do so is required by some other principle which also has great weight. *Which* principle we ought to allow to override the others in a particular case is a matter for critical thought.

Review and Discussion Questions

1. Why are logic and the study of language important aspects of philosophy?

2. Hare writes that his approach to ethics applies the insights of utilitarianism and Kantianism and that it is also compatible with the Golden Rule and other moralities. What do you see as the gist of that approach?

3. What are the two levels of moral thinking that Hare distinguishes? Give an example that illustrates the difference.

4. Explain why you agree or disagree with Hare's contention that the market requires or presupposes ethics.

5. What is the prisoners' dilemma, and how is it relevant to the operation of the market? What are the advantages and disadvantages of self-regulation as a response to the dilemma?

6. Explain the two ways in which the fact that something is against the law can, according to Hare, make a difference to its morality. In your view, is it always wrong to break the law? If an action is legal, does that make it morally permissible? Explain your answers.

WHEN IS "EVERYBODY'S DOING IT" A MORAL JUSTIFICATION?

RONALD M. GREEN

People often give "Everybody's doing it" as a justification for engaging in conduct that is undesirable but widespread. That is certainly true in business, where the actions of competitors can pose difficult choices for managers. When does the claim that "Everybody's doing it" provide a sound moral reason for one's doing the same thing? In this essay, Ronald M. Green, professor of religion at Dartmouth College, proposes five conditions as a guide for determining when the existence of a prevalent but otherwise undesirable pattern of behaviour provides a moral justification for engaging in such behaviour oneself. He then tests those conditions by applying them to a series of business cases.

The fact that "Everyone's doing it" is frequently appealed to as a reason why people feel morally justified in acting in less than ideal ways. This is particularly true in business matters, where competitive pressures often conspire to make perfectly upright conduct seem difficult if not impossible. . . .

The "Everyone's doing it" claim usually arises when we encounter a more or less prevalent form of behavior that is morally undesirable because it involves a practice that, on balance, causes harms people would like to avoid. Although it is rare that literally "everyone else" is engaged in this behavior, the "Everyone's doing it" claim is meaningfully made whenever a practice is widespread enough to make one's own forbearing from this conduct seem pointless or needlessly self-destructive. . . . In the commercial sphere, practices of bribery, cheating, and deception are common examples. Other things being equal, we and others would

From *Business Ethics Quarterly,* Volume 1, Number 1 (January 1991). Reprinted with permission of Philosophy Documentation Center.

prefer that no one act in these ways, but the practices are widespread and our failing to participate in them can cause us serious loss or injury.

In what follows I want to focus on the use of the "Everyone's doing it" claim as a *justification* for conduct. This is not the only way this claim is used in our moral discourse. Sometimes the fact that many others are engaging in a form of conduct is offered as proof that the conduct is not really harmful or undesirable. Prevalent patterns of behavior may be offered as evidence for differing moral intuitions on a matter of dispute, as when Catholic liberals point to the use of birth control by many faithful believers as evidence for error in the Church's official moral teaching. Or prevalent behavior may be offered as an evidence for the existence (or nonexistence) of some morally relevant convention, as when the widespread and open giving of gifts at the closing of business deals is taken as a sign that this behavior is not regarded as bribery. Sometimes, as well, the "Everyone's doing it" claim is used to mitigate punishment for admittedly wrongful behavior, as when people argue that the prevalence of a certain form of immoral conduct renders it unjust to single out any one person for punishment.

The specific employment of the "Everyone's doing it" claim on which I want to focus differs from these situations in that there is no question that the behavior at issue is generally harmful and, hence, morally undesirable. If others were not acting in this way, I would not seek to justify doing so myself. Nor am I merely seeking to avoid being singled out for punishment for wrongful past acts. Because others are acting in this undesirable way, and because I may suffer serious harm or loss if I do not follow their lead, the "Everyone's doing it" claim is made as a way of defending the moral permissibility of my (even prospectively) imitating their behavior.

Facing situations of this sort, where the prospect of injury or serious loss is present, I believe, the five conditions listed on the following table guide our thinking about when it is morally permissible to adopt an otherwise undesirable but prevalent practice ourselves. If all five of these conditions, or at least the first four, are met, it is morally permitted to act as others are doing. If any of the first four are not satisfied, we'll see, moral decision becomes more complex.

1. Refraining from this behavior will unavoidably cause you (or those you care for or for whom you are responsible) serious harm or loss.
2. Your engaging in this behavior will not also cause significantly more harm or loss to others.
3. Your engaging in this behavior will not lead others to engage in it in ways that are equally or more harmful, *and this would be true if your engaging in this behavior were to become public knowledge.*
4. Your refraining from this behavior will not lead others to refrain from it, *and this would be true if your refraining from this behavior were to become public knowledge.*
5. Your refraining from this behavior will unavoidably lead others to engage in it in ways that are substantially more harmful than would have been the case had you chosen to engage in it yourself *and this would be true if your refraining from this behavior were to become public knowledge.*

The first four of these conditions constitute *prima facie* reasons for one's allowably acting as others are doing in situations of this kind. If all four conditions are met one may morally choose either to act or *not* act as others are doing. If these first four conditions are satisfied, one is not *required* to act as others are doing. For personal reasons or reasons of prudence, one may forbear from doing what these conditions morally permit. Similarly, these conditions say nothing about supererogatory behavior that seeks to resist moral compromise. Thus, although one who follows others' lead when these conditions are satisfied may do so without blame, depending on further considerations he or she may also be praiseworthy for choosing not to do so. Only the fifth condition carries us over into a realm of possible moral requiredness. If this condition is met and no other way reasonably exists to forestall the harm involved, I may be called on to do what "Everyone else is doing" and may be faulted if I refrain from doing so, although this will depend on the degree of harm my conduct helps prevent. In the ensuing discussion, I will explore none of these finer distinctions, but it is important to recognize that the first four conditions do not ordinarily identify mandatory behavior. So long as the fifth condition is not involved, individuals whose scruples lead them to object to any form of moral compromise may well choose not to act in ways these conditions otherwise allow them to do.

As we might expect, it is rare for all these conditions to be met and equally rare for all *not* to be met. Hence, moral decision in cases where others are acting in undesirable ways frequently requires us to balance condition against condition and to assess the harms identified by each condition. Although there is no magical solution to this balancing problem, a key requirement is impartiality in reasoning. This is a fundamental feature of the "moral point of view." It requires us to evaluate the harms created or avoided by our conduct independently of the knowledge of how they affect ourselves (or those we care for). In some cases, this will be an extraordinarily difficult task, compounded by the confusion of personal information and motives with impartial reasoning in any actual instance of choice. Nevertheless, these five conditions can at least preliminarily assist us in this complex process by identifying the morally relevant matters we must address.

Why are these considerations the important ones? We may think of them as arising out of and expressing the more basic logic of the moral reasoning process. In keeping with this logic, morality aims at minimizing the infliction of harm on persons against their will. Morality also seeks to provide a public forum of appeal concerning disputed modes of conduct. This means that moral choice, however private in fact, is always inherently public and requires us, at least in principle, to submit the rule implicit in our conduct to the approval of all persons it might affect. Finally, because of its public and rule-oriented character, moral reasoning supports conduct whose disclosure and expression as a public rule of allowable behavior would tend to discourage rather than encourage harmful behavior. Each of our five conditions is designed to express one or more aspects of this basic logic. The first and second conditions, for example, address the matter of proportionate harm. The third, fourth, and fifth conditions express our concern with the impact of our example on others' behavior, and the publicity clause in the third, fourth, and fifth conditions identifies the fact that it is the public rule implicit in our behavior that is morally relevant, not just the immediate impact of the behavior itself.

Do these conditions provide a complete and accurate guide to reasoning our way through "Everyone's doing it"–type situations? One way of answering this question is to see how thoroughly and well these conditions express the underlying logic of the moral reasoning process. A complementary approach is to see how well these conditions guide our thinking in specific cases of moral choice. In what follows, I want to take the second course, applying these conditions to a series of typical cases drawn from the business sector. If these conditions are consistently able to guide our thinking about complex choices in ways that correspond to, or at least do not seriously defy, our settled moral judgments about such matters, then we may assume that these conditions are an appropriate expression of the basic moral reasoning process applied to cases of this sort.

CASE 1

You are the Philippines general manager of HAL, a large, multinational computer firm. Some months ago, the Philippine government placed an order for several of your firm's largest mainframe computers. The computers have arrived and are being held dockside by a regional office of the Customs Bureau. You learn that the reason for this delay is that a mid-level customs official is demanding a bribe to release the units for shipment. The sum involved is not large, but paying the bribe will violate HAL's policies and will require special authorization from the home office. You are reasonably confident that the payment is unnecessary. High officials in the government agencies who have ordered the units can soon be expected to bring pressure to bear on the Customs Bureau to have the units released. At worst, therefore, if you refuse to pay the bribe you face several more weeks of waiting. You know that bribery of customs officials is commonplace in the Philippines. May you appeal to this fact to expedite your shipment?

We have here a form of behavior that normally raises the "Everyone's doing it" claim. It is morally undesirable because it causes harm that, on balance, people would like to avoid, but it is nevertheless widely practiced. Bribery undermines economic rationality and stalls rather than expedites economic or political transactions. Nor is this a case of a harmless convention that only seems undesirable because of its unfamiliarity, for example, like the practice of petty "baksheesh" involving small payments to minor officials who earn their living this way in lieu of salaries. We may assume that the extortion involved here is substantial and genuinely impedes economic activity and development.

Despite the prevalence of this conduct in the Philippines your firm should not pay the bribe in this case because of the practice's undesirability and because not one of our five conditions is satisfied. Let's look at this in some detail, taking as our guide these five conditions expressed as a series of questions.

1. Will refraining from bribery cause you (or those you care for or for whom you are responsible) serious and unavoidable harm or loss?

For bribery to be justified in terms of this consideration, you must be able to answer this question "yes." However, in the case as described, the answer to this question seems to be "no." The harms and losses involved in not paying the bribe are minimal.

2. Will your engaging in bribery also cause significantly more harm or loss to others?

For bribery to be justified in terms of this consideration, the appropriate answer to this question is "no." This seems to be true, although, in view of the absence of harm to you or your firm in this case, the question itself does not seem applicable, as it would be in a case where harm to you had to be balanced against possible direct injury to others. If we think of the first of our five conditions as the driving force legitimating moral compromise, the failure to meet the first condition means that satisfying any of the restraining considerations represented by conditions 2 through 4 is morally irrelevant.

3. Will your engaging in bribery lead others to engage in it in ways that are equally or more harmful, and would this still be true if your engaging in bribery were to become public knowledge?

For bribery to be justified in terms of this consideration, the appropriate answer to this question must be "no." In this case, the answer is unclear. A large multinational

firm's acquiescence to extortion of this sort may set an example for other firms, including many smaller and less powerful organizations. Furthermore, rewarding the extortionary activities of petty officials may encourage them to repeat this behavior in the future. This suggests an affirmative answer to the question. However, if we assume that bribery is already endemic in this environment, it may be reasonable to argue that one firm's conduct will have little or no impact on the prevalence of the practice. Note that because of the requirement that this encouragement not occur if this behavior were (even only hypothetically) to become public knowledge, this conclusion would hold even if the payment were made secretly.

4. *Will your refraining from bribery lead others to refrain from it*, and would this still be true if your refraining from bribery were to become public knowledge?

For bribery to be permissible in terms of this consideration, you must, again, be able to answer this question "no." As was true for the previous question, it is hard to determine whether a large multinational firm's decision actively to resist extortion of this sort will encourage others to follow its lead, although it is reasonable to suppose some effect of this sort. Corrupt customs officers may become more wary in the future about putting the squeeze on powerful multinational firms, especially if they find themselves subject to disciplinary action as a result. Hence, we can give a somewhat affirmative answer to this question, although the prevalence of this practice may mitigate the discouragement effect. Again, because of this condition's hypothetical requirement of publicity, this equivocal conclusion would hold even if HAL's resistance to extortion were not publicized in any way or if news of it were suppressed. . . .

5. Will your refraining from bribery unavoidably lead others to engage in it in ways that are substantially more harmful than would have been the case had you chosen to engage in it yourself, and would this still be true if your refraining from bribery were to become public knowledge?

There seems to be no reason to believe in this case that your refusing to pay the bribe will have this effect. Since a strongly affirmative answer is required here for complicity in this practice to be permissible (or required) this consideration lends no support to paying a bribe in this case.

Overall, although our second condition is not violated, none of the other conditions needed to justify acquiescence to extortion are clearly met in this case, and we can reasonably consider it morally impermissible to participate in this practice.

CASE 1′

We can change this case slightly by invoking the possibility of serious harm to you, your firm, or the Philippine government as a result of a refusal to pay the bribe. Suppose, for example, that additional weeks of delay on the dock expose the computers to damage for which your division is financially responsible and which will seriously reduce profits.

In that case, our first question receives the requisite affirmative answer: refusing to pay the bribe causes serious harm or loss, but this must still be weighed against the harm or stimulus to wrongdoing uncovered by our answers to the remaining four questions.

The second question is answered negatively, as it must be if paying the bribe is allowable in this case. You probably do not directly cause more harm to others than your firm is likely to suffer. However, the answers to questions 3, 4, and 5 remain the same as in the previous version of the case, and the possibly affirmative answers to 3 and 4, in particular, continue to provide good reasons for not paying the bribe. Although there is no simple formula for adjudicating the conflict here, these considerations suggest that even in the face of significant annoyance and injury, there is substantial moral reason for not acquiescing to extortion.

CASE 1″

We can take this case one step farther and assume that at some point the harm incurred by resisting involvement in bribery increases significantly. This might be true, for example, if HAL's ability to do business in the Philippines were threatened by its refusal to pay bribes of this sort. Not only would this represent a substantial increment in the degree of harm experienced by the firm, but the fact that HAL's efforts are not supported by the government suggests that its refusal to engage in bribery is not significantly contributing to a reduction in bribery and extortion by others. Hence, condition 4 and (we may suppose) condition 3 are met in ways that increase the justifiability of involvement in this common but undesirable behavior.

CASE 1‴

Finally, we might make one further change in the case to develop a far more compelling justification for involvement in bribery. Imagine, now, that instead of your firm's being a large and powerful multinational corporation, it is a small joint partnership whose economic survival depends on retaining a toehold in the Philippine market. Failure to pay the bribe in this case will represent economic disaster and loss for you and all the constituencies you represent.

Here we can give a strong affirmative answer to the first question. You suffer serious harm or loss if you refuse to pay the bribe. The second question is answered negatively as it must be for complicity to be allowable: no one is directly harmed by your bribery more than you and your firm are by not bribing. The third and fourth questions must also be answered negatively, and there is good reason to think that in this case they are. Given the pervasiveness of bribery and your firm's small size and lack of influence, paying or refusing to pay will likely have no impact on the prevalence of this behavior. Indeed, if you falter economically because of refusing to pay the bribe, other firms will surely step into your place and the practice will continue unabated. Although there is no suggestion here that your refusing to pay the bribe will accentuate the incidence or level of wrongdoing—and hence that condition 5 is met—the first

four conditions are satisfied and, according to our conditions, bribery is morally permissible in this instance.

Of course, this is not the end of the matter. If it is true that the practice of bribery is generally undesirable, even though in this case you might be morally justified in participating in it, this does not relieve you of any moral obligation you might have, whether as a member of society generally or as a person in a specific social role with corresponding duties, to seek to abate the practice as a whole. To the extent that you have some kind of obligation to help prevent or reduce harm to others, for example, you are called on to speak out publicly against extortion and bribery and you should also perhaps join industry-wide or civic efforts at reform. It is not necessarily true that if you choose to do this you must also morally refrain from paying bribes until they are more effectively banned. If you become prominent in the anti-bribery effort, your continued payment of bribes may be tactically unwise and it may also be wrong if you deceive people and lead them to think you are resisting bribery and extortion. But it is not clear so long as you are open about your conduct that you are wrong in continuing to pay bribes when they are a condition of doing business in the country and our other conditions are met.

CASE 2

You are Vice President, Corporate Communications, of a large food processing firm, one of whose principal products is infant formula. A large share of your firm's formula sales take place in third world nations in Africa, Latin America, and the Caribbean where, along with your competitors, you actively engage in promoting formula used among new mothers. You all sample heavily in village health centers and urban hospitals and rely on medical professionals and paraprofessionals to promote your product.

Within the past year, an important international protest movement has developed against these policies. Critics point out that even under the best conditions, breastfeeding is superior to bottle feeding, both because of the balanced nutrition and antibodies it provides and because of its value in infant-mother bonding. Furthermore, they say, in the third world environment, bottle feeding can be very harmful because water supplies are often contaminated and women are too poor to afford the level of formula purchases needed for adequate infant nutrition. Critics blame your marketing practices for the epidemic of fatal newborn diarrhea in these regions and some have begun to use words like "genocide" to describe your conduct.

Infant formula sales overseas constitute roughly 25 percent of your firm's total revenues and, because of the return to breast-feeding in North America, are the fastest growing sector of its business. Shortly, you will participate in a meeting of your firm's Executive Committee where a strategy to respond to the rising tide of criticism will be discussed. At that meeting, you will be called on to articulate the moral issues involved here. You are aware that many persons in your firm believe that your conduct is ethical. Some feel you are making an option available to women in these countries they would not otherwise have.

They point out that no one is being forced to adopt bottle feeding and that some women unable to nurse would be seriously harmed if you withdrew from the market. Finally, whatever their views on these other matters, many in your firm believe that if you were to withdraw from this business or to market less aggressively, nothing would be accomplished. Competitors (some based in other countries and not subject to your domestic laws or codes) would merely step into the void your departure creates. Those who argue this way concede that your present practices have probably contributed to the rise in infant mortality in the third world. But they see a change in policy as accomplishing nothing while economically damaging your firm.

Once again we have a case to which our five conditions are meant to apply. On balance, in its present form the marketing practices of infant formula firms are undesirable. Even if these practices have some beneficial aspects, they inflict unnecessary harm on many third world children. Nevertheless, "Everyone's doing it," in the sense that the practice is prevalent, and if your firm does not, others will. How would you answer each of the five relevant questions in this case?

1. Will refraining from aggressive marketing of infant formula in the third world unavoidably cause your firm serious harm or loss?

Assuming that third world sales represent a substantial and growing share of your company's business, and that all the relevant alternatives are even more costly for the firm, it seems that this question receives an affirmative answer. On this count, then, continuing your policy might be justifiable.

2. Will your aggressive marketing of infant formula in the third world cause significantly more harm to others?

I think the answer to this question is almost certainly "yes." If the critics are right—and for our purposes here we may assume they are—many thousands of third world children will die or be subject to the ravages of malnutrition as a direct result of your current marketing practices. Since few people would argue that profit considerations of this sort justify inflicting death and suffering on so many children, your conduct here seems morally unjustifiable.

Whichever way you answer questions 3 and 4 will only sustain or reinforce this judgment. If your continued marketing of formula this way encourages other firms to do so, then this conduct becomes even more unjustifiable, whereas its having no effect still leaves you directly involved in the imposition of disproportionate harm on children. If your refraining from these practices causes others to follow suit, this constitutes a further reason for altering your conduct, but even if this doesn't occur, ceasing this marketing would at least prevent your firm from being an agent of disproportionate harm to others.

Incidentally, we may think of this second condition as a kind of damper on the spread of disproportionately harmful behavior. Permitting people to engage in such behavior merely because others are (or inevitably will) do so and

because the net balance of harm will remain unaffected if one withdraws is an open invitation to the proliferation of harmful conduct. This second condition rules out such complicity. Only if conditions 3, 4, and 5 are further satisfied—that is, if one's behavior does not encourage others to engage in it, if one's refraining would not discourage them, and if the net harm created by one's refraining from a practice can be shown to be unavoidably and substantially greater than one's engaging in it—may involvement in the infliction of direct, disproportionate harm be justified.

About the only way the case for continuing these practices could be made, therefore, is if condition 5 were met. This would require a strongly affirmative answer to the following question, *"Will your refraining from aggressive marketing of infant formula in the third world lead others to engage in it in ways that are substantially more harmful than would have been the case had you chosen to engage in it yourselves?"* In the next case, we'll encounter a situation where there might arguably be an affirmative answer to this question, but nothing presented in this case suggests such an answer here. Thus, the condition implicit in this question is not satisfied and your current practices are probably morally unjustifiable. Only the first consideration of financial loss supports your continued involvement, and few people believe that this is a good enough reason to inflict suffering and death on children.

This suggests the need for an alternative strategy if your firm is to preserve any kind of involvement in this market. Earlier we saw that when an otherwise morally undesirable practice exists, we always have some measure of moral responsibility to discourage it. This is true even when the conditions for one's complicity in the practice are fully satisfied, but this responsibility is magnified by prudential considerations when these conditions prohibit our involvement. In the case at hand, this recommends a complex strategy for your firm: forthright alignment of your public position with that of the formula marketing critics and active involvement or leadership in international efforts to regulate marketing practices by *all* infant formula firms in the third world environment. . . .

CASE 3

You are Vice President, Corporate Communications, of one of the largest brewing firms in North America. Like most other large brewers . . ., your company engages in a substantial marketing effort aimed at the college age population. This effort has more than immediate sales as its object since studies show that brand preferences for beer are firmly established during the college years. In order to capture a large share of this important market, your firm, like its competitors, advertises heavily in college publications and national print and broadcast media aimed at college students. You also engage in substantial promotional activities on campuses where this is allowed. These range from matching grants for student-run charitable telethons and sports activities to "wet tee shirt contests" and other forms of social activity.

Recently, these practices have come under attack. Critics maintain they help create a "culture of alcohol" that has contributed to a dramatic rise of drinking problems among younger people. They point to the growing incidence of alcohol abuse on college campuses . . . and to studies linking such abuse during the college years to alcoholism later in life. Some of these critics have called on brewers to eliminate these marketing activities voluntarily, while others have demanded an outright legal ban on these activities.

In an interview reported in the national press, the CEO of your company recently went on record as being concerned about these practices. Although he did not agree that alcohol abuse can be blamed on the availability or promotion of alcoholic beverages, he conceded that many of the promotional efforts you and your competitors engage in are "distasteful." He expressed the wish that the industry as a whole could somehow "get its act together" to improve its record in this area. But he added that without an industry-wide agreement, no single firm could withdraw from the college market. "As things now stand," he observed, "the college market is the name of the game." At the close of this interview, your CEO pointed out that the promotional activities of your firm are significantly better than most of its competitors. Your marketing people take special care to see that your campus-based activities involve only students of legal drinking age and are adequately supervised by responsible authorities. Your print and broadcast ads aimed at college students also stress moderation in the use of alcohol. Whenever practicable, print ads contain explicit warnings about the dangers of alcohol abuse. Finally, you have been committed for several years to devoting a significant portion (10 percent) of your marketing budget to the support of alcohol education programs on college campuses. . . .

Not entirely satisfied with the course of this interview, your CEO subsequently designated a committee of senior officers to study alternatives for the company in this area. You are a member of that committee. As you would expect, the discussions have been vigorous. Some members have argued strongly that they see nothing wrong in current promotional activities. These are aimed, they maintain, at college age adults who should be free to make their own decisions in this area. One member of the committee summed up this view when he stated that "Prohibition is over."

Other members of the committee are less sure that your activities have not unintentionally contributed to problems of alcohol abuse on campus and beyond. They argue, however, that it would be pointless for your firm to withdraw from this market. Competitors would be eager to step in and assume the market share you lose. One committee member who argues this way goes farther: she contends that your withdrawing from this market will be morally counterproductive. "We are the most ethically responsible firm in this area," she insists. "Our ads and campus-based activities are not only responsible, they make a positive contribution to alcohol education. None of our competitors has shown equivalent responsibility. If we get out, college students will be the losers."

You are puzzled by this gamut of arguments. How do our five conditions bear on the issue? In view of the fact that college age students constitute such an important part of a brewer's market, there is probably no doubt that a unilateral withdrawal from these activities will financially damage your firm. Our first condition, therefore, seems reasonably satisfied in this case. The meaning of the second condition for this case is less clear. Although there is controversy over whether beer advertising and promotion contribute to alcohol abuse, even your CEO has expressed concern here by stating his belief that it would probably be better if all members of the industry showed more restraint.

The answers to the questions implicit in our third and fourth conditions are also less than clear. Does your firm's engaging in the gamut of its marketing activities contribute to other firms' following its lead? Would its publicly announced withdrawal from this market or specific marketing activities put pressure on leading competitors to follow suit? An argument can be made for positive answers to both questions, especially the second one. In view of the developing public reaction against these practices, a unilateral move by an industry leader might have a significant impact on industry-wide practice or on the legal environment.

In view of the opposing set of considerations exposed by a review of conditions 1 through 4, the fifth condition becomes especially important. To what extent will your firm's withdrawal from this market be a victory for personal moral purity gained at the expense of a real and adverse impact on college populations as a whole? Will your refraining from involvement in this area unavoidably cause a net and significant increase in irresponsible advertising and promotional activities by others who will step into the place your departure creates?

The answer to this question is itself unclear and probably cannot be determined apart from a specific investigation of the dynamics of this industry and the effect of your involvement *versus* that of others. Nevertheless, to this point, our analysis reveals several things. First, that the fifth condition may legitimately be introduced as a consideration in "Everyone's doing it"–type situations. Members of the committee who urge this matter are not wrong to do so and there will be situations when satisfying this condition will clearly justify complicity and continued involvement in less than ideal practices. This situation may not be one of them, however, and this illustrates a second point: that it is not enough to claim the applicability of condition 5. One must show that it is satisfied beyond reasonable doubt in order to justify involvement in practices markedly violating other conditions. It is thoroughly predictable that those engaged in prevalent but undesirable conduct will seek to justify their doing so on the grounds that others' involvement will somehow increase the net level of harm. In view of this, condition 5 must be thought to impose an especially severe constraint on decision makers: they must show beyond reasonable doubt that their continued involvement helps avoid a significant level of increased harm, and they must show that the harm avoided clearly outweighs any immediate harms and relevant encouragement or discouragement effects governed by conditions 2, 3, and 4.

Is this stern standard met in this case? I personally think it is not. I am not persuaded by the bare facts of this case that whatever positive effects result from this firm's college marketing program really offset the immediate injury inflicted on some college students by the stimulus to excessive alcohol consumption. Nor am I convinced that the powerful example of an industry leader publicly withdrawing from involvement in these activities, perhaps hand-in-hand with its assuming the role of leadership in an industry-wide drive for self-restraint, would not in the long run prove effective in reducing the harms associated with current practices.

The point here, however, is not to resolve this case, which involves complex factual matters beyond our reach, so much as it is to illustrate the way in which these five conditions focus discussion and inquiry. Frequently in the course of moral debate one or another of these conditions is appealed to, but often only in an implicit or oblique fashion that impedes thorough analysis. By taking these conditions separately, each condition may be given the degree of logical and factual examination appropriate to it in the case at hand. In this instance, for example, the potentially strongest argument in the firm's favor, its claim that its marketing activities relatively benefit college age students, seems less persuasive when brought to the fore and exposed to critical investigation than it does when it is an undifferentiated part of complex argument. This points up the value of analyzing an "Everyone's doing it" situation in terms of each of these five conditions. By proceeding carefully, condition by condition, we are better able to identify the facts and claims relevant to each aspect of what are usually complex arguments about a form of behavior.

CONCLUSION

The task of identifying a set of justifying conditions for complex cases of moral choice points in two different directions. On the one hand, these conditions must be shown to reflect and adequately express the relevant considerations governing all moral choice, what I earlier called the basic "logic" of the moral reasoning process. On the other hand, a list of justifying conditions must also adequately guide judgement through both familiar and novel cases for decision and it must do so without violating some of our firmest and most settled judgments about these cases. When these two sides of the task are adequately accomplished, we can say that an exercise of this sort is successful and that we are in a position of "reflective equilibrium" before the issues at hand.

The foregoing investigation sought only to accomplish a fragment of this task. Although I suggested the conformity of these five conditions to the basic logic of the moral reasoning process, I did not develop this point. Instead, I chose to focus on the second part of the task: applying these conditions to a series of complex cases. I have tried to suggest that these conditions furnish a useful guide to judgment. Showing this to be consistently true for all cases, using these conditions to assess and adequately respond to competing intuitions about concrete cases, and seeing if we can go beyond a listing of conditions to a more precise adjudication of conflicts among them are tasks that lie ahead. For now I hope we have made a beginning in addressing one of ethics' most persistent and puzzling questions.

Review and Discussion Questions

1. How common do you think it is for people to try to justify their conduct by the argument that "Everybody's doing it"? Give examples from your own experience.

2. Restate in your own words the five conditions that Green identifies. What's the difference between satisfying the first four conditions and satisfying the fifth? Assess his claim that his five conditions arise out of and express the basic logic of the moral reasoning process.

3. Carefully examine Case 1 in this Reading and the three variations on it in light of Green's five conditions. Do you agree with the moral conclusions he draws?

4. Do you agree with Green that in cases of morally permissible bribery, one may still have an obligation to combat the practice? If so, what would that imply in practical terms?

5. Under what circumstances, if any, would a firm be justified in marketing infant formula in a developing country?

6. Analyze the application of condition 5 to Case 3. Is it plausible to believe that it might justify the company's remaining in the college market?

7. In your view, is drinking by college students a serious problem, or is the issue exaggerated? Do you believe that marketing helps to create a "culture of alcohol" on campus? If so, what does morality require the makers of beer, wine, and other alcoholic beverages to do?

8. Do you believe that Green's five conditions provide a useful framework for determining when "Everybody's doing it" provides a legitimate justification for engaging in conduct that is undesirable but widespread? Explain why or why not.

Further Reading for Chapter 2

Tom L. Beauchamp, *Philosophical Ethics*, 3rd ed. (New York: McGraw-Hill, 2001) is an introductory text with selected readings covering classical ethical theories, rights, and the nature of morality.

Bernard Gert, *Common Morality: Deciding What to Do* (New York: Oxford University Press, 2004) provides a lucid account of the moral system that implicitly guides thoughtful people's everyday moral decisions.

Hugh LaFollette, ed., *The Blackwell Guide to Ethical Theory* (Oxford: Blackwell, 2000) and **Peter Singer**, ed., *A Companion to Ethics* (Oxford: Blackwell, 1991) are comprehensive reference works with survey essays by many individual authors.

William H. Shaw, *Contemporary Ethics: Taking Account of Utilitarianism* (Oxford: Blackwell, 1999) sympathetically examines the utilitarian approach to ethics.

Christina Hoff Sommers, ed., *Right and Wrong* (New York: Harcourt Brace Jovanovich, 1986), **Judith A. Boss**, ed., *Perspectives on Ethics*, 2nd ed. (New York: McGraw-Hill, 2003), and **Mark Timmons**, ed., *Conduct and Character*, 4th ed. (Belmont, CA: Wadsworth, 2003) provide good selections of readings on egoism, relativism, utilitarianism, Kantianism, and other normative theories.

Mark Timmons, *Moral Theory: An Introduction* (Lanham, MD: Rowman & Littlefield, 2002) provides a clear and accessible survey of all the major moral theories.

(See also the readings suggested at the end of Chapter 1.)

3

Justice and Economic Distribution

It seems strange to recall that until almost the first quarter of the twentieth century (until the *Income War Tax Act*, 1917), there was no federal tax on personal or corporate income in Canada. (In the U.S. it was only four years earlier that the Congress was granted the right to collect taxes on income.) Since then, the income tax laws have grown enormously complex, taking up thousands of pages in the statute books. Lawyers study for years to master the intricacies of the system, and most people with middle incomes or better require professional assistance to file their annual tax forms.

Because the tax rules do so much to shape the character of our economy and the distribution of income and wealth across the country, their fairness is frequently a political issue—hence, the usual controversy over income tax changes proposed by a government with the opposition parties contending that one or the other measure is unfair since it favours the well-to-do while penalizing the have-nots.

Although some tax cuts benefit mostly the well-to-do, still the wealthiest among us pay the bulk of the country's income taxes—for the simple reason that most of the country's income goes to them (and because of the principle of "progressive" taxation in our system—that is, the idea that higher incomes should be taxed at higher rates). In 2004, the average earnings of the richest 10 percent of Canada's families with children was 82 times that earned by the poorest 10 percent of Canada's families.[1] In another measure, the lowest quintile (measuring the poorest 20 percent of Canadian income earners) earned just 5 percent of total income, as against the highest quintile (the wealthiest 20 percent), which earned 44 percent of the total income. Perhaps a more telling feature is that the highest quintile received 71 percent of the total increase in wealth—and it was considerable—experienced in Canada between 1999 and 2005.[2] This is part of a trend in recent years, especially since the mid-1990s, toward an increasingly unequal distribution of the national income and wealth in our country, with well-off Canadians getting increasingly bigger slices of the pie.

Although real wages for production and nonsupervisory workers have gone up, middle-level managers have fared much better, and top executives have done spectacularly well. The average of the top-paid CEOs pocketed $9,059,113 in 2005. The top 100 ranged from $2,870,118 (number 100) to $74,824,355 (number one). The average weekly earnings (wages and salaries) of Canadian workers, as calculated from Statistics Canada's measure of average weekly earnings (wages and salaries) for 2005, was $728.17, for an annual total (52.2 working weeks) of $38,010.[3] Canadian corporate executives are among the highest-paid in the world. Japan's CEOs, for example, earn a salary of only $300,000 to $500,000 a year, with far fewer bonuses and stock options than their North American counterparts.[4]

While those on top do better than ever, life continues to be a struggle for people in the middle and lower echelons. Although our economy has created millions of new jobs in the last two decades, most of them pay relatively low wages. Productivity gains have gone predominantly to investors, not to wage earners, with capitalists grabbing a larger share of the national income at the expense of workers. A great many Canadians work at jobs that do not pay enough to support a full household, or at least to have what most people feel are necessities. No great deal of statistical information is really needed to see the point. Consider this. In 2005, the before-tax Low Income Cut-Offs (LICOs) for a family of four, residing in communities of the population size indicated in the parentheses, were as follows: $38,610 (500,000+); $33,251 (100,000–499,999); $33,046 (30,000–99,999); $30,238 (less than 30,000); $26,579 (in rural areas).[5] Persons and families living below these income levels are considered to live "in straitened circumstances" or, less euphemistically, "below the poverty line." We saw above that the average annual earnings for Canadian workers in 2005 were $38,010.[6]

The increasing inequality in the distribution of income and, especially, of wealth in Canada does not bode well for people's prospects of moving up the intergenerational income mobility (the extent to which children move up or down the income spectrum relative to their parents' generation), since with increasing inequality one usually gets an economy that is more rigid and class-bound. Though one's prospects of upward mobility are much better in Canada than in the United States or Britain, they are not as good as in a lot of the countries of the European Union.[7] Further, there is evidence that there is more mobility occurring at the higher quartiles than at the bottom ones,[8] which suggests that it is a lot easier to get ahead if your parental economic situation is already doing well. It does certainly look as though the "apple falls close to the tree."[9]

Education is a crucial determinant of future income. And these days socioeconomic class increasingly determines access to university or college. Statistics Canada reports that students from low-income families are less than half as likely to go to university than those from high-income families. Tuition fees are steadily increasing as universities seek to offset government cuts in funding by increasing student fees. This trend will certainly magnify the existing barriers to access to higher education on the part of prospective student from low-income families.[10]

There is nothing inevitable about declining social mobility or about large inequalities in income and wealth. They are not brute facts of nature, even in market-oriented societies. For example, the distribution of income in Germany and Japan is far more equal than in the United States, even though both are just as thoroughly capitalist, and an American is three times more likely to be poor than is someone in Italy.[11] Rather, political choices determine how income and wealth are distributed and what sort of assistance is given to those struggling to get by. Some countries simply choose to spend a smaller percentage of their GDP than other countries do combating inequality and pursuing policies intended to assist the bottom half of society to advance. That is why, according to some people, the gap between the wealthiest 10 percent and the poorest 10 percent is greater in the United States than in any industrialized country except Russia.[12] How much inequality and what sort of socioeconomic disparities a society is willing to accept reflect both its moral values and the relative strength of its contending social and political forces.

This chapter focuses on the subject of economic justice, which concerns the constellation of moral issues raised by a society's distribution of wealth, income, status, and power. Ethical questions arise daily about these matters. Is it just, for example, that CEOs pull in astronomical salaries and help themselves to enormous benefits when this reduces the profits of stockholders who, after all, own the company? Or, to take another issue, thanks to modern technology today's hospitals are able to perform life-prolonging feats of medicine that were undreamed of only a couple of decades ago, but these services are often extraordinarily costly. Who, then, should have access to them? Those who can afford them? Any who need them? Those who are most likely to benefit?

Chapter 2 discussed several basic moral theories and the general principles of right and wrong associated with them. This chapter focuses on the more specific topic of justice and economic distribution—that is, on the principles that are relevant to the moral assessment of society's distribution of economic goods and services. Although the topic is an abstract one, it is particularly relevant to the study of business ethics, because it concerns the moral standards to be used in evaluating the institutional frameworks within which both business and non-business organizations operate. Specifically, this chapter will examine these topics:

1. The concept of justice, its relation to fairness, equality, rights, and what people deserve, and some rival principles of economic distribution

2. The utilitarian approach to justice in general and economic justice in particular

3. The libertarian theory, which places a moral priority on liberty and free exchange

4. The contractarian and egalitarian theory of John Rawls

THE NATURE OF JUSTICE

Justice is an old concept with a rich history, one that is fundamental to any discussion of how society ought to be organized. Philosophical concern with justice goes back at least to ancient Greece. For Plato (427–347 BCE) and some of his contemporaries, justice seems to have been the paramount virtue or, more precisely, the sum of virtue with regard to our relations with others. Philosophers today, however, generally distinguish justice from the whole of morality. The complaint that something is "unjust" is more specific than that it is "bad" or "immoral." What, then, makes an act, policy, or institution unjust? Unfortunately, the terms *just* and *unjust* are vague, and different people use them in different ways. Still, talk of justice or injustice typically focuses on at least one of several related ideas—fairness, equality, desert, or rights.

First, justice is often used to mean *fairness*. Justice frequently concerns the fair treatment of members of groups of people or else looks backward to the fair compensation of prior injuries. Exactly what fairness requires is difficult to say, and different standards may be pertinent in different cases. If corporate manager Smith commits bribery, he is justly punished under our laws. If other managers commit equally serious crimes but are allowed to escape punishment, then Smith suffers a comparative injustice because he was unfairly singled out. On the other hand, Smith and other white-collar criminals are treated unfairly and thus unjustly, although this time for the opposite reason, if stiffer sentences are meted out to common criminals for less grave offences.

One way unfairness creates injustice occurs when like cases are not treated in the same fashion. Following Aristotle, most philosophers believe that we are required, as a formal principle of justice, to treat similar cases alike except where there is some relevant difference. This principle emphasizes the role of impartiality and consistency in justice, but it is a purely formal principle because it is silent about which differences are relevant and which are not. Furthermore, satisfying this formal requirement does not guarantee that justice is done. For example, a judge who treats similar cases alike can succeed in administering fairly and non-arbitrarily a law that is itself unjust (like a statute requiring racial segregation).

Related to Aristotle's fairness requirement is a second idea commonly bound up with the concept of justice, namely, that of *equality*. Justice is frequently held to require that our treatment of people reflect their fundamental moral equality. While Aristotle's formal principle of justice does not say whether we are to assume equality of treatment until some difference between cases is shown or to assume the opposite until some relevant similarities are demonstrated, a claim of injustice based on equality is meant to place the burden of proof on those who would endorse unequal treatment. Still, the premise that all persons are equal does not establish a direct relationship between justice and economic distribution. We all believe that some differences in the treatment of persons are consistent with equality (punishment, for example), and neither respect for equality nor a commitment to equal treatment necessarily implies an equal distribution of economic goods.

Despite equality, then, individual circumstances—in particular, what a person has done—make a difference. We think it is unjust, for example, when a guilty person goes free or an innocent person hangs, regardless of how others have been treated. This suggests that justice sometimes involves, as a third aspect, something in addition to equal or impartial treatment. Justice also requires that people get what they *deserve* or, as a number of ancient moralists put it, that each receive his or her due.

This is closely related to a fourth and final idea, namely, that one is treated unjustly when one's moral *rights* are violated. John Stuart Mill, in fact, made this the defining characteristic of injustice. In his view, what distinguishes injustice from other types of wrongful behaviour is that it involves a violation of the rights of some identifiable person:

Whether the injustice consists in depriving a person of a possession, or in breaking faith with him, or in treating him worse than he deserves, or worse than other people who have no greater claims—in each case the supposition implies two things: a wrong done, and some assignable person who is wronged. . . . It seems to me that this feature in the case—a right in some person, correlative to the moral obligation—constitutes the specific difference between justice and generosity or beneficence. Justice implies something which it is not only right to do, and wrong not to do, but which some individual person can claim from us as a moral right.[13]

Rival Principles of Distribution

Justice, then, is an important subclass of morality in general, a subclass that generally involves appeals to the overlapping notions of fairness, equality, desert, and rights. Turning to the topic of distributive justice—that is, to the proper distribution of social benefits and burdens (in particular, economic benefits and burdens)—a number of rival principles have been proposed. Among the principles most frequently recommended as a basis of distribution are: to each an equal share, to each according to individual need, to each according to personal effort, to each according to social contribution, and to each according to merit. Every one of these principles has its advocates, and each seems plausible in some circumstances. But only in some. There are problems with each. For example, if equality of income were guaranteed, then the lazy would receive as much as the industrious. On the other hand, effort is hard to measure and compare, and what one is able to contribute to society may depend on one's luck in being at the right place at the right time. And so on. No single principle seems to work in enough circumstances to be defended successfully as the sole principle of justice in distribution.

It often seems that we simply employ different principles of distributive justice in different circumstances. For example, corporations in certain industries may be granted tax breaks because of their social contribution; welfare programs operate on the basis of need; and business firms award promotions for meritorious performance. Moreover, multiple principles may often be relevant to a single situation. Sometimes they may pull in the same direction, as when wealthy professionals such as doctors defend their high incomes simultaneously on grounds of superior effort, merit, social contribution, and even (because of the high cost of malpractice insurance) need. Or the principles may pull in different directions, as when a teacher must balance effort against performance in assigning grades to pupils. Some philosophers are content to leave the situation here. As they see it, there are various equally valid, prima facie principles of just distribution—equality, need, effort, and so on—and one must try to find the principle that best applies in the given circumstances. If several principles seem to apply, then one must simply weigh them the best one can.

In his book *Spheres of Justice*, Michael Walzer pursues a more sophisticated version of this pluralistic approach.[14] Skeptical of the assumption that justice requires us to implement (in different contexts) some basic principle or set of principles, Walzer argues

that different goods ought to be distributed for different reasons, in accordance with different procedures, by different agents; and that all these differences derive from different understandings of the social goods themselves—the inevitable product of historical and cultural particularism.[15]

Different norms and principles govern different distributive spheres, and these norms and principles are shaped by the implicit social meanings of the goods in question. He continues:

Every social good or set of goods constitutes, as it were, a distributive sphere within which only certain criteria and arrangements are appropriate. Money is inappropriate in the sphere of ecclesiastical office. . . . There is no single standard [against which all distributions are to be measured]. But there are standards (roughly knowable even when they are also controversial) for every social good and every distributive sphere in every particular society.[16]

As Walzer sees it, distributive criteria are determined by the particular, historically shaped social meanings of the goods in question. The philosophical task is to tease out the inner logic of each type of good, thus revealing the tacit, socially shared values that govern (or should govern) its distribution.

Walzer's historically informed discussion of topics like medical care or dirty and degrading work is rich and intriguing, but his view implies that when it comes to issues of distributive justice, the best philosophers can do is to try to unravel the implicit, socially specific norms that govern the distribution of different goods in a particular society. Many contemporary philosophers disagree. They believe that we should step further back than Walzer does from existing norms and social arrangements and seek some general theory of justice in economic distribution, on the basis of which we can assess current social practices. Three such positions are reviewed below: the utilitarian, the libertarian, and the Rawlsian (egalitarian) position.

THE UTILITARIAN VIEW

For utilitarians, as Chapter 2 explained, happiness is the overarching value. Whether one assesses the rightness and wrongness of actions in terms of how much happiness they produce, as an act utilitarian does, or uses happiness as the standard for deciding what moral principles a society should accept as the basis for determining right and wrong, as a rule utilitarian does, happiness is the only thing that is good in and of itself. On that tenet all utilitarians agree.

Earlier we considered John Stuart Mill's idea that injustice involves the violation of the rights of some identifiable person. This is what distinguishes it from other types of immoral behaviour. But if injustice involves the violation of moral rights, the question arises of how a utilitarian like Mill understands talk of rights. Mill's position was that saying I have a right to something is saying I have a valid claim on society to protect me in the possession of that thing, either by the force of law or through education and opinion. And I have that valid claim in the first place because society's protection of my possession of that thing is warranted on utilitarian grounds. "To have a right, then, is . . . to have something which society ought to defend me in the possession of. If the objector goes on to ask why it ought, I can give him no other reason than general utility."[17] What utilitarianism identifies as rights are certain moral rules, the observance of which is of the utmost importance for the long run, overall maximization of happiness.

Accordingly, Mill summed up his view of justice as follows:

> Justice is a name for certain classes of moral rules which concern the essentials of human well-being more nearly, and are therefore of more absolute obligation, than any other rules for the guidance of life; and the notion which we have found to be of the essence of the idea of justice—that of a right residing in an individual—implies and testifies to this more binding obligation.
>
> The moral rules which forbid mankind to hurt one another (in which we must never forget to include wrongful interference with each other's freedom) are more vital to human well-being than any maxims, however important, which only point out the best mode of managing some department of human affairs.[18]

Although justice for Mill was ultimately a matter of promoting social well being, not every issue of social utility was a matter of justice. The concept of justice identifies certain important social utilities, that is, certain rules or rights, the upholding of which is crucial for social well being.

For utilitarians, then, justice is not an independent moral standard, distinct from their general principle. Rather, the maximization of happiness ultimately determines what is just and unjust. Critics of utilitarianism contend that knowing what will promote happiness is always difficult. People are bound to estimate consequences differently, thus making the standard of utility an inexact and unreliable principle for determining what is just. Mill, however, did not see much merit in this criticism. For one thing, it presupposes that we all agree about what the principles of justice are and how to apply them. This is far from the case, Mill argued. Indeed, without utilitarianism to provide a determinate standard of justice, one is always left with a plethora of competing principles, all of which seem to have some plausibility but are mutually incompatible.

As an example, Mill pointed to the conflict between two principles of justice that occurs in the realm of economic distribution. Is it just or not, he asked, that more talented workers should receive a greater remuneration? There are two possible answers to this question:

> On the negative side of the question it is argued that whoever does the best he can deserves equally well, and ought not in justice to be put in a position of inferiority for no fault of his own; that superior abilities have already advantages more than enough . . . without adding to these a superior share of the world's goods; and that society is bound in justice rather to make compensation to the less favored for this unmerited inequality of advantages than to aggravate it.[19]

This argument sounds plausible, but then so does the alternative answer:

> On the contrary side it is contended that society receives more from the more efficient laborer; that, his services being more useful, society owes him a larger return for

them; that a greater share of the joint result is actually his work, and not to allow his claim to it is a kind of robbery; that, if he is only to receive as much as others, he can only be justly required to produce as much.[20]

Here we have two conflicting principles of justice. How are we to decide between them? The problem, Mill said, is that both principles seem plausible:

> Justice has in this case two sides to it, which it is impossible to bring into harmony, and the two disputants have chosen opposite sides; the one looks to what it is just that the individual should receive, the other to what it is just that the community should give.[21]

Each disputant is, from his or her own point of view, unanswerable. "Any choice between them, on grounds of justice," Mill continued, "must be perfectly arbitrary." What, then, is the solution? For Mill, the utilitarian, the answer was straightforward: "Social utility alone can decide the preference."[22] The utilitarian standard must be the ultimate court of appeal in such cases. Only the utilitarian standard can provide an intelligent and satisfactory way of handling controversial questions of justice and of resolving conflicts between two competing principles of justice.

Utilitarianism and Economic Distribution

The utilitarian theory of justice ties the question of economic distribution to the promotion of social well-being or happiness. Utilitarians want an economic system that will bring more good to society than any other system. But what system is that? Utilitarianism itself, as a normative theory, provides no answer. The answer depends on the relevant social, economic, and political facts. A utilitarian must understand the various possibilities, determine their consequences, and assess the available options. Obviously, this is not a simple task. Deciding what sort of economic arrangements would best promote human happiness requires the utilitarian to consider many things, including (1) the type of economic ownership (private, public, mixed); (2) the way of organizing production and distribution in general (pure laissez faire, markets with government planning and regulation, fully centralized planning); (3) the type of authority arrangements within the units of production (worker control versus managerial prerogative); (4) the range and character of material incentives; and (5) the nature and extent of social security and welfare provisions.

As a matter of historical fact, utilitarians in the early nineteenth century tended to favour free trade and the laissez-faire view of Adam Smith that unregulated market relations and free competition best promote the total social good.[23] Today it is probably fair to say that few, if any, utilitarians believe happiness would be maximized by a pure nineteenth-century-style capitalism, without any welfare arrangements. However, they are not in agreement on the question of what economic arrangements would in fact maximize happiness. Nonetheless, many utilitarians would view favourably increased worker participation in industrial life and more equal distribution of income.

Worker Participation   In his *Principles of Political Economy*, originally published in 1848, Mill argued for the desirability of breaking down the sharp and hostile division between the producers, or workers, on the one hand, and the capitalists, or owners, on the other. Not only would this be a good thing, it was also something that the advance of civilization was tending naturally to bring about: "The relation of masters and workpeople will be gradually superseded by partnership, in one or two forms: in some cases, association of the labourers with the capitalist; in others, and perhaps finally in all, association of labourers among themselves."[24] These developments would not only enhance productivity but also—and more importantly—promote the fuller development and well being of the people involved. The aim, Mill thought, should be to enable people "to work with or for one another in relations not involving dependence."[25]

By the association of labour and capital, Mill had in mind different schemes of profit sharing. For example, "in the American ships trading to China, it has long been the custom for every sailor to have an interest in the profits of the voyage; and to this has been ascribed the general good conduct of those seamen."[26] This sort of association, however, would eventually give way to a more complete system of worker cooperatives:

> The form of association, however, which if mankind continue to improve, must be expected in the end to predominate, is not that which can exist between a capitalist as chief, and workpeople without a voice in the management, but the association of the labourers themselves on terms of equality, collectively owning the capital with which they carry on their operations, and working under managers elected and removable by themselves.[27]

In *Principles* Mill discussed several examples of successful cooperative associations and viewed optimistically the future of the cooperative movement:

> Eventually, and in perhaps a less remote future than may be supposed, we may, through the cooperative principle, see our way to a change in society, which would combine the freedom and independence of the individual, with the moral, intellectual, and economical advantages of aggregate production; and which . . . would realize, at least in the industrial department, the best aspirations of the democratic spirit.[28]

What that transformation implied for Mill was nothing less than "the nearest approach to social justice, and the most beneficial ordering of industrial affairs for the universal good, which it is possible at present to foresee."[29]

Greater Equality of Income Utilitarians are likely to be sympathetic to the argument that steps should be taken to reduce the great disparities in income that characterize our society. That is, they are likely to believe that making the distribution of income more equal is a good strategy for maximizing happiness. The reason for this goes back to what economists would call "the declining marginal utility of money." This phrase simply means that successive additions to one's income produce, on average, less happiness or welfare than did earlier additions.

The declining utility of money follows from the fact, as Professor Richard Brandt explains it, that the outcomes we want are preferentially ordered, some being more strongly wanted than others:

> So a person, when deciding how to spend his resources, picks a basket of groceries which is at least as appealing as any other he can purchase with the money he has. The things he does not buy are omitted because other things are wanted more. If we double a person's income, he will spend the extra money on items he wants less (some special cases aside), and which will give less enjoyment than will the original income. The more one's income, the fewer preferred items one buys and the more preferred items one already has. On the whole, then, when the necessities of life have been purchased and the individual is spending on luxury items, he is buying items which will give less enjoyment. . . . This conclusion corresponds well with common-sense reflection and practice.[30]

The obvious implication is that a more egalitarian allocation of income—that is, an allocation that increases the income of those who now earn less—would boost total happiness. Brandt, for one, therefore defends equality of after-tax income on utilitarian grounds, subject to the following exceptions: supplements to meet special needs, supplements necessary for incentives or to allocate resources efficiently, and variations to achieve other socially desirable ends, such as population control.[31] Brandt states that this guiding principle of distribution is of only prima facie force and may have to be balanced against other principles and considerations. Still, it illustrates the point that utilitarians today are likely to advocate increased economic equality.

THE LIBERTARIAN APPROACH

Whereas utilitarians associate justice with social utility, philosophers who endorse what is called *libertarianism* identify justice with an ideal of liberty. For them, liberty is the prime value, and justice consists in permitting each person to live as he or she pleases, free from the interference of others. Accordingly, one libertarian asserts: "We are concerned with the condition of men in which coercion of some by others is reduced as much as possible in society."[32] Another maintains that libertarianism is "a philosophy of personal liberty—the liberty of each person to live

according to his own choices, provided he does not attempt to coerce others and thus prevent them from living according to their choices."[33] Such views show clearly the libertarian's association of justice with liberty and of liberty itself with the absence of interference by other persons.

Libertarians firmly reject utilitarianism's concern for total social well-being. Utilitarians are willing to restrict the liberty of some, to interfere with their choices, if doing so will promote greater net happiness than not doing so. Libertarians cannot stomach that approach. As long as you are not doing something that interferes with anyone else's liberty, then no person, group, or government should disturb you in living the life you choose—not even if its doing so would maximize social happiness.

Although individual liberty is something that all of us value, it may not be the only thing we value. For the libertarian, however, liberty takes priority over other moral concerns. In particular, justice consists solely of respect for individual liberty. A libertarian world, with a complete commitment to individual liberty, would be a very different world from the one we now live in. Consider the following. Until 1969 Canadian laws forbade sodomy between consenting male homosexuals; some countries conscript their young men and/or women into military service, while other countries register them for military service and can, if they choose, draft them; most countries have laws preventing adults from ingesting substances that are deemed harmful or immoral (such as marijuana and cocaine); and the state imposes taxes on our income to—among many other things—support needy citizens, provide loans to college and university students, and fund various projects for the common good. From a libertarian perspective, none of these policies is just.

Given the assumption that liberty means noninterference, libertarians generally agree that liberty allows only a minimal or "night watchman" state. Such a state is limited to the narrow functions of protecting its citizens against force, theft, and fraud; enforcing contracts; and performing other such basic maintenance functions. In this view, a more extensive state—in particular, one that taxes its better-off citizens to support the less-fortunate ones—violates the liberty of individuals by forcing them to support projects, policies, or persons they have not freely chosen to support.

Nozick's Theory of Justice

Although libertarians differ in how they formulate their theory, the late Harvard professor Robert Nozick's *Anarchy, State, and Utopia* is a very influential statement of the libertarian case.[34] Nozick's challenging and powerful advocacy of libertarianism has stimulated much debate, obliging philosophers of all political persuasions to take the libertarian theory seriously. His views are thus worth presenting in detail.

Nozick begins from the premise that people have certain basic moral rights, which he calls "Lockean rights." By alluding to the political philosophy of John Locke

(1632–1704), Nozick wishes to underscore that these rights are both negative and natural. They are negative because they require only that people forbear from acting in certain ways—in particular, that we refrain from interfering with others. Beyond this, we are not obliged to do anything positive for anyone else, nor is anyone required to do anything positive for us. We have no right, for example, to be provided with satisfying work or with any material goods that we might need. These negative rights, according to Nozick, are natural in the sense that we possess them independently of any social or political institutions.

These individual rights impose firm, virtually absolute restrictions (or, in Nozick's phrase, "side constraints") on how we may act. We cannot morally infringe on someone's rights for any purpose. Not only are we forbidden to interfere with a person's liberty in order to promote the general good, we are prohibited from doing so even if violating that individual's rights would somehow prevent other individuals' rights from being violated. Each individual is autonomous and responsible, and should be left to fashion his or her own life free from the interference of others—as long as doing so is compatible with the rights of others to do the same. Only an acknowledgment of this almost absolute right to be free from coercion, Nozick argues, fully respects the distinctiveness of individuals, each with a unique life to lead.

A belief in these rights shapes Nozick's theory of economic justice, which he calls the "entitlement theory." Essentially, Nozick maintains that people are entitled to their holdings (that is, goods, money, and property) as long as they have acquired them fairly. Stated another way, if you have obtained your possessions without violating other people's Lockean rights, then you are entitled to them and may dispose of them as you choose. No one else has a legitimate claim on them. If you have secured a vast fortune without injuring other people, defrauding them, or otherwise violating their rights, then you are morally permitted to do with your fortune whatever you wish—bequeath it to a relative, endow a university, or squander it in riotous living. Even though other people may be going hungry, justice imposes no obligation on you to help them.

The first principle of Nozick's entitlement theory concerns the original acquisition of holdings—that is, the appropriation of unheld goods or the creation of new goods. If a person acquires a holding in accordance with this principle, then he or she is entitled to it. If, for example, you retrieve minerals from the wilderness or make something out of materials you already legitimately possess, then you have justly acquired this new holding. Nozick does not spell out this principle or specify fully what constitutes a just original acquisition, but the basic idea is clear and reflects the thinking of John Locke.

Property is a moral right, said Locke, because individuals are morally entitled to the products of their labour. When they mix their labour with the natural world, they are entitled to the resulting product. Thus, if a man works the land, then he is entitled to the land and its products because through his labour he has put something of himself into them. This investment of self through labour is the moral basis of ownership, Locke wrote, but there are limits to this right:

> In the beginning . . . men had a right to appropriate, by their labour, each one of himself, as much of the things of nature, as he could use. . . . Whatsoever he tilled and reaped, laid up and made use of, before it spoiled, that was his peculiar right; whatsoever he enclosed, and could feed, and make use of, the cattle and product was also his. But if either the grass of his inclosure rotted on the ground, or the fruit of his planting perished without gathering, and laying up, this part of the earth . . . was still to be looked on as waste, and might be the possession of any other.[35]

In this early "state of nature" prior to the formation of government, property rights were limited not only by the requirement that one not waste what one claimed, but also by the restriction that "enough and as good" be left for others—that is, that one's appropriation not make others worse off. Later, however, with the introduction of money, Locke thought that both these restrictions were overcome. You can pile up money beyond your needs without its spoiling; and if your property is used productively and the proceeds offered for sale, then your appropriation leaves others no worse off than before.

Nozick's second principle concerns transfers of already-owned goods from one person to another: how people may legitimately transfer holdings and how they may legitimately get holdings from others. If a person possesses a holding because of a legitimate transfer, then he or she is entitled to it. Again, Nozick does not work out the details, but it is clear that acquiring something by purchase, as a gift, or through exchange would constitute a legitimate acquisition. Gaining it through theft, force, or fraud would violate the principle of justice in transfer.

Nozick's third and final principle states that one can justly acquire a holding only in accord with the two principles just discussed. If you come by a holding in some other way, you are not entitled to it. Nozick sums up his theory this way:

1. A person who acquires a holding in accordance with the principle of justice in acquisition is entitled to that holding.

2. A person who acquires a holding in accordance with the principle of justice in transfer, from someone else entitled to the holding, is entitled to the holding.

3. No one is entitled to a holding except by (repeated) applications of 1 and 2.

In short, the distribution of goods in a society is just if and only if all are entitled to the holdings they possess. Nozick calls his entitlement theory "historical" because what matters is how people come to have what they have. If people are entitled to their possessions, then the distribution of economic holdings is just, regardless of what the actual distribution happens to look like (for instance, how far people are above or below the average income) or what its consequences are.

The Wilt Chamberlain Example

Nozick argues that respect for liberty inescapably leads one to repudiate other conceptions of economic justice in favour of his entitlement approach. One of his most ingenious examples features Wilt Chamberlain, the late basketball star. Suppose, Nozick says, that things are distributed according to your favourite nonentitlement theory, whatever it is. (He calls this distribution D_1.) Now imagine that Wilt Chamberlain signs a contract with a team that guarantees him \$5 from the price of each ticket. Whenever people buy a ticket to a game, they drop \$5 into a special box with Chamberlain's name on it. To them it is worth it to see him play. Imagine then that in the course of a season one million people attend his games and Chamberlain ends up with far more than the average income—far more, indeed, than anyone else in the society earns. This result (D_2) upsets the initial distributional pattern (D_1).

Can the proponent of D_1 complain? Nozick thinks not:

Is [Chamberlain] entitled to this income? Is this new distribution, D_2, unjust? If so, why? There is *no* question about whether each of the people was entitled to the control over the resources they held in D_1; because that was the distribution (your favorite) that (for the purposes of the argument) we assumed was acceptable. Each of these persons *chose* to give [\$5] of their money to Chamberlain. . . . If D_1 was a just distribution, and people voluntarily moved from it to D_2, transferring parts of their shares they were given under D_1 . . . isn't D_2 also just? If the people were entitled to dispose of the resources to which they were entitled (under D_1), didn't this include their being entitled to give it to, or exchange it with, Wilt Chamberlain? Can anyone else complain on grounds of justice?[36]

Having defended the legitimacy of Chamberlain's new wealth, Nozick pushes his case further, arguing that any effort to maintain some initial distributional arrangement like D_1 will interfere with people's liberty to use their resources as they wish. To preserve this original distribution, he writes, society would have to "forbid capitalist acts between consenting adults:"

The general point illustrated by the Wilt Chamberlain example . . . is that no [non-entitlement] principle of justice can be continuously realized without continuous interference with people's lives. Any favored pattern would be transformed into one unfavored by the principle, by people choosing to act in various ways; for example, by people exchanging goods and services with other people, or giving things to other people. . . . To maintain a pattern one must either continually interfere to stop people from transferring resources as they wish to, or continually (or periodically) interfere to take from some persons resources that others for some reason chose to transfer to them.[37]

The Libertarian View of Liberty

Libertarianism clearly involves a commitment to leaving market relations—buying, selling, and other exchanges—totally unrestricted (Chapter 4 examines the nature of market economies and in particular capitalism). Force and fraud are forbidden, of course, but there should be no interference with the uncoerced exchanges of consenting individuals. Not only is the market morally legitimate, but any attempt to interfere with consenting and nonfraudulent transactions between adults will be unacceptable. Thus, libertarians are for economic laissez faire and against any governmental economic activity that interferes with the marketplace, even if the point of the interference is to enhance the performance of the economy.

It is important to emphasize that libertarianism's enthusiasm for the market rests on this commitment to liberty. By contrast, utilitarian defenders of the market defend it on the ground that an unregulated market works better than either a planned, socialist economy or the sort of regulated capitalism with some welfare benefits that we in fact find in most developed countries, including Canada and the United States. That is, if a utilitarian defends laissez faire, he or she does so because of its consequences. Convince a utilitarian that some other form of economic organization better promotes human well-being, and the utilitarian will advocate that instead. With libertarians this is definitely not the case. As a matter of fact, libertarians typically agree with Adam Smith that unregulated capitalist behaviour best promotes everyone's interests. But even if, hypothetically, someone like Nozick were convinced that some sort of socialism or welfare capitalism outperformed laissez-faire capitalism economically—greater productivity, shorter working day, higher standard of living—he or she would still reject this alternative as morally unacceptable. To tinker with the market, however beneficial it might be, would involve violating someone's liberty.

Libertarians say that their commitment to an unrestricted market reflects the priority of liberty over other values. However, libertarians do not value liberty in the mundane sense of people's freedom to do what they want to do. Rather, libertarians understand freedom in terms of their theory of rights, thus building a commitment to private property into their concept of liberty. According to them, being able to do what you want does not automatically represent an increase in your liberty. It does so only if you remain within the boundaries set by the Lockean rights of others. Likewise, one is unfree or coerced only when one's rights are infringed.

Imagine, for example, that having purchased the forest in which I occasionally stroll, the new owner bars my access to it. It would seem that my freedom has been reduced because I can no longer ramble where I wish. But libertarians deny that this is a restriction of my liberty. My liberty is restricted if and only if someone violates my Lockean rights, which no one has done. Suppose that I go for a hike in the forest anyway. If the sheriff's deputies arrest me, they prevent me from doing what I want to do. But according to libertarianism, they do not restrict my liberty, nor do they coerce me. Why not? Because my hiking in the forest violates the landowner's rights.

Here libertarians seem driven to an unusual use of familiar terminology, but they have no choice. They cannot admit that abridging the landowner's freedom to do as he wants with his property would expand my freedom. If they did, then their theory would be in jeopardy. They would have to acknowledge that restricting the liberty or property rights of some could enhance the liberty of others. In other words, if their theory committed them simply to promoting as much as possible the goal of people doing what they want to do, then libertarians would be in the position of balancing the freedom of some against the freedom of others. But this sort of balancing and trading off is just what libertarians dislike about utilitarianism.

If liberty means being free to do what you want, it's not true that libertarians value it above everything else. What they value are Lockean property rights, which then set the parameters of liberty. Libertarians frequently contend (1) that private property is necessary for freedom and (2) that any society that doesn't respect private property rights is coercive. But libertarianism makes 1 true by definition, and 2 is incorrect. Any system of property (whether Lockean, socialist, or something in between) necessarily puts restrictions on people's conduct; its rules are coercive. What one system of property permits, another forbids. Society X prevents me from hiking in your woods, whereas society Y prevents you from stopping me. Both systems of rules are coercive. Both grant some freedoms and withhold others.

Markets and Free Exchange

Libertarians defend market relations, then, as necessary to respect human liberty (as their theory understands liberty). However, in doing so, libertarians do not assert that, morally speaking, people deserve what they receive from others through gift or exchange, only that they are entitled to whatever they receive. The market tends generally, libertarians believe, to reward people for skill, diligence, and successful performance. Yet luck plays a role, too. Jack makes a fortune from having been in the right place at the right time with his beanie babies, while Jill loses her investment because the market for bottled water collapses. The libertarian position is not that Jack deserves to be wealthy and Jill does not; rather, it is that Jack is entitled to his holdings if he has acquired them in accordance with the principles of justice.

The same point comes up with regard to gifts and inheritance. Inheritance strikes many people as patently unfair. How can it be just, they ask, that one child inherits a vast fortune, the best schooling, and social, political, and business connections that will ensure his or her future, while another child inherits indigence, inferior schooling, and connections with crime? At birth neither youngster deserves anything—a fact suggesting, perhaps, that an equal division of holdings and opportunities would be the only fair allocation. For his part, Nozick contends that deserving has no bearing on the justice of inherited wealth; people are simply entitled to it as long as it is not ill gotten. Or looking at it the other way, if one is entitled to one's holdings, then one has a right to do with them as one wishes, including using them to benefit one's children.

According to libertarians, a totally free market is necessary for people to exercise their fundamental rights. Sometimes, however, unregulated market transactions can lead to disastrous results. Unfortunately, this is more than just a theoretical possibility. Amartya Sen, the Nobel Prize–winning economist, has shown how in certain circumstances changing market entitlements have led to mass starvation. Although the average person thinks of famine as caused simply by a shortage of food, Sen and other experts have established that famines are frequently accompanied by no shortfall of food in absolute terms. Indeed, even more food may be available during a famine than in non-famine years—if one has the money to buy it. Famine occurs because large numbers of people lack the financial wherewithal to obtain the necessary food.[38]

For example, drought may cause food output in one area to decline and the peasants in that area to starve because they lack the means to buy food from elsewhere, even though there is no dearth of food in the country as a whole (Ethiopia in 1973). Or famine may result when the purchasing power of one occupational group shoots up, ruining the chances of other groups, whose nominal incomes have not changed, to buy food (Bengal in 1943). A reduction of food output because of potato blight triggered the great Irish famine of the 1840s, which killed a higher proportion of the population than any other famine in recorded history. But if one looks at the United Kingdom as a whole, there was no shortage of food. Food could certainly have moved from Britain to Ireland if the Irish could have afforded to purchase it. As it was, at the height of the famine, food was exported from Ireland to England because the prosperous English could pay a higher price for it.[39]

Libertarians would find it immoral and unjust to force people to aid the starving or to tax the affluent in order to set up programs to relieve hunger or prevent famines in the first place. Nor does justice require that a wealthy merchant assist the hungry children in his community to stay alive. And it would certainly violate the merchant's property rights for the children to help themselves to his excess food. Nevertheless, although justice does not require that one assist those in need, libertarians would generally acknowledge that we have some humanitarian obligations toward others. Accordingly, they would not only permit but also presumably encourage people to voluntarily assist others. Justice does not require the merchant to donate, and it forbids us from forcing him to do so, but charity on his part would be a good thing. This reflects the libertarian's firm commitment to property rights: what you have legitimately acquired is yours to do with as you will.

Property Rights

Nozick's theory makes property rights virtually sacrosanct. From the perspective of libertarianism, property rights grow out of one's basic moral rights, either reflecting one's initial creation or appropriation of the product, some sort of exchange or transfer between consenting persons, or a combination of these. Property rights exist prior to any social arrangements and are morally antecedent to any legislative decisions that a society might make. However, Nozick's critics argue that it is a mistake to think of property as a simple, pre-social relation between a person and a physical thing.

First, property is not restricted to material objects like cars, watches, or houses. In developed societies, it may include more abstract goods, interests, and claims. For instance, property may include the right to pay debts with the balance in a bank account, the right to dividends from a corporate investment, and the right to collect from a pension plan one has joined. In fact, the courts have counted as property a wide range of items such as new life forms, an original idea, pension payments, the news, or a place on the welfare rolls.[40]

Second, property ownership involves a bundle of different rights—for instance, to possess, use, manage, dispose of, or restrict others' access to something in certain specified ways. The nature of this bundle differs among societies, as do the types of things that can be owned. In any society, property ownership is structured by the various implicit or explicit rules and regulations governing the legitimate acquisition and transfer of various types of goods, interests, and claims. Not only do property rights differ between societies, but the nature of ownership can also change over time in any given society. As a general trend, the social restrictions on property ownership in most countries have increased dramatically during our history (much to the displeasure of libertarians).

For these reasons, most nonlibertarian social and political theorists view property rights as a function of the particular institutions of a given society. This is not to say that a society's property arrangements cannot be criticized. On the contrary, their morality can be assessed just as the morality of any other institution can.

RAWLS'S THEORY OF JUSTICE

A Theory of Justice by John Rawls (1921–2002) is generally thought to be the most influential work of the post–World War II period in social and political philosophy, at least in the English language.[41] Not only has Rawls's elegant theory touched a responsive chord in many readers, but also his book has helped rejuvenate serious work in normative theory. Even those who are not persuaded by

Rawls find themselves obliged to come to terms with his thinking. Although Rawls's basic approach is not difficult to explain (and Rawls himself had sketched out his key concepts in earlier articles), A Theory of Justice elaborates his ideas with such painstaking care and philosophical thoroughness that even vigorous critics of the book (such as his colleague Robert Nozick) pay sincere tribute to its many virtues.

By his own account, Rawls presents his theory as a modern alternative to utilitarianism, one that he hopes will be compatible with the belief that justice must be associated with fairness and the moral equality of persons. Rawls firmly wishes to avoid reducing justice to a matter of social utility. At the same time, his approach differs fundamentally from Nozick's. Rawls conceives of society as a cooperative venture among its members, and he elaborates a conception of justice that is thoroughly social. He does not base his theory, as Nozick does, on the postulate that individuals possess certain natural rights prior to any political or social organization.

Two features of Rawls's theory are particularly important: his hypothetical-contract approach and the principles of justice that he derives with it. Rawls's strategy is to ask what we would choose as the fundamental principles to govern society if, hypothetically, we were to meet for this purpose in what he calls the "original position." He then elaborates the nature of this original position, the constraints on the choice facing us, and the reasoning that he thinks people in the original position would follow. In this way, Rawls offers a modern variant of social contract theory, in the tradition of Hobbes, Locke, Rousseau, and other earlier philosophers. Rawls argues that people in the original position would agree on two principles as the basic governing principles of their society, and that these principles are, accordingly, the principles of justice. These principles are examined at some length in a later section. But briefly, the first is a guarantee of certain familiar and fundamental liberties to each person, and the second—more controversial—holds in part that social and economic inequalities are justified only if those inequalities benefit the least advantaged members of society.

The Original Position

Various principles of economic justice have been proposed, but an important question for philosophers is whether, and how, any such principles can be justified. Thinking of possible principles of economic distribution is not very difficult, but proving the soundness of such a principle, or at least showing it to be more plausible than its rivals, is a challenging task. After all, people seem to differ in their intuitions about what is just and unjust, and their sentiments are bound to be influenced by their social position. Nozick's entitlement theory, for example, with its priority on property rights, is bound to seem more plausible to a corporate executive than to a migrant farm worker. The justice of a world in which some children are born into wealth while other children struggle by on welfare is unlikely to seem as obvious to the poor as it may to the well-to-do.

The strategy Rawls employs to identify and justify some basic principles of justice is to imagine that people come together for the purpose of deciding on the ground rules for their society, in particular on the rules governing economic distribution. Although in the past groups of people have written down constitutions and similar political documents, never have the members of a society decided from scratch on the basic principles of justice that should govern them. Nor is it even remotely likely that people will do this in the future. What Rawls imagines is a thought experiment. The question is hypothetical: What principles would people choose in this sort of original position? If we can identify these principles, Rawls contends, then we will have identified the principles of justice just because they are the principles that we would all have agreed to.

The Nature of the Choice On what basis are we to choose these principles? The most obvious answer is that we should select principles that strike us as just. But this won't work. Even if we are all agreed on what is just and unjust, we would be relying on our already existing ideas about justice as a basis for choosing the principles to govern our society. Philosophically, this approach doesn't accomplish anything. We would simply be going in a circle, using our existing conception of justice to prove the principles of justice.

Rawls suggests instead that we imagine people in the original position choosing solely on the basis of self-interest. That is, each individual chooses the set of principles for governing society that will be best for himself or herself (and loved ones). We don't have to imagine that people are antagonistic or that outside of the original position they are selfish; we just imagine that they hope to get the group to choose those principles that will, more than any other possible principles, benefit them. If people in the original position can agree on some governing principles on the basis of mutual self-interest, then these principles will be, Rawls thinks, the principles of justice. Why? Because the principles are agreed to under conditions of equality and free choice. By analogy, if we make up a game and all agree ahead of time, freely and equally, on how the game is to be played, nobody can later complain that the rules are unfair.

The Veil of Ignorance If people in the original position are supposed to choose principles on the basis of self-interest, agreement seems unlikely. If Carolyn has vast real estate holdings, she will certainly want rules that guarantee her extensive property rights, whereas her tenants are likely to support rules that permit rent control. Likewise, the wealthy will tend to advocate rules rather like Nozick's entitlement theory, whereas those without property will, on the basis of their self-interest, desire a redistribution of property. Conflicts of self-interest seem bound to create totally irreconcilable demands. For instance, artists may contend that they should be rewarded more than professional people, men that they should earn more than women, and labourers that they merit more than people with desk jobs.

Agreement seems unlikely, given that some rules would benefit one group while other rules would benefit another. As a way around this problem, Rawls asks us to imagine that people in the original position do not know what social position or status they hold in society. They do not know whether they are rich or poor, and they do not know their personal talents and characteristics—whether, for example, they are athletic or sedentary, artistic or tone-deaf, intelligent or not very bright, physically sound or handicapped in some way. They do not know their race or even their sex. Behind what Rawls calls the "veil of ignorance," people in the original position know nothing about themselves personally or about what their individual situation will be once the rules are chosen and the veil is lifted. They do, however, have a general knowledge of history, sociology, and psychology—although no specific information about the society they will be in once the veil is lifted.

Under the veil of ignorance, the people in Rawls's original position have no knowledge about themselves or their situation that would lead them to argue from a partial or biased point of view. No individual is likely to argue that some particular group—such as white men, property owners, star athletes, philosophers—should receive special social and economic privileges when, for all that the individual knows, he or she might be nonwhite, propertyless, unathletic or bored by philosophy when the veil is lifted. Because individuals in the original position are all equally ignorant of their personal situation and they are all trying to advance their self-interest, agreement is possible. The reasoning of any one person will be the same as the reasoning of each of the others, for each is in identical circumstances and each has the same motivation. As a result, no actual group has to perform Rawls's thought experiment. People who read Rawls's book can imagine that they are in the original position and then decide whether they would choose the principles Rawls thinks they would.

The veil of ignorance, in effect, makes agreement possible by forcing people in the original position to be objective and impartial. Also, according to Rawls, the fact that people have no special knowledge that would allow them to argue in a biased way accords with our sense of fairness. The circumstances of the original position are genuinely equal and fair, and hence, the principles agreed to under these conditions have a good claim to be considered the principles of justice.

Choosing the Principles

Although people in the original position are ignorant of their individual circumstances, they know that whatever their particular goals, interests, and talents turn out to be, they will want more, rather than less, of what Rawls calls the "primary social goods." These include not just income and wealth but also rights, liberties, opportunities, status, and self-respect. Of course, once the veil of ignorance is lifted, people will have more specific ideas about what is good for them—they may choose a life built around religion, one spent in commerce and industry, or one devoted to academic study. But whatever these particular individual goals, interests, and plans turn out to be, they will almost certainly be furthered, and definitely never limited, by the fact that people in the original position secured for themselves more rather than less in the way of primary goods.

How, then, will people in the original position choose their principles? A *Theory of Justice* explores in depth the reasoning that Rawls thinks would guide their choice. At the heart of Rawls's argument is the contention that people in the original position will be conservative, in the sense that they will not wish to gamble with their future. In setting up the ground rules for their society, they are determining their own fate and that of their children. This exercise is not something to be taken lightly, a game to be played and replayed. Rather, with so much at stake, people will reason cautiously.

Consider, for example, the possibility that people in the original position will set up a feudal society: 10 percent of the population will be nobles, living a life of incredible wealth, privilege, and leisure; the other 90 percent will be serfs, toiling away long hours to support the extravagant lifestyles of the aristocracy. Perhaps some people would consider the joy of being a pampered noble so great that they would vote for such an arrangement behind the veil of ignorance, but they would be banking on a long shot. When the veil of ignorance is lifted, the odds are nine to one that they will be poor and miserable serfs, not lords. Rawls thinks that people in the original position will not, in fact, gamble with their futures. They will not agree to rules that make it overwhelmingly likely that they will have to face a grim life of hardship.

Rawls argues that for similar reasons people in the original position will not adopt the utilitarian standard to govern their society, because the utilitarian principle might sacrifice the well-being of some to enhance society's total happiness. People in the original position, Rawls argues, will not be willing to risk sacrificing their own happiness, once the veil of ignorance is lifted, for the greater good.

What people in the original position would actually do, Rawls believes, is follow what game strategists call the *maximin rule* for making decisions. This rule says that you should select the alternative under which the worst that could happen to you is better than the worst that could happen to you under any other alternative; that is, you should try to *maximize* the *minimum* that you will receive. This rule makes sense when you care much more about avoiding an unacceptable or disastrous result (such as being a serf) than about getting the best possible result (being a noble) and when you have no real idea what odds you are facing. It is a conservative decision principle, but Rawls thinks that people in the original position will find it a rational and appropriate guideline for their deliberations.

Rawls's Two Principles

Rawls argues that people in the original position considering various alternatives will eventually endorse two principles as the most basic governing principles of their society. These principles, because they are agreed to in an initial situation of equality and fairness, will be the principles of justice. Once these two principles of justice have been decided, the people in the original position can gradually be given more information about their specific society. They can then go on to design their basic social and political institutions in more detail.

Rawls states the two basic principles of justice as follows:

1. Each person is to have an equal right to the most extensive total system of equal basic liberties compatible with a similar system of liberty for all.[42]

2. Social and economic inequalities are to satisfy two conditions: first, they are to be attached to positions and offices open to all under conditions of fair equality of opportunity; and second, they are to be to the greatest expected benefit of the least advantaged members of society.[43]

According to Rawls, the first principle takes priority over the second, at least for societies that have attained a moderate level of affluence. The liberties Rawls has in mind are the traditional democratic ones of freedom of thought, conscience, and religious worship, as well as freedom of the person and political liberty. Explicitly absent are "the right to own certain kinds of property (e.g., means of production), and freedom of contract as understood by the doctrine of laissez-faire." The first principle guarantees not only equal liberty to individuals but also as much liberty to individuals as possible, compatible with others having the same amount of liberty. There is no reason why people in the original position would settle for anything less.

All regulations could be seen as infringing on personal liberty, because they limit what a person may do. The law that requires you to drive on the right-hand side of the road denies you the freedom to drive on either side whenever you wish. Some would argue that justice requires only an equal liberty. For example, as long as every motorist is required to drive on the right-hand side of the road, justice is being served; or if everyone in a dictatorial society is forbidden to criticize the leader's decisions, then all are equal in their liberty. But Rawls argues that if a more extensive liberty were possible, without inhibiting the liberty of others, then it would be irrational to settle for a lesser degree of liberty. In the case of driving, permitting me to drive on either side of the road would only interfere with the liberty of others to drive efficiently to their various destinations, but introducing right-turn-on-red laws enhances everyone's liberty. In the dictatorship example, free speech could be more extensive without limiting anyone's liberty.

The second principle concerns social and economic inequalities. Regarding inequalities, Rawls writes:

> It is best to understand not *any* differences between offices and positions, but differences in the benefits and burdens attached to them either directly or indirectly, such as prestige and wealth, or liability to taxation and compulsory services. Players in a game do not protest against there being different positions, such as batter, pitcher, catcher, and the like, nor to there being various privileges and powers as specified by the rules; nor do the citizens of a country object to there being the different offices of government such as president, senator, governor, judge, and so on, each with their special rights and duties.[44]

Rather, at issue are differences in wealth and power, honours and rewards, privileges and salaries that attach to different roles in society.

Rawls's second principle states that insofar as inequalities are permitted—that is, insofar as it is compatible with justice for some jobs or positions to bring greater rewards than others—these positions must be open to all. In other words, there must be meaningful equality of opportunity in the competition among individuals for those positions in society that bring greater economic and social rewards. This, of course, is a familiar ideal, but what exactly a society must do to achieve not just legal but full and fair equality of opportunity will be a matter of debate.

The other part of the second principle is less familiar and more controversial. Called the *difference principle*, it is the distinctive core of Rawls's theory. It states that inequalities are justified only if they work to the benefit of the least advantaged group in society. By "least advantaged," Rawls simply means those who are least well off. But what does it mean to require that inequalities work to the benefit of this group?

Imagine that we are back in the original position. We wish to make sure that under the principles we choose, the worst that can happen to us once the veil of ignorance is lifted is still better than the worst that might have happened under some other arrangement. We might, therefore, choose strict social and economic equality. With an equal division of goods, there's no risk of doing worse than anyone else, no danger of being sacrificed to increase the total happiness of society. In the case of liberty, people in the original position do insist on full equality, but with social and economic inequality, the matter is a little different.

Suppose, for instance, that as a result of dividing things up equally, people lack an incentive to undertake some of the more difficult work that society needs done. It might then be the case that allowing certain inequalities—for example, paying people more for being particularly

productive or for undertaking the necessary training to perform some socially useful task—would work to everyone's benefit, including those who would be earning less. If so, then why not permit those inequalities? Compare the two diagrams:

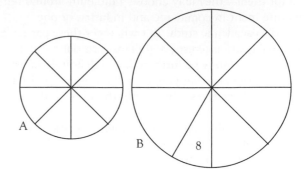

Each pie represents a possible social and economic distribution among eight basic groups (the number eight is arbitrary) in society. In Figure A, things are divided equally; in Figure B, unequally. Imagine that if a society permits inequalities as an incentive to get people to work harder or to do work that they would not have wanted to do otherwise, then the overall amount to be distributed among its members will be greater. That is, the economic pie will increase in size from A to B, and the people with the thinnest slice of B will be better off than they would have been with an equal slice of A.

Which society will people in the original position prefer? Obviously the one represented by Figure B, because the minimum they can attain in B (the slice labelled 8) is bigger than any of the eight equal slices in A. People in the original position do not care about equality of distribution as a value in and of itself; they want the social and economic arrangement that will provide them with the highest minimum.

Rawls is not trying to prove that the benefits received by the better-off will always, or even usually, trickle down to the least advantaged (although, of course, some people believe that). Rather, his point is simply that people in the original position would not insist on social and economic equality at all costs. If permitting some people to be better off than the average resulted in the least-well-off segment of society being better off than it would have been under a strictly equal division, then this is what people in the original position will want. Rawls's difference principle is intended to capture this idea. Rawls's principles permit economic inequalities only if they do in fact benefit the least advantaged.

Consider the recurrent proposal to further lower or even eliminate the income tax on capital gains (that is, on personal income from the sale of assets like stocks, bonds, and real estate). Proponents claim that the tax break will spur trading in financial assets, which will in turn lead to growth in tax revenues, and that the cut will trigger more long-term investment, helping revitalize the economy. Critics of the proposal contest both claims. Still, everyone agrees that the tax break would certainly increase the income of the rich, for example in the United States, because the wealthiest 1.4 percent of households receive 73.2 percent of all capital-gains income.[45] Will lowering taxes on the rich benefit the least advantaged members of society more in the long run than any alternative tax policy?

This question illustrates the application of Rawls's difference principle in a practical context, but we must remember that Rawls intends his principles to be used not as a direct guide to day-to-day policy decisions but rather as the basis for determining what form society's primary social, political, and economic institutions should take in the first place. What will these institutions look like? More specifically, what sort of economic system will best satisfy Rawls's difference principle? Rawls does not answer this question. He sees it as primarily a question for economists and other social scientists, whereas the task of philosophers like himself is the preliminary one of working out a satisfactory conception of justice. Rawls does appear to believe, however, that a liberal form of capitalism, with sufficient welfare provisions, would satisfy his principles, but he does not rule out the possibility that a democratic socialist system could as well.

Fairness and the Basic Structure

Rawls intends his theory as a fundamental alternative to utilitarianism, which he rejects on the grounds that maximizing the total well-being of society could permit an unfair distribution of burdens and benefits. Utilitarianism, in Rawls's view, treats people's pleasures and pains as completely interchangeable: a decrease of happiness here is justified by greater happiness there. Within a person's own life, such tradeoffs are sensible. An increase of pain now (as the dentist fills a cavity in my tooth) is justified in terms of greater happiness later (no painful, rotted tooth). But between individuals, as when Jack's happiness is decreased to provide Jill with a more-than-compensating gain, such tradeoffs are morally problematic.

Thus Rawls stresses that, in his view,

each person possesses an inviolability founded on justice that even the welfare of society as a whole cannot override. . . . Therefore . . . the rights secured by justice are not subject to political bargaining or to the calculus of social interests.[46]

And he emphasizes that the difference principle

excludes, therefore, the justification of inequalities on the grounds that the disadvantages of those in one position are outweighed by the greater advantages of those in another position. This rather simple restriction is the main modification I wish to make in the utilitarian principle as usually understood.[47]

On the other hand, Rawls is equally unsympathetic to the approach adopted by Nozick. Contrary to the entitlement theory, he argues that the primary subject of justice is not, in the first instance, transactions between individuals but rather "the basic structure, the fundamental social institutions and their arrangement into one scheme." Why? As Rawls explains:

Suppose we begin with the initially attractive idea that the social circumstances and people's relationships to one another should develop over time in accordance with free agreements fairly arrived at and fully honored. Straightaway we need an account of when agreements are free and the social circumstances under which they are reached are fair. In addition, while these conditions may be fair at an earlier time, the accumulated results of many separate and ostensibly fair agreements . . . are likely in the course of time to alter citizens' relationships and opportunities so that the conditions for free and fair agreements no longer hold. The role of the institutions that belong to the basic structure is to secure just background conditions against which the actions of the individuals and associations take place. Unless this structure is appropriately regulated and adjusted, an initially just social process will eventually cease to be just, however free and fair particular transactions may look when viewed by themselves.[48]

Additional considerations support taking the basic structure of society as the primary subject of justice—in particular, the fact that the basic structure shapes the wants, desires, hopes, and ambitions of individuals. Thus, Rawls continues:

Everyone recognizes that the institutional form of society affects its members and determines in large part the kind of person they want to be as well as the kind of person they are. The social structure also limits people's ambitions and hopes in different ways. . . . So an economic regime, say, is not only an institutional scheme for satisfying existing wants but a way of fashioning desires and aspirations in the future.[49]

Rawls stresses that because the basic structure is the proper focus of a theory of justice, we cannot expect the principles that apply to it to be simply an extension of the principles that govern everyday individual transactions:

The justice of the basic structure is, then, of predominant importance. The first problem of justice is to determine the principles to regulate inequalities and to adjust the profound and long-lasting effects of social, natural, and historical contingencies, particularly since these contingencies combined with inequalities generate tendencies that, when left to themselves, are sharply at odds with the freedom and equality appropriate for a well-ordered society. In view of the special role of the basic structure, we cannot assume that the principles suitable to it are natural applications, or even extensions, of the familiar principles governing the actions of individuals and associations in everyday life which take place within its framework. Most likely we shall have to loosen ourselves from our ordinary perspective and take a more comprehensive viewpoint.[50]

Benefits and Burdens

The passages quoted here touch on a theme that is central to Rawls's theory. Inevitably, there will be natural differences among human beings—in terms of physical prowess, mental agility, and so on—but there is nothing natural or inevitable about the weight attached by society to those differences. For Rawls, a desirable feature of any account of justice is that it strives to minimize the social consequences of purely arbitrary, natural differences. He stresses that no one deserves his or her particular natural characteristics. We cannot say that Robert Redford deserves to be handsome or that Albert Einstein deserved to be blessed with an excellent mind any more than we can say that Fred merits his shortness or Pamela her nearsightedness. Their attributes are simply the result of a genetic lottery. But Rawls goes beyond this to argue that even personal characteristics, like diligence and perseverance, reflect the environment in which one was raised:

> We do not deserve our place in the distribution of native endowments, any more than we deserve our initial starting place in society. That we deserve the superior character that enables us to make the effort to cultivate our abilities is also problematic; for such character depends in good part upon fortunate family and social circumstances in early life for which we can claim no credit. The notion of desert does not apply here.[51]

Accordingly, Rawls thinks we cannot really claim moral credit for our special talents or even our virtuous character. In Rawls's view, then, if our personal characteristics are not something that we deserve, we have no strong claim to the economic rewards they might bring. On the contrary, justice requires that the social and economic consequences of these arbitrarily distributed assets be minimized.

> The difference principle represents, in effect, an agreement to regard the distribution of natural talents as in some respects a common asset and to share in the greater social and economic benefits made possible by the complementarities of this distribution. Those who have been favored by nature, whoever they are, may gain from their good fortune only on terms that improve the situation of those who have lost out. The naturally advantaged are not to gain merely because they are more gifted, but only to cover the costs of training and education and for using their endowments in ways that help the less fortunate as well. No one deserves his greater natural capacity nor merits a more favorable starting place in society. But, of course, this is no reason to ignore, much less to eliminate these distinctions. Instead, the basic structure can be arranged so that these contingencies work for the good of the least fortunate. Thus we are led to the difference principle if we wish to set up the social system so that no one gains or loses from his arbitrary place in the distribution of natural assets or his initial position in society without giving or receiving compensating advantages in return.[52]

This important passage from *A Theory of Justice* reflects well Rawls's vision of society as a cooperative project for mutual benefit.

SUMMARY

1. Justice is one important aspect of morality. Talk of justice and injustice generally involves appeals to the related notions of fairness, equality, desert, and rights. Economic or distributive justice concerns the principles appropriate for assessing society's distribution of social benefits and burdens, particularly wealth, income, status, and power.

2. Economic distribution might be based on pure equality, need, effort, social contribution, or merit. Each of these principles is plausible in some circumstances but not in others. In some situations, the principles pull us in different directions. Dissatisfied with a pluralistic approach, some moral philosophers have sought to develop more general theories of justice.

3. Utilitarianism holds that the maximization of happiness ultimately determines what is just and unjust. Mill contended, more specifically, that the concept of justice identifies certain very important social utilities and that injustice involves the violation of the rights of some specific individual.

4. Utilitarians must examine a number of factual issues in order to determine for themselves which economic system and principles will best promote social well being or happiness. Many utilitarians favour increased worker participation and a more equal distribution of income.

5. The libertarian theory identifies justice with liberty, which libertarians understand as living according to our own choices, free from the interference of others. They reject utilitarianism's concern for total social well-being.

6. The libertarian philosopher Robert Nozick defends the entitlement theory. His theory holds that the distribution of goods, money, and property is just if people are entitled to what they have—that is, if they have acquired their possessions without violating the rights of anyone else.

7. In the Wilt Chamberlain example, Nozick argues that theories of economic justice not in accord with his inevitably fail to respect people's liberty.

8. Libertarians operate with a distinctive concept of liberty, defend free exchange and laissez-faire markets without regard to results, put a priority on freedom over all other values, and see property rights as existing prior to any social arrangements. Critics contest each of these features of libertarianism.

9. John Rawls's approach lies within the social-contract tradition. He asks us to imagine people meeting in the "original position" to choose the basic principles that are to govern their society. Although in this original position people choose on the basis of self-interest, we are to imagine that they are behind a veil of ignorance, with no personal information about themselves. Rawls contends that any principles agreed to under these circumstances have a strong claim to be considered the principles of justice.

10. Rawls argues that people in the original position would follow the maximin rule for making decisions. They would choose principles guaranteeing that the worst that could happen to them is better than the worst that could happen to them under any rival principles. Rawls argues that they would agree on two principles. The first states that each person has a right to the most extensive scheme of liberties compatible with others having the same amount of liberty. The second principle states that to be justified, any inequalities must be to the greatest expected benefit of the least advantaged and open to all under conditions of fair equality of opportunity.

11. Rawls rejects utilitarianism because it might permit an unfair distribution of burdens and benefits. Contrary to the entitlement theory, he argues that the primary focus of justice should be the basic social structure, not transactions between individuals. He contends that society is a cooperative project for mutual benefit and that justice requires us to reduce the social and economic consequences of arbitrary natural differences among people.

CASE 3.1

Eminent Domain

Note: Though this case study pertains to a strictly American context, the substantive issues it raises are very much similar to issues that might arise and have arisen in Canadian jurisdictions. For example, the City of Winnipeg used the notion of "eminent domain" (better known in Canada as "expropriation") in the 1980s to claim a part of downtown Winnipeg for redevelopment. The Canadian company TransCanada Pipelines Ltd. is involved in "eminent domain" proceedings with farmers in South Dakota (see Scott Waltman, "Pipeline Leading to Court," Aberdeen American News, October 6, 2007). There are fears that in line with NAFTA agreements for super-transportation corridors, the national governments might use in the near future "eminent domain" to expropriate thousands of square kilometres of land. (For more information on Canadian "expropriation," start with www.cga.ct.gov/2005/rpt/2005-R-0321.htm.)

Susette Kelo's nondescript, pink clapboard house sits above the Thames River in the Fort Trumbull area of New London, Connecticut. Vacant lots surround it, where neighbours once lived. One by one, these neighbours have left, and their homes have been razed. Their property has been taken over by the City of New London, which has used its power of eminent domain to clear the land where dozens of homes once stood in order to prepare the way for new development.[53]

Eminent domain is the ancient right of government to take property from an individual without consent for the common good—for example, to build a highway, an airport, a dam, or a hospital. The U.S. Constitution recognizes that right, permitting private property to be taken for "public use" as long as "just compensation" is paid. In this case, however, New London is taking land from one private party and giving it to another. By tearing down Susette Kelo's old neighbourhood, the city hopes to attract new development, which, in turn, will help revitalize the community and bring in more tax revenue. "This isn't for the public good," says Kelo, a nurse who works three jobs. "The public good is a firehouse or a school, not a hotel and a sports club."

Connecticut officially designates New London a blighted area. When the Navy moved its Undersea Warfare Center away from New London in 1996, taking 1,400 jobs with it, the city's already high rate of unemployment only got worse. Much of its housing stock is old and second-rate. The Fort Trumbull area, in particular, is—or was, anyway—a rather gritty neighbourhood, where earlier generations of immigrants struggled to get a start. But New London saw a chance to turn things around when Pfizer pharmaceutical company built a $350 million research centre along the river below historic Fort Trumbull. Since then, city and state governments have created a park around the fort, cleaned up the Navy's old asbestos-laden site, and opened the riverfront to public access. Now the city wants to build a hotel, office buildings, and new homes to fill the riverfront blocks around Fort Trumbull. And it's not talking about new homes for people like Susette Kelo.

"We need to get housing at the upper end, for people like the Pfizer employees," says Ed O'Connell, the lawyer for the New London Development Corporation, which is in charge of the city's redevelopment efforts. "They are the professionals, they are the ones with the expertise and the leadership qualities to remake the city—the young urban professionals who will invest in New London, put their kids in school, and think of this as a place to stay for 20 or 30 years." And housing developers want open space to work with; they don't want to build around a few old properties such as Ms. Kelo's and that of her neighbours, Wilhelmina and Charles Dery.

Aged 87 and 85, respectively, they live in the house Wilhelmina was born in. The city is willing to pay a fair price for their home, but it's not an issue of money. "We get this all the time," says their son Matt. "'How much did they offer? What will it take?' My parents don't want to wake up rich tomorrow, they just want to wake up in their own home."

Unfortunately for the Derys, the U.S. Supreme Court recently upheld the city's condemnation rights. In a close, 5-to-4 decision, it ruled that compulsory purchase to foster economic development falls under "public use" and is thus constitutionally permissible. "Promoting economic development is a traditional and long accepted function of government," Justice John Paul Stevens wrote for the majority. Intended to increase jobs and tax revenues, New London's plan "unquestionably serves a public purpose." In her dissenting opinion, however, Justice Sandra Day O'Connor objected: "Under the banner of economic development, all private property is now vulnerable to being taken and transferred to another private owner, so long as it might be upgraded. . . . Nothing is to prevent the state from replacing any Motel 6 with a Ritz-Carlton, any home with a shopping mall, or any farm with a factory."

The Supreme Court's decision pushes the debate over eminent domain back to the states and local communities, where political and legal battles are being fought far beyond Susette Kelo's home in New London. For example, in Highland Park, New Jersey, the owners of a photography studio worry that a plan to redevelop their street will force them out of the location they've occupied for 25 years. In Port Chester, New York, a state development agency wants the site of a small furniture plant for a parking lot for Home Depot, and its owners are resisting. And in Salina, New York, 29 little businesses—with names like Butch's Automotive and Transmission, Syracuse Crank and Machine, Gianelli's Sausage, and Petersen Plumbing—are battling local government's use of eminent domain to pave the way for DestiNY's proposed 325-acre (about 131.5 ha), 2.67-billion-dollar research and development park.

Like New London, Salina desperately needs big ideas and big development, and it may not get another chance soon. But is tearing down these businesses fair? "We're here," says Philip Jakes-Johnson, who owns Solvents & Petroleum Service, one of the 29 businesses in question. "We pay our taxes. We build companies and run them without tax breaks." Brian Osborne, another owner, adds: "Everything I and my family have worked for over the past 25 years is at stake because of the way eminent domain is being used in this state and across the country."

Discussion Questions

1. Is New London treating Susette Kelo and her neighbours fairly? Assuming that the proposed development will help to revitalize New London, is it just for the city to appropriate private property around Fort Trumbull?

2. Assuming that what they are doing is constitutionally permissible, are towns such as New London and Salina pursuing wise, beneficial, and progressive social policies, or are their actions socially harmful and biased against ordinary working people and small-business owners?

3. Do you believe that eminent domain is a morally legitimate concept? Explain why or why not.

4. "If 'just compensation' is paid, then by definition those who lose their property cannot claim that they have been treated unjustly." Assess this argument. Can compensation be just if one of the parties is unwilling to accept it?

5. Is it fair to the community if an individual refuses payment and blocks a socially useful project? Putting legal issues aside, are there situations in which it would be morally permissible for government to seize private property for the public good with less than full compensation or even with no compensation at all?

6. Assess the concept of eminent domain, in general, and the plight of Susette Kelo and her neighbours, in particular, from the point of view of the different theories of justice discussed in this chapter. Is it possible to square the government's exercise of eminent domain with a libertarian approach to justice?

CASE 3.2

Battling over Bottled Water

Water is the lifeblood of the earth, but by 2025, according to the UN, two-thirds of the world's population could face chronic shortages of water. In fact, some countries are already importing huge supertankers of freshwater from other countries. But one place that's definitely not short of water is the state of Michigan, which has 11,000 lakes and is surrounded by Lakes Michigan, Huron, Superior, and Erie. So it came as a surprise to some that the Nestlé company's new Ice Mountain bottled-water plant in Mecosta County, Michigan, dredged up so much controversy when it began pumping water from a local spring.[54]

Nestlé's willingness to invest $100 million to build a new 410,000-square-foot (about 38,000 m²) bottling plant in Mecosta reflects the fact that bottled water is big business, with annual sales of $6 billion (up 35 percent since 1997). Many county residents, in fact, are thrilled about Nestlé's being there. The Ice Mountain plant employs about a hundred people at $12 to $23 per hour, significantly more than many local jobs pay. And the company shells out hundreds of thousands of dollars in local taxes. Township supervisor Maxine McClellan says, "This is probably the best project we've ever brought into Mecosta County." She adds that she wants "a diversified economy where our kids don't have to move away to find jobs."

The problem, as some local residents see it, is that Nestlé has also built a 12-mile stainless steel pipeline from the plant to Sanctuary Spring, which sits on an 850-acre (about 340 ha) private deer-hunting ranch and is part of the headwaters of the Little Muskegon River, which flows into the Muskegon and then into Lake Michigan. The company started pumping 130 gallons of water every minute from the spring, with plans to increase that to 400 gallons per minute, or about 262 million gallons a year. But whose water is Nestlé pumping? That's the question being asked by Michigan Citizens for Water Conservation (MCWC), a local Mecosta group that has filed suit contesting Nestlé's right to the spring's waters. Although the company has a 99-year lease on the land, MCWC contends that the water itself is a public resource. As Jim Olson, MCWC's lawyer, explains it, under the doctrine of "reasonable use" the owners of a stream can use its water for drinking, boating, swimming, or anything else "as long as it's in connection with their land." But, he argues, "this does not include the right to transport water to some distant land for [some other] use. We're arguing that the same is true with groundwater—you can't sever it from the estate."

Michigan State Senator Ken Sikkema, who chaired a task force on Michigan water issues, rejects that argument: "A farmer pumps water out of the ground, waters potatoes, and sends the potatoes to Illinois—there's no real difference. The water in those potatoes is gone." This reasoning hasn't assuaged the fears of three American Indian tribes who have joined the fray. Citing an 1836 treaty that protects their fishing and hunting rights in the Great Lakes region, they have brought a federal lawsuit against Nestlé and the state of Michigan to stop what they see as a massive water grab. "Our fear," says a spokesperson for the Little Traverse Bay Bands of Odawa Indians, "is that the export could significantly and permanently damage the fishery."

However, David K. Ladd, head of the Office of Great Lakes, argues that bottled water is a special case. Legally, he contends, it's a "food," regulated by the Food and Drug Administration. "There's no difference between Perrier bottling water, Gerber making baby food, or Miller brewing beer. When you incorporate water from the basin into a product, it's no longer water per se." And Brendan O'Rourke, an Ice Mountain plant manager, adds that the 262 million gallons it wants to pump are less than 1 percent of the annual recharge rate of the local watershed, equivalent to just 14 minutes of evaporation from the surface of Lake Michigan.

For their part, scientists opposed to the project argue that Nestlé's pumping has already lowered the local water table and that northern pike are having trouble spawning in a stream fed by Sanctuary Spring. Jim Olson argues that the Ice Mountain plant should reduce its water consumption to 100 gallons per minute or less, not increase it to 400 gallons. "Every gallon removed is needed for the stream to sustain itself," he states. "The right to withdraw groundwater does not include the right to diminish . . . existing or future uses."

In 2003, to the surprise of many, Michigan state court judge Lawrence Root bought that argument and upheld the MCWC's lawsuit. Ruling that the environment is at risk no matter how much water Nestlé draws out, he ordered the pumps turned off. The company, however, won a reprieve. This permits it to continue pumping but limits it to 250 gallons per minute, pending its appeal of the case. Meanwhile, the political climate in Michigan has begun changing with the election of a new governor, Jennifer M. Granholm.

Believing that the Ice Mountain project didn't receive enough scrutiny under her predecessor, in 2004 she proposed the Water Legacy Act, which would protect all the state's groundwater. A year later, after the state legislature repeatedly failed to act on her bill, Granholm issued an executive order, instructing Michigan's Department of Environmental Quality to begin regulating operations such as the Ice Mountain plant. She then slapped a moratorium on all new or expanded bottled-water operations in the state until the legislature acts.

Discussion Questions

1. Should people in Michigan be concerned about how, and by whom, the state's groundwater is used? In your view, what issues of justice does this case raise?

2. Does Nestlé's pumping 262 million gallons of water per year from Sanctuary Spring constitute "reasonable use"? Is the company treating either local residents or the Native American tribes unfairly, or would it be unfair to restrict Nestlé's use of water from the spring?

3. Is groundwater a public resource, the use of which is appropriate for society to regulate? Or is it the property of those who own the land to use as they see fit? Who has the strongest claim on groundwater—the owners of the land from which it is pumped, the original inhabitants of the area (that is, the local Indian tribes), local residents, citizens of the whole Great Lakes region, or all citizens of the country?

4. Assess this case from the perspective of the utilitarian, libertarian, and Rawlsian theories of justice. How would each address the case? Which theory's approach do you find the most helpful or illuminating?

CASE 3.3

Poverty in Canada

Canadians as a whole are doing pretty well. Despite a slight downturn since 2000, for some years now the median after-tax income of Canadian households has been increasing at a fairly steady pace. In 2004, Canadian families with two or more people had an estimated median income after taxes of $54,100, up about 2 percent from 2003 in real terms after adjusting for inflation. (The *median* is the point at which half of families had higher income and half less.) The Canadian economy, as measured by real gross domestic product, grew 2.9 percent in 2004. This gain extended to the labour market as employment rose during the year, all in full-time jobs, and the unemployment rate declined.

The increase in after-tax income was not shared by all family types, however. It was also virtually unchanged among "unattached individuals," or single people, whose median

after-tax income amounted to $21,300, and among female lone-parent families who had a median of $27,700. Among female lone-parent families, median earnings (pre-tax) have risen dramatically from $8,400 in 1996 to about $19,000 in 2004. For every $100 in total income, single mothers received $65 from earnings, $11 more than in 1996. This increase led to a reduction in their dependence on government transfers. And this is the point to remember. The female lone-parent family's after-tax income includes about $7,000 in government transfers. However, the pre-tax income is well under the poverty line or LICO—which is a measure of the income thresholds below which an individual or family unit in Canada would spend 20 percent more than average of their before tax income on the necessities of *food*, *shelter* and *clothing*. The addition of the

Selected Median Income Concepts by Main Family Types, 2004 Constant Dollars

	Market Income	Government Transfers	Income Taxes	After–Tax Income
Economic families, two persons or more	55,800	4,000	8,600	54,100
Senior families	20,700	21,600	2,900	38,500
Non-senior couples without children	59,200	400	10,100	53,000
Two-parent families with children	71,700	2,300	11,700	64,100
Female lone-parent families	19,000	6,700	300	27,700
Single persons	17,400	700	2,300	21,300

Source: From Statistics Canada, *The Daily*, Thursday, March 30, 2006. Retrieved from http://www.statcan.gc.ca/daily-quotidien/060330/dq060330a-eng.htm.

government transfers barely brings the after-tax income over the LICO level for, say, a female lone-parent with two children living anywhere in Canada. If you add another child and move them to any of the big metropolitan centres, the family unit would almost certainly be at or below the LICO for their particular size (for the different LICOs, see Statistics Canada, "Low Income Before Tax Cut-Offs," 2006 *Census Dictionary*).

These harsh economic conditions do not apply just to female lone-parent families. In 2004, about 3.5 million people were living on low income. They accounted for 11.2 percent of all Canadians, well below the peak of 15.7 percent in 1996. Among families, the proportion living on low income after taxes declined to 7.8 percent in 2004 from 8.5 percent in 2003 and a high of 12.1 percent in 1996. But it still left 684,000 families below the LICO in 2004. These families faced an average income gap of $7,200, which represents the amount of income they required to bring their income above the cut-off. The average income gap was $7,400 in 1996. Some 865,000 children under 18 were in low-income families, 12.8 percent of the total.

The National Council of Welfare, Poverty Facts 2003, puts the number of people living in poverty in 2003 at 4.9 million (or 15.9 percent) and the number of children in poverty in 2003 at 1.2 million (or 17.6 percent). It also claims that 47 percent of poor families and 57 percent of poor singles received more than half of their income from working, and that employment is the primary source of income for 12.9 percent of food bank clients.

Discussion Questions

1. Does the existence of poverty imply that our socio-economic system is unjust? Does the concentration of poverty in certain groups make it more unjust than it would be otherwise?

2. What are the causes of poverty? Are they structural or individual? How is one's answer to this question likely to affect one's view of the justice or injustice of poverty?

3. What moral obligation, if any, do we have individually and as a society to reduce poverty? What steps could be taken? What role should business play?

4. How would a utilitarian view the facts about poverty? What are the implications for our society of the concept of the declining utility of money?

5. How would our economy be assessed from the point of view of Rawls's difference principle? Can it be plausibly maintained that, despite poverty, our system works to "the greatest expected benefit of the least advantaged"? Is this an appropriate standard?

Notes to Chapter 3

1. See Canadian Centre for Policy Alternatives, "Alternative Federal Budget 2007," www.policyalternatives.ca.

2. See TD Bank Financial Group, Special Reports, "Lifestyles of the Rich and Unequal: An Investigation into Wealth Inequality in Canada," December 13, 2006, pp. 1–2, www.td.com/economics/special/dt1206_wealth.jsp; also *The Daily*, "Wealth Inequality," February 22, 2002, www.statcan.ca/Daily/English/020222/d020222a.htm.

3. The source of the data is the survey of the top 100 CEOs for 2005 published in *The Globe and Mail* on May 6, 2006. See Hugh Mackenzie, "Timing is Everything" (Toronto: Canadian Centre for Policy Alternatives, January 2007), amillionreasons.ca/Timing_is_Everything.pdf, accessed November 8, 2008.

4. "Learning How to Talk About Salary in Japan," *New York Times*, April 7, 2002, sec. 3, 12.

5. These figures reproduce in part the table of all 35 different LICOs (varying according to the size of the family unit and of the community) prepared by the Canadian Council for Social Development using Statistics Canada measures. See www.ccsd.ca/factssheet/fs_lico05_bt.htm.

6. For a useful discussion of different measures of poverty, see Canadian Council for Social Development, *The Canadian Fact Book on Poverty 2000*, ch. 2, www.ccsd.ca/pubs/2000/fbpov00/chapter2.pdf.

7. See the report "Economic Mobility: Is the American Dream Alive and Well?," p. 8, n. 13, from The Pew Charitable Trusts' Economic Mobility Project, www.economicmobility.org, which offers the following intergenerational income elasticities (the smaller the figure the higher the likelihood of upward mobility): United Kingdom—0.50; United States—0.47; France—0.41; Germany—0.32; Sweden—0.27; Canada—0.19; Finland—0.18; Norway—0.17; Denmark—0.15. See also Centre for Economic Performance, "Intergenerational Mobility in Europe and North America," April 2005, www.suttontrust.com/reports/IntergenerationalMobility.pdf, p. 6, Table 2.

8. See N. M. Fortin and S. Lefebvre, "Intergenerational Income Mobility in Canada" in Miles Corak, ed., *Labour Markets, Social Institutions, and the Future of Canada's Children* (Ottawa: Statistics Canada, November 1998), www.econ.ubc.ca/nfortin/chapt4a.pdf.

9. For the applicability of this saying to the American context, see "Rich-Poor Gap Widens in U.S.," *Wall Street Journal*, A7.

10. See Statistics Canada, "Participation in Postsecondary Education and Family Income," *The Daily*, December 7, 2001; also "Tuition Fees in Canada" by the Canadian Federation of Students, www.reducetuitionfees.ca.

11. Tony Judt, "Europe vs. America," *New York Review of Books*, February 10, 2005, 38.

12. "Would You Like Your Class War Shaken?," *Economist*, 28. See also Andrew Hacker, *Money: Who Has How Much and Why* (New York: Simon & Schuster, 1997), 54, and John Isbister, *Capitalism and Justice: Envisioning Social and Economic Fairness* (Bloomfield, CT: Kumarian Press, 2001), 55.

13. John Stuart Mill, *Utilitarianism* (Indianapolis: Bobbs-Merrill, 1957), 71.

14. Michael Walzer, *Spheres of Justice* (New York: Basic Books, 1983). See also Jon Elster, *Local Justice: How Institutions Allocate Scarce Goods and Necessary Burdens* (New York: Russell Sage, 1992).

15. Walzer, *Spheres of Justice*, 6.

16. Ibid., 10.

17. Mill, *Utilitarianism*, 66.

18. Ibid., 73.

19. Ibid., 71.

20. Ibid.

21. Ibid.

22. Ibid.

23. Smith's ideas are discussed further in Chapter 4.

24. John Stuart Mill, *Principles of Political Economy*, ed. Donald Winch (Harmondsworth, Middlesex: Penguin, 1970), 129.

25. Ibid., 128.

26. Ibid., 129.

27. Ibid., 133.

28. Ibid., 139–140.

29. Ibid., 140–141.

30. Richard B. Brandt, *A Theory of the Good and the Right* (New York: Oxford University Press, 1979), 312–313.

31. Ibid., 310.

32. F. A. Hayek, *The Constitution of Liberty* (Chicago: University of Chicago Press, 1960), 11.

33. John Hospers, *Libertarianism* (Los Angeles: Nash, 1971), 5.

34. Robert Nozick, *Anarchy, State, and Utopia* (New York: Basic Books, 1974).

35. John Locke, *Second Treatise of Government* (Indianapolis: Hackett Publishing, 1980), 23–24.

36. Nozick, *Anarchy, State, and Utopia*, 161.

37. Ibid., 163.

38. Amartya Sen, *Development as Freedom* (New Delhi: Oxford University Press, 1999), ch. 7. See also Amartya Sen, *Poverty and Famines* (New York: Oxford University Press, 1981), and Jean Drèze and Amartya Sen, *Hunger and Public Action* (Oxford: Oxford University Press, 1989).

39. Sen, *Development as Freedom*, 167, 170–171.

40. Lawrence C. Becker and Kenneth Kipnis, eds., *Property: Cases, Concepts, Critiques* (Englewood Cliffs, NJ: Prentice Hall, 1984), 3–5.

41. John Rawls, *A Theory of Justice*, rev. ed. (Cambridge: Harvard University Press, 1999). For subsequent developments in Rawls's thinking, see John Rawls, *Political Liberalism* (New York: Columbia University Press, 1993), and *Justice as Fairness: A Restatement* (Cambridge: Harvard University Press, 2001).

42. Rawls, *A Theory of Justice*, 266; cf. *Political Liberalism*, 291.

43. Rawls, *Political Liberalism*, 6; cf. *A Theory of Justice*, 53, 72, 266.

44. John Rawls, "Justice as Fairness," *Philosophical Review* 67 (April 1958): 167.

45. Arthur MacEwan, "Ask Mr. Dollar," *Dollars & Sense*, November/December 1997, 39; and Michelle Cottle, "The Real Class War," *Washington Monthly*, July/August 1997, 12.

46. Rawls, *A Theory of Justice*, 3–4. Reprinted by permission of the publisher from A THEORY OF JUSTICE by John Rawls, pp. 3–4, Cambridge, Mass.: The Belknap Press of Harvard University Press, Copyright © 1971, 1999 by the President and Fellows of Harvard College.

47. Rawls, "Justice as Fairness," 168. Reprinted by permission of the publisher from JUSTICE AS FAIRNESS: A RESTATEMENT by John Rawls, p. 168, Cambridge, Mass.: The Belknap Press of Harvard University Press, Copyright © 2001 by the President and Fellows of Harvard College.

48. Rawls, *Political Liberalism*, 265–266.

49. Ibid., 269.

50. Rawls, "A Kantian Conception of Equality," *Cambridge Review* 96 (February 1975): 95

51. Rawls, *A Theory of Justice*, 89. Reprinted by permission of the publisher from A THEORY OF JUSTICE by John Rawls, pp. 3–4, Cambridge, Mass.: The Belknap Press of Harvard University Press, Copyright © 1971, 1999 by the President and Fellows of Harvard College.

52. Ibid., 87. Reprinted by permission of the publisher from A THEORY OF JUSTICE by John Rawls, pp. 3–4, Cambridge, Mass.: The Belknap Press of Harvard University Press, Copyright © 1971, 1999 by the President and Fellows of Harvard College.

53. This case study is based on "Government Says It's Too Nice for Them to Call Home," *New York Times*, January 30, 2005, sec. 1, 25; "Case for the Public Good Collides with Private Rights," *Financial Times*, February 14, 2005, 14; "Clear the Way, Fellows," *New York Times*, May 8, 2005, sec. 1, 25; and "Justice Uphold Taking Property for Developing," *New York Times*, June 24, A1.

54. This case study is based on "Where They're Boiling over Water," *Business Week*, May 27, 2002; "Fight over Bottled Water," *Detroit Free Press*, May 5, 2003; "No New Bottled Water Operations for Now," *Detroit Free Press*, May 27, 2005 (online); and "Ice Mountain Hopes Court Will Increase Flow," *Grand Rapids Press*, June 12, 2005 (online).

INCOME DISTRIBUTION

JOHN ISBISTER

The distribution of income in all capitalist countries is unequal, though it is more so in some countries (like the U.S. and Britain) than in others. Taking as his starting point Plato's suggestion that in a just society the rich should possess no more than four times as much as the poor, economics professor John Isbister explores what limits there should be to inequality and what a just distribution of income would look like. He explains why perfect equality of income would be inefficient and argues that pay differentials are necessary to compensate for training, as incentives for hard work, and to acknowledge status differences. However, a wage differential ratio of eight to one would probably be sufficient for these purposes, and with that in mind, he sketches a model of what a just income range would be for a country such as the United States.

People living in capitalist countries may have equal moral standing, but they do not have equal access to the goods and services provided by their economies. Their incomes are vastly unequal.

A good way of looking at the income distribution in a country is to compare the portion of total national income going to the poorest 20 percent of the population with the portion going to the richest 20 percent. Each group of 20 percent is called a "quintile." According to calculations by the World Bank, in fifteen industrialized countries, including much of western Europe plus Canada, the United States, and Australia, the bottom quintile of households earns an average of about 8 percent of the national income, while the top quintile earns around 39 percent.[1] Of those countries, the United States has the most skewed distribution of incomes, with the lowest and highest quintiles earning 5 percent and 45 percent, respectively. In the United States, the most prosperous one-tenth of the population earn 29 percent of total income. As far as one can tell (data from before the 1970s are skimpy on this topic), the income distribution in the United States became more equal throughout the twentieth century until about 1973, and the proportion of people living in poverty fell. After 1973, however, incomes became less equal, and the proportion of people in poverty fluctuated without a trend. The huge increases in national income since 1973 have gone overwhelmingly to the rich, while the incomes of most Americans, when corrected for inflation, have fallen.[2] Some evidence exists that the poorest began to benefit from the long economic expansion at the end of the 1990s.[3]

Uneven as these figures for household income are, they are egalitarian compared to the figures for the distribution of wealth in the United States (income is what you earn, while wealth is what you own). According to data compiled by Edward N. Wolff, the share of wealth held by the top quintile was 85 percent at last count.[4]

The average pay of a CEO in a major corporation was $11.9 million in 2000.[5] The latest estimates are that the poverty line is about $20,000 for a family of four in the United States, and almost 17 percent of families fall below that threshold. The ratio of these two figures—11.9 million divided by 20,000—is almost 600, and this of course understates the ratio between the richest and the poorest Americans, since some earned much more than $11.9 million and many took in less than the poverty threshold. To avoid being accused of alarmism, however, let us take this as the ratio between the "typical" rich and poor families in the United States: 600:1.

What spread of incomes is consistent with social justice? This chapter proposes an answer. . . . The reasoning supporting my answer is, I hope, defensible, but in some respects it is unavoidably intuitive. I will try to be explicit about the intuitions; readers with different intuitions may wish to adjust my conclusions. . . .

PLATO'S COLONY

Economists are typically reluctant to say just what distribution of incomes is morally justified; it all depends, they say, on one's values and assumptions. We do, however, have one carefully thought out and precise recommendation. It comes from Plato's *Laws*, written in the fourth century B.C., a dialogue on the principles to govern a new colony. In book 5 of *Laws*, Plato says that the colony should consist of 5,040 households, each household given a lot of equal size. The purpose of the laws in the new society is "that our people should be supremely happy and devotedly attached to one another, but citizens will never be thus attached where there are many suits at law between them, and numerous wrongs committed, but where both are rarest and of least consequence." This leads him, a few sentences later, to consider the optimal income distribution. . . . Plato is clear: no hiding behind the veil of value-neutrality for him. Each man shall have at a minimum a lot of equal size and equal opportunity. Because of different personal characteristics, some will earn more than this. Because of equal opportunity, men may move up and down the income ladder. The maximum allowable is four times the value of the lot, because anything higher will induce jealousy, crime, strife, and conflict. Any income or property earned above this limit is forfeit to the state or to the gods.

It is a good answer. . . . Equality of opportunity—which we have taken to be the most basic meaning of equality in justice—is provided for. Citizens have a guaranteed income, so they will not fall into dire poverty. They have the right to be rewarded for their hard work and talents, but not so much that they will induce envy, which would rupture the attachment of one citizen to another. It is a reasonable balancing act between different components of justice.

Classical Greece was a different world from today's advanced capitalism. Is it possible that 4:1 is no longer the right ratio and that it should be replaced by something like 600:1?

From John Isbister, *Capitalism and Justice: Envisioning Social and Economic Fairness.* © 2001 Kumarian Press. Reprinted by permission of Copyright Clearance Center. Some notes omitted.

WHAT DIFFERENCES IN LABOR INCOMES ARE NEEDED FOR EFFICIENCY?

. . . Since we are of equal moral worth, our incomes should be as equal as possible—not because justice requires equality of outcomes but because if incomes vary from family to family, the children in our families will have unequal opportunities. Let us begin the discussion of an optimal income distribution, therefore, by assuming a utopian society in which all incomes are equal and no barriers of class, race, gender, sexual preference, nationality, or anything else impede equality of opportunity.

Such a society would, unfortunately, be inefficient, because people would have no financial incentive to be productive. Their incomes, being equal, would be unrelated to their contributions to society. People are motivated by many factors, not just money, but money matters. Efficiency, therefore, conflicts with equality, and we must compromise. We should ask what are the *minimum departures from equality* necessary to bring about the efficiency that we really need. The departures should be minimal because every concession to income differences in support of efficiency will take us further down the road of unequal opportunity for children.

People get their income from different sources, principal among them wages and salaries from labor, rents from land and improvements on the land, interest and dividends from investments, profits from entrepreneurship, transfers from the government, and gifts and inheritances. The most important source is wages and salaries, which account for over two-thirds of personal income in the United States. We begin, therefore, by thinking about the relationship between employees' incomes and efficiency. Why might we want firms and other organizations to pay people at unequal rates?

Many of the wage differences that exist in the real world are obviously unjust. Differences caused by discrimination based on race, gender, or other personal characteristics, or by family connections or monopoly power, have no place in a just world. Some of the existing wage differences cannot be so easily dismissed, however, because they are signals that lead to the efficient employment of labor.

Take a simple example. A society has just two jobs, server at a fast-food establishment and high-tech engineer, each with its own employer. It has two workers, Mary and George. Mary is technically adept while George is inept in most pursuits. Both employers would prefer to hire Mary. If the wages in both positions were equal, Mary might choose the less-demanding job of food server, leaving George to take the engineering post, and that would be an inefficient allocation of labor. If, however, the employers are allowed to set their own rates of pay, the high-tech employer will likely raise Mary's rate to such a level that she chooses the engineering job. The fast-food employer will not be able to match the offer, although she would like to hire Mary, because Mary, although she is worth more behind the counter than George is, is not worth as much behind the counter as she is in the lab. The high-tech employer

will be able to outbid the fast-food employer for Mary's services. The resulting allocation of labor will be efficient: Mary in the engineering job and George behind the food counter. The story shows that sometimes, not always, wages are an indicator of productivity. When wages differ, and when people try to get jobs with the highest possible wages, they may sort themselves out among the available jobs in such a way as to promote efficiency.

What departures from equal wages should we want, on grounds of efficiency? We probably have different answers—depending upon the weights we give to equality and efficiency—but we can narrow our disagreement by identifying some of the specific reasons for thinking that inequality promotes efficiency.

The first efficiency-related justification for unequal wages is to persuade some people to undertake education, apprenticeships, and training programs so that they will enhance their skills. Consider an eighteen-year-old who has just graduated from high school and is choosing between two careers, one as a clerk, a job she can start immediately, the other as a doctor. In the just world of equal opportunity that we are assuming, she has not already been tracked by her race or class or by her high school counselor into choosing one or the other career; she can make an autonomous choice. If she chooses the medical career, she faces twelve more years of training—four years of college, four years of medical school, and four years of residency—during all of which time, let us assume, she will earn no income at all, before she can start earning a doctor's income. (This is an oversimplification, since residents typically earn a low salary.) If the society wants some doctors, it may have to pay her an income, once she finishes her residency, sufficient to persuade her that she was right to give up the clerical job. How much more does she need to earn?

She expects to retire at age sixty-five, so if she chooses to be a clerk she will have forty-seven years of income-earning work, and if she chooses the medical career she will have thirty-five years. She may reason that she needs to make at least as much during her thirty-five years of doctoring as she would have during her forty-seven years of clerking. On these grounds, the annual income of a doctor would need to be 34 percent above that of a clerk; that is, the ratio of incomes would be 1.34:1. One way to think of this is that she would go in debt for the first twelve years, by the amount of the clerical salary forgone each year, then would pay off the debt during her earning years and still have the same income during those years, net of debt repayments, as the clerk. The two lifetime incomes would be the same, just arranged differently over time.

Actually the ratio would have to be higher than 1.34:1 because of time preference and the interest rate. For a variety of reasons, people prefer to have their income earlier rather than later. Perhaps it is a fear of death, a fear that they may not be around to enjoy the later income, or perhaps it is a failure of imagination, a failure to understand that they will want income as much in the future as they do now. Whatever the reason, it is normal for people to prefer income earlier rather than later. Put differently, if they are going to have to put off their income, they need to be compensated for the wait, by earning interest. So part of the dilemma facing our high school graduate is that if she chooses a clerical career, she will begin earning income now, when she most wants it. To persuade her to choose medicine, a career whose rewards will come later, we will need to sweeten the pot. By how much? Suppose her rate of time preference is 5 percent a year—that is, she would be indifferent between receiving $100 today and $105 a year from now; and suppose also that 5 percent is the interest rate she would have to pay on funds that she borrows while she is in her twelve years of medical education. Under these circumstances, a calculation discounting future income at a 5 percent annual rate demonstrates that the doctor's annual pay rate would have to be roughly double that of the clerk's, or a ratio of 2:1.

It was not by chance that a doctor's career was used in this example, but because medicine has the longest training period of any profession. Even the longest training period can justify an earnings ratio in the neighborhood of only 2:1. In a way, of course, there is no income difference in this example. Thought of in terms of lifetime earnings or, more accurately, in terms of the present value of lifetime earnings when discounted for time preference, the two earnings figures are the same.

A second reason for thinking that earnings differences promote efficiency is that many people need the prospect of higher earnings, or the fear of lower earnings, as an incentive to work hard and effectively. A good deal of evidence on this subject comes from the experience of agricultural communes in communist China and the former Soviet Union. They were very large farms, sometimes with a membership of tens of thousands of workers. In many cases, each worker was paid the same amount, calculated as a portion of the earnings of the commune. When the commune did well, earnings rose, and vice versa. The contribution that any one worker made to the success of the overall operation was too small to be noticed and had no perceptible effect on that worker's compensation. Agricultural economist D. Gale Johnson, writing about the Soviet communes in 1983, said, "The farm worker sees little or no relationship between his or her work and the pay received. Consequently there is little incentive to do any particular job well, to work hard, or to work long hours during busy seasons of the year."[6] . . .

We know, therefore, that equal wages, unrelated to a worker's effort, cause major problems in overall efficiency. When we try to quantify the effect of merit pay on actual performance, however, we find conflicting evidence. Some studies show a substantial impact, others only a weak one. The difference in findings may be related to the difficulty that organizations have in assessing meritorious performance. In any case, many organizations establish a salary range for each position and attempt to locate people within that range according to their performance. The range varies from position to position and from organization to

organization, but it seldom exceeds 50 percent of the base pay for the position.[7]

I have personal experience, however, of a merit range of approximately 100 percent. On the university campus where I teach, tenured full professors are typically promoted to that rank in their early forties and can look forward to twenty to twenty-five more working years before retirement. Since they are in the privileged position of holding tenure, they are in no danger of being fired. What keeps them working hard—and most of them do work hard—over those twenty-five years? Part of the answer is pride in their work. Beyond that, material incentives are provided. Approximately every three years, each professor goes through a rigorous peer review. Success in one of these merit reviews normally results in a pay increase of about 5 percent; there are a number of cases, however, of no increase, on the one hand, or 10 percent or even greater increases, on the other. The net result of all these personnel actions is that, at any time, the gap between the highest and lowest paid full professor is about 2:1. I can report, from many years of having been subject to this system of merit pay and having helped to administer it, that the professors take it very seriously. The increments provide not only income but, equally if not more importantly, recognition of the value of their work.

This is just one observation, and it probably lies at the extreme range of what is needed to keep people working effectively. People with less job security, who face the prospect of being fired if their performance is unsatisfactory, probably need less incentive pay: hence the more typical range of 50 percent or less. In a few cases, the ratio may need to be as high as 2:1.

A third connection between wage inequality and efficiency comes from organizational hierarchies. Most of us work in organizations with many layers of status and function. From the president at the top through all the vice presidents and assistant vice presidents to the section chiefs and the assistant chiefs, the professionals and the quasi professionals, the technicians and the clericals, the custodians and the cleaners, the number of layers is often quite large in big organizations. It seems to be important that each superior layer in the organization carry a higher rate of pay than the layer below it, since most people find it hard to supervise people with higher salaries or to be supervised by people with lower. This is not a universal phenomenon; for example, some professional sports stars play under coaches who earn lower salaries. Still, it is the convention that a higher rank carry higher compensation, and probably for good reason. How much total differential is required? In the real world, the gap between the top and the bottom is often enormous, reflecting a significant difference between each separate position. In a just world that honored the goal of equality as well as efficiency, the gap would not have to be as great. A ratio of 2:1 between top and bottom, for example, would allow for at least twenty separate gradations of 5 percent or fifty gradations of 2 percent.

Some people think the gap needs to be greater; not surprisingly, they tend disproportionately to be people with higher incomes.[8] The *New York Times* records a conversation between its reporter and several top corporate executives, including L. Dennis Kozlowski, CEO of Tyco International.

> Q. It's often said that at a certain level it no longer matters how much any of you make, that you would be doing just as good a job for $100 million less or $20 million less.
>
> Kozlowski: Yeah, all my meals are paid for, for as long as I'm around. So, I'm not working for that any longer. But it does make a difference in the charities I ultimately leave monies behind to, and it's a way of keeping score.[9]

It does not take an overly active imagination to think of better ways of funding charities and cheaper ways of keeping score.

Combining the reasons for pay differences among employees that we have discussed so far—compensation for training, incentives for hard work, and status differences in the hierarchy—and assuming that the reasons for pay differences are completely independent one from another, we come up with a maximum ratio between the top and the bottom of the labor force of 8:1, that is, $2 \times 2 \times 2$.

Factors exist that could reduce or increase this ratio. There are at least two reasons for reducing it. First, the justifications for pay differentials sometimes overlap. A person who is highly trained is likely to qualify for a more senior position in the hierarchy. One way a person is rewarded for good job performance is often by being promoted to a job at the next status level. To a certain extent, therefore—not totally—the three categories collapse into a single category.

Second, the discussion so far has taken no account of what is sometimes called "psychic income." In a free labor market, people get to choose their jobs, at least to a certain extent, and they often choose them because they like them. The young woman who was deciding between a clerical and a medical career might have had a strong preference for medicine. She might have chosen to be a doctor even if it paid less over her lifetime than a clerical job; the difference is her psychic income. Suppose Michael Jordan—who became the world's greatest and highest-paid basketball player—had figured out at the age of eighteen that he could have had a clerical career paying $30,000 a year or a basketball career paying $20,000. There is a good chance he would have chosen basketball, because he loved it. The same sort of reasoning is true of the other categories. Many of my professor colleagues work hard because they enjoy research and teaching; money is not the main issue. . . . In organizational hierarchies, many people simply want to be boss; the fact that the next position up comes with a higher salary is an added bonus, but it is not the only incentive. In other words, the added psychic income that usually attaches to higher-status positions reduces although it does not eliminate the need for pay differentials.

On the other side, an argument for increasing the ratio is that we have not exhausted the reasons for thinking that pay differentials signal an efficient allocation of labor. In the first example, both employers preferred Mary over George, not

necessarily because she was more highly trained or because she was a more conscientious worker—she may not have been—but because she was more skilled and effective.

In the real world, the gap in effectiveness between some of the most-skilled people like Mary and some of the least-skilled people like George is enormous. Think, for example, about the difference between a Nobel Prize–winning scientist and a typical high school dropout—or, along a different dimension of competency, about the difference between Michael Jordan and an athletic klutz like, say, me. If compensation packages are kept within a ratio of about 8:1, they may be insufficient, in some cases, to direct people to their most efficient employment. In fact, any restriction on the spread of incomes is likely to have some negative effect on efficiency. We must arrive at a compromise, therefore, achieving neither as much equality as we would like nor as much efficiency. If we opt for complete equality, our productive system will collapse. If we opt for the most efficient possible system, we will suffer from extreme inequality, as we do now.

A salary ratio of 8:1 is a good compromise. A range between, say, $20,000 and $160,000 a year would provide a great deal of room for wages to be related to effectiveness. It would probably constrain some labor contracts that would otherwise be efficient, but surely not many, particularly in view of the points made above about the narrowing effects of both psychic income and the overlapping of categories. Moreover, since equality is so important, I think the distribution of labor incomes should be bell-shaped, with many more people in the middle than at the extremes. . . .

Differences in Nonlabor Incomes

What about nonlabor income, including interest, dividends, rent, profits, and appreciation in the value of assets? Much of this is income earned by people in return for providing capital. Capital is defined as a means of production that has itself been produced: for the most part, although not entirely, buildings, plant, and equipment. It is essential to the production process, so a way must be found of providing it.

. . . In capitalism, the capital is owned privately. Suppose we start with a situation of absolutely equal distribution of income. Some people consume all their income and have nothing left at the end of the year. Others consume only half their income, save the rest, and purchase capital with it. In each successive year they do the same. Essentially they are postponing their consumption in the hope of increasing it in the long run. In the first year, they consume only half the goods they might have. In each successive year, though, their income grows if their investments turn out successfully, because they earn increasing amounts of capital income as the capital stock they own grows. Eventually their income is so large, because of the capital income they are adding each year, that not only their income but their consumption exceeds that of their nonsaving neighbors. They save a portion of their income each year and create capital with it because they expect they will be compensated with capital income in the future. If they did not expect this capital income, they would not continue to save. In a capitalist system, therefore, a limit on the income that can be earned from capital will likely reduce the amount of capital available to the society. The citizens may decide that this is a worthwhile limit to impose, but they will have to reckon with the loss in efficiency.

In a noncapitalist society, the answer may be different. If savings were made from the profits of firms structured as worker cooperatives, say, or from the profits of state-owned enterprises, or from the excess of a government's tax receipts over its expenditures, capital would not be in individual hands and the income accruing to capital could be shared in any way. The world in which we live is, however, capitalist.

Profits can be thought of as the return to entrepreneurship, to organization, or, if you will, to risk taking. A person, a group, or a company with a new idea invests some money in developing that idea in the hope that it will be commercially successful. If they fail, they lose their money and time; if they succeed, they reap profits. The prospect of profits is, therefore, an engine of growth. If profits are restricted in a capitalist society, there is a chance that risk taking, innovation, and growth will be reduced.

FREEDOM, EFFICIENCY, AND INCOMES

We have uncovered problems with a strict income ratio of 8:1. This sort of spread, or less, is all that is required to compensate us for our merits and to provide most of the incentives that are needed for efficiency. Neither this limit nor any limit, however, will allow us the most efficient possible economy. Some unusual people are so productive that virtually any restriction on their labor income will lead to the possibility that they will not be employed in the most efficient way. Limits on the incomes of capital owners and entrepreneurs may induce some of them to reduce their contributions to economic growth.

A second sort of problem inheres in any limit on incomes. If the limit is applied rigidly, it may violate the norm of freedom, and freedom is an important component of justice. . . . Freedom requires not just the absence of constraints. In its broadest sense, it moves us toward a fairly egalitarian income distribution, so that everyone can have an equal capacity to do what she wants to do. Therefore, in the name of freedom, one can justify taking some resources from people with means in order to redistribute them to people without. The high-income earners among us do not deserve to keep all their income, as a matter of freedom, because they depend upon so many other people in the earning of it. They do, however, deserve to keep some of it. Confiscation of all their income, or all their income over a fixed limit, would violate their freedom. The concept of freedom surely includes a certain security, a right to be free from arbitrary seizure of one's property. One does not have to go as far as the libertarian philosopher Robert Nozick, who claims that virtually any taxation of one's wealth is a violation of justice, to assert that people have the right to hold on to *some* of what they have created and earned.

It follows that a binding limit on the top incomes that people can earn will create problems of either efficiency or freedom. Consider the example of Bill Gates, who amassed the world's greatest fortune by innovating in microelectronics.

Confronted by the news that he would have to forfeit all his annual income above $160,000, he could take one of two steps: he could stop innovating or he could continue. If he stopped, the society would become less efficient. The products he has developed have, after all, improved the productivity and increased the enjoyment of millions of people. We may not care much what income he takes home to his family, but we do care about continued improvements in the quality of our lives. If, on the other hand, he continued to innovate, and thereby earned income above the $160,000 limit only to see all of it confiscated by the tax collector, his freedom to at least some security in his holdings would be violated.

AN ETHICALLY DEFENSIBLE DISTRIBUTION OF INCOMES

Let's summarize where we have gotten so far. The idea of equal incomes is initially attractive because it would ensure equal opportunity for succeeding generations. Completely equal incomes would, however, lead to a society that most of us would not be willing to tolerate. We would not be compensated for the autonomous use of our will, we would have no financial incentive to work efficiently, we would suffer from a shortage of capital and entrepreneurship, and our right to some security in our possessions would be violated. So we must retreat from complete equality. We should not, however, retreat as far as the inequality in, for example, the current American economy. The inequality in such a society egregiously violates the standards of both equal opportunity and equal freedom. For almost all of us, a ratio of something like 8:1 in earned incomes should be more than sufficient to recognize the differences in desert among us and to persuade us to work efficiently. Most of us need only a 2:1 ratio. The criteria of equality, freedom, and efficiency conflict, and we should try to arrive at a compromise that honors all of them as much as possible, but none of them completely. In a small number of cases, I think we will want to permit incomes to rise above the 8:1 limit, in the interests of both freedom and efficiency.

So we will have to abandon Plato's idea that we can specify an exact ratio between the highest and lowest incomes that is compatible with justice. Fortunately we have another measure, the share of total personal incomes accruing to different percentiles of the population. Some of the current data were given at the beginning of this [reading]. The latest figures for the United States show the lowest 20 percent of the population receiving 5 percent of the income, and the highest 20 percent 45 percent.

No overall distribution of incomes guarantees social justice, of course, since what looks like a defensible array of incomes may hide individual injustices. We can speculate, however, about what the distribution of incomes might look like if justice were achieved.

Begin with an average family income of about $90,000, which is the range that existed in the United States at the end of the twentieth century. This may seem high to readers, but remember it is the average income per family, not per person. The median family income in the United States—the

Table 1 Hypothetical Income Distribution for a Country of 1,000 People

Annual Income (in $ Thousands)	Average Income of Families in Range (in $ Thousands)	Number of Families	Income Earned by Group (in $ Thousands)
20	20	100	2,000
20–40	30	50	1,500
40–60	50	50	2,500
60–80	70	220	15,400
80–100	90	310	27,900
100–120	110	220	24,200
120–140	130	40	5,200
140–160	150	9	1,350
Over 160	300	1	300
Total		1,000	80,350

income below which half the families are found—is about half the average, approximately $45,000.[10] The gap between the median and the average is a measure of how skewed the current distribution is, with a small number of exceptionally rich people pulling the average above the median. If the population were concentrated near the center of the income distribution, with symmetrical tails on either side, the median and average would roughly coincide.

A just distribution of family incomes would, I think, follow these principles. First, no family would fall below the poverty line, no matter what the contribution of its members to overall production. . . . In a world of justice, no child suffers the disadvantage of growing up poor. The figure of $20,000 is the poverty cutoff for a family of four; we simplify the discussion by taking $20,000 as the cutoff for all families. Second, most families would be within a 2:1 ratio of incomes. This is sufficient to provide most of the incentives needed for economic efficiency. Third, except for a small number of people, the maximum ratio of incomes would be 8:1. Fourth, a few incomes would rise above the 8:1 ratio.

One expression of these principles is in Table 1, which shows 75 percent of the families within a 2:1 ratio, earning between $60,000 and $120,000 a year. Another 10 percent are right at the poverty line of $20,000; most of these are families whose adult members either cannot or choose not to earn the subsistence level of income, and they are brought up to this level by transfers from the government. Ten percent are above the poverty line but below the middle-income range, and 5 percent are above the middle-income range. Among the latter group, 0.1 percent of the families in the country earn incomes above the 8:1 ratio.

In Table 1, total personal income is $80,350,000, so with 1,000 families, the average personal income is $80,350, a little below the actual figure in the United States in recent years and well within the range of average incomes in most advanced capitalist countries. The median income is close to the average, a result of the facts that families are bunched

near the center of the distribution and that incomes are not severely skewed at either end. The bottom 20 percent of the population earn 7.5 percent of the income while the top 20 percent earn 29 percent of the income, both figures indicating a more egalitarian distribution than currently exists in the United States.

This is not the only array of incomes consistent with justice—for example, the portion of the population just at the poverty line might be lower. It is, however, a fair array, allowing as it does considerable differences in personal incomes to reflect differences in accomplishments and incentives, while responding to the fact of moral equality by restricting most incomes within a narrow 2:1 band.

Notes

1. World Bank, *World Development Report 1999/2000* (New York: Oxford University Press, 1999).

2. Frank Levy, *The New Dollars and Dreams* (New York: Russell Sage Foundation, 1998).

3. Jeff Madrick, "How New Is the New Economy?," *New York Review of Books* 46 (September 23, 1999): 42–50.

4. Edward N. Wolff, *Top Heavy: The Increasing Inequality of Wealth in America and What Can Be Done About It* (New York: New Press, 1996).

5. David Leonhardt, "Executive Pay Drops Off the Political Radar," *New York Times*, April 16, 2000, Week in Review, 5.

6. D. Gale Johnson and Karen McConnell Brooks, *Prospects for Soviet Agriculture in the 1980s* (Bloomington: Indiana University Press, 1983), 199.

7. Frederick W. Cook, "Merit Pay and Performance Appraisal," in *The Compensation Handbook: A State-of-the-Art Guide to Compensation Strategy and Design*, ed. Milton L. Rock and Lance A. Berger (New York: McGraw-Hill, 1991), 542–66.

8. Alan Wolfe, "The Pursuit of Autonomy," *New York Times Magazine*, May 7, 2000, 53–56.

9. Reed Abelson, "A Leader's-Eye View of Leadership," *New York Times*, October 10, 1999, sec. 3, 1.

10. The figures in this paragraph may be found in or calculated from United States Census Bureau, *Statistical Abstract of the United States: 1999*, 119th ed. (Washington, DC: 1999), Tables 70, 732, and 750.

Review and Discussion Questions

1. Why does Plato wish to limit inequality? Does inequality of income have negative social consequences?

2. Restate and critically assess the three efficiency-related justifications for unequal wages that Isbister presents. Explain "psychic income" and the other factors that could reduce or increase the 8:1 ratio that Isbister comes up with.

3. Isbister's Table 1 outlines what he takes to be an ethically defensible distribution of income. Assess his proposed distribution from the point of view of utilitarianism, libertarianism, and Rawls's theory of justice.

4. Does justice require our society to attempt to move toward a more equal distribution of income? How might it attempt to do so? How equal should the distribution of income be? Does respect for freedom limit the pursuit of equality?

Is Inheritance Justified?

D. W. Haslett

Many people support inheritance because they believe it is an essential and necessary feature of capitalism. After reviewing some facts about wealth distribution and inheritance in the United States today, D. W. Haslett argues against this view. He contends not only that inheritance is not essential to capitalism but also that it is inconsistent with the fundamental values underlying capitalism. In particular, inheritance violates the capitalistic ideals of "distribution according to productivity," "equal opportunity," and "freedom." Haslett maintains, accordingly, that the practice of inheritance, as it exists today, should be abolished. (The points made in the paper regarding the concentration of wealth in the United States can be made even more forcefully in connection with the Canadian context, since wealth is even more concentrated in Canada.)

I. BACKGROUND INFORMATION

Family income in the United States today is not distributed very evenly. The top fifth of American families receives 57.3 percent of all family income, while the bottom fifth receives only 7.2 percent.

But, for obvious reasons, a family's financial well-being does not depend upon its income nearly as much as it does upon its wealth, just as the strength of an army does not depend upon how many people joined it during the year as much as it does upon how many people are in it altogether. So if we really want to know how unevenly economic well-being is distributed in the United States today, we must look at the distribution not of income, but of wealth.

Although—quite surprisingly—the government does not regularly collect information on the distribution of wealth, it has occasionally done so. The results are startling. One to two percent of American families own from around 20 to 30 percent of the (net) family wealth in the United States; 5 to 10 percent own from around 40 to 60 percent. The top fifth owns almost 80 percent of the wealth, while the bottom fifth owns only 0.2 percent. So while the top fifth has, as we saw, about eight times the income of the bottom fifth, it has about 400 times the wealth. Whether deliberately or not, by regularly gathering monumental amounts of information on the distribution of income, but not on the distribution of wealth, the government succeeds in directing attention away from how enormously unequal the distribution of wealth is, and directing it instead upon the less unequal distribution of income. But two things are clear: wealth is distributed far more unequally in the United States today than is income, and this inequality in the distribution of wealth is enormous. These

are the first two things to keep in mind throughout our discussion of inheritance.

The next thing to keep in mind is that, although estate and gift taxes in the United States are supposed to redistribute wealth, and thereby lessen this inequality, they do not do so. Before 1981 estates were taxed, on an average, at a rate of only 0.2 percent—0.8 percent for estates over $500,000—hardly an amount sufficient to cause any significant redistribution of wealth. And, incredibly, the *Economic Recovery Act* of 1981 *lowered* estate and gift taxes.

Of course the top rate at which estates and gifts are *allegedly* taxed is far greater than the 0.2 percent rate, on the average, at which they are *really* taxed. Prior to 1981, the top rate was 70 percent, which in 1981 was lowered to 50 percent. Because of this relatively high top rate, the average person is led to believe that estate and gift taxes succeed in breaking up the huge financial empires of the very rich, thereby distributing wealth more evenly. What the average person fails to realize is that what the government takes with one hand, through high nominal rates, it gives back with the other hand, through loopholes in the law. . . . Indeed, as George Cooper shows, estate and gift taxes can, with the help of a good attorney, be avoided so easily they amount to little more than "voluntary" taxes.[1] As such, it is not surprising that, contrary to popular opinion, these taxes do virtually nothing to reduce the vast inequality in the distribution of wealth that exists today.

Once we know that estate and gift taxes do virtually nothing to reduce this vast inequality, what I am about to say next should come as no surprise. This vast inequality in the distribution of wealth is (according to the best estimates) due at least as much to inheritance as to any other factor. Once again, because of the surprising lack of information about these matters, the extent to which this inequality is due to inheritance is not known exactly. One estimate, based upon a series of articles appearing in *Fortune* magazine, is that 50 percent of the large fortunes in the United States were derived basically from inheritance. But by far the most careful and thorough study of this matter to date is that of John A. Brittain. Brittain shows that the estimate based upon the *Fortune* articles actually is too low,[2] that a more accurate estimate of the amount contributed by inheritance to the wealth of "ultrarich" males is 67 percent.[3] In any case, it is clear that, in the United States today, inheritance plays a large role indeed in perpetuating a vastly unequal distribution of wealth. This is the final thing to keep in mind throughout the discussion which follows.

II. INHERITANCE AND CAPITALISM

Capitalism (roughly speaking) is an economic system where (1) what to produce, and in what quantities, is determined essentially by supply and demand—that is, by people's "dollar votes"—rather than by central planning, and (2) capital goods are, for the most part, privately owned. In the minds of many today, capitalism goes hand in hand

From *PAPA/Philosophy and Public Affairs*, Vol. 15, 2, Spring 1986, pp. 122–155. Reprinted with permission from Blackwell Publishing.

with the practice of inheritance; capitalism without inheritance, they would say, is absurd. But, if I am right, the exact opposite is closer to the truth. Since, as I shall try to show in this section, the practice of inheritance is incompatible with basic values or ideals that underlie capitalism, what is absurd, if anything, is capitalism *with* inheritance. . . .

I do not try to show here that the ideals underlying capitalism are worthy of support; I only try to show that inheritance is contrary to these ideals. And if it is, then from this it follows that, *if* these ideals are worthy of support (as, incidentally, I think they are), then we have prima facie reason for concluding that inheritance is unjustified. What then are these ideals? For an answer, we can do no better than turn to one of capitalism's most eloquent and uncompromising defenders: Milton Friedman.

Distribution According to Productivity

The point of any economic system is, of course, to produce goods and services. But, as Friedman tells us, society cannot very well *compel* people to be productive and, even if it could, out of respect for personal freedom, probably it should not do so. Therefore, he concludes, in order to get people to be productive, society needs instead to *entice* them to produce, and the most effective way of enticing people to produce is to distribute income and wealth according to productivity. Thus we arrive at the first ideal underlying capitalism: "To each according to what he and the instruments he owns produces."[4]

Obviously, inheritance contravenes this ideal. For certain purposes, this ideal would require further interpretation; we would need to know more about what was meant by "productivity." For our purposes, no further clarification is necessary. According to *any* reasonable interpretation of "productivity," the wealth people get through inheritance has nothing to do with their productivity. And one need not be an adherent of this ideal of distribution to be moved by the apparent injustice of one person working eight hours a day all his life at a miserable job, and accumulating nothing, while another person does little more all his life than enjoy his parents' wealth, and inherits a fortune.

Equal Opportunity

But for people to be productive it is necessary not just that they be *motivated* to be productive, but that they have the *opportunity* to be productive. This brings us to the second ideal underlying capitalism: equal opportunity—that is, equal opportunity for all to pursue, successfully, the occupation of their choice. According to capitalist ethic, it is OK if, in the economic game, there are winners and losers, provided everyone has an "equal start." As Friedman puts it, the ideal of equality compatible with capitalism is not equality of outcome, which would *discourage* people from realizing their full productive potential, but equality of opportunity, which *encourages* people to do so.[5]

Naturally this ideal, like the others we are considering, neither could, nor should, be realized fully; to do so would

require, among other things, no less than abolishing the family and engaging in extensive genetic engineering. But the fact that this ideal cannot and should not be realized fully in no way detracts from its importance. Not only is equal opportunity itself an elementary requirement of justice but, significantly, progress in realizing this ideal could bring with it progress in at least two other crucial areas as well: those of productivity and income distribution. First, the closer we come to equal opportunity for all, the more people there will be who, as a result of increased opportunity, will come to realize their productive potential. And, of course, the more people there are who come to realize their productive potential, the greater overall productivity will be. Second, the closer we come to equal opportunity for all, the more people there will be with an excellent opportunity to become something other than an ordinary worker, to become a professional or an entrepreneur of sorts. And the more people there are with an excellent opportunity to become something other than an ordinary worker, the more people there will be who in fact become something other than an ordinary worker or, in other words, the less people there will be available for doing ordinary work. As elementary economic theory tells us, with a decrease in the supply of something comes an increase in the demand for it, and with an increase in the demand for it comes an increase in the price paid for it. An increase in the price paid for it would, in this case, mean an increase in the income of the ordinary worker vis-à-vis that of the professional and the entrepreneur, which, surely, would be a step in the direction of income being distributed more justly.

And here I mean "more justly" even according to the ideals of capitalism itself. As we have seen, the capitalist ideal of distributive justice is "to each according to his or her productivity." But, under capitalism, we can say a person's income from some occupation reflects his or her productivity only to the extent there are no unnecessary limitations upon people's opportunity to pursue, successfully, this occupation—and by "unnecessary limitations" I mean ones that either *cannot* or (because doing so would cause more harm than good) *should not* be removed. According to the law of supply and demand, the more limited the supply of people in some occupation, then (assuming a healthy demand to begin with) the higher will be the income of those pursuing the occupation. Now if the limited supply of people in some high-paying occupation . . . is the result of unnecessary limitations upon people's opportunity to pursue that occupation, then the scarcity is an "artificial" one, and the high pay can by no means be said to reflect productivity. The remedy is to remove these limitations; in other words, to increase equality of opportunity. To what extent the relative scarcity of professionals and entrepreneurs in capitalist countries today is due to natural scarcity, and to what extent to artificial scarcity, no one really knows. I strongly suspect, however, that a dramatic increase in equality of opportunity will reveal that the scarcity is far more artificial than most professionals and entrepreneurs today care to think—*far* more artificial. . . .

That inheritance violates the (crucial) second ideal of capitalism, equal opportunity, is, once again, obvious. Wealth *is* opportunity, and inheritance distributes it very unevenly indeed. Wealth is opportunity for realizing one's potential, for a career, for success, for income. There are few, if any, desirable occupations that great wealth does not, in one way or another, increase—sometimes dramatically—one's chances of being able to pursue, and to pursue successfully. And to the extent that one's success is to be measured in terms of one's income, nothing else, neither intelligence, nor education, nor skills, provides a more secure opportunity for "success" than does wealth. Say one inherits a million dollars. All one then need do is purchase long-term bonds yielding a guaranteed interest of ten percent and (presto!) one has a yearly income of $100,000, an income far greater than anyone who toils eight hours a day in a factory will probably ever have. If working in the factory pays, relatively, so little, then why, it might be asked, do not all these workers become big-time investors themselves? The answer is that they are, their entire lives, barred from doing so by a lack of initial capital which others, through inheritance, are simply handed. With inheritance, the old adage is only too true: "The rich get richer, and the poor get poorer." Without inheritance, the vast fortunes in America today, these enormous concentrations of economic power, would be broken up, allowing wealth, and therefore opportunity, to become distributed far more evenly.

Freedom

But so far I have not mentioned what many, including no doubt Friedman himself, consider to be the most important ideal underlying capitalism: that of liberty or, in other words, freedom. This ideal, however, takes different forms. One form it takes for Friedman is that of being able to engage in economic transactions free from governmental or other types of human coercion. The rationale for this conception of freedom—let us call it freedom in the "narrow" sense—is clear. As Friedman explains it, assuming only that people are informed about what is good for them, this form of freedom guarantees that ". . . no exchange will take place unless both parties benefit from it."[6] If at least the parties themselves benefit from the transaction, and it does not harm anyone, then, it is fair to say, the transaction has been socially valuable. So people with freedom of exchange will, in doing what is in their own best interests, generally be doing what is socially valuable as well. In other words, with this form of freedom, the fabled "invisible hand" actually works.

All of this is a great oversimplification. For one thing, a transaction that benefits both parties may have side effects, such as pollution, which harm others and, therefore, the transaction may not be socially valuable after all. So freedom, in the narrow sense, should certainly not be absolute. But the fact that freedom, in this sense, should not be absolute does not prevent it from serving as a useful ideal. . . .

There are [those] whose conception of freedom is that of not being subject to any governmental coercion (or other

forms of human coercion) for any purposes whatsoever—a conception sometimes referred to as "negative" freedom. It is true that governmental (or other) coercion for purposes of enforcing the abolition of inheritance violates this ideal, but then, of course, so does any such coercion for purposes of *maintaining* inheritance. So this "anticoercion" ideal . . . neither supports nor opposes the practice of inheritance, and therefore this conception of freedom need not concern us further here. . . .

A very popular variation of the anticoercion conception of freedom is one where freedom is, once again, the absence of all governmental (or other human) coercion, *except for any coercion necessary for enforcing our fundamental rights*. Prominent among our fundamental rights, most of those who espouse such a conception of freedom will tell us, is our right to property. So whether this conception of freedom supports the practice of inheritance depends entirely upon whether our "right to property" should be viewed as incorporating the practice of inheritance. But whether our right to property should be viewed as incorporating the practice of inheritance is just another way of stating the very point at issue in this investigation. . . . Consequently, this popular conception of freedom cannot be used here in support of the practice of inheritance without begging the question.

But there is still another conception of freedom espoused by many: that which we might call freedom in the "broad" sense. According to this conception of freedom, to be free means to have the ability, or the opportunity, to do what one wants. For example, according to this conception of freedom, rich people are, other things being equal, freer than poor people, since their wealth provides them with opportunities to do things that the poor can only dream about. . . .

Let us now see whether inheritance and freedom are inconsistent. Consider, first, freedom in the narrow sense. Although inheritance may not be inconsistent with this ideal, neither is the *abolishment* of inheritance. This ideal forbids governmental interference with free exchanges between people; it does not necessarily forbid governmental interference with *gifts* or *bequests* (which, of course, are not *exchanges*). Remember, Friedman's rationale for this ideal is, as we saw, that free exchange promotes the "invisible hand"; that is, it promotes the healthy functioning of supply and demand, which is at the very heart of capitalism. Supply and demand hardly require gifts, as opposed to exchanges, in order to function well.

If anything, gifts and bequests, and the enormous concentrations of economic power resulting from them, hinder the healthy functioning of supply and demand. First of all, gifts and bequests, and the enormous concentrations of economic power resulting from them, create such great differences in people's "dollar votes" that the economy's demand curves do not accurately reflect the needs of the population as a whole, but are distorted in favor of the "votes" of the rich. And inheritance hinders the healthy functioning of supply and demand even more, perhaps, by interfering with supply. As we have seen, inheritance (which, as I am using the term, encompasses large gifts) is responsible for some starting out in life with a vast advantage over others; it is, in other words, a major source of unequal opportunity. As we have also seen, the further we are from equal opportunity, the less people there will be who come to realize their productive potential. And, of course, the less people there are who come to realize their productive potential, the less overall productivity there will be or, in other words, the less healthy will be the economy's *supply* curves. So, while inheritance may not be *literally* inconsistent with freedom in the narrow sense, it does, by hindering indirectly both supply and demand, appear to be inconsistent with the "spirit" of this ideal. . . .

So we may conclude that, at best, inheritance receives no support from freedom in the narrow sense. But it remains for us to consider whether inheritance receives any support from the other relevant ideal of freedom, an ideal many, including myself, would consider to be the more fundamental of the two: freedom in the broad sense—being able to do, or having the opportunity to do, what one wants. So we must now ask whether, everything considered, there is more overall opportunity throughout the country for people to do what they want with inheritance, or without it.

On the one hand, without inheritance people are no longer free to leave their fortunes to whomever they want and, of course, those who otherwise would have received these fortunes are, without them, less free to do what they want also.

But to offset these losses in freedom are at least the following gains in freedom. First, as is well known, wealth has, generally speaking, a diminishing marginal utility. What this means is that, generally speaking, the more wealth one already has, the less urgent are the needs which any given increment of wealth will go to satisfy and, therefore, the less utility the additional wealth will have for one. This, in turn, means that the more evenly wealth is distributed, the more overall utility it will have.* And since we may assume that, generally speaking, the more utility some amount of wealth has for someone, the more freedom in the broad sense it allows that person to enjoy, we may conclude that the more evenly wealth is distributed, the more overall freedom to which it will give rise. Now assuming that abolishing inheritance would not lessen *overall* wealth . . . and that it would indeed distribute wealth more evenly, it follows that, by abolishing inheritance, there would be some gain in freedom in the broad sense attributable to the diminishing marginal utility of wealth. Next, abolishing inheritance would also increase freedom by increasing equality of opportunity. Certainly those who do not start life having inherited significant funds (through either gift or bequest) start life, relative to those who do, with what amounts to a significant handicap. Abolishing inheritance, and thereby starting everyone at a more equal level, would

obviously leave those who otherwise would have suffered this handicap (which would be the great majority of people) more free in the broad sense.

I, for one, believe these gains in freedom—that is, those attributable to the diminishing marginal utility of wealth and more equality of opportunity—would *more* than offset the loss in freedom resulting from the inability to give one's fortune to whom one wants. Abolishing inheritance is, I suggest, analogous to abolishing discrimination against blacks in restaurants and other commercial establishments. By abolishing discrimination, the owners of these establishments lose the freedom to choose the skin color of the people they do business with, but the gain in freedom for blacks is obviously greater and more significant than this loss. Likewise, by abolishing inheritance the gain in freedom for the poor is greater and more significant than the loss in freedom for the rich. So to the list of ideals that inheritance is inconsistent with, we can, if I am right, add freedom in the broad sense.

To recapitulate: three ideals that underlie capitalism are "distribution according to productivity," "equal opportunity," and "freedom," the latter being, for our purposes, subject to either a narrow or a broad interpretation. I do not claim these are the *only* ideals that may be said to underlie capitalism; I do claim, however, that they are among the most important. Inheritance is inconsistent with both "distribution according to productivity," and "equal opportunity." Perhaps it is not, strictly speaking, inconsistent with the ideal of freedom in the narrow sense, but neither is the abolishment of inheritance. On the other hand, it probably *is* inconsistent with what many would take to be the more fundamental of the two relevant ideals of freedom: freedom in the broad sense. Since these are among the most important ideals that underlie capitalism, I conclude that inheritance not only is not essential to capitalism, but is probably inconsistent with it. . . .

III. A PROPOSAL FOR ABOLISHING INHERITANCE

First, my proposal for abolishing inheritance includes the abolishment of all large gifts as well—gifts of the sort, that is, which might serve as alternatives to bequests. Obviously, if such gifts were not abolished as well, any law abolishing inheritance could be avoided all too easily.

Of course we would not want to abolish along with these large gifts such harmless gifts as ordinary birthday and Christmas presents. This, however, raises the problem of where to draw the line. I do not know the best solution to this problem. The amount that current law allows a person to give each year tax free ($10,000) is too large a figure at which to draw the line for purposes of a law abolishing inheritance. We might experiment with drawing the line, in part at least, by means of the distinction between, on the one hand, consumer goods that can be expected to be, within ten years, either consumed or worth less than half their current value and, on the other hand, all other goods. We can be more lenient in allowing gifts of goods falling within the former category since, as they are consumed or

---

*The more evenly wealth is distributed, the more overall utility it will have since any wealth that "goes" from the rich to the poor, thereby making the distribution more even, will (given the diminishing marginal utility of wealth) have more utility for these poor than it would have had for the rich, thus increasing overall utility.

quickly lose their value, they cannot, themselves, become part of a large, unearned fortune. The same can be said about gifts of services. But we need not pursue these technicalities further here. The general point is simply that, so as to avoid an obvious loophole, gifts (other than ordinary birthday presents, etc.) are to be abolished along with bequests.

Next, according to my proposal, a person's estate would pass to the government, to be used for the general welfare. If, however, the government were to take over people's property upon their death then, obviously, after just a few generations the government would own virtually everything—which would certainly not be very compatible with capitalism. Since this proposal for abolishing inheritance *is* supposed to be compatible with capitalism, it must therefore include a requirement that the government sell on the open market, to the highest bidder, any real property, including any shares in a corporation, that it receives from anyone's estate, and that it do so within a certain period of time, within, say, one year from the decedent's death. This requirement is, however, to be subject to one qualification: any person specified by the decedent in his will shall be given a chance to *buy* any property specified by the decedent in his will before it is put on the market (a qualification designed to alleviate slightly the family heirloom/business/farm problem . . .). The price to be paid by this person shall be whatever the property is worth (as determined by governmental appraisers, subject to appeal) and any credit terms shall be rather lenient (perhaps 10 percent down, with the balance, plus interest, due over the next 30 years).

Finally, the abolishment of inheritance proposed here is to be subject to three important exceptions. First, there shall be no limitations at all upon the amount a person can leave to his or her spouse. A marriage, it seems to me, should be viewed as a joint venture in which both members, whether or not one stays home tending to children while the other earns money, have an *equally* important role to play; and neither, therefore, should be deprived of enjoying fully any of the material rewards of this venture by having them taken away at the spouse's death. And unlimited inheritance between spouses eliminates one serious objection to abolishing inheritance: namely, that it is not right for a person suddenly to be deprived, not only of his or her spouse, but also of most of the wealth upon which he or she has come to depend—especially in those cases where the spouse has, for the sake of the marriage, given up, once and for all, any realistic prospects of a career.

The second exception to be built into this proposal is one for children who are orphaned, and any other people who have been genuinely dependent upon the decedent, such as any who are mentally incompetent, or too elderly to have any significant earning power of their own. A person shall be able to leave funds (perhaps in the form of a trust) sufficient to take care of such dependents. These funds should be used only for the dependent's living expenses, which would include any educational or institutional expenses no matter how much. They should not, of course, be used to provide children with a "nest egg" of the

sort others are prohibited from leaving their children. And at a certain age, say twenty-one (if the child's formal education has been completed), or upon removal of whatever disability has caused dependency, the funds should cease. This exception eliminates another objection to abolishing inheritance—the objection that it would leave orphaned children, and other dependents, without the support they needed.

The third and final exception to be built into this proposal is one for charitable organizations—ones created not for purposes of making a profit, but for charitable, religious, scientific, or educational purposes. And, in order to prevent these organizations from eventually controlling the economy, they must, generally, be under the same constraint as is the government with respect to any real property they are given, such as an operating factory: they must, generally, sell it on the open market within a year. . . .

IV. AN OBJECTION

We turn next to what is, I suppose, the most common objection to abolishing inheritance: the objection that, if people were not allowed to leave their wealth to their children, they would lose their incentive to continue working hard, and national productivity would therefore fall. In spite of the popularity of this objection, all the available evidence seems to indicate the contrary. For example, people who do not intend to have children, and therefore are obviously not motivated by the desire to leave their children a fortune, do not seem to work any less hard than anyone else. And evidence of a more technical nature leads to the same conclusion: people, typically, do not need to be motivated by a desire to leave their children (or someone else) great wealth in order to be motivated to work hard.[7]

Common sense tells us the same thing. The prospect of being able to leave one's fortune to one's children is, no doubt, for some people one factor motivating them to be productive. But even for these people, this is only *one* factor; there are usually other factors motivating them as well, and motivating them to such an extent that, even if inheritance were abolished, their productivity would be unaffected. Take, for example, professional athletes. If inheritance were abolished, would they try any less hard to win? I doubt it. For one thing, abolishing inheritance would not, in any way, affect the amount of money they would be able to earn for use during their lives. So they would still have the prospect of a large income to motivate them. But there is something else which motivates them to do their best that is, I think, even more important, and is not dependent on money: the desire to win or, in other words, to achieve that which entitles them to the respect of their colleagues, the general public, and themselves. Because of the desire to win, amateur athletes compete just as fiercely as professionals. Abolishing inheritance would in no way affect this reason for doing one's best either. Athletes would still have the prospect of winning to motivate them. Businessmen, doctors, lawyers, engineers, artists, researchers—in general, those who contribute most to society—are not, with respect to what in the most general sense motivates them, really very different from professional athletes. Without inheritance, these people would still be motivated by the prospect of a sizable income for themselves and, probably even more so, by the prospect of "winning"; that is, by the prospect of achieving, or continuing to achieve, that which entitles them to the respect of their colleagues, the general public, and themselves.

Notes

1. George A. Cooper, *A Voluntary Tax? New Perspectives on Sophisticated Estate Tax Avoidance* (Washington, DC: Brookings Institution, 1979).

2. John A. Brittain, *Inheritance and the Inequality of National Wealth* (Washington, DC: Brookings Institution, 1978), pp. 14–16.

3. Ibid., p. 99.

4. Milton Friedman, *Capitalism & Freedom* (Chicago: University of Chicago Press, 1962), pp. 161–162.

5. Milton & Rose Friedman, *Freedom to Choose* (New York: Harcourt Brace Jovanovich, 1979), pp. 131–140. . . .

6. Friedman, *Capitalism & Freedom*, p. 13.

7. See, for example, D. C. McClelland, *The Achieving Society* (Princeton: Van Nostrand, 1961), pp. 234–235; and Seymour Fiekowsky, *On the Economic Effects of Death Taxation in the United States* (unpublished doctoral dissertation, Harvard University, 1959), pp. 370–371.

Review and Discussion Questions

1. Has Haslett correctly identified the fundamental ideals underlying capitalism? Would you agree that inheritance is contrary to capitalism's fundamental values?

2. Distinguish freedom in the narrow sense from freedom in the broad sense. Which is the more useful concept? How would the abolition of inheritance affect freedom (in both senses)?

3. How would a utilitarian, a libertarian, and a Rawlsian evaluate inheritance?

4. How feasible do you find Haslett's proposal for abolishing inheritance? Would it be just?

5. Suppose that adopting Haslett's proposal would make it possible to abolish federal and provincial taxes on income. Which system would you prefer—Haslett's or our present one? Which would be fairer?

Further Reading for Chapter 3

John Arthur and **William H. Shaw**, eds., *Justice and Economic Distribution*, 2nd ed. (Englewood Cliffs, NJ: Prentice Hall, 1991) contains substantial extracts from Rawls's *A Theory of Justice* and Nozick's *Anarchy, State, and Utopia*, contemporary presentations of the utilitarian approach, and various recent essays discussing the topic of economic justice.

Joel Feinberg, *Social Philosophy* (Englewood Cliffs, NJ: Prentice Hall, 1973), ch. 7, discusses the different types of justice and injustice.

Stephen Holmes and **Cass R. Sunstein**, *The Cost of Rights: Why Liberty Depends on Taxes* (New York: Norton, 1999) argues that because all legally enforceable rights cost money, freedom is not violated by a government that taxes and spends, but requires it.

John Isbister, *Capitalism and Justice: Envisioning Social and Economic Fairness* (Bloomfield, CT: Kumarian Press, 2001) discusses a number of questions of justice in the real world, such as income distribution, taxation, welfare, and foreign aid, in a readable but thoughtful way.

David Cay Johnston, *Perfectly Legal* (New York: Penguin, 2003) argues that the U.S. tax system has been corrupted to favour the rich and powerful at the expense of the vast majority.

Will Kymlicka, *Contemporary Political Philosophy*, 2nd ed. (Oxford: Oxford University Press, 2001) covers the major schools of contemporary political thought and their competing views of justice and community.

Liam Murphy and **Thomas Nagel**, *The Myth of Ownership: Taxes and Justice* (New York: Oxford University Press, 2002) explores the justice of different tax policies in the light of contemporary moral and political philosophy.

Various authors discuss economic inequality in the United States in special issues of *Social Philosophy and Policy* 19 (Winter 2002): "Should Differences in Income and Wealth Matter?" and *Daedalus* (Winter 2002): "On Inequality." See also **Kevin Phillips**, *Wealth and Democracy* (New York: Broadway Books, 2002) for a historical perspective. The plight of the middle class today is discussed in **Elizabeth Warren and Amelia Warren Tyagi**, "What's Hurting the Middle Class," *Boston Review*, September/October 2005, with critical responses from 12 other experts.

Part Two

Capitalist Business and Its Basis

4

The Nature of Capitalism

In March 1996 the U.S. Department of Labor issued a report that most Americans took to be very good news, indeed: after months of concern about layoffs and declining economic prospects, the economy had added 700,000 jobs the previous month—more jobs than in any month since 1983. Further, the unemployment rate had fallen from 5.8 percent to 5.5 percent. This report wasn't considered good news, however, at the New York Stock Exchange, the heart of international capitalism. The day the report was issued, the Dow Jones industrial average plunged over 171 points, at the time its third-largest point decline ever. Why? The reason is complicated. Although economic expansion and increased employment are good for ordinary people, they also raise the spectre of inflation. American traders had been counting on the U.S. Federal Reserve Board to lower short-term interest rates and thus add fuel to a bull market, but any hint of inflation, traders feared, would prevent the Board from doing so.

As it turned out, the sharp drop in the stock market that day was only a minor dip in the upward growth of a long bull market that still had four more years to run. And the brief pain investors felt then was nothing compared with the pain they were to feel in the early years of the present century as the air leaked gradually, but inexorably, out of what, by the end of the 1990s, had clearly become a speculative bubble in the stock market. High-flying dot-com and other technology stocks suffered the most as the laws of capitalist reality—which many pundits thought had been suspended as the United States was supposedly leading the world into a "new economy"— reasserted themselves, reducing the nominal value of American stocks by trillions of dollars. Experts disagree on the exact causes of the long run-up in stock prices (the Dow Jones Industrial Average had grown from 875 in 1982 to 11,497 in early 2000, and the technology-heavy NASDAQ index from 196 to 4,069). They also disagree on the causes of the stock market's subsequent decline. But they agree that Wall Street's troubles reverberated around the globe, with stocks suffering in every major market from Toronto to Tokyo and from London to Johannesburg. The same is true of the current world economic crisis, which started in 2007 with the collapse of the sub-prime mortgage market in the U.S.

That is not surprising. Capitalism is a worldwide system, multinational firms operate without regard for traditional political boundaries, and the economies of capitalist nations are intricately interconnected. But what exactly is the nature of the economic system called capitalism? What is its underlying economic philosophy? What has it accomplished and what are its prospects for the future? This chapter examines these and related questions.

Looking back in history, one must definitely credit capitalism with helping break the constraints of medieval feudalism, which had severely limited individual possibilities for improvement. In place of a stifling economic system, capitalism offered opportunities for those blessed with imagination, an ability to plan, and a willingness to work. Capitalism must also be credited with enhancing the abundance and diversity of consumer goods beyond Adam Smith's wildest dreams. It has increased our material wealth and our standard of living and has converted our cities from modest bazaars into treasure troves of dazzling merchandise.

In the light of such accomplishments and the acculturation process that tends to glorify them, it is possible to overlook capitalism's theoretical and operational problems, which have serious moral import. This chapter attempts to identify some of these problems and their moral implications. It provides some basic historical and conceptual categories for understanding the socioeconomic framework within which business transactions occur and moral issues arise. In particular, this chapter addresses the following topics:

1. The definition of capitalism and its major historical stages

2. Four of the key features of capitalism: companies, profit motive, competition, and private property

3. Two classical moral justifications of capitalism—the first based on the right to property, the second on Adam Smith's concept of the "invisible hand"

4. Fundamental criticisms of capitalism—in particular, the persistence of inequality and poverty, capitalism's implicit view of human nature, the rise of economic oligarchies, the shortcomings of competition, and the employee's experience of alienation and exploitation on the job

5. Some specific socioeconomic challenges facing Canada today: (1) the decline in Canadian manufacturing; (2) the "hollowing" of corporate Canada; (3) the shortage of skilled labour; and (4) improving the workers' work–life balance.

CAPITALISM

Capitalism can be defined ideally as an economic system in which the major portion of production and distribution is in private hands, operating under what is termed a profit or market system. All manufacturing firms are privately owned, including those that produce military hardware for the government. The same applies to banks, insurance companies, and most transportation companies. All businesses—small, medium, and large—are also privately owned, as are power companies. With the possible exception of government expenditures for certain sectors thought to be intimately connected to the national interest (for example, health, education, welfare, highways, or military equipment) no central governing body dictates to these private owners what or how much of anything will be produced. They are free to determine what products they will produce, to set their own production goals, and set prices according to anticipated consumer demand and other market forces.

The private ownership and market aspects of capitalism contrast with its polar opposite, socialism. Ideally, *socialism* is an economic system characterized by public ownership of property and a planned economy. Under socialism, a society's productive equipment is not owned by individuals (capitalists) but by public bodies. Socialism depends primarily on centralized planning rather than on the market system for both its overall allocation of resources and its distribution of income; crucial economic decisions are made not by individuals but by government. In the former Soviet Union, for example, government agencies decided the number of automobiles—including models, styles, and colours—to be produced each year. Top levels of government formulated production and cost objectives, which were then converted to specific production quotas and budgets that individual plant managers had to follow.

Contemporary countries have by and large adopted what is called a *mixed economy*; that is, an economic system that combines features of both capitalism and socialism, with the principal difference among the various countries being the degree to which they may resemble or deviate from one or the other of the two ideal types. For example, the U.S. economy is closer to the ideal capitalism system, China is closer to the ideal socialist system—though no one knows for how long—while Canada is somewhere in between the two. Remember that Canada still has dozens of federal and provincial Crown corporations involved in various aspects of economic activity.

Historical Background of Capitalism

What we call capitalism did not fully emerge until the Renaissance in Europe during the fifteenth and sixteenth centuries. Before the Renaissance, business exchanges in medieval Europe were organized through *guilds*, which were associations of individuals of the same trade.

Today, if you want a pair of shoes, you head for a shoe store, where you find an array of shoes. If nothing strikes your fancy, you set out for another shop, and perhaps another, until at last you find what you want. Or, if still disappointed, you might ask the store clerk to order a pair in your size from the manufacturer or its distributor. You certainly wouldn't ask the clerk to have someone make you a pair of shoes. Under the guild organization, shoemakers, who were also shoe sellers, made shoes only to fill orders. If they had no orders, they made no shoes. The shoemaker's sole economic function was to make shoes for people when they wanted them. His labour allowed him to maintain himself, not advance his station in life. When the shoemaker died, his business went with him—unless he had a son to inherit and carry on the enterprise. As for shoe quality and cost, the medieval shopper could generally count on getting a good pair of shoes at a fair price because the cobblers' guild strictly controlled quality and price.

Weaving was another big medieval trade. In fact, in the fourteenth century weaving was the leading industry in the German town of Augsburg. Little wonder, then, that an enterprising young man named Hans Fugger became a weaver when he settled there in 1367. But young Hans had ambitions that stretched far beyond the limits of the weaving trade and the handicraft guild system. And they were grandly realized, for within three short generations a family of simple weavers was transformed into a great German banking dynasty.[1]

Not content with being a weaver, Hans Fugger began collecting and selling the products of other weavers. Soon he was employing lots of weavers, paying them for their labour, and selling their products as his own. His son, Jacob Fugger, continued the business, which was expanded by Jacob Fugger II, the foremost capitalist of the Renaissance. Under his direction, the family's interests expanded into metals and textiles. Jacob Fugger II also lent large sums of money to the Hapsburg emperors to finance their wars, among other things. In return, he obtained monopoly rights on silver and copper ores, which he then traded. When Fugger bought the mines themselves, he had acquired all the components necessary to erect an extraordinary financial dynasty.

Like latter-day titans of international capitalist industry, Fugger employed thousands of workers and paid them wages, controlled all his products from raw material to market, set his own quality standards, and charged whatever the traffic would bear. In one brief century, what was once a handicraft inseparable from the craftsperson had become a company that existed outside any family members. What had once motivated Hans Fugger—maintenance of his station in life—had given way to gain for gain's sake, the so-called *profit motive*. Under Jacob Fugger II, the company amassed profits, a novel concept, that well exceeded the needs of the Fuggers. And the profits were measured not in goods or in land but in money.

Capitalism has undergone changes since then.[2] For example, the kind of capitalism that emerged in the Fuggers' time is often termed *mercantile capitalism*, because it was based on mutual dependence between state and commercial (merchant) interests. Implicit in mercantile capitalism are the beliefs that national wealth and power are best served by increasing exports and collecting precious metals in return, and that the role of government is to provide laws and economic policies designed to encourage production for foreign trade, keep out imports, and promote national supremacy.

In North America, *industrial capitalism*, which is associated with the development of large-scale industry, emerged in the period following Confederation in Canada (1867) and the Civil War (1861–1865) in the United States. A confluence of factors in each country contributed to the expansion of industry: protectionist policies (certainly in Canada) in reaction to British laissez-faire practices, the expansion of the railway system, an ample, cheap and willing labour force, a sound financial base, the technology for mass production, and expanding markets for cheaply manufactured goods. Exploiting these fortuitous conditions in the U.S. was a group of hard-driving, visionary entrepreneurs called robber barons by their critics and captains of industry by their supporters: Cornelius Vanderbilt, Cyrus McCormick, Andrew Carnegie, John D. Rockefeller, Jay Gould, and others.

As industrialization increased, so did the size and power of business. The private fortunes of a few individuals could no longer underwrite the accelerated growth of business activity. The large sums of capital necessary could be raised only through a corporate form of business, in which risk and potential profit were distributed among numerous investors.

As competition intensified, an industry's survival came to depend on its financial strength to reduce prices and either eliminate or absorb competition. To shore up their assets, industries engaged in *financial capitalism*, characterized by pools, trusts, holding companies, and an interpenetration of banking, insurance, and industrial interests. Hand in hand with this development, the trend continued toward larger and larger corporations, controlling more and more of the country's economic capacity.

The economic and political challenges of the Great Depression of the 1930s helped usher in still another phase of capitalism, often called *state welfare capitalism*, in which government plays an active role in regulating economic activities in an effort to smooth out the boom-and-bust pattern of the business cycle. In addition, government programs like the old age pension plan and unemployment insurance seek to enhance the welfare of the workforce, and legislation legitimizes the existence of trade unions. Conservative politicians sometimes advocate less government control of business, but in reality the governments of all capitalist countries are deeply involved in the management of their economies.

These days capitalism increasingly operates on a worldwide scale, leading many contemporary commentators to see *globalized capitalism* as a new stage or level of capitalist development. Although capitalism has always involved international trade, today—thanks to the computer, the Internet, satellites, cell phones, and other technological advances—the economies of most countries are becoming more and more integrated, a process labelled *globalization*. Although the world is still far from constituting a single global economy, investment capital is more mobile than ever, and the currencies, stock exchanges, and economic fortunes of all capitalist countries are bound together in a single financial system. The business operations of a growing number of companies take place on a world stage. Capitalist enterprises are more likely than ever before to utilize foreign components and draw on foreign labour or services, to export products or provide services abroad, and to acquire or start foreign subsidiaries or engage in joint ventures with overseas companies. Many apparently national companies produce one component in one country and another component in a different country, assemble them in a third country, and market them throughout the world.

Although the study of capitalism's evolution is best left to economic historians, it is important to keep in mind capitalism's dynamic nature. There is nothing fixed and immutable about this or any other economic system; it is as susceptible to the social forces of change as any other institution. Nevertheless, the capitalism we know does have some prominent features that were evident in the earliest capitalistic businesses.

KEY FEATURES OF CAPITALISM

Complete coverage of capitalism's features has filled many a book. Four features of particular significance—the existence of companies, profit motive, competition, and private property—will be discussed briefly here.

Companies

Chapter 2 mentioned the Firestone case, in which a media misrepresentation was left uncorrected. When asked why Firestone had not corrected the error, a spokesperson said that it was Firestone's policy to ask for corrections only when it was beneficial to the company to do so. Expressions like "Firestone's policy" and "beneficial to the company" reflect one key feature of capitalism: the existence of companies or business firms separate from the human beings who work for and within them.

"It's not in the company's interests," "The company thinks that," "From the company's viewpoint," "As far as the company is concerned"—all of us have heard, perhaps even used, expressions that treat a business organization like a person or at least like a separate and distinct entity. Such personifications are not mere lapses into the figurative but bespeak a basic characteristic of capitalism: capitalism permits the creation of companies or business organizations that exist separately from the people associated with them. We take the existence of companies for granted, but some experts believe that it is not church or state but the company that is "the most important organization in the world."[3]

Today the big companies we're familiar with—BCE, RBG, General Electric, AT&T, Ford, IBM—are, in fact, incorporated businesses, or corporations. Chapter 5 discusses the nature of the modern corporation, including its historical evolution and its social responsibilities. Here it's enough to observe that, in the nineteenth century, U.S. Chief Justice John Marshall defined a *corporation* as "an artificial being, invisible, intangible, and existing only in the contemplation of law." Although a corporation is not something that can be seen or touched, it does have prescribed rights and legal obligations within the community. Like you or me, a corporation may enter into contracts and may sue or be sued in courts of law. It may even do things that the corporation's members disapprove of. The corporations that loom large on our economic landscape harken back to a feature of capitalism evident as early as the Fugger dynasty: the existence of the company.

Profit Motive

A second characteristic of capitalism lies in the motive of the company: to make profit. As dollar-directed and gain-motivated as our society is, most of us take for granted that the human being is by nature an acquisitive creature who, left to his or her own devices, will pursue profit with all the instinctual vigour of a cat chasing a mouse. However, as economist Robert Heilbroner points out, the "profit motive, as we understand it, is a very recent phenomenon. It was foreign to the lower and middle classes of Egyptian, Greek, Roman, and medieval cultures, only scattered throughout the Renaissance times, and largely absent in most Eastern civilizations." The medieval church taught that no Christian ought to be a merchant. Heilbroner concludes: "As a ubiquitous characteristic of society, the profit motive is as modern an invention as printing."[4]

Modern or not, profit in the form of money is the lifeblood of the capitalist system. Companies and capitalists alike are motivated by a robust appetite for money profit. Indeed, the profit motive implies and reflects a critical assumption about human nature: that human beings are basically economic creatures, who recognize and are motivated by their own economic self-interests.

Competition

If self-interest and an appetite for money profit drive individuals and companies, then what stops them short of holding up society for exorbitant ransom? What stops capitalists from bleeding society dry?

Adam Smith provided an answer in his monumental treatise on political economy, *An Inquiry into the Nature and Causes of the Wealth of Nations* (1776). Free competition, said Smith, is the regulator that keeps a community activated only by self-interest from degenerating into a mob of ruthless profiteers. When traditional restraints are removed from the sale of goods and from wages and when all individuals have equal access to raw materials and markets (the doctrine of *laissez faire*, from the French meaning "to let do"), we are all free to pursue our own interests. In pursuing our own interests, however, we come smack up against others similarly motivated. If any of us allow blind self-interest to dictate our actions—for example, by price gouging or employee exploitation—we will quickly find ourselves beaten out by a competitor who, let's say, charges less and pays a better wage. Competition thus regulates individual economic activity.

To sample the flavour of Smith's argument, imagine an acquisitive young woman in a faraway place who wants to pile up as much wealth as possible. She looks about her and sees that people need and want strong-twilled cotton trousers, so she takes her investment capital and sets up a jeans factory. She charges $45 for a pair of jeans and soon realizes handsome profits. The woman's success is not lost on other business minds, especially manufacturers of formal slacks and dresses, who observe a sharp decline in those markets. Wanting a piece of the jeans action, numerous enterprises start up jeans factories. Many of these start selling jeans for $40 a pair. No longer alone in the market, our hypothetical businesswoman must either check her appetite for profit by lowering her price or risk folding. As the number of jeans on the market increases, their supply eventually overtakes demand, and the price of jeans declines further and further. Inefficient manufacturers start dropping like flies. As the competition thins out, the demand for jeans slowly balances with the supply, and the price regulates itself. Ultimately, an equilibrium is reached between supply and demand, and the price of jeans stabilizes, yielding a normal profit to the efficient producer.

In much this way, Adam Smith tried to explain how economic competition steers individuals pursuing self-interest in a socially beneficial direction. By appealing to their self-interest, society can induce producers to provide it with what it wants—just as manufacturers of formal slacks and dresses were enticed into jeans production. But competition keeps prices for desired goods from escalating; high prices are self-correcting because they call forth an increased supply.

Private Property

In its discussion of the libertarian theory of justice, Chapter 3 emphasized that property should not be identified only with physical objects like houses, cars, and videorecorders. Nor should ownership be thought of as a simple relationship between the owner and the thing owned. First, one can have property rights over things that are not simple physical objects, as when one owns stock in a company. Second, property ownership involves a generally complex bundle of rights and rules governing how, under what circumstances, and in what ways both the owner and others can use, possess, dispose of, and have access to the thing in question.

Private property is central to capitalism. To put it another way, capitalism as a socioeconomic system is a specific form of private property. What matters for capitalism is not private property simply in the sense of personal possessions, because a socialist society can certainly permit people to own houses, television sets, and jogging shoes. Rather, capitalism requires private ownership of the major means of production and distribution. The means of production and distribution include factories, warehouses, offices, machines, computer systems, trucking fleets, agricultural land, and whatever else makes up the economic resources of a nation. Under capitalism, private hands control these basic economic assets and productive resources. Thus, the major economic decisions are made by individuals or groups acting on their own in pursuit of profit. These decisions are not directly coordinated with those of other producers, nor are they the result of some overall plan. Any profits (or losses) that result from these decisions about production are those of the owners.

Capital, as an economic concept, is closely related to private property. Putting it simply, capital is money that is invested for the purpose of making more money. Individuals or corporations purchase various means of production or other related assets and use them to produce goods or provide services, which are then sold. They do this not for the purpose of being nice or of helping people out but rather to make money—more money, hopefully, than they spent to make the goods or provide the services in the first place. Using money to make money is at the heart of the definition of capitalism.

MORAL JUSTIFICATIONS OF CAPITALISM

People tend to take for granted the desirability and moral legitimacy of the political and economic system within which they live. Canadians and Americans are no exception. We are raised in a society that encourages individual competition, praises capitalism, promotes the acquisition of material goods, and worships economic wealth. Newspapers, television, recordings, movies, and other forms of popular culture celebrate these values, though we are, but rarely, presented with fundamental criticisms of or possible alternatives to our socioeconomic order. Small wonder, then, that most of us blithely assume, without ever bothering to question, that our capitalist economic system is a morally justifiable one.

Yet as thinking people and moral agents, it is important that we reflect on the nature and justifiability of our social institutions. The proposition that capitalism is a morally acceptable system is very much open to debate. Whether we decide that capitalism is morally justified will depend, at least in part, on which general theory of justice turns out to be the soundest. Chapter 3 explored in detail the utilitarian approach, the libertarian alternative, and the theory of John Rawls. Now, against that background, this chapter looks at two basic ways defenders of capitalism have sought to justify their system: first, the argument that the moral right to property guarantees the legitimacy of capitalism and, second, the utilitarian-based economic argument of Adam Smith. The chapter then considers some criticisms of capitalism.

The Natural Right to Property

We live in a socioeconomic system that guarantees us certain property rights. Although we are no longer permitted to own other people, we are certainly free to own a variety of other things, from livestock to stock certificates, from our own homes to whole blocks of apartment buildings. A common defence of capitalism is the argument that people have a fundamental moral right to property and that our capitalist system is simply the outcome of this natural right.

In Chapter 3, we saw how Locke attempted to base the right to property in human labour. When individuals mix their labour with the natural world, they are entitled to the results. This idea seems plausible in many cases. For example, if Carl diligently harvests coconuts on the island he shares with Adam, while Adam himself idles away his days, then most of us would agree that Carl has an entitlement to those coconuts that Adam lacks. But property ownership as it actually exists in the real world today is a very complex, socially shaped phenomenon. This is especially true in the case of sophisticated forms of corporate and financial property—for example, bonds or stock options.

One could, of course, reject the whole idea of a natural right to property as a fiction, as, for example, utilitarians do. In their view, although various property systems exist, there is no natural right that things be owned privately, collectively, or in any particular way whatsoever. The moral task is to find that property system, that way of organizing production and distribution, with the greatest utility. Yet even if one believes that there is a natural right to property, at least under some circumstances, one need not believe that this right leads to capitalism or that it is a right to have a system of property rules and regulations just like the one we find in Canada or the United States. That is, even if Carl has a natural right to his coconuts, there may still be moral limits on how many coconuts he can rightfully amass and what he can use them for. When he takes his coconuts to the coconut bank and receives further coconuts as interest, his newly acquired coconuts are not the result of any new labour on his part. When we look at capitalistic property—that is, at socioeconomic environments in which people profit from ownership alone—then we have left Locke's world far behind.

A defender of capitalism may reply, "Certainly, there's nothing unfair about Carl's accruing these extra coconuts through his investment; after all, he could have eaten his original coconuts instead." And, indeed, within our system this reasoning seems perfectly correct. It is the way things work in our society. But this fact doesn't prove that Carl has some *natural* right to use his coconuts to make more coconuts—that is, that it would be unfair or unjust to set up a different economic system (for example, one in which he had a right to consume his coconuts but no right to use them to earn more coconuts). The argument here is simply that the issue is not one of the all-or-nothing variety. There may be certain fundamental moral rights to property, but those rights need not be unlimited or guarantee capitalism as we know it.

Adam Smith's Concept of the Invisible Hand

Relying on the idea of a natural right to property is not the only way and probably not the best way to defend capitalism. Another, very important argument defends capitalism in terms of the many economic benefits the system brings, claiming that a free and unrestrained market system, which exists under capitalism, is more efficient and more productive than any other possible system and is thus to be preferred on moral grounds. Though this is essentially a utilitarian argument, one need not be a utilitarian to take it seriously. As mentioned in Chapter 2, almost every normative theory puts some moral weight on the consequences of actions. Thus if capitalism does indeed work better than other ways of organizing economic life, then this will be a very relevant moral fact—one that will be important, for instance, for Rawlsians.

This section sketches Adam Smith's economic case for capitalism, as presented in *The Wealth of Nations*. Smith argues that when people are left to pursue their own interests, they will, without intending it, produce the greatest good for all. Each person's individual and private pursuit of wealth results—as if, in Smith's famous phrase, "an invisible hand" were at work—in the most beneficial overall organization and distribution of economic resources. Although the academic study of economics has developed greatly since Smith's times, his classic arguments remain extraordinarily influential.

Smith took it for granted that human beings are acquisitive creatures. Self-interest and personal advantage, specifically in an economic sense, may not be all that motivate people, but they do seem to motivate most people much of the time. At any rate, they are powerful enough forces that any successful economic system must strive to harness them. We are, Smith thought, strongly inclined to act so as to acquire more and more wealth.

In addition, humans have a natural propensity for trading—"to truck, barter, and exchange." Unlike other species, we have an almost constant need for the assistance of others. Yet because people are creatures of self-interest, it is folly for us to expect others to act altruistically toward us. We can secure what we need from others only by offering them something they need from us:

> Whoever offers to another a bargain of any kind, proposes to do this. Give me that which I want, and you shall have this which you want, is the meaning of every such offer; and it is in this manner that we obtain from one another the far greater part of those good offices which we stand in need of. It is not from the benevolence of the butcher, the brewer, or the baker that we expect our dinner, but from their regard to their own interest. We address ourselves, not to their humanity but to their self love, and never talk to them of our own necessities but of their advantages.[5]

This disposition to trade, said Smith, leads to the division of labour—dividing the labour and production process into areas of specialization, which is the prime means of increasing economic productivity.

Thus, Smith reasoned that the greatest utility will result from unfettered pursuit of self-interest. Individuals should be allowed unrestricted access to raw materials, markets, and labour. Government interference in private enterprise should be eliminated, free competition encouraged, and economic self-interest made the rule of the day. Because human beings are acquisitive creatures, we will, if left free, engage in labour and exchange goods in a way that results in the greatest benefit to society. In our efforts to advance our own economic interests, we inevitably act to promote the economic well-being of society generally:

> Every individual is continually exerting himself to find the most advantageous employment for whatever capital he can command. It is his own advantage, indeed, and not that of the society, which he has in view . . . . [But] by directing that industry in such a manner as its produce may be of the greatest value, he [is] . . . led by an invisible hand to promote an end that was no part of his intention . . . . By pursuing his own interest he frequently promotes that of society more effectually than when he really intends to promote it.[6]

To explain why pursuit of self-interest necessarily leads to the greatest social benefit, Smith invoked the law of supply and demand, which was alluded to in discussing competition. The law of supply and demand tempers the pursuit of self-interest exactly as competition keeps the enterprising capitalist from becoming a ruthless profiteer. The law of supply and demand similarly solves the problems of adequate goods and fair prices.

Some think the law of supply and demand even solves the problem of fair wages, for labour is another commodity up for sale like shoes or jeans. Just as the price of a new product at first is high, like the jeans in our earlier hypothetical example, so, too, are the wages of labour in a new field. But as labour becomes more plentiful, wages decline. Eventually they fall to a point at which inefficient labourers are eliminated and forced to seek other work, just as the inefficient manufacturers of jeans were forced out of that business and into others. And like the price of jeans, the price of labour then stabilizes at a fair level. As for the inefficient labourers, they find work and a living wage elsewhere. In seeking new fields of labour, they help maximize the majority's opportunities to enjoy the necessities, conveniences, and trifles of human life.

Some modern defenders of capitalism claim that it operates as Smith envisioned and can be justified on the same utilitarian grounds. But not everyone agrees.

CRITICISMS OF CAPITALISM

The two major defences of capitalism have not persuaded critics that it is a morally justifiable system. Their objections to capitalism are both theoretical and operational. Theoretical criticisms challenge capitalism's fundamental values, basic assumptions, or inherent economic tendencies. Operational criticisms focus more on capitalism's alleged deficiencies in actual practice (as opposed to theory)—in particular, on its failure to live up to its own economic ideals.

The following criticisms are a mix of both theoretical and operational concerns. They raise political, economic, and philosophical issues that cannot be fully assessed here. The debate over capitalism is a large and important one; the presentation that follows should be viewed as a stimulus to further discussion and not as the last word on the pros and cons of capitalism.

Inequality

Chapter 3 gave some evidence of the great economic inequality that exists in our capitalist society. The disparity in personal incomes is enormous; a tiny minority of the population owns the vast majority of the country's productive assets; and at the beginning of the twenty-first century, our society continues to be marred by poverty and homelessness. With divisions of social and economic class comes inequality of opportunity. A child born to a working-class family, let alone to an unwed teenager in an inner-city ghetto, has life prospects and possibilities that pale beside those of children born to wealthy, stock-owning parents. This reality challenges capitalism's claim of fairness, and the persistence of poverty and economic misfortune provides the basis for a utilitarian objection to it.

Few doubt that poverty and inequality are bad things, but defenders of capitalism make several responses to those who criticize it on these grounds:

1. A few extreme supporters of capitalism simply deny that it is responsible for poverty and inequality. Rather, they say, government interference with the market causes these problems. Left to itself, the market would eliminate unemployment and poverty while ultimately lessening inequality. But neither theoretical economics nor the study of history supports this reply. Most economists and social theorists would agree that in the past seventy years

or so activist government policies have done much, in all the Western capitalist countries, to reduce poverty and (to a lesser extent) inequality.

2. More moderate defenders of capitalism concede that in its pure laissez-faire form, capitalism does nothing to prevent and may even foster inequality and poverty. However, they argue that the system can be modified or its inherent tendencies corrected by political action, so that inequality and poverty are reduced or even eliminated. Critics of capitalism reply that the policies necessary to seriously reduce inequality and poverty are either impossible within a basically capitalist economic framework or unlikely to be carried out in any political system based on capitalism.

3. Finally, defenders of capitalism argue that the benefits of the system outweigh this weak point. Inequality is not so important if living standards are rising and even the poor have better lives than they did in previous times. This contention rests on an implicit comparison with what things would be like if society were organized differently and is, accordingly, difficult to assess. Naturally, it seems more plausible to those who are relatively favoured by, and content with, the present economic system than it does to those who feel disadvantaged by it.

Some critics of capitalism go on to maintain that, aside from inequalities of income and ownership, the inequality inherent in the worker-capitalist relationship is itself morally undesirable. John Stuart Mill found capitalism inferior in this respect to more cooperative and egalitarian economic arrangements. "To work at the bidding and for the profit of another," he wrote, "is not . . . a satisfactory state to human beings of educated intelligence, who have ceased to think themselves inferior to those whom they serve."[7] The ideal of escaping from a system of "superiors" and "subordinates" was well expressed by the great German playwright and poet Bertolt Brecht when he wrote that "He wants no servants under him/And no boss over his head."[8]

Human Nature and Capitalism

The theory of capitalism rests on a view of human beings as rational economic creatures, individuals who recognize and are motivated largely by their own economic self-interests. Adam Smith's defence of capitalism, for instance, assumes that consumers have full knowledge of the diverse choices available to them in the marketplace. They are supposed to know the price structures of similar products, to be fully aware of product differences, and to be able to make the optimal choice regarding price and quality.

But the key choices facing today's consumers are rarely simple. From foods to drugs, automobiles to appliances, fertilizers to air conditioners, the modern marketplace is a cornucopia of products whose nature and nuances require a high level of consumer literacy. Even with government agencies and public interest groups to aid them, today's consumers are rarely a match for the powerful industries which influence prices and create and shape markets. The effectiveness of advertising, in particular, is difficult to reconcile with the picture of consumers as the autonomous, rational, and perfectly informed economic maximizers that economics textbooks presuppose in their attempts to demonstrate the benefits of capitalism. Consumers frequently seem to be pawns in the play of social and economic forces beyond their control.

According to some critics of capitalism, however, what is objectionable in the capitalist view of human beings as essentially economic creatures is not this gap between theory and reality but rather the fact that it presents little in the way of an ideal to which either individuals or societies may aspire. As George Soros puts it, "Humans are capable of transcending the pursuit of narrow self-interest. Indeed, they cannot live without some sense of morality. It is market fundamentalism, which holds that the social good is best served by allowing people to pursue their self-interest without any thought for the social good . . . that is a perversion of human nature."[9] Not only does capitalism rest on the premise that people are basically acquisitive, individualistic, and materialistic, but in practice capitalism strongly reinforces those human tendencies. Capitalism, its critics charge, presents no higher sense of human mission or purpose, whereas other views of society and human nature do.

Christianity, for example, has long aspired to the ideal of a truly religious community united in *agape*, selfless love. And socialism, because it views human nature as malleable, hopes to see people transformed from the "competitive, acquisitive beings that they are (and that they are *encouraged* to be) under all property-dominated, market-oriented systems." In the more "benign environment of a property-less, non-market social system," socialists believe that more cooperative and less selfish human beings will emerge.[10] Such positive ideals and aspirations are lacking in capitalism—or so its critics charge.

Finally, it is an implicit assumption of capitalism that human beings find increased well-being through greater material consumption. That's why the avid pursuit of economic gain, as mediated through the invisible hand of the market, is supposed to make us all better off. Moreover, contemporary capitalism needs people to keep on buying and consuming goods for the system to continue running. Consumer demand makes the economic wheels turn. And that, in turn, requires people in general to choose working more so they can consume more rather than working less, having more leisure, and buying fewer things. However, this bias in favour of material consumption runs up against the fact, according to social psychologists, that people today—in America, Europe, and Japan—are no more pleased with their lives than they were in the 1950s despite the very substantial increase in standard of living that all these societies have enjoyed.[11]

Competition Isn't What It's Cracked Up to Be

As we have seen, one of the key features of capitalism is competition. Unfettered competition supposedly serves the collective interest while offering rich opportunities for the individual. But competition is one of the targets of capitalism's critics. They contend that capitalism breeds oligopolies which eliminate competition and concentrate economic power; that a system of corporate welfare protects many businesses from true marketplace competition; and finally, that competition is neither generally beneficial nor desirable in itself.

Capitalism Breeds Oligopolies As early as the middle of the nineteenth century, the German philosopher and political economist Karl Marx (1818–1883) argued that capitalism leads to a concentration of property and resources, and thus economic power, in the hands of a few. High costs, complex and expensive machinery, intense competition, and the advantages of large-scale production all work against the survival of small firms, said Marx. Many see proof of Marx's argument in today's economy.

Before the Industrial Revolution, capitalism was characterized by comparatively free and open competition among a large number of small firms. Since then the economy has come to be dominated by a relatively small number of enormous companies that can, to a distressing extent, conspire to set prices, eliminate competition, and monopolize an industry. The U.S. food industry is a perfect example, with four or fewer firms controlling the vast majority of sales of almost any given product.[12]

Today, the 500 largest U.S. firms constitute at least three-quarters of the American economy. In Canada, the picture is even more extreme. The revenues in 2006 of the 50 largest corporations in Canada accounted for about 80 percent of the country's gross domestic product. Most of the giant corporations in the U.S. or even in the Canadian economy have annual revenues greater than provincial or state governments do and which exceed the GDP of the majority of the countries in the world today. Increasingly multinational in character, these giant corporations do business around the globe, disavowing allegiance to any particular nation. In fact, more than a quarter of the world's economic activity comes from the two hundred largest corporations.[13] Since the 1980s, wave after wave of corporate takeovers and mergers have further accelerated the trend toward oligopoly and ever-greater economic concentration. Since the mid-1990s merger and acquisition activity in the United States has grown sevenfold to around US$1.5 trillion annually.[14] In Canada, during 2006 alone, there were announcements regarding merger and acquisition activities totalling about $265 billion, while the first quarter of 2007 has already seen announcements totalling about $70 billion.[15]

It is admittedly true that governments have used statutory measures (for example, the *Competition Act* in Canada, the *Sherman Antitrust Act* and the *Clayton Act* in the U.S., the *Competition Law* in the European Union) to foster competition and break up monopolies. For example, in 1998 the Canada Competition Bureau and the then federal Minister of Finance foiled the planned merger between the Royal Bank of Canada and the Bank of

Montreal. The *Sherman Act* was used in the past to break up such U.S. corporate behemoths as Standard Oil Company (in 1914) and AT&T (in 1982). More recently, the U.S. government went after Microsoft for "exclusionary and predatory" businesses practices, while the European Union fined the same corporation US$613 million for violating its *Competition Law*. On the whole, however, such actions by governments have proved ineffectual in halting the concentration of economic power. Because of their sway over the market and their political clout, the gigantic corporations that we know today have so altered the face of capitalism that Adam Smith would have trouble recognizing it. As a result, in terms of competition our present-day economic system differs significantly from the textbook model of capitalism. One expert puts it this way:

> In surveying the American business system it is obvious that competition still exists; however, it is not a perfect competition. Often it is not price competition at all. With the possible exception of some farm markets where there are still large numbers of producers of similar and undifferentiated products (wheat, for instance), virtually every producer of goods and services has some control over price. The degree of control varies from industry to industry and between firms within an industry. Nevertheless, it does exist and it amounts to an important modification in our model of a free-enterprise economy.[16]

Corporate Welfare Programs Protect Businesses

"Corporate welfare" refers to government programs that provide unique benefits or advantages to private business corporations or industries. Such programs may involve direct grants, research and other services, subsidized loans, and financial guarantees. Included by some in "corporate welfare" are also protective tariffs or quotas on imported goods and tax breaks to specific industries. In Canada, all levels of governments (federal, provincial, territorial and municipal) may and do have programs of "assistance" to businesses and industries. Here are a few examples. From 1999 to 2002, Canadian taxpayers supported Canadian farmers—in the form of either direct farm subsidies or of paying artificially inflated prices—to the tune of about $25 billion. Between 1982 and 2005, the federal Industry Canada alone authorized $18.4 billion in grants and loans to various companies and organizations. According to some estimates, certain categories of subsidies to the forest industry by the provincial government of British Colombia translate to between $3 and $6 billion a year. In 2004, the governments of Canada and the province of Ontario contributed $164 million in subsidies to the expansion and renovation of the Ford auto plant in Oakville, Ontario.

Corporate welfare programs are even more active and pervasive in the United States, the very bastion of capitalism. In 2002 U.S. President Bush slapped tariffs ranging from 8 percent to 30 percent on imported steel, continuing a thirty-year tradition of cosseting the steel industry with various subsidies and protections that have cost the U.S. a small fortune. These tariffs were held to be necessary because of a surge of imported steel, even though foreign steel imports had declined 27.5 percent in the preceding four years.[17] Unfortunately, what's good for one industry can be bad for the rest of the country. Businesses that use steel, for example, employ roughly forty times more people than do steel producers. According to the U.S. Institute for International Economics, until the cancellation of the tariffs, between 45,000 and 75,000 jobs were lost because higher steel prices made U.S. steel-using industries less competitive.[18] Similarly, U.S. quotas on sugar imports have, in recent years, resulted in the domestic price of sugar being three-and-a-half times the world market price. As a result, to survive, American candy makers have been forced to move production to countries where sugar is cheaper, at the cost of 7,500 to 10,000 jobs.[19]

From 1995 to 2002, U.S. taxpayers spent more than $114 billion on subsidies to farmers. In 2002 the U.S. Congress increased agricultural subsidies to an estimated $180 to $190 billion over the next ten years. Indeed, as this section is being written, Canada is lodging a complaint with the World Trade Organization alleging that the United States is exceeding legitimate levels of farm subsidies.[20] In a single year, U.S. spending on farm subsidies exceeds the gross domestic product of more than seventy nations.[21] Most of that money goes to the largest and wealthiest farmers, with 10 percent of the recipients receiving 65 percent of the loot.[22] Subsidies for farmers and tariffs on steel and sugar are just the most blatant examples of the way corporate welfare programs assist business and protect it from competition. The list goes on.[23] Every year the U.S. federal government doles out an estimated $85 billion to private business in direct subsidy programs. Some estimates put the total U.S. federal spending on corporate welfare at over $167 billion a year, which is far more than combined U.S. state and federal spending on social welfare programs for the poor.[24]

Competition Is Not a Good Because the profit motive governs capitalism, it should not be surprising that even those companies that preach the doctrine of free competition are willing to shelve it when collusion with other firms, or government tariffs and subsidies, make higher profits possible. How else to explain the fact that the United States forbids foreign companies from owning airlines in America and prevents foreign airlines from picking up passengers at more than one American city? In these ways, capitalism fails to live up to its own ideal. This was something that worried Adam Smith, who once wrote, "People of the same trade seldom meet together, even for merriment or diversion, but the conversation ends in a conspiracy against the public, or in some contrivance to raise prices."[25]

Unlike Adam Smith, however, some critics of capitalism repudiate competition as an ideal, arguing that it is neither beneficial in general nor desirable in itself. They point to empirical studies establishing that in business there is frequently a negative correlation between performance and individual competitiveness.[26] In other words, it is often cooperation, rather than competitiveness, that best enhances both individual and group achievement. According to Alfie Kohn, the reason is simple: "Trying to do well and trying to beat others are two different things."[27] Competition is an extrinsic motivator; not only does it not produce the kind of results that flow from enjoying the activity itself, but also the use of extrinsic motivators can undermine intrinsic motivation and thus adversely affect performance in the long run. The unpleasantness of competition can also diminish people's performance.

The critics also contend that competition often precludes the more efficient use of resources that cooperation allows. When people work together, coordination of effort and an efficient division of labour are possible. By contrast, competition can inhibit economic coordination, cause needless duplication of services, retard the exchange of information, foster copious litigation, and lead to socially detrimental or counterproductive results such as business failures, mediocre products, unsafe working conditions, and environmental neglect. When presented with examples of the beneficial results of competition, the critics argue that on closer inspection the supposed advantages turn out to be shortlived, illusory, or isolated instances.

Exploitation and Alienation

Marx argued that as the means of production become concentrated in the hands of the few, the balance of power between capitalists (bourgeoisie) and labourers (proletariat) tips further in favour of the bourgeoisie. Because workers have nothing to sell but their labour, said Marx, the bourgeoisie is able to exploit them by paying them less than the true value created by their labour. In fact, Marx thought, it is only through such an exploitative arrangement that capitalists make a profit and increase their capital. And the more capital they accumulate, the more they can exploit workers. Marx predicted that eventually workers would revolt. Unwilling to be exploited further, they would rise and overthrow their oppressors and set up an economic system that would truly benefit all.

The development of capitalist systems since Marx's time belies his forecast. Legal, political, and economic changes have tempered many of the greedy, exploitative dispositions of early capitalism. The twentieth century witnessed legislation curbing egregious worker abuse, guaranteeing a minimum wage, and ensuring a safer and more healthful work environment. The emergence of labour unions and their subsequent victories significantly enlarged the worker's share of the economic pie. Indeed, many of the specific measures proposed by Marx and his collaborator Friedrich Engels in the Communist Manifesto (1848) have been implemented in capitalist countries: a program of graduated income tax, free education for all

children in public schools, investiture of significant economic control in the state, and so on.

Still, many would say that although democratic institutions may have curbed the excesses of capitalism, they could do nothing to prevent the alienation of workers that results from having to do unfulfilling work. Again, because of the unequal positions of capitalist and worker, labourers must work for someone else—they must do work imposed on them as a means of satisfying the needs of others. As a result, they must eventually feel exploited and debased. And this is true, critics of capitalism claim, not just of manual labourers but also of white-collar workers, many of who identify with the cubicle dwellers of the cartoon strip Dilbert.

But what about workers who are paid handsomely for their efforts? They, too, said Marx, remain alienated, for their work ultimately proves meaningless to them, since someone else enjoys the fruits of their labour. The following selection from Marx's "Economic and Philosophic Manuscripts" (1844) summarizes his notion of alienation as the separation of individuals from the objects they create, which in turn results in one's separation from other people, from oneself, and ultimately from one's human nature:

> The worker is related to the *product of his labor* as to an *alien* object. For it is clear . . . that the more the worker expends himself in work the more powerful becomes the world of objects which he creates in face of himself, the poorer he becomes in his inner life, and the less he belongs to himself . . . . The worker puts his life into the object, and his life then belongs no longer to himself but to the object . . . . What is embodied in the product of his labor is no longer his own. The greater this product is, therefore, the more he is diminished. The *alienation* of the worker in his product means not only that his labor becomes an object, assumes an *external* existence, but that it exists independently, *outside himself*, and alien to him, and that it stands opposed to him as an autonomous power . . . .
>
> What constitutes the alienation of labor? First, that the work is *external* to the worker, that it is not part of his nature; and that, consequently, he does not fulfill himself in his work but denies himself . . . . His work is not voluntary but imposed, *forced labor*. It is not the satisfaction of a need, but only a *means* for satisfying other needs. Its alien character is clearly shown by the fact that as soon as there is no physical or other compulsion it is avoided like the plague. External labor, labor in which man alienates himself, is a labor of self-sacrifice . . . . Finally, the external character of work for the worker is shown by the fact that it is not his own work but work for someone else, that in work he does not belong to himself but to another person . . . .
>
> We have now considered the act of alienation of practical human activity, labor, from two aspects: (1) the relationship of the worker to the *product of labor* as an alien object which dominates him . . . [and] (2) the

relationship of labor to the *act of production* within *labor*. This is the relationship of the worker to his own activity as something alien and not belonging to him . . . . This is *self-alienation* as against the above-mentioned alienation of the *thing*.[28]

In Marx's view, when workers are alienated they cannot be truly free. They may have the political and social freedoms of speech, religion, and governance, but even with these rights, individuals still are not fully free. Freedom from government interference and persecution does not necessarily guarantee freedom from economic exploitation and alienation, and it is for this kind of freedom that Marx and Engels felt such passion.

Some might say that one need not wade through Marxist philosophy to get a feel for what Marx and others mean by worker alienation. Just talk to workers themselves, as writer Studs Terkel did. In different ways the hundreds of workers from diverse occupations whom Terkel interviewed speak of the same thing: dehumanization.

> Mike Fitzgerald . . . is a laborer in a steel mill. "I feel like the guys who built the pyramids. Somebody built 'em. Somebody built the Empire State Building, too. There's hard work behind it. I would like to see a building, say the Empire State, with a footwide strip from top to bottom and the name of every bricklayer on it, the name of every electrician. So when a guy walked by, he could take his son and say, 'See, that's me over there on the 45th floor. I put that steel beam in.' . . . Everybody should have something to point to."
>
> Sharon Atkins is 24 years old. She's been to college and acidly observes, "The first myth that blew up in my face is that a college education will get you a worthwhile job." For the last two years she's been a receptionist at an advertising agency. "I didn't look at myself as 'just a dumb broad' at the front desk, who took phone calls and messages. I thought I was something else. The office taught me differently."
>
> . . . Harry Stallings, 27, is a spot welder on the assembly line at an auto plant. "They'll give better care to that machine than they will to you. If it breaks down, there's somebody out there to fix it right away. If I break down, I'm just pushed over to the other side till another man takes my place. The only thing the company has in mind is to keep that machine running. A man would be more eager to do a better job if he were given proper respect and the time to do it."[29]

TODAY'S ECONOMIC CHALLENGES

Capitalism faces a number of important critical questions, both theoretical and operational. These criticisms are a powerful challenge, especially to capitalism in its pure laissez-faire form. But, as we have seen, today's capitalism is a long way from the laissez-faire model. Corporate behemoths able to control markets and sway governments have replaced the small-scale entrepreneurs and free-wheeling competition of an earlier day. And governments in all capitalist countries actively intervene in the economic realm; they endeavour to assist or modify the so-called invisible hand; and over the years they have reformed or supplemented capitalism with programs intended to enhance the security of the workforce and increase the welfare of their citizens.

This reality complicates the debate over capitalism. Its defenders may be advocating either the pure laissez-faire ideal or the modified state welfare capitalism that we in fact have. Likewise, those who attack the laissez-faire ideal may do so on behalf of a modified, welfarist capitalism, or they may criticize both forms of capitalism and defend some kind of socialism, in which private property and the pursuit of profit are no longer governing economic principles. We thus have a three-way debate over the respective strengths and weaknesses of laissez-faire capitalism, state welfare capitalism, and socialism.

The rest of this chapter leaves this fundamental debate behind. Instead of looking at criticisms of capitalism in general and at issues relevant to any capitalist society, it examines some of the more specific socioeconomic challenges facing Canada today. These include (1) the recent decline in Canadian manufacturing; (2) the so-called "hollowing" of corporate Canada; (3) the shortage, present and projected, of skilled labour; and (4) improving the workers' work–life balance.

The Decline of Canadian Manufacturing

"Manufacturing" refers to all large-scale (usually industrial) activity that utilizes tools and labour to transform raw materials into finished products for consumption. The manufacturing sector is normally a vitally important element in modern advanced economies. For capitalists have traditionally made money by producing goods on a large scale. The manufacturing sector has certainly been the backbone of the U.S. economy and a very important, though by no means primary, element of the Canadian economy. As of 2006, it employed 12.6 percent of Canada's workforce, while it accounted for 15.7 percent of the gross domestic product. According to the Canadian Manufacturing Coalition, "Every dollar in value generated in manufacturing adds an estimated $3.05 in total economic activity."[30] However, since 2002, despite the overall strong economy, our manufacturing sector has been experiencing what some experts regard as a crisis. Perhaps the most dramatic symptom of the "crisis" is to be seen in the workforce front. Between November 2002 and February 2007 the sector has lost 247,000 jobs, almost all of them in Ontario and Quebec, the main locations of Canadian manufacturing.

The reasons for the decline in the fortunes of the manufacturing sector are many and various, including escalating energy costs, a high Canadian dollar, the importation of much cheaper manufactured goods from low-wage Asian countries, not to mention the ripple effect of the Free Trade Agreement (1988, between Canada and the U.S.) and its sequel, the North American Free Trade Agreement (1994, among Canada, the U.S., and Mexico).[31] It is true that the jobs lost in manufacturing have been made up by new jobs created in other areas of the economy. However, the overwhelming majority of the new jobs are of much lower remunerative quality than jobs in the manufacturing sector. The February 2007 report by the CIBC World Markets on its Canadian Employment Quality Index noted that the Index has fallen to its lowest level since the early 1990s partly due to the fact that most of the recently created jobs are in self-employment and in "low-paying sectors such as personal services, repair and maintenance, retailing and textiles."[32]

The "Hollowing" of Corporate Canada

The metaphor of "hollowing out" may refer to different phenomena within the business world or within different countries. In the United States, for example, the term is most frequently used to refer to the transformation of companies in the manufacturing sector from their traditional structure (in which a single company performs all aspects of the production-distribution process) to companies that lack their own production base (instead they may either "relocate" or "outsource" their production base, in part or in whole, offshore). In Canada the term is mainly used to refer to the foreign control of Canadian business and corporations, an issue that Canadians have been debating intermittently for generations. In the 1960s and 1970s, concerns over issues of national policy and sovereignty led to the introduction in 1973 of FIRA (the Foreign Investment Review Agency, by the Liberal federal government of Pierre Trudeau), which was supposed to determine whether foreign takeovers of Canadian companies would promote the national interest. In 1985 FIRA was replaced by Investment Canada (brought in by the Progressive Conservative federal government of Brian Mulroney), which was supposed to be more receptive of foreign investment than FIRA (which was perceived by its critics as obstructionist and slow-moving). Since that time, in the context of the North American free-trade agreements and under the growing impact of globalization, concerns over foreign control of Canadian companies had subsided and tended to dwell mainly on issues of economic growth, competitive advantage, job creation, and consumer benefit or choice. However, the recent and current[33] spate of acquisitions of Canadian companies by foreign interests has not only rekindled the debate but brought back concerns over "national policy" and "national pride."[34]

Inco Ltd., Falconbridge Ltd., Dofasco Ltd., Stelco Ltd., The Hudson's Bay Co., Sleeman Breweries, and Fairmont Hotels & Resorts Inc. make up a small, and readily recognizable, sample of Canadian companies taken over by foreign (and not exclusively American) interests over the last few years. Some may point out that over the past twenty years or

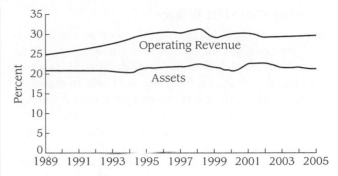

Figure 4.1 Share of Assets and Operating Revenue Under Foreign Control, 1989–2005, All Industries[35]

so the level of foreign control of Canadian companies has remained fairly constant (see Figure 4.1). True, but what may be of concern to Canadians is the fact that in certain sectors of the economy (manufacturing, oil and gas, mining), foreign, and particularly American, control of Canadian companies amounts to nearly 50 percent.

Shortage of Skilled Labor

Canada is among the top three nations worldwide which are currently experiencing serious shortages in skilled labour, especially in health care, construction, and education.[36] The percentage of companies reporting a shortage of both skilled and unskilled labour as an "impediment to business" doubled over the last few years. The reasons for the current shortage are multiple: steadily increasing economic growth (especially in Western Canada), an aging workforce with a shrinking 15–64 years-of-age cohort (especially in Atlantic Canada), difficulties in the accreditation of foreign-trained labour, etc. Statistics Canada reports large-scale changes, between 2001 and 2006, in the age distribution of Canada's population that show a rapidly aging population, a phenomenon caused largely by our low birth rates and an increasing life expectancy. If present trends continue, it is inevitable that our country will experience in the not-too-distant future what some experts call "catastrophic" shortages not only of skilled but also of unskilled labour. For example, if present trends continue, it is estimated that by 2017 there will be more "seniors" (over the age of 65) than "juniors" (under the age of 15) in Canada.[37] Admittedly, labour shortages turn not merely on the demographic features in the workforce or the population of a country but also on the growth or decline of economic activity, the gains or losses in labour or management efficiency, the willingness or unwillingness to employ technological innovation (for example, automation), governmental rules and policies regarding education and training regimes, immigration, the accreditation of foreign-trained labour, and a host of other areas of civic and personal life. But precisely because the issue is so complex and multifaceted—with some factors in possible solutions taking almost a whole generation to show their effect—it is imperative that business, labour, and governments undertake now to redouble their efforts to understand and offer solutions to the problem.

Improving Work–Life Balance

Some commentators believe that the socioeconomic problems facing us today include also the challenge of coming to grips with people's changing attitudes toward government, social institutions, business, and work. In regards to work, there's little question that over recent decades, people's ideas about its value and the role it should play in their lives have been evolving. Fewer and fewer people nowadays believe entirely in the so-called "Protestant" or "Puritan" work ethic, which values work for its own sake and regards hard work as the most important ingredient in the quest to fulfill a person's wishes and dreams in life.[38] Although it is extremely hard to pin down the shifting attitudes of workers toward work today, basically they seem willing to work hard on a job they find interesting and rewarding as long as they have the freedom to influence the nature of their jobs and pursue their own lifestyles. They have a growing expectation that work should provide self-respect, nonmaterial rewards, and substantial opportunities for personal growth. And they have a growing willingness to demand individual rights, justice, and equality on the job.[39]

While the workforce's values are changing to a perspective which places one's work within the broader context of one's own idiosyncratic aspirations and familial relations and duties, the pressures in the workplace and at home have been increasing: "Throughout the nineties, technological change and the need to be competitive increased the pressures on organizations and employees alike. Time in employment increased for many, as did the use of non-standard types of employment. Non-work demands also increased over the decade as family structures continued to change and the percentage of working Canadians with childcare, eldercare or both (the sandwich generation) continued to rise."[40]

Inevitably workers begin to feel the squeeze of the conflicting and equipotent demands on them and, as it is natural, problems arise. More and more workers report stress and fatigue. Absenteeism and time off for illness are on the rise. It is not uncommon for operative workers to balk at doing the monotonous tasks their ancestors once accepted, albeit grudgingly. Loyalty to employers seems to be on the decline. Turnover rates in many industries are enough to make discontinuity an expensive problem. Organizational plans, schedules, and demands no longer carry the authoritative clout they once did; workers today often subordinate them to personal needs. Employee sabotage and violence, once unheard of, occur frequently enough today to worry management. Leaving aside the high cost in human mental and physical suffering, work–life imbalance has a staggering economic cost. Consider the costs, according to some estimates, attributable to certain consequences of work–life imbalance: absenteeism, $6 to $10 billion; visits to family physician, $6 billion; overnight stays at hospital, $17 billion.[41]

If Canada is to improve productive capacity and be competitive, business, labour, and all levels of government must all seriously confront the many problems arising out of our changing attitudes to work–life balance and our organizational and management practices. As Paul Bernstein argues, it is counterproductive to compare today's worker with an idealized worker of yesteryear. Rather, we must acknowledge that we have a new work ethic, which is, in Bernstein's words,

> part and parcel of the individual desire for meaningful and challenging labor in which some autonomy is an integral feature. An increasingly professionalized work force will not accept a golden embrace unless it is accompanied by fulfilling jobs that have been designed for a labor force that sees work in relation to family, friends, leisure and self-development. Work, for most of us, continues as an important part of our lives, but only in relation to our total experience.[42]

SUMMARY

1. Capitalism is an economic system in which the major portion of production and distribution is in private hands, operating under a profit or market system. Socialism is an economic system characterized by public ownership of property and a planned economy.

2. Capitalism has gone through several stages: mercantile, industrial, financial, and state welfare.

3. Four key features of capitalism are the existence of companies, profit motive, competition, and private property.

4. One basic defence of capitalism rests on a supposed natural moral right to property. Utilitarians deny the existence of such rights; other critics doubt that this right entitles one to have a system of property rules and regulations identical to the one we now have Canada and the United States.

5. Utilitarian defence of capitalism is associated with the classical economic arguments of Adam Smith. Smith believed that human beings are acquisitive and that they have a natural propensity for trading, and he insisted that when people are left free to pursue their own economic interests, they will, without intending it, produce the greatest good for all.

6. Critics question the basic assumptions of capitalism (theoretical challenges) and whether it has delivered on its promises (operational challenges). Specifically, they raise the following issues: Can capitalism eliminate poverty and reduce inequality? Are humans basically economic creatures? Does capitalism breed oligopolies that thwart competition? Is competition valuable? Does capitalism exploit and alienate?

7. As the twenty-first century begins, our capitalist socioeconomic system faces a number of challenges. These include the decline of the manufacturing sector, the increasing takeover of Canadian companies by foreign interests and the current and anticipated shortage of especially skilled workforce. In addition, we must come to grips with our society's changing attitudes toward work.

CASE 4.1

Licensing and Laissez Faire

The United States is a capitalist country, and their system of medical care is, to a significant extent, organized for profit. True, many hospitals are nonprofit, but the same cannot be said of doctors, who, judged as a whole, form an extremely affluent and privileged occupational group.

Sometimes physicians themselves seem a little uncomfortable about the business aspect of their professional lives or worry that outsiders will misinterpret their attention to economic matters. For example, the professional journal *Medical Economics*, which discusses such pocketbook issues as malpractice insurance, taxes, fees, and money management (a recent cover story was titled "Are You Overpaying Your Staff?"), works hard at not being available to the general public. When a subscriber left his copy on a commercial airliner, another reader found it and sent the mailing label to the magazine; the magazine's editor sent a cautionary note to the subscriber. The editor advises readers to "do your part by restricting access to your personal copies of the magazine. Don't put them in the waiting room, don't leave them lying about in the examination rooms, and don't abandon them in public places."[43]

Medical Economics probably suspects that even in our capitalist society many people, including probably most doctors, would not like to think of physicians simply as medical entrepreneurs who are in it for the money. And, indeed, many people in the U.S. and many more in other countries criticize the American medical system for being profit-oriented. They think medical care should be based on need, and that ability to pay should not affect the quality of medical treatment one receives. Interestingly, though, some people criticize medical practice in the United States as being insufficiently market-oriented; University of Chicago professor of economics Milton Friedman is one of them.

Friedman has been a longstanding critic of occupational licensure in all fields. His reasoning is straightforward. Licensure—the requirement that one obtain a licence from a recognized authority in order to engage in an occupation—restricts entry into the field. Licensure thus permits the occupational or professional group to enjoy a monopoly in the provision of services. In Friedman's view, this contravenes the principles of a free market to the disadvantage of us all.

Friedman has no objection to certification; that is, to public or private agencies certifying that an individual has certain skills. But he rejects the policy of preventing people who do not have such a certificate from practising the occupation of their choice. Such a policy restricts freedom and keeps the price of the services in question artificially high. When one reads the long lists of occupations for which some states require a licence—librarians, tree surgeons, pest controllers, well diggers, barbers, carpet installers, movie projectionists, florists, upholsterers, makeup artists, even potato growers, among many others[44]—Friedman's case gains plausibility. But Friedman pushes his argument to include all occupations and professions.

Does this mean we should let incompetent physicians practise? Friedman's answer is yes.[45] In his view the American Medical Association (AMA) is simply a trade union, though probably the strongest one in the United States. It keeps the wages of its members high by restricting the number of those who can practise medicine.

The AMA does this not just through licensure but also, even more effectively, through controlling the number of medical schools and the number of students admitted to them. Today, for instance, over 45,000 applicants vie every year for roughly 16,000 vacancies in U.S. medical schools.[46] The medical profession, Friedman charges, limits entry into the field both by turning down applicants to medical school and by making standards for admission and licensure so difficult as to discourage many young people from ever trying to gain admission.

Viewed as a trade union, the AMA has been singularly effective. As recently as the 1920s, physicians were far down the list of professionals in terms of income; the average doctor made less than the average accountant. American physicians constitute the profession that arguably has the highest status and the best pay in their country. The median income for primary-care physicians is $157,000. For general surgeons it is $265,000. And in certain specialties, it is a great deal higher. Cardiologists, pain specialists, radiologists, hand surgeons, and others often earn over half a million dollars a year.[47] American doctors earn far more than their foreign counterparts do, even in countries where average wages are similar to those in the United States. Still, the medical establishment remains worried. It believes that there are too many doctors in the United States, and that "this surplus breeds inefficiency and drives up costs."[48]

The economic logic behind this proposition is murky. An increase in the supply of barbers, plumbers, or taxi drivers does not drive up the cost of getting a haircut, having your pipes fixed, or taking a cab. Why should it be different with doctors? Critics of the medical profession believe that its real worry is the prospect of stabilizing or even declining incomes. In any case, the doctors have written two prescriptions.

The first is to reduce the number of medical students by closing down some medical schools; the second is to make it more difficult for foreign doctors to practise in the U.S. Although the medical establishment has often expressed concern about the quality of foreign medical training, today the worry is strictly a matter of quantity. "We've got to stop the pipeline of foreign medical graduates," says Dr. Ed O'Neil of the Center for the Health Professions at the University of California, San Francisco. "They are a big chunk of physician oversupply . . . . We're just trying to be rational."[49] As for homegrown doctors, the U.S. Congress is following medical advice. To stem the supposed glut, it decided to pay hospitals around the country hundreds of millions of dollars to decrease the number of physicians they train. It turns out, however, that the United States has fewer doctors per 1,000 than do Germany, Sweden, France, and many other developed countries.[50] In fact, the United States is now predicted to have a shortage of 200,000 physicians by 2020.[51]

Medical licensure restricts the freedom of people to practise medicine and prevents the public from buying the medical care it wants. Nonetheless, most people would probably defend the principle of licensure on the grounds that it raises the standards of competence and the quality of care. Friedman contests this. By reducing the amount of care available, he contends, licensure also reduces the average quality of care people receive. (By analogy, suppose that automobile manufacturers were forbidden to sell any car that did not have the quality of a Mercedes Benz. As a result, people who owned cars would have cars of higher average quality than they do now. But because fewer people could afford cars and more of them would, therefore, have to walk or ride bicycles, such a regulation would not raise the quality of transportation enjoyed by the average person.) Friedman charges, furthermore, that the monopoly created by the licensing of physicians has reduced the incentive for research, development, and experimentation, both in medicine and in the organization and provision of services.

Since Friedman initially presented his argument forty years ago, some of the alternatives to traditional practice that he proposed have come to pass; prepaid services have emerged, and group and clinic-based practices are on the increase. But what about his main contention that instead of licensure we should allow the marketplace to sort out the competent from the incompetent providers of medical services?

Friedman's critics contend that even if the licensing of professionals "involves violating a moral rule" against restricting individuals' "freedom of opportunity," it is still immoral to allow an unqualified person to engage in potentially harmful activities without having subjected the person to adequate tests of competence.[52] Despite the appeal of Friedman's arguments on behalf of free choice, the danger still remains, they say, that people will be victimized by the incompetent.

Consider, for example, the quack remedies and treatments peddled to AIDS patients all over the world. Bottles of processed pond scum and concoctions of herbs, injections of hydrogen peroxide or of cells from the glands of unborn calves, the eating of bee pollen and garlic, $800 pills containing substances from mice inoculated with the AIDS virus, and even whacking the thymus gland of patients to stimulate the body's immune system—all these are among the treatments that have been offered to desperate people by the unscrupulous and eccentric. Deregulation of the medical field seems most unlikely to diminish such exploitation.

Discussion Questions

1. What explains the fact that licences are required for so many occupations? What do you see as the pros and cons of occupational licensure in general? Does it have benefits that Friedman has overlooked?

2. Do you believe that licensure in medicine or any other field is desirable? In which fields and under what circumstances? What standards would you use to determine where licensure is needed?

3. Is occupational licensure consistent with the basic principles and values of capitalism? Is it a violation of the free-market ideal? How would you respond to the argument that licensure illegitimately restricts individual freedom to pursue a career or a trade?

4. Does licensure make the market work more or less effectively? Would you agree that as long as consumers are provided accurate information, then they should be permitted to make their own choices with regard to the services and products they purchase—even when it comes to medical care? Or is licensing necessary to protect them from making incorrect choices?

5. Like Friedman, some may view the AMA or the CMA as a trade union, and they believe that the high incomes of doctors are due more to artificial restrictions on the free market than to the inherent value of their services. Is this an accurate or fair picture of the medical profession?

6. Is licensing an all-or-nothing issue, or is it possible that although there are certain services that we should permit only licensed practitioners to perform, there are other services now monopolized by the same practitioners that could be performed less expensively but equally competently by paraprofessionals or laypersons?

Hucksters in the Classroom

Increased student loads, myriad professional obligations, and shrinking school budgets have sent many public school teachers scurrying for teaching materials to facilitate their teaching.

They don't have to look far. Into the breach has stepped business, which is ready, willing, and able to provide print and audiovisual materials for classroom use.[53] These industry-supplied teaching aids are advertised in educational journals, distributed directly to schools, and showcased at educational conventions. Clearasil, for example, distributes a teaching aid and colour poster called "A Day in the Life of Your Skin." Its message is hard to miss: Clearasil is the way to clear up your pimples. Domino's Pizza supplies a handout that is supposed to help kids learn to count by tabulating the number of pepperoni wheels on one of the company's pizzas. Chef Boyardee sponsors a study program on sharks based on its "fun pasta," which is shaped like sharks and pictured everywhere on its educational materials.

The list goes on. General Mills supplies educational pamphlets on Earth's "great geothermic 'gushers'" along with the company's "Gushers" snack (a candy filled with liquid). The pamphlets recommend that teachers pass the "Gushers" around and then ask the students as they bite the candy, "How does this process differ from that which produces erupting geothermic phenomena?" In an elementary school in Texas, teachers use a reading program called "Read-A-Logo." Put out by Teacher Support Software, it encourages students to use familiar corporate names such as McDonald's, Hi-C, Coca-Cola, or Cap'n Crunch to create elementary sentences, such as, "I had a hamburger and a Pepsi at McDonald's." In other grade schools, children learn from Exxon's Energy Cube curriculum that fossil fuels pose few environmental problems and that alternative energy is costly and unattainable. Similarly, materials from the American coal foundation teach them that the "earth could benefit rather than be harmed from increased carbon dioxide." Courtesy of literature from the Pacific Lumber Company, students in California learn about forests; they also get Pacific Lumber's defence of its forest-clearing activities: "The Great American Forest . . . is renewable forever." At Pembroke Lakes elementary school in Broward County, Florida, ten-year-olds learned how to design a McDonald's restaurant, and how to apply and interview for a job at McDonald's, thanks to a seven-week company-sponsored class intended to teach them about the real world of work.

"It's a corporate takeover of our schools," says Nelson Canton of the National Education Association in the U.S. "It has nothing to do with education and everything to do with corporations making profits and hooking kids early on their products." "I call it the phantom curriculum," adds Arnold Fege of the National PTA, "because the teachers are often unaware that there's subtle product placement." There's nothing subtle, however, about the product placement in

Mathematics Applications and Connections, a textbook used by many sixth graders in the U.S. It begins its discussion of the coordinate system with an advertisement for Walt Disney: "Have you ever wanted to be the star of a movie? If you visit Walt Disney–MGM Studios Theme Park, you could become one." Other math books are equally blatant. They use brand-name products like M&Ms, Nike shoes, and Kellogg's Cocoa Frosted Flakes as examples when discussing surface area, fractions, decimals, and other concepts.

All this is fine with Lifetime Learning Systems, a marketing firm in the U.S. that specializes in pitching to students the products of its corporate customers. "[Students] are ready to spend and we reach them," the company brags, touting its "custom-made learning materials created with your [company's] specific marketing objectives in mind." Today's 43 million schoolchildren in the U.S. have tremendous buying power. Elementary schoolchildren spend $15 billion a year and influence another $160 billion in spending by parents. Teenagers spend $57 billion of their own money and $36 billion of their families' money. It's not surprising, then, that many corporations clearly see education marketing as a cost-effective way to build brand loyalty.

Corporate America's most dramatic venture in the classroom, however, began in 1990, when Whittle Communications started beaming into classrooms around the country its controversial Channel One, a television newscast for middle and high school students. The broadcasts are twelve minutes long—ten minutes of news digest with slick graphics and two minutes of commercials for Levi's jeans, Gillette razor blades, Head & Shoulders shampoo, Snickers candy bars, and other familiar products. Although a handful of states have banned Channel One, 40 percent of American teens see it every school day.

Primedia, which now owns Channel One, provides cash-hungry schools with thousands of dollars worth of electronic gadgetry, including TV monitors, satellite dishes, and videorecorders, if the schools agree to show the broadcasts. In return, the schools are contractually obliged to broadcast the program in its entirety to all students at a single time on 90 to 95 percent of the days that school is in session. The show cannot be interrupted, and teachers do not have the right to turn it off.

For their part, students seem to like Channel One's fast-paced MTV-like newscasts. "It was very interesting and it appeals to our age group," says student Angelique Williams. "One thing I really like was the reporters were our own age. They kept our attention." But educators wonder how much students really learn. A University of Michigan study found that students who watched Channel One scored only 3.3 percent better on a 30-question test of current events than did students in schools without Channel One. Although researchers called this gain so small as to be educationally unimportant, they noted that all the Channel One students remembered the commercials. That, of course, is good news for Primedia, which charges advertisers $157,000 for a 30-second spot. That price sounds high, but companies are willing to pay it because Channel One delivers a captive, narrowly targeted audience.

That captive audience is just what worries the critics. Peggy Charren of Action for Children's Television calls the project a "great big, gorgeous Trojan horse. . . . You're selling the children to the advertisers. You might as well auction off the rest of the school day to the highest bidders." On the other hand, Principal Rex Stooksbury of Central High School in Knoxville, which receives Channel One, takes a different view. "This is something we see as very, very positive for the school," he says. And as student Danny Diaz adds, "We're always watching commercials" anyway.

Discussion Questions

1. What explains industry's thrust into education? Is it consistent with the basic features of capitalism?

2. Have you had any personal experience with industry-sponsored educational materials? What moral issues, if any, are involved in the affiliation between education and commercial interests? Does commercial intrusion into schools change the nature of education? What values and beliefs does it instill in children?

3. Do you think students have a "moral right" to an education free of commercial indoctrination? If you were a parent of school-age children, would you be concerned about their exposure to commercials and corporate propaganda?

4. If you were a member of a school board contemplating the use of either industry-sponsored materials or Channel One, what would you recommend?

5. Do you think industry in general and Channel One in particular are intentionally using teachers and students as a means to profit? Or do they have a genuine concern for the education process? On the other hand, if teachers and students benefit from these educational materials or from viewing Channel One, is there any ground for concern?

CASE 4.3

Immigrant Workers in Canada[54]

(A) IMMIGRANT UNEMPLOYMENT RATES REMAIN HIGH

It can be hard for newcomers to get a foot in the door with Canadian employers but it becomes easier with time, a new report shows. Immigrants are more highly educated on average than their Canadian-born counterparts but their unemployment rates are significantly higher, according to Statistics Canada. However, that employment gap narrows and ultimately disappears after more years in the country.

Last year, almost 12% of immigrants who had been in Canada five years or less were unemployed—more than double the 5% jobless rate of native-born Canadians. After five to 10 years here, just over 7% of immigrants didn't have jobs. Eventually, "established" immigrants with over a decade in the country level off at the same unemployment rates as Canadian-born workers. "It is difficult for most new immigrants to break into the workforce right away, especially in a professional field," says Laurie Sing, program manager in career services with the Immigrant Services Society of B.C. "The foreign credentials and lack of work experience are still major barriers." Language skills also pose a challenge, she says, because even foreigners who've taken advanced lessons can have a hard time with the subtleties and cultural references that help them fit in at a potential workplace.

Employment challenges persist for immigrants despite the fact that they tend to have more education than Canadian-born workers, Statistics Canada numbers show. While 36 per cent of immigrants aged 25 to 54 have at least a bachelor's degree, just 22 per cent of Canadian-born do. Within the immigrant population, women—especially those under 24—have a harder time finding jobs than men, regardless of how long they've been in the country.

However, Alberta's hot job market means that in that province, even brand-new immigrants enjoy a six per cent unemployment rate—the lowest of any region of the country. That's still double the unemployment rate for Canadian-born Albertans, but half the national average for newcomers. On the other hand, immigrants in Quebec have the highest unemployment rates in the country, with 18 per cent of very recent arrivals unable to find a job. The data comes from the Labour Force Survey, and this report focused on the "core working age group" of 25 to 54 years.

"Canada needs to be known as a place where newcomers can succeed or it risks losing the best and brightest to an increasingly competitive global labour market," says Elizabeth McIsaac, executive director of Toronto Region Immigrant Employment Council. "When we select immigrants and give them the visas to come as permanent residents to Canada, there is an implied promise that there is opportunity," she says.

Enrique Maglanque is one of the success stories. The 45-year-old emigrated from the Philippines in May with his wife, Erlinda, and their children Louise, 13, Patricia, 11, and nine-year-old Andrew. A mechanical engineer by training, Maglanque worked on government mining and geosciences projects for 17 years before leaving Manila. He stayed with his brother in North Vancouver when he first arrived in Canada, but as soon as he was able to rent a house, he launched his job search with a 10-day workshop at the Immigrant Services Society (ISS). Maglanque reworked his résumé and sent it out to 50 employers as far away as Yukon in hopes of finding a job in his field.

He credits his years of experience and demand for his skills with the fact that he landed a job after less than two months in Canada, but Maglanque knows his experience isn't typical. "I was just lucky," he says. "Most of my friends and acquaintances had a harder time and they had to take on a survival job before they were able to later take a job which was more suitable to their training and experience."

Still, Sing at ISS has seen encouraging signs in the last six months. Her clients are getting better jobs and getting them faster, she says, and that effect isn't limited to B.C. "I think that upswing in the labour market is meaning there are more jobs open, there are better jobs open, there's less competition for those jobs than there was in the past, and that's good for new immigrants," she says.

(B) WHY A VETERAN MD WORKS AS AN ORDERLY

When patients with eye injuries come into the crowded emergency ward at Toronto East General hospital, Dr. Jorge Pena knows he could make a quick diagnosis. Once or twice, emergency-room physicians have even turned to him for advice. But Dr. Pena, who has more than 15 years experience as an ophthalmologist, is not licensed to perform cataract surgery, treat acute glaucoma or retinal detachment. Instead, he is stuck wheeling patients down hallways, working as an orderly for $16 an hour. He is one of more than 4,000 doctors in Ontario alone who are unable to use their medical expertise because Canada does not recognize their foreign credentials.

It is especially ironic for Dr. Pena, who trained at a world-renowned clinic in Bogota, Colombia, where Canadian medical residents have studied. "It is terrible, so frustrating for me. But this is the Canadian way," said Dr. Pena, 47. "I would feel so useful and happy if I could just be an ophthalmologist again." Dr. Pena fled Villavicencio, a city on the western coast of Colombia, three years ago after armed groups who have been waging a civil war in Colombia for four decades threatened his life. They said they would kidnap family members if he didn't pay kickbacks. He, his wife and two teenage children were accepted as political refugees in Toronto, where Dr. Pena, who had run a successful clinic back home, assumed he could practise medicine.

The clinic he trained at in Colombia, Instituto Barraquer de Americas, is famous for pioneering laser and cataract surgery techniques, recognized by ophthalmologists such as Harold Stein, co-owner of Toronto's Bochner Eye Institute. "He was with a very famous clinic in Bogotá run by a guy I know well. We sit on various boards and committees in the U.S. The clinic is renowned," Dr. Stein said. However, none of this mattered to the Royal College of Physicians and Surgeons. The college did not accept Dr. Pena's credentials because Colombia is not one of the 13 countries whose medical education systems have been deemed acceptable (the college has ruled the systems in 28 countries inconclusive or rejected them outright).

Dr. Pena then discovered it would take more than two years and cost about $3,000 to write the Medical Council of Canada's qualifying exams, a process which is less expensive and much faster in the United States. If he passed, he had only a 10-per-cent chance of being accepted in a residency program to retrain. (In Ontario, unlike other provinces, foreign-trained physicians cannot compete directly with Canadian medical students.)

Discouraged, Dr. Pena had to accept the reality: the family could not afford for him to re-qualify as an ophthalmologist—not that he believed he should have to. He decided to retrain as a nurse in a special one-year program at Mohawk College in Hamilton for foreign-trained doctors. He, along with 160 other international medical graduates—Chinese anesthesiologists, Iranian general practitioners and Pakistani gynecologists—studied pill dispensing and clinical nursing techniques. "I am glad to have retrained as nurse. But I still believe I should be able to use my high-tech skills and knowledge here," Dr. Pena said. He knows other foreign doctors have been forced to pick fruit or clear tables for minimum wage. Not only that, Mohawk College recently closed its doors to foreign-trained doctors, because the College of Nurses of Ontario now requires nurses to have bachelor of science degrees. Dr. Pena was one of the last to get in.

Joan Atkin, executive director of the Association of International Physicians and Surgeons of Ontario, said many international medical graduates are in a similar position as Dr. Pena—except for those lucky enough to have trained in fields in which Canada has a shortage. "For mid-career specialists, their only option is to go back to the beginning and retrain in a different specialty," she said.

Provinces are aware of the difficulty foreign doctors face and have launched initiatives to assist them. The provincial government in Quebec, which has a shortage of 1,000 doctors, recently launched a program to help foreign-trained physicians pass provincial medical exams. Michelle Courchesne, provincial health minister, noted that many foreign-trained doctors were in precarious financial situations, even collecting social assistance, which she described as "a waste of important talent." In Ontario, the government has created a separate stream for international medical graduates with 50–75 spots in specific specialties, although ophthalmology is not one. In addition, the province recently announced a program to allow international doctors in certain specialties to complete six-month qualifying rotations in hospitals, although again, ophthalmology is not one of them.

Dr. Pena recently began working as a scrub nurse at the Bochner Eye Institute. He is grateful for the job—but finds it routine and wishes he could operate on patients, instead of hand instruments to doctors: "I am not used to being on the other side of the operating table."

(C) ONTARIO PROPOSES CHANGES TO GET FOREIGN DOCTORS WORKING SOONER

The Ontario government announced Friday [June 6, 2008] that it plans to lift restrictions on foreign-trained doctors and to fast-track applications to help them start practising as soon as they enter Canada.

The move is designed to reduce the province's critical shortage of physicians. . . . But critics said the push to bring more foreign doctors to Canada won't help physicians who already live here and are stuck doing odd jobs. One medical association also criticized the changes as a flawed and potentially immoral approach. "I think we have to seriously look at the ethics," said Karl Stobbe, president of the Society of Rural Physicians of Canada. "We lure them over here and a lot of times the countries we're taking them from . . . have a bigger problem than we have and we're actually making their problem worse."

Under the proposed changes, doctors licensed in the United States and Commonwealth countries, as well as the other provinces, would be eligible to begin practising in Ontario without having to go through onerous assessments and evaluation periods. That would bring Ontario in line with other provinces, such as Alberta and British Columbia, which already have programs to tap into the talented pool of foreign doctors whose training is equivalent to Canadian requirements.

The province will also create a new "transitional licence" that would eliminate the need for foreign-trained physicians to wait years before being allowed to practise. The changes would let foreign specialists whose credentials differ substantially from Canadian requirements practise in a supervised setting. The transitional licence would last between two and five years, during which the doctors would be responsible for undergoing training to meet Canadian requirements. . . .

Mr. Smitherman [Ontario's minister of health] said it's impossible to say how many new doctors this program could generate because it focuses on streamlining the registration process for foreign-trained physicians, not adding spots for medical residents. "It's not about simply creating more residency positions," Mr. Smitherman said. "This is about transitioning those specialists into opportunities without having to go through residency, and they would be supervised by existing physicians in those environments."

Although the changes may offer some help to doctors who want to move to Canada, Conservative health critic Elizabeth Witmer criticized the government for failing to create more residency positions to help foreign-trained doctors who already live in Canada and are stuck in dead-end jobs.

Discussion Questions

1. Are there indications in article A that the higher rates of unemployment among immigrants are also due to some forms of discrimination? Explain your reasons fully.

2. What, if anything, do you consider wrong with the Medical Council of Canada's qualifying exams for foreign-trained physicians (article B)? Explain your reasons and suggest remedies for whatever aspect you consider wrong.

3. On what grounds, if any, can one justify Ontario's position that foreign-trained physicians, even after they have passed their MCC's qualifying exams, cannot compete for residency positions with Canadian-trained medical students (article B)?

4. Is the Ontario program outlined by Mr Smitherman in article C an effective and fair way to address the shortage of physicians in Ontario (and Canada)? Explain.

Notes to Chapter 4

1. For a succinct treatment of the rise of the Fugger dynasty, see Ned M. Cross, Robert C. Lamm, and Rudy H. Turk, *The Search for Personal Freedom* (Dubuque, IA: W. C. Brown, 1972), 12.

2. Ibid., 13. See also Robert B. Carson, *Business Issues Today: Alternative Perspectives* (New York: St. Martin's Press, 1982), 3–30.

3. John Micklethwait and Adrian Wooldridge, *The Company: A Short History of a Revolutionary Idea* (New York: Modern Library, 2003), xv.

4. Robert Heilbroner, *The Worldly Philosophers*, 5th ed. (New York: Simon & Schuster, 1980), 22–23.

5. Adam Smith, *The Wealth of Nations* (New York: Modern Library, 1985), 16.

6. Ibid., 223–225.

7. As quoted by G. A. Cohen, *History, Labour, and Freedom* (Oxford: Oxford University Press, 1988), 273.

8. Ibid., 265.

9. Quoted by Joseph E. Stiglitz, "A Fair Deal for the World," *New York Review of Books*, May 23, 2002, 28.

10. Robert Heilbroner, *The Economic Problem* (Englewood Cliffs, NJ: Prentice Hall, 1972), 725.

11. Ed Diener et al., "Subjective Well-Being: Three Decades of Progress," *Psychological Bulletin* 125, no. 2 (1999): 228; Richard A. Easterlin, "The Economics of Happiness," *Daedalus*, Spring 2004, 31; and Robert H. Frank, "How Not to Buy Happiness," *Daedalus*, Spring 2004, 70.

12. For illustration, see Jim Hightower, "Food Monopoly: Who's Who in the Thanksgiving Business?," *Texas Observer*, November 17, 1978; Deborah Baldwin, "The Cornflake Cartel," *Common Cause Magazine*, Summer 1993; and "The Wal-Mart of Meat," *Business Week*, September 20, 2004, 90.

13. Sarah Anderson and John Cavanagh, "The Top 200: The Rise of Corporate Global Power" (Washington, DC: Institute for Policy Studies, December 2000), www.ips-dc.org.

14. Adrian Slywotsky and Richard Wise, "Resist the Urge to Merge," *Wall Street Journal*, July 16, 2002, B2.

15. See "Canadian Mergers and Acquisition Activity—Fourth Quarter 2006," crosbieco.com.

16. Carson, *Business Issues Today*, 29.

17. David E. Sanger, "Bush Puts Tariffs of as Much as 30% on Steel Imports," *New York Times*, March 6, 2002. A1; and "Rust Never Sleeps," *Economist*, March 9, 2002, 61. President Bush cancelled the tariffs in December 2003 under pressure from the WTO and the European Union.

18. Daniel W. Drezner, "The Outsourcing Bogeyman," *Foreign Affairs* 83, no. 2 (May/June 2004): 33–34.

19. Ibid., 33; Dennis Byrne, "A Bitter Lesson About Sugar," *Chicago Tribune*, January 26, 2004, sec. 1, 11; and George F. Will, "Lethal Quotas," *San Francisco Chronicle*, February 13, 2004, A31.

20. See *The Globe and Mail* or the *Toronto Star* for June 23–24, 2007.

21. Nicolas Heidorn, "The Enduring Political Illusion of Farm Subsidies," *San Francisco Chronicle*, August 18, 2004, B9.

22. Matthew Miller, "Campaign Rhetoric," *Forbes*, September 6, 2004, 65.

23. Thomas A. Hemphill, "Confronting Corporate Welfare," *Business Horizons* 40 (November/December 1997): 5.

24. Timothy Taylor, "Corporate 'Welfare' Is Tricky," *San Jose Mercury News*, September 21, 1995, 7F.

25. Quoted in "Economic Focus: Competition Is All," *Economist*, December 6, 2003, 70.

26. Alfie Kohn, *No Contest: The Case Against Competition* (Boston: Houghton Mifflin, 1986), 46–55. This paragraph and the next are based on ch. 3, "Is Competition More Productive?"

27. Ibid., 55.

28. This extract is from *Karl Marx: Early Writings*, translated by T. B. Bottomore, 1963. Used with permission of McGraw-Hill Book Company.

29. Studs Terkel, "How I Am a Worker," in Leonard Silk, ed., *Capitalism: The Moving Target* (New York: Quadrangle, 1974), 68–69. Reprinted by permission of the *New York Times*.

30. In a letter to Prime Minister Stephen Harper dated November 6, 2006. See the coalition website.

31. See the report of the House of Commons Standing Committee on Industry, Science and Technology, "Manufacturing: Moving Forward—Rising to the Challenge," ch. 2 entitled "Canadian Manufacturing Sector, Trends and Challenges."

32. On September 13, 2007, federal Liberal Opposition Leader Stephane Dion mailed out to households a pamphlet entitled "Conservatives Ignoring Struggling Manufacturing Sector."

33. For a list of Canadian companies acquired by foreign concerns since 2002, see cbc.ca/news/background/mergers, February 2007; also thestar.com, May 13, 2007.

34. See thestar.com, June 25, 2007, September 7, 2007; see also letter of July 13, 2007 from the Canadian Labour Congress to the federal Ministers of Industry and Finance at www.canadianlabour.ca/Index.php/Letters_to_Government/1203.

35. Source: Statistics Canada. See *Corporations Returns Act—2005*, File 61-220-XWE, Chart 1.3; see also Chart 1.4 for the American share of the foreign control.

36. See Statistics Canada, *Business Conditions Survey* (in the manufacturing sector) for February 4, 2003 (statcan.ca/Daily/English/030204/d030204a.htm) and for July 27, 2007 (statcan.ca/Daily/English/070727/d070727a.htm).

37. See statcan.ca/Daily/English/070717/d070717a.htm.

38. In a U.S. survey only one in three people believes this, down from 60 percent in a 1960 survey. See A. Alvarez, "Learning from Las Vegas," *New York Review of Books*, January 11, 1996, 16.

39. See L. W. Roberts et al., *Recent Social Trends in Canada: 1960–2000* (Montreal & Kingston: McGill-Queen's University Press, 2005), ch. 7.4 on "values," 649–652 in the light of pp. 7–16; also Darrel Bricker & John Wright, *What Canadians Think*, (Doubleday Canada, 2005), 91–2; 132.

40. L. Huxbury et al, *Voices of Canadians: Seeking Work-Life Balance*, (Human Resources Canada: Ottawa, 2003) p. 1. See also L.W. Roberts et al., *Recent Social Trends in Canada*, 219; D. Bricker and J. Wright, *What Canadians Think*; www.cbc.ca/background/work, October 24, 2006; see also www.stacan.ca/Daily/English/070213/d070212b.htm for a summary of Martin Turcotte's "Time Spent with Family During a Typical Workday, 1986 to 2005."

41. See L. Huxbury, *Dealing with Work–Life Issues in the Workplace* (Kingston, ON: Queen's University Industrial Relations Centre, 2005), 13–17.

42. Paul Bernstein, "The Work Ethic That Never Was," *Wharton Magazine* 4 (Spring 1980): 19–25.

43. "Memo from the Editor," *Medical Economics*, November 7, 2004.

44. For more examples, see "Informer," *Forbes*, April 26, 2004.

45. See chapter entitled "Occupational Licensure" in Milton Friedman, *Capitalism and Freedom* (Chicago: University of Chicago Press, 1962), esp. 149.

46. "Medical Schools Are Urged to Cut Admissions by 20%," *New York Times*, November 17, 1995, C2.

47. Atul Gawarde, "Piecework," *New Yorker*, April 4, 2005, 44.

48. "Competition and Cutbacks Hurt Foreign Doctors in U.S.," *New York Times*, November 7, 1995, B15.

49. Ibid.

50. U.S. Census Bureau, *Statistical Abstract of the United States 2004–05* (Washington, DC: U.S. Government Printing Office, 2004), Table 1324.

51. Jay Greene, "Now Forecast Is for Shortage of Physicians," amednews.com, January 21, 2002.

52. B. Gert, "Licensing Professions," *Business and Professional Ethics Journal* 1 (Summer 1982): 52; and Donald Weinert, "Commentary" on it on p. 62.

53. This case study draws on "The Stepford Kids," *Business Week*, September 27, 2004, 26; "Gripes Grow over Rampant Textbook Ads," *San Francisco Chronicle*, June 26, 1999, A1; "Knowing the Score," *California Educator*, December 1998; "This Lesson Is Brought to You by…," *Business Week*, June 30, 1997; "This Lesson Is Brought to You by…," *Good Housekeeping*, February 1996; and Alex Molnar, "Learning to Ad," *New Republic*, March 22, 1993. "Mixed Reviews on Classroom Commercials," *San Francisco Chronicle*, March 8, 1989, is the source of the quotations in the final two paragraphs.

54. Source: (A) Shannon Proudfoot, "Immigrant Unemployment Rates Remain High," *CanWest News Service*, September 10, 2007; (B) Marina Jimenez, "Why a Veteran MD Works as an Orderly: Rules Trap Eye Doctor Trained at Top Clinic," *The Globe and Mail*, December 2, 2003; (C) Carly Weeks, "Ontario Proposes Changes to Get Foreign Doctors Working Sooner," *The Globe and Mail*, June 7, 2008, A12.

BUDDHIST ECONOMICS

E. F. SCHUMACHER

When thinking about economic matters, people in our society make a number of assumptions. These assumptions have important theoretical and practical consequences, but we simply take their truth for granted. Author and economist E. F. Schumacher exposes several of these implicit dogmas simply by showing how the thinking of a Buddhist economist would differ from that of a modern Western economist on some basic issues: the nature of work, the benefits of mechanization, the relation between material wealth and human well-being, and the use of natural resources.

"Right Livelihood" is one of the requirements of the Buddha's Noble Eightfold Path. It is clear, therefore, that there must be such a thing as Buddhist economics.

Buddhist countries have often stated that they wish to remain faithful to their heritage. So Burma: "The New Burma sees no conflict between religious values and economic progress. Spiritual health and material well-being are not enemies: they are natural allies." Or: "We can blend successfully the religious and spiritual values of our heritage with the benefits of modern technology." Or: "We Burmans have a sacred duty to conform both our dreams and our acts to our faith. This we shall ever do."

All the same, such countries invariably assume that they can model their economic development plans in accordance with modern economics, and they call upon modern economists from so-called advanced countries to advise them, to formulate the policies to be pursued, and to construct the grand design for development, the Five-Year Plan or whatever it may be called. No one seems to think that a Buddhist way of life would call for Buddhist economics, just as the modern materialist way of life has brought forth modern economics.

Economists themselves, like most specialists, normally suffer from a kind of metaphysical blindness, assuming that theirs is a science of absolute and invariable truths, without any presuppositions. Some go as far as to claim that economic laws are as free from "metaphysics" or "values" as the law of gravitation. We need not, however, get involved in arguments of methodology. Instead, let us take some fundamentals and see what they look like when viewed by a modern economist and a Buddhist economist.

There is universal agreement that a fundamental source of wealth is human labour. Now, the modern economist has been brought up to consider "labour" or work as little more than a necessary evil. From the point of view of the employer, it is in any case simply an item of cost, to be reduced to a minimum if it cannot be eliminated altogether, say, by automation. From the point of view of the workman, it is a "disutility"; to work is to make a sacrifice of one's leisure and comfort, and wages are a kind of compensation for the sacrifice. Hence the ideal from the point of view of the employer is to have output without employees, and the ideal from the point of view of the employee is to have income without employment.

The consequences of these attitudes both in theory and in practice are, of course, extremely far-reaching. If the ideal with regard to work is to get rid of it, every method that "reduces the work load" is a good thing. The most potent method, short of automation, is the so-called division of labour and the classical example is the pin factory eulogised in Adam Smith's *Wealth of Nations*. Here it is not a matter of ordinary specialisation, which mankind has practised from time immemorial, but of dividing up every complete process of production into minute parts, so that the final product can be produced at great speed without anyone having had to contribute more than a totally insignificant and, in most cases, unskilled movement of his limbs.

The Buddhist point of view takes the function of work to be at least threefold: to give a man a chance to utilise and develop his faculties; to enable him to overcome his ego-centredness by joining with other people in a common task; and to bring forth the goods and services needed for a becoming existence. Again, the consequences that flow from this view are endless. To organise work in such a manner that it becomes meaningless, boring, stultifying, or nerve-racking for the worker would be little short of criminal; it would indicate a greater concern with goods than with people, an evil lack of compassion, and a soul-destroying degree of attachment to the most primitive side of this worldly existence. Equally, to strive for leisure as an alternative to work would be considered a complete misunderstanding of one of the basic truths of human existence, namely that work and leisure are complementary parts of the same living process and cannot be separated without destroying the joy of work and the bliss of leisure.

From the Buddhist point of view, there are therefore two types of mechanisation which must be clearly distinguished: one that enhances a man's skill and power and one that turns the work of man over to a mechanical slave, leaving man in a position of having to serve the slave. How to tell the one from the other? "The craftsman himself," says Ananda Coomaraswamy, a man equally competent to talk about the modern west as the ancient east, "can always, if allowed to, draw the delicate distinction between the machine and the tool. The carpet loom is a tool, a contrivance for holding warp threads at a stretch for the pile to be woven round them by the craftsmen's fingers; but the power loom is a machine, and its significance as a destroyer of culture lies in the fact that it does the essentially human part of the work." It is clear, therefore, that Buddhist economics must be very different from the economics of modern materialism, since the Buddhist sees the essence of civilisation not in a multiplication of wants but in the purification of human character. Character, at the same time, is formed primarily by a man's work. And work, properly conducted in conditions of human dignity and freedom, blesses those who do it and equally their products. The Indian

From SMALL IS BEAUTIFUL by E.F. Schumacher, published by Hutchinson. Reprinted by permission of Random House Group Ltd.

philosopher and economist J. C. Kumarappa sums the matter up as follows:

> If the nature of the work is properly appreciated and applied, it will stand in the same relation to the higher faculties as food is to the physical body. It nourishes and enlivens the higher man and urges him to produce the best he is capable of. It directs his free will along the proper course and disciplines the animal in him into progressive channels. It furnishes an excellent background for man to display his scale of values and develop his personality.

If a man has no chance of obtaining work he is in a desperate position, not simply because he lacks an income but because he lacks this nourishing and enlivening factor of disciplined work which nothing can replace. A modern economist may engage in highly sophisticated calculations on whether full employment "pays" or whether it might be more "economic" to run an economy at less than full employment so as to ensure a greater mobility of labour, a better stability of wages, and so forth. His fundamental criterion of success is simply the total quantity of goods produced during a given period of time. "If the marginal urgency of goods is low," says Professor Galbraith in *The Affluent Society*, "then so is the urgency of employing the last man or the last million men in the labour force." And again: "If . . . we can afford some unemployment in the interest of stability—a proposition, incidentally, of impeccably conservative antecedents—then we can afford to give those who are unemployed the goods that enable them to sustain their accustomed standard of living."

From a Buddhist point of view, this is standing the truth on its head by considering goods as more important than people and consumption as more important than creative activity. It means shifting the emphasis from the worker to the product of work, that is, from the human to the subhuman, a surrender to the forces of evil. The very start of Buddhist economic planning would be a planning for full employment, and the primary purpose of this would in fact be employment for everyone who needs an "outside" job: it would not be the maximisation of employment nor the maximisation of production. Women, on the whole, do not need an "outside" job, and the large-scale employment of women in offices or factories would be considered a sign of serious economic failure. In particular, to let mothers of young children work in factories while the children run wild would be as uneconomic in the eyes of a Buddhist economist as the employment of a skilled worker as a soldier in the eyes of a modern economist.

While the materialist is mainly interested in goods, the Buddhist is mainly interested in liberation. But Buddhism is "The Middle Way" and therefore in no way antagonistic to physical well-being. It is not wealth that stands in the way of liberation but the attachment to wealth; not the enjoyment of pleasurable things but the craving for them. The keynote of Buddhist economics, therefore, is simplicity and non-violence. From an economist's point of view, the marvel of the Buddhist way of life is the utter rationality of its pattern—amazingly small means leading to extraordinarily satisfactory results.

For the modern economist this is very difficult to understand. He is used to measuring the "standard of living" by the amount of annual consumption, assuming all the time that a man who consumes more is "better off" than a man who consumes less. A Buddhist economist would consider this approach excessively irrational: since consumption is merely a means to human well-being, the aim should be to obtain the maximum of well-being with the minimum of consumption. Thus, if the purpose of clothing is a certain amount of temperature comfort and an attractive appearance, the task is to attain this purpose with the smallest possible effort, that is, with the smallest annual destruction of cloth and with the help of designs that involve the smallest possible input of toil. The less toil there is, the more time and strength is left for artistic creativity. It would be highly uneconomic, for instance, to go in for complicated tailoring, like the modern west, when a much more beautiful effect can be achieved by the skillful draping of uncut material. It would be the height of folly to make material so that it should wear out quickly and the height of barbarity to make anything ugly, shabby or mean. What has just been said about clothing applies equally to all other human requirements. The ownership and the consumption of goods is a means to an end, and Buddhist economics is the systematic study of how to attain given ends with the minimum means.

Modern economics, on the other hand, considers consumption to be the sole end and purpose of all economic activity, taking the factors of production—land, labour, and capital—as the means. The former, in short, tries to maximise human satisfactions by the optimal pattern of consumption, while the latter tries to maximise consumption by the optimal pattern of productive effort. It is easy to see that the effort needed to sustain a way of life which seeks to attain the optimal pattern of consumption is likely to be much smaller than the effort needed to sustain a drive for maximum consumption. We need not be surprised, therefore, that the pressure and strain of living is very much less in, say, Burma than it is in the United States, in spite of the fact that the amount of labour-saving machinery used in the former country is only a minute fraction of the amount used in the latter.

Simplicity and non-violence are obviously closely related. The optimal pattern of consumption, producing a high degree of human satisfaction by means of a relatively low rate of consumption, allows people to live without great pressure and strain and to fulfill the primary injunction of Buddhist teaching: "Cease to do evil; try to do good." As physical resources are everywhere limited, people satisfying their needs by means of a modest use of resources are obviously less likely to be at each other's throats than people depending upon a high rate of use. Equally, people who live in highly self-sufficient local communities are less likely to get involved in large-scale violence than people whose existence depends on worldwide systems of trade.

From the point of view of Buddhist economics, therefore, production from local resources for local needs is the most rational way of economic life, while dependence on imports from afar and the consequent need to produce for export to unknown and distant peoples is highly uneconomic and justifiable only in exceptional cases and on a small scale. Just as the modern economist would admit that a high rate of consumption of transport services between a man's home and his place of work signifies a misfortune and not a high standard of life, so the Buddhist economist would hold that to satisfy human wants from faraway sources rather than from sources nearby signifies failure rather than success. The former tends to take statistics showing an increase in the number of ton/miles per head of the population carried by a country's transport system as proof of economic progress, while to the latter—the Buddhist economist—the same statistics would indicate a highly undesirable deterioration in the *pattern* of consumption.

Another striking difference between modern economics and Buddhist economics arises over the use of natural resources. Bertrand de Jouvenel, the eminent French political philosopher, has characterised "western man" in words which may be taken as a fair description of the modern economist:

> He tends to count nothing as an expenditure, other than human effort; he does not seem to mind how much mineral matter he wastes and, far worse, how much living matter he destroys. He does not seem to realise at all that human life is a dependent part of an ecosystem of many different forms of life. As the world is ruled from towns where men are cut off from any form of life other than human, the feeling of belonging to an ecosystem is not revived. This results in a harsh and improvident treatment of things upon which we ultimately depend, such as water and trees.

The teaching of the Buddha, on the other hand, enjoins a reverent and non-violent attitude not only to all sentient beings but also, with great emphasis, to trees. Every follower of the Buddha ought to plant a tree every few years and look after it until it is safely established, and the Buddhist economist can demonstrate without difficulty that the universal observation of this rule would result in a high rate of genuine economic development independent of any foreign aid. Much of the economic decay of south-east Asia (as of many other parts of the world) is undoubtedly due to a heedless and shameful neglect of trees.

Modern economics does not distinguish between renewable and non-renewable materials, as its very method is to equalise and quantify everything by means of a money price. Thus, taking various alternative fuels, like coal, oil, wood, or water-power: the only difference between them recognised by modern economics is relative cost per equivalent unit. The cheapest is automatically the one to be preferred, as to do otherwise would be irrational and "uneconomic." From a Buddhist point of view, of course, this will not do; the essential difference between non-renewable fuels like coal and oil on the one hand and renewable fuels like wood and water-power on the other cannot be simply overlooked. Non-renewable goods must be used only if they are indispensable, and then only with the greatest care and the most meticulous concern for conservation. To use them heedlessly or extravagantly is an act of violence, and while complete non-violence may not be attainable on this earth, there is nonetheless an ineluctable duty on man to aim at the ideal of non-violence in all he does.

Just as a modern European economist would not consider it a great economic achievement if all European art treasures were sold to America at attractive prices, so the Buddhist economist would insist that a population basing its economic life on non-renewable fuels is living parasitically, on capital instead of income. Such a way of life could have no permanence and could therefore be justified only as a purely temporary expedient. As the world's resources of non-renewable fuels—coal, oil, and natural gas—are exceedingly unevenly distributed over the globe and undoubtedly limited in quantity, it is clear that their exploitation at an ever-increasing rate is an act of violence against nature which must almost inevitably lead to violence between men.

This fact alone might give food for thought even to those people in Buddhist countries who care nothing for the religious and spiritual values of their heritage and ardently desire to embrace the materialism of modern economics at the fastest possible speed. Before they dismiss Buddhist economics as nothing better than a nostalgic dream, they might wish to consider whether the path of economic development outlined by modern economics is likely to lead them to places where they really want to be. Towards the end of his courageous book *The Challenge of Man's Future*, Professor Harrison Brown of the California Institute of Technology gives the following appraisal:

> Thus we see that, just as industrial society is fundamentally unstable and subject to reversion to agrarian existence, so within it the conditions which offer individual freedom are unstable in their ability to avoid the conditions which impose rigid organisation and totalitarian control. Indeed, when we examine all of the foreseeable difficulties which threaten the survival of industrial civilisation, it is difficult to see how the achievement of stability and the maintenance of individual liberty can be made compatible.

Even if this were dismissed as a long-term view there is the immediate question of whether "modernisation," as currently practised without regard to religious and spiritual values, is actually producing agreeable results. As far as the masses are concerned, the results appear to be disastrous—a collapse of the rural economy, a rising tide of unemployment in town and country, and the growth of a city proletariat without nourishment for either body or soul.

It is in the light of both immediate experience and long-term prospects that the study of Buddhist economics could be recommended even to those who believe that economic growth is more important than any spiritual or religious values. For it is not a question of choosing between "modern growth" and "traditional stagnation." It is a question of finding the right path of development, the Middle Way between materialist heedlessness and traditionalist immobility, in short, of finding "Right Livelihood."

Review and Discussion Questions

1. From the Buddhist point of view, what is the function of work? What do you see as the main social and economic implications of the Buddhist perspective?

2. Schumacher sees simplicity as a keynote of Buddhist economics. What's the connection between simplicity and nonviolence? Why does Buddhism value simplicity? Does capitalism promote needless complexity?

3. How do Buddhism and capitalism differ in their understanding of the nature and purpose of human existence? Is the Buddhist view of the role of women sexist?

4. What distinguishes Buddhist economics from modern economics in its approach to material wealth? To natural resources? With which approach are you more sympathetic and why?

5. Is a capitalist economic system compatible with a Buddhist perspective? Is any other economic system?

6. Would you agree that Buddhism has something to teach us about economics?

MARKETS AND THE ROLE OF ETHICS IN CAPITALISM

AMARTYA SEN

In this extract from his book, Development as Freedom, *Amartya Sen, winner of the Nobel Prize in economics, discusses the advantages and limitations of markets and the important, but overlooked, role of business ethics in the successful functioning of a capitalist system. Like other economists, Sen appreciates the beneficial results of markets, but he also emphasizes the importance of the freedom they provide. Interest groups that attempt to restrict market competition for their own benefit should be resisted, but Sen acknowledges that markets do have shortcomings, which may justify our interfering with their operation. This is particularly true with respect to issues of equity, public goods, and other cases where the private pursuit of gain runs counter to social interests. In the final sections of the reading, Sen goes on to argue that for its successful operation capitalism requires more than self-interested, profit-maximizing behaviour. Rather, it depends on mutual trust and adherence to certain norms—that is, on business ethics.*

MARKETS, LIBERTY AND LABOR

Even though the merits of the market mechanism are now very widely acknowledged, the *reasons* for wanting markets are often not fully appreciated . . . . In recent discussions, the focus in assessing the market mechanism has tended to be on the *results* it ultimately generates, such as the incomes or the utilities yielded by the markets. This is not a negligible issue, and I shall come to it presently. But the more immediate case for the freedom of market transaction lies in the basic importance of that freedom itself. We have

good reasons to buy and sell, to exchange, and to seek lives that can flourish on the basis of transactions. To deny that freedom in general would be in itself a major failing of a society. This fundamental recognition is *prior* to any theorem . . . showing . . . the . . . outcomes of markets . . . in terms of incomes, utilities and so on.

The ubiquitous role of transactions in modern living is often overlooked precisely because we take them for granted. There is an analogy here with the rather underrecognized—and often unnoticed—role of certain behavioral rules (such as basic business ethics) in developed capitalist economies (with attention being focused only on aberrations when they occur). But when these values are not yet developed, their general presence or absence can make a crucial difference. In the analysis of development, the role of elementary business ethics thus has to be moved out of its obscure presence to a manifest recognition. Similarly, the absence of the freedom to transact can be a major issue in itself in many contexts.

This is, of course, particularly so when the freedom of labor markets is denied by laws, regulations or convention. Even though African American slaves in the pre–Civil War South may have had pecuniary incomes as large as (or even larger than) those of wage laborers elsewhere and may even have lived longer than the urban workers in the North, there was still a fundamental deprivation in the fact of slavery itself (no matter what incomes or utilities it might or might not have generated). The loss of freedom in the absence of employment choice and in the tyrannical form of work can itself be a major deprivation.

The development of free markets in general and of free seeking of employment in particular is a much appreciated fact in historical studies. Even that great critic of capitalism Karl Marx saw the emergence of freedom of employment as momentous progress . . . . But this issue concerns not just history but the present as well, since this freedom is critically important right now in many parts of the world. Let me illustrate this point with four quite different examples.

First, various forms of labor bondage can be found in many countries in Asia and Africa, and there are persistent denials of basic freedom to seek wage employment away from one's traditional bosses . . . . The situation has been more studied in India than elsewhere . . . , but there is enough evidence that similar problems are present in several other countries as well.

Second (to turn now to a very different illustration), the failure of bureaucratic socialism in Eastern Europe and the Soviet Union cannot be fully grasped merely in terms of the economic problems in generating incomes or other results, such as life expectancies. Indeed, in terms of life expectancies, the communist countries often did quite well, relatively speaking (as is readily checked from the demographic statistics of the Soviet Union, pre-reform China, Vietnam and Cuba, among others). In fact, several of the ex-communist countries now are in a significantly *worse* position than they were under communist rule—perhaps nowhere more so than in Russia itself (where the life expectancy at birth of Russian men has dropped now to about fifty-eight years—considerably below those in India or Pakistan). And yet the population is unwilling to vote to return to the previous arrangements . . . .

In assessing what happened, the economic inefficiency of the communist system must, of course, be recognized. But there is also the more immediate issue of the denial of freedom in a system where markets were simply ruled out in many fields . . . .

Third, . . . in the distressing subject of child labor (as prevalent, for example, in Pakistan, or India, or Bangladesh), there is an embedded issue of slavery and bondage, since many of the children working in exacting tasks are forced to perform them. The roots of such servitude may go back to the economic deprivation of the families from which they come—sometimes the parents are themselves under some kind of bondage vis-à-vis the employers—and on top of the nasty issue of laboring children, there is also the barbarity of children being *forced* to do things. The freedom to go to school, in particular, is hampered not only by the weakness of primary educational programs in these regions, but in some cases also by the lack of any choice that the children (and often their parents) have in deciding what they want to do.

The issue of child labor tends to divide South Asian economists. Some have argued that merely abolishing child labor without doing anything to enhance the economic circumstances of the families involved may not serve the interest of the children themselves. There is certainly a debatable issue here, but the frequent congruence of child labor with what effectively is slavery does make it, in those cases, a simpler choice. The starkness of slavery yields a forceful case for more vigorous enforcement of antislavery as well as anti-child-labor legislation. The system of child labor—bad enough on its own—is made much beastlier still through its congruence with bondage and effective slavery.

Fourth, the freedom of women to seek employment outside the family is a major issue in many third world countries. This freedom is systematically denied in many cultures, and this in itself is a serious violation of women's liberty and gender equity. The absence of this freedom militates against the economic empowerment of women, and also has many other consequences. Aside from the direct effects of market employment in adding to the economic independence of women, outside work is also causally important in making women have a better "deal" in intrahousehold distributions. Needless to say, women's work at home can be backbreaking, but it is rarely honored or even recognized (and certainly not remunerated), and the denial of the right to work outside the home is a rather momentous violation of women's liberty.

The prohibition of outside employment for women can sometimes be brutally executed in an explicit and fierce way (as, for example, in . . . Afghanistan [under the Taliban]). In other cases, the prohibition may work more implicitly through the power of convention and conformity. Sometimes there may not even be, in any clear sense, a ban on women's seeking employment, and yet women reared with traditional values may be quite afraid to break with the tradition and to shock others. The prevailing perceptions of "normality" and "appropriateness" are quite central to this question . . . .

MARKETS AND EFFICIENCY

The labor market can be a liberator in many different contexts, and the basic freedom of transaction can be of central importance, quite aside from whatever the market mechanism may or may not achieve in terms of incomes or utilities or other results. But it is important also to examine those consequential results, and I turn now to that—rather different—issue.

In assessing the market mechanism, it is important to take note of the forms of the markets: whether they are competitive or monopolistic (or otherwise uncompetitive), whether some markets may be missing (in ways that are not easily remediable) and so on. Also, the nature of factual circumstances (such as the availability or absence of particular kinds of information, the presence or absence of economies of large scale) may influence the actual possibilities and impose real limitations on what can be achieved through various institutional forms of the market mechanism.

In the absence of such imperfections (including the nonmarketability of some goods and services), classical models of general equilibrium have been used to demonstrate the merits of the market mechanism in achieving economic efficiency. This is standardly defined in terms of what economists call "Pareto optimality": a situation in which the utility (or welfare) of no one can be raised without reducing the utility (or welfare) of someone else. This efficiency achievement . . . the so-called Arrow-Debreu theorem . . . is of real importance despite the simplifying assumptions.

The Arrow-Debreu results show, inter alia, that—given some preconditions—the results of the market mechanism are not improvable in ways that would enhance everyone's utility (or enhance the utility of some without reducing the utility of anyone else) . . . .

These efficiency results do not say anything about the equity of outcomes, or about the equity in the distribution of freedoms. A situation can be efficient in the sense that no one's utility or substantive freedom can be enhanced without cutting into the utility or freedom of someone else, and yet there could be enormous inequalities in the distribution of utilities and of freedoms.

The problem of inequality, in fact, gets magnified as the attention is shifted from income inequality to the inequality in the *distribution of substantive freedoms and capabilities*. This is mainly because of the possibility of some "coupling" of income inequality, on the one hand, with unequal advantages in converting incomes into capabilities, on the other. The latter tends to intensify the inequality problem already reflected in income inequality. For example, a person who is disabled, or ill, or old, or otherwise handicapped may, on the one hand, have problems in *earning* a decent income, and on the other, also face greater difficulties in *converting* income into capabilities and into living well. The very factors that may make a person unable to find a good job and a good income (such as a disability) may put the person at a disadvantage in achieving a good quality of life even with the same job and with the same income. This relationship between income-*earning* ability and income-*using* ability is a well-known empirical phenomenon in poverty studies. The interpersonal income inequality in the market outcomes may tend to be magnified by this "coupling" of low incomes with handicaps in the conversion of incomes into capabilities.

The freedom-efficiency of the market mechanism, on the one hand, and the seriousness of freedom-inequality problems, on the other hand, are worth considering *simultaneously*. The equity problems have to be addressed, especially in dealing with serious deprivations and poverty, and in that context, social intervention including governmental support may well have an important role. To a great extent, this is exactly what the social security systems in welfare states try to achieve, through a variety of programs including social provision of health care, public support of the unemployed and the indigent and so on. But the need to pay attention *simultaneously* to efficiency and equity aspects of the problem remains, since equity-motivated interference with the working of the market mechanism can weaken efficiency achievements even as it promotes equity. It is important to be clear about the need for simultaneity in considering the different aspects of social evaluation and justice . . . .

MARKETS AND INTEREST GROUPS

The role that markets play must depend not only on what they can do, but also on what they are allowed to do. There are many people whose interests are well served by the smooth functioning of markets, but there are also groups whose established interests may be hurt by such functioning. If the latter groups are politically more powerful and influential, then they can try to see that markets are not given adequate room in the economy. This can be a particularly serious problem when monopolistic production units flourish—despite inefficiency and various types of ineptitude—thanks to insulation from competition, domestic or foreign. The high product-prices or the low product-qualities that are involved in such artificially propped-up production may impose significant sacrifice on the population at large, but an organized and politically influential group of "industrialists" can make sure that their profits are well protected . . . .

It is one of the ironies of the history of ideas that some who advocate radical politics today often fall for old economic positions that were so unequivocally rejected by Smith, Ricardo and Marx . . . . It is not surprising that the protected bourgeoisie often do their best to encourage and support the illusion of radicalism and modernity in dusting up generically anti-market positions from the distant past.

It is important to join these arguments through open-minded criticisms of the claims made in favor of general restriction of competition. This is not to deny that attention must also be paid to the political power of those groups that obtain substantial material benefits from restricting trade and exchange. Many authors have pointed out, with good reason, that the advocacies involved must be judged by identifying the vested interests involved, and by taking note of the influence of "rent-seeking activities" implicit in keeping competition away. As Vilfredo Pareto pointed out, in a famous passage, if "a certain measure A is the cause of the loss of one franc to each of a thousand persons, and of a thousand franc gain to one individual, the latter will expend a great deal of energy, whereas the former will resist weakly; and it is likely that, in the end, the person who is attempting to secure the thousand francs via A will be successful." Political influence in search of economic gain is a very real phenomenon in the world in which we live.

Confronting such influences has to occur not merely through resisting—and perhaps even "exposing" (to use an old-fashioned word)—the seekers of profit from captive markets, but also from taking on their intellectual arguments as proper subjects of scrutiny. Economics does have a long tradition in that critical direction, going back at least to Adam Smith himself, who simultaneously pointed his accusing finger at the perpetrators, and went on to debunk their claims in favor of the thesis of social benefits from disallowing competition. Smith argued that the vested interests tend to win because of their "better knowledge of their own interest" (*not* "their knowledge of publick interest"). He wrote:

> The interest of the dealers, however, in any particular branch of trade or manufactures, is always in some respects different from, and even opposite to that of the publick. To widen the market and to narrow the competition, is always the interest of the dealers. To widen the market may frequently be agreeable enough to the interest of the publick; but to narrow the competition must always be against it, and can serve only to enable the dealers, by raising their profits above what they naturally would be, to levy for their own benefit, an absurd tax upon the rest of their fellow-citizens. The proposal of any new law or

regulation of commerce which comes from this order, ought always to be listened to with great precaution, and ought never to be adopted till after having been long and carefully examined, not only with the most scrupulous, but with the most suspicious attention.

There is no reason why vested interests must win if open arguments are permitted and promoted . . . . This is an ideal field for more public discussion of the claims and counter-claims on the different sides, and in the test of open democracy, public interest may well have excellent prospects of winning against the spirited advocacy of the small coterie of vested interests . . . .

NEED FOR CRITICAL SCRUTINY OF THE ROLE OF MARKETS

Indeed, critical public discussion is an inescapably important requirement of good public policy since the appropriate role and reach of markets cannot be predetermined on the basis of some grand, general formula—or some all-encompassing attitude—either in favor of placing everything under the market, or of denying everything to the market. Even Adam Smith, while firmly advocating the use of markets where it could work well (and denying the merits of any *general* rejection of trade and exchange), did not hesitate to investigate economic circumstances in which particular restrictions may be sensibly proposed, or economic fields in which non-market institutions would be badly needed to supplement what the markets can do.

It must not be presumed that Smith's critique of the market mechanism was always gentle, or, for that matter, that he got his critical points invariably right. Consider, for example, his advocacy of legal restriction on usury. Smith was, of course, opposed to any kind of general ban on charging interest on loans (as some antimarket thinkers had advocated). However, he wanted to have legal restrictions imposed by the state on the maximum rates of interest that could be charged:

> In countries where interest is permitted, the law, in order to prevent the extortion of usury, generally fixes the highest rate which can be taken without incurring a penalty . . . .
>
> The legal rate, it is to be observed, though it ought to be somewhat above, ought not to be much above the lowest market rate. If the legal rate of interest in Great Britain, for example, was fixed so high as eight or ten per cent, the greater part of the money which was to be lent, would be lent to prodigals and projectors, who alone would be willing to give this high interest. Sober people, who will give for the use of money no more than a part of what they are likely to make by the use of it, would not venture into the competition. A great part of the capital of the country would thus be kept out of the hands which were most likely to make a profitable and advantageous use of it, and thrown into those which were most likely to waste and destroy it.

In Smith's interventionist logic the underlying argument is that market signals can be misleading, and the consequences of the free market may be much waste of capital, resulting from private pursuit of misguided or myopic enterprises, or private waste of social resources . . . .

It is not particularly important to assess these specific arguments of Smith, but it is important to see what his general concerns are. What he is considering is the possibility of social loss in the narrowly motivated pursuit of private gains. This is the opposite case to the more famous remark of Smith: "It is not from the benevolence of the butcher, the brewer, or the baker that we expect our dinner, but from their regard to their own interest. We address ourselves, not to their humanity but to their self-love . . . ." If the butcher-brewer-baker example draws our attention to the mutually beneficial role of trade based on self-interest, the prodigal-projector argument points to the possibility that under certain circumstances private profit motives may indeed run counter to social interests. It is this general concern that remains relevant today . . . .

The lesson to draw from Smith's analysis of the market mechanism is not any massive strategy of jumping to policy conclusions from some general "pro" or "anti" attitude to markets. After acknowledging the role of trade and exchange in human living, we still have to examine what the other consequences of market transactions actually are. We have to evaluate the actual possibilities critically, with adequate attention being paid to the contingent circumstances that may be relevant in assessing all the results of encouraging markets, or of restraining their operation. If the butcher-brewer-baker example points to a very common circumstance in which our complementary interests are mutually promoted by exchange, the prodigal-projector example illustrates the possibility that this may not work in quite that way in every case. There is no escape from the necessity of critical scrutiny . . . .

Those who have tended to take the market mechanism to be the best solution of every economic problem may want to inquire what the limits of that mechanism may be. I have already commented on issues of equity and the need to go beyond efficiency considerations . . . . But even in achieving efficiency, the market mechanism may sometimes be less than effective, particularly in the presence of what are called "public goods."

One of the assumptions standardly made to show the efficiency of the market mechanism is that every commodity—and more generally everything on which our welfares depend—can be bought and sold in the market. It can all be marketed (if we want to place it there), and there is no "nonmarketable" but significant influence on our welfare. In fact, however, some of the most important contributors to human capability may be hard to sell exclusively to one person at a time. This is especially so when we consider the so-called public goods, which people consume *together* rather than separately.

This applies particularly in such fields as environmental preservation, and also epidemiology and public health care. I may be willing to pay my share in a social program of malaria eradication, but I cannot buy my part of that protection in the form of "private good" (like an apple or a shirt). It is a "public good"—malaria-free surroundings—which we have to consume together. Indeed, if I do manage somehow to organize a malaria-free environment where I live, my neighbor too will have that malaria-free environment, without having to "buy" it from anywhere.

The rationale of the market mechanism is geared to private goods (like apples and shirts), rather than to public goods (like the malaria-free environment), and it can be shown that there may be a good case for the provisioning of public goods, going beyond what the private markets would foster. Exactly similar arguments regarding the limited reach of the market mechanism apply to several other important fields as well, where too the provision involved may take the form of a public good. Defense, policing and environmental protection are some of the fields in which this kind of reasoning applies.

There are also rather mixed cases. For example, given the shared communal benefits of basic education, which may transcend the gains of the person being educated, basic education may have a public-good component as well (and can be seen as a semipublic good). The persons receiving education do, of course, benefit from it, but in addition a general expansion of education and literacy in a region can facilitate social change (even the reduction of fertility and mortality...) and also help to enhance economic progress from which others too benefit. The effective reach of these services may require cooperative activities and provisioning by the state or the local authorities. Indeed, the state has typically played a major role in the expansion of basic education across the world. The rapid spread of literacy in the past history of the rich countries of today (both in the West and in Japan and the rest of East Asia) has drawn on the low cost of public education combined with its shared public benefits.

It is in this context rather remarkable that some market enthusiasts recommend now to the developing countries that they should rely fully on the free market even for basic education—thereby withholding from them the very process of educational expansion that was crucial in rapidly spreading literacy in Europe, North America, Japan, and East Asia in the past. The alleged followers of Adam Smith can learn something from his writings on this subject, including his frustration at the parsimony of public expenditure in the field of education:

> For a very small expence the publick can facilitate, can encourage, and can even impose upon almost the whole body of the people, the necessity of acquiring those most essential parts of education.

The "public goods" argument for going beyond the market mechanism supplements the case for social provisioning that arises from the need of basic capabilities, such as elementary health care and basic educational opportunities. Efficiency considerations thus supplement the argument for equity in supporting public assistance in providing basic education, health facilities and other public (or semipublic) goods . . . .

BUSINESS ETHICS, TRUST, AND CONTRACTS

While capitalism is often seen as an arrangement that works only on the basis of the greed of everyone, the efficient working of the capitalist economy is, in fact, dependent on powerful systems of values and norms. Indeed, to see capitalism as nothing other than a system based on a conglomeration of greedy behavior is to underestimate vastly the ethics of capitalism, which has richly contributed to its redoubtable achievements.

The use of formal economic models to understand the operation of market mechanisms, as is the standard practice in economic theory, is to some extent a double-edged sword. The models can give insight into the way the real world operates. On the other hand, the structure of the model can conceal some implicit assumptions that produce the regular relations that the models build on. Successful markets operate the way they do not just on the basis of exchanges being "allowed," but also on the solid foundation of institutions (such as effective legal structures that support the rights ensuing from contracts) and behavioral ethics (which makes the negotiated contracts viable without the need for constant litigation to achieve compliance). The development and use of trust in one another's words and promises can be a very important ingredient of market success . . . .

Despite its effectiveness, capitalist ethics is, in fact, deeply limited in some respects, dealing particularly with issues of economic inequality, environmental protection and the need for cooperation of different kinds that operate outside the market. But within its domain, capitalism works effectively through a system of ethics that provides the vision and the trust needed for successful use of the market mechanism and related institutions.

Successful operation of an exchange economy depends on mutual trust and the use of norms—explicit and implicit. When these behavioral modes are plentiful, it is easy to overlook their role. But when they have to be cultivated, that lacuna can be a major barrier to economic success. There are plenty of examples of the problems faced in precapitalist economies because of the underdevelopment of capitalist virtues. Capitalism's need for motivational structures that are more complex than pure profit maximization has been acknowledged in various forms, over a long time, by many leading social scientists, such as Marx, Weber, Tawney and others. That nonprofit motives have a role in the success of capitalism is not a new point, even though the wealth of historical evidence and conceptual arguments in that direction is often neglected in contemporary professional economics.

A basic code of good business behavior is a bit like oxygen: we take an interest in its presence only when it is absent . . . . What may not cause wonder or surprise in Zurich or London or Paris may, however, be quite problematic in Cairo or Bombay or Lagos (or Moscow), in their challenging struggle to establish the norms and institutions of a functioning market economy. Even the problem of political and economic corruption in Italy, which has been much discussed in recent years (and has also led to radical changes in the political equilibrium in Italy), relates a good deal to the somewhat dualist nature of the Italian economy, with elements of "underdevelopment" in some parts of the economy and the most dynamic capitalism elsewhere in the same economy.

In the economic difficulties experienced in the former Soviet Union and countries in Eastern Europe, the absence of institutional structures and behavioral codes that are central to successful capitalism has been particularly important. There is need for the development of an alternative system of institutions and codes with its own logic and loyalties that may be quite standard in the evolved capitalist economies, but that are relatively hard to install suddenly as a part of "planned capitalism." Such changes can take quite some time to function—a lesson that is currently being learned rather painfully in the former Soviet Union and in parts of Eastern Europe. The importance of institutions and behavioral experiences was rather eclipsed there in the first flush of enthusiasm about the magic of allegedly automatic market processes.

The need for institutional developments has some clear connection with the role of codes of behavior, since institutions based on interpersonal arrangements and shared understandings operate on the basis of common behavior patterns, mutual trust and confidence in the other party's ethics. The reliance on rules of behavior may typically be implicit rather than explicit—indeed so implicit that its importance can be easily overlooked in situations where such confidence is not problematic. But wherever it *is* problematic, overlooking the need for it can be quite disastrous . . . .

VARIATIONS OF NORMS AND INSTITUTIONS WITHIN THE MARKET ECONOMY

Behavioral codes vary even among the developed capitalist economies, and so does their effectiveness in promoting economic performance. While capitalism has been very successful in radically enhancing output and raising productivity in the modern world, it is still the case that the experiences of different countries are quite diverse. The successes of East Asian economies (in recent decades), and most notably of Japan (stretching further back), raise important questions about the modeling of capitalism in traditional economic theory. To see capitalism as a system of pure profit maximization based on individual ownership of capital is to leave out much that has made the system so successful in raising output and in generating income.

Japan has frequently been seen as the greatest example of successful capitalism, and despite the longish period of recent recession and financial turmoil, this diagnosis is unlikely to be completely washed away. However, the motivation pattern that dominates Japanese business has much more content than would be provided by pure profit maximization. Different commentators have emphasized distinct motivational features in Japan. Michio Morishima has outlined the special characteristics of the "Japanese ethos" as emerging from particular features of the history of Japan and its tendency toward rule-based behavior patterns. Ronald Dore and Robert Wade have identified the influence of "Confucian ethics." . . .

Indeed, there is some truth even in the apparently puzzling claim made in *The Wall Street Journal* that Japan is "the only communist nation that works." That enigmatic remark points to the nonprofit motivations underlying many economic and business activities in Japan. We have to understand and interpret the peculiar fact that one of the most successful capitalist nations in the world flourishes economically with a motivation structure that departs, in some significant spheres, from the simple pursuit of self-interest, which—we have been told—is the bedrock of capitalism.

Japan does not, by any means, provide the only example of a special business ethics in promoting capitalist success. The merits of selfless work and devotion to enterprise in raising productivity have been seen as important for economic achievements in many countries in the world, and there are many variations in these behavioral codes even among the most developed industrial nations.

CONCLUSION

To conclude the discussion of different aspects of the role of values in capitalist success, we must see the system of ethics underlying capitalism as involving a good deal more than sanctifying greed and admiring cupidity. The success of capitalism in transforming the general level of economic prosperity in the world has drawn on morals and codes of behavior that have made market transactions economical and effective. In making use of the opportunities offered by the market mechanism and greater use of trade and exchange, the developing countries have to pay attention not only to the virtues of prudential behavior, but also to the role of complementary values, such as the making and sustaining of trust, avoiding the temptations of pervasive corruption, and making assurance a workable substitute for punitive legal enforcement. In the history of capitalism there have been significant variations within the basic capitalist behavioral codes, with divergent achievements and experiences, and there are things to be learned there as well.

The big challenges that capitalism now faces in the contemporary world include issues of inequality (especially that of grinding poverty in a world of unprecedented prosperity) and of "public goods" (that is, goods that people share together, such as the environment). The solution to these problems will almost certainly call for institutions that take us beyond the capitalist market economy. But the reach of the capitalist market economy itself is, in many ways, extendable by an appropriate development of ethics sensitive to these concerns. The compatibility of the market mechanism with a wide range of values is an important question, and it has to be faced along with exploring the extension of institutional arrangements beyond the limits of the pure market mechanism.

Review and Discussion Questions

1. Sen believes that the market is valuable both for the freedom it provides and for the results it delivers. Give examples of each. Which is the more important rationale for capitalism—freedom or efficiency?

2. Give your own examples of the efforts of interest groups to restrict market competition for their own benefit. What point does Vilfredo Pareto make in this context? What factors determine whether an interest group succeeds in protecting itself from competition?

3. Why did Adam Smith advocate legal restrictions on usury? What lesson does Sen draw from this example?

4. What are "public goods"? Give some examples. How do they show the limits of the market mechanism? Is education a public good? Explain why or why not.

5. What does Sen mean when he writes that capitalism needs "motivational structures that are more complex than pure profit maximization"? Why does capitalism require business ethics for its successful operation? In your view, what values and motivational structures are the most important for capitalism's functioning?

IN DEFENSE OF INTERNATIONAL SWEATSHOPS

IAN MAITLAND

These days, contractors in Third World countries such as Indonesia and China manufacture most of the shoes, shirts, and other clothing that large American footwear and apparel companies sell. Because working conditions in these factories are poor and the wages they pay are exceedingly low, critics call them "sweatshops" and condemn American companies such as Nike and Levi Strauss for using them. Although these critics believe that international sweatshops represent capitalism at its worse, Ian Maitland, a management professor at the University of Minnesota, defends them against the charge of exploitation on both factual and ethical grounds. He examines and rejects the idea that sweatshops pay unconscionable wages, that they impoverish local workers and widen the gap between rich and poor, and that American companies collude with repressive regimes that stifle dissent and repress workers. Arguing that interfering with the market can have terrible results, he concludes not only that paying market wages in developing countries is morally permissible but also that it may be morally wrong for companies to pay wages that exceed market levels.

In recent years, there has been a dramatic growth in the contracting out of production by companies in the industrialized countries to suppliers in developing countries. This globalization of production has led to an emerging international division of labor in footwear and apparel in which companies like Nike and Reebok concentrate on product design and marketing but rely on a network of contractors in Indonesia, China, Central America, etc., to build shoes or sew shirts according to exact specifications and deliver a high quality good according to precise delivery schedules. As Nike's vice president for Asia has put it, "We don't know the first thing about manufacturing. We are marketers and designers."

From *The Great Non-Debate over International Sweatshops* by Ian Maitland, Carlson School Of Management, University of Minnesota. Reprinted by permission of the author.

The contracting arrangements have drawn intense fire from critics—usually labor and human rights activists. The "critics" (as I will refer to them) have charged that the companies are (by proxy) exploiting workers in the plants (which I will call "international sweatshops") of their suppliers. Specifically, the companies stand accused of chasing cheap labor around the globe, failing to pay their workers living wages, using child labor, turning a blind eye to abuses of human rights, and being complicit with repressive regimes in denying workers the right to join unions and failing to enforce minimum labor standards in the workplace, and so on.

The campaign against international sweatshops has largely unfolded on television and, to a lesser extent, in the print media. What seems like no more than a handful of critics has mounted an aggressive, media-savvy campaign that has put the publicity-shy retail giants on the defensive. The critics have orchestrated a series of sensational "disclosures" on prime time television exposing the terrible pay and working conditions in factories making jeans for Levi's or sneakers for Nike or Pocahontas shirts for Disney . . . .

OBJECTIVE OF THIS ESSAY

In this confrontation between the companies and their critics, neither side seems to have judged it to be in its interest to seriously engage the issue at the heart of this controversy, namely: What are appropriate wages and labor standards in international sweatshops? . . . The companies have treated the charges about sweatshops as a public relations problem to be managed so as to minimize harm to their public images. The critics have apparently judged that the best way to keep public indignation at boiling point is to oversimplify the issue and treat it as a morality play featuring heartless exploiters and victimized third world workers . . . .

This essay takes up the issue of what are appropriate wages and labor standards in international sweatshops. Critics charge that the present arrangements are exploitative. I proceed by examining the specific charges of exploitation from the standpoints of both (a) their factual and (b) their ethical sufficiency . . . .

WHAT ARE ETHICALLY APPROPRIATE LABOR STANDARDS IN INTERNATIONAL SWEATSHOPS?

What are ethically acceptable or appropriate levels of wages and labor standards in international sweatshops? The following four possibilities just about run the gamut of standards or principles that have been seriously proposed to regulate such policies.

1. *Home-country standards:* It might be argued (and in rare cases has been) that international corporations have an ethical duty to pay the same wages and provide the same labor standards regardless of where they operate. However, the view that home-country standards should apply in host countries is rejected by most business ethicists and (officially at least) by the critics of international sweatshops. Thus, . . . Richard De George makes . . . the . . . argument: If there were a rule that said "that American MNCs [multinational corporations] that wish to be ethical must pay the same wages abroad as they do at home . . . . [then] MNCs would have little incentive to move their manufacturing abroad; and if they did move abroad they would disrupt the local labor market with artificially high wages that bore no relation to the local standard or cost of living."1

2. *"Living wage" standard:* It has been proposed that an international corporation should, at a minimum, pay a "living wage." Thus, De George says that corporations should pay a living wage "even when this is not paid by local firms."2 However, it is hard to pin down what this means operationally. According to De George, a living wage should "allow the worker to live in dignity as a human being." In order to respect the human rights of its workers, he says, a corporation must pay "at least subsistence wages and as much above that as workers and their dependents need to live with reasonable dignity, given the general state of development of the society." As we shall see, the living wage standard has become a rallying cry of the critics of international sweatshops. Apparently, De George believes that it is preferable for a corporation to provide no job at all than to offer one that pays less than a living wage.

3. *Donaldson's test:* Thomas Donaldson believes that "it is irrelevant whether the standards of the host country comply or fail to comply with home country standards; what is relevant is whether they meet a universal, objective minimum." He tries to specify "a moral minimum for the behavior of all international economic agents." However, he concedes . . . that "many rights . . . are dependent for their specification on the level of economic development of the country in question." Accordingly, he proposes a test to determine when deviations from home-country standards are unethical. That test provides as follows: "The practice is permissible if and only if the members of the home country would, under conditions of economic development relevantly similar to those of the host country, regard the practice as permissible."3 Donaldson's test is vulnerable to Bernard Shaw's objection to the Golden Rule, namely that we should not do unto others as we would they do unto us, because their tastes may be different. The test also complicates matters by introducing counterfactuals and hypotheticals (if I were in their place [which I'm not] what would I want?). This indeterminacy is a serious weakness in an ethical code: It is likely to confuse managers who want to act ethically and to provide loopholes for those who don't.

4. *Classical liberal standard:* Finally, there is what I will call the classical liberal standard. According to this standard a practice (wage or labor practice) is ethically acceptable if it is freely chosen by informed workers. For example, in a recent report the World Bank invoked this standard in connection with workplace safety. It said: "The appropriate level is therefore that at which the costs are commensurate with the value that informed workers place on improved working conditions and reduced risk."4 Most business ethicists reject this standard on the grounds that there is some sort of market failure or the "background conditions" are lacking for markets to work effectively. Thus, for Donaldson full (or near-full) employment is a prerequisite if workers are to make sound choices regarding workplace safety: "The average level of unemployment in the developing countries today exceeds 40 percent, a figure that has frustrated the application of neoclassical economic principles to the international economy on a score of issues. With full employment, and all other things being equal, market forces will encourage workers to make trade-offs between job opportunities using safety as a variable. But with massive unemployment, market forces in developing countries drive the unemployed to the jobs they are lucky enough to land, regardless of the safety."5 . . . De George, too, believes that the necessary conditions are lacking for market forces to operate benignly. Without what he calls "background institutions" to protect the workers and the resources of the developing country (e.g., enforceable minimum wages) and/or greater equality of bargaining power, exploitation is the most likely result.6 . . .

THE CASE AGAINST INTERNATIONAL SWEATSHOPS

To many of their critics, international sweatshops exemplify the way in which the greater openness of the world economy is hurting workers. According to one critic, "as it is now constituted, the world trading system discriminates against workers, especially those in the Third World." Globalization means a transition from (more or less) regulated domestic economies to an unregulated world economy. The superior mobility of capital, and the essentially fixed, immobile nature of world labor, means a fundamental shift in bargaining power in favor of large international corporations. Their global reach permits them to shift production almost costlessly from one location to another. As a consequence, instead of being able to exercise some degree of control over companies operating within their borders, governments are now locked in a bidding war with one another to attract and retain the business of large multinational companies.

The critics allege that international companies are using the threat of withdrawal or withholding of investment to pressure governments and workers to grant concessions. "Today [multinational companies] choose between workers in developing countries that compete against each other to depress wages to attract foreign investment." The result is a race for the bottom—a "destructive downward bidding spiral of the labor conditions and wages of workers throughout the world . . . ." Thus, critics charge that in Indonesia wages are deliberately held below the poverty level or subsistence in order to make the country a desirable location. The results of this competitive dismantling of worker protections, living standards and worker rights are predictable: deteriorating work conditions, declining real incomes for workers, and a widening gap between rich and poor in developing countries. I turn next to the specific charges made by the critics of international sweatshops.

Unconscionable Wages

Critics charge that the companies, by their proxies, are paying "starvation wages" and "slave wages." They are far from clear about what wage level they consider to be appropriate. But they generally demand that companies pay a "living wage." . . . According to Tim Smith, wage levels should be "fair, decent or a living wage for an employee and his or her family." He has said that wages in the maquiladoras of Mexico averaged $35 to $55 a week (in or near 1993) which he calls a "shockingly substandard wage," apparently on the grounds that it "clearly does not allow an employee to feed and care for a family adequately."[7] In 1992, Nike came in for harsh criticism when a magazine published the pay stub of a worker at one of its Indonesian suppliers. It showed that the worker was paid at the rate of $1.03 per day which was reportedly less than the Indonesian government's figure for "minimum physical need."

Immiserization Thesis

Former Labor Secretary Robert Reich has proposed as a test of the fairness of development policies that "[l]ow-wage workers should become better off, not worse off, as trade and investment boost national income." He has written that "[i]f a country pursues policies that . . . limit to a narrow elite the benefits of trade, the promise of open commerce is perverted and drained of its rationale."[8] A key claim of the activists is that companies actually impoverish or immiserize developing country workers. They experience an absolute decline in living standards. This thesis follows from the claim that the bidding war among developing countries is depressing wages . . . .

Widening Gap Between Rich and Poor

A related charge is that international sweatshops are contributing to the increasing gap between rich and poor. Not only are the poor being absolutely impoverished, but trade is generating greater inequality within developing countries. Another test that Reich has proposed to establish the fairness of international trade is that "the gap between rich and poor should tend to narrow with development, not widen." Critics charge that international sweatshops flunk that test. They say that the increasing GNPs of some developing countries simply mask a widening gap between rich and poor. "Across the world, both local and foreign elites are getting richer from the exploitation of the most vulnerable." And, "The major adverse consequence of quickening global economic integration has been widening income disparity within almost all nations . . . ." There appears to be a tacit alliance between the elites of both first and third world to exploit the most vulnerable, to regiment and control and conscript them so that they can create the material conditions for the elites' extravagant lifestyles.

Collusion with Repressive Regimes

Critics charge that, in their zeal to make their countries safe for foreign investment, third world regimes, notably China and Indonesia, have stepped up their repression. Not only have these countries failed to enforce even the minimal labor rules on the books, but they have also used their military and police to break strikes and repress independent unions. They have stifled political dissent, both to retain their hold on political power and to avoid any instability that might scare off foreign investors. Consequently, critics charge, companies such as Nike are profiting from political repression. "As unions spread in [Korea and Taiwan], Nike shifted its suppliers primarily to Indonesia, China and Thailand, where they could depend on governments to suppress independent union-organizing efforts."

EVALUATION OF THE CHARGES AGAINST INTERNATIONAL SWEATSHOPS

The critics' charges are undoubtedly accurate on a number of points: (1) There is no doubt that international companies are chasing cheap labor. (2) The wages paid by the international sweatshops are—by American standards—shockingly low. (3) Some developing country governments have tightly controlled or repressed organized labor in order to prevent it from disturbing the flow of foreign investment. Thus, in Indonesia, independent unions have been suppressed. (4) It is not unusual in developing countries for minimum wage levels to be lower than the official poverty level. (5) Developing country governments have winked at violations of minimum wage laws and labor rules. However, most jobs are in the informal sector and so largely, outside the scope of government supervision. (6) Some suppliers have employed children or have subcontracted work to other producers who have done so. (7) Some developing country governments deny their people basic political rights. China is the obvious example; Indonesia's record is pretty horrible . . . . But on many of the other counts, the critics' charges appear to be seriously inaccurate. And, even where the charges are accurate, it is not self-evident that the practices in question are improper or unethical, as we see next.

Wages and Conditions

Even the critics of international sweatshops do not dispute that the wages they pay are generally higher than—or at least equal to—comparable wages in the labor markets where they operate. According to the International Labor Organization (ILO), multinational companies often apply standards relating to wages, benefits, conditions of work, and occupational safety and health that both exceed statutory requirements and those practised by local firms. The ILO also says that wages and working conditions in so-called Export Processing Zones (EPZs) are often equal to or higher than jobs outside.[9] The World Bank says that the poorest workers in developing countries work in the informal sector where they often earn less than half what a formal sector employee earns. Moreover, "informal and rural workers often must work under more hazardous and insecure conditions than their formal sector counterparts."[10]

The same appears to hold true for the international sweatshops. In 1996, young women working in the plant of a Nike supplier in Serang, Indonesia, were earning the Indonesian legal minimum wage of 5,200 rupiahs or about $2.28 each day. As a report in the *Washington Post* pointed out, just earning the minimum wage put these workers among higher-paid Indonesians: "In Indonesia, less than half the working population earns the minimum wage, since about half of all adults here are in farming, and the typical farmer would make only about 2,000 rupiahs each day." . . . Also in 1996, a Nike spokeswoman estimated that an entry-level factory worker in the plant of a Nike supplier made five times what a farmer makes. Nike's chairman, Phil Knight, likes to teasingly remind critics that the average worker in one of Nike's Chinese factories is paid more than a professor at Beijing University. There is also plentiful anecdotal evidence from non-Nike sources. A worker at the Taiwanese-owned King Star Garment Assembly plant in Honduras told a reporter that he was earning seven times what he earned in the countryside.[11] In Bangladesh, the country's fledgling garment industry was paying women who had never worked before between $40 and $55 a month in 1991. That compared with a national per capita income of about $200 and the approximately $1 a day earned by many of these women's husbands as day laborers or richshaw drivers.[12] . . .

There is also the mute testimony of the lines of job applicants outside the sweatshops in Guatemala and Honduras. According to Lucy Martinez-Mont, in Guatemala the sweatshops are conspicuous for the long lines of young people waiting to be interviewed for a job.[13] Outside the gates of an industrial park in Honduras . . . "anxious onlookers are always waiting, hoping for a chance at least

to fill out a job application [for employment at one of the apparel plants]."[14]

The critics of sweatshops acknowledge that workers have voluntarily taken their jobs, consider themselves lucky to have them, and want to keep them . . . . But they go on to discount the workers' views as the product of confusion or ignorance, and/or they just argue that the workers' views are beside the point. Thus, while "it is undoubtedly true" that Nike has given jobs to thousands of people who wouldn't be working otherwise, they say that "neatly skirts the fundamental human-rights issue raised by these production arrangements that are now spreading all across the world." Similarly, Charles Kernaghan says that "[w]hether workers think they are better off in the assembly plants than elsewhere is not the real issue." Kernaghan, and Jeff Ballinger of the AFL-CIO, concede that the workers desperately need these jobs. But "[t]hey say they're not asking that U.S. companies stop operating in these countries. They're asking that workers be paid a living wage and treated like human beings."[15] Apparently these workers are victims of what Marx called false consciousness, or else they would grasp that they are being exploited. According to Barnet and Cavanagh, "For many workers . . . exploitation is not a concept easily comprehended because the alternative prospects for earning a living are so bleak."[16]

Immiserization and Inequality

The critics' claim that the countries that host international sweatshops are marked by growing poverty and inequality is flatly contradicted by the record. In fact, many of those countries have experienced sharp increases in living standards—for all strata of society. In trying to attract investment in simple manufacturing, Malaysia and Indonesia and, now, Vietnam and China are retracing the industrialization path already successfully taken by East Asian countries such as Taiwan, Korea, Singapore, and Hong Kong. These four countries got their start by producing labor-intensive manufactured goods (often electrical and electronic components, shoes, and garments) for export markets. Over time they graduated to the export of higher value-added items that are skill-intensive and require a relatively developed industrial base.

As is well known, these East Asian countries have achieved growth rates exceeding eight percent for a quarter-century . . . . The workers in these economies were not impoverished by growth. The benefits of growth were widely diffused: These economies achieved essentially full employment in the 1960s. Real wages rose by as much as a factor of four. Absolute poverty fell. And income inequality remained at low to moderate levels. It is true that in the initial stages the rapid growth generated only moderate increases in wages. But once essentially full employment was reached, . . . the increased demand for labor resulted in the bidding up of wages as firms competed for a scarce labor supply.

Interestingly, given its historic mission as a watchdog for international labor standards, the ILO has embraced this development model. It recently noted that the most successful developing economies, in terms of output and employment growth, have been "those who best exploited emerging opportunities in the global economy."[17] An "export-oriented policy is vital in countries that are starting on the industrialization path and have large surpluses of cheap labour." Countries that have succeeded in attracting foreign direct investment (FDI) have experienced rapid growth in manufacturing output and exports. The successful attraction of foreign investment in plant and equipment "can be a powerful spur to rapid industrialization and employment creation." . . .

According to the World Bank, the rapidly growing Asian economies (including Indonesia) "have also been unusually successful at sharing the fruits of their growth."[18] In fact, while inequality in the West has been growing, it has been shrinking in the Asian economies. They are the only economies in the world to have experienced high growth *and* declining inequality, and they also show shrinking gender gaps in education . . . .

Profiting from Repression?

What about the charge that international sweatshops are profiting from repression? It is undeniable that there is repression in many of the countries where sweatshops are located. But economic development appears to be relaxing that repression rather than strengthening its grip. The companies are supposed to benefit from government policies (e.g., repression of unions) that hold down labor costs. However, as we have seen, the wages paid by the international sweatshops already match or exceed the prevailing local wages. Not only that, but incomes in the East Asian economies, and in Indonesia, have risen rapidly. Moreover, even the sweatshops' critics admit that the main factor restraining wages in countries like Indonesia is the state of the labor market . . . . The high rate of unemployment and underemployment acts as a brake on wages: Only about 55 percent of the Indonesian labor force can find more than thirty-five hours of work each week, and about two million workers are unemployed.

The critics, however, are right in saying that the Indonesian government has opposed independent unions in the sweatshops out of fear they would lead to higher wages and labor unrest. But the government's fear clearly is that unions might drive wages in the modern industrial sector *above* market-clearing levels—or, more exactly, farther above market . . . . I think we can safely take at face value its claims that its policies are genuinely intended to help the economy create jobs to absorb the massive numbers of unemployed and underemployed.

LABOR STANDARDS IN INTERNATIONAL SWEATSHOPS: PAINFUL TRADE-OFFS

Who but the grinch could grudge paying a few additional pennies to some of the world's poorest workers? There is no doubt that the rhetorical force of the critics' case against international sweatshops rests on this apparently self-evident proposition. However, higher wages and improved labor standards are not free. After all, the critics themselves attack companies for chasing cheap labor. It follows that, if labor in developing countries is made more expensive (say, as the result of pressure by the critics), then those countries will receive less foreign investment, and fewer jobs will be created there. Imposing higher wages may deprive these countries of the one comparative advantage they enjoy, namely low-cost labor . . . .

By itself that may or may not be ethically objectionable. But these higher wages come at the expense of the incomes and the job opportunities of much poorer workers. As economists explain, higher wages in the formal sector reduce employment there and (by increasing the supply of labor) depress incomes in the informal sector. The case against requiring above-market wages for international sweatshop workers is essentially the same as the case against other measures that artificially raise labor costs, such as the minimum wage. In Jagdish Bhagwati's words: "Requiring a minimum wage in an overpopulated, developing country, as is done in a developed country, may actually be morally wicked. A minimum wage might help the unionized, industrial proletariat, while limiting the ability to save and invest rapidly which is necessary to draw more of the unemployed and nonunionized rural poor into gainful employment and income."[19] The World Bank makes the same point: "Minimum wages may help the most poverty-stricken workers in industrial countries, but they clearly do not in developing nations . . . . The workers whom minimum wage legislation tries to protect—urban formal workers—already earn much more than the less favored majority . . . . And inasmuch as minimum wage and other regulations discourage formal employment by increasing wage and non-wage costs, they hurt the poor who aspire to formal employment."[20]

The story is no different when it comes to labor standards other than wages. If standards are set too high, they will hurt investment and employment. The World Bank report points out that "[r]educing hazards in the workplace is costly, and typically the greater the reduction the more it costs. Moreover, the costs of compliance often fall largely on employees through lower wages or reduced employment. As a result, setting standards too high can actually lower workers' welfare . . . ." Perversely, if the higher standards advocated by critics retard the growth of formal sector jobs, then that will trap more informal and rural workers in jobs that are far more hazardous and insecure than those of their formal sector counterparts . . . .

Of course it might be objected that trading off workers' rights for more jobs is unethical. But, so far as I can determine, the critics have not made this argument. Although they sometimes implicitly accept the existence of the trade-off (we saw that they attack Nike for chasing cheap labor), their public statements are silent on the lost or forgone jobs from higher wages and better labor standards. At other times, they imply or claim that improvements in workers' wages and conditions are essentially free: According to Kernaghan, "Companies could easily double their employees' wages, and it would be nothing."

In summary, the result of the ostensibly humanitarian changes urged by critics are likely to be (1) reduced employment in the formal or modern sector of the economy, (2) lower incomes in the informal sector, (3) less investment and so slower economic growth, (4) reduced exports, (5) greater inequality and poverty . . . .

CONCLUSION: THE CASE FOR NOT EXCEEDING MARKET STANDARDS

. . . The business ethicists whose views I summarized at the beginning of this essay—Thomas Donaldson and Richard De George—objected to letting the market alone determine wages and labor standards in multinational companies. Both of them proposed criteria for setting wages that might occasionally "improve" on the outcomes of the market.

Their reasons for rejecting market determination of wages were similar. They both cited conditions that allegedly prevent international markets from generating ethically acceptable results. Donaldson argued that neoclassical economic principles are not applicable to international business because of high unemployment rates in developing countries. And De George argued that, in an unregulated international market, the gross inequality of bargaining power between workers and companies would lead to exploitation.

But this essay has shown that attempts to improve on market outcomes may have unforeseen tragic consequences. We saw how raising the wages of workers in international sweatshops might wind up penalizing the most vulnerable workers (those in the informal sectors of developing countries) by depressing their wages and reducing their job opportunities in the formal sector . . . . As we have seen, above-market wages paid to sweatshop workers may discourage further investment and so perpetuate high unemployment. In turn, the higher unemployment may weaken the bargaining power of workers vis-à-vis employers. Thus, such market imperfections seem to call for more reliance on market forces rather than less. Likewise, the experience of the newly industrialized East Asian economies suggests that the best cure for the ills of sweatshops is more sweatshops. But most of the well-intentioned policies proposed by critics and business ethicists are likely to have the opposite effect.

Where does this leave the international manager? If the preceding analysis is correct, then it follows that it is ethically acceptable to pay market wage rates in developing countries (and to provide employment conditions appropriate for the level of development). That holds true even if the wages pay less than so-called living wages or subsistence or even (conceivably) the local minimum wage. The appropriate test is not whether the wage reaches some predetermined standard but whether it is freely accepted by (reasonably) informed workers. The workers themselves are in the best position to judge whether the wages offered are superior to their next-best alternatives. (The same logic applies *mutatis mutandis* to workplace labor standards.)

Indeed, not only is it ethically acceptable for a company to pay market wages, but it may be ethically unacceptable for it to pay wages that exceed market levels. That will be the case if the company's above-market wages set precedents for other international companies that raise labor costs to the point of discouraging foreign investment. Furthermore, companies may have a social responsibility to transcend their own narrow concern with protecting their brand image and to publicly defend a system that has improved the lot of millions of workers in developing countries.

Notes

1. Richard De George, *Competing with Integrity in International Business* (New York: Oxford University Press, 1993), 79.
2. De George, *Competing with Integrity*, 356–57.
3. Thomas Donaldson, *Ethics of International Business* (New York: Oxford University Press, 1989), 101, 103, 145.
4. World Bank, "Workers in an Integrating World Economy" (World Development Report 1995) (New York: Oxford University Press, 1995), 77.
5. Donaldson, *Ethics of International Business*, 115.
6. De George, *Competing with Integrity*, 48.
7. Tim Smith, "The Power of Business for Human Rights," *Business & Society Review*, January 1994: 36.
8. Robert B. Reich, "Escape from the Global Sweatshop: Capitalism's Stake in Uniting the Workers of the World," *Washington Post*, May 22, 1994. Reich's test is intended to apply in developing countries "where democratic institutions are weak or absent."
9. International Labor Organization, *World Employment 1995* (Geneva: ILO, 1995), 73.
10. World Bank, "Workers in an Integrating World Economy," 5.
11. Larry Rohter, "To U.S. Critics, a Sweatshop; for Hondurans, a Better Life," *New York Times*, July 18, 1996.
12. Marcus Brauchli, "Garment Industry Booms in Bangladesh," *Wall Street Journal*, August 6, 1991.
13. Lucy Martinez-Mont, "Sweatshops Are Better Than No Shops," *Wall Street Journal*, June 25, 1996.
14. Rohter, "To U.S. Critics, a Sweatshop."
15. William B. Falk, "Dirty Little Secrets," Newsday, June 16, 1996.
16. Richard J. Barnet and John Cavanagh, "Just Undo It: Nike's Exploited Workers," *New York Times*, February 13, 1994.
17. ILO, *World Employment 1995*, 75.
18. World Bank, *The East Asian Miracle* (New York: Oxford University Press, 1993), 2.
19. Jagdish Bhagwati and Robert E. Hudec, eds., *Fair Trade and Harmonization* (Cambridge: MIT Press, 1996), vol. 1, p. 2.
20. World Bank, "Workers in an Integrating World Economy," 75.

Review and Discussion Questions

1. What are the four different standards that have been proposed for setting wages and labour standards in international sweatshops? Critically assess each standard. Are you persuaded by Maitland's criticism of Donaldson's test? Why do Donaldson and De George believe the classical liberal standard is inapplicable to poor, developing countries? Explain why you agree or disagree with their arguments.

2. By North American standards, wages in international sweatshops are very low, and working conditions appear terrible. Does the fact that foreign workers are eager to take these jobs establish that those wages and conditions are morally acceptable?

3. Maitland appears to believe that with regard to wages, "the appropriate test is . . . whether [the wage] [is] accepted by (reasonably) informed workers." Is that the only morally relevant test? Can wages be exploitative even if workers accept them?

4. Critics of international sweatshops believe that their wages and working conditions are morally inadequate, that international sweatshops impoverish local workers and increase inequality between rich and poor, and that the companies that use them end up colluding with repressive regimes. Maitland disputes each of those points. With regard to each point, with whom do you agree and why?

5. Business ethicists such as Donaldson and De George believe that multinational companies operating in the Third World should not leave it to the market alone to determine wages and working conditions. Maitland, to the contrary, argues that interfering with the market may have tragic consequences. With whom do you agree and why?

6. Assess international sweatshops from a utilitarian point of view, taking into account not just their effect on foreign workers and countries but also their consequences in terms of cheaper prices and lost jobs for the home country. What non-utilitarian moral considerations are also relevant to this issue?

7. Maitland believes that North American companies act rightly by paying market wages in developing countries and that it may even be wrong for them to pay wages that exceed market levels. What would you do if you were an international manager of a North American company?

8. Assess the following response to Maitland: "I agree that a law forcing companies to raise sweatshop wages would have bad results because it would discourage foreign investment. But this doesn't imply that an individual company has no moral obligation to raise its own wages, and it certainly doesn't imply that it would be wrong for the company to choose to do so."

9. Research in a number of countries shows (contrary to what one might expect) that increasing the minimum wage hasn't led to higher unemployment in the jurisdictions that have done so and that the most profitable firms pay the best wages. Is this evidence relevant to the assessment of Maitland's argument?

Further Reading for Chapter 4

Denis G. Arnold and **Norman E. Bowie**, "Sweatshops and Respect for Persons," *Business Ethics Quarterly* 13, no. 1 (April 2003), and **Chris Meyers**, "Wrongful Beneficence: Exploitation and Third World Sweatshops," *Journal of Social Philosophy* 35, no. 3 (Fall 2004) provide moral analyses of international sweatshops different from and critical of that of Ian Maitland.

John Douglas Bishop, ed., *Ethics and Capitalism* (Toronto: University of Toronto Press, 2000) is a collection of thought-provoking essays. Bishop's own contribution to the volume, "Ethics and Capitalism: A Guide to the Issues," is a valuable survey of the nature of capitalism and the key ethical issues it gives rise to.

Todd G. Buchholz, *New Ideas from Dead Economists*, rev. ed. (New York: Penguin, 1999), is a balanced and readable guide to modern economic thought applied to today's economy.

John Kenneth Galbraith, *The Economics of Innocent Fraud* (Boston: Houghton Mifflin, 2004) is a brief, masterly critique of our economic system by the famous economist.

Robert L. Heilbroner and **Lester C. Thurow**, *Economics Explained*, rev. ed. (New York: Simon & Schuster, 1994), is two respected economists' analysis of how our economy works, what its current difficulties are, and where it is headed.

Tibor R. Machan, ed., *The Main Debate: Communism Versus Capitalism* (New York: Random House, 1986) is a collection of accessible essays that debate the relative merits of capitalism and socialism.

David Schweickart, *After Capitalism* (Lanham, MD: Rowman & Littlefield, 2002) is an argument for worker-control socialism.

"A Survey of Globalisation," *Economist*, September 29, 2001; "A Survey of Capitalism and Democracy," *Economist*, June 28, 2003; and "A Survey of the World Economy," *Economist*, September 24, 2005 are intelligent, balanced discussions of the capitalist system.

5

Corporations

Nearly fifty years ago the vice-president of Ford Motor Company described the modern business corporation as the dominant institution of American society. Today few observers would disagree. As one of them puts it, "The modern corporation is *the* central institution of contemporary society."[1] As an aggregate, corporations wield awesome economic clout. While the Canadian gross domestic product (GDP, the total market value of all the goods and services produced) for the year ending in July 2007 was about $1.1 trillion, the total revenues for the 16 Canadian companies that made it into the Fortune Global 500 were about $300 billion. The 500 largest U.S. companies constitute at least three-quarters of the American economy. But the dominant role of corporations in our society extends well beyond that. Not only do they produce almost all the goods and services we buy, but also they and their ethos permeate everything from politics and communications to athletics and religion. And their influence is growing relentlessly around the world.

By any measure, the biggest corporations worldwide are colossi that dominate the earth. Many of them employ tens of thousands of people, and the largest have hundreds of thousands in their ranks. In Canada, George Weston Ltd. employs about 155,000 people and the Big Five (banks) together about 220,000 people, However impressive, these figures pale before the workforces of some of the world's economic behemoths: General Electric's approximately 340,000 and General Motors's 388,000—not to mention the 1.7 million people who work for Wal-Mart, the world's largest private-sector employer. And their revenues are dazzling. For example, General Motors takes in more than $193 billion a year, Wal-Mart $288 billion, Ford $172 billion, and IBM $96 billion. By comparison, the GDP of, say, Turkey is about $185 billion; that of Norway $124 billion; and that of New Zealand $68 billion. The province of Ontario in 2006 contained 38 percent of Canada's population and accounted for about 41 percent of the country's annual GDP. Yet the provincial GDP was less than the total revenues in that year of the top 25 companies.[2]

And corporations throughout the globe are growing larger and wealthier every year. For example, in 1989 Time Inc. merged with Warner Communications to form Time Warner. Seven years later Time Warner combined with Turner Broadcasting. Then in January 2001, in a move that shook up Wall Street, Time Warner and America Online merged. At a stroke, the new company they created was valued at $350 billion. What does $350 billion mean? It is equivalent to the GDP of India, the 15th-highest in the world. It is more than the combined GDPs of Hungary, Ukraine, the Czech Republic, New Zealand, Peru, and Pakistan. And it is more than the industrial output of the United Kingdom or the manufacturing output of China.

Modern corporations are in principle three-part organizations, made up of stockholders, who provide the capital, own the corporation, and enjoy liability limited to the amount of their investments; managers, who run the business operations; and employees, who produce the goods and services. However, a corporate giant such as AOL Time Warner, Exxon Mobil, or Citigroup is less like a single company and more like "a fabulously wealthy investment club with a limited portfolio." Such companies invest in subsidiaries, whose heads, writes business analyst Anthony J. Parisi, "oversee their territories like provincial governors, sovereigns in their own lands but with an authority stemming from the power center. . . . The management committee exacts its tribute (the affiliate's profits from current operations) and issues doles (the money needed to sustain and expand those operations)."[3] In the best-run organizations the management system is highly structured and impersonal. It provides the corporation's overall framework, the formal chain of command that ensures that the company's profit objectives are pursued.

The emergence of corporate behemoths is one of the more intriguing chapters in the evolution of capitalism. Certainly the political theory of John Locke and the economic theory of Adam Smith admitted no such conglomerates of capital as those that originated in the nineteenth century—as late as 1832 hardly any private firms had ten or more employees[4]—and today dominate the world's economic, political, and social life. This book isn't the place to analyze why a people committed by and large to an individualistic social philosophy and a free-competition market economy allowed vast oligopolistic organizations to develop. Rather, the concern here is with the problem of applying moral standards to corporate organizations and with understanding their social responsibilities. After a brief review of the history of the corporation, this chapter looks at the following specific topics:

1. The debate over whether corporations are moral agents and can be meaningfully said to have moral responsibilities

2. The controversy between the narrow and the broad views of corporate social responsibility

3. Three key arguments in this debate: the invisible-hand argument, the let-government-do-it argument, and the business-can't-handle-it argument

4. The importance of institutionalizing ethics within corporations and how this may be done

THE LIMITED-LIABILITY COMPANY

If you ask a lawyer for a definition of *corporation*, you will probably get something like the following: a corporation is an organization that can endure beyond the natural lives of its members and that has incorporators who may sue and be sued as a unit and who are able to consign part of their property to the corporation for ventures of limited liability. *Limited liability* is a key feature of the modern corporation. It means that the members of the corporation are financially liable for corporate debts only up to the extent of their investments.

In addition, limited-liability companies, or corporations, differ from partnerships and other forms of business association in two ways. First, a corporation is not formed simply by an agreement entered into among its first members. It becomes incorporated by being publicly registered or in some other way having its existence officially acknowledged by the law (either provincial or federal statutes). Second, although a partner is automatically entitled to his or her share of the profits as soon as they are ascertained, the shareholder in a corporation is entitled to a dividend from the company's profits only when it has been "declared." Under Canadian and U.S. law, dividends are usually declared by the directors of a corporation.

When we think of corporations, we naturally think of corporate giants that exert enormous influence over their national economy and indeed the international economic and social context: such American giants as General Motors, Microsoft and Wal-Mart, or our own mini-giants like the Royal Bank, Manulife Financial or Power Corp. But the local independently owned convenience store may be a corporation, and historically the concept of a corporation has been broad enough to encompass churches, trade guilds, and local governments. Corporations may be either *for* profit or *non*-profit-making. Princeton University, for example, is a nonprofit corporation. Companies like Eastman Kodak or Magna International, by contrast, aim to make money for shareholders. Corporations may be privately owned or owned (in part or whole) by the government. Though the federal or provincial governments own numerous corporations (known as either federal or provincial Crown corporations, for example, VIA Rail, CBC, Hydro One), the overwhelming majority of Canadian corporations are privately owned, while in the U.S. corporations are almost entirely privately owned. In connection with privately-owned, profit-making corporations, it may be that only a small group of investors own all of its outstanding shares (a "privately held" corporation), or its stock may be traded among the general public (a "publicly held" corporation). All companies whose stocks are listed on stock exchanges are publicly held corporations.

Several stages mark the evolution of the corporation. The corporate form itself developed during the early Middle Ages, and the first corporations were towns, universities, and ecclesiastical orders. They were chartered by government and regulated by public statute. As corporate bodies, they existed independently of the particular individuals who constituted their membership at any given time. By the fifteenth century, the courts of England had evolved the principle of limited liability—thus setting limits, for example, on how much an alderman of the Liverpool Corporation might be required to pay if the city went bankrupt. During the medieval period, however, the law did not grant corporate status to purely profit-making associations. In those days, something besides economic self-interest had to be seen as uniting the members of the corporation: religion, a trade, shared political responsibilities.

This state of affairs changed during the Elizabethan era, as the actual incorporation of business enterprises began. European entrepreneurs were busy organizing trading voyages to the East and to North America. The East India Company, which epitomizes the great trading companies of this period, was formed in 1600, when Queen Elizabeth I granted to a group of merchants the right to be "one body corporate" and bestowed on it a trading monopoly to the East Indies. In the following decades, numerous other incorporated firms were granted trading monopolies and colonial charters. Much of North America's settlement, in fact, was initially underwritten as a business venture. A key player in that business venture was our own Hudson's Bay Company which was incorporated by Royal Charter from King Charles II in 1670.

Although the earliest corporations typically held special trading rights from the government, their members did not pool capital. Rather, they individually financed voyages using the corporate name and absorbed the loss individually if a vessel sank or was robbed by pirates. But as ships became larger and more expensive, no single buyer could afford to purchase and outfit one, and the loss of a ship would have been ruinous to any one individual. The solution was to pool capital and share liability. Thus emerged the prototype of today's corporations.[5]

The movement toward the corporate organization of business began in earnest only after Confederation in Canada and the end of Civil War in the U.S. The loosening of government restrictions on corporate chartering procedures in the nineteenth century marks this final stage of corporate evolution. Until the mid-1800s, prospective corporations had to apply for charters. Government officials carefully studied applications, rejecting some and burdening others with special conditions (for example, limits on the amount of property that might be owned or restrictions on where it might be held) in order to promote the public good. Critics of the incorporation system charged that it really promoted favouritism, corruption, and unfair monopolies. Gradually, the old system of incorporation was replaced by the system we know today, in which corporate status is granted essentially to any organization that fills out the forms and pays the fees.

Lurking behind this change were two important theoretical shifts. First, underlying the old system was the mercantilist idea that a corporation's activities should advance some specific public purpose. But Adam Smith and, following him, Alexander Hamilton, the first U.S. Secretary of the Treasury, challenged the desirability of a direct tie between business enterprise and public policy. Their idea was that businesspeople should be encouraged to explore their own avenues of enterprise. The "invisible hand" of the market would direct their activities in a socially beneficial direction more effectively than any public official could.

Second, when nineteenth-century reformers argued for changes in incorporation procedures, they talked not only about government favouritism and the advantages of a laissez-faire approach but also about the principle of a corporation's right to exist.[6] Any petitioning body with the minimal qualifications, they asserted, has the right to receive a corporate charter. By contrast, the early Crown-chartered corporations were clearly creations of the state, in accordance with the legal-political doctrine that all corporate status was a privilege bestowed by the state as it saw fit. According to the reformers, however, incorporation is a byproduct of the people's right of association, not a gift from the state.

Even though the right of association supports relaxed incorporation procedures, the state must still incorporate companies and guarantee their legal status. Corporations must be recognized by the law as a single agent in order for them to enjoy their rights and privileges. To a large extent, then, the corporation remains, as U.S. Chief Justice John Marshall put it in 1819, "an artificial being, invisible, intangible, and existing only in the contemplation of the law."[7]

Corporations are clearly legal agents. But are they also moral agents? And whereas corporations have definite legal responsibilities, what, if any, social and moral responsibilities do they have?

CORPORATE MORAL AGENCY

Corporations are of course recognized as legal entities. In recent years courts have also began to recognize them as protected under legislation intended in the first place to protect the rights of human individuals. In their attempt to facilitate and regulate human interactions, courts may well find it necessary to treat abstract entities like corporations as if they were, as we might say, "human." But legal decisions do not automatically decide the issue of whether corporate entities are properly to be regarded as "persons." There may be larger philosophical and logical objections to so treating them. One of the immediate problems is, of course, that corporations are not human. To quote Lord Thurlow, an eighteenth-century lawyer, how can you "expect a corporation to have a conscience, when it has no soul to be damned and no body to be kicked?"[8] We might express Thurlow's point differently as follows. Although corporations are indeed collective entities that in some sense really exist, with an identity distinct from that of the people whom they comprise at any given time, it is questionable whether they have moral obligations just as individual human beings do. Can they be held morally responsible, not just legally liable, for the things they do? The answer to this question hangs on another question, namely: Does it make sense to view corporations as moral agents, that is, as entities capable of making moral decisions? If so, then corporations can be held morally responsible for their actions. They—and not just the individual human beings who make them up—can be seen as having moral obligations and as being blameworthy for failing to meet those obligations. They can, accordingly, be praised or blamed, even punished, for the decisions they make and the actions and policies they undertake.

The task of determining whether corporations can make moral decisions is anything but simple. Immediately, we must ponder whether it makes sense to say that any entity other than an individual person can make decisions in the first place, moral or otherwise.

Can Corporations Make Moral Decisions?

Corporate internal decision (CID) structures amount to established procedures for accomplishing specific goals. For example, consider ExxonMobil's system, as depicted by Anthony J. Parisi:

> All through the Exxon system, checks and balances are built in. Each fall, the presidents of the 13 affiliates take their plan for the coming year and beyond to New York for review at a meeting with the management committee and the staff vice presidents. The goal is to get a perfect corporate fit. Some imaginary examples: The committee might decide that Exxon is becoming too concentrated in Australia and recommend that Esso Eastern move more slowly on that continent. Or it might conclude that if the affiliates were to build all the refineries they are proposing, they would create

more capacity than the company could profitably use. One of the affiliates would be asked to hold off, even though, from its particular point of view, a new refinery was needed to serve its market.[9]

The implication here is that any decisions coming out of ExxonMobil's annual sessions are formed and shaped to effect corporate goals, "to get a perfect corporate fit." Metaphorically, all data pass through the filter of corporate procedures and objectives. The remaining distillation constitutes the decision. Certainly the participants actively engage in decision making. But in addition to individual persons, the other major component of corporate decision making consists of the framework within which policies and activities are determined.

The CID structure lays out lines of authority and stipulates under what conditions personal actions become official corporate actions. Some philosophers have compared the corporation to a machine or have argued that because of its structure it is bound to pursue its profit goals single-mindedly. As a result, they claim, it is a mistake to see a corporation as being morally responsible or to expect it to display such moral characteristics as honesty, considerateness, and sympathy. Only the individuals within a corporation can act morally or immorally; only they can be held responsible for what it does.

Others have argued the contrary. The CID structure, like an individual person, collects data about the impact of its actions. It monitors work conditions, employee efficiency and productivity, and environmental impacts. Professors Kenneth E. Goodpaster and John B. Matthews argue that as a result, there is no reason a corporation cannot show the same kind of rationality and respect for persons that individual human beings can. By analogy, they contend, it makes just as much sense to speak of corporate moral responsibility as it does to speak of individual moral responsibility.[10] Thomas Donaldson agrees. He argues that a corporation can be a moral agent if moral reasons enter into its decision making and if its decision-making process controls not just the company's actions but also its structure of policies and rules.[11]

Philosopher Peter French arrives at the same conclusion in a slightly different way.[12] The CID structure, says French, in effect absorbs the intentions and acts of individual persons into a "corporate decision." Perhaps no corporate official intended the course or objective charted by the CID structure, but, French contends, the corporation did. And he believes that these corporate intentions are enough to make corporate acts "intentional" and thus make corporations "morally responsible." Professor of philosophy Manuel Velasquez demurs. An act is intentional, says Velasquez, only if the entity that formed the intention brings about the act through its bodily movements. But it is only the people who make up the corporation who carry out the acts attributed to it. Velasquez concludes that only corporate members, not the corporation itself, can be held morally responsible.[13]

Corporate Punishment The debate over corporate moral agency bears on the question of punishment. If corporations are not moral actors, the law can, of course, still fine them, monitor and regulate their activities, and require the people who run them to do one thing or another. But one can talk in a literal sense about punishing corporations only if they are entities or "persons" capable of making moral decisions. However, even if they are, not all the usual goals and methods of punishment make sense when applied to corporations. If corporations are moral agents, then the law can deter them with the threat of punishment, and it can force them to make restitution. Punishment can, perhaps, even rehabilitate a corporation, viewed as a moral agent. Retribution, as a goal of punishment, however, seems to have little application to corporations. And obviously corporations cannot be jailed for breaking the law. Even imposing fines on them can be problematic. Financial penalties stiff enough to have an impact can easily injure innocent parties, for example, if they lead to layoffs, plant closures, or higher prices for consumers.

Vanishing Individual Responsibility

Some might argue that whether or not corporations as artificial entities can properly be held morally responsible, the nature and structure of a modern corporate organization allows virtually everyone in it to share moral accountability for what it does. But in practice this diffusion of responsibility can mean that no particular person or persons are held morally responsible. For example, does responsibility for an injury caused by a defective product fall on the shoulders of the worker who last handled the product, the foreman overseeing the running of the assembly line, the factory supervisor, the quality control team, the engineers who designed and tested the equipment, the regional managers who decided to produce the item, or the company's CEO, whose office is in another city? Indeed, each of these individuals may have been only following established procedures and decision-making guidelines. Inside a corporation it may often be difficult, even impossible, to assign responsibility for a particular outcome to any single individual because so many different people, acting within a given CID framework, contributed to it in small ways.

This masking of moral accountability may not seem so surprising: after all, in situations that don't involve corporations, assigning praise and blame can also be problematic. But it raises the troubling possibility that the size and impersonal bureaucratic structure of the corporation may so envelop its members that it becomes vacuous to speak of individual moral agency. This, in turn, raises the spectre of actions without actors in any moral sense—of defective products, broken laws, or flouted contracts, without any morally responsible parties.

There are two ways to escape this uncomfortable conclusion. One is to attribute moral agency to corporations just as we do to individual persons. The other, not necessarily incompatible with the first, is to realize that these days too many people are willing, even eager, to duck personal responsibility—"it's not my job," "there's nothing I can do about it," "I was just following procedure"—by submerging it in the protoplasmic CID structures of the modern corporation. Perhaps until CID structures are reconstituted to deal explicitly with non-economic matters, we can expect more of the same evasion of personal responsibility.

The issue of corporate moral agency undoubtedly will continue to exercise scholars. Meanwhile, the inescapable fact is that corporations are increasingly being accorded the status of biological persons, with all the rights and responsibilities implied by that status. Before it was gobbled up by another corporation, the Continental Oil Company expressed in an in-house booklet the public perception and its implications as follows:

No one can deny that in the public's mind a corporation can break the law and be guilty of unethical and amoral conduct. Events . . . such as corporate violation of federal laws and failure of full disclosure [have] confirmed that both our government and our citizenry expect *corporations* to act lawfully, ethically, and responsibly.

Perhaps it is then appropriate in today's context to think of Conoco as a *living corporation*; a sentient being whose conduct and personality are the collective effort and responsibility of its employees, officers, directors, and shareholders.[14]

Today many companies and many of the people inside them accept without hesitation the idea that corporations are moral agents with genuinely moral, not just legal, responsibilities.

This point was illustrated recently when Colonial Pipeline of Atlanta published full-page advertisements in several newspapers headlined "We Apologize." The company used the ads to take responsibility for having spilled oil into the Reedy River of South Carolina three years before. True, the ads were part of a plea agreement with the Justice Department for having violated the *Clean Water Act* (the company also agreed to pay a $7 million fine). Yet the company's words had ethical overtones. As Laura Nash of the Harvard Divinity School comments, they put "moral emotion into what is essentially a legal statement" because "the word 'apologize' . . . admits a sense of shame and humility."[15] Shame and humility were evident, too, when in 2004 the world saw photographs of Charles Prince, the chief executive of Citigroup, and Douglas Petersen, Citibank Japan CEO, bowing their heads at a press conference in Tokyo in a public act of remorse for Citigroup's illegal actions in that country.

If, then, it makes sense to talk about the social and moral responsibilities of corporations, either in a literal sense or as a shorthand way of referring to the obligations of the individuals that make up the corporation, what are these responsibilities?

RIVAL VIEWS OF CORPORATE RESPONSIBILITY

In 1963 Tennessee Iron & Steel, a subsidiary of United States Steel, was by far the largest employer, purchaser, and taxpayer in Birmingham, Alabama. In the same city at the same time, racial tensions exploded in the bombing of an African-American church, killing four black children. The ugly incident led some to blame U.S. Steel for not doing more to improve race relations, but Roger Blough, chairman of U.S. Steel, defended his company:

I do not either believe that it would be a wise thing for United States Steel to be other than a good citizen in a community, or to attempt to have its ideas of what is right for the community enforced upon the community by some sort of economic means. . . .

When we as individuals are citizens in a community we can exercise what small influence we may have as citizens, but for a corporation to attempt to exert any kind of economic compulsion to achieve a particular end in the racial area seems to me quite beyond what a corporation can do.[16]

Not long afterward, Sol M. Linowitz, chairman of the board of Xerox Corporation, declared in an address to the U.S. National Industrial Conference Board: "To realize its full promise in the world of tomorrow, American business and industry—or, at least, the vast portion of it—will have to make social goals as central to its decisions as economic goals; and leadership in our corporations will increasingly recognize this responsibility and accept it."[17] But, just what responsibilities does a corporation have? Is its responsibility to be construed narrowly as merely profit-making? Or is it to be construed more broadly so as to include refraining from harming society and even contributing actively and directly to the public good?

Narrow View: Profit Maximization

As it happened, the year preceding the Birmingham incident had seen the publication of *Capitalism and Freedom*, in which author Milton Friedman forcefully argued that business has no social responsibilities other than to maximize profits:

The view has been gaining widespread acceptance that corporate officials and labor leaders have a social responsibility that goes beyond serving the interest of their stockholders or their members. This view shows a fundamental misconception of the character and nature of a free economy. In such an economy, there is one and only one social responsibility of business—to use its resources and engage in activities designed to increase its profits so long as it stays within the rules of the game, which is to say, engages in open and free competition, without deception or fraud . . . . Few trends could so thoroughly undermine the very foundations of our free society as the acceptance by corporate officials of a social responsibility other than to make as much money for their stockholders as possible.[18]

Although from Friedman's perspective the only responsibility of business is to make money for its owners, obviously a business may not do literally anything whatsoever to increase its profits. Gangsters pursue profit maximization when they ruthlessly rub out their rivals, but such activity falls outside what Friedman referred to as "the rules of the game." Harvard professor Theodore Levitt echoed this point when he wrote, "In the end business has only two responsibilities—to obey the elementary canons of face-to-face civility (honesty, good faith, and so on) and to seek material gain."[19]

What, then, are the rules of the game? Obviously, elementary morality rules out deception, force, and fraud, and the rules of the game are intended to promote open and free competition. The system of rules in which business is to pursue profit is, in Friedman's view, one that is conducive to the laissez-faire operation of Adam Smith's "invisible hand" (which was discussed in Chapter 4). Friedman is a conservative economist who believes that by allowing the market to operate with only the minimal restrictions necessary to prevent fraud and force, society will maximize its overall economic well-being. Pursuit of profit is what makes our system go. Anything that dampens this incentive or inhibits its operation will weaken the ability of Smith's invisible hand to deliver the economic goods.

Because the function of a business organization is to make money, the owners of corporations employ executives to accomplish that goal, thereby obligating these managers always to act in the interests of the owners. According to Friedman, to say that executives have social responsibilities beyond the pursuit of profit means that at least sometimes they must subordinate owner interests to some social objective, such as controlling pollution or fighting inflation. They must then spend stockholder money for general social interests—in effect, taxing the owners and spending those taxes on social causes. But taxation is a function of government, not private enterprise; executives are not public employees but employees of private enterprise. The doctrine of social responsibility thus transforms executives into civil servants and business corporations into government agencies, thereby diverting business from its proper function in the social system.

Friedman is critical of those who would impose on business any duty other than that of making money, and he is particularly harsh with those business leaders who themselves take a broader view of their social responsibilities. They may believe that they are defending the free-enterprise system when they give speeches proclaiming that profit isn't the only goal of business or affirming that business has a social conscience and takes seriously its responsibility to provide employment, refrain from polluting, eliminate discrimination, and so on. But these business leaders are short-sighted; they are helping to undermine capitalism by implicitly reinforcing the view that the pursuit of profit is wicked and must be regulated by external forces.[20]

Friedman acknowledges that corporate activities are often described as an exercise of "social responsibility" when, in fact, they are intended simply to advance the company's self-interest. For example, it might be in the long-term self-interest of a corporation that is a major employer in a small town to spend money to enhance the local community by helping to improve its schools, parks, roads, or social services, thereby attracting good employees to the area, reducing the company's wage bill, or improving worker morale and productivity. By portraying its actions as dictated by a sense of social responsibility, the corporation can generate good will as a byproduct of expenditures that are entirely justified by self-interest. Friedman has no problem with a company pursuing its self-interest by these means, but he rues the fact that "the attitudes of the public make it in the self-interest [of corporations] to cloak their actions in this way."[21] Friedman's bottom line is that the bottom line is all that counts, and he firmly rejects any notion of corporate social responsibility that would hinder a corporation's profit maximization.

The Broader View of Corporate Social Responsibility

The rival position to that of Friedman and Levitt is simply that business has other obligations in addition to pursuing profits. The phrase *in addition to* is important. Critics of the narrow view do not as a rule believe there is anything wrong with corporate profit. They maintain, rather, that corporations have other responsibilities as well—to consumers, to employees, to suppliers and contractors, to the surrounding community, and to society at large. They see the modern corporation as a social institution that should consider the interests of all the groups it has an impact on. Sometimes called the "social entity model" or the "stakeholder model," this broader view of corporate social responsibility maintains that a corporation has obligations, not just to its stockholders, but also to all the other constituencies that affect or are affected by its behaviour, that is, to all parties that have a stake in what a corporation does or doesn't do.

If the adherents of the broader view share one belief, it is that corporations have responsibilities beyond simply enhancing their profits because, as a matter of fact, they have such great social and economic power in our society. With that power must come social responsibility. As professor of business administration Keith Davis puts it:

One basic proposition is that *social responsibility arises from social power.* Modern business has immense social power in such areas as minority employment and environmental pollution. If business has the power, then a just relationship demands that business also bear responsibility for its actions in these areas. Social responsibility arises from concern about the consequences of business's acts as they affect the interests of others. Business decisions do have social consequences. Businessmen cannot make decisions that are solely economic decisions, because they are interrelated with the whole social system. This situation requires that businessmen's thinking be broadened beyond the company gate to the whole social system. Systems thinking is required.

Social responsibility implies that a business decision maker in the process of serving his own business interests is obliged to take actions that also protect and enhance society's interests. The net effect is to improve the quality of life in the broadest possible way, however quality of life is defined by society. In this manner, harmony is achieved between business's actions and the larger social system. The businessman becomes concerned with social as well as economic outputs and with the total effect of his institutional actions on society.[22]

Proponents of the broader view, such as Davis, stress that modern business is intimately integrated with the rest of society. Business is not some self-enclosed world, like a private poker party. Rather, business activities have profound ramifications throughout society, and their influence on our lives is hard to escape. Business writer John Kay makes this point with reference to General Electric: "The company's activities are so extensive that you necessarily encounter them daily, often without knowing you are doing so. GE's business is our business even if we do not want it to be."[23]

As a result, although society permits and expects corporations to pursue their economic interests, they have other responsibilities as well. Thus, for example, it is wrong for corporations to raid the pension funds of their employees, as many have done,[24] or to evade taxes through creative accounting or by reincorporating in tax havens such as Bermuda,[25] even if doing so is legal and enhances the bottom line. "We reasonably expect that GE should care that its engines are safe," writes John Kay, "not just that they comply with FAA procedures; that if there is a problem with its medical equipment the company will try to put it right, not cover it up; that GE financial statements are true and fair and not just compliant with accounting standards."[26]

Melvin Anshen has cast the case for the broader view in a historical perspective.[27] He maintains that there is always a kind of "social contract" between business and society. This contract is, of course, only implicit, but it represents a tacit understanding within society about the proper goals and responsibilities of business. In effect, in Anshen's view, society always structures the guidelines within which business is permitted to operate in order to derive certain benefits from business activity. For instance, in the nineteenth century, society's prime interest was rapid economic growth, which was viewed as the source of all progress, and the engine of economic growth was identified as the drive for profits by unfettered, competitive, private enterprise. That attitude was reflected in the then-existing social contract.

Today, however, society has concerns and interests other than rapid economic growth—in particular, a concern for the quality of life and for the preservation of the environment. Accordingly, the social contract is in the process of being modified. In particular, Anshen writes, "it will no longer be acceptable for corporations to manage their affairs solely in terms of the traditional internal costs of doing business, while thrusting external costs on the public."

In recent years we have grown more aware of the possible deleterious side effects of business activity, or what economists call *externalities*. Externalities are the unintended negative (or in some cases positive) consequences that an economic transaction between two parties can have on some third party. Industrial pollution provides the clearest illustration. Suppose, for example, that a factory makes widgets and sells them to your firm. A by-product of this economic transaction is the waste that the rains wash from the factory yard into the local river, waste that damages recreational and commercial fishing interests downstream. This damage to third parties is an unintended side-effect of the economic transaction between the seller and the buyer of widgets.

Defenders of the new social contract, like Anshen, maintain that externalities should no longer be overlooked. In the jargon of economists, externalities must be "internalized." That is, the factory should be made to absorb the cost, either by disposing of its waste in an environmentally safe (and presumably more expensive) way or by paying for the damage the waste does downstream. On one hand, basic fairness requires that the factory's waste no longer be dumped onto third parties. On the other hand, from the economic point of view, requiring the factory to internalize the externalities makes sense, for only when it does so will the price of the widgets it sells reflect their true social cost. The real production cost of the widgets includes not just labour, raw materials, machinery, and so on but also the damage done to the fisheries downstream. Unless the price of widgets is raised sufficiently to reimburse the fisheries for their losses or to dispose of the waste in some other way, then the buyer of widgets is paying less than their true cost. Part of the cost is being paid by the fishing interests downstream.

Advocates of the broader view go beyond requiring business to internalize its externalities in a narrow economic sense. Keith Davis, for example, maintains that in addition to considering potential profitability, a business must weigh the long-range social costs of its activities as well. Only if the overall benefit to society is positive should business act:

The expectation of the social responsibility model is that a detailed cost/benefit analysis will be made prior to determining whether to proceed with an activity and that social costs will be given significant weight in the decision-making process. Almost any business action will entail some social costs. The basic question is whether the benefits outweigh the costs so that there is a net social benefit. Many questions of judgment arise, and there are no precise mathematical measures in the social field, but rational and wise judgments can be made if the issues are first thoroughly explored.[28]

Stockholders and the Corporation

On the broad view of its aims, business must, in addition to maximizing profit for its shareholders, take care to address the concerns and interests of other stakeholders, such as the employees, consumers, suppliers, the local and even national community. Perhaps surprisingly, even a majority of managers rejects a profit-only philosophy of corporate management.[29] Advocates of the narrow view of business aims, however, believe that these views and attitudes reflect a misunderstanding of the proper relationship between management and stockholders. Stockholders own the company. They entrust management with their funds, and in return management undertakes to make as much money for them as it can. As a result, according to proponents of the narrow view, management has a fiduciary duty to maximize shareholder wealth, a duty that is inconsistent with any social responsibility other than the relentless pursuit of profit.

The managers of a corporation do indeed have a fiduciary responsibility to look after the interests of shareholders, a duty that is clearly violated by those corporate executives who take advantage of their position to enrich themselves at company expense with extravagant bonuses, stock options, and retirement packages or to waste corporate money on jets, apartments, private parties, and various personal services that lack any plausible business rationale. But it doesn't follow from this, as proponents of the narrow view maintain, that the corporation should be run entirely for the benefit of stockholders, that their interests always take priority over the interests of everyone else. To the contrary, argue critics of the narrow view, management has fiduciary responsibilities to other constituencies as well—for example, to employees, bondholders, and consumers. The duty to make money for shareholders is real, but it doesn't trump all of a company's other responsibilities. Indeed, it's debatable whether most shareholders believe that it does. Many of them may want the company they "own" to act in a morally responsible manner—say, by not contributing to environmental pollution or by treating employees with respect—even if that means less profit.

Against that point of view, however, Milton Friedman argues, "The whole justification for permitting the corporate executives to be selected by the shareholders is that the executive is an agent serving the interests of his principal."[30] This justification disappears, he believes, when executives expend corporate resources in ways that don't necessarily enhance the bottom line. They are then acting more like public servants than employees of a private enterprise. But even if one agrees that stockholders select corporate managers to act as their agents and advance their interests, this doesn't prove that those executives are bound to act

solely to increase shareholder wealth, ignoring all other moral considerations. Undertaking to look after other people's interests or promising to try to make money for them creates a genuine obligation, but that obligation is not absolute. It doesn't eliminate all other moral responsibilities. By analogy, promising to meet someone at a certain time and place for lunch creates an obligation, but that obligation doesn't override one's duty to assist someone having a heart attack. And something that it would be immoral for you to do (such as making a dangerous product) doesn't become right just because you're acting on behalf of someone else or because you promised him that you would do it.

Friedman believes that if executives "impose taxes on stockholders and spend the proceeds for 'social' purposes, they become 'civil servants,' and thus should be selected through a political process."[31] He considers such a proposal absurd or, at best, socialistic. And yet others contend that corporations are too focused on profits and fear the damage to society when firms are willing to sacrifice all other values on the altar of the bottom line. They don't think it absurd at all that corporations should take a broader view of their social role and responsibilities. They see nothing in the management–stockholder relationship that would morally forbid corporations from doing so.

Who Controls the Corporation? According to the narrow view of corporate social responsibility, stockholders own the corporation and select managers to run it for them. Although that model may make sense for some small firms or when venture capitalists invest in a startup company, it doesn't accurately reflect modern corporate reality. To begin with, most stockholders purchase shares in a company from current stockholders, who acquired their shares the same way. Very few investors put their money directly into a corporation; rather, they buy second-hand shares that were initially issued years before. They pick companies that look profitable or likely to grow or whose products or policies appeal to them, or they may simply be following the advice of their broker. And they are generally prepared to resell their shares, perhaps even the same day they bought them, if it is profitable to do so. Stockholders have no legal obligation to the company. They are a far-flung, diverse, and ever-changing group. They come and go, and rarely, if ever, have direct contact with the managers of the company or even know or care who they are.

For those reasons, then, it's implausible to see stockholders in, say, Home Depot or Procter & Gamble as being genuine owners or proprietors of the company. "A share of stock," write two legal experts, "does not confer ownership of the underlying assets owned by the corporation. Instead, it provides the holder with a right to share in the financial returns produced by the corporations' business." It is a financial instrument, more akin to a bond, than to a car or building.[32]

Few economists or business theorists believe that stockholders are really in charge of the companies whose shares they hold or that they select the managers who run them. As long ago as 1932, Adolf Berle and Gardiner Means showed that because stock ownership in large corporations is so dispersed, actual control of the corporation has passed to management.[33] Today, as most business observers acknowledge, management handpicks the board of directors, thus controlling the body that is supposed to police it. "The CEO puts up the candidates; no one runs against them, and management counts the votes," says Nell Minow of the Corporate Library, a corporate watchdog website. "We wouldn't deign to call this an election in a third-world country."[34] Even in those rare cases when shareholders put up their own candidates, such proxy fights are expensive, and the incumbent management has the corporate coffers at its disposal to fight them.

As a result, the board of directors typically rubber-stamps the policies and recommendations of management. That's why it's not surprising that in 2000 the directors of Enron ignored shareholder interests and approved paying out $750 million in executive compensation—$140 million of it to its chairman—when the company's entire net income was only $975 million. And how else to explain the lavish retirement packages that boards lavish on former CEOs; these often include a million-dollar annual pension, an expensive apartment, a car and driver, and free use of the company aircraft.[35] True, in the past couple of decades, institutional investors like pension funds and large mutual funds have increased their sway over corporate policies, but it's still exceedingly difficult for shareholders to change policies they don't like because the voting rules are rigged in management's favour.[36]

DEBATING CORPORATE RESPONSIBILITY

We can pursue the debate over corporate social responsibility further by examining three arguments in support of the narrow view: the invisible-hand argument, the let-government-do-it argument, and the business-can't-handle-it argument. Advocates of the broader view of corporate responsibility reject all three arguments.

The Invisible-Hand Argument

Adam Smith claimed that when each of us acts in a free-market environment to promote our own economic interests we are led by an "invisible hand" to promote the general good. Like-minded contemporary thinkers such as Friedman agree. They point out that corporations, in fact, were chartered by states precisely with utility in mind. If businesses are permitted to seek self-interest, their activities will inevitably yield the greatest good for society as a whole. To invite corporations to base their policies and activities on anything other than profit-making is to politicize business's unique economic function and to hamper its ability to satisfy our material needs. Accordingly, corporations should not be invited to fight racial injustice, poverty, or pollution, to broaden competition, or to help reduce prices or increase accessibility to products, except insofar as these activities enhance corporate profits.

Yet this argument allows that corporations may still be held accountable for their actions. To the degree that they fulfill or fail to fulfill their economic role, they can be praised or blamed. And they can rightly be criticized for breaking the law or violating the rules of the game, for example, by shady accounting practices that mislead investors about company assets. But corporations should not be held morally responsible for non-economic matters; to do so would distort the economic mission of business in society and undermine the foundations of the free enterprise system.

The invisible-hand argument, however, runs up against the fact that modern corporations bear about as much resemblance to Smith's self-sufficient farmers and crafts-persons as today's military bears to the militia regiments of the seventeenth century. Given the sway they have over our economy and society, the enormous impact they have on our lives, our communities, and our environment, today's gigantic corporations are more like public enterprises than private ones. They constitute powerful economic fiefdoms, far removed from the small, competitive producers of classical economics. Perhaps within a restricted area of economic exchange, when the parties to the exchange are roughly equal, then each party pursuing its own self-interest can result in the greatest net good. But in the real world of large corporations, the concept of an invisible hand orchestrating the common good does often stretch credulity. For example, the state of California deregulated its electricity market to promote competition and give the invisible hand room to operate. But the result was a disaster. Instead of cheaper energy, the state got power blackouts and soaring prices as energy companies adroitly and greedily manipulated the market. Each time the state tried to make the market work better, energy sellers devised new ways to exploit the system. The state government only stanched the crisis by a costly intervention that has basically put it in the power business.[37]

The invisible-hand argument in favour of the narrow view of corporate responsibility is thus open to criticism as theoretically unsound and economically unrealistic. Moreover, in practice the argument is complicated by the fact that corporations today find themselves in a social and political environment in which they are pressured by public opinion, politicians, the media, and various activist groups to act—or at least be perceived to be acting—as responsible corporate citizens, as socially conscious enterprises that acknowledge other values besides profit and that seek to make a positive contribution to our society. Few if any corporations can afford to be seen as exploiters of foreign labour, as polluters of the environment, or as indifferent to consumer welfare or the prosperity of our communities. Companies today religiously guard their name and their brands against the slander that they care only about profits. And the larger the corporation, the more susceptible it is to the demand that it behave with a developed sense of moral responsibility, the more it needs to guard its image and to take steps to assure the public that it is striving to make the world a better place.

Admittedly, this is in part a matter of public relations, but it's also true that in today's world, business success requires companies to respond to society's demand that they act as morally responsible agents. For purely self-interested reasons, even corporations that take a very narrow view of their responsibilities may have to behave as if they held a broader view. For example, in a world in which 88 percent of young people believe that companies have a responsibility to support social causes and 86 percent of them say that they switch brands on the basis of social issues, a world in which 72 percent of job seekers prefer to work for a company that supports social causes,[38] corporate philanthropy promotes the bottom line. Moreover, almost all studies indicate that socially responsible corporate behaviour is positively correlated with financial success and that the most profitable companies treat their consumers, employees, and business partners ethically.[39] Ironically, then, this gives companies a self-interested reason not merely to pretend to have a broad sense of social responsibility but also to become the kind of company that really does want to make a positive mark in the world. Of course, whether we are talking about individuals or about corporations, there's no guarantee that acting morally will always pay off, and indeed if that is one's only motivation for doing the right thing, then one can hardly be said to be acting morally. On the other hand, there's little reason for either individuals or companies to believe that acting selfishly or doing what they know to be wrong will pay off for them in the long run.

The Let-Government-Do-It Argument

According to the narrow view of corporate social responsibility, business's role is purely economic, and corporations should not be considered moral agents. Some adherents of this view, however, such as (Canadian-born) economist and social critic John Kenneth Galbraith, reject the assumption that Smith's invisible hand will solve all social and economic problems or that market forces will moralize corporate activities. Left to their own self-serving devices, Galbraith and others warn, modern corporations will enrich themselves while impoverishing society. If they can get away with it, they will pollute, exploit workers, deceive customers, and strive to eliminate competition and keep prices high through oligopolistic practices. They will do those things, the argument continues, because as economic institutions they are naturally and quite properly profit-motivated. But what is profitable for them is not necessarily useful or desirable for society, and what is socially useful or desirable is not always profitable.

Then how is the corporation's natural and insatiable appetite for profit to be controlled? Through government regulation. The strong hand of government, through a system of laws and incentives, can and should bring

corporations to heel. "I believe in corporations," former U.S. President Teddy Roosevelt once proclaimed. "They are indispensable instruments of our modern civilization; but I believe that they should be so supervised and so regulated that they shall act for the interests of the community as a whole."[40]

"Do not blame corporations and their top executives" for things like layoffs or urge them to acknowledge obligations beyond the bottom line, writes Robert Reich, Secretary of Labor under former U.S. President Clinton. "They are behaving exactly as they are organized to behave." He pooh-poohs moral appeals and rejects the idea that CEOs should seek to balance the interests of shareholders against those of employees and their communities. Rather, Reich says, "if we want corporations to take more responsibility" for the economic well-being of Americans, then government "will have to provide the proper incentives."[41]

This advice sounds realistic and is intended to be practical, but the let-government-do-it argument rejects the notion of broadening corporate social responsibility just as firmly as the invisible-hand argument does. That argument puts the focus on the market. Galbraith's and Reich's argument puts it on the visible hand of government. The two positions agree, however, in thinking it misguided to expect or demand that business firms do anything other than pursue profit.

Critics of the let-government-do-it argument contend that it is a blueprint for big, intrusive government. Moreover, they doubt that government can control any but the most egregious corporate immorality. They fear that many questionable activities will be overlooked, safely hidden within the labyrinth of the corporate structure. Lacking intimate knowledge of the goals and sub-goals of specific corporations, as well as of their daily operations, government simply can't anticipate a specific corporation's moral challenges. Rather, it can prescribe behaviour only for broad, cross-sectional issues, such as bribery, price-fixing, and unfair competition.

Finally, is government a credible custodian of morality? If recent experience around the world has taught anything, it is that government officials are not always paragons of virtue. Looked at as another organization, government manifests many of the same structural characteristics that test moral behaviour inside the corporation. Furthermore, given the awesome clout of corporate lobbyists, one wonders whether, as moral police, government officials will do anything more than impose the values and interests of their most generous financiers. Can we seriously expect politicians to bite the hand that feeds them?

The Business-Can't-Handle-It Argument

In support of the narrow view of corporate social responsibility, some argue that it is misguided to encourage corporations to address non-business matters. They are the wrong group for us to entrust with a broad responsibility for promoting the well-being of society. They can't handle the job, first, because they lack the necessary expertise and, second, because in addressing non-economic matters, they will inevitably impose their own materialistic values on the rest of society.

Corporations Lack the Expertise Those who develop the first point contend that business can't handle the job, that it is the wrong group to rely on to promote the well-being of society, because corporate executives lack the moral and social expertise to make other than economic decisions. To assign them non-economic responsibilities would be to put social welfare in the hands of inept custodians. Thus, business analyst Walter Goodman writes, "I don't know of any investment adviser whom I would care to act in my behalf in any matter except turning a profit."[42] In his view, corporate leaders lack the moral insight or social know-how that a broader view of corporate social responsibility would seem to require of them.

Against that, however, one can argue that we don't normally restrict the moral responsibilities of individuals, professional bodies, or other organizations to matters that fall within the narrow confines of their business or other expertise. We see nothing wrong, for example, with physicians advocating AIDS awareness or trying to promote the use of seat belts in automobiles, or with a teachers' union involving itself in a campaign to combat the use of illegal drugs. And ordinary citizens may sometimes have a duty to educate themselves about, and do what they can to address, social issues that fall outside their usual sphere of knowledge and activity. What if anything, asks the critic, makes the social role of the corporation unique, so that its responsibilities and that of those it employs should be confined solely to profit-making?

The argument that corporations aren't up to addressing social issues because they lack the necessary expertise runs up against the fact that, often, it is only business that has the know-how, talent, experience, and organizational resources to tackle certain problems. If society wants, for example, to eradicate malaria in Africa or increase longevity at home, to reduce diesel engine emissions or retard global warming, to increase agricultural productivity while reducing the risks from pesticides, or to see that inner-city youth learn entrepreneurship or that community groups have the business skills necessary for success, then society will need the assistance of business. To take a specific illustration, Citibank supports microfinance programs in Mexico and India, intended to give poor rural women, in particular, the tiny loans they need, say, to buy a sewing machine and start their own business. True, as a Citigroup executive says, "there is not going to be a huge short-term profit" for the company.[43] But who is better able to help these women than a company like Citigroup?

Corporations Will Impose Their Values on Us Others argue that corporations are the wrong group to address social issues, that business can't handle the assignment, for a different reason. They fear that if permitted to stray from strictly economic matters, corporate officials will impose their materialistic values on all of society. Thus, broadening corporate responsibility will "materialize" society instead of "moralizing" corporate activity.

More than forty-five years ago, Theodore Levitt expressed this concern:

> The danger is that all these things [resulting from having business pursue social goals other than profit making] will turn the corporation into a twentieth-century equivalent of the medieval church . . . . For while the corporation also transforms itself in the process, at bottom its outlook will always remain materialistic. What we have then is the frightening spectacle of a powerful economic functional group whose future and perception are shaped in a tight materialistic context of money and things but which imposes its narrow ideas about a broad spectrum of unrelated non-economic subjects on the mass of man and society. Even if its outlook were the purest kind of good will, that would not recommend the corporation as an arbiter of our lives.[44]

This argument seems to assume that corporations do not already exercise enormous discretionary power over us. But as Keith Davis points out, business already has immense social power. "Society has entrusted to business large amounts of society's resources," says Davis, "and business is expected to manage these resources as a wise trustee for society. In addition to the traditional role of economic entrepreneurship, business now has a new social role of trusteeship. As trustee for society's resources, it serves the interests of all claimants on the organization, rather than only those of owners, or consumers, or labor."[45]

As Paul Camenisch notes, business is already using its privileged position to propagate, consciously or unconsciously, a view of humanity and the good life.[46] Implicit in the barrage of advertisements to which we are subjected daily are assumptions about happiness, success, and human fulfillment. In addition, corporations or industry groups sometimes speak out in unvarnished terms about social and economic issues. For example, ExxonMobil disputes the notion that fossil fuels are the main cause of global warming and lobbies against the Kyoto accord capping global-warming emissions, while drug companies such as Eli Lilly, Procter & Gamble, and Bristol-Myers Squibb contribute to conservative think tanks that seek to reduce the regulatory powers of the U.S. Food and Drug Administration.

The point here is that business already promotes consumerism and materialistic values. It doesn't hesitate to use its resources to express its views and influence our political system on issues that affect its economic interests. If corporations take a broader view of their social responsibilities, are they really likely to have a more materialistic effect on society, as Levitt suggests, than they do now? It's hard to believe they could. Levitt's view implies that there is some threat to society's values when corporations engage in philanthropy or use their economic and political muscle for other than purely self-interested ends. But society's values are not endangered when the Canadian Imperial Bank of Commerce sponsors and supports the CIBC Run for the Cure in aid of the Canadian Breast Cancer Foundation, or the Royal Bank of Canada donates 1 percent of its pre-tax profits (about $43 million in 2006) to community and charitable causes,[47] or (to turn to the more generous American corporations) when Sara Lee donates 2 percent of its pre-tax profits (nearly $13 million) to charitable causes, mostly cultural institutions and organizations serving disadvantaged people,[48] or when General Mills gives away 3 percent of its domestic pre-tax earnings ($45 million) to community organizations, donates food to people in need, and helps inner-city companies to get up and running.[49] And where is the "materialization of society" if, instead of advertising on a silly situation comedy that reaches a large audience, a corporation spends the same amount underwriting a science program with fewer viewers solely out of a sense of social responsibility?

INSTITUTIONALIZING ETHICS WITHIN CORPORATIONS

The criticisms of these three arguments in support of the narrow view of corporate responsibility have led many people inside and outside business to adopt the broader view—that the obligations of the modern business corporation extend beyond simply making money for itself. Society grants corporations the right to exist, gives them legal status as separate entities, and permits them to use natural resources. It does this not to indulge the profit appetites of owners and managers but, as Camenisch says, because it needs "the available raw materials transformed into needed goods and services, and because business in its contemporary form has been conspicuously successful in doing just that."[50] In return for its sufferance of corporations, society has the right to expect corporations not to cause harm, to take into account the external effects of their activities, and whenever possible to act for the betterment of society.

The list of corporate responsibilities goes beyond such negative injunctions as "Don't pollute," "Don't misrepresent products," and "Don't bribe." Included also are affirmative duties like "See that your product or service makes a positive contribution to society," "Improve the skills of your employees," "Seek to hire the disabled," "Give special consideration to the needs of historically disadvantaged groups," "Contribute to the arts and education," "Locate plants in economically depressed areas," and "Improve working conditions." This class of affirmative responsibilities includes activities that are not intrinsically related to the operations of the corporation but are rather responsibilities that each of us, whether individuals or institutions, has simply by virtue of our being members of society. Precisely how far each of us must go to meet these responsibilities depends largely on our capacity to

fulfill them, which, of course, varies from person to person, institution to institution. But given their considerable power and resources, large corporations seem better able to promote the common good than most individuals or small businesses.

How corporations are to promote the common good cannot be answered very specifically; methods will depend on the type of firm and its particular circumstances. Proponents of broadening corporate responsibility probably would agree that the first step is to create an ethical atmosphere within the corporation. This means making ethical behaviour a high priority. How to do this? At least four actions seem called for:

1. Corporations should acknowledge the importance, even necessity, of conducting business morally. Their commitment to ethical behaviour should be unequivocal and highly visible, from top management down.

2. Corporations should make a real effort to encourage their members to take moral responsibilities seriously. This commitment would mean ending all forms of retaliation against those who buck the system and rewarding employees for evaluating corporate decisions in their broader social and moral contexts.

3. Corporations should end their defensiveness in the face of public discussion and criticism. Instead, they should actively solicit the views of stockholders, managers, employees, suppliers, customers, local communities, and even society as a whole. Corporations should invite outside opinions and conduct a candid ethical audit of their organizational policies, priorities, and practices.

4. Corporations must recognize the pluralistic nature of the social system of which they are a part. Society consists of diverse, interlocked groups, all vying to maintain their autonomy and advance their interests. These groups are so related that the actions of one inevitably affect the standing of another on a variety of levels: economic, political, educational, cultural. As part of society, corporations affect many groups, and these groups affect corporations. Corporations that fail to realize this certainly run the risk of losing sight of the social framework that governs their relationship with the external environment.

Undoubtedly, other general directives could be added to this list. Still, if corporate responsibility should be expanded, then something like the preceding approach seems basic.

Limits to What the Law Can Do

Critics of the let-government-do-it argument question Galbraith's and Reich's view that society should not expect business to behave morally but rather should simply use government to direct business's pursuit of profit in socially acceptable directions. This issue is worth returning to in the present context. All defenders of the broad view of corporate social responsibility believe that more than laissez faire is necessary to ensure that business behaviour is socially and morally acceptable. Yet there is a tendency to believe that law is a fully adequate vehicle for this purpose.

Law professor Christopher Stone has argued, however, that there are limits on what the law can be expected to achieve.[51] Three of his points are particularly important. First, many laws, such as controls on the disposal of toxic waste, are passed only after there is general awareness of the problem; in the meantime, damage has already been done. The proverbial barn door has been shut only after the horse has left.

Second, formulating appropriate laws and designing effective regulations are difficult. It is hard to achieve consensus on the relevant facts, to determine what remedies will work, and to decide how to weigh conflicting values. In addition, our political system gives corporations and their lobbyists significant input into the writing of laws.[52] Not only that, but the specific working regulations and day-to-day interpretation of the law require the continual input of industry experts. This is not a conspiracy but a fact of life. Government bureaus generally have limited time, staffing, and expertise, so they must rely on the cooperation and assistance of those they regulate.[53] Third, enforcing the law is often cumbersome. Legal actions against corporations are expensive and can drag on for years, and the judicial process is often too blunt an instrument to use as a way of managing complex social and business issues. In fact, recourse to the courts can be counterproductive, and Stone argues that sometimes the benefits of doing so may not be worth the costs. Legal action may simply make corporations more furtive, breeding distrust, destruction of documents, and an attitude that "I won't do anything more than I am absolutely required to do."

What conclusion should be drawn? Stone's argument is not intended to show that regulation of business is hopeless. Rather, what he wants to stress is that the law cannot do it alone. We do not want a system in which businesspeople believe that their only obligation is to obey the law and that it is morally permissible for them to do anything not (yet) illegal. With that attitude, disaster is just around the corner. More socially responsible business behaviour requires, instead, that corporations and the people within them not just respond to the requirements of the law but also hold high moral standards—and that they themselves monitor their own behaviour.

Ethical Codes and Economic Efficiency

It is, therefore, important that corporations examine their own implicit and explicit codes of conduct and the moral standards that are being propagated to their employees. As mentioned earlier in this chapter and in Chapter 1,[54] there is no necessary tradeoff between profitability and ethical corporate behaviour. Indeed, the contrary appears to be true: the most morally responsible companies are consistently among the most profitable companies. Yet ethical behaviour in the business world is often assumed to come at the expense of economic efficiency. Defenders of the broader view, such as Anshen, as well as defenders of the narrow view, such as Friedman, seem to make this assumption. Anshen believes that other values should take priority over economic efficiency, whereas Friedman contends business should concern itself only with profit and, in this way, maximize economic well-being. In his important essay "Social Responsibility and Economic Efficiency," Nobel Prize–winning economist Kenneth Arrow has challenged this assumption.[55]

To begin with, any kind of settled economic life requires a certain degree of ethical behaviour, some element of trust and confidence. Much business, for instance, is conducted on the basis of oral agreements. In addition, says Arrow, "there are two types of situation in which the simple rule of maximizing profits is socially inefficient: the case in which costs are not paid for, as in pollution, and the case in which the seller has considerably more knowledge about his product than the buyer."

The first type of situation relates to the demand that corporations "internalize their externalities." In the second situation, in which the buyer lacks the expertise and knowledge of the seller, an effective moral code, either requiring full disclosure or setting minimal standards of performance (for example, the braking ability of a new automobile), enhances rather than diminishes economic efficiency. Without such a code, buyers may purchase products or services they don't need. Or because they don't trust the seller, they may refrain from purchasing products and services they do need. Either way, from the economist's point of view the situation is inefficient.

An effective professional or business moral code—as well as the public's awareness of this code—is good for business. Most of us, for example, have little medical knowledge and are thus at the mercy of doctors. Over hundreds of years, however, a firm code of ethical conduct has developed in the medical profession. As a result, people generally presume that their physician will perform with their welfare in mind. They rarely worry that their doctor might be taking advantage of them or exploiting them with unnecessary treatment. By contrast, used-car dealers have historically suffered from a lack of public trust.

For a code to be effective it must be realistic, Arrow argues, in the sense of connecting with the collective self-interest of business. And it must become part of the corporate culture, "accepted by the significant operating institutions and transmitted from one generation of executives to the next through standard operating procedures [and] through education in business schools."

For both Arrow and Stone, then, the development of feasible and effective business and professional codes of ethics must be a central focus of any effort to enhance or expand corporate responsibility. The question is how to create a corporate atmosphere conducive to moral decision making.

Corporate Moral Codes

What can be done to improve the organizational climate so individual members can reasonably be expected to act ethically? If those inside the corporation are to behave morally, they need clearly stated and communicated ethical standards that are equitable and enforced. This development seems possible only if the standards of expected behaviour are institutionalized—that is, only if they become a fixture in the corporate organization. To institutionalize ethics within corporations, professor Milton Snoeyenbos suggests that top management should (1) articulate the firm's values and goals, (2) adopt an ethical code applicable to all members of the company, (3) set up a high-ranking ethics committee to oversee, develop, and enforce the code, and (4) incorporate ethics training into all employee-development programs.[56]

The company's code of ethics should not be window dressing or so general as to be useless. It should set reasonable goals and sub-goals, with an eye on blunting unethical pressures on subordinates. In formulating the code, the top-level ethics committee should solicit the views of corporate members at all levels regarding goals and sub-goals, so that the final product articulates "a fine-grained ethical code that addresses ethical issues likely to arise at the level of sub goals."[57] Moreover, the committee should have full authority and responsibility to communicate the code and decisions based on it to all corporate members, clarify and interpret the code when the need arises, facilitate the code's use, investigate grievances and violations of the code, discipline violators and reward compliance, and review, update, and upgrade the code.

To help employees in ethically difficult situations, a good corporate ethics program must be user-friendly. It should provide a support system with a variety of entry points, one that employees feel confident about using.[58] In addition, part of all employee-training programs should be devoted to ethics. At a minimum, this should include study of the code, review of the company's procedures for handling ethical problems, and discussion of employer and employee responsibilities and expectations. Snoeyenbos and others believe that institutionalizing ethics within the corporation in these ways, when supplemented by the development of industry-wide codes of ethics to address issues beyond a particular firm, will go far toward establishing a corporate climate conducive to individual moral decision making.

Corporate Culture

During the past two decades, organizational theorists and writers on business management have increasingly emphasized "corporate culture" as the factor that makes one company succeed while another languishes. Although intangible in comparison with things like sales revenue and profit margin, corporate culture is often the key to a firm's success. According to one study, 30 percent of the difference in performance between companies can be attributed to differences in culture, but only 5 percent to differences in strategy.[59]

What is corporate culture? One writer describes it as "the shared beliefs top managers have in a company about how they should manage themselves and other employees, and how they should conduct their business(es). These beliefs are often invisible to the top managers but have a major impact on their thoughts and actions."[60] Another writer puts it this way: "Culture is the pattern of shared values and beliefs that gives members of an institution meaning and provides them with rules for behavior in their organization."[61] W. Brooke Tunstall, an assistant vice-president of AT&T, provides a fuller definition. He describes corporate culture as "a general constellation of beliefs, mores, customs, value systems and behavioural norms, and ways of doing business that are unique to each corporation, that set a pattern for corporate activities and actions, and that describe the implicit and emergent patterns of behaviour and emotions characterizing life in the organization."[62]

Corporate culture may be both explicit and implicit. The formal culture of a corporation, as expressed in idealized statements of values and norms, should also be distinguished from the informal culture that shapes beliefs, values, and behaviour. In addition, there may be multiple and overlapping cultures within an organization because employees have different backgrounds, work in different divisions of the organization, and may be subject to different systems of rewards and sanctions.

Organizational theorists emphasize the importance of monitoring and managing corporate culture—beginning with an attempt to understand each corporation's distinctive culture—to prevent dysfunctional behaviour and processes. As one consultant puts it, "A corporation's culture is what determines how people behave when they are not being watched."[63] If management does not make explicit the values and behaviour it desires, the culture will typically develop its own norms, usually based on the types of behaviour thought to lead to success within the organization. Thus, the desired values must be communicated and transmitted throughout the organization. Conduct congruent with them must be rewarded and conduct inconsistent with them penalized. Overlooking behaviour that contradicts the desired norms can have the effect of encouraging and even rewarding it.

William Donaldson, former chairman of the U.S. Securities and Exchange Commission, emphasizes the importance of ethical leadership, of the example set by upper management. "The tone is set at the top," he says. "You must have an internal code that goes beyond the letter of the law to encompass the spirit of the company. Does that concept exist in all companies? No. All you have to do is look at executive compensation to recognize that we still have a long way to go."[64]

These points are crucial when it comes to corporate social responsibility. Management needs to understand the real dynamics of its own organization. At Sears, for example, new minimum work quotas and productivity incentives at its auto centres created a high-pressure environment that led employees to mislead customers and sell them unnecessary parts and services, from brake jobs to front-end alignments.[65] Thus, it is necessary for socially responsible executives to ask: How do people get ahead in our company? What conduct is actually rewarded, what values are really being instilled in our employees? Andrew C. Sigler, chairman of Champion International, stresses this point: "Sitting up here in Stamford, there's no way I can affect what an employee is doing today in Texas, Montana, or Maine. Making speeches and sending letters just doesn't do it. You need a culture and peer pressure that spells out what is acceptable and isn't and why. It involves training, education, and follow-up."[66]

Johnson & Johnson is widely seen as a model of corporate responsibility, especially because of its decisive handling of the Tylenol crisis of 1982, when seven people in the Chicago area died from cyanide-laced Extra-Strength Tylenol capsules. The company immediately recalled 31 million bottles of Tylenol from store shelves across the nation and notified 500,000 doctors and hospitals about the contaminated capsules. A toll-free consumer hotline was set up the first week of the crisis, and consumers were offered the opportunity to replace Tylenol capsules with a free bottle of Tylenol tablets. Johnson & Johnson was also open with the public instead of being defensive about the deaths. Accurate information was promptly released, and domestic employees and retirees were kept updated on developments. The chairman of the company appeared on the talk show *Donahue* and on *60 Minutes* to answer questions about the crisis, and other executives were interviewed by *Fortune* and *The Wall Street Journal*.

Despite the setback—the recall alone cost Johnson & Johnson $50 million after taxes—Tylenol rebounded within a year, in large part because the public never lost faith in Johnson & Johnson. The company itself credits its sixty-year-old, one-page statement of values, known as the Credo, with enabling it to build the employee trust necessary for maintaining a firm corporate value system. The Credo acknowledges the company's need to make a sound profit while addressing its obligations to provide a quality product, to treat its employees fairly and with respect, and to be a good corporate citizen, supporting the community of which it is a member.

The Credo is "the most important thing we have in this company," says chairman Ralph Larsen. But creating and maintaining a morally sound corporate culture is an ongoing task, and Johnson & Johnson hasn't always been able to live up to its own values. In 1995, for instance, the company agreed to pay $7.5 million in fines and costs after admitting that wayward employees had shredded papers to hinder a federal probe into the marketing of an acne cream. "There was no excuse," admits Larsen. "But it is a huge undertaking to spread our values around the world."[67]

SUMMARY

1. What we know as the modern business corporation has evolved over several centuries, and incorporation is no longer the special privilege it once was.
2. Corporations are legal entities, with legal rights and responsibilities similar but not identical to those enjoyed by individuals. Business corporations are limited-liability companies—that is, their owners or stockholders are liable for corporate debts only up to the extent of their investments.
3. The question of corporate moral agency is whether corporations are the kind of entity that can have moral responsibilities. If corporations can make rational and moral decisions, then they can be held morally blameworthy or praiseworthy for their actions. Philosophers disagree about whether the corporate internal decision (CID) structure makes it reasonable to assign moral responsibility to corporations.
4. This problem is compounded by the difficulty of assigning moral responsibility to individuals inside corporations.
5. Despite these controversies, the courts and the general public find the notion of corporate responsibility useful and intelligible—either in a literal sense or as shorthand for the obligations of individuals in the corporation.
6. The debate over corporate responsibility is whether it should be construed narrowly to cover only profit maximization or more broadly to include acting morally, refraining from socially undesirable behaviour, and contributing actively and directly to the public good.
7. Proponents of the narrow view, such as Milton Friedman, contend that diverting corporations from the pursuit of profit makes our economic system less efficient. Business's only social responsibility is to make money within the rules of the game. Private enterprise should not be forced to undertake public responsibilities that properly belong to government.
8. Defenders of the broader view maintain that corporations have additional responsibilities because of their great social and economic power. Business is governed by an implicit social contract that requires it to operate in ways that benefit society. In particular, corporations must take responsibility for the unintended side effects of their business transactions (externalities) and weigh the full social costs of their activities.
9. Advocates of the narrow view stress that management has a duty to the owners (stockholders) of a corporation, which takes priority over any other responsibilities and obligates it to focus on profit maximization alone. Critics challenge this argument.
10. Three arguments in favour of the narrow view are the invisible-hand argument, the let-government-do-it argument, and the business-can't-handle-it argument. Finding flaws in each of these arguments, critics claim there is no solid basis for restricting corporate responsibility to profit-making.

11. Those proposing broader corporate responsibilities see the creation of an ethical atmosphere within the corporation as an important first step. Essential to this atmosphere are acknowledging the critical importance of ethics, encouraging morally responsible conduct by all employees, recognizing the pluralistic nature of our social system, and an openness to public discussion and review.

12. Corporations and the people who make them up must have high moral standards and monitor their own behaviour because there are limits to what the law can do to ensure that business behaviour is socially and morally acceptable.

13. All settled economic life requires trust and confidence. The adoption of realistic and workable codes of ethics in the business world can actually enhance business efficiency. This is particularly true when there is an imbalance of knowledge between the buyer and the seller.

14. To improve the organizational climate so individuals can reasonably be expected to act ethically, corporations should adopt an ethical code, set up a high-ranking ethics committee, and include ethics training in their employee-development programs. Attention to corporate culture is also crucial to the successful institutionalization of ethics inside an organization.

CASE 5.1

Living and Dying with Asbestos

Asbestos is a fibrous mineral used for fireproofing, electrical insulation, building materials, brake linings, and chemical filters. If exposed long enough to asbestos particles—usually ten or more years—people can develop a chronic lung inflammation called asbestosis, which makes breathing difficult and infection easy. Also linked to asbestos exposure is mesothelioma, a cancer of the chest lining that sometimes doesn't develop until forty years after the first exposure. Although the first major scientific conference on the dangers of asbestos was not held until 1964, the asbestos industry knew of its hazards more than seventy years ago.[68]

As early as 1932, the British documented the occupational hazards of asbestos dust inhalation. Indeed, on September 25, 1935, the editors of the trade journal *Asbestos* wrote to Sumner Simpson, president of Raybestos-Manhattan, a leading asbestos company, asking permission to publish an article on the dangers of asbestos. Simpson refused and later praised the magazine for not printing the article. In a letter to Vandivar Brown, secretary of Johns-Manville, another asbestos manufacturer, Simpson observed: "The less said about asbestosis the better off we are." Brown agreed, adding that any article on asbestosis should reflect American, not English, data.

In fact, American data were available, and Brown, as one of the editors of the journal, knew it. Working on behalf of Raybestos-Manhattan and Johns-Manville and their insurance carrier, Metropolitan Life Insurance Company, Anthony Lanza had conducted research between 1929 and 1931 on 126 workers with three or more years of asbestos exposure. But Brown and others were not pleased with the paper Lanza submitted to them for editorial review. Lanza, said Brown, had failed to portray asbestosis as milder than silicosis, a lung disease caused by long-term inhalation of silica dust and resulting in chronic shortness of breath. Under the then-pending Workmen's Compensation law, silicosis was categorized as a compensable disease. If asbestosis were worse than silicosis or indistinguishable from it, then it, too, would have to be covered. Apparently Brown didn't want this and thus requested that Lanza depict asbestosis as less serious than silicosis. Lanza complied and also omitted from his published report the fact that more than half the workers examined—67 of 126—were suffering from asbestosis.

Meanwhile, Sumner Simpson was writing F. H. Schulter, president of Thermoid Rubber Company, to suggest that several manufacturers sponsor additional asbestos experiments. The sponsors, said Simpson, could exercise oversight prerogatives; they "could determine from time to time after the findings are made whether we wish any publication or not." Added Simpson: "It would be a good idea to distribute the information to the medical fraternity, providing it is of the right type and would not injure our companies." Lest there be any question about the arbiter of

publication, Brown wrote to officials at the laboratory conducting the tests:

> It is our further understanding that the results obtained will be considered the property of those who are advancing the required funds, who will determine whether, to what extent and in what manner they shall be made public. In the event it is deemed desirable that the results be made public, the manuscript of your study will be submitted to us for approval prior to publication.

Industry officials were concerned with more than controlling public information flow. They also sought to deny workers early evidence of their asbestosis. Dr. Kenneth Smith, medical director of a Johns-Manville plant in Canada, explained why seven workers he found to have asbestosis should not be informed of their disease:

> It must be remembered that although these men have the X-ray evidence of asbestosis, they are working today and definitely are not disabled from asbestosis. They have not been told of this diagnosis, for it is felt that as long as the man feels well, is happy at home and at work, and his physical condition remains good, nothing should be said. When he becomes disabled and sick, then the diagnosis should be made and the claim submitted *by the Company*. The fibrosis of this disease is irreversible and permanent so that eventually compensation will be paid to each of these men. But as long as the man is not disabled, it is felt that he should not be told of his condition so that he can live and work in peace and the Company can benefit by his many years of experience. Should the man be told of his condition today there is a very definite possibility that he would become mentally and physically ill, simply through the knowledge that he has asbestosis.

When lawsuits filed by asbestos workers who had developed cancer reached the industry in the 1950s, Dr. Smith suggested that the industry retain the Industrial Health Foundation to conduct a cancer study that would, in effect, squelch the asbestos–cancer connection. The asbestos companies refused, claiming that such a study would only bring further unfavourable publicity to the industry and that there wasn't enough evidence linking asbestos and cancer industry-wide to warrant it.

Shortly before his death in 1977, Dr. Smith was asked whether he had ever recommended to Johns-Manville officials that warning labels be placed on insulation products containing asbestos. He testified as follows:

> The reasons why the caution labels were not implemented immediately, it was a business decision as far as I could understand. Here was a recommendation, the corporation is in business to make, to provide jobs for people and make money for stockholders and they had to take into consideration the effects of everything they did, and if the application of a caution label identifying a product as hazardous would cut out sales, there would be serious financial

implications. And the powers that be had to make some effort to judge the necessity of the label vs. the consequences of placing the label on the product.

Dr. Smith's testimony and related documents have figured prominently in hundreds of asbestos-related lawsuits. In the 1980s these lawsuits swamped Manville (as Johns-Manville is now called) and forced the company into bankruptcy. A trust fund valued at $2.5 billion was set up to pay Manville's asbestos claimants. To fund the trust, shareholders were required to surrender half the value of their stock, and the company had to give up much of its projected earnings over the next 25 years. Claims, however, soon overwhelmed the trust, which ran out of money in 1990. After various legal delays, the trust fund's stake in Manville was increased to 80 percent, and Manville was required to pay it an additional $300 million in dividends. The trust fund itself was restructured to pay the most seriously ill victims first, but average payments to victims were lowered significantly—from $145,000 to $43,000.[69]

In 1997 the U.S. Supreme Court struck down a landmark $1.3 billion class-action settlement between some twenty former asbestos producers and their injured workers. A few years earlier, the companies involved had approached the workers' lawyers and agreed to settle thousands of existing health complaints, in a deal that netted the lawyers millions of dollars in fees. Then the lawyers and companies devised a settlement agreement involving people who had not filed claims against the company by a specified date. It was this aspect of the settlement that was the main sticking point. Although a lower court had praised the settlement for "forging a solution to a major social problem," the Supreme Court balked at the fact that future claimants were not allowed to opt out of the agreement. A class-action agreement, the Court said, was not the best way to resolve thousands of different claims involving different factual and legal issues.[70] In 1999, the Court rejected a second proposed settlement. As a result, thousands of lawsuits that would have been settled by the agreements continue to clog U.S. federal dockets.

The situation is made worse by the fact that in the last few years asbestos-related litigation has expanded exponentially—spun out of control, some would say—as workers who did not make asbestos, but only handled it every now and then or worked in the vicinity of those who did, are suing companies that never made the stuff but only used or distributed products containing asbestos or (purchased companies that did). With cases now pending against more than 1,000 companies, no one disputes the awfulness of asbestos. More than 100,000 workers (300,000 according to trial lawyers) have died from exposure to it. But critics charge that the legal claims of two-thirds of the approximately 850,000 asbestos plaintiffs are largely groundless.[71] In fact, of the 91,000 cases filed in a recent year, only 6 percent of the claimants actually suffered from asbestos-related diseases. Almost all the others are seeking compensation for anxiety they have experienced over the risk that they might have asbestosis.[72] Meanwhile, the U.S. Congress continues to struggle unsuccessfully to craft a solution to the problem and end what has become a thirty-year battle over asbestos liability.

Discussion Questions

1. How is this case relevant to the debate over corporate social responsibility? Assess the actions of the asbestos companies from the perspective of both the narrow and the broad views of corporate social responsibility.

2. Should the asbestos companies be seen as moral agents capable of making moral decisions and deserving of praise or blame? Or should only the individual people involved be considered morally responsible agents?

3. Simpson and Brown presumably acted in what they thought were the best financial interests of their companies. Nothing they did was illegal. On what grounds, if any, are their actions open to criticism?

4. If you were a stockholder in Raybestos-Manhattan or Johns-Manville, would you have approved of Simpson's and Brown's conduct? If not, why not?

5. Proponents of the let-government-do-it view would say that it's the responsibility of government, not the asbestos industry, to ensure health and safety with respect to asbestos—that in the absence of appropriate government regulations, asbestos manufacturers have no responsibility other than to operate efficiently and profitably. Do you agree?

6. Assess Dr. Smith's decision to conceal from workers the nature of their health problems. Did he do all he was morally obliged to do as an employee of an asbestos company? What about Lanza's suppression of data in his report?

7. Do you think a corporate ethical code, together with an industry-wide code, a corporate ethics committee, and training in ethics for management personnel, would have made a difference in this case?

8. What responsibilities do asbestos manufacturers now have to their injured workers? Should the companies be punished in some way for their past actions, or is their liability to civil lawsuits sufficient?

9. What are the moral and legal responsibilities of companies that simply used or sold asbestos products? How should society respond to claims for restitution by workers who handled asbestos products?

10. Do you see any parallels between this case and the tobacco industry's response to the health risks of smoking?

CASE 5.2

Selling Infant Formula Overseas

In the mid-1860s Henri Nestlé developed infant formula to save the life of an infant who couldn't be breastfed. According to officials at Nestlé—a Swiss-based corporation that is now the world's third-largest food company, with annual sales of nearly $39 billion—the Frenchman's concoction has been saving lives ever since, especially in developing countries. They point to relief organizations such as the International Red Cross, which has used the formula to feed thousands of starving infants in refugee camps, for example. Without its infant formula, the Nestlé people say, Third World mothers considering use of a breast-milk substitute would use less nutritious local alternatives. Maybe so. But a hundred years after it was first developed, Henri Nestlé's sweet idea turned sour.[73]

The infant formula controversy began to heat up back in 1970 at a United Nations–sponsored meeting on infant feeding in Bogotá, Colombia. Meeting to discuss different aspects of world hunger, the Protein Advisory Group (PAG)—made up of nutritionists, paediatricians, and food-industry representatives—were especially concerned about the worldwide decline in breastfeeding, despite the demonstrated superiority of mother's milk over infant formula. But some PAG members bristled at what they thought was PAG's failure to engage a critical issue: the implications of marketing infant formula in Third World countries.

Straightaway the media began reporting some of the common marketing practices of infant-formula companies:

Item—Dressed as health care professionals, representatives of formula companies visited villages to promote the use of infant formula.

Item—While interned in clinics and hospitals, new mothers were given free samples of infant formula.

Item—Free or low-cost supplies of infant formula were given to health institutions, thus routinizing bottle-feeding within hospitals and discouraging breastfeeding.

Item—Product labels failed to warn of potential dangers from incorrect use of infant formula.

Most damaging from the industry's viewpoint was infant formula's alleged complicity in the death of Third World infants. Dr. Derrick B. Jelliffe, then director of the Caribbean Food and Nutrition Institute, claimed that millions of infants suffered and died as a result of bottle-feeding. A major reason was that Third World mothers could not take sterilization and storage precautions commonplace in homes with modern kitchens.

Outraged by these allegations, the Infant Formula Action Coalition (INFACT) was formed in the late 1970s. It focused its indignation on Nestlé, the largest producer of infant formula worldwide. Chaired by Douglas A. Johnson and joined by a hundred other religious and health organizations, INFACT instituted an international boycott against the Nestlé Company, charging it with aggressive marketing tactics designed to pressure mothers in underdeveloped countries to switch from breastfeeding to bottle-feeding, thus contributing to high infant-mortality rates.

INFACT's and Jelliffe's bold charges were weakened by a shortage of reliable information—as Nestlé's defenders were quick to point out. Was breastfeeding really decreasing in developing nations? Were infant morbidity and mortality in fact increasing? No one really knew. And even if bottle-feeding was increasing and even if there was a connection between it and increased infant mortality, no one could claim for certain that Nestlé's promotional practices had much, if anything, to do with it. Also overlooked was the fact that Third World mothers who cannot nurse are also more likely to be subject to the economic factors that make bottle-feeding risky.[74]

In May 1981, the World Health Organization (WHO) adopted a "Code of Marketing of Breastmilk Substitutes," which called on governments to prohibit advertising of infant formula that discourages breastfeeding. The code would prohibit, for example, sending women dressed as nurses to rural villages or paying local health workers to push infant formula. Of the 119 WHO members who voted, 118 voted for adoption. The sole opposition vote was cast by the United States, which invoked the principles of free trade and free speech. The United States said that WHO had no business telling private business how to sell its products and that it didn't want to make WHO an international Federal Trade Commission.

Although Nestlé branded the code unacceptably ambiguous, the company said it would support it. INFACT and others identified four areas for Nestlé to review: educational materials dealing with infant formula, hazard warnings and labels, gifts to health professionals, and free supplies to hospitals. Until Nestlé complied, INFACT threatened to pursue its campaign against the company. Nestlé said it already was complying and that the charges of noncompliance were based on subjective interpretations of the code. To safeguard its reputation as well as its infant-formula market, Nestlé dipped into its war chest to fight the boycott—to the tune, some say, of $40 million.

While on one front Nestlé was waging a battle to preserve its reputation, on another it was moving toward a more constructive resolution to the problem. Because WHO had no enforcement authority, there was no neutral party to monitor compliance with its "Code of Marketing of Breastmilk Substitutes." So Nestlé formed the Nestlé Infant Formula Audit Commission (NIFAC). NIFAC, which was chaired by former Senator Edmund S. Muskie, was asked to review Nestlé's instructions to field personnel to see if they could be improved. NIFAC laboured for 18 months, issuing quarterly reports to the public and requesting from WHO/UNICEF several clarifications of the code. Its efforts eventually bore fruit. The international boycott against Nestlé was suspended in 1984 when Nestlé developed procedures for dealing with the four specific points of the code in dispute.

Regarding educational material, Nestlé agreed to include in all materials dealing with the feeding of infants information on (1) the benefits and superiority of breast-feeding, (2) maternal nutrition and preparation for maintenance of breastfeeding, (3) the negative effect on breastfeeding of introducing partial bottle-feeding, (4) the difficulty of reversing the decision not to breastfeed, (5) possible health hazards of inappropriate food or feeding methods, and (6) the social and financial consequences of the decision to use infant formula.

Regarding hazard warning labels, Nestlé agreed to test different statements in Third World countries, with the help of specialized consultants recommended by WHO and UNICEF. It specifically promised to ensure that product users fully understood the consequences of inappropriate or incorrect use arising from unclean water, dirty utensils, improper dilution, and storage of prepared foods without refrigeration.

Regarding gifts to health professionals, Nestlé agreed not to give gifts such as chocolate, keyrings, and pens to health professionals. It also agreed to avoid product advertising in technical and scientific publications.

Regarding low-cost supplies of infant formula to health institutions, Nestlé recognized that this might inadvertently discourage breastfeeding. Accordingly, it agreed to restrict the distribution of supplies to situations in which infants had to be fed on breast-milk substitutes and to help specify the conditions that would warrant such substitutes.

After a verification period of eight months, boycott leaders were satisfied that Nestlé had begun to put into place the agreed-on changes, and the "suspended" boycott was officially ended. Unfortunately, the story of Nestlé and infant formula does not come to a happy end there. It wasn't many years before Douglas A. Johnson and his Minneapolis-based organization Action for Corporate Accountability charged Nestlé with noncompliance. They urged a resumption of the boycott against Nestlé as well as an expansion of the boycott to include American Home Products (AHP), the second-largest distributor of infant formula in developing nations. Action for Corporate Accountability accused both companies of violating at least the spirit—and, according to Johnson, also the letter—of the WHO code.

Specifically, Nestlé and AHP were accused of continuing to dump free supplies of formula on hospitals to induce mothers to bottle-feed their infants. The code permits donations of formula for infants needing breast-milk substitutes, but it prohibits distributing free formula solely for sales promotion. The effectiveness of free samples is well known in the advertising world. Mothers who receive free samples are far more likely to bottle-feed than those who do not. By the time the mother and baby have been discharged from the hospital, the mother's milk will have begun to dry up. She and the baby will have become hooked on the formula, Action for Corporate Accountability argued, just when the companies' donations stop and profit-making begins.

Thad Jackson, a Washington spokesperson for Nestlé, insisted that the company was in "total compliance" with national and international codes. He also said that the company never gave the product directly to mothers. "We do not dump supplies in hospitals," he stated. Carol Emerling, an official of AHP, also challenged the boycott. "This whole activity is based on allegations that we violate the WHO code—and we flat out deny that."[75]

Monitoring by the United Methodist Church, however, concluded that the industry continued to violate restrictions on supplies to hospitals. One study of 45 hospitals in four Asian countries found that Nestlé was supplying formula to 80 percent of them—in enough quantity to feed over 110 percent of their infants. AHP supplied formula to 64 percent of the hospitals. Moreover, the companies' own data suggested that the practice was designed to produce sales. In Brazil, for instance, where Nestlé had a monopoly on infant formula, it distributed no free supplies to hospitals. When the government of the Ivory Coast conducted a campaign to promote breastfeeding, Nestlé stepped up its donations of formula to that nation's hospitals.[76]

Boycotts are difficult to organize and sustain, and Johnson's efforts to mount a second one against Nestlé had little effect. But there was some progress. In March 1992, UNICEF and WHO joined forces to launch a new "Baby-Friendly Hospital Initiative." Nestlé is one of the parties that pledged to coordinate efforts on behalf of this initiative, designed to encourage breastfeeding and halt the distribution of free or low-cost samples of infant formula to hospitals in developing nations.

Unfortunately, though, the problem is not limited to the Third World. To secure a contract allowing it to be the only company to provide free formula samples to all mothers giving birth in New York City hospitals, AHP paid $1 million to the New York City Health and Hospital Corporation. New York's plan was to spend the entire sum on promoting breastfeeding. Would this counteract the influence of those free samples to mothers? AHP was willing to gamble $1 million that it wouldn't.[77]

UPDATE

UNICEF estimates that 1.5 million babies die every year because they are not breastfed. And over twenty years after WHO adopted a code of conduct for the marketing of infant formula, International Baby Food Action Network and affiliated organizations like Baby Milk Action continue to campaign against Nestlé and other infant-formula companies, charging that they violate the code by marketing their product aggressively to young mothers and pregnant women in the Third World.[78] These charges gained support from a *British Medical Journal* report published in 2003, which found that the infant formula marketing code was being ignored in the two African countries it studied, with companies failing to include a statement about the health benefits of breastfeeding, instructions for the appropriate preparation and storage of formula, or a warning against the health hazards of inappropriate use. According to the study, 90 percent of health providers had never heard of the code, and two-thirds of mothers using formula had never received any advice on breastfeeding. For its part, Nestlé insists that it has always respected the code and would take "the necessary steps" to remedy any local problems.[79]

Meanwhile, the company has been making a concerted effort to market baby formula to Hispanic mothers in the United States. One can easily see why. Hispanic households, which tend to be larger and have a growing birth rate, are expected to constitute 20 percent of the U.S. population by 2020. Some doctors and breastfeeding advocates, however, believe that infant formula should not be regarded as a growth area for any company, and they're especially concerned about marketing the product to low-income immigrant mothers, who may lack fluency in English or won't receive sufficient medical advice to make an informed choice between formula and breastfeeding their infants. True, many Hispanic mothers must work and can't be with their babies all day, and some find that their infants do better with formula. Still, medical studies consistently show that breast milk protects infants from allergies, infections, and other illnesses and that raising the rate of breastfeeding would save families, insurance companies, and the government millions of health care dollars annually.[80]

Discussion Questions

1. What moral issues are raised by the controversy over infant formula? Do you find anything objectionable in the marketing techniques used to sell infant formula? What moral rights, if any, are at stake in this controversy? How would you respond to the argument that all Nestlé was doing was selling a high-quality product at its normal price to willing buyers?

2. In the light of this case, do you think it makes sense to talk of a corporation like Nestlé as a moral agent, or is it only the people in it who can be properly described as having moral responsibility?

3. Identify the views of corporate social responsibility held by the different actors and organizations in this case. In what ways does this case raise questions about the social and moral responsibility of corporations?

4. Appraise Nestlé's actions from the perspective of both the narrow and the broader view of corporate social responsibility.

5. How would you assess Nestlé's conduct throughout the whole controversy? Has Nestlé acted in good faith? Do you think it is sincerely concerned about the drawbacks and dangers of using infant formula?

6. Given the health benefits of breastfeeding, is it morally responsible for any company to try to increase demand for infant formula?

7. Can boycotts be effective in pressuring corporations to exercise social responsibility? When, if ever, does an individual have a moral obligation to participate in a corporate boycott?

CASE 5.3

Free Speech or False Advertising?

With annual sales of over $10.5 billion and annual profits of around $475 million, Nike is one of the giants in the sports apparel business, and its trademark "Swoosh" logo is recognized around the world. However, for a company its size, Nike directly employs surprisingly few workers—only about 22,000. That is because overseas contractors manufacture all Nike's products. These independent contractors employ approximately 600,000 workers at 910 factories, mostly in China, Indonesia, Vietnam, and Thailand.

Like many other firms, Nike outsources its manufacturing to take advantage of cheap overseas labour. But the price of doing so began getting higher for Nike in the late 1990s, when anti-sweatshop activists started campaigning against the company, charging that the Third World workers making its products were exploited and abused. Activists on many college campuses, for instance, encouraged their peers to boycott Nike shoes and clothing and tried to pressure their universities' athletic departments not to sign deals with Nike for team sports apparel.

Instead of ducking the issue, as other companies might have, Nike responded vigorously to the criticisms. At the University of North Carolina, for example, Nike ran full-page ads in the student newspaper, asserting that it was a good corporate citizen and upheld humane labour standards. It sent representatives to meet with student activists, and the company CEO Philip Knight took the unusual step of showing up at an undergraduate seminar on corporate globalization to defend his company. Nike issued press releases and sent letters to many college presidents and athletic departments, asserting, among other things, that Nike paid "on average, double the minimum wage as defined in countries where its products are produced" and that its workers "are protected from physical and sexual abuse."

Enter Marc Kasky, a 59-year-old San Francisco activist. He thought Nike's campaign was misleading the public about working conditions inside its factories, so he sued the company for false advertising under California's consumer protection law. In Kasky's view, the case is simply a matter of protecting consumers from corporate deceit. In response, Nike argues that the statements in question are protected by the First Amendment because they were made in news releases, letters to the editor, and op-ed essays and because they related to the company's labour practices—which are a matter of public concern—and not the products it sells. Two lower courts agreed with Nike, but then the California Supreme Court overturned their verdict, ruling in a 4–3 decision that the company's campaign was essentially commercial speech (which generally receives less First Amendment protection than political or personal speech) even though Nike was not specifically talking about shoes. In the court's view, Nike's speech was directed at customers and dealt with its business operations; the form in which the

information was released was irrelevant. The judges, however, didn't determine whether Nike really did abuse workers or mislead consumers; it left those factual questions for a trial court to decide.

Nike then appealed the case to the U.S. Supreme Court. California Attorney General Bill Lockyer filed a brief in support of Kasky, which 17 other states joined. The brief contends that the case is not about free speech but rather "Nike's ability to exploit false facts to promote commercial ends." Harvard law professor Laurence Tribe, however, defended the company, arguing that treating Nike's letters and press releases as equivalent to advertising would undercut the ability of companies to speak out on political issues. He believes the California decision will have a "chilling effect on freedom of speech." To this, however, the chief author of the California brief, deputy attorney general Roland Reiter responds: "I believe the concerns expressed are really overblown. We have a company talking about itself. It's difficult to see why holding them to the truth would cause any kind of calamity." USC law professor Erwin Chemerinsky agrees. He argues that it doesn't matter whether Nike issued the information in the form of a press release: "If a company makes false statements about its product or practices with the intent of increasing profits, that's commercial speech."

After having heard the case, however, the U.S. Supreme Court declined to decide the substantive legal issues at stake. Instead, in June 2003 it dismissed the case on a technicality and sent it back to California for trial. Before the trial began, however, Nike settled out of court with Kasky. As part of the deal, Nike will donate $1.5 million to the Fair Labor Association, a sweatshop-monitoring group, and in a joint statement, Kasky and Nike "mutually agreed that investments designed to strengthen workplace monitoring and factory worker programs are more desirable than prolonged litigation." A happy ending? Not in everyone's eyes. Friends of Nike argue that because the Supreme Court did not act forthrightly to protect corporate speech, companies will be reluctant to discuss public issues involving their products. Those on the other side, however, respond that when disclosing information about wages and working conditions, companies should be held to the same standards of truth and accuracy as when they disclose financial data.[81]

Discussion Questions

1. In this case, was Nike engaged in commercial speech, or were its statements political or social speech? What determines whether speech is commercial or not?

2. Was the out-of-court settlement a reasonable resolution of this case? What would have been the good or bad consequences of the U.S. Supreme Court's deciding in Nike's favour? Of its deciding in Kasky's favour?

3. Do corporations have the same moral rights as individual human beings? Should they have the same political rights? Is it morally permissible to limit the speech of corporations in ways that it would be wrong to limit that of individual citizens? If it is permissible, is it good public policy?

4. Does Nike have a social responsibility to address matters of public concern such as the working conditions in its overseas operation? If it chooses to do so, does it have an obligation to make its statements as truthful and accurate as it can? Under what circumstances should corporations be held liable for the truth of their public statements?

Notes to Chapter 5

1. John McDermott, *Corporate Society: Class, Property, and Contemporary Capitalism* (Boulder, CO: Westview, 1991), 4.

2. See www.reportonbusines.com/top1000.

3. Anthony J. Parisi, "How Exxon Rules Its Great Empire," *San Francisco Chronicle*, August 5, 1980, 27. For an update, see "Inside the Empire of Exxon the Unloved," *Economist*, March 15, 1994.

4. "The Next Society: A Survey of the Near Future," *Economist*, November 3, 2001, 16.

5. Thomas Donaldson, *Corporations and Morality* (Englewood Cliffs, NJ: Prentice Hall, 1982), 4.

6. Ibid., 5.

7. Ibid., 3.

8. "Prosecutor's Dilemma," *Economist*, June 15, 2002, 76.

9. Parisi, "How Exxon Rules," 38.

10. See Kenneth Goodpaster and John B. Matthews, Jr., "Can a Corporation Have a Conscience?," *Harvard Business Review* 60 (January/February 1982): 132–141.

11. Donaldson, *Corporations and Morality*, 10.

12. See Peter A. French, "The Corporation as a Moral Person," *American Philosophical Quarterly* 16 (July 1979): 207–215; and French, "Corporate Moral Agency" in *The Blackwell Encyclopedia of Management, Vol. II: Business Ethics*, 2nd ed., P. H. Werhane and R. E. Freeman, eds. (Malden, MA: Blackwell, 2005).

13. See Manuel G. Velasquez, "Why Corporations Are Not Morally Responsible for Anything They Do," *Business and Professional Ethics Journal* 2 (Spring 1983), and Velasquez, "Debunking Corporate Moral Responsibility," *Business Ethics Quarterly* 13 (October 2003).

14. Quoted in Goodpaster and Matthews, "Can a Corporation Have a Conscience?," 141.

15. Jeffrey L. Seglin, "A Safer World for Mea Culpas," *New York Times*, March 21, 1999, sec. 3, 4.

16. Quoted in Clarence C. Walton, *Corporate Social Responsibilities* (Belmont, CA: Wadsworth, 1967), 169–170.

17. Quoted in Bernard D. Nossiter, *The Mythmakers: An Essay on Power and Wealth* (Boston: Houghton Mifflin, 1964), 100.

18. Milton Friedman, *Capitalism and Freedom* (Chicago: University of Chicago Press, 1962), 133.

19. Theodore Levitt, "The Dangers of Social Responsibility," *Harvard Business Review* 36 (September/October 1958).

20. Milton Friedman, "The Social Responsibility of Business Is to Increase Its Profits," *New York Times Magazine*, September 13, 1970, 33, 126

21. Ibid., 124.

22. Reprinted from Keith Davis, "Five Propositions for Social Responsibility," *Business Horizons* 18 (June 1975): 20. © 1975 by the Foundation for the School of Business at Indiana University. Used with permission.

23. John Kay, "Business Leaders Have No Natural Authority," *Financial Times*, April 5, 2005, 17.

24. Robert Kuttner, "The Great American Pension-Fund Robbery," *Business Week*, September 8, 2003, 24.

25. "The Corporate Tax Game," *Business Week*, March 31, 2003, 79–83.

26. Kay, "Business Leaders," 17.

27. Melvin Anshen, "Changing the Social Contract: A Role for Business," *Columbia Journal of World Business* 5 (November/December 1970). See also James E. Post, Anne T. Lawrence, and James Weber, *Business and Society: Corporate Strategy, Public Policy, Ethics*, 10th ed. (New York: McGraw-Hill, 2002), 16–17.

28. Davis, "Five Propositions for Social Responsibility," 22.

29. Thomas Donaldson, "Defining the Value of Doing Good Business," *Financial Times*, June 3, 2005, Supplement, 3.

30. Friedman, "The Social Responsibility of Business," 122.

31. Ibid.

32. When Companies Put Shareholders Second," *Financial Times*, February 28, 2005, 10.

33. Adolf A. Berle, Jr., and Gardiner C. Means, *The Modern Corporation and Private Property* (New York: Macmillan, 1932).

34. "Design by Committee," *Economist*, June 15, 2002, 71. See also Alan Murray, "Political Capital," *Wall Street Journal*, July 16, 2002, A4, and July 13, 2004, A4.

35. Joann S. Lublin, "How CEOs Retire in Style," *Wall Street Journal*, September 13, 2002, B1. See also Arthur Levitt, Jr., "Money, Money, Money," *Wall Street Journal*, November 22, 2004, A14.

36. Louis Lavelle, "How Shareholder Votes Are Legally Rigged," *Business Week*, May 20, 2002, 48; "CEO Elections out of Shareholders' Control," *Financial Times*, August 17, 2004, 8; and "No Democracy Please, We're Shareholders," *Economist*, May 1, 2004, 13.

37. "As California Starved for Energy, U.S. Business Had a Feast," *Wall Street Journal*, September 16, 2002, A1; and "How Energy Traders Turned Bonanza into an Epic Bust," *Wall Street Journal*, December 31, 2002, A1. The deregulation in Ontario of electricity and gas utilities has certainly resulted in sharply rising prices for both commodities and shortages in the former.

38. "The Corporate Givers," *Business Week*, November 29, 2004, 102–103.

39. Donaldson, "Defining the Value of Doing Good Business," 2.

40. Quoted by John Micklethwait and Adrian Wooldridge, *The Company* (New York: Modern Library, 2003), 182.

41. Robert B. Reich, "How to Avoid These Layoffs," *New York Times*, January 4, 1996, A13. See also George F. Will, "Capable Candidate in Waiting," *San Jose Mercury News*, February 10, 2002, 7P.

42. Walter Goodman, "Stocks Without Sin," *Harper's*, August 1971, 66.

43. "From a Handout to a Hand Up," *Financial Times*, February 3, 2005, 3.

44. Levitt, "The Dangers of Social Responsibility," 44. See also George G. Brenkert, "Private Corporations and Public Welfare," *Public Affairs Quarterly* 6 (April 1992): 155–168.

45. Davis, "Five Propositions for Social Responsibility," 20.

46. Paul F. Camenisch, "Business Ethics: On Getting to the Heart of the Matter," *Business and Professional Ethics Journal* 1 (Fall 1981).

47. For a list of "caring" corporations, see www.imaginecanada.ca/?q=en/node/119.

48. "The Cecil Rhodes of Chocolate-Chip Cookies," *Economist*, May 25, 1996, 74.

49. "Good Citizens of the Community," *Business Ethics*, March/April 2002, 9; and "The Corporate Donors," *Business Week*, December 1, 2003, 92.

50. Camenisch, "Business Ethics."

51. See Christopher D. Stone, *Where the Law Ends* (New York: Harper & Row, 1975), Chapter 11.

52. In case you think lobbyists operate only in the American political scene, see www.politicswatch.com/lobbyists-dec12-2005.htm.

53. See Ted Schrecker, "Risks Versus Rights: Economic Power and Economic Analysis in Environmental Politics", in D.C. Poff and W.J. Waluchow, eds., *Business Ethics in Canada*, 3rd ed. (Englewood Cliffs, NJ: Prentice Hall, 1999), 321–25.

54. See n. 9 to Chapter 1. See also Robert H. Frank, *What Price the Moral High Ground?* (Princeton, NJ: Princeton University Press, 2004), ch. 4.

55. Kenneth J. Arrow, "Social Responsibility and Economic Efficiency," *Public Policy* 21 (Summer 1973).

56. Milton Snoeyenbos and Barbara Caley, "Managing Ethics," in Milton Snoeyenbos, Robert Almeder, and James Humber, eds., *Business Ethics*, 3rd ed. (Buffalo, NY: Prometheus, 2001), 143.

57. Ibid., Snoeyenbos and Caley, "Managing Ethics," 141.

58. Gillian Flynn, "Make Employee Ethics Your Business," *Personnel Journal*, June 1995.

59. "Organisations, Too, Can Be Put on the Couch," *Financial Times*, June 20, 2003, 12.

60. Donald P. Robin and R. Eric Reidenbach, *Business Ethics: Where Profits Meet Value Systems* (Englewood Cliffs, NJ: Prentice Hall, 1989), 59.

61. Ibid.

62. Quoted by Robin and Reidenbach, *Business Ethics*, 59.

63. "When Something Is Rotten," *Economist*, July 27, 2002, 53.

64. "Donaldson Laments U.S. Chiefs' Lack of Ethical Leadership," *Financial Times*, September 20, 2004, 1.

65. Lynn Sharp Paine, "Managing for Organizational Integrity," *Harvard Business Review* 72 (March/April 1994): 107–108.

66. "Businesses Are Signing Up for Ethics 101," *Business Week*, February 15, 1988, 56.

67. *Economist*, April 8, 1995, 57, and August 19, 1995, 56.

68. Samuel S. Epstein, "The Asbestos 'Pentagon Papers,'" in Mark Green and Robert Massie, Jr., eds., *The Big Business Reader: Essays on Corporate America* (New York: Pilgrim Press, 1980) is the primary source of the facts and quotations reported here.

69. See "Asbestos Claims to Be Reduced Under New Plan," *Wall Street Journal*, November 20, 1990, A4, and "Court Rejection of Asbestos Trust Means More Delay," *Santa Cruz Sentinel*, December 8, 1992, B4.

70. "Asbestos Settlement Tossed," *San Jose Mercury News*, May 11, 1996, 1D; and "Voiding of Class-Action Asbestos Settlement Upheld," *New York Times*, June 26, 1997, C25.

71. "A Bid to Bypass the Lawyers," *Economist*, January 29, 2005, 69. See also "Asbestos Quagmire," *Wall Street Journal*, January 27, 2003, B1.

72. "Outlandish Claims," *Economist*, May 25, 2002, 75; and "Spreading Out of Control," *Economist*, September 21, 2002, 71–72. See also David Stout, "Railways Held Liable for Workers' Fear of Deadly Disease," *New York Times*, March 10, 2003 (online).

73. For further, more detailed discussions of the marketing of infant formula, see Lisa H. Newton and David P. Schmidt, *Wake-Up Calls: Classic Cases in Business Ethics* (Belmont, CA: Wadsworth, 1996), ch. 3, and Robert F. Hartley, *Business Ethics* (New York: John Wiley, 1993), ch. 10. See also Lisa H. Newton, "A New Power Agenda: Tracking the Emergence of a New Global Polity in the Infant Formula Controversy," *Business and Professional Ethics Journal* 2, no. 2 (Summer 2000).

74. Newton and Schmidt, *Wake-Up Calls*, 65–67.

75. "New Boycott Plea in Infant Formula Fight," *San Francisco Chronicle*, October 5, 1988, A9.

76. Carol-Linnea Salmon, "Milking Deadly Dollars from the Third World," *Business and Society* 68 (Winter 1989).

77. Salmon, "Milking Deadly Dollars."

78. See, in particular, www.babymilkaction.org.

79. See "Baby Milk Marketing 'Breaks Rules,'" *BBC News*, January 17, 2003 (available online at www.bbc.co.uk) and the *British Medical Journal*, January 18, 2003.

80. "Nestlé Markets Baby Formula to Hispanic Mothers in U.S.," *Wall Street Journal*, March 4, 2004, B1.

81. For more on this case, see "Just How Far Does First Amendment Protection Go?," *Wall Street Journal*, January 10, 2003, B1; "Suit Against Nike Raises Free Speech Questions," *San Jose Mercury News*, April 21, 2003, 1A; "Free Speech or False Advertising?," *Business Week*, April 28, 2003, 69; and Robert J. Samuelson, "The Tax on Free Speech," *Newsweek*, July 24, 2003, 41.

The Greed Cycle: How Corporate America Went out of Control

John Cassidy

In this essay, John Cassidy, author of Dot.Con and a staff writer for The New Yorker, tells the story of how the stock market boom of the 1990s collapsed amid the debris of business failures and corporate scandals. Since the emergence of the modern publicly held corporation in the nineteenth century, there has been a "principal–agent" problem—namely, how to ensure that managers act in the interest of the shareholders. An attempt to deal with this problem, the stockholder-value movement led to the 1980s wave of leveraged buyouts and then in the 1990s to the increased use of stock options as executive compensation. This, however, created an environment in which CEOs had an incentive to mislead investors, and thus keep stock prices high, by inflating corporate earnings through accounting skulduggery that exaggerated revenues and understated costs.

There are many ways to take the measure of what has happened to corporate America in recent years. As good a way as any is to flip through some back copies of the *Financial Times*, which recently published a remarkable series of articles on what it termed the "barons of bankruptcy—a privileged group of top business people who made extraordinary personal fortunes even as their companies were heading for disaster." The *F.T.* examined the twenty-five biggest business collapses since the start of [2001]. From the beginning of 1999 to the end of 2001, senior executives and directors of these doomed companies walked away with some $3.3 billion in salary, bonuses, and the proceeds from sales of stock and stock options. Some of the names on the list were familiar to anybody who reads the papers: Global Crossing's Gary Winnick ($512.4 million); Enron's Kenneth Lay ($246.7 million); and WorldCom's Scott Sullivan ($49.4 million). However, there were also many names that haven't received much public attention, such as Clark McLeod and Richard Lumpkin, the former chairman and the former vice-chairman, respectively, of McLeodUSA, a telecommunications company based in Cedar Rapids, Iowa. These two corporate philanthropists cashed in stock worth ninety-nine million dollars and a hundred and sixteen million dollars, respectively, before the rest of the stockholders were wiped out.

Even veteran observers have been taken aback by recent events. "It became a competitive game to see how much money you could get," Paul Volcker, the former chairman of the Federal Reserve Board, told me when I visited him at his office in Rockefeller Center. . . . Earlier . . . Volcker [had] tried and failed to rescue Arthur Andersen, Enron's accounting firm, which ended up going out of business. "Corporate greed exploded beyond anything that could have been imagined in 1990," Volcker went on. "Traditional norms didn't exist. You had this whole culture where the only sign of worth was how much money you made."

Economists from Adam Smith to Milton Friedman have seen greed as an inevitable and, in some ways, desirable feature of capitalism. In a well-regulated and well-balanced economy, greed helps to keep the system expanding. But it is also kept in check, lest it undermine public faith in the entire enterprise. The extraordinary thing about the last few years is not the mere presence of greed but the way it was systematically encouraged and then allowed to careen out of control. Kenneth Lay, in quietly selling stock and exercising stock options worth more than two hundred million dollars shortly before Enron collapsed, wasn't just being a selfish, unscrupulous individual: he was defying the social contract that underpins a system, which, despite its faults, has lasted almost two hundred years.

I

In 1814, Francis Cabot Lowell, a Boston merchant, founded the first public company, when he built a textile factory on the banks of the Charles River in Waltham, Massachusetts, and called it the Boston Manufacturing Company. Lowell had smuggled a plan of a power loom out of England, and he intended to compete with the Lancashire mills. But he couldn't afford to pay for the construction and installation of expensive machinery by himself, so he sold stock in his company to ten associates. Within seven years, these stockholders had received a cumulative return of more than a hundred per cent, and Lowell had established a new business model. Under its auspices, mankind has invented cures for deadly diseases, extracted minerals from ocean floors, extended commerce to all corners of the earth, and generated unprecedented rates of economic expansion.

Initially, most economists were skeptical of Lowell's innovation. At the heart of any public company there is an implicit bargain: the managers promise to run the company in the owners' interest, and the stockholders agree to hand over day-to-day control of the business to the managers. Unfortunately, there is no easy way to make sure that the managers don't slack off, or divert some of the stockholders' money into their own pockets. Adam Smith was among the first to identify this problem. "The directors of such companies . . . being the managers rather of other people's money than of their own, it cannot well be expected that they should watch over it with the same anxious vigilance with which the partners in a private [company] frequently watch over their own," Smith wrote in "The Wealth of Nations." And he went on, "Negligence and profusion, therefore, must always prevail, more or less, in the management of the affairs of such a company."

Smith thought that private companies would remain the normal way of doing business, but technological change and financial necessity proved him wrong. With the development of the railroads, for example, companies like the New York Central and the Union Pacific needed to raise tens of millions of dollars from outside investors to lay track and buy rolling stock. And because the administrative complexity of the railroads was too much for a single entrepreneur to handle, a new class of full-time executives . . . emerged to run them. Though the emerging industry attracted dubious financiers like Jay Gould, most of the professional managers were content to collect generous salaries and pensions rather than habitually attempt to rob the stockholders and bondholders . . . .

Alas, by the late nineteen-twenties it was clear that corporate perfidy was prospering in an impressive variety of forms, most of them involving insiders exploiting their position to fleece outsiders. After the stock-market crash of 1929, congressional investigators uncovered widespread insider trading, stock-price manipulation, and diversion of corporate funds to personal use. Then, as now, the revelations of corporate wrongdoing prompted the federal government to respond. The Securities Act of 1933 imposed extensive disclosure requirements on any company wanting to issue stock, and outlawed insider dealing and other attempts to manipulate the market. In 1934, the Securities and Exchange Commission was set up to enforce the new regulations.

Public confidence in business eventually recovered, but the potential conflict of interest at the heart of public companies was never fully resolved. During the nineteen-sixties and early seventies, corporate managers were often cavalier about the interests of stockholders. Back then, the chief executive's compensation was usually linked to the size of the firm he ran—the bigger the company, the bigger the paycheck. This encouraged business leaders to build sprawling empires rather than focus on their firms' profitability and stock price. Many of them spent heavily on perquisites of office, such as lavish headquarters and corporate retreats, and they kept on spending even when their companies ran into trouble.

In theory, the stockholders could have joined together to force out managers, but organizing such a collective effort was costly and time consuming, and it rarely happened. Nor was managerial waste constrained by competition from rival firms that didn't splurge on pink marble for the office bathrooms. Companies like General Motors saw their businesses decimated by foreign competition, but C.E.O.s, such as G.M.'s Roger Smith, rarely suffered. From a stockholder's perspective, something more potent was required to get those who ran the companies to serve the interests of those who owned the companies. When the solution materialized, it would turn out to be more potent than anybody had imagined.

II

Thirty years ago, two obscure young financial economists provided the spark for reform. Michael Jensen and William Meckling had graduate degrees from the University of Chicago . . . . They began with the supposition that senior managers, faced with competition from other firms, would do the best they could for their stockholders, by cutting costs and trying to make as big a profit as possible. "But the more we thought about it the more we realized that what we had been taught in Chicago and believed most of our lives wasn't true," Jensen recalled recently. "It wasn't automatically true that corporations would maximize value."

Jensen and Meckling . . . planted the idea that the most important people in any company are not the employees or the managers but the owners—the stockholders and bondholders. This model provided an intellectual rationale, of sorts, for the controversial explosion in C.E.O. pay that began in the nineteen-eighties; and it justified the widespread adoption of executive stock options.

Jensen and Meckling analyzed the relationship between stockholders and managers as a "principal–agent problem"—a dilemma that arises whenever one party (the principal) employs another (the agent) to do a job for him. It might be a family hiring a contractor to renovate its house, a company hiring a brokerage firm to manage its retirement fund, or even an electorate choosing a government. In all these cases, the same issue arises: How can the principal insure that the agent acts in his or her interest? As anybody who has dealt with a contractor knows, there is no simple solution. One option is to design a contract that rewards the contractor for doing the job well. Municipal-construction projects, for example, have a chronic tendency to overrun, snarling traffic and infuriating the public. So when the City of New York, say, puts out tenders for roadwork, its contracts often include financial incentives for finishing the work early and penalties for being late.

Jensen and Meckling were the first economists to apply this idea to corporations. They argued that there was no perfect way to align the interests of the owners and the managers. In any firm that relied on outsiders for financing, the senior executives would make some damaging decisions. If the firm issued stock, they would waste some of the proceeds on perks like corporate jets. If the firm issued debt, the managers, knowing that the bondholders would be the main losers if anything went wrong, would make too many risky investments. The "agency costs" that the business incurred as a result of these actions were unavoidable. It didn't matter whether the firm was a cosseted monopoly or a company facing extensive competition: managers would destroy value.

. . . Eventually . . . most economists accepted Jensen and Meckling's logic, and they began to ask more questions: How should the performances of senior executives be measured? Was it better to give them money, in the form of salaries or bonuses, or company stock? If some managerial inefficiency was inevitable, how could it be minimized? Principal–agent theory provided a clear answer to these questions: treat chief executives just like plumbers, contractors, or any other truculent agent, and reward them for acting in the best interest of the principal—i.e., the stockholders.

At the time, many chief executives saw their main task as overseeing the welfare of their employees and customers. As long as the firm made a decent profit every year and raised the dividend it paid its stockholders, this was considered good enough. But, once C.E.O.s were viewed as merely the agents of the firm's owners, they were urged to live by a new, simpler credo: shareholder value. Henceforth, economists and management gurus agreed, their overriding aim should be to maximize the value of the firm, as it was determined in the stock market.

The shareholder-value movement soon attracted rich and aggressive investors who used the economists' arguments to justify attacks on corporate America. During the hostile-takeover wave of the nineteen-eighties, controversial figures like T. Boone Pickens and Carl Icahn bought stakes in public companies they considered undervalued and, claiming to represent the ordinary stockholder, often tried to seize control. Since the corporate raiders financed their attacks with borrowed money, their takeovers became known as "leveraged buyouts," or LBOs. In a typical LBO, the acquirer would buy out the public stockholders and run the company as a private concern, slashing costs and slimming it down. The ultimate aim was to refloat the company on the stock market at a higher valuation. Individual raiders weren't the only force behind LBOs. Wall Street firms like Kohlberg Kravis Roberts and Hicks, Muse also got in on the game. Nearly half of all major public corporations received a takeover offer in the eighties. Many companies were forced to lay off workers and sell off underperforming divisions in order to boost their stock price and fend off potential bidders. Raiders were popularly denounced as speculators and predators, which, of course, most of them were . . . .

Still, many economists defended LBOs as an effective way to overcome the agency problems that Jensen and Meckling had identified. The stockholders who sold out often made considerable profits, and the managers of bought-out companies were usually given large chunks of equity. Senior executives would be forced to run the firms more efficiently, it was argued, because of all the debt that had been taken on, and, if they boosted the value of the firm, they should make a lot of money themselves.

. . . When the economy went into a recession during the early nineteen-nineties, many of the firms that had gone private, such as Macy's and Revco, couldn't keep up their interest payments, and the resulting wave of bankruptcies discredited the LBO as a business model. Far from creating value, many LBOs had ended up wiping out the investors and bondholders who financed them. The only people who consistently made money were the stockholders and senior managers who sold out early on. The enduring economic lesson of the LBO era was that unleashing greed wasn't enough to raise efficiency. But the message that corporate America took from its ordeal was quite different: senior executives who converted to the new religion of shareholder value tended to get very rich, while those who argued that corporations ought to consider their employees and customers as well as their stockholders often ended up without a job.

At the same time, corporations came to realize that leveraged buyouts weren't the only way to align the interests of managers and shareholders. There was a much simpler tool available, which didn't involve going to all the trouble of a multibillion-dollar takeover: the executive stock option. Once endowed with a generous grant of these magical instruments, a senior executive would no longer think of himself as a mere hired hand but as a proprietor who had the long-term health of the firm at heart. That was the theory, anyway.

III

An executive stock option is a legal contract that grants its owner the right to buy a stock in his or her company at a certain price (the "strike price") on a certain date in the future. Take a company with a stock price of fifty dollars that grants its chief executive the right to buy a million shares three years hence at the current market price. Assume the stock price rises by ten per cent per year, so that after three years it is trading at about sixty-six dollars and fifty cents. At that point, the chief executive can "exercise" his option and make the company sell him a million shares at fifty dollars. Then he can sell the shares in the open market, and clear a profit of sixteen and a half million dollars . . . .

In 1980, fewer than a third of chief executives of public companies were granted stock options. Most firms still depended on bonuses and profit sharing to motivate and reward their senior managers. As the nineteen-eighties progressed, and the Dow tripled, stock options began to look much less risky. Thanks to the startling growth of firms that used them heavily, such as Microsoft and Intel, they also became fashionable . . . . Yet the real benefit of granting stock options—or so economists insisted—was that they solved the problem of providing incentives to senior executives . . . .

By 1994, seven in ten chief executives received option grants, and stock options made up about half of their average take-home pay. In the second half of the nineties, so-called "mega-options"—options grants worth at least ten million dollars—became the norm. In 1997, according to the executive-compensation consulting firm Pearl Meyer & Partners, ninety-two of America's top two hundred chief executives received mega-options, with an average value of thirty-one million dollars. A year later, two Harvard economists, Brian J. Hall and Jeffrey Liebman, took another look at managerial pay and confirmed what anybody who followed the financial pages already knew: C.E.O.s weren't paid anything like bureaucrats. They were paid more like rock stars.

Wittingly and unwittingly, Washington encouraged the great giveaway. During the 1992 election campaign, Bill Clinton and Al Gore made a political issue out of lavish C.E.O. pay. A year later, the new Administration limited to a million dollars the tax deductions that corporations could take for executive salaries. The reform turned out to be counterproductive. Since executive stock options weren't counted as regular compensation, corporations had yet another reason to pay their senior managers less in salary and more in options. In 1994, the Financial Accounting Standards Board (F.A.S.B.), the descendant of the Accounting Principles Board, set out to force companies to deduct the value of the stock options they granted from their earnings. Following an intense lobbying campaign by Silicon Valley companies, several leading members of Congress, including Joseph Lieberman and Dianne Feinstein, threatened to put the F.A.S.B. out of business if it went ahead with the change. The board backed down, and the latest official attempt to control corporate avarice came to an end.

IV

The rise of the stock option revolutionized the culture of corporate America. The chief executives of blue-chip companies, who in the nineteen-eighties had portrayed Icahn, Pickens, and their ilk as corporate vandals, now embraced the values of the raiders as their own. For decades, the Business Roundtable, a lobbying group that represents the C.E.O.s of dozens of major companies, had stressed the social role that corporations played in their communities, as well as the financial obligations they owed their stockholders. In 1997, the Business Roundtable changed its position statement to read, "The paramount duty of management and board is to the shareholder."

In many cases, the C.E.O.s turned into corporate raiders themselves, albeit internal raiders. Companies like I.B.M., Xerox, and Procter & Gamble, acting on their own volition, fired tens of thousands of workers. Their chief executives insisted that the "downsizing" was necessary to compete effectively, and that was sometimes true. But once the C.E.O.s were in possession of mega-options, they had another motivating factor: an enormous vested interest in boosting their firms' stock price. For the first time, they had an opportunity to create fortunes on a scale hitherto reserved for industrial pioneers like Rockefeller, Morgan, and Gates. In 1997, Michael Eisner, the chairman and chief executive of Walt Disney, earned five hundred and seventy million dollars. A year later, Mel Karmazin, the chief executive of CBS, exercised options worth almost two hundred million dollars.

The scattered protests at these startling payouts notwithstanding, many economists credited the doctrine of shareholder value for reinvigorating American business. In spite of fears that downsizing would devastate communities, the economy thrived, and the total number of jobs in the country increased. Far from being pilloried, ruthless businessmen ended up being lauded . . . .

As long as the economy kept expanding and the stock market kept going up, most Americans were content to avert their eyes from the lopsided manner in which the rewards of the long boom were being distributed. For those who looked closely, though, there was already evidence that executive stock options were sometimes being abused . . . .

As the Nasdaq headed for 5,000, even some leading advocates of the shareholder-value movement called for changes in the design of stock options. In early 1999, Alfred Rappaport, a consultant who wrote the management text "Creating Shareholder Value," published an article in the

Harvard Business Review in which he pointed out, "Under current compensation schemes, senior managers are rewarded even when their companies underperform." The vertiginous rise in the Nasdaq and the Dow meant that nearly anybody who was lucky enough to be in charge of a public company stood to get very rich, however lacklustre his performance. Rappaport proposed indexing the strike price of executive stock options to the Dow or the Nasdaq. This way, he explained, the options would rise in value only if the stock outperformed the market, and chief executives would have to earn their fortunes.

Despite the eminent sense of this proposal, nobody in corporate America paid any heed to it. Under the nonsensical accounting rules covering options, the value of indexed options had to be deducted from earnings, whereas the value of ordinary options didn't. Businesses weren't willing to reduce their earnings by making the switch . . . .

Worse still, many companies repriced their senior executives' stock options at a lower level whenever the stock price fell. The chip company Advanced Micro Devices, for example, repriced the options of its founder, Jerry Sanders III, no fewer than six times, allowing him to make untold millions of dollars while his firm's stock performed modestly. The software company Oracle followed the same practice. In 2000, Larry Ellison, Oracle's already wealthy founder, made seven hundred million dollars by cashing in some low-priced options shortly before his firm's stock price collapsed.

It is hard to think of a better example of what is wrong with corporate America. When the firm's stock price does well, the people in charge make out like lottery winners. When the stock price plummets, they get another set of chances to win. The scheme, in its audacity, and its logic, is almost beautiful. Graef Crystal, an expert on executive pay, who wrote the book "In Search of Excess: The Overcompensation of American Executives," told me recently that if you combine a volatile stock with a willingness to reprice the stock options "then you have created a money machine, an antigravity device, which guarantees that the senior executives will get super-rich."

V

The most insidious aspect of executive stock options is that—especially in tough times—they give senior managers a strong incentive to mislead investors about the true condition of their companies. Even before the current raft of financial scandals, more and more firms were resorting to accounting skullduggery, exaggerating their revenues and understating their costs.

Economists like Michael Jensen largely ignored this disturbing development, but inside the accounting world it was well known. Under the American system of corporate governance, which hasn't changed much since the nineteen-thirties, public companies provide an earnings update every quarter, and release a more detailed, audited report every twelve months. In preparing their financial results, firms rely on the Generally Accepted Accounting

Principles, a lengthy set of rules that the S.E.C. and the big accounting firms agree upon. The rules are designed to provide a fair picture of how much money a company is making after subtracting its expenses from its revenues, but a determined management can interpret them in many different ways.

In 1993, Howard Schilit, a professor of accounting at American University, in Washington, D.C., published a book about the tricks that companies use to boost their earnings. Back then, most people who weren't C.P.A.s assumed that (outside Hollywood, anyway) accounting standards were clear and exacting, but Schilit had uncovered dozens of ways in which firms can manipulate their results. His book, "Financial Shenanigans: How to Detect Accounting Gimmicks and Fraud in Financial Reports," identified seven accounting dodges ranging from sleight of hand to outright fraud: (1) recording revenue too soon or of questionable quality; (2) recording bogus revenue; (3) boosting income with one time gains; (4) shifting current expenses to a later or an earlier period; (5) failing to record liabilities or improperly reducing them; (6) shifting current revenue to a later period; (7) shifting future expenses to the current period as a special charge.

The following year, Schilit founded the Center for Financial Research & Analysis, a company that monitors corporate financial statements and issues warnings to its clientele of institutional investors. As the decade progressed, the number of warnings increased. "The accounting problems didn't suddenly happen in the last six months or twelve months," Schilit told me not long ago. "They were horrendous in the period from 1997 onward." Schilit and his colleagues often received a hostile reaction when they publicly questioned a company's earnings. "People got very angry," Schilit recalled. "The amount of money that C.E.O.s were making from out-of-control option plans was astounding, but everybody who was around them was happy, because they were also getting rich. They didn't want somebody raising questions." . . .

Cendant was a major financial scandal. Almost twenty billion dollars of shareholder value was wiped out, and the company ended up paying $2.8 billion to settle shareholder suits, but the story rarely made it out of the business section. Schilit told me, "When a bull market is raging, investors lose a lot of money on Cendant, and the advisers, the investment bankers, say, 'O.K., Joe. Fraud can happen. But you made a lot of money on the previous five deals I brought you.' Investors tend to grit their teeth and say, 'Yes, I got nailed on this one, but I did make money on the five other deals.'"

Around the time that the truth about Cendant emerged, an accounting scandal forced Al Dunlap to resign from Sunbeam, the appliance maker . . . . Dunlap denied any wrongdoing, but in 2001 the S.E.C. charged him and four of his former colleagues with fraud, claiming that they had given a false impression of Sunbeam's business by inflating its "stock price and thus improving its value as an acquisition target." Sunbeam eventually filed for bankruptcy, and its stockholders . . . ended up with nothing.

The frauds at Cendant and Sunbeam were dwarfed by an even bigger accounting scandal, at Waste Management, the largest trash-hauling company in the country . . . . The S.E.C. launched an investigation, which discovered that between 1992 and 1996 Waste Management had exaggerated its profits by $1.43 billion.

Cendant and Waste Management were both scrappy firms trying to crash their way into the financial establishment. Lucent Technologies, the former equipment-making division of A.T.&T., was the bluest of blue chips. Lucent went public in April, 1996; within three years its stock had risen eightfold, and it had become the most widely held stock in America. In 1998, Lucent generated about a billion dollars in net income. Investors were expecting the firm's rapid growth to continue over the next year, and the company was doing nothing to dispel the idea that it would. But in reality Lucent's sales were slowing, and its inventories were rising. The company included in its earnings gains from its corporate pension plan (shenanigan No. 3), started capitalizing software expenditures (shenanigan No. 4), and created new reserves related to acquisitions (shenanigan No. 7). In February and May of 1999, the Center for Financial Research & Analysis issued two warnings about Lucent's financial condition. "There wasn't one thing that leaped out at you," Howard Schilit recalled. "There was just a whole series of little tricks here and there."

As usual, investors didn't pay much attention. That November, Lucent's stock hit eighty dollars. On January 6, 2000, Schilit and his colleagues issued a third warning, detailing how Lucent had artificially boosted its earnings by reversing a previous restructuring charge. A week later, Lucent announced that it would miss Wall Street's earnings estimates for the last quarter of 1999, and its stock fell sharply. Two and a half years later, it is trading below two dollars.

"What Lucent taught a lot of people, me included, was that this could happen anywhere," Schilit said. "These blue-chip companies were just as susceptible to accounting trickery as the small ones."

VI

If investors had been paying more attention, they would have seen that Schilit wasn't the only one warning that something was wrong with the upbeat figures corporate America was releasing. Between the fourth quarter of 1996 and the fourth quarter of 2000, the firms in the S. & P. 500 reported that their earnings per share had increased from $38.73 to $54.78, with not a single down quarter. Even at the end of 2000, most big companies were predicting further rises in profits. But according to the Commerce Department, which measures the gross domestic product and its components, corporate profits peaked in 1997, at close to eight hundred billion dollars. Thereafter, they fell sharply, to just above seven hundred and twenty billion dollars in 1998. Profits didn't recover their 1997 level until 2000, whereupon they slumped again in 2001.

There are two possible ways to explain the glaring difference between the Commerce Department's numbers and corporate America's. The government calculates profits from corporate tax filings, which often contain lower estimates of earnings than the filings that firms present to Wall Street. (For some reason, firms feel no urge to exaggerate their profits to the I.R.S.) Moreover, the government gathers numbers from all types of enterprises, big and small, whereas the S. & P. 500 is composed of the largest corporations in the country. It is at least conceivable that the decline in profitability that the Commerce Department detected was concentrated among tax avoiders and small firms. But a far more convincing explanation is that the vast majority of major corporations were artificially inflating their profits. Instead of admitting that rising wages and intense competition were corroding their earnings, they were resorting to subterfuge.

The men heading these companies faced an unenviable dilemma. At the stock market's peak, many of them had options worth tens of millions of dollars. But this wealth was alarmingly evanescent: with a plunge in the company's stock price, their options would be rendered worthless. In these circumstances, it would have taken a brave man to tell the truth about what was happening to corporate earnings. Such corporate statesmen were in short supply. Far more common were senior executives, who, in Alan Greenspan's words, sought to "harvest" some of their stock-market gains before it was too late.

Even Michael Jensen, the great defender of big payouts for C.E.O.s, now concedes that the design of enormous stock-options packages had a disastrous effect on corporate ethics. If he had his way, Jensen told me recently, every standard executive stock option would be scrapped. Instead, managers would receive options with a strike price that went up every year. "I was a defender of the move toward stock options and more liberal rewards for C.E.O.s. But I'm now a critic of where we got to," Jensen said. "For a long time now, we've had a situation in which the stock prices of many firms have been too high," he explained. "That is to managers what heroin is to a drug addict." When stock prices are overvalued, managers get into an elaborate game with Wall Street to try and justify them. "But if they are too high you can't possibly justify them. So you keep struggling for ways to get the earnings up, to generate the reports that the market is expecting to see." Whenever a company does admit that its earnings aren't growing as rapidly as investors are expecting, its stock price gets crushed and its management gets pilloried. "Once you train managers by penalizing them for telling the truth and rewarding them for lying, then that kind of unethical behavior gets extended to all sorts of things," Jensen said.

Jensen's discovery that executive stock options can have perverse results is rather belated, but his analysis of the last few years is hard to fault. Stock options, instead of spurring corporate leaders to build businesses that would create wealth for decades to come, encouraged them to manage for the short term, tailoring their actions to the demands of Wall Street stock analysts; and, in all too many cases, the practice turned them into crooks. WorldCom, for example, the second-biggest long-distance phone company in the country, classed billions of dollars in routine expenditures, such as payments the firm made to other telephone companies for connecting calls, as capital investments, which made it look a lot more profitable than it really was. Global Crossing, a startup company that built a transatlantic communications network, swapped fibre-optic capacity with other telecommunications companies in order to create fake revenues. Dynegy, an energy-trading firm, recorded phantom trades to do the same thing. Xerox, Qwest, and Rite Aid are all accused of inflating their revenues.

None of these accounting shenanigans emerged until after the Nasdaq crashed, in April, 2000, but they were all similar to the ones Schilit had identified in the nineties. At Enron, the finagling was more complicated. The wrongdoing appears to have begun in earnest toward the end of 1997, when the credit-rating agencies (Moody's and Standard & Poor's) became increasingly concerned about the debt that Enron had taken on as it expanded from a gas-pipeline company into areas like energy trading and online commerce. If the credit-rating agencies had downgraded Enron's debt, its stock price would have fallen, which would have had a disastrous impact on the massive stock-option packages that virtually all the firm's senior executives owned. In order to forestall this eventuality, Andrew Fastow, Enron's chief financial officer, set up a series of investment partnerships, with names like Chewco and LJM1, which were used to reduce Enron's debt and disguise its losses on new ventures. An investigative committee appointed by Enron's board later concluded that "the transactions between Enron and the LJM partnerships resulted in Enron increasing its reported financial results by more than a billion dollars, and enriching Fastow and his co-investors by tens of millions of dollars at Enron's expense." Just as important, the partnerships helped to maintain Enron's stock price long enough for the firm's senior management to cash in hundreds of millions of dollars of stock options.

Jensen has been looking closely at Enron. In a recent working paper, he and another economist, Joseph Fuller, pointed out that "Enron was in many ways an extraordinary company. It boasted significant global assets, true achievements, dramatic innovations, and a promising long-run future." The firm's one big problem was its outsize stock-market valuation, which in August, 2001, reached almost seventy billion dollars. In order to justify this outlandish figure, Wall Street analysts were demanding higher earnings, and Enron's top executives were casting around for ways to meet these demands. "If Enron's management had confronted the analysts with courage and conviction and resisted their relentless focus on outsize earnings growth, the company could have avoided questionable actions taken to please the analysts and the markets," Jensen and Fuller conclude. "The result could well have been a lower-valued but stable and profitable company."

A corollary of this argument is that Kenneth Lay and his colleagues were not necessarily deceitful or venal people; nor were the heads at WorldCom, Dynegy, and Global

Crossing: they were all victims of circumstance. "It is important to recognize that this doesn't come about as a result of crooks," Jensen insisted. "This comes about as a result of honest people being subjected to forces that they don't understand. The forces are very strong, and this evolves over a period of time. You end up with highly moral, honest people doing dishonest things. It wasn't as if the Mafia had taken over corporate America. We are too quick to say—and the media feed this—that if a bad thing happens it's because a bad person did it, and that person had evil intentions. It is much more likely that there were some bad systems in place."

VII

What Jensen doesn't say, of course, is that he and other economists were at least partly responsible for the compensation systems that unleashed an orgy of self-enrichment. In retrospect, Jensen and his colleagues were hopelessly naïve in assuming that executive stock options wouldn't be abused. If the past thirty years have demonstrated anything, it is that the avarice of America's corporate leaders is practically unlimited, and so is their power to run companies in their own interest. "When I did my first study, in 1973, the average C.E.O. of a major company was making about forty-five times the average pay of the workers," Graef Crystal reminded me recently. "When I wrote my book, in 1991, the pay ratio was a hundred and forty. Now it's five hundred." Under the light-handed regulation of public companies that has been fashionable since the Reagan era, the onus has fallen on auditors, boards of directors, and outside stockholders to restrain the selfishness of senior executives, but none of these groups have proved up to the task.

Even before the Enron scandal, it was clear that many auditors were not doing their jobs properly. In the case of Waste Management, for example, Arthur Andersen complained about many of the bookkeeping ruses that the senior managers were using, but it approved the company's financial statements nonetheless. Had Andersen done otherwise, it would have risked losing a lucrative client. Between 1991 and 1997, Andersen billed Waste Management $7.5 million in audit fees and $11.8 million in fees for other services, such as work on tax and regulatory issues. Meanwhile, Andersen Consulting billed Waste Management six million dollars, $3.7 million of which was related to a strategic review designed to "increase shareholder value."

Boards of directors often end up as patsies for the senior managers they are supposed to be monitoring. As Graef Crystal has been pointing out for years, the typical American board is composed of ten friends of the chairman, a token woman, and a token representative of a minority group. All too often, chief executives largely determined their own compensation arrangements, and the board rubber-stamped them.

"I think there were some people who were greedy, and who felt nobody was watching and they could get away with anything," Carl McCall, the state comptroller of New York, said when I spoke to him last month. McCall recently served on a New York Stock Exchange panel that recommended a set of reforms for companies wanting to list themselves on the Exchange. After the reforms are adopted, every company on the N.Y.S.E. must have a majority of independent directors on its board, and three of the company's committees—the audit committee, the compensation committee, and the nominating and governance committee—must be made up solely of independent directors. (At the moment, members of the audit committee have to be independent, but companies are not even required to have compensation, nominating, or governance committees.)

These are worthwhile reforms, but, as Paul Volcker points out, "There's a limit on the supervisory, skeptical role that you can expect a board of directors to provide. In a successful company, the directors are going to have a collegial feeling. They have been appointed by the C.E.O. They are going to be heavily influenced by what he says. They are going to give him the benefit of the doubt." Moreover, a management team that is determined to act crookedly can often hide its fraud. At Enron, the outside directors included a former accounting professor and a former federal energy regulator, but neither of them was aware of the extent of what had been happening to the company until they read it in the newspapers.

Of course, senior executives are ultimately responsible to the owners of the company: the stockholders. But it was the weakness of the stockholders that justified the use of executive stock options to begin with, and little has changed in this regard. Most investors will simply sell their stock in a company if they see something they don't like. During the nineteen-nineties, there was another reason that investors were reluctant to police rapacious executives: most were too greedy themselves to question the startling earnings growth that supported the bull market. They gleefully accepted the optimistic line that Wall Street and corporate America fed to them, pausing only to inspect their monthly statements from Fidelity and Charles Schwab. It was only after the bubble burst that they were shocked to discover that many of the schemes they had been sold were illusory, and that some senior executives were dishonest.

VIII

. . . There are at least two ways that C.E.O.s could be reined in. In Germany, most big firms have two boards: an operating board, which deals with the day-to-day running of the company, and a supervisory board, which oversees the actions of the senior managers. The chief executive doesn't even have a seat on the supervisory board. In Britain, the post of chairman and chief executive is often split, so the company has two powerful figures at the top, who can keep an eye on each other. Americans often presume that their system of corporate governance is the best in the world, but there are things to be learned from practices elsewhere. Above all, it is time to downsize the myth of the all-powerful C.E.O. Effective leadership is one aspect of corporate success, but it is by no means the only one.

History, competition, and luck also play crucial roles. And most C.E.O.s are eminently replaceable.

In recent weeks, senior executives of WorldCom and Adelphia Communications have been paraded before the cameras in handcuffs . . . . These pictures . . . sent a salutary message to other senior executives: public companies are social organizations with social responsibilities. Unless this message is heeded, the furor over Kenneth Lay and his fellow corporate scoundrels will gradually fade. And, once the economy and the stock market revive, the greed cycle will start up again.

Review and Discussion Questions

1. What is a publicly held corporation, and how does it differ from a private company? Why did publicly held corporations eventually replace private companies as the dominant form of capitalist economic organization?

2. What is the principal–agent problem, and how does it apply to corporate managers?

3. What are leveraged buyouts? What economic benefit are they supposed to bring, and what negative effects do they have?

4. What factors encouraged the rapid expansion of stock options as a form of executive compensation? How did they lead to both the financial boom of the 1990s and its collapse?

5. Do the issues discussed by Cassidy denote deep, permanent flaws in our corporate system, or are they only transient problems? What future do you foresee for corporate America? Are there ways in which our corporate system can and should be reformed?

6. What effect has the "greed cycle" discussed by Cassidy had on the rest of the economy and on our society generally? Can we avoid future greed cycles or are they an inevitable part of our system?

THE ETHICS OF CORPORATE DOWNSIZING

JOHN ORLANDO

In recent years corporations have been downsizing their workforces at an unprecedented rate. Although this business trend may have benefited the economy overall, its human price has been high as hardworking employees suffer the emotional and financial repercussions of losing their jobs. In this essay John Orlando argues that downsizing is often morally wrong. He begins by challenging the assumption that the interests of shareholders take priority over those of employees, arguing instead for their moral equality. This equality implies that for downsizing to be permissible it must be justifiable from a utilitarian perspective, which takes into account the interests of both shareholders and workers. However, Orlando argues that the utilitarian case for it is unproved. Moreover, there are at least three moral arguments against downsizing. Although downsizing may be justified in extreme cases, for example, if it is necessary to save the corporation, Orlando concludes that downsizing merely to increase profit will usually be wrong.

I. THE ISSUE

. . . Many workers, especially manufacturing workers, would place corporate downsizing—the closing of whole plants or divisions in order to increase profits—at the head of their list of ethically contentious business practices. Though the issue has provoked considerable debate in the popular press, the philosophical community has largely ignored it.

This oversight is curious given that downsizing is arguably the major business trend of our era . . . . The statistics on downsizing's human costs are sobering. One study found that 15 percent of downsized workers lost their homes, and another that the suicide rate among laid-off workers is thirty times the national average.[1] Despite the rosy picture of the economy painted by the popular media, where attention is constantly drawn to the growth of the stock market, evidence suggests that trends such as downsizing have led to a general decline in employee earnings, as well as a widening of the gulf between rich and poor in America.[2] Added to this is the fact that since the loss of jobs is concentrated in a relatively small geographic area, these closings affect the entire community. Businesses that rely upon workers' spending will feel the pinch, often leading to secondary layoffs. Consequently, communities as a whole have been devastated by such closings. Downsizing also carries with it serious nonquantifiable harms. News of mass layoffs sends psychological tremors across the nation, leading to general worker apprehension about job security and less job satisfaction. Worse yet, the anxiety of unemployment often leads to psychological symptoms such as depression, or expresses itself through a variety of unpleasant behaviors: i.e., crime, domestic violence, child abuse, and alcohol and drug abuse.[3] . . .

I will argue that acts of downsizing are very often morally wrong. I will begin by demonstrating that the business ethics literature has yet to identify a morally relevant distinction between the situation of the shareholder and that of the worker in relation to the corporation. This means that the corporate manager has no naturally greater duty to shareholders than to workers. I will make my case by examining, and dismissing, the various arguments advanced for privileging the interests of shareholders above all other parties. I then advance arguments against the moral

From John Orlando, "The Fourth Wave: The Ethics of Corporate Downsizing", *Business Ethics Quarterly*, Volume 9, Number 2 (April 1999), pp. 295–314.

permissibility of acts of downsizing. I will finish with a few words about how the concerns I raise might [guide corporate managers and] provide direction for future investigations into the ethical status of [downsizing in particular business circumstances] . . .

II. THE MORAL EQUALITY OF WORKERS AND SHAREHOLDERS

Property Rights

First, it must be understood that one cannot justify the position that shareholder concerns take precedence over all other groups simply by appeal to the fact that the shareholders are the legal owners of the corporation. In that case, all one has done is provide a definition of the term *shareholder*; one has yet to provide a morally relevant reason for privileging the interests of that group . . . .

The natural tack at this point is to assert that a legal owner has property rights that allow her to dispose of her property in any manner she sees fit. But this justification skews the issue in the shareholder's favor by appealing to a paradigm that does not apply in the case of corporate ownership. The term *property rights* conjures up images of property for personal *use*, not *profit*. For instance, property rights advocates normally worry about laws that place restrictions on the use of one's homestead, such as laws regulating the appearance of one's home . . . . We may harbor a deep-seated intuition that property is sacred, but that intuition is tied to property with which we are in some respect intimately connected, such as a home.

To avoid glossing over the distinction between property for private use and property for profit, we will need to narrow our inquiry to an example of property for profit. Imagine that I own an apartment which I have rented to a couple for ten or fifteen years (think Fred and Ethel from "I Love Lucy"). I discover that I can make more money by dividing up the apartment and renting it to college students. My intuition is that I have a responsibility to the people who rent from me. At the very least, I should assure the couple, who might be frightened about the prospect of being thrown into the street, that I will not have them leave until they have procured similar housing elsewhere at a similar cost. I would also feel obligated to ensure that their transition is as easy as possible by, for instance, helping them move. Moreover, the purpose of the money will have a bearing on the moral status of the act. The act is far easier to justify if it is needed to pay for my wife's extended medical care, than if it merely allows me to buy a longer sailboat. Thus, the general appeal to property rights breaks down when the property in question is for profit, and when we turn to scenarios closer to the practice of downsizing itself.

Fiduciary Duties

Many theorists and business managers defend the moral superiority of shareholders on grounds that corporate managers are bound by a fiduciary duty to their shareholders that trumps any competing duties. The burden of proof is then taken to fall on the shoulders of those arguing against this position to demonstrate that the manager has equally strong duties to others as well . . . .

But this characterization of the issue misconstrues the lines of justification for the duties of an agent in a fiduciary relationship. The fiduciary duty does not establish the obligations of the agent . . . . We must look to the particularities of the relationship to identify the contours of the manager's duty to her shareholders. The term *fiduciary duty* is merely a label for whatever obligations the manager owes to the shareholder; it does not create those duties, and thus cannot justify them . . . .

There is considerable evidence that the fiduciary duty of a corporate manager has been historically justified as a means of protecting the owner from that manager . . . . The legal basis of fiduciary duties of corporate managers to shareholders has been construed as the obligation to not advance their own interests against those of the shareholders. Adopting this view of the fiduciary relationship would mean that when a corporate manager takes into account the interests of [other] stakeholders, even where that comes at the expense of profits, this does not conflict with a manager's fiduciary duty to shareholders.

Risk

Ian Maitland provides two justifications for the position that corporate managers have duties to shareholders over those to other parties. The first appeals to the fact that shareholders have invested capital in the corporation. Why is this fact morally relevant? According to Maitland, shareholders have taken a risk in placing their money in the hands of the corporation, and are thereby due compensation in the form of having their interests given privilege over those of other parties. Maitland states that:

> As a practical matter, no stakeholder is likely to agree to bear the risk associated with the corporation's activities unless it gets the commitment that the corporation will be managed for its benefit. That is logical because the stockholder alone stands to absorb any costs of mismanagement.[4]

It is strange, however, to think that the worker who loses his job has not absorbed any costs of mismanagement. Maitland's point must be that while workers stand to lose their jobs due to corporate mismanagement, they only lose future potential earnings, whereas shareholders lose something they have placed into the corporation. However, workers too have placed something at risk when accepting a job. At the very least, the worker has bypassed other possible job opportunities, opportunities that may have turned out to be financially more rewarding. Also, some have gone to school in the hopes of pursuing a career in the field, thereby investing substantial sums of money (or accruing substantial debt) in the process. Even more importantly, many workers have purchased homes in the expectation of a steady income, and in this manner have risked their homes on the corporation. We can also add to our list the various ways in which workers plant roots in the community which are disrupted when they are forced to relocate, such as placing their children in local schools or having their spouses accept jobs. While the worker's investment in a corporation is not of the same sort as the shareholder's, it constitutes a risk nevertheless, and so the worker's position is not dissimilar to that of the shareholder. The only difference between the risks taken by the two parties is one of degree, and the degree of that risk will depend upon the particular situation of each individual.

Contracts

Maitland's second argument is that corporations are fundamentally a "freely chosen . . . nexus . . . of contracts" between its stakeholders, which establish both the "rights" and the "obligations" of each party.[5] These contracts stipulate that the worker will give the corporation her labor in return for a fixed wage, while the shareholder will receive all of the profits of the corporation in return for investing capital in it. When third parties tinker with that arrangement, they violate the right of self-determination of the members of the contract, who have determined the terms of the contracts under "free," "voluntary," and "uncoerced" bargaining circumstances . . . .

However, Maitland's picture of the corporation simply does not square with reality. It turns out that most shareholders expect corporate managers to take into account the interests of other constituencies when making decisions about the welfare of the corporation.[6] More importantly, shareholders tend to think of themselves not as owners of the corporation, but rather as investors in it . . . . For the vast majority of shareholders, dabbling in the stock market is thought of as one means among many of investing one's money, something chosen for its high rate of return, not in order to become a corporate owner. Thus, it is hard to understand how the investor can be acting under the assumption of an unstated contract between himself, management, and the company's employees. On the other side, employees have traditionally assumed that taking a job meant having it for life as long as they perform their duties well. Given these considerations, if we are basing such contracts on the implicit understandings and expectations of the parties involved, the evidence actually points in the very opposite direction to which Maitland argues.

Finally, one can raise serious doubts about the assertion that the worker/manager/shareholder relationship has been established under "free, voluntary, and uncoerced" circumstances. For one, the parties are by no means in an equal bargaining position. Despite Maitland's insistence that the disgruntled employee can always "fire his boss by resigning," employees often find that they have very few job options given their skills, the labor market, and the costs of moving to another area. Shareholders, however, have thousands of companies from which to choose, and a variety of mechanisms specifically designed to make movement in and out of the stock market as easy as possible . . . .

Other People's Money

Milton Friedman also [argues] against the position that corporations have a responsibility to parties other than shareholders. Friedman's . . . objection is that "the corporation is an instrument of the stockholders who own it," meaning that the manager is acting with other people's money, and thus serving the public interest at the expense of profits is an impermissible use of that money.[7] Another way to put it is that any action that diminishes profits to aid other parties constitutes a "tax" on the shareholders' income.

However, such a use of the shareholders' income is only impermissible if it is unauthorized, and as I have noted, most shareholders expect managers to take into account considerations beyond maximizing profits. Moreover, shareholders in a modern corporation can withdraw their money from that corporation with a simple phone call, and thus the manager who announces his intention to act for the public good gives shareholders plenty of time to remove their money before such a "tax" is levied. More importantly, . . . an act of downsizing cannot be morally justified in virtue of the fact that it is done in the interests of the shareholders of the corporation, since if it is wrong for the shareholder to perform that act, then it is equally wrong for the manager to do so for them. The fact that a manager is an agent of others cannot itself make the action morally right, and therefore the moral status of the act will turn on other considerations . . . .

I have argued that no philosophically sound argument has yet been advanced for privileging the interests of shareholders over those of workers simply by virtue of the fact that they are shareholders. This is not to say that no such argument may someday appear, but rather that in the absence of compelling reasons to the contrary, we must assume that the worker has an equal moral standing as the shareholder since they are, after all, both humans. Cast in this manner, the burden of proof in the debate runs contrary to what has been up to now believed by its participants. It has been tacitly assumed that it is the job of those arguing for the moral status of nonshareholders to establish their position, perhaps due to the earlier-mentioned view of fiduciary duties. But one of our most deeply felt convictions is that two human beings have equal moral status until morally relevant considerations can distinguish between them. Thus, it is really on the shoulders of those arguing for privileging the interests of the shareholders to make their case. This, I have argued, they have yet to do, leaving us to default to the presumption of equality.

III. THE UTILITARIAN ARGUMENT

I now wish to examine the utilitarian defense of downsizing. It seems to me that once the moral equality of workers and shareholders has been granted, the only considerations that could justify acts of downsizing would be consequentialist in nature. At the very least, arguments currently advanced to justify acts of downsizing, when they do not rely upon the premise of a moral superiority of shareholders, have been utilitarian. Thus, if I can establish that the utilitarian case has yet to be made, I will have demonstrated that we have yet to find an adequate defense of downsizing.

. . . Utilitarianism is generally construed as the principle that the act that maximizes total utility is morally right. Thus, one could argue that downsizing benefits the majority of the population, and though it leaves some individuals by the wayside, the benefit to the whole outweighs the harm to the few. The entire economy, it might be argued, is becoming more efficient. Moreover, the stock market has skyrocketed, benefiting all those who have investments in mutual funds.

But there is reason to doubt whether downsizing has generated a net gain in utility. A group of researchers recently concluded a fifteen-year study which found that when acts of downsizing are not accompanied by careful restructuring of the corporation—in other words, when people are simply laid off in order to lower costs of production without thought of how the remaining employees will sustain levels of productivity—downsizing has always hurt the corporation in the long run.[8] Reich also notes that the downsizing trend has caused a general drop in employee loyalty in the United States.[9] Workers are far less likely to go the extra mile for firms who treat them as disposable cogs in the corporate machine. While loyalty is not easily quantifiable, and thus does not show up in a corporate ledger, it will affect the company's overall performance . . . .

But even if the case could be made that downsizing improves the overall health of the economy, there would still be a gap between this fact and the conclusion that overall utility has risen. If the argument were to terminate at this point, it would be assuming that one can equate well-being with financial gain; however, far more things go into determining one's well-being. For instance, it is indisputable that the anxiety from job loss has a profoundly negative influence upon one's psychic health. The harm of unemployment cannot simply be measured by the total loss of income; it produces fear for one's own well-being as well as the well-being of one's family, not to mention the anxiety experienced by those other groups themselves. When these factors are taken into account, it becomes clear that utilitarian considerations do not clearly point in favor of downsizing. It might in fact be determined that downsizing improves net utility in the long run, but the empirical evidence is inconclusive. Our position on the issue, therefore, will need to be informed by other considerations.

IV. ARGUMENTS AGAINST DOWNSIZING

Harming Some to Benefit Others

Up to this point I have argued only that defenders of downsizing have failed to establish that downsizing is morally permissible. Here I will present reasons for thinking that downsizing is often morally wrong. The first argument appeals to the widely held intuition . . . that causing a great harm for a lesser benefit, even to a great number of people, cannot be morally justified. Most people would even consider it wrong to incur a great harm to a few in order to produce a great benefit to the many, such as removing the eyes from a sighted man and implanting them in two blind persons so that they can now see (with only a drop off in peripheral vision and depth perception distinguishing them from those with two eyes). There are even some who believe that no amount of harm to an individual can be justified on grounds that it will benefit others, since harms and benefits are incommensurable commodities. Given that statistics demonstrate that downsizing often leads to the loss of home and even suicide, it seems hard to deny that at least some downsized workers incur a significant harm from the practice. On the other side, since investors in a large corporation tend to diversify their assets, they incur only a minor benefit when any one stock price rises. Thus, if the act of downsizing is not done as a means of saving the corporation—preventing more workers from losing their jobs—but rather to increase profits, it involves causing a great harm for a minor benefit.

We can also draw a distinction within the practice of downsizing which will serve to amplify its wrongfulness in certain circumstances . . . . Consider the case where a CEO downsizes under the knowledge that the mere news of these layoffs will be greeted favorably by the stock market, and thus cause stock prices to rise . . . as opposed to the case where downsizing will improve profits by increasing productivity. Here the very act that harms the workers—the loss of their jobs—itself produces the benefit to shareholders. Harm is not a simple byproduct of an act which independently brings benefit, but rather is the means to that benefit. This grates even more deeply against our intuitions that it is wrong to use individuals for others' benefit.

Legitimate Expectations

We might also approach the issue from the perspective of the legitimate expectations of the individuals involved. To illustrate this notion, consider the possibility that the federal government repeals the home interest tax break without any other modifications in the tax code. While I see no reason why homeowners, and not renters, deserve such a break, one could question the action on grounds that homeowners have made plans under the assumption that this break would continue. Those who lose their homes because of the change in the tax laws would have a legitimate complaint, even though there was never a written guarantee that current tax laws would remain forever unchanged. Similarly, workers have made plans under the assumption of a continued source of income. These are not simply plans for leisure activities such as vacations, but rather plans that impinge upon their fundamental well-being as well as the well-being of their families. There are, however, no similar expectations on the part of the shareholder. For one, shareholders know that stock prices are volatile and that they take a risk when entering the market. Thus, no reasonable investor backs her home on the future performance of her securities. Investors may expect a certain average rate of return, but this is over the long term and they budget accordingly . . . . Also, as mentioned earlier, shareholders tend to consider the companies in which they invest to have obligations to parties other than themselves. Hence, one cannot plead that shareholders entered the market expecting that the company would be run solely for their own benefit.

Fairness

We may also appeal to the work of John Rawls to provide critical perspective on the issue . . . . I will draw upon what I consider his more central intuition: that the arbitrary conditions of one's situation ought not to count against one's life prospects. The idea here is that the individual does not deserve the rewards or punishments that come via things for which she is not responsible. At the very least, these factors include genetic endowments and the social institutions of the society in which she lives . . . .

To apply the principle here, we would first note that the worker who loses his job does so through no fault of his own. Someone fired due to incompetence is not downsized. Downsizing does not involve a surgical removal of all employees in a firm whose work is not up to snuff; instead, whole divisions are removed by virtue of their overall profitability, with no effort made to determine if individual members of those divisions are at fault. In fact, if a division or plant is unprofitable it is most likely due to mismanagement on the part of those running the corporation. This is perhaps one of the reasons why downsized workers feel betrayed, as no attempt is made by management to judge their actual job performance. Downsized workers find themselves harmed due to forces outside of their control. Moreover, these forces have conspired to selectively harm them since upper management tends to be insulated from these harms, by devices such as receiving a sizable "golden parachute" when dismissed. True, there are a variety of ways in which natural and social forces reward and punish arbitrarily but this does not make those harms permissible or release us from obligations to mitigate them.

On the other side, shareholders have done nothing to merit the sharp gains that downsizing produces. Perhaps they are owed good faith efforts at sound management by the corporation in virtue of their investment, but they cannot claim to deserve the special increases in the value of their investments due solely to laying off workers. The fact that we happen to live in a world where canning large numbers of workers is a quick means of increasing profits is not any of their doing. Note also that those shareholders who have invested through mutual funds have not themselves chosen to invest in this particular firm. These investors most likely have little idea as to which stocks their mutual funds actually hold, since one of the appeals of these funds is that they allow individuals to enter the market without the need to concern themselves with the intricacies of investing, or the day-to-day fluctuations of the market . . . .

V. APPLYING THE RESULTS AND RELATED CONCERNS

. . . Business managers will need to examine the actual situations of their shareholders and workers, as well as that of the company, in order to ascertain if a decision to downsize is morally permissible. While this grants that some acts of downsizing may be morally permissible, simply establishing that corporate managers cannot lay claim to a special duty to shareholders that trumps any competing duties cuts against the grain of much of corporate America's current philosophy . . . . While many business persons would agree that corporations have some obligations to persons besides shareholders, all but the most socially conscious would likely consider anathema the position that these obligations stand on equal footing with obligations to shareholders . . . .

How might the corporate manager apply the insights gathered here to a particular situation? First and foremost, an act of downsizing that prevents the collapse of the corporation can be justified on grounds that the organism is saved by amputating a limb. However, we must keep in mind that bankruptcy does not always mean the complete shutting down of shop. Bankruptcy courts make every effort to find a way of restructuring the debts of the corporation to keep it in business . . . . But an act of downsizing that merely increases profits, which seems increasingly the case, requires a careful analysis of the harms and benefits it will incur to the parties involved. For a small firm, such as a fast-food franchise with a single proprietor, the owner may be at greater risk than her employees. The owner most likely has a large percentage of her personal fortune wrapped up in the company, whereas the workers are usually (but not always) high school students just earning extra spending money. However, with a large corporation, the results are likely to be quite different. It bears mention that . . . the owner of a corporation is not personally liable for its debts; if IBM dissolves, shareholders need not fear that IBM's creditors will come knocking at their doors. Legal protection to the shareholder is built into the corporation's charter. More importantly, since investors tend not to risk money that is required for their sustenance, their losses do not normally affect their immediate well-being. By contrast, the worker who banks his home on his job places his immediate well-being, as well as the well-being of his family, in far greater peril. Finally, investors today diversify their assets through mutual funds which own shares in thousands of corporations. Thus, losses from one stock create only a minor shift in the fund's overall value. This means that acts of downsizing can cause great harm to a few for a minor benefit to the many, something that I have argued is not morally permissible. Also, one can argue that the sole proprietor who has nursed the business from the ground up merits greater consideration than the mutual fund investor who may not even know that he or she owns shares in the corporation. Moreover, the worker who has purchased a home, and started a family, based on the assumption of the continued source of income, is deserving of greater consideration than the investor who finds that unprecedented gains in the stock market allow him to extend his vacation to Aruba by a week.

Notes

1. Richard L. Bunning, "The Dynamics of Downsizing," *Personnel Journal* 69, no. 9 (Sept. 1990): 69.

2. Interview with Secretary of Labor Robert Reich in *Challenge*, July/August 1996, 4. Reich notes that while the *average* wage is up, the *median* wage (the wage of the individual in the middle) is down. The discrepancy is due to the unprecedented rise in compensation for top executives during the 1980s and 1990s.

3. David Dooley, Ralph Catalano, and Karen S. Rook, "Personal and Aggregate Unemployment and Psychological Symptoms," *Journal of Social Issues* 44 (1988): 107–23; David Dooley, Ralph Catalano, and Georjeanna Wilson, "Depression and Unemployment: Panel Findings from the Epidemiologic Catchment Area Study," *American Journal of Community Health* 22 (1994): 745–65.

4. Ian Maitland, "The Morality of the Corporation: An Empirical or Normative Disagreement?," *Business Ethics Quarterly* 4, no. 4 (1994): 445–57.

5. Maitland, op. cit., 449.

6. Larry D. Sonderquist and Robert P. Vecchio, "Reconciling Shareholders' Rights and Corporate Responsibility: New Guidelines for Management," *Duke Law Journal* (1978): 840.

7. Friedman, "The Social Responsibility of Business Is to Increase Its Profits," *New York Times Magazine*, September 1970.

8. Wayne F. Cascio, interview on National Public Radio, November 14, 1997.

9. Reich, op. cit.

Review and Discussion Questions

1. Orlando distinguishes property for private use and property for profit, using the example of a landlord renting an apartment. Do you find the example persuasive? Explain why or why not.

2. Orlando discusses five arguments intended to show that the interests of shareholders take priority over those of other groups. State each of these arguments in one or two sentences and critically assess it. Which of the arguments are the strongest? Which do you see as the weakest? How convincing are Orlando's responses to each?

3. Do you agree that there is moral equality between workers and shareholders? If so, what does this imply?

4. Can downsizing be supported on utilitarian grounds? Explain why or why not.

5. Is downsizing wrong because it is an instance of "harming some to benefit others," as Orlando argues?

6. Orlando's "legitimate expectations" argument against downsizing rests on the premise that "workers have made plans under the assumption of a continued source of income." Is that premise true and, if so, was it reasonable for workers to make that assumption?

7. Orlando argues that downsizing is unfair by appealing to the principle that people do not deserve rewards or punishments for things for which they are not responsible. Do you accept Orlando's principle? If so, does it show that downsizing is wrong?

ETHICAL DILEMMAS FOR MULTINATIONAL ENTERPRISE: A PHILOSOPHICAL OVERVIEW

RICHARD T. DE GEORGE

Corporations today are increasingly multinational in their business activities. This fact has stirred up controversy about the effects of those activities on foreign countries and about what sort of moral responsibilities multinational corporations have. In this essay, Professor De George clarifies these issues by explaining and defending five basic theses, which provide a useful framework for discussing the moral dilemmas that multinationals can face. Although De George defends multinationals against some of their critics, he maintains that there are definite moral standards to which they must adhere.

First World multinational corporations (MNCs) are both the hope of the Third World and the scourge of the Third World. The working out of this paradox poses moral dilemmas for many MNCs. I shall focus on some of the moral dilemmas that many American MNCs face.

Third World countries frequently seek to attract American multinationals for the jobs they provide and for the technological transfers they promise. Yet when American MNCs locate in Third World countries, many Americans condemn them for exploiting the resources and workers of the Third World. While MNCs are a means for improving the standard of living of the underdeveloped countries, MNCs are blamed for the poverty and starvation such countries suffer. Although MNCs provide jobs in the Third World, many criticize them for transferring these jobs from the United States. American MNCs usually pay at least as high wages as local industries, yet critics blame them for paying the workers in underdeveloped countries less than they pay American workers for comparable work. When American MNCs pay higher than local wages, local companies criticize them for skimming off all the best workers and for creating an internal brain-drain. Multinationals are presently the most effective vehicle available for the development of the Third World. At the same time, critics complain that the MNCs are destroying the local cultures and substituting for them the tinsel of American life and the worst aspects of its culture. American MNCs seek to protect the interests of their shareholders by locating in an environment in which their enterprise will be safe from destruction

by revolutions and confiscation by socialist regimes. When they do so, critics complain that the MNCs thrive in countries with strong, often right-wing, governments.

The dilemmas the American MNCs face arise from conflicting demands made from opposing, often ideologically based, points of view. Not all of the demands that lead to these dilemmas are equally justifiable, nor are they all morally mandatory. We can separate the MNCs that behave immorally and reprehensibly from those that do not by clarifying the true moral responsibility of MNCs in the Third World. To help do so, I shall state and briefly defend five theses.

Thesis 1: Many of the moral dilemmas MNCs face are false dilemmas which arise from equating United States standards with morally necessary standards.
Many American critics argue that American multinationals should live up to and implement the same standards abroad that they do in the United States and that United States mandated norms should be followed.* This broad claim confuses morally necessary ways of conducting a firm with United States government regulations. The FDA sets high standards that may be admirable. But they are not necessarily morally required. OSHA specifies a large number of rules which in general have as their aim the protection of the worker. However, these should not be equated with morally mandatory rules. United States wages are the highest in the world. These also should not be thought to be the morally necessary norms for the whole world or for United States firms abroad. Morally mandatory standards that no corporation—United States or other—should violate, and moral minima below which no firm can morally go, should not be confused either with standards appropriate to the United States or with standards set by the United States government. Some of the dilemmas of United States multinationals come from critics making such false equations.

This is true with respect to drugs and FDA standards, with respect to hazardous occupations and OSHA standards, with respect to pay, with respect to internalizing the costs of externalities, and with respect to foreign corrupt practices. By using United States standards as moral standards, critics pose false dilemmas for American MNCs. These false dilemmas in turn obfuscate the real moral responsibilities of MNCs.

Thesis 2: Despite differences among nations in culture and values, which should be respected, there are moral norms that can be applied to multinationals.
I shall suggest seven moral guidelines that apply in general to any multinational operating in Third World countries and that can be used in morally evaluating the actions of MNCs. MNCs that respect these moral norms would escape the legitimate criticisms contained in the dilemmas they are said to face.

Reprinted by permission of the publisher from W. Michael Hoffman, Ann E. Lange, and David A. Fredo, *Ethics and the Multinational Enterprise* (Lanham, MD: University Press of America, 1986). © 1986 by University Press of America. Notes omitted.

*The position I advocate does not entail moral relativism, as my third thesis shows. The point is that although moral norms apply uniformly across cultures, U.S. standards are not the same as moral standards, should themselves be morally evaluated, and are relative to American conditions, standard of living, interests, and history.

1. MNCs *should do no intentional direct harm*.

   This injunction is clearly not peculiar to multinational corporations. Yet it is a basic norm that can be usefully applied in evaluating the conduct of MNCs. Any company that does produce intentional direct harm clearly violates a basic moral norm.

2. MNCs *should produce more good than bad for the host country*.

   This is an implementation of a general utilitarian principle. But this norm restricts the extent of that principle by the corollary that, in general, more good will be done by helping those in most need, rather than by helping those in less need at the expense of those in greater need. Thus the utilitarian analysis in this case does not consider that more harm than good might justifiably be done to the host country if the harm is offset by greater benefits to others in developed countries. MNCs will do more good only if they help the host country more than they harm it.

3. MNCs *should contribute by their activities to the host country's development*.

   If the presence of an MNC does not help the host country's development, the MNC can be correctly charged with exploitation, or using the host country for its own purposes at the expense of the host country.

4. MNCs *should respect the human rights of their employees*.

   MNCs should do so whether or not local companies respect those rights. This injunction will preclude gross exploitation of workers, set minimum standards for pay, and prescribe minimum standards for health and safety measures.

5. MNCs *should pay their fair share of taxes*.

   Transfer pricing has as its aim taking advantage of different tax laws in different countries. To the extent that it involves deception, it is itself immoral. To the extent that it is engaged in to avoid legitimate taxes, it exploits the host country, and the MNC does not bear its fair share of the burden of operating in that country.

6. *To the extent that local culture does not violate moral norms, MNCs should respect the local culture and work with it, not against it.*

   MNCs cannot help but produce some changes in the cultures in which they operate. Yet, rather than simply transferring American ways into other lands, they can consider changes in operating procedures, plant planning, and the like, which take into account local needs and customs.

7. MNCs *should cooperate with the local government in the development and enforcement of just background institutions*.

   Instead of fighting a tax system that aims at appropriate redistribution of incomes, instead of preventing the organization of labor, and instead of resisting attempts at improving the health and safety standards of the host country, MNCs should be supportive of such measures.

Thesis 3: Wholesale attacks on multinationals are most often overgeneralizations. Valid moral evaluations can be best made by using the above moral criteria for context-and-corporation-specific studies and analysis.

Broadside claims, such that all multinationals exploit underdeveloped countries or destroy their culture, are too vague to determine their accuracy. United States multinationals have in the past engaged—and some continue to engage—in immoral practices. A case by case study is the fairest way to make moral assessments. Yet we can distinguish five types of business operations that raise very different sorts of moral issues: (1) banks and financial institutions; (2) agricultural enterprises; (3) drug companies and hazardous industries; (4) extractive industries; and (5) other manufacturing and service industries.

If we were to apply our seven general criteria in each type of case, we would see some of the differences among them. Financial institutions do not generally employ many people. Their function is to provide loans for various types of development. In the case of South Africa they [did] not do much—if anything—to undermine apartheid, and by lending to the government they usually strengthen[ed] the government's policy of apartheid. In this case, an argument can be made that they [did] more harm than good . . . . Financial institutions can help and have helped development tremendously. Yet the servicing of debts that many Third World countries face condemns them to impoverishment for the foreseeable future. The role of financial institutions in this situation is crucial and raises special and difficult moral problems, if not dilemmas.

Agricultural enterprises face other demands. If agricultural multinationals buy the best lands and use them for export crops while insufficient arable land is left for the local population to grow enough to feed itself, then MNCs do more harm than good to the host country—a violation of one of the norms I suggested above.

Drug companies and dangerous industries pose different and special problems. I have suggested that FDA standards are not morally mandatory standards. This should not be taken to mean that drug companies are bound only to local laws, for the local laws may require less than morality requires in the way of supplying adequate information and of not producing intentional, direct harm. The same type of observation applies to hazardous industries. While an asbestos company will probably not be morally required to take all the measures mandated by OSHA regulations, it cannot morally leave its workers completely unprotected.

Extractive industries, such as mining, which remove minerals from a country, are correctly open to the charge of exploitation unless they can show that they do more good than harm to the host country and that they do not benefit only either themselves or a repressive elite in the host country.

Other manufacturing industries vary greatly, but as a group they have come in for sustained charges of exploitation of workers and the undermining of the host country's culture. The above guidelines can serve as a means of sifting the valid from the invalid charges.

Thesis 4: On the international level and on the national level in many Third World countries the lack of adequate just background institutions makes the use of clear moral norms all the more necessary.

American multinational corporations operating in Germany and Japan, and German and Japanese multinational corporations operating in the United States, pose no special moral problems. Nor do the operations of Brazilian multinational corporations in the United States or Germany. Yet First World multinationals operating in Third World countries have come in for serious and sustained moral criticism. Why?

A major reason is that in the Third World the First World's MNCs operate without the types of constraints and in societies that do not have the same kinds of redistributive mechanisms as in the developed countries. There is no special difficulty in United States multinationals operating in other First World countries because in general these countries *do* have appropriate background institutions.

More and more Third World countries are developing controls on multinationals that insure the companies do more good for the country than harm. Authoritarian regimes that care more for their own wealth than for the good of their people pose difficult moral conditions under which to operate. In such instances, the guidelines above may prove helpful.

Just as in the nations of the developed, industrial world the labor movement serves as a counter to the dominance of big business, consumerism serves as a watchdog on practices harmful to the consumer, and big government serves as a restraint on each of the vested interest groups, so international structures are necessary to provide the proper background constraints on international corporations.

The existence of MNCs is a step forward in the unification of mankind and in the formation of a global community. They provide the economic base and substructure on which true international cooperation can be built. Because of their special position and the special opportunities they enjoy, they have a special responsibility to promote the cooperation that only they are able to accomplish in the present world.

Just background institutions would preclude any company's gaining a competitive advantage by engaging in immoral practices. This suggests that MNCs have more to gain than to lose by helping formulate voluntary, UN (such as the code governing infant formulae), and similar codes governing the conduct of all multinationals. A case can also be made that they have the moral obligation to do so.

Thesis 5: The moral burdens of MNCs do not exonerate local governments from responsibility for what happens in and to their country. Since responsibility is linked to ownership, governments that insist on part or majority ownership incur part or majority responsibility.

The attempts by many underdeveloped countries to limit multinationals have shown that at least some governments have come to see that they can use multinationals to their own advantage. This may be done by restricting entry to those companies that produce only for local consumption, or that bring desired technology transfers with them. Some countries demand majority control and restrict the export of money from the country. Nonetheless, many MNCs have found it profitable to engage in production under the terms specified by the host country.

What host countries cannot expect is that they can demand control without accepting correlative responsibility. In general, majority control implies majority responsibility. An American MNC, such as Union Carbide, which had majority ownership of its Indian Bhopal plant, should have had primary control of the plant. Union Carbide, Inc. can be held liable for the damage the Bhopal plant caused because Union Carbide, Inc. did have majority ownership. If Union Carbide did not have effective control, it is not relieved of its responsibility. If it could not exercise the control that its responsibility demanded, it should have withdrawn or sold off part of its holdings in that plant. If India had had majority ownership, then it would have had primary responsibility for the safe operation of the plant.

This is compatible with maintaining that if a company builds a hazardous plant, it has an obligation to make sure that the plant is safe and that those who run it are properly trained to run it safely. MNCs cannot simply transfer dangerous technologies without consideration of the people who will run them, the local culture, and similar factors. Unless MNCs can be reasonably sure that the plants they build will be run safely, they cannot morally build them. To do so would be to will intentional, direct harm.

The theses and guidelines that I have proposed are not a panacea. But they suggest how moral norms can be brought to bear on the dilemmas American multinationals face and they suggest ways out of apparent or false dilemmas. If MNCs observed those norms, they could properly avoid the moral sting of their critics' charges, even if their critics continued to level charges against them.

Review and Discussion Questions

1. Explain each of De George's five theses in your own words. Do you agree with them? Are any open to doubt or possible objection? Explain.

2. What do you see as the most important moral dilemmas that face MNCs operating overseas? With regard to the five types of business operations distinguished by De George (in his discussion of Thesis 3), do you think that MNCs operating in Third World countries do more good than harm?

3. De George offers seven moral guidelines for multi-nationals operating in the Third World. Do you agree with them? What would a proponent of the narrow view of corporate responsibility say about them? Has De George overlooked any other responsibilities that multinationals have?

4. De George denies that MNCs should live up to and implement the same standards abroad as they do at home. Do you agree? Does De George's position imply some kind of ethical relativism?

BUSINESS ETHICS: ON GETTING TO THE HEART OF THE MATTER

PAUL F. CAMENISCH

It is common in discussions of business ethics to make one of two assumptions. The first is that business ethics is essentially the prevailing moral code of the society applied to business. The second is that business ethics is essentially a matter of applying certain standards of social responsibility to corporations. Paul F. Camenisch argues in the following essay that neither approach gets to the heart of business ethics. To do this, we must inquire about the fundamental nature of business—what it is, what it claims to do, and what distinctive functions it performs. Camenisch keys on two essential elements of business: profit and the provision of goods and services. By Milton Friedman's account, the profit goal takes precedence over the other: If business makes a profit, it meets its responsibility to society. Camenisch demurs; whereas profit may be an adequate criterion for assessing a business undertaking, he says it is an inadequate ethical ideal. Camenisch goes on to argue that the business activity itself must be scrutinized according to how it affects "human flourishing directly through the kind of products or services it provides, and through the responsible or irresponsible use of limited and often nonrenewable resources."

THE HEART OF BUSINESS ETHICS

Many current discussions of business ethics seem in the end to locate the ethical concern some distance from the central and essential activity of business. One way this is done is to assume that the content of business ethics is no more and no less than the prevailing moral code of the society as applied to business activities. Business persons and institutions, like all other citizens, are expected to refrain from murder, from fraud, and from polluting the environment. But we cannot limit business ethics to such matters. In fact, perhaps we ought not even call this *business* ethics for the same reasons that we do not say that parental ethics

prohibits my brutalizing my children. This is not parental ethics but just ethics plain and simple. This constraint arises from what it means to be a decent human being, not from what it means to be a parent. Similarly, the prohibition upon murdering to eliminate a business competitor is not part of a *business* ethic, for it does not arise from what it means to be engaged in business, nor does it apply to one simply because one is engaged in business. It too arises from what it means to be a decent, moral human being.

The second way of moving ethical issues to the edge of business's activities usually occurs under the rubric of "business's social responsibilities." The most remote of the issues raised here involve the question of whether corporations should devote any of their profits to philanthropic, educational and other sorts of humanitarian undertakings. This is a controversial issue which will not be easily resolved, but even if we concluded that this was a social responsibility of business, it would again fail to be business ethics in any specific and distinctive sense. It would simply be the application to this corporate member of a general societal expectation that members of a society existing in extensive interdependence with and benefitting from that society ought, if able, to contribute some portion of their wealth to such worthy causes. It should in passing be noted that there are persuasive grounds for rejecting this form of social responsibility for business.

Another class of social responsibilities urged upon business is somewhat closer to business activity as such since they can be fulfilled in the course of business's central activity of producing and marketing goods and services. These are the negative duties of neither creating nor aggravating social ills which might arise from business activity such as discriminatory employment, advancement and remuneration along racial, sexual, or other irrelevant lines, dangerous working conditions, and avoidable unemployment or worker dislocation.

Still we have not yet reached the heart of business ethics because we have said nothing of the ethics which come to bear on business *as business*, on business at its very heart and essence. But what is this "heart" of the business enterprise, and how and why are business ethics to be grounded in it?

Paul F. Camenisch, "Business Ethics: On Getting to the Heart of the Matter," *Business and Professional Ethics Journal* 1 (Fall 1981): 59–69. Reprinted by permission of the author. Section titles added.

*I am not prepared to enter here into the current debate concerning the existence and/or nature of corporate moral agency. For my present point it is sufficient to note that the moral stances, decisions and actions of various persons engaged in business and working together, as or through a corporation, do have impacts on the life of society and of its members of the sort I here have in mind. Whether these impacts are to be credited to those individual persons or to the corporation seems to make little difference in the present analysis.

Imagine a corporation which observes all the moral claims already noted—it does not commit fraud or murder, it freely contributes from its profits to various community "charities," its employment practices are above reproach, and it sells quality products at a fair and competitive price while securing for its investors a reasonable return on their investment. So far so good. Its moral record is impeccable. But imagine that the only conceivable use of its products is for human torture. Can we say that here there are no moral or ethical judgments to be made? That the kind of service or product which is at the heart of the enterprise is entirely inconsequential in any and all moral assessments of that enterprise? I do not see how morally sensitive persons or societies can set aside their moral perceptions at this point.

Of course one good reason for resisting this suggestion is the great difficulty in making such assessments of goods and services. *Whose* assessments will prevail? We might get general agreement on instruments of human torture—although even here I would not expect unanimity. But what of other goods such as napalm, Saturday-night specials, pornographic materials, junk foods, tobacco, liquors, etc., and services such as prostitution, the training of military mercenaries, or even the provision of such, or the training of the armed forces of repressive regimes, offensive-oriented "survival" courses, the construction of the usually redundant fast-food outlets along suburban slurp strips? In addition to these items in which virtually everyone should be able to see some detrimental elements, there is an additional class of items which some would list here because of their use of limited, even nonrenewable, resources for no purpose beyond momentarily satisfying the whimsey of the indiscriminate wealthy, the bored, the vain, or of increasing corporate profits . . . .

But how do we carry business ethics to the very heart of the business enterprise? I would argue that we can begin by asking the question of what the business sector is and claims to do, what its distinctive function is in the larger society of which it is a part. The norms, both moral and otherwise, for the conduct of an agent, whether individual or corporate,* can be determined only after we have established what that agent's relations are to other agents in the moral community, what role the agent plays in relation to them, what the agent's activities in the context of that community aim at . . . .

TWO ESSENTIAL ELEMENTS OF BUSINESS

In looking for the essential or definitive element in business I would suggest that it is necessary and helpful to see business as one form of that activity by which humans have from the beginning sought to secure and/or produce the material means of sustaining and then of enhancing life. It is plausible to assume that in earlier times individuals and small groups did this for themselves in immediate and direct ways such as gathering, hunting and fishing, farming, producing simple tools and weapons, etc. With the passage of time developments such as co-operative efforts, barter and monetary exchange modified this simple and idyllic situation.

Business, I would suggest, enters this picture as that form of such activities in which the exchanges engaged in are no longer motivated entirely by the intention of all participants to secure goods or services immediately needed to sustain and/or enhance their own lives, but by the design of at least some of the participants to make a profit, i.e., to obtain some value in excess of what they had before the exchange which is sufficiently flexible that it can be put to uses other than the immediate satisfaction of the recipient's own needs and desires. It should be noted that this last point is as much or more a matter of defining business, as it is of charting its historical emergence.

In the above statement I am suggesting that there are two essential elements in any adequate definition of business, the *provision of goods and services,* and the fact that this is done with the intention of making a *profit.* The first of these shows business's continuity with the various other human activities just noted by which life has been sustained and enhanced throughout the ages and enables us to understand business in relation to the larger society. The second is a more specific characteristic and sets business off from these other activities by revealing its distinctive internal dynamic. But this element does *not* sever business's connection with those predecessors. The crucial moral points to be made here are that moral/ethical issues arise around both of these elements and that the most important ones concern the "goods and services" element, i.e., the connection between business and the larger society of which it is part.

This appears to put me in definite tension with Milton Friedman who attempts to ground business ethics, or at least that portion of it which he calls the social responsibility of business, in the profit element only: "In . . .[a free] economy, there is one and only one social responsibility of business—to use its resources and engage in activities designed to increase its profits so long as it stays within the rules of the game, which is to say, engages in open and free competition, without deception or fraud."[1]

Of course it is unfair to Friedman to say that for him the maximization of profit is business's only moral duty since he may assume that playing by the rules of the game and that even conducting oneself so as to make a profit in such a "game" would bring additional restraints to bear on business, restraints which many of us would consider to be *moral* restraints. Nevertheless, Friedman's statement does seem to put undue emphasis on business's profit-making function in answering the question of its social and/or moral responsibility.

But however one interprets Friedman's statement, we do here encounter a question fundamental to our present point. This is the question of whether, in defining business and understanding it as a moral reality, we should focus primarily on its goal of producing goods and services or of generating a profit. One can attempt to resolve this question in several ways. There is the rather common sense way of looking at the way most persons generally apply the label "business." A producer of goods and services intending to make a profit but failing to do so is still, by most accounts, engaged in business. Of course some might respond that the concept of profit is still crucial to this activity's being considered business even though here it is present in intention only. But consider the other side. What if profit is present but the provision of goods and services is entirely absent as in a bank robbery? Most, I take it, would deny that here we have just another instance of business, or even an instance of business of a rather unusual sort. Most would simply want to deny that the bank robber was engaged in business at all. Of course one might salvage the position that business is defined by profit-making and yet avoid having to consider the bank robber a businessman by arguing that profit is not just any kind of gain at all, but is a particular sort of gain or is gain realized only under certain circumstances. But even this move would tend to support my position that a single simple concept of profit is not by itself sufficient to define what we mean by business. Whether these additional defining characteristics are written into a more complex definition of profit or are seen as additional to profit is a matter of indifference in terms of the present argument.

Secondly, one could take a more reflective, analytical approach and ask what the relation between these two elements—providing goods and services and profit-making—is, to see if that relation grants a kind of priority to either of them. I would argue, consistent with the above scenario of the emergence of business, that business's primary function, like that of the activities it supplants, is the producing of goods and services to sustain and enhance human existence. Profit then, given the way business functions in the marketplace, becomes one of the necessary means by which business enables itself to continue supplying such goods and services. This would mean that the goods and services element must be given priority in our understanding of business as a social reality and in our moral/ethical response to it. For in the absence of goods and services which are really *goods* and *services*, the making of a profit is at best morally irrelevant. In the absence of the end sought, the means for achieving it are otiose . . . .

Finally, in trying to settle the question of the relation between profits on the one hand and goods and services on the other, one might look at business in terms of its social function and ask why societies have generated and now support and sustain business. Surely it is not for business's own sake, nor for the sake of the few who own and manage businesses so that they can make a profit. Society has no need for profit-making as such. But rather, societies generate, encourage and sustain business because societies need the available raw materials transformed into needed goods and services, and because business in its contemporary form has been conspicuously successful in doing just that. In fact, in the current setting it may be that only business has the resources and the know-how to do that job on the needed scale.

All three of these ways of addressing the relation between these two elements would seem to confirm my position that the provision of goods and services can, perhaps must, be given priority over the profit element in our understanding of business. The major implication of this position for the resulting business ethics would be that the assessment of business as such and of specific business enterprises would begin with the question of whether the goods and services produced thereby serve to enhance or detract from the human condition, whether they contribute to or obstruct human flourishing. Implicit here is the suggestion that businesses engaged in producing goods and services which do not contribute to human flourishing are engaged in a morally questionable enterprise, and those engaged in producing goods and services inimical to human flourishing are engaged in immoral activity . . . .

ASSESSING BUSINESS'S CONTRIBUTION TO HUMAN FLOURISHING

Of course this suggestion concerning the heart of business ethics is rife with problems. Chief among them is the question of how we define the human flourishing which business is to serve. While we cannot resolve this question here, raising it at least serves to demonstrate that business ethics, like any serious ethics, will need to develop a philosophical or theological anthropology, a view of humanity and what its proper pursuit, its appropriate fulfillment is.

Some, of course, will argue that the only proper answers to such questions are the ones given by consumers in the marketplace as they use their purchasing power to vote for or against the various answers business implicitly offers in the form of diverse goods and services. While this may be an acceptable answer when one focuses exclusively on the relation between the individual consumer and the marketplace, it is clearly inadequate when we focus on the marketplace in relation to the total society, its present condition and needs and its future prospects. And clearly it is unrealistic, even irresponsible, to attempt to view an enterprise as large and as extensively intertwined with the total fabric of the society as is business only in its relation to individual consumers and their choices. Furthermore, the "marketplace as voting booth" answer to these questions is a costly trial and error method. And given advertising and other forms of demand formation, the significance of consumer "votes" is very unclear. Yet to have such judgments made by any agency outside the marketplace has serious implications for citizen-consumer freedom and rights in a free society.

In light of these difficult problems it might be tempting to give up the search for criteria by which to assess the performance of business at the level of its central function. And yet there are at least three important reasons for attempting this assessment in spite of the obvious problems. As we become increasingly aware of the limits of the earth and its resources within which all of humanity both present and future must live, and of the fact that in our present setting only business has the means and the know-how to transform those resources on any significant scale into the needed goods and services, it becomes increasingly clear that the total society has a crucial stake in, and should therefore have a say about, what business does with this our common legacy. As Keith Davis has suggested, " . . . business now has a new social role of . . . trustee for society's resources . . . ."[2]

The knowing use of nonrenewable resources to make products of little or no human value and/or with short useful life solely for the sake of an immediate profit thus becomes a serious disservice to the larger society. An ethic of the sort here proposed provides a framework within which we could raise the question of how this trusteeship can best be exercised.

Secondly, this enterprise of assessing business in terms of its contribution to human flourishing is called for and legitimated by the fact that business in its various activities is already propagating, whether consciously or not, a view of humanity and of what human flourishing consequently means, views which of course assign a major role to the consumption of the goods and services business produces. Even if this view of humanity is only implicit or perhaps especially if it is implicit, its content and potential impact call for assessment by parties outside the business sector.

Finally, the difficult task of responding to business on these central issues is worth undertaking because of the role business plays in contemporary America and similar societies. In observing the role of business and related economic matters in contemporary America one might almost suggest that we have moved from a sacralized society dominated by religious concerns, through a secularized one in which various major sectors attained considerable autonomy in their own spheres, to a commercialized or an economized culture in which the common denominators which unify and dominate all areas of activity are business related or business grounded considerations such as dollar-value, profitability, marketability, efficiency, contribution to the gross national product, etc. And as Thomas Donaldson and Patricia Werhane have written:

> There may be nothing inherently evil about the goals of economic growth, technological advance, and a higher material standard of living; but critics such as Galbraith have argued that when these become the primary goals of a nation there is a significant lowering in the quality of human life. Economic goals are able to distract attention from crucial human issues, and freedom, individuality, and creativity are lost in a society dominated by large corporations and economic goals.[3]

If the above is a plausible interpretation of the role of business, broadly understood, in contemporary America, and of some of its implications for human flourishing, then it should be obvious that we have need for an ethic which responds to the central activity of business, since the crucial human implications of such cultural domination by business arise from this central function and not from the less central concerns often raised in business ethics . . . .

But why should business submit to the scrutiny and recommendations of an ethic such as is proposed here? One answer would be because such an ethic is predicated on what business *is*—one important part of society's efforts to enable its members to flourish, specifically that part which deals with the provision of the material means for sustaining and enhancing life.

"Of course," the critic might respond, "this answer works *if* we agree on what you say business is. But if we maintain that business must be defined and understood in terms of its own internal dynamics and goals, e.g., profit-making, rather than in terms of society's needs and goals, then the answer falls apart." True enough. But given business's extensive interdependence with society—its reliance on society's educational system to provide educated workers, on society's maintenance of transportation systems, of a stable social and political setting in which to do business, of a legal system by which business can adjudicate its disputes with competitors and customers, of what E. F. Schumacher has called the "infrastructure"[4]—it is naive to suggest that business is a self-sufficient and self-contained entity which can define its own goals and functions entirely independently of the society's goals and needs. As Robert A. Dahl has written:

> Today it is absurd to regard the corporation simply as an enterprise established for the sole purpose of allowing profit making. We the citizens give them special rights, powers, and privileges, protection, and benefits on the understanding that their activities will fulfill purposes. Corporations exist only as they continue to benefit us . . . . Every corporation should be thought of as a social enterprise whose existence and decisions can be justified only insofar as they serve public or social purposes.[5]

Furthermore, anyone who argues that business should be permitted to define its own goals and purposes and thus its own ethics independently of societal interests will have to explain why business should be granted latitude at this point that is denied to other major sectors of societal activity such as politics, education, or the traditional professions such as law and medicine . . . .

There are numerous varied matters which are legitimately included in any adequate definition of business ethics. In fact, in a nascent field such as this it is as yet impossible to say with any certainty what is within and what is without its borders. But it does seem clear that any business ethic that does not respond first and foremost to business's contribution to or detraction from human flourishing through its essential and definitive activity of generating life sustaining and enhancing goods and services will have failed to lay a foundation from which to address all other questions for it will not yet have gotten to the heart of the matter.

Notes

1. Milton Friedman, *Capitalism and Freedom* (Chicago: University of Chicago Press, 1962), 133.

2. Keith Davis, "Five Propositions for Social Responsibility," in Tom L. Beauchamp and Norman E. Bowie, eds., *Ethical Theory and Business* (Englewood Cliffs, N.J.: Prentice-Hall, 1979), 170.

3. Thomas Donaldson and Patricia H. Werhane, eds., *Ethical Issues in Business* (Englewood Cliffs, N.J.: Prentice-Hall, 1979), 330.

4. E. F. Schumacher, *Small Is Beautiful* (New York: Harper & Row, 1975), 273–274.

5. Robert A. Dahl, "A Prelude to Corporate Reform," in Robert L. Heilbroner and Paul London, eds., *Corporate Social Policy* (Reading, Mass.: Addison-Wesley Publishing Company, 1975), 18–19, as cited in Norman E. Bowie, "Changing the Rules," in Tom L. Beauchamp and Norman E. Bowie, eds., *Ethical Theory and Business* (Englewood Cliffs, N.J.: Prentice-Hall, 1979), 148.

Review and Discussion Questions

1. Explain the two ways, according to Camenisch, in which discussions of business ethics often fail to connect with the central activity of business.

2. How would you assess a company that is "socially responsible" but that makes products for human torture? What about companies that make cigarettes, cheap guns, pornographic movies, or junk food?

3. What are Camenisch's three reasons for maintaining that the business goal of providing goods and services takes priority over making a profit? Do you agree with them?

4. Camenisch argues that business should promote "human flourishing." What does that mean to you? Do you think that there is any means other than the marketplace itself to decide what goods and services promote human flourishing?

5. Why does Camenisch believe that it is justified and important to develop criteria for assessing business in terms of human flourishing?

6. Would you agree that Camenisch has taken us to the "heart" of business ethics? What practical implications does his approach have?

Further Reading for Chapter 5

John R. Danley, "Corporate Moral Agency," in Robert E. Frederick, ed., *A Companion to Business Ethics* (Malden, MA: Blackwell, 1999) reviews the philosophical literature on this difficult topic with particular attention to the influential views of Peter French.

Thomas Donaldson, *Corporations and Morality* (Englewood Cliffs, NJ: Prentice Hall, 1982) discusses the moral status of corporations, arguments for and against corporate social responsibility, and the idea of a social contract for business, among other issues.

Peter A. French, *Collective and Corporate Responsibility* (New York: Columbia University Press, 1984) analyzes the philosophical issues involved in assigning moral responsibility to corporations and other collectivities, whereas his *Corporate Ethics* (Fort Worth, TX: Harcourt Brace, 1996) looks at a wider range of moral issues involving corporations.

Thomas M. Jones, Andrew C. Wicks, and **R. Edward Freeman**, "Stakeholder Theory: The State of the Art," in Norman E. Bowie, ed., *The Blackwell Guide to Business Ethics* (Malden, MA: Blackwell, 2002) discusses one influential way of thinking about the obligations of managers to stockholders and other stakeholders.

John McDermott, *Corporate Society: Class, Property, and Contemporary Capitalism* (Boulder, CO: Westview, 1991) analyzes the modern business corporation's impact on society.

John Micklethwait and **Adrian Wooldridge**, *The Company: A Short History of a Revolutionary Idea* (New York: Modern Library, 2003) is a readable, well-informed history of the corporation from its earliest beginnings to recent scandals.

David E. Schrader, "The Oddness of Corporate Ownership," *Journal of Social Philosophy* 27 (Fall 1996) argues that stockholders do not own the corporation.

Thomas I. White, ed., *Business Ethics: A Philosophical Reader* (New York: Macmillan, 1993) contains useful essays on corporate personhood and responsibility in ch. 6 and on the punishing of corporations in ch. 7.

"The Good, the Bad, and Their Corporate Codes of Ethics: Enron, Sarbanes-Oxley, and the Problems with Legislating Good Behavior," *Harvard Law Review* 116 (May 2003) discusses the negative impact of recent legislation on corporate codes of conduct.

Part Three

The Organization and the People in It

6

The Workplace (1):
Basic Issues

Scientists first described acquired immune deficiency syndrome, commonly known as AIDS, in 1981. Apparently the result of a new infection of human beings, AIDS probably stems originally from central or west Africa, where several subspecies of chimpanzees carry a closely related virus. Within three years scientists in France and the United States had isolated human T-lymphotropic virus III, now known as HIV, for "human immunodeficiency virus." HIV is the parent virus of AIDS and a couple of related diseases. To be infected with the virus is not automatically to have AIDS, but most of those infected go on to develop AIDS symptoms and often die from them. After identifying the virus, scientists quickly developed blood tests for its presence, but they have yet to discover a vaccine. The stakes are high. It is estimated that 39 million people worldwide are infected with HIV. Nearly 5 million people are infected worldwide every year, and since the pandemic began, AIDS has killed over 24 million people. At the end of 2002, an estimated 56,000 people in Canada were living with HIV and AIDS, a number representing a 12 percent increase since 1999.[1] Our neighbours to the south are relatively worse off. Approximately 800,000 Americans are infected, and over 450,000 have already died. Researchers estimate that there are 40,000 newly infected Americans every year.[2]

No one today can doubt the seriousness of AIDS. Media attention has ensured that the public is aware of its deadliness and the threat it poses, and this is a good thing. But when fear of danger combines with ignorance about a disease's nature and causes, panic is often the result. This has sadly been the case with AIDS—not least in the workplace.

Take what is, unfortunately, a typical case. John L. is a white-collar employee, working in the downtown branch of a firm operating in a major West Coast city. He had been feeling generally run-down and complained of various small ailments to his physician. When a routine checkup didn't reveal anything specific, John's doctor encouraged him to undergo a blood test for AIDS. He tested positive, which means that the antibodies for HIV are present in his body. Their presence means that he is infected by the virus and that it is probable, given his symptoms, that he has AIDS.

A few of John's friends in the office know of his recent ill health, and gradually word of his test results has circulated. And now problems have begun—not just for John but also for his coworkers and for management. John's colleagues feel uneasy around him; they're not sure what to do or to say, and some of them are very worried about possible contagion. A few coworkers feel strongly that John should not be permitted to go on working there. The boss is concerned not just with the prospect of declining work performance from John but also with the effects of his presence on office morale. She may herself also have doubts about the wisdom or even the safety of allowing John to continue to interact with the public, which is part of his job.

The myriad problems, doubts, tensions, possibly even mild hysteria that the mere presence of John L. can create in a business or some other organization are easy to imagine, but sorting out the morally relevant factors and deciding how the situation ought to be dealt with is less easy. What are John's rights and interests? How are these to be weighed against the interests and rights of both his coworkers and the organization itself? What responsibilities does an organization have to one of its members who may be facing a terminal illness? Given the size and organizational structure of John's workplace and the type of work in question, how—morally speaking—should management respond?

Those are questions that more and more firms must answer. Reliable figures are difficult to come by, but given the continent-wide statistics and the ever-increasing business travel, virtually every large company can be assumed to have had cases of AIDS among its employees or their dependents. For the foreseeable future, the problems posed by AIDS in the workplace can only continue to increase. Yet in Canada and worldwide only a modest percentage of firms have or are planning to formulate a policy on AIDS.[3]

Traditionally, the obligations between a business organization and its employees could be boiled down to "A fair wage for an honest day's work." Business's primary, if not sole, obligation to its employees was to pay a decent wage. In return, employees were expected to work efficiently and to be loyal and obedient to their employer. This model of employer–employee relations is obviously too simple and fails to come to terms not just with the dilemmas facing John's office but also with many other major moral issues that arise in today's workplace. This chapter looks at some of these issues, in particular:

1. The state of civil liberties in the workplace

2. The efforts of some successful companies to respect the rights and moral dignity of their employees

3. Moral issues that arise with respect to personnel matters—namely, hiring, promotions, discipline and discharge, and wages

4. The role and history of unions in our economic system, their ideals and achievements, and the moral issues they raise

CIVIL LIBERTIES IN THE WORKPLACE

Employees have all sorts of job-related concerns. Generally speaking, they want to do well at their assignments, to get along with their colleagues, and to have their contributions to the organization recognized. Their job tasks, working conditions, wages, and possibility of promotion are among the many things that occupy their day-to-day thoughts. Aside from the actual work that they are expected to perform, employees are naturally concerned about the way their organizations treat them. Frequently they find such treatment to be morally deficient and complain that the organizations for which they work violate their moral rights and civil liberties.

Consider the following cases in the Canadian and American workplace context. Jim Christie, a member of the World Wide Church of God, worked for the Central Alberta Dairy Pool. Christie requested to take unpaid leave for two days in order to observe two holy days of his religion. He was allowed one day off but was required to work on the other day "for reasons of plant operating needs." Christie reiterated his request and the reasons for it to his supervisor, his shop steward, and the branch manager. All parties concerned had a meeting, at which time the branch manager told Christie that if he failed to show up for work on the day in question he would be fired. True to his beliefs, Christie did not show up for work, and he was immediately dismissed. Christie launched a complaint that the company refused to continue to employ him because of his religion, contrary to the Alberta *Individual's Rights Protection Act, R.S.A. 1980*. The Board of Inquiry upheld his complaint but the Board's decision was subsequently overturned by the Alberta Court of Queen's Bench. The Alberta Court of Appeal upheld the Queen's

Bench decision. The case went to the Supreme Court of Canada (see *Alberta Central Milk Pool v. Alberta (Human Rights Commission)* [1990] 2 S.C.R 489). When the Canadian National Railway Co. introduced a work rule that all employees had to wear a hard hat at a certain work site, Mr. Bhinder, a Sikh employee, refused to comply because his religion did not allow the wearing of headgear other than the turban. Bhinder's employment was terminated because the company refused to make exceptions to the rule and Bhinder refused to accept other work not requiring a hard hat. This case too went to the Supreme Court (see *Bhinder v. CN* [1985] 2 S.C.R. 561).

Louis V. MacIntire worked for the DuPont Company in Orange, Texas, for 16 years. As a chemical engineer he was well paid, and during the course of his career at DuPont he received several promotions. MacIntire also had literary ambitions and wrote a novel, *Scientists and Engineers: The Professionals Who Are Not*. Several characters in the novel inveigh against various management abuses at the novel's fictional Logan Chemical Company and argue for a union for technical employees. Logan Chemical at least superficially resembles MacIntire's real-life employer, DuPont, and some of MacIntire's supervisors were unhappy with his thinly veiled criticisms. He was fired. MacIntire sued DuPont, claiming that his constitutional right of free speech had been violated. A Texas district judge threw that charge out of court.[4]

It is interesting to see how Canadian companies doing business with American companies, especially Canadian subsidiaries of U.S. companies, and ultimately Canadian courts will handle attempts by American companies to apply provisions of several U.S. laws (for example, the *Patriot Act*) and the U.S. International Traffic in Arms Regulations (ITAR) to certain groups of Canadians workers (or citizens) working in Canada for Canadian companies. For example, under pressure from U.S. banking institutions, the Royal Bank of Canada will not allow Canadians to hold a U.S.-dollar account if they also hold citizenship from any one of six U.S.-sanctioned countries (Iran, Iraq, Sudan, North Korea, Myanmar, and Cuba). A group of Canadian citizens, also holding citizenships from various countries sanctioned by the United States, working for Bell Helicopter Textron Canada Ltd., were refused access to U.S. defence data that was crucial to completing projects they were working on. Indeed, a Venezuelan-born permanent resident of Canada has filed Quebec's first human rights complaint against his former employer, Bell Helicopter, over issues arising out of Bell's adherence to U.S. laws and regulations. On the face of it, the intrusion of U.S. laws into the lives of Canadian workers seems to violate the Canadian *Charter* and the various federal and provincial privacy acts.[5]

The above cases illuminate what many workers see as the widespread absence of civil liberties in the workplace. Many believe that we enjoy an extensive array of civil liberties until we go to our workplace. David W. Ewing, former editor of the *Harvard Business Review*, agrees.

He sees the corporate invasion of employees' civil liberties as rampant and attacks it in scathing terms:

> In most . . . [corporate] organizations, during working hours, civil liberties are a will-o'-the-wisp. The Constitutional rights that employees have grown accustomed to in family, school, and church life generally must be left outdoors, like cars in the parking lot. As in totalitarian countries, from time to time a benevolent chief executive or department head may encourage speech, conscience, and privacy, but these scarcely can be called rights, for management can take them away at will . . . . It is fair to say that an enormous corporate archipelago has grown which, in terms of civil liberties, is as different from the rest of America as day is from night. In this archipelago . . . the system comes first, the individual second.[6]

Two historical factors, in Ewing's view, lie behind the absence of civil liberties and the prevalence of authoritarianism in the workplace. One of these factors was the rise of professional management and personnel engineering at the turn of the twentieth century, following the emergence of large corporations. This shaped the attitudes of companies toward their employees in a way hardly conducive to respecting their rights. As Frederick Winslow Taylor (1856–1915), generally identified as the founder of "scientific management," bluntly put it, "In the past, the man has been first. In the future, the system must be first." The second historical factor is that in North America the law has traditionally given employers a free hand in hiring and firing employees. Up to the latter part of the nineteenth century, Britain and its colonies (including Canada) regulated "employment issues" through "masters and servants law," a compendium of statutory enactments, common law, and social practices the origins of which went back to Elizabethan times. Though it varied widely from place to place, masters and servants law invariably displayed the following three characteristics:

> The first was the idea that the employment relation was a matter of *private contract* or agreement for work and wages between an employer who thereby acquired the right to command and an employee who undertook to obey. The second was the provision for *summary enforcement* of these private agreements by lay justices of the peace or other magistrates, largely unsupervised by the senior courts. The third was *punishment* of the uncooperative worker: not damages to remedy the breach of contract, but whipping, imprisonment, forced labor, fines, the forfeit of all wages earned. This distinctive conjuncture of civil contract, informal justice, and effective criminalization of the worker's breach was enacted in thousands of statutes, enforced around the globe in a web of closely related language, doctrine, and social practice.[7]

Over a century ago, a court in the state of Tennessee expressed this doctrine in memorable form. Employers, the court held, "may dismiss their employees at will . . . for good cause, for no cause, or even for cause morally wrong, without thereby being guilty of legal wrong."

In addition, common law requires that an employee be loyal to an employer, acting solely for the employer's benefit in matters connected to work. The employee is also duty-bound "not to act or speak disloyally," except in pursuit of his own interests outside work. It's no wonder, then, that traditional employer–employee law has hardly been supportive of employee's concerns or rights. According to common law, then, unless there is an explicit contractual provision to the contrary, every employment is employment "at will," and either side is free to terminate it at any time without advance notice or reason. The common law has, of course, been modified in important ways by statutory provisions and more employee-friendly case law. The *Canadian Charter of Rights and Freedoms* (which forms Part I of the *Constitution Act, 1982*) and subsequent federal and provincial legislation and case law[8] prohibit discrimination on the basis of race, creed, nationality, religion, age, sex , disability or sexual orientation. Equally importantly, employees are more and more protected by law against arbitrary or unjust dismissal, though in general employers have the right to terminate the employment of their employees and employees have the right to terminate their employment with their employer. Many workers are of course protected by their union contracts from unjust dismissals.

Thus, today working people have protection against some forms of unjust termination, and many of them enjoy the assurance that they can expect due process and that at least some of their civil liberties and other moral rights will be respected on the job. "But," writes Clyde Summers in the *Harvard Business Review*, "random individuals who are unjustly terminated are isolated and without organizational or political voice. For them the harsh common law rule remains."[9]

Companies That Look Beyond the Bottom Line

Although the law seems to be gradually changing, leaving the common-law heritage of employer–employee doctrine behind, recent legal developments are complicated and not entirely consistent, as courts deliver their judgments depending on the peculiar details of each case and the requirements of different provincial and territorial jurisdictions. As argued in Chapter 1, however, our moral obligations extend beyond merely keeping within the law.

True, some businesspeople not only support employment at will as a desirable legal policy but also embrace it as a moral doctrine. They reject the normative principle—accepted by most ordinary people—that employees should be fired only for just cause, and they deny that employers have any obligations to their employees beyond those specified by law or by explicit legal contract. Their actions, if not their words, suggest that they view the people who work for them as lacking any meaningful moral rights, seeing them as fungible assets—as means rather than ends in themselves—to be used in whatever way is profitable. But nowadays that is a minority perspective. More and more corporations are coming to acknowledge, and to design institutional procedures that respect, the rights and moral dignity of their employees. Moreover, the firms taking the lead in this regard are often among the most successful companies.

This fact undermines the old argument that corporate efficiency requires employees to sacrifice their civil liberties and other rights between 9 and 5. Without strict discipline and the firm maintenance of management prerogatives, the claim was, our capitalist economic system would come apart at the seams. An increasing body of evidence, however, suggests just the opposite. As Ewing writes:

> Civil liberties are far less of a threat to the requirements of effective management than are collective bargaining, labor–management committees, job enrichment, work participation, and a number of other schemes that industry takes for granted. Moreover, the companies that lead in encouraging rights—organizations such as Polaroid, IBM, Donnelly Mirrors, and Delta Airlines—have healthier-looking bottom lines than the average corporation does.[10]

Although under no legal compulsion to do so, a small but growing number of companies encourage employee participation in company policies affecting the welfare of employees and the community. Some companies foster open communication through regular, informal or even formal (through joint management–labour committees) exchanges between management and other employees. Others, for example, Delta Air Lines, have top officials answer questions submitted anonymously by employees—in the absence of supervisors. Still others, such as General Electric and New England Telephone, have a hotline for questions, worries, and reports of wrongdoing. Finally, some, like Dow Chemical, open the pages of company publications to employee questions and criticisms.

Union contracts frequently require companies to set up grievance procedures and otherwise attempt to see that their members are guaranteed due process on the job. Some enlightened nonunionized companies have done the same. Polaroid, for instance, has a well-institutionalized committee whose job it is to represent an employee with a grievance. The committee members are elected from the ranks, and reportedly a fair number of management decisions are overruled in the hearings. If the decision goes against the aggrieved employee, he or she is entitled by company rules to submit the case to an outside arbitrator.

Some companies go further by following a policy of no layoffs. Consider Hewlett-Packard. A recession once reduced orders so much that HP management was considering a 10 percent cut in the workforce. Because laying off people was anathema, HP went a different route. It set up a working schedule of nine days out of ten for everybody in the company, from the CEO on down. The program stayed in place for six months, when orders picked up, and the full ten-day schedule was resumed. "The net result of this program," said William Hewlett, "was that effectively all shared the burden of the recession, good people were not turned out on a very tough job market, and, I might observe, the company benefited by having in place a highly qualified work force when business returned."[11]

Not only, then, is it a moral duty of companies to respect the rights and dignity of their employees, in particular by acknowledging their civil liberties and guaranteeing them due process, but doing so can also work to the company's benefit by enhancing employee morale and, thus, the company's competitive performance. Hence, there is little basis for the widespread belief that efficient management is incompatible with a fair workplace environment.[12]

Consider the case of Spruceland Millworks, a maker of wooden moldings and trim work, in Acheson, Alberta. In 1992, Spruceland's main plant burned down and the 48 staff expected to be out of work. But rather than laying his staff off, owner Ben Sawatzky put them to work rebuilding the 50,000-square-foot-facility (about 4,645 square metres), which was operational again in just over three months. Over the following years Sawatzky provided low-cost loans to allow his workers to buy a 20 percent stake in the business. He also instituted the practice of giving his workers a daily production target, and if it is met in less than eight hours, they are free to go home with full pay as reward for a good day's work. The business has now expanded to almost 150 staff and more than $70 million in annual sales. Last year, Sawatzky paid his staff a "prosperity bonus"—$1,000 for every year of service—and flew the whole company to Mexico for an annual meeting.[13] "What I absolutely believe is that honoring the people who do the work can produce stunning results for the company," says Sidney Harmon, CEO of Harmon International Industries. "If the people in the factory believe there's a real effort to help improve their skills, provide opportunities for advancement and job security, they can do things that will blow your mind."[14] Some business writers push this point even further. For example, Robert Levering and Milton Moskowitz argue that

> The authoritarian work style—long the standard operating procedure in business—has failed. That failure is at the root of the poor performance of U.S. companies and massive layoffs in the '80s and '90s. When management is disconnected from the people who work in the company, it becomes easy to fire those people. And when workers are disconnected from what they do, it becomes easy not to care about the product or service.[15]

Of course, a company that does not sincerely consider employee rights of inherent moral importance is not likely to reap the benefits of enhanced business performance. Trust, as more and more management theorists are saying,[16] is the key here, and employees can tell the difference between a company that has a genuine regard for their welfare and a company that only pretends to have moral concern.[17]

As mentioned in Chapter 1 and elsewhere, whether we are speaking of companies or of individuals, acting morally is generally in one's long-term interest even though there is no guarantee that one will always benefit by doing so. However, people or organizations that worry about whether doing the right thing will profit them or who act fairly and treat people decently only because they believe that doing so will advance their self-interest are unlikely to enjoy the benefits that accrue to those whose lives are genuinely governed by moral principle. People or businesses that act ethically only because they believe it will pay off are liable to act unethically when they think that acting so will pay off.

So far, this chapter has suggested that the workplace should provide an environment in which employees are treated fairly and their inherent dignity respected, and it has argued that doing so can be perfectly compatible with a firm's business goals. Although important, those points are generalities. They do not provide much guidance for dealing with the specific moral issues and dilemmas that arise day in and day out on the job. The remainder of this chapter and the chapter that follows take a closer look at some of these issues.

PERSONNEL POLICIES AND PROCEDURES

People make up organizations, and how an organization impinges on the lives of its own members is a morally important matter. One obvious and very important way organizational conduct affects the welfare and rights of employees and potential employees is through personnel policies and procedures; that is, how the organization handles the hiring, firing, paying, and promoting of the people who work for it. These human-resources procedures and policies structure an organization's basic relationship with its employees. This section looks at some of the specific, morally relevant concerns to which any organization must be sensitive. Speaking generally, though, a company's personnel decisions must, if they are to be fair, reflect policies and procedures that are based on criteria that are job-related, clear and accessible, and applied equally.

Hiring

A basic task of the employer or personnel manager is hiring. Employers strive to hire people who will enable the organization to produce the products or services it seeks to provide or to promote its other goals. Bad hiring decisions are bound to harm the bottom line. In addition, the actions of unqualified, dishonest, or careless employees may impact adversely customers, clients and other third parties. Such actions may render the company legally liable, even when the company itself does nothing wrong. Recent decisions by the Supreme Court have highlighted the conditions under which corporations (including the Crown and nonprofit organizations) may be held negligent or simply "vicariously liable" for harms caused by the actions of their employees or their volunteers or even outside contractors they may hire to do a job. For example, *Lewis (Guardian ad litem of) v. British Columbia*, [1997] 3 S.C.R. 1145; *Balzey v. Curry*, [1999] 2 S.C.R. 534; *Jacobi v. Griffiths*, [1999] 2 S.C.R. 570. Courts in the United States have used the principle of negligent hiring to broaden the liability of an employer for damage or injury caused by its employees—even after regular hours and away from the job site. For instance, Avis Rent-A-Car was required to pay $800,000 after a male employee raped a female employee; the jury found that the company had been negligent in hiring the man without thoroughly investigating his background.[18]

Nevertheless, in making hiring decisions, employers must be careful to treat job applicants fairly and with due regard to their civil rights. As one might imagine, determining the fair thing to do is not always easy. Balancing issues of privacy with security or safety concerns is an extremely delicate task, and one that changing social and legal perspectives make ever more difficult. One useful way to approach some of the moral aspects of hiring is to examine the principal steps involved in the process: screening, testing, and interviewing.

Screening   When firms recruit employees, they attempt to screen them—that is, to attract applicants who have a good chance of qualifying for the job and to weed out applicants or potential applicants who are unlikely to succeed at the job. When done properly, screening ensures a pool of competent candidates and guarantees that everyone has been dealt with fairly; when done improperly, it undermines effective recruitment and invites injustices into the hiring process.

Screening begins with a job description and a job specification. A *job description* lists all pertinent details about the content of a job, including its duties, responsibilities, working conditions, and physical requirements. A *job specification* describes the qualifications an employee needs, such as skills, background, education, and work experience. Job descriptions and specifications must be complete and accurate. Otherwise, job candidates lack the necessary information for making informed decisions and can waste time and money pursuing jobs they are not suited for. In addition, disappointment and unfairness can result if a position is inaccurately described or wrongly classified.

That sounds simple enough. But in an effort to attract strong job candidates, hiring officers can easily, perhaps even unintentionally, begin to exaggerate what the job offers in regard to opportunities, travel, the ability to work from home, the budget one will control, and so on. And exaggeration can grow into blatant distortion. One recruiter offers this sample lexicon: "Character building" means that the job stinks, "mentoring" translates into babysitting your staff, "expense account" signifies a bagged lunch at your desk, and "work team environment" denotes noisy cubicles.[19] Exaggerations like these may start innocently, but some businesses clearly and intentionally cross the line—for example, by deliberately misclassifying hourly workers as salaried employees to avoid paying them overtime.

One of the main moral concerns in screening is to avoid wrongful discrimination. For several decades now, the law has forbidden discrimination against individuals on the basis of various characteristics (for example, age, race, national origin, religion, sex, etc.) and such features should never appear in job specifications or recruitment advertisements. Chapter 9 discusses the moral issues surrounding job discrimination, but it's clear that basing employment decisions on such factors almost always excludes potential employees on non-job-related grounds. Firms must therefore be careful to avoid job specifications that discriminate subtly ("excellent opportunity for college student") or employ gender-linked job terminology (for example, "salesman" rather than "salesperson" or "waiter" rather than "server") that may discourage qualified candidates from applying.

Bona fide occupational qualifications, or BFOQs, are job specifications to which the protection against discrimination afforded by the *Charter* or the *Canada Human Rights Act* (1977, 1998) (or the civil rights legislation in the U.S.) does not apply. Still BFOQs are limited in scope and open to dispute. The Supreme Court case (cited earlier) of *Bhinder v. CN* is interesting here. Though the Court did not allow Bhinder's appeal on the grounds that wearing a helmet was a BFOQ, the Court's decision was split. The dissenting judges held that an occupational requirement that had a discriminatory effect on the appellant was not a BFOQ and hence contrary to the provisions of the Charter.[20] There are no BFOQs for race or colour, and in the case of sex, BFOQs exist only to allow for authenticity (for example, where only a male model will do) and modesty (for example, hire only women as a women's locker room attendant).

In validating job specifications, firms are not permitted to rely on the preferences of their customers as a reason for discriminatory employment practices. For example, the fact that for decades airline passengers were accustomed to being attended to by young female flight attendants and may even have preferred them could not legally justify excluding men from this occupation. Both Canadian and U.S. courts have ruled that a negative reaction to an employee on the part of customers does not constitute a substantial justification for the company to restrict the employee's freedom to, say, wear a beard.

Section 15 (1–2) of the *Canadian Charter* guarantees equality, in process and in substance, before the law "without discrimination based on race, national or ethnic origin, colour, religion, sex, age or mental or physical disability," while the *Canada Human Rights Act* specifically prohibits employment discrimination on these and other grounds. Similarly, in the States, the *Americans with Disabilities Act* (ADA, 1994) prohibits employers from screening out disabled applicants who have the capacity to carry out the job. All these statutory provisions are intended to protect, among other things, the right of people with disabilities to obtain gainful employment, and

do forbid employers from discriminating against employees or job applicants with disabilities when making employment decisions. These provisions also require employers to make "reasonable accommodations" for an employee or a job applicant with a disability as long as doing so doesn't inflict "undue hardship" on the business. Although the general moral imperative here is clear, in practice applying these concepts and making the appropriate determinations can be difficult. Respect for the rights of people with disabilities may sometimes have to be balanced against expense to the company or inconvenience to other employees. Such expense or inconvenience, however, has to be very great indeed if it is to outweigh the moral injury and financial loss being borne by the person who is denied a job opportunity because of disability.

When screening potential employees, companies must also be careful to avoid unfairly excluding applicants on the basis of language, physical appearance, or lifestyle. And they should not automatically screen out potential employees because they lack qualifications that aren't really necessary or, contrariwise, because they are "overqualified," or because they have a gap in their employment history.

To begin with language, bilingual ability (English–French or English–another language) may be a justifiable job specification in some areas of the country, where such skills can be essential for successful job performance. But employers need to be aware of the danger of creating unnecessary specifications for a position, especially if they unfairly discriminate on the basis of national origin. Similarly, although the ability to communicate effectively in English is a common workplace requirement, it can seriously impede the employment prospects of some workers. Again, one must remember that a person's appearance is very rarely an indicator of their ability to perform the job. Similarly, one's stature or weight may be thought to be problematic in satisfying BFOQs for the job, but employers may first try to reexamine whether the required range for height or weight is reasonably set in view of the demands of the job. In its "Guide to Screening and Selection in Employment," the Canadian Human Rights Commission suggests that with respect to "weight" and "height," employers should make "no inquiry unless there is evidence they are genuine occupational requirements."

Some employers may wade into morally troubling waters by screening job applicants on the basis of lifestyle. For example, some companies will not hire anyone who admits to being even an occasional alcoholic drinker or who engages in recreational activities that are "high-risk"—like motorcycling, skydiving, motor racing, mountain-climbing, or flying one's own plane. Ill-considered educational requirements are also potentially objectionable. Requiring more formal education than is truly needed for a job is unfair to less-educated candidates who, as a result, aren't even considered for the position. One of them might, in fact, turn out to the best person for the job, which means that the firm also stands to lose. The other side of the coin is to deny an applicant consideration because he or she is "overqualified" in terms of education or experience. To avoid hiring someone who may become bored or frustrated by the job or who is likely to jump ship at the first opportunity, firms are justified in raising the issue. But they shouldn't proceed on the basis of assumptions that may be unwarranted. The employment ranks are filled with people successfully doing jobs for which they are technically overqualified.

Tests   Testing is an integral part of the hiring process, especially with large firms. Tests are generally designed to measure the applicant's verbal, quantitative, and logical skills. Aptitude tests help determine an applicant's suitability for a job; skill tests measure the applicant's proficiency in specific areas, such as typing, shorthand, or arithmetic; personality tests help determine the applicant's maturity and sociability. In addition, some firms in the business of designing and assembling precision equipment administer dexterity tests to determine how nimbly applicants can use their hands and fingers.

To be successful, a test must be valid. *Validity* refers to whether test scores correlate with performance in some other activity—that is, whether the test measures the skill or ability it is intended to measure. Just as important, tests must also be reliable. *Reliability* refers to whether test results are replicable, that is, whether a subject's scores will remain relatively consistent from test to test (so that a test-taker won't score high one day and low the next). Clearly, not all tests are both valid and reliable. Many tests are not able to measure desired qualities, and others exhibit a woefully low level of forecast accuracy. Some companies use tests that haven't been designed for the company's particular situation. Legitimizing tests can be an expensive and time-consuming project, but if tests are used, the companies using them are obliged to ensure their validity and reliability.

But even when they are valid and reliable, tests can be unfair—for example, if they are culturally biased or if the skills they measure are irrelevant to job performance. The U.S. Supreme Court took a stand on this issue in the famous, and internationally influential, case of *Griggs v. Duke Power Company* [401 U.S. 424 (1971)]. The case involved 13 African-American labourers who were denied promotions because they scored low on a company-sponsored intelligence test involving verbal and mathematical puzzles. In its decision, the Court found that the *Civil Rights Act* prohibits employers from requiring a high school education or the passing of a general intelligence test as a prerequisite for employment or promotion without demonstrating that the associated skills relate directly to job performance. The *Griggs* decision makes it clear that if an employment practice such as testing has an adverse impact (or unequal effect) on minority groups, then the burden of proof is on the employer to show the job-relatedness or business necessity of the test or other procedure. Duke Power Company couldn't do that.

Today, hundreds of thousands of job applicants are putting pencil to paper, or sitting down in front of a computer screen, to take skills tests, leadership tests, personality tests and even tests to predict what an applicant's coworkers will think of him or her after a year on the job.[21] By means of all these tests, management seeks to gain a potentially more productive group of workers whose skills match more closely the requirements of the job. The supposed objectivity of tests is often illusory, however. Chapter 7 will have more to say about testing when it discusses privacy, but clearly putting too much faith in tests can lead to arbitrary employment decisions, decisions that are unfair to candidates and not in the best interests of the company. Test results should therefore be treated merely as one measure in the overall evaluative process. Indeed, most experts believe that even the best tests cannot substitute for face-to-face interviews.

Interviews   When moral issues arise in interviewing, they almost always relate to the manner in which the interview was conducted. Human-resources experts rightly caution against rudeness, coarseness, hostility, and condescension in interviewing job applicants. In guarding against these qualities, personnel managers would do well to focus on the humanity of the individuals who sit across the desk from them, mindful of the very human need that has brought those people into the office. This is especially true when the interviewer might not otherwise identify closely with the person being interviewed because of cultural or other differences. Interviewers must exercise care to avoid thoughtless comments that may hurt or insult the person being interviewed—for instance, a passing remark about a person's physical disability or personal situation (a single parent, for instance). A comment that an unthinking interviewer considers innocent or even friendly might be experienced as distressing or intrusive by the person across the table. For example, it may be very uncomfortable for candidates when interviewers ask about their political affiliation or how they intend to vote.

Roland Wall, a job placement counsellor for individuals with disabilities in the United States, describes taking a developmentally disabled client, with an IQ of about 70, for a job interview. The personnel manager emerged from the room in which Wall's client was taking an initial test along with several other job applicants. The personnel manager asked Wall where his client was and was amazed to learn that she had gone in along with the others for testing. "Really?" he said. "I didn't see one in there." This personnel manager is probably more sensitive about people with disabilities than many employers, given his willingness to interview Wall's client, yet he assumed that because she was mentally retarded, the applicant would look a certain way—she would look like "one."[22]

Even though everyone suffers from conscious and unconscious biases and stereotypes, interviewers should strive to free themselves as much as possible from these "idols of the mind," as the English philosopher Francis Bacon (1561–1626) called them. As Bacon put it: "The human understanding is like a false mirror, which, receiving rays irregularly, distorts and discolors the nature of things by mingling its own nature with it."[23] In short, we view things, people included, through the lens of our own preconceptions. Interviewers need to keep this fact in mind. Panel interviews with a uniform list of questions for all applicants can also help increase objectivity. That technique, however, wouldn't have helped the exceptionally well-qualified applicant who was turned down for a vice-presidential position at a West Coast sports company because he wore a dark, three-piece suit to the interview. His casually dressed interviewers simply took it for granted that he wouldn't fit into their laid-back operation.[24]

Proponents of the new but increasingly popular "situational interview" claim that it predicts future job performance more accurately than a standard interview does and also more accurately than résumé analysis, personality assessments, or pen-and-paper tests.[25] In situational interviews, job candidates have to engage in role-playing in a mock office scenario. For example, they might have to face a company manager pretending to be a disgruntled customer. Meanwhile the company's interviewers watch and assess the candidates' performance: how they process the information given by "the customer," how they decide to handle the situation, the words they choose, even their body language. Proponents of the technique believe that job candidates have a harder time putting on a false front than in a standard interview, but there's no escaping the fact that bias and preconceptions can still affect the interviewers' assessment of the likely job performance of different candidates based on their role-playing skills.

Promotions

It's no secret that factors besides job qualifications often determine promotions. How long you've been with a firm, how well you're liked, whom you know, even when you were last promoted—all these influence promotions in the real business world. As with hiring, the key moral ideal here is fairness. Nobody would seriously argue that promoting the unqualified is fair or justifiable. It's a breach of duty to owners, employees, and ultimately the general public. But many reasonable people debate whether promoting by job qualification alone is the fairest thing to do. Are other criteria admissible? If so, when, and how much weight should those criteria carry? These are tough questions with no easy answers. To highlight the problem we consider seniority, inbreeding, and nepotism, three factors that sometimes serve as bases for promotions.

Seniority *Seniority* refers to longevity on a job or with a firm. Frequently job transfers or promotions are made strictly on the basis of seniority, but problems can occur with this promotion method. Imagine that personnel manager Manuel Rodriguez needs to fill the job of quality-control supervisor. Carol Martin seems slightly better qualified for the job than Jim Turner, except in one respect: Turner has been on the job for three years longer than Martin. Whom should Rodriguez promote to quality-control supervisor?

The answer isn't easy. Those who'd argue for Carol Martin—opponents of seniority—would undoubtedly claim that the firm has an obligation to fill the job with the most qualified person. In this way, the firm is best served and the most qualified are rewarded. Those advancing Turner's promotion—proponents of seniority—would contend that the company should be loyal to its senior employees, that it should reward them for faithful service. In this way, employees have an incentive to work hard and to remain with the firm.

When company policies indicate what part seniority should play in promotions and job transfers, the problem abates but does not vanish. We can still wonder about the morality of the policy itself. In cases in which no clear policy exists, the problem begs for an answer.

The difficulty of the question is compounded by the fact that seniority in itself does not necessarily indicate competence or loyalty. Just because Jim Turner has been on the job three years longer than Carol Martin does not necessarily mean he is more competent or more loyal. Of course, in some instances seniority may be a significant indicator of job qualifications. A pilot who has logged hundreds of hours of flying time with an airline is much more likely to be better qualified for captaincy than one who hasn't.

Then there's the question of employee expectations. If employees expect seniority to count substantially, management can injure morale and productivity by overlooking it. True, worker morale might suffer equally should seniority alone determine promotions. Ambitious and competent workers might see little point in refining skills and developing talents when positions are doled out strictly on the basis of longevity.

It seems impossible, then, to say precisely what part, if any, seniority ought to play in promotions. But this is just all the more reason for management to consider carefully its seniority policies. Of paramount importance in any decision is that management remembers its twin responsibilities of promoting on the basis of qualifications and of recognizing prolonged and constructive contributions to the firm. A policy that provides for promotions strictly on the basis of qualifications seems heartless, whereas one that promotes by seniority alone seems mindless. The challenge for management is how to merge these dual responsibilities in a way that is beneficial to the firm and fair to all concerned.

Inbreeding All the cautions about seniority apply with equal force to *inbreeding*, the practice of promoting exclusively from within the firm. In theory, whenever managers must fill positions they should look only to competence. The most competent, whether within or outside the firm, should receive the position. In this way responsibilities to owners are best served.

In practice, however, managers must seriously consider the impact of outside recruitment on in-house morale. Years of loyal service, often at great personal expense, invariably create a unique relationship between employer and employee and, with it, unique obligations of gratitude. The 18 years that Christina Zhuy has worked for National Textile create a relationship between her and the firm that does not exist between the firm and an outsider it may wish to hire for the job Zhuy seeks. Some would argue that management has a moral obligation to remember this loyalty when determining promotions, especially when outside recruitment departs from established policy.

Nepotism *Nepotism* is the practice of showing favouritism to relatives and close friends. Suppose a manager promoted a relative strictly because of the relationship between them. Such an action would raise a number of moral concerns, chief among them disregard of managerial responsibilities to the organization and of fairness to other employees.

Not all instances of nepotism need raise serious moral concerns. For example, when a firm is strictly a family operation and has as its purpose providing work for family members, nepotistic practices are generally justified. Many people believe that it is unfair to exclude a person from consideration for a job just because he or she is a relative or friend of someone in the company. But Advest Group, a U.S. brokerage firm, traditionally brings sons and daughters into the organization. "Good work ethics seem to run throughout families," says senior vice-president Robert Rulevich.[26] But that is probably a minority view. Today, it is more common for companies to prohibit the employment of relatives, or at least to restrict such employment in order to avoid situations in which one relative is supervising another.

On the other hand, when it comes to senior executives the matter may be different. In the United States there's a long list of well-known, publicly traded companies that employ in lucrative positions the wives, children, and in-laws of their top managers or board members.[27] In Canada, it is estimated that "roughly 40% of the largest 100 companies by market cap on the TSX have handed down control to a second, or even later, generation."[28] The companies in question may well contend that they hire and promote only on the basis of merit. Adam Bellow claims, "it's well established that talents and abilities run in families." Still, it is rather difficult to disagree with Charles Elson of the Weinberg Center for Corporate Governance at the University of Delaware (U.S.), who says, "It just doesn't look right." "It creates the appearance of a conflict of interest," adds Nell Minnow of the Corporate Library, a U.S. research firm focusing on corporate governance issues. "The burden of proof is on the company to prove it's an arm's-length transaction, and that's hard to do."[29]

Even when a friend, a relative, or a spouse of a manager or some other high-ranking employee is qualified for a position or deserving of promotion, the decision can hurt company morale, breed resentment and jealousy, and create problems with regard to future placement, scheduling, or dismissal of the person. It can make him or her an object of distrust and hostility within the organization and even discourage qualified outsiders from seeking

employment with the firm. Such undesirable consequences are apt to happen especially when there are "family feuds" during succession to top positions. To add oil to the fire, recent research seems to indicate that family-controlled companies tend to outperform their non-nepotistic peers.[30]

Discipline and Discharge

For an organization to function in an orderly, efficient, and productive way, managers and personnel departments establish guidelines for behaviour based on such factors as appearance, punctuality, dependability, efficiency, and cooperation. This is not the place to examine the morality of specific rules and regulations, only the organization's treatment of employees when infractions occur.

For example, it's one thing to speak with a person privately about some infraction and quite another to chastise or punish the person publicly. Also, trying to correct someone's behaviour on a graduated basis, from verbal warning to dismissal, is different from firing someone for a first infraction. The point is that discipline, although desirable and necessary, raises concerns about fairness, non-injury, and respect for persons in the way it's administered. To create an atmosphere of fairness, one in which rules and standards are equally applied, the principles of just cause and due process must operate.

Just cause requires that reasons for discipline or discharge deal directly with job performance. AIC Securities in Chicago, for example, lacked just cause for terminating with one day's notice an experienced employee with a good record because he had been diagnosed as having brain cancer.[31] And it's difficult to see why smoking in your car on company property is just cause for dismissal, even though you can be fired for it at two Motorola plants in Illinois.[32] Of course, distinguishing between a job-related and a non-job-related issue is not always easy and can be controversial.

In addition, how a person behaves outside work is often incompatible with the image a company wishes to project. Does the organization have a right to discipline its employees for off-the-job conduct? The answer depends largely on the legitimate extent of organizational influence over individual lives—that is, on where precisely a company's legitimate interests stop and a worker's private life begins. Such concerns raise complex questions about privacy that are explored further in Chapter 7.

The second principle related to fair worker discipline and discharge is *due process*, which refers to the fairness of the procedures an organization uses to impose sanctions on employees. Of particular importance is that the rules be clear and specific, that they be administered consistently and without discrimination or favouritism, and that workers who have violated them be given a fair and impartial hearing. Due process requires both the hearing of grievances and the setting up of a step-by-step procedure by which an employee can appeal a managerial decision.

It is useful to distinguish among four types of discharge. *Firing* is for-cause dismissal—the result of employee theft, gross insubordination, release of proprietary information, and so on. *Termination* results from an employee's poor performance—that is, from his or her failure to fulfill expectations. *Layoff* usually refers to hourly employees and implies that they are "subject to recall," whereas *position elimination* designates the permanent elimination of a job as a result of workforce reduction, plant closing, or departmental consolidation.

Before dismissing an employee, management should follow a rational and unbiased decision-making process and analyze carefully the reasons leading to that decision. The organization must ask itself if its treatment of the employee follows the appropriate procedures for that type of discharge, as those procedures are outlined in the employee handbook, collective bargaining agreement, or corporate policy statement. In addition, the company must guard against preferential treatment. Have there been employees who behaved in the same way but were not let go?

Evenhandedness and strict compliance with established procedures may not guarantee fairness. For example, unless it is stated in the contract or employees have union representation, a company may not (depending on the type of case and where it occurs) be legally obligated to give reasons for firing an employee, and it may not be legally obligated to give advance notice. When employers terminate someone without notice or cause, they may have been strictly faithful to contractual agreement or established practice, but have they been just? Have they acted morally?

In answering that question, it's helpful to distinguish between two employer responsibilities. Employers bear the responsibility of terminating the employment of workers who fail to fulfill their contractual obligations, but they are also obliged to terminate these workers as painlessly as possible. In other words, although employers have the right to fire, this does not mean they have the right to fire an employee in whatever way they choose. Because firing can be so materially and psychologically destructive to employees, management should take steps to ease its effects. Moreover, crass firings hurt a company's reputation and impair its ability to attract top-notch employees.[33]

The literature on personnel management provides many suggestions for handling the discharge of employees more compassionately and humanely, ranging from the recommendation not to notify employees of termination on Fridays, birthdays, wedding anniversaries, or the day before a holiday, to various steps to respect the terminated employee's privacy and dignity.[34] A company should not notify employees of their dismissal by email,[35] nor should it give a longtime employee a pink slip, as General Dynamics did, on the day he returns to work after burying his six-year-old son.[36] And, certainly, no employer should do what John Patterson, former head of NCR, a U.S. computer company, once did. He fired an underperforming executive by taking his desk and chair outside, dousing it with kerosene and setting it on fire in front of the poor man.[37] Even when an employee is fired for misconduct, the company must be careful not to defame the person.

One obvious thing employers can do to ease the trauma of firing is to provide sufficient notice. Morally speaking, what constitutes sufficient notice of termination or discharge depends primarily on the nature of the job, the type of skill involved, the availability of similar jobs, and the employee's length of service. Whenever employers have reason to suspect that employees will react to notice of their terminations in a hostile, destructive way, sufficient notice might merely take the form of severance pay. Ideally, the length of notice should be spelled out in a work contract.

For most people who have to do it, firing a worker is painfully difficult, at times impossible. In part to help managers perform the dirty job of terminating, enlightened organizations sometimes enlist the services of displacement companies. For a fee, the displacement company sends in a counsellor who assists the displaced employee to assess personal strengths and weaknesses, analyze the causes of the dismissal, and start planning a job search. This makes the distasteful task of firing a little more palatable than it would otherwise be. And to be sure, it protects the company from being sued by the seasoned, middle-aged executive who may feel trifled with. Self-serving interests notwithstanding, companies using displacement experts deserve recognition for their attempt to ease the anguish of those who must fire and to help those terminated salvage both their interrupted careers and their self-respect.

Today, with frequent downsizing and outsourcing, moral management requires careful study of responsibilities to workers in times of job elimination. It's debatable whether Valiant Networks, a U.S. consulting company, did that. After laying off nearly one hundred workers, it asked them to return half of the bonuses they'd received six months earlier. Those bonuses were contingent on the employees staying with the company for a year—which the axed employees hadn't done.[38] When weighing their responsibilities to terminated employees, companies need to remember that termination of employment affects not only workers but their families and the larger community as well. It is impossible here to specify further what measures can or should be taken to ease the effects of displacement. Different circumstances suggest different approaches. Whatever the specific circumstances, though, firms have a moral obligation to terminate workers only for just cause and as a last resort, to follow due process and fair organizational procedures, and to treat dismissed employees with dignity and compassion.

Wages

Every employer faces the problem of setting wage rates and establishing salaries. From the moral point of view, it is very easy to say that firms should pay a fair and just wage, but what constitutes such a wage? So many variables are involved that no one can say with mathematical precision what a person should be paid for a job. The employee's contribution to the firm, the market for labour and products, the competitive position of the company, the bargaining power of the firm and unions, seasonal labour fluctuations, and individual needs conspire to make a simple answer impossible. The issue is further complicated by the fact that remuneration can also include health care, retirement programs, perquisites like tips or a company car, and bonuses, commissions, and other incentive awards.

Although some writers believe that a fair wage is whatever an employee is willing to accept,[39] the moral issues involved are more complex than that. In an ethical organization the basis of remuneration should be distributive justice, with a wage and salary system that centres on the employee's value to the business—his or her contribution to the organization—and not on extrinsic, non-job-related considerations such as being a single parent or a relative of the CEO.[40] In addition, salary judgments should be made on criteria which are clear, publicly available and objectively applied. Consideration of the following more specific factors can provide the well-intentioned business manager with some ethical guidelines and help minimize the chances of setting unfair wages and salaries:

1. *What is the law?* Provincial and territorial laws require businesses to pay their employees at least the minimum wage set for their jurisdictions (which ranges from $8.50 per hour in Nunavut to $7 in Newfoundland). An organization can, of course, satisfy the minimum requirements of the law and still not act morally, especially if one considers that a minimum wage of $10 per hour would earn one an annual pay of only $20,000, which is below the current poverty line.

2. *What is the prevailing wage in the industry?* The salaries given for similar positions in the industry can provide some direction for arriving at a fair wage, but this factor is not a moral barometer, and relying on it can be problematic.

3. *What is the community wage level?* This point recognizes that some communities have a higher cost of living than others. For example, it is more expensive to live in Vancouver or Toronto than, say, in Paris, Ontario. To ignore the cost of living would be to jeopardize worker welfare.

4. *What is the nature of the job itself?* Some jobs require more training, experience, and education than others. Some are physically or emotionally more demanding. Some jobs are downright dangerous, others socially undesirable. Risky or unskilled jobs often attract the least educated and the most desperate for work, thus leading to possible worker exploitation. Although it is impossible to draw a precise correlation between the nature of the job and what someone should be paid, a relationship exists that must be taken into account.

5. *Is the job secure? What are its prospects?* Employment that promises little or no security fails to fulfill a basic need of employees. In such cases employers should seek to compensate workers for this deprivation through higher pay, better fringe benefits, or both. On the other hand, a secure job with a guarantee of regular work and excellent retirement benefits (for example, a civil service position) may justify a more moderate wage. In addition, a relatively low salary may be acceptable for a job that is understood to be a stepping-stone to better positions inside the organization.

6. *What are the employer's financial capabilities?* What can the organization afford to pay? A startup company with minimal cash flow and a narrow profit margin may be unable to pay more than a minimum wage. A mature company with a secure market position might easily afford to pay better wages.

7. *What are other employees inside the organization earning for comparable work?* To avoid discrimination and unfairness in setting wage rates, it is important to look at what the organization is already paying its present employees for work of a similar nature. Gross salary disparities that are not warranted by the nature of the work, the experience required, or other objective considerations can also hurt employee morale.

Guidelines 6 and 7 have recently drawn widespread attention as both employees and stockholders have begun scrutinizing the benefits and perks paid to top management. Studies have found that huge salary imbalances between those at the top and their employees create resentment.[41] The greater the differential grows, the more employee loyalty declines and the more turnover increases.[42] That information will come as no surprise to employees of ITT in the United States, who saw the company lavish $10.4 million on Chairman Rand Araskog and $5.3 million on President Bob Rowman the very same year that it fired 125 of the 200 workers at company headquarters in order to save $20 million.[43] At the same time, many stockholders are getting tired of seeing company profits going to its executives and not to them; hence, the uproar when the Walt Disney Company awarded CEO Michael Eisner a ten-year pay package that yielded him about $771 million. Eisner's handsome reward came only two months after the company had granted Michael Ovitz a severance package of $38.9 million in cash plus options on 3 million shares worth $54 million—for having served as Disney's president for 14 months.[44]

Canadian corporate executives did not do too badly either. Tony Comper retired as CEO of the BMO Financial Group in the spring of 2007 with stock options, shares and share units worth about $80 million, in addition to his S13 million salary.[45] Within months of his retirement, BMO was announcing 15 percent year-to-date losses in net income and earnings per share due to the impact of

$829 million loss in the commodities business and a $135 million restructuring charge.[46] Of the 270 executives listed as reporting their compensation in the *Globe and Mail's* annual review of CEO compensation (for 2006), 210 made salaries ranging from $1 million to just under $55 million.[47]

Two final factors are of equal importance with guidelines 1 through 7. The first is job performance. Some people work harder or are more talented, and thus accomplish more for the organization. Most businesses rightly seek to recognize and award achievement. As with an employee's base salary, however, bonuses and other awards must relate to business performance and be a function of criteria that are measurable and objectively applied. This point is clearly made with regard to executive compensation in a recent proposal by the Institute of Corporate Directors.[48] The second factor is how the wage agreement was arrived at. A fair wage presupposes a fair work contract, and the fairness of a work contract requires free negotiation and the informed and mutual consent of both employer and employee. Where a surplus exists of workers who are willing and able to perform a given job, the employer enjoys a strong bargaining advantage. In situations where that advantage is great and workers are desperate for employment, the fairness of the work contract may be called into question.

Employees are motivated by many things. One of them is the desire to be fairly treated. Feeling that they have been reasonably rewarded for their efforts is crucial to people's self-esteem. Thus, besides helping management discharge one of its prime responsibilities, the establishment of fair wages may enhance the work environment and remove a potential source of job dissatisfaction. This fact may help explain why economists have found that, year in and year out, firms paying the highest wages are the most profitable.[49] Costco, for example, which pays significantly better wages and provides more generous benefits than does Wal-Mart, is also more profitable, and its employees more loyal and productive.[50] Likewise, business is booming at the clothing company American Apparel, which, in an industry characterized by sweatshops, pays its workers $13 an hour along with overtime, health insurance, and subsidized lunches. (It even pays its mostly Latino workers while they take English classes on the premises.)[51] But nobody surpasses Semco, the Brazilian company, which lets workers set their own hours and pay. Its revenue increased from $35 million to $212 million in just six years.[52]

UNIONS

This chapter and Chapter 7 are concerned with a number of moral issues that arise in the workplace between employer and employees. However, no discussion of the workplace should overlook one of the basic institutions structuring employer–employee relations, determining the terms and conditions of employment, and shaping the environment in which people work—namely, labour unions. Accordingly, this section briefly examines the history and economic role of unions, the ideals that motivate them, and some of the moral dilemmas they raise.

History of the Union Movement

Many economists, sociologists and students of the union movement give it primary credit for raising the standard of living and increasing the security of working people throughout the world. Certainly almost all the benefits enjoyed by employees today in the more advanced nations, whether they happen to be in unions or not, can be traced to union victories or to union-backed legislation. At the same time, the benefits that unions brought to workers—higher wages, paid vacations, health benefits, retirement pensions, and increased job security—have contributed, in turn, to social stability and, through enhanced demand, to economic growth itself. Yet, as the history of the labour movement in Canada and the United States[53] reveals, employers have opposed unionization and union demands almost every step of the way—often with deadly violence.

Just as the roots of capitalism can be traced to the handicraft guilds, so the earliest efforts of Canadian unionism can be found in the craft unions of the early nineteenth century. At that time, groups of skilled artisans formed "crowds," loosely structured but disciplined groups, who came together for two basic reasons: to equalize their relationship with their employers and to professionalize their crafts. They agreed on acceptable wages and working hours and pledged not to work for any employer who didn't provide them. They also set minimal admission standards for their crafts. One of the earliest records of such "union" activities is to be found in an act of the Nova Scotia legislature aimed at controlling the "great numbers of . . . Journeymen and Workmen, in the Town of Halifax, and other parts of the province, [who] have, by unlawful Meetings and Combinations, endeavour to regulate the rate of wages, and to effectuate illegal purposes."[54]

Despite the hostile attitude of employers and the law, skilled workers—printers in Toronto, Montreal, Hamilton, or Halifax; shoemakers in Hamilton and Montreal—formed their own groups to deal with issues specific to their own trade as they arose from time to time. Some of these groups were even prepared to strike in support of their demands. The most famous and significant of these was the Printers' Strike of 1872 in Toronto. By the early 1870s craftsmen in many towns were pressing for a reduction in the normal ten- or twelve-hour workday. In the face of employer inflexibility, workers' leagues decided to launch a series of strikes beginning in Hamilton, Ontario in May 1872. But the Toronto Typographical Union jumped the gun and went on strike on March 25, after its demand for a nine-hour workday (in a six-day work week) was rejected. Though centred on George Brown's *Globe* (the forerunner of today's *Globe and Mail*), the strike engulfed almost all of Toronto's newspapers. On April 15, the Toronto Trades Assembly organized a huge march and rally in support of the strikers' demands. Next day a group of anti-union newspaper owners, led by George Brown (yes, one of the fathers of Confederation) secured the arrest of the entire 24-member strike committee on charges of conspiracy. Partly in response to the public outcry against Brown's heavy-handedness, Prime Minister John A. Macdonald introduced the *Trade Unions Act* (1872) by the provisions of which trade unions were exempt from liability to conspiracy charges. Trade Unions were now legal, though they did not achieve their goal of a nine-hour workday. Further, employers did not have to recognize them or negotiate with them, while certain amendments to the *Criminal Code*, sponsored again by Macdonald, put severe restrictions on union organizing efforts and workers' protest activities like picketing and demonstrations.[55]

Still, the legalization, at least on paper, of union activity encouraged union leaders to try and develop a broader and more permanent working-class presence in Canadian public life. The Canadian Labour Union was formed in 1873 but lasted for only five years. In 1881 attempts to revive a national labour organization led to the formation of the Canadian Labour Congress but whose life was even briefer than that of the Labour Union. In the meantime, an important development was taking place in the Canadian labour movement. Local trades councils at first in Ontario (especially in the Hamilton–Toronto area) and later Canada-wide, were increasingly coming under the influence of and developing connections with the first truly national labour movement in the United States, established in 1869, known as the Knights of Labor. The interests of the Knights were not merely "bread-and-butter," as their platform included programs for raising the educational level and social awareness of their members as well as sustained efforts to influence socially progressive legislation. They were also inclusive in that they called together all workers, skilled and unskilled, black and white, male and female, into one mighty association (though they did exclude the Chinese and turn a blind eye to the segregation of blacks!). Though its appeal was forceful and popular in Canada for many years, the movement fizzled out by the mid-1890s, partly due to internal frictions and largely due to the downturn in the economy starting in the late 1870s.

In 1883 the Toronto Trades Council (an association of five different trades which had played a very important role in the Printers' Strike of 1872) and the Knights of Labor called a meeting of various unionists at which the Trades and Labour Congress of Canada (TLC) was established. The TLC would go through many changes and face critical challenges to develop at the beginning of World War II as a labour organization that represented primarily the skilled (trades or craft) workers. In 1926 the All-Canadian Congress of Labour was formed in opposition to the TLC which was dominated by Canadian affiliates of American trades unions. The ACCL platform objected to the American domination of Canadian labour affairs and pledged to cater to the interests of industrial

workers (whose numbers were increasing rapidly to keep up with the demands of industrial expansion) most of whom were unskilled.

In 1940 the ACCL merged with the Canadian section of the Congress of Industrial Organizations (affiliates of American industrial unions) to form the Canadian Congress of Labour (CCL). The CCL had some 360,000 members by 1956 when it joined the Trades and Labour Congress of Canada to form the Canadian Labour Congress. Today the CLC is the umbrella organization for Canada's national and international unions, the provincial and territorial federations of labour, and 136 district labour councils, which represent over 3 million members.

The cause of unionism was significantly advanced during World War II, when in response to labour unrest, the government issued *Order-in-Council* P.C. 1003 of 1944, which in effect gave Canadian workers and their unions even more protections than their American counterparts had been enjoying for almost a decade under the *U.S. National Labor Relations Act, 1935* (called the *Wagner Act*). Among other items, P.C. 1003 included: union recognition by certification; right of union to represent all employees in a bargaining unit; the duty of employer and unions to meet and negotiate in good faith; prohibition on strikes and lockouts during the term of a collective agreement; and the maintenance of a labour relations board to administer all the provisions. When the new federal *Industrial Relations and Disputes Investigation Act* was adopted in 1948 to replace the wartime emergency regulations, it contained all the provisions of P.C. 1003 together with provisions for the compulsory conciliation of disputes. In 1967 the *I.R.D.I. Act* was consolidated with other labour statutes into the *Canada Labour Code*. Amendments to the *Code* in 1973 made collective bargaining easier and extended the right to previously excluded groups (for example, supervisors, employed professionals, private police). It should be mentioned that the *Canada Labour Code* covers workers under federal jurisdiction but comparable provincial and territorial statutes apply to other workers.[56]

In recent years, unions have been more and more on the defensive, as the industries in which they have been traditionally based have declined. The number of days lost to strikes, for instance, has been at a record low, and many unions have been forced to go along with decreases in wages and benefits. Meanwhile, the general political climate has been unfavourable to labour for the past two decades as politicians and electorates veer more and more to the economic right. In the States the federal government, under President George W. Bush, has moved to tighten its regulation of unions and to restrict their ability to organize.[57] On the legal front, labour unions in the United States suffered a major setback when the U.S. Supreme Court ruled that private employers could "replace permanently" striking workers, even though the 1935 *Wagner Act* makes it illegal for employers to retaliate against workers who go on strike by "firing" them. In Canada too the picture is a bit murky. Two provincial jurisdictions

(B.C. and Quebec) prohibit "replacement" workers ("scabs") but the *Canada Labour Code* does not. There is, however, an important vote coming up in Parliament in November 2007 on an amendment to the *Code* (known as Bill C-252) that would make the hiring of replacement workers illegal.

Whatever happens, as long as workers risk losing their jobs because they go on a strike, then the balance of power in collective bargaining is dramatically altered. Instead of negotiating in good faith, a company might now provoke a strike, hire new workers to replace the pickets, and cut costs. And management has done exactly that in a number of cases, as many corporations have grown increasingly and aggressively anti-union. Employers hire anti-union management consultants, hold mandatory anti-union meetings, show anti-union videos at work, have supervisors meet individually with employees to disparage unions, and distribute anti-union leaflets at work or mail them to employees' homes.[58] They try to break existing unions or prevent their formation by harassing and even firing pro-union workers and by waging vigorous, often illegal anti-union campaigns.[59] For example, Wal-Mart Stores Inc. generally regarded as extremely anti-union, in 2005 closed down its store in Jonquière, Quebec, on the grounds that demands from the workers' union would make it impossible for the store to sustain itself. In response, Michael Fraser, national director of the United Food & Commercial Workers Canada, said, "Wal-Mart has fired these workers not because the store was losing money but because the workers exercised their right to join a union." Later the same year, the Quebec Labour Relations Board confirmed Fraser's view by ruling in favour of former Wal-Mart workers on the grounds that the company had acted illegally in dismissing them for engaging in union activity. A few years earlier in the United States, when the meat-cutting department of a Texas Wal-Mart voted to join the Union of Food and Commercial Workers, the company responded by closing the department and firing the offending employees.[60]

Union Ideals

From the beginning, unions have been driven by an attempt to protect workers from abuses of power at the hands of employers. This effort is based on the indisputable premise that employers have tremendous power over individual workers. They can hire and fire, relocate and reassign, set work hours and wages, create rules and control working conditions. Acting individually, a worker rarely is an employer's equal in negotiating any of these items. The position of most workers acting independently is further weakened by their lack of capital, occupational limitations, and personal and family needs. Furthermore, whereas employers obviously need workers, they rarely need any particular worker. They can, generally speaking, select whomever they want, for whatever reasons they choose.

Interestingly, Adam Smith himself recognized this fundamental imbalance in his classic *The Wealth of Nations*. Regarding the respective bargaining power of workers and their "masters," or employers, he wrote that "upon all ordinary occasions" employers "have the advantage in the dispute, and force the other into a compliance with their terms."

> The masters, being fewer in number, can combine much more easily . . . . We have no acts of parliament against combining to lower the price of work; but many against combining to raise it. In all such disputes the masters can hold out much longer . . . . Though they did not employ a single workman, [employers] could generally live a year or two upon the stocks which they have already acquired. Many workmen could not subsist a week, few could subsist a month, and scarce any a year without employment. In the long run the workman may be as necessary to his master as his master is to him, but the necessity is not so immediate.[61]

In an attempt, then, to redress the balance of power in their dealings with employers, workers band together. In acting as a single body, a union, workers in effect make employers dependent on them in a way that no individual worker can. The result is a rough equality or mutual dependence, which serves as the basis for collective bargaining—negotiations between the representatives of organized workers and their employers over things such as wages, hours, rules, work conditions, and, increasingly, participation in decisions affecting the workplace. As the World Bank and others have recognized, by giving workers a collective voice, unions do not just push up wages. They can also improve productivity and efficiency, promote stability in the workforce, and make government less likely to meddle in the labour market.[62]

Certainly no one can object to unionism's initial and overriding impulse: to protect workers from abuse and give them a voice in matters that affect their lives. Indeed, those two goals reflect two lofty moral ideals: non-injury and autonomy. Ironically, it is out of respect for these ideals that some individuals criticize modern unions.

The critics argue that union shops infringe on the autonomy and right of association of individual workers. Even if workers are not required to join the union but only to pay some equivalent to union dues, the critics contend that this still infringes on their freedom. In addition, evidence suggests that companies in alliance with unions sometimes treat non-union personnel less favourably than union members. Some people contend that such treatment is discriminatory. Whether or not it is, it certainly raises a moral question about the right to determine for oneself organizational membership and participation.

Taking the union's viewpoint reveals competing ideals and other consequences that must be considered. First, there is organized labour's ideal of solidarity, which is vital to collective bargaining and to winning worker equality. Union proponents point to the fact that unionized workers earn more than other workers. For example, Statistics Canada found that the average union worker (in 2003) is paid $21.05 an hour in contrast to the average non-union worker rate of $16.65 an hour. The per capita personal income is higher in American states with free collective bargaining than in right-to-work states. For instance, of the twenty-two right-to-work states, only Nevada and Virginia have personal incomes above the U.S. national average. Practically speaking, if workers receive union benefits without having to belong or pay dues, then they lack an incentive to join the union, which greatly weakens the union's ability to improve wages and strengthen workers' rights.

Second, there is a question of fairness. Is it fair for a non-union worker to enjoy the benefits won by union members—often at great personal and organizational expense? This question arises most forcefully when unions are attempting to establish an *agency shop*, in which all employees must pay union dues but are not required to join the union. The agency shop is designed to eliminate free-riders while respecting the individual worker's freedom of choice. Opponents claim that an agency shop does not so much eliminate free-riders as create forced passengers.

Union Tactics

The tactics unions use to try to get management to accept their demands also raise moral issues.

Direct Strikes The legal right to strike is labour's most potent tool in labour–management negotiations. A strike occurs when an organized body of workers withholds its labour to force the employer to comply with its demands. Because strikes can cause financial injuries to both employer and employee, inconvenience and perhaps worse to consumers, and economic dislocations in society, they always raise serious moral questions. On the other hand, sometimes workers cannot obtain justice and fair play in the workplace in any other way. Austin Fagothey and Milton A. Gonsalves suggest the following conditions of a justified strike:[63]

1. *Just cause*. "Just cause" refers to job-related matters. Certainly, inadequate pay, excessive hours, and dangerous and unhealthful working conditions are legitimate worker grievances and provide just cause for a strike. Revenge, personal ambition, petty jealousies, and the like do not constitute just cause and thus cannot justify a strike.

2. *Proper authorization*. For a strike to be legitimate it must be duly authorized. This means, first, that workers themselves must freely reach the decision without coercion and intimidation. Second, if the workers are organized, then the proposed strike must receive union backing (although this condition becomes difficult to apply when the local union chapter and the national organization don't see eye to eye).

3. *Last resort*. To be justified a strike must come as a last resort. This condition acknowledges the serious potential harm of strikes. A basic moral principle is that we should always use the least injurious means available to accomplish the good we desire. Since there is an array of less drastic collective-bargaining tactics that can and usually do achieve worker objectives, all these should be exhausted before a strike is called.

Even when a strike is warranted, however, not every means of implementing it is morally justified. Peaceful picketing and an attempt by striking workers to publicize their cause and peacefully persuade others not to cross the picket line are typically considered moral means of striking. Physical violence, threats, intimidation, and sabotage are not.

The preceding discussion deals with direct strikes—that is, cessation of work by employees with the same industrial grievance. There is, however, another kind of strike, far more controversial than the direct strike: the sympathetic strike.

Sympathetic Strikes A sympathetic strike occurs when workers who have no particular grievance of their own and who may or may not have the same employer decide to strike in support of others. The bigger unions become and the more diverse the workers they count among their members, the more likely are sympathetic strikes aimed at different employers. Indeed, the sympathetic strike can take on global proportions, as when American dockside workers refused to unload freighters from the Soviet Union to show support of the Solidarity movement in Poland.

Sometimes the sympathetic strike involves several groups of workers belonging to different unions but employed by the same company. Acting on a grievance, one group strikes. But because it is so small, it enlists the aid of the other groups; it asks them to engage in a sympathetic strike. Cases like these do not seem to differ in any morally significant way from direct strikes. Indeed, it might be argued that the affiliated groups have obligations of loyalty and beneficence to join the strike. It is true, of course, that the sympathetic strikers do not have personal grievances, but they do have the same unjust employer, and they are in a unique position to help remedy that injustice by withholding their labour.[64]

Sympathetic strikes involving groups of employees working for different employers differ significantly from direct strikes or sympathetic strikes against the same employer. For one thing, the employers being struck out of sympathy may be perfectly innocent victims whose treatment of workers is beyond reproach. They have lived up to their end of the work contract, only to have their workers break it.

On the other hand, such sympathetic strikes can be very effective. J. P. Stevens & Co., the second-largest company in the U.S. textile industry, fought unionization for decades. The company engaged in a variety of flagrantly unfair labour practices and refused to recognize or bargain collectively with the union, despite various court orders to do so.[65] During the boycott of J. P. Stevens products, United Auto Workers members at a General Motors plant in Canada refused to install J. P. Stevens carpeting in the cars they were producing, thus shutting down the assembly line. In less than half a day, J. P. Stevens carpeting was gone from the plant. Had U.S. workers done something similar, both they and the textile workers union would have been subject to legal action, but J. P. Stevens would not have been able to refuse to bargain as long as it did.

Boycotts and Corporate Campaigns   Besides strikes, unions also use boycotts to support their demands. A primary boycott occurs when union members and their supporters refuse to buy products from a company being struck. A secondary boycott occurs when people refuse to patronize companies that handle products of struck companies. Although the *Taft-Hartley Act* in the United States prohibits secondary boycotts, they still occur when unions urge American shoppers not to buy from stores that purchase products from companies being struck. In a recent decision, the Supreme Court of Canada upheld, on the basis of the *Charter*, the right of unions to engage in secondary picketing and other protests provided that such conduct does not involve "tortuous or criminal conduct."[66]

The express purpose of any boycott is the same as a strike: to hurt the employer or company financially and thus strengthen the union's bargaining position. In general, a boycott is justifiable when it meets the same conditions as a strike. In the case of the secondary boycott, which is like a sympathetic strike, the damage is extended to those whose only offence may be that they are handling the products of the unjust employer—and perhaps they are handling them out of financial necessity. In such cases, Fagothey and Gonsalves reject secondary boycotts. But this assessment seems too automatic and doesn't allow us to weigh the likely harms and benefits in particular cases.[67]

A relatively new pressure tactic in the United States is the so-called corporate campaign, in which unions enlist the cooperation of a company's creditors or corporate customers to pressure the company to unionize or comply with union demands. The tactic first gained widespread recognition after it was successfully used to help the U.S. Amalgamated Clothing & Textile Workers Union win contracts with Farah Manufacturing Company, a Texas-based men's garment maker. Union representatives persuaded retailers in Birmingham, Alabama, to stop selling Farah slacks by threatening them with a consumer boycott and then persuaded Farah's major creditors to help mediate the dispute.

Another version of this tactic is the one initiated in 2002 by the Graphic Communications International Union (GCIU) to get a neutrality agreement with Quebecor World, a Canadian company and one of the world's largest commercial printing companies (and whose Chairman of the Board at the time and currently is Brian Mulroney, the former Prime Minister of Canada). The agreement sought was to the effect that the company would remain neutral and not interfere or oppose efforts by its employees to unionize. As part of its campaign, the union targeted and asked for the support of major Quebecor customers (for example, IKEA and Victoria's Secret, for whom Quebecor printed catalogues and flyers); union members attended Quebecor shareholders meetings where they raised the issue; and they tried to mobilize support from labour unions in other countries and, through them, support from their national companies who were Quebecor customers.[68]

In another conflict, several unions in the United States cooperated in order to mount a corporate campaign to force Washington Gas Company to settle a dispute with the International Union of Gasworkers. The Teamsters, the Service Employees International Union, the Laborers' International Union, and the Communications Workers of America joined forces with several local unions to pressure Crestar Bank—where Washington Gas has a line of credit—to intervene on the union side. To lean on Crestar, the unions had at their disposal pension funds, payroll accounts, normal operating capital for their organizations, and even the mortgages on their buildings. Crestar complained that it was only caught in the middle. "We are not a party to the dispute," said spokesman Barry Koling. "We are neutral with respect to the issues between them." But union spokesman Jorge Rivera responded, "We judge our business partners by their actions concerning workers."[69]

At the heart of the corporate campaign is the issue of corporate governance. In pressuring financial institutions with mass withdrawals and cancellations of policies, unions and administrators of public-employee pension funds are trying to influence those institutions' policies and business relationships. And when the financial institutions accede to union demands, they in turn pressure the recalcitrant company to change its business policies. The harshest critics of the corporate campaign call it corporate blackmail. Its champions view it as an effective way to get financial institutions and companies to become good corporate citizens. Such tactics, they say, are necessary at a time when union wages are stagnating and when management has been so successful at exploiting labour laws and regulations to undermine unions and thwart their recruitment efforts.

SUMMARY

1. A number of thinkers believe that too many corporations routinely violate the civil liberties of their employees. Historically, this authoritarianism stems from (a) the rise of professional management and personnel engineering and (b) the common-law doctrine that employees can be discharged without cause ("employment at will").

2. Some very successful companies have taken the lead in respecting employees' rights and human dignity. Corporate profits and efficient management are compatible with a fair workplace environment.

3. Fairness in personnel matters requires, at least, that policies, standards, and decisions affecting workers be directly job-related, based on clear and available criteria, and applied equally.

4. Misleading job descriptions and inaccurate job specifications can injure applicants by denying them information they need to reach informed occupational decisions.

5. Ordinarily, questions of sex, age, race, national origin, and religion are non-job-related and thus should not enter into personnel decisions. Discrimination against the disabled is now expressly forbidden by law. Screening on the basis of language, physical appearance, lifestyle, or ill-considered educational requirements may also be unfair.

6. A test is valid if it measures precisely what it is designed to determine and reliable when it provides reasonably consistent results. Tests that lack validity or reliability are unfair. Tests may also be unfair if they are culturally biased or if the performance they measure does not relate directly to job performance.

7. Most moral concerns in interviewing relate to how the interview is conducted. Interviewers should focus on the humanity of the candidate and avoid allowing their personal biases to colour their evaluations.

8. A key issue in promotions is whether job qualification alone should determine who gets promoted. Seniority, or longevity on the job, is not necessarily a measure of either competency or loyalty. The challenge for management is to accommodate its twin responsibilities of promoting on the basis of qualifications and recognizing long-term contributions to the company.

9. Inbreeding, or promoting exclusively within the organization, presents challenges similar to those presented by seniority. Nepotism—showing favouritism to relatives or close friends—is not always objectionable, but it may overlook managerial responsibilities to the organization and may result in unfair treatment of other employees.

10. Most moral issues in employee discipline and discharge concern how management carries out these unpleasant tasks. Just cause and due process are necessary for fair treatment. Due process requires that there be procedures for workers to appeal discipline and discharge. To ease the trauma associated with discharge, employers should provide sufficient warning, severance pay, and perhaps displacement counselling.

11. The factors that bear on the fairness of wages include the law, the prevailing wage in the industry, the community wage level, the nature of the job, the security of the job, the company's financial capabilities, and the wages it is paying other employees for comparable work. Also important are job performance and the manner in which the wage is established. Fairness requires a legitimate work contract, one arrived at through free negotiation and informed and mutual consent.

12. Unions attempt to protect workers from abuse and give them a voice in matters that affect their lives. Critics charge that forcing workers to join unions infringes on autonomy and the right of association. They allege that union workers receive discriminatory and unlawful favouritism.

13. A direct strike is justified, argue some moral theorists, when there is just cause and proper authorization and when it is called as a last resort.

14. Sympathetic strikes involve the cessation of work in support of other workers with a grievance. When the companies involved are different, questions arise concerning possible injury and injustice to innocent employers, consumers, and workers.

15. Primary boycotts—refusing to patronize companies being struck—seem morally comparable to direct strikes. Secondary boycotts—refusing to patronize companies handling products of struck companies—are morally analogous to sympathetic strikes.
    In corporate campaigns, unions enlist the cooperation of a company's creditors or corporate customers to pressure the company to permit unionization or to comply with union demands.

CASE 6.1

AIDS in the Workplace

Carla Lombard always worked well with people. So when she opened her bagel shop Better Bagels seven years ago, she anticipated that managing her employees would be the easy part. She had worked for enough different bosses herself, she thought, to know what it took to be a good employer. Whether she was up to the financial side of running a business was her worry. As it turned out, however, Better Bagels flourished. Not only had Carla gone on to open three smaller branches of Better Bagels, but her bakery also made daily wholesale deliveries to dozens of coffee shops and restaurants around the city. No, the business was prospering. It was just that the personnel issues were more difficult than she had ever expected. Take this week, for example.

On Tuesday, Carla was in the main bagel shop when around noon Tom Walters's ex-wife, Frances, came in. Tom oversaw a lot of the early morning baking at that shop, and like most of Carla's employees put in his share of time working the sales counter. He was a good worker, and Carla had been considering promoting him next month to manager of one of the branch shops. After ordering a bagel, Frances took Carla aside. She beat around the bush for a few minutes before she got to her point, because she was there to tell Carla that Tom had AIDS. Frances said she was telling Carla because she "always liked her and thought she was entitled to know because she was Tom's employer." Carla barely knew Frances, and she was so taken aback that she was at a loss for words. She was shocked and embarrassed and didn't know whether she should even discuss Tom with Frances. While Carla was still trying to recover herself, Frances took her bagel and left.

Carla was still concerned and upset when she saw Tom the next day. Perhaps he had been thinner and looked tired more often the last few months, Carla thought to herself. But she couldn't be sure, and Tom seemed to be his usual upbeat self. Carla wanted to discuss Frances's visit with Tom, but she couldn't bring herself to mention it. She had always liked Tom, but—face it, she thought—he's my employee, not my friend. And it's his business. If I were an employee, I wouldn't want my boss asking me about my health.

Later, however, she began to wonder if it wasn't her business after all. She overheard some customers saying that people were staying away from the local Stenny's franchise because one of its cooks was reported to have AIDS. The rumour was that some of his fellow employees had even circulated a petition saying that the cook should go, but a local AIDS support group had intervened, threatening legal action. So the cook was staying, but the customers weren't. Carla knew something about AIDS and thought some of what her customers were saying was bigoted and ill informed. She was pretty sure that you couldn't transmit HIV through food—including bagel—preparation, but she thought that maybe she should double-check her information. But what was really beginning to worry her were the business implications. She didn't want a Stenny's-like situation at Better Bagels, but in her customers' comments she could see the possibility of something like that happening once the word got out about Tom, especially if she made him a manager. Carla was running a business, and even if her customers' fears might be irrational or exaggerated, she couldn't force them to visit her shops or eat her bagels.

Carla knew it was illegal to fire Tom for having AIDS, and in any case that's not the kind of person she was. But she couldn't afford to skirt the whole problem, she realized, as some large companies do, by simply sending the employee home at full pay. To be sure, doing that deprives the employee of meaningful work, but it removes any difficulties in the workplace, and the employee has no legal grounds for complaint if he or she is left on the payroll. And then, of course, there was always the question of Tom's future work performance. Putting the question of promotion aside, if he really was ill, as Frances had said, his work performance would probably decline, she thought. Shouldn't she begin developing some plan for dealing with that?

UPDATE

Frances was ill informed. Tom didn't have AIDS, but he had developed multiple sclerosis, a degenerative disease of the central nervous system. It's not fatal, but the course of the disease is unpredictable. Attacks can occur at any time and then fade away. A person can feel fine one day, only to have an attack the next day that causes blurred vision, slurred speech, numbness, or even blindness and paralysis. Tom was never worried about losing his job, and he was pretty sure he could continue to perform well at it, maybe even move higher in the business either with Carla or with another employer. But he kept his condition to himself, hiding his symptoms and covering up occasional absences and trips to the doctor, because he was worried that customers and colleagues would perceive him differently. He didn't want looks of pity if he stumbled or constant questions about how he was feeling.

Discussion Questions

1. What are the moral issues in this case? What ideals, obligations, and consequences must Carla Lombard consider? What rights, if any, are at stake? Will it make a difference whether Carla adopts a Kantian approach or a utilitarian approach to this situation?

2. Would it be wrong of Carla to ask Tom Walters about his health? Why or why not? Defend your answer by appeal to moral principle.

3. Suppose Tom has AIDS. What should Carla do? Is an employee's HIV status a job-related issue? In particular, is it a factor Carla should consider in deciding whether to promote Tom? What part, if any, should the attitudes of Tom's coworkers play in Carla's decision?

4. How should companies address the problem of public fear and prejudice when employees with AIDS have direct contact with customers?

5. Should companies develop programs or policies that deal specifically with AIDS? If so, what characteristics should they have? Or should they deal with the problem only on a case-by-case basis? Should large corporations develop AIDS-awareness programs? Or should AIDS be treated no differently than any other disease?

6. Does Tom have a moral obligation to disclose his medical condition to Carla—and, if so, at what point? Suppose a job applicant has a chronic, potentially debilitating medical condition. Should he or she reveal that fact before being hired? Would it be wrong not to mention the disease if the interviewer inquires about the applicant's health?

CASE 6.2

Web Porn at Work

Al Smetana is the founding president of a medium-sized, Saskatchewan-based manufacturing firm, Layburn Unlimited. He's proud of the way his company has grown, and done so on the basis of an organizational culture committed to honesty, integrity, and the intrinsic value of each individual. But now those values are being put to the test.

It began when Al learned that an employee had tapped into the company's computer system and figured out how to read people's email and to learn what websites they visited. Determining who the culprit was wasn't difficult. When confronted about it, the employee admitted what he had done. Al immediately terminated his employment. But as he left, the employee said angrily, "Just ask Lindley about his computer usage," referring to Craig Lindley, the director of human resources and an old friend of Al's. Although Al didn't trust the discharged employee, he was disturbed by his comment and reluctant to let it go. So he called Craig Lindley into his office and asked him about it.

After a few minutes of gentle questioning, Craig started weeping. When he recovered himself, he explained that for the past year or so he had been hooked on pornography on the Web, and at the office sometimes spent an hour or so a day looking at it. Al asked him whether his wife knew. Craig said she didn't. He was too ashamed of his habit to talk to her or anybody about it. Al then told him to take the rest of the day off, to think the matter over, and to return to Al's office the next morning. When Craig left, Al stood and looked out the window, silently asking himself what he should do.[70]

Discussion Questions

1. Is Craig Lindley's behaviour a sign of some psychological problem that Layburn Unlimited should help him overcome, perhaps with psychological counselling? Or is dismissal called for? Should Al Smetana fire Craig to send a message to other employees not to misuse company time and resources?

2. Does Al have just cause for dismissing Craig? Does it matter whether Layburn Unlimited has an explicit policy regarding computer use? Suppose it has such a policy and Craig violated it. Does that settle the matter? Would it affect your judgment of the case if Craig had helped draw up that policy?

3. Does the fact that Craig is a valued member of the company with a long record of service make a difference? Or that he is a personal friend of Al's?

4. Was it right for Al to have asked Craig about his computer usage in the first place? Did he violate Craig's privacy or civil liberties?

5. Because he fired the employee who violated the company's computer system, would it be inconsistent or unfair of Al to treat Craig any differently?

6. Al Smetana and Layburn Unlimited are committed to honesty and integrity (the upholding of which seems to support dismissal) and the intrinsic worth of each individual (which might argue for more lenient treatment). Are these values in conflict? What would you do if you were Al?

CASE 6.3

Speaking Out About Malt

When Mary Davis, associate vice-president for plant management at Whitewater Brewing Company, wrote an article for a large metropolitan newspaper in her state, she hadn't realized where it would lead. At first she was thrilled to see her words published. Then she was just worried about keeping her job.

It all started when her husband, Bob, who was working on his MBA, talked her into taking an evening class with him. She did, and to her surprise really got into the course, spending most of her weekends that semester working on her term project—a study of wine and beer marketing. Among other things her essay discussed those respectable wine companies like F. & J. Gallo that market cheap, fortified wines such as Thunderbird and Night Train Express. With an alcohol content 50 percent greater than regular wine and selling for around $1.75 a pint, these screw-top wines are seldom advertised and rarely seen outside poor neighbourhoods, but they represent a $125-million-a-year industry. Skid-row winos are their major consumers, a fact that evidently embarrasses Gallo, because it doesn't even put its company name on the label.[71]

Mary's essay went on to raise some moral questions about the marketing of malt liquor, a beer brewed with sugar for an extra punch of alcohol. It has been around for about thirty years; what is relatively new is the larger size of the container. A few years ago, the industry introduced malt liquor in 40-ounce bottles that sell for about two dollars. Packing an alcohol content roughly equivalent to six 12-ounce beers or five cocktails, 40s quickly became the favourite high of many inner-city teenagers. Ads for competing brands stress potency—"It's got more" or "The Real Power"—and often use gang slang. Get "your girl in the mood quicker and get your jimmy thicker," raps Ice Cube in a commercial for St. Ides malt liquor. Like baggy pants and baseball caps turned backward, 40s soon moved from the inner city to the suburbs. Teenage drinkers like the quick drunk, and this worries drug counsellors. They call 40s "liquid crack" and "date rape brew."[72]

Mary's instructor liked her article and encouraged her to rewrite it for the newspaper. The problem was that Whitewater also brews a malt liquor, called Rafter, that it had recently started offering in a 40-ounce bottle. True, Mary's article mentioned Whitewater's brand only in passing, but top management was distressed by her criticisms of the whole industry, which, they thought, damaged its image and increased the likelihood of further state and federal regulation. The board of directors thought Mary had acted irresponsibly, and Ralph Jenkins, the CEO, had written her a memo on the board's behalf instructing her not to comment publicly about malt liquor without first clearing her remarks with him. Mary was hurt and angry.

"I admit that the way the newspaper edited my essay and played up the malt liquor aspect made it more sensationalistic," Mary explained to her colleague Susan Watts, "but everything I said was true."

"I'm sure it was factual," replied Susan, "but the company thought the slant was negative. I mean, lots of ordinary people drink Rafter."

"I know that. Bob even drinks it sometimes. I don't know why they are so upset about my article. I barely mentioned Rafter. Anyway, it's not like Rafter is a big moneymaker. Most of our other beers outsell it."

"Well," continued Susan, "the company is really touchy about the whole issue. They think the product is under political attack these days and that you were disloyal."

"That's not true," Mary replied. "I'm no troublemaker, and I have always worked hard for Whitewater. But I do think they and the other companies are wrong to market malt liquor the way they do. It only makes a bad situation worse."

The next day Mary met with Ralph Jenkins and told him that she felt Whitewater was "invading," as she put it, her rights as a citizen. In fact, she had been invited to speak about wine and beer marketing at a local high school as part of its anti-drug campaign. She intended to keep her speaking engagement and would not subject her remarks to company censorship.

Jenkins listened but didn't say much, simply repeating what he had already written in his memo. But two days later Mary received what was, in effect, an ultimatum. She must either conform with his original order or submit her resignation.

Discussion Questions

1. Do you think Mary Davis acted irresponsibly or disloyally? Does Whitewater have a legitimate concern about her speaking out on this issue? Does the company have a right to abridge her freedom of expression?

2. Is your answer to question 1 affected by whether you agree or disagree with the views Mary Davis expressed?

3. Should there be any limits on an employee's freedom of expression? If not, why not? If so, under what circumstances is a company justified in restricting an employee's right to speak out?

4. The case presentation doesn't specify whether the newspaper article identified Mary Davis as an employee of Whitewater. Is that a relevant issue? Does it matter what position in the company Mary Davis holds?

5. What do you think Mary Davis ought to do? What moral considerations should she weigh? Does she have conflicting obligations? If so, what are they?

6. Is the company right to be worried about what Mary Davis writes or says, or is the board of directors exaggerating the potential harm to Whitewater of her discussing these issues?

7. Assume a CEO like Ralph Jenkins is legitimately worried that an employee is making damaging statements about the company. How should the CEO handle the situation? Is discharge or some sort of discipline called for? Should the company adopt a formal policy regarding employee speech? If so, what policy would you recommend that it adopt?

Notes to Chapter 6

1. See Public Health Agency of Canada, "State of the HIV/AIDS Pandemic," www.phac-aspc.gc.ca/media/nr-rp/2005/2005_1bk2_e.html.

2. "U.S. Rise in HIV Catches the Least Aware," *Wall Street Journal,* July 8, 2002, A17; and the Centers for Disease Control and Prevention, www.cdc.gov/hiv.stats.htm.

3. Of 75 Canadian and 52 American companies surveyed in 2003-04, only 7 percent of the Canadian and 8 percent of the American respondents indicated that they had a written policy on HIV/AIDS. See www.amfar.org/binary-data/AMFAR_PDF/pdf/97.pdf. "Business and HIV/AIDS: Who Me?," *A Global Review of the Business Response to HIV/AIDS, 2003–2004,* Table 23 (prepared for the World Economic Forum); see also Archie B. Carroll and Ann K. Buchholtz, *Business and Society: Ethics and Stakeholder Management,* 6th ed. (Mason, OH: Thomson South-Western, 2006), 558.

4. See David W. Ewing, "Civil Liberties in the Corporation," in Tom L. Beauchamp and Norman E. Bowie, eds., *Ethical Theory and Business,* 2nd ed. (Englewood Cliffs, NJ: Prentice Hall, 1983), 141.

5. See Don MacDonald and Allison Lampert, "U.S. Rules Reach into Canada," *The Gazette* (Montreal), February 3, 2007, C.1; Allison Lampert, "ITAR Cost Technician Job at Bell Helicopter," *The Gazette* (Montreal), February 7, 2007, B.2.

6. Ewing, "Civil Liberties," 139–140.

7. Douglas Hay and Paul Craven, *Masters, Servants, and Magistrates in Britain and the Empire 1562–1955* (Chapel Hill: University of North Carolina Press, 2004), iii.

8. For example, *The Employment Equity Act, 1995; Canada Labour Code; KcKinley v. BC Tel,* [2001] 2 S.C.R. 161; 2001 SCC 38. In the United States, the *Wagner Act* of 1935 was a watershed, as it prohibited firing workers because of union membership or union activities. The *Civil Rights Act* of 1964 entitled Americans to much the same liberties as are found in our *Charter.*

9. Clyde W. Summers, "Protecting All Employees Against Unjust Dismissal," *Harvard Business Review* 58 (January/February 1980).

10. Ewing, "Civil Liberties," 148.

11. See Tad Tuleja, *Beyond the Bottom Line* (New York: Penguin, 1987), ch. 5.

12. See Robert Levering and Milton Moskowitz, "The 100 Best Companies to Work For," *Fortune,* January 24, 2005, 61–97; and Jeffrey Pfeffer, "Practices of Successful Organizations: Employment Security," in Joseph R. DesJardins and John J. McCall, eds., *Contemporary Issues in Business Ethics,* 5th ed. (Belmont, CA: Wadsworth, 2005).

13. See www.macleans.ca/business/companies/article.jsp?content=2006101 6_134445_13445.

14. Richard W. Stevenson, "Do People and Profits Go Hand in Hand?," *New York Times,* May 9, 1996, C1.

15. "The Work Place 100," *USA Weekend,* January 22–24, 1993, 4.

16. See "Trust in Me," *Economist,* December 16, 1995, 61.

17. Sue Shellenbarger, "Workers Leave If Firms Don't Stick to Values," *San Francisco Sunday Examiner & Chronicle,* June 27, 1999, CL31.

18. See Marian M. Extejt and William N. Bockanic, "Issues Surrounding the Theories of Negligent Hiring and Failure to Fire," *Business and Professional Ethics Journal* 8 (Winter 1989).

19. "Short Hours, Big Pay and Other Little Lies," *Wall Street Journal,* October 22, 2003, B1.

20. For an updated and useful information on BFOQs, see the website for the Canadian Human Rights Commission at www.chrc-ccdp.ca/discrimination/occupational-en.asp.

21. "Employers Score New Hires," *USA Today,* July 9, 1997, 1B; "Put Applicants' Skills to the Test," *HR Magazine,* January 2000, 75–80; and "Job Applicants' First Screener Is . . . a Screen," *San Francisco Chronicle,* May 31, 2004, D3.

22. Roland Wall, "Discovering Prejudice Against the Disabled," *ETC* 44 (Fall 1987): 236.

23. Francis Bacon, *The New Organon* (New York: Bobbs-Merrill, 1960), 48.

24. Kris Maher, "The Jungle," *Wall Street Journal,* December 9, 2003, D6.

25. "Improv at the Interview," *Business Week,* February 3, 2003, 63.

26. "Work Week," *Wall Street Journal,* May 21, 1996, A1. See also Adam Bellow, *In Praise of Nepotism* (New York: Doubleday, 2003), 12.

27. "Family Ties," *San Francisco Chronicle,* April 4, 2004, J1.

28. See canadianbusiness.com/managing/article.jsp?content=200050523_68657_68657.

29. "Family Ties."

30. Danny Miller and Isabelle Le Breton-Miller, *Managing for the Long Run: Lessons in Competitive Advantage from Great Family Businesses* (Boston: Harvard Business School Press, 2005).

31. "Disability Act's First Lawsuit," *San Jose Mercury News,* November 8, 1992, 3C.

32. *San Francisco Chronicle,* July 3, 1996, B5.

33. "An Alternative to Cocker Spaniels," *Economist,* August 25, 2001, 49.

34. See, for example, "Termination with Dignity," *Business Horizons* 43 (September/October 2000): 4–10, and Jathan W. Janove, "Don't Add Insult to Injury," *HR Magazine,* May 2002, 113–120.

35. John Challenger, "Downsize with Dignity," *Executive Excellence,* March 2002, 17.

36. "Waging War in the Workplace," *Newsweek,* July 19, 1993.

37. "Special Report: Corporate Governance," *Economist,* June 15, 2002, 70.

38. "Axed Workers Asked to Return Bonuses," *San Jose Mercury News,* November 6, 2001, 1C.

39. For example, Tibor R. Machan and James E. Chester, *A Primer on Business Ethics* (Lanham, MD: Rowman & Littlefield, 2002), 88.

40. Elizabeth Vallance, *Business Ethics at Work* (Cambridge: Cambridge University Press, 1995), 71.

41. Richard Blackwell, "How Much Money Is Too Much for a CEO?," *The Globe and Mail,* Report on Business, January 16, 2006.

42. "High CEO Pay Can Damage Workers' Morale, Reports Says," *San Francisco Examiner,* May 4, 1997, CL11.

43. "Zapping the Little Folks," *Newsweek,* May 26, 1997, 54.

44. Eisner's Pay Package Incites Protest by Disney Stockholders," *San Francisco Chronicle,* February 24, 1997, D6. See also "Who Profits If the Boss Is Overfed?," *New York Times,* June 20, 1999, sec. 3, 9.

45. Janet McFarland, "'Big Leavers' Lever Bigger Pay Packages," *Globe and Mail,* Report on Business, Monday, June 4, 2007.

46. See BMO Financial Group, *Third Quarter 2007 Report to Shareholders.*

47. See www.reportonbusiness.com/ceocompensation20006.

48. See www.icd.ca/content/navigationmenu/library/
blueribboncommission07/default.htm.

49. Robert H. Frank, "Why Is Cost-Benefit Analysis So Controversial?,"
Journal of Legal Studies 29 (June 2000): 920.

50. "The Costco Way," *Business Week*, April 12, 2004, 76–77; and "How
Costco Became the Anti-Wal-Mart," *New York Times*, July 17, 2005,
sec. 3, 1.

51. "Living on the Edge at American Apparel," *Business Week*, June 27,
2005, 88–90.

52. Dave Murphy, "Set Your Own Pay and Hours," *San Francisco Chronicle*,
May 15, 2004, C1.

53. For a brief account of the rich history of the American union movement, see W. H. Shaw and V. Barry, *Moral Issues in Business*, 10th ed.
(Thomson, 2007), 291–293.

54. Quoted in C. Heron, *The Canadian Labour Movement*, 2nd ed.
(Toronto: James Lorimer & Co, 1996), 6.

55. Ibid., 16–17.

56. For the brief outline of the history of the labour movement in
Canada, I relied on: Heron's book
(see n. 52 above); Desmond Morton, *Working People: An illustrated
History of the Canadian Labour Movement*, 4th ed. (Montreal &
Kingston: McGill-Queen's University Press, 1998); the federal
government site www.canadianeconomy.gc.ca/english/economy/
1873Canadian_Labour_Union.html; and the CLC's "Canadian
Labour History" at www.canadianlabour.ca/updir/
labourhistory.pdf.

57. "Critics Claim Union Clampdown Is Latest
Washington Concession to Big Business," *Financial Times*, April 4,
2005, 1. See also "The Rush to Squash a Promising Union Tactic,"
Business Week, August 2, 2004, 87, and "Brothers at Arms," *Economist*,
May 14, 2005, 32.

58. "Can This Man Save Labor?," *Business Week*, September 24, 2004, 84.

59. Robert Kuttner, "Labor and Management—Will They Ever Wise
Up?," *Business Week*, May 9, 1994, 16.

60. Simon Head, "Inside the Leviathan," *New York Review of Books*,
December 16, 2004, 88. See also "How Wal-Mart Keeps Unions
at Bay," *Business Week*, October 28, 2002, 96, and Karen Olsson,
"Up Against Wal-Mart," *Mother Jones*, March/April 2003,
54–59.

61. Adam Smith, *An Inquiry into the Nature and Causes of the Wealth of
Nations* (New York: Modern Library, 1985), 68.

62. See "The Future of Unions" and "Unions for the Poor," *Economist*,
July 1, 1995, 16, 56.

63. Austin Fagothey and Milton A. Gonsalves, *Right and Reason: Ethics in
Theory and Practice* (St. Louis: Mosby, 1981), 428–429.

64. Ibid., 429.

65. See ch. 4 of Mary Gibson, *Workers' Rights* (Totowa, NJ: Rowman &
Allanheld, 1983). The film *Norma Rae* portrays the dogged resistance
of a company like J. P. Stevens to unionization.

66. In R.W.D.S.U., *Local 558 v. Pepsi-Cola Canada Beverages (West) Ltd.*
[2002] 1 SCR 156, 2002 SCC 8.

67. Fagothey and Gonsalves, *Right and Reason*, 428–429.

68. For a detailed account, see Alan Tate, "The Justice @ Quebecor
Campaign: Lessons For Canadian Unions," *Just Labour* 8 (2006):
40–49.

69. "Unions Threaten Huge Bank Withdrawal," *San Jose Mercury News*,
April 10, 1996, 1C.

70. This case is based on Willard P. Green, "Pornography at Work," *Business Ethics*, Summer 2003, 19.

71. David Dietz, "The Bottom of the Barrel," *San Francisco Chronicle*, July
7, 1996, in "Sunday," 1.

72. "The Drink of Choice," *Santa Cruz Sentinel*, May 26, 1996, D1.

EMPLOYMENT AT WILL AND DUE PROCESS

PATRICIA H. WERHANE AND TARA J. RADIN

According to the common-law principle of employment at will (EAW), a U.S. employer may hire, fire, promote, or demote any employee (not covered by contract or statute) when and for whatever reason the employer wishes. Unlike public-sector employees, most workers in the private sector are "at will" employees and thus have no right to appeal employment decisions. Werhane and Radin critically assess several justifications for the principle of EAW. Urging that the right to procedural and substantive due process be extended to all employees, they argue that even if the principle of EAW is justified, it does not condone arbitrary employment decisions. They argue, further, that the distinction between public and private institutions is not sufficiently clear-cut to justify the denial of constitutional guarantees to employees in the private sector. Canada has statutory provisions requiring employers to show good cause for dismissal.

. . . The principle of EAW is a common-law doctrine that states that, in the absence of law or contract, employers have the right to hire, promote, demote, and fire whomever and whenever they please . . . .

In the United States, EAW has been interpreted as the rule that, when employees are not specifically covered by union agreement, legal statute, public policy, or contract, employers "may dismiss their employees at will . . . for good cause, for no cause, *or even for causes morally wrong*, without being thereby guilty of legal wrong."[1] At the same time, "at will" employees enjoy rights parallel to employer prerogatives, because employees may quit their jobs for any reason whatsoever (or no reason) without having to give any notice to their employers. "At will" employees range from part-time contract workers to CEOs, including all those workers and managers in the private sector of the economy not covered by agreements, statutes, or contracts. Today at least 60% of all employees in the private sector in the United States are "at will" employees. These employees have no rights to due process or to appeal employment decisions, and the employer does not have any obligation to give reasons for demotions, transfers, or dismissals. Interestingly, while employees in the *private* sector of the economy tend to be regarded as "at will" employees, *public*-sector employees have guaranteed rights, including due process, and are protected from demotion, transfer, or firing without cause.

Due process is a means by which a person can appeal a decision in order to get an explanation of that action and an opportunity to argue against it. Procedural due process is the right to a hearing, trial, grievance procedure, or appeal when a decision is made concerning oneself. Due process is also substantive. It is the demand for rationality and fairness: for good reasons for decisions. EAW has been widely interpreted

as allowing employees to be demoted, transferred or dismissed without due process, that is, without having a hearing and without requirement of good reasons or "cause" for the employment decision. This is not to say that employers do not have reasons, usually good reasons, for their decisions. But there is no moral or legal obligation to state or defend them. EAW thus sidesteps the requirement of procedural and substantive due process in the workplace, but it does not preclude the institution of such procedures or the existence of good reasons for employment decisions.

EAW is still upheld in the state and federal courts of this country . . . , although exceptions are made when violations of public policy and law are at issue . . . .

[Recently] a number of positive trends have become apparent in employment practices and in state and federal court adjudications of employment disputes. Shortages of skilled managers, fear of legal repercussions, and a more genuine interest in employee rights claims and reciprocal obligations have resulted in a more careful spelling out of employment contracts, the development of elaborate grievance procedures, and in general less arbitrariness in employee treatment.[2] While there has not been a universal revolution in thinking about employee rights, an increasing number of companies have qualified their EAW prerogatives with restrictions in firing without cause. Many companies have developed grievance procedures and other means for employee complaint and redress . . . .

These are all positive developments. At the same time, there has been neither an across-the-board institution of due process procedures in all corporations nor any direct challenges to the *principle* (although there have been challenges to the practice) of EAW as a justifiable and legitimate approach to employment practices. Moreover, as a result of mergers, downsizing, and restructuring, hundreds of thousands of employees have been laid off summarily without being able to appeal those decisions.

"At will" employees, then, have no rights to demand an appeal to such employment decisions except through the court system. In addition, no form of due process is a requirement preceding any of these actions. Moreover, unless public policy is violated, the law has traditionally protected employers from employee retaliation in such actions. It is true that the scope of what is defined as "public policy" has been enlarged so that "at will" dismissals without good reason are greatly reduced. It is also true that many companies have grievance procedures in place for "at will" employees. But such procedures are voluntary, procedural due process is not *required*, and companies need not give any reasons for their employment decisions.

In what follows we shall present a series of arguments defending the claim that the right to procedural and substantive due process should be extended to all employees in the private sector of the economy. We will defend the claim partly on the basis of human rights. We shall also argue that the public/private distinction that precludes the application of constitutional guarantees in the private sector has sufficiently broken down so that the absence of a due process requirement in the workplace is an anomaly.

EMPLOYMENT AT WILL

EAW is often justified for one or more of the following reasons:

1. The proprietary rights of employers guarantee that they may employ or dismiss whomever and whenever they wish.

2. EAW defends employee and employer rights equally, in particular the right to freedom of contract, because an employee voluntarily contracts to be hired and can quit at any time.

3. In choosing to take a job, an employee voluntarily commits herself to certain responsibilities and company loyalty, including the knowledge that she is an "at will" employee.

4. Extending due process rights in the workplace often interferes with the efficiency and productivity of the business organization.

5. Legislation and/or regulation of employment relationships further undermine an already over-regulated economy.

Let us examine each of these arguments in more detail. The principle of EAW is sometimes maintained purely on the basis of proprietary rights of employers and corporations. In dismissing or demoting employees, the employer is not denying rights to *persons*. Rather, the employer is simply excluding that person's *labor* from the organization . . . .

In dismissing an employee, a well-intentioned employer aims to rid the corporation of the costs of generating that employee's work products. In ordinary employment situations, however, terminating that cost entails terminating that employee. In those cases the justification for the "at will" firing is presumably proprietary. But treating an employee "at will" is analogous to considering her a piece of property at the disposal of the employer or corporation. Arbitrary firings treat people as things. When I "fire" a robot, I do not have to give reasons, because a robot is not a rational being. It has no use for reasons. On the other hand, if I fire a person arbitrarily, I am making the assumption that she does not need reasons either. If I have hired people, then, in firing them, I should treat them as such, with respect, throughout the termination process. This does not preclude firing. It merely asks employers to give reasons for their actions, because reasons are appropriate when people are dealing with other people.

This reasoning leads to a second defense and critique of EAW. It is contended that EAW defends employee and employer rights equally. An employer's right to hire and fire "at will" is balanced by a worker's right to accept or reject employment. The institution of any employee right that restricts "at will" hiring and firing would be unfair unless this restriction were balanced by a similar restriction controlling employee job choice in the workplace. Either program would do irreparable damage by preventing both employees and employers from continuing in voluntary employment arrangements. These arrangements are guaranteed by "freedom of contract," the right of persons or organizations to enter into any voluntary agreement with which all parties of the agreement are in accord.[3] Limiting EAW practices or requiring due process would negatively affect freedom of contract. Both are thus clearly coercive, because in either case persons and organizations are forced to accept behavioral restraints that place unnecessary constraints on voluntary employment agreements.[4]

This second line of reasoning defending EAW, like the first, presents some solid arguments. A basic presupposition upon which EAW is grounded is that of protecting equal freedoms of both employees and employers. The purpose of EAW is to provide a guaranteed balance of these freedoms. But arbitrary treatment of employees extends prerogatives to managers that are not equally available to employees, and such treatment may unduly interfere with a fired employee's prospects for future employment if that employee has no avenue for defense or appeal. This is also sometimes true when an employee quits without notice or good reason. Arbitrary treatment of employees *or* employers therefore violates the spirit of EAW—that of protecting the freedoms of both employees and employers.

The third justification of EAW defends the voluntariness of employment contracts. If these are agreements between moral agents, however, such agreements imply reciprocal obligations between the parties in question for which both are accountable. It is obvious that, in an employment contract, people are rewarded for their performance. What is seldom noticed is that, if part of the employment contract is an expectation of loyalty, trust, and respect on the part of an employee, the employer must, in return, treat the employee with respect as well. The obligations required by employment agreements, if these are free and noncoercive agreements, must be equally obligatory and mutually restrictive on both parties. Otherwise one party cannot expect—morally expect—loyalty, trust, or respect from the other.

EAW is most often defended on practical grounds. From a utilitarian perspective, hiring and firing "at will" is deemed necessary in productive organizations to ensure maximum efficiency and productivity, the goals of such organizations. In the absence of EAW unproductive employees, workers who are no longer needed, and even troublemakers, would be able to keep their jobs. Even if a business *could* rid itself of undesirable employees, the lengthy procedure of due process required by an extension of employee rights would be costly and time-consuming, and would likely prove distracting to other employees. This would likely slow production and, more likely than not, prove harmful to the morale of other employees . . . .

Such an argument assumes that due process increases costs and reduces efficiency, a contention that is not documented by the many corporations that have grievance procedures . . . . Procedural due process demands a means of appeal, and substantive due process demands good reasons, both of which are requirements for other managerial decisions and judgments. Neither demands benevolence, lifetime employment, or prevents dismissals. In fact, having good reasons gives an employer a justification for getting rid of poor employees.

In summary, arbitrariness, although not prohibited by EAW, violates the managerial ideal of rationality and consistency. These are independent grounds for not abusing EAW. Even if EAW itself is justifiable, the practice of EAW, when interpreted as condoning arbitrary employment decisions, is not justifiable. Both procedural and substantive due process are consistent with, and a moral requirement of, EAW. The former is part of recognizing obligations implied by freedom of contract, and the latter, substantive due process, conforms with the ideal of managerial rationality that is implied by a consistent application of this common law principle.

EMPLOYMENT AT WILL, DUE PROCESS, AND THE PUBLIC/PRIVATE DISTINCTION

The strongest reasons for allowing abuses of EAW and for not instituting a full set of employee rights in the workplace, at least in the private sector of the economy, have to do with the nature of business in a free society. Businesses are privately owned voluntary organizations of all sizes from small entrepreneurships to large corporations. As such, they are not subject to the restrictions governing public and political institutions. Political procedures such as due process, needed to safeguard the public against the arbitrary exercise of power by the state, do not apply to private organizations. Guaranteeing such rights in the workplace would require restrictive legislation and regulation. Voluntary market arrangements, so vital to free enterprise and guaranteed by freedom of contract, would be sacrificed for the alleged public interest of employee claims . . . .

Due process is . . . guaranteed for permanent full-time workers in the public sector of the economy, that is, for workers in local, state and national government positions. The Fifth and Fourteenth Amendments protect liberty and property rights such that any alleged violations or deprivation of those rights may be challenged by some form of due process. According to recent Supreme Court decisions, when a state worker is a permanent employee, he has a property interest in his employment. Because a person's productivity contributes to the place of employment, a public worker is entitled to his job unless there is good reason to question it, such as poor work habits, habitual absences, and the like. Moreover, if a discharge would prevent him from obtaining other employment, which often is the case with state employees who, if fired, cannot find further government employment, that employee has a right to due process before being terminated.

This justification for extending due process protections to public employees is grounded in the public employee's proprietary interest in his job. If that argument makes sense, it is curious that private employees do not have similar rights. The basis for this distinction stems from a tradition in Western thinking that distinguishes between the public and private spheres of life. The public sphere contains that part of a person's life that lies within the bounds of government regulation, whereas the private sphere contains that part of a person's life that lies outside those bounds. The argument is that the portion of a person's life that influences only that person should remain private and outside the purview of law and regulation, while the portion that influences the public welfare should be subject to the authority of the law . . . .

The public/private distinction was originally developed to distinguish individuals from the state and to protect individuals and private property from public—i.e., governmental—intrusion . . . . There are some questions, however, with the justification of the absence of due process with regard to the public/private distinction. Our economic system is allegedly based on private property, but it is unclear where "private" property and ownership end and "public" property and ownership begin. In the workplace, ownership and control is often divided. Corporate assets are held by an ever-changing group of individual and institutional shareholders. It is no longer true that owners exercise any real sense of control over their property and its management. Some do, but many do not. Moreover, such complex property relationships are spelled out and guaranteed by the state. This has prompted at least one thinker to argue that "private property" should be defined as "certain patterns of human interaction underwritten by public power."[5]

This fuzziness about the "privacy" of property becomes exacerbated by the way we use the term "public" in analyzing the status of businesses and in particular corporations. For example, we distinguish between privately owned business corporations and government-owned or -controlled public institutions. Among those companies that are not government owned, we distinguish between regulated "public" utilities whose stock is owned by private individuals and institutions; "publicly held" corporations whose stock is traded publicly, who are governed by special SEC regulations, and whose financial statements are public knowledge; and privately held corporations and entrepreneurships, companies and smaller businesses that are owned by an individual or group of individuals and not available for public stock purchase.

There are similarities between government-owned, public institutions and privately owned organizations. When the air controllers went on strike in the 1980s, [U.S. President] Ronald Reagan fired them, and declared that, as public employees, they could not strike because it jeopardized the public safety. Nevertheless, both private and public institutions run transportation, control banks, and own property. While the goals of private and public institutions differ in that public institutions are allegedly supposed to place the public good ahead of profitability, the simultaneous call for businesses to become socially responsible and the demand for governmental organizations to become efficient and accountable further question the dichotomy between "public" and "private."

Many business situations reinforce the view that the traditional public/private dichotomy has been eroded, if not entirely, at least in large part. For example, in 1981, General Motors (GM) wanted to expand by building a plant in what is called the "Pole-town" area of Detroit. Poletown is an old Detroit Polish neighborhood. The site was favorable because it was near transportation facilities and there was a good supply of labor. To build the plant, however, GM had to displace residents in a nine-block area. The Poletown Neighborhood Council objected, but the Supreme Court of Michigan decided in favor of GM and held that the state could condemn property for private use, with proper compensation to owners, when it was in the public good. What is particularly interesting about this case is that GM is not a government-owned corporation; its primary goal is *profitability*, not the common good. The Supreme Court nevertheless decided that it was in the *public* interest for Detroit to use its authority to allow a company to take over property despite the protesting of the property owners. In this case the public/private distinction was thoroughly scrambled.

The overlap between private enterprise and public interests is such that at least one legal scholar argues that "developments in the twentieth century have significantly undermined the 'privateness' of modern business corporations, with the result that the traditional bases for distinguishing them from public corporations have largely disappeared."[6] Nevertheless, despite the blurring of the public and private in terms of property rights and the status and functions of corporations, the subject of employee rights appears to remain immune from conflation.

The expansion of employee protections to what we would consider just claims to due process gives to the state and the courts more opportunity to interfere with the private economy and might thus further skew what is seen by some as a precarious but delicate balance between the private economic sector and public policy. We agree. But if the distinction between public and private institutions is no longer clear-cut, and the traditional separation of the public and private spheres is no longer in place, might it not then be better to recognize and extend constitutional guarantees so as to protect all citizens equally? If due process is crucial to political relationships between the individual and the state, why is it not central in relationships between employees and corporations since at least some of the companies in question are as large and powerful as small nations? Is it not in fact inconsistent with our democratic tradition *not* to mandate such rights?

The philosopher T. M. Scanlon summarizes our intuitions about due process. Scanlon says,

> The requirement of due process is one of the conditions of the moral acceptability of those institutions that give some people power to control or intervene in the lives of others.[7]

The institution of due process in the workplace is a moral requirement consistent with rationality and consistency expected in management decision-making. It is not precluded by EAW, and it is compatible with the overlap between the public and private sectors of the economy. Convincing business of the moral necessity of due process, however, is a task yet to be completed.

Notes

1. Lawrence E. Blades, "Employment at Will Versus Individual Freedom: On Limiting the Abusive Exercise of Employer Power," *Columbia Law Review*, 67 (1967), p. 1405, quoted from *Payne v. Western*, 81 Tenn. 507 (1884), and *Hutton v. Watters*, 132 Tenn. 527, S.W. 134 (1915).

2. See David Ewing, *Justice on the Job: Resolving Grievances in the Nonunion Workplace* (Boston: Harvard Business School Press, 1989).

3. See *Lockner v. New York*, 198 U.S. (1905), and Adina Schwartz, "Autonomy in the Workplace," in Tom Regan, ed., *Just Business* (New York: Random House, 1984), pp. 129–40.

4. Eric Mack, "Natural and Contractual Rights," *Ethics* 87 (1977), pp. 153–59.

5. Morris Cohen, "Dialogue on Private Property," *Rutgers Law Review* 9 (1954), p. 357. See also *Law and the Social Order* (1933) and Robert Hale, "Coercion and Distribution in a Supposedly Non-coercive State," *Political Science Quarterly* 38 (1923), p. 470; John Brest, "State Action and Liberal Theory," *University of Pennsylvania Law Review* (1982), pp. 1296–1329.

6. Gerald Frug, "The City As a Legal Concept," *Harvard Law Review* 93 (1980), p. 1129.

7. T. M. Scanlon, "Due Process," in J. Roland Pennock and John W. Chapman, eds., *Nomos XVIII: Due Process* (New York: New York University Press, 1977), p. 94.

Review and Discussion Questions

1. What is the principle of employment at will? What are the two aspects of due process?

2. Examine and critically assess each of the five justifications for EAW, as stated on page 219. Which of these arguments is the strongest? How persuasive are Werhane and Radin's rejoinders to them? Are there arguments for EAW that the authors have overlooked or not answered adequately?

3. The authors contend that due process is both "consistent with, and a moral requirement of, EAW." Assess both aspects of this assertion.

4. How is the public/private distinction relevant to the debate over EAW and due process? Why do the authors believe that the distinction is blurred? Do you agree?

Bringing Minimum Wages Above the Poverty Line

Stuart Murray and Hugh Mackenzie

The living-wage movement campaigns for higher minimum wage laws to improve the lot of low-income workers, many of whom struggle to support families or even just to get by as individuals on poverty-level wages. A number of provinces have responded by raising or by promising to raise the minimum wage in their jurisdictions. The Province of Ontario intends to gradually increase the minimum wage to $10 per hour by 2010. However, many economists and businesspeople view the living-wage movement with disfavour. They oppose minimum wage laws on the grounds that they reduce employment, work against the interests of less-skilled employees, and raise business costs. In this reading selection, Stuart Murray and Hugh Mackenzie try to counter these and similar arguments by using not only a formidable array of statistics but also by insisting that increasing the minimum wage is morally the fair thing to do.

SECTION TWO: REAL MINIMUM WAGES OVER TIME

In this section we review the overall trend in minimum wages from 1968 to 2005 in Canada. We look at real (inflation-adjusted) minimum wages for each province and the federal government. The nominal minimum wage is the rate using dollars that were current at the time. For example, the nominal minimum wage in BC in 1968 was $1.25 an hour. The real minimum wage, however, is calculated by adjusting the nominal figure for inflation using the Consumer Price Index. After the adjustment, the real minimum wage reflects current dollar figures. For example, the real minimum wage in BC in 1968 was $7.03 an hour in 2005 dollars.

The only meaningful way to compare minimum wages over time is to use the inflation-adjusted minimum wage as the basis for comparison. Movements in the real minimum wage over time capture both the periodic minimum wage increases introduced by governments, from time to time, and the impact that changes in the cost of living have on the buying power of a minimum-wage income. Every Canadian province has, periodically, increased their minimum wage—in some cases at a rate that exceeds inflation, in other cases not. Governments almost never reduce the minimum wage. One of the only exceptions to this rule was BC's introduction of a "training wage" (or "first job wage") in 2001, which reduced the minimum wage from $8.00 to $6.00 per hour for those workers who had completed fewer

than 500 hours of work. However, it is common for provinces to allow several years to pass without a minimum wage increase, allowing inflation to erode the value of the real minimum wage over time—effectively reducing the minimum wage without actually doing anything.

Although minimum wage patterns vary from province to province, some general trends are evident from the data for all provinces. Minimum wages tended to increase, in real terms, from the beginning of our study period in 1968 until they reached a peak in the mid-to-late 1970s. After the late 1970s, minimum wages declined steadily reaching a low point between 1984 and 1990. Since then, minimum wages have remained flat or increased slightly. Table 1 shows the highest and lowest real minimum wage between 1968 and 2005 in every province and at the federal level. We see that in every jurisdiction real minimum wages peaked in 1976 or 1977 at between $8.46 and $10.15 per hour depending on the province. The lowest minimum wage for each province is either in the earliest years (i.e. the late 1960s), or during the period 1985 to 1995, when most provinces' minimum wages reached new lows. The one exception to this rule is the federal government, which froze its minimum wage during the 1990s. As a result, the federal minimum wage reached its record low in 1995 before it was effectively eliminated by linking it to the provincial minimum wage in each province. Depending on the province, the lowest real minimum wages observed in the study period are between $4.90 and $6.75 an hour. These rates help to put into perspective the call for increases in minimum wages to $10 per hour. Real minimum wages close to the $10 target are by no means without precedence in Canada. In BC, the real minimum wage reached $10.15 per hour in 1976, and a number of other jurisdictions have had real minimum wages close to that level.

It is important to note that current minimum wages are by no means near their historic peaks in real dollar terms. . . . Minimum wages effective February 2007 were below peak levels by between $0.96 in Ontario and $2.47 in New Brunswick.

SECTION THREE: PROFILE OF MINIMUM WAGE EARNERS

Critics typically make three types of arguments against increasing minimum wages: that there are so few people working at the minimum wage the problem is trivial; that because most minimum wage earners are teenagers living at home, we shouldn't be worried about what they are paid; and that negative employment effects from increases in minimum wages are so substantial that higher minimum wages will actually hurt their intended beneficiaries more than they will help. This section focuses on the first two of these arguments. The next section focuses on the third.

Across Canada, according to 2003 Statistics Canada data, 4.1% of all employees worked for the minimum wage or less: one worker in 25. There are slight variations in the percentage among provinces. . . . While 4.1% of employees does not represent an overwhelming number, neither that

Table 1 Highest and Lowest Real Minimum Wage Between 1968 and 2005

	Highest Real Minimum Wage	Year in Effect	Lowest Real Minimum Wage	Year in Effect
British Columbia	$10.15	1976	$5.66	1987
Alberta	$9.31	1977	$5.82	1991
Saskatchewan	$9.47	1976	$5.90	1968
Manitoba	$9.98	1976	$6.24	1993
Ontario	$8.96	1976	$5.62	1968
Quebec	$9.78	1977	$6.75	1985
New Brunswick	$9.47	1976	$5.41	1969
Nova Scotia	$8.54	1977	$5.96	1988
Prince Edward Island	$8.46	1976	$5.82	1995
Newfoundland and Labrador	$8.46	1976	$5.72	1990
Federal	$9.81	1976	$4.90	1995

Source: Minimum wage data is effective in November of each year. Data come from the Human Resources Development Canada website.
Note: Real dollar figures are indexed to 2005 dollars.

percentage nor the 547,000 employees it represents could be said to be trivial.

The assertion that minimum wage employment largely involves teenagers who work part-time raises both a policy question—is it appropriate to dismiss the economic situation of teenage employees in this fashion—and a factual question. Even without considering the constitutional legitimacy of discriminating in minimum wage policy on the basis of age, the idea that an important component of our labour market regulatory framework would be based on who you are rather than on what you do is difficult to justify. The fact that an employee is a young person does not, by itself, mean that his or her work is less valuable or that the income that his or her work generates is less important. Indeed, in an environment in which students and their families are expected to contribute a greater and greater share of the costs of their own education, such an argument is even more difficult to sustain today than it might have been in the past.

In addition, when you look closely at who low-wage workers actually are, it is clear that it is simply not valid to assume that low-wage employment is limited to teenagers living at home . . . .

In this section of the report, we provide data on the characteristics of minimum wage workers. We look at the age, sex, educational attainment, and family situation of those earning a minimum wage. We also look at the wage distribution of those with low wages, in order to gain an understanding of how minimum wage increases would affect low-wage workers who are paid slightly above the minimum wage.

This profile is based on data from Statistics Canada's Labour Force Survey effective November 2003. When describing minimum wage workers, we include those workers whose wage is within 25 cents of (i.e. above or below) the respective province's minimum wage. We include all Canadian provinces in our data sample, and we use each province's minimum wage at the time of the survey . . . .

A majority of minimum wage workers are teens; 53% of female minimum wage workers and 64% of male minimum wage workers are between the ages of 15 and 19. For both sexes, 19% of minimum wage workers are youth aged 20–24.

However, a significant minority of workers earning a minimum wage are over age 25. Among women workers, 28% of minimum wage workers are over 25, and among male workers, 17% of minimum wage workers are over 25.

Among the broader population, minimum wage work is a common experience for those starting work for the first time, primarily those starting work in their teens. However, these data show that in many cases minimum wage work persists into adulthood during the prime earning years of some workers . . . . For all workers over age 15, two-thirds (66%) of minimum wage workers are women. Among teen workers, 62% of minimum wage workers are women, but as workers age, women make up an increasing share of minimum wage workers. For young adults aged 20–24, 66% of minimum wage workers are women. For adults age 25 and older, women make up over three quarters (76%) of minimum wage workers.

[Statistical data] indicate that 40% of minimum wage workers have less than a high school diploma, while another 23% have graduated from high school. Those with post secondary education make up another 37% of minimum wage workers combined, including 19% with some post secondary, 13% with a post secondary certificate, and 5% with a university degree. While it is true that a large fraction of minimum wage workers have low levels of education, 37% of minimum wage workers have education beyond high school. It is evident that many minimum wage workers have skills that would warrant a higher level of pay . . . .

[According to statistical data on the family status of minimum wage workers in Canada], for both sexes combined, 51% of minimum wage workers are teens living with their parents. Another 11% of minimum wage workers are young adults aged 20–24 who live with their parents. Combined, 63% of minimum wage workers are people under age 25 who live with their parents.

Within the two younger categories, those living at home make up a majority of minimum wage workers. Among teens working for the minimum wage, 91% live at home. Meanwhile, 58% of young adults working for the minimum wage live at home.

Other research has confirmed that young adults are more likely to live at home than they were in the past. While there are several factors influencing this trend, economic circumstances are seen as a major factor contributing to the increasing trend of youth living at home. For example, living at home becomes increasingly common during recessions, and is more pronounced among youth who have lower incomes. We can reasonably surmise that low minimum wages are a contributing factor to young adults staying home and postponing establishing an independent residence.

Among adults age 25 and over, married people make up the largest component of their age group. Another 4% of females and 1% of males are adults age 25 and over who are lone parents. Indeed married or lone parent status also occurs among young adults age 20–24, making up 4% of females and 1% of males. If we combine all age groups for both sexes, we find that married people and single parents make up 21% of minimum wage workers. Meanwhile, 6% of minimum wage workers are living alone and are attempting to support themselves on their limited earnings. We know from other studies that, while half of low-wage workers live with families and are protected from poverty by other family income, 30 percent of those full-time workers earning less than $10 an hour lived in a low-income household in 2000. For many minimum wage workers—even though they may live with other income earners—their wages represent vital income for getting their families nearer to or just over the poverty line. The proportion of workers earning less than $10 an hour who lived in a low-income household is distinctly higher among unattached individuals (78.4%), lone mothers (55.9%), lone fathers (52.6%) and recent immigrants who are visible minorities (43.7%).

While it is true that a majority of minimum wage workers are teens and youth living with parents, a large fraction of minimum wage workers are supporting themselves and their families. So for a significant proportion of Canada's workforce, the idea that full-time minimum wage work should pay well enough to stay out of poverty is more than an abstract principle of justice. It is a matter of financial survival . . .

. . . In the broadest terms, minimum wage work is relatively uncommon, making up 5.5% of waged workers over age 15 for both sexes. However, when we focus on sub-groups of the population, we find that some categories of workers are far more likely to work for the minimum wage. For example, 52.2% of female teens who work earn the minimum wage, as do 31.3% of teen males. A much smaller percentage of young adults aged 20–24 earn the minimum wage; 10.6% of young women and 6% of young men. Among adults aged 25 and over, minimum wage work is less common, occurring among 3.1% of women and 1.1% of males. There is also a whole category of workers who earn less than the minimum wage. However, just above the minimum wage we find a large number of workers (13.7% of the total) who earn a rate that is between 25 cents per hour above the minimum wage and $10 an hour. While these workers are making more than the minimum wage, it is important to note that these wages are still low, and are below the $10 minimum wage currently under discussion. Workers in this low wage category include 44.1% of teens, 31.1% of workers age 20–24, and 8.6% of workers aged 25+. [In the data on the age distribution of those earning less than $10 an hour], we see that 52% of the females and 34% of the males are aged 25 and older. Because adults are more likely to be living alone or supporting their families, the large number of adults working below $10 an hour is of particular concern.

Taken together, we find that there are two general categories of low-wage workers: 1) those working near or below the minimum wage; and 2) those working between 25 cents above the minimum wage and $10 an hour.

If we look at these two categories of worker [combined] in comparison to the remainder of the waged work force, we develop some interesting insights. For example, . . . low wage work affects 85.8% of teens, 39.4% of young adults, and 10.6% of adults aged 25+. A total of 19.2% of workers in all age categories, for both sexes, works below $10 an hour.

This is a significant portion of the workforce. It is worthwhile to question whether we would choose to organize our society in a way that leaves almost one in five waged workers earning less than $10 an hour. We can expect that such a high incidence of low wage work would be a major contributing factor to worker poverty.

[The evidence] drives home another important point. While only a small share of workers over 25 years of age are working at or near the current minimum wage (2.1%), a significant share (10.6%) are working between the current minimum wage and the proposed new minimum wage of $10. Once the debate shifts to a consideration of the merits of a $10 minimum wage, the issue is no longer one dominated by teens and young workers.

We can surmise that many minimum wage workers are teens and youth living with parents as they build work experience, apply for more highly paid jobs, or go to school. Yet minimum wage work and low wage work persists for many categories of workers who should have already been able to get ahead. We know from other studies that once someone starts working for low pay "half will not move up to better wages within five years. Most of them are women and have low education." By education level, 37% of minimum wage workers have education beyond high school. Minimum wages and low wages disproportionately affect women and youth, as well as recent immigrants. A large fraction of minimum wage workers must support themselves and their families on limited earnings.

Minimum wage work may be an important transitional first step into the labour market for many workers. For many others, minimum wage and low wage work have become a long-term reality.

SECTION FOUR: THE IMPACT OF MINIMUM WAGES ON EMPLOYMENT RATES

The impact of minimum wage increases on employment has been the subject of vigorous debate in the academic literature for decades. Surveys of this literature identify two broad types of studies of the impact of minimum wages on employment.

One is based on the basic principle in economics that if you increase the price of something, other things equal and under competitive market conditions, demand for that thing will go down. Translating that proposition to the labour market, these studies postulate that if the price of minimum wage labour goes up, less of that labour will be demanded.

These types of studies look at employment patterns over time to develop estimates of the labour demand response to a given percentage increase in minimum wages. These studies typically find a small negative employment effect of approximately 1/5 of the percentage change in the minimum wage for teenage minimum wage workers, a reduced impact for workers in their early 20s, and little or no impact of statistical significance on the employment of workers over age 25.

What this means is that, for example, for a 10% increase in the minimum wage, these studies would predict a 2% reduction in employment among young workers.

Not all of these studies arrive at the same conclusions. In general, the results vary in the 1% to 3% range with a 10% increase in minimum wage. The most detailed models found the lowest disemployment effects, predicting disemployment effects in the neighbourhood of 1%.

The principal difficulty with these studies is that, while they confidently predict fairly substantial employment impacts for young workers resulting from increases in minimum wages, actual employment data fail to show any observable negative impacts resulting from actual increases in minimum wages . . . .

The traditional econometric studies that have pointed to disemployment effects also suffer from other limitations. They often fail to capture dynamic positive effects that come from increasing the minimum wage . . .

There is also a concern about publication bias. Through some interesting statistical analysis, David Card and Alan Krueger (in *Myth and Measurement*, 1995, 192), show published reports that make up the consensus range are quite predictable in the degree to which they narrowly meet the statistical threshold necessary to get a study published. The authors note that the most likely explanation was that "early literature was affected by specification searching"; that is, hunting for the right model to get the desired publishable results, as well as publication biases.

The empirical debate is also disproportionately focused on disemployment effects, when a more relevant topic is the impact on the wage bill. After all, if minimum wage workers as a whole receive higher wages after a minimum wage increase, then minimum wage increases are a policy success. These are the findings from Green and Goldberg (*Raising the Floor*, 1999) All changes in public policy have costs and benefits, and while the "consensus range" has focused on a narrowly-defined negative impact, in a broader sense the benefits outweigh the costs.

There is also the problem that regression models show the disemployment effect of minimum wage increases "all other things being equal." While it is helpful to look at the stand-alone impacts of minimum wage increases on employment, the consensus range regression data isolates discussion to one very narrow cause and effect.

The reality in economics is that there is a wide variety of causes and effects, such that the isolated impact of any one phenomenon can easily be swamped by other, more important, policy variables. While it is helpful to know the disemployment effect, "all other things being equal," in reality the minimum wage exists in a context that is constantly changing.

A second type of study attempts to address these problems. Based on the premise that minimum wage impacts are virtually invisible over time because they are swamped by other more significant economic changes, these studies compare employment in jurisdictions where minimum wages have increased with employment in neighbouring US jurisdictions where minimum wages have not increased. Using this approach, these studies suggest that, if there are disemployment effects from increases in minimum wages, they should reveal themselves in differences in employment patterns between neighbouring jurisdictions.

These studies, conducted using data from the US in the late 1980s and 1990s, tended to find employment effects that either were substantially below the range of 1–3%, were statistically insignificant, or were so small as to be immaterial.

The best known of these studies were published by Princeton University economists David Card and Alan Krueger (and particularly their 1995 book *Myth and Measurement*). Their studies generally found that minimum wage increases resulted in either no effect on employment, or in some cases resulted in job growth.

While studies continue to be produced using more sophisticated versions of the time series methodologies that find disemployment effects for young workers in the 1–3% range, the general view among economists of the impact of minimum wage increases on employment has changed fundamentally.

As Economic Policy Institute economist Liana Fox notes in her November 2006 review of the literature on employment impacts: "Some distinguished economists have acknowledged their change of opinion on the issue. Former [U.S.] Federal Reserve Vice Chairman and current Princeton economist Alan Blinder commented, 'My thinking on this has changed dramatically. The evidence appears to be against the simple-minded theory that a modest increase in the minimum wage causes substantial job loss.'"

The latest version of his popular introductory economics textbook reflects his change in thinking:

> Elementary economic reasoning . . . suggests that setting a minimum wage . . . above the free-market wage . . . must cause unemployment . . . . Indeed, earlier editions of this book, for example, confidently told students that a higher

minimum wage must lead to higher unemployment. But some surprising economic research published in the 1990s cast serious doubt on this conventional wisdom.

This lack of a strong relationship between minimum wages and employment is best illustrated by looking at the broader employment rate over time. [Looking at data which track employment rates over time for the four largest provinces—BC, Alberta, Ontario and Quebec] . . . When comparing the broad trends in the employment rate with changes in the real minimum wage, a vital observation is evident: there is no obvious relationship between employment levels and the minimum wage. Sometimes employment rates fall after a minimum wage increase, and sometimes they rise. For the most part, larger-scale changes in the economy drive the employment rate, and the major trends—such as recessions, the growth of female labour participation, economic growth—upstage any impact the minimum wage has on employment.

SECTION FIVE: POLICY CONSIDERATIONS

The fundamental purpose of a minimum wage is to intervene in the labour market to prevent the wages of low-paid employees from sinking below a socially acceptable floor. In other words, it is explicitly intended to offset an imbalance of economic power in the labour market between low-paid employees and their employers. The role of the minimum wage as a counterweight to imbalances of economic power in employment relationships is reflected in the fact that employees whose economic power in the employment relationship is relatively weaker—women, recent immigrants, people of colour—tend to be overrepresented among employees working for low pay. In this respect, minimum wage policy has more in common with other policies that have the effect of altering the balance of power in employment relationships than with policies specifically aimed at alleviating poverty. Such policies cover a wide range of issues in the employment relationship, from employment standards such as hours of work; to health and safety regulation; to the Canada/Quebec Pension Plan (essentially a mandatory jointly funded workplace pension plan); to medicare (essentially an universal substitute for employer health benefits); to the legislative framework for union organization and collective bargaining.

The relationship between the minimum wage and other legislated employment standards and union organization is particularly important. Minimum standards legislation is often seen as a mechanism for ensuring that all employees, whether covered by a collective bargaining agreement or not, are guaranteed at least a minimum set of the working conditions that would otherwise be the subject of collective bargaining in a unionized environment. Indeed, historically, improvements in employment standards have been established by unions in collective bargaining long before they became recognized in legislation. Furthermore, the current focus on minimum wage legislation is at least in part a response to a combination of changes in the structure of the labour market and recent legislative changes intended to discourage union organization.

Ultimately, minimum wage legislation serves as a form of "collective agreement" between society at large and vulnerable/low-wage workers. It ensures a floor below which even those without the benefits of unionization and collective representation cannot or should not fall.

SETTING AND MAINTAINING THE MINIMUM WAGE

We now look more closely at what the $10 an hour target is based on. In the past, minimum wage levels have been set periodically with a view to the relationship between the minimum wage and the average wage, or the relationship between changes in the minimum wage and the cost of living. Such approaches are essentially arbitrary, in that there is no internal logic that leads one to select one percentage of the average wage over another, or to select one base year for a comparison with inflation over another. The approach adopted in the late 1990s in Great Britain was a sharp departure from that type of approach, in a number of respects. First, and most important, the Low-Pay Commission, which is responsible for making minimum wage recommendations to the government, advanced a rationale for its recommendations that paid work should enable those in low-paid work to feel that they belong to the mainstream of society, and not force them to live in poverty. As the chair of the Low-Pay Commission stated on the release of its first report in November 1998:

> Poverty wages cannot encourage people to move from benefits to work. We were struck by a comment made to us in Northern Ireland, and echoed in other visits, that the low paid were often on "the margins of degradation." We hope that our recommendations will play some part in giving workless households and those in low-paid employment more opportunities to participate fully in the economic and social life of society. The introduction of a statutory floor for wage levels must encourage feelings of belonging not to the margins, but to the mainstream of society.

The argument for a $10 minimum wage in Canada is based on a similar logic: namely the proposition that someone working full-time for a full year should not be forced to live in poverty. Although Statistics Canada takes pains to stress that it is not a "poverty line", poverty in Canada is most commonly measured by using Statistics Canada's Low Income Cut-Off (LICO). The cut-off is based on the concept that people in poverty live in "straitened circumstances"—that is, they spend a disproportionate amount of their income on food, clothing and shelter. The Survey of Household Spending conducted by Statistics Canada shows that the average family spends 34.3% of its income from all sources before taxes on food, clothing and shelter. Families are considered to be in "straitened circumstances" if they spend 54.3% or more of their income on these three items. . . . In this case, we are calculating a hypothetical wage at which someone could earn the LICO if they worked full-year at 40 hours per week. It should be noted that while this wage level would enable a full-time worker to earn at the low-income cutoff, many of the low-paid work less than full-time hours. For example, among those earning less than $10 an hour, teenagers work an average of 18 hours per week, young adults aged 20–24 work 27.4 hours a week, and adults aged 25+ work 32.2 hours per week. While those working full-time at the wages listed above would be able to live above poverty, many part-time workers would need either a higher wage or more work hours per week to get by.

We should note that the $10 target is based on a call for increases linked to the 2005 LICO. Therefore, we need to take note of inflation since that date. Assuming 2.1% annual inflation between 2005 and 2010 (based on the average rate of inflation for the past 10 years), we see that the $10 figure actually represents $10.42 in 2007 dollars and $11.10 in 2010 dollars . . . . The government of Ontario has recently set a minimum wage target of $10.25 in 2010. However, a LICO-equivalent figure for 2010 will be closer to $11.10. Once the $10 target has been met (in 2005 dollars), the minimum wage should be indexed to inflation, and rise each year to keep pace with the rising cost of living

[Though] there is no strong, discernable connection between minimum wage and employment impacts . . . there is a strong connection between low minimum wage and the working poor. It is common for researchers analyzing the minimum wage to note that minimum wages are a "blunt instrument for dealing with poverty." There are two things we would note about this traditional complaint about minimum wages. First, higher minimum wages do increase the wage bill of those who are affected by the minimum wage. Not all of those affected have poverty-level family incomes. [True, but] the minimum wage does increase the wages of low-wage workers.

It's true that raising the minimum wage tends to have a push effect on wages of those workers whose incomes are just above the minimum. But just because a higher minimum wage may help workers who are not working at the minimum wage does not mean minimum wages are without merit. Rather, it raises questions about how we value the work effort of all workers, including those at the bottom end of the income spectrum. Second, policy analysts and anti-poverty advocates rarely argue that minimum wages are a cure-all for alleviating poverty. Minimum wages are simply one tool in a toolbox of policy options which, taken as a whole, can go a long way to addressing Canada's persistent poverty problem. In addition to higher minimum wages, the poor would benefit from, for example, better income assistance (both high rates and easier access), income supplements for the working poor, employer policies to improve pay and working conditions, increased coverage of drugs and dental benefits, improved access to affordable child care and home support, improved Employment Insurance, improved access to education learning opportunities, and reduced claw-backs for government programs.

Increasing the minimum wage would have other positive impacts:

- Minimum wages affect more than those who are working at the minimum wage. For example, one study found that increases in the minimum wage resulted in wage increases for workers whose earnings were a dollar or more above the new minimum wage. If a certain job pays $1 above the minimum wage, an employer will want to maintain that differential after the minimum wage has increased. As a result, we can expect that a higher minimum wage would reduce inequality in wages and generally increase hourly earnings of a variety of workers.

- Given that minimum-wage workers are more likely to be members of more vulnerable parts of the labour market, a higher minimum wage would be a key element of a broader policy to fight poverty and promote greater wage fairness—social justice goals our governments should be pursuing in any case.

- Employers that pay well but compete with firms that don't will find themselves on a level playing field

- Employers will also benefit from less turnover and easier recruitment. Workers can easily be lured away from employers that provide low pay. The negative consequences of high turnover include added staffing and training costs, administrative costs, operational disruption, lost productivity, and low morale.

- A higher minimum wage can also increase the independence and self-sufficiency of teens and youth—perhaps enabling young adults who wish to leave home to be able to handle such a move financially.

- Increasing the total wage bill for those at the bottom-end of the labour market can also lead to positive health implications. The broader trend is that "[p]eople who are living at a socioeconomic disadvantage are biologically more susceptible to becoming sick and dying." Healthy workers spend less time away from work due to sickness.

- Finally, by making the minimum wage a living wage, we can restore a sense of fairness and equality in communities and improve well-being among those making difficult choices. A higher minimum wage makes hard decisions easier to make, and makes life generally less harsh . . . .

A real $10 minimum wage is a powerfully symbolic way of rewarding hard-working Canadians who are doing all they can to contribute to the nation's growing economy and keep their households financially afloat. Raising the minimum wage is not only do-able, it's the only fair thing to do.

Review and Discussion Questions

1. Explain the authors' reasons for thinking that increasing the minimum wage to $10 (and thereafter indexing it to inflation) will not have adverse effects on employment rates ("disemployment effect"). Do you agree/disagree with them? Explain fully.

2. Outline and expand on the authors' grounds for claiming that increasing the minimum wage to $ 10 is the "fair thing to do." (You may wish to consult Chapter 3.)

The Libertarian Critique of Labor Unions

Peter Levine

Perhaps because of their inclination to individualism, many people worldwide (not just Americans, to whom the essay is specifically addressed) tend to be skeptical of, or even opposed to, labour unions. At the more philosophical level, this sentiment is reflected in the libertarian critique of unions. Libertarians contend that unions violate individual rights, restrict people's freedom, and harm outsiders. In this essay, however, Peter Levine argues that unions have the potential to safeguard freedom and due process and even to protect the property interests of workers in their jobs. Although the purely economic effects of unions are open to debate, unions make an important contribution to civic society—a contribution that libertarians in particular, with their enthusiasm for nongovernmental associations, should appreciate.

Many Americans, including some who would benefit economically from union membership, view unions with ambivalence or even hostility. Fewer than half of respondents to a poll recently conducted by Fox News thought that unions were good for the country. This skepticism may reflect disapproval with the alienating style and performance of the AFL-CIO in modern times. But American individualism also plays a role. Americans tend to distrust organizations that seem to put solidarity, security, and fraternity above personal liberty, innovation, and competition. Therefore, despite generations of struggle, labor unions remain cultural anomalies. Labor lawyer Thomas Geoghegan describes union meetings as events at which "paunchy, middle-aged men, slugging down cans of beer, come to hold hands, touch each other, and sing 'Solidarity Forever.' O.K., that hardly ever happens, but most people in this business, somewhere, at some point, see it once, and it is the damnedest un-American thing you will ever see."

Most prominent union supporters take for granted that the labor movement benefits workers. They often assume that opponents have selfish economic motives, while anti-union workers must be victims of coercion of misinformation. This attitude ignores the possibility that moral values (such as liberty, self-reliance, and efficiency) motivate distrust of unions. Meanwhile, public figures on the other side of the debate generally assume that unions are harmful and talk darkly about bosses, strike-related violence, and rent-seeking bureaucracies.

To their credit, libertarians approach the question with less partisanship. While they are receptive to unions as non-governmental associations, they are also skeptical of institutions that interfere with "free" markets. Since the libertarian position captures certain widespread American attitudes in a refined (and radical) form, it is a good starting point for philosophical analysis. If libertarian arguments against unions are strong, then maybe public skepticism is justified. If, however, libertarians employ flawed arguments, then perhaps the widespread distrust of unions is misguided.

UNIONS AGAINST INDIVIDUAL RIGHTS

Libertarians strongly defend freedom of choice and association. Thus, when workers choose to act collectively, negotiate together, or voluntarily walk off the job, libertarians have no reasonable complaint—even if other people are harmed—because they support the right to make and exit voluntary partnerships.

But unions gain strength by overriding private rights. They routinely block anyone from working under a non-union contract, and they prevent employers from making offers—even advantageous ones—to individual workers unless the union is informed and consents. Unions declare strikes and establish picket lines to prevent customers and workers from entering company property; they may fine employees who cross these lines. They also extract fees from all workers who are covered by their contracts. Although covered workers may avoid paying for certain union functions (such as lobbying) that are not germane to contract issues, they must pay for strikes and other activities that some of them oppose.

The great libertarian theorist Friedrich Hayek concluded that unions "are the one institution where government has signally failed in its first task, that of preventing coercion of men by other men—and by coercion I do not mean primarily the coercion of employers but the coercion of workers by their fellow workers." Hayek may have been thinking mainly of corrupt and unaccountable union leaders. But even a completely democratic union sometimes supplants private rights. As libertarians like Morgan O. Reynolds point out, majorities within a union are able to ignore minorities' preferences.

Libertarians are especially critical of "closed shop" contracts (which require businesses to hire only union members) and "union shop" contracts (which require all employees to join a specified union after they are hired). Libertarians see such arrangements as state-sanctioned violations of private contract rights. Both closed shops and genuine union shops are now illegal in the United States, but if libertarian arguments are flawed, then perhaps these institutions deserve reconsideration.

In any case, "agency shops" remain in the 29 states that have not passed so called "right-to-work" legislation that bans this kind of contract. In an agency shop, the union negotiates one collective-bargaining agreement that covers a whole class of employees. Workers do not have to join the union, but they must pay dues and work under the union contract. Proponents argue that employees ought to pay fees for a service (union representation) that benefits them tangibly, just as they may be required to pay for food in the company canteen. But this also means that workers in agency shops cannot avoid their union's jurisdiction.

Although organized labor is popular among covered workers—only 8 percent would vote to "get rid of" their unions—libertarians insist that if even *one person* pays dues but opposes the existence of her union, then she is not a member of a voluntary association. As Senator Barry Goldwater (R-AZ) told the union leader Walter Reuther in 1953: "There is only one question in this whole field in my mind. What about the man who does not want to belong to the union?" Goldwater spoke in the days of the "closed shop," when union membership could be compulsory. But more recently, Representative Ron Goodlatte (R-VA) claimed that even an "agency shop" violates individual rights, because "compelling a man or woman to pay fees to a union in order to work violates the very principle of individual liberty upon which this nation was founded."

At times, unions have overridden some of their own members' economic interests. In one important case, African American workers, dissatisfied by their union's efforts to end discrimination at a department store, attempted to picket without the union's approval. The Supreme court ruled 8–1 (in a decision written by Justice Thurgood Marshall) that only the union could take such actions, because the principles of *organized* labor and *collective* bargaining implied that unions were entitled to gain power from disciplined action.

Unions have also abridged their members' individual freedom of conscience. Justice Potter Stewart once noted that a worker's "moral or religious views about the desirability of abortion may not square with the union's policy in negotiating a medical benefits plan. One person might disapprove of unions negotiating limits on the right to strike, believing that such policies guarantee the serfdom of the working class, while another person might object to unions on purely economic grounds."

Unions can harm outsiders, too, including the customers, managers, and owners of any company involved in a labor dispute. In general, libertarians believe that non-governmental organizations should be able to act freely in the marketplace, even if their behavior imposes costs on others. For instance, firms are within their rights to run competitors out of business or to lay off their employees. By the same token, it would seem that unions should not be stopped just because their tactics cost other people money. However, American unions owe some of their power to government recognition, so libertarians view any harms that they cause as impermissible violations of liberty. In particular, the libertarian economist Milton Friedman complains that unions raise labor costs and thus increase unemployment, to the detriment of poor people who are not their members. He insists that unions have "made the incomes of the working class more unequal by reducing the opportunities available to the most disadvantaged workers." Although unions often strive to protect poor people in order to narrow the pay differential between their own members and the rest of the workforce, Friedman's hypothesis is true in some cases.

UNIONS IN DEFENSE OF RIGHTS

Libertarians cite natural or individual rights, such as freedom of property and choice, that militate against unions. But unions also have the potential to *safeguard* freedom and due process. Some workers may see the job market as a "state of nature," a ruthless competition that endangers legitimate individual rights, and they may believe that a lone individual cannot secure through her own efforts a living wage, job tenure, freedom to criticize and dissent, and some measure of self-rule. Such workers may view their employer as a despot with absolute and arbitrary power. Although one way to guarantee rights is to pass and enforce appropriate legislation, employees may trust another strategy: unionization. A worker who is treated unfairly cannot expect her fellow workers to take effective action in defense of her (and their) rights unless they are organized into a disciplined organization such as a union.

This argument hinges on the notion that employers are "despots," since their power to discipline and fire workers is comparable to the police powers of a state. Charles E. Lindblom, a Yale professor of economics and political science, writes that the "mere threat of termination can be as constraining, as coercive, as menacing as an authoritative governmental command." Losing one's livelihood, especially through layoff or demotion, can be catastrophic and arbitrary, entirely lacking in due process or rational justification. Thus, unskilled workers in a glutted labor market may need a union to give them any semblance of rights. But workers who command a high price in the market may feel that they are more free without a union—which will impose its own rules, officials, and bureaucracies.

In addition to the balance of power between labor and capital, a second factor is also relevant: the degree to which supervisors act in the overall interest of their companies. Assume that you can trust your boss to help maximize the firm's profits. Then you may be happy without a union if your skills give you some leverage in contract negotiations. But your own supervisor may not be competent or responsible. He may be lazy, arbitrary, discriminatory, or motivated by completely selfish goals (as in cases of sexual harassment). Since it is dangerous to challenge a supervisor directly and difficult to change jobs, even workers with high market value may want enforceable and inflexible rules to govern salaries, promotion prospects, grievance procedures, and job descriptions. For people who distrust managers, a union is not an unwelcome bureaucracy but an independent institution to which they can appeal in defense of their rights.

Although unions support due process, fair treatment, and other rights for workers, they are typically seen as the enemy of *property* rights. However, some have argued that jobs should be seen as the property of workers, since their labor creates value. Late in the nineteenth century, political economist Henry C. Adams contended that, in appropriate circumstances, employees should "be given tenure of employment," so that they "cannot be discharged except for cause that satisfies a commission of arbitrators." Further, he believed that workers ought to be "consulted whether hours of work or the numbers employed shall be reduced," and given preference over those outside the industry. These steps would make jobs into "workmen's property." Adams added that the state could not be trusted to intervene fairly and, consequently, unions were the best means to redefine property.

As Adams (among others) realized, "property" admits of no universal, self-evident definition. Some have claimed that a class of objects should be defined as property because doing so encourages such positive consequences as increased investment and effort, or the efficient use and distribution of goods. At present, jobs are considered the alienable property of employers, who use them to maximize profits. If instead jobs were seen as the (non-transferable) property of workers, then although investment and innovation might suffer, employees might also feel deep satisfaction when positions became *theirs* because of their work. In short, Adams' proposal has both positive and negative implications, and the net change would be difficult to assess.

In my view, only the state has the authority to decide what is the best system of ownership in the labor market. The marketplace itself cannot make such decisions, because any market presupposes the existing system of property. Nor should we allow unions to determine property rights unilaterally, since they do not allow outsiders to vote. But elected legislatures could decide that jobs shall become workers' property under certain circumstances, and an appropriate means to that end would be to strengthen unions. After all, if investors can create entities such as corporations, with a well-defined set of property rights, then perhaps workers ought to be able to form entities such as bargaining units, with similar claims to property.

UNIONS AND COMPETITIVE MARKETS

Mainstream economic theory contends that a competitive market generally produces the greatest possible quantity and desired goods and services; in this sense, it is efficient. However, unions reduce competition in labor markets by preventing employers from firing unionized employees and by blocking job-seekers from accepting offers below the union rate. They may thus protect unproductive workers, raise costs, distort incentives, and frustrate entrepreneurship. Furthermore, organized labor is specifically exempted from antitrust laws whose general goal is to promote competition. Judge Richard A. Posner (who is often called a libertarian, although his views are idiosyncratic) concludes that American labor law is a device to promote the "cartelization of the labor supply by unions." Because it confers power on unions, the law "is founded on a policy that is the opposite of the policies of competition and economic efficiency that most economists support."

One economist has calculated that unions cost the country 4.9 percent of GDP annually. Other estimates are much lower, and some cite evidence that unions are good for the economy—boosting morale and trust, reducing turnover, offering senior workers incentives to share knowledge with novices, and improving the flow of information between workers and managers. One recent study by Sandra E. Black and Lisa M. Lynch found that productivity in unionized firms was ten percent higher than in comparable non-unionized firms. Still, unions must at least sometimes reduce the nation's supply of goods and services. Of course, the same could be said of many private activities (smoking, gambling, early retirement) that libertarians consider well within the bounds of personal liberty. But Hayek distinguished between harms—which free people inevitably cause as they pursue their own interests—and coercion, which is impermissible. Hayek thought that unions acted coercively, so whenever they caused economic damage, they also violated rights and freedoms.

Contrary to what libertarians assume, freedom is not just a matter of selecting among choices in a marketplace. Imagine that workers have won some leverage over an employer because of a union. As a result, they can lay claim to a larger portion of the profits that their work generates. Now they must decide how tough to be in contract negotiations (considering possible damage to the company) and how seriously to risk a strike. They must also decide whether they want to use their collective muscle to pursue salary increases, equity among their membership, additional leisure time, job security, or insurance against catastrophic losses that would only affect their least fortunate members. This type of political deliberation and self-government is a form of freedom that is impossible without the union.

Libertarians sometimes argue that unions damage people's interests in a different way: by diminishing wealth or the supply of consumer goods and services. As economists David G. Blanchflower and Andrew J. Oswald note, "The idea that income buys happiness is one of the assumptions—made without evidence but rather for deductive reasons—in microeconomics textbooks." However, actual data reveal that, while money has a positive effect on happiness, its impact is "not as large as some would expect." Other variables—such as marriage, employment, and race—have more powerful effects. Indeed, while Americans have grown much wealthier in the aggregate since 1945, according to political scientist Robert Putnam, we have also seen a tenfold increase in the depression rate, a quadrupling of the teenage suicide rate, and dramatic increases in "headaches, indigestion, and sleeplessness" among younger people, even affluent ones.

Putnam argues these maladies can be traced to a decline in social connectedness. Interpreting data on self-reported happiness, he finds that "getting married is the 'happiness equivalent' of quadrupling your income" and that "regular club attendance, volunteering, entertaining, or church attendance is the happiness equivalent of getting a college degree or more than doubling your income." If the goal is the maximization of happiness or welfare, then one should strongly favor unions—even if they reduce aggregate money income—because they provide civic connections, which "rival marriage and affluence as predictors of life happiness."

UNIONS AS PARTS OF CIVIL SOCIETY

Unions are more than economic actors that negotiate with employers; they are also communities of workers, forums for debate, and lobbying organizations. They can thus be described as parts of "civil society," a social sector that enjoys strong support from libertarians—and most other ideological groups as well. However, this terminology raises a new set of questions about the proper role and scope of civil society.

Libertarians believe that civil society should consist of institutions that people can join and exit freely depending on their values and preferences. But Americans usually join unions because the company where they want to work happens to be unionized—not because they support the labor movement or want to frequent the union hall. Quitting the union would then mean waiving their right to vote without escaping the obligation to pay dues and to work under the union contract. Therefore, unions serve the goal of free association less well than other organizations do.

However, libertarians' equation of civil society with freedom of association overlooks some of its most attractive features. For instance, some people argue that the purpose of civil society is to offer the moral and psychological advantages of *community*, which are missing in a competitive market. Unions commonly meet political theorist Thomas Bender's definition of a "community," which involves a limited number of people in a restricted social space who are "held together by shared understandings and a sense of obligation." Bender observes that relationships are "close, often intimate, and usually face to face," with individuals bound together by emotional ties rather than individual self-interest. He concludes that "there is a 'we-ness' in a community; one is a member." As philosopher Richard Rorty notes, "You would never guess, from William Bennett's and Robert Bork's speeches about the need to overcome liberal individualism, that the labor unions provide by far the best examples in America's history of the virtues these writers claim we must recapture. The history of the unions provides the best examples of comradeship, loyalty, and self-sacrifice." . . .

A third understanding of "civil society" views this sector as the source of "social capital." Robert Putnam and his colleagues use this phrase to refer to habits, skills, and attitudes—especially trust and a propensity to join organizations—that expedite collective action and lessen the burdens on government.

Union members have much more social capital than those who belong to no groups at all. According to the General Social Survey, union members are 10 percent more likely to trust other people, 19 percent more likely to express an interest in politics, 16 percent more likely to vote, 17 percent more likely to influence others about elections, and 22 percent more likely to talk to several people about important issues—a pattern that remains even when one controls for income, education, and employment status. Further, large numbers of union members report having contacted the government (18.3 percent), attended conferences (56.5 percent), or served as committee members (49 percent) and officers (36.8 percent) as a result of their membership.

However, union members are not very active in civil society compared to people who belong to at least one association, but not to a union. Union members perform at least five percent worse than these other participants on all the measures listed above except "influencing people about elections" (where union members are more active than other members). It seems, then, that unions boost civic participation, but to a lesser extent than the average association. Union membership is also a weak predictor of overall associational membership—unionized workers are not avid joiners the way that Rotarians and PTA volunteers are. Thus, although unions contribute to civil society and cultivate civic behavior, they are not outstanding contributors of civic life.

A fourth theory views "civil society" as the domain of interest groups, political factions, or lobbies. This definition clearly covers unions, since they lobby government officials, litigate, communicate to their own members about elections and issues, spend money on grassroots political campaigns, buy advertising, make endorsements, and donate to candidates and parties. Especially in recent decades (and especially in the United States), these political activities have been much more effective than such traditional tactics of labor unions as organizing workers, bargaining with employers, and striking . . . .

Indeed, unions often enhance public deliberation about national priorities by adding a disciplined, well-funded alternative to the influential views of corporations. In some cases, speech is a public good that cannot be produced by uncoordinated, individual action. Since many employees may be tempted to act as free riders, relying on others to speak for the interests of workers as a class, the few who do speak (or voluntarily pay for speech) will see weak results from their efforts. But if workers form a union for collective-bargaining purposes, and if it can *compel* everyone to pay for political activities, then all workers will gain a strong voice at a small cost to each. In many poor communities, unions are among the only institutions that have the power to fund themselves without outside assistance from either government or philanthropy. The benefit to the larger community is robust public debate, which libertarians prize . . . .

Unions also force other institutions, such as the mass media and legislatures, to debate issues that may otherwise be ignored. And by protecting freedom of association and criticism inside the workplace, unions give workers a means to *act* on their deliberate beliefs in ways that influence the wider society. As scholar-activists Harry Boyte and Nanci Kari argue in *Building America*, many "deliberative theorists put citizens in the role of judicious audience." That is, they assume a distinction between judgment—the citizens' role—and work or action, which is what rulers do. But when union members debate a contract, decide to strike, and then provide food and childcare for their fellow strikers, they fruitfully combine judgment, work, and action.

CONCLUSION

These arguments will not satisfy pure libertarians, but they do suggest that unions are compatible with personal liberty. To be sure, the powers and prerogatives of unions must be balanced against individual rights. Workers should be free to avoid union membership and dues beyond those necessary for contract negotiations, and all members ought to have enforceable rights against discrimination by their unions. But these qualifications (which are enshrined in current law) would not prevent strong unions from forming.

Unfortunately, the actual rate of union membership—15 percent of all employees; less in the private sector—is much lower than in other democracies and below half the level reached in America around 1950. About one third of non-unionized American workers believe that, "were an election held tomorrow, workers at their firm would support a union," but they are unlikely ever to have the opportunity to cast a vote.

Congress could respond to the current situation by legalizing "agency shops" nationwide. Research by economist David T. Ellwood and lawyer Glenn Fine suggests that this reform would allow about five percent of the population in current "right-to-work" states to join unions, for a total increase of millions of members.

Federal law could also approach corporate resistance differently. Companies typically rely on illegal tactics to stop an organizing drive by, for instance, intimidating union supporters and firing employees involved in organizing the union. Although federal judges may declare automatic certification of a union if they believe that laws have been broken, in practice, unions arising in this way are weak from the start and managers feel free not to make them serious contract offers. A better solution is to recognize a union as the sole legitimate bargaining agent of a workforce as soon as a majority of the covered workers signs a petition to unionize. Then employees would be spared a struggle against management intimidation, and neither side would know how deeply the rank-and-file was committed to the union or how well the union could weather a strike. This uncertainty would encourage management to negotiate seriously with the union leadership, which (for its part) would have dues money and other resources to use during the bargaining process.

Since this reform is untested in the U.S., one can only speculate on the results. But the proposal is consistent with the philosophical considerations explored in this article. As labor lawyer Thomas Geoghegan observes, "I can think of nothing, no law, no civil rights act, that would radicalize this country more, democratize it more…, than to make this one tiny change in the law: to let people join unions if they like, freely and without coercion, without threat of being fired, just as people are permitted to do in Europe and in Canada."

Review and Discussion Questions

1. On what grounds are libertarians critical of labour unions? Do unions infringe on people's rights or do they safeguard those rights?

2. Do unions interfere with the right to property as libertarians believe? Assess the idea that jobs are the property of employees. What are its implications?

3. In your view, do unions have on balance positive or negative economic effects? Do they have positive or negative social effects? Do you agree with Levine that unions make an important contribution to civic society? Explain why or why not.

4. Today unions represent a smaller percentage of the workforce than they have in the past. Is this a good thing—for workers, the economy, or society as a whole?

Further Reading for Chapter 6

Ronald Duska, "Employee Rights," in Robert E. Frederick, ed., *A Companion to Business Ethics* (Malden, MA: Blackwell, 1999) discusses the nature of rights in general and the specific rights claimed for employees in recent times.

Thomas Geoghegan, *Which Side Are You On? Trying to Be for Labor When It's Flat on Its Back*, rev. ed. (New York: New Press, 2004) is the insightful and entertaining memoir of a labour lawyer.

Gerard Hunt and **David Rayside**, eds., *Equity, Diversity, and Canadian Labour* (Toronto: University of Toronto Press, 2007) contains different essays which examine the response of Canada's organized labour to issues of gender, race, disability, and sexual orientation in the workplace.

Andrew Jackson, *Work and Labour in Canada* (Toronto: Canadian Scholars' Press Inc., 2005) is an informative and accessible account and assessment of specific issues within the Canadian workplace based on research conducted originally for the Canadian Labour Congress.

Reed Larson and **William L. Clay** debate right-to-work laws in "Does America Need a National Right-to-Work Law?," *Insight on the News* 14 (August 17, 1998).

Paul Le Blanc, *A Short History of the U.S. Working Class* (Amherst, NY: Prometheus, 1999) is an informative but short and readable account of working people in America.

Richard L. Lippke, *Radical Business Ethics* (Lanham, MD: Rowman & Littlefield, 1995), ch. 6, discusses the right to freedom of speech and conscience in the workplace.

David Sirota, **Louis A. Mischkind**, and **Michael Irwin Meltzer**, *The Enthusiastic Employee: How Companies Profit by Giving Workers What They Want* (Philadelphia: Wharton School Publishing, 2005) presents years of research demonstrating the relationship between high employee morale and strong financial performance.

Patricia Werhane, "Individual Rights in Business," in Tom Regan, ed., *Just Business: New Introductory Essays in Business Ethics* (New York: Random House, 1984), provides a useful overview of many basic moral issues in the workplace.

7

The Workplace (2): Today's Challenges

It was a routine business day for Eastern Airlines—until it received an anonymous tip that some of its baggage handlers at Miami International Airport were using drugs. Eastern quickly sprang into action, ordering security guards to round up the ten employees then at work in the airport's plane-loading area. The employees were marched between two rows of guards and into waiting vans—"like terrorists," a lawsuit later claimed—all in full view of other employees and passengers. After questioning the workers, suspicious supervisors put them on board a bus, once again in front of onlookers, and took them to a hospital. There the employees were given an ultimatum: Either take a urine test or be fired on the spot.[1]

The baggage handlers were union members, but they caved in and took the test. All ten of them tested negative (that is, free of drugs), but they weren't happy about what they'd been through. Not long afterward, they filed suit against the airline in federal court, seeking damages of $30,000 each on charges of invasion of privacy, defamation, and intentional infliction of emotional distress. Eastern has since gone out of business, but the case represents in dramatic form one of the major issues dividing employers and employees today: privacy. Companies in all parts of the world are delving further into employees' personal lives than ever before, claiming the need to monitor their behaviour and probe into their health and habits. Workers are resisting ever more adamantly, fighting back for the right to be left alone.

Chapter 6 examined personnel policies and procedures, trade unions, the state of civil liberties on the job, and the efforts of some successful companies to respect the rights, dignity, and moral integrity of their workers. This chapter also focuses on moral issues that emerge in the workplace. It looks in detail at one crucial civil liberty—the right to privacy—and at the ethical choices it poses inside the organization. The remainder of the chapter examines several other topics that are stirring up controversy in today's workplace. More specifically, this chapter explores the following:

1. The nature of privacy and the problems of organizational influence over private decisions

2. The moral issues raised by the use of polygraph and personality tests, employee monitoring, and drug testing in the workplace

3. Working conditions—in particular, health and safety, styles of management, and provision of day-care facilities and maternity leave

4. Job satisfaction and dissatisfaction and the prospects for enhancing the quality of work life

ORGANIZATIONAL INFLUENCE IN PRIVATE LIVES

Privacy is widely acknowledged today to be a fundamental right, yet corporate behaviour and policies often threaten privacy, especially in the case of employees. One way this happens is through the collection of personal information about employees. Another, and the most prevalent, way is the release of personal information. The data banks and personnel files of business and non-business organizations contain an immense amount of private information, the disclosure of which can seriously violate employees' rights. Most firms guard their files closely and restrict the type of material that they can contain in the first place, but the potential for abuse is still great. There is of course nowadays a complicated set of laws and court rulings that limits the collection of or access to such information. For example, just to mention a few, the *Privacy Act*, 1983, covering institutions of the federal government; the *Personal Information Protection and Electronic Documents Act*, 2000, covering also the private sector; and the Supreme Court decision in *R v. Dyment* [1988] 2 S.C.R. 417, which emphasizes privacy as a value worthy of constitutional protection.[2] Despite all that, a wide range of snoops still manage, legitimately or illegitimately, to get their hands on private information (even by searching through one's garbage, by email spying, etc.).

As a related matter, more employees are suing their former bosses for passing on damaging information to prospective employers. The courts have traditionally considered this sort of information exchange between employers to be "privileged," but companies can lose this protection by giving information to too many people or by making false reports. Through fear of defamation or invasion of privacy suits,[3] many organizations now refuse to reveal anything about former employees except their dates of employment.

More significant are the threats to privacy that can arise on the job itself. For example, some bosses unhesitatingly rummage through the files of their workers, even when they are marked "private." Some companies routinely eavesdrop on their employees' phone calls, and a majority of them read their employees' email and monitor their use of the Internet.[4] Voice mail isn't safe either, as Michael Huttcut, a manager of a McDonald's outlet in St. Louis, learned the hard way. He was having an affair with a coworker, and the romantic voice-mail messages he sent her were retrieved and played by his boss. When Huttcut complained, he was fired.[5] Other companies secretly quiz managers—or even call in private investigators—to gain knowledge about the personal habits and behaviour of workers who call in sick.[6] Meanwhile, Global Positioning System (GPS) technology lets companies track employees when they are in their company vehicles—often without their knowledge.[7]

Equally important is the way organizations attempt to influence behaviour that ought properly to be left to the discretion of their employees—in particular, efforts to impose their own values on their workers. For example, Wal-Mart fired Lauren Allen, who was married but separated from her husband, for dating a coworker, who was single. Wal-Mart says that it "strongly believes in and supports the 'family unit'" and that the conduct of Allen and her coworker violated the company's rules.[8] Or consider the case of Virginia Rulon-Miller, a marketing manager in IBM's office products division. A week after receiving a 13.3 percent pay raise, she was called on the carpet for dating Matt Blum, a former IBM account manager who had gone to a competitor. She and Blum had begun dating when Blum was at IBM, and he still played on the IBM softball team. IBM told Rulon-Miller to give up Blum or be demoted. "I was so steeped in IBM culture," she says, "that I was going to break up with Matt." But the next day, before she had a chance to do anything, she was dismissed. It's not only in affairs of the heart that companies sometimes intrude into the personal sphere of employees by imposing their values on them or telling them what to think or do in matters that bear little relation to their jobs. Some executives, for example, find themselves pressured to contribute cash to their company's political action committee.[9] Other corporations ask their employees for partisan political contributions. By bundling these together as one gift, companies can circumvent the ban on corporate campaign giving.

Both in the workplace and in general, our concern for privacy seems to have at least three dimensions to it. First, we want to control intimate or personal information about ourselves and not permit it to be freely available to everyone. We are concerned to restrict who has certain kinds of knowledge about us, the means by which they can acquire it, and those to whom they may disclose it. Second, we wish to keep certain thoughts, feelings, and behaviour free from the scrutiny, monitoring, or observation of strangers. We don't want our private selves to be on public display. Third, related to the second point, we value being able to make certain personal decisions autonomously. We seek to preserve and protect a sphere in which we can choose to think and act for ourselves, free from the illegitimate influence of our (prying) employers and others.

Our concern over privacy, especially in an age of computer technology, goes to the core of our being as individuals. The extent and kind of information about ourselves that we are prepared to share with others mediates the *kind* of relationships with have with them and the variety or *diversity* of relationships we may have with different people. Consider what sorts of information you share with your mother, your teacher or your banker, as opposed to your sister, your best friend or your lover. Researchers have noticed that people, when they think they are being observed by others, tend generally to behave as they believe the observer would like them to behave. Think of the main reason behind the use of cameras at main traffic intersections in some of our bigger cities. There is an important sense then in which our being observed by others leads to *conformity* with the views and practices of the observer. Life under a general climate of conformity has deleterious effects on both the individual and society: individuals become passive and society stagnates. Indeed, some thinkers argue that passive, conformist individuals are not fit subjects for a democracy, since democracy requires active citizens who are ready to exercise their autonomy, to express freely their own views, especially when these views are novel, and criticize the views of others.[10] Though there is no consensus among philosophers or lawyers about how precisely to define the concept of privacy, how far the right to privacy extends, or how to balance a concern for privacy against other moral considerations, all of us would agree, nonetheless, that we have a clear right to keep private certain areas of our lives and that we need to have our privacy respected if we are to function as complete, self-governing agents.

Even when a genuine privacy right is identified, the strength of that right depends on circumstances—in particular, on competing rights and interests. Privacy is not an absolute value. The *Canadian Charter of Rights and Freedoms* does not recognize such a right as "a right to privacy" (though the *Code Civil du Quebec* does in section 3). Corporations and other organizations often have legitimate interests that may conflict with the privacy concerns of employees. Determining when organizational infringement on a person's private sphere is morally justifiable is, of course, precisely the question at issue.

As a general rule, though, whenever an organization infringes on what would normally be considered the personal sphere of an individual, it bears the burden of establishing the legitimacy of that infringement. The fact that a firm thinks an action or policy is justifiable does not, of course, prove that it is. The firm must establish both that it has some legitimate interest at stake and that the steps it is taking to protect that interest are reasonable and morally permissible. But what are the areas of legitimate organizational influence over the individual?

Legitimate and Illegitimate Influence

The demands of the work contract, the firm's responsibilities to owners, consumers or to society at large, the very purpose of the firm itself, all these support the proposition that the firm is legitimately interested in whatever significantly influences work performance. However, what constitutes a significant influence on work performance eludes precise definition, because the connection between an act or policy and the job is often fuzzy.

Take, for example, the area of dress and grooming. A roofing company has a legitimate interest in the type and quality of shoes its workers wear, because footwear affects safety and job performance. Similarly, one may argue, specialty-clothing stores such as Gap, Polo, Ralph Lauren, and Abercrombie & Fitch have legitimate grounds for requiring their employees to dress in the store's latest styles. Enterprise Rent-A-Car also puts a high priority on employee grooming and appearance. It lays down thirty dress-code guidelines for female employees (no denim or skirts more than two inches above the knee) and twenty-six rules for male employees (no beards; dress shirts with coordinated ties). More debatable is the company's requiring employee Angela Garrett to remove the red tints from her hair because they weren't appropriate for her ethnic group (she's African-American).[11] Or consider the ticket agent who was fired by an airline for refusing to wear makeup. Perhaps that was a legitimate demand in the name of good public relations, but maybe it was arbitrary and narrow-minded.[12]

An employer's concern with dress can interfere with an employee's personal choices in other ways. Consider the case of Margaret Hasselman, who worked as a lobby attendant in a New York City high rise. Wearing the new uniform provided by her employer—a poncho with large openings under the arms, dancer's underpants, and white pumps—she repeatedly encountered sexual harassment. She complained about the outfit to her boss, but to no avail. When she eventually refused to wear it, she was fired. Issues of morality, of course, differ from questions of legality. But it is interesting that when Hasselman filed suit, the court ruled that no employer has the right to force workers to wear revealing or sexually provocative clothing.

The general proposition that a firm has a legitimate interest only in employee behaviour that significantly influences work performance applies equally to off-the-job conduct. BankAmerica probably fell afoul of this guideline when it fired Michael Thomasson, a legal secretary, for working as a gay stripper during his off hours. After a coworker read a personal letter Thomasson had written on a company computer that mentioned his job as an exotic dancer, a group of bank employees, including several of Thomasson's supervisors, went to see him perform. Two weeks later he was dismissed—despite a record of positive job evaluations and a recent merit raise.[13]

Some years ago, the city of Longueuil, Quebec, required all its permanent employees to sign an employment contract that obliged them to reside within the city limits of Longueuil itself. One of the employees took the issue all the way to the Supreme Court, which decided that the city had violated its employees' constitutional rights in imposing upon them the obligation to reside within the city. The Court also found that employees did not waive their residency rights by signing an employment contract that contained the restrictive residency conditions.[14]

Years ago, Henry Ford made his autoworkers' wages conditional on their good behaviour outside the factory. He had 150 inspectors whose job it was to keep tabs on his employees' hygiene and housekeeping habits. And Milton Hershey, another famous business leader, used to tour Hershey, Pennsylvania, the chocolate-manufacturing town, to make sure his workers were keeping up their lawns, and he even hired private detectives to find out who was throwing trash in Hershey Park.[15] These days it's easy to say Ford and Hershey crossed the line and were poking their noses into aspects of their employees' lives that had nothing to do with their work performance.

In other cases, though, determining when off-the-job conduct bears on job performance can be difficult. For example, how would you decide the following case? In an off-the-job fight, a plant guard drew his gun on his antagonist. Although no one was injured, the guard's employer viewed the incident as grounds for dismissal. The employer reasoned that such an action indicated a lack of judgment on the part of the guard. Do you think the employer had a right to fire the guard under those circumstances? Again, consider the employee who sold a small amount of marijuana to an undercover police officer, or the employee who made obscene phone calls to the teenage daughter of a client. Their employers fired them, but they were reinstated by an arbitrator.

Then there's the amorphous area of company image and the question of whether it can be affected by off-the-job conduct. The political activities of a corporate executive, for example, could significantly affect the image a firm wishes to project, whereas what an obscure worker on the firm's assembly line does politically might have a comparatively insignificant impact on the company's image. Companies and other organizations have an interest in protecting their good names. The off-duty conduct of employees might damage an organization's reputation, but in practice damage is often difficult to establish. For example, two agents of the U.S. Internal Revenue Service were suspended for "mooning" a group of women after leaving a bar. Would you agree with their suspension? An arbitrator didn't and revoked it. He couldn't see that their conduct damaged the IRS's reputation.[16]

Obviously we can't spell out exactly when off-duty conduct affects company image in some material way, any more than we can say precisely what constitutes a significant influence on job performance. But that doesn't prevent us from being able to judge that in many cases organizations step beyond legitimate boundaries and interfere with what should properly be personal decisions by their employees. That interference can take many forms, but two are worth looking at more closely.

Involvement in Civic Activities To enhance their image in the community, businesses and other organizations have long prodded employees to donate to charitable causes during company-led fundraising drives, or encouraged them to participate in public-spirited activities off the job—for example, by running for the local school board or joining civic service organizations, such as Kiwanis, Lions, or Rotary. Moreover, since the 1990s there has been a boom in corporate-sponsored employee volunteer programs, with more and more firms encouraging employees to spend off-duty hours helping out at designated charities or donning a company T-shirt and pitching in on Saturdays at some company-run charitable project.

There's no doubt that the trend toward corporate volunteer programs has been good for society. But such programs can collide with ever-increasing job demands, forcing employees to spend valued off-duty time away from their families and fuelling employee resentment and burnout. Moreover, such programs can raise moral questions, especially as the pressure to participate increases. Some employers have "unwritten rules" requiring volunteer work; other companies award employees points for approved volunteer work on their performance evaluations. And employees have been downgraded, disciplined, or even fired for not contributing the "suggested" amount of money to the United Way or other charitable cause sponsored by the firm. I still remember the time when my own employer would send out a letter to all employees soliciting contributions to the United Way (a practice I had no trouble with) but also asking them to return the response card, even when they did not wish to contribute, with a tick on the appropriate box (a practice I did object to).

By striving too hard for a do-gooder image, a company can thus be guilty of attempting to influence the personal choices and off-the-job behaviour of employees in ways that constitute an invasion of privacy. By explicitly or implicitly requiring employees to associate themselves with a particular activity, group, or cause, firms are telling workers what to believe, what values to support, and what goals to promote outside work.

Health Programs Sometimes organizations pressure employees in certain directions for "their own good." Recently, for example, a group of employers led by Ford, PepsiCo, and General Mills launched a campaign to get their overweight employees to slim down.[17] Consider also the aggressive "wellness" programs that some companies are mounting to push employees toward healthier lifestyles. These paternalistic (after a fashion) programs are aimed at helping employees live longer and improve their health and productivity. The programs teach employees about nutrition, exercise, stress, and heart disease and encourage them to give up smoking, eat more healthfully, moderate their drinking, and work out in the company gym or join a company sports team after work.[18]

Wellness programs try to make fitness part of the corporate culture, and that seems not only innocent enough but beneficial as it is conducive to health. But some companies are making employees pay more for their health care benefits if they are overweight, have high blood pressure, or don't exercise.[19] And employees have been fired for smoking or taking a drink at home[20] or for refusing to take a test to prove they're nonsmokers.[21] One organization offers employees a financial incentive for agreeing to undergo a comprehensive health assessment and working with a health coach who telephones periodically to check up on them and who may or may not report back to the boss. Critics charge that this is a kind of "privacy tax." Those with good salaries have enough money to pay it, but what low-wage workers? Can they afford to protect their privacy by refusing to participate?[22] "I think employers are going to get deeper and deeper into the wellness business," says Professor Alan F. Westin of Columbia University. "This is going to throw up a series of profound ethical and legal dilemmas about how they should do it and what we don't want them to do."[23]

OBTAINING INFORMATION

Canadian employers are legally allowed to collect only personal information that is appropriate for the specific transaction they wish to collect it for. They must also explain the need for collecting the information, how that information will be used, and whether they plan to disclose it to anyone else. The law also includes provisions under which an employer may collect personal information without the employee's knowledge. It is of course no secret that firms do frequently seek, store, and communicate information about employees without their consent. Canadian Pacific Railway did, and workers brought a complaint against the company that eventually went to the Federal Court of Canada (*Erwin Eastmond v. Canadian Pacific Railway*, 2004 FC 852). A firm may bug employee lounges, hoping to discover who's responsible for pilfering. Another firm may use a managerial grapevine, with supervisors meeting once a month to exchange anecdotal material about employees, some of it obtained in confidence, all of it gathered with the hope of anticipating potential trouble-makers. Still another company may keep detailed files on the personal lives of its employees to ensure compatibility with organizational image and reputation.

Of special interest here are two common practices organizations engage in: subjecting employees to various tests and monitoring employees on the job to discover sundry information. Before beginning the discussion, however, we need to take a brief look at the concept of informed consent and how it connects with these topics.

Informed Consent

Certainly no employee is ever compelled to take a lie-detector, personality, or genetic screening test in the sense that someone puts a loaded revolver to the person's head and says, "Take the test or else." But compulsion, like freedom, comes in degrees. Although an employee may not be compelled to take a test in the same way that a prisoner of war, for example, is compelled to cooperate with a captor, enough coercion may be present to significantly diminish the worker's capacity to consent freely to privacy-invading procedures.

Obviously if workers submit to an honesty exam or to a test for genetic disorders, they agree to do so. But was their consent valid and legitimate? Was it informed consent? That's the issue, and it is an altogether reasonable issue to raise, because information collected on workers is often intimately personal and private and, when used carelessly, can injure them.

Informed consent implies deliberation and free choice. Workers must understand what they are agreeing to, including its full ramifications, and must voluntarily choose it. Deliberation requires not only the availability of facts but also a full understanding of them. Workers must be allowed to deliberate on the basis of enough usable information, information that they can understand. But usable information is not of itself enough to guarantee informed consent. Free choice is also important—the *consent* part is as significant as the *informed* part of informed consent.

Everyone agrees that for consent to be legitimate, it must be voluntary. Workers must willingly agree to the privacy-invading procedure. They must also be in a position to act voluntarily. One big factor that affects the voluntariness of consent is the pressures, express and implied, exerted on employees to conform to organizational policy. Especially when those pressures to conform are reinforced with implicit reprisals, they can effectively undercut the voluntariness of consent. That is obvious in the case of job applicants asked to undergo some invasion of their privacy. They can either submit or look for work elsewhere.

Polygraph Tests

When an individual is disturbed by a question, certain detectable physiological changes occur. The person's heart may begin to race, blood pressure may rise, respiration may increase. The polygraph simultaneously records changes in these physiological processes and, thus, is often used in lie detection. Such tests would be very useful in all sorts of situations and contexts where one wanted to know whether information or testimony was credible or not; for example, in police investigations, counterintelligence or . . . in screening employees. Polygraph tests are used much more frequently and broadly in the United States (where, some claim, polygraph testing is a "growth industry") than in Canada, though some organizations in Canada also use them.

Businesses may cite several reasons for using polygraph tests. First, the polygraph is a fast and economical way to verify information provided by a job applicant and to screen candidates for employment. So used, it can help reveal personal philosophy, behavioural patterns, and character traits incompatible with the organization's purpose, function, and image.

Second, the polygraph allows employers to identify dishonest employees or job candidates, at a time when many companies are suffering staggering annual losses through in-house theft. Third, companies argue that the use of polygraphs permits business to abolish audits and oppressive controls. They say the use of polygraphs actually increases workers' freedom.

However, the defenders of the use of polygraphs rely on three assumptions all of which are open to question.[24] The first assumption is that lying triggers an involuntary, distinctive response that truth telling does not. But this is not necessarily the case. What the polygraph can do is record that the respondent was more disturbed by one question than by another, but it cannot determine why the person was disturbed. Perhaps the question made the person feel guilty or angry or frightened, but deception does not necessarily lurk behind the emotional response.

Second, it is assumed that polygraphs are extraordinarily accurate. Lynn March, president of the American Polygraph Association, claims that "when administered correctly by qualified operators, the tests are accurate more than 90 percent of the time."[25] But David T. Lykken, a psychiatry professor, claims that these boasts are not borne out by three scientifically credible studies of the accuracy of polygraphs used on actual criminal suspects. The accuracies obtained by qualified operators in these experiments were 63 percent, 39 percent, and 55 percent.[26] Whether the polygraph is accurate 90 percent of the time or less, the conclusion is the same: it cannot reveal with certainty that a person is or is not telling the truth.

The third major assumption about polygraphs is that they cannot be beaten. Lykken, for one, suggests otherwise. The easiest way to beat the polygraph, the psychiatrist claims, is by augmenting your response to the control question by some form of covert self-stimulation, like biting your tongue. Not everybody believes this. Defenders of the polygraph contend that liars can't fool skilled operators of the machine. But even if the polygraph generally catches the guilty, it will also generate a disturbing number of "false positives"—that is, it will falsely identify as liars people who are telling the truth.

To see this, imagine that the polygraph is 95 percent accurate and suppose, for the sake of illustration, that at a large corporation with an in-house theft problem one out of every fifty employees is stealing from their employer. If the corporation has a thousand employees, then twenty will be crooks and 980 will be honest. If every employee is tested, then the test, being only 95 percent accurate, will identify nineteen of the twenty crooks; one will escape detection. But the test will also identify as liars 5 percent of the company's 980 innocent employees; that is, forty-nine people will be falsely accused. By firing all those who fail the polygraph, a company might well succeed in weeding out the guilty, but it would also seriously harm many innocent employees.

It might be well to quote from the majority decision of the Supreme Court of Canada in *R. v. Béland*, [1987] 2 S.C.R. 398, March 31, 1987, October 15, 1987, which rejected the results of polygraph testing as evidence in court:

> The results of a polygraph examination are not admissible as evidence. The polygraph has no place in the judicial process where it is employed as a tool to determine or to test the credibility of witnesses. The admission of such evidence would offend well-established rules of evidence, in particular, the rule against oath-helping, which prohibits a party from presenting evidence solely for the purpose of bolstering a witness' credibility . . . and the character evidence rule. The polygraph evidence is also inadmissible as expert evidence. The issue of credibility is an issue well within the experience of judges and juries and one in which no expert evidence is required. Further, ... It will also lead to numerous complications which will result in no greater degree of certainty in the process than that which already exists. The results recorded by the polygraph instrument, their nature and significance will reach the trier of fact through the mouth of the operator. Human fallibility will thus still be present, but now fortified with the mystique of science.

Of course, in addition to the above considerations, polygraph tests infringe on privacy. As professor of politics Christopher Pyle says, they violate "the privacy of beliefs and associations, the freedom from unreasonable searches, the privilege against self-accusation, and the presumption of innocence."[27] That is not to say employers never have the right to abridge privacy or employees never have an obligation to reveal themselves. In important cases of in-house theft, employers may be justified in using a polygraph as a last resort. But the threat to privacy remains.

The moral concerns embedded in the use of polygraphs suggest three points—in addition to the question of informed consent—to consider in evaluating their use in the workplace:

1. The information the organization seeks should be clearly and significantly related to the job. This caveat harks back to a determination of the legitimate areas of organizational influence over the individual.

2. Because the polygraph intrudes on psychic freedom, those administering it should consider whether they have compelling job-related reasons for doing so. Some persons contend that among the reasons must be the fact that the polygraph is the only way the organization can get information about a significant job-related matter. They believe that a firm should not subject employees to polygraph tests without having first exhausted all other means of preventing pilferage.

3. We must be concerned with how the polygraph is being used, what information it's gathering, who has access to this information, and how it will be disposed of.

Scientists, however, are experimenting with new techniques for detecting honesty, such as magnetic-resonance imaging, "cognosensors," and electroencephalography (EEG), all of which look directly at brain activity to see who is lying and who is not.[28] Although these techniques are not yet foolproof, their proponents believe that they promise to prove far more accurate than the antiquated polygraph. Look for them soon at a workplace near you.

Personality Tests

Companies often wish to determine whether prospective employees are emotionally mature, get along well with others, have a good work ethic, or would fit in with the organization. So they sometimes administer personality tests. One of the most popular of these tests, the Myers-Briggs Type Indicator, is used widely by private companies and various level of governments both in Canada and the United States. Personality tests such as the Myers-Briggs can reveal highly personal information, and they often intrude into areas of our lives and thoughts that we normally consider private. Consent is usually less than fully voluntary because personality tests are generally part of a battery of tests that job applicants must take if they wish to be considered for a position.

Used properly, personality tests serve two purposes in the workplace. First, they help screen applicants for jobs by indicating areas of adequacy and inadequacy. Second, in theory they simplify the complexities of business life by reducing the amount of decision making involved in determining whether an individual has the personal characteristics appropriate for a given job. For example, if a firm knows Wendy is an introvert, it would hardly place her in public relations.

But one key premise underlying such tests is questionable. That premise is that all individuals can usefully and validly be placed into a relatively small number of categories of personality types and character traits. The test designers typically believe that one's overall personality is shaped by only five factors and that these factors, which they seek to measure, account for "99 percent of the differences in human behavior."[29] However, people rarely represent pure personality types, such as the classic introvert or extrovert. Nor is the possession of a character trait an all-or-nothing thing. Most of us possess a variety of personality traits in various degrees, and social circumstances often influence the characteristics we display and the talents we develop. When organizations attempt to categorize employees, they oversimplify both human nature and their employees' potential and force people into artificial arrangements that may do justice neither to employees nor to the firms they work for.

Personality tests also screen for organizational compatibility, sometimes functioning to eliminate prospective employees whose individuality or creativity may be exactly what the firm needs. Some companies, for example, seek employees who are extremely submissive to authority. Thus, when writer Barbara Ehrenreich submitted to a personality test for a job at Wal-Mart, she was reprimanded for getting the "wrong" answer when she agreed only "strongly" with the proposition "All rules have to be followed to the letter at all times." The correct answer was "totally agree."[30] When used this way, personality tests raise a pressing moral issue in the employer–employee relationship: conformity of the individual to organizational ideals. Organizations by nature represent a danger to individual freedom and independence. When personality tests are used to screen for conformity to organizational values, goals, and philosophy, they can catalyze this natural tendency into a full-blown assault.

Then, of course, there's the intrusive nature of the questions. Questions like "Does driving give you a sense of power?" "Do you like a lot of excitement in your life?" or "If you could, would you work as an entertainer in Las Vegas?" may seem innocuous, but what about a personality test that delves into your love life or that asks men, "Was there ever a time in your life when you liked to play with dolls?" One disgruntled test-taker complains about "questions you wouldn't even answer for your own mother, if she asked you."[31] Worse, many of the tests asking these questions have little or no research to back them up or have not been validated for use in pre-employment situations. Even those who favour testing admit as much. John Kamp, an industrial psychologist, points out that even intelligent businesspeople can be swayed by a good marketing pitch from the companies that peddle invalid or unreliable tests. "That's the unfortunate thing," he says. "A person with a slick pitch and no real research behind their tests can have a good business."[32]

Monitoring Employees on the Job

In the past decade, most major employers have gained the technical ability to monitor the performance of their employees through the computers and telephones they use. In businesses with phone-in customers, the practice is especially prevalent as a way of ensuring better and more efficient service. The law restricts the government from eavesdropping on your cellular car phone, email, computer-to-computer transmissions, or private video conferences, but it permits employers to intercept employee communications. Workers don't necessarily resent this monitoring, if it is in the open. "I don't think people mind having their work checked," says Morton Bahr, president of the Communications Workers of America. "It's the secretiveness of it" that bothers employees.[33]

A great number of employers record employees' voice mail, email, or phone calls; review their computer files; or even videotape them—often without their knowledge. Overseeing customer service is not the only reason companies monitor their employees. Some companies, for example, check employees' computers or their Global Positioning System to see whether they exceed the allotted time for lunch or work breaks; others listen in on phone conversations and examine email messages to catch employees conducting personal business on company time.

"What are they going to think up to do to us next?" wonders one employee. "It's scary. I'll bet no one monitors the phones or email of CEOs and other top executives."[34] Nancy Flynn, executive director of ePolicy Institute, agrees with that sentiment. "In a lot of organizations," she says, "the senior executives are immune from [electronic] monitoring."[35] If so, this raises a basic moral objection. As explained in Chapter 1, and again in Chapter 2's discussion of Kant, if we make a moral judgment, we must be willing to make the same judgment in any similar set of circumstances. These executives, however, are apparently willing to apply to others a policy that they are unwilling to apply to themselves.

When in-house theft, sabotage, or other threatening conduct occurs, organizations frequently install monitoring devices—mirrors, cameras, and electronic recorders—to apprehend the employees who are responsible. But monitoring suspected trouble spots or private acts may create morally difficult situations. Consider the two male employees of Boston Sheraton Hotel who, during a hunt for a drug dealer, were secretly videotaped changing clothes in the locker room. They weren't suspects, just bystanders.[36]

As with personality and polygraph tests, monitoring can gather information about employees without their informed consent. Organizations frequently confuse notification of such practices with employee consent, but notification does not constitute consent. When employee restrooms, dressing rooms, locker rooms, and other private places are bugged, an obvious and serious threat to privacy exists—posted notices notwithstanding. It's true that in some cases surveillance devices may be the only way to apprehend the guilty. Nevertheless, they may often do more harm than good by violating the privacy of the vast majority of innocent employees. Obviously, even more serious moral questions arise when monitoring devices are not used exclusively for the purposes intended but also for cajoling, harassing, or snooping on employees.

Drug Testing

Political, legal and philosophical battles over the drug testing of employees have raged for years. Many U.S. companies have warmly embraced testing. A study published in the *Journal of the American Medical Association* supports doing so. It showed that postal workers who tested positive for drug use in a pre-employment urine test were at least 50 percent more likely to be fired, injured, disciplined, or absent than those who tested negative.[37] Although many companies remain skeptical of the benefits of testing, 67 percent of large U.S. corporations now test either current employees or job applicants for illegal substances.[38]

Canadian companies are more circumspect in testing for drugs especially since the Ontario Court of Appeal decision in *Entrop v. Imperial Oil Ltd.*, 2000 CanLII 16800

(ON C.A.). The decision struck down random drug tests partly on the ground that presently such tests detect the presence of drugs in the body but do not measure impairment from such drugs, though the Court did allow random tests for alcohol (breathalyzer tests) since there is a direct connection between the result of such tests and actual impairment at the time of testing. The Court treated alcohol testing as a Bona Fide Occupational Requirement. The Court also allowed that testing for drugs or alcohol was justified under the *Ontario Human Rights Code* after a significant work accident and in the presence of reasonable cause.

In principle, testing employees to determine whether they are using illegal drugs raises the same questions that other tests raise: Is there informed consent? How reliable are the tests? Is testing really pertinent to the job in question? Are the interests of the firm significant enough to justify encroaching on the privacy of the individual? But rather than reiterate these issues, all of which are important and relevant, this section limits itself to four additional remarks:

1. The issue of drug testing by corporations and other organizations arises in the broader context of the drug-abuse problem in our society today (which includes the abuse not just of illegal street drugs but of alcohol and prescription medicines as well). To discuss this problem intelligently, one needs good information, reliable statistics, and sociological insight; yet these are difficult to come by. The problems alcohol and drug abuse pose for businesses and other organizations are real and serious, even though the use of illegal drugs, at least, appears to have dropped significantly among workers since the mid-1980s. Excessive media attention and political posturing can create a false sense of crisis, leading people perhaps to advocate extreme or unnecessary measures.

2. Since drugs differ, one must carefully consider both what drugs one is testing for and why. Steroids, for instance, may be a problem for the NCAA but not for Manulife Financial. To be defensible, drug testing must be pertinent to employee performance and there must be a lot at stake. Testing airline pilots for alcohol consumption is one thing; testing the baggage handlers is something else. To go on a fishing trip in search of possible employee drug abuse, when there is no evidence of a problem or of significant danger, seems unreasonable.

3. Drug abuse by an individual is a serious problem, generally calling for medical and psychological assistance rather than punitive action. The moral assessment of any program of drug testing must rest in part on the potential consequences for those taking the test: Will they face immediate dismissal and potential legal penalties, or therapy and a chance to retain their positions? To put the issue another way, when an organization initiates a testing program, does it treat is as a kind of police function or as a way to respond to the needs and problems of its

employees? Some business writers argue that voluntary, non-punitive drug-assistance programs are far more cost-effective for companies, in any case, than testing initiatives.[39]

4. Any drug-testing program, assuming it is warranted, must be careful to respect the dignity and rights of the persons to be tested. Some alternatives to body fluid testing are less invasive of employee privacy. Due process must also be followed, including advance notification of testing as well as procedures for retesting and appealing test results. All possible steps should be taken to ensure individual privacy.

WORKING CONDITIONS

In a broad sense, the conditions under which people work include personnel policies and procedures, as well as the extent to which an organization is committed to respecting the rights and privacy of its employees. This section, however, examines three other aspects of working conditions: health and safety on the job, styles of management, and the organization's maternity and day-care arrangements.

Health and Safety

In Canada both the federal and the provincial or territorial governments have in place so-called "modern" occupational health and safety legislation which embodies in statute and regulatory practice the following three principles: the right of workers to be informed of known or foreseeable health or safety hazards in the workplace; the right of workers to participate in the prevention of occupational injuries; and the right of workers to refuse to do dangerous work and to be protected against dismissal or disciplinary action for such refusal. The federal *Canada Labour Code* and the various provincial or territorial occupational health and safety acts, along with the various provincial or territorial health and safety commissions or boards, have been in place for at least a generation and one would have thought that they would have contributed to an increasingly safer and healthier Canadian workplace. In some respects they have, but in others they have not.

The Canadian workplace is not safe or healthy enough. During 2005 there were 1,097 workplace fatalities in Canada as against 758 in 1993, an increase of 44 percent in absolute numbers or an increase from 5.9 fatalities per 100,000 workers in 1993 to 6.8 per 100,000 in 2005 (the increase is equivalent to 1 fatality per 15,000 workers). These are the finding of a recent study by the Centre for the Study of Living Standards. The very title of the study tells the sad story: "Five Deaths a Day: Workplace Fatalities in Canada, 1993–2005." According to its authors, the study brings out two messages: "First, despite the problems associated with the definition and measurement of workplace fatalities, the number and rate of workplace fatalities in Canada, even from accidents, is unacceptably high. Second, insufficient progress is being made in reducing the number and rate of workplace fatalities. Canada can do much better."[40] On the other hand, according to the Association for Workers' Compensation Boards of Canada the number of accepted time-loss injuries (injuries accepted and paid for by Compensation Boards) have been on the decline since the mid-1990s.[41] This would be gratifying news if it were not for allegations from many quarters that some WCBs doctor their statistics for a variety of reasons.[42] Critics claim that it is odd to have an increase in workplace fatalities at the same time as we have a decrease in workplace injuries. It does sound odd. However, one must bear in mind that a great percentage of the increase in fatalities is accounted for, not by an increase in accidents, but by occupational diseases, especially those associated with asbestos. This very fact may bode ill for future developments in the workplace as more and more of the older workers are diagnosed with occupational diseases that may take over 20–30 years to develop. The more real and serious health and safety problems in the workplace are those stemming, not from specific and identifiable events on the job, but from long years of labour or long-term exposure to hazardous substances.

Employers clearly have a moral obligation not to expose their workers to needless risks or to endanger their lives or health negligently or recklessly. In the case of a drilling company that lowered a 23-year-old worker to the bottom of a 34-foot-deep, 18-inch-wide hole, where he then suffocated, a Los Angeles county prosecutor put it this way: "Our opinion is you can't risk somebody's life to save a few bucks. That's the bottom line."[43] Issues of legal liability aside, however, employers are not morally responsible for all workplace accidents. Sometimes coworkers are negligent or act irresponsibly, and sometimes the victims themselves may have behaved stupidly or failed to exercise due care. Sometimes, as people often say, accidents "just happen." Moreover, nothing in life is free of risk, and we often judge the risk worth taking (for example, when we choose to drive a car). And in some circumstances or in certain occupations, an injured worker can reasonably be said to have voluntarily assumed the risk. Although there is some truth in all these points, they are also somewhat misleading about the nature of accidents.

To begin with assumption of risk, the proposition that, for example, the young Los Angeles man who died at the bottom of the shaft can be inferred to have freely and knowingly decided to gamble with his life is dubious, to say the least. Voluntary assumption of risk presupposes informed consent. As we have seen, that would require the worker to have been fully informed of the danger and to have freely chosen to assume it, which is rarely true of workers who are just doing what the boss tells them to do. Informed consent entails that employees have a moral right to refuse work when it exposes them to "danger" or "imminent danger" or "unusual danger" or "undue hazard," and employers are wrong to reprimand or otherwise retaliate against them for doing so.[44] Of course, what constitutes an "imminent" danger (or the other variants one finds in the statutes or regulations of different jurisdictions) may sometimes be open to debate, and workers should always behave reasonably and, when trying to avoid a perceived danger, take the least disruptive course of action open to them.

Employers, for their part, should inform workers of any life-threatening hazards, as they are, of course, legally obliged to do.[45] Still, employees are often unaware of the dangers they face, many of which may be long-term, rather than imminent, hazards. Take, for example, Suncor Energy Products Inc. and Tornado Insulation Ltd., who were fined by the Ontario Court of Justice in Sarnia, Ontario, for failing, among other things, to "ensure workers wore appropriate personal protective equipment when removing the materials both after the suspected asbestos was discovered and after it was confirmed."[46] Again, consider the electronics industry. It might look safe in comparison with other occupations, but behind its clean, high-tech image lurk health hazards for workers—in particular, the chemical toxins indispensable to the manufacture of computer chips.[47] One workplace toxin causing concern recently is beryllium, a miracle metal—one-third the weight of aluminum, yet six times stiffer than steel—which is used in a number of products these days, including computers, cell phones, and golf clubs. More toxic than plutonium, a few millionths of a gram of beryllium can trigger an immune system attack and fatally damage the lungs and other organs. Current legal standards suffice to keep workers handling the stuff from dying after a few days or weeks on the job, but they don't adequately protect them from developing chronic beryllium disease, which may take up to twenty-five years to develop. The same is true of a lot of other dangerous substances workers have been handling for years and years, like asbestos, uranium, crystalline silica, etc., exposure to which leads to serious and often fatal conditions many years after exposure.[48]

Putting aside the assumption of risk and the right to know about and refuse hazardous work, we turn now to the causes of workplace accidents. As previously stated, it seems that accidents often result not from direct employer malfeasance but, rather, from employee blunders, coworker negligence, or just plain bad luck with nobody at fault. According to safety experts, though, this way of thinking is inaccurate. Industrial accidents don't just happen. They are caused—by inadequate worker training, sloppy procedures, lack of understanding of the job, improper tools and equipment, hazardous work environments, poor equipment maintenance, and overly tight scheduling.[49] And these are all matters that fall within the purview of the employer. For example, when some heavy machinery crushed his ankle, Michael Rodriguez was unable to leave his workplace and get to the hospital for several hours. That's because, until unfavourable publicity forced a policy change, Wal-Mart would lock its employees in at night, and there was no one on duty with a key.[50] A worker at an Oakville, Ontario, plant had the fingers of one hand crushed in the rollers of a silicone rubber mill which the employer had failed to equip with a proper guarding device. An electrician was electrocuted while fixing an electrical relay switch at a Napanee, Ontario, manufacturing plant because, among other things, the facility had no lockout in place to ensure that the circuit remained de-energized while work was performed.[51]

Workplace injuries, most experts believe, are related not to shortcomings in technology, but to unsafe human behaviour resulting from poor job practices and a workplace environment that fails to put safety first. The key to a safer workplace is not so much engineering as changing the company's "hidden culture"—the unspoken rules and practices followed—to one that is proactively oriented toward safety. In addition, governments at all levels must invest more in field inspections to ensure proper enforcement of the existing legislation and compliance with regulations. The Ontario government is doing something about it, as it is currently going through a hiring program that will see the number of Ministry of Labour inspectors increase from 230 in 2004 to 430 by 2008.

At the same time, however, the practice of field inspections must adapt itself to the changing trends in work schedules and to the increasing violence in the workplace. Inspectors have traditionally visited mines, forestry fields, or construction and manufacturing sites, and have done so following a traditional five-day, nine-to-five schedule. But an increasing number of people work outside the traditional schedule (for example, during weekends or after hours). Furthermore, there has been an increase in the occurrence of violent incidents in the Canadian workplace. Statistics Canada reports that there were 356,000 violent incidents in the workplace during 2004. A third of all workplace violence took place against workers in the field of social assistance or health care, including hospitals and nursing homes, while there was also a high number of incidents involving workers in the accommodation and food services, the retail trade, and educational services. "I think what is really shocking about this report," said Jessie Callaghan, a specialist on workplace violence, "is that they [Statistics Canada] are just talking about physical assault, sexual assault and robbery." The problem becomes much more extensive if we also take into account other acts of violence such as verbal abuse or psychological harassment.[52] Accordingly, inspectors should perhaps start visiting also health care facilities, educational institutions of all level, and office environments. For example, 73,000 nurses were assaulted in hospitals or care homes in Canada during 2005 (that's one in three of all nurses involved in direct patient care).[53]

New Health Challenges One problem that governments, business, and labour unions will have to address in the future is the epidemic of occupational injury and illness known as musculoskeletal disorders. In offices and factories across the country, hundreds of thousands of workers suffer from aching backs, crippled

fingers, sore wrists, and other problems caused or aggravated by their jobs. Telephone operators, court stenographers, and supermarket checkout clerks are just a few of the workers who have to live with numb fingers, swollen knuckles, and aching wrists from the constant repetition of awkward hand and arm movements. The ailments in question may sound minor, but they are anything but trivial to those who suffer from them. After years and years of doing such repetitive tasks, some of them cannot even pick up a cup of coffee without feeling excruciating pain in their finger joints. The breaking up of jobs into smaller and smaller units, with each worker performing fewer tasks but repeating them thousands of times a day, has contributed to the problem in manufacturing industries. However, musculoskeletal disorders are also rampant among white-collar office workers, especially those who spend all day at the video display screen. The redesign of jobs, adjustable chairs, training in the proper use of computer terminals, and other preventive measures can often reduce the problem. In the meantime, it is not only the employees who are suffering. Musculoskeletal disorders decrease productivity and dampen morale, and having a skilled worker go out on long-term disability and vocational rehabilitation can cost a company a small fortune.[54]

Another aspect of work with health and economic implications concerns the shifts people work. A team of scientists from Harvard and Stanford universities believes that the health and productivity of workers whose work hours change regularly can be measurably improved if employers schedule shift changes to conform with the body's natural and adjustable sleep cycles. This is particularly important given that sleep deprivation and fatigue are prime causes of industrial accidents.[55]

Related to fatigue is an aspect of work we have only recently begun to appreciate fully—the health implications of stress. It is estimated that 50 percent of Canadians view their workplace as a major contributor to stress,[56] while another estimate places the annual cost to the Canadian economy of all stress-related injuries at between $16 and $33 billion.[57] Many factors contribute to workplace stress: workload, work schedule, conflicting job demands, job security, level of responsibility, safety or security or health concerns, management style, and so on.[58] Furthermore, technology leashes many employees to the job even when they're at home. As a result, says Donald I. Tepas, a professor of industrial psychology, "the distinction between work and non-work time is getting fuzzier all the time."

The relation between workplace stress and ill health is now well established. In fact, scientists have even ascertained that stressful job conditions diminish mental health and damage physical functioning as much as smoking does.[59] Revamping working environments that produce stress and helping employees learn to cope with it are among the major health challenges facing Canadian business (and indeed business worldwide) now and in the years to come.

Management Styles

How managers conduct themselves on the job can do more to enhance or diminish the work environment than any other facet of employer–employee relations. "Management creates the conditions in which most adults spend half their waking lives," writes Thomas A. Stewart, editor of the *Harvard Business Review*. "Bad management makes lives miserable."[60] In their survey of Canadians workers, Darrell Bricker and John Wright[61] found that about 11 percent of them (roughly about 1.75 million workers) either "hated" their boss or "dreaded going to work" because of their boss. Now, that's a lot of unhappy people in the Canadian workplace. The survey did not go into the behaviour of the bosses, but Harvey Hornstein has identified "bullying" bosses who are abusive, dictatorial, devious, dishonest, manipulative, and inhumane.[62]

This workplace reality runs contrary to the teachings of almost all management theorists. For example, in his classic work *The Human Side of Enterprise*, Douglas McGregor formulated "Theory X" to describe the management style premised on the belief that workers dislike work and will do everything they can to avoid it.[63] These managers insist that the average person wishes to avoid responsibility, lacks ambition, and values security over everything else. Accordingly, he or she has to be coerced and bullied into conformity with organizational objectives. McGregor advocated "Theory Y," which assumes that employees basically like work and view it as something natural and potentially enjoyable. Workers are seen as motivated as much by pride and a desire for self-fulfillment as by money and job security. They don't dodge responsibility but accept it and even seek it out.

Since McGregor's book, other management writers have pursued this line of thought and recommended countless other management styles—including "Theory Z," which touts Japanese-style respect for workers. More recently, some theorists have advocated an alternative management style that eschews a masculine, hierarchical, aggressive, analytic, winner-take-all approach in favour of a more personal, empathetic, and collaborative style, thought to be characteristic of, and more congenial to, women. This is not the place to discuss different theories of management, but clearly the management styles recommended by different writers, as well as the management styles actually adopted by different bosses, rest on implicit or explicit assumptions about human nature.

However, no set of assumptions about human nature is absolutely correct or incorrect, nor is there one perfectly right way to manage. But that's precisely the point. Problems inevitably arise when managers routinize their leadership style, regardless of the needs, abilities, and predilections of their particular employees. When managers ignore individual differences, they risk creating a work atmosphere that's distressing to workers and less productive than it might be. Moreover, implicit assumptions about human nature can easily become self-reinforcing because people tend to behave as they are treated. Thus, managers who treat employees as if they were incapable of taking initiative will probably end up with employees who don't take initiative. As a result managers must carefully examine their preconceptions when determining the most appropriate leadership style to adopt in their workplace. That is easier said than done for many successful managers. "With the success they've achieved," says Michael Feiner of the Columbia Business School, "bosses can come to believe that their way is the right way, the best way—perhaps the only way."[64]

Day Care and Maternity Leave

One area often overlooked in discussions of working conditions is the provision of maternity or paternity leave and child care services for workers with children. The need for such services is steadily growing, as certain social and economic trends are changing. For example, in 1976, women accounted for 37 percent of the employed workforce in Canada, while in 2006 they made up 47 percent of it, or nearly half of it. In 1976, only 39 percent of all women with children under age 16 living at home were part of the employed workforce. By 2006 their percentage had grown to 73, though women with children were still less likely to be employed than women without children.[65] At the same time, there have been increases in the proportion of single-parent families with young children and in the incidence of non-traditional working schedules (with most workers in such schedules being women). Also, the proportion of dual-earner families among husband/wife families with children under 16 has nearly doubled between 1976 and 2005, from 36 to 69 percent. All these factors have contributed to an increased demand for non-parental care of young children. Nor is that demand likely to diminish in the future. The trend of dual-earner families (especially during their childbearing years) is likely to keep growing. Many families are unable to make satisfactory child care arrangements either because the services are unavailable or for the simple reason that the parent(s) cannot afford them.

Though the federal and provincial governments have made some progress in this area (especially in the province of Quebec), there is still a great deal to be done, especially by the private sector in cooperation with labour unions. It is true that, despite their traditional support of public child care, some unions have also started bargaining with employers to establish work-related child care services. The notable case here is the Canadian Auto Workers union with its CAW Community Child Care and Developmental Services. It is also true that a number of private and public sector employers have already established work-related (either onsite or in locations near work) childcare centres. In 2000, there were 336 such centres in Canada, with over half of them in Quebec. In total, 55 percent of these child care centres were sponsored by public-sector employers, 41 percent by private-sector employers, and 4 percent were private/public ventures. By the way, none of these services are free, as parents are charged considerable fees per child.[66] Still these efforts, however salutary, are not enough. "While the number of day care centre places has increased dramatically, it is estimated that only 20% of children whose mothers work can be accommodated. Whether because of choice or necessity, the majority of children in non-parental care in Canada continue to be cared for in unregulated homes."[67]

Some business writers have argued that offering child care as a fringe benefit and dealing as flexibly as possible with employees' family needs can prove advantageous for most employers. Such policies can be cost-effective in the narrower sense by decreasing absenteeism, boosting morale and loyalty to the firm, and enhancing productivity. This is an important consideration. But even more important are the underlying moral issues.

First, women have a right to compete on an equal footing with men, or, to put the point more generally, parents of young children have a right to compete for jobs on an equal footing with childless workers. Surely, their contribution to the collective (that is, their producing future citizens and workers) cannot itself be a barrier to their enjoying rights open to all (in this case, equal opportunity in seeking and maintaining fruitful and meaningful employment). Or one might defend such a policy on the utilitarian ground that it would enhance total social welfare. In fact, many organizations find it in their self-interest to provide paid leave and flexible work arrangements so they can attract better and more-talented employees.

Second, from various ethical perspectives, the development of our potential capacities is a moral ideal—perhaps even a human right. For that reason, or from the point of view of promoting human well-being, many theorists would contend that women or men should not be forced to choose between, on the one hand, childbearing or meaningful parenting and, on the other, the successful pursuit of their careers. Nor should they be forced to reduce the quality of their commitment either to their children or to their careers. If employment circumstances force them to do so, and if those circumstances could reasonably be changed, then we have not lived up to the ideal of treating those women or men as persons whose goals are worthy of respect.

The moral value here is not to promote any single vision of the good life but rather to permit individuals, couples, and families as much autonomy as possible, given other social goals. They should be able to define the good life for themselves and to seek the arrangement of work and personal relations that makes that life possible. Firm-affiliated child care services and other institutional arrangements that accommodate parental needs can clearly play a key role in the overall redesigning of work to enhance workers' well-being.

REDESIGNING WORK

Chapter 4 looked at alienation under capitalism and changing attitudes toward work. It remains true that many, perhaps even most, employees are dissatisfied with their jobs to some extent. Any investigation of the moral issues arising around the workplace and any discussion of the challenges facing business today must confront this basic problem and consider ways of improving the quality of work life.

Dissatisfaction on the Job

As early as the 1920s, researchers began to realize that workers would be more productive if management met those needs of the workers that money cannot buy. Managers at the Hawthorne factory of Western Electric Company were conducting experiments to determine the effect of the work environment on worker productivity. In the literature of work motivation, these studies have become known as the Hawthorne studies. What they discovered has been termed the "Hawthorne effect."

Researchers in the Hawthorne studies chose a few employees to work in an experimental area, apart from the thousands of employees in the rest of the factory. Every effort was made to improve working conditions, from painting walls a cheerful colour to making lights brighter. Worker productivity increased with each improvement. Then the experimenters decided to reverse the process. For example, lights were made dimmer. To everyone's surprise, productivity continued to increase.

The conclusion the researchers drew was that workers were producing more because they were receiving attention. Instead of feeling that they were spokes in an organizational wheel, they felt important and recognized. The attention had the effect of heightening their sense of personal identity and feeling of control over their work environment. Recognition of this effect can help management increase worker motivation and job satisfaction and also increase the organization's productivity.

Subsequent research corroborates and deepens the Hawthorne results.[68] In studying the problem of poor worker motivation, the influential management theorist Frederick Herzberg discovered that factors producing job satisfaction differed from those producing job dissatisfaction. Herzberg found that although job dissatisfaction frequently arises from extrinsic problems (such as pay, supervision, working conditions, and leadership styles), resolving those extrinsic problems does not necessarily produce satisfied workers. They can still express little or no job satisfaction. The reason, Herzberg contends, is that worker satisfaction depends on such factors as a sense of accomplishment, responsibility, recognition, self-development, and self-expression.[69] Recent surveys in the United States support Herzberg's findings. When employees at all occupational levels are asked to rank what is important to them, they list interesting work; sufficient help, support, and information to accomplish the job; enough authority to carry out the work; good pay; the opportunity to develop special skills; job security; and a chance to see the results of their work. Other research shows that what makes people content is being respected by members of groups they respect. In line with this, Roger Martin, dean of the school of management at the University of Toronto, argues that employees are happiest when they're respected members of a team they admire and when the team and company are respected by the outside world.[70]

In light of the above points, things are not well in the Canadian workplace. In a recent survey, Canadians were asked to grade their employers with respect to five work-environment conditions, namely the extent to which their employers make them feel that they "fit in" their work role and the extent to which they feel "supported in" their role, "clear" in their role, "valued" at their work, and "inspired." Canadian workers gave their employers an overall grade of "C+."[71] The issue of workers dissatisfaction or satisfaction is probably more keenly felt in countries which, like Canada, are officially egalitarian and multicultural societies but in which minority groups of various kinds are still discriminated against in the workplace.

Numerous mental health problems stem from a lack of job satisfaction—low self-esteem, anxiety, impaired interpersonal relations, and psychosomatic ailments such as ulcers and hypertension—especially in low-status, boring, unchallenging jobs that offer little autonomy. Furthermore, such jobs tend to inhibit intellectual growth and the pursuit of richer, more fulfilling activities outside work.[72] Even worse, researchers have found that workers in boring, passive jobs are 33 to 35 percent more likely to die prematurely than workers in active jobs. Stressful work that offers little decision-making opportunity (like assembly-line work) makes an untimely demise even more likely.[73] Those findings are of particular relevance to today's workforce, in which many persons of relatively high educational achievement occupy comparatively low-status jobs.

One of the most intriguing studies not only suggests a correlation between longevity and job satisfaction but also contends that job satisfaction is the strongest predictor of longevity.[74] The second major factor for longevity is happiness. Both of these factors predict longevity better than either the physical health or the genetic inheritance of individuals.

Because the design of work materially affects the total well-being of workers, work content and job satisfaction are paramount moral concerns. But if we also assume that a happier, more contented worker is generally a more productive one, then it follows that business has an economic reason as well as a moral obligation to devise ways, in concert with labour and perhaps even government, to improve the quality of work life (QWL).

Quality of Work Life (QWL)

This book isn't the place for determining precisely what QWL measures firms should take. For some firms QWL may mean providing workers with less supervision and more autonomy. For others it may mean providing work opportunities to develop and refine skills. Still other firms might try to provide workers with greater participation in the conception, design, and execution of their work—that is, with greater responsibility and a deeper sense of achievement. It is interesting in this connection to consider the managerial format Magna International uses for greater productivity and worker satisfaction in its (non-union) plants.[75]

Granting workers new responsibilities and respect can benefit the entire organization. Randy Pennington, vice-president of Performance Systems Corporation, tells of a friend who showed an ad for a new American car to a Japanese businessperson. The ad said that the car "set a new standard for quality because it was examined by 34 different quality inspectors." "Now, *this*," he said to his Japanese colleague, "is what we need to compete with you. Imagine: 34 quality inspectors!" The Japanese looked at the ad, smiled, and said, "You don't need 34 inspectors to get quality. You just need everyone who works on the car to be proud of the work. Then you'll need only one inspector."[76]

Thawing the antagonistic worker–boss relations that characterize many plants isn't always easy. Some union members are wary, worried about "being co-opted and looking like management flunkies."[77] Investigators believe that the success of QWL programs and other workplace reform efforts depends on the ability of the organization to reinforce high levels of trust. To the extent that it does so, organizational performance can improve. But, warns William Cooke, professor at Wayne State University and author of a book on workplace reform, "if [workers] perceive management as doing this without due consideration for the welfare of employees . . . it will have the potential of destroying the efforts altogether."[78]

After Gerard Arpey took over as CEO of American Airlines in 2003, the company began the arduous but ambitious process of developing better and more stable working relations between managers and employees, something that had long eluded American. In an apparently successful effort to end adversarial relations with the unions, Arpey created new structures of consultancy across the company, captured in the slogans "Involve before Deciding. Discuss before Implementing. Share before Announcing." "We are trying to make our unions our business partners," Arpey says. "It is not about sitting around the campfire singing Kumbaya."[79]

These days, closer union–management relations also characterize many GM plants. Mike Spitzley, manager of GM's 5,300-worker car-truck plant in Janesville, Wisconsin, for example, says "most of the things we talk about, it's 'we.' It's not us versus them. We've pretty much realized that our goals are the same" as the union's. Mike O'Brien, president of the local chapter of the United Auto Workers, agrees. "There's something different going on," he says. "Years ago, it wasn't any of our business what went on in the business." The most striking example is GM's Saturn Corporation, where union and management share all big decisions, from choosing suppliers to picking the company's advertising agency.[80]

At GM and American, the ideals of improved job atmosphere, employee participation, and worker job security appear to have meshed nicely with the goal of increased productivity. Studies provide evidence of this compatibility in many other cases, too. Not only is productivity 5 to 10 percent higher in companies with profit sharing, but productivity is also consistently higher in enterprises with an organized program of worker participation.[81] This is in line with the views of many experts, who insist that worker-friendly companies outperform traditional command-and-control employers. They argue that new organizational structures and work practices that put a premium on collaboration and cooperation are fundamental to the nation's future economic success.[82]

Although a range of social and economic research supports that conclusion, there is no watertight guarantee that worker participation and an improved quality of work life will always boost productivity. For example, although diversifying tasks may make work more satisfying, Japanese carmakers reduced the number of rejects on their assembly line not by diversifying but by standardizing the cars produced. And Volkswagen found that its productivity and quality were higher when production consisted solely of the standard Rabbit than when other models were introduced. Job-enlargement programs, by definition, add to the variety of tasks the worker is assigned; job-enrichment programs add some planning, designing, and scheduling to the operative worker's tasks. Both programs may slow output in some cases. Worker involvement in production management may not fit well, some argue, with the two other ingredients that managers and management consultants see as essential for manufacturing efficiency: a just-in-time approach to eliminating waste, and rigorous statistical process control to improve quality.

On the other hand, employee involvement is essential to work elimination programs—programs that eliminate wasteful and unnecessary tasks, thus enhancing job satisfaction while making the organization leaner and more productive. Still, the possibility of a conflict between the obligation to make work more satisfying and the goal of increasing productivity will likely be at the heart of moral decisions in this area for years to come. To resolve them will require a cooperative effort by labour and management, rooted in the recognition that tradeoffs are inevitable.

SUMMARY

1. Individuals have a right to privacy, in particular a right to control certain information about themselves, to shelter aspects of their lives from public scrutiny, and to make personal decisions autonomously, free from illegitimate influence. Whenever an organization infringes on an individual's personal sphere, it must justify that infringement.

2. A firm is legitimately interested in whatever significantly influences job performance, but there is no precise definition of "significant influence." Organizations may be invading privacy when they coerce employees to contribute to charities, do volunteer work, or participate in wellness programs.

3. Information-gathering on employees can be highly personal and subject to abuse. The critical issue here is *informed consent*, which implies deliberation and free choice. Deliberation requires that employees be provided all significant facts concerning the information-gathering procedure and understand their consequences. Free choice means that the decision to participate must be voluntary and uncoerced.

4. Polygraph tests, personality tests, drug tests, and the monitoring of employees on the job can intrude into employee privacy. The exact character of these devices, the rationale for using them to gather information in specific circumstances, and the moral costs of doing so must always be carefully evaluated.

5. Health and safety remain of foremost moral concern in the workplace. Employers have a moral obligation not to expose their workers to needless risk, and employees have a right to know about and refuse hazardous work. The scope of occupational hazards, including shift work and stress, and the number of employees harmed by work-related injuries and diseases are greater than many people think. Enforcement of existing regulations has too often been lax.

6. Management style greatly affects the work environment. Managers who operate with rigid assumptions about human nature or who devote themselves to infighting and political manoeuvring damage employees' interests.

7. Day-care services and reasonable parental-leave policies also affect working conditions. Despite the genuine need for and the ethical importance of both day care and flexible work arrangements for parents, only a handful of companies make serious efforts to provide them.

8. Studies report extensive job dissatisfaction at all levels. Various factors influence satisfaction and dissatisfaction on the job. Redesigning the work process can enhance the quality of work life, the well-being of workers, and even productivity.

CASE 7.1

Testing for Honesty

"Charity begins at home." If you don't think so, ask the Salvation Army. Some years ago, one of the Army's local branches discovered that it had a problem with theft among its kettle workers, the people who collect money for the Army during the Christmas season. Some of the Army's kettlers were helping themselves to the Army's loot before the organization had a chance to dole it out. To put a stop to the problem, Army officials sought the assistance of Dr. John Jones, director of research for London House Management Consultants.

London House is one of several companies that market honesty tests for prospective employees. Some of these tests, such as London House's Personnel Selection Inventory (PSI), also measure the applicant's tendency toward drug use and violence. All three categories—honesty, drugs, and violence—play a major part in company losses, according to the makers of these tests.

The company losses in question are astronomical. The U.S. Chamber of Commerce estimates that employee theft costs U.S. companies $40 billion annually; some unofficial estimates run three times as high. Moreover, 20 percent of the businesses that fail do so because of employee crime.[83] Compounding the problem is the cost of employee drug use in terms of absenteeism, lost initiative, inattentiveness, accidents, and diminished productivity. Employee violence also costs companies millions of dollars in damage, lost productivity, and lawsuits.

Honesty-test makers say that the only way to deal with these problems is before workers are hired, not after—by subjecting them to a pre-employment psychological test that will identify those prospective employees who will be likely to steal, who have a history of violence or emotional instability, or who have used illegal drugs on a regular basis.

James Walls, one of the founders of Stanton Corporation, which has offered written honesty tests for twenty-five years, says that dishonest job applicants are clever at hoodwinking potential employers in a job interview. "They have a way of conducting themselves that is probably superior to the low-risk person. They have learned what it takes to be accepted and how to overcome the normal interview strategy," he says. "The high-risk person will get hired unless there is a way to screen him." For this reason, Walls maintains, written, objective tests are needed to weed out the crooks.[84]

Millions of written honesty tests are given annually, thanks to congressional restrictions on polygraph testing. In addition to being legal, honesty tests are also more economical than polygraph tests. They cost between $7 and $14 per test, compared with $90 or so for a polygraph. Furthermore, the tests are easily administered at the workplace and can be quickly evaluated by the test maker. The tests are also non-discriminatory because the race, gender, or ethnicity of applicants has no significant impact on scores.

A typical test begins with some cautionary remarks. Test-takers are told to be truthful because dishonesty can be detected, and they are warned that incomplete answers will be considered incorrect, as will any unanswered questions. Then applicants ordinarily sign a waiver permitting the results to be known to their prospective employer and authorizing the testing agency to check out their answers. Sometimes, however, prospective employees are not told that they are being tested for honesty, only that they are being asked questions about their background. James Walls justifies this less-than-frank explanation by saying that within a few questions it is obvious that the test deals with attitudes toward honesty. "The test is very transparent, it's not subtle."[85]

Some questions do indeed seem transparent—for example, "If you found $100 that was lost by a bank truck on the street yesterday, would you turn the money over to the bank, even though you knew for sure there was no reward?" But other questions are more controversial: "Have you ever had an argument with someone and later wished you had said something else?" If you were to answer no, you would be on your way to failing. Other questions that may face the test-taker are: "How strong is your conscience?" "How often do you feel guilty?" "Do you always tell the truth?" "Do you occasionally have thoughts you wouldn't want made public?" "Does everyone steal a little?" "Do you enjoy stories of successful crimes?" "Have you ever been so intrigued by the cleverness of a thief that you hoped the person would escape detection?" Or consider questions like "Is an employee who takes it easy at work cheating his employer?" or "Do you think a person should be fired by a company if it is found that he helped employees cheat the company out of overtime once in a while?" These ask you for your reaction to hypothetical dishonest situations. "If you are a particularly kind-hearted person who isn't sufficiently punitive, you fail," says Lewis Maltby, director of the workplace rights office at the American Civil Liberties Union. "Mother Teresa would never pass some of these tests."[86]

A big part of some tests is a behavioural history of the applicant. Applicants are asked to reveal the nature, frequency, and quantity of specific drug use, if any. They also must indicate if they have ever engaged in drunk driving, illegal gambling, traffic violations, forgery, vandalism, and a host of other unseemly behaviours. They must also state their opinions about the social acceptability of drinking alcohol and using other drugs.

Some testing companies go further in this direction. Instead of honesty exams, they offer tests designed to draw a general psychological profile of the applicant, claiming that this sort of analysis can predict more accurately than either the polygraph or the typical honesty test how the person will perform on the job. Keith M. Halperin, a psychologist with Personnel Decision, Inc. (PDI), a company that offers such tests, complains that most paper-and-pencil honesty tests are simply written equivalents of the polygraph. They ask applicants whether they have stolen from their employers, how much they have taken, and other questions directly related to honesty. But why, asks Halperin, "would an applicant who is dishonest enough to steal from an employer be honest enough to admit it on a written test?" It is more difficult for applicants to fake their responses to PDI's tests, Halperin contends.[87]

Not everyone is persuaded. Phyllis Bassett, vice-president of James Bassett Company of Cincinnati, believes tests developed by psychologists that do not ask directly about the applicant's past honesty are poor predictors of future trustworthiness.[88] This may be because, as some psychologists report, "it is very difficult for dishonest people to fake honesty." One reason is that thieves tend to believe that "everybody does it" and that therefore it would be implausible for them to deny stealing.[89] In general, those who market honesty exams boast of their validity and reliability, as established by field studies. They insist that the tests do make a difference; they enable employers to ferret out potential troublemakers—as in the Salvation Army case.

Dr. Jones administered London House's PSI to eighty kettler applicants, which happened to be the number that the particular theft-ridden centre needed. The PSIs were not scored, and the eighty applicants were hired with no screening. Throughout the fundraising month between Thanksgiving and Christmas, the centre kept a record of each kettler's daily receipts. After the Christmas season, the tests were scored and divided into "recommended" and "not recommended" for employment. After accounting for the peculiarities of each collection neighbourhood, Jones discovered that those kettlers the PSI had not recommended turned in on the average $17 per day less than those the PSI had recommended. Based on this analysis, he estimated the centre's loss to employee theft during the fund drive at $20,000.

The list of psychological-test enthusiasts is growing by leaps and bounds, but the tests have plenty of detractors. Many psychologists have voiced concern over the lack of standards governing the tests; the American Psychological Association favours the establishment of federal standards for written honesty exams. But the chief critics of honesty and other psychological exams are the people who have to take them. They complain about having to reveal some of the most intimate details of their lives and opinions.

For example, until an employee filed suit, Rent-A-Center, a Texas corporation, asked both job applicants and employees being considered for promotion true-false questions like these: "I have never indulged in any unusual sex practices," "I am very strongly attracted by members of my own sex," "I go to church almost every week," and "I have difficulty in starting or holding my bowel movements."

A manager who was fired for complaining about the test says, "It was ridiculous. The test asked if I loved tall women. How was I supposed to answer that? My wife is 5 feet 3 inches." A spokesman for Rent-A-Center argues that its questionnaire is not unusual and that many other firms use it.[90]

Firms who use tests like Rent-A-Center's believe that no one's privacy is being invaded because employees and job applicants can always refuse to take the test. Critics disagree. "Given the unequal bargaining power," says former ACLU official Kathleen Bailey, "the ability to refuse to take a test is one of theory rather than choice—if one really wants the job."[91]

Discussion Questions

1. Describe how you'd feel having to take a psychological test or an honesty test either as an employee or as a precondition for employment. Under what conditions, if any, would you take such a test?

2. How useful do you think such tests are? Assuming that tests like those described are valid and reliable, are they fair? Explain.

3. Do you think tests like these invade privacy? Explain why or why not.

4. What ideals, obligations, and effects must be considered in using psychological tests as pre-employment screens? In your view, which is the most important consideration?

5. If you were an employer, would you require either employees or job applicants to pass an honesty exam? Explain the moral principles that support your position.

6. What do you think a business's reaction would be if the government required its executive officers to submit to a personality test as a precondition for the company's getting a government contract? The tests would probe attitudes about questionable business practices, such as bribery, product misrepresentation, unfair competition, and so forth. If, in your opinion, the business would object, does it have any moral grounds for subjecting workers to comparable tests?

7. Utilitarians would not find anything inherently objectionable about psychological tests as long as the interests of all parties were taken into account and given equal consideration before such tests are made a pre-employment screen. Do you think this is generally the case?

8. Should there be a law prohibiting or regulating psychological tests as a pre-employment screen? Should a decision to use these tests be made jointly by management and labour, or is testing for employment an exclusive employer right?

CASE 7.2

Protecting the Unborn at Work

The unobtrusive factory sits behind a hillside shopping centre in the small college town of Bennington, Vermont. The workers there make lead automobile batteries for Sears, Goodyear, and other companies. Of the 280 workers employed there a decade or so ago, only twelve were women, none of whom was able to have children. The company, Johnson Controls, Inc., refused to hire any who could.[92]

Why? Because tiny toxic particles of lead and lead oxide fill the air inside the plant. According to the company, the levels of lead are low enough for adults, but too high for children and fetuses. Numerous scientific studies have shown that lead can damage the brain and central nervous system of a fetus; moreover, lead lingers in the bloodstream, which means that fetuses can be affected by it even if a woman limits her exposure to lead once she learns she is pregnant. Because of this, Johnson Controls decided that it would exclude women at all fourteen of its factories from jobs that entail high exposure to lead—unless they could prove that they couldn't become pregnant. The company made no exceptions for celibate women or women who used contraceptives. The company's position was simple: "The issue is protecting the health of unborn children."

Johnson Controls's stance was in line with the U.S. National Centers for Disease Control's recommendation that women of childbearing age be excluded from jobs involving significant lead exposure. Because by law its standards must be "feasible," the U.S. Occupational Safety and Health Administration (OSHA) regulations permit chemicals in the workplace that are known to cause harm both to fetuses and to some adult employees. But OSHA holds that employers have a general duty to reduce the hazards of the workplace as far as possible. On this basis, employers such as Olin Corporation, American Cyanamid, General Motors, Monsanto, Allied Chemical, Gulf Oil, and B. F. Goodrich also adopted policies excluding women from chemical plant jobs judged to be hazardous to their potential offspring.

Scientific studies of the effect of exposure to toxic manufacturing chemicals on workers' reproductive health are, unfortunately, few. Only a small percentage of the workplace chemicals with a potential for damaging reproduction have been evaluated, and every year many new chemicals are introduced into factories. Although employers are obviously dealing with many unknowns, no one doubts that they have a moral and legal obligation to control and limit these risks as best they can. Lawsuits and even criminal sanctions have battered companies that have managed hazardous chemicals irresponsibly. Monsanto Chemical Company, for example, agreed to pay $1.5 million to six employees because exposure to a chemical additive used for rubber production allegedly gave them bladder cancer. Fetal protection policies aren't just dictated by management, though. "Women who become pregnant," the *New York Times* reports, "are beginning to demand the right to transfer out of jobs they believe to be hazardous, even when there is only sketchy scientific evidence of any hazard."

But many women were unhappy about the decision of Johnson Controls. They worried that fetal protection policies would be used to exclude women from more and more workplaces on the grounds that different chemical substances or certain tasks such as heavy lifting might be potential causes of miscarriage and fetal injury. In line with this, the United Automobile Workers, which represents many of the Johnson employees, sought to overturn the U.S. Court of Appeals decision that judged Johnson's policy to be "reasonably necessary to the industrial safety-based concern of protecting the unborn child from lead exposure." The union contends, to the contrary, that the policy discriminates against women, jeopardizing their hard-won gains in male-dominated industries.

Many women's advocates see the issue in slightly different terms. They believe policies like that of Johnson Controls challenge a woman's right not only to control her fetus but to control her unfertilized eggs as well. In addition, such policies infringe on privacy: by taking a job at Johnson, a woman was in effect telling the world that she was sterile. And there is also the fundamental question of who knows what is best for a woman.

After bearing two children, Cheryl Chalifoux had a doctor block her fallopian tubes so that she couldn't become pregnant again. Although career advancement wasn't the reason she made her decision, it did enable her to switch from a factory job paying $6.34 an hour to one at Johnson's Bennington plant paying $15 an hour. Still, she says that the policy was unfair and degrading. "It's your body," she complains. "They're implying they're doing it for your own good." Cheryl Cook, also a mother of two who had surgery for the same reason, joined Chalifoux in leaving the other company to work for Johnson Controls. She says, "I work right in the lead. I make the oxide. But you should choose for yourself. Myself, I wouldn't go in there if I could get pregnant. But they don't trust you."

Isabelle Katz Pizler, director of women's rights at the American Civil Liberties Union, agrees. "Since time immemorial," she says, "the excuse for keeping women in their place has been because of their role in producing the next generation. The attitude of Johnson Controls is: 'we know better than you. We can't allow women to make this decision. We have to make it for them.'" And the ACLU has argued in court that "since no activity is risk-free, deference to an employer's analysis of fetal risk could limit women's participation in nearly every area of economic life."

To this the company responded that it has a moral obligation to the parties that cannot participate in the woman's decisions—namely, the unfertilized ovum and the fetus. In addition, the company has an obligation to stockholders, who would bear the brunt of lawsuits brought by employees' children born with retardation, nervous system disorders, or other disorders that lead can cause.

Joseph A. Kinney, executive director of the National Safe Workplace Institute in Chicago, sides with Johnson Controls, but only because he believes that letting women assume the burden of their safety undermines OSHA's responsibility to mandate workplace safety rules. "The discrimination side of the issue needs to be resolved," Kinney says. "But the ideal thing is to regulate lead out of the workplace and any other toxin that poses fetal damage."

However, the U.S. Supreme Court has ruled unanimously that the fetal protection policy at Johnson Controls violated the *Civil Rights Act* of 1964, which prohibits sex discrimination in employment.[93] Pointing to evidence that lead affects sperm and can thus harm the offspring of men exposed to it at the time of conception, the Court stated:

> Respondent does not seek to protect the unconceived children of all its employees. Despite evidence in the record about the debilitating effect of lead exposure on the male reproductive system, Johnson Controls is concerned only with the harms that may befall the unborn offspring of its female employees . . . . [The company's policy is] discriminatory because it requires only a female employee to produce proof that she is not capable of reproducing.

On the other hand, the Court was divided over whether fetal protection policies could ever be legally justified. Justice Harry A. Blackmun, writing for a majority of the Court, declared that they could not, that the *Civil Rights Act* prohibited all such policies:

> Decisions about the welfare of future children must be left to the parents who conceive, bear, support and raise them rather than to the employers who hire those parents. Women as capable of doing their jobs as their male counterparts may not be forced to choose between having a child and having a job.

Referring to the *Pregnancy Discrimination Act* of 1978, which amended the 1964 *Civil Rights Act* and prohibits employment discrimination on the basis of pregnancy or potential pregnancy, Blackmun added:

> Employment late in pregnancy often imposes risks on the unborn child, but Congress indicated that the employer may take into account only the woman's ability to get her job done.

A minority of the justices, however, were unwilling to go so far, and in a concurring opinion, Justice Byron R. White wrote, "common sense tells us that it is part of the normal operation of business concerns to avoid causing injury to third parties as well as to employees." But he added that, in his view, a fetal protection policy would not be defensible unless an employer also addressed other known occupational health risks.

Discussion Questions

1. Do you agree that Johnson Controls's fetal protection policy discriminated against women? Do pregnant women have a moral—not just a legal—right to work with lead?

2. Suppose exposure to lead did not affect sperm or the male reproductive system. Would Johnson's policy still have been discriminatory? Would it hamper women's efforts to win equality in the workplace?

3. Can there be a nondiscriminatory fetal protection policy? Is Justice White correct in arguing that companies have an obligation to avoid causing injury to fetuses just as they do other "third parties"?

4. Suppose a company forbids any employee capable of reproducing from working with lead. Would such a policy wrongly interfere with employees' freedom of choice? Would it be an invasion of their privacy? Would it be fair to employees who are fertile but plan to have no children?

5. Evaluate fetal protection policies from the egoistic, utilitarian, and Kantian perspectives. What rights are involved? What are the likely benefits and harms of such policies?

6. Assuming they are fully informed, do employees with a certain medical condition have a right to work at jobs that can be hazardous to the health of people in their condition? Or can company policy or government regulations justifiably prevent them from doing so for their own good?

7. Would you agree with Joseph Kinney that the real issue is to remove toxins from the workplace? Is this a realistic goal?

CASE 7.3

The Mommy Track

"The cost of employing women in management is greater than the cost of employing men. This is a jarring statement, partly because it is true, but mostly because it is something people are reluctant to talk about." So begins a provocative article by Felice N. Schwartz.[94] Schwartz goes on to contend that the rate of turnover in management positions is two-and-a-half times higher among top-performing women than it is among men. Moreover, one-half of the women who take maternity leave return to their jobs late or not at all. "We know that women also have a greater tendency to plateau or to interrupt their careers," she writes. "But we have become so sensitive to charges of sexism and so afraid of confrontation, even litigation, that we rarely say what we know to be true."

Schwartz's article exploded like a bombshell. What really upset her critics was the distinction Schwartz drew between two types of women: the career-primary woman and the career-and-family woman.[95] Those in the first category put their careers first. They remain single or childless, or if they do have children, they are satisfied to have others raise them. The automatic association of all women with babies is unfair to these women, according to Schwartz—after all, some 90 percent of executive men but only 35 percent of executive women have children by age forty. "The secret to dealing with such women," Schwartz writes, "is to recognize them early, accept them, and clear artificial barriers from their path to the top."

The majority of women fall into Schwartz's second category. They want to pursue genuine careers while participating actively in the rearing of their children. Most of them, Schwartz contends, are willing to trade some career growth and compensation for freedom from the constant pressure to work long hours and weekends. By forcing these women to choose between family and career, companies lose a valuable resource and a competitive advantage. Instead, firms must plan for and manage maternity, they must provide the flexibility to help career-and-family women be maximally productive, and they must take an active role in providing family support and in making high-quality, affordable child care available to all women.

Schwartz's various suggestions of ways for organizations to serve the needs of working mothers and benefit from their expertise seem humane and practical. But her feminist critics see her as distinguishing between the strivers and the breeders, between women who should be treated as honorary males and those who should be shunted onto a special lower-paid, low-pressure career track—the now-notorious "mommy track." Former congresswoman Patricia Schroeder of Colorado says that Schwartz actually "reinforces the idea that you can either have a family or a career, but not both, if you're a woman."[96] And other women worry that Schwartz's article will encourage corporations to reduce pay and withhold promotions in exchange for the parental leave, flextime, and child care that they will sooner or later have to provide as they become more and more dependent on female talent.[97]

Barbara Ehrenreich and Deirdre English challenge Schwartz's data and call her article "a tortured muddle of feminist perceptions and sexist assumptions, good intentions and dangerous suggestions—unsupported by any acceptable evidence at all." What they resent is that Schwartz makes no mention of fathers or of shared parental responsibility for child raising. Schwartz is also accused of assuming that mothers don't need top-flight careers and of taking for granted the existing values, structures, and biases of a corporate world that is still male-dominated. "Bumping women—or just fertile women, or married women, or whomever—off the fast track may sound smart to cost-conscious CEOs," they write. "But eventually it is the corporate culture itself that needs to slow down to a human pace . . . [and end] work loads that are incompatible with family life."[98]

"What's so disturbing about Felice Schwartz's article," adds Fran Rodgers, president of Work-Family Directions, a Massachusetts research and referral group, "is that it is devoted to fitting women into the existing culture, instead of finding ways to change that culture." And Rodgers rejects the idea of "dividing women into two groups, but completely ignoring the diversity among men."[99]

Other observers fear that men will simply leave the mommy trackers in the dust. "In most organizations, the mommy track is a millstone around your neck," says Richard Belous, an economist at the National Planning Association. "CEOs and rainmakers don't come out of the mommy track," he warns. "If you go part-time, you're signaling to your employer you're on the B-team."[100] Traditionally, men who make it to the upper ranks have relied on their wives to raise the kids and to take full responsibility at home. A fast-track woman who wants children, however, gets caught in a time and energy squeeze, even if her husband is an equal partner at home. And even though more men today are willing to share child-raising responsibilities, most still seem hesitant about making significant career sacrifices for spouse and family. There's no analogous "daddy track," it seems.

In fact, the evidence points to what's been called a "daddy penalty"—at least for dads in dual-career families. Two recent studies have shown that male managers whose wives stay home to care for their children earn more than their counterparts with working wives. Even when differences in the numbers of hours worked, years of experience, field of employment, and career interruptions are taken into account, men who are the sole breadwinners for their families enjoy incomes at least 20 percent higher than those of married men with children whose wives have careers.[101]

Why? No one knows for sure. Some observers suggest that men who are the sole income earners work more, produce more, and push harder for raises and promotions. Others suggest that having a wife at home is a significant career resource, allowing the man to perform more effectively in his job. Yet others speculate that men who are strongly career-oriented choose wives who support that choice in the first place, whereas men who want more balance between work and family are more likely to marry women who want to work. And, finally, there are those who believe that the data reflect a corporate prejudice in favour of traditional families.

Discussion Questions

1. Do you think Schwartz is correct to assert that the cost of employing women in management is greater than that of employing men? If you agree, what are the implications for corporate policy?

2. Can working women accurately be divided into Schwartz's two categories? Is it desirable for companies to distinguish the different types of career paths followed by female employees?

3. Do you think there already is such a thing as a "mommy track"? Is the idea a good one? Is it somehow discriminatory against women? Against men?

4. Should special organizational arrangements be made for workers who wish to combine career and child raising? Identify the steps companies can take to accommodate parental needs more effectively.

5. Does a firm have an obligation to give employees the flexibility to work out the particular balance of career and family that is right for them? Or does this go beyond the social responsibilities of business?

Notes to Chapter 7

1. The facts reported here are from "Privacy," *Newsweek*, March 28, 1988, 61–68.

2. For a succinct and clear review of the *Personal Information Protection and Electronic Documents Act*, see the report by the House of Commons Standing Committee on Access to Information, Privacy and Ethics at www.cmte.parl.gc.ca/content/hoc/committee/391/ethi/reports/rp2891060/ethirp04/05-rep-e.htm.

3. See the decision by the Ontario Superior Court of Justice in *Somwar v. McDonald's Restaurants of Canada Ltd.*, 2006 CanLII 202 (ON S.C.). Quoted in "Privacy" (see n. 1).

4. "Snooping E-Mail by Software Is Now a Workplace Norm," *Wall Street Journal*, March 9, 2005, B1. See also Eilene Zimmerman, "HR Must Know When Employee Surveillance Crosses the Line," *Workforce*, February 2002, 38.

5. "Is Office Voice Mail Private?," *Wall Street Journal*, February 28, 1995, B1.

6. "As Abuse of Sick Leave Continues, Crackdown Raises Issues of Privacy," *New York Times*, November 30, 1992, A1.

7. "On the Road Again, but Now the Boss Is Sitting Beside You," *Wall Street Journal*, May 14, 2004, A1.

8. Charles Reich, "The Corporate Control of Big Government," *Business and Society Review* 95 (1996): 61.

9. "Up Front," *Business Week*, August 16, 2004, 10.

10. For the classic treatment of the evils of conformity, see J. S. Mill, *On Liberty* (1859). On the effects of being observed, see Jeffrey Reiman, "Privacy, Intimacy, and Personhood," *Philosophy and Public Affairs* 6 (1976): 31–36. On the disconnect between conformity and democracy (and on privacy as a social good) see Deborah G. Johnson, *Computer Ethics*, 3rd ed. (Upper Saddle River, NJ: Prentice-Hall, 2000).

11. "Enterprise Takes Idea of Dressed for Success to a New Extreme," *Wall Street Journal*, November 20, 2002, B1.

12. *Dollars and Sense*, April 1989, 4; and *San Francisco Examiner*, May 12, 1994, A14.

13. "Legal Secretary Fired over Gay Stripper Job," *Santa Cruz Sentinel*, June 7, 1992, A10.

14. See *Godbout v. Longueuil (City)* [1997] 3 S.C.R. 844 (October 31, 1997).

15. Laura P. Hartman, "Technology and Ethics," in Laura P. Hartman, ed., *Perspectives in Business Ethics*, 3rd ed. (New York: McGraw-Hill, 2005), 730–731.

16. Terry L. Leap, "When Can You Fire for Off-Duty Conduct?," *Harvard Business Review* 66 (January/February 1988): 36.

17. "Firms Aim to Trim Fat, Literally," *International Herald Tribune*, June 19, 2003, 12; "Cutting the Fat at Work," *Monterey County Herald*, January 18, 2004, A2; and "Trimming the Fat," *American Way*, January 15, 2004, 80–81.

18. See Scott Campbell, "Better Than the Company Gym," *HR Magazine*, June 1995, and "Wellness Becomes an Issue in the Workplace," *Santa Cruz Sentinel*, April 28, 2002, D-1.

19. Greg Jaffe, "Weighty Matters," *San Francisco Examiner*, February 22, 1998, J1; and "Companies Get Tough with Smokers, Obese to Trim Costs," *Wall Street Journal*, October 12, 2004, B1.

20. Shape Up—Or Else," *Newsweek*, July 1, 1991, 42; and "If You Light Up on Sunday, Don't Come In on Monday," *Business Week*, August 26, 1991, 68–70.

21. "Why Wellness Is Making Employees Feel Sick," *Financial Times*, February 17, 2005, 9.

22. Ibid.

23. "Privacy," 68 (see n. 1).

24. See David T. Lykken, "Three Big Lies About the Polygraph," *USA Today*, February 17, 1983, 10A. See also William A. Nowlin and Robert Barbato, "The Truth About Lie Detectors," *Business and Society Review* 66 (Summer 1988), and "Scientists Say Lie Detector Doesn't Always Tell Truth," *Wall Street Journal*, October 9, 2002, B1.

25. Lynn March, "Lie Detectors Are Accurate and Useful," *USA Today*, February 17, 1983, 10A.

26. Lykken, "Three Big Lies."

27. Christopher H. Pyle, "These Tests Are Meant to Scare People," *USA Today*, February 17, 1983, 10A.

28. "Making Windows in Men's Souls," *Economist*, July 10, 2004, 71–72.

29. "Personality Counts," *HR Magazine*, February 2, 2002, 30–31. See also Gladwell, "Personality Plus"; Graham Lawton, "Let's Get Personal," *New Scientist*, September 13, 2003; and Annie Murphy Paul, *The Cult of Personality* (New York: Free Press, 2004).

30. Barbara Ehrenreich, "Two-Tiered Morality," *New York Times*, June 30, 2002, sec. 4, 15.

31. "Trying to Get a Job? Check Yes or No," *New York Times*, November 28, 1997, B1.

32. Ibid.

33. "Privacy," 68 (see n. 1).

34. Kleiman, "The Boss May Be Listening," *San Jose Mercury News*, February 25, 1996, 1PC.

35. Jared Sandberg, "Monitoring of Workers Is Boss's Right but Why Not Include the Top Brass?," *Wall Street Journal*, May 18, 2005, B1.

36. "What the Boss Knows About You," *Fortune*, August 9, 1993.

37. "Study May Spur Job-Applicant Drug Screening," *Wall Street Journal*, November 28, 1990, B1.

38. Kris Maher, "The Jungle," *Wall Street Journal*, April 13, 2004, B4.

39. James T. Wrich, "Beyond Testing: Coping with Drugs at Work," *Harvard Business Review* 66 (January/February 1988).

40. For the full study see www.csls.ca/reports/csls2006-04.pdf.

41. See Association of Workers' Compensation Boards of Canada, National Work Injuries Statistics Program, December 2006.

42. See Jeremy Loome, "Numbers Don't Lie—or Do They?," *Edmonton Sun*, September 10, 2006. You can also find it (free) on the website of the Canadian Injured Workers Society at www.ciws.ca/articles_alberta_workplace_injury_rate.htm.

43. Quoted in John R. Boatright, *Ethics and the Conduct of Business*, 4th ed. (Upper Saddle River, NJ: Prentice-Hall, 2003), 316.

44. The *Canada Labour Code* (Part II, #128) and all similar provincial statutes allow employees such refusal.

45. See, for example, Ontario's *Occupational Health and Safety Act* R.R.O. 1990, Regulation 860, "Workplace Hazardous Materials Information System," Sect. 6–7, 8–16.

46. See the Ontario Ministry of Labour's website under "News Releases," May 15, 2007. The case I cite here is one of 11 involving fines for "Health and Safety" violations just for the month of May 2007, in just one province.

47. See Joseph LaDoc, "The Not-So-Clean Business of Making Chips," *Technological Review* 87 (May/June 1984), and "Chip Makers Promise Action on Toxics," *San Jose Mercury News*, December 4, 1992, 1A.

48. See the website of the Canadian Centre for Occupational Health and Safety at www.ccohs.ca/ohsanswers/diseases.

49. Myron I. Peskin and Francis J. McGrath, "Industrial Safety: Who Is Responsible and Who Benefits?," *Business Horizons* 35 (May/June 1992). See also Alan Tidwell, "Ethics, Safety, and Managers," *Business & Professional Ethics Journal* 19 (Fall/Winter 2000).

50. Steven Greenhouse, "Workers Assail Night Lock-Ins by Wal-Mart," *New York Times*, January 18, 2004 (online).

51. See Ontario Ministry of Labour's website under "News Releases" for October 5, 2007, and September 20, 2007.

52. See CBC News at www.cbc.ca/canada/story/2007/02/16workplace-violence.html; Human Resources and Social Development Canada, "Prevention of Violence in the Workplace," www.hrsdc.gc.ca/en/lp/spila/clli/ohslc/07prevention_violence_in_workplace.html; Derrick

Hynes, "Preventing Workplace Violence: Towards an Aggression-Free Workplace," Conference Board of Canada, August 2001.

53. See CBC News at www.cbc.ca/news/background/workplace-safety, January 17, 2007; also CBC News at www.cbc.ca/news/background/workplace-safety/outofsync.html.

54. "Make Ergonomics," *HR Magazine*, April 2000, 37–42.

55. See "Fatigue: The Hidden Culprit," *USA Weekend*, January 29–31, 1993, and "Worker Fatigue Can Be Deadly," *San Jose Mercury News*, March 3, 1996.

56. See "Stress and the Workplace," Public Health Agency of Canada, Canadian Health Network, at www.canadian-health-network.ca.

57. See CBC News at www.cbc.ca/news/background/workplace-safety/dyingforajob.html, 7.

58. See Cara Williams, "Sources of Workplace Stress," *Respectives on Labour and Income* 4, no, 6 (June 2003) (publication of Statistics Canada, Catalogue No. 75-001-XIE); and Karen A. Blotnicky, "Should There Be Caution Tape Around the Office Door?," *The Workplace Review*, November 2006, at www.stmarys.ca/academic/sobey/workplacereview/nov2006/TacklingWorkplaceStress.pdf.

59. Yawen Cheng et al., "Association Between Psychosocial Work Characteristics and Health Functioning in American Women," *British Medical Journal* 30 (May 27, 2000): 1432–1436.

60. Thomas Stewart, "Managers Look for the Moral Dimension," *Financial Times*, August 27, 2004, 7.

61. Darrell Bricker and John Wright, *What Canadians Think* (Scarborough, ON: Doubleday Canada, 2005), 124–125.

62. Harvey Hornstein, *Brutal Bosses and Their Prey* (New York: Putnam, 1996).

63. Douglas McGregor, *The Human Side of Enterprise* (New York: McGraw-Hill, 1960).

64. "How to Influence Your Boss and Keep Your Friends," *Financial Times*, February 26, 2005, 8.

65. Statistics Canada, "Spotlight: Working Women," at www42.statcan.ca/smr04/2007/10/smr04_27407_04_e.htm.

66. For useful statistics, reasons for and against work-related centres, and general information, see Human Resources and Social Development Canada at www.hrsdc.gc.ca/en/lp/spila/wlb/wrccc/06chapter_1.shtml; see also CBC News, "Day Care in Canada" at www.cbc.ca/news/background/daycare.

67. Human Resources and Social Development Canada, "1. Introduction," *A Study of Family, Child Care and Well-Being in Young Canadian Families*, at www.hrsdc.gc.ca/en/cs/sp/sdc/pkrf/publications/research/2001-000148/page04.shtml.

68. But for a criticism of the original study, see "Scientific Myths That Are Too Good to Die," *New York Times*, December 9, 1998, sec. 4, 2.

69. For an accessible discussion of Herzberg's ideas, see J. Michael Syptak, David M. Marsland, and Deborah Ulmer, "Job Satisfaction: Putting Theory into Practice," *Family Practice Management*, October 1999, 26.

70. Michael Skapinker, "Money Can't Make You Happy but Being in a Trusted Team Can," *Financial Times*, June 1, 2005, 8.

71. *What Canadians Think*, 131–132 (see n. 61).

72. A. R. Gini and T.J. Sullivan, *It Comes with the Territory* (New York: Random House, 1989), 27–29.

73. "Bored to Death at Work—Literally," *Business Week*, July 1, 2002, 16.

74. E. Palmore, "Predicting Longevity: A Follow-Up Controlling for Age," *Gerontologist* 9 (1960): 247–250.

75. See Wayne Lewchuk and Don Wells, "Transforming Worker Representation: The Magna Model in Canada and Mexico," *Labour/Le Travail*, 2007, 60: 109–38.

76. Randy Pennington, "Collaborative Labor Relations: The First Line Is the Bottom Line," *Personnel*, March 1989, 78.

77. "A Top-Flight Employee Strategy," *Financial Times*, April 4, 2005, 8.

78. Sharon Cohen, "Management Unions Join Forces," *San Francisco Examiner*, December 9, 1990, D3.

79. "A Top-Flight Employee Strategy," 8.

80. Cohen, "Management, Unions." See also "Japanese Plants in the U.S. Lose Edge to the Big Three," *International Herald Tribune*, June 17–18, 2000, 14, and "The NUMMI Road to Japan," *San Jose Mercury News*, May 18, 2002, 1C.

81. Alan S. Blinder, "Want to Boost Productivity? Try Giving Workers a Say," *Business Week*, April 17, 1989, 10; and "A Firm of Their Own," *Economist*, June 11, 1994, 59. See also "United We Own," *Business Week*, March 18, 1996, 96.

82. See Roger E. Alcaly, "Reinventing the Corporation," *New York Review of Books*, April 10, 1997.

83. Samuel Greengard, "Theft Control Starts with HR Strategies," *Personnel Journal*, April 1993, 81–88; and "The Thief on the Payroll," *San Jose Mercury News*, April 14, 1996, 1PC. See also "Taking at the Office Reaches New Heights," *New York Times*, July 12, 2000, C8, and "Amid the Recession, More Employees Are Stealing from Work," *Santa Cruz Sentinel*, March 24, 2002, D1.

84. Judith Crossen, "Job Applicants Would Disappoint Diogenes," *San Francisco Examiner*, December 18, 1988, D15.

85. Crossen, "Job Applicants."

86. "Trying to Get a Job?" *New York Times*, B1.

87. "Honest Answers—Postpolygraph," *Personnel*, April 1988, 8.

88. Ibid.

89. "Searching for Integrity," *Fortune*, March 8, 1993, 140.

90. "Texas Company Settles over Nosy Questions to Employees," *San Francisco Chronicle*, July 8, 2000, A3.

91. Susan Tempor, "More Employers Attempt to Catch a Thief by Giving Job Applicants 'Honesty' Exams," *Wall Street Journal*, August 3, 1981, 15.

92. Peter T. Kilborn, "Who Decides Who Works at Jobs Imperiling Fetuses?," *New York Times*, September 2, 1990, 1, is the main source for this case study.

93. *New York Times*, March 21, 1991, A1. Excerpts from *Automobile Workers v. Johnson Controls* quoted in the following paragraphs are from page A14.

94. Felice N. Schwartz, "Management Women and the New Facts of Life," *Harvard Business Review* 67 (January/February 1989): 65.

95. Ibid., 69.

96. Tamar Lewin, "New Look at Working Moms," *San Francisco Chronicle*, March 8, 1989, A1.

97. Barbara Ehrenreich and Deirdre English, "Blowing the Whistle on the 'Mommy Track,'" *Ms.*, July/August 1989, 56.

98. Ibid., 58.

99. Lewin, "New Look at Working Moms."

100. "The Mommy Track," *Newsweek*, March 20, 1989, 132.

101. "Primary Sources," *Atlantic Monthly*, November 2004, 58. See also "Men Whose Wives Work Earn Less, Studies Show," *New York Times*, October 11, 1994, A1, and "Marriage's 'Unique Effect,'" *Business Week*, May 13, 2002, 32.

DRUG TESTING IN EMPLOYMENT

JOSEPH R. DESJARDINS AND RONALD DUSKA

If drug testing of employees is not to violate privacy, the information it seeks must be relevant to the employment contract. DesJardins and Duska examine two arguments used to establish that knowledge of drug use is job-relevant information: first, that drug use adversely affects job performance and, second, that it can harm the employer, other employees, and the public. Although they reject the first argument, they grant that the second can, in certain limited circumstances, justify drug testing. But even in these cases, strict procedural limitations should be placed on drug testing—despite the fact that drug use itself is illegal. They conclude by raising the question of whether employee consent to drug testing is voluntary.

We take privacy to be an "employee right," by which we mean a presumptive moral entitlement to receive certain goods or be protected from certain harms in the workplace.[1] Such a right creates a prima facie obligation on the part of the employer to provide the relevant goods or, as in this case, refrain from the relevant harmful treatment. These rights prevent employees from being placed in the fundamentally coercive position where they must choose between their jobs and other basic human goods.

Further, we view the employer–employee relationship as essentially contractual. The employer–employee relationship is an economic one and, unlike relationships such as those between a government and its citizens or a parent and a child, exists primarily as a means for satisfying the economic interests of the contracting parties. The obligations that each party incurs are only those that it voluntarily takes on. Given such a contractual relationship, certain areas of the employee's life remain his or her own private concern, and no employer has a right to invade them. On these presumptions we maintain that certain information about an employee is rightfully private, in other words, that the employee has a right to privacy.

THE RIGHT TO PRIVACY

George Brenkert has described the right to privacy as involving a three-place relation between a person A, some information X, and another person B. The right to privacy is violated only when B deliberately comes to possess information X about A and no relationship between A and B exists that would justify B's coming to know X about A.[2] Thus, for example, the relationship one has with a mortgage company would justify that company's coming to know

From DESJARDINS/MCCALL, *Contemporary Issues in Business*, 5E. © 2005 Wadsworth, a part of Cengage Learning, Inc. Reproduced by permission, www.cengage.com/permissions. Notes abridged.

about one's salary, but the relationship one has with a neighbor does not justify the neighbor's coming to know that information.

Hence, an employee's right to privacy is violated whenever personal information is requested, collected, or used by an employer in a way or for any purpose that is *irrelevant to* or *in violation of* the contractual relationship that exists between employer and employee.

Since drug testing is a means for obtaining information, the information sought must be relevant to the contract if the drug testing is not to violate privacy. Hence, we must first decide whether knowledge of drug use obtained by drug testing is job relevant. In cases in which the knowledge of drug use is *not* relevant, there appears to be no justification for subjecting employees to drug tests. In cases in which information of drug use is job relevant, we need to consider if, when, and under what conditions using a means such as drug testing to obtain that knowledge is justified.

IS KNOWLEDGE OF DRUG USE JOB-RELEVANT INFORMATION?

Two arguments are used to establish that knowledge of drug use is job-relevant information. The first argument claims that drug use adversely affects job performance, thereby leading to lower productivity, higher costs, and consequently lower profits. Drug testing is seen as a way of avoiding these adverse effects. According to some estimates $25 billion are lost each year in the United States through loss in productivity, theft, higher rates in health and liability insurance, and similar costs incurred because of drug use. Since employers are contracting with an employee for the performance of specific tasks, employers seem to have a legitimate claim upon whatever personal information is relevant to an employee's ability to do the job.

The second argument claims that drug use has been and can be responsible for considerable harm to individual employees, to their fellow employees, and to the employer, and third parties, including consumers. In this case, drug testing is defended because it is seen as a way of preventing possible harm. Further, since employers can be held liable for harms done to employees and customers, knowledge of employee drug use is needed so that employers can protect themselves from risks related to such liability. But how good are these arguments?

THE FIRST ARGUMENT: JOB PERFORMANCE AND KNOWLEDGE OF DRUG USE

The first argument holds that drug use lowers productivity and that, consequently, an awareness of drug use obtained through drug testing will allow an employer to maintain or increase productivity. It is generally assumed that the performance of people using certain drugs is detrimentally affected by such use, and any use of drugs that reduces productivity is consequently job relevant. If knowledge of such drug use allows the employer to eliminate production losses, such knowledge is job relevant.

On the surface this argument seems reasonable. Obviously some drug use, in lowering the level of performance, can decrease productivity. Since the employer is entitled to a certain level of performance and drug use adversely affects performance, knowledge of that use seems job relevant.

But this formulation of the argument leaves an important question unanswered. To what level of performance are employers entitled? Optimal performance, or some lower level? If some lower level, what? Employers have a valid claim upon some *certain level* of performance, such that a failure to perform at this level would give the employer a justification for disciplining, firing, or at least finding fault with the employee. But that does not necessarily mean that the employer has a right to a maximum or optimal level of performance, a level above and beyond a certain level of acceptability. It might be nice if the employee gives an employer a maximum effort or optimal performance, but that is above and beyond the call of the employee's duty and the employer can hardly claim a right at all times to the highest level of performance of which an employee is capable . . . .

If the person is producing what is expected, knowledge of drug use on the grounds of production is irrelevant since, by this hypothesis, the production is satisfactory. If, on the other hand, the performance suffers, then to the extent that it slips below the level justifiably expected, the employer has preliminary grounds for warning, disciplining, or releasing the employee. But the justification for this action is the person's unsatisfactory performance, not the person's use of drugs. Accordingly, drug use information is either unnecessary or irrelevant and consequently there are not sufficient grounds to override the right of privacy. Thus, unless we can argue that an employer is entitled to optimal performance, the argument fails.

This counterargument should make it clear that the information that is job relevant, and consequently is not rightfully private, is information about an employee's level of performance and not information about the underlying causes of that level. The fallacy of the argument that promotes drug testing in the name of increased productivity is the assumption that each employee is obliged to perform at an optimal or at least quite high level. But this is required under few if any contracts. What is required contractually is meeting the normally expected levels of production or performing the tasks in the job description adequately (not optimally). If one can do that under the influence of drugs, then on the grounds of job performance at least, drug use is rightfully private. An employee who cannot perform the task adequately is not fulfilling the contract, and knowledge of the cause of the failure to perform is irrelevant on the contractual model.

Of course, if the employer suspects drug use or abuse as the cause of the unsatisfactory performance, then she might choose to help the person with counseling or rehabilitation. However, this does not seem to be something morally required of the employer. Rather, in the case of unsatisfactory performance, the employer has a prima facie justification for dismissing or disciplining the employee . . . .

THE SECOND ARGUMENT: HARM AND THE KNOWLEDGE OF DRUG USE TO PREVENT HARM

The performance argument is inadequate, but there is an argument that seems somewhat stronger. This is an argument that takes into account the fact that drug use often leads to harm. Using a variant of the Millian argument, which allows interference with a person's rights in order to prevent harm, we could argue that drug testing might be justified if such testing led to knowledge that would enable an employer to prevent harm.

Drug use certainly can lead to harming others. Consequently, if knowledge of such drug use can prevent harm, then knowing whether or not an employee uses drugs might be a legitimate concern of an employer in certain circumstances. This second argument claims that knowledge of the employee's drug use is job relevant because employees who are under the influence of drugs can pose a threat to the health and safety of themselves and others, and an employer who knows of that drug use and the harm it can cause has a responsibility to prevent it.

Employers have both a general duty to prevent harm and the specific responsibility for harms done by their employees. Such responsibilities are sufficient reason for any employer to claim that information about an employee's drug use is relevant if that knowledge can prevent harm by giving the employer grounds for dismissing the employee or not allowing him or her to perform potentially harmful tasks. Employers might even claim a right to reduce unreasonable risks, in this case the risks involving legal and economic liability for harms caused by employees under the influence of drugs, as further justification for knowing about employee drug use.

This second argument differs from the first, in which only a lowered job performance was relevant information. In this case, even to allow the performance is problematic, for the performance itself, more than being inadequate, can hurt people. We cannot be as sanguine about the prevention of harm as we can about inadequate production. Where drug use may cause serious harm, knowledge of that use becomes relevant if the knowledge of such use can lead to the prevention of harm and drug testing becomes justified as a means for obtaining that knowledge.

Jobs with Potential to Cause Harm

In the first place, it is not clear that every job has a potential to cause harm—at least, not a potential to cause harm sufficient to override a prima facie right to privacy. To say that employers can use drug testing where that can prevent harm is not to say that every employer has the right to know about the drug use of every employee. Not every job poses a threat serious enough to justify an employer coming to know this information.

In deciding which jobs pose serious-enough threats, certain guidelines should be followed. First the potential for harm should be *clear* and *present*. Perhaps all jobs in some extended way pose potential threats to human well-being.

We suppose an accountant's error could pose a threat of harm to someone somewhere. But some jobs—like those of airline pilots, school bus drivers, public transit drivers, and surgeons—are jobs in which unsatisfactory performance poses a clear and present danger to others. It would be much harder to make an argument that job performances by auditors, secretaries, executive vice-presidents for public relations, college teachers, professional athletes, and the like could cause harm if those performances were carried on under the influence of drugs. They would cause harm only in exceptional cases.[3]

Not Every Person Is to Be Tested

But, even if we can make a case that a particular job involves a clear and present danger for causing harm if performed under the influence of drugs, it is not appropriate to treat everyone holding such a job the same. Not every jobholder is equally threatening. There is less reason to investigate an airline pilot for drug use if that pilot has a twenty-year record of exceptional service than there is to investigate a pilot whose behavior has become erratic and unreliable recently, or one who reports to work smelling of alcohol and slurring his words. Presuming that every airline pilot is equally threatening is to deny individuals the respect that they deserve as autonomous, rational agents. It is to ignore their history and the significant differences between them. It is also probably inefficient and leads to the lowering of morale. It is the likelihood of causing harm, and not the fact of being an airline pilot per se, that is relevant in deciding which employees in critical jobs to test.

So, even if knowledge of drug use is justifiable to prevent harm, we must be careful to limit this justification to a range of jobs and people where the potential for harm is clear and present. The jobs must be jobs that clearly can cause harm, and the specific employee should not be someone who has a history of reliability. Finally, the drugs being tested should be those drugs that have genuine potential for harm if used in the jobs in question.

LIMITATIONS ON DRUG-TESTING POLICIES

Even when we identify those situations in which knowledge of drug use would be job relevant, we still need to examine whether some procedural limitations should not be placed upon the employer's testing for drugs. We have said when a real threat of harm exists and when evidence exists suggesting that a particular employee poses such a threat, an employer could be justified in knowing about drug use in order to prevent the potential harm. But we need to recognize that so long as the employer has the discretion for deciding when the potential for harm is clear and present, and for deciding which employees pose the threat of harm, the possibility of abuse is great. Thus, some policy limiting the employer's power is called for.

Just as criminal law imposes numerous restrictions protecting individual dignity and liberty on the state's pursuit of its goals, so we should expect that some restrictions be placed on employers to protect innocent employees from harm (including loss of job and damage to one's personal and professional reputation). Thus, some system of checks upon an employer's discretion in these matters seems advisable.

A drug-testing policy that requires all employees to submit to a drug test or to jeopardize their jobs would seem coercive and therefore unacceptable. Being placed in such a fundamentally coercive position of having to choose between one's job and one's privacy does not provide the conditions for a truly free consent. Policies that are unilaterally established by employers would likewise be unacceptable. Working with employees to develop company policy seems the only way to ensure that the policy will be fair to both parties. Prior notice of testing would also be required in order to give employees the option of freely refraining from drug use. Preventing drug use is morally preferable to punishing users after the fact, because this approach treats employees as capable of making rational and informed decisions.

Further procedural limitations seem advisable as well. Employees should be notified of the results of the test, they should be entitled to appeal the results (perhaps through further tests by an independent laboratory), and the information obtained through tests ought to be kept confidential. In summary, limitations upon employer discretion for administering drug tests can be derived from the nature of the employment contract and from the recognition that drug testing is justified by the desire to prevent harm, not the desire to punish wrongdoing.

THE ILLEGALITY CONTENTION

At this point critics might note that the behavior which testing would try to deter is, after all, illegal. Surely this excuses any responsible employer from being overprotective of an employee's rights. The fact that an employee is doing something illegal should give the employer a right to that information about his or her private life. Thus, it is not simply that drug use might pose a threat of harm to others, but that it is an *illegal* activity that threatens others. But again, we would argue that illegal activity itself is irrelevant to job performance. At best, *conviction* records might be relevant, but since drug tests are administered by private employers we are not only ignoring the question of conviction, we are also ignoring the fact that the employee has not even been arrested for the alleged illegal activity.

Further, even if the due process protections and the establishment of guilt are acknowledged, it still does not follow that employers have a claim to know about all illegal activity on the part of their employees.

Consider the following example: Suppose you were hiring an auditor whose job required certifying the integrity of your firm's tax and financial records. Certainly, the personal integrity of this employee is vital to adequate job performance. Would we allow the employer to conduct, with or without the employee's consent, an audit of the employee's own personal tax return? Certainly if we discover that this person has cheated on a personal tax return we will have evidence of illegal activity that is relevant to this person's ability to do the job. Given one's own legal liability for filing falsified statements, the employee's illegal activity also poses a threat to others. But surely, allowing private individuals to audit an employee's tax returns is too intrusive a means for discovering information about that employee's integrity. The government certainly would never allow this violation of an employee's privacy. It ought not to allow drug testing on the same grounds. Why tax returns should be protected in ways that urine, for example, is not, raises interesting questions of fairness. Unfortunately, this question would take us beyond the scope of this paper.

VOLUNTARINESS

A final problem that we also leave undeveloped concerns the voluntariness of employee consent. For most employees, being given the choice between submitting to a drug test and risking one's job by refusing an employer's request is not much of a decision at all. We believe that such decisions are less than voluntary and thereby hold that employers cannot escape our criticisms simply by including within the employment contract a drug-testing clause. Furthermore, there is reason to believe that those most in need of job security will be those most likely to be subjected to drug testing. Highly skilled, professional employees with high job mobility and security will be in a stronger position to resist such intrusions than will less skilled, easily replaced workers. This is why we should not anticipate surgeons and airline pilots being tested and should not be surprised when public transit and factory workers are. A serious question of fairness arises here as well.

Drug use and drug testing seem to be our most recent social "crisis." Politicians, the media, and employers expend a great deal of time and effort addressing this crisis. Yet, unquestionably, more lives, health, and money are lost each year to alcohol abuse than to marijuana, cocaine, and other controlled substances. We are well advised to be careful in considering issues that arise from such selective social concern. We will let other social commentators speculate on the reasons why drug use has received scrutiny while other white-collar crimes and alcohol abuse are ignored. Our only concern at this point is that such selective prosecution suggests an arbitrariness that should alert us to questions of fairness and justice.

In summary, then, we have seen that drug use is not always job relevant, and if drug use is not job relevant, information about it is certainly not job relevant. In the case of performance it may be a cause of some decreased performance, but it is the performance itself that is relevant to an employee's position, not what prohibits or enables that employee to do the job. In the case of potential harm being done by an employee under the influence of drugs, the drug use seems job relevant, and in this case drug testing

to prevent harm might be legitimate. But how this is practicable is another question. It would seem that standard motor dexterity or mental dexterity tests given immediately prior to job performance are more effective in preventing harm, unless one concludes that drug use invariably and necessarily leads to harm. One must trust the individuals in any system for that system to work. One cannot police everything. Random testing might enable an employer to find drug users and to weed out the few to forestall possible future harm, but are the harms prevented sufficient to override the rights of privacy of the people who are innocent and to overcome the possible abuses we have mentioned? It seems not.

Clearly, a better method is to develop safety checks immediately prior to the performance of a job. Have a surgeon or a pilot or a bus driver pass a few reasoning and motor-skill tests before work. The cause of the lack of a skill, which lack might lead to harm, is really a secondary issue.

Notes

1. "A Defense of Employee Rights," Joseph DesJardins and John McCall, *Journal of Business Ethics* 4 (1985). We should emphasize that our concern is with the *moral* rights of privacy for employees and not with any specific or prospective *legal* rights . . . .

2. "Privacy, Polygraphs, and Work," George Brenkert, *Journal of Business and Professional Ethics*, vol. 1, no. 1 (Fall 1981).

3. Obviously we are speaking here of harms that go beyond the simple economic harm that results from unsatisfactory job performance. These economic harms are discussed in the first argument above. Further, we ignore such "harms" as providing bad role models for adolescents, harms often used to justify drug tests for professional athletes. We think it unreasonable to hold an individual responsible for the image he or she provides to others.

Review and Discussion Questions

1. DesJardins and Duska consider two arguments intended to show that knowledge of drug use is job-relevant information. What are their reasons for rejecting the first argument and what are the limitations of the second argument? Are you persuaded by their reasoning?

2. Do you agree that the crucial question regarding drug testing in employment is whether the information sought is job relevant? Are there other reasons for drug testing that don't turn on this issue?

3. What, if any, procedural limitations should be placed on drug testing in those cases in which it is justified? Are DesJardins and Duska right to maintain that the illegality of drug use is irrelevant?

4. How voluntary do you think employee consent to drug testing really is?

5. What steps do you think employers should take to deal with the problem of employee drug use?

WORK, PRIVACY, AND AUTONOMY

RICHARD L. LIPPKE

Lippke argues that privacy is valuable because of its importance for human autonomy. Rejecting analyses of privacy in the workplace that focus on whether information is "job relevant" as this is defined by the work contract, Lippke sets the question of workplace privacy in the broader context of the imbalance of power that actually exists between employers and employees. He contends that this power imbalance and the accompanying authoritarian organization of work already deprive employees of any significant input into the decisions that affect their working lives. As a result, information-gathering techniques such as surveillance and drug testing are to be resisted as further eroding what little autonomy employees have left.

Employees today face what many believe are unjustified assaults on their privacy. At present, the most well-known and controversial such assault is the urine test. Estimates are that about 30% of the Fortune 500 companies in the United States require a urine test as part of the employment application process. Proponents of such testing warn of the dangers of rampant drug use and abuse in our society. They insist on the need to safeguard co-worker and consumer health and safety, and the need to maintain productivity. Opponents of testing conjure up images of Orwell's *1984*—of large and powerful institutions run amok, forcing innocent people to urinate while under the intense (and let us hope not prurient) supervision of official inspectors. Opponents lambast testing as an invasion of privacy and as a form of self-incrimination. Their most effective tactic has been to raise the specter of inaccurate tests; of persons unfairly scored with the scarlet letter of drug use.

Unfortunately, in the public debate over these issues there is little in the way of patient and careful analysis . . . . I will maintain that the philosophical defenses of employee privacy that have been offered are either incomplete or misguided. At times, they say too little about the value of privacy. Or, they offer suspect models of the employer/ employee relationship. Or, they fail to convincingly show how we should deal with the conflict between privacy and other, competing values.

I will begin my analysis by arguing that privacy is valuable because of its relation to autonomy. For the purposes of this discussion, I will define autonomy as the capacity of persons to make rationally reflective choices about their ends and activities. All areas of persons' lives are assumed to be fit subjects for the exercise of their autonomy. Unless the relation between privacy and autonomy is kept clearly in view, we will not be able to establish the need for restrictions

on the information employers may gather or on the means they may use. More importantly, I will argue that we must examine the privacy issue in the context of an understanding of how the contemporary organization of work in the United States affects the autonomy of workers. Simply put, workers in the U.S. face myriad assaults to their autonomy. I will show how failure to recognize this and to incorporate it into philosophical analyses of employee privacy inevitably weakens the case that can be made on behalf of employees. I will argue that when the reality of work is ignored, workers are more likely to be blamed for behavior that arguably stems (at least in part) from the system of private property rights in productive resources that deprives them of control over their working lives . . . .

THE VALUE OF PRIVACY

There are difficulties in defining what privacy is. However, I do not think we need to be detained by them.[1] Generally, there is a consensus that it involves two things: (1) control over some information about ourselves; and (2) some control over who can experience or observe us. In the abstract, it is hard to further specify how much control privacy involves and over what types of information it ranges. This is because whether any given piece of information about me is private in relation to someone else depends on the type of relationship I have to that individual. What is private in relation to my spouse is very different from what is private in relation to an employer or working associate.

Joseph Kupfer has recently offered a compelling analysis of the value of privacy.[2] Two of the ways in which privacy is valuable are especially relevant to the employer/employee relationship, so I will concentrate on them. First, Kupfer argues that privacy plays an essential role in individuals coming to have an "autonomous self-concept," that is, a concept of themselves as in control of their own lives:

> An autonomous self-concept requires identifying with a particular body whose thoughts, purposes, and actions are subject to one's control . . . . [A]utonomy requires awareness of control over one's relation to others, including their access to us . . . . [P]rivacy contributes to the formation and persistence of autonomous individuals by providing them with control over whether or not their physical and psychological existence becomes part of another's experience.[3]

Kupfer does not argue that privacy is intrinsically good. He argues that it is causally related to the formation and maintenance of an autonomous self-concept. An autonomous self-concept is, in turn, a necessary condition of the basic good of autonomy. In other words, unless individuals conceive of themselves as able to determine their own courses of action, their own life-plans, they cannot be autonomous. If individuals are to develop and maintain an autonomous self-concept, others must grant them control over information about themselves and control over who can experience them and when. Kupfer offers some empirical evidence to

From *Public Affairs Quarterly* 3 (April 1989). Copyright 1989 by Public Affairs Quarterly. Reprinted with permission. Section titles added; some notes omitted.

substantiate the claim that lack of privacy defeats the formation and maintenance of an autonomous self-concept . . . .

A second way in which privacy is valuable is that individuals subjected to invasions of their privacy seem less likely to conceive of themselves as *worthy* of autonomy:

> Privacy is a trusting way others treat us, resulting in a conception of ourselves as worth being trusted. In contrast, monitoring behavior or collecting data on us, projects a disvaluing of the self in question.[4]

Close, intrusive supervision and constant correction (or the threat of it) are inimical to individuals developing and maintaining a sense of themselves as worthy of autonomy. In contrast, social practices that respect privacy give the individual a chance to make mistakes or do wrong, and thus convey the message that the individual is worthy of acting autonomously. The sense that they are worthy of acting autonomously may, as Kupfer notes, increase the confidence of individuals in themselves, and so they may exercise their autonomy to an even greater extent . . . .

JOB RELEVANCE AND THE CONTRACTUAL MODEL

With this brief characterization of some of the ways in which privacy is valuable in hand, I turn first to consider the issues raised by the *content* of information that businesses might acquire about employees or prospective employees. Both George Brenkert and Joseph DesJardins offer arguments designed to restrict the types of information employers may justifiably gather about employees to information that is "job relevant." Both also construe the employer/employee relationship in contractual terms . . . .

DesJardins argues that the contractual model is a marked improvement over the old principal/agent model, where the moral and legal rights seemed to be largely on the side of the employer and the moral and legal duties on the side of the employee. The contractual model presumes the existence of a legal framework to enforce the contract. More importantly, "contracts also must be noncoercive, voluntary agreements between rational and free agents."[5] And, they must be free from fraud and deception.

DesJardins . . . argues that the employer is entitled to make sure that the contract is free from fraud and deception. The employer can legitimately acquire information about the prospective employee's job qualifications, work experience, educational background, and "other information relevant to the hiring decision."[6] Information is "relevant" if it has to do with determining whether or not the employee is capable of fulfilling her part of the contract. In a similar vein, Brenkert argues that the "job relevance" requirement limits the information sought "to that which is directly connected with the job description."[7] Brenkert admits that aspects of a person's social and moral character (for example, honesty, ability and willingness to cooperate with others) are job relevant. What both Brenkert and

DesJardins want to rule out as job relevant is information about such things as a prospective employee's political or religious beliefs and practices, her sexual preferences, marital status, credit or other financial data, and the like . . . .

I am sympathetic with the idea of such content restrictions, but I believe the arguments of DesJardins and Brenkert are seriously flawed. In the first place, we should be wary of the contractual model of the employer/employee relationship . . . .

The danger in using this model is that it may lead us to ignore a crucial imbalance of power that exists in the marketplace. Individual employees rarely have bargaining power equal to that of their prospective employers. First, there are typically more potential employees available to firms than there are job openings available. Many jobs require little training or pre-existing expertise, and so workers can often be easily replaced. The threat that "there is always someone to take your place" is not an idle one for most workers . . . . Second, firms seem able to absorb underemployment more easily than workers can absorb unemployment. While firms need employees, they rarely need them as desperately as workers need jobs. As a result of these two factors, individual workers are rarely in a position to bargain on anything like equal terms with their prospective employers.

This imbalance of power renders most workers practically unable to resist the demands for information that precede and accompany employment offers, and makes all the more urgent the content restrictions DesJardins and Brenkert advocate. After all, what is the point of urging such restrictions if the wage-labor agreement is one between relative equals? Why not just leave the sorts of information to be exchanged up to the negotiations between employer and employee?

. . . My point is that the contractual model is very misleading if used as a way to conceive of the reality of work in the U.S. It suggests a type of equality that does not exist, and if its descriptive and normative functions are run together, it distorts our perception of where the balance of power lies in the relationship between workers and employers.

Leaving aside the problems with the contractual model, it does not seem that DesJardins and Brenkert help us to understand the moral basis for the content restrictions they advocate. The appeal to the notion of "job relevance" raises more questions than it answers. Lots of information both would prevent employers from obtaining is, arguably, job relevant. For instance, if all of my employees are politically and religiously conservative, knowing where prospective employees stand on these matters may very well be job relevant if my employees have to work closely together . . . .[8]

A DIFFERENT PERSPECTIVE

Even if the notion of "job relevance" was unproblematic, the argument would be incomplete. What we want is an argument that connects job relevance up with some moral value or values. In other words, why (morally speaking) limit employer access to only job relevant information? What is at stake in doing so?

If we turn back to the analysis of the value of privacy, the answer emerges. Suppose that employers are allowed to gather all of the sorts of information that the notion of "job relevance" is meant to exclude, and to use that information in making employment-related decisions. The result might be that business hiring and promotion decisions will wind up shaping people's lives in rather dramatic ways. Consider the likely chilling effects on employees. They may be reluctant to try out any new ideas or activities that may, at some future date, come back to haunt them. As we saw, privacy vitally contributes to our concept of ourselves as in control of our own lives. Part of this is that it protects our sense of self-determination by enabling us to engage in a "no holds barred" examination of all aspects of our lives. It allows us to experiment with different courses of our lives, if only in thought. These different courses may not be popular, especially to employers who are very conscious of the bottom line.

There is also the very real danger that all sorts of mistaken inferences about employee behavior will be made from access to such information. For instance, suppose that a polygraph test uncovers the fact that a person sometimes fantasizes about theft. It seems clear that a person who fantasizes about theft may be a long way from behaving as a thief. We do not understand the connections between the "inner workings" of people's minds and their behavior anywhere near well enough to allow employers to make such predictions in an accurate fashion.

In short, the content restrictions DesJardins and Brenkert favor are morally justified as ways of limiting the perceived power that businesses have over the lives of their employees. We should discourage invasions of privacy that will likely result in individuals narrowing the exploration and examination of their lives, or that will decrease their sense that they control and are responsible for their lives. In a work environment without such restrictions, and where employers are already in a position to impose their wills on employees in other ways, it seems unlikely that employees will have as rich and lively a sense of their own autonomy. In turn, they will be less prone to exercise their autonomy.

It seems clear that many of the most controversial *means* of acquiring information about employees may provide employers with information that is, on any reasonable interpretation of the notion, job relevant. Surveillance to prevent theft or to maintain productivity provides such information. Urine tests will provide such information, though they will also provide information about off-the-job drug or alcohol use that is, less obviously, job relevant. Searches of employee desks or lockers, and even polygraph tests (where the questions are suitably restricted), will provide such information. Physical exams and skills tests will do so, though few have seen these as controversial.

Numerous writers have argued against the use of at least some of these means. One popular objection to some of these means is that they are so inaccurate. Polygraph tests,

in particular, seem gravely defective in this way, and to a lesser extent, so do urine tests. The concern about accuracy is a concern about fairness, about the possibility of unfairly accusing individuals of actions they are innocent of. I think that the inaccuracy issue is a very serious one, but I do not believe we should base our case against such tests on it alone, or even primarily. The reason for this is simple: suppose through various technological developments such tests are made *very* accurate. Are we then to conclude that there is nothing objectionable about them? I think not. I will try to show that there are other objectionable features to such tests.

A second objection might be that such means of acquiring information are somehow too intrusive. It is important to ask what this means. Is it that such methods come too close to us, crossing some physical or psychological boundary that is morally significant? . . . Physical contact does not seem to be a necessary condition of intrusiveness. It might be a sufficient condition, but we need to know precisely what is so objectionable about such contact . . . [especially] where the concern is with shielding individuals from physical harm . . . .

What all of these methods of acquiring information seem to have in common is that they are ways of checking on the things employees say about themselves or the ways employees present themselves. In this regard, I do not see how a urine test or surveillance is all that much different than the required disclosure of information about work experience or educational background. Perhaps some methods are more intrusive, as a matter of degree, than others. Employees are increasingly finding that not even their own bodies are safe havens, let alone their desks and lockers. At every turn, they are hounded by employer efforts to catch them speaking or acting in ways contrary to what are deemed the employer's interests.

The proliferation of these methods of acquiring contradicting information seems likely to have two sorts of effects on workers. First, all such methods implicitly remind the worker where the balance of power lies in the working world. Again, most workers are not in a position to refuse to cooperate with the use of such methods and workers are highly vulnerable to any negative employer reactions to the information so gleaned. The more a worker is checked on, tested, spied upon, and so on, the less likely she is to feel that she controls her own life in the working world. The aggregate and cumulative effects of many (by themselves seemingly innocent) attempts to check on workers might be an increased sense on the part of workers that the workplace is an oppressive environment. It is distressing that so many employees apparently submit to polygraph or urine tests without any reluctance. Can this be because they have already internalized the message that in the workplace their lives are not their own?

Second, random or across-the-board drug testing, or surveillance without "reasonable cause," implicitly tells employees that they are not trustworthy. It is important to keep in mind that in spite of statistics on the use of drugs by workers (estimates as high as one in six use drugs either on or off the job), the vast majority of workers are probably "clean" and honest. However, instead of there being a presumption that employees will act responsibly, the presumption behind the use of these methods of gathering information is that they cannot be trusted to act responsibly. Individuals who find themselves with a presumption of doubt against them may simply react with resentment. That is bad enough and a potential cost to employers. What is worse is the tendency such methods might have to undermine the employees' sense of trustworthiness, and therefore their sense that they are worthy of acting autonomously. Again, one valuable thing about privacy is that it affirms an individual's sense that she is worthy of autonomy. The more she lacks that sense, the more she is prone to tolerate invasions of her privacy, with the resulting debilitating effects on her autonomy.

THE ORGANIZATION OF WORK

In the abstract, concerns about the effects of such methods on employee autonomy might appear legitimate, but not of a sufficiently compelling nature to convince us that their use is wholly objectionable. If they are employed in a work environment that is otherwise supportive of employee autonomy, they might be only minor threats. Therefore, in order to strengthen the case against the use of such methods, it will help here to focus attention on how the organization of work in the U.S. *already* undermines the autonomy of most workers to an extraordinary extent.

As numerous critics of the organization of work in the U.S. have pointed out, the majority of workers are routinely subjected to a hierarchical, authoritarian management structure that deprives them of any significant input into the economic decisions directly affecting their working lives. Most have very little input into decisions about the organization of work at even the shop-floor level, let alone at levels above it. As Adina Schwartz argues, most workers are subjected to a division of labor where they are confined to increasingly narrowly defined tasks determined and supervised by others:

> These routine jobs provide people with almost no opportunities for formulating aims, for deciding on means for achieving their ends, or for adjusting their goals and methods in light of experience.[9]

Work technology is decided by others, as are productivity quotas, criteria for evaluation, discipline procedures, and plant closings or employee lay-offs. Even the attitudes with which work is to be done are prescribed and pressures are put on workers to "be a loyal member of the team" or to "please the customer at all costs." . . .

Thus, each concession made to management's desire to gather information using the methods we have been discussing adds to an already impressive arsenal of weapons at its disposal for the assault on employee autonomy. The question is *not* whether we should endorse the use of methods that undermine employee autonomy in a setting where that autonomy is otherwise affirmed and nurtured.

The question is whether we should endorse the use of methods that might further erode employee autonomy. For instance, random or across-the-board urine tests do not send a message to workers that they are untrustworthy in a context where their trustworthiness is normally affirmed. Instead, it sends a message that is likely repeated to workers in a thousand different ways throughout their working lives. A verdict wholly in favor of employees on all of the privacy issues we have been considering will, by itself, come nowhere near establishing working conditions supportive of employee autonomy.

Another way to put the preceding point about the organization of work in the U.S. is to say that property rights, with their supporting political-social institutions and practices, give some individuals a considerable amount of *power* over the lives of others. It is with this in mind that we should consider attempts to override the privacy of employees by appeals to the property rights of the owners and stockholders.

Proponents of gathering information about employees may admit that privacy is a value and that it is threatened by the means employers want to use to gather information. But, they will argue, the property rights of the owners and stockholders are valuable as well. They will rightly demand to be shown that the privacy rights of workers ought to prevail over these property rights . . . .

What this plausible-sounding argument ignores is how property rights in productive resources differ from privacy rights. The right to privacy is such that respecting it provides individuals with an increased sense of control (a necessary condition of autonomy) over their own lives. Respecting it does *not* provide individuals with increased control over the lives of others. Property rights as they exist in the U.S. are, as we have seen, not like this. They do give some power over the lives of others. And, importantly, a verdict in favor of the owners and stockholders will mean a further extension of that already considerable control.

Hence, the issue is not the rather abstract one of whether privacy rights are more or less important than property rights in relation to the autonomy of the bearers of those rights. Rather, since property rights as currently institutionalized give some power over the lives of others, the issue is whether to preserve or increase that power, *or* curtail it. Indeed, once the connection between property rights and power is revealed in this way, those rights become fit subjects for critical scrutiny. If we are concerned about the autonomy of workers, we can hardly ignore the existence of working conditions that systematically and pervasively undermine it.

A second reason for not allowing the issues to be framed simply in terms of conflicting rights is that this is likely to exonerate the existing organization of work from any blame for generating the employee behavior that is viewed as irresponsible. This irresponsible behavior is taken as a *given*, and various methods for collecting information about employees are proposed. The need to gather such information is implicitly attributed solely to defects in the character of employees. Those who seek to defend workers against invasions of their privacy are likely to be portrayed as condoning dishonesty, drug use, and the like. This portrayal is, of course, unfair, but it gains credence from the implicit assumption that such behaviors simply exist and must be countered. Thus, the debate about conflicting rights begins, and employers are all too easily depicted as the innocent victims of their unscrupulous, irresponsible, and ungrateful employees.

Many critics of the organization of work in the U.S. will argue that it is the character of that work itself which is a very significant factor in producing such "problem" behaviors. The research that exists in this area strongly suggests that this is a possibility we should not ignore.[10] It is surprising that in the popular and philosophical discussions of these issues, the following sorts of questions are so rarely asked: Why is it that employees show up drunk or drugged for work? Why is it that they shirk work and responsibility? Why is it that they lie about their credentials or exaggerate them? Why is it that they engage in theft or sabotage? When the question asked is whether the employee privacy that is violated in order to counter such behaviors outweighs or is outweighed by the right to property, the preceding sorts of questions are suppressed. Behaviors which may be symptomatic of a morally sick organization of work are viewed as the underlying cause of the conflict. Then, in a twist of bitter irony, the property rights in which that organization of work is anchored are brought in to beat back the challenge posed by the employees' privacy rights.

Appeals to co-worker health and safety, or to the health and safety of consumers and members of the general public, are also used to justify invasions of worker privacy. No one wants their airline pilot to be high on cocaine or their nuclear power plant operator to be blitzed on Jim Beam. Moreover, protecting people's health and safety does *not* ipso facto give them power over the lives of others. Health and safety are obviously essential conditions for the preservation and exercise of autonomy, perhaps more essential than privacy. So, it would seem that health and safety considerations ought to prevail over privacy considerations.

In response to this, I begin by noting that we should not isolate the issue of whether or not we can invade the privacy of workers to protect health and safety from the larger issue of the role of the current organization of work in generating dangerous behavior. The issue is not simply whether health and safety outweighs privacy, but also whether fundamental changes in the organization of work would lessen or eliminate the behavior that makes overriding privacy seem so reasonable. It is hard to say whether and to what extent the means many would now use to gather information about employees would be used in a more democratically and humanely organized economy. Such an economy would eliminate or at least lessen the specter of unemployment, and so the felt need to lie about or exaggerate credentials in order to obtain work might be eliminated. Such an economy would give workers more real control over their working lives, and would eliminate the division between those who make decisions at work and those who simply implement the decisions of others. Such an economy

would give workers more control over the products of their labor, and give them the power to discipline other workers. How such changes would affect employee morale, productivity, and the sense of responsibility for work performed are things we can only speculate about.

It seems likely that such changes will *not* eliminate all dangerous or destructive behavior on the part of workers. I do not wish to rule out, once and for all, the use of means of acquiring information that encroach on privacy. What I do want to suggest, in closing, is that in a more democratically and humanely organized economy, decisions about what measures to use and when to use them would not be made unilaterally by some people and then simply imposed on others. If we are going to respect the autonomy of persons, then we must give them input into decisions like this that vitally affect their lives.

Notes

1. For a useful discussion of the difficulties in defining privacy, see H. J. McCloskey, "Privacy and the Right to Privacy," *Philosophy,* vol. 55 (1980), pp. 17–38.

2. Joseph Kupfer, "Privacy, Autonomy, and Self-Concept," *American Philosophical Quarterly,* vol. 24 (1987), pp. 81–89. For a similar analysis, see Jeffrey H. Reiman, "Privacy, Intimacy, and Personhood," *Philosophy and Public Affairs,* vol. 6 (1976), pp. 26–44.

3. Kupfer, "Privacy, Autonomy, and Self-Concept," p. 82.

4. Ibid., p. 85.

5. Joseph R. DesJardins, "Privacy in Employment," in *Moral Rights in the Workplace,* Gertrude Ezorsky (ed.) (Albany: State University of New York Press, 1987), pp. 127–139, 131.

6. Ibid., p. 132.

7. George G. Brenkert, "Privacy, Polygraphs, and Work," in *Contemporary Issues in Business Ethics,* Joseph R. DesJardins and John J. McCall (eds.) (Belmont, CA: Wadsworth, 1985), pp. 227–237, 231.

8. Ibid., p. 231. Brenkert admits that the criterion of job relevance is "rather vague," yet proceeds to use it.

9. Adina Schwartz, "Meaningful Work," *Ethics,* vol. 92 (1982), pp. 634–646. Cf. also Edward Sankowski, "Freedom, Work, and the Scope of Democracy," *Ethics,* vol. 91 (1981), pp. 228–242.

10. See, for instance, *Work in America: Report of a Special Task Force to the Secretary of Health, Education, and Welfare* (Cambridge, MA: MIT Press, 1973); Harry Braverman, *Labor and Monopoly Capital: The Degradation of Work in the Twentieth Century* (New York: Monthly Review Press, 1974).

Review and Discussion Questions

1. Lippke maintains that privacy is valuable because of its relation to autonomy and (following Joseph Kupfer) highlights two ways in which privacy contributes to autonomy. Explain the connections between privacy and autonomy. Do you agree that autonomy is the reason privacy is valuable?

2. Relying on a contractual model of employer–employee relations, some writers like DesJardins and Duska use the concept of "job relevance" to restrict the information employers may justifiably gather about employees. What are Lippke's reasons for

rejecting this approach? Are you persuaded by his arguments?

3. By contrast with the contractual model, what are Lippke's reasons both for opposing employers' acquiring certain sorts of information and for objecting to certain methods of gathering it?

4. Do you agree with Lippke that there is a grave imbalance in power between employers and employees and that the workplace is characterized by authoritarian management structures that deprive employees of much of their autonomy? What are the implications of viewing privacy rights in this context?

5. How does Lippke respond to the argument that the property rights of owners and stockholders should take precedence over the privacy rights of employees? Do you agree that the existing organization of work contributes significantly to problems like drug use and dishonesty?

WORKPLACE WARS: HOW MUCH SHOULD I BE REQUIRED TO MEET THE NEEDS OF YOUR CHILDREN?

CLAUDIA MILLS

Many companies these days are endeavouring to be more "family-friendly," but this can be a burden on the childless employees who must sometimes take up the slack when, say, a parent has to leave work early to pick up children. In addition, some employees without children find it unfair that colleagues with children receive benefits that are denied to them. In this essay, Claudia Mills discusses the special needs of parents, what obligations these needs impose on others, and what workplace policies would be fair to employees both with and without children. Although she believes we all have an interest in the successful raising of the next generation, she contends that companies should, as far as possible, treat parents and non-parents alike.

Johnny's mom leaves work early to coach Johnny's soccer team; Katie's dad leaves work early to attend Katie's kindergarten graduation—while other, childless (or, alternatively, childfree) workers stay late to pick up the slack. Johnny's mom and Katie's dad both receive, as part of their benefit packages, health insurance for Johnny and Katie, as well as the opportunity to contribute to a tax-free childcare account—benefits not available to colleagues without children. While many applaud such company efforts to assist working parents, struggling under a dual burden of employment and parenthood, recently a chorus of voices has been raised to challenge "family-friendly" policies, charging that they are friendly to families at the expense of unfairness to fellow workers without children.

Are the special needs of parents ones we should be seeking to meet? If so, who is this "we"—the government, employers, fellow workers? What policies in the workplace are most fair to parents and non-parents alike?

RESPONSIBILITIES, CHOICES, AND NEEDS

One first answer here, which I hear from some of my most environmentally conscious friends, is that the rest of us should bear no responsibility whatsoever for parents' special needs, because people shouldn't be becoming parents in the first place. In a world as crowded as ours, and as environmentally threatened, people should not be having children at all. Admittedly, those in Western, developed nations are not currently reproducing at greater than replacement rates; nonetheless, it is these children who have the heaviest and most destructive "ecological footprint." One of my friends, environmentally outraged, refused to speak to his own brother after his third nephew was born! Few of us subscribe to this draconian environmental ethic, however. Children provide such a great part of the good of life that it seems unreasonable to expect people to forgo the central life experience of parenthood in exchange for environmental benefits that are speculative and diffuse.

On the other end of the spectrum, it is claimed that the continued production of children is a positive good for all of us, and parents are thus to be congratulated, and heartily and humbly assisted in their endeavor. According to this view, those who do not have children, far from being paragons of environmental virtue, are parasites on those who do. Sylvia Ann Hewlett, chairman of the National Parenting Association, is quoted in the *Denver Rocky Mountain News* as saying, "Children are 100 percent of the future and we are all stakeholders in their future because they are the folks who will be paying our Social Security. If you are a childless adult you are kind of a free rider on the effort of raising children." But this view as well seems overstated. Collectively we may need and want *some* people to be having children, but we hardly feel the more, the better. And most of those who have children don't approach the having of children in this light, as a duty grimly assumed for the benefit of humankind generally.

We are left, then, with a middle position. Having children, I claim, is a morally permissible but not morally

From *Philosophy & Public Policy Quarterly 21* (Winter 2001). Reprinted with permission of the author. References omitted.

mandatory choice that persons make to enrich their own lives. This would seem to support the view that the consequences of this choice—the increased needs that parenthood brings—should be regarded by and large as the responsibility of the parents alone. After all, if they didn't want to assume those burdens, they could have refrained from having children. We see a similar reaction in other areas of life in which special needs flow from voluntary choices rather than from the vagaries of chance and the uncertainties of fortune. We question whether we should be collectively providing medical care for those whose medical problems arise from poor lifestyle choices: smoking, overeating, risky sexual behaviors. Moving closer to our current topic, some question whether welfare payments should be provided to poor mothers who repeatedly bear children out of wedlock.

However, even as we question the provision of assistance in such cases, by and large we do continue to provide it, and to feel morally uncomfortable with the refusal to provide it. Our response to need, we hope, is not in the first place dictated by a detached judgment regarding the cause of that need; we aspire to be more open-hearted than that. However, as the need in question becomes chronic rather than acute, and poses a less dire threat to life and health, we rethink our willingness to offer aid. We would rescue a child drowning in a pond, however she came to be floundering there; we don't feel the same way about repeatedly picking up our neighbor's child from day care, when he *could* leave work on time but chooses to stay late. In the latter case, we may wonder whether we have left the realm of "needs" behind altogether.

Yet it may be a mistake to press too heavily on the voluntariness of the choice to bear and raise children. While this is indeed a choice we make, it seems to be misrepresented as a (mere) "lifestyle choice." Having children is such a central part of a full human life, something Aristotle felt comfortable including as a fundamental element in *eudaimonia*, human flourishing. While some—and perhaps a growing number—obviously define flourishing for themselves differently, it is hardly eccentric to view a full human life as including children of one's own (biological or adopted) to love and care for. Life without children seems importantly similar, in my view, to life without sex. There are those who live a full and joyous life without sex; yet most of us don't feel that sex is something we can simply ask people to renounce, as the price of absolving themselves of responsibility for any future offspring (although some of us do). So, while we can consider the bearing and raising of children as a choice, it is not a choice which most people feel blithely free to take or leave, especially given heavy societal pressures and expectations to reproduce.

It is not clear how relevant this concession is, however, to the question we are pursuing here. For even if we accept that parents' special needs don't flow from choices we can reasonably ask them to forgo, we may be wary of workplace policies which place too much weight on the meeting of particular, personal needs. To be blunt, "To each according to his needs" is not, contrary to what many Americans in a recent opinion poll reported believing, a creed enshrined in the American Constitution. While I will argue below that allocation according to need *is* an important principle at the level of government policy, in the workplace other competing principles—such as allocation according to effort, or to accomplishment—command greater allegiance.

In the case of meeting parental need, it would seem strikingly unfair to most of us to pay parents more than non-parents for the same work, on the grounds that they have greater income requirements. In the past considerations such as this provided the rationale for paying men higher salaries (as family "breadwinners") than women without dependents. It is not only the sexism here that troubles us, but also the unfairness of giving greater pay to one employee than to another for the same contribution.

If we move toward the other extreme, however, of disregarding need, we can arrive at some seemingly ludicrous results. Should one worker complain that another, who suffers a heart attack, receives considerably greater benefits from his company-provided health insurance policy than she does from hers? Lisa Benenson, editor of *Working Mother* magazine, is quoted in the *New York Times* as asking, "If the person at the desk next to you gets cancer, do you think of them as 'earning' more because their health dollar costs are higher?" However, the health insurance case is a special one, which can't be generalized too far. The whole idea of health insurance is based on a commitment to risk-sharing; if we were just going to pay for our own health-care needs, unwilling to take a chance on having to pay for anybody else's, we wouldn't have gotten health insurance in the first place. We recognize that health insurance is in some respects a lottery, in which we may emerge as either winners or losers.

A better example to test our willingness to match benefits to needs might be: Suppose a company provides each employee with three days of bereavement leave annually, as needed. Would it make sense to allow the non-bereaved to use this leave to enjoy summer barbecues or time at the spa? Here, while intuitions may differ, this doesn't seem to me absurd. As we shall see below, many employers are moving in precisely this direction, of providing an extensive and variable menu of benefits from which both parents and non-parents can choose at will. Of course, what employers are willing and financially able to provide for all may fall considerably short of what employees in special circumstances need. But here it may be unreasonable for the needy to expect their plight to be addressed by their employer rather than by a general societal safety net.

My conclusion so far, then, is that greater parental need is an insecure foundation for greater parental benefits—partly because the need flows from a voluntary choice (although one that is hardly trivial or eccentric), partly because we are only moderately willing to apportion workplace benefits according to need, in any case.

A more promising approach, I suggest, proceeds as follows. Whatever we decide about the choice to have children, and our appropriate response to the needs generated by it, nobody benefits when children are not raised well. It may or may not be in my interest that you have children; but it is definitely in my interest that your children, once here to share the planet with me, grow up to be as happy, loving, good, and decent as possible. This is one kind of argument that supports the provision of free public education to all children, financed by the contributions of tax-paying parents and non-parents alike. What good does it do anyone to have children growing up uneducated? And, we can also ask, what good does it do anyone to have children growing up with poor parenting? So even if we understand the choice to have children as one that implies the responsibility to assume at least some of the additional burdens involved in raising these children, we all—parents and non-parents alike—have a stake in seeing these children raised well. We all share an interest in the optimal raising of our future citizens, neighbors, colleagues, and friends.

Now, this argument appeals to the enlightened self-interest of non-parents, regarding the raising of other people's children. It may therefore seem to fall short of grounding actual moral obligations. What if someone were to listen to the argument just offered, and shrug and say, "Maybe I'm being foolishly shortsighted in not wanting to assist you with the raising of your children, but, frankly I just don't care"? Here my response is that one of the deepest problems of political philosophy is to establish actual obligations on the part of those who profess not to care about the collective benefits to be generated by collective cooperation: those who don't want to pay their share for national defense, or environmental protection, or other public goods. It is simply not feasible to permit individuals to opt out at will on the provision of collective benefits, while still remaining full-fledged citizens and members of our common life. Moreover, I argue that it is morally imperative (and not merely optional) for us to ensure that all persons' *basic* needs are met, simply out of respect for basic human rights. Thus, we all bear some responsibility for meeting all children's most basic needs (for food, shelter, health care, and education), not as a duty owed to these children's parents, but as a duty owed to the children, as our fellow human beings, themselves. However, current workplace policies aim beyond the bare meeting of basic, universal human needs, toward facilitating good, rather than just minimally adequate, parenting.

Now, the appeal to the widely shared benefits of optimal child rearing can take us only so far. Raising happy, healthy children is an important societal goal, but it is not our only societal goal. Indeed, raising happy, healthy children is not even the only goal of those children's parents, who presumably continue to care about other aspects of their lives as well: their work, their marriages, their contributions to the larger community. So we need now to consider actual policy proposals regarding the treatment of parents and non-parents in the workplace, and in the community beyond.

HOW FAR DO WE GO?

If we recognize compelling reasons to provide at least some assistance to parents in child rearing, what does this mean in practice? Who should be assisting parents, and how?

There is currently a wide range of options possible. The federal government provides tax breaks for parents by giving a $2,800 tax deduction for each dependent in a family, as well as an additional dependent-care credit (up to $4,800), and has recently added a $500 per child tax credit. There are calls for greater governmental subsidization of day care, and for stricter governmental regulation of day care. Employers can provide more or less "family-friendly" policies, ranging from the provision of health insurance benefits for family members, to tax-free dependent-care accounts, to on-site, company-sponsored day care, to flextime and other ways of structuring a more accommodating workplace. And fellow workers and neighbors also lend various amounts of informal assistance: staying late when working parents need to be at home, watching children when working parents need to be at work.

Note that some family-friendly policies make it easier for parents *not* to work (by easing the financial burden imposed by children, and so reducing the need for parents to generate additional income); some make it easier for parents *to* work (by, for example, providing high-quality, affordable day care). Which kind of policies we favor will depend on our other views about how children are best raised: by stay-at-home parents or by working parents. I will not enter that debate here, except to say that, just as children are an important part of a flourishing, full human life, so is work. Just as I am reluctant to ask workers to forgo being parents, so am I reluctant to ask parents to forgo being workers. I do happen to think it is beneficial for children to see both male and female parents as making some (paid or unpaid) contribution to the world beyond the home. But even if I didn't, I would not want to insist that parents—or any of the rest of us—are required to do *everything possible* to raise the *best possible* children. I will return to this issue below.

At this point, our question is, given the desirability of some family-friendly policies, who should bear the cost of putting family-friendly policies in place? I want to argue that it is best if this cost is shared as widely as possible, by all members of society. For the good in question—the raising of healthy, happy children—is a public good, equally shared by all. Thus, it is preferable, in my view, to provide family benefits through general governmental revenues. This would include tax deductions for dependents (I would limit this to deductions for *two* children, to address the environmental concerns raised above), deductions for child care as a legitimate business expense, and (in an ideal society) provision of welfare services and health care to all children, as to all persons generally.

I find it more problematic when differential benefits are provided to parents not by the government, but by employers (and more problematic still when working parents, through their own informal arrangements, simply impose a greater share of work on childless workers). Here it does seem to me that the provision of differential benefits to working parents violates our strong, long-standing commitment to the principle of equal pay for equal work. Elinor Burkett, author of *The Baby Boon: How Family-Friendly America Cheats the Childless*, says (in a *Denver Post* article), "If compensation packages given to parents are worth $10,000 more than those given to non-parents, then we're compensating parents for their fertility and not their work."

Thus I would argue for company policies that, as far as possible, treat parents and non-parents alike, by extending to all the benefits needed primarily by parents. This would mean offering a mix-and-match menu of benefits from which all workers could choose: health insurance for dependents, additional vacation time, flextime, and so forth. The case for uniform (but more generous) benefits goes like this. Employees have many needs, beyond the need to care for small children. As we move through the cycle of life, the need to care for growing children is replaced by the need to care for aging parents (though some, in the so-called "sandwich generation," may face both needs simultaneously). Employees who struggle with poor health would welcome a less strenuous schedule. Benefits such as flextime and enhanced personal leave (e.g., the typical European worker receives six weeks of annual leave, to our two weeks) would greatly enrich the lives of all workers, parents and non-parents alike. Many commentators have observed the extent to which the early twenty-first century workplace deforms and degrades human life. Juliet Schor, in *The Overworked American*, argues that leisure time has declined steeply for Americans in the past three decades. We work longer for less satisfaction, neglecting other passions and interests. It would be in the interest of all of us to adopt, as Jerome Segal has recently argued, a more graceful and humane pace of life. Theda Skocpol, Professor of Government and Sociology at Harvard, suggests that the solution to the workplace wars lies in looking for "ways to modify working conditions to facilitate both family and community involvements by everyone. In that way, contributions by parents can be considered one of a range of ways in which people engage in caring work and civic involvements." Even now some employers allow, and encourage, their employees to do a certain amount of community service on company time; employers could offer employees a choice of release time for *either* community service *or* family commitments.

Extending this idea still further, we might suggest that government offer tax benefits to its citizens for a range of important and life-enhancing activities: for dependent care generally, rather than child care more narrowly (as is the case with most of the deductions in the current tax code); for continuing education; and even for various other rewarding activities. The core idea here is to permit, and indeed to promote, the seeking of our own flourishing in our own chosen way.

HAVING IT ALL

Would uniformly more benign workplace (and tax) policies solve the conflict between working parents and non-parents?

It may seem that uniform policies here would do violence to Aristotle's famous injunction to treat likes alike, and unlikes differently. Working parents may still complain that uniform policies would continue to leave them significantly disadvantaged at the end of the day. They have the same health stresses of their own as non-parents, the same obligations to elderly parents, the same need for a more graceful and humane pace of life. Plus, they have *kids*. So they need financial support and release time to meet parental obligations in addition to what they need just to *live*. Moreover, in our society at the present time, this double burden (triple burden? quadruple burden?) is especially likely to fall on women, who still assume a disproportionate share of childcare and other domestic responsibilities.

Here, though, is where I think working parents go too far. Part of maturity, indeed part of living gracefully, is to accept that all resources, including life itself, are finite. Quite simply, the time I spend doing x will be time I will not spend doing y. It would be unreasonable for parents to expect to face no consequences whatsoever for their choice to become parents. While the gendered inequities here trouble me deeply—mothers generally face greater consequences for their choice to become mothers than fathers do for their choice to become fathers—I don't think the best way to address these is to introduce further divisive inequities between parents and non-parents.

While I cannot document this, I suspect that some of the most bitter conflicts with working parents comes from those who consciously chose not to have children so as to pursue other valued objectives. Workers who are not currently parents, but were in the past, may be able to sympathize with working parents, even as they may mourn that certain benefits were not in place when they were struggling to balance home and work. (Of course, some are not: "I struggled without affordable day care; you should have to struggle, too.") Workers who are not currently parents, but will be someday, have a clear interest in seeing family-friendly policies put firmly in place, though this may not be an interest they are able fully to recognize (many of us have stories of friends who made a comically abrupt turn-around here on the day they discovered *they* were about to become parents). Those unable to have children may have less sympathy for working parents' laments: they would give anything to be able to assume such a double "burden." And those who made the decision not to have children just so that they could concentrate on professional success, or a strong marital relationship, or other interests, may well think: I made my choice and I'm living with it; why can't you live with yours?

A memory from my adolescent years comes to mind here. In the days before backpacks, I would limp home every day from school under the groaning weight of a huge armful of heavy textbooks. My best friend Debbie skipped and scampered beside me, unencumbered with any books whatsoever. Finally, one especially hot and weary afternoon, I asked her if she might want to help me out by carrying a few of my books. Her answer stayed with me for the next thirty years. "Claudia," Debbie told me, "if *I* wanted to carry home textbooks, *I'd* carry home textbooks, and *I'd* study, and *I'd* get good grades, but I don't want to carry home textbooks, so I don't." Her message was clear: if I wanted the good grades so badly, I would have to carry the weight of books that went with it.

To learn to live with our choices, and the inescapable limits they impose on us, is to give up the pipe dream of having it all. Yet one of the cruel paradoxes of our time is that just as parents are entering the work force in record numbers, the expectations for what counts as adequate parenting are also increasing. The less time parents have to give to parenting, the more we have come to expect of them as parents. Recent years have seen a staggering proliferation of extracurricular activities for children, all of which require parental chauffeuring, zealous attendance at games, endless recognition ceremonies. We not only have to be dutiful soccer moms, cheering at every soccer game, but, with children playing in two sports simultaneously, and studying two musical instruments, we have to cheer at every soccer game *and* every swim meet and every piano recital *and* every violin recital, as well as coach their Destination Imagination teams and plan extravaganzas for Vacation Bible School. We have seen the rise of what has been called "hyper-parenting"; we have taken too seriously the goal of *optimal* child rearing, as opposed simply to good parenting.

Now, it is admittedly difficult for individuals to act alone to buck societal trends. Working parents do feel intense pressures today—both to parent as if they were not workers, and to work as if they were not parents. But the sad, or perhaps not so sad, perhaps liberating and joyous, truth is that this can't be done. The sooner we accept this truth, the better it will be for us as workers, as parents, as human beings.

A rich and full life is a great good. I for one do not want to force people to choose between work and parenthood; and we all share some responsibility for meeting children's basic needs and assisting parents in raising tomorrow's citizens. It is best when this responsibility is met by broadly shared tax policies and governmental programs, and by workplace policies that offer a more humane and graceful way of working to parents and non-parents alike. But working parents also need to be realistic and non-hubristic, to accept the limitations of time and life, and experience the distinctive joy that such acceptance can bring.

Review and Discussion Questions

1. Do family-friendly workplace policies sometimes impose a burden on childless people? Is it unfair for corporations to provide special benefits for employees with children and thus spend more money on them than they do on employees without children?

2. Mills seeks a middle way between the view that producing children is a positive social good that we should all support and the view that it is an environmentally irresponsible choice. Explain. Is the decision to have children simply a "lifestyle choice"?

3. Assess the argument that because parents choose to have children, they are not entitled to any special benefits or consideration in the workplace. Are you persuaded by her argument that it is in the enlightened self-interest of all of us to support the raising of healthy, happy children? What implications, if any, does this argument have for the workplace?

4. Explain why Mills finds it "problematic when differential benefits are provided to parents . . . by employers." Do you agree or disagree with her reasoning? Should companies try to treat parents and nonparents alike, or should they take into account the special needs of parents?

5. Are the income-tax breaks that parents receive fair or unfair? Mills apparently favors the government's providing special benefits to people with families. If so, why don't corporations have a similar social responsibility?

6. Is it in the self-interest of corporations to adopt family-friendly workplace policies? What policies do you think companies should adopt with regard to maternity/paternity leave, release time for family matters, and day care? Would it ever be appropriate to pay an employee more because of his or her family responsibilities?

PARTICIPATION
IN EMPLOYMENT

JOHN J. MCCALL

After distinguishing different types of worker participation, John J. McCall presents five moral reasons that argue in favour of strong worker participation in the codetermination of policy. All of these reasons derive from a need to protect centrally important human goods. McCall contends that, in practice, protection for these goods is most effective when there are strong forms of employee participation. McCall also considers some traditional arguments against participation, none of which, he concludes, are of sufficient weight for rejecting it.

Until recently, worker participation in corporate decision making was a topic largely ignored in American management training and practice. Even in recent years, the attention usually given to worker participation by management theory has been confined to small-scale experiments aimed at increasing labor productivity. Little, if any, attention has been given to the possibility that there is a moral basis for extending a right to participation to all workers.

Numerous explanations for this lack of attention are possible. One is that management sees worker participation as a threat to its power and status. Another explanation may be found in a pervasive ideology underlying our patterns of industrial organization. The ruling theory of corporate property distinguishes sharply between the decision-making rights of ownership and its management representatives on the one hand, and employee duties of loyalty and obedience on the other. The justification for that distinction lies partly in a view of the rights of property owners to control their goods and partly in a perception that nonmanagement employees are technically unequipped to make intelligent policy decisions. The perceived threat to power and this dominant ideology of employment provide for strong resistance even to a discussion of broad worker participation in corporate decisions. But perhaps as strong a source of this resistance comes from a confusion about the possible meanings of and moral justifications for worker participation. The primary aim of this essay is to clarify those meanings and justifications. If the essay is successful, it might also suggest that the above sources of resistance to participation should be abandoned.

What people refer to when they use the term "participation" varies widely. We can get a better grasp of that variation in meaning if we recognize that it is a function of variety in both the potential issues available for participatory decisions and the potential mechanisms for that decision making. The potential issues for participation can be divided into three broad and not perfectly distinct categories. First, employees could participate in decisions involving shop-floor operations. Characteristic shop-floor issues are the schedule of employee work hours, assembly line speed, and the distribution of work assignments. Second, employees could participate in decisions that have been the traditional prerogative of middle management. Issues here are hiring or discharge decisions, grievance procedures, evaluations of workers or supervisors, the distribution of merit wage increases, etc. Finally, employees might participate in traditional board-level decisions about investment, product diversification, pricing or output levels, and the like. Simply put, employee participation might refer to participation in decision making over issues that arise at any or all levels of corporate policy.

The mechanisms for participation vary as widely as do the potential issues. These participatory mechanisms vary both in terms of their location within or outside the corporation and in terms of the actual power they possess. For instance, some see employees participating in the shaping of corporate policy by individual acceptance or rejection of employment offers and by collective bargaining through union membership. These mechanisms are essentially external to the particular business institution. Internal mechanisms for participation in corporate policy making include employee stock ownership plans, "quality circle" consulting groups, and bodies that extend employees partial or total effective control of the enterprise. Employee participation through stock ownership might exist either through union pension fund holdings or through individual employee profit sharing plans.

Internal participation can also exist in ways more directly related to the day-to-day functioning of the corporation. For example, quality circle participation is a recent adaptation of some Japanese approaches to the management of human resources. Employees in these quality circles are invited to participate in round-table discussions of corporate concerns such as improving productivity. It is important to note that these quality circle groups are advisory only; their function within the corporation is consultative and they have no actual authority to implement decisions.

Distinct from these advisory bodies are those mechanisms by which employees share in the actual power to make corporate policy. Among the mechanisms for such partial effective control are worker committees with authority to govern selected aspects of the work environment or worker representatives on the traditional organs of authority. An example of the former would be an employee-run grievance board; an example of the latter received significant notice in the United States when United Auto Workers' President Douglas Fraser assumed a seat on Chrysler's Board of Directors. Either of these mechanisms provides for only partial control, since one has a highly defined area of responsibility and the other provides employees with only one voice among many.

A final form of participation provides employees with full control of the operations of the corporation. Examples of this extensive participation are rare in North America, although some midwest farm and northwest lumber cooperatives are organized in this way.

. . . This brief survey should indicate that discussions of employee participation must be pursued with care, since arguments criticizing or supporting participation might be sufficient grounds for drawing conclusions about one form of participation but not sufficient grounds for conclusions about other forms. That caution brings us to the second major aim of this essay—the clarification of moral arguments in favor of broad extensions of worker rights to participate in corporate decisions. Five justifications, or arguments, for participation will be sketched. Comments about the issues of mechanisms required by each justification will follow each argument sketch.

Argument 1

The first . . . justification for employee participation . . . takes its cue from the fundamental objective of any morality—the impartial promotion of human welfare. That requirement of impartiality can be understood as a requirement that we try to guarantee a fair hearing for the interests of every person in decisions concerning policies that centrally affect their lives. Certainly, many decisions at work can have a great impact on the lives of employees. For instance, an employee's privacy and health, both mental and physical, can easily be threatened in his or her working life. Morality, then, requires that there be some attempt to guarantee fair treatment for workers and their interests. We might attempt to institutionalize that guarantee through government regulation of business practices. However, regulation, while helpful to some degree, is often an insufficient guarantee of fair treatment. It is insufficient for the following reasons:

1. Regulation, when it does represent the interests of workers, often does so imprecisely because it is by nature indirect and paternalistic.

2. Business can frequently circumvent the intent of regulations by accepting fines for violations or by judicious use of regulatory appeal mechanisms.

3. Perhaps most importantly, corporate interests can emasculate the content of proposed legislation or regulation through powerful lobbying efforts.

So it seems that an effective guarantee that worker interests are represented fairly requires at least some mechanisms additional to regulation.

We might avoid many of the difficulties of legislation and regulation if workers were allowed to represent their interests more directly whenever crucial corporate decisions are made. Thus, a fair hearing for workers' interests might have a more effective institutional guarantee where workers have available some mechanisms for participation in those decisions. In practice, then, morality's demand for impartiality presumptively may require worker input in the shaping of corporate policies . . . .

Clearly, if worker interests are to be guaranteed as much fair treatment as possible, the participatory mechanisms must have actual power to influence corporate decisions. For while workers might receive fair treatment even where they lack such power, possession of real power more effectively institutionalizes a *guarantee* of fairness. Thus, internal participatory mechanisms that serve in a purely advisory capacity (e.g., quality circle groups) are obviously insufficient vehicles for meeting the fairness demands of morality.

Less obvious are the weaknesses of individual contract negotiations, union membership, and stock ownership as devices for guaranteeing fairness. None of these devices, in practice, can provide enough power to protect fair treatment for workers. Individual contract decisions often find the prospective employee in a very poor bargaining position. The amount of effective power possessed through union membership varies with the changing state of the economy and with changes in particular industrial technologies. In addition, the majority of workers are not unionized; the declining proportion of union membership in the total work force now stands at about one-fifth. Stock ownership plans provide employees very little leverage on corporate decisions because, commonly, only small percentages of stock are held by workers. Moreover, all three of these participation mechanisms most often have little direct power over the important operating decisions which affect worker interests . . . .

Thus, a serious moral concern for fairness, a concern central to any moral perspective, presumptively requires that mechanisms for employee participation provide workers with at least partial effective control of the enterprise. And since decisions that have important consequences for the welfare of workers are made at every level of the corporation, employees ought to participate on issues from the shop floor to the board room. Moreover, since a balanced and impartial consideration of all interests is more probable when opposing parties have roughly equal institutional power, employees deserve more than token representation in the firm's decision-making structure. Rather, they should possess an amount of authority that realistically enables them to resist policies that unfairly damage their interests. This first moral argument, then, provides strong presumptive support for the right of employees to co-determine corporate policy.

Argument 2

The second moral argument . . . derives from points that . . . are similar to those of the preceding argument. Any acceptable moral theory must recognize the inherent value and dignity of the human person. One traditional basis for that belief in the dignity of the person derives from the fact that persons are agents capable of free and rational deliberation. We move towards respect for the dignity of the person when we protect individuals from humanly alterable interferences that jeopardize important human goods and when we allow them, equally, as much freedom from other interferences as possible. Persons with this freedom from interference are able to direct the courses of their own lives without threat of external control or coercion. (Such a view of persons provides for the moral superiority of self-determining, democratic systems of government over oppressive or totalitarian regimes.)

This moral commitment to the dignity of persons as autonomous agents has significant implications for corporate organization. Most of our adult lives are spent at our places of employment. If we possess no real control over that portion of our lives because we are denied the power to participate in forming corporate policy, then at work we are not autonomous agents. Instead we are merely anonymous and replaceable elements in the production process, elements with a moral standing little different from that of the inanimate machinery we operate . . . . The moral importance of autonomy in respecting the dignity of persons should make us critical of these traditional patterns of work and should move us in the direction of more employee participation. However, since autonomy is understood as an ability to control one's activities, the preferred mechanisms of participation should allow employees real control at work. Thus, a commitment to the autonomy and the dignity of persons, just as a commitment to fairness, appears to require that workers have the ability to co-determine policy that directs important corporate activity.

Argument 3

These first two arguments for broad worker participation rights have ended in an explicit requirement that workers have real and actual power over corporate policy. The final three arguments focus not on actual power but on the worker's *perception* of his or her ability to influence policy. All of these last arguments concern the potential for negative consequences created when workers see themselves as having little control over their working lives.

The third argument warns that workers who believe themselves powerless will lose the important psychological good of self-respect. Moral philosophers have contended that since all persons should be treated with dignity, all persons consequently deserve the conditions that generally contribute to a sense of their own dignity or self-worth. Psychologists tell us that a person's sense of self is to a large degree conditioned by the institutional relationships she has and the responses from others that she receives in those relationships. A person will have a stronger sense of her own worth and will develop a deeper sense of self-respect when her social interactions allow her to exercise her capacities in complex and interesting activities and when they reflect her status as an autonomous human being. Of course, in contemporary America the development of the division of labor and of hierarchical authority structures leaves little room for the recognition of the worker's autonomy or for the ordinary worker to exercise capacities in complex ways. The consequence of such work organization is the well-documented worker burnout and alienation; workers disassociate themselves from a major portion of their lives, often with the psychological consequence of a sense of their own unimportance. Contemporary American patterns of work, then, often fail to provide individuals with those conditions that foster a strong sense of self-respect; instead, they more often undermine self-respect. Numerous studies have indicated that a reversal of these trends is possible where workers are provided greater opportunities for exercising judgment and for influencing workplace activities.

If we take seriously a demand for the universal provision of the conditions of self-respect, we ought to increase opportunities for satisfying work by allowing workers to participate in corporate policy decisions. It would seem, however, that this argument for worker participation need not conclude that workers be given actual power. All that the argument requires is that a worker's *sense* of self-respect be strengthened, and that is at least a possible consequence of participation in an advisory capacity. In fact, worker satisfaction has been shown to increase somewhat when employees are involved in Japanese-style quality circles that offer suggestions for improving production. Nor does it appear that the self-respect argument requires that workers be able to influence all aspects of corporate activity, since an increased sense of one's own significance could be had through participation only on immediate shop-floor issues.

However, we must be careful to estimate the long-range effects on worker alienation and self-respect of these less extensive forms of participation. Some evidence indicates that, over time, workers can grow more dissatisfied and alienated than ever if they perceive the participatory program as without real power or as simply a management attempt to manipulate workers for increased productivity.[1] We should consider, then, that a concern for long-run and substantial increases in self-respect might require workers to exercise some actual authority, of a more than token amount, over the workplace.

Argument 4

The fourth argument supporting participation also takes its cue from the studies that show repetitive work without control over one's activities causes worker alienation. The specific consequence that this argument focuses on, however, is not a lessening of self-respect but a potential threat to the mental and physical health of workers. Certainly, everyone is now aware that alienated individuals suffer from more mental disturbances and more stress-related physical illnesses. Workers who are satisfied because they feel able to contribute to corporate policy are held to suffer from less alienation. Since mental and physical health are undoubtedly very central human goods, there seems strong presumptive moral reason for minimizing any negative effects on them that institutional organizations might have. Since broader powers apparently help to minimize such effects, we again have an argument for an expansion of worker rights to participate in corporate decisions.

As with the self-respect argument, however, the issues and mechanisms of participation that this requires are unclear. It could be that negative health effects are minimized in the short run through advisory bodies of participation. On the other hand, minimizing threats to mental or physical well-being in the long run might require more actual authority. Which sorts of mechanisms help most is a question only further empirical research can answer. However, since we have already seen presumptive reasons for actual power to co-determine policy from the first two arguments and since that power can have positive effects on self-respect and health, we perhaps have reasons for preferring the stronger forms of participation if we are presented with a choice between alternatives.

Argument 5

The fifth argument for worker participation also derives from the purported negative consequences of hierarchical and authoritarian organizations of work. This argument, however, focuses on broader social consequences—the danger to our democratic political structures if workers are not allowed to participate in corporate decisions.

Many political theorists are alarmed by contemporary voter apathy. They worry that with that apathy the political process will be democratic in name only, and that the actual business of government will be controlled by powerful and private economic interests. To reverse this trend that threatens democratic government demands that individual citizens become more involved in the political process. However, increased individual involvement is seen as unlikely unless citizens believe themselves to have political power. But an initial increased sense of one's own political power does not seem possible from involvement in the large macroscopic political institutions of contemporary government. Rather, involvement in smaller, more local and immediate social activities will nurture a sense of political efficacy. Since so much time and attention is devoted to one's work life, the place of employment appears a prime candidate for that training in democracy necessary for development of civic involvement. In fact, powerless and alienated workers can bring their sense of powerlessness home and offer their children lessons in the futility of involvement. Allowing those lessons to continue would only exacerbate the threat to vital democratic institutions. This fifth argument, then, sees participation at work as a necessary condition for the existence of a healthy and lasting system of democracy where citizens have the confidence to engage in self-determining political activities.

Again, since this argument focuses on the worker's perception of his or her own power, it provides presumptive support for those mechanisms that would increase both that sense of power and the tendency for political activity. Just what mechanisms these are can be open to argument. However, as before, if workers feel that their participatory mechanisms lack power, there is the danger that they will become even more cynical about their ability to influence political decisions. And since we have already seen arguments supporting participation with actual power to co-determine policy, there should be a presumption in favor of using mechanisms with real power.

SOURCES OF RESISTANCE

We have, then, five significant reasons for extending to workers a broad right to co-determine corporate policy. Now, in order to determine whether the presumption in favor of worker participation can be overridden, we need only to consider some of the common reasons for resisting this employee right to participate. Common sources of resistance to worker participation are that managers perceive it as a threat to their own status or power, that owners feel entitled to the sole control of their property, and that ordinary employees are believed incompetent to make corporate decisions. We shall consider briefly each of these sources of resistance in turn. Our evaluation of these claims will show them to be unacceptable sources of resistance when measured against the above moral reasons in favor of broad participation.

First, in order for management's perception that participation threatens its power to count as an acceptable moral reason for resistance, management power must have some moral basis of its own. According to even traditional conservative theories of corporate property, management has no basic moral right of its own to control the corporation. Rather, management's authority stems from its position as an agent of the economic interests of shareholders, who are seen as the ultimate bearers of a right to use, control, or dispose of property. On the traditional theory, then, management can find a legitimate moral reason for resisting participation only if it can show that schemes of employee participation are real threats to the economic interests of shareholders . . . .

Does participation damage the interests of ownership in a morally unacceptable way? To answer this question, we need to consider what interests ownership has and to what benefits property ownership should entitle one. In the process of confronting these issues, we will also see reasons for suspicion about claims that workers are not capable of participating in the intelligent setting of corporate policy.

In legally incorporated businesses, shareholders commonly have a monetary return on their investment as their principal desire. Moreover, corporate property owners generally have surrendered their interest in day-to-day control of the corporation. The usual owner interest, then, concerns the profitability of the business. Worker participation does not pose a serious threat to this interest in monetary return. Evidence shows that worker participation schemes often improve the economic condition of the business by increasing the interest, motivation, and productivity of employees.[2] In addition, corporations seeking qualified and motivated workers in the future might, out of self-interest, have to construct mechanisms for participation to satisfy the demands of a more slowly growing but more highly educated entry-level labor force. And even in those cases where experiments at worker participation have not succeeded, the failures can often be explained by shortcomings of the particular program that are not generic to all forms of participation. In fact, some of those with experience in constructing participatory work schemes believe that employees can be trained to operate most efficiently with expanded responsibilities.[3] When programs are designed carefully and when time is invested in training both former managers and employees, the competence of workers has not been seen as a crucial reason behind examples of participation's lack of success. Thus, in light of both the marked economic successes of broader worker participation programs and the apparent absence of any *generic* threats to profitability (such as employee incompetence), the economic interests of owners do not appear to provide a substantial basis for a justified resistance to an employee right to participate in corporate decision making.

Some might object, however, that corporate property owners have other interests at stake. Many see a right to control one's goods as fundamental to the concept of property ownership, for example. Thus, they might claim that shareholders have, because of their property ownership, rights to retain control of the business enterprise even if they fail to exercise those rights on a day-to-day basis. This right to control one's property would effectively eliminate the possibility of an employee right to co-determine policy.

There are two reasons, however, to question whether a right to control property can provide a moral basis for denying workers a right to participate in corporate decisions. First, corporate property owners have been granted by society a limit on their legal liability for their property. If a legally incorporated business is sued, owners stand to lose only the value of their investment; an owner of an unincorporated business can lose personal property beyond the value of the business. Part of the motivation behind making this legal limit on liability available was that society would thereby encourage investment activity that would increase the welfare of its members.[4] It is not unreasonable to suggest that this justification for the special legal privilege requires that corporations concern themselves with the welfare of persons within the society in exchange for limited liability. Society, then, places limits on the extent to which owners can direct the use of their corporate property. For example, society can require that corporations concern themselves with the environmental health effects of their waste disposal policies. Failure to require such concern is tantamount to allowing some to profit from harms to others while preventing those others from obtaining reasonable compensation for grievous harms. However, if the legal limitation on liability requires corporations to have some moral concern for the welfare of others, it can also require corporations to protect the welfare of its employees. We have already seen, though, that morally serious goods are at stake when employees are unable to participate significantly in corporate decisions. Thus, if in exchange for limited liability the control of the corporation is to be limited by a concern for others, then the shareholders' interest in controlling corporate property could be limited to allow for an employee right to participate.

A second reason for rejecting the claim that an ownership right to control prohibits employee participation looks not on the legal privileges associated with corporate property but on the very concept of property itself . . . . It is certainly true that property ownership is meaningless without some rights to control the goods owned. It is equally true, however, that no morally acceptable system of property rights can allow unlimited rights to control the goods owned. You, for example, are not allowed to do just anything you

please with your car; you cannot have a right to drive it through my front porch. We accept similar restrictions on the control of business property; we prohibit people from selling untested and potentially dangerous drugs that they produce. The point of these examples is to illustrate that control of property, corporate or not, has to be limited by weighing the constraints on owners against the significance of the human goods that would be jeopardized in the absence of the constraints. Acceptable institutions of property rights, then, must mesh with a society's moral concern for protecting the fundamental human goods of all its members.

We have seen in the first part of this essay that there are significant reasons for thinking that important moral values are linked to a worker's ability to participate in corporate decision making. If control of property, personal or corporate, is to override these moral concerns, we need to be presented with an argument showing what more central goods would be jeopardized if employees were granted strong participation rights. The burden of proof, then, is on those who want to deny an employee right to co-determine corporate policy. They must show that an owner's interest in broad control of corporate policy can stand as an interest worthy of protection as a moral right even when such protection would threaten the dignity, fair treatment, self-respect, and health of workers, as well as the continued viability of a democratic polity with an actively self-determining citizenship.

SUMMARY

To summarize: We have seen that there are various understandings of worker participation. The difference between these various understandings is a function of the workplace issues addressed and the participatory mechanisms that address them. We have also seen sketches of five arguments that purport to show a moral presumption in favor of strong worker participation in the form of an ability to actually co-determine policy. We have seen, further, that some traditional sources of resistance to worker participation (a threat to management or owner prerogatives of control, a belief in the incompetence of workers, a fear that profits will suffer) are either not supported by the evidence or are incapable of sustaining a moral basis for rejecting participation. The provisional conclusion we should draw, then, is that our society ought to move vigorously in the direction of a broader authority for all workers in their places of employment.

Notes

1. Cf. Daniel Zwerdling, *Workplace Democracy* (New York: Harper & Row, 1980).

2. Additional evidence is found in the experiences of the small but highly publicized Volvo experiments and of Donnelly Mirrors, Inc. Interviews with heads of both Volvo and Donnelly can be found in *Harvard Business Review*, 55:4 (1977) and 55:1 (1977), respectively. In West Germany, co-determination is mandated by law in some major industries that have been highly competitive with their American counterparts.

3. The Donnelly interview, *op cit.*, and Nancy Foy and Herman Gadon, "Worker Participation: Contrasts in Three Countries," *Harvard Business Review*, v. 54, no. 3 (1976).

4. Cf. W. Michael Hoffman and James Fisher, "Corporate Responsibility: Property and Liability," in *Ethical Theory and Business*, 1st ed., T. Beauchamp and N. Bowie, eds. (Englewood Cliffs, N.J.: Prentice Hall, 1979), pp. 187–196.

Review and Discussion Questions

1. What are the different forms that employee participation can take? Which do you see as the most valuable forms? In your experience, how extensive is employee participation today?

2. McCall argues for participation in terms of the values of fair treatment, human dignity, self-respect, physical and mental health, and the promotion of a democratic society. Explain how each of these values, according to him, supports the case for participation. Are you persuaded by his reasoning?

3. On what grounds does management typically resist worker participation? How sound are its reasons for doing so? Does participation violate the rights of the owners of corporate property?

4. Is worker participation compatible with the efficient functioning of a free-enterprise system?

5. Do you think that more extensive worker participation would make companies more socially responsible? Do you agree with McCall's conclusion "that our society ought to move vigorously in the direction of a broader authority for all workers in their places of employment"?

Further Reading for Chapter 7

David Barstow and **Lowell Bergman,** "Dangerous Business," *New York Times*, January 8, 9, and 10, 2003, is a disturbing, detailed investigative report on the company with the worst safety record in the United States.

Douglas Birsch, "The Universal Drug Testing of Employees," *Business and Professional Ethics Journal* 14 (Fall 1995), **Michael Cranford,** "Drug Testing and the Right to Privacy," *Journal of Business Ethics* 17 (November 1998), and **John R. Rowan,** "Limitations on the Moral Permissibility of Employee Drug Testing," *Business and Professional Ethics Journal* 19 (Summer 2000) examine the ethics of drug-testing employees.

Gertrude Ezorsky, ed., *Moral Rights in the Workplace* (Albany: State University of New York Press, 1987) is a good collection of articles on the right to meaningful work, occupational health and safety, employee privacy, unions, industrial flight, and related topics.

Ben Hamper, *Rivethead* (New York: Warner Books, 1992) is a riotous look at life on a GM assembly line.

Sylvia Ann Hewlett, "Executive Women and the Myth of Having It All," *Harvard Business Review* 80 (April 2002) discusses the factors that prevent successful career women from having children.

John Kaler, "Understanding Participation," *Journal of Business Ethics* 21 (September 2000) discusses different types of employee participation.

Scott O. Lilienfeld, "Do 'Honesty' Tests Really Measure Honesty?," *Skeptical Inquirer* 18 (Fall 1993) is a critique of honesty exams.

Robert Mayer, "Is There a Right to Workplace Democracy?," *Social Theory and Practice* 26 (Summer 2000) argues on nonlibertarian grounds against such a right.

John J. McCall, "Employee Voice in Corporate Governance," *Business Ethics Quarterly* 11 (January 2001) argues for a strong employee right to co-determine corporate policy.

Adam D. Moore, "Employee Monitoring and Computer Technology," *Business Ethics Quarterly* 10 (July 2000), discusses the tension between privacy and evaluative surveillance.

Social Philosophy and Policy 17 (Summer 2000), special issue on "The Right to Privacy," is an insightful but advanced collection of readings.

8

Moral Choices Facing Employees

When his eldest daughter asked him, "Why don't you just do what they want?" George Betancourt wasn't sure how he should answer. Betancourt was a senior engineer at Northeast Utilities, which operates five nuclear plants in the New England states of America, and all he had done was to speak up and express his professional judgment. Now Northeast wanted him to shut up. First, Northeast's human-resources officer had called him in. After complaining that Betancourt wasn't being a "team player," she described to him the company's termination policies. Three weeks later, Betancourt was informed he was being reassigned. "We'd like to help you, George," Eric DeBarba, vice-president of technical services, told him. "But you've got to start thinking company."[1]

George Galatis was the Northeast engineer on whose behalf George Betancourt had spoken up. Galatis had discovered what he considered to be a glaring safety problem at Northeast's Millstone No. 1 nuclear power plant. In an effort to save downtime (and hence money) during the refuelling process, the plant's procedures routinely violated federal guidelines and pushed its spent-fuel pool well beyond its design capacity. For eighteen months, Galatis's supervisors denied the problem existed and refused to report it to the U.S. Nuclear Regulatory Commission (NRC). Northeast brought in a series of outside experts to prove Galatis wrong, but the consultants ended up agreeing with him. Within the company, Betancourt backed up Galatis's safety concerns. When Northeast finally began to acknowledge a possible problem, it didn't move fast enough to satisfy Galatis. Two years after having initially raised his safety concerns, he finally took the case directly to the NRC, only to learn that it had known about the unsafe procedures for years. He also discovered evidence that suggested collusion between Northeast and NRC officials to subordinate safety to profitability.

As a result of going to the NRC, Galatis says he experienced "subtle forms of harassment, retaliation, and intimidation." He wasn't just being paranoid. Two dozen Millstone No. 1 employees claimed they were fired or demoted for raising safety concerns. Some of his colleagues sided with the company, however, accusing Galatis of aiding antinuclear activists and trying to take away their livelihood. But Galatis didn't stop. He hired a lawyer who specializes in representing whistleblowers and kept after the NRC. With the lawyer's help, the public spotlight was focused on Millstone No. 1. Local politicians began asking questions. Even though the NRC ignored Galatis, it ended up validating his concerns, and Millstone No. 1 was shut down. Citing chronic safety concerns, employee harassment, and a "historic emphasis on cost savings vs. performance," the NRC also put Northeast's other two Millstone plants on its high-scrutiny "watch list." And a new NRC head vowed to shake up the regulatory body itself.

Galatis and Betancourt have managed to hang on to their jobs, but their careers are at a standstill. "The two Georges had better watch their backs," says one engineer. "Up at Northeast, they've got long memories." A disillusioned Galatis says, "If I had it to do over again, I wouldn't."

For someone in the shoes of George Galatis or George Betancourt, two general issues come up. First, there is the question of where an employee's overall moral duty lies. For a professional engineer to go public with documented safety concerns may seem to be a more straightforward moral decision than that faced by an employee who suspects irregularities, unsafe procedures, or wrongdoing in an area unrelated to his or her own job. In that case, the employee may possibly have conflicting moral obligations. Furthermore, if an employee reports irregularities to the appropriate authority, the employee must then decide whether he or she is morally obligated to pursue the matter further. Again other moral considerations come into play.

Second, once they have decided that they ought to blow the whistle, employees must face the possible negative consequences of their action. Galatis and Betancourt are skilled, mature, and respected professionals, with established records and good credentials; in terms of employment options, they may have less to risk than do potential whistleblowers who are just starting their careers or who have restricted job options or heavy financial obligations. Nor is this simply a tug of war between moral duty and self-interest. Most moral theorists would agree that depending on the circumstances, certain personal sacrifices might be so great that we cannot reasonably be morally obliged to make them.

These two themes—determining one's moral responsibility amid a welter of conflicting demands and paying the personal costs that may be involved in living up to one's obligations—recur throughout this chapter. In particular, this chapter looks at the following topics:

1. The obligations employees have to the firm, company loyalty, and the problem of conflicts of interest

2. Illegitimate use of one's official position for private gain, through insider trading or access to proprietary data

3. Domestic and foreign bribery and the factors to consider in determining the morality of giving and receiving gifts in a business context

4. The obligations employees have to third parties and the considerations they should weigh in cases of conflicting moral duties or divided loyalties

5. What whistleblowing is and the factors relevant to evaluating its morality

6. The problem of how considerations of self-interest are to be weighed by an employee facing a tough moral choice

OBLIGATIONS TO THE FIRM

When you accept employment, you generally agree to perform certain tasks, usually during certain specified hours, in exchange for financial remuneration. Whether it is oral or written, implicit or explicit, a contract governs your employment relationship and provides the basic framework for understanding the reciprocal obligations between you and your employer. Your employment contract determines what you are supposed to do or accomplish for your employer, and it may cover a variety of other matters from parking privileges to your dress and deportment while carrying out your responsibilities. The terms of your employment contract may be specific and detailed or vague and open-ended.

Loyalty to the Company

Because you are hired to work for your employer, you have an obligation, when acting on behalf of the organization, to promote your employer's interests. Insofar as you are acting as an agent of your employer, the traditional law of agency places you under a legal obligation to act loyally and in good faith and to carry out all lawful instructions. But it would be morally benighted to view employees merely as agents of their employers and thus expect them to subordinate entirely their autonomy and private lives to the organization. Morality requires neither blind loyalty nor total submission to the organization.

Some writers, however, have gone to the opposite extreme, denying that employees have any obligation of loyalty to the company, even a prima facie obligation, "because companies are not the kind of things that are properly objects of loyalty." Why not? Because a firm's function is to make money, the argument goes, self-interest is all that binds it together. But "loyalty depends on ties that demand self-sacrifice with no expectation of reward."[2] From this perspective, then, one can owe loyalty to family, friends, or country, but not to a corporation. Employees simply work to get paid, and they are misguided if they see themselves as owing loyalty to the company. It may well be true that corporations in the abstract may not be fit subjects of one's loyalty, but they may be such subjects when considered as collections of various people all working for a common goal, in much the same way that a member of a military unit might feel loyalty toward the group (the collection of all the individuals making up the unit).

The above point is consistent with the fact that the notion of company loyalty is commonplace, and that most people not only find it a coherent and legitimate concept but also feel it naturally in their soul. For the many employees who willingly make sacrifices for the organization above and beyond their job descriptions, loyalty is a real and important value. Loyalty, though, is a two-way street, and most employees believe it's up to the company to earn and retain their loyalty to it. That is, loyalty is a reciprocal relation. Indeed, it is not clear how well any business or organization could function without winning employee loyalty, and certainly most companies want more than minimal time and effort from their employees.

Arguably, some obligations of loyalty simply come with the job—for example, the obligation to warn the organization of danger, the obligation to act in a way that protects its legitimate interests, and the obligation to cooperate actively in the furtherance of legitimate corporate goals.[3] To be sure, many businesses demand more than this in the name of loyalty. They may expect employees to defend the company if it is maligned, to work overtime when the company needs it, to accept a transfer if necessary for the good of the organization, or to demonstrate their loyalty in countless other ways. Displaying loyalty in those ways certainly seems morally permissible, even if it is not morally required.[4] In addition, employees, like other individuals, can come to identify with the groups they are part of, accepting group goals and norms as their own. Some moral theorists believe not only that loyalty to the group can become an important value for the individual employee, but also that in the appropriate circumstances the process of group identification can create an additional obligation of loyalty that the employee would not otherwise have.[5]

Conflicts of Interest

Of course, even the most loyal employees can find that their interests collide with those of the organization. You want to dress one way, the organization requires you to dress another way; you'd prefer to show up for work at noon, the company expects you to be present at 8 a.m.; you'd like to receive $75,000 for your services, the organization pays you a fraction of that figure. The reward, autonomy, and self-fulfillment that workers seek aren't always compatible with the worker productivity that the organization desires. Whatever the matter in question, the perspectives of employee and employer may differ.

Sometimes this clash of goals and desires can take the serious form of a *conflict of interest*. In an organization, a conflict of interest arises when employees at any level have special or private interests that are substantial enough to interfere with their job duties; that is, when their personal interests lead them, or might reasonably be expected to lead them, to make decisions or act in ways that are detrimental to their employer's interests. That was certainly the case when Enron's chief financial officer, Andrew Fallon, represented the company in negotiations with firms of which he was a managing partner (and, as such, he eventually earned millions of dollars from the deals).

As we have seen, the work contract is the primary source of an organization's right to expect employees to act on its behalf in a way that is unprejudiced by their personal interests. In general, if the contents of the work agreement are legal and if the employee freely consents to them, then he or she is under an obligation to fulfill the terms of the agreement. Implicit in any work contract is the assumption that employees will not sacrifice the interests of the organization for personal advantage. Of course, individuals may seek to benefit from being employed with a certain business or organization, but in discharging their contractual duties, employees should not subordinate the welfare of the organization to their own gain.

When in a certain situation an employee's private interests run counter to the interests of his or her employer in some significant way—or, to put the point differently, when those interests are likely to interfere with the employee's ability to exercise proper judgment on behalf of the organization—a conflict of interest exists. The danger, then, is that those interests will lead the employee to sacrifice the interests of his or her employer. For example, Bart Williams, sales manager for Leisure Sports World, gives all his firm's promotional work to Impact Advertising because its chief officer is Bart's brother-in-law. As a result, Leisure Sports World pays about 15 percent more in advertising costs than it would if its work went to another agency. Here Bart has allowed his decisions as an employee to be influenced by his personal interests, to the detriment of Leisure Sports World. Note that Williams's interest is not financial; a conflict of interest can take various forms.

Suppose Bart Williams does not throw all of his company's promotional work to his brother-in-law; rather, he gives the firm's business to his brother-in-law only when he sincerely believes that doing so is best for Leisure Sports World. Nevertheless, a conflict of interest can still be said to exist. Because of his brother-in-law, Bart Williams still has a private interest in his business dealings for Leisure

Sports World that could possibly lead him to act against the interests of the company. In other words, there is a danger that Bart's judgment may not be as objective as it should be.

Conflicts of interest are morally worrisome not only when an employee acts to the detriment of the organization but also when the employee's private interests are significant enough that they might tempt the person to do so. Indeed, research shows that conflicts of interest can unconsciously distort the decisions of even very honest people.[6] That's why alarm bells went off when *Business Week* disclosed that two members of the audit committee at Qwest Communications, which was already under fire for its dubious accounting practices, directed companies with million-dollar contracts with Qwest, raising questions about their ability to exercise independent and objective judgment.[7]

By definition, to have a conflict of interest is to be in a morally risky situation; that is why employees should promptly extricate themselves from them or avoid them in the first place. But deciding when an employee's private interests are substantial enough for the situation to constitute a conflict of interest can be difficult. Equally difficult is one's decision of exactly how one should deal with a specific conflict. Sometimes people are encouraged simply to disclose the conflict to those relying on their judgment, thus preventing deception and allowing those relying on them to adjust their reliance accordingly. That is good counsel, but it doesn't end the conflict of interest. Moreover, it's no panacea. Supposedly, if I tell you that I have a financial reason for skewing my advice to you, then you'll take that into account and everything will be fine. Unfortunately, however, experimental evidence suggests that even when informed that the advice may be biased, people fail to discount it as much as they should.[8]

Financial Investments Conflicts of interest may exist when employees have financial investments in suppliers, customers, or distributors with whom their organizations do business. For example, Monica Walters, purchasing agent for Trans-Can Trucking, owns a substantial amount of stock with Timberline Office Works. When ordering office supplies, Walters buys exclusively from Timberline, even though she could get equivalent supplies cheaper from another supplier. In this case, Walters has acted against Trans-Can's interests. But even if Walters never acts in this way to benefit herself, a conflict of interest still exists.

During the dot-com boom, executives at high-tech firms often owned stock in other young companies in the same or closely related fields. Those tangled financial relationships sometimes produced conflicts of interest. For example, eight executives at EMC were heavily invested in the startup StorageNetworks. They recommended it to their clients, and those referrals quickly grew to 40 percent of the younger company's business. But as StorageNetworks got larger and as EMC expanded its own services division, the two companies found themselves competing, leading some at EMC to complain that the other firm was poaching its employees and interfering with its customer relationships. Today EMC says the impact on business was negligible. But a former board member maintains that instead of recommending StorageNetworks, the eight executives should have been pushing EMC equipment: "No question, it had an impact on their day-to-day decisions. It was a tremendous financial incentive."[9]

How much of a financial investment does it take to create a conflict of interest? There's no simple answer. Certainly it is acceptable to own stock in large publicly held corporations, such BCE, RBC, or Hewlett-Packard, that are listed on the stock exchange and whose stock price is unlikely to be influenced by your company's buying their products or not. Sometimes companies limit the percentage of outstanding stock their employees may own in a potential supplier, customer, distributor, or competitor (usually up to 10 percent). But in the EMC case, the eight executives owned shares of StorageNetworks before the company went public, and with the latter's stock rocketing from 50 cents a share to over $90, adhering to the 10 percent rule wouldn't have prevented the problem. Frequently companies require key officials to make a full disclosure of all outside interests that could cloud their judgment or adversely affect their ability to promote the organization's interests. That's important, but as previously mentioned, full disclosure alone doesn't make the conflict disappear. Other steps might still need to be taken (for example, divestment, withdrawal, etc). Organizations need a detailed policy, customized to reflect their needs and interests, that spells out the limits of permissible outside financial investments and what employees should do when they have possible conflicts of interest. Because such a policy can affect the financial well-being of those who fall under it, however, it should be open to negotiation just as employee compensation is.

ABUSE OF OFFICIAL POSITION

The use of one's official position for personal gain always raises moral concerns and questions because of the likelihood that one is violating one's obligations to the firm or organization. Examples range from misusing expense accounts to billing the company for unnecessary travel, from using subordinates for non-organization-related work to abusing a position of trust within an organization to enhance one's own financial leverage and holdings. Executives who use corporate funds for private purposes like health club memberships, extravagant parties, vacation travel, or remodelling their homes are guilty of abusing their official position. There are, unfortunately, many, many examples. But some of the more notable ones are Bernard J. Ebbers of WorldCom, John Legere of Global Crossing, or L. Dennis Kozlowski of Tyco International, who used their high positions to borrow huge amounts of money at below-market rates—in Ebbers's case over $400 million—from the companies they worked for;[10] or Lord Conrad Black, who allegedly diverted funds arising out of no-compete business deals to his own accounts instead of having them go to the company's shareholders.

Insider Trading

One common way of abusing one's official position is through insider trading. *Insider trading* refers to the buying or selling of stocks (or other financial securities) by business "insiders" on the basis of information that "has not been generally disclosed and could reasonably be expected to significantly affect the market price or value of a security." For example, as soon as he learned that the U.S. Food and Drug Administration (FDA) was not going to approve his company's highly touted cancer drug Erbitux, Dr. Sam Waksal, the CEO of ImClone Systems at the time, knew its stock would plummet. Before the FDA's decision was made public, Waksal quickly but quietly sold his stock in the company and told his father and one of his daughters to do so as well. He is also alleged to have passed the word on to his friend Martha Stewart, who dumped her ImClone stock the day before the FDA announced its decision. One doesn't have to profit personally to cross the line, however. For example, the wife of the president and chief executive of Genentech in the United States was charged with insider trading for providing confidential information to her brother. Before the biotechnology firm was partly acquired by another company, she told her brother that "some good things were about to happen" to the company and suggested that he buy a few thousand dollars' worth of stock, even if he had to borrow the funds. She also advised him to keep the purchase secret and make it in the name of a "trustworthy" friend.

In case anyone might think that, since all the above examples concern U.S. executives, Canadian executives are immune to insider trading, note that in 2001–2002 there were 289 insider trading cases opened in Canada.[11] Some of the better known cases of insider trading in Canada involve John Felderhof of Bre-X Minerals, Michael Cowpland of Corel Corp., Scott Paterson of Yorkton Securities Inc., and Andrew Rankin of RBC Dominion Securities Inc. ("tipping").[12] In addition, a recent study points to patterns in the "repurchase" of shares that strongly suggest that there is a lot more illegal insider trading than security regulators are able to detect.[13] The same study also reveals that between 1980 and 2002 there was on average just one prosecution per year for illegal insider trading in the whole of Canada.

Inside traders ordinarily defend their actions by claiming that they don't injure anyone. It's true that trading by insiders on the basis of nonpublic information seldom directly harms anyone. But moral concerns arise from indirect injury, as well as from direct. As one author puts it, "What causes injury or loss to outsiders is not what the insiders knew or did; rather it is what [the outsiders] themselves did not know. It is their own lack of knowledge which exposes them to risk of loss or denies then an opportunity to make a profit."[14] Case in point: the famous Texas Gulf Sulphur stock case.

When test drilling by the U.S. company Texas Gulf indicated a rich ore body near Timmins, Ontario, some officials at Texas Gulf attempted to play down the potential worth of the Timmins property in a press release by describing it as only a prospect. But four days later a second press release termed the Timmins property a major discovery. In the interim, inside investors made a handsome personal profit through stock purchases. At the same time, stockholders who unloaded stock after the first press release or who sold the stock short, anticipating its price would fall, lost money.[15]

Insider dealings raise intriguing questions. When can employees buy and sell securities in their own companies? How much information must they disclose to stockholders about the firm's plans and prospects? When must this information be disclosed? There's also the question, Who is considered an insider? Corporate executives, directors, officers, and other key employees are certainly insiders. But what about outsiders whom a company temporarily employs, such as accountants, lawyers, and contractors? Or what about those who just happen upon inside information?

In Canada both the provinces and the federal government have jurisdiction over the regulation of insider trading. Provinces do so through their corporation and securities laws. For example, in Ontario the activity is regulated through the *Ontario Securities Act*, the *Ontario Business Corporations Act* and the *Canada Criminal Code*, while all the other provinces and territories have analogous structures in place. The federal government regulates insider trading in corporations under its jurisdiction through the *Canada Business Corporations Act* and the *Canada Criminal Code* (for better or worse, Canada, unlike the U.S., does not have a federal regulatory system for securities).[16]

In reaction to the flurry of corporate scandals around the turn of the century, the Canadian government amended the *Criminal Code* in 2004 by passing Bill C-13. Among other things, the amendments made insider trading and tipping (conveying insider information to another) criminal offences carrying maximum sentences of ten and five years in prison respectively (*Criminal Code*, part X, section 382, 1–4). The amended *Criminal Code* defines an inside trader in a broader way than existing provincial or territorial securities legislation; for example, a person is liable to prosecution if he or she buys or sells a security "knowingly using" inside information that they possess by virtue of being a shareholder of the issuer, or even by virtue of, or obtained in the course of, their business or professional relationship with the issuer, etc. At the same time, the stipulation that the offender must "knowingly use" the inside information would make it much more difficult for the Crown to prove its case. Aspects of the legislation are unclear and will almost certainly be challenged in court. In any case, the efforts of the Canadian government to use the *Criminal Code* to deal with "the most egregious cases" of insider trading and tipping are to be applauded because the offences do, after all, have "victims": the outside investors are victims of unfair treatment (they have no equality of opportunity in accessing market information); capital markets themselves are victims of practices that undermine their efficiency, their integrity, and hence their sustainability.

A number of thinkers have defended what is normally considered illegal insider trading. For example, law professor and economist Henry Manne not only sees nothing inherently wrong with insider trading but argues that it is good for the market and the outsiders. For, under unhindered insider trading, stock prices would reflect the actual fiscal condition of the affected corporation or set of corporations, leading thus to a more fair market and, hence, benefiting all stock traders. For this reason, he thinks that regulators (that is, the state) should stay totally out of the insider-trading field. "The use of insider information should be governed by private contractual relationships," he believes, such as those between corporations and their personnel or between a law firm and its members.[17]

At the core of the disagreement as to the nature and outcomes of insider trading are two opposed perspectives on what makes the market work. One the one side, some analysts and regulators contend that the marketplace can work only if it is perceived as being honest and offering equal investment opportunity. Insider trading, they argue, makes that impossible. On the other side, those who think like Manne believe that permitting insiders to trade is good for the market because it accelerates the flow of positive or negative information about the stock to other shareholders and investors. As a result, this information is more quickly reflected in the stock's price, which is healthy for the market. They also believe that permitting insider trading can benefit a company by providing employees an incentive to invent new products, put together deals, or otherwise create new information that will increase the value of a company's stock.

Philosophy professor Jennifer Mills Moore agrees with Manne that it is difficult to prove that insider trading harms ordinary investors or to show that there is something unfair about it. However, she argues that insider trading is wrong because it undermines the fiduciary relationship central to business management. Employees have a duty to act in the interests of the firm and its shareholders, but many ways of profiting from insider information do not benefit the company at all—indeed, they may seriously damage its interests.[18] Another philosophy professor, Patricia Werhane, contends that insider trading undermines the efficiency of free, laissez-faire markets; in consequence, furthermore, it violates the economic, and hence the moral, justification of the free system.[19]

The information that employees garner within the company is not always the kind that affects stock prices. Sometimes the information concerns highly sensitive data related to company research, technology, product development, and so on. How employees treat such secret or classified data can also raise important moral issues.

Proprietary Data

Companies guard information that can affect their competitive standing with all the zealousness of a bulldog guarding a ham bone. This is especially true when it comes to high-tech firms. A typical example is Lexar Media, which recently sued Toshiba for abusing its business relation with Lexar and passing the latter's confidential flash-memory technology to SanDisk, one of its competitors.[20] But even in the low-tech world, spats over proprietary data break out all the time. Procter & Gamble, for example, once sued three rival food chains for allegedly using the patented baking technique in its Duncan Hines brand of chocolate-chip cookies to make "infringing cookies." P&G further claimed that these companies had spied at a sales presentation and at cookie plants. One of the defendants, Frito-Lay, admitted to sending a worker to photograph the outside of a Duncan Hines bakery. But it denied telling the man's college-age son to walk into the plant and ask for some unbaked cookie dough—which the enterprising youth did, and got.[21]

When novel information is patented or copyrighted, it is legally protected but not secret. Others may have access to the information, but they are forbidden to use it (without permission) for the life of the patent or copyright. When a company patents a process, as Kleenex did with pop-up tissues, for example, the company has a monopoly on that process. Until the patent expires, no other firm may compete in the production of pop-up facial tissues. Although on the face of it this rule violates the ideal of a free market and would appear to slow the spread of new processes and technology, patents and copyrights are generally defended on the ground that without them technological innovation would be hampered. Individuals and companies would not be willing to invest in the development of a new process if other firms could then immediately exploit any new invention without having themselves invested in developing it. Although patent law is complicated and patents are not easy to acquire, what it means for something to be patented is well defined legally.

By contrast, the concept of a *trade secret* is broad and imprecise. There is no specific statute on "trade secrets" in Canada, they are under provincial or territorial jurisdiction, and are addressed entirely through case law, following either the *Civil Code* in Quebec (*Code civil du Quebec*) or English common law in the other provinces or territories.[22] It is generally true to say that in common law something (for example, a formula, pattern, design, etc.) is a "trade secret" provided that information about it is commercially valuable, not in the public domain, and the subject of reasonable efforts to maintain its secrecy. That is, virtually any information not generally known (or whose utility is not recognized) is eligible for classification as a trade secret, as long as such information is valuable to its possessor and is treated confidentially. By contrast with patents and copyrights, one does not have to declare or register something a "trade secret" for it to be protected. Trade secrets, however, do not enjoy the same protection as patented information. The formula for Coca-Cola, for instance, is secret but not patented. No competitor has yet succeeded in figuring it out by "reverse engineering," but if your

company managed to do so, then it would be entitled to use the formula itself.

There are at least three arguments for legally protecting trade secrets: (1) trade secrets are the intellectual property of the company; (2) the theft of trade secrets is unfair competition; and (3) employees who disclose trade secrets violate the confidentiality owed to their employers.[23] In individual cases, what constitutes intellectual property, unfair competition, or a violation of confidentiality can often be controversial. But clearly one of the biggest challenges facing an organization can be to prevent its trade secrets and proprietary data from being misused by its own employees.

This is an especially troublesome problem in high-tech firms, in which employees who are privy to sensitive information are especially prone to job-hopping. (For example, the average job tenure of an executive in the software industry is a scant twenty-two months.)[24] Two factors conspire to make this a morally complicated problem: (1) the individual's right to seek new employment and (2) the difficulty of separating trade secrets from the technical know-how, experience, and skill that are part of the employee's own intellect and talents. The latter issue was addressed in *Faccenda Chicken Ltd. v. Fowler* [1984] ICR 589. The presiding judge drew a threefold classification of the information an employee may pick up in the course of his or her employment and which is not the subject of any relevant express agreement: (1) information which is of trivial nature or is easily accessible from public sources; (2) information that the employee must treat as confidential but which, once acquired, remains in one's head and becomes part of one's skill and knowledge (it must be treated as confidential either because the employee is expressly told that it is confidential, or because it is obvious from the nature of the information that it is confidential); and (3) specific trade secrets (for example, a secret process). The Court held that: information in (a) may be used or disclosed to anyone at any time; information in (b) cannot be used or disclosed while the employment relationship continues, but once the employment is over, the employee can use or disclose such information to anyone unless restrained by a valid contract; and information in (c) is so confidential that it cannot lawfully be used for anyone's benefit but the employer's. These distinctions are useful but they only go so far. Later courts have challenged the distinctions in categories (a) and (b).[25]

A widely known case involved Donald Wohlgemuth, who worked in the spacesuit department of B. F. Goodrich in Akron, Ohio.[26] Eventually Wohlgemuth became general manager of the spacesuit division and learned Goodrich's highly classified spacesuit technology for the U.S. *Apollo* flights. Shortly thereafter, Wohlgemuth, desiring a higher salary, joined Goodrich's competitor, International Latex Corporation in Dover, Delaware, as manager of engineering for the industrial area that included making spacesuits in competition with Goodrich. Goodrich protested by seeking an order restraining Wohlgemuth from working for Latex or for any other company in the space field. The Court of

Appeals of Ohio denied Goodrich's request for an injunction, respecting Wohlgemuth's right to choose his employer, but it did provide an injunction restraining Wohlgemuth from revealing Goodrich's trade secrets.

Cases like Wohlgemuth's are fundamentally different from those involving insider trading, for they pit a firm's right to protect its secrets against an employee's right to seek employment wherever he or she chooses. As a result, the moral dilemmas that arise in proprietary-data cases are not easily resolved. For one thing, the trade secrets that companies seek to protect have often become an integral part of the departing employee's total job skills and capabilities. These may, for instance, manifest themselves simply in a subconscious or intuitive sense of what will or will not work in the laboratory. Wohlgemuth's total intellectual capacity included the information, experience, and technical skills acquired at his former workplace. Goodrich might be justified in claiming much of Wohlgemuth's intellectual capacity as its corporate property, but it is difficult to see how he could divest himself of it.

Disputes like this are frequent when an employee leaves a company to join, or become, a competitor. Sometimes companies require employees to sign contracts restricting their ability to get a job with, or start, a competing company within a certain geographical radius or for a certain time. Not all such "noncompete" or "nondisclosure" contracts are legally valid, however. But even without one, companies sometimes sue departing employees as Essex Temporary Services did when Frank Cumbo and ten colleagues left the organization to start a competing business. It filed a second suit against six other employees who quit a few months later to join the new firm of Lerner, Cumbo, and Associates.[27]

The underlying issue of fairness isn't, of course, just a legal question. Frank Cumbo claims that he didn't take any information from Essex that couldn't be found in a phone book. That's relevant to assessing the morality of his conduct, but one would have to know all the details to determine if he wrongly took advantage of information, connections, or business know-how that he had acquired at Essex. In the Goodrich case, it appears that Donald Wohlgemuth didn't take this moral question very seriously. When asked whether he had acted ethically in leaving Goodrich for a competitor, he replied, "Loyalty and ethics have their price, and International Latex has paid the price."[28]

BRIBES AND KICKBACKS

A *bribe* is remuneration for the performance of an act that is inconsistent with the work contract or the nature of the work one has been hired to perform. The remuneration can be money, gifts, entertainment, preferential treatment, or, in general, any object or activity of value.

A typical but blatant case was that of Norman Rothberg, an accountant working at ZZZZ Best Carpet Cleaning Company in the Los Angeles area. When he learned that ZZZZ Best had falsified accounts on insurance restoration jobs, he gave the information to the accounting firm of Ernst & Whinney, which was overseeing ZZZZ Best's planned multimillion-dollar acquisition of another carpet-cleaning chain. When an investigation began, Rothberg accepted $17,000 from ZZZZ Best officials to back off from his initial reports.[29] A more subtle case of attempted bribe is the one involving rookie constable Daniel Chagnon of the Edmonton Police Service. When he saw the flash of photo radar behind him last March, he went up to the officer on duty and asked, "Would a bottle make this fine go away?" The officer on duty was not amused, and Chagnon was suspended for 10 hours without pay.[30]

Rothberg's conduct was wrong because he accepted money in exchange for violating his responsibilities as an accountant, and Chagnon's because he tried to entice another to violate his job responsibilities. By contrast, a server who accepts a gratuity for providing good service to a restaurant customer is not accepting a bribe, for she is not violating her duties. However, the situation would be different if she took money in exchange for not charging the customer for the drinks he ordered. Of course, bribery can occur in more subtle forms than in the Rothberg case. For instance, in exchange for a "sympathetic reading of the books," a company gives a provincial auditor week for two at the Ottawa Fairmont Château Laurier Hotel plus a private box at a Senators game. Or a sporting goods company provides the child of one of its retailers with free summer camp in exchange for preferred display space for its products. In both instances, individuals have received payments inconsistent with their job contract or the nature of the work they are expected to perform.

Bribery sometimes takes the form of *kickbacks*, a practice that involves a percentage payment to a person able to influence or control a source of income. Thus, Alice Farnsworth, sales representative for Sisyphus Books, offers a book-selection committee member a percentage of the handsome commission she stands to make if a Sisyphus civics text is adopted. The money the committee member receives for the preferred consideration is a kickback. A flagrant case of kickbacks involved American executives of the Honda Motor Company. For years they pocketed millions in bribes and kickbacks from local car dealers; in return, the dealers received permission to open lucrative dealerships and had no trouble obtaining models (such as the Acura) that were in scarce supply and could be sold at a large profit.[31]

Canada and Corruption of Foreign Officials

Canada has signed the Convention on Combating Bribery of Foreign Public Officials in International Business Transactions and enacted the *Corruption of Foreign Public Officials Act* (CFPO Act, 1998).[32] The Convention deals with the offence of promising or giving a bribe and of receiving a bribe. It is an offence for a person to bribe in order to obtain or retain business or "other improper advantage." "Other improper advantage" refers to situations in which the briber was not clearly entitled to the benefits—for example, where a person obtains a permit or licence even though he or she does not satisfy the statutory requirements. But the law does not treat all bribes as equal. In certain societies, such payments are necessary—even mandatory—to conduct business. Thus, the law does not prohibit "facilitation payments" (the term used on the marginal notations to the text of section 3(4) of the *Act*) to get an official to perform his normal duties and functions. For example, one can pay a foreign official a small amount to issue a permit, licence, visa, or work permit, or offer police protection in the normal course of their duties. Furthermore, the *CFPO Act* does not make a distinction between bribery and extortion. A company is extorted by a foreign official if, for instance, the official threatens to violate the company's rights, perhaps by closing down a plant on some legal pretext, unless the official is paid off.

Critics of Canada's legislative commitments to curb international bribery and corruption contend that if Canadian firms do not "bribe" or "grease" foreign officials, the firms of other nations will, and Canadian firms will lose lucrative deals. Such reasoning, however, can be a way of rationalizing morally indefensible conduct. For one thing, as a matter of fact competition is often not a factor at all. Indeed, studies in the United States have shown that the enactment of the U.S. *Foreign Corrupt Practices Act* (FCPA) in 1977 has been at most a minor disincentive to American export expansion. Even in nations where the FCPA is alleged to have hurt American business, there has been no statistically discernible effect on U.S. market share. In fact, since passage of the FCPA, U.S. trade with bribe-prone countries has outpaced its trade with other countries.[33] For another, there is evidence that governments worldwide are increasing their efforts to combat corruption within their own borders, especially in high places. South Korea convicted two of its former presidents for taking millions in bribes from various companies. Japan brought down Prime Minister Noburu Takeshita in the 1980s, and in 1994 Prime Minister Morihiro Hosokawa resigned amid allegations of payments from Nippon Telegraph and Telephone. Similarly, Ireland's Prime Minister Charles Haughey was brought down by corruption charges in 1992, and so was Italy's Silvio Berlusconi in 1995. Canada has successfully prosecuted only one case so far under the *CFPO Act*. A Canadian company was fined $25,000 for bribing a U.S. immigration official—Hector Ramirez Garcia—working at the Calgary International Airport.

Since the establishment of the Convention by the OECD countries and the 2005 pact on "zero tolerance" on bribes signed by the world's largest construction and natural-resources companies,[34] it is increasingly much less likely that Canadian companies (and indeed companies of other nations) will be at a competitive disadvantage in the future. But even if adherence to the Convention or compliance with the *CFPO Act* does handicap Canadian firms and cause them to lose lucrative deals, that fact would have to be carefully weighed against the ample documentary evidence of the serious harm done to individuals, companies, and governments as a result of systematic bribery overseas.

Another argument, of a different sort, is also frequently heard against legislation on bribery of foreign officials, namely that the law imposes our standards on foreign countries and that bribery and payoffs are common business practices in other nations. But that argument is too glib, especially when it comes from those who don't really have a working knowledge of another culture. In some other nations, to be sure, bribery is more widespread than it is here, but that doesn't imply that bribery is considered morally acceptable even in those nations. (Drug dealing is not morally acceptable here, even though it is, unfortunately, widespread.) If other countries really did consider bribery and related practices to be morally acceptable, then presumably the people engaging in them would not mind having that fact publicized. But it is difficult to find a real-life example of foreign officials willing to let the public know they accept bribes.

Certainly our legislation and conventions do reflect our own moral standards, but those standards are not simply matters of taste (like clothing styles) or completely arbitrary (like our decision to drive on the right, whereas the British drive on the left). Good, objective arguments can be given against bribery and related corrupt practices, because such practices are intended to induce people inside business or other organizations to make decisions that would not be justifiable according to normal business or other criteria. For example, by encouraging the purchase of inferior goods or the payment of an exorbitant price on non-market grounds, bribery can, and does, clearly injure a variety of legitimate interests—from stockholders to consumers, from taxpayers to other businesses. It subverts market competition by giving advantage in a way that is not directly or indirectly product- or market-related. Indeed, if business activity in a free, competitive setting is only possible under the standard (moral) values inherent in business activity itself (for example, fulfillment of contracts, honesty, truthfulness, respect for the equality and autonomy of the contacting parties), then we have an argument that there can be no "business transactions" between culturally different societies unless they all observe and adhere by the (moral) values of the marketplace. The phenomenon of so-called "globalization" is aiding and abetting the recognition of such a common "moral code" across culturally (and even morally) diverse societies.

In any case, there is nothing "relative" about the damage that such corruption can do to a society. Studies show that the more corrupt a nation is, the less it invests and the slower its economic growth.[35] If we or the other signatories to the Convention were to permit our firms to engage in bribery overseas, we would be encouraging practices in other countries that we consider too harmful to tolerate at home. Moreover, even an occasional corporate bribe overseas can foster bribery and kickbacks at home and lead employees to subordinate the interest of the organization to their own private gain. Corruption is difficult to cordon off; once a company engages in it, corruption can easily spread throughout the organization.

The multiple impacts of bribery can be succinctly drawn out in one final case, which involved Bethlehem Steel Corporation, the second-largest steel company in the United States. Bethlehem was fined $325,000 by a U.S. federal judge for bribery and other corrupt practices stretching over four years. Bethlehem admitted paying bribes to shipowners' representatives, including officers of the Colombian Navy. The bribes were paid to ensure that ships needing repairs would be steered into Bethlehem's eight shipyards. Thus, competitive bidding for the contracts was effectively eliminated, various members of the Colombian Navy were corrupted, and the Colombian government presumably ended up paying more for the repair work than it had to. Beyond that, Bethlehem generated more than $1.7 million for the payoffs by padding bills and skimming profits from legitimate shipyard repair work. Thus, unsuspecting clients of Bethlehem were made to pay the bill for Bethlehem's bribery.

GIFTS AND ENTERTAINMENT

Business gifts and entertainment of clients and business associates are a familiar part of the business world. Still, both practices can raise conflict-of-interest problems and even border on bribery, but knowing where to draw the line is not always easy. One thing is clear: those who cross that line, wittingly or not, might end up in big trouble.

The issue is more urgent in the public sector, as national and taxpayer interests may be implicated. In fulfilling their duties to their constituents, federal, provincial, and territorial governments have to solicit the services of and sign contacts with private companies worth billions of dollars every year. All such contracts are examined by and arranged through the services of public servants on behalf of the nation. In this expenditure of public funds, it is imperative, both from a moral and a business point of view, that the methods and practices used in seeing through all necessary transactions are objective, fair, transparent, efficient, and beneficial to the public good. In order to safeguard these qualities, public servants must not allow their own personal interests, financial or otherwise, to interfere with and cloud their judgment. The federal government regulates its procurement practices through an array of statutes and regulations, from the *Criminal Code* to the *Financial Administration Act*, from the *Lobbyist Registration Act* to the latest addition to the legislative arsenal, the *Federal Accountability Act* (2006). Provincial and territorial governments have their own acts and regulations, plus legislation requiring municipal governments to put in place their own regulations. Moreover, Canada is bound by international agreements like the World Trade Organization's *Agreement on Government Procurement*.

For example, the *Conflict of Interest Act* (as emended in the *Federal Accountability Act*) requires all members of parliament and public office holders to report to the Conflict of Interest and Ethics Commissioner all personal trusts and private interests from which they derive benefit. The Commissioner has the power to fine violators and hold them accountable for their actions. In performing their various activities, including defining requirements and evaluating bids, public servant are obliged to adhere to the laws, regulations, and policies established by the government. In addition, they are required to commit themselves to uphold the democratic, professional, ethical, and social values of the *Values and Ethics Code for the Public Service* of Canada. At the time of signing their letter of offer, public servants acknowledge that compliance with this Code is a condition of employment. In addition, public servants "must arrange their private affairs so that public confidence and trust in the integrity, objectivity and impartiality of government are conserved and enhanced."[36]

For people in the business world, the rules are not so cut and dried. In fact, some of them manage to ignore altogether that acceptance of gifts may and very often does give rise to conflict-of-interest issues. But most companies and most businesspeople consider such behaviour as morally problematic, to say the least. Of course, determining the morality of giving or receiving gifts in a business situation is not always or even usually an easy matter. After all, it is human nature to feel the pull of gratitude in wishing to give gifts and of pleasure in receiving them.

Nevertheless, there are several factors a conscientious businessperson should take into account:

1. *What is the value of the gift?* Is the gift of nominal value, or is it substantial enough to influence a business decision? Undoubtedly, definitions of "nominal" and "substantial" are open to interpretation and are often influenced by situational and cultural variables. Nevertheless, many organizations consider a gift worth twenty-five dollars or less given infrequently—perhaps once a year—only nominal, but anything larger or more frequent would constitute a substantial gift. Although this standard won't fit all cases, it does indicate that accepting even a rather inexpensive gift might be deemed inappropriate.

2. *What is the purpose of the gift?* Dick Randall, a department store manager, accepts small gifts such as pocket calculators from an electronics firm. He insists that the transactions are harmless and that he doesn't intend to give the firm any preferential treatment in terms of advertising displays in the store. As long as the gift is not intended or received as a bribe and remains nominal, there doesn't appear to be any serious problem. But it would be important to ascertain the electronics firm's intention in giving the gift. Is it to influence how Randall lays out displays? Does Randall himself expect it as a palm-greasing device before he'll ensure that the firm receives equal promotional treatment? If so, extortion may be involved. Important to this question of purpose is a consideration of whether the gift is directly tied to an accepted business practice. For example, appointment books, calendars, or pens and pencils with the donor's name clearly imprinted on them serve to advertise a firm. Trips to Hawaii rarely serve this purpose.

3. *What are the circumstances under which the gift was given or received?* A gift given during the holiday season, for a store opening, or to signal other special events is circumstantially different from one unattached to any special event. Whether the gift was given openly or secretly should also be considered. An open gift, say, with the donor's name embossed on it, raises fewer questions than a gift known only to the donor and the recipient.

4. *What is the position and sensitivity to influence of the person receiving the gift?* Is the person in a position to affect materially a business decision on behalf of the gift giver? In other words, might the recipient's opinion, influence, or decision result in preferential treatment for the donor? Another important point is whether the recipients have made it abundantly clear to the donors that they don't intend to allow the gift to influence their action one way or the other.

5. *What is the accepted business practice in the industry?* Is this the customary way of conducting this kind of business? Monetary gifts and tips are standard practice in numerous service industries. Their purpose is not only to reward good service but to ensure it again. But it's not customary to tip the head of the produce department in a supermarket so the person will put aside the best tomatoes for you. When gratuities are an integral part of customary business practice, they are far less likely to pose moral questions.

6. *What is the company's policy?* Many firms explicitly forbid the practice of giving and receiving gifts to minimize even the suspicion that a conflict may exist. Kmart, for example, adopted such a policy, which it requires not only its managers but also its vendors, suppliers, and real estate associates to sign, after one of its corporate directors was indicted for accepting kickbacks.[37] When such a policy exists, the giving or receiving of a gift would normally be wrong.

7. *What is the law?* Certain federal, provincial, territorial, or municipal government employees, for example, may be forbidden by law from receiving any gifts from firms with which they do business. When gift transactions violate the law, they are clearly unacceptable.

Related to gift giving is the practice of entertaining. Some companies distinguish entertainment from gifts as follows: if you can eat or drink it on the spot, it's entertainment. In general, entertainment should be interpreted more sympathetically than gifts, because it usually occurs within the context of doing business in a social situation. Still, the morality of entertainment should be evaluated along the same lines as gifts—that is, with respect to value, purpose, circumstances, position, and sensitivity

to influence of the recipient, accepted business practice, company policy, and the law. In each case the ultimate moral judgment hinges largely on whether an objective party could reasonably suspect that the gift or entertainment might lead the recipient to sacrifice the interest of the firm for his or her personal gain.

OBLIGATIONS TO THIRD PARTIES

Consider the following situations:

> An employee knows that a coworker occasionally sips whiskey on the job. Should she inform the boss?
>
> A dishwasher knows that the restaurant's chef typically reheats three- or four-day-old food and serves it as fresh. When he informs the manager, he is told to forget it. What should the dishwasher do?
>
> A consulting engineer discovers a defect in a structure that is about to be sold. If the owner will not disclose the defect to the potential purchaser, should the engineer do so?
>
> A clerical worker learns that the personnel department has authorized hirings that violate the firm's anti-nepotism rules and neglect its affirmative action commitments. What should she do about it?
>
> On a regular basis, a secretary is asked by her boss to lie to his wife about his whereabouts. "If my wife telephones," he tells her, "don't forget that 'I'm calling on a client.'" In fact, as the secretary well knows, the boss is having an affair. What should the secretary do?

Such cases are not unusual, but they are different from the ones previously considered in this chapter because they involve workers caught in the crossfire of competing ethical concerns and moral responsibilities. Should the employee ensure the welfare of the organization by reporting the fellow worker who drinks, or should she be loyal to her coworker and say nothing? Should the dishwasher go public with what he knows or should he simply forget the matter? Should the secretary carry out her boss's instructions, or should she tell his wife the truth? In each case the employee may experience conflicting obligations, diverging ideals, and divided loyalties.

Many of the difficult moral decisions that employees sometimes face involve such conflicts. How are they to be resolved? According to the procedure recommended in Chapter 2, our moral decisions should take into account our specific obligations, any important ideals that our actions would support or undermine, and, finally, the effects or consequences of the different options open to us. To begin with the last consideration, remember that even staunch non-consequentialists acknowledge that the likely results of our actions are relevant to their moral assessment and that we have some duty to promote human well-being. In general, the fuller our understanding of the possible results of the different actions we might take in the specific situation before us—that is, the better we understand the exact ramifications of the alternatives—the more likely we are to make a sound moral decision. Reflecting on the effects of these different courses of action can help us understand what ideals are at stake and determine the exact strength of the more specific obligations we have.

The impact of our actions on significant moral ideals is the second consideration to be weighed. Any serious moral decision should take into account the various ideals advanced or respected, ignored or hindered, by the alternative courses of conduct open to us. In addition, our moral choices are often strongly influenced by the personal weight we put on the different values at stake in a specific situation. Sometimes those values can point in different directions, as when our simultaneous commitment to professional excellence, personal integrity, and loyalty to friends pulls us in different ways.

Finally, any responsible moral decision must, of course, take into account the more specific obligations we have—in particular, those obligations that are a function of the particular relationships, roles, or circumstances we happen to be in. This chapter has already discussed the obligations employees have to the organization based on a freely negotiated work contract, and it is easy to see that employees have moral obligations arising from the business, professional, or organizational roles they have assumed. For example, teachers have an obligation to grade fairly, bartenders to refrain from serving intoxicated customers, engineers to guarantee the safety of their projects, and accountants to certify that financial statements present data fairly and according to generally accepted accounting principles. Because of his or her role responsibilities, an auditor who suspects some irregularity has an obligation to get to the bottom of the matter, whereas an ordinary employee who has a hunch that something is not in order in another department probably would not have that responsibility.

Thus, employees have certain general duties to their employers, and because of the specific business, professional, or organizational responsibilities they have assumed, they may have other more precise role-based obligations. In addition, employees are human beings with moral responsibilities to friends, family, and coworkers—to those flesh-and-blood people with whom their lives are intertwined, both inside and outside the workplace. These ongoing relationships are the source of important moral obligations.

What about the obligations of employees to other parties or to society in general? In particular, what obligations do employees have to people with whom they have no relationship and for whom they have no specific professional, organizational, or other role responsibility? Here different moral theories may steer us in slightly different directions, but simply as a matter of ordinary common-sense morality it is clear that employees—like everyone else—have certain elementary duties to other people. Of particular significance are the obligations to avoid injuring others and to be truthful and fair.

When faced with a moral decision, then, employees should follow the two-step procedure set forth in Chapter 2: Identify the relevant obligations, ideals, and effects and then try to decide where the emphasis should lie among these considerations. There is nothing mechanical about this process, but when we as employees weigh moral decisions, two simple things can help keep our deliberations free from the various rationalizations to which we are all prone. First, we can ask ourselves whether we would be willing to read an account of our actions in the newspaper. That is, when we have made our decisions, are the contemplated actions ones that we would be willing to defend publicly? Second, discussing a moral dilemma or ethical problem with a friend can often help us avoid bias and gain a better perspective. People by themselves, and especially when emotionally involved in a situation, sometimes focus unduly on one or two points, ignoring other relevant factors. Input from others can keep us from overlooking pertinent considerations, thus helping us make a better, more objective moral judgment.

As the preceding discussion mentioned, employees sometimes learn about the illegal or immoral actions of a supervisor or firm. When an employee tries to correct the situation within institutional channels and is thwarted, a central moral question emerges: Should the employee go public with the information? Should a worker who is ordered to do something illegal or immoral, or who knows of the illegal or immoral behaviour of a supervisor or organization, inform the public?

WHISTLEBLOWING

Morris H. Baslow, a forty-seven-year-old biologist and father of three, won't forget the day he dropped an envelope in the mail to Thomas B. Yost, an administrative law judge with the U.S. Environmental Protection Agency (EPA). For later that day, Baslow was fired from his job with Lawler, Matusky & Skelly, an engineering consulting firm that had been hired by Consolidated Edison of New York to help it blunt EPA demands. The EPA was insisting that the power company's generating plants on the Hudson River had to have cooling towers to protect fish from excessively warm water that it was discharging into the river.

Baslow claimed that the documents he sent showed that Con Ed and Lawler, Matusky & Skelly had knowingly submitted to the EPA invalid and misleading data, giving the false impression that the long-term effects of the utility's effluent on fish were negligible. On the basis of his own research, Baslow believed that the fish could be significantly harmed by the warm-water discharge. He said that for two years he tried to get his employers to listen, but they wouldn't.

Shortly after being fired, Baslow sent dozens of company documents supporting his allegation to the EPA, the U.S. Energy Regulatory Commission, and the U.S. Justice Department. In the month following those disclosures, Baslow's employers accused him of stealing the documents and sued him for defamation. Baslow countersued, citing the *Clean Water Act,* which protects consultants from reprisals for reporting findings prejudicial to their employers and clients.

A year later, Lawler, Matusky & Skelly dropped all legal action against Baslow and gave him a cash settlement, reportedly of around $100,000. In return, Baslow wrote to the EPA and other government agencies, withdrawing his charges of wrongdoing and perjury but not recanting his own scientific conclusions. Asked why he finally accepted the cash payment, the unemployed Baslow said, "I've had to bear the brunt of this financially by myself . . . . I just wish somebody had listened to me six months ago."[38]

Other whistleblowers express similar sentiments, even when they have been proved right. Talk to David Graham, a researcher at the U.S. Food and Drug Administration (FDA), who endured rebukes and harassment from superiors for first investigating and then exposing the risk of heart attack posed by the painkiller Vioxx. "I can guarantee you, there are other whistleblowers at FDA," says Graham. "Fear has them by the throat. And they struggle with their conscience and they struggle with the wrong they see, and they are paralyzed by their fear. They are looking to see—can that Graham fellow get away with committing the truth? It remains to be seen whether I can." He adds, "Please understand, I am not a hero, and I'm not endowed with extraordinary courage."[39] For his part, David Franklin offers the following advice to potential whistleblowers: "People who are in the position I was need to think about their own futures and how they feel about themselves and what their kids look up to and why they got into this business in the first place," he says. "That's where the endurance of the thing comes into play."[40]

Or ask Denise Revine, an employee with the Human Resources of the Royal Canadian Mounted Police (RCMP), who in 2003 alerted her immediate superiors regarding improper spending in the force's pension fund. (Auditor-General Sheila Fraser later found that $3.4 million had been improperly spent on non-pension items—though later repaid—and that $1.3 million had gone on hiring employees' relatives or for services that provided little or no value). Revine's post was declared surplus. Her boss, Chief Superintendent Fraser Macaulay, was reassigned when he brought her revelations to the RCMP chief executive. An internal investigator, Staff Sergeant Mike Frizzell, was ordered off the case. In 2007 an independent investigator appointed by the federal government recommended that Revine, Macaulay, and Frizzell receive commendations.[41]

The Baslow and Graham-Revine cases illustrate the ethical issues and personal risks facing employees who blow the whistle on what they perceive as organizational misconduct. We now address two more-specific questions from a logical and moral perspective: What exactly is whistleblowing? And when is one morally justified in blowing the whistle?

The Definition of Whistleblowing

Whistleblowing refers, in general, to an employee's informing the public about the illegal or immoral behaviour of an employer or an organization. One expert defines whistleblowing more fully as

> A practice in which employees who know that their company is engaged in activities that (a) cause unnecessary harm, (b) are in violation of human rights, (c) are illegal, (d) run counter to the defined purpose of the institution, or (e) are otherwise immoral, inform the public or some governmental agency of those activities.[42]

Another business ethicist spells out the concept this way:

> Whistle-blowing is the voluntary release of nonpublic information, as a moral protest, by a member or former member of an organization outside the normal channels of communication to an appropriate audience about illegal and/or immoral conduct in the organization or conduct in the organization that is opposed in some significant way to the public interest.[43]

These definitions limit the scope of what constitutes whistleblowing. Whistleblowing is something that can be done only by a (past or present) member of an organization. An investigative reporter, for example, who exposes corporate malfeasance is not a whistleblower. Nor is an employee who spreads gossip about in-house gaffes and indiscretions, thus abusing confidentiality and acting disloyally to colleagues and to the organization. By contrast, whistleblowing refers to exposing activities that are harmful, immoral, or contrary to the public interest or to the legitimate goals and purposes of the organization. It does not encompass sabotage or taking retaliatory action against the employer or firm, but it does require going outside normal channels. (This doesn't imply, however, that whistleblowing must be external. Most writers on the subject hold that there can also be internal whistleblowing, in which disclosure of inappropriate conduct is made to someone inside the organization.)

When Is Whistleblowing Justified?

Although the motivations of whistleblowers may and most often are honourable and praiseworthy, whistleblowing itself is a morally problematic action, as Professor Sissela Bok reminds us.[44] The whistle can be blown in error or malice, privacy invaded, and trust undermined. Not least, publicly accusing others of wrongdoing can be very destructive and brings with it an obligation to be fair to the persons accused. In addition, internal prying and mutual suspicion make it difficult for any organization to function. And, finally, one must bear in mind that whistleblowers are only human beings, not saints, and they can sometimes have their own self-serving agenda.[45]

Professor of philosophy Norman Bowie has correctly pointed out that today's discussions of whistleblowing parallel those on civil disobedience in the United States of the 1960s. Just as civil disobedients of that era felt that their duty to obey the law was overridden by other, higher moral obligations, so the whistleblower overrides loyalty to colleagues or the corporation in favour of higher duties in the service of the public good.[46] In developing his analogy with civil disobedience, Bowie proposes several conditions that must be met for an act of whistleblowing to be morally justified. These conditions may not be the last word on this controversial subject, but they do provide a good starting point for further debate over the morality of whistleblowing. According to Bowie, whistleblowing is morally justified if and only if

1. *It is done from an appropriate moral motive.* For an act of whistleblowing to be justified, it must be motivated by a desire to expose unnecessary harm, illegal or immoral actions, or conduct counter to the public good or the defined purpose of the organization. Desire for attention or profit or the exercise of one's general tendency toward stirring up trouble is not a justification for whistleblowing.

Although, as Chapter 2 explained, the question of motive is an important one in Kantian ethics, not all moral theorists would agree with Bowie's first condition. Might not an employee be justified in blowing the whistle on serious wrongdoing by the employer, even if the employee's real motivation was the desire for revenge? Granted that the motivation was ignoble, the action itself might nonetheless have been the morally right one. An action can still be morally justified, say some theorists, even when it is done for the wrong reason. Still, many people were troubled to learn that the whistleblowing paralegal who provided anti-tobacco lawyers with crucial documents about a tobacco company's secret studies on the health dangers of cigarettes was paid more than $100,000 by the lawyers.[47]

2. *The whistleblower, except in special circumstances, has exhausted all internal channels for dissent before going public.* The duty of loyalty to the firm obligates workers to seek an internal remedy before informing the public of a misdeed. This is an important consideration, but in some cases the attempt to exhaust internal channels may result in dangerous delays or expose the would-be whistleblower to retaliation.

3. *The whistleblower has compelling evidence that wrongful actions have been ordered or have occurred.* Spelling out what constitutes "compelling evidence" is difficult, but employees can ask themselves whether the evidence is strong enough that any reasonable person in a similar situation would be convinced that the activity is illegal or immoral. Although this may not be a decisive guideline, the standard of what a reasonable person would believe is commonly invoked in other cases, such as deceptive advertising and negligence lawsuits.

4. *The whistleblower has acted after careful analysis of the danger: How serious is the moral violation? How immediate is the problem? Can the whistleblower point to specific misconduct?* These criteria focus on the nature of the wrongdoing. Owing loyalty to employers, employees should blow the whistle only for grave legal or moral matters. The greater the harm or the more serious the wrongdoing, the more likely is the whistleblowing to be justified. Indeed, in some circumstances, whistleblowing may not only be morally justified; it may be morally required. Additionally, employees should consider the time factor. The greater the time before the violation is to occur, the more likely the firm's own internal mechanisms will prevent it; and the more immediate a violation, the more justified the whistleblowing. Finally, the whistleblower must be specific. General allegations, such as that a company is "not operating in the best interests of the public" or is "systematically sabotaging the competition," won't do. Concrete examples are needed that can pass the other justificatory tests.

5. *The whistleblowing has some chance of success.* This criterion recognizes that the chances of remedying an immoral or illegal action are an important consideration. Sometimes the chances are good; sometimes they're slim. Probably most cases fall somewhere between these extremes. In general, given the potential harmful effects, whistleblowing that stands no chance of success is less justified than that with some chance of success. Even so, sometimes merely drawing attention to an objectionable practice, although it may fail to improve the specific situation, encourages government and society to be more watchful of certain behaviour.

SELF-INTEREST AND MORAL OBLIGATION

For many employees, protecting themselves or safeguarding their jobs is the primary factor in deciding whether to put third-party interests above those of the firm. Concern with self-interest in cases that pit loyalty to the company against other obligations is altogether understandable and even warranted. After all, workers who subordinate the organization's interests to an outside party's expose themselves to charges of disloyalty, disciplinary action, freezes in job status, forced relocations, and even dismissal. Furthermore, even when an employee successfully blows the whistle, he or she can be blacklisted in an industry. Given the potential harm to self and family that employees risk in honouring third-party obligations, it is perfectly legitimate to inquire about the weight considerations of self-interest should be given in resolving cases of conflicting obligations.

Sadly, there is no clear, unequivocal answer to this question. Moral theorists and society as a whole do distinguish between prudential reasons and moral reasons. "Prudential" (from the word *prudence*) refers here to considerations of self-interest; "moral" refers here to considerations of the interests of others and the demands of morality. Chapter 1 explained that it is possible for prudential and moral considerations to pull us in different directions. One way of looking at their relationship is this: if prudential concerns outweigh moral ones, then employees may do what is in their own best interest. If moral reasons override prudential ones, then workers should honour their obligations to others.

Consider the case of a cashier at a truck stop who is asked to write up phoney chits so truckers can get a larger expense reimbursement from their employers than they really deserve. The cashier doesn't think this is right, so she complains to the manager. The manager explains that the restaurant is largely dependent on trucker business and that this is a good way to ensure it. The cashier is ordered to do the truckers' bidding and is thus being told to violate at least three duties owed to any outside party (in this case, the trucking firms): truth, non-injury, and fairness. Given these moral considerations, the cashier ought to refuse, and perhaps she should even report the conduct to the trucking companies.

But let's suppose that the cashier happens to be a recent divorcée with no formal education. She lacks occupational skills and stands little chance of getting another job in an economy that happens to be depressed—for months she was unemployed before landing her present position. With no other means of support, the consequences of job loss for her would be serious indeed. Now, given this scenario and given that the wrongdoing at issue is relatively minor, prudential concerns would probably take legitimate precedence over moral ones. In other words, the cashier would be justified in "going along," at least on a temporary basis.

Some moral theorists would agree with this conclusion but analyze the case somewhat differently. They think it is incorrect to say that in some circumstances we may permit prudential considerations to outweigh moral considerations. There is no neutral perspective outside both morality and self-interest from which one can make such a judgment. Furthermore, they would say that, by definition, nothing can outweigh the demands of morality.

Does that mean the cashier should refuse to do what her manager wants and, thus, lose her job? Not necessarily. Morality does not, these theorists contend, require us to make large sacrifices in order to right small wrongs. Writing up phoney chits does violate some basic moral principles, and the cashier has some moral obligation not to go along with it. But morality does not, all things considered, require her—under the present circumstances—to take a course of action that would spell job loss. She should, however, take less drastic steps to end the practice (like continuing to talk to her boss and the truckers about it) and perhaps eventually find other work. Thus, according to this way of thinking, the cashier is not sacrificing morality to self-interest in "going along" for a while. The idea is that morality does not impose obligations on us without regard to their cost; it does not, under the present circumstances, demand an immediate resignation by the cashier.

Whichever way one looks at it, the question of balancing our moral obligations to others and our own self-interest is particularly relevant to whistleblowing. In situations in which whistleblowing threatens one's livelihood and career, prudential concerns may properly be taken into account in deciding what one should do, all things considered. This doesn't mean that if the worker blows the whistle despite compelling prudential reasons not to, he or she is not moral. On the contrary, such an action could be highly moral. (As Chapter 2 explained, ethical theorists term such actions "supererogatory," meaning that they are, so to speak, above and beyond the call of duty.) On the other hand, when the moral concerns are great (for example, when the lives of others are at stake), elementary morality and personal integrity can require people to make substantial sacrifices.

Two further points are pertinent here. First, an evaluation of prudential reasons obviously is coloured by one's temperament and perceptions of self-interest. Each of us has a tendency to magnify potential threats to our livelihood or career. Exaggerating the costs to ourselves of acting otherwise makes it easier to rationalize away the damage we are doing to others. In the business world, for instance, people talk about the survival of the firm as if it were literally a matter of life and death. Going out of business is the worst thing that can happen to a firm, but the people who make it up will live on and get other jobs. Keeping the company alive (let alone competitive or profitable) cannot justify seriously injuring innocent people.

Not only do we tend to exaggerate the importance of self-interested considerations, but also most of us have been socialized to heed authority. As a result, we are disinclined to question the orders of someone above us, especially when the authority is an employer or supervisor with power to influence our lives for better or worse. It's easy for us to assume that any boat-rocking will be very harmful, even self-destructive.

It follows, then, that each of us has an obligation to perform a kind of character or personality audit. Do we follow authority blindly? Do we suffer from moral tunnel vision on the job? Do we mindlessly do what is demanded of us, oblivious to the impact of our cooperation and actions on outside parties? Have we given enough attention to our possible roles as accomplices in the immoral undoing of other individuals, businesses, and social institutions? Do we have a balanced view of our own interests versus those of others? Do we have substantial evidence for believing that our livelihoods are really threatened, or is that belief based more on an exaggeration of the facts? Have we been imaginative in trying to balance prudential and moral concerns? Have we sought to find some middle ground, or have we set up a false self-other dilemma in which our own interests and those of others are erroneously viewed as incompatible? These are just some of the questions that a personal inventory should include if we are to combat the all-too-human tendency to stack the deck in favour of prudential reasons whenever they are pitted against moral ones.

A second point about the relationship between prudential and moral considerations concerns our collective interest in protecting the welfare of society by encouraging people to act in non-self-interested ways. As we have seen, in some cases considerations of self-interest may mean that one does not have an overriding obligation to blow the whistle. When that is the case, how can society be protected from wrongdoing? Is its welfare to be left to those few heroic souls willing to perform supererogatory actions? And even when employees have a clear duty to blow the whistle, the personal risk involved may, human nature being what it is, keep them from doing the right thing. Who protects society then? The only realistic and reasonable approach, it seems, is to restructure our legal, business, and social institutions so that acting in a morally responsible way no longer brings the severe penalty that it often does these days. Whether people do what they know to be right—whether they act in a way that respects others and protects their important interests—is not simply a matter of their conscience and the strength of their moral convictions. It is also a function of the environment in which they must act and the incentives and disincentives they face.

Protecting Those Who Do the Right Thing

For many years now there have been several different statutory measures to protect whistleblower in Canada; for example, in the *Competition Act*, in various health and safety legislation and environmental legislation. Also, there is protection against reprisal in a number of employment-related contexts (for example, in employment standards, workplace safety, and human rights legislation). However, as numerous examples attest, this legislative protection has not alleviated fears on the part of prospective whistleblowers regarding reprisals nor deterred employers or managers from retaliating or threatening to retaliate against actual whistleblowers. But in 2003 the Canadian government took certain measures that increased substantially the protection afforded by law to "those who do the right thing." The amendments that year to the *Canada Criminal Code*, contained in Bill C-13, made retaliation against whistleblowers a criminal offence. The law now prohibits an employer (or a person in a position of authority in respect of an employee) "from taking any disciplinary measure against or adversely affecting in any way the employment of an employee, or threatening to do so, with the intent to: Compel the employee to abstain from providing information to a law enforcement authority about an offence that the employee believes has been or is being committed by the employer, an officer, director or employee of the employer; or Retaliate against the employee because the employee has provided information to a law enforcement authority." The new protection in the *Criminal Code* is much broader than other existing protection, especially since the meaning of "information"

or how it is obtained is left open. No doubt, in time courts will have something to say about it. The penalty for violating the provisions of the *Code* on whistleblowing carry a maximum penalty of five years' imprisonment, in addition to any provincial or regulatory sanctions under securities legislation—including imprisonment in a federal penitentiary.

The U.S. *Sarbanes-Oxley Act* of 2002 is an even more radical statute. This act provides sweeping new legal protection for employees who report possible securities fraud, making it unlawful for companies to "discharge, demote, suspend, threaten, harass, or in any other manner discriminate against" them. Fired workers can sue, and they are guaranteed the right to a jury trial instead of having to endure months or years of administrative hearings. In addition, the U.S. Labor Department can order companies to rehire terminated whistleblowers with no court hearings whatsoever. Moreover, executives who retaliate against employees who report possible violations of *any* federal law now face imprisonment for up to ten years.

However, it is not enough merely to change the law. Corporate attitudes need to change as well. Often managers or employers consider it cheaper to fire employees than to listen to their legitimate concerns.[48] Reprisals may take forms the law may have hard time punishing (for example, from the cold-shoulder treatment in the office to the promotion that takes one to an undesirable destination). Kris Kolesnik, director of the National Whistleblower Center in the United States, is pessimistic. "No matter how many protections whistleblower laws have created over the years," he says, "the system always seems to defeat them."[49] In the long run, however, organizations benefit more from encouraging employees to come forward with their ethical concerns than they do from ignoring possible wrongdoing and retaliating against those who raise awkward queries. Openness and a receptive attitude toward moral questioning by employees give the organization a chance to take corrective action. This can save it money (by rooting out embezzlement, say, or forestalling litigation) or at least—as recent scandals make clear—help it to head off worse trouble when the problems bothering employees eventually leak out to the public.

To discharge their moral responsibilities and safeguard their own interests, companies need to develop explicit, proactive whistleblowing policies. At minimum, these policies should state that employees aware of possible wrongdoing have a responsibility to disclose that information; specific individuals or groups outside the chain of command should be designated to hear those concerns; employees who in good faith disclose perceived wrongdoing should be protected from adverse employment consequences; and there should be a fair and impartial investigative process. In these ways, management can create organizational procedures and a corporate culture that make it less likely that employees will be forced to blow the whistle externally.

SUMMARY

1. The employment contract creates various obligations to one's employer. In addition, employees often feel loyalty to the organization. Conflicts of interest arise when employees have a personal interest in a transaction substantial enough that it might reasonably be expected to affect their judgment or lead them to act against the interests of the organization.

2. When employees have financial investments in suppliers, customers, or distributors with whom the organization does business, conflicts of interest can arise. Company policy usually determines the permissible limits of such financial interests.

3. *Insider trading* refers to buying or selling stocks based on nonpublic information likely to affect stock prices. Insider trading seems unfair; it can injure other investors and undermine public confidence in the stock market. In practice, determining what counts as insider trading is not always easy, but it typically involves misappropriating sensitive information. Some writers defend insider trading as performing a necessary and desirable economic function.

4. *Proprietary data* refers to an organization's classified or secret information. Increasingly, problems arise as employees in high-tech occupations with access to sensitive information and trade secrets quit and take jobs with competitors. Proprietary-data issues pose a conflict between two legitimate rights: the right of employers to keep certain information secret and the right of individuals to work where they choose.

5. A *bribe* is payment in some form in return for an act that runs counter to the work contract or the nature of the work one has been hired to perform. Bribery generally involves injury to individuals, competitors, or political institutions and damage to the free-market system.

6. The following considerations are relevant in determining the moral acceptability of gift giving and receiving: the value of the gift, its purpose, the circumstances under which it is given, the position and sensitivity to influence of the person receiving the gift, accepted business practice, company policy, and what the law says.

7. Employees have duties to their employers, and they may also have more specific obligations based on the business or professional roles and responsibilities they have assumed. In addition, they have the same elementary moral obligations that all human beings have—including the obligation not to injure others and to be truthful and fair.

8. Balancing our obligations to employer or organization, to friends and coworkers, and to third parties outside the organization can create conflicts and divided loyalties. In resolving such moral conflicts, we must identify the relevant obligations, ideals, and effects and decide where the emphasis among them should lie.

9. *Whistleblowing* refers to an employee's informing the public about the illegal or immoral behaviour of an employer or organization.

10. An act of whistleblowing can be presumed to be morally justified if it is done from a moral motive; if the whistleblower has, if possible, exhausted internal channels before going public; if the whistleblower has compelling evidence; if the whistleblower has carefully analyzed the dangers; and if the whistleblowing has some chance of success.

11. Prudential considerations based on self-interest can conflict with moral considerations, which take into account the interests of others. Some sacrifices of self-interest would be so great that moral considerations must give way to prudential ones. But employees must avoid the temptation to exaggerate prudential concerns, thereby rationalizing away any individual moral responsibility to third parties. Legislation and changes in corporate culture can reduce the personal sacrifices that whistleblowers must make.

CASE 8.1

Changing Jobs and Changing Loyalties

Cynthia Martinez was thrilled when she first received the job offer from David Newhoff at Crytex Systems. She had long admired Crytex, both as an industry leader and as an ideal employer, and the position the company was offering her was perfect. "It's just what I've always wanted," she told her husband, Tom, as they uncorked a bottle of champagne. But as she and Tom talked, he raised a few questions that began to trouble her.

"What about the big project you're working on at Altrue right now? It'll take three months to see that through," Tom had reminded her. "The company has a lot riding on it, and you've always said that you're the driving force behind the project. If you bolt, Altrue is going to be in a real jam."

Cynthia explained that she had mentioned the project to David Newhoff. "He said he could understand I'd like to see it through, but Crytex needs someone right now. He gave me a couple of days to think it over, but it's my big chance."

Tom looked at her thoughtfully and responded, "But Newhoff doesn't quite get it. It's not just that you'd like to see it through. It's that you'd be letting your whole project team down. They probably couldn't do it without you, at least not the way it needs to be done. Besides, Cyn, remember what you said about that guy who quit the Altrue branch in Baltimore."

"That was different," Cynthia responded. "He took an existing account with him when he went to another firm. It was like ripping Altrue off. I'm not going to rip them off, but I don't figure I owe them anything extra. It's just business. You know perfectly well that if Altrue could save some money by laying me off, the company wouldn't hesitate."

"I think you're rationalizing," Tom said. "You've done well at Altrue, and the company has always treated you fairly. Anyway, the issue is what's right for you to do, not what the company would or wouldn't do. Crytex is Altrue's big competitor. It's like you're switching sides. Besides, it's not just a matter of loyalty to the company, but to the people you work with. I know we could use the extra money, and it would be a great step for you, but still . . ."

They continued to mull things over together, but the champagne no longer tasted quite as good. Fortunately, she and Tom never really argued about things they didn't see eye to eye on, and Tom wasn't the kind of guy who would try to tell her what she should or shouldn't do. But their conversation had started her wondering whether she really should accept that Crytex job she wanted so much.

Discussion Questions

1. What should Cynthia do? What ideals, obligations, and effects should she take into account when making her decision?

2. Would it be unprofessional of Cynthia to drop everything and move to Crytex? Would it show a lack of integrity? Could moving abruptly to Crytex have negative career consequences for her?

3. Is it morally wrong, morally permissible, or morally required for Cynthia to take the new job? Examine Cynthia's choice from a utilitarian point of view. How would Kant and Ross look at her situation?

4. What does loyalty to the company mean, and how important is it, morally? Under what circumstances, if any, do employees owe loyalty to their employers? When, if ever, do they owe loyalty to their coworkers?

Profiting on Columns
Prior to Publication

In an otherwise unmemorable issue of *Money* magazine, managing editor Frank Lalli wrote a column criticizing the magazine's rival, *Smart Money*, for permitting one of its writers to tout stocks in which he had a personal investment. Seven months later, Lalli's righteousness turned to embarrassment when *Business Week* reported that the SEC was investigating Dan Dorfman, *Money*'s star columnist and syndicated stock tipster, based on reports of conflicts of interest and possible insider trading. *Money* subsequently dismissed Dorfman. Dorfman denies any wrongdoing, but the allegations against him brought to mind the famous and controversial case of R. Foster Winans.

Along with their morning cup of coffee, readers of the *Wall Street Journal* got a shock one day when the paper announced that it had fired Winans, author of its highly influential stock market column "Heard on the Street." This was immediately after the thirty-six-year-old business analyst admitted to federal investigators that he had leaked information about upcoming columns to associates who were then able to profit from the information by buying or selling stock.

A month later the SEC charged Winans with violating federal law by failing to disclose to readers that he had financial interests in the securities he wrote about. Winans, whose tips about columns prior to publication helped two stockbrokers net about half a million dollars, also was charged with personally profiting from the material.

The basis of the charges was an SEC rule that prohibits anyone from omitting to state a material fact regarding the purchase or sale of securities. But the applicability of the SEC rule to the Winans case is unclear. Professor of journalism Gilbert Cranberg phrases the ambiguity this way: "Is the ownership by a reporter of stock in a company about which he writes a 'material fact' to readers sufficient to require disclosure, or must the reporter also intend to profit from the story?"[50] Ambiguous or not, the SEC's action has convinced some legal scholars that the media must disclose the financial holdings of their financial analysts.

Even before the Winans case, some publications had formulated explicit policies designed to leave no doubt in reporters' minds about the impropriety of trading on knowledge of stories. For example, the *Washington Post* requires that all its financial and business reporters submit to their editors a confidential statement outlining their stock holdings. *Post* policy prohibits writers from either writing about companies in which they have an interest or buying stock in companies they have written about. The *New York Times* has a similar policy, and *Forbes* magazine and the *Chicago Tribune* require editorial employees to divulge their corporate investments. Ralph Schulz, senior vice-president at McGraw-Hill's publication unit, says his company has a conflict-of-interest policy based on the premise that "nobody who writes about a company ought to own stock in it."[51] The *Wall Street Journal*'s three-and-a-half-page conflict-of-interest policy warns employees against trading in companies immediately before or after a *Journal* piece on that company. The policy reads in part:

> It is not enough to be incorruptible and act with honest motives. It is equally important to use good judgment and conduct one's outside activities so that no one—management, our editors, an SEC investigator with power of subpoena, or a political critic of the company—has any grounds for even raising the suspicion that an employee misused a position with the company.[52]

But such written policies remain the exception, as shown by an informal survey of the country's media conducted by the *Wall Street Journal*. Although many newspapers have formal dress codes, few have formal rules about stock trading. Moreover, few news executives show any concern about insider trading by non-editorial employees, although sensitive investigative reports generally are accessible to any employee in the newsroom.

The *Wall Street Journal* survey also reveals general indifference among media executives to stock trading by subjects of interviews, as in the case of G. D. Searle & Co. The SEC began investigating unusual activity in options on that company's stock just before the broadcast of a *CBS Evening News* report that raised questions about NutraSweet, Searle's new low-calorie sweetener. The SEC charged that an Arizona scientist interviewed by CBS for the report bought "put" options in Searle's NutraSweet before the story aired in order to profit when the stock tumbled as a result of negative comments by himself and others. "I honestly believe I had a right to do it," says the Arizona scientist. He adds, "I don't think it's unethical. It's the American way."[53] The scientist's lawyer and some CBS employees also were targets of the SEC investigation.

Dan Dorfman admits that his stories may affect the price of stocks, and by implication, shrewd subjects of interviews could stand to benefit on the stories. But he doesn't think there's anything he can do about that. "It's not my job to police," Dorfman says. "My job is to get information." John G. Craig, Jr., editor of the *Pittsburgh Post Gazette*, agrees. In his view, preventing sources from trading on an article "is an ethical responsibility a newspaper can't assume."[54] And yet James Michaels, the editor of *Forbes*, recalls once pulling a story when he learned that one of the sources had sold stock short, betting the article would have a negative impact. Likewise, the *Wall Street Journal* admits to killing stories when learning that investors were using their knowledge of them to wheel and deal on Wall Street.

In the case of R. Foster Winans, the U.S. government took a strong stand against such wheeling and dealing, with the Justice Department filing a sixty-one-count indictment for fraud and conspiracy against him and two alleged collaborators. Among other things, the indictment charged that Winans and his roommate speculated on stocks about to be mentioned in forthcoming columns. They made about a $4,500 profit on a $3,000 investment.[55] Although Winans described his role in these deals as "stupid" and "wrong," he denied he broke any law. After a long and technical legal battle, the U.S. Supreme Court upheld the Justice Department's contention that what he did was not just imprudent but criminal.

Professor Cranberg fears that the Winans case may make bad law. Although he thinks that the time has come for reporters and editors to report outside compensation and financial interests, he worries that the SEC and the courts may equate business-news reporters with investment advisers and, as a result, wield undue influence on the press.

Cranberg fears that such a development not only threatens freedom of the press but also would have a chilling effect on press coverage of corporate America. "Not every problem has, or should have, a legal solution," Cranberg points out. "Most problems involving the press are best handled by voluntary measures. The way for the press to show that it can keep its house in order is to do it. More actions and less self-satisfied ridicule of concern about conflicts of interest would be signs that the press can and will."[56]

Michael Missal, a lawyer for the SEC, thinks such fears are unfounded. "We don't expect every journalist to disclose all financial relationships," he says. Instead, the government wishes to prevent profiteering on advance knowledge of stories. That, Missal says, is what the Winans case is all about.[57]

Discussion Questions

1. In your opinion, did Winans engage in insider trading? Did he do something wrong? Explain why or why not.

2. Did Winans violate some duty owed to his employer? What obligations, ideals, and effects should he have considered before acting as he did?

3. Do you believe that media financial analysts should disclose to their audience any financial interests they have in the securities they write about? Do you think they should be required to make such disclosures? If so, should the requirement take the form of an institutional policy, a law, or both?

4. Does it make a difference to your assessment whether it is only the reporter who profits from prior knowledge of his or her financial story? Morally speaking, is it better or worse if the reporter does not profit but others do?

5. Do you think McGraw-Hill's policy—that "nobody who writes about a company ought to own stock in it"—is fair? Or do you think it is an unreasonable encroachment on the employee's right to profit through investments?

6. Do you agree that the Arizona scientist had a right to trade on the information before it was broadcast?

7. What do you think Kant's position on insider trading would be? How would utilitarians look at it? What about libertarians?

8. Under what circumstances does a company have a right to know about the financial investments of its employees?

The Housing Allowance

Wilson Mutambara grew up in the slums outside Stanley, capital of the sub-Saharan African country of Rambia.[58] Through talent, hard work, and luck he made it through secondary school and won a scholarship to study in the United States. He eventually received an MBA and went to work for NewCom, a cellular telephone service. After three years in the company's Atlanta office, Wilson was given an opportunity to return to Rambia, where NewCom was setting up a local cellular service. Eager to be home, Wilson Mutambara couldn't say yes fast enough.

NewCom provides its employees in Rambia with a monthly allowance of up to $2,000 for rent, utilities, and servants. By Western standards, most of the housing in Stanley is poor quality, and many of its neighbourhoods are unsafe. By providing the allowance, NewCom's intention is to see that its employees live in areas that are safe and convenient and that they live in a style appropriate to the company's image.

To claim their housing allowance, NewCom's employees in Rambia are supposed to turn in receipts, and every month Wilson Mutambara turned in an itemized statement for $2,000 from his landlord. Nobody at NewCom thought it unusual that Wilson never entertained his coworkers at home. After all, he worked long hours and "travelled frequently on business. However, after Wilson had been in Rambia for about fifteen months, one of his coworkers, Dale Garman, was chatting with a Rambian customer, who referred in passing to Wilson as a person living in Old Town. Garman knew Old Town was one of the slums outside Stanley, but he kept his surprise to himself and decided not to mention this information to anyone else until he could independently confirm it. This wasn't difficult for him to do. Wilson was indeed living in Old Town in the home of some relatives. The house itself couldn't have rented for more than $300, even if Wilson had the whole place to himself, which he clearly didn't. Dale reported what he had learned to Wilson's supervisor, Barbara Weston.

When Weston confronted him about the matter, Wilson admitted that the place did rent for a "little less" than $2,000, but he vigorously defended his action this way: "Every other NewCom employee in Rambia receives $2,000 a month. If I live economically, why should I be penalized? I should receive the same as everyone else." In response, Weston pointed out that NewCom wanted to guarantee that its employees had safe, high-quality housing that was in keeping with the image that the company wanted to project. Wilson's housing arrangements were "unseemly," she said, and not in keeping with his professional standing. Moreover, they reflected poorly on the company. To this, Wilson Mutambara retorted: "I'm not just a NewCom employee; I'm also a Rambian. It's not unsafe for me to live in this neighbourhood, and it's insulting to be told that the area I grew up in is 'unseemly' or inappropriate for a company employee."

Barbara Weston pointed out that the monthly receipts he submitted had been falsified. "Yes," he admitted, "but that's common practice in Rambia. Nobody thinks twice about it." However, she pressed the point, arguing that he had a duty to NewCom, which he had violated. As the discussion continued, Mutambara became less confident and more and more distraught. Finally, on the verge of tears, he pleaded, "Barbara, you just don't understand what's expected of me as a Rambian or the pressure I'm under. I save every penny I have to pay school fees for eight nieces and nephews. I owe it to my family to try to give those children the same chance I had. My relatives would never understand my living in a big house instead of helping them. I'm just doing what I have to do."

Discussion Questions

1. Did Wilson Mutambara act wrongly? Explain why or why not. Assess each of the arguments he gives in his own defence. What other courses of action were open to him? What would you have done in his place?

2. Was Dale Garman right to confirm the information he had received and to report the matter? Was it morally required of him to do so?

3. What should Barbara Weston and NewCom do? Should Wilson be ordered to move out of Old Town and into more appropriate housing? Should he be terminated for having falsified his housing receipts? If not, should he be punished in some other way?

4. Is NewCom unfairly imposing its own ethnocentric values on Wilson Mutambara? Is the company's housing policy fair and reasonable? Is it culturally biased?

Ethically Dubious Conduct

Brenda Franklin has worked at Allied Tech for nearly eight years. It's a large company, but she likes it and enjoys the friendly work environment. When she tacked her list onto the bulletin board outside her office, she didn't intend to make things less friendly. In fact, she didn't expect her list to attract much attention at all.

It had all started the week before when she joined a group of coworkers for their weekly lunch get-together, where they always talked about all sorts of things. This time they had gotten into a long political discussion, with several people at the table going on at great length about dishonesty, conflicts of interest, and shady dealings among politicians and corporate leaders. "If this country is going to get on the right track, we need people whose integrity is above reproach," Harry Benton had said to nods of approval around the table, followed by a further round of complaints about corruption and corner-cutting by the powerful.

Brenda hadn't said much at the time, but she thought she sniffed a whiff of hypocrisy. Later that night, after pondering the group's discussion, she typed up her list of "Ethically Dubious Employee Conduct." The next day she posted it outside her door.

Harry Benton was the first one to stick his head in the office. "My, my, aren't we smug?" was all he said before he disappeared. Later that morning, her friend Karen dropped by. "You don't really think it's immoral to take a pad of paper home, do you?" she asked. Brenda said no, but she didn't think one could just take it for granted that it was okay to take company property. She and Karen chatted more about the list. On and off that week, almost everyone she spoke with alluded to the list or commented on some of its items. They didn't object to her posting it, although they seemed to think it was a little strange. One day outside the building, however, an employee she knew only by sight asked Brenda sarcastically whether she was planning on turning people in for "moral violations." Brenda ignored him.

Now she was anticipating her group's weekly lunch. She had little doubt about what the topic of discussion would be, as she again glanced over her list:

Ethically Dubious Employee Conduct

1. Taking office supplies home for your personal use.
2. Using the telephone for personal, long-distance phone calls.
3. Making personal copies on the office machine.
4. Charging the postage on your personal mail to the company.
5. Making non-business trips in a company car.
6. On a company business trip: staying in the most expensive hotel, taking taxis when you could walk, including wine as food on your expense tab, taking your spouse along at company expense.
7. Using your office computer to shop online, trade stocks, view pornography, or email friends on company time.
8. Calling in sick when you need personal time.
9. Taking half the afternoon off, when you're supposedly on business outside the office.
10. Directing company business to vendors who are friends or relatives.
11. Providing preferential service to corporate customers who have taken you out to lunch.

Discussion Questions

1. Review each item on Brenda's list and assess the conduct in question. Do you find it morally acceptable, morally unacceptable, or somewhere in between? Explain.
2. Examine Brenda's list from both the utilitarian and the Kantian perspectives. What arguments can be given for and against the conduct on her list? Is the rightness or wrongness of some items a matter of degree? Can an action (such as taking a pad of paper) be both trivial and wrong?
3. Someone might argue that some of the things listed as ethically dubious are really employee entitlements. Assess this contention.
4. How would you respond to the argument that if the company doesn't do anything to stop the conduct on Brenda's list, then it has only itself to blame? What about the argument that none of the things on the list is wrong unless the company has an explicit rule against it?
5. What obligations do employees have to their employers? Do companies have moral rights that employees can violate? What moral difference, if any, is there between taking something that belongs to an individual and taking something that belongs to a company?
6. What, if anything, can we learn about an employee's character on the basis of whether he or she does the things on Brenda's list? Would you admire someone who scrupulously avoids doing any of these ethically dubious things?
7. What should Brenda do when she finds a fellow employee engaging in what she considers ethically dubious conduct?

Notes to Chapter 8

1. See "Nuclear Warriors," *Time*, March 4, 1996, 47–54, from which the details that follow are taken.

2. Ronald Duska, "Whistleblowing and Employee Loyalty," in Tom L. Beauchamp and Norman E. Bowie, eds., *Ethical Theory and Business*, 6th ed. (Upper Saddle River, NJ: Prentice Hall, 2001), 328.

3. John H. Fielder, "Organizational Loyalty," *Business and Professional Ethics Journal* 11 (Spring 1992): 87.

4. Richard T. De George, *Business Ethics*, 6th ed. (Upper Saddle River, NJ: Prentice Hall, 2006), 412.

5. Fielder, "Organizational Loyalty," 80–84.

6. Mahzarin R. Banaji et al., "How (Un)Ethical Are You?," *Harvard Business Review*, December 2003, 61.

7. "A Case of Conflicts at Qwest," *Business Week*, April 22, 2002, 37.

8. "Conflict-of-Interest Disclosures May Not Protect the Unsophisticated," *Wall Street Journal*, January 13, 2005, A2.

9. "Tech's Kickback Culture," *Business Week*, February 10, 2003, 76.

10. "Loans to Corporate Officers Unlikely to Cease Soon," *Wall Street Journal*, July 2, 2002, A8.

11. See www.cbc.ca/news/background/crime/insider_trading.html; also www.cbc.ca/money/story/2007/05/11/fpi-insider.html on the provincial government of Newfoundland and Labrador filing an insider trading complaint about sales of stock by George Armoyan, a former senior official of Fishery Products International.

12. See "Collected Woes" at www.globeadvisor.com/servlet/ArticleNews/story/gam/20061124/RO12COLLECTED.

13. See William J. McNally and Brian F. Smith, "Do Insiders Play by the Rules?," *Canadian Public Policy*, 29 (2003), 125–144. Among other things, the study compared the number of repurchased shares as reported, if reported at all, to the Ontario Securities Commission (as firms must do under the law) with the number of such shares recorded in the transactions of the Toronto Stock Exchange. The comparison revealed a significantly larger number of shares recorded at the TSX than reported to the OSC.

14. John A. C. Hetherington, "Corporate Social Responsibility, Stockholders, and the Law," *Journal of Contemporary Business*, Winter 1973, 51.

15. The U.S. Securities and Exchange Commission, the regulator of the U.S. stock market, subsequently charged that a group of insiders—including Texas Gulf directors, officers, and employees—had violated the disclosure section of the U.S. *Securities Exchange Act* of 1934 by purchasing stock in the company while withholding information about the rich ore strike the company had made. The courts upheld the charge, finding that the first press release was "misleading to the reasonable investor using due care." See "Texas Gulf Ruled to Lack Diligence in Minerals Case," *Wall Street Journal*, Midwest edition, February 9, 1970, 1.

16. For a full discussion of insider trading along with the regulatory controls and problems, see the report "Illegal Insider Trading in Canada: Recommendations on Prevention, Detection and Deterrence" (November 2003) by the Insider Trading Task Force, which was established in 2002 by the Ontario, British Columbia and Alberta Securities Commissions, the Commission des valeurs mobilieres du Quebec, the Investment Dealers Association of Canada, the Bourse de Montréal, and Market Regulation Services Inc. One may access it at www.csa-acvm.ca/pdfs/ITTF_Report.pdf.

17. See Henry Manne, *Insider Trading and the Stock Market* (New York: The Free Press, 1966), chh. 10–11; also "SEC, Professor Split on Insider Trades," *Wall Street Journal*, March 2, 1984, 8; and Henry G. Manne, "The Case for Insider Trading," *Wall Street Journal*, March 17, 2003, A14. See also James Altucher, "The case for legalising insider trades" at www.ft.com/cms/s/2/46a756a8-2e61-11dc-821c-0000779fd2ac.html.

18. Jennifer Moore, "What Is Really Unethical About Insider Trading?," *Journal of Business Ethics* 9 (March 1990). Reprinted at the end of this chapter.

19. See her "The Ethics of Insider Trading," *Journal of Business Ethics*, 8 (1989), 841–845.

20. "Lexar Wins Millions in Damages," *San Francisco Chronicle*, March 23, 2005, C1.

21. See "Cookie Cloak and Dagger," *Time*, September 10, 1984, 44.

22. An important and often cited case in the handling of issues involving "trade secrets" is a case decided by the Queen's Bench in England: *Fraser v. Thames Television Ltd.* [1984] Q.B. 44. For the handling of cases in Quebec, see Francois M. Grenier, "The Law of Trade Secrets and Confidential Information in the Province of Quebec" at www.robic.ca/publications/Pdf/141-FMG.pdf, and Marie-Eve Cote, "The Limited Protection of Trade Secrets Under Quebec Law" at www.robic.ca/publications/Pdf/238-04MEC.pdf.

23. John R. Boatright, *Ethics and the Conduct of Business*, 4th ed. (Upper Saddle River, NJ: Prentice Hall, 2003), 128–136.

24. Rory J. O'Connor, "Trade-Secrets Case Casts Chill," *San Jose Mercury News*, March 7, 1993, 1A.

25. See, for example, the decision by the Court of Appeal in *Faccenda v. Fowler* [1987] Ch 117, and the decision in *Ocular Sciences Ltd. v. Aspect Vision Care Ltd* [1997] RPC 289.

26. See Michael S. Baram, "Trade Secrets: What Price Loyalty?," *Harvard Business Review* 46 (November/December 1968).

27. Kris Mahler, "The Jungle," *Wall Street Journal*, June 8, 2004, B4.

28. Baram, "Trade Secrets."

29. Kim Murphy, "Accountant for ZZZZ Best Convicted of Fraud," *Los Angeles Times*, December 20, 1988, II-1.

30. *Edmonton Journal*, September 29, 2007.

31. "Prosecutors Link Honda Fraud Cases to U.S. Executives," *New York Times*, March 15, 1994, A1.

32. The Convention was agreed upon and signed by the member countries to the Organization for Economic Development and Cooperation in 1997. Canada's CFPO Act implemented in law the obligations Canada had undertaken by signing the Convention.

33. Bartley A. Brennan, "The Foreign Corrupt Practices Act Amendments of 1988: 'Death' of a Law," *North Carolina Journal of International Law and Commerce Regulation* 15 (1990): 229–247; and Wesley Cragg and William Woof, "The U.S. Foreign Corrupt Practices Act: A Study of Its Effectiveness," *Business and Society Review* 107 (Spring 2002): 99.

34. "Global Heavyweights Vow 'Zero Tolerance' for Bribes," *Wall Street Journal*, January 27, 2005, A2.

35. "A Global War Against Bribery," *Economist*, January 16, 1999, 22–23; and "The Worm That Never Dies," *Economist*, March 2, 2002, 12.

36. See the *Code*, ch. 1 at www.tbs-sct.gc.ca/pubs_pol/hrpubs/TB_841/vec-cve1_e.asp#_Toc46202800.

37. "New Kmart Code Bans Gifts, Bribes," *San Jose Mercury News*, April 12, 1996, 6C.

38. "Speaking Up Gets Biologist into Big Fight," *Wall Street Journal*, November 26, 1980, sec. 2, 25.

39. "Behind the Vioxx Headlines," *Business Ethics*, Winter 2004, 7.

40. "Question of Conscience," *San Francisco Chronicle*, May 14, 2004, C3.

41. See David Brown QC, "A Matter of Trust: Report of the Independent Investigator into Matters Relating to RCMP Pension and Insurance Plans" at www.publicsafety.gc.ca/rcmppension-retaitegrc/_fl/report-en.pdf.

42. Ronald F. Duska, "Whistleblowing," in R. Edward Freeman and Patricia H. Werhane, eds., *The Blackwell Encyclopedic Dictionary of Business Ethics* (Oxford: Blackwell, 1998), 654.

43. Boatright, *Ethics and the Conduct of Business*, 106.

44. Sissela Bok, *Secrets* (New York: Vintage, 1983), ch. 14.

45. Dan Seligman, "Blowing Whistles, Blowing Smoke," *Forbes*, September 6, 1999.

46. Norman Bowie, *Business Ethics* (Englewood Cliffs, NJ: Prentice Hall, 1982), 142.

47. "Tobacco Whistle-Blower Acknowledges He's Paid," *New York Times*, May 1, 1996, A12.

48. "Peep and Weep," *Economist*, January 12, 2002, 56.

49. Ibid.

50. Gilbert Cranberg, "*Wall Street Journal* Case Could Bring Overreaction," *Los Angeles Times*, June 4, 1984, II-5.

51. See "Media Policies Vary on Preventing Employees and Others from Profiting on Knowledge of Future Business Stories," *Wall Street Journal*, March 2, 1984, 8.

52. Ibid.

53. "Market Leaks: Illegal Insider Trading Seems to Be on Rise," *Wall Street Journal*, March 2, 1984, 8.

54. "Media Policies," *Wall Street Journal*, 8.

55. See "Impropriety or Criminality?," *Time*, September 10, 1984, 45.

56. Cranberg, "Case Could Bring Overreaction," II-5.

57. "Impropriety or Criminality?," *Time*, 43.

58. This case study was inspired by one in *Across the Board* 36 (January 1999).

FOUR CONCEPTS OF LOYALTY

DAVID E. SOLES

Loyalty is an ambiguous concept, and discussions of company loyalty and of whether employees owe loyalty to their employers are frequently hampered by the absence of a shared understanding of the meaning of loyalty. In this essay, David E. Soles explains and critically assesses four different concepts of loyalty: the idealist account, the commonsense conception, loyalties as norms, and the minimalist account. Each has different implications for business ethics.

Loyalty has figured prominently in recent discussions of business ethics and there seems to be a general consensus that loyalty is to be ranked among the virtues of a good employee. That employees have obligations of loyalty to their employers is largely assumed without question within the business community; the major concern there is how to strengthen and retain the bonds of loyalty.[1] It is not only representatives of business interests, however, who maintain that employees have obligations of loyalty to their employers; such a view is popular among philosophers writing on business ethics. Norman Bowie, for instance, articulates the majority opinion when he asserts that, "[o]ne of the chief duties of an employee is loyalty to an employer."[2] Though prevalent, this view has been challenged by a few distinguished philosophers like Richard De George who maintains that "[o]ne has no general, moral obligation of loyalty to one's employer, even though employers would like to have loyal employees."[3]

In the absence of a shared, fairly precise understanding of loyalty, it is very difficult, perhaps impossible, to adjudicate between the competing positions advocated by Bowie and De George. Yet it is just such an agreed-upon and

From *The International Journal of Applied Philosophy* 8 (Summer 1993). Reprinted with permission of Philosophy Documentation Center.

precise conception of loyalty that is missing from current discussions. Participants appear to be employing vague and very different conceptions of loyalty and, thus, talking at cross purposes. My objective in this essay is to examine some of the different conceptions of loyalty embedded in current discussions and assess the relevance of each to employer/employee relations. In three of the cases I conclude that the notion of loyalty is such that we have no reason for saying that employees have general obligations of loyalty. In the fourth case, the notion of loyalty is sufficiently attenuated to warrant the advocacy of employee loyalty; it is so attenuated, however, that such advocacy cannot bear the weight placed upon it.

THE IDEALIST ACCOUNT

The first view of loyalty may be called an idealist account because of the close resemblance it bears to the position developed by the American idealist, Josiah Royce. According to Royce, loyalty is

[t]he willing and practical and thorough-going devotion of a person to a cause. A man is loyal when, first, he has some cause to which he is loyal; secondly, he willingly and thoroughly devotes himself to this cause; and when, thirdly, he expresses his devotion in some sustained and practical way, by acting steadily in the service of his cause. Instances of loyalty are: The devotion of a patriot to his country, when this devotion leads him to actually live and perhaps to die for his country; the devotion of a martyr to his religion; the devotion of a ship's captain to the requirements of his office when, after a disaster, he works steadily for his ship and for the saving of the ship's company until the last possible service is accomplished, so that he is the last man to leave the ship, and is ready if need be to go down with his ship.[4]

As Royce realizes, each of the aspects of his analysis requires further elucidation. To begin with the object of loyalty: that to which one is loyal must be something objective, external to the individual, and possessed of its own inherent value; "[i]t does not get its value merely from your being pleased with it. You believe, on the contrary, that you love it just because of its own value, which it has by itself, even if you die" (19).

By saying that loyalty requires *willing* devotion, Royce is maintaining that loyalty must be freely given; while obedience can be demanded, loyalty cannot. In part, this follows from Royce's thesis that loyalty entails devotion: devotion is a mental state not reducible to behavior, and while behavior can be demanded, mental states cannot. But while loyalty may entail devotion, devotion is never sufficient for loyalty: "[l]oyalty is never mere emotion. Adoration and affection may go with loyalty, but can never alone constitute loyalty" (18).

This follows from the claim that loyalty is practical—to be loyal is to serve a cause. Furthermore, this service is thorough-going and sustained; a loyal person does whatever is necessary to promote the cause, "ready to live or die as the cause directs" (18).

This idealist conception of loyalty is germane to discussions of business ethics in the following way. If this is the accepted conception of loyalty and if it can be established that employees ought to be loyal to their employers, then the stringent obligations sometimes placed upon employees in the name of loyalty would be perfectly justified. A loyal employee would be one thoroughly dedicated to serving the interests of his principal, ready to live or die as directed, and to say that employees should be loyal would be to advocate such dedication. It is instructive to consider some examples of the sorts of obligations this conception of loyalty could require of a loyal employee. A loyal employee would always be willing to place the interests of the principal before purely private interests, even in matters unrelated to employment; a loyal employee would be willing to sacrifice the interests of uninvolved third parties or even society at large, if doing so served the employer's interest; a loyal employee would never advocate or vote for social policies or legislation that might damage the interests of the employer; a loyal employee would never publicly criticize or oppose the actions of the employer; a loyal employee would never consider leaving the employer. That something akin to the idealist conception of loyalty is operative in some quarters is evidenced by the frequent endorsements of these claims.

Lest it be thought that I am constructing a straw man here, consider the following case which Marcia Baron discusses in *The Moral Status of Loyalty*.

> In a 1973 CBS report on Phillips Petroleum, Inc., one of its chief executives was asked to describe what sort of qualities his company looks for in prospective employees. He responded without hesitation that above all else, what Phillips wants and needs is loyalty on the part of its employees. A loyal employee, he elaborated, would buy only Phillips products . . . . Moreover, a loyal employee would vote in local, state, and national elections in whatever way was most conducive to the growth and flourishing of Phillips. And, of course, a loyal employee would never leave Phillips unless it was absolutely unavoidable. To reduce the likelihood of that happening, prospective employees were screened to make sure their respective wives did not have careers which might conflict with life-long loyalty to Phillips.[5]

Is it true that employees have an obligation to so thoroughly dedicate themselves to the interests of their employers and, if so, what are the grounds of that obligation? One might begin to address this question by asking a more general question: is there any reason to so thoroughly dedicate oneself to any one thing?

Royce has an answer to this latter question, but it is one which will provide little comfort for those who advocate idealistic loyalty to employers. According to him, such dedication is demanded by the human predicament, for human beings are incapable of finding any meaning or significance to their lives within themselves . . . .

Thus, on Royce's account, because human life can be made meaningful and significant only through the total dedication of that life to the service of some external cause, loyalty becomes the highest moral virtue. One should totally dedicate oneself to the service to some cause because such dedication is necessary to make one's life meaningful.

There are, of course, myriad problems with such an account . . . . For the moment we can grant Royce his dubious views about human nature, for there is a more serious problem confronting the idealist account; its thorough-going, total dedication to a cause requires an abdication of moral autonomy that can be neither demanded nor given.

It is morally irresponsible to be willing to perform any conceivable action that would further the interests of one's chosen cause; one must always reserve the option of saying that one can no longer serve a cause if it requires the performance of certain sorts of actions . . . .

Royce . . . is right about one thing. If loyalty requires such total, thorough-going dedication to a cause, there are very few things worthy of loyalty; furthermore, since the interests of any two causes could conceivably come into conflict, one can be loyal to only one object. Therefore, it is incumbent upon each person to ensure that the object of his loyalty is of the highest inherent worth.

It is very unlikely that business institutions qualify as objects of the most inherent worth. To begin with, business institutions are instrumentally, not inherently, valuable; they are valued because they are means for providing goods and services which are valued. If we no longer cared for those goods and services or if we found better ways to obtain them, the institutions which provide them would lose much of their value. Furthermore, not all business institutions possess instrumental value: some produce more harm than good by manufacturing dangerous, inferior products, polluting the environment, engaging in illegal business practices, etc. But whether instrumentally good or evil, a business institution is not the sort of thing worthy of loyalty in the idealist sense.

In summary, if the idealist conception of loyalty were accepted as our working notion of loyalty, and if it could be established that employees ought to be loyal to their employers, then the demands placed upon employees in the name of loyalty would be justified: employees would have an obligation to place the interests of their employers before all other interests. However, it is not clear that we should accept this as our working conception of loyalty and, more importantly, even if we did, we must conclude that business institutions could not be appropriate objects of loyalty.

THE COMMON SENSE CONCEPTION

The common sense view of loyalty more satisfactorily captures the everyday conception of loyalty with which most of us are familiar. Most of us are untroubled by statements to the effect that someone is a loyal fan of the Kansas City Royals, a loyal member of the Republican party, or loyal to her alma mater, and when we hear such claims we are not inclined to suppose that the person is totally dedicated to the cause, "willing to live or die as the cause directs."

A version of the common sense view of loyalty has been formulated by Andrew Oldenquist in "Loyalties."[6] According to Oldenquist,

> . . . [w]hen I have a loyalty to something I have somehow come to view it as *mine*. It is an object of non-instrumental value to me in virtue (but not only in virtue) of its being mine, and I am disposed to feel pride when it prospers, shame when it declines, and anger or indignation when it is harmed. In general, people care about the objects of their loyalties, and they acknowledge obligations that they would not acknowledge were it not for their loyalties. (175)
> . . . [L]oyalty is positive and is primarily characterized by esteem and concern for the common good of one's group. (177)

On this view, there are three essential features of loyalty. First, loyalty entails having a positive attitude towards the objects of one's loyalty; a loyalty is to "an object of non-instrumental value," people "care about" the objects of their loyalties. Second, loyalty entails a disposition to serve the interests of the object to which one is loyal; loyal persons "acknowledge obligations that they would not acknowledge were it not for their loyalties." Third, both the concern and the obligations are rooted in the individual's belief that he stands in some personal relationship to the object of his loyalty; to have a loyalty to something is to somehow come to view it as one's own.

The first thing to note about this conception of loyalty is that it is not sufficient to distinguish loyalty from many other virtues.[7] While caring, acknowledging obligations, and feeling a personal relationship may be necessary features of loyalty, they also are necessary features of virtues such as love and friendship and may even characterize the relationship between some professionals and their patients, clients, students, etc. Many dedicated teachers consider their students to be objects of non-instrumental value, care about them, acknowledge supererogatory obligations, and both the concern and the obligations stem from the fact that these students are their students. Similar remarks may be made about doctors, nurses, lawyers, social workers, etc. To characterize their attitude as one of loyalty seems to be stretching the common sense notion of loyalty too far . . . .

In conflating loyalty with other, distinct, virtues, Oldenquist has failed to provide the promised analysis of loyalty. Nevertheless, while this common sense account should not be construed as providing a definition of "loyalty" in terms of necessary and sufficient conditions, it may be acceptable as a rough characterization of some essential features of loyalty. Loyalty, like friendship, love, and professional interest, entails concern, obligations, and a feeling of personal identification with the object of one's loyalty. The questions that need to be asked, then, are: (1) does one have any obligation to have such attitudes to one's employer, and (2) does the having of such attitudes justify always acting in the interests of the object of one's loyalty?

Beginning with the first question, on the common sense account, the mere fact that one happens to have been born in a particular country, happens to have attended a particular school, or happens to work for a particular institution is not sufficient for saying that one should be loyal to it. Oldenquist makes this point in maintaining that ". . . a loyalist doesn't value something simply because it is his. It must have features which make it worth having, and it could deteriorate to the extent that shame ultimately kills his loyalty" (178). On this conception of loyalty, one should bestow one's loyalty only on those objects which are worthy of it and loyalty bestowed upon some nations, schools or institutions would be misguided.

Furthermore, if this is our working conception of loyalty, no one has an obligation to be loyal to anything; to suppose that one has an obligation to be loyal to anything is to make a fundamental category mistake. On this view, being loyal entails having certain sorts of attitudes; to be loyal to an object one must care about it. But while persons can have moral obligations to perform certain actions and while certain attitudes may be morally desirable or indesirable, we do not have moral obligations to have certain attitudes and beliefs. Just as no one has an obligation to have feelings of love or friendship to another, no one has an obligation to have feelings of loyalty to anything. Thus, one can have no obligation to be loyal to her nation, school, or employer even if they are worthy of loyalty.

Turning to the second question, does loyalty require one to always act in the interest of that to which one is loyal? It is often suggested that loyalty is inconsistent with certain sorts of actions, for example, whistleblowing is alleged to be incompatible with loyalty. Sissela Bok, for instance, sets up the dichotomy this way.

> . . . [T]he whistleblower hopes to stop the game; but since he is neither referee nor coach, and since he blows the whistle on his own team, his act is seen as a violation of loyalty. In holding his position, he has assumed certain obligations to his colleagues and clients. He may even have subscribed to a loyalty oath or a promise of confidentiality. Loyalty to colleagues and clients comes to be pitted against loyalty to the public interest, to those who may be injured unless the revelation is made.
> *Not only is loyalty violated in whistleblowing,* hierarchy as well is often opposed . . . . If the facts warrant whistleblowing, how can the second element—*breach of loyalty*—be minimized?[8] (my italics)

On the common sense conception, this is a very misleading way of presenting the problem for it implies that whistleblowing is a breach of loyalty, that one cannot both be loyal to an institution and blow the whistle on it. But, on the common sense view, this is surely wrong; one can view an institution as one's own, care deeply about it, assume obligations towards it, and still publicly and strenuously oppose what one takes to be unethical or illegal actions on its part. This is a feature of loyalty explicitly recognized in British politics as "the loyal opposition."

Setting up a dichotomy between loyalty and whistleblowing is not merely a misleading way to present the problem of whistleblowing, it is dangerous. Loyalty is generally perceived as a virtue and disloyalty is perceived as a vice. To say that loyalty demands a certain action is to give a prima facie reason for performing that action and to label a particular action as disloyal is to give a prima facie reason for not performing that action. Under those conditions, potential whistleblowers are encouraged to construe themselves as choosing between performing a wrong act themselves (being disloyal) or remaining silent about the performance of wrongs committed by others. When presented this way, it is not surprising that many individuals choose silence. But if whistleblowing is not construed as an instance of disloyalty, the whole complexion of the problem changes. If loyalty does not require acquiescence in wrong doing, the refusal to remain silent about known wrongs cannot be construed as an ipso facto instance of disloyalty.

Acceptance of the common sense view of loyalty, thus, would justify two conclusions both of which are anathema to many discussions of business and professional ethics. First, it is simply a mistake to suppose that individuals have an obligation to be loyal to their employers and second, loyalty is compatible with strenuously opposing actions of one's employer.

LOYALTIES AS NORMS

While he does not appear to be aware that he is doing so, Oldenquist formulates a second conception of loyalty radically different from his common sense account. According to this second view, "loyalties are norms that define the domains within which we accept the moral machinery of universalizable reasons and relevant differences" (182); alternatively, "loyalties define moral communities or domains within which we are willing to universalize moral judgments, treat equals equally, protect the common good, and in other ways adopt the familiar machinery of impersonal morality . . . . A loyalty defines a moral community in terms of a conception of a common good and a special commitment to the members of the group who share this good" (177). This seems to be incompatible with the common sense account Oldenquist formulates. Attitudes, definitions and norms are different sorts of things. If loyalty is an attitude as the common sense account maintains, then it is neither a norm nor a definition.

Perhaps the confusion here is merely verbal. Perhaps Oldenquist's claim is something like this: the class of objects to which one is loyal is delineated by, or co-extensive with, the moral communities or domains "within which we are

willing to universalize moral judgments, treat equals equally, protect the common good, and in other ways adopt the familiar machinery of impersonal morality." On this reading, loyalty is not literally a norm which defines a moral community; rather, one has attitudes of loyalty towards the moral community determined by the norms.

There are two ways of interpreting this talk of loyalty to the moral community: (1) we might have feelings of loyalty to each of the members of the community defined by the norm, or (2) we might have feelings of loyalty to the community, but not necessarily to each of its members. Either alternative faces serious difficulties.

Beginning with the first interpretation, if loyalty is characterized by positive feelings of esteem and concern, a disposition to feel pride when the object of loyalty prospers, shame when it declines, and anger or hurt when it is harmed, then the moral community defined by the norms and the objects of one's loyalty might not be co-extensive. One might, for instance, define the moral community as rational, sentient beings; this would define the domain within which we are willing to universalize moral judgments, etc. One might not, however, have positive feelings of concern, esteem, etc. for all the members of this community. In that case, the community of objects to which one is loyal would not be coextensive with the moral community.

The second interpretation would avoid this conclusion by arguing that on the above example one is loyal to the class of rational sentient beings, not individual rational sentient beings; that communities and not individuals are the proper objects of loyalty. That this might be Oldenquist's position is implied by statements such as the following.

> A loyalty defines a moral community in terms of a conception of a common good and a special commitment to the members of the group who share this good. The members, along with certain conventional, institutional structures, and often a geographical location, together constitute the community that is the object of my loyalty. (177)

On this account, then, one is loyal to communities and to be loyal to a community just is to "adopt the familiar procedures of impersonal morality" in one's dealings with members of that community. Thus, according to Oldenquist, a Kantian who maintains that rationality is an end in itself is advocating loyalty to the class of rational beings (179) and a utilitarian who maintains that the happiness of all human beings is to count equally is advocating loyalty to the class of human beings (180–181). But to come to this conclusion is to trivialize talk of loyalty: as a moral category, loyalty has become vacuous, it no longer draws any moral distinctions.

If any moral norm to which one is committed defines a moral community to which one is loyal, then loyalty can never come into conflict with any other moral standard. Suppose that I am loyal to the institution where I am employed; it is a community towards which I have positive attitudes, I have assumed special obligations to promote its interests, I treat the members of that community according to the procedures of impersonal morality, recognizing universalizable reasons, and relevant differences, etc. Suppose that I am also committed to the principle that rational beings should always be treated as ends in themselves. Suppose, finally, that I come to perceive certain policies pursued by my institution as being grossly exploitive and am torn between a desire to protect the institution and an obligation to act on my moral principles. In choosing what course of action to pursue, it would be natural to describe myself as choosing between considerations of loyalty to the institution and some other principle of morality.

On Oldenquist's view, however, the choice is merely one between a wide and a narrow loyalty; on the one hand I am loyal to the institution and on the other hand I am loyal to the moral community defined by the norm. If any moral standard which I accept defines a moral community to which I am loyal, then loyalty can never come into conflict with any other moral standard, there can only be conflicts between wide and narrow loyalties. At precisely that point loyalty becomes a vacuous, trivial moral notion.

Furthermore, to say that loyalty is a norm does not answer any ethical questions nor provide moral guidance . . . . In particular, characterizing loyalties as norms which define moral communities provides no guidance in ascertaining whether we should be loyal to our employers nor does it provide any insight into what loyalty would demand should we decide that loyalty is appropriate. Consequently, such an analysis is useless for deciding the interesting questions about loyalty that arise in the context of business and professional ethics.

THE MINIMALIST ACCOUNT

There is a fourth conception of loyalty which maintains that a loyal individual is one who meets reasonable expectations of trust; to be loyal just is to discharge one's obligations and responsibilities conscientiously. Such an attenuated view of loyalty does not demand positive feelings of affection, devotion, or respect nor does it expect one to perform supererogatory actions in promoting the interests of the object of one's loyalty. At most, loyalty demands that one act in a way that does not betray reasonable expectations of trust.

The Restatement of the Law of Agency is subject to a minimalist interpretation.[9] That Restatement maintains that a loyal agent has a duty ". . . to act solely for the benefit of the principal in all matters connected with his agency" (387). This claim that the agent is to act solely for the benefit of the principal is qualified in several important respects by the Restatement. First, an agent may act against the interests of his principal when doing so is necessary for the protection of his own interests or those of others (387b). Second, an agent has no obligation to perform acts which are illegal or unethical and ". . . in determining whether or not the orders of the principal are reasonable . . . business or professional ethics . . . are considered" (385-1a). Third, an agent is not "prevented from acting in good faith outside his employment in a manner which injuriously affects his principal's business" (387b). Finally, "[a]n agent is privileged to reveal information confidentially acquired . . . in the protection of a superior interest of himself or of a third person. Thus, if the confidential information is to the effect that the principal is committing or is about to commit a crime, the agent is under no duty not to reveal it" (395f).

Like most documents, the Restatement of Agency is subject to competing interpretations. As Blumberg has noted, the Restatement

> . . . is drafted in terms of economic activity, economic motivation, and economic advantage and formulates duties of loyalty and obedience for the agent to prevent the agent's own economic interest from impairing his judgment, zeal, or single-minded devotion to the furtherance of his principal's economic interests. The reference in section 395, Comment f permitting the agent to disclose confidential information concerning a criminal act committed or planned by the principal is the sole exception to a system of analysis that is otherwise exclusively concerned with matters relating to the economic position of the parties.[10] . . .

As Blumberg rightly emphasizes, the Restatement is concerned almost exclusively with conflicts of economic interests; nevertheless, if interpreted liberally, the Restatement can be quite useful in responding to the broader issues. The discussion of criminal activity at 395f could be treated as an example of a case where the revelation of confidential material is justified by the need to protect a superior interest; it need not be read as limiting the revelation of confidential material to cases involving criminal activity. By the same token, 387b could be interpreted as maintaining that an agent is justified in acting against the interests of the principal when doing so is necessary to protect important non-economic interests of himself or others. Interpreted thusly, either 395f or 387b could be appealed to in justifying the claim that loyalty is consistent with acting against the interests of one's employer.

On the minimalist account, loyalty would not entail a willingness to participate in, condone or remain silent about illegal activities. It would not entail willingness to participate in unethical conduct if doing so promoted the interests of one's principal. It would be compatible with acting against the interests of one's employer, even revealing confidential information, if doing so were necessary to protect important interests of the public. Finally, contrary to the opinion of the Phillips executive, loyalty would be compatible with voting in ways not conducive to the growth and flourishing of one's principal and even compatible with seeking employment elsewhere. In this minimalist sense, simply meeting reasonable expectations of trust is sufficient for loyalty.

This, of course, raises the issue of what responsibilities it is reasonable for employers to entrust to employees. Many of these are defined and clearly stipulated in job descriptions, contracts, and codes of professional ethics and many more are informally recognized as standard acceptable practices within a profession; and, while there are bound to be grey areas and points of disagreement, there are some activities which loyalty does not enjoin.

If the minimalist conception of loyalty is accepted, it seems clear that employees ought to be loyal to their employers. That, however, merely amounts to the claim that they ought to meet reasonable, legitimate expectations of trust; it does not impose upon them the sorts of obligations that often are urged in the name of loyalty.

CONCLUSION

Much of the confusion and disagreement infecting discussions of the role of loyalty in business and professional ethics has been engendered by equivocation and ambiguity in the concept itself. This essay has briefly considered four different conceptions of loyalty and examined some of the implications of each. If the idealist conception of loyalty is accepted, loyalty to one's employer would demand the sort of behavior sometimes advocated in its name. It is not clear, however, that this account should be accepted and, if we do accept it, employers would not be appropriate objects of loyalty. If the common sense conception of loyalty is accepted, two conclusions follow: first, since loyalty is supererogatory, no one has an obligation to feel loyal to anything; second, loyalty, in this sense, does not entail placing the interests of one's principal before all other considerations and, in fact, is compatible with opposing some of the interests of one's principal. The third conception, which maintains that the adoption of any norm regulating conduct generates a loyalty, trivializes the notion of loyalty to the point where it is useless for guiding conduct. Finally, on the minimalist conception, one can justify saying that employees ought to be loyal to their employers; the minimalist view is sufficiently attenuated, however, that such a claim does not amount to much.

Notes

1. See, for example, R. Rowan, "Rekindling Corporate Loyalty," *Fortune*, Fall, 1981, or P. C. Lederer, "Management's Right to Loyalty of Supervisors," *Labor Law Review*, Fall, 1981, or "The End of Corporate Loyalty?" *Business Week*, Aug. 4, 1986.

2. Norman Bowie, *Business Ethics*, Prentice Hall, Inc., Englewood Cliffs, New Jersey, 1982, p. 13.

3. Richard De George, *Business Ethics*, MacMillan, New York, 1982, p. 154.

4. Josiah Royce, *The Philosophy of Loyalty*, The MacMillan Co., New York, 1916, pp. 16–17. Subsequent references to this work are provided as page numbers in the text.

5. Marcia Baron, *The Moral Status of Loyalty*, Kendal Hunt, Dubuque, Iowa, 1984, p. 1.

6. Andrew Oldenquist, "Loyalties," *The Journal of Philosophy*, April, 1982, pp. 173–193. Subsequent references to this work are provided as page numbers in the text.

7. This should not be construed as a criticism of Oldenquist. His objective seems to be to advocate loyalty, not explicate the conception.

8. Sissela Bok, "Whistleblowing and Professional Responsibility," *New York University Education Quarterly*, Vol. II, 4 (1980), 2–7. Reprinted in Beauchamp and Bowie, *Ethical Theory and Business*, 2nd ed., Prentice Hall, Inc., Englewood Cliffs, New Jersey, pp. 261–269.

9. *Restatement of the Law, Second, Agency*, Vol. 2, American Law Institute Publishers, St. Paul, Minn., 1958.

10. Phillip J. Blumberg, "Corporate Responsibility and the Employee's Duty of Loyalty and Obedience," in Beauchamp and Bowie, *Ethical Theory and Business*, Prentice Hall, Inc., Englewood Cliffs, New Jersey, 1979, pp. 309–310.

Review and Discussion Questions

1. Explain the key features of each of the four concepts of loyalty that Soles discusses. What do you see as the strong and weak points of each? Are there aspects of loyalty that all four concepts overlook?

2. What do you think is the best way to define loyalty? Is loyalty only a feeling, or is it a source of moral obligation? When and under what conditions do we owe loyalty?

3. Examine the following two questions from the perspective of each of the four concepts of loyalty; then give your own answer: (a) Do employees owe loyalty to their employers? (b) What does loyalty to one's employer require?

4. What are you loyal to? What determines your loyalties? Is loyalty important? Does it give meaning to our existence? Is it a necessary component of the moral life?

What Is Really Unethical About Insider Trading?

Jennifer Moore

In this article Jennifer Moore examines the principal ethical arguments against insider trading: the claim that the practice is unfair, the claim that it involves a "misappropriation" of information, and the claim that it harms ordinary investors. She concludes that each of these arguments has serious deficiencies and that none of them suffices to outlaw insider trading. Instead, she argues that the real reason for prohibiting insider trading is that it undermines the fiduciary relationship that lies at the heart of business management.

This essay is divided into two parts. In the first part, I examine critically the principal ethical arguments against insider trading. The arguments fall into three main classes: arguments based on fairness, arguments based on property rights in information, and arguments based on harm to ordinary investors or the market as a whole. Each of these arguments, I contend, has some serious deficiencies. No one of them by itself provides a sufficient reason for outlawing insider trading. This does not mean, however, that there are no reasons for prohibiting the practice. Once we have cleared away the inadequate arguments, other, more cogent reasons for outlawing insider trading come to light. In the second part of the essay, I set out what I take to be the real reasons for laws against insider trading.

The term *insider trading* needs some preliminary clarification. Both the SEC and the courts have strongly resisted pressure to define the notion clearly. In 1961, the SEC stated that corporate insiders—such as officers or directors—in possession of material, non-public information were required to disclose that information or to refrain from trading. But this "disclose or refrain" rule has since been extended to persons other than corporate insiders. People who get information from insiders ("tippees"), and those who become "temporary insiders" in the course of some work they perform for the company, can acquire the duty of insiders in some cases. Financial printers and newspaper columnists, not "insiders" in the technical sense, have also been found guilty of insider trading. Increasingly, the term *insider* has come to refer to the kind of information a person possesses rather than to the status of the person who trades on that information. My use of the term will reflect this ambiguity. In this essay, an "insider trader" is someone who trades in material, nonpublic information—not necessarily a corporate insider.

From *Journal of Business Ethics*, Volume 9, Issue 3, March 1990, pp. 171–182.

I. ETHICAL ARGUMENTS AGAINST INSIDER TRADING

Fairness

Probably the most common reason given for thinking that insider trading is unethical is that it is "unfair." For proponents of the fairness argument, the key feature of insider trading is the disparity of information between the two parties to the transaction. Trading should take place on a "level playing field," they argue, and disparities in information tilt the field toward one player and away from the other. There are two versions of the fairness argument: the first argues that insider trading is unfair because the two parties do not have *equal* information; the second argues that insider trading is unfair because the two parties do not have equal *access* to information. Let us look at the two versions one at a time.

According to the equal information argument, insider trading is unfair because one party to the transaction lacks information the other party has, and is thus at a disadvantage. Although this is a very strict notion of fairness, it has its proponents, and hints of this view appear in some of the judicial opinions. One proponent of the equal information argument is Saul Levmore, who claims that "fairness is achieved when insiders and outsiders are in equal positions. That is, a system is fair if we would not expect one group to envy the position of the other." As thus defined, Levmore claims, fairness "reflects the 'golden rule' of impersonal behavior—treating others as we would ourselves."[1] If Levmore is correct, then not just insider trading, but *all* transactions in which there is a disparity of information are unfair, and thus unethical. But this claim seems overly broad. An example will help to illustrate some of the problems with it.

Suppose I am touring Vermont and come across an antique blanket chest in the barn of a farmer, a chest I know will bring $2,500 back in the city. I offer to buy it for $75, and the farmer agrees. If he had known how much I could get for it back home, he probably would have asked a higher price—but I failed to disclose this information. I have profited from an informational advantage. Have I been unethical? My suspicion is that most people would say I have not. While knowing how much I could sell the chest for in the city is in the interest of the farmer, I am not morally obligated to reveal it. I am not morally obligated to tell those who deal with me *everything* that it would be in their interest to know . . . .

In general, it is only when I owe a *duty* to the other party that I am legally required to reveal all information that is in his interest. In such a situation, the other party believes that I am looking out for his interests, and I deceive him if I do not do so. Failure to disclose is deceptive in this instance because of the relationship of trust and dependence between the parties. But this suggests that trading on inside information is wrong, *not* because it violates a general notion of fairness, but because a breach of fiduciary duty is involved. Cases of insider trading in which no fiduciary duty of this kind is breached would not be unethical . . . .

The "equal information" version of the fairness argument seems to me to fail. However, it could be argued that insider trading is unfair because the insider has information that is not *accessible* to the ordinary investor. For proponents of this second type of fairness argument, it is not the insider's information advantage that counts, but the fact that this advantage is "unerodable," one that cannot be overcome by the hard work and ingenuity of the ordinary investor. No matter how hard the latter works, he is unable to acquire non-public information, because this information is protected by law.[2]

This type of fairness argument seems more promising, since it allows people to profit from informational advantages of their own making, but not from advantages that are built into the system. Proponents of this "equal access" argument would probably find my deal with the Vermont farmer unobjectionable, because information about antiques is not in principle unavailable to the farmer. The problem with the argument is that the notion of "equal access" is not very clear. What does it mean for two people to have equal access to information?

Suppose my pipes are leaking and I call a plumber to fix them. He charges me for the job, and benefits by the informational advantage he has over me. Most of us would not find this transaction unethical. True, I don't have "equal access" to the information needed to fix my pipes in any real sense, but I could have had this information had I chosen to become a plumber. The disparity of information in this case is simply something that is built into the fact that people choose to specialize in different areas. But just as I could have chosen to become a plumber, I could have chosen to become a corporate insider with access to legally protected information . . . .

One might argue that I have easier access to a plumber's information than I do to an insider trader's, since there are lots of plumbers from whom I can buy the information I seek. The fact that insiders have a strong incentive to keep their information to themselves is a serious objection to insider trading. But if insider trading were made legal, insiders could profit not only from trading on their information, but also on selling it to willing buyers. Proponents of the practice argue that a brisk market in information would soon develop—indeed, it might be argued that such a market already exists, though in illegal and clandestine form.[3] . . .

The most interesting thing about the fairness argument is not that it provides a compelling reason to outlaw insider trading, but that it leads to issues we cannot settle on the basis of an abstract concept of fairness alone. The claim that parties to a transaction should have equal information, or equal access to information, inevitably raises questions about how informational advantages are (or should be) acquired, and when people are entitled to use them for profit . . . .

Property Rights in Information

As economists and legal scholars have recognized, information is a valuable thing, and it is possible to view it as a type of property. We already treat certain types of information as

property: trade secrets, inventions, and so on—and protect them by law. Proponents of the property rights argument claim that material, non-public information is also a kind of property, and that insider trading is wrong because it involves a violation of property rights.

If inside information is a kind of property, whose property is it? How does information come to belong to one person rather than another? This is a very complex question, because information differs in many ways from other, more tangible sorts of property. But one influential argument is that information belongs to the people who discover, originate or "create" it. As Bill Shaw put it in a recent article, "the originator of the information (the individual or corporation that spent hard-earned bucks producing it) owns and controls this asset just as it does other proprietary goods."[4] Thus, if a firm agrees to a deal, invents a new product, or discovers new natural resources, it has a property right in that information and is entitled to exclusive use of it for its own profit.

It is important to note that it is the firm itself (and/or its shareholders), and not the individual employees of the firm, who have property rights in the information. To be sure, it is always certain individuals in the firm who put together the deal, invent the product, or discover the resources. But they are able to do this only because they are backed by the power and authority of the firm. The employees of the firm—managers, officers, directors—are not entitled to the information any more than they are entitled to corporate trade secrets or patents on products that they develop for the firm. It is the firm that makes it possible to create the information and that makes the information valuable once it has been created. As Victor Brudney puts it,

> The insiders have acquired the information at the expense of the enterprise, and for the purpose of conducting the business for the collective good of all the stockholders, entirely apart from personal benefits from trading in its securities. There is no reason for them to be entitled to trade for their own benefit on the basis of such information . . . .[5]

If this analysis is correct, then it suggests that insider trading is wrong because it is a form of theft. It is not exactly like theft, because the person who uses inside information does not deprive the company of the use of the information. But he does deprive the company of the *sole* use of the information, which is itself an asset. The insider trader "misappropriates," as the law puts it, information that belongs to the company and uses it in a way in which it was not intended—for personal profit. It is not surprising that this "misappropriation theory" has begun to take hold in the courts, and has become one of the predominant rationales in prosecuting insider trading cases. In *U.S. v. Newman*, a case involving investment bankers and securities traders, for example, the court stated:

> In *U.S. v. Chiarella*, Chief Justice Burger . . . said that the defendant "misappropriated"—stole to put it bluntly— "valuable nonpublic information entrusted to him in the utmost confidence." That characterization aptly describes

the conduct of the connivers in the instant case . . . . By sullying the reputations of [their] employers as safe repositories of client confidences, appellee and his cohorts defrauded those employers as surely as if they took their money.[6]

The misappropriation theory also played a major role in the prosecution of R. Foster Winans, a *Wall Street Journal* reporter who traded on and leaked to others the contents of his "Heard on the Street" column.[7]

This theory is quite persuasive, as far as it goes. But it is not enough to show that insider trading is always unethical or that it should be illegal. If insider information is really the property of the firm that produces it, then using that property is wrong *only when the firm prohibits it*. If the firm does not prohibit insider trading, it seems perfectly acceptable.* Most companies do in fact forbid insider trading. But it is not clear whether they do so because they don't want their employees using corporate property for profit or simply because it is illegal. Proponents of insider trading point out that most corporations did not prohibit insider trading until recently, when it became a prime concern of enforcement agencies . . .

A crucial factor here would be the shareholders' agreement to allow insider information. Shareholders may not wish to allow trading on inside information because they may wish the employees of the company to be devoted simply to advancing shareholder interests. We will return to this point below. But if shareholders did allow it, it would seem to be permissible. Still others argue that shareholders would not need to "agree" in any way other than to be told this information when they were buying the stock. If they did not want to hold stock in a company whose employees were permitted to trade in inside information, they would not buy that stock. Hence they could be said to have "agreed."

Manne and other proponents of insider trading have suggested a number of reasons why "shareholders would voluntarily enter into contractual arrangements with insiders giving them property rights in valuable information."[8] Their principal argument is that permitting insider trading would serve as an incentive to create more information—put together more deals, invent more new products, or make more discoveries. Such an incentive, they argue, would create more profit for shareholders in the long run. Assigning employees the right to trade on inside information could take the place of more traditional (and expensive) elements in the employee's compensation package. Rather than giving out end of the year bonuses, for example, firms could allow employees to put together their own bonuses by cashing in on inside information, thus saving the company money. In addition, proponents argue, insider trading would improve the efficiency of the market. We will return to these claims below.

If inside information really is a form of corporate property, firms may assign employees the right to trade on it if they choose to do so. The only reason for not permitting firms to allow employees to trade on their information would be that doing so causes harm to other investors or to society at large. Although our society values property rights very highly, they are not absolute. We do not hesitate to restrict property rights if their exercise causes significant harm to others. The permissibility of insider trading, then, ultimately seems to depend on whether the practice is harmful.

Harm

There are two principal harm-based arguments against insider trading. The first claims that the practice is harmful to ordinary investors who engage in trades with insiders; the second claims that insider trading erodes investors' confidence in the market, causing them to pull out of the market and harming the market as a whole. I will address the two arguments in turn.

Although proponents of insider trading often refer to it as a "victimless crime," implying that no one is harmed by it, it is not difficult to think of examples of transactions with insiders in which ordinary investors are made worse off. Suppose I have placed an order with my broker to sell my shares in Megalith Co., currently trading at $50 a share, at $60 or above. An insider knows that Behemoth Inc. is going to announce a tender offer for Megalith shares in two days, and has begun to buy large amounts of stock in anticipation of the gains. Because of his market activity, Megalith stock rises to $65 a share and my order is triggered. If he had refrained from trading, the price would have risen steeply two days later, and I would have been able to sell my shares for $80. Because the insider traded, I failed to realize the gains that I otherwise would have made.

But there are other examples of transactions in which ordinary investors *benefit* from insider trading. Suppose I tell my broker to sell my shares in Acme Corp., currently trading at $45, if the price drops to $40 or lower. An insider knows of an enormous class action suit to be brought against Acme in two days. He sells his shares, lowering the price to $38 and triggering my sale. When the suit is made public two days later, the share price plunges to $25. If the insider had abstained from trading, I would have lost far more than I did. Here, the insider has protected me from loss . . . .

The truth about an ordinary investor's gains and losses from trading with insiders seems to be not that insider trading is never harmful, but that it is not systematically or consistently harmful. Insider trading is not a "victimless crime," as its proponents claim, but it is often difficult to tell exactly who the victims are and to what extent they have been victimized. The stipulation of the law to "disclose *or* abstain" from trading makes determining victims even more complex. While some investors are harmed by the insider's trade, to others the insider's actions make no difference at all; what harms them is simply *not having complete information* about the stock in question. Forbidding insider trading will not prevent these harms. Investors who neither buy nor sell, or who buy or sell for reasons independent of share price, fall into this category.

---

*Unless there is some other reason for forbidding it, such as that it harms others. See [the following section].

Permitting insider trading would undoubtedly make the securities market *riskier* for ordinary investors. Even proponents of the practice seem to agree with this claim. But if insider trading were permitted openly, they argue, investors would compensate for the extra riskiness by demanding a discount in share price.[9] . . . If insider trading were permitted, in short, we could expect a general drop in share prices, but no net harm to investors would result. Moreover, improved efficiency would result in a bigger pie for everyone. These are empirical claims, and I am not equipped to determine if they are true. If they are, however, they would defuse one of the most important objections to insider trading, and provide a powerful argument for leaving the control of inside information up to individual corporations.

The second harm-based argument claims that permitting insider trading would cause ordinary investors to lose confidence in the market and cease to invest there, thus harming the market as a whole. As former SEC Chairman John Shad puts it, "if people get the impression that they're playing against a marked deck, they're simply not going to be willing to invest."[10] Since capital markets play a crucial role in allocating resources in our economy, this objection is a very serious one.

The weakness of the argument is that it turns almost exclusively on the *feelings* or *perceptions* of ordinary investors, and does not address the question of whether these perceptions are justified. If permitting insider trading really does harm ordinary investors, then this "loss of confidence" argument becomes a compelling reason for outlawing insider trading. But if, as many claim, the practice does not harm ordinary investors, then the sensible course of action is to educate the investors, not to outlaw insider trading. It is irrational to cater to the feelings of ordinary investors if those feelings are not justified. We ought not to outlaw perfectly permissible actions just because some people feel (unjustifiably) disadvantaged by them. More research is needed to determine the actual impact of insider trading on the ordinary investor.[11]

II. IS THERE ANYTHING WRONG WITH INSIDER TRADING?

My contention has been that the principal ethical arguments against insider trading do not, by themselves, suffice to show that the practice is unethical and should be illegal. The strongest arguments are those that turn on the notion of a fiduciary duty to act in the interest of shareholders, or on the idea of inside information as company "property." But in both arguments, the impermissibility of insider trading depends on a contractual understanding among the company, its shareholders, and its employees. In both cases, a modification of this understanding could change the moral status of insider trading.

Does this mean that there is nothing wrong with insider trading? No. If insider trading is unethical, it is so *in the context* of the relationship among the firm, its shareholders, and its employees. It is possible to change this context in a way that makes the practice permissible. But *should* the

context be changed? I will argue that it should not. Because it threatens the fiduciary relationship that is central to business management, I believe, permitting insider trading is in the interest neither of the firm, its shareholders, nor society at large.

Fiduciary relationships are relationships of trust and dependence in which one party acts in the interest of another. They appear in many contexts, but are absolutely essential to conducting business in a complex society. Fiduciary relationships allow parties with different resources, skills, and information to cooperate in productive activity. Shareholders who wish to invest in a business, for example, but who cannot or do not wish to run it themselves, hire others to manage it for them. Managers, directors, and to some extent, other employees, become fiduciaries for the firms they manage and for the shareholders of those firms.

The fiduciary relationship is one of moral and legal obligation. Fiduciaries, that is, are bound to act in the interests of those who depend on them even if these interests do not coincide with their own. Typically, however, fiduciary relationships are constructed as far as possible so that the interests of the fiduciaries and the parties for whom they act *do* coincide. Where the interests of the two parties compete or conflict, the fiduciary relationship is threatened . . . .

Significantly, proponents of insider trading do not dispute the importance of the fiduciary relationship. Rather, they argue that permitting insider trading would *increase* the likelihood that employees will act in the interest of shareholders and their firms.[12] We have already touched on the main argument for this claim. Manne and others contend that assigning employees the right to trade on inside information would provide a powerful incentive for creative and entrepreneurial activity. It would encourage new inventions, creative deals, and efficient new management practices, thus increasing the profits, strength, and overall competitiveness of the firm. Manne goes so far as to argue that permission to trade on insider information is the only appropriate way to compensate entrepreneurial activity, and warns: "[I]f no way to reward the entrepreneur within a corporation exists, he will tend to disappear from the corporate scene."[13] The entrepreneur makes an invaluable contribution to the firm and its shareholders, and his disappearance would no doubt cause serious harm.

If permitting insider trading is to work in the way proponents suggest, however, there must be a direct and consistent link between the profits reaped by insider traders and the performance that benefits the firm. It is not at all clear that this is the case—indeed, there is evidence that the opposite is true. There appear to be many ways to profit from inside information that do not benefit the firm at all. I mention four possibilities below. Two of these (2 and 3) are simply ways in which insider traders can profit without benefiting the firm, suggesting that permitting insider trading is a poor incentive for performance and fails firmly to link the interests of managers, directors and employees to those of the corporation as a whole. The others (1 and 4) are actually harmful to the corporation, setting up conflicts of interest and actively undermining the fiduciary relationship.

1. Proponents of insider trading tend to speak as if all information were positive. "Information," in the proponents' lexicon, always concerns a creative new deal, a new, efficient way of conducting business, or a new product. If this were true, allowing trades on inside information might provide an incentive to work even harder for the good of the company. But information can also concern *bad* news—a large lawsuit, an unsafe or poor quality product, or lower-than-expected performance. Such negative information can be just as valuable to the insider trader as positive information. If the freedom to trade on positive information encourages acts that are beneficial to the firm, then by the same reasoning the freedom to trade on negative information would encourage harmful acts. At the very least, permitting employees to profit from harms to the company decreases the incentive to avoid such harms. Permission to trade on negative inside information gives rise to inevitable conflicts of interest. Proponents of insider trading have not satisfactorily answered this objection.[14]

2. Proponents of insider trading also assume that the easiest way to profit on inside information is to "create" it. But it is not at all clear that this is true. Putting together a deal, inventing a new product, and other productive activities that add value to the firm usually require a significant investment of time and energy. For the well-placed employee, it would be far easier to start a rumor that the company has a new product or is about to announce a deal than to sit down and produce either one—and it would be just as profitable for the employee. If permitting insider trading provides an incentive for the productive "creation" of information, it seems to provide an even greater incentive for the nonproductive "invention" of information, or stock manipulation. The invention of information is in the interest neither of the firm nor of society at large.

3. Even if negative or false information did not pose problems, the incentive argument for insider trading overlooks the difficulties posed by "free riders"—those who do not actually contribute to the creation of the information, but who are nevertheless aware of it and can profit by trading on it . . . . Unless those who do not contribute can be excluded from trading on it, there will be no incentive to produce the desired information; it will not get created at all.

4. Finally, allowing trading on inside information would tend to deflect employees' attention from the day-to-day business of running the company and focus it on major changes, positive or negative, that lead to large insider trading profits. This might not be true if one could profit by inside information about the day-to-day efficiency of the operation, a continuous tradition of product quality, or a consistently lean operating budget. But these things do not generate the kind of information on which insider traders can reap large profits. Insider profits come from dramatic changes, from "news"—not from steady, long-term performance. If the firm and its shareholders have a genuine interest in such performance, then permitting insider trading creates a conflict of interest for insiders. The ability to trade on inside information is also likely to influence the types of information officers announce to the public, and the timing of such announcements, making it less likely that the information and its timing is optimal for the firm. And the problems of false or negative information remain.[15]

If the arguments given above are correct, permitting insider trading does not increase the likelihood that insiders will act in the interest of the firm and its shareholders. In some cases, it actually causes conflicts of interest, undermining the fiduciary relationship essential to managing the corporation. This claim, in turn, gives corporations good reason to prohibit the practice. But insider trading remains primarily a private matter among corporations, shareholders, and employees. It is appropriate to ask why, given this fact about insider trading, the practice should be *illegal*. If it is primarily corporate and shareholder interests that are threatened by insider trading, why not let corporations themselves bear the burden of enforcement? Why involve the SEC? There are two possible reasons for continuing to support laws against insider trading. The first is that even if they wish to prohibit insider trading, individual corporations do not have the resources to do so effectively. The second is that society itself has a stake in the fiduciary relationship . . . .

The notion of the fiduciary duty owed by managers and other employees to the firm and its shareholders has a long and venerable history in our society. Nearly all of our important activities require some sort of cooperation, trust, or reliance on others, and the ability of one person to act in the interest of another—as a fiduciary—is central to this cooperation. The role of managers as fiduciaries for firms and shareholders is grounded in the property rights of shareholders. They are the owners of the firm, and bear the residual risks, and hence have a right to have it managed in their interest. The fiduciary relationship also contributes to efficiency, since it encourages those who are willing to take risks to place their resources in the hands of those who have the expertise to maximize their usefulness. While this "shareholder theory" of the firm has often been challenged in recent years, this has been primarily by people who argue that the fiduciary concept should be widened to include other "stakeholders" in the firm. I have heard no one argue that the notion of managers' fiduciary duties should be eliminated entirely, and that managers should begin working primarily for themselves.

III. CONCLUSION

I have argued that the real reason for prohibiting insider trading is that it erodes the fiduciary relationship that lies at the heart of our business organizations. The more frequently heard moral arguments based on fairness, property rights in information, and harm to ordinary investors are not compelling. Of these, the fairness arguments seem to me the least persuasive. The claim that a trader must reveal everything that it is in the interest of another party to know seems to hold up only when the other is someone to whom he owes a fiduciary duty. But this is not really a "fairness" argument at all. Similarly, the "misappropriation" theory is only persuasive if we can offer reasons for corporations not to assign the right to trade on inside information to their employees. I have found these in the fact that permitting insider trading threatens the fiduciary relationship. I do believe that lifting the ban against insider trading would cause harms to shareholders, corporations, and society at large. But again, these harms stem primarily from the cracks in the fiduciary relationship caused by permitting insider trading, rather than from actual trades with insiders. Violation of fiduciary duty, in short, is at the center of insider trading offenses.

Notes

1. Saul Levmore, "Securities and Secrets: Insider Trading and the Law of Contracts," 68 *Virginia Law Review* 117.

2. The equal access argument is perhaps best stated by Victor Brudney in his influential article, "Insiders, Outsiders, and Informational Advantages Under the Federal Securities Laws," 93 *Harvard Law Review* 322.

3. Manne, *Insider Trading and the Stock Market* (Free Press, New York, 1966), p. 75.

4. Bill Shaw, "Should Insider Trading Be Outside the Law?" *Business and Society Review* 66, p. 34. See also Macey, "From Fairness to Contract: The New Direction of the Rules Against Insider Trading," 13 *Hofstra Law Review* 9 (1984).

5. Brudney, "Insiders, Outsiders, and Informational Advantages," 344.

6. *U.S. v. Newman*, 664 F. 2d 17.

7. *U.S. v. Winans*, 612 F. Supp. 827. The Supreme Court upheld Winans' conviction, but was evenly split on the misappropriation theory. As a consequence, the Supreme Court has still not truly endorsed the theory, although several lower court decisions have been based on it . . . .

8. Carlton and Fischel, "The Regulation of Insider Trading," 35 *Stanford Law Review* 857. See also Manne, *Insider Trading and the Stock Market*.

9. Kenneth Scott, "Insider Trading: Rule 10b-5, Disclosure and Corporate Privacy," 9 *Journal of Legal Studies* 808.

10. "Disputes Arise over Value of Laws on Insider Trading," *The Wall Street Journal*, November 17, 1986, p. 28.

11. One area that needs more attention is the impact of insider trading on the markets (and ordinary investors) of countries that permit the practice. Proponents of insider trading are fond of pointing out that insider trading has been legal in many overseas markets for years, without the dire effects predicted by opponents of the practice. Opponents reply that these markets are not as fair or efficient as U.S. markets, or that they do not play as important a role in the allocation of capital.

12. See Frank Easterbrook, "Insider Trading as an Agency Problem," *Principals and Agents: The Structure of Business* (Cambridge, MA: Harvard University Press, 1985). I speak here as if the interests of the firm and its shareholders are identical, even though this is sometimes not the case.

13. Manne, *Insider Trading and the Stock Market*, p. 129.

14. Manne is aware of the "bad news" objection, but he glosses over it by claiming that bad news is not as likely as good news to provide large gains for insider traders. *Insider Trading and the Stock Market*, p. 102.

15. There are ways to avoid many of these objections. For example, Manne has suggested "isolating" non-contributors so that they cannot trade on the information produced by others. Companies could also forbid trading on "negative" information. The problem is that these piecemeal restrictions seem very costly—more costly than simply prohibiting insider trading as we do now. In addition, each restriction brings us farther and farther away from what proponents of the practice actually want: unrestricted insider trading.

Review and Discussion Questions

1. Do you agree with Moore's criticism of the fairness argument, or is there something unethical about transactions between parties that lack equal information or equal access to information?

2. If insider trading were legal, then it would be up to individual companies and their shareholders to decide whether to permit it. Would it be in their interest to do so?

3. Critics of insider trading argue that it harms ordinary investors and that permitting it would cause them to lose confidence in the market. Is Moore right to reject these arguments?

4. What are fiduciary relationships, and what is their role in business? Would insider trading undermine such relationships, as Moore argues? Is this a sufficient reason for outlawing insider trading?

5. Are there any arguments against or for insider trading that Moore has overlooked or paid insufficient attention to? Do you believe that insider trading is wrong? Should it remain illegal?

Some Paradoxes of Whistleblowing

Michael Davis

In this essay, Michael Davis, professor of philosophy at the Illinois Institute of Technology, challenges the standard theory of justified whistleblowing, arguing that it gives rise to three paradoxes—the paradox of burden, the paradox of missing harm, and the paradox of failure. In its place he advocates what he calls the complicity theory. In contrast to the standard theory, which focuses on the whistleblower's obligation to prevent harm, the complicity theory justifies whistleblowing on the basis of the whistleblower's obligation to avoid complicity in wrongdoing. Davis tests his theory against a classic case of whistleblowing, Roger Boisjoly's testimony before the U.S. commission investigating the Challenger disaster. (A senior engineer at Morton-Thiokol, Boisjoly had recommended that the space shuttle Challenger *not be launched because the temperature at the launch site had fallen below the safety range for the O-ring seals in the rocket boosters. Top management overrode the recommendation, and the next day, shortly after being launched, the* Challenger *exploded, killing all seven members of its crew.)*

INTRODUCTION

By "paradox" I mean an apparent—and, in this case, real—inconsistency between theory (our systematic understanding of whistleblowing) and the facts (what we actually know, or think we know, about whistleblowing). What concerns me is not a few anomalies, the exceptions that test a rule, but a flood of exceptions that seems to swamp the rule.

This essay has four parts. The first states the standard theory of whistleblowing. The second argues that the standard theory is paradoxical, that it is inconsistent with what we know about whistleblowers. The third part sketches what seems to me a less paradoxical theory of whistleblowing. The fourth tests the new theory against one classic case of whistleblowing, Roger Boisjoly's testimony before the presidential commission investigating the *Challenger* disaster ("the Rogers Commission"). I use that case because the chief facts are both uncontroversial enough and well-known enough to make detailed exposition unnecessary. For the same reason, I also use that case to illustrate various claims about whistleblowing throughout the essay.

JUSTIFICATION AND WHISTLEBLOWING

The standard theory is not about whistleblowing, as such, but about justified whistleblowing—and rightly so. Whether this or that is, or is not, whistleblowing is a question for lexicographers. For the rest of us, mere moral agents, the question is—when, if ever, is whistleblowing justified?

From *Business and Professional Ethics Journal* 15 (Spring 1996). Reprinted by permission of the author. Some notes omitted.

We may distinguish three (related) senses in which an act may be "justified." First, an act may be something morality permits. Many acts, for example, eating fruit at lunch, are morally justified in this weak sense. They are (all things considered) morally all right, though some of the alternatives are morally all right too. Second, acts may be morally justified in a stronger sense. Not only is doing them morally all right, but doing anything else instead is morally wrong. These acts are *morally* required. Third, some acts, though only morally justified in the weaker sense, are still required all things considered. That is, they are mandatory because of some non-moral consideration. They are *rationally* (but not morally) required.

I shall be concerned here only with *moral* justification, that is, with what morality permits or requires. I shall have nothing to say about when other considerations, for example, individual prudence or social policy, make (morally permissible) whistleblowing something reason requires.

Generally, we do not *need* to justify an act unless we have reason to think it wrong (whether morally wrong or wrong in some other way). So, for example, I do not need to justify eating fruit for lunch today, though I would if I were allergic to fruit or had been keeping a fast. We also do not need a justification if we believe the act in question wrong. We do not need a justification because, insofar as an act is wrong, justification is impossible. The point of justification is show to be right an act the rightness of which has been put in (reasonable) doubt. Insofar as we believe the act wrong, we can only condemn or excuse it. To condemn it is simply to declare it wrong. To excuse it is to show that, while the act was wrong, the doer had good reason to do it, could not help doing it, or for some other reason should not suffer the response otherwise reserved for such a wrongdoer.

Most acts, though permitted or required by morality, need no justification. There is no reason to think them wrong. Their justification is too plain for words. Why then is whistleblowing so problematic that we need *theories* of its justification? What reason do we have to think whistleblowing might be morally wrong?

Whistleblowing always involves revealing information that would not ordinarily be revealed. But there is nothing morally problematic about that; after all, revealing information not ordinarily revealed is one function of science. Whistleblowing always involves, in addition, an actual (or at least declared) intention to prevent something bad that would otherwise occur. There is nothing morally problematic in that either. That may well be the chief use of information.

What seems to make whistleblowing morally problematic is its organizational context. A mere individual cannot blow the whistle (in any interesting sense); only a member of an organization, whether a current or a former member, can do so. Indeed, he can only blow the whistle on his own organization (or some part of it). So, for example, a police officer who makes public information about a burglary ring, though a member of an organization, does not blow the whistle on the burglary ring (in any interesting sense).

He simply alerts the public. Even if he came by the information working undercover in the ring, his revelation could not be whistleblowing. While secret agents, spies, and other infiltrators need a moral justification for what they do, the justification they need differs from that which whistle-blowers need. Infiltrators gain their information under false pretenses. They need a justification for that deception. Whistleblowers generally do not gain their information under false pretenses.

What if, instead of being a police officer, the revealer of information about the burglary ring were an ordinary member of the ring? Would such an informer be a (justified) whistleblower? I think not. The burglary ring is a criminal organization. The whistleblower's organization never is, though it may occasionally engage in criminal activity (knowingly or inadvertently). So, even a burglar, who, having a change of heart, volunteers information about his ring to the police or the newspaper, does not need to justify his act in the way the whistleblower does. Helping to destroy a criminal organization by revealing its secrets is morally much less problematic than whistleblowing.

What then is morally problematic about the whistle-blower's organizational context? The whistleblower cannot blow the whistle using just any information obtained in virtue of membership in the organization. A clerk in Accounts who, happening upon evidence of serious wrong-doing while visiting a friend in Quality Control, is not a whistleblower just because she passes the information to a friend at the *Tribune*. She is more like a self-appointed spy. She seems to differ from the whistleblower, or at least from clear cases of the whistleblower, precisely in her relation to the information in question. To be a whistleblower is to reveal information with which one is *entrusted*.

But it is more than that. The whistleblower does not reveal the information to save his own skin (for example, to avoid perjury under oath). He has no excuse for revealing what his organization does not want revealed. Instead, he claims to be doing what he should be doing. If he cannot honestly make that claim—if, that is, he does not have that intention—his revelation is not whistleblowing (and so, not justified as whistleblowing), but something analogous, much as pulling a child from the water is not a rescue, even if it saves the child's life, when the "rescuer" merely believes herself to be salvaging old clothes. What makes whistle-blowing morally problematic, if anything does, is this high-minded but unexcused misuse of one's position in a generally law-abiding, morally decent organization, an organization that *prima facie* deserves the whistleblower's loyalty (as a burglary ring does not).

The whistleblower must reveal information the organization does not want revealed. But, in any actual organization, "what the organization wants" will be contested, with various individuals or groups asking to be taken as speaking for the organization. Who, for example, did what Thiokol wanted the night before the *Challenger* exploded? In retrospect, it is obvious that the three vice presidents, Lund, Kilminster, and Mason, did not do what Thiokol wanted—or, at least, what it would have wanted. At the time, however,

they had authority to speak for the company—the conglomerate Morton-Thiokol headquartered in Chicago—while the protesting engineers, including Boisjoly, did not. Yet, even before the explosion, was it obvious that the three were doing what the company wanted? To be a whistle-blower, one must, I think, at least temporarily lose an argument about what the organization wants. The whistleblower is disloyal only in a sense—the sense the winners of the internal argument get to dictate. What can justify such disloyalty?

THE STANDARD THEORY

According to the theory now more or less standard,[1] such disloyalty is morally permissible when:

(S1) The organization to which the would-be whistle-blower belongs will, through its product or policy, do serious considerable harm to the public (whether to users of its product, to innocent bystanders, or to the public at large);

(S2) The would-be whistleblower has identified that threat of harm, reported it to her immediate superior, making clear both the threat itself and the objection to it, and concluded that the superior will do nothing effective; and

(S3) The would-be whistleblower has exhausted other internal procedures within the organization (for example, by going up the organizational ladder as far as allowed)—or at least made use of as many internal procedures as the danger to others and her own safety make reasonable.

Whistleblowing is morally required (according to the standard theory) when, in addition:

(S4) The would-be whistleblower has (or has accessible) evidence that would convince a reasonable, impartial observer that her view of the threat is correct; and

(S5) The would-be whistleblower has good reason to believe that revealing the threat will (probably) prevent the harm at reasonable cost (all things considered).

Why is whistleblowing morally required when these five conditions are met? According to the standard theory, whistleblowing is morally required, when it is required at all, because "people have a moral obligation to prevent serious harm to others if they can do so with little cost to themselves."[2] In other words, whistleblowing meeting all five conditions is a form of "minimally decent Samaritanism" (a doing of what morality requires) rather than "good Samaritanism" (going well beyond the moral minimum) . . . .

THREE PARADOXES

That's the standard theory—where are the paradoxes? The first paradox I want to call attention to concerns a commonplace of the whistleblowing literature. Whistleblowers are not minimally decent Samaritans. If they are Samaritans at all, they are good Samaritans. They always act at considerable risk to career, and generally, at considerable risk to their financial security and personal relations.

In this respect, as in many others, Roger Boisjoly is typical. Boisjoly blew the whistle on his employer, Thiokol; he volunteered information, in public testimony before the Rogers Commission, that Thiokol did not want him to volunteer. As often happens, both his employer and many who relied on it for employment reacted hostilely. Boisjoly had to say goodbye to the company town, to old friends and neighbors, and to building rockets; he had to start a new career at an age when most people are preparing for retirement.

Since whistleblowing is generally costly to the whistleblower in some large way as this, the standard theory's minimally decent Samaritanism provides *no* justification for the central cases of whistleblowing.[3] That is the first paradox, what we might call "the paradox of burden."

The second paradox concerns the prevention of "harm." On the standard theory, the would-be whistleblower must seek to prevent "serious and considerable harm" in order for the whistleblowing to be even morally permissible. There seems to be a good deal of play in the term *harm*. The harm in question can be physical (such as death or disease), financial (such as loss of or damage to property), and perhaps even psychological (such as fear or mental illness). But there is a limit to how much the standard theory can stretch "harm." Beyond that limit are "harms" like injustice, deception, and waste. As morally important as injustice, deception, and waste can be, they do not seem to constitute the "serious and considerable harm" that can require someone to become even a minimally decent Samaritan.

Yet, many cases of whistleblowing, perhaps most, are not about preventing serious and considerable physical, financial, or psychological harm. For example, when Boisjoly spoke up the evening before the *Challenger* exploded, the lives of seven astronauts sat in the balance. Speaking up then was about preventing serious and considerable physical, financial, and psychological harm—but it was not whistleblowing. Boisjoly was then serving his employer, not betraying a trust (even on the employer's understanding of that trust); he was calling his superiors' attention to what he thought they should take into account in their decision and not publicly revealing confidential information. The whistleblowing came after the explosion, in testimony before the Rogers Commission. By then, the seven astronauts were beyond help, the shuttle program was suspended, and any further threat of physical, financial, or psychological harm to the "public" was—after discounting for time—negligible. Boisjoly had little reason to believe his testimony would make a significant difference in the booster's redesign, in safety procedures in the shuttle program, or even in reawakening concern for safety among NASA employees and contractors. The *Challenger*'s explosion was much more likely to do that than anything Boisjoly could do. What Boisjoly could do in his testimony, what I think he tried to do, was prevent falsification of the record.

Falsification of the record is, of course, harm in a sense, especially a record as historically important as that which the Rogers Commission was to produce. But falsification is harm only in a sense that almost empties "harm" of its distinctive meaning, leaving it more or less equivalent to "moral wrong." The proponents of the standard theory mean more by "harm" than that. De George, for example, explicitly says that a threat justifying whistleblowing must be to "life or health."[4] The standard theory is strikingly more narrow in its grounds of justification than many examples of justified whistleblowing suggest it should be. That is the second paradox, the "paradox of missing harm."

The third paradox is related to the second. Insofar as whistleblowers are understood as people out to prevent harm, not just to prevent moral wrong, their chances of success are not good. Whistleblowers generally do not prevent much harm. In this too, Boisjoly is typical. As he has said many times, the situation at Thiokol is now much as it was before the disaster. Insofar as we can identify cause and effect, even now we have little reason to believe that—whatever his actual intention—Boisjoly's testimony actually prevented any harm (beyond the moral harm of falsification). So, if whistleblowers must have, as the standard theory says, (S5), (beyond the moral wrong of falsification) "good reason to believe that revealing the threat will (probably) prevent the harm," then the history of whistleblowing virtually rules out the moral justification of whistleblowing. That is certainly paradoxical in a theory purporting to state sufficient conditions for the central cases of justified whistleblowing. Let us call this "the paradox of failure."

A COMPLICITY THEORY

As I look down the roll of whistleblowers, I do not see anyone who, like the clerk from Accounts, just happened upon key documents in a cover-up.[5] Few, if any, whistleblowers are mere third-parties like the good Samaritan. They are generally deeply involved in the activity they reveal. This involvement suggests that we might better understand what justifies (most) whistleblowing if we understand the whistleblower's obligation to derive from *complicity* in wrongdoing rather than from the ability to prevent harm.

Any complicity theory of justified whistleblowing has two obvious advantages over the standard theory. One is that (moral) complicity itself presupposes (moral) wrongdoing, not harm. So, a complicity justification automatically avoids the paradox of missing harm, fitting the facts of whistleblowing better than a theory which, like the standard one, emphasizes prevention of harm.

That is one obvious advantage of a complicity theory. The second advantage is that complicity invokes a more demanding obligation than the ability to prevent harm does. We are morally obliged to avoid doing moral wrongs. When, despite our best efforts, we nonetheless find ourselves engaged in some wrong, we have an obligation to do what we reasonably can to set things right. If, for example, I cause a traffic accident, I have a moral (and legal) obligation to call help, stay at the scene until help arrives, and render first aid (if I know how), even at substantial cost to myself and those to whom I owe my time, and even with little likelihood that anything I do will help much. Just as a complicity theory avoids the paradox of missing harm, it also avoids the paradox of burden.

What about the third paradox, the paradox of failure? I shall come to that, but only after remedying one disadvantage of the complicity theory. That disadvantage is obvious—we do not yet have such a theory, not even a sketch. Here, then, is the place to offer a sketch of such a theory.

Complicity Theory   You are morally required to reveal what you know to the public (or to a suitable agent or representative of it) when:

(C1) what you will reveal derives from your work for an organization;

(C2) you are a voluntary member of that organization;

(C3) you believe that the organization, though legitimate, is engaged in serious moral wrongdoing;

(C4) you believe that your work for that organization will contribute (more or less directly) to the wrong if (but *not* only if) you do not publicly reveal what you know;

(C5) you are justified in beliefs C3 and C4; and

(C6) beliefs C3 and C4 are true.

The complicity theory differs from the standard theory in several ways worth pointing out here. The first is that, according to C1, what the whistleblower reveals must derive from his work for the organization. This condition distinguishes the whistleblower from the spy (and the clerk in Accounts). The spy seeks out information in order to reveal it; the whistleblower learns it as a proper part of doing the job the organization has assigned him. The standard theory, in contrast, has nothing to say about how the whistleblower comes to know of the threat she reveals (S2). For the standard theory, spies are just another kind of whistleblower.

A second way in which the complicity theory differs from the standard theory is that the complicity theory (C2) explicitly requires the whistleblower to be a *voluntary* participant in the organization in question. Whistleblowing is not—according to the complicity theory—an activity in which slaves, prisoners, or other involuntary participants in an organization engage. In this way, the complicity theory makes explicit something implicit in the standard theory. The whistleblowers of the standard theory are generally "employees." Employees are voluntary participants in the organization employing them.

What explains this difference in explicitness? For the Samaritanism of the standard theory, the voluntariness of employment is extrinsic. What is crucial is the ability to prevent harm. For the complicity theory, however, the voluntariness is crucial. The obligations deriving from complicity seem to vary with the voluntariness of our participation in

the wrongdoing. Consider, for example, a teller who helps a gang rob her bank because they have threatened to kill her if she does not; she does not have the same obligation to break off her association with the gang as someone who has freely joined it. The voluntariness of employment means that the would-be whistleblower's complicity will be more like that of one of the gang than like that of the conscripted teller.

A third way in which the complicity theory differs from the standard theory is that the complicity theory (C3) requires moral wrong, not harm, for justification. The wrong need not be a new event (as a harm must be if it is to be *prevented*). It might, for example, consist in no more than silence about facts necessary to correct a serious injustice.

The complicity theory (C3) does, however, follow the standard theory in requiring that the predicate of whistleblowing be "serious." Under the complicity theory, minor wrongdoing can no more justify whistleblowing than can minor harm under the standard theory. While organizational loyalty cannot forbid whistleblowing, it does forbid "tattling," that is, revealing minor wrongdoing.

A fourth way in which the complicity theory differs from the standard theory, the most important, is that the complicity theory (C4) requires that the whistleblower believe that her work will have contributed to the wrong in question if she does nothing, but it does *not* require that she believe that her revelation will prevent (or undo) the wrong. The complicity theory does not require any belief about what the whistleblowing can accomplish (beyond ending complicity in the wrong in question). The whistleblower reveals what she knows in order to prevent complicity in the wrong, not to prevent the wrong as such. She can prevent complicity (if there is any to prevent) simply by publicly revealing what she knows. The revelation itself breaks the bond of complicity, the secret partnership in wrongdoing, that makes her an accomplice in her organization's wrongdoing. The complicity theory thus avoids the third paradox, the paradox of failure, just as it avoided the other two.

The fifth difference between the complicity theory and the standard theory is closely related to the fourth. Because publicly revealing what one knows breaks the bond of complicity, the complicity theory does not require the whistleblower to have enough evidence to convince others of the wrong in question. Convincing others, or just being able to convince them, is not, as such, an element in the justification of whistleblowing.

The complicity theory does, however, require (C5) that the whistleblower be (epistemically) justified in believing both that his organization is engaged in wrongdoing and that he will contribute to that wrong unless he blows the whistle. Such (epistemic) justification may require substantial physical evidence (as the standard theory says) or just a good sense of how things work. The complicity theory does not share the standard theory's substantial evidential demand (S4).

In one respect, however, the complicity theory clearly requires more of the whistleblower than the standard theory does. The complicity theory's C6—combined with C5—requires not only that the whistleblower be *justified* in her beliefs about the organization's wrongdoing and her part in it, but also that she be *right* about them. If she is wrong about either the wrongdoing or her complicity, her revelation will not be justified whistleblowing. This consequence of C6 is, I think, not as surprising as it may seem. If the would-be whistleblower is wrong only about her own complicity, her revelation of actual wrongdoing will, being otherwise justified, merely fail to be justified *as whistleblowing* (much as a failed rescue, though justified as an attempt, cannot be justified as a rescue). If, however, she is wrong about the wrongdoing itself, her situation is more serious. Her belief that wrong is being done, though fully justified on the evidence available to her, cannot justify her disloyalty. All her justified belief can do is *excuse* her disloyalty. Insofar as she acted with good intentions and while exercising reasonable care, she is a victim of bad luck. Such bad luck will leave her with an obligation to apologize, to correct the record (for example, by publicly recanting the charges she publicly made), and otherwise to set things right.

The complicity theory says nothing on at least one matter about which the standard theory says much—going through channels before publicly revealing what one knows. But the two theories do not differ as much as this difference in emphasis suggests. If going through channels would suffice to prevent (or undo) the wrong, then it cannot be true (as C4 and C6 together require) that the would-be whistleblower's work will contribute to the wrong if she does not publicly reveal what she knows. Where, however, going through channels would *not* prevent (or undo) the wrong, there is no need to go through channels. Condition C4's if-clause will be satisfied. For the complicity theory, going through channels is a way of finding out what the organization will do, not an independent requirement of justification . . . .

A last difference between the two theories worth mention here is that the complicity theory is only a theory of morally required whistleblowing while the standard theory claims as well to define circumstances when whistleblowing is morally permissible but not morally required. This difference is another advantage that the complicity theory has over the standard theory. The standard theory, as we saw, has trouble making good on its claim to explain how whistleblowing can be morally permissible without being morally required.

TESTING THE THEORY

Let us now test the theory against Boisjoly's testimony before the Rogers Commission. Recall that under the standard theory any justification of that testimony seemed to fail for at least three reasons: First, Boisjoly could not testify without substantial cost to himself and Thiokol (to whom he owed loyalty). Second, there was no serious and substantial harm his testimony could prevent. And, third, he had little reason to believe that, even if he could identify a serious and considerable harm to prevent, his testimony had a significant chance of preventing it.

Since few doubt that Boisjoly's testimony before the Rogers Commission constitutes justified whistleblowing, if anything does, we should welcome a theory that—unlike the standard one—justifies that testimony as whistleblowing. The complicity theory sketched above does that:

(C1) Boisjoly's testimony consisted almost entirely of information derived from his work on booster rockets at Thiokol.

(C2) Boisjoly was a voluntary member of Thiokol.

(C3) Boisjoly believed Thiokol, a legitimate organization, was attempting to mislead its client, the government, about the causes of a deadly accident. Attempting to do that certainly seems a serious moral wrong.

(C4) On the evening before the *Challenger* exploded, Boisjoly gave up objecting to the launch once his superiors, including the three Thiokol vice presidents, had made it clear that they were no longer willing to listen to him. He also had a part in preparing those superiors to testify intelligently before the Rogers Commission concerning the booster's fatal field joint. Boisjoly believed that Thiokol would use his failure to offer his own interpretation of his retreat into silence the night before the launch, and the knowledge that he had imparted to his superiors, to contribute to the attempt to mislead Thiokol's client.

(C5) The evidence justifying beliefs C3 and C4 consisted of comments of various officers of Thiokol, what Boisjoly had seen at Thiokol over the years, and what he learned about the rocket business over a long career. I find this evidence sufficient to justify his belief both that his organization was engaged in wrongdoing and that his work was implicated.

(C6) Here we reach a paradox of *knowledge*. Since belief is knowledge if, but only if, it is *both* justified *and* true, we cannot *show* that we know anything. All we can show is that a belief is now justified and that we have no reason to expect anything to turn up later to prove it false. The evidence now available still justifies Boisjoly's belief both about what Thiokol was attempting and about what would have been his part in the attempt. Since new evidence is unlikely, his testimony seems to satisfy C6 just as it satisfied the complicity theory's other five conditions.

Since the complicity theory explains why Boisjoly's testimony before the Rogers Commission was morally required whistleblowing, it has passed its first test, a test the standard theory failed.

Notes

1. Throughout this essay, I take the standard theory to be Richard T. De George's version in *Business Ethics*, 3rd Edition (New York: Macmillan, 1990), pp. 200–214 (amended only insofar as necessary to include non-businesses as well as businesses). Why treat De George's theory as standard? There are two reasons: first, it seems the most commonly cited; and second, people offering alternatives generally treat it as the one to be replaced. The only obvious competitor, Norman Bowie's account, is distinguishable from De George's on no point relevant here. See Bowie's *Business Ethics* (Englewood Cliffs, NJ: Prentice Hall, 1982), p. 143.

2. De George, *op. cit* . . . .

3. Indeed, I am tempted to go further and claim that, where an informant takes little or no risk, we are unlikely to describe her as a whistleblower at all. So, for example, I would say that using an internal or external "hot-line" is whistleblowing only when it is risky. We are, in other words, likely to consider using a hot-line as disloyalty (that is, as "going out of channels") only if the organization (or some part of it) is likely to respond with considerable hostility to its use.

4. De George, p. 210: "The notion of *serious* harm might be expanded to include serious financial harm, and kinds of harm other than death and serious threats to health and body. But as we noted earlier, we shall restrict ourselves here to products and practices that produce or threaten serious harm or danger to life and health."

5. See Myron Peretz Glazer and Penina Migdal Glazer, *The Whistleblowers: Exposing Corruption in Government and Industry* (New York: Basic Books, 1989) for a good list of whistleblowers (with detailed description of each); for an older list (with descriptions), see Alan F. Westin, *Whistleblowing! Loyalty and Dissent in the Corporation* (New York: McGraw-Hill, 1981).

Review and Discussion Questions

1. What makes whistleblowing morally problematic—that is, why does it need to be justified? According to Davis, why isn't the police officer, the criminal informant, or the clerk who happens upon evidence of wrongdoing in another department a whistleblower?

2. According to the standard theory, when is whistleblowing morally permissible and when is it morally required? Do you see any problems with conditions S1 through S5?

3. Explain the three paradoxes that Davis claims the standard theory gives rise to. If you were a defender of the standard theory, how might you respond to Davis's arguments?

4. Explain Davis's complicity theory. What are the most important differences between it and the standard theory? Is Davis's theory of justified whistleblowing an improvement over the standard theory? Explain why or why not.

5. Does the example of Roger Boisjoly fit the complicity theory better than it does the standard theory? If it does, is that a good argument for the complicity theory? Can you think of any examples of whistleblowing that favour the standard theory over the complicity theory?

6. Are there any aspects of whistleblowing that Davis's theory neglects or fails to do full justice to?

Further Reading for Chapter 8

Sissela Bok, *Secrets* (New York: Vintage, 1983) includes insightful writing on trade secrets and patents in Chapter 10 and on whistleblowing in Chapter 14.

Thomas L. Carson, "Conflicts of Interest," *Journal of Business Ethics*, May 1994, analyzes the concept and discusses the wrongness of conflicts of interest. Also useful is **Michael Davis**, "Conflict of Interest Revisited," *Business and Professional Ethics Journal* 12 (Winter 1993).

Natalie Dandekar, "Can Whistle-Blowing Be Fully Legitimated? A Theoretical Discussion," *Business and Professional Ethics Journal* 10 (Fall 1990).

Tibor Machan, "What Is Morally Right with Insider Trading," *Public Affairs Quarterly* 10 (April 1996) is a succinct libertarian defence of insider trading.

Mike W. Martin, "Whistleblowing: Professionalism, Personal Life, and Shared Responsibility for Safety in Engineering," *Business and Professional Ethics Journal* 11 (Summer 1992), and **C. Fred Alford**, "Whistleblowers and the Narrative of Ethics," *Journal of Social Philosophy* 32 (Fall 2001) are good studies of the moral complexity of whistleblowing.

Brian Schrag, "The Moral Significance of Employee Loyalty," *Business Ethics Quarterly* 11 (January 2001) discusses the meaning of loyalty and whether it is good for either the employee or the employer.

Martin Snoeyenbos, **Robert Almeder**, and **James Humber**, eds., *Business Ethics*, 3rd ed. (Buffalo: Prometheus, 2001), part 3, provides essays and cases on conflict of interest, gifts and payoffs, patents, and trade secrets.

9

Job Discrimination

Discrimination against persons raises its ugly head in every aspect of our society. People may experience discrimination in education, in health care, in the justice system, in their dealings with civil servants or the police, or in their ordinary dealings with fellow citizens. Discrimination issues are complex and take different forms in different contexts, including different cultural-social contexts, though ultimately the underlying philosophical-ethical issues are the same. Here we are going to concentrate on discrimination in the Canadian workplace.[1]

The *Canadian Human Rights Act* (1977) prohibits discrimination on the basis of race, national or ethnic origin, colour, religion, age, sex, sexual orientation, marital status, family status, disability, and criminal conviction for which a pardon has been granted. The *Charter of Rights and Freedoms* (1982)—along with some Supreme Court decisions—guarantees constitutionally the right of all people in Canada not to be discriminated against on such grounds. However, for just over a generation now the federal government, in cooperation with business, labour unions, non-government organizations and provincial governments, has been trying to improve conditions in employment opportunities for four specific groups of people who have traditionally been subject to discrimination in our country: Aboriginal peoples (First Nations, Métis, and Inuit), women, visible minorities, and persons with disabilities. In 1986 the federal *Employment Equity Act* came into force whose provisions require employers to take positive measures to improve the employment opportunities of the four groups listed above. In order to set this progressive legislation in its proper context, it will help to review, ever so briefly, the history of institutional discrimination against the four groups it covers.

1. *Women.* The history of the contact between men and women is of course much too long for our brief outline. One irony in this case is that the discriminated group constitutes and, in all probability, has constituted from time immemorial not a minority but the majority of humankind. Another tragic irony is that the discriminated group

was, by and large, not forced into their position of servitude to men but they themselves piously accepted it through a long process of enculturation. As far as the lot of women in Canada is concerned, suffice it to say that: women (but not Aboriginal women) were granted the right to vote in federal elections only in 1918, and even then it was not a right enjoyed by all women across Canada until 1940 (since the *Dominion Elections Act* of 1900 allowed persons to vote federally only if they had the legal right to vote provincially, and a lot of provinces had not yet given women the right to vote in provincial elections); it was only in 1928 that women were accepted as "qualified persons" to be named to the Senate, as stipulated in article 24 of the *British North America Act* (1867), despite the fact that they might have satisfied all the qualifications stipulated under article 23; women were not allowed to be jurors in Québec until 1971, and it would take another year for the federal government to abolish sex discrimination against potential jurors in criminal cases; women were not allowed into the RCMP until 1974; Canada did not get its first female coeducational university president (Pauline Jewett) or Governor-General (Jeanne Sauvé) or Chief Justice of the Supreme Court (Beverley McLachlin) or leader of a federal political party (Audrey McLaughlin) until 1973, 1984, 1989, and 1999 respectively.[2]

2. *Aboriginal peoples.* On the whole, and especially after the *Royal Proclamation of 1763*, the history of the contacts between the Aboriginal peoples and the white European settlers details the white man's lies, broken promises, deception, exploitation, hypocritical piety, cultural jingoism, and use of brute force. From the 1850s on, every aspect of the life of Aboriginal peoples was regulated by a hodgepodge of legislative measures enacted by various levels of government. In 1876 the federal government consolidated all these different measures into the *Indian Act*, and this *Act*, though amended numerous times since, remains the legislative fountainhead of federal policy and practice regarding Aboriginal peoples.

For many Canadians, the *Indian Act* has not only retained its original name but is still animated by some of the assumptions that governed its first enactment 130 years ago: that Aboriginal peoples are inferior and incapable of governing themselves; that, hence, Aboriginal peoples need some one else *in loco parentis* who will decide what is good for them without their consent or their involvement in design or implementation; that the concept of personal or community development could and should be defined by non-Aboriginal values alone; and that treaties signed with Aboriginal peoples are not contracts of mutual trust that confer obligations and rights, but merely "memoranda of understanding which may be conveniently ignored." These assumptions were behind the practices of residential schools and of relocating entire Aboriginal communities,[3] not to mention the fact that the *Indian Act* invaded and regulated just about every aspect of the life of Aboriginal peoples, or the fact that Aboriginals did not get a clear, unqualified right to vote federally until 1960.[4]

3. *Visible minorities.* Most of us have heard of the black Loyalists who were given freedom and promised land grants on their coming into Canada during the American War of Independence, of Governor Simcoe's *Abolition Act*[5] of 1793, of the Osgoode decision[6] of 1803, of the black militia fighting on the side of the British in the War of 1812, of the "Underground Railroad," of William Hall, the first black and first Nova Scotian to win the Victoria Cross . . . . and other feel-good stories. But one may well wonder how many Canadians[7] know that of the land grants promised to black Loyalists, some never did materialize, some took years to materialize, and, when they did, they amounted on average to one-third those given to white Loyalists; that about 1,200 Blacks (around a quarter of all Blacks in Nova Scotia at the time), fed up with an unwelcoming Promised Land, embarked on four ships in 1792 and sailed to Africa and there founded the city of Freetown in Sierra Leone; that when he died in 1904, William Hall was buried in an unmarked grave without military honours; that in 1911 a federal order-in-council was prepared (but never proclaimed) that stipulated: "landing in Canada . . . is prohibited of any immigrants belonging to the Negro race, which is deemed unsuitable to the climate and the requirements of Canada." It is true that slavery became illegal in Canada in 1834, but it is also true that the last segregated school in Ontario closed down only in 1965.

Or consider the plight of Chinese people in Canada. During the last quarter of the nineteenth century, Chinese men (but not women) were allowed into Canada as labourers for the railroad construction projects going on at the time. But after such projects came to an end, so did Canada's willingness to allow in Chinese. The *Chinese Immigration Act* of 1885 made immigration into Canada not merely extremely difficult for Chinese immigrants but also profitable for the Canadian government, as it placed a head tax on all Chinese entering Canada.[8] The *Chinese Immigration Act* of 1923 (known among the Chinese as the "Chinese Exclusion Act") put an end to the head tax, but only because it banned Chinese immigrants, purely on racial grounds, from entering Canada unless they were diplomats, merchants, or foreign students. The 1923 *Act* was not repealed until 1947. But still, Chinese people wishing to enter the country were treated differently from other immigrants until 1967, when the Canadian government introduced the point system in the selection of immigrants.[9]

Around the turn of the twentieth century, small numbers of East Indians, predominantly Sikhs, were admitted to British Columbia in order to work in the mines, forestry, or the railroad. By 1907 there were no more than 3,500 East Indians in the entire province, but the popular press, under the influence of local politicians and labour organizers, was warning Canadians of a "Hindu invasion." After a 1907 riot in Vancouver against primarily Chinese and Japanese workers, the provincial and federal governments introduced anti-immigration measures that were aimed specifically at Chinese and Japanese workers but also encompassed East Indians, if only because the legislation required immigrants to take a "continuous" journey or passage from their country of origin or citizenship to Canada and also that they bear on them the amount of $200. Since no shipping company had a direct service from India to Canada at the time, or since few if any had that kind of money, East Indians found it impossible to satisfy the requirements. The irony in the sordid treatment of East Indian people is that at the time they were (and were led to believe they were) British subjects having equal rights with all the other subjects of the Empire. Well . . . apparently not in Canada.[10]

The underlying reasons for such treatment of all these visible minorities were partly connected to the view of many Anglo-European workers that East Indian, Chinese, or Japanese labourers were taking away jobs and pushing wages down. But a great deal of the hostility is attributable simply to racial prejudice. The Premier of British Columbia at the time, Sir Richard McBride, expressed a sentiment shared by a lot of his white contemporaries when he said, "To admit orientals in large numbers would mean in the end the extinction of the white peoples and we have always in mind the necessity of keeping this a white man's country."[11]

4. *Persons with disabilities.* One might say with some justice that as a group people with disabilities have no history, because, unlike women who were supposed to be seen but not heard, people with disabilities were, until relatively recently, neither seen nor heard. This applied to people with serious physical (missing limbs, in wheelchairs, blind, etc.) or mental (psychoses, severe depression, bipolar disorder, etc.) or developmental disabilities, who routinely either stayed or were kept at home, or were put in institutions. Social attitudes to people with disabilities in general have changed for the better, though one might wonder how much they have really changed apropos serious disabilities.[12] Serious or not, disability was involved in one-third of the discrimination complaints received by the Human Rights Commission between 1995 and 1998. Nowadays we are inclined to understand disability from what is often called the "functional perspective"; that is, we understand disability as a restriction in one's ability to perform certain standard tasks in a way considered "normal" (that the majority can do).[13] The "restriction" may be the result of one or more conditions or causes, be they physical (hearing impairment, chronic pain, paralysis, etc.), mental (certain phobias, depression, etc.) or developmental (mental retardation, etc.). From this perspective on disability, there were 3.6 million Canadians living with activity limitations in 2001. This represents a disability rate of 12.4 percent, a significant minority. More importantly for our purposes, among persons between the ages of 15 and 64 the disability rate was 9.9 percent, while among those between the ages of 64 and 75 the rate jumped to 31.2 percent.[14] These numbers are important, as the first rate concerns those in the active workforce, while the second refers to people who may be called back into the active workforce in view of the expected labour shortages or who may simply wish to continue working beyond the traditional age(s) of retirement (as more and more provinces introduce legislation to ban mandatory retirement).

Most people, of course, oppose racial or sexual bias and reject job discrimination as immoral. In fact, upon learning of the record of the treatment of minorities in the past, most people would surely condemn it as a sad chapter of our national history. However, explicit prejudice and overt discrimination are just part of the problem. Even open-minded people may operate on implicit assumptions that work to the disadvantage of the four groups in question, and many who nowadays believe themselves to be unprejudiced harbour unconscious racist or sexist attitudes. It is well, therefore, that whatever our avowed feelings and views might be, we bear in mind the past record and the attitudes underneath it as we explore the area of job discrimination. In particular, in this chapter we will examine the following topics:

1. The meaning of job discrimination and its different forms

2. The legislative and legal context of "employment equity" ("affirmative action")

3. The moral arguments for and against "employment equity"

4. The doctrine of comparable worth and the controversy over it

5. The problem of sexual harassment in employment—what it is, what forms it takes, what the law says about it, and why it's wrong

THE MEANING OF JOB DISCRIMINATION

In the morally significant sense of the term, for person P to "discriminate against" person P_2 means that: (i) P engages in behaviour "B" that treats P_2 in an adverse way, and (ii) P does "B" because P_2 has a certain characteristic "C," and (iii) "C" is irrelevant to P's doing "B." Examples of behaviour "B" would be P's eliminating P_2 from consideration for a job or a promotion, or P's excluding P_2 from the list of possible tenants or buyers of his or her house. Typically, characteristic "C" would be a feature of P_2 related to his or her gender or sexual orientation or race or looks etc. There are two points to be raised in connection with the definition given above. First, discriminatory behaviour in many cases, and certainly when it enters into employment issues, involves a third party, what some thinkers have called "beneficiaries" of discrimination. If P does not give the job to P_2 (because of discrimination), some other person, P_3, gets the job, who presumably, in the view of the discriminator, does not possess the characteristic "C" of being, say, gay, lesbian, black, Aboriginal, etc. This point, regarding "beneficiaries" of one's discriminatory behaviour, becomes important in discussions of so-called "affirmative action" programs in the employment of groups that have traditionally been discriminated against. The second point concerns part (ii) of the definition. For the adverse behaviour "B" to be "discriminatory," P must do it *because* P_2 has the characteristic "C"; that is, P *intentionally* singles out P_2 for adverse treatment because P_2 is black or gay or Seventh Day Adventist or what have you.

Like discrimination in general, job discrimination can take different forms. It can be individual or institutional, and it can be either intentional or unwitting. Individuals, for instance, sometimes intentionally discriminate out of personal prejudice or on the basis of stereotypes. For example, a manager may purposely disregard job applications from women because he believes that they "should be home taking care of their husbands and children." On the other hand, individuals may discriminate because they unthinkingly or unconsciously accept traditional practices or stereotypes. For example, suppose that the merit-pay recommendations of a manager are influenced by his implicit assumption that male employees are career-oriented and have families to support, whereas female employees are there just to make a little extra money. If the manager were unaware that this bias affects his decisions, his actions would fall into this category.

Job discrimination may also occur at the institutional level. Sometimes institutions do so explicitly and intentionally—for example, employment agencies that screen out Blacks, Latinos, older workers, and others at the request of their corporate customers. On the other hand, the routine operating procedures of a company or an organization may reflect stereotypes and prejudiced practices that it is not fully aware of. For example, for years the FBI routinely transferred its Hispanic agents around the United States on temporary, low-level assignments where knowledge of Spanish was needed; the agents functioned as little more than assistants to their non-Hispanic colleagues. Hispanic agents dubbed this the "taco circuit" and claimed it adversely affected their opportunities for promotion. A U.S. federal court agreed with them that the practice was indeed discriminatory.[15] In addition, institutional practices that appear neutral and nondiscriminatory may harm members of groups that are traditionally discriminated against. The requirement that RCMP officers wear the Stetson hat was, on the face of it, neutral until the early 1990s when it threatened the job of RCMP Constable Dhillon who refused to wear it in place of his Sikh's turban. Again, when USAir had a special backdoor hiring channel for pilots recommended by employees or friends of the company, only white pilots were ever hired this way.[16] So, although an institutional policy may look neutral and may thus not involve job discrimination in the narrow sense, it may nevertheless work to the disadvantage of minority groups, denying them full equality of opportunity.

From the moral point of view, only intentional and direct discrimination is morally culpable. There are compelling moral arguments, from a variety of moral perspectives, against direct job discrimination on racial, sexual, or disability grounds. Since such discrimination involves false assumptions about the inferiority of a certain group and harms individual members of that group, utilitarians would reject it because of its ill effects on total human welfare. Kantians would clearly repudiate it, since it fails to respect people as ends in themselves. Universalizing the maxim underlying discriminatory practices is virtually impossible. No people who now discriminate would be willing to accept such treatment themselves. Discrimination on grounds of sex, race, age, etc. also violates people's basic moral rights and mocks the ideal of human moral equality. Furthermore, such discrimination is unjust. To use Rawls's theory as an illustration, parties in the original position would clearly choose for themselves the principle of equal opportunity. From a practical point of view, discrimination denies people a job or a position or a promotion or an award they may well deserve more than the persons who actually got it. The discriminator denies a person a job or a promotion not because the applicant failed to meet criteria relevant to the performance of the job, but because she or he failed to meet the discriminator's perceptions or feelings regarding the applicant's colour, gender, ethnic background, etc., which are irrelevant to the job.

However, one may still be held morally culpable if the adverse effects of one's unintentional discriminatory behaviour were foreseeable by a "reasonable" person, or were made known but not rectified. In fact, it is debatable whether the distinction between "unintentional" and "intentional" discrimination is ultimately tenable, since determining motives is notoriously difficult. Indeed, from the point of view of social and political programs aimed at promoting substantive equality among all citizens by eliminating discrimination, the distinction between intentional and "adverse effect" discrimination is irrelevant. This is the view suggested by Judge Rosalie Abella in "Equality in Employment," excerpts from which are reproduced in one of the readings for this chapter. It is also the view of the Supreme Court of Canada in *Ont.*

Human Rights Commission v. Simpson's-Sears Ltd. [1985] 2 S.C.R. 536:

> An employment rule, honestly made for sound economic and business reasons and equally applicable to all to whom it is intended to apply, may nevertheless be discriminatory if it affects a person or persons differently from others to whom it is intended to apply. The intent to discriminate is not a governing factor in construing human rights legislation aimed at eliminating discrimination. Rather, it is the result or effect of the alleged discriminatory action that is significant.[17]

"EMPLOYMENT EQUITY"

Concerned about the slow progress in the "employability and productivity of women, Native people, disabled persons and visible minorities," the federal government appointed in 1980 a Royal Commission to look into the problem. The single member of the Commission, Judge (now Puisne Judge of the Supreme Court) Rosalie Silberman Abella, produced her report in 1984. Among other things, the report suggested that we concentrate our attention on "systemic discrimination," that is, on the "unjustifiably negative effect on certain groups in society" of "the systems and practices we customarily and often unwittingly adopt." Systemic discrimination in the workplace produces high unemployment rates, lower-than-average salaries, and concentrations in low-status jobs for the affected groups. In order to remedy "systemic discrimination," the report recommended that we adopt a particular systemic measure, similar to the American "preferential treatment," but which it called "employment equity." "Employment equity" does not refer simply to the equality of opportunity in employment that comes about when we treat people the same despite their differences, but also to that equality in opportunity that comes about when we treat people as equals by accommodating their differences. "Employment equity" requires that we not only eliminate discrimination but also overcome barriers in employment that unjustifiably prevent the affected groups from participating equally in employment.

The Abella report formed the basis for the federal *Employment Equity Act* of 1986, later amended as the *Employment Equity Act* of 1995. It is to be noted that the Act applies only to the four specified groups it covers. Individuals not in those groups are protected against employment discrimination under the *Canadian Human Rights Act* (1985, s. 7–10).

The purpose of the *Employment Equity Act* (1995, s. 2) is

> to achieve equality in the workplace so that no person shall be denied employment opportunities or benefits for reasons unrelated to ability and, in the fulfilment of that goal, to correct the conditions of disadvantage in employment experienced by women, aboriginal peoples, persons with disabilities and members of

visible minorities by giving effect to the principle that employment equity means more than treating persons in the same way but also requires special measures and the accommodation of differences.

To this effect, every employer must identify and eliminate employment barriers that "result from the employer's employment systems, policies and practices that are not authorized by law." In addition, employers must institute "such positive policies and practices and making such reasonable accommodations as will ensure that persons in designated groups achieve a degree of representation in each occupational group in the employer's workforce that reflects their representation" in the "Canadian workforce, or those segments of the Canadian workforce that are identifiable by qualification, eligibility or geography and from which the employer may reasonably be expected to draw employees." However, in implementing employment equity, employers are not required to take any measure "where the taking of that measure would cause undue hardship to the employer"; nor are they required to hire or promote persons who "do not meet the essential qualifications for the work to be performed."[18] In determining the limits of an employer's capacity to "accommodate" an employee from the designated groups, the Act simply states "up to the point of undue hardship." This means presumably that an employer is not expected to provide accommodation if doing so would bring about unreasonable difficulties based on health, safety, or financial considerations. The concept of "undue hardship" in unclear, and there is no standard formula for determining what amounts to undue hardship. Each case should be assessed individually, and in time case law will establish some principles for employers to follow.

EMPLOYMENT EQUITY: A GENERATION LATER

If the members of a group have higher unemployment rates, have lower levels of income, and tend to cluster in jobs with lower occupational status, there is every chance the group is subject to job discrimination. If one goes by these "social indicators" of systemic discrimination in employment, the four groups covered by the Employment Equity Act are currently doing, on the whole, much better than a generation ago. Still, the progress is not enviable.

There is currently a much higher participation of women in the workforce. In 1976, 42 percent of all women aged 15 and over were part of the workforce. By 2004 that percentage had gone up to 58 percent. As a result, women accounted for 47 percent of the employed workforce in 2004, up from 37 percent in 1976. Partly because of the increased participation, women have higher profiles in many professional fields (especially the health care and education fields) now than they did thirty years ago. Women have also done relatively well in nontraditional occupations of management and the professions. Their participation in these sectors has risen by 93 percent since 1980 (okay, but 93 percent of what?). They

have also had a great deal of success in the federal public service sector. By March 2005, the representation of women in the federal public service was 1.3 percentage points higher than their workforce availability (they made up 53.5 percent of the federal public service, as against 52.2 percent of their workforce availability).[19]

While in 1980 women earned on average about 51.8 percent of the average earnings for men, by 2005 the ratio had gone up to 64 percent. That's not anything to write to mother about, but it is an improvement. Further, despite the overall improvement, certain subgroups of women are not doing well at all. The percentage of Aboriginal women living in poverty is more than double the percentage of non-Aboriginal women who are poor. At the time of the 2001 Census, based on before-tax incomes, more than 36 percent of Aboriginal women and 29 percent of visible minority women were living in poverty, as compared with 17 percent of non-Aboriginal women. While the poverty rate for all foreign-born women was 23 percent, women who immigrated to Canada between 1991 and 2000 had a poverty rate of 35 percent.[20] The significant point about this particular cohort is that the majority was also from visible minority groups, and it is suspected that job discrimination might be an important contributing factor to their predicament.

According to a 2005 annual report of Human Resources and Social Development Canada, in the period 1987 to 2004 members of visible minority groups have almost tripled their participation in the various private sectors of employment covered by the Employment Equity Act, with the result that in 2004 they made up 13.3 percent of the workforce in all relevant sectors of the economy.[21] This seems to fit very well with the representation targets set by the Act, given that, in 2001, 13 percent of the population (not of the workforce) identified themselves as belonging to a visible minority group as defined in the Employment Equity Act.[22] However, visible minorities have not done nearly as well in the federal public service sector, where they are still seriously underrepresented. As of June 2006 their representation was 2.3 percentage points lower than their workforce availability (8.1 percent of the federal public service, as against 10.4 percent of their workforce availability). Also, visible minorities have not done well in the Greater Toronto Area where they constitute 37 percent of the population (according to the 2001 Census).[23]

In general, according to a survey conducted in 2002, about 20 percent of self-identified members of visible minorities indicated that they had experienced discrimination or unfair treatment either "sometimes" or "often" in the previous five years, because of their ethnicity, culture, race, skin colour, language, accent, or religion. An additional 15 percent of visible minorities reported such treatment occurring "rarely." Experiences of discrimination in general were reported by 50 percent of Blacks, 43 percent of Japanese, and 35 percent of South Asians. The most frequently cited location of discrimination was the workplace or when applying for a job. Second-generation visible minority members who were born in Canada to immigrant parents reported a much higher incidence of discriminatory experience than did second-generation non-visible minorities. Of the people who did not identify as a visible minority, only 5 percent said that they had experienced discrimination or unfair treatment "sometimes" or "often," because of their ethnicity, culture, race, skin colour, language, accent, or religion. In addition, another 5 percent of non-visible minorities said that this had occurred "rarely."[24]

Aboriginal peoples have done fairly well in the federal public service where, as of 2005, they were at +1.7 percent of their workforce availability (4.2 percent of the federal public service, as against 2.5 percent of their workforce availability). Their situation vis-à-vis the private sector under the *Act* has improved, but slowly, and their level of participation in this workforce is still not anywhere near the level of their availability in the Canadian workforce. Their representation in the workforce reached 65.4 percent of their labour market availability in 2002. They are significantly underrepresented in ten occupations (below 80 percent of availability), and severely underrepresented in one occupation, namely, senior management, at 32.0 percent of their labour market availability. The conditions for Aboriginal peoples in western Canada are crucial, since most of the off-reserve Aboriginal people live in Western Canada. Statistics Canada reports improvement in their participation in private sector employment, especially in Alberta. One very encouraging feature of the picture in the west is that Aboriginal people with a university degree had an employment rate of 84 percent in 2005, in contrast to 77 percent among the non-Aboriginal population. Still, Aboriginal youths (18–24 years of age) have difficulties entering the workforce, and in general Aboriginal peoples have more than double the unemployment rates for non-Aboriginal people.[25]

Despite very slow progress in the 1990s, persons with disabilities have done very well in the federal public service. As of 2005, people with disabilities were at +2.2 percent (5.8 percent of the federal public service, in contrast to 3.6 percent workforce availability). They have also done well within this sector in terms of executive positions and promotions. On the whole, however, people with disabilities do not seem to have made very much progress over the last generation. Their unemployment rate ranges from three to ten times higher (across all age groups) than that of people without disabilities, while their average and median earnings are at 72 and 64 percent of the average and median earnings of the people without disabilities. Further, the situation of women and Aboriginal people with disabilities is especially bad, even by comparison to that of other women and Aboriginals.[26] There have certainly been improvements in the lot of the four designated groups over the past thirty years, though it is hard to determine whether it has come about as the direct result of the *Employment Equity Act*. Take the considerable improvement in the lot of women. One may well be tempted to think that demographics and market forces had more to do with it than anything else. For example,

there are just a lot more women now in the workforce and more women than men obtain university degrees nowadays. They would thus be more likely to get employment in a wider range of sectors, since the possession of a degree or diploma is now almost a standard requirement of all jobs other than low-status ones (with low wages). Again, the improvement in the employment prospects of Aboriginal peoples in the west may well be the result of the pressures exerted on the marketplace by the shortage of labour. Still, the *Act* seems to have helped a great deal in relation to the sectors it covers, even though, contrary to what one might have expected, the private sector covered by it has performed much better than governmental agencies and departments. The general progress, however, is slow, and the four designated groups still bear the brunt of poverty in our country.

EMPLOYMENT EQUITY: THE MORAL ISSUES

The ever-evolving legislative or legal positions on employment equity are of course important, since they set the context in which business operates and let employers know what they are and are not legally permitted to do. But these positions by themselves do not exhaust the relevant moral issues. Employers—as well as women, minorities, and white men—want to know whether the programs and practices carried out in the name of employment equity are morally right. Indeed, part of the rationale underpinning legislative and judicial decisions is surely influenced not just by technical issues in the management of human resources or in jurisprudence but also by how politicians and judges answer this moral question.

Before evaluating arguments for and against employment equity, one needs to know what is being debated. "Employment equity" here means programs taking the race or sex of employees or job candidates into account as part of an effort to correct imbalances in employment that exist as a result of past discrimination, either in the particular employment sector itself or in the larger society. Bear in mind that employment equity excludes programs that establish quotas or that hire and promote unqualified persons. However, it may allow programs that hire or promote a woman or a Black or an Aboriginal person who might not otherwise be, according to already established and, presumably, fair criteria, the best-qualified candidate.

Arguments for Employment Equity

1. *Compensatory Justice Demands Employment Equity Programs.*

Point. "As groups, women and minorities have historically been discriminated against, often viciously. As individuals and as a nation, we can't ignore the sins of our fathers and mothers. In fact, we have an obligation to do something to help repair the wrongs of the past. Employment equity is one sound way to do this."

Counterpoint. "People today can't be expected to atone for the sins of the past. We're not responsible for them, and in any case, we wouldn't be compensating those who rightly deserve it. Young Blacks or women coming now for their first job have never suffered employment discrimination. Their parents and grandparents may deserve compensation, but why should today's candidates receive any special consideration? No one should discriminate against them, of course, but they should have to compete openly and on their merits, just like everybody else."

2. *Employment Equity Is Necessary to Permit Fairer Competition.*

Point. "Even if young Aboriginal persons or women today have not themselves suffered job discrimination, Aboriginal peoples in particular have suffered all the disadvantages of growing up in families that have been affected by discrimination. In our racist society, they have suffered from inferior schools and poor environment. In addition, as victims of society's prejudiced attitudes, young Aboriginals and young women have been hampered by a lack of self-confidence and self-respect. Taking race and sex into account makes job competition fairer by keeping white men from having a competitive edge that they don't really deserve."

Counterpoint. "Your point is better when applied to Aboriginals than to women, it seems to me, but I'm still not persuaded. You overlook the fact that there are a lot of disadvantaged whites out there, too. Is an employer going to have to investigate everyone's life history to see who had to overcome the most obstacles? I think an employer has a right to seek the best-qualified candidate without trying to make life fair for everybody. And isn't the best-qualified person entitled to get the job or the promotion?"

3. *Employment Equity Is Necessary to Break the Cycle That Keeps Minorities and Women Locked into Low-Paying, Low-Prestige Jobs.*

Point. "You advocate neutral, non-discriminatory employment practices, as if we could just ignore our whole history of racial and sexual discrimination. Statistics show that Aboriginal peoples and visible minorities in particular have been trapped in a socioeconomically subordinate position. If we want to break that pattern and eventually heal the racial rifts in our country, we've got to adopt vigorous employment equity programs that allow more of these minorities into middle-class jobs. Even assuming racism was dead in our society, with mere nondiscrimination alone it would take a hundred years or more for some minorities to equalize their position."

Counterpoint. "You ignore the fact that employment equity has its costs, too. You talk about healing the racial rifts in our country, but employment equity programs make everybody more racially conscious. They also cause resentment and frustration among white men. Many members of the minority groups themselves resent being advanced on grounds that may appear not to be based on merit."

Arguments Against Employment Equity

1. *Employment Equity Injures White Men and Violates Their Rights.*

Point. "Even moderate employment equity programs injure the white men who are made to bear their brunt. Other people design the programs, but it is specific white males who find their career opportunities hampered. Moreover, such programs violate the right of white men to be treated as individuals and to have racial or sexual considerations not affect employment decisions."

Counterpoint. "I'm not sure that white males have the rights you are talking about. Racial and sexual considerations are often relevant to employment decisions. Jobs, especially in lucrative positions, are scarce resources, and society may distribute these in a way that furthers its legitimate ends—like breaking the cycle of poverty for minorities. I admit that with employment equity programs white men do not have as many advantages as they did before, and I'm against extreme programs that disregard their interests altogether. But their interests have to be balanced against society's interest in promoting these programs."

2. *Employment Equity Itself Violates the Principle of Equality.*

Point. "Employment equity programs are intended to enhance racial and sexual equality, but you can't do that by treating people unequally. If equality is the goal, it must be the means, too. With employment equity programs, you use racial and sexual considerations—but that is the very thing that has caused so much harm in the past and that employment equity itself is hoping to get rid of."

Counterpoint. "First, I admit that it would be distasteful to have to take racial or sexual considerations into account when dealing with individuals in employment situations. I would not wish to be in a position to have to do so. However, it is unfortunately true that in the real world racial or sexual factors go a long way toward determining an individual's life prospects. We can't wish that reality away by pretending the world is colour- or gender-blind when it is not. Formal, colour- or gender-blind equality might have to be infringed if we are ever to achieve real, meaningful racial and sexual equality. Second, in any case, employment equity does not require that we base our decisions on racial or gender considerations independently of issues of qualification. It rather requires us to ask of any particular qualification whether it is a genuine Bona Fide Occupational Requirement and, if it is, whether it is set at a level that arbitrarily or unnecessarily or unjustifiably excludes particular groups of prospective employees."

3. *Nondiscrimination Will Achieve Our Social Goals; Stronger Employment Equity Is Unnecessary.*

Point. "The *Canadian Human Rights Act* unequivocally outlaws job discrimination, and numerous employees and job candidates have won discrimination cases before the

Canadian Human Rights Commission or in the courts. We need to insist on rigorous enforcement of the law. Also, employers should continue to recruit in a way that attracts minority applicants and to make sure that their screening and review practices do not involve any implicit racist or sexist assumptions. And they should monitor their internal procedures and the behaviour of their white male employees to root out any discriminatory behaviour. Stronger employment equity programs or what I call 'affirmative action' measures, in particular taking race or sex into account in employment matters, are unnecessary. They only bring undesirable results."

Counterpoint. "Without what you call 'affirmative action' measures, progress often stops. The percentage of minorities and women employed by those sectors subject to the *Employment Equity Act* has risen much higher than it has elsewhere. Take the example of women. When Catalyst Canada began tracking representation of females on boards in 1997, women held only 8.2 percent of board positions in Fortune 500 companies. In 2006, that number had grown to about 12.5 percent. While this is an improvement, it is not all that good. Not only that, but some experts believe that the Catalyst percentages for 2006 may be too optimistic, and that the actual overall representation of women on executive boards of firms not covered by the *Act* is nearer 9 percent.[27] By contrast, women's share of positions in the executive group of the Canadian public service, which is covered by the *Act*, continues to increase. Women now occupy 38.8 percent of executive jobs, up from 25.1 percent in 1997."[28]

The debate over employment equity is not the only controversy connected with job discrimination. Two other issues, both primarily concerning women, have been the topic of recent moral, legal, and political discussion: the issue of comparable worth and the problem of sexual harassment on the job.

COMPARABLE WORTH AND PAY EQUITY

In essence, the doctrine of *comparable worth* holds that women and men should be paid on the same scale, not just for doing the same or equivalent jobs (for which one should get "equal pay"), but also for doing different jobs involving equal skill, effort, and responsibility (which results in "pay equity").[29] Almost all jurisdictions in Canada have some form of pay equity legislation or policy with a view to establishing compensation practices that are based on the value of the work performed and not on the gender of the performer. The provinces and territories include pay equity provisions in their pay equity acts or human rights codes and they cover public and private sectors of employment. Employment sectors under federal jurisdiction are covered by the *Canadian Human Rights Act* and its companion *Equal Wages Guidelines* as administered by the Canadian Human Rights Commission.

Advocates of comparable worth point to the substantial statistical evidence demonstrating that women are in more low-paying jobs than men. They also note the consistent relationship between the percentage of women in an occupation and the salary of that occupation: the more women dominate an occupation, the less it pays. Comparable-worth advocates contend that women have been shunted into a small number of pink-collar occupations and that a biased and discriminatory wage system has kept their pay below that of male occupations requiring a comparable degree of skill, education, responsibility, and so on.

As comparable-worth advocates see it, justice demands that women receive equal pay for doing work of comparable value. Jobs should be objectively evaluated in terms of the education, skills, and experience required and in terms of responsibilities, working conditions, and other relevant factors. Equivalent jobs should receive equivalent salaries, even if discriminatory job markets would otherwise put them on different pay scales. Some comparable-worth advocates further argue that when women have not received equivalent pay for jobs of comparable worth, justice requires that employers pay them reparation damages for the money they have lost. That would be expensive. But whether pay adjustments are retroactive or not, all comparable-worth programs envision adjusting the salary schedules of women upward rather than the pay of men downward.

Opponents of comparable worth insist that women, desiring flexible schedules and less taxing jobs, have freely chosen lower-paying occupations and thus are not entitled to any readjustment in pay scales. Phyllis Schlafly, for one, calls comparable worth "basically a conspiracy theory of jobs . . . . It asserts that, first, a massive societal male conspiracy has segregated or ghetto-ized women into particular occupations by excluding them from others; and then, second, devalued the women's job by paying them lower wages than other occupations held primarily by men." She adds: "For two decades, at least, women have been free to go into any occupation . . . . But most women continue to choose traditional, rather than nontraditional, jobs. This is their own free choice. Nobody makes them do it."[30] Others who are sympathetic to the concept of comparable worth worry about its implementation. How are different jobs to be evaluated and compared, they wonder. "How do you determine the intrinsic value of one job and then compare it to another?" asks Linda Chavez, former staff director of the U.S. Commission on Civil Rights. She points out that "for 200 years, this has been done by the free marketplace. It's as good an alternative as those being suggested by comparable-worth advocates. I'm not sure the legislative bodies or courts can do any better."[31] On the other hand, job evaluation studies are common in the public sector, and many private companies also utilize them to determine the skill, effort, responsibility, and working conditions that characterize different job categories and, hence, the wages appropriate to them. However, even if reasonably objective judgments of comparability are possible, opponents worry about the price tag: revising salaries could cost a medium-sized company millions of dollars in increased pay and benefits.

Advocates of comparable worth respond to those criticisms by pointing to statistical evidence demonstrating gender-linked pay inequities, as well as the reality of visceral sexism in the workplace and to the thousands of cases every year involving workplace discrimination against women. They reject the idea that women end up in jobs that pay less than comparable jobs held by men because of their free choice. Rather, discrimination distorts the operation of the labour market and needs to be corrected. Moreover, proponents of comparable worth reject the argument that implementing comparable worth would be prohibitively expensive. They point to jurisdictions where comparable-worth programs were phased in over several years so that the costs were spread out over long periods of time. But the core of their argument remains an appeal to fairness and equity, which, they insist, cannot be sacrificed on the altar of economy.

SEXUAL HARASSMENT

Some men may find the term *sexual harassment* amusing and have a difficult time taking it seriously. "It wouldn't bother me," they feel certain. "In fact," they chuckle, "I wouldn't mind being harassed a little more often." Others shrug it off, saying, "What's the big deal? You know what the world is like. Men and women, love and sex, they make it go 'round. Only uptight women are going to complain about sexual advances." But for thousands of working women, the reality of sexual harassment is not something to be shrugged off. In 2002 the Ontario Human Rights Commission alone received over 15,000 calls for information about sexual harassment, though only just over 4,000 callers decided to speak to someone about their issue.[32] For these women the issue is no laughing matter. Harassed women feel stress, loss of self-esteem, guilt, or they exhibit a number of abnormal physical symptoms (for example, pain, nausea), not to mention the fact that 25 percent of them leave their jobs after the occurrence of the harassment.

Issues of sexual harassment fall under the purview of the various federal or provincial or territorial human rights acts or codes, which in certain circumstances impose liability on employers for the discriminatory acts of their employees—including sexual harassment. In *Robichaud v. Canadian Treasury Board*, [1987] 2 S.C.R. 84, the Supreme Court held that employers are vicariously liable for sexual harassment on the part of their supervisors. In another landmark decision, *Janzen v. Platy Enterprises Ltd.* [1989] 1 S.C.R. 1252, the Supreme Court generalized the principle of vicarious liability from government departments to private employers, and overturned the ruling by the Manitoba Court of Appeal that Janzen, the waitress who was sexually assaulted, was not a victim of sexual discrimination because the attack was motivated by her physical attractiveness, not her sex.

Critics may find it odd that the legislation and courts view sexual harassment as a kind of sex discrimination. If an infatuated supervisor harasses only the female employee who is the object of his desire, is his misconduct really best understood as discrimination against women? He does not bother women in general, just this particular individual. In viewing sexual harassment as a violation of the *Canadian Human Rights Act*, however, legislators and judges rightly acknowledge that such behaviour, and the larger social patterns that reinforce it, rest on male attitudes and assumptions that work against women.

Accepting this viewpoint still leaves puzzles, however. Assume that the infatuated supervisor is a woman and the employee a man. Are we to interpret this situation as sex discrimination, considering that it does not take place against a social backdrop of exploitation and discrimination against men? Or imagine a bisexual employer who sexually harasses both male and female employees. Because he discriminates against neither sex, is there no sexual harassment? These conceptual puzzles have to do with the law's interpretation of sexual harassment as a kind of sex discrimination. Practically speaking, this interpretation has benefited women and brought them better and fairer treatment on the job, but it clearly has its limits. Legally speaking, the most important aspect of sexual harassment may be that it represents discrimination, but it is doubtful that discrimination is morally the worst aspect of sexual harassment. Morally, there is much more to be said about the wrongness of sexual harassment.

The Definition of Sexual Harassment

What exactly is sexual harassment? In its *Janzen v. Platy Enterprises* decision (cited above), the Supreme Court stated that "sexual harassment in the workplace is unwelcome conduct of a sexual nature that detrimentally affects the work environment or leads to adverse job-related consequences for the victims of the harassment." In an attempt to be practically helpful to prospective complainants, the Ontario Human Rights Commission explains, "'sexual harassment' means that someone is bothering you by saying or doing unwanted or unwelcome things of a sexual or gender-related nature. For example, someone who makes unwelcome sexual or gender-related remarks and gestures by: touching you inappropriately; making offensive jokes or remarks about women or men; making sexual requests or suggestions; staring at or making unwelcome comments about your body; displaying sexually offensive pictures."[33]

Sexual harassment divides into two types: "quid pro quo" and "hostile work environment." The phrase *quid pro quo* refers to giving something in return for something else. Quid-pro-quo sexual harassment, then, occurs when a supervisor makes an employee's employment opportunities conditional on the employee's entering into a sexual relationship with, or granting sexual favours to, the supervisor. Sexual threats are an example—in its crudest form, "You'd better agree to sleep with me if you want to keep your job." The immorality of such threats seems clear. In threatening harm, they are coercive and violate the rights of the person being threatened, certainly depriving her or him of equal treatment on the job. Obviously such threats can be seriously damaging, psychologically and otherwise, and hence are morally wrong.

Sexual offers are another species of quid-pro-quo sexual harassment: "If you sleep with me, I'm sure I can help you advance more quickly in the firm." Often such offers harbour an implied threat, and, unlike with genuine offers, the employee may risk something by turning them down. Larry May and John Hughes have argued that such offers by a male employer to a female employee put her in a worse position than she was before and are therefore coercive. Even sexual offers without hint of retaliation, they contend, change the female employee's working environment in an undesirable way.[34] In the case of both threats and offers, the supervisor is attempting to exploit the power imbalance between him and the employee.

The second kind of sexual harassment—hostile work environment—is broader, but it may be more important because it is so pervasive. This form of sexual harassment refers to behaviour of a sexual nature that is distressing to women and interferes with their ability to perform on the job, even when the behaviour is not an attempt to pressure the woman for sexual favours. Sexual innuendos; leering or ogling at a woman; sexist remarks about women's bodies, clothing, or sexual activities; the posting of pictures of nude women; and unnecessary touching, patting, or other physical conduct can all constitute sexual harassment. Such behaviour is humiliating and degrading to its victim. It interferes with her peace of mind and undermines her work performance.

Legally, a woman is not required to prove that she was psychologically damaged or unable to work in order to establish sexual harassment. On the other hand, an isolated or occasional sexist remark or innuendo does not constitute harassment. Harassment of the second type requires that the objectionable behaviour be persistent. Human beings are sexual creatures, and when men and women work together, there may be sexual undertones to their interactions. Women as well as men can appreciate, with the right persons and at the appropriate times, sexual references, sex-related humour, and physical contact with members of the opposite sex. Flirting, too, is often appreciated by both parties. It is not necessary that a serious and professional work environment be entirely free from sexuality, nor is this an achievable goal.

When, then, is behaviour objectionable or offensive enough to constitute harassment? What one person views as innocent fun or a friendly overture may be seen as objectionable and degrading by another. Comments that one woman appreciates or enjoys may be distressing to another. Who can decide what is right? In the case of sexual harassment, who determines what is objectionable or offensive? To answer that question, the courts may ask what the hypothetical "reasonable person" would find offensive if the person were a woman in that situation. What matters morally, however, is to respect each person's choices and wishes. Even if the other women in the office like it when the boss gives them a little hug, it would still

be wrong to hug the one woman who is made uncomfortable. If the behaviour is unwanted—that is, if the woman doesn't like it—then persisting in it is wrong. The fact that objectionable behaviour must be persistent and repeated to be sexual harassment allows for the possibility that people can honestly misread coworkers' signals or misjudge their likely response to a sexual innuendo, a joke, or a friendly pat. That may be excusable; what is not excusable is persisting in the behaviour once you know it is unwelcome.

Dealing with Sexual Harassment

Neither the wrongness nor the illegality of sexual harassment requires that the harassing conduct be by the employee's supervisor. This is particular relevant in hostile-work-environment cases, in which the harassment a woman endures may come from coworkers. Furthermore, companies can be held legally liable for harassing behaviour by their employees even if they are unaware of it, especially in cases of quid-pro-quo harassment by supervisors. In cases of hostile work environment, companies can escape liability or be subject to reduced liability if they can show (1) that they took reasonable steps to prevent and promptly correct sexually harassing behaviour and (2) that the employee unreasonably failed to take advantage of the preventive or corrective procedures established by the company. This fact gives companies an incentive to be proactive, and many of them have responded by developing comprehensive programs to educate employees about, and to protect them from, sexual harassment. Legal issues aside, companies clearly have a moral obligation to provide a work environment in which employees are free from sexual harassment. They need to be alert to the possibility of sexual harassment, take reasonable steps to prevent it, and deal with it swiftly and fairly should it occur.

Practically speaking, what should a female employee do if she encounters sexual harassment? First, she must make it clear that the behaviour is unwanted. That may be more difficult to do than it sounds, because most of us like to please others and do not want to be thought to be prudes or to lack a sense of humour. The employee may wish to be tactful and even pleasant in rejecting behaviour she finds inappropriate, especially if she thinks the offending party is well-intentioned. But in any case, she has to make her feelings known clearly and unequivocally. Second, if the behaviour persists, she should try to document it by keeping a record of what has occurred, who was involved, and when it happened. If others have witnessed some of the incidents, then that will help her document her case.

The third thing the female employee must do when faced with sexual harassment is to complain to the appropriate supervisor, sticking to the facts and presenting her allegations as objectively as possible. She should do this immediately in the case of sexual threats or offers by supervisors; in the case of inappropriate behaviour by coworkers, she should generally wait to see if it persists despite her having told the offending party that she objects. If complaining to her immediate supervisor does not bring quick action, then she must try whatever other channel is available to her in the organization—the grievance committee, for example, or the chief executive's office.

Fourth, if internal complaints do not bring results, then the employee should seriously consider seeing a lawyer and learning in detail what legal options are available. Many women try to ignore sexual harassment, but the evidence suggests that in most cases it continues or grows worse. When sexual threats or offers are involved, a significant number of victims are subject to unwarranted reprimands, increased work loads, or other reprisals. The employee must remember, too, that she has both a moral and a legal right not only to work in an environment free from sexual harassment but also not to be subjected to retaliatory actions for opposing the harassing behaviour.

SUMMARY

1. Discrimination in employment involves adverse decisions against employees or job applicants based on their membership in a group that is an object of prejudice or viewed as inferior or deserving of unequal treatment. Discrimination can be intentional or unintentional, institutional or individual.

2. The *Canadian Human Rights Act* forbids discrimination in employment on the basis of race, colour, sex, religion, national origin, etc., while the *Employment Equity Act* enjoins agencies and private corporations under federal jurisdiction to implement programs to correct imbalances in employment opportunities existing as a result of past discrimination against four specific groups: women, Aboriginal peoples, visible minorities and disabled person.

3. The application of the notion of "employment equity" in the workplace seems to have improved the lot of the four specified groups in the public service and the private sector under federal jurisdiction. Progress has been made in the private sector not under federal regulations, but it has been very slow.

4. The moral issues surrounding "employment equity" are controversial. Its defenders argue that compensatory justice demands employment-equity programs; that employment equity is needed to permit fairer competition; and that employment equity is necessary to break the cycle that keeps the four specified groups locked into poor-paying, low-prestige jobs.

5. Critics of employment equity argue that affirmative action injures white men and violates their rights; that it itself violates the principle of equality; and that nondiscrimination on its own (without employment equity) will suffice to achieve our social goals.

6. The doctrine of comparable worth holds that women and men should be paid on the same scale for doing different jobs if they involve equivalent skill, effort, and responsibility.

7. Advocates of comparable worth say that women have been shunted into low-paying jobs, that they suffer from a discriminatory labour market, and that justice requires that they receive equal pay for doing jobs of equal worth. Some contend further that monetary reparations are due to women who in the past have not received equal pay for work of equal value.

8. Opponents of comparable worth claim that women have freely chosen their occupations and are not entitled to compensation. They contend that only the market can and should determine the value of different jobs. Revising pay scales would also be expensive.

9. Sexual harassment is widespread. It includes unwelcome sexual advances and other conduct of a sexual nature in which submission to such conduct is a basis for employment decisions (quid pro quo) or such conduct substantially interferes with an individual's work performance (hostile work environment). Sexual harassment is a kind of discrimination and is illegal.

10. Employees encountering sexually harassing behaviour from coworkers should make it clear that the behaviour is unwanted. If it persists, harassed employees should document the behaviour and report it to the appropriate person or office in the organization. In the case of sexual threats or offers from supervisors, they should do this immediately. If internal channels are ineffective, employees should seek legal advice.

CASE 9.1

Hoop Dreams[35]

In basketball, talent plus hard work equals success. That's an equation that holds true for women as well as men, and in recent years dedicated female athletes have raised women's basketball to new heights and won the allegiance of many new fans. But what about their coaches? Do any obstacles stand between them and their dreams? Marianne Stanley didn't think so when she began coaching women's basketball for the University of Southern California, where she earned $64,000 a year—a fair sum, one might think, but less than half that of her counterpart, George Raveling, who coached the men's team. True, Raveling had been coaching for thirty-one years, had been an assistant on the U.S. Olympic team, and had twice been named coach of the year. But Stanley was no slouch either. She had been a head coach for sixteen years and won three national championships. In her last two years at USC, she had win–loss records of 23–8 and 22–7, which compared favourably with Raveling's 19–10 and 24–6.

So when her initial four-year contract expired, Marianne Stanley sought pay parity with Raveling. Stanley knew that Raveling was also earning tens of thousands of dollars in perks, but she was willing to overlook that and settle for an equal base salary of $135,000. Instead, USC offered Stanley a three-year contract starting at $88,000 and increasing to $100,000. When she rejected that offer, USC countered with a one-year contract for $96,000. Stanley declined the offer and left USC, her hoop dreams diminished, although she later began coaching at UC Berkeley, where her salary was equivalent to that of the men's coach.

For his part, George Raveling didn't mind Stanley's making as much money as he did. But he understood why USC paid him more. He was, after all, a hot property, and if USC was going to prevent his being lured away by some other university trying to boost its basketball program, then it had to pay him a high salary. By contrast, Marianne Stanley didn't have any other job offers.

Too bad, one might say, but that's how the market works in a capitalist society. But what if the market itself is discriminatory? Defenders of comparable worth argue that it is, and that coaches like Stanley can't negotiate for comparable salaries because women's basketball isn't valued as highly as men's. And it's college administrators, they argue, who are to blame for that. As one feminist puts it:

> The women didn't get the advertising and marketing dollars. They didn't get the PR. Then when fans weren't showing up, the TV stations weren't carrying the games and other universities weren't fighting over the best coaches, administrators told the women that, because they and their sport didn't draw as much attention as men, they shouldn't be paid as much.

In response, defenders of USC deny that it or any other university is responsible for the fact that men's sports are big revenue earners and women's are not. The higher pay for those who coach men simply reflects that social and cultural reality, which is something college administrators have no control over. If someone like Marianne Stanley wants to enter the big leagues, then she should coach men.

UPDATE

Sadly, sometimes even those who have fought against discrimination can discriminate against others. In 2002 Sharrona Alexander, formerly an assistant women's basketball coach at UC Berkeley, filed suit against the university, alleging that head coach Marianne Stanley told her to get an abortion or lose her job. Stanley denies the abortion allegation, but admits that she did ask Alexander to resign because of her pregnancy. Either way, a champion of women's rights was guilty of trampling on someone else's hoop dreams. Ironically, Stanley herself played college basketball when she was pregnant (returning to practice eleven days after her daughter was born) and went on, single and with a toddler, to coach Old Dominion University to three national championships. Moreover, some sports commentators believe that, far from being a handicap, motherhood can give a coach an edge in recruiting because the parents of prospective recruits prefer their daughters to be coached by women who, when they say they treat their teams as family, know what they are talking about. In addition, Arizona State coach Charli Turner Thorne says, because "you're taking young ladies at a very formative time, you have to play the parent role." She adds, "There's absolutely no doubt [motherhood] makes me a better coach."

Discussion Questions

1. The doctrine of comparable worth holds that men and women should be paid the same wage for doing jobs of equal skill, effort, and responsibility. Were Marianne Stanley and George Raveling doing work of comparable value?

2. Was Stanley treated unfairly or in some way discriminated against? Should USC have offered to pay her more?

3. Why do sports played by men tend to be more popular and generate more revenue than sports played by women? Are female athletes—and their coaches—disadvantaged? Are they discriminated against? If so, who is responsible for this discrimination, and do colleges and universities have an obligation to do something about it?

4. Should universities like USC base their coaching salaries entirely on market considerations? Or should they pay the coaches of men's and women's sports comparable salaries based on experience, skill, and performance?

5. Respond to the argument that because men are free to coach women's teams and women to coach men's teams, there is nothing discriminatory in the fact that one job pays more than the other.

6. Was Sharrona Alexander's pregnancy likely to have adversely affected her coaching performance? If so, was Marianne Stanley wrong to ask her to resign? How should Stanley have handled the situation?

CASE 9.2

Raising the Ante

Having spearheaded the women's cause on behalf of equal pay for jobs of equal value, Phyllis Warren was elated when the board decided to readjust salaries. Its decision meant Phyllis and the other women employed by the crafts firm would receive pay equivalent to men doing comparable jobs. But in a larger sense it constituted an admission of guilt on the part of the board, acknowledgment of a history blemished by sexual discrimination.

In the euphoria that followed the board's decision, neither Phyllis nor any of the other activists thought much about the implied admission of female exploitation. But some weeks later, Herm Leggett, a sales dispatcher, half-jokingly suggested to Phyllis over lunch that she shouldn't stop with equal pay now. Phyllis asked Herm what he meant.

"Back pay," Herm said without hesitation. "If they're readjusting salaries for women," he explained, "they obviously know that salaries are out of line and have been for some time." Then he asked her pointedly, "How long you been here, Phyl?" Eleven years, she told him. "If those statistics you folks were passing around last month are accurate," Herm said, "then I'd say you've been losing about $2,000 a year, or $22,000 over eleven years." Then he added with a laugh, "Not counting interest, of course."

"Why not?" Phyllis thought. Why shouldn't she and other women who'd suffered past inequities be reimbursed?

That night Phyllis called a few of the other women and suggested that they press the board for back pay. Some said they were satisfied and didn't think they should force the issue. Others thought the firm had been fair in readjusting the salary schedule, and they were willing to let bygones be bygones. Still others thought that any further efforts might, in fact, roll back the board's favourable decision. Yet a nucleus agreed that workers who had been unfairly treated in the past ought to receive compensation. They decided, however, that because their ranks were divided, they shouldn't wage as intense an in-house campaign as previously but instead take the issue directly to the board, while it might still be inhaling deeply the fresh air of social responsibility.

The following Wednesday, Phyllis and four other women presented their case to the board, intentionally giving the impression that they enjoyed as much support from other workers as they had the last time they appeared before it. Although this wasn't true, Phyllis suggested it as an effective strategic ploy.

Phyllis's presentation had hardly ended when board members began making their feelings known. One called her proposal "industrial blackmail." "No sooner do we try to right an injustice," he said testily, "than you take our good faith and threaten to beat us over the head with it unless we comply with your request."

Another member just as vigorously argued that the current board couldn't be held accountable for the actions, policies, and decisions of previous boards. "Sure," he said, "we're empowered to alter policies as we see fit and as conditions change to chart new directions. And we've done that. But to expect us to bear the full financial liability of decisions we never made is totally unrealistic—and unfair."

Still another member wondered where it would all end. "If we agree," he asked, "will you then suggest we should track down all those women who ever worked for us and provide them compensation?" Phyllis said no, but the board should readjust retirement benefits for those affected.

At this point the board asked Phyllis if she had any idea what her proposal would cost the firm. "Whatever it is, it's a small price to pay for righting wrong," she said firmly.

"But is it a small price to pay for severely damaging our profit picture?" one of the members asked. Then he added, "I needn't remind you that our profit outlook directly affects what we can offer our current employees in terms of salary and fringe benefits. It directly affects our ability to revise our salary schedule." Finally, he asked Phyllis whether she'd accept the board's reducing everyone's current compensation to meet what Phyllis termed the board's "obligation to the past."

Despite its decided opposition to Phyllis's proposal, the board agreed to consider it and render a decision at its next meeting. As a final broadside, Phyllis hinted that, if the board didn't comply with the committee's request, the committee was prepared to pursue legal action.

Discussion Questions

1. If you were a board member, how would you vote? Why?

2. What moral principles are involved in this case?

3. Do you think Phyllis Warren was unfair in taking advantage of the board's implied admission of salary discrimination on the basis of sex? Why?

4. Do you think Phyllis was wrong in giving the board the impression that her proposal enjoyed broad support? Why?

5. If the board rejects the committee's request, do you think the committee ought to sue? Give reasons.

CASE 9.3

Facial Discrimination

Scene. A conference room of a branch office of Allied Products, Inc., where Tom, Frank, and Alice have been interviewing college students for summer internships.

Tom: Did you see that last candidate? Jeez, was he sorry looking.

Frank: Too ugly to work here, that's for sure. And those thick glasses didn't help. Still, he wasn't as ugly as that young woman you hired last summer. What was her name . . . Allison? Boy, she was enormous, and remember that hair of hers. It wasn't surprising we had to let her go.

Alice: Come on, Frank. Don't be so hung up on looks. That last guy seemed to know his stuff, and he certainly was enthusiastic about working for Allied.

Frank: Hey, don't get me wrong, Alice. I know you don't have to be beautiful to work for Allied—after all, look at Tom here. Still, with a face like that guy's, you got to wonder.

Tom: Wisecracks aside, Alice, Frank's got a point. Studies show that it's natural for people to discriminate on the basis of looks. I've read that even babies will look at a pretty face longer than an ugly face.

Alice: I know that. Studies also show that people attribute positive characteristics to people they find attractive and that they treat unattractive people worse than other people in lots of ways. Strangers are less likely to do small favours for unattractive people than they are for attractive people, and even parents and teachers have lower expectations for ugly, fat, or odd-looking children. But what this really boils down to is implicit discrimination.

Tom: That's what I'm saying. It's natural. Besides, it's not illegal to discriminate on the basis of appearance.

Frank: That's right. You wouldn't want us to hire somebody with green hair and rings in his nose and put him out at the front desk, would you? This is a business, not a freak show.

Alice: Hey, slow down, guys. First, it may be natural and it may even be legal to favour good-looking people, but that doesn't make it right. And second, I'm not talking about grooming or dress. It's your choice to dye your hair and decorate your face, and if you don't fit in because of that, that's your fault. But the guy we talked to today didn't choose to be ugly, so why hold it against him?

Frank: I suppose next you'll be telling us that we should have kept Allison on last summer just because she was fat.

Alice: No, I'm not saying you have to give preferential treatment to overweight people. But I think that nobody in the office cut her any slack. If she'd been normal size, things would have worked out okay, but people took one look at her and pre-judged her to be a loser. You know, Frank, some courts may hold that discrimination against the obese violates the *Charter of Rights and Freedoms*, since obesity may be a handicap.

Tom: That's only if it's a medical condition.

Frank: Yeah, Allison's only problem was that she liked to eat.

Alice: You don't know that. You don't know anything about her.

Frank: I suppose her hair was a medical condition, too.

Tom: Okay, you two, take it easy. Seriously, though, Alice, a number of our interns have to interact with the public, and people can be put off by having to deal with ugly people, fat people, or even very short people. So why aren't an employee's looks a job-relevant issue?

Alice: No, I think that as long as the person is clean and well groomed, then the public shouldn't be put off by having to deal with someone who is unattractive or unusual looking. It's unreasonable.

Tom: That's what you say. But what if the public is "unreasonable"? What if they prefer companies with attractive or at least normal-looking employees?

Alice: It's still irrelevant. It's the same as if a company had customers who didn't like dealing with blacks. That's no reason for it not to hire blacks.

Tom: Yeah, I can see that.

Frank: Okay, but what about this ugly guy? Do we have to offer him an internship?

Discussion Questions

1. Assess the argument that there is nothing wrong with "facial discrimination"—that it simply reflects the fact that human beings are naturally attracted to, or repelled by, other human beings on the basis of their physical characteristics.

2. Under what circumstances is physical attractiveness a job-related employment criterion? Is it relevant to being a salesperson, a flight attendant, or a receptionist?

3. What arguments can be given for and against a law preventing job discrimination on the basis of immutable aspects of one's appearance?

4. Assess the argument that because fat, ugly, or strange-looking people have it tougher throughout their lives than do attractive people, we should give them preferential treatment whenever we can—for example, in job situations—to make up for the disadvantages they've suffered and to help level the playing field.

5. Are businesses morally obligated to try to prevent or reduce appearance discrimination in the workplace? What steps can they take?

Notes to Chapter 9

1. For a brief look at discrimination in the American context, see ch. 9 of W. Shaw and V. Barry's *Moral Issues in Business*, 10th ed. (Belmont, CA: Thomson Wadsworth, 2007).

2. For important events in the history of women in Canada, one may find useful the website of Status of Women Canada at www.swc-cfc.gc.ca/index_e.html under "Women's History Month."

3. Aboriginal children were taken away from their families and traditions and put into faraway schools with a view to assimilating them into non-Aboriginal society. A 1905 amendment to the *Indian Act* allowed the removal of Aboriginal people from a reserve near towns with a population of more than 8,000 inhabitants.

4. For this section I relied heavily on "The Report of the Royal Commission on Aboriginal Peoples" (November 1996), vol. 1, chh. 8–9. One may access the report through the website of Indian and Northern Affairs Canada at www.ainc-inac.gc.ca/ch/rcap/sg/sgm8_e.html. It is interesting to note that at the time the *Indian Act* was first enacted (1876) it was a common assumption even among liberal Victorian thinkers that "barbarians" or "savages" were in need of "guardians." Even as sensitive a thinker as J. S. Mill could claim in his essay *On Liberty* (1859) that freedom of thought and action applies "only to human beings in the maturity of their faculties," thereby excluding children and "those backward states of society in which the race itself may be considered as in its nonage."

5. It freed slaves over the age of 25 and made it illegal to bring slaves into Upper Canada (Ontario).

6. Whereby the Chief Justice of Lower Canada (Quebec) abolished in effect slavery in Lower Canada.

7. See Royson James, "Are We in Denial over Slave Role?," February 5, 2007, at www.thestar.com/News/article/178264; also the brief submitted by the Canadian Civil Liberties Association to Dave Cooke, Minister of Education for Ontario, 1994 at www.ccla.org/pos/briefs/educate.html.

8. The head tax was set at $50 in 1885 and by 1903 it was up to $500 a head. Such an amount represented about two years of pay, and made it practically impossible for Chinese workers to enter Canada or to bring in their wives or children.

9. For a brief history of the Chinese immigration into Canada and the treatment of Chinese immigrants, see "Chinese Immigration: Gold Mountain I, Gold Mountain II" at www.cbc.ca/news/background/china/chinese_immigration.html#top.

10. It is instructive to follow the events preceding, during and after the "Komagata Maru" incident which took place in the Vancouver harbour between May and July 1914, when 376 British subjects of Indian origin aboard a Japanese steamer of that name were denied entry and forced to sail back to India. For a brief account, see www.sikhpioneers.org/koma.html.

11. Quoted at www.sikhspectrum.com/052004/lions_r_k.htm

12. See the stories on the CBC News, Disability Matters series, by Ed Smith ("Death, Not Disability, Is the End of the World") and Helena Katz ("Disability Matters in the Workforce") at www.cbc.ca/news/viewpoint/vp_disabilitymatters/index.html.

13. Though what group should constitute the "majority," in relation to the ability to do a given activity, is sometimes a legitimate and debatable issue.

14. See Statistics Canada, "A Profile of Disability in Canada, 2001" at www.statcan.ca/english/freepub/89-577-XIE/index.htm. The survey covered persons residing in private and some collective households in the ten provinces but excluded persons living in the Yukon, Northwest Territories, and Nunavut; in institutions; and on First Nations reserves. The rates may therefore be a bit higher than reported.

15. Philip Shenon, "Judge Finds F.B.I. Is Discriminatory," *New York Times*, October 1, 1988, 1.

16. Tom L. Beauchamp and Norman E. Bowie, *Ethical Theory and Business*, 4th ed. (Englewood Cliffs, NJ: Prentice Hall, 1993), 437.

17. See also the Supreme Court decision in *British Columbia (Public Service Employee Relations Commission) v. BCGSEU*, [1999] 3 S.C.R. 3. The Court offers six different reasons as to why the "conventional approach of categorizing discrimination as 'direct' or 'adverse effect' discrimination should be replaced by a unified approach."

18. For the text of the *Act*, see www.laws.justice.gc.ca/en/H-6/index.html. "Employment equity" is not a synonym for "nondiscrimination," nor is it a measure for achieving "workplace diversity" or "pay equity."

19. See "Employment Equity in the Federal Public Service—Not There Yet," preliminary findings of the Standing Senate Committee on Human Rights, February 2007, 11, at www.parl.gc.ca/39/1/parlbus/commbus/senate/com-e/huma-e/rep-e/rep07feb07-e.pdf.

20. Monica Townson, "Poverty Issues for Canadian Women" at www.swc-cfc.gc.ca/resources/consultations/ges09-2005/poverty_e.html#_edn7.

21. These sectors include principally communications, transportation, media, banking and financial services. See www.hrsdc.gc.ca/en/lp/lo/lswe/we/ee_tools/reports/annual/2005/chapter1-4.shtml.

22. See *The Daily*, March 22, 2005 at www.statcan.ca/Daily/English/050322/d050322b.htm. According to the *Act*, "'visible minorities' means persons, other than aboriginal peoples, who are non-Caucasian in race or non-white in colour."

23. See the literature review on "Socioeconomic Integration of Visible Minorities and Aboriginal Peoples in Toronto," Human Resources and Social Development Canada, at www.hrsdc.gc.ca/en/lp/lo/lswe/we/special_projects/RacismFreeInitiative/Goerge-Doyle.shtml.

24. See "Ethnic Diversity Survey: Portrait of a Multicultural Society" at www.statcan.ca/english/freepub/89-593-XIE/89-593-XIE2003001.pdf, 17–21.

25. Statistics Canada, "Labour Force Survey: Western Canada's Off-Reserve Aboriginal Population," *The Daily*, June 13, 2005; and "Study: The Aboriginal Labour Force in Western Canada," *The Daily*, January 25, 2007.

26. For the first part of the paragraph, see "Employment Equity in the Federal public Service—Not There Yet," preliminary findings of the Standing Senate Committee on Human Rights, February 2007, 14, at www.parl.gc.ca/39/1/parlbus/commbus/senate/com-e/huma-e/rep-e/rep07feb07-e.pdf. For the latter part of the paragraph, see Statistics Canada, *The 2001 Participation and Activity Limitation Survey*; also Human Resources and Social Development Canada, "Advancing the Inclusion of People with Disabilities 2006," Appendix A, Tables A3 and A4.

27. See Denise Deveau, "What Do Women Want?," *Financial Post*, at www.canada.com/nationalpost/financialpost/smallbusiness/story.html?id=fef20678-0bf5-485c-91b3-cd29cf535bd4.

28. See the report by the Canadian Human Rights Commission at www.chrc-ccdp.ca/publications/ar_2006_ra/page4-en.asp.

29. For some celebrated cases of pay equity see www.cbc.ca/newsinreview/Dec%2099/Pay%20-Equity/Intro.html.

30. Caroline E. Mayer, "The Comparable Pay Debate," *Washington Post National Weekly Edition*, August 6, 1984, 9

31. Ibid.

32. See *The Globe and Mail*, "Careers," September 8, 2004.

33. See www.ohrc.on.ca/en/sexual_harassment.

34. Larry May and John C. Hughes, "Sexual Harassment," in Ezorsky, ed., *Moral Rights in the Workplace* (Albany: State University of New York Press, 1987).

35. This case study is based on Joan Ryan, "Playing Field Is Still Not Level," *San Francisco Chronicle*, June 13, 1999, "Sunday," 1, and Ann Killion, "Belief That Coach Can't Be Pregnant Outdated," *San Jose Mercury News*, September 17, 2002, 1A.

EQUALITY IN EMPLOYMENT

ROSALIE SILBERMAN ABELLA

Concerned over the fact that "the measures taken by Canadian employers to increase the employability and productivity of women, native people, disabled persons and visible minorities have as yet not resulted in nearly enough change in the employment practices which have the unintended effect of screening a disproportionate number of those persons out of opportunities for hiring and promotion," the Government of Canada appointed Judge Rosalie Abella (then of the Ontario Provincial Court—Family Division) to inquire into "the opportunities for employment" of the four groups "in certain crown corporations and corporations wholly owned by the Government of Canada." Judge Abella conducted a far-ranging inquiry and presented in October 1984 her findings and recommendations in the "Report of the Commission on Equality in Employment." The selection that follows is a collection of excerpts from Chapter 1 of the report, in which Abella discusses her working definition of "equality" and explains the essence and purpose of the notion of "employment equity," and Chapter 2, in which she outlines the various problems faced by members of designated groups.

CHAPTER 1

Defining Equality in Employment

Equality is, at the very least, freedom from adverse discrimination. But what constitutes adverse discrimination changes with time, with information, with experience, and with insight. What we tolerated as a society 100, 50, or even 10 years ago is no longer necessarily tolerable. Equality is thus a process—a process of constant and flexible examination, of vigilant introspection, and of aggressive open-mindedness. One hundred years ago, the role for women was almost exclusively domestic; 50 years ago, some visible minorities were disenfranchised; 25 years ago, native people lacked a policy voice; and 10 years ago, disabled persons were routinely kept dependent. Today, none of these exclusionary assumptions is acceptable. But the goal of equality is more than an evolutionary intolerance to adverse discrimination. It is to ensure, too, that the vestiges of these arbitrarily restrictive assumptions do not continue to play a role in our society.

If in this ongoing process we are not always sure what "equality" means, most of us have a good understanding of what is "fair." And what is happening today in Canada to women, native people, disabled persons, and visible minorities is not fair. It is not fair that many people in these groups have restricted employment opportunities, limited access to decision-making processes that critically affect them, little public visibility as contributing Canadians, and a circumscribed range of options generally. It may be understandable, given history, culture, economics, and even human nature, but by no standard is it fair.

To attempt to unravel the complex tapestries that hang as a background to discriminatory attitudes can be an unproductive exercise. It is undoubtedly of interest to know why certain attitudes or practices were allowed to predominate; but in devising remedies to redress patently unfair realities, sorting through the malevolent, benevolent, or pragmatic causes of these realities is of little assistance. One can assume that the unfair results would not have occurred without the nourishing environment of limited sensitivities. But as we have these sensitivities educated, we must concentrate not on the motives of the past but on the best way to rectify their impact. And one of those ways is to appeal to our collective sense of fairness.

Equality in employment means that no one is denied opportunities for reasons that have nothing to do with inherent ability. It means equal access free from arbitrary obstructions. Discrimination means that an arbitrary barrier stands between a person's ability and his or her opportunity to demonstrate it. If the access is genuinely available in a way that permits everyone who so wishes the opportunity to fully develop his or her potential, we have achieved a kind of equality. It is equality defined as equal freedom from discrimination.

From *The Royal Commission on Equality in Employment*. Reproduced with the permission of the Minister Of Public Works and Government Services, 2008, and courtesy of the Privy Council Office. Footnotes omitted.

Discrimination in this context means practices or attitudes that have, whether by design or impact, the effect of limiting an individual's or a group's right to the opportunities generally available because of attributed rather than actual characteristics. What is impeding the full development of the potential is not the individual's capacity but an external barrier that artificially inhibits growth. It is not a question of whether this discrimination is motivated by an intentional desire to obstruct someone's potential, or whether it is the accidental by-product of innocently motivated practices or systems. If the barrier is affecting certain groups in a disproportionately negative way, it is a signal that the practices that lead to this adverse impact may be discriminatory.

This is why it is important to look at the results of a system. In these results one may find evidence that barriers which are inequitable impede individual opportunity. These results are by no means conclusive evidence of inequity, but they are an effective signal that further examination is warranted to determine whether the disproportionately negative impact is in fact the result of inequitable practices, and therefore calls for remedial attention, or whether it is a reflection of a non-discriminatory reality.

Equality in employment is not a concept that produces the same results for everyone. It is a concept that seeks to identify and remove, barrier by barrier, discriminatory disadvantages. Equality in employment is access to the fullest opportunity to exercise individual potential.

Sometimes equality means treating people the same, despite their differences, and sometimes it means treating them as equals by accommodating their differences. Formerly, we thought that equality only meant sameness and that treating persons as equals meant treating everyone the same. We now know that to treat everyone the same may be to offend the notion of equality. Ignoring differences may mean ignoring legitimate needs. It is not fair to use the differences between people as an excuse to exclude them arbitrarily from equitable participation. Equality means nothing if it does not mean that we are of equal worth regardless of differences in gender, race, ethnicity, or disability. The projected, mythical, and attributed meaning of these differences cannot be permitted to exclude full participation.

Ignoring differences and refusing to accommodate them is a denial of equal access and opportunity. It is discrimination. To reduce discrimination, we must create and maintain barrier-free environments so that individuals can have genuine access free from arbitrary obstructions to demonstrate and exercise fully their potential. This may mean treating some people differently by removing the obstacles to equality of opportunity they alone face for no demonstrably justifiable reason. People are disadvantaged for many reasons and may be disadvantaged in a variety of ways— economically, socially, politically, or educationally. Not all disadvantages derive from discrimination. Those that do demand their own particular policy responses.

At present, society's disadvantages are disproportionately assumed by the four designated groups. Clearly, some distinctions have been made or overlooked in the past that have resulted in the disproportionate representation of native people, visible minorities, disabled persons, and women on the lower rungs of the ladder to society's benefits. By reversing our approach and by using these same distinctions to identify, confront, and eliminate barriers these distinctions have caused in the past, we can reverse the trends, provide access, and open the door to equality. To create equality of opportunity, we have to do different things for different people. We have to systematically eradicate the impediments to these options according to the actual needs of the different groups, not according to what we think their needs should be. And we have to give individuals an opportunity to use their abilities according to their potential and not according to what we think their potential should be. The process is an exercise in redistributive justice. Its object is to prevent the denial of access to society's benefits because of distinctions that are invalid.

Unless we reject arbitrary distinctions, these four groups will remain unjustifiably in perpetual slow motion. The objectives of breathing life into the notion of equality are to rectify as quickly as possible the results of parochial perspectives which unfairly restrict women, native people, disabled persons, and visible minorities . . . .

Employment Equity/Affirmative Action

The achievement of equality in employment depends on a double-edged approach. The first concerns those pre-employment conditions that affect access to employment. The second concerns those conditions in the workplace that militate against equal participation in employment.

Efforts to overcome barriers in employment are what have generally been called in North America affirmative action measures. These include making recruitment, hiring, promotion, and earnings more equitable. They concentrate on making adjustments in the workplace to accommodate a more heterogeneous workforce.

The Commission was told again and again that the phrase "affirmative action" was ambiguous and confusing. Not surprisingly, those who favoured government intervention to create more equitably distributed employment opportunities had less objection to the term, even if they were unclear as to its precise meaning. On the other hand, those who rejected intervention opposed the term, no matter how it was defined.

The language that has collected around the issue of equality often produces overwhelmingly emotional responses. Positions are frequently taken that have not been thought through either to their logical origins or conclusions, and this is true regardless of which side of the argument is being presented; yet they are so strongly held that they leave little room for the introduction of information or contrary judgements.

Often the words themselves rather than the issues trigger intellectual resistance. Their use almost instantly produces a protective wall through which reason cannot easily penetrate. In such cases it is sometimes worth changing the language in order to allow the debate to unfold on a more reasonable level. The duel should be between principles and not between reflexes.

People generally have a sense that "affirmative action" refers to interventionist government policies, and that is enough to prompt a negative reaction from many. For others, however, much depends on the degree and quality of the intervention. They may never agree to the concept, however reasonably argued, but at least a discussion of the issues will not have been foreclosed by the waving of the semantic red flag. In other words, there may be a willingness to discuss eliminating discriminatory employment barriers but not to debate "affirmative action" as it is currently misunderstood.

The Commission notes this in order to propose that a new term, "employment equity," be adopted to describe programs of positive remedy for discrimination in the Canadian workplace. No great principle is sacrificed in exchanging phrases of disputed definition for newer ones that may be more accurate and less destructive of reasoned debate . . . .

In default of some new verbal coinage, where this Report refers to affirmative action in the Canadian context, it is no more than a convenient way of identifying positive steps to correct discrimination in the workplace. Ultimately, it matters little whether in Canada we call this process employment equity or affirmative action, so long as we understand that what we mean by both terms are employment practices designed to eliminate discriminatory barriers and to provide in a meaningful way equitable opportunities in employment.

Purpose of Employment Equity

Much legislative attention has been paid remedying discriminatory behaviour. Human rights acts, labour codes, and the Charter of Rights and Freedoms contain provisions to address the problem. By and large these provisions have been limited in two respects: they are restricted to individual allegations of discrimination; and they are potentially restricted, except under the Ontario Human Rights Code and the Canadian Human Rights Act, to cases of intentional discrimination.

This approach to the enforcement of human rights, based as it is on individual rather than group remedies, and perhaps confined to allegations of intentional discrimination, cannot deal with the pervasiveness and subtlety of discrimination.

Neither, by itself, can education. Education has been the classic crutch upon which we lean in the hopes of coaxing change in prejudicial attitudes. But education is an unreliable agent, glacially slow in movement and impact, and often completely ineffective in the face of intractable views. It promises no immediate relief despite the immediacy of the injustice.

The traditional human rights commission model, which valiantly signalled to the community that redress was available for Individuals subjected to deliberate acts of discrimination, is increasingly under attack for its statutory inadequacy to respond to the magnitude of the problem. Resolving discrimination caused by malevolent intent on a case-by-case basis puts human rights commissions in the position of stamping out brush fires when the urgency is in the incendiary potential of the whole forest . . . .

It is sometimes exceptionally difficult to determine whether or not someone intends to discriminate. This does not mean that there is no need for processes that provide remedies to individuals when intentional discrimination can be proven. On the contrary, the need is manifest, but these processes do not sufficiently address the complexity of the problem. There are those who are prejudiced in attitude but not in deed, and others who commit acts of flagrant discrimination out of obliviousness or misplaced benevolence. What we intend is sometimes far less relevant than the impact of our behaviour on others . . .

Systemic discrimination requires systemic remedies. Rather than approaching discrimination from the perspective of the single perpetrator and the single victim, the systemic approach acknowledges that by and large the systems and practices we customarily and often unwittingly adopt may have an unjustifiably negative effect on certain groups in society. The effect of the system on the individual or group, rather than its attitudinal sources, governs whether or not a remedy is justified.

Remedial measures of a systemic and systematic kind are the object of employment equity and affirmative action. They are meant to improve the situation for individuals who, by virtue of belonging to and being identified with a particular group, find themselves unfairly and adversely affected by certain systems or practices.

Systemic remedies are a response to patterns of discrimination that have two basic antecedents: (a) a disparately negative impact that flows from the structure of systems designed for a homogeneous constituency; and (b) a disparately negative impact that flows from practices based on stereotypical characteristics ascribed to an individual because of the characteristics ascribed to the group of which he or she is a member.

The former usually results in systems primarily designed for white able-bodied males; the latter usually results in practices based on white able-bodied males' perceptions of everyone else.

In both cases, the institutionalized systems and practices result in arbitrary and extensive exclusions for persons who, by reason of their group affiliation, are systematically denied a full opportunity to demonstrate their individual abilities . . . .

CHAPTER 2: THE DESIGNATED GROUPS

Women

According to 1982 data, about 52 per cent of Canadian women are in the paid labour force. They constitute 41 per cent of the workforce. Year after year, women make the case for better childcare facilities, equal pay for work of equal value, equitable benefits, equal employment opportunities, unbiased educational options, and an end to job segregation. Year after year, they are told by governments that measures are being looked into and solutions being devised. Every year, progress is largely chimerical. The lack of progress results in a perpetuation of losses that become increasingly irreversible . . . .

One of the major impediments to women having adequate employment opportunities, articulated by both women and employers, has to do with the education choices made by females. If these choices are based on an assumption by females that they need not seek paid employment, that their economic security will flow from a marriage, then clearly they will not address the issue of which educational options will provide them with better employment skills. Where they are interested, and most are, in seeking employment, they must participate in the full range of available educational opportunities. This will require dramatic changes in the school system . . . .

What precedes employment may be just as important as what occurs once employment is obtained. The cultural ambience from which men and women emerge affects what takes place in the workplace. How men and women perceive one another as spouses and how children perceive their parents both determine what happens to women in the workforce. If women are considered economic and social dependants in the home, they will continue to be treated as subservient in the workplace. If, on the other hand, they are perceived as social and economic equals in a partnership in the home, this will be translated into the practices of the workplace. Two issues must therefore be addressed simultaneously: the way women are perceived generally in society, and the employment practices that affect women in any given corporation.

The problem is one of assumptions, almost religiously held, about the role and ability of women in Canada. Many men and women seem unable to escape from the perceptual fallout of the tradition that expects women to behave dependently and supportively toward men.

The historic and legally sanctioned role of women in Canada has been as homemaker. For more than a century, in every province, the legal doctrines around marriage required that the legal personae of husband and wife merge into that of the husband. This obliterated the wife's identity as an independent legal entity. It also required, rather than permitted, the husband to be the breadwinner, resulting in the allocation of the homemaking function to the wife.

Only in the recent past have provinces begun to impose an equal obligation on husband and wife to be responsible for their own support. The right of one spouse to support from the other now flows mainly from economic need arising from the spousal relationship and its division of labour rather than from gender. Marriage is to be considered a partnership of social and economic equals, and the division of labour in marriage between breadwinner and homemaker is to be considered a division of two equally valuable contributions to this partnership . . . .

At the same time, it would be wrong to undervalue the role of homemaking and to ignore its economic contribution simply because it is not "employment" as it has been traditionally defined. Homemakers, who have made choices authorized by law and justified by their own spousal relationships, should not be penalized economically because the majority of women are now making different choices.

The essence of equality for women, now and in the future, is that in their options, which may or may not include the selection of a "traditional" role, they face no greater economic liability than would a man, and that in whatever "employment" environment they choose, they receive the same benefit for their contribution as would a man. Particular efforts must be made to provide the necessary human and financial supports to those women who, in the absence of a spouse's household assistance, hold two full-time jobs: one in the paid labour force and one unpaid as the spouse with the primary responsibility for homemaking functions.

A number of harmful consequences to women of traditional stereotypical assumptions must be addressed. The first involves an approach to the family that treats it as a single indivisible unit for policy purposes. The family as a unit performs a private function for its individual members in providing intersecting emotional, social, and often financial services. As a carapace from external circumstances, it can be a source of comfort and protection. But beyond this sweeping and idealized generalization, it is a mistake to presume that there is a standardized social or economic formula governing the way families operate. The mistake tends to work to the detriment of both women and men, who are categorized as playing assigned roles.

Although women have the same right to work and stay home as do men, until the legal directive In modern family law that each spouse is responsible for his or her own support takes root and inspires routinely in young girls and women the realization that they themselves, no less than any future spouse, must be financially self-reliant, women will likely be the gender performing the homemaking responsibilities.

. . . Eighty-five per cent of single-parent families in 1981 were headed by a woman, and Statistics Canada data show that three out of five female-headed families were living below the poverty line. Women who have functioned primarily as homemakers may suffer enormously heavy economic penalties when their marriages unravel, and they should be assisted in the form of tax and pension measures as well as enforceable maintenance and support systems to help them resist poverty and achieve financial viability. When they apply for jobs, their homemaking and volunteer work should be considered legitimate work experience. If they work part-time, they should not bear the unfair financial brunt of a perception that part-time work is not serious work. They should be remunerated and receive benefits on a prorated basis with workers employed full-time.

But for all women, whether they work at home or in the paid labour force, it is crucial that they not be deemed for policy purposes as economic satellites of their partners. Tax laws, pension schemes, the public perception of parental responsibilities—all these need to be examined, and in some cases drastically revised, to confirm for women their status as independent individuals. to negate the perception of their dependency, and to discredit the assumption that they have a different range of options than men have . . . .

The care of children needs to be seen as a parental rather than a maternal responsibility. We are unfairly overburdening and restricting both men and women if we fail to base practices, employment and otherwise, on a policy of shared responsibility between men and women for the care of their children. Because responsibility for childcare used to be an exclusively maternal one, the greatest psychological pressure for the care of children is still felt by women. Childcare is thus a critical access route for women. Unless it is provided in adequate quality and quantity, the debate about the right to equal employment opportunity is academic for most women . . . .

Most women work in the clerical, sales, and support services of any corporation. These are not only the lowest paying jobs, they also tend to be jobs limited in opportunities for promotion. Even where women perform managerial functions, as many secretaries do, they are not given credit for these responsibilities when candidates for promotion to management are sought. Nor do women get the same educational or training leaves in corporations as do men, and they are rarely selected by corporations for significant corporate policy task forces or committees. Women must train for, be hired in, and given opportunities for the full range of occupational categories in order to break out of the economically limiting job segregation they now experience. This means more than an occasional token appointment of a woman to a management position; it means the routine hiring of qualified women throughout the occupational layers of a workforce.

Their work, wherever they perform it, should be valued and remunerated no less differently than work done by men. There is no excuse for excluding paid domestic workers from the protection of human rights or employment legislation. At the workplace, women should be free from sexual harassment. When sexual harassment has been proven, women should have available an effective and early remedy. They should be encouraged to qualify and apply for the widest range of jobs and careers, but where they choose to work in jobs traditionally held by women they should not, by virtue of working in a predominantly female occupation, be paid less than is paid for work that is no more valuable but is done predominantly by men.

Women should be encouraged to set up their own businesses and be assisted by banks and other lending institutions with no less serious consideration than that accorded men and no more onerous proof of their business potential than that required of men.

Native People

Native people in Canada include Status and non-Status Indians, Metis, and Inuit. It is not new that their economic conditions are poor. Study after study has documented the facts. The unemployment rate of native people is more than twice that of other Canadians. Those in the labour force are concentrated in low-paid, low-skill jobs. The average employment income in 1980 for native men was 60.2 per cent of the average income for non-native men; for native women it was 71.7 per cent of the average income for non-native women.

Their economic plight has taken its inevitable toll on social conditions. Native people are angry over the disproportionate numbers of native people who drop out of school, who are in prison, who suffer ill-health, who die young, who commit suicide. They are saddened by the personal, communal, and cultural dislocation of their people . . . .

. . . Notwithstanding efforts of numerous levels of government, native people do not have anything that begins to approximate equality in a country they inhabited before any others. They feel that the funding of an elaborate bureaucracy, ostensibly created for their benefit, would be more productively spent if directly allocated to their own administrative agencies. Many look to the settlement of land claims to release them from economic dependency.

The essence of the concerns expressed by native people was the need to participate in the decision-making process in areas that affect them. They are concerned that in all aspects of programming relating to native people—education, training, and social services—they are sometimes consulted but have no determinative say in the nature of the systems or institutions designed for their benefit.

Another major frustration is with the fragmentation of the system that delivers services to them. Not only are there three layers of government providing them with economic and social assistance pursuant to various statutes, there are a number of government agencies within every level. The result is that native people are often unaware of what programs exist or they spend so much time trying to find out what initiatives are available that their energy is deflected from more urgent needs . . . .

It is the perception of many native people that their lack of influence, the instability of funding, the fragmentation of government services, and the dearth of autonomy all undercut the development of a meaningful strategy to build the conditions of equality. One of the desired priorities in this strategy would be obtaining more funds and assistance for economic self-development. Although native people spent hours with this Commission discussing employment practices that tend to exclude native people, they stressed that ultimately economic self-sufficiency would make them better able to provide job opportunities for native people and develop the bargaining power necessary to realize the goals of their communities. They explained that they have difficulty getting credit from traditional lending institutions such as banks, and therefore find themselves in a position where, except for government assistance, they are unable to develop the economic structures to make them financially secure.

Many of their apprehensions are focused on an education system they feel is not accountable to the people it serves. There are insufficient numbers of native people teaching, resulting in an absence of role models for young children. Curricula in the public and high schools do not reflect the cultural differences of native persons, and therefore a sense of either alienation or unreality inhibits the development of the minds of children who are being taught about a world that often seems inhospitable or irrelevant to them.

There is an inadequate supply of relevant training programs. Training programs designed with insufficient input from native people often result in skills developed for jobs that are either unavailable or low-paying. Waiting lists are often as long as two years, There is a strong unmet demand for trades and technical training, as well as for basic literacy training and for upgrading and preparatory courses, such as basic job readiness. The lack of training programs specially designed for native people means that many existing programs are ineffective for them. Educational requirements for many of these training programs are felt to be unrealistically and inappropriately high and therefore arbitrarily exclude less educated native people from participating. They are concerned that they are being streamed into training for low-paid and low-skill jobs . . . .

For those native people living on reserves, or in rural and remote areas, the location of training programs or employment opportunities is a problem. Native people find that training courses tend to be too short to learn adequately the offered skills but too long for them to be comfortably away from families and communities. Transportation and communication costs are inadequate to allow visits home if the employment or training opportunity is far from the community.

Native women feel that they are doubly disadvantaged—on one level because they are women and on another level because they are native people. They feel that they are being constantly streamed into low-paying and irrelevant job opportunities.

For native women, particularly those living on reserves and in rural and remote areas, the lack of childcare acts as a barrier to training and employment opportunities. These women are also concerned that where childcare facilities do exist they tend not to be run by native people who can enhance the cultural environment found in the child's home . . . .

Moreover, the government agencies that provide services to adult native people are generally staffed by non-native persons who are often unable to understand the needs of native persons. The most frequent use of native persons is made in the Outreach program, whose workers perform many of the same functions as do regular government employees but are employed on a year-to-year contract position, with no benefits or security. They are perceived by native people to be critical to the delivery of government-run services for native people. There is resentment that native Outreach workers are being paid at a lesser rate than government employees, most of whom are not native people.

Native people living in urban areas encounter numerous difficulties. For Status Indians, some of these difficulties stem from the fact that they are not entitled to benefits that accrue to them if they live on reserves. This limits their options and is a disincentive to seeking job opportunities off the reserves, even if job opportunities are severely limited on the reserves. Status Indians requested amendments to the tax system to soften the impact of living off the reserves . . . .

Some native people indicated that once they were hired by corporations, they were denied promotions. They feel the psychological burden of having to perform better than a non-native worker in a given job; if they do less well, they fear being perceived as paradigmatic of all native people.

Some also complained that corporations often transport southern, non-native workers to sites in northern and remote areas rather than hire native people who live in the area. Native people feel that they are an underutilized source of labour in the north and are tapped only for the lowest-paid and lowest-status jobs. They pointed out the successful experiments of a number of corporations that introduced flexible work patterns to accommodate cultural differences and needs.

Native people acknowledged that programs to recruit and train them for the public service exist but criticized the lack of significant results. They find educational requirements for these programs unnecessarily high and opportunities few . . . .

Native people need better housing, services, and medical care. The Indian people want the paternalistic Indian Act abolished; it controls who can belong to Indian bands, the administration of reserves and reserve lands and resources, the ownership of reserve lands, and education. Although they explained that these were not, strictly speaking, employment issues, they felt they were fundamental to their well-being. Poor social and economic conditions and the absence of control over or contribution to the basic decision-making processes have undermined their ability to avail themselves of educational and employment opportunities . . . .

The central issues for native people are their exclusion from relevant decision-making, the fragmented and uncoordinated programming, the problem of uncoordinated policy approaches, the absence of federal/provincial/municipal coordination of service delivery systems, and the constant sense that they are forever subject to the discretion of people who do not understand their culture. As much as any group, they complained of the proliferation of discussion and research, and of the absence of corresponding political action. They feel a sense of urgency that is intense—the human cost of their political and economic positions has been enormously and inexcusably high.

Disabled Persons

Because the range of concerns among persons who are disabled varies with the nature of the disability, it is impossible to itemize every measure that must be taken to eliminate barriers for disabled persons.

What is possible, however, is to suggest an overall approach from which certain consistent steps will inevitably flow. It is also possible to identify certain aspects of the approach that will require flexibility in order to accommodate the full range of disabilities.

The World Health Organization (WHO) distinguishes among "impairment," "disability," and "handicap." An "impairment" embraces any disturbance of or interference with the normal structure and function of the body, including the systems of mental function. Health and Welfare Canada statistics place the number of Canadians who have some form of mental or physical impairment at 5.5 million.

"Disability," according to WHO, "is the loss or reduction of functional ability and activity" that results from an impairment. In other words, an impairment does not necessarily produce a disability, a fact reflected in the Health and Welfare Canada statistics estimating that fewer than half (2.3 million) of impaired Canadians can be termed disabled.

A "handicap" is defined by WHO as the disadvantage that is consequent upon impairment and disability.

The language of disability was very much a preoccupation of disabled persons across Canada. Many were particularly concerned because the language of disability often reinforces the perception of their incapacities rather than their capacities.

Persons with disabilities experience some limitation of their work functioning because of their physical or mental impairment. But the extent to which their disability affects their lives on a daily basis—that is, handicaps them—is very often determined by how society reacts to their disability. A disabled person need not be handicapped.

The significance of these distinctions lies in the fact that we have tended to consider disabled persons as a uniformly incapacitated group of people. Disability mayor may not lead to a handicap affecting employment.

It is therefore essential to develop an approach to the employment problems of disabled persons that treats disability as tangential to, rather than definitive of, the individual.

The issue must be examined from the point of view of the individual who has the disability rather than from the point of view of the assumptions of the employer. This is not to suggest that an employer's needs and concerns are not relevant; in fact, they may be critically so. But it is to suggest that the way one deals with this issue is first to determine whether or not the disabled person is qualified or qualifiable, and secondly to determine what measures are necessary to maximize the ability of a qualified disabled individual to perform the job for which he or she is being employed. The determination must be made individual by individual. Disabled persons do not expect to be hired for a job they cannot or could not be trained to do. What they are entitled to expect, however, is that wherever reasonably possible employers make adjustments to workplaces so that disabled persons are not handicapped in their ability to perform the job . . . .

The Commission was made aware of the formidable combination of a public perception that disabled persons have limited capacities and the uncertainty many disabled persons have about whether, in fact, they will be welcome and able to perform to maximum capacity in a work environment. More employment training must exist, and on-the-job support in the form of technical aids, personnel assistance, and a sensitized able-bodied workforce must all

be offered to make employment possible for disabled persons. Transportation systems have to be devised to ensure that physical access to employment is possible, and buildings must be constructed or retrofitted to be physically accessible in all respects to disabled persons.

Concern was expressed that certain job requirements demand irrelevant qualifications which have the effect of excluding disabled people from employment opportunity. The problem of irrelevant requirements all four designated groups. Job requirement that have a disparate impact on certain groups need to be analyzed to determine whether or not they are justified. Employment practices resulting in disparate impact are justifiable only if no reasonable alternative exists or if the practice is dictated by business necessity.

A related issue is the question of when an employer should be required to reasonably accommodate a disabled employee. Incentives must be given to employers to ensure that in those circumstances where accommodations should be made, it is economically feasible for the employer to make them. Amendments should be made to the Income Tax Act in order to permit employers to fully deduct these costs.

Although there was general agreement that wherever possible incentives should be provided to employers to accommodate people with disabilities, including tax deductions to retrofit premises, hire support personnel, and make available technical aids, there was also general agreement that wage subsidies were degrading. Moreover, from a practical point of view, the majority of such job opportunities appeared to end with the termination of the wage subsidy.

But whether or not an employer continues the employment of an individual originally hired with the assistance of a wage subsidy, disabled individuals felt strongly that no employer should be subsidized to hire qualified people. They generally find that this is debilitating psychologically, and that it undermines their confidence in their qualifications. They feel there are other ways to assist employers in making job opportunities available that do not border so perilously close to charity . . . .

For disabled persons, as for other individuals, two stages in employment equality are called for. The first stage is the preparation for their eligibility to compete fairly and equally for jobs—qualifying the qualifiable candidate for employment. In the education of the disabled child, for instance, the child should be made to feel that he or she is an equal social participant, with access to whatever services and systems exist for the general public.

The second stage is in preparing the work environment itself, where the effectiveness of the disabled person's performance may be determined by the extent to which the disability is either ignored, accommodated, or over-emphasized.

This emphasis on integration should be carried into an examination of which institutions are properly providing the care disabled persons need and which are unfairly isolating them from general opportunities. In addition, the public should be educated against making stereotypical judgements about disabled persons which prevent them from gaining access to those things to which they are otherwise entitled. The best education is the employment of a qualified disabled person who can, by doing the job, teach able-bodied fellow employees and employers that what was thought impossible is not only possible but inevitable.

Visible Minorities

Visible minorities were defined by this Commission for purposes of the questionnaire requesting data from the designated crown corporations as "non-whites." It is undoubtedly possible to define this category by country of origin, by race, or by some other criterion, but arguably it is as reasonable to approach this ambiguous categorization from the point of view of what problem was meant to be addressed. The issue was to attempt to ascertain the extent to which people who were visibly non-white were excluded thereby from employment opportunities available to whites.

It is by no means a definitive approach. Some non-whites face more serious employment barriers than others. Although it is unquestionably true that many non-whites face employment discrimination, the degree to which different minorities suffer employment and economic disadvantages varies significantly by group and by region. To combine all non-whites together as visible minorities for the purpose of devising systems to improve their equitable participation, without making distinctions to assist those groups in particular need, may deflect attention from where the problems are greatest. In devising ameliorative programs, therefore, the emphasis should be on concentrating efforts on those minorities in those regions where the need has been demonstrated. At present, data available from Statistics Canada are not sufficiently refined by race or region as to occupational segregation, income levels, job promotions, or other indicators of disadvantage to make determinative judgements as to which visible minorities appear not to be in need of employment equity programs. Any such exclusionary judgements should be made not only on the basis of better data, but also on the basis as well of consultations with the relevant minorities . . . .

Focusing on visible minority groups through employment equity programs does not relieve society of the responsibility to eradicate discrimination for all minority groups. It does not cancel the duty to provide for immigrants adequate language and skill training, biasfree mechanisms for determining the validity of foreign credentials and experience, and vigilant regard for whether employers are unreasonably making Canadian experience a job requirement. Nor does it absolve the school systems of their responsibility to ensure that minorities—visible or otherwise—are not being streamed routinely into certain types of courses. These are examples of the kind of measures that should be undertaken in any event to protect Canada's minorities from arbitrarily exclusionary systems.

Non-whites all across Canada complained of racism. They undeniably face discrimination, both overt and indirect.

Those who had been in Canada for many years particularly attributed their lack of employment opportunities to discrimination. They were people with recognized qualifications and proven job skills who found, nonetheless, that they were simply not promoted or given the same opportunities as whites with similar qualifications.

More recent immigrants did not as readily identify the problem as one of prejudice. Their attention focused primarily on the weaknesses in the services and facilities established to integrate them into Canadian life.

In both groups there was a sense that in Canada there is little understanding of and only slightly more tolerance of other cultures, and that newly arrived immigrants have difficulty understanding the Canadian culture.

The problems for newly arrived immigrants are enormous. There is little information given to them prior to their emigrating to prepare them for living in Canada, and they often arrive completely unfamiliar with Canadian life and institutions.

This has critical implications in employment contexts. In the interviewing process, for example, people are often hired on the basis of, among other things, an interviewer's perception of their ability to integrate easily into a given labour force. This may not be relevant either to the candidate's actual ability to integrate or to his or her qualifications.

Consistently across Canada the Commission heard that the language training an immigrant receives upon arrival is inadequate. The training tends to be too short; it tends to be English or French immersion which, for many immigrants, is an impossible pedagogical style; it is usually not taught by someone who speaks their own language; and it rarely provides instruction sufficient for them to be able to communicate with any degree of fluency. Moreover, an individual almost never receives language training in his or her own skill or profession. The absence of technical language training practically guarantees that the immigrant's job opportunities are severely restricted and that whatever qualifications he or she brought to this country will be underutilized . . . .

Many immigrants find, too, that when they apply for employment they are told that the job requires Canadian experience, an impossible qualification for recently arrived immigrants. Often the requirement has no objective relevance to the proper performance of the job.

The problem of professional or career credentials from other countries is a serious one for many who try without success to find ways of satisfying an employer that their educational qualifications match those required to perform the job.

Many skilled and professional immigrants are frustrated by the absence of a mechanism to determine whether or not the professional qualifications they bring to this country qualify them to practise their profession in Canada or to determine what upgrading courses are necessary. The examinations and licencing requirements for many occupations and professions across Canada are prohibitively expensive. There is an additional problem of portability from province to province of professional qualifications. A system of qualification and credential assessment should be available so that recent as well as prospective immigrants can be advised accurately about exactly what is necessary in order to qualify them to practise their professions. It is a waste of human and intellectual resources that these people are consistently underemployed for reasons that have less to do with their professional qualifications or qualifiability and more to do with the insularity of some professional organizations. Having been selected as immigrants to Canada, many on the strength of these very qualifications, it is unfair to put insurmountable impediments in the way of their practising the professions they may be qualified to practise. Standardized testing, as well as the elimination of requirements for Canadian citizenship in most jobs and professions, would do much to reduce these barriers . . . .

Career mobility was stressed as a problem. Even when individuals from visible minority groups are hired for jobs, many find that after a certain point they are unable to move up through the corporation with the same ease as are whites . . . .

Paid domestic workers, an occupation in which visible minorities are heavily represented, are inexplicably excluded from employment and human rights legislation . . . .

There are few role models for visible minorities in key public positions and members of visible minorities are not widely portrayed in the media as being an integral part of the community.

The problem is essentially one of racism. Strong measures are therefore needed to remedy the impact of discriminatory attitudes and behaviour flowing from this problem.

What is clear is that many groups of people living in Canada despair about ever being able to avail themselves of the economic, political, or social opportunities that exist in this country. They increasingly experience a sense of futility. Nothing short of strong legislative measures is necessary to reverse, or at least inhibit, the degree to which members of visible minorities are unjustifiably excluded from the opportunity to compete as equals.

Review and Discussion Questions

1. Abella claims that "Equality is, at the very least, freedom from adverse discrimination." She also claims that even if "we are not always sure what 'equality' means, most of us have a good understanding of what is 'fair.' And what is happening today in Canada to women, native people, disabled persons, and visible minorities is not fair." What does Abella mean by "fairness" and in what sense are issues of "equality" also issues of "fairness"?

2. Explain the difference between "disability" and "handicap" and discuss the relevance of the difference in cases of employment. Illustrate your discussion with the example of a blind person applying for a teaching position at a college of university.

3. For any one of the four designated groups, compare their position nowadays relative to their position as depicted by Abella in 1981–82. Offer documented evidence (studies, statistics from Statistics Canada, parliamentary or ministry reports, advocacy groups etc).

THE SANITIZED WORKPLACE

VICKI SCHULTZ

Since the 1980s, Canadian and American courts have interpreted sexual harassment to be a kind of sex discrimination and thus in violation of the provisions in civil rights legislation. No one doubts that this legal development has greatly improved the lot of working women. In this article, however, Vicki Schultz, a Yale Law School professor, argues that sexual harassment law and the corporate policies intended to implement it have gone too far. She criticizes them for (1) targeting even harmless sexual conduct as harassment whether or not it involves discrimination against women, (2) focusing on the misconduct of individual males rather than on larger structural issues that work against gender equality, and (3) endeavouring to drive sexuality entirely out of the workplace.

From *The Yale Law Journal*, Volume 112 (2003). Reprinted by permission of The Yale Law Journal Company, Inc. and William S. Hein Company.

INTRODUCTION

Does sex have a place in the workplace? According to most management theorists and feminist lawyers, the answer is a resounding no. Progress, they say, means precisely driving sex out of the workplace—whether in the name of efficiency or equality.

It may seem paradoxical that such strange bedfellows would endorse the same sanitizing impulse; feminists are rarely viewed as close companions of corporate management. But upon further examination, it isn't ironic or strange at all. One of American society's most cherished beliefs is that the workplace is—or should be—asexual. The dominant ethic says, "Work is work, and sex is sex, and never the twain shall meet." Call it the ethic of workplace asexuality.

One may be tempted to attribute this ethic to Americans' prudishness, and, of course, conservative sexual sensibilities probably have played a role. But our commitment to workplace asexuality is, even more directly, a legacy of our historic commitment to a certain conception of organizational rationality. It wasn't Victorian churchwomen, but twentieth-century organization men who took the lead in creating the asexual imperative: men like

Frederick Winslow Taylor, who saw managers as rational "heads" who would control the unruly "hands" and irrational "hearts" of those who assumed their places as workers in the modern organization. Although the necessity of bureaucratic organization has come under challenge in recent years, the drive toward asexuality is not fading along with it. Today, as much as ever, sexuality is seen as something "bad"—or at least beyond the bounds of professionalism—that should be banished from organizational life. If sexuality cannot be banished entirely, then those who embody or display it must be brought under tight control and subjected to discipline.

Although the drive to sanitize the workplace raises a range of fascinating issues about the place of sexuality and other affective elements of human life in contemporary organizations, it is beyond the scope of this Article to deal with most of them here. My goal is more modest: to show how sexual harassment law, as envisioned by some feminist reformers and implemented by many human resource (HR) managers, has become an important justification for a neo-Taylorist project of suppressing sexuality and intimacy in the workplace. To put it plainly, sex harassment policies now provide an added incentive and an increased legitimacy for management to control and discipline relatively harmless sexual behavior without even inquiring into whether that behavior undermines gender equality on the job.

. . . Although organizations are the main actors driving the sanitization process, the legal system has played an important role in providing incentive and cover for sanitization. In the United States, sex harassment has been viewed primarily as a form of sex discrimination under Title VII of the Civil Rights Act, the federal statute that prohibits sex discrimination in employment. Title VII says nothing about sexuality; it simply prohibits discrimination based on sex. Thus, under the statute, the concept of sex harassment might have been elaborated to cover the full range of hostile and discriminatory actions—both sexual and nonsexual—that tend to keep women (or men who fail to conform to prescribed gender roles) in unequal jobs or work roles . . . .

Instead, the federal agency and the lower courts charged with interpreting the Title VII defined harassment primarily in terms of sexual advances and other sexual conduct—an approach I call the sexual model. In earlier work, I showed that this sexual model is too narrow, because the focus on sexual conduct has obscured more fundamental problems of gender-based harassment and discrimination that are not primarily "sexual" in content or design. In this Article, I show that the sexual model is also too broad, because the same focus on sexual conduct that has led *courts* to ignore these larger patterns of sexism and discrimination is also leading *companies* to prohibit a broad range of relatively harmless sexual conduct, even when that conduct does not threaten gender equality on the job. In the name of preventing sexual harassment, many companies are proscribing sexual conduct that would not amount to sexual harassment, let alone sex discrimination, under the law. Many firms are even banning or discouraging intimate relation-ships between their employees. Worst of all, companies are disciplining (and even firing) employees for these perceived sexual transgressions without bothering to examine whether they are linked to sex discrimination in purpose or effect.

. . . How can we understand the campaign to sanitize the workplace that employers are undertaking in the name of sexual harassment law? Libertarian critics claim that the threat of employer liability under Title VII, combined with a vague definition of harassment, gives employers an incentive to go overboard in regulating employee conduct. But this explanation fails to account for the central puzzle of this reform effort: Why are employers cracking down on *sexual* conduct, rather than equally serious *nonsexual* forms of harassment and discrimination for which they are also liable? Firms often simply go through the motions or even resist legal mandates; why have they responded so enthusiastically, even overzealously, to this body of law?

The answer lies in the fact that sexual harassment law resonated with a widely shared conception of organizational rationality. The legal system's focus on the harmfulness of sexual conduct tapped into an age-old view of sexuality that was deeply ingrained in managerial ideology and successfully exploited by feminist leaders. Classical organizational theory holds that sexuality and other "personal" forces are at odds with productivity and out of place in organizational life. Rather than challenging this conception, many feminists who campaigned against sexual harassment explicitly drew on it. They argued that men's sexual conduct subverted women's equal standing as employees, while at the same time undermining organizational productivity. Like classical organizational theory, feminist arguments pitted workplace sexuality, and professional competence and productivity, against each other . . . .

As I elaborate, . . . the confluence of legal, feminist, managerial, and popular ideals created an environment in which organizational actors have been able to steer the law to serve their own ends. As sociologists of law have shown, human resource managers—the inside managers and outside consultants who specialize in helping organizations handle personnel matters—and management-side labor lawyers consistently shape understandings of law and compliance with it in a direction that emphasizes organizational aims, especially efficiency. In the context of a legal system that highlighted the harm of workplace sexual conduct, a feminist campaign that condemned it as inconsistent with women's equality, a managerial tradition that defined it as in conflict with organizational rationality, and a news media that sensationalized it, it was almost predictable that HR managers and lawyers would mobilize sexual harassment law in the service of suppressing sexual conduct . . . . These experts have encouraged companies to punish sexual conduct without attending to the larger structures of gender inequality in which genuine harassment flourishes. They urge "zero-tolerance" policies and "cultural sensitivity" approaches that err on the side of prohibiting sexual conduct that might subjectively be perceived as offensive (such as sexual jokes and remarks), or that might even conceivably lead to sexual harassment claims (such as office romances).

Aided by extensive press coverage that has popularized the idea of harassment-as-sexual-conduct and generated an intense fear of legal liability, these experts' views are taking hold in organizational life . . . . The motivations of these experts, and the employers who rely on their advice, are complex. Obviously, it is in the experts' self-interest to interpret the law in a way that allows them to create a market for their own services (such as sexual harassment policies and training programs). But self-interest can coexist with idealistic, or at least ideological, impulses. Perhaps, like early feminists, many professionals and managers genuinely believe that workplace sexual conduct harms women. Perhaps many of them see sexual harassment law as an acceptable—even progressive—justification for imposing prohibitions that serve other management interests. Perhaps both. Troublingly, . . . there are hints that employers sometimes seize on accusations of sexual harassment as a pretext for less benign motives for firing employees, such as age discrimination or sexual orientation discrimination. In other cases, employers seem to be acting in good faith to enforce sexual harassment policies that simply reach too far. Either way, no effort is made to determine whether the alleged harassment was linked to sex discrimination. In the hands of organizational actors, the concept of sex harassment has been given a direction of its own, diverted from the larger goals of employment discrimination law.

. . . The focus on sexual conduct has encouraged organizations to treat harassment as a stand-alone phenomenon—a problem of bad or boorish men who oppress or offend women—rather than as a symptom of larger patterns of sex segregation and inequality. As a result, companies can feel good about punishing individual employees for sexual offenses while doing little or nothing to address the overarching dynamics of harassment and discrimination that preserve gender hierarchy at work. By displacing attention away from genuine problems of sex discrimination and associating feminism with a punitive stance toward sexuality, I believe the drive toward sexual sanitization may even undercut the goal of achieving gender equality.

To add to the problem, the emphasis on eliminating sexual conduct encourages employees to articulate broader workplace harms as forms of sexual harassment, obscuring more structural problems that may be the true source of their disadvantage. Thus, women may complain about sexual jokes, when their real concern is a caste system that relegates them to low-status, low-pay positions . . . . Even more worrying is the prospect that some employees may make allegations of sexual harassment that disproportionately disadvantage racial and sexual minorities . . . . White women who enjoy sexual banter and flirtation with their white male coworkers may regard the same conduct as a form of sexual harassment when it comes from men of color . . . .

The truth is that managers cannot succeed in banishing sexuality from the workplace: They can only subject particular expressions of it to surveillance and discipline. Although some groups suffer more than others when this occurs, everyone loses . . . . I am . . . concerned about the threats to human intimacy and the negative politics of

sexuality that are ushered in by the drive toward sanitization. With the decline of civil society, the workplace is one of the few arenas left in our society where people from different walks of life can come to know one another well. Because people who work together come into close contact with each other for extended periods for the purpose of achieving common goals, work fosters extraordinarily intimate relationships of both the sexually charged and the more platonic varieties. When managers prohibit or discourage employees from dating each other, they deprive people of perhaps the single most promising avenue available for securing sexual partners. And, when managers punish employees for sexualized interactions with each other, they create a climate that may stifle workplace friendships and solidarity more generally . . . .

Even more is at stake than whether or not people can form close friendships at work: The larger question is whether we as a society can value the workplace as a realm alive with personal intimacy, sexual energy, and "humanness" more broadly . . . . The old Taylorist dream of the workplace as a sterile zone in which workers suspend all their human attributes while they train their energies solely on production doesn't begin to reflect the rich, multiple roles that work serves in people's lives. For most people, working isn't just a way to earn a livelihood. It's a way to contribute something to the larger society, to struggle against their limits, to make friends and form communities, to leave their imprint on the world, and to know themselves and others in a deep way . . . .

. . . The drive to sanitize the workplace assumes that sexuality is properly a private element that will assume a destructive quality if unleashed in a public setting. But . . . sexuality isn't . . . always discriminatory or destructive to organizational life: It can serve a variety of positive ends. Just as individual employees may express themselves or embroider intimate relations through sexual language and conduct, so too may employees as a group resort to sexual interactions to alleviate stress or boredom on the job, to create vital forms of community and solidarity with each other, or to articulate resistance to oppressive management practices. Research suggests that workplace romance may even increase productivity in some circumstances.

Contrary to prevailing orthodoxy, such uses of workplace sexuality do not always harm or disadvantage women: A lot depends on the larger structural context in which the sexuality is expressed . . . . As a well-accepted body of systematic social science research demonstrates, women who enter jobs in which they are significantly underrepresented often confront hostility and harassment from incumbent male workers, and in some settings the men use sexual conduct as a means of marking the women as "different" and out of place. However, a new body of sociological research suggests that women who work in more integrated, egalitarian settings often willingly participate and take pleasure in sexualized interactions—probably because their numerical strength gives them the power to help shape the sexual norms and culture to their own liking. Rather than presuming that women will always find sexual conduct offensive, this research suggests that we should ensure that women are fully integrated into equal jobs and positions of authority, thus giving them the power to decide for themselves what kind of work cultures they want to have.

This analysis leads me to the conclusion that, in a pluralistic society, we should neither encourage nor cede to management the unilateral power to censor sexual conduct. Instead, we should strive to create structurally egalitarian work settings in which employees can work with management to forge their own norms about sexual conduct . . . .

The contemporary drive to sanitize the workplace came about through a complex interplay of forces in which feminists, judges, HR managers, lawyers, and the news media all helped create an understanding that sexuality disadvantages women and disrupts productivity. In my view, we can only hope to halt the sanitization process by articulating a more appealing vision in which sexuality and intimacy can coexist with, and perhaps even enhance, gender equality and organizational rationality. This is a tremendous task, but, for reasons I hope emerge clearly from this Article, one I believe is worthy of the efforts of the next generation of scholars, feminists, lawyers, and managers . . . .

EQUATING SEXISM AND SEXUALITY

. . . Instead of challenging the ethic of asexuality, a powerful strand of the [American women's] movement mounted a legal campaign to curb men's sexual conduct. Feminist activists and lawyers invented a claim for sexual harassment, which holds companies responsible for unwanted sexual conduct as a form of sex discrimination in employment. Through this approach, feminists joined management's traditional drive to desexualize the workplace and demanded its contemporary completion. Management might believe the workplace was asexual, feminists claimed, but women's entrance had occasioned overt displays of heterosexual male predation. Men's sexual overtures subverted gender equality, feminists contended, for women could never be respected as employees so long as they were regarded as sexual objects. Not only did male sexuality threaten women's interests, it also interfered with everyone's productivity—men and women alike. Thus, feminists could claim, rationalizing the workplace required reining in male sexuality.

The centerpiece of this feminist strategy was equating unwanted sexual conduct with sex discrimination—a powerful maneuver that has crowded out other notions of workplace harassment and justified the drive to root sex out of the work-world. Feminist lawyers focused on Title VII of the Civil Rights Act, which holds employers liable for sex discrimination and other forms of discrimination in employment. But Title VII does not mention sexuality or even sex harassment; its purpose was to end discriminatory job segregation. Thus, feminists might have pushed for a broad concept of sex harassment that encompassed the entire range of hostile and discriminatory actions—both sexual and nonsexual—through which supervisors and coworkers labeled women workers "different" and inferior, thereby

helping to preserve historic patterns of sex segregation in employment that consigned women to lower-status, lower-paying, female-dominated jobs . . . .

But . . . most feminists did not pursue this path. Instead, feminist activists and lawyers pushed for a narrower understanding of sex harassment, defining the concept in terms of unwanted male-female sexual advances. They argued that such sexual advances were discriminatory and harmful to women—an argument that inspired sympathy among both liberal and socially conservative judges. Courts first accepted this line of argument in an early group of cases commonly known as quid pro quo harassment cases, in which male supervisors fired female subordinates for refusing their sexual advances. Although alternative lines of reasoning were available, the lower courts located the source of sex discrimination in the *sexual desire* presumed to motivate the supervisor's sexual advances. A heterosexual male boss's sexual come-on toward a female employee is discriminatory, said the courts, because the boss would not have been attracted to—and thus would not have made a sexual advance toward—a male employee . . . . Over time, the sexualized understanding of harassment that arose out of the quid pro quo cases came to overwhelm the concept of hostile work environment harassment as well. As a result, courts have tended to single out sexual advances and other conduct of a sexual nature for disapproval, and have tended to exonerate even serious patterns of sexist misconduct that could not be easily characterized as sexually motivated . . . .

THE LEGAL AND CULTURAL ENVIRONMENT

. . . My reading of the available evidence is that the libertarian critics of sexual harassment law are partly right: In the name of preventing sexual harassment, many companies *are* punishing benign forms of sexual conduct that would not amount to sexual harassment or sex discrimination under the law. These critics claim that the threat of strict liability for sex harassment, combined with uncertainty about when individual instances of conduct might combine to create an actionable environment, creates an incentive for companies to go overboard in curtailing sexual conduct, as noted above. Yet these factors cannot explain why organizations are curtailing *sexual* conduct, as opposed to equally serious *nonsexual* forms of harassment and discrimination. Only the fact that the legal system has highlighted the harm of sexual conduct helps explain this trend. The sexual model is the engine of sanitization.

Thus, although the libertarian critics are right about *what* is happening, they are wrong about *why*: There *is* organizational overreaching, but it is not an inevitable consequence of treating sex harassment as a violation of Title VII. Instead, it is an example of a process that is more akin to what sociologist Lauren Edelman has termed the "managerialization of law." Sociologists of law have emphasized how organizations respond to legal environments by reinterpreting legal ideals and infusing them with managerial values. They have shown that, particularly when the law is ambiguous, managerial actors will actively work to shape the meaning of the law and compliance "through a set of managerial lenses chiefly designed to encourage smooth employment relations and high productivity." They have highlighted the role of HR managers, and, to a lesser extent, lawyers, in this translation process, showing how these professionals interpret the law to maximize their own self-interest while at the same time serving organizational ends. They have also shown how the press contributes to the process, by bringing lawsuits to the attention of HR professionals and managers and generating a fear of bad publicity that is perhaps as powerful as the fear of liability itself . . . .

PROHIBITING SEXUAL CONDUCT

. . . Surveys confirm that the overwhelming majority of American companies have policies prohibiting sexual harassment, and these policies tend to reach broadly to forbid many forms of potentially harmless sexual conduct without demanding inquiry into the surrounding factors that would determine legal liability. To begin with, the policies define harassment exclusively in terms of sexual conduct (as opposed to conduct that discriminates on the basis of sex more generally). In fact, most of the surveys and policies track the language of the EEOC guidelines, which . . . define harassment in terms of "[u]nwelcome sexual advances, requests for sexual favors, and other verbal or physical conduct of a sexual nature." . . .

. . . My review of numerous sex harassment policies adopted by companies or proposed by experts confirms that most prohibit a broad range of sexual conduct that would not necessarily be legally actionable. Most policies begin by citing the EEOC guidelines' definition, and then expand upon it by listing various forms of covered conduct, including sexual joking and banter, visual displays, and various forms of touching. The Bureau of National Affairs book, *Preventing Employment Lawsuits*, for example, includes a sample sexual harassment policy that begins by quoting the definition from the EEOC guidelines. The policy elaborates on the definition by stating that sexual harassment includes, but is not limited to, "sexual innuendoes, sexual propositions, jokes of a sexual nature, sexually suggestive cartoons, suggestive or insulting sounds, leers, sexually related whistles, and obscene gestures. In addition, pinching, brushing against another person's body, and subtle pressure for sexual favors is [sic] considered harassment." . . .

Just as many sexual harassment policies have been crafted in an overzealous spirit, many are being enforced in a similar spirit. When sexual harassment is defined in terms of conduct of a sexual nature with no understanding of how harassment is linked to larger forms of inequality such as job segregation by sex, there is no incentive for companies to engage in structural reforms that might reduce the incidence of harassment, such as integrating their workforces. Instead, current law sets up incentives for employers to punish individual employees for engaging in any sexual conduct that might be seen as contributing to a hostile work environment—incentives that mesh well with many employers' preexisting inclinations to

view sexual conduct as disruptive and out of place in the workplace . . . .

Sexual harassment law has also provided new momentum for policing consensual intimate relationships between employees. In the name of preventing harassment, employers are not simply prohibiting employees' sexual misconduct on the job: They are also policing employees' sexual relationships off the job. Not only has workplace flirting become suspect, so too has falling in love (and lust).

Although there are a number of reasons why companies might have concerns about workplace romance, a growing literature pinpoints fear of sexual harassment liability as the reason companies must take action. [Consider, for example,] consultants Laurie Jones (who advocates telling employees, "You don't date! There's a million other people out there!"), Holly Culhane (who argues that "any type of dating relationship is a potential sexual harassment situation"), and Craig Pratt (whose model handbook strongly discourages even fully consensual employee relationships). The "how-to-avoid-liability" literature generally confirms the view that employee relationships are dangerous—even explosive—because they can land companies in trouble for sexual harassment. "[O]ffice romances . . . [may] lead to sexual harassment, which is illegal and for which employers can be held liable to the tune of millions of dollars in legal fees, settlements, and penalties—enough to cripple or bankrupt most companies," warned one business journal . . . .

DISREGARDING DISCRIMINATION

Underneath this avalanche of no-dating policies, . . . zero-tolerance policies, self-policing, and discipline for conduct with sexual overtones, the most fundamental goal of employment discrimination law has been lost. Title VII should not be used to police sexuality; it was meant to guarantee women and men equal work roles. The drive to eliminate sexuality from the workplace has detracted from this important goal—and may even encourage organizations to act in ways that undermine genuine workplace equality.

At the level of individual complaint, companies do not attempt to determine whether the alleged sexual harassment was linked to sex discrimination. They simply *assume* that any sexual conduct covered by their policies is discriminatory or harmful. Yet, in many of the cases in which men have been fired or disciplined for violating sexual harassment policies, the women who were the alleged targets of the harassment did not even object (or voiced only vague objections) to the conduct for which the offenders were punished . . . .

At the organizational level, sexual harassment policies have taken on a life of their own, divorced from the larger goal of dismantling sex discrimination. As I have emphasized above, . . . sex harassment is integrally linked to such sex segregation in employment. Sex segregation structures work environments in which harassment flourishes because numerical dominance encourages male job incumbents to associate their work with masculinity and to police their jobs by treating women and gender-nonconforming men as "different" and out of place. By the same token, sex harassment preserves segregation by driving away or denigrating the newcomers who would integrate the job. As a tool of segregation, sex harassment assumes many forms—not all of which can be easily or even best characterized as "sexual" in content or design.

Despite this linkage between sex harassment and sex segregation, few companies are taking steps to incorporate their sex harassment policies into more comprehensive plans to integrate women equally into all levels of the organization. Indeed, most experts do not even see harassment as a problem that might be alleviated by taking steps to achieve gender integration. Among consultants, the typical approach is represented by Beverly R. Davis, a consultant in San Diego, who regards sex harassment as unrelated to the larger structural forms of discrimination that result in segregation . . . . Her recommendations for how to prevent harassment do not include recommendations for how to prevent other forms of sex discrimination (such as discrimination in hiring, promotion, training, and evaluation). Indeed, when asked if she believes sex harassment is linked to any of these other structural forms of discrimination, she said, "No."

Instead, like a number of other consultants interviewed, Davis saw harassment as a "power issue" that afflicts individual men. "It's usually a coworker, male against female thing . . . . [I]t's a way to pick on that employee," a way of saying, "'I'm better than you, I have power over you.'" . . .

Once harassment is attributed to the psychosexual proclivities of individual male workers or the external cultural insensitivities of the men as a group, rather than linked to larger organizational structures, it makes sense to deal with it through stand-alone policies that regulate sexual conduct through the threat (and reality) of employer discipline. Throughout America, as we have seen, companies seek to prevent harassment by prohibiting various forms of sexual conduct, conducting training sessions to "sensitize" supervisors and workers, and warning employees of the disciplinary consequences applied to those who fail to comply. Companies seek to remedy harassment by setting up machinery to process individual complaints and by undertaking investigations to identify and punish the harassers, one by one . . . .

CONCLUSION

No recent legal campaign for equality has seemed to achieve more immediate and complete success than the one against sexual harassment. Yet, the idea that the law has succeeded in creating egalitarian workplaces is largely an illusion. Early on, as we have seen, the promise of sex harassment law to help dismantle sex segregation and inequality was lost and replaced with an emphasis on eradicating workplace sexuality. In the process, sexual harassment law has bestowed new life and increased legitimacy on an age-old managerial dream of achieving a perfectly rational workplace devoid of sexuality and other distracting passions.

As the sexual sanitization campaign advances, some people are harmed more than others, but we all lose. In the name of preventing sexual harassment, employers increasingly ban or discourage employee romance, chilling intimacy and solidarity among employees of both a sexual and nonsexual variety. Many companies are punishing employees for behavior that does not meet the legal definition of sex harassment, costing many workers their jobs and undercutting their ability to express themselves and create their own cultures and sexual norms. Women are encouraged to translate—and perhaps even to understand—broader forms of discrimination and managerial abuse as sexual harms. Perhaps most disturbingly, managers sometimes invoke sex harassment law as a pretext for firing people on discriminatory or otherwise suspect grounds, and employees use it to legitimate their bias against coworkers of a different race, sexual orientation, or class whose sexuality threatens or offends them.

In the face of these developments, neither managers nor their advisers are considering the all-important question that Title VII demands we ask: Is the sexual conduct in question being used to discriminate in purpose or effect? As I hope to have persuaded readers, workplace sexual conduct isn't necessarily discriminatory or harmful; employees often use sexuality in the service of benign and even empowering ends. The sexual model of sex harassment and the resulting sanitization campaign are based on a false premise that sexuality is an individual attribute that can be isolated and purged from institutions.

Review and Discussion Questions

1. What is the "sexual model" of sexual harassment? Why does Schultz believe that it is both too narrow and too broad? According to her, in what way do management interests coincide with current interpretations of sexual harassment law?

2. Do you agree that corporate sexual harassment policies go too far in trying to eliminate sexuality from the workplace? Explain why or why not. Do companies today punish employees too severely for perceived sexual misconduct?

3. Should the workplace be an asexual environment, or is Schultz right that sexuality has a positive role to play inside the organization?

4. What sort of formal policies, if any, should companies have regarding sexual harassment and sexual conduct by employees? Should companies discourage dating and office romances?

5. Are corporations genuinely concerned about sexual harassment? Is it a moral issue for them, or are they only trying to reduce their legal liability? Is Schultz right that corporations tend to focus on sexual misconduct while ignoring larger questions of sex equality? If so, what explains this?

HOMOSEXUALITY, PREJUDICE, AND DISCRIMINATION

RICHARD D. MOHR

Mohr addresses his paper specifically to the U.S. legal situation regarding sexual orientation and job discrimination on its basis. Canadian legislation is more progressive in this regard, as the Canadian Human Rights Act forbids discrimination also on the basis of sexual discrimination. Still, Mohr's paper is worth reading since not only does he describe the discrimination that homosexuals suffer, both on and off the job, but he also attacks some of the myths and stereotypes surrounding homosexuality and rebuts the contention that it is immoral or unnatural. He argues that civil rights legislation should be extended to protect lesbians and gay men from private-sector discrimination because doing so will permit them to enter the mainstream, thus enriching society and confirming our commitment to human rights.

STEREOTYPES

Who are gays anyway? Though the number of gays in America is hotly disputed, studies agree that gays are distributed through every stripe and stratum of Americans. Who are homosexuals? They are your friends, your minister, your teacher, your bankteller, your doctor, your mailcarrier, your officemate, your roommate, your congressional representative, your sibling, parent, and spouse. They are we. We are everywhere, virtually all ordinary, virtually all unknown.

Ignorance about gays, however, has not stopped people's minds from being filled with stereotypes about gays. Society holds two oddly contradictory groups of anti-gay stereotypes. One revolves around an individual's allegedly confused gender identity: lesbians are females who want to be, or at least look and act like, men—bulldykes, diesel dykes; while gay men are males who want to be, or at least look and act like, women—queens, fairies, nances, limp-wrists, nellies, sissies, aunties. These stereotypes of mismatches between biological sex and socially defined gender provide the materials through which lesbians and gay men become the butts of ethnic-like jokes. These stereotypes and jokes, though derisive, basically view lesbians and gay men as ridiculous . . . .

The other set of stereotypes revolves around gays as a pervasive sinister conspiratorial threat. The core stereotype here is that of the gay person—especially the gay man—as child molester, and more generally as sex-crazed maniac. Homosexuality here is viewed as a vampire-like corruptive contagion. These stereotypes carry with them fears of the very destruction of family and civilization itself. Now, that

which is essentially ridiculous can hardly have such a staggering effect. Something must be afoot.

Clarifying the nature of stereotypes can help make sense of this incoherent amalgam. Stereotypes are not simply false generalizations from a skewed sample of cases examined. Admittedly, false generalizing plays some part in the stereotypes society holds about gays and other groups. If, for instance, one takes as one's sample gay men who are in psychiatric hospitals or prisons, as was done in nearly all early investigations, not surprisingly one will probably find them to be of a crazed or criminal cast. Such false generalizations, though, simply confirm beliefs already held on independent grounds, ones that likely led the investigator to the prison and psychiatric ward to begin with. Evelyn Hooker, who in the late 1950s carried out the first rigorous studies of non-clinical gay men, found that psychiatrists, when presented with case files including all the standard diagnostic psychological profiles—but omitting indications of sexual orientation—were unable to distinguish gay files from non-gay ones, even though they believed gay men to be crazy. These studies proved a profound embarrassment to the psychiatric establishment, which has profited throughout the century by attempting to "cure" allegedly insane gays. The studies led eventually to the decision by the American Psychiatric Association in 1973 to drop homosexuality from its registry of mental illnesses. Nevertheless, the stereotype of gays as "sick" continues to thrive in the mind of America.

False generalizations help maintain stereotypes; they do not form them. As the history of Hooker's discoveries shows, stereotypes have a life beyond facts; their origin lies in a culture's ideology—the general system of beliefs by which it lives—and they are sustained across generations by diverse cultural transmissions, including slang and jokes, which usually don't even purport to have a scientific basis. Stereotypes, then, are not the products of bad science, but reflections of society's conception of itself.

Understanding this much, it is easy to see how stereotypes about gays as gender-confused reinforce still powerful gender roles in American society. What these stereotypes presume about gays and condemn is the notion that freely choosing one's social roles independently of one's biological sex might threaten many guiding social divisions, both domestic and commercial. Blurred would be the socially sex-linked distinctions between breadwinner and homemaker, boss and secretary, doctor and nurse, protector and protected, even God and His world. The accusations "fag" and "dyke" serve in significant part to keep women in their place and to prevent men from breaking ranks and ceding away theirs.

The stereotypes of gays as destroyers of civilization function to displace (possibly irresolvable) social problems from their actual source to a remote and (society hopes) manageable one. For example, the stereotype of the gay person as child molester functions to give the traditionally defined family unit a false sheen of innocence. It keeps the unit from being examined too closely for incest, child abuse, wife-battering, and the terrorizing of women and children by a father's constant threats. The stereotype teaches that the problems of the family are not internal to it, but external.

If this account of stereotypes holds, society has been profoundly immoral. For its treatment of gays is a grand-scale rationalization, a moral sleight-of-hand. The problem is not that society's usual standards of evidence and procedure in decision making have been misapplied to gays, rather when it comes to gays, the standards themselves have simply been ruled out of court and disregarded in favor of mechanisms that encourage unexamined fear and hatred.

DISCRIMINATION AGAINST GAYS

Partly because lots of people suppose they don't know any gay people and partly through the maintaining of stereotypes, society at large is unaware of the many ways in which gays are subject to discrimination in consequence of widespread fear and hatred. Contributing to this social ignorance of discrimination is the difficulty for gay people, as an invisible minority, even to complain of discrimination. If one is gay, the act of registering a complaint suddenly targets oneself as a stigmatized person, and so, especially in the absence of any protection against discrimination, simply invites additional discrimination. So, discrimination against gays, like rape, goes seriously underreported. Even so, known discrimination is massive.

Annual studies by the National Gay and Lesbian Task Force have consistently found that over 90 percent of gay men and lesbians have been victims of violence or harassment in some form on the basis of their sexual orientation. Greater than one in five gay men and nearly one in ten lesbians have been punched, hit, or kicked; a quarter of all gays have had objects thrown at them; a third have been chased; a third have been sexually harassed, and 14 percent have been spit on, all just for being perceived to be gay . . . .

Gays are also subject to widespread discrimination in employment. Governments are leading offenders here. They do a lot of discriminating themselves, require that others do it, and set precedents favoring discrimination in the private sector. First and foremost, the armed forces discriminate against lesbians and gay men. The federal government has also denied gay men and lesbians employment in the CIA, FBI, and the National Security Agency—and continues to defend such discrimination in the courts. The government refuses to give security clearances to gays and so forces the country's considerable private sector military and aerospace contractors to fire employees known to be gay and to avoid hiring those perceived to be gay. State and local governments regularly fire gay teachers, policemen, firemen, social workers, and anyone who has contact with the public. Further, state licensing laws (though frequently honored only in the breach) officially bar gays from a vast array of occupations and professions—everything from doctors, lawyers, accountants, and nurses to hairdressers, morticians, even used-car dealers.

Gays are subject to discrimination in a wide variety of other ways, including private-sector employment, public accommodations, housing, insurance of all types, custody, adoption, and zoning regulations that bar "singles" or "nonrelated" couples from living together. A 1988 study by the Congressional Office of Technology Assessment found that a third of America's insurance companies openly admit that they discriminate against lesbians and gay men. In nearly half the states, same-sex sexual behavior is illegal.

Legal sanctions, discrimination, and the absorption by gays of society's hatred all interact to impede and, for some, block altogether the ability of gay men and lesbians to create and maintain significant personal relations with loved ones. Every facet of life is affected by discrimination. Only the most compelling reasons could possibly justify it.

BUT ISN'T HOMOSEXUALITY IMMORAL?

Many people suppose society's treatment of gays is justified because they think gays are extremely immoral. To evaluate this claim, different senses of "moral" must be distinguished. Sometimes "morality" means the values generally held by members of a society—its mores, norms, and customs. On this understanding, gays certainly are not moral: lots of people hate them, and social customs are designed to register widespread disapproval of gays. The problem here is that this sense of morality is merely a descriptive one. Every society has this kind of morality—even Nazi society, which had racism and mob rule as central features of its "morality" understood in this sense. Before one can use the notion of morality to praise or condemn behavior, what is needed is a sense of morality that is prescriptive or normative.

As the Nazi example makes clear, the fact that a belief or claim is descriptively moral does not entail that it is normatively moral. A lot of people in a society saying that something is good, even over aeons, does not make it so. The rejection of the long history of the socially approved and state-enforced institution of slavery is another good example of this principle at work. Slavery would be wrong even if nearly everyone liked it. So consistency and fairness require that one abandon the belief that gays are immoral simply because most people dislike or disapprove of gays.

Furthermore, recent historical and anthropological research has shown that opinion about gays has been by no means universally negative. It has varied widely even within the larger part of the Christian era and even within the Church itself. There are even current societies—most notably in Papua New Guinea—where compulsory homosexual behavior is integral to the rites of male maturity. Within the last thirty years, American society has undergone a grand turnabout from deeply ingrained, nearly total condemnation to nearly total acceptance on two emotionally charged "moral" or "family" issues—contraception and divorce. Society holds its current descriptive morality of gays not because it has to, but because it chooses to.

Clearly popular opinion and custom are not enough to ground moral condemnation of homosexuality. Religious arguments are also frequently used to condemn homosexuality. Such arguments usually proceed along two lines. One claims that the condemnation is a direct revelation of God, usually through the Bible. The other sees condemnation in

God's plan as manifested in nature; homosexuality (it is claimed) is "contrary to nature."

One of the more remarkable discoveries of recent gay research is that the Bible may not be as univocal in its condemnation of homosexuality as many have believed. Christ never mentions homosexuality. Recent interpreters of the Old Testament have pointed out that the story of Lot at Sodom is probably intended to condemn inhospitality rather than homosexuality. Further, some of the Old Testament condemnations of homosexuality seem simply to be ways of tarring those of the Israelites' opponents who happen to accept homosexual practices when the Israelites themselves did not. If so, the condemnation is merely a quirk of history and rhetoric rather than a moral precept.

What does seem clear is that those who regularly cite the Bible to condemn an activity like homosexual sex do so by reading it selectively. Do clergy who cite what they take to be condemnations of homosexuality in Leviticus maintain in their lives all the hygienic, dietary, and marital laws of Leviticus? If they cite the story of Lot at Sodom to condemn homosexuality, do they also cite the story of Lot in the Cave to condone incestuous rape? It seems then not that the Bible is being used to ground condemnations of homosexuality as much as society's dislike of homosexuality is being used to interpret the Bible.

Even if a consistent portrait of condemnation could be gleaned from the Bible, what social significance should it be given? One of the guiding principles of society, enshrined in the Constitution as a check against the government, is that decisions affecting social policy are not made on religious grounds. The Religious Right has been successful in thwarting sodomy law reform, in defunding gay safe-sex literature and gay art, and in blocking the introduction of gay materials into school curriculums. If the real ground of the alleged immorality invoked by governments to discriminate against gays is religious (as it seems to be in these cases), then one of the major commitments of our nation is violated. Religious belief is a fine guide around which a person might organize his own life, but an awful instrument around which to organize someone else's life.

BUT ISN'T HOMOSEXUALITY UNNATURAL?

In the second kind of religious argument, people try to justify society's treatment of gays by saying they are unnatural. Though the accusation of unnaturalness looks whimsical, it is usually hurled against homosexuality with venom of forethought. It carries a high emotional charge, usually expressing disgust and evincing queasiness. Probably it is nothing but an emotional charge. For people get equally disgusted and queasy at all sorts of things which are perfectly natural and which could hardly be fit subjects for moral condemnation. Two typical examples in current American culture are some people's responses to mothers breastfeeding in public and to women who do not shave body hair. Similarly people fling the term "unnatural" at gays in the same breath and with the same force as when they call gays "sick" and "gross." When people have strong emotional reactions, as they do in

these cases, without being able to give good reasons for them, they can hardly be thought of as operating morally, but more likely as obsessed and manic.

When "nature" is taken in technical rather than ordinary usages, it also cannot ground a charge of homosexual immorality. When unnatural means "by artifice" or "made by humans," it can be pointed out that virtually everything that is good about life is unnatural in this sense. The chief feature that distinguishes people from other animals is people's very ability to make over the world to meet their needs and desires. Indeed people's well-being depends upon these departures from nature. On this understanding of human nature and the natural, homosexuality is perfectly unobjectionable; it is simply a means by which some people adapt nature to fulfill their desires and needs.

Another technical sense of natural is that something is natural and so, good, if it fulfills some function in nature. On this view, homosexuality is unnatural because it violates the function of genitals, which is to make babies. One problem with this view is that lots of bodily parts have lots of functions and just because some one activity can be fulfilled by only one organ (say, the mouth for eating), this activity does not condemn other functions of the organ as immoral (say, the mouth for talking, licking stamps, or blowing bubbles). So the possible use of the genitals to produce children does not, without more, condemn the use of the genitals for other purposes, say, achieving ecstasy and intimacy.

The notion of function seemed like it might ground moral authority, but instead it turns out that moral authority is needed to define "proper function." If God is the moral authority, we are back to square one—holding others accountable to our own religious beliefs.

Finally, people sometimes attempt to establish authority for a moral obligation to use bodily parts in a certain fashion simply by claiming that moral laws are natural laws and vice versa. On this account, inanimate objects and plants are good in that they follow natural laws by necessity, animals follow them by instinct, and persons follow them by a rational will. People are special in that they must first discover the laws that govern them. Now, even if one believes the view— dubious in the post-Newtonian, post-Darwinian world— that natural laws in the usual sense ($e = mc^2$, for instance) have some moral content, it is not at all clear how one is to discover the laws in nature that apply to people.

On the one hand, if one looks to people themselves for a model—and looks hard enough—one finds amazing variety, including homosexual relations as a social ideal (as in upper-class fifth-century Athens) and even as socially mandatory (as in some Melanesian initiation rites today). When one looks to people, one is simply unable to strip away the layers of social custom, history, and taboo in order to see what's really there to any degree more specific than that people are the creatures that make over their world and are capable of abstract thought. That this is so should raise doubts that neutral principles are to be found in human nature that will condemn homosexuality.

On the other hand, if one looks to nature apart from people for models, the possibilities are staggering. There are fish that change sex over their lifetimes: should we "follow nature" and be operative transsexuals? Orangutans, genetically our next of kin, live completely solitary lives without social organization of any kind among adults: ought we to "follow nature" and be hermits? There are many species where only two members per generation reproduce: shall we be bees? The search in nature for people's purpose far from finding sure models for action is likely to leave one morally rudderless.

SEXUAL ORIENTATION AND CHOICE

But (it might also be asked) aren't gays willfully the way they are? It is widely conceded that if sexual orientation is something over which an individual—for whatever reason—has virtually no control, then discrimination against gays is presumptively wrong, as it is against racial and ethnic classes.

Attempts to answer the question whether or not sexual orientation is something that is reasonably thought to be within one's own control usually appeal simply to various claims of the biological or "mental" sciences. But the ensuing debate over genes, hormones, hypothalamuses, twins, early child- hood development, and the like is as unnecessary as it is currently inconclusive. All that is needed to answer the question is to look at the actual experience of lesbians and gay men in current society, and it becomes fairly clear that sexual orientation is not likely a matter of choice.

On the one hand, the "choice" of the gender of a sexual partner does not seem to express a trivial desire which might as easily be fulfilled by a simple substitution of the desired object. Picking the gender of a sex partner is decidedly dissimilar, that is, to such activities as picking a flavor of ice cream. If an ice cream parlor is out of one's flavor, one simply picks another. And if people were persecuted, threatened with jail terms, shattered careers, loss of family and housing, and the like for eating, say, Rocky Road ice cream, no one would ever eat it. Everyone would pick another easily available flavor. That gay people abide in being gay even in the face of persecution suggests that being gay is not a matter of easy choice.

On the other hand, even if establishing a sexual orientation is not like making a relatively trivial choice, perhaps it is like making the central and serious life choices by which individuals try to establish themselves as being of some type or having some occupation. Again, if one examines gay experience, this seems not to be the general case. For one virtually never sees anyone setting out to become a homosexual, in the way one does see people setting out to become doctors, lawyers, and bricklayers. One does not find gays-to-be picking some end—"At some point in the future, I want to become a homosexual"—and then setting about planning and acquiring the ways and means to that end, in the way one does see people deciding that they want to become lawyers, and then sees them plan what courses to take and what sort of temperaments, habits, and skills to develop in order to become lawyers. Typically, gays-to-be simply find themselves having homosexual encounters and yet, at least

initially, resisting quite strongly the identification of being homosexual. Such a person even very likely resists having such encounters, but ends up having them anyway. Only with time, luck, and great personal effort, but sometimes never, does the person gradually come to accept her or his orientation, to view it as a given material condition of life, coming as all materials do with certain capacities and limitations. The person begins to act in accordance with his or her orientation and its capacities, seeing its actualization as a requisite for an integrated personality and as a central component of personal well-being. As a result, the experience of coming out to oneself has for gays the basic structure of a discovery, not the structure of a choice. And far from signaling immorality, coming out to others affords one of the few remaining opportunities in ever more bureaucratic, technological, and socialistic societies to manifest courage.

CIVIL RIGHTS

Current federal civil rights law bars private-sector discrimination in housing, employment, and public accommodations on the basis of race, national origin, ethnicity, gender, religion, age, and disability, but not sexual orientation. Where city councils and state legislatures have passed protections for gay men and lesbians, the protections have been under concerted and frequently successful attack through referendum initiatives . . . . [But there are strong] moral arguments for protecting lesbians and gay men from private-sector discrimination.

Even though civil rights legislation restricts somewhat the workings of free enterprise, it promotes other core American values that far outweigh this slight loss of entrepreneurial freedom. These values are self-respect, self-sufficiency, general prosperity, and individual flourishing.

No one in American society can have much self-respect or maintain a solid sense of self, if she is, in major ways affecting herself, subject to whimsical and arbitrary actions of others. Work, entertainment, and housing are major modes through which people identify themselves to themselves. Indeed in modern culture, work and housing rank just after personal relationships and perhaps (for some) religion, as the chief means by which people identify themselves to themselves. A large but largely unrecognized part of the misery of unemployment is not merely poverty and social embarrassment, but also a sense of loss of that by which one defined oneself, a loss which many people also experience upon retirement, even when their income and social esteem are left intact. People thrown out of work frequently compare this loss to the loss of a family member, especially to the loss of a child. Here the comparison is not simply to the intensity of the emotion caused by the loss, but to the nature of the loss: what was lost was a central means by which one constituted one's image of oneself.

Work is also the chief means by which people in America identify themselves to others. Indeed in America, one's job is tantamount to one's social identity. Socially one finds out who a person is by finding out what she or he does. At social gatherings, like parties, asking after a person's employment is typically the first substantive inquiry one makes of a person to whom one has been introduced. America is a nation of doers. When job discrimination is directed at lesbians and gay men, say, as a child care worker or museum director, it is a way of branding them as essentially un-American, as alien. It is a chief mode of expatriation from the national experience . . . .

In a nonsocialist, noncommunist society like America, there is a general expectation that each person is primarily responsible for meeting his or her own basic needs and that the government becomes an active provider only when all else fails. It is largely noncontroversial that people ought to have their basic needs met. For meeting basic needs is a necessary condition for anyone being able to carry out a life plan. If government aims at enhancing the conditions in which people are able to carry out their life plans, then enhancing the conditions in which basic needs are met will be a high government priority, all the more so if the means to this end themselves avoid greatly coercing people's life plans.

Current civil rights legislation tries to unclog channels between an individual's efforts and the fulfillment of the individual's needs. For it is chiefly through employment, in conjunction with access to certain public accommodations and housing, that people acquire the things they need to assure their continued biological existence—food, shelter, and clothing. Importantly, these are also the chief means by which people satisfy those various culturally relative needs which maintain them as credible players in the ongoing social, political, and economic "games" of the society into which they are born—say, needs for transportation and access to information. Civil rights legislation then helps people discharge their presumptive obligation to meet through their own devices their basic biological needs and other conditions required for human agency.

If gays were barred only from buying rocks at Tiffany's, eating truffles at "21," and holding seats on the Board of Trade, their inclusion in civil rights laws on the ground that such laws help meet needs would not be very compelling. And indeed America holds a stereotype of gays, especially gay men, as wealthy, frivolous, selfish, conspicuous consumers. Based on this stereotype, some people claim that gays are not in need of civil rights protections. But the stereotype is false. One of the surprising findings of Alfred Kinsey's 1948 study of male sexuality was that more male homosexual behavior occurs among the economically disadvantaged and among the uneducated than among the wealthy and college educated. And it is generally acknowledged that lesbians on average fall well below the national average for income, if for no other reason than that women are so far below the national average for income . . . .

Extending civil rights protection to gay men and lesbians is also justified as promoting general prosperity. Such legislation tends to increase the production of goods and services for society as a whole. It does so in three ways.

First, by eliminating extraneous factors in employment decisions, such legislation promotes an optimal fit between a worker's capacities and the tasks of her prospective work. Both the worker and her employer are advantaged because a worker is most productive when her talents and the requirements of her job mesh. Across the business community as a whole, such legislation further enhances the prospects that talent does not go wasting and that job vacancies are not filled by second bests.

In response to prospective discrimination, gays are prone to take jobs which only partially use their talents. Many gays take dead-end jobs; they do so in order to avoid reviews which might reveal their minority status and result in their dismissal. Many gay men and lesbians go into small business because big business will not have them. In turn, many small businesses or dead-end occupations, like being a florist, hairdresser, male nurse, female trucker or construction worker, have in society's mind become so closely associated with homosexuality that nongays who might otherwise go into these lines of employment do not do so out of fear that they will be socially branded as gay. In these circumstances, the talents of people—both gay and nongay—are simply wasted both to themselves and to society. Rights for gays are good for everyone.

Second, human resources are wasted if one's energies are constantly diverted and devoured by fear of arbitrary dismissal. The cost of life in the closet is not small, for the closet permeates and largely consumes the life of its occupant. In the absence of civil rights legislation for gays, society is simply wasting the human resources which are expended in the day-to-day anxiety—the web of lies, the constant worry—that attends leading a life of systematic disguise as a condition for continued employment.

Third, employment makes up a large part of what happiness is. To a large extent, happiness is job satisfaction. When one's employment is of a favorable sort, one finds a delight in its very execution—quite independently of any object which the job generates, whether product or wage. People whose work on its own is rich enough and interesting enough to count as a personal flourishing, people, for instance, employed in human services, academics, and other professionals, and people whose jobs entail a large element of craft, like editors and artisans, are indeed likely to view job satisfaction as a major constituent of happiness and rank it high both qualitatively and quantitatively among the sources of happiness. And even people who are forced by necessity or misfortune to take up employment which does not use their talents, or which is virtually mechanical, or positively dangerous, or which has other conditions that make the workplace hateful—even these people are likely to recognize that the workplace, if properly arranged, would be a locus of happiness, and this recognition of opportunity missed is part of the frustration which accompanies jobs which are necessarily unsatisfying to perform. Permitting discriminatory hiring practices reduces happiness generally by barring access to one of its main sources . . . .

CONCLUSION

If discrimination ceased, gay men and lesbians would enter the mainstream of the human community openly and with self-respect. The energies that the typical gay person wastes in the anxiety of leading a day-to-day existence of systematic disguise would be released for use in personal flourishing. From this release would be generated the many benefits that accrue to a society when its individual members thrive.

Society would be richer for acknowledging another aspect of human diversity. Families with gay members would develop relations based on truth and trust rather than lies and fear. And the heterosexual majority would be better off for knowing that they are no longer trampling their gay friends and neighbors.

Finally and perhaps paradoxically, in extending to gays the rights and benefits it has reserved for its dominant culture, America would confirm its deeply held vision of itself as a morally progressing nation, a nation itself advancing and serving as a beacon for others—especially with regard to human rights. The words with which our national pledge ends—"with liberty and justice for all"—are not a description of the present, but a call for the future. America is a nation given to a prophetic political rhetoric which acknowledges that morality is not arbitrary and that justice is not merely the expression of the current collective will. It is this vision that led the black civil rights movement to its successes. Those senators and representatives who opposed that movement and its centerpiece, the 1964 Civil Rights Act, on obscurantist grounds, but who lived long enough and were noble enough, came in time to express their heartfelt regret and shame at what they had done. It is to be hoped and someday to be expected that those who now grasp at anything to oppose the extension of that which is best about America to gays will one day feel the same.

Review and Discussion Questions

1. What are the two chief types of antigay stereotypes? Is Mohr correct in contending that antigay stereotypes are a means of reinforcing gender roles in society? What do you think explains violence against, and harassment of, homosexuals?

2. That something is descriptively moral (or immoral) does not make it normatively moral (or immoral). What is the relevance of this point to homosexuality?

3. How does Mohr respond to the argument that homosexuality is unnatural because it violates the function of the genitals, which is to produce babies? Why does Mohr believe that sexual orientation is not a matter of choice? How is this point relevant to the issue of discrimination? Are there moral arguments against homosexuality that Mohr has overlooked or not done justice to?

4. What arguments does Mohr give in favor of legislation banning job discrimination against homosexuals? Do you find them persuasive? Can any arguments be given against extending civil rights legislation to protect homosexuals? Would such legislation have any practical problems or bad effects?

5. For a period in the early 1990s, the Cracker Barrel Old Country Store, a restaurant and gift-shop chain in the Southeast, adopted a policy of firing homosexual employees and refusing to hire homosexuals. Supposedly based on the company's commitment to "traditional American values" and the "perceived values of [its] customers," Cracker Barrel's policy violated no laws. Critically assess its policy both from a business point of view and from the moral point of view. If a private employer believes that homosexuality is immoral, is it wrong of the employer to choose not to hire homosexuals?

6. Do companies have a moral obligation to discourage antigay sentiment among their employees? How might they do so?

Further Reading for Chapter 9

Tom L. Beauchamp and **Norman E. Bowie**, eds., *Ethical Theory and Business*, 4th ed. (Englewood Cliffs, NJ: Prentice Hall, 1993). The papers by **Helen Remick** and **Ronnie J. Steinberg**, "Comparable Worth and Wage Discrimination," and by **Robert L. Simon**, "Comparable Pay for Comparable Work?," provide a clear and thorough introduction to the comparable-worth debate.

Steven M. Cahn, ed., *The Affirmative Action Debate*, 2nd ed. (New York: Routledge, 2002); **Francis Beckwith** and **Todd E. Jones**, eds., *Affirmative Action: Social Justice or Reverse Discrimination?* (Buffalo, NY: Prometheus, 1997) are good sources of essays both for and against affirmative action.

Karen A. Crain and **Kenneth A. Heischmidt**, "Implementing Business Ethics: Sexual Harassment," *Journal of Business Ethics* 14 (April 1995) is a useful essay that discusses what actions companies should take.

D. W. Haslett, "Workplace Discrimination, Good Cause, and Color Blindness," *Journal of Value Inquiry* 36 (March 2002), provides a helpful theory of what constitutes unethical discrimination in the workplace.

Andrew Jackson, *Work and Labour in Canada* (Toronto: Canadian Scholars' Press Inc., 2005) is an informative and accessible account and

assessment of specific issues within the Canadian workplace based on research conducted originally for the Canadian Labour Congress. Part II deals with issues of discrimination.

Elizabeth Kristen, "Addressing the Problem of Weight Discrimination in Employment," *California Law Review* 90 (January 2002) argues that job discrimination against the overweight is a serious problem that the law should address.

Linda LeMoncheck and **Mane Hajdin**, *Sexual Harassment: A Debate* (Totowa, NJ: Rowman & Littlefield, 1997) probes the philosophical and ethical issues. See also **Linda L. Peterson**, "The Reasonableness of the Reasonable Woman Standard," *Public Affairs Quarterly* 13 (April 1999).

Glenn Loury, *The Anatomy of Racial Inequality* (Cambridge, MA: Harvard University Press, 2002) examines the complex reality of "racial stigma" and the self-replicating patterns of racial stereotypes that rationalize and sustain discrimination.

Laura Pincus and **Bill Shaw**, "Comparable Worth: An Economic and Ethical Analysis," *Journal of Business Ethics* 17 (April 1998) presents opposing views on adopting comparable worth as a public policy.

Part Four

Business and Society

10

Consumers

The "Marlboro man" has long mesmerized people around the world, and few can deny the glamour of the ruggedly good-looking Marlboro cowboy, with boots, hat, chaps—and, of course, a cigarette in his mouth. Product of one of the most successful advertising campaigns in history, the Marlboro man revolutionized the image of Marlboro cigarettes, making it the best-selling brand in the United States and one of the best international brands around the world. Very few people, however, know or remember that the actor who originally portrayed the Marlboro man died of lung cancer as a result of smoking.

Everybody, of course, knows that smoking is hazardous to one's health—everyone, that is, but the tobacco industry. It continues, publicly at least, to deny any cause-and-effect relationship between smoking and disease, even though smoking has been shown time and time again to be a major risk factor for respiratory and cardiovascular diseases and several forms of cancer, and is responsible for one-quarter of all deaths among adults between 35 and 84 years of age.[1] Although the percentage of Canadians who smoke is dropping,[2] smoking-related diseases exact a terrible toll on Canadians in terms of premature loss of life, of pain and suffering, and of medical expenditures. Virtually no other consumer good compares to cigarettes in terms of individual injury and social cost.

Because of this, starting in the late 1980s the federal and provincial levels of government have introduced a series of legislative measures which restrict severely the advertising of tobacco products and restrict their use in public places or places of work. Furthermore, the province of British Columbia passed the *Tobacco Damages and Health Care Costs Recovery Act* under which it sued, in 2001, a number of tobacco companies in order to recover costs incurred by the provincial health care system in taking care of people suffering from tobacco-related diseases. The case is in limbo, as the defendants have challenged the province's case on constitutional and jurisdictional grounds.[3] Similar actions have been taken by federal and state governments in the United States.

Indeed, the U.S. federal government filed suit against the large tobacco companies on anti-racketeering legislation, on the grounds that cigarette manufacturers "have engaged in and executed . . . a massive 50-year scheme to defraud the public" by suppressing evidence that cigarette smoke contains carcinogens and that nicotine is addictive. In addition, the suit accused tobacco companies of marketing cigarettes to teenagers, agreeing among themselves not to develop safer cigarettes, and manipulating nicotine levels in cigarettes to create and sustain addiction. The U.S. government sought an astounding $280 billion in damages—a sum equivalent to all the profits of the top six cigarette manufacturers from sales to smokers addicted as youths from 1971 to 2000, plus interest. But after several legal setbacks, in 2005 the U.S. government scaled back its demand to a relatively modest $10 billion, intended to fund a five-year anti-smoking program.

The slow progress or mitigated victories of governmental legal actions against cigarette manufacturers hasn't, of course, prevented smokers from suing them for injuries allegedly caused by their deadly habit. Despite the warnings that have been required on cigarette packs and ads since the early 1970s, smokers—or their estates—contend that they were addicted and couldn't stop. Many of these lawsuits are large class-action suits involving dozens of law firms with the collective resources to take on the big tobacco companies.[4] Cigarettes are an especially dangerous product, and their manufacture, marketing, advertising, and sale raise a number of acute questions relevant to the consumer issues discussed in this chapter. For instance, what are the responsibilities to consumers of companies that sell potentially or (in the case of cigarettes) inherently harmful products? To what extent do manufacturers abuse advertising? When is advertising deceptive? Can advertisers create or at least stimulate desires for products that consumers would not otherwise want or would not otherwise want as much? How, if at all, should advertising be restricted?

Are consumers sufficiently well informed about the products they buy? Are they misled by deceptive labelling and packaging? In general, how far should society go in controlling the claims of advertisers, in regulating product packaging and labels, in monitoring product quality and price, and in upholding explicit standards of reliability and safety? What are the moral responsibilities of businesses in these matters? In a market-oriented economic system, how do we balance the interests of business with the rights of consumers? How do we promote social well-being while still respecting the choices of individuals? These are among the issues probed in this chapter—in particular:

1. Product safety—the legal and moral responsibilities of manufacturers and the pros and cons of government regulations designed to protect consumers

2. The responsibilities of business to consumers concerning product quality, prices, labelling, and packaging

3. Deceptive and morally questionable techniques used in advertising

4. The choice between the "reasonable" consumer and "ignorant" consumer standards as the basis for identifying deceptive advertisements

5. Advertising and children

6. The social desirability of advertising in general: Is it a positive feature of our economic system? Does it manipulate, or merely respond to, consumer needs?

PRODUCT SAFETY

Business's responsibility for understanding and providing for consumer needs derives from the fact that citizen-consumers depend on business to satisfy their needs. This dependence is particularly true in our highly technological society, characterized as it is by a complex economy, intense specialization, and urban concentration. These conditions contrast with those prevailing in Canada when the country was primarily agrarian, composed of people who could themselves satisfy most of their own needs. Today, however, we rely on others to provide the wherewithal for our survival and prosperity. We rarely make our own clothing, supply our own fuel, manufacture our own tools, or construct our own homes, and our food is more likely to come from thousands of miles away than from our own gardens.

The increasing complexity of today's economy and the growing dependence of consumers on business for their survival and enrichment have heightened business's responsibilities to consumers—particularly in the area of product safety. From toys to tools, cars to baby cribs, consumers use countless products every day believing that neither they nor their loved ones will be harmed or injured by them. Consumers, however, lack the expertise to judge many of the sophisticated products they utilize. Being human, they also make mistakes in handling the things they buy—mistakes that the manufacturers of those products can often anticipate and make less likely. For these reasons, society must rely on the conscientious efforts of business to promote consumer safety.

The Legal Liability of Manufacturers

Statistics suggest that faith in the conscientiousness of business is sometimes misplaced. Every year thousands of Canadians require medical treatment from product-related accidents. If any of us is injured by a defective product, we can sue the manufacturer of that product under the area of law called "products liability," and we can do so in two general ways: through tort law or contract law.

A consumer's action under contract law is usually brought against the distributor or supplier of a product (as opposed to its manufacturer), as the law deems that the manufacturer of a product is not typically close enough to the selling-buying transaction to be considered a "party" to a contract with the buyer. The contractual relationship in question is simply the sale—that is, the exchange of money for a commodity of a certain description. But that contractual relationship is an important source of moral and legal responsibilities for the seller or seller-producer. It obligates business firms to provide customers with a product that lives up to the claims the firm makes about it. Those claims shape customers' expectations about what they are buying and lead them to enter into the contract in the first place. So, if a consumer purchases a defective product, he or she may have a case against the seller based on the seller's breach of express or implied terms of the purchase contract. Common law has developed implied warranties of reasonable fitness and of merchantable quality (= satisfactory quality) to protect consumers from defective products. Further, each province and territory has in place legislation that assumes or implies certain conditions in contracts for the sale of goods. A condition of reasonable fitness is implied, "Where the buyer, expressly or by implication, makes known to the seller the particular purpose for which the goods are required so as to show that the buyer relies on the seller's skill or judgment, and the goods are of a description that it is in the course of the seller's business to supply (whether the seller is the manufacturer or not). . . ."[5] The implied condition that the goods are of merchantable quality is wider in scope. For the condition to be implied, the sale must be "by description": "Where goods are bought by description from a seller who deals in goods of that description (whether the seller is the manufacturer or not), there is an implied condition that the goods will be of merchantable quality, but if the buyer has examined the goods, there is no implied condition as regards defects that such examination ought to have revealed."[6]

Cases of liability in tort require merely that the plaintiff and the defendant be sufficiently close for the defendant to have a legal duty of care toward the plaintiff. Accordingly, this sort of case is usually brought against manufacturers of products (who normally do not enter into contractual relationships with the buyers of the products they produce). "Duty of care" or "due care" is the idea that consumers and sellers do not meet as equals and that the consumer's interests are particularly vulnerable to being harmed by the manufacturer, who has knowledge and expertise the consumer does not have. Thus, manufacturers have an obligation, above and beyond any contract, to exercise due care not only to prevent the consumer from being injured by defective products but also to warn consumers of dangers inherent in the use of the product. In *Hollis v. Dow Corning Corp.*, [1995] 4 S.C.R. 634, the Supreme Court held:

> A manufacturer of a product has a duty in tort to warn consumers of dangers it knows or ought to know are inherent in the product's use. This duty is a continuing one, requiring manufacturers to warn not only of dangers known at the time of sale, but also of dangers discovered after the product has been sold and delivered. All warnings must be reasonably communicated, and must clearly describe any specific dangers that arise from the ordinary use of the product. The duty to warn serves to correct the knowledge imbalance between manufacturers and consumers by alerting consumers to any dangers and allowing them to make informed decisions concerning the safe use of the product. The nature and scope of this duty varies with the level of danger entailed by the ordinary use of the product.

The concept of the duty to care has definitely moved legal policy beyond the old doctrine of *caveat emptor* or "Let the buyer beware." Although legally the doctrine was never upheld across the board, it still symbolizes a period, before the 1920s, in which consumers themselves had a greater legal responsibility to accept the consequences of their product choices. Consumers at that time were held to the ideal of being knowledgeable, shrewd, and skeptical. It was their free choice whether to buy a certain product. Accordingly, they were expected to take the claims of manufacturers and salespeople with a grain of salt, to inspect any potential purchase carefully, to rely on their own judgment, and to accept any ill results of their decision to use a given product. In the first part of the twentieth century, however, courts repudiated this doctrine, largely on grounds of its unrealistic assumptions about consumer knowledge, competence, and behaviour.

The duty to care doctrine, with its broader view of a manufacturer's liability, may still leave an injured consumer with the burden of proving that the manufacturer had been negligent. Not only might such an assertion be difficult to prove, but also a product might be dangerously defective despite the manufacturer's having taken reasonable steps to avoid such a defect. The issue in such cases is what to do about liability or, if you like, who is going to pay for the mess? American jurisdictions and to a much lesser extent Canadian jurisdictions have moved to the concept of *strict product liability*. According to this notion, the manufacturer of a product has legal responsibilities to compensate the user of that product for injuries suffered because the product's defective condition made it unreasonably dangerous, even though the manufacturer has not been negligent in permitting that defect to occur. Under this doctrine, a judgment for the recovery of damages could conceivably be won even if the manufacturer adhered to strict quality-control procedures. Strict liability, however, is not absolute liability. The manufacturer is not responsible for any injury whatsoever that might befall the consumer. The product must be defective, and the consumer always has the responsibility to exercise care.

Strict product liability is not without its critics, however. They contend that the doctrine is unfair. If a firm has exercised due care and taken reasonable precautions to avoid or eliminate foreseeable dangerous defects, they argue, then it should not be held liable for defects that are not its fault—that is, for defects that happen despite its best efforts to guard against them. To hold the firm liable anyway seems unjust.

The argument for strict liability is basically utilitarian. Its advocates contend, first, that only such a policy leads firms to bend over backward to guarantee product safety. Because they know that they will be held liable for injurious defects no matter what, they make every effort to enhance safety. Second, proponents of strict liability contend that the manufacturer is best able to bear the cost of injuries due to defects. Naturally, firms raise the price of their products to cover their legal costs (or pay for liability insurance). Defenders of strict liability do not disapprove of this. They see it as a perfectly reasonable way of spreading the cost of injuries among all consumers of the product, rather than letting it fall on a single individual—a kind of insurance scheme.

Government Safety Regulation

These developments in the common law of product liability set the general legal framework within which manufacturers must operate today. In addition, a great number of federal, provincial, and territorial pieces of legislation (estimated to be around 400) and a number of regulatory agencies have become involved in monitoring and regulating product safety: for example, the *Food and Drugs Act*, the *Hazardous Products Act*, Industry Canada, Health Canada, the Canada Transportation Agency, the Canadian Food Inspection Agency, and so on.

In undertaking their regulatory and monitoring functions, the various government bodies aid consumers in evaluating product safety, develop uniform standards, gather data, conduct research, and recall unsafe or dangerous products. Although most product safety regulations bring obvious benefits, critics worry about the economic costs. New safety standards add millions of dollars to the cumulative price tag of various goods. Often economists can estimate how many lives a regulation saves and then compare that with the cost of implementing the rule. For example, research in the United States estimates that the cost of requiring labels showing the trans-fat content of foods is only $3,000 per life saved, whereas the cost of insulation to protect against fire in airplane cabins is $300,000. For other regulations, the cost to save one life is considerably higher: stronger automobile doors $500,000; flame-retardant children's sleepwear $2.2 million; and reducing the asbestos exposure of factory workers $5.5 million.[7] And what about recalls of products? Automobile recalls cost auto manufacturers millions of dollars every year. Is the expense worth it?

In addition to cost is the issue of consumer choice. Sometimes consumers dislike mandated safety technology. In 1974, for example, the U.S. Congress legislated an interlock system that would require drivers to fasten their seat belts before their car could move. No doubt the law would have saved lives, but a public outcry forced lawmakers to rescind it. Apparently, many drivers saw interlock systems as a nuisance and believed their inconvenience outweighed any gain in safety. In other cases, safety regulations may prevent individuals from choosing to purchase a riskier, though less expensive, product. A case in point concerns the notorious Ford Pinto with its unsafe gas tank. In 1978, after all the negative publicity, scores of lawsuits, and the trial of Ford Motor Company in the United States for reckless homicide, the sale of Pintos fell dramatically. Consumers evidently preferred a safer car for comparable money. However, when the state of Oregon took all the Pintos out of its fleet because of safety concerns and sold them, at least one dealer reported brisk sales of the turned-in Pintos at their low, secondhand price.[8] Some consumers were willing to accept the risks of a Pinto if the price was right.

Economists worry about the inefficiencies of preventing individuals from balancing safety against price. Philosophers worry about interfering with people's freedom of choice. Take automobile safety again. Because smaller cars provide less protection than larger ones, people in small cars are less likely to survive accidents. Bigger, safer cars are more expensive, however, and many would prefer to spend less on their cars despite the increased risk. If only those cars that were as safe as, say, a Mercedes-Benz were allowed on the market, then there would be fewer deaths on the highways. But then fewer people could afford cars.

This example touches on the larger controversy over *legal paternalism*, which is the doctrine that the law may justifiably be used to restrict the freedom of individuals for their own good. No one doubts that laws justifiably restrict people from harming other people, but a sizable number of moral theorists deny that laws should attempt to prevent people from running risks that affect only themselves. Requiring your car to have brakes protects others; without brakes, you are more likely to run over a pedestrian. On the other hand, requiring you to wear a seat belt when you drive affects only you. Anti-paternalists would protest that your being forced to wear a seat belt despite your wishes fails to respect your moral autonomy.

Paternalism is a large issue that can't be done justice here, but in regard to safety regulations, three comments are in order. First, the safety of some products or some features of products (such as a car's brakes) affects not just the consumer who purchases the product but third parties as well. Regulating these products or product features can be defended on non-paternalistic grounds. Second, anti-paternalism gains plausibility from the view that individuals know their own interests better than anyone else and that they are fully informed and able to advance those interests. But in the increasingly complex consumer world, that assumption is often doubtful. Whenever citizens lack knowledge and are unable to make intelligent comparisons and safety judgments, they may find it in their collective self-interest to set minimal safety standards. Such standards are particularly justifiable when few, if any, reasonable persons would want a product that did not satisfy those standards.

Finally, the controversy over legal paternalism pits the values of individual freedom and autonomy against social welfare. Requiring people to wear seat belts may infringe the former but saves thousands of lives each year (not to mention the reduction in health care costs). We may simply have to acknowledge the clash of values and be willing to make tradeoffs. This doesn't imply a defence of paternalism across the board. Arguably, some paternalistic regulations infringe on autonomy more than laws about seat belts do but bring less gain in social welfare. In the end, one may have to examine paternalistic product safety legislation case by case and weigh the conflicting values and likely results.

How Effective Is Regulation?

As with anything else in our lives, protective legislation and regulatory agencies do not and cannot guarantee product safety. All we may demand of governmental bodies charged with our protection is that they are vigilant, that they act conscientiously and without undue delay in correcting anything amiss, that they respond quickly and effectively to consumer complaints, and that they enforce the law and regulations strictly and thoroughly. Such actions will go a long way in minimizing harm to consumers. In fact, the breakdowns in consumer protection involved in the tainted blood scandal (covered in Case Study 10.1) and the Walkerton water scandal were failures on the part of officials to discharge one or more of the duties mentioned above. The remedy to such failures is, again, vigilance and severe legal punishment for officials who do not carry out properly their assigned duties.

Canadian public regulatory agencies do, by and large, an effective job of monitoring product safety. However, as is well known, "An ounce of prevention is worth a pound of cure." And the best place for prevention is at the very source of a given product, the producing firm. In addition to government regulation, however, other forms of societal pressure must also be brought to bear on companies in order for them to take product safety seriously; for example, public opinion, media attention, pressure from consumer advocacy groups, and the willingness of individuals to take part in class-action lawsuits. Businesspeople, however, tend to be hostile to both regulation and consumer lawsuits. When it comes to safety, they generally prefer self-regulation, competition, and voluntary, industry-determined safety standards. Their point of view is certainly in keeping with the tenets of classical capitalism, and self-regulation is arguably an attractive ideal on both moral and economic grounds. However, self-regulation can easily become an instrument for subordinating consumer interests to profit making when the two goals clash. Under the guise of self-regulation, businesses can end up ignoring or minimizing their responsibilities to consumers.

Consider the auto industry, which has a long history of fighting against safety regulations. For example, it successfully lobbied the U.S. federal government to delay the requirement that new cars be equipped with air bags or automatic seat belts. Each year of the delay saved the industry millions of dollars. But the price paid by consumers was high: according to the U.S. National Highway Traffic Safety Administration, driving with your seat belt on in a car with air bags cuts in half your chance of dying in a crash.

When the U.S. law finally required passive restraint systems in new vehicles, Chrysler Motors became (in 1989) the first U.S. auto manufacturer to install driver-side air bags in all its new models. Only five years earlier, Chrysler chairman Lee Iacocca had boasted in his autobiography of fighting against air bags since their invention in the mid-1960s. In 1971, he and Henry Ford II (then the top executives at Ford) met secretly with U.S. President Richard Nixon to persuade him to kill a pending Department of Transportation regulation requiring air bags in every new car sold in the United States.[9] Had air bags been made standard equipment in 1974, more than 70,000 deaths and many times that number of severe injuries would have been avoided in the United States.

As car buyers have become better informed, automobile manufacturers are rethinking Iacocca's old bromide "Safety doesn't sell." But even if safety does sometimes sell, for an industry to wait for marketplace demand before increasing safety standards can be irresponsible. If society always waited for demand before insisting on public health and safety regulations, pasteurization of milk and sprinkler systems to suppress fires in public places would still be "options."

The Responsibilities of Business

Simply obeying laws and regulations does not exhaust the moral responsibilities of business in the area of consumer safety. When it comes to product safety, the exact nature of business's moral responsibilities is difficult to specify in general, because much depends on the particular product or service being provided. But abiding by the following steps would go a long way in helping business behave morally with respect to consumer safety:

1. *Business should give safety the priority warranted by the product.* This injunction is important because businesses often base safety considerations strictly on cost. If the margin of safety can be increased without significantly insulting budgetary considerations, fine; if not, then safety questions are shelved.

Cost cannot be ignored, of course, but neither can two other factors. One is the seriousness of the injury the product can cause. A police officer may seldom have to rely on a bulletproof vest, but the potential harm from a defective one is obvious. Yet Second Chance Body Armor in the United States suppressed evidence of a defect in its product, because company executives feared that it would hurt plans for an initial stock offering.[10] The second factor to consider is the frequency of occurrence. Is a design flaw on a lawnmower, for example, likely to result in one customer out of a thousand—or one out of two million—cutting off a finger? The higher a product's score on the seriousness or the frequency test (or both), the greater the priority that needs to be given to safety issues.

2. *Business should abandon the misconception that accidents occur exclusively as a result of product misuse and that it is thereby absolved of all responsibility.* At one time such a belief may have been valid, but in using today's highly sophisticated products, even people who follow product instructions explicitly sometimes still suffer injuries. In any case, the point is that the company shares responsibility for product safety with the consumer. Rather than insisting that consumers' abuse of product leads to most accidents and injuries, firms would probably accomplish more by carefully pointing out how their products can be used safely.

Both manufacturers and retailers have an obligation to try to anticipate and minimize the ways their products can cause harm, whether or not those products are misused. For example, a four-year-old girl was seriously injured when she stood on an oven door to peek into a pot on top of the stove and her weight caused the stove to tip over. A manufacturer can reasonably foresee that a cook might place a heavy roasting pan on the oven door. If doing so caused the stove to tip over, a court would almost certainly find the stove's design defective. But should the manufacturer have foreseen the use of the door not as a shelf but as a stepstool? Probably yes. If a product poses a serious potential threat, a company may need to take extraordinary measures to ensure continued safe use of it. Determining the extent to which the company must go, however, isn't an easy task. Sometimes a firm's moral responsibility for ensuring safety doesn't reach much beyond the sale of the product. Other times it may extend further. Consider, for example, a company that produces heavy machinery. Workers using its products could easily fall into bad habits. Some would argue, therefore, that the company has an obligation to follow up the sale of such a product, perhaps by visiting firms using its machinery to see if they've adopted dangerous shortcuts.

3. *Business must monitor the manufacturing process itself.* Frequently firms fail to control key variables during the manufacturing process, resulting in product defects. Companies should periodically review working conditions and the competence of key personnel. At the design stage of the process, they need to predict ways the product might fail and the consequences of such failure. For production, companies ordinarily can select materials that have been pre-tested or certified as flawless. If a company fails to do this, then we must question its commitment to safety. Similar questions arise when companies do not make use of available research about product safety. To answer some questions a company may have to generate its own research. However, independent research groups ensure impartial and disinterested analysis and are usually more reliable than in-house studies.

Testing should be rigorous and simulate the toughest conditions. Tests shouldn't assume that the product would be used in just the way the manufacturer intends it to be used. Even established products should be tested. U.S. courts have repeatedly held that a trouble-free history does not justify the assumption that the product is free of defects.[11]

When a product moves into production, it is often changed in various ways. These changes should be documented and referred to some appropriate party, such as a safety engineer, for analysis. The firm must be scrupulous about coordinating department activities so manufacturing specifications are not changed without determining any potential dangers related to these changes.

4. *When a product is ready to be marketed, companies should have their product safety staff review their market strategy and advertising for potential safety problems.* This step is necessary because both product positioning and advertising influence how a product is used, which in turn affects the likelihood of safety problems. For example, ATVs (all-terrain vehicles) are marketed in a way that appeals to young people, who have comparatively little driving experience and a propensity to take risks. According to U.S. statistics, ATVs result in more injuries per vehicle than cars do, and they cause more deaths and injuries than snowmobiles or personal watercraft. At the same time, a third of those injured are under sixteen while children under twelve account for 14 percent of ATV deaths.[12] Or consider the case of a U.S. feeder auger

manufacturer whose promotional brochure stated that "even a child can do your feeding." The brochure had a photograph of the auger with its safety cover removed to show the auger's inner workings. When a young boy was injured while using the feeder auger with the safety cover removed, a U.S. jury found the promotional brochure misleading with respect to operating conditions and product safety.[13]

5. *When a product reaches the marketplace, firms should make available to consumers written information about the product's performance.* This information should include operating instructions, the product's safety features, conditions that will cause it to fail, a complete list of the ways the product can be used, and a cautionary list of the ways it should not be used. Warnings must be specific.

But no matter how specific they are, warnings are of little value if a consumer cannot read them. For example, St. Joseph Aspirin for Children is marketed in Spanish-speaking areas of the U.S. and is advertised in the Spanish-language media. But you have to know English to read the crucial warning: "Children and teenagers should not use this medicine for chicken pox or flu symptoms before a doctor is consulted about Reye's Syndrome, a rare but serious illness reported to be associated with aspirin." Because his mother spoke only Spanish and couldn't read the label on the St. Joseph's box, little Jorge Ramirez of Modesto, California, contracted Reye's Syndrome. Today, he is blind, quadriplegic, and mentally impaired.[14]

6. *Companies should investigate consumer complaints.* This process encourages firms to deal fairly with consumers and to use the most effective source of product improvement: the opinions of those who use it.

Even if firms seriously attended to these safety considerations, they couldn't guarantee an absolutely safe product. Some hazards invariably attach to certain products, heroic efforts notwithstanding. But business must acknowledge and discharge its responsibilities in this area. Morally speaking, no one's asking for an accident- and injury-proof product, only that manufacturers do everything reasonable to approach that ideal.

OTHER AREAS OF BUSINESS RESPONSIBILITY

Product safety is naturally a dominant concern of consumers. No one wants to be injured by the products he or she uses. But safety is far from the only interest of consumers. The past forty years have seen a general increase in consumer awareness and an increasingly stronger consumer advocacy movement. One chief consumer issue has been advertising and its possible abuse, which will be discussed in subsequent sections. Three other areas of business responsibility—product quality, pricing, and packaging and labelling—are equally important and are taken equally seriously by the consumer movement.

Product Quality

The demand for high-quality products is closely related to a number of themes mentioned in the discussion of safety. Most people would agree that business bears a general responsibility to ensure that the quality of a product measures up to the claims made about it and to reasonable consumer expectations. They would undoubtedly see this responsibility as deriving primarily from the consumer's basic right to get what he or she pays for.

One way that business assumes responsibilities to consumers for product quality and reliability is through *warranties*, which are obligations to purchasers that sellers assume. People generally speak of two kinds of warranties, express and implied. *Express warranties* are the claims that sellers explicitly state—for example, that a product is "shrinkproof" or will require no maintenance for two years. The moral concern, of course, is whether a product lives up to its billing. Express warranties include assertions about the product's character, assurances of product durability, and other statements on warranty cards, labels, wrappers, and packages or in the advertising of the product. Many companies offer detailed warranties that are very specific about what defects they cover. Few go as far as L. L. Bean does with its "100% guarantee," which allows customers to return any purchase at any time for a full refund if it proves unsatisfactory.

Implied warranties include the claim, implicit in any sale, that a product is fit for its ordinary, intended use. The law calls this the implied warranty of *merchantability*. It's not a promise that the product will be perfect; rather, it's a guarantee that it will be of passable quality or suitable for the ordinary purpose for which it is used. Implied warranties can also be more specific—for example, when the seller knows that a buyer has a particular purpose in mind and is relying on the seller's superior skill or judgment to furnish goods adequate for that purpose.

The concept of an implied warranty is relevant to the case of Kodak's instant cameras in the United States. When Polaroid won a patent violation judgment against it, Kodak was forced not only to stop selling its instant cameras but also to compensate previous purchasers, who could no longer obtain film for their cameras. Those purchasers had relied on the implicit claim that Kodak would not make its products obsolete.[15] With or without warranties, however, consumers today are more militant than ever in their insistence on product quality and on getting exactly what they paid for.

Prices

Have you ever wondered why a product sells at three for a dollar or is priced at $6.99 rather than simply $7? Or why a product that retails for $9.80 on Monday is selling for $11.10 on Friday? The answer may have little to do with the conventional determinants of product price such as overhead, operating expenses, and the costs of materials and labour. More and more frequently, purely psychological factors enter into the price-setting equation.

For example, why would a retailer price T-shirts at $9.88 instead of $9.99? "When people see $9.99, they say, 'That's $10,'" explains the general sales manager of one company. "But $9.88 isn't $10. It's just psychological."[16] Similar psychological considerations are at work when airlines advertise one-way fares that are available only with the purchase of a round-trip ticket for twice the price.

For many consumers, higher prices mean better products, so manufacturers arbitrarily raise the price of a product to give the impression of superior quality or exclusivity. But as often as not, the price is higher than the product's extra quality. For example, a few years ago Proctor-Silex's most expensive fabric iron sold in the United States for $54.95, a price $5 higher than the company's next most expensive. Its wholesale price was $26.98 against $24.20, a difference of only $2.78. Moreover, the extra cost of producing the top model was less than $1 for a light that signalled when the iron was ready.[17]

Manufacturers trade on human psychology when they sell substantially identical products at different prices. An especially good example is afforded by the actions of the U.S. company Heublein which raised the price of its Popov brand vodka from about $3.80 to $4.10 a fifth (750 millilitres) without altering the vodka that went into the fifth. Why the price increase? Heublein sales representatives believed that consumers wanted a variety of vodka prices to choose from. Apparently they were right: Even though Popov lost 1 percent of its market share, it increased its profits by 30 percent. Applying its theory further, Heublein offers vodka drinkers an even more expensive vodka: Smirnoff. Analysts insist that there is no qualitative difference among vodkas made in the United States.[18] In this case, the use of psychological pricing is closely related to the problem of pricing branded products higher than generic products that are otherwise indistinguishable. Consumers pay more assuming that the brand name or the higher price implies a better product.

Sometimes consumers are misled by prices that conceal a product's true cost. Hidden charges, surcharges, and other stealth fees can boost the consumer's actual cost significantly above announced price: for example, charges for mounting and balancing when you buy tires; multiple taxes and services fees on cell phone plans; "visitor" taxes and collision insurance on rental cars; and "convenience" charges, processing fees, and shipping charges on concert or sports event tickets. In addition, manufacturers often disguise price increases by reducing the quality or the quantity of the product—downsizing a pound of coffee to 13 ounces, for example, or shrinking a candy bar or doughnut but not its price. Another ethically dubious practice is printing on packages a suggested retail price that is substantially higher than what retailers are known to charge. When retailers mark a new, lower price over the "suggested price," customers receive the false impression that the item is selling below its usual price. Retailers themselves are on questionable ethical ground when they use special pricing codes or fail to post a price on or near products, thus hindering consumers from easily comparing prices. And too many electronic scanners these days ring up prices incorrectly.

Many practical consumers think of these pricing practices and gimmicks as a nuisance or irritant that they must live with, not as something morally objectionable. But tricky or manipulative pricing does raise moral questions—not least about business's view of itself and its role in the community—that businesspeople and ethical theorists are now beginning to take seriously.

Price Fixing Much more attention has been devoted to price fixing, which despite its prevalence is widely recognized as a violation of the rules of the game in a market system whose ideal is open and fair price competition. For example, it was disclosed in 2003 that about two dozen Mercedes-Benz dealers in New York, New Jersey, and Connecticut conspired not to undercut one another with discounts.[19] In another case, a U.S. federal judge found Toys "R" Us guilty of conspiring to keep prices for Barbie, Mr. Potato Head, and other popular toys artificially high. The retail giant used its market clout to force Mattel, Hasbro, and other major toymakers not to sell their toys to warehouse clubs like Sam's Club and Costco. Toys "R" Us threatened not to buy any toy that a manufacturer sold to a cost-cutting competitor, and it would use the acquiescence of one toymaker to force other manufacturers to go along.[20]

Often, of course, it is the manufacturer, not the retailer, that engages in price fixing. For example, Panasonic was found guilty of pressuring retailers such as Circuit City, Kmart, and Montgomery Ward in the United States into selling its products at the company's suggested retail price and not at a discount. Although manufacturers often suggest prices to their retailers, the retailers are supposed to be free to set their own prices, depending on the profit they foresee in the market. Any agreement between a manufacturer and a retailer to fix a price is illegal. Panasonic sales executives, however, badgered stores that did not honour the manufacturer's minimum prices and threatened to stop doing business with retailers that didn't comply. Until one large New York retailer finally complained to the New York State Attorney General's office, not only did the stores and chains go along, but they also reported uncooperative competitors to Panasonic.[21]

When a few companies gain control of a market, they are often in a position to force consumers to pay artificially high prices. To take a notorious example, in 1960 General Electric, Westinghouse, and twenty-seven other U.S. companies producing electrical equipment were found guilty of fixing prices in that billion-dollar industry. The companies were made to pay about $2 million in fines and many more millions to their corporate victims.[22] Given the oligopolistic nature of the electrical equipment market, consumers could not reasonably be said to have had the option to take their business elsewhere and thus drive down prices. (In fact, until it was exposed, they had no reason to believe they were being victimized by price

fixing.) More recently, U.S. federal and state investigators have established that executives at the largest national and regional dairy companies in the United States have conspired—sometimes for decades—to rig bids on milk products sold to schools and military bases. Forty-three companies, among them Borden, Pet, Dean, and Flav-O-Rich, have been convicted of price fixing and bid rigging.[23]

Of course, controlling prices need not be done so blatantly. Firms in an oligopoly can tacitly agree to remain uncompetitive with one another, thereby avoiding losses that might result from price-cutting competition. They can then play "follow the leader": let the lead firm in the market raise its prices, and then the rest follow suit. The result is a laundered form of price fixing. Nobody, they say to themselves, wants a price war, as if price competition were a threat to our market system rather than its life-blood. Familiar rivals such as Pepsi and Coca-Cola or McDonald's and Burger King usually prefer to compete in terms of image and jingles rather than price.

Price Gouging From the moral point of view, prices, like wages, should be just or fair. Merchants cannot morally charge whatever they want or whatever the market will bear any more than employers can pay workers whatever they (the employers) wish or can get away with. In particular, price gouging is widely viewed as unethical, although what exactly constitutes price gouging is often debated. Some define it as charging what the market will bear regardless of production costs. But that definition doesn't take into account supply and demand. Because they are in short supply, tickets for the World Series or houses in a popular neighbourhood may command an extremely high price relative to their production costs, and yet this does not constitute price gouging. Price gouging is better understood as a seller's exploiting a short-term situation in which buyers have few purchase options for a much-needed product by raising prices substantially. New York hotels that doubled or tripled their prices in the aftermath of the September 11, 2001, attacks were guilty of this, and indeed some jurisdictions do make it illegal for retailers to raise their prices during a natural disaster or some other emergency. However, the morality or immorality of some instances of possible gouging seems open to debate. Is it unethical for a hardware store to boost the price of snow shovels from $15 to $20 after a large snowstorm or for a car dealer to mark up the price of a popular car model that is temporarily in short supply?

When a gas station raises the price of its current stock of gasoline because the wholesale price is scheduled to go up or when the big oil companies set the wholesale price of gasoline 5 to 10 cents a litre higher in Town X than in Town Y because average household income is greater in X, that may not fit the definition of price gouging, but it strikes many people as unfair. So does the fact that Americans have to pay substantially more for medicines than Canadians or Europeans. This is not a matter of cheap generics or illegal knockoffs. Brand-name drugs such as Lipitor, Zoloft, Vioxx, and Nexium cost 30 to 100 percent more in the United States than in Canada or Europe.[24]

In the end, the question "What is a fair price?" probably defies a precise answer. Still, one can approach an answer by assessing the factors on which the price is based and the process used to determine it. Certainly factors such as the costs of material and production, operating and marketing expenses, and profit margin are relevant to price setting. One can also ask whether a seller's pricing practices treat buyers as ends in themselves (that is, treat buyers as moral agents) or try to exploit them by taking advantage of a lack of competition or some other buyer vulnerability. Also relevant is whether it would be good for our socioeconomic system as a whole if a particular pricing practice were widespread or generally followed.

In a market-oriented society, of course, consumer choice is a key variable affecting price. Product price, in other words, reflects in part the consuming public's judgment of the relative value of the article. This judgment is formed in the open market in a free interplay between sellers and buyers. However, for this process to function satisfactorily, buyers must be in a position to exercise informed consent. As discussed in Chapter 7, informed consent calls for deliberation and free choice, which require in turn that buyers understand all significant relevant facts about the goods and services they are purchasing. But consumers are at least sometimes, perhaps often, denied informed consent. They do not always receive the clear, accurate, and complete information about product quality and price that they need to make prudent choices.

Labelling and Packaging

Business's general responsibility to provide clear, accurate, and adequate information undoubtedly applies to product labelling and packaging. The reason is that, despite the billions of dollars spent annually on advertising, a product's label and package remain the consumer's primary source of product information.

In addition to many other federal statutes covering specific sectors (for example, the *Textile Labelling Act*), the federal *Consumer Packaging and Labelling Act* (or "An Act respecting the packaging, labelling, sale, importation and advertising of prepackaged and certain other products") and the *Food and Drugs Act* (or "An Act respecting food, drugs, cosmetics and therapeutic devices") oblige manufacturers of packaged foods to provide information pertinent to the product, and especially nutritional information, that is clear, specific, and of benefit to health-conscious consumers. Despite the litany of statutes and thousands of regulations and specifications, federal regulatory agencies secure the conviction of at least two dozen firms every year under these two acts.[25] Of course, one may wonder how many more offenders are out there who, for one reason or another, will never be caught.

Even when product labels provide pertinent information, they are often difficult to understand or even unclear, and what they omit may be more important than what they say. For example, nothing is more confusing than environmental labelling. Manufacturers label products "biodegradable," "environmentally safe," or "recyclable" without defining those terms or providing any scientific evidence to back them up. And even the most socially and environmentally conscious consumers have difficulty distinguishing among "fair-trade certified," "fairly traded," "Rainforest Alliance certified," "sustainable," and "certified sustainable."

In addition to unclear or misleading labels, package shape can trick consumers by exploiting certain optical illusions. Tall and narrow cereal boxes look larger than short, squat ones that actually contain more cereal; shampoo bottles often have pinched waists to give the illusion of quantity; fruits are packed in large quantities of syrup; and dry foods often come in tins or cartons stuffed with cardboard. Package terms such as *large, extra large, jumbo, economy size,* and *value pack* frequently confuse or mislead shoppers about what they are buying and how good a deal they are getting. Although in theory unit pricing helps shoppers to compare the relative prices of items, in practice the spread of bar codes thwarts their ability to do so. By eliminating price tags from packages, bar codes make it harder for time-pressed buyers to recall specific prices for individual items.

This is part of the explanation of why many retailers are able to sell "economy size" items for a higher per-unit price than their smaller counterparts. These "quantity surcharges" are a much wider-spread phenomenon than most people realize. For example, one can often buy the two-kilogram container of a certain margarine for, say, $4.27 while the four-kilogram container of the same brand goes for $8.65. Although consumers frequently compare prices between brands, they generally neglect to make intra-brand comparisons, because they take it for granted that the larger the volume, the better the deal. "You assume 'bigger' is a better deal," says Tom Pirko, president of a beverage and food consulting company, "and that gives marketers an open door to take advantage of people."[26] Because quantity surcharges exploit a common consumer error, the practice raises at least two moral questions: Can it be justified as a conscious pricing policy, and can retailers ethically remain silent about its existence?[27]

In general, the moral issues involved in packaging and labelling, as in marketing as a whole, relate primarily to truth telling and consumer exploitation. Sound moral conduct in this matter must rest on a strong desire to provide consumers with clear and usable information about the price, quality, and quantity of a product so they can make intelligent comparisons and choices. When marketers are interested primarily in selling a product and only secondarily in providing relevant information, morally questionable practices are bound to follow. Those responsible for labelling and packaging would be well advised to consider at least the following questions, a negative answer to any of which could signal a moral problem: Is there anything about the packaging that is likely to mislead consumers? Have we clearly and specifically identified the exact nature of the product in an appropriate part of the label? Is the net quantity prominently displayed? Is it readily understandable to those wishing to compare prices? Are ingredients listed so they can be readily recognized and understood? Have we indicated and represented the percentage of the contents that is filler, such as the bone in a piece of meat?

These questions represent only some that a morally responsible businessperson might ask. In addition, we must not forget people whose health necessitates certain dietary restrictions. They often have great difficulty determining what products they can safely purchase.

DECEPTION AND UNFAIRNESS IN ADVERTISING

We tend to take advertising for granted; yet it is enormously important from the sociological and economic point of view. Ads dominate our environment. Famous ones become part of our culture; their jingles dance in our heads, and their images haunt our dreams and shape our tastes. Advertising is also big business. Firms and corporations based in Canada spent an estimated US$8.3 billion in advertising during 2006 (or roughly US$260 per person). This is a lot of money, though it pales to insignificance before the $250 billion spent by Americans on all forms of media advertising (or $800 for every American).

When people are asked what advertising does, their first thought is often that it provides consumers with information about goods and services. In fact, advertising conveys very little information. Nor are most ads intended to do so. Except for classified ads (by amateurs!) and newspaper ads reporting supermarket prices, very few advertisements offer any information of genuine use to the consumer. (Those wanting useful product information must go to a magazine like *Consumer Reports*, which publishes objective and comparative studies of various products.) Instead, advertisements offer us jingles, rhymes, and attractive images.

The goal of advertising, of course, is to persuade us to buy the products that are being touted. Providing objective and comparative product information may be one way to do that, but it is not the only way or a very common way, if one were to judge from ads these days—which frequently say nothing at all about the product's qualities. The similarity among many competing products may be the explanation. One writer identifies the effort to distinguish among basically identical products as the "ethical, as well as economic, crux of the [advertising] industry"; another refers to it as the "persistent, underlying bad faith" of much American advertising.[28]

Deceptive Techniques

Because advertisers are trying to persuade people to buy their products and because straight product information is not necessarily the best way to do that, there is a natural temptation to obfuscate, misrepresent, or even lie. In an attempt to persuade, advertisers are prone to exploit ambiguity, conceal facts, exaggerate, and use psychological appeals.

Ambiguity When ads are ambiguous, they can be deceiving. For example, the Continental Baking Company was charged with such ambiguity by the U.S. Federal Trade Commission (FTC). In advertising its Profile bread, Continental implied that eating the bread would lead to weight loss. The fact was that Profile had about the same number of calories per ounce as other breads; each slice contained seven fewer calories but only because it was sliced thinner than most breads. Continental issued a corrective advertisement.

Ambiguous ads can mislead the consumer. The Profile ad is a good example. A large number of people interpreted that ad to mean that eating Profile bread would lead to weight loss. Likewise, for years consumers inferred from its advertisements that Listerine mouthwash effectively fought bacteria and sore throats. Not so; accordingly, the FTC ordered Listerine to run a multimillion-dollar disclaimer. And when Sara Lee began promoting its Light Classics desserts, the implicit implication was that "light" meant the products contained fewer calories than other Sara Lee desserts. When pressed by investigators to support this implied claim, Sara Lee contended that "light" referred only to the texture of the product. In cases like these, advertisers and manufacturers invariably deny that they intended consumers to draw false inferences. Admittedly, there is a difference between "lying" and "creating a false belief." X is lying to Y if X communicates with the intention of creating a false belief in Y. But if X's communication is not intended or expected to create a false belief, then X is not lying, though his/her communication may well create a false belief in Y. In such cases, we may say that the communication was "ambiguous." However, sometimes the ambiguity is such that a reasonable person wouldn't infer anything else but the false belief.

Aiding and abetting ambiguity is the use of "weasel" words, words used to evade or retreat from a direct or forthright statement. Consider the weasel word *help*. "Help" means "aid" or "assist" and nothing else. Yet as one author has observed, "'help' is the one single word which, in all the annals of advertising, has done the most to say something that couldn't be said."[29] Because the word *help* is used to qualify, almost anything can be said after it. Thus we're exposed to ads for products that "help us keep young," "help prevent cavities," "help keep our houses germ-free." Consider for a moment how many times a day you hear or read phrases like these: helps stop, helps prevent, helps fight, helps overcome, helps you feel, helps you look. And, of course, *help* is hardly the only weasel word. *Like, virtual,* or *virtually, can be, up to* (as in "provides relief up to eight hours"), *as much as* (as in "saves as much as one gallon of gas"), and numerous other weasel words are used to imply what can't be said. Sometimes weasel words deprive the message of any meaning whatsoever, as when *up to* and *more* come together in "save up to 40 to 50 percent and more."

The fact that ads are open to interpretation doesn't exonerate advertisers from the obligation to provide clear information. Indeed, this fact intensifies their responsibility, because the danger of misleading through ambiguity increases as the ad is subject to interpretation. At stake are not only people's money but also their health, loyalties, and expectations. The potential harm a misleading ad can cause is great, not to mention its cavalier treatment of the truth. For these reasons ambiguity in ads is of serious moral concern.

Concealed Facts When advertisers conceal facts, they suppress information that is unflattering to their products. That is, they neglect to mention or distract consumers' attention away from information knowledge of which would probably make their products less desirable.

Shell, for example, used to advertise that its gasoline had "platformate" but neglected to mention that all other brands did too. And Kraft advertised its Philadelphia Cream Cheese as having "half the calories of butter," but didn't tell consumers that it is also high in fat. When peanut butter makers advertise their products as cholesterol-free, they omit the fact that only animal products contain cholesterol and that peanut butter is rich in fat. Weight Watchers tells consumers that its frozen meals are without butter, chicken fat, or tropical oils but not that they are high in salt. Caverject promotes itself as an alternative to Viagra as a treatment for male impotence. Its ads say that "Caverject can help you and your partner enjoy renewed spontaneity and sexual satisfaction." But they don't say that Caverject is a prescription medicine that must be injected with a needle inserted directly into the penis.

Advertisements for painkillers routinely conceal relevant information. For years, Bayer aspirin advertised that it contained "the ingredient that doctors recommend most." What is that ingredient? Aspirin. The advertising claim that "last year hospitals dispensed ten times as much Tylenol as the next four brands combined" does not disclose the fact that Johnson & Johnson supplies hospitals with Tylenol at a cost well below what consumers pay. Interestingly, American Home Products sued Johnson & Johnson on the grounds that the Tylenol ad falsely implies that it is more effective than competing products. But at the same time, American Home Products was advertising its Anacin-3 by claiming that "hospitals recommended acetaminophen, the aspirin-free pain reliever in Anacin-3, more than any other pain reliever"—without telling consumers that the acetaminophen hospitals recommend is, in fact, Tylenol.

Concealment of relevant facts and information can exploit people by misleading them; it also undermines truth telling. Unfortunately, truth rarely seems foremost in the minds of advertisers. For example, Coors continued to advertise its beer as brewed from "Rocky Mountain spring water" even after it opened plants outside Colorado that use local water. And Perrier advertised its bottled water as having bubbled up from underground springs decades after it had begun pumping the water up from the ground through a pipe and combining it with processed gas.

As one U.S. advertising-industry insider writes: "Inside the agency the basic approach is hardly conducive to truth telling. The usual thinking in forming a campaign is first what can we say, true or not, that will sell the product best? The second consideration is, how can we say it effectively and get away with it so that (1) people who buy won't feel let down by too big a promise that doesn't come true, and (2) the ads will avoid quick and certain censure by the [regulators]."[30] This observation shows the common tendency to equate what's legal with what's moral. It's precisely this outlook that leads to advertising behaviour of dubious morality.

Examples of ads that conceal important facts are legion. An old Colgate-Palmolive ad for its Rapid Shave Cream used sandpaper to demonstrate the cream's effect on tough beards. Colgate concealed the fact that the "sandpaper" in the ad was actually Plexiglas and that actual sandpaper had to be soaked in Rapid Shave for about eighty minutes before it came off in one stroke. A few years ago, Campbell vegetable soup ads showed pictures of a thick, rich brew calculated to whet even a gourmet's appetite. What the ads didn't show were clear glass marbles deposited in that bowl to give the soup the appearance of solidity. Similarly, a television ad for Volvo showed a row of cars being crushed by a big-wheel truck, with only a Volvo remaining intact. What the ad neglected to say was that the Volvo had been reinforced and the other cars weakened. More recently, ads run in travel magazines to encourage Americans to vacation in Bermuda have pictured people swimming or diving or sunning themselves on the beach—in Hawaii!

If business has an obligation to provide clear, accurate, and adequate information, we may certainly wonder if it does discharge that duty when it hides facts relevant to the consumer's purchase of a product. Concealing information raises serious moral concerns relative to truth telling and consumer exploitation. When consumers are deprived of comprehensive knowledge about a product, their choices are constricted and distorted.

If pushed further, the moral demand for full information challenges almost all advertising. Even the best advertisements never point out the negative features of their products or that there is no substantive difference between the product being advertised and its competitors, as is often the case. In this sense, they could be accused of concealing relevant information. Most advertisers would be shocked at the suggestion that honesty requires an objective presentation of the pros and cons of their products, and in fact consumers don't expect advertisers or salespeople to be impartial. Nevertheless, it is not clear why this moral value should not be relevant to assessing advertising. And it can be noted that retail salespeople, despite a sometimes negative reputation, often do approach this level of candour—at least when they are fortunate enough to sell a genuinely good and competitive product or when they do not work on commission.

Exaggeration Advertisers can mislead through exaggeration—that is, by making claims unsupported by evidence. For example, claims that a pain reliever provides "extra pain relief," is "50 percent stronger than aspirin," or is "superior to any other nonprescription painkiller on the market" contradict evidence that all analgesics are effective to the same degree. Manufacturers of vitamins and other dietary supplements are notorious for exaggerating the possible benefits of their products. Some drug companies do the same. Ads for Propecia tell men, "Starting today, you need not face the fear of more hair loss." But while Propecia can slow hair loss, it doesn't necessarily stop it.

Nabisco's advertising of its 100-percent-bran cereal as being "flavored with two naturally sweet fruit juices" is typical of exaggerated product claims. Although fig juice and prune juice have indeed been added to the product, they are its least significant ingredients in terms of weight; the primary sweetener is sugar. As in this case, exaggeration often goes hand in hand with concealed information. Until stopped by legal action, General Electric advertised its 90-watt Energy Choice bulb as an energy-saving replacement for a conventional 100-watt bulb. But there is nothing special about the GE bulb; it simply produces fewer lumens than a 100-watt bulb. Trident chewing gum, to take another example, has long advertised that it helps fight cavities, but its ads (which describe Trident as a "dental instrument") clearly exaggerate the benefits of chewing Trident. Chewing gum can indeed help dislodge debris on dental enamel, but so can eating an apple or rinsing one's mouth with water. And the sugar substitute used by Trident (sorbitol) can indirectly promote tooth decay: it nurtures the normally harmless bacteria that sugar activates into decay-producing microorganisms.

"Anti-aging" skin-care products are one of the fastest-growing segments of the cosmetic industry, partly because the baby boom generation is getting older. Here exaggeration is rampant, as advertisers make claims for their products that are, to put it as gently as possible, scientifically unfounded. For example, Face Lift asserts that it boosts collagen production and "reduces deep wrinkles up to 70%"; L'Oréal brags that its "dermo-smoothing complex" called "d-contraxol" significantly reduces wrinkles, and Procter & Gamble touts Regenerist, an "amino peptide complex" that supposedly provides "revolutionary cell care" to "regenerate" skin.[31] When it comes to exaggeration, though, few products surpass weight-loss pills, powders, and patches. So many of these products take advantage of gullible, often desperate consumers by promising them that they can shed unwanted pounds and excess inches without reducing their caloric intake or exercising more.

The line between such deliberate deception and so-called *puffery* is not always clear. Puffery is the supposedly harmless use of superlatives and subjective praise in advertisements. Thus advertisers frequently boast of the merits of their products by using words such as *best*, *finest*, or *most*, or phrases and slogans like *king of beers*, *breakfast of champions*, or *the ultimate driving machine*. In most instances, puffery appears innocuous, but sometimes it's downright misleading, as in the Dial soap ad that claimed Dial was "the most effective deodorant soap you can buy." When asked to substantiate that claim, the Armour-Dial company insisted that it was not claiming product superiority; all it meant was that Dial soap was as effective as any other soap.

The law permits puffery on the grounds that it doesn't deceive people. University of Wisconsin professor Ivan L. Preston, however, argues that puffery shouldn't be immune from regulation. Why? Because the public is often taken in by it. Consider the following pieces of puffery: "State Farm is all you need to know about life insurance," "Ford has a better idea," and "It's the real thing [Coca-Cola]." Although these statements may seem like meaningless verbal posturing, in one survey 22 percent of those sampled thought the first claim was "completely true" while 36 percent considered it "partly true." The second claim was judged "completely true" by 26 percent and "partly true" by 42 percent while 35 percent believed the third claim was "completely true" and 29 percent "partly true."[32] Moreover, argues Preston, if puffery didn't work, salespeople and advertisers wouldn't use it.[33]

Psychological Appeals A psychological appeal is one that aims to persuade by appealing primarily to human emotional needs and not to reason. This is potentially the area of greatest moral concern in advertising. An automobile ad that presents the product surrounded by people who look wealthy and successful appeals to our need and desire for status. A life insurance ad that portrays a destitute family woefully struggling in the aftermath of a provider's death tries to persuade through pity and fear. Reliance on such devices, although not unethical per se, raises moral concerns because rarely do such products fully deliver what the ads promise.

Ads that rely extensively on pitches to power, prestige, sex, masculinity, femininity, acceptance, approval, and the like aim to sell more than a product. They are peddling psychological satisfaction. Perhaps the best example is the increasingly explicit and pervasive use of sexual pitches in ads:

Scene:	An artist's sky lit studio. A young man lies nude, the bed sheets in disarray. He awakens to find a tender note on his pillow. The phone rings and he gets up to answer it.
Woman's Voice:	You snore.
Artist (smiling):	And you always steal the covers.

More cozy patter between the two. Then a husky-voiced announcer intones: "Paco Rabanne. A cologne for men. What is remembered is up to you."

Although sex has always been used to sell products, it has never before been used as explicitly in advertising as it is today—as the nudes in the ads for Calvin Klein products demonstrate. And the sexual pitches are by no means confined to products like cologne or clothes. The California Avocado Commission supplemented its "Love Food from California" recipe ads with a campaign featuring a leggy actress sprawled across two pages of some eighteen national magazines to promote the avocado's nutritional value. The copy line reads: "Would this body lie to you?" Similarly, Dannon yogurt ran ads featuring a bikini-clad beauty and this message: "More nonsense is written on dieting than any other subject—except possibly sex."

Some students of marketing claim that ads like these appeal to the subconscious mind of both marketer and consumer. Purdue University psychologist and marketing consultant Jacob Jacoby contends that marketers, like everyone else, carry around sexual symbols in their subconscious that, intentionally or not, they use in ads. A case in point: the Newport cigarette "Alive with Pleasure" campaign. One campaign ad featured a woman riding the handlebars of a bicycle driven by a man. The main strut of the bike wheel stands vertically beneath her body. In Jacoby's view, such symbolism needs no interpretation.

Author Wilson Bryan Key, who has extensively researched the topic of subconscious marketing appeals, claims that many ads take a subliminal form. *Subliminal advertising* is advertising that communicates at a level beneath our conscious awareness, where, some psychologists claim, the vast reservoir of human motivation primarily resides. Most marketing people would deny that such advertising occurs. Key disagrees. Indeed, he goes so far as to claim: "It is virtually impossible to pick up a newspaper or magazine, turn on a radio or television set, read a promotional pamphlet or the telephone book, or shop through a supermarket without having your subconscious purposely massaged by some monstrously clever artist, photographer, writer, or technician."[34]

Concern with the serious nature of psychological appeals appears to have motivated the California Wine Institute to adopt an advertising code of standards. The following restrictions are included:

No wine ad shall present persons engaged in activities with appeal particularly to minors. Among those excluded: amateur or professional sports figures, celebrities, or cowboys; rock stars, racecar drivers.

No wine ad shall exploit the human form or "feature provocative or enticing poses or be demeaning to any individual."

No wine ad shall portray wine in a setting where food is not presented.

No wine ad shall present wine in "quantities inappropriate to the situation."

No wine ad shall portray wine as similar to another type of beverage or product such as milk, soda, or candy.

No wine ad shall associate wine with personal performance, social attainment, achievement, wealth, or the attainment of adulthood.

No wine ad shall show automobiles in a way that one could construe their conjunction.

In adopting such a rigorous code of advertising ethics, the California Wine Institute rightly acknowledged the subtle implications and psychological nuances that affect the message an ad communicates.

Ads Directed at Children

Advertising to children is big business in both Canada and the United States. Indeed on this particular aspect (if not on the entire issue) of advertising, it is rather pointless to try to regard the Canadian picture in isolation from the U.S. picture. For the overwhelming majority of Canadians live along the U.S.-Canada border and thus have ready access to American television and radio broadcasting. Every year children under twelve and teenagers spend themselves billions of dollars in the marketplace. In addition one must take into account the billions of adult purchases for gifts, clothes, and groceries that are influenced by children. In recent years advertising aimed specifically at children has grown exponentially. American advertisers now spend more than $1.5 billion a year on ads for children, and there are more and more venues for such ads—with new magazines, websites, and entire television channels aimed at children.[35]

Furthermore, it's no longer just cereal, candy, and toys that are being advertised. Advertisers of other products are wooing children in an effort to create customers for the future. As Jackie Pate of Delta Air Lines puts it, "By building brand-loyalty in children today, they'll be the adult passengers of the future." Ann Moore, Chairperson and CEO of Time Inc., which publishes *Sports Illustrated for Kids*, adds, "We believe children make brand decisions that will carry into their adult lives."[36] Although the magazine attracts mostly eight-to-fourteen-year-old boys as readers, a recent issue featured a two-page spread for the Chevy Venture minivan.

Of course, advertisers admit that it's not just future consumers they want. "We're relying on the kid to pester the mom to buy the product, rather than going straight to the mom," says Barbara A. Martino of Grey Advertising. And Karen Francis, brand manager for the Chevy Venture, reports that even she was surprised how often parents tell her that their kids played a tie-breaking role in deciding which car to buy. Naturally, advertisers argue that parents still have ultimate control over what gets purchased and what doesn't. But is the strategy of selling to parents by convincing the children a fair one? As one parent complains, "Brand-awareness has been an incredibly abusive experience—the relentless requests to go to McDonald's [or] to see movies that are inappropriate for six-year-olds [but] that are advertised on kids' shows."

Television and advertising play a large role in most children's lives. At age seven a typical child sees 20,000 television commercials a year, and children remember what they see. For example, in the 1990s researchers found that the frogs in the Budweiser beer commercials were more widely recognized among children than any cartoon characters other than Bugs Bunny. The problem is that children, particularly young children, are naive and gullible and thus particularly vulnerable to advertisers' enticements. Consider, for example, ads in which children are shown, after eating a certain cereal, to have enough power to lift large playhouses. No adult would be misled by that ad, but children lack experience and independent judgment. This provides at least a prima facie case for protecting them.

"Kids are the most pure consumers you could have," says one advertising expert. "They tend to interpret your ad literally. They are infinitely open." This problem is growing greater because the line between children's shows and the commercials that come with them is fading away. Children's entertainment features characters whose licensed images are stamped on toys, sheets, clothes, and food. Moreover, at the same time that movies and television shows are ever more tightly linked to the selling of toys and other items, commercials are becoming more like entertainment. Is it any wonder that many children perceive little difference between ads and television shows? As one nine-year-old sees it, the only distinction is that "commercials are shorter."

Some writers contend that it is "ethical to advertise toys, sugar-loaded cereal or non-violent games to children . . . as long as it is *truthful* and as long as children understand the message."[37] But that overlooks children's special susceptibilities and the need to protect them from manipulation and endless commercial enticement. After all, the ads directed at them for cereals, snacks, and soft drinks say nothing untrue, and children understand their message all too well. But few youngsters understand much about nutrition or are aware that obesity among children is reaching epidemic proportions. Advertising to children thus raises important ethical issues, issues that also lead to the larger question of the nature and desirability of advertising's role in today's media-dominated society, which is our next topic.

THE DEBATE OVER ADVERTISING

The controversy over advertising does not end with the issue of deceptive techniques and unfair advertising practices. Advertising provides little usable information to consumers. Advertisements almost always conceal relevant negative facts about their products, and they are frequently based on subtle appeals to psychological needs, which the products they peddle are unlikely to satisfy. These realities are the basis for some critics' wholesale repudiation of advertising on moral grounds. They also desire a less commercially polluted environment, one that does not continually reinforce materialistic values.

Consumer Needs

Some defenders of advertising take these points in stride. They concede that images of glamour, sex, or adventure sell products, but they argue that these images are what we, the consumers, want. We don't want just blue jeans; we want romance or sophistication or status with our blue jeans. By connecting products with important emotions and feelings, advertisements can also satisfy our deeper needs and wants. As one advertising executive puts it,

> Advertising can show a consumer how a baby powder helps affirm her role as a nurturing mother—Johnson & Johnson's "The Language of Love." Or it can show a teenager how a soft drink helps assert his or her emerging independence—Pepsi's "The Choice of a New Generation."[38]

Harvard business professor Theodore Levitt has drawn an analogy between advertising and art. Both take liberties with reality, both deal in symbolic communication, and neither is interested in literal truth or in pure functionality. Rather, both art and advertising help us repackage the otherwise crude, drab, and generally oppressive reality that surrounds us. They create "illusions, symbols, and implications that promise more." They help us modify, transform, embellish, enrich, and reconstruct the world around us. "Without distortion, embellishment, and elaboration," Levitt writes, "life would be drab, dull, anguished, and at its existential worst." Advertising helps satisfy this legitimate human need. Its handsome packages and imaginative promises produce that "elevation of the spirit" that we want and need. Embellishment and distortion are therefore among advertising's socially desirable purposes. To criticize advertising on these counts, Levitt argues, is to overlook the real needs and values of human beings.[39]

Levitt's critics contend that even if advertising appeals to the same deep needs that art does, advertising promises satisfaction of those needs in the products it sells, and that promise is rarely kept. At the end of the day, blue jeans are still just blue jeans, and your love life will be unaffected by which soap you shower with. The imaginative, symbolic, and artistic content of advertising, which Levitt sees as answering real human needs, is viewed by critics as manipulating, distorting, and even creating those needs.

In his influential books *The Affluent Society* and *The New Industrial State*, John Kenneth Galbraith has criticized advertising on just this point. Galbraith argues that the process of production today, with its expensive marketing campaigns, subtle advertising techniques, and sophisticated sales strategies, creates the very wants it then satisfies. Producers, that is, create both the goods and the demand for those goods. If a new breakfast cereal or detergent were so much wanted, Galbraith reasons, why must so much money be spent trying to get the consumer to buy it? He thinks it is obvious that "wants can be synthesized by advertising, catalyzed by salesmanship, and shaped by" discreet manipulations.

Accordingly, Galbraith rejects the economist's traditional faith in "consumer sovereignty": the idea that consumers should and do control the market through their purchases. Rather than independent consumer demand shaping production, as classical economic theory says it does, nowadays it is the other way around. Galbraith dubs this the "dependence effect": "As a society becomes increasingly affluent, wants are increasingly created by the process by which they are satisfied."[40]

One consequence, Galbraith thinks, is that our system of production cannot be defended on the ground that it is satisfying urgent or important wants. We can't defend production as satisfying wants if the production process itself creates those wants. "In the absence of the massive and artful persuasion that accompanies the management of demand," Galbraith argues,

> increasing abundance might well have reduced the interest of people in acquiring more goods. They would not have felt the need for multiplying the artifacts— autos, appliances, detergents, cosmetics—by which they were surrounded.[41]

Another consequence is our general preoccupation with material consumption. In particular, Galbraith claims, our pursuit of private goods, continually reinforced by advertising, leads us to neglect public goods and services. We need better schools, parks, artistic and recreational facilities; safer and cleaner cities and air; more efficient, less crowded transportation systems. We are rich in the private production and use of goods, Galbraith thinks, and starved in public services. In 2004 Galbraith summarized his long-held views this way:

> Belief in a market economy in which the consumer is sovereign is one of our most pervasive forms of fraud. Let no one try to sell without consumer management, control. As power over the innovation, manufacture, and sale of goods and services has passed to the producer and away from the consumer, the aggregate of this production has been the prime test of social achievement . . . . Not education or literature or the arts but the production of automobiles, including SUVs: Here is the modern measure of economic and therefore social achievement.[42]

Galbraith's critics have concentrated their fire on a couple of points. First, Galbraith never shows that advertising has the power he attributes to it. Despite heavy advertising, most new products fail to win a permanent place in the hearts of consumers. Advertising campaigns like that for Listerine in the 1920s, which successfully created the problem of "halitosis" in order to sell the new idea of "mouthwash," are rare.* Although it is true that we are inundated with ads, experiments suggest we no

longer care much about them. Each of us sees an average of 1,600 advertisements a day, notices around 1,200 of them, and responds favourably or unfavourably to only about 12. We also appear to pay more attention to ads for products that we already have.[43]

Second, critics have attacked Galbraith's assumption that the needs supposedly created by advertisers and producers are, as a result, "false" or "artificial" needs and therefore less worthy of satisfaction. Human needs, they stress, are always socially influenced and are never static. How are we to distinguish between "genuine" and "artificial" wants, and why should the latter be thought less important? Ads might produce a want that we would not otherwise have had without that want being in any way objectionable.

Although conclusive evidence is unavailable, critics of advertising continue to worry about its power to influence our lives and shape our culture and civilization. Even if producers cannot create wants out of whole cloth, many worry that advertising can manipulate our existing desires—that it can stimulate certain desires, both at the expense of other, non-consumer-oriented desires and out of proportion to the likely satisfaction that fulfillment of those desires will bring.

Market Economics

Defenders of advertising are largely untroubled by these worries. They see advertising as an aspect of free competition in a competitive market, which ultimately works to the benefit of all. But this simple free-market defense of advertising has weaknesses. First, advertising doesn't fit too well into the economist's model of the free market. Economists can prove, if we grant them enough assumptions, that free-market buying and selling lead to optimal results.* One of those assumptions is that everyone has full and complete information, on the basis of which they then buy and sell. But if that were so, advertising would be pointless.

One might argue that advertising moves us closer to the ideal of full information, but there is good reason to doubt this. Even if we put aside the question of whether ads can create, shape, or manipulate wants, they do seem to enhance brand loyalty, which generally works to thwart price competition. A true brand-name consumer is willing to pay more for a product that is otherwise indistinguishable from its competitors. He or she buys a certain beer despite being unable to taste the difference between it and other beers.

More generally, critics of advertising stand the invisible-hand argument on its head. The goal of advertisers is to sell you products and to make money, not to maximize your well-being. Rational demonstration of how a product will in fact enhance your well-being is not the only way advertisers can successfully persuade you to buy their products. Indeed, it is far from the most common technique. Critics charge, accordingly, that there is no reason to think that advertising even tends to maximize the well-being of consumers.

---

*Given that the saliva in one's mouth is completely replenished every fifteen minutes or so anyway, no mouthwash can have an effect longer than that.

*Technically, they lead to *Pareto optimality*, which means that no one person can be made better off without making someone else worse off.

Defenders of advertising may claim that, nonetheless, advertising is necessary for economic growth, which benefits us all. The truth of this claim, however, is open to debate. Critics maintain that advertising is a waste of resources and serves only to raise the price of advertised goods. Like Galbraith, they may also contend that advertising in general reinforces mindless consumerism. It corrupts our civilization and misdirects our society's economic effort toward private consumption and away from the public realm. The never-ending pursuit of material goods may also divert us as a society from the pursuit of a substantially shorter workday.[44]

Free Speech and the Media

Two final issues should be briefly noted. Defenders of advertising claim that, despite criticisms, advertising enjoys protection under the *Charter* in Canada (or the First Amendment in the U.S.) as a form of speech. But that right is not absolute under the *Charter* (see Limitations under s. 1; see also *R v. Keegstra* [1990] 3 S.C.R. 697; *R. v. Butler* [1992] 1 S.C.R. 452). But even if one were to concede to advertisers the legal right to free speech, not every exercise of that legal right need be morally justifiable. If advertisements in general or of a certain type or for certain products were shown to have undesirable social consequences, or if certain sorts of ads relied on objectionable or non-rational persuasive techniques, then there would be a strong moral argument against such advertisements regardless of their legal status.

Advertising subsidizes the media, and that is a positive but far from conclusive consideration in its favour. But the very fact that it is free to the consumer results in far more consumption than would otherwise be the case and probably, as many think, far more than is good for us. Although satellite and cable television have improved things, the mediocrity of much television fare is hardly accidental. The networks need large audiences. Obviously they can't run everyone's favourite type of program, because people's tastes differ; consequently, they seek to reach a common denominator. If viewers instead of advertisers paid for each show they watched, things would be different.

SUMMARY

1. The complexity of today's economy and the dependence of consumers on business increase business's responsibility for product safety.
2. The legal liability of manufacturers for injuries caused by defective products has evolved over the years. Today the courts have moved to the doctrine of *strict liability*, which holds the manufacturer of a product responsible for injuries suffered as a result of defects in the product, regardless of whether the manufacturer was negligent.
3. Government agencies, such as the Consumer Product Safety Commission, have broad powers to regulate product safety. Critics contend that these regulations are costly and that they prevent individuals from choosing to purchase a riskier but less expensive product. This argument touches on the controversy over *legal paternalism*, the doctrine that the law may justifiably be used to restrict the freedom of individuals for their own good.
4. Although there are exceptions, regulations generally help ensure that business meets its responsibilities to consumers. Businesspeople, however, tend to favour self-regulation and government deregulation.
5. To increase safety, companies need to give safety the priority necessitated by the product, abandon the misconception that accidents are solely the result of consumer misuse, monitor closely the manufacturing process, review the safety implications of their marketing and advertising strategies, provide consumers with full information about product performance, and investigate consumer complaints. Some successful companies already put a premium on safety.
6. Business also has other obligations to consumers: product quality must live up to express and implied warranties; prices should be fair, and business should refrain from price fixing, price gouging, and manipulative pricing; and product labelling and packaging should provide clear, accurate, and adequate information.
7. Advertising tries to persuade people to buy products. Ambiguity, the concealment of relevant facts, exaggeration, and psychological appeals are among the morally dubious techniques that advertisers use.
8. The Federal Trade Commission protects us from blatantly deceptive advertising. But it is debatable whether the FTC should ban only advertising that is likely to deceive reasonable people or whether it should protect careless or gullible consumers as well. The FTC now seeks to prohibit advertising that misleads a significant number of consumers, regardless of whether it was reasonable for them to have been misled.
9. Advertising to children is big business, but children are particularly susceptible to the blandishments of advertising. Advertisers contend that parents still control what gets purchased and what doesn't. However, critics doubt the fairness of selling to parents by appealing to children.
10. Defenders of advertising view its imaginative, symbolic, and artistic content as answering real human needs. Critics maintain that advertising manipulates those needs or even creates artificial ones. John Kenneth Galbraith contends that today the same process that produces products also produces the demand for those products (the dependence effect). Galbraith argues, controversially, that advertising encourages a preoccupation with material goods and leads us to favour private consumption at the expense of public goods.
11. Defenders of advertising see it as a necessary and desirable aspect of competition in a free-market system, a protected form of free speech, and a useful sponsor of the media, in particular television. Critics challenge all three claims.

CASE 10.1

Hemophilia and the Tainted Blood Scandal[45]

A. *Time Line in Steven's Life.* In 1982 the first case of acquired immune deficiency syndrome (AIDS) was diagnosed in Canada. That same year Steven Holmes turned 21 years old. Steven suffered from moderate hemophilia A. Hemophilia is a disorder affecting, almost exclusively, males who have a deficiency in or lack one of two proteins in their blood that contribute to the blood-clotting process. These proteins are called either coagulation factor VIII or IX. Hemophilia A is associated with factor VIII problems and hemophilia B with factor IX problems.

These unfortunate males then have a bleeding disorder and can experience hemorrhaging into their joints and muscles, easy bruising, and severe, prolonged hemorrhaging after trauma or surgery. The modern treatment for hemophilia has been to replace these deficient or absent clotting factors by the same ones obtained from plasma donors. The plasma from thousands of donors is pooled and the factor VIII or XI proteins are then extracted, freeze-dried, and packaged in easily transportable vials. They are then stored in the hemophiliac's home and administered as needed.

Steven required infusions of factor VIII at a rate of approximately one infusion every two months for bleeding episodes. He had a relatively normal life with no serious bleeding episodes and was able to play non-contact sports, of which tennis was his forte. In early 1985, Steven's doctor recommended human immunodeficiency virus (HIV) testing because of his risk of HIV infection from use of the factor VIII concentrate. The tests showed that Steven was free of the virus at that time. In July 1985, he started to use heat-treated factor VIII concentrates, since they had become available in Canada at that time. Heat treatment was believed to inactivate the HIV. Steven was tested again for HIV in early 1986; this time he tested positive. In June 1988, along with all other hemophiliacs, he began using factor VIII concentrate that was treated with the new method of "wet-heat." Steven went for a few years without any significant symptoms, but he began to feel unwell in late 1988 at which time he was diagnosed with AIDS. Steven Holmes died of complications caused by AIDS in 1993 at the age of 32.

B. *The Canadian Red Cross and the Time Line for AIDS.* The first North American case of AIDS was diagnosed in the United States in June 1981. The first Canadian case of AIDS was diagnosed in March 1982. By June 1982 the scientific community generally believed that AIDS was caused by an infectious agent yet to be identified. The AIDS epidemic in Canada was one-and-a-half years behind that of the United States and Canadian officials had an opportunity to learn from the early U.S. experiences of its spread across the country and of the people at highest risk of contracting it. Canada also had the opportunity of scrutinizing the U.S.'s early attempts at screening blood donors at risk for

AIDS. In the summer of 1982 three hemophiliacs in different parts of the United States developed AIDS-like symptoms, and hemophiliacs quickly became the next risk "group" for developing AIDS, after homosexuals, intravenous drug users, and Haitian immigrants. By January 1983, it was widely believed by the scientific community that AIDS could be transmitted by blood, while by January 1984 there was scientific proof that the AIDS virus could be transmitted by blood and blood products.

In January 1983, the American Red Cross, the American Association of Blood Banks, and the U.S. Council of Community Blood Centers released a joint statement which recommended that blood donor screening should be implemented and that specific questions be asked of donors to detect possible exposure to AIDS, in particular questions that would elicit early symptoms of AIDS such as a history of night sweats, unexplained fevers, unexpected weight loss, and swollen lymph glands. This statement was shared with Canadian Red Cross officials the same month. In March 1983, the relevant U.S. organizations implemented enhanced donor-screening practices by questioning blood donors for symptoms of AIDS and providing pamphlets listing high-risk groups.

No similar changes were made at the time to the then-existing CRC protocol regarding the screening of blood donors. Instead, the CRC issued a press release in which it asked people with a high risk of contracting AIDS not to donate blood or blood products. In the same press release the CRC announced that expansion of current donor screening practices would be implemented to include questions related to symptoms of AIDS. No donor screening or donor education related to AIDS would take place at most of the Canadian blood clinics for another year. In May 1984, the CRC published a pamphlet to be given to all blood donors. But the pamphlet did not include "persons with symptoms of AIDS" in the groups of people who should not donate blood, nor did it list groups of people who were at risk for AIDS infection. In January 1986, the CRC revised its 1984 pamphlet in order to improve screening of possible HIV-infected donors. The pamphlet now included the symptoms of AIDS and defined at high risk any male who had had sex with another male since 1977.

In April 1984, scientists discovered the virus that causes AIDS. By August 1984, the CRC had become aware that scientists (primarily in the U.S.) were developing AIDS virus test kits, which would be available within a year. In March 1985, the U.S. Food and Drug Administration granted licences to firms to distribute HIV antibody test kits. U.S. organizations began testing within weeks, and by May 1985 all blood and plasma centres in the United States were testing all donations for the HIV antibody. Australia began testing in April 1985. Testing on blood donations in Canada began in November of 1985. The delays in the implementation of testing were apparently caused by long consultations with the National Advisory Committee on AIDS, funding delays by the Canadian Blood Committee, and delays in the CRC implementation period.

At the end of October 1984, the U.S. Centre for Disease Control in Atlanta reported that a process called "heat treatment" could inactivate the HIV. In mid-November 1984, the Bureau of Biologics at Health Canada recommended that the CRC replace non-heat-treated factor concentrates with heat-treated ones. The CRC, however, was concerned about the existing inventory of non-heat-treated concentrates and formulated an implementation plan for initiating the recommended heat-treated products after exhausting its inventory of non-heat-treated products. The conversion to heat-treated products started in July 1, 1985.

The Canadian Red Cross got its supplies of heat-treated factor concentrates from two U.S. manufacturers, the Armour Pharmaceutical Company and Cutter Pharmaceuticals. The CRC then distributed them to hemophiliacs throughout Canada. These suppliers were required to keep the Bureau of Biologics at Health Canada informed of any matter relating to the safety of products for which they have received a licence in Canada. The Bureau of Biologics was the regulator of the manufacture, importation, and distribution of blood products in Canada. It was responsible for setting minimum standards of quality and safety in the blood industry and making reasonable efforts to ensure that those standards were met. In carrying out its mandate, the Bureau depended largely on the reports and studies from the firms it was supposed to regulate. Neither of the suppliers informed the Bureau of anything untoward about their products. However, Armour was aware of problems with their heat-treated factor concentrates in the United Kingdom and the Netherlands since the summer of 1985.

Articles about the efficacy of heat treatment of factor concentrates began to appear in peer-reviewed journals as early as the summer of 1985. There were concerns that heat treatment does not effectively kill or inactivate the virus in the blood or blood products. In 1986 there were reports linking positive tests for HIV antibodies to the use of (heat-treated) factor concentrate marketed by the Armour Pharmaceutical Company. In the fall of 1987, six hemophiliac persons in British Columbia suddenly became HIV-antibody positive. They had all used heat-treated factor concentrates exclusively. It was soon established that tainted concentrate units from Armour Pharmaceutical had infected all six.

Shortly after that, the completely effective treatment known as "wet-heat" was implemented.

Discussion Questions

1. Compare the time line of events in Steven's life (A) with the time line of events in the life of CRC (B). Can you find a particular event in (B) that might account for Steven's contracting HIV?

2. Getting rid of existing inventory before you start trading your new stock may well be a good and prudent business practice. Are there any conditions under which you might be prepared to think that the CRC acted properly in delaying the use of "heat-treated" products until they had used up the non-heat-treated ones? Was the CRC negligent? In your answer, explain what it is normally meant by "negligent."

3. Would you hold Armour Pharmaceuticals responsible either "causally" or "morally" (or both) for the six persons in British Columbia who contracted HIV in 1987?

CASE 10.2

Sniffing Glue Could Snuff Profits

The H. B. Fuller Company is now a leading manufacturer of industrial glues, coatings, and paints, with operations worldwide. The company's 10,000 varieties of glue hold together everything from cars to cigarettes to disposable diapers. However, some of its customers don't use Fuller's glues in the way they are intended to be used.

That's particularly the case in Central America, where Fuller derives 27 percent of its profits and where tens of thousands of homeless children sniff some sort of glue. Addicted to glue's intoxicating but dangerous fumes, these unfortunate children are called *resistoleros* after Fuller's Resistol brand. Child-welfare advocates have urged the company to add a noxious oil to its glue to discourage abusers, but the company has resisted, either because it might reduce the glue's effectiveness or because it will irritate legitimate users.[46]

Either way, the issue is irritating H. B. Fuller, which has been recognized by various awards, honours, and socially conscious mutual funds as a company with a conscience. Fuller's mission statement says that it "will conduct business legally and ethically, support the activities of its employees in their communities and be a responsible corporate citizen." The St. Paul–based company gives 5 percent of its profits to charity; it has committed itself to safe environmental practices worldwide (practices that are "often more stringent than local government standards," the company says); and it has even endowed a chair in business ethics at the University of Minnesota. Now Fuller must contend with dissident stockholders inside, and demonstrators outside, its annual meetings.

The glue-sniffing issue is not a new one. In 1969 the Testor Corporation added a noxious ingredient to its hobby glue to discourage abuse, and in 1994 Henkel, a German chemical company that competes with Fuller, stopped making certain toxic glues in Central America. However, Fuller seems to have been singled out for criticism not only because its brand dominates Central America but also because—in the eyes of its critics, anyway—the company has not lived up to its own good-citizen image. Timothy Smith, executive director of the Interfaith Center for Corporate Responsibility, believes that companies with a reputation as good corporate citizens are more vulnerable to attack. "But as I see it," he says, "the hazard is not in acting in a socially responsible way. The hazard is in over-marketing yourself as a saint."

Saintly or not, the company has made matters worse for itself by its handling of the issue. In 1992 H. B. Fuller's board of directors acknowledged that "illegal distribution was continuing" and that "a suitable replacement product would not be available in the near future." Accordingly, it voted to stop selling Resistol adhesives in Central America. "We simply don't believe it is the right decision to keep our solvent product on the market," a company spokesman said.

The Coalition on Resistoleros and other corporate gadflies were ecstatic, but their jubilation turned to anger when they learned a few months later that Fuller had not in fact stopped selling Resistol in Central America, and did not intend to. True, Fuller no longer sold glue to retailers and small-scale users in Honduras and Guatemala, but it continued to sell large tubs and barrels of it to industrial customers in those countries and to a broader list of commercial and industrial users in neighbouring countries.

The company says that it has not only restricted distribution but also taken other steps to stop the abuse of its product. It has altered Resistol's formula, replacing the sweet-smelling but highly toxic solvent toluene with the slightly less toxic chemical cyclohexane. In addition, the company has tried—without success, it says—to develop a nonintoxicating water-based glue, and it contributes to community programs for homeless children in Central America. But the company's critics disparage these actions as mere image-polishing. Bruce Harris, director of Latin American programs for Covenant House, a nonprofit child-welfare advocate, asserts that Resistol is still readily available to children in Nicaragua and El Salvador and, to a lesser extent, in Costa Rica. "If they are genuinely concerned about the children," he asks, "why haven't they pulled out of all the countries—as their board mandated?"

Discussion Questions

1. What are H. B. Fuller's moral obligations in this case? What ideas, effects, and consequences are at stake? Have any moral rights been violated? What would a utilitarian recommend? A Kantian?

2. What specifically should H. B. Fuller do about Resistol? Are the critics right that the steps the company has taken so far are mere image-polishing? Is the company's only moral option to withdraw from the Central American market altogether?

3. When, if ever, is a company morally responsible for harm done by the blatant misuse of a perfectly legitimate and socially useful product? Does it make a difference whether the abusers are adults or children? Is it relevant that other companies market similar products?

4. Given H. B. Fuller's conduct in other matters, would you judge it to be a morally responsible company, all things considered? Are companies that pride themselves on being morally responsible likely to be held to a higher standard than other companies? If so, is this fair?

CASE 10.3

Brain Damage[47]

Robin Savage is worried about her son Jarret. He can hardly read. He can barely write. And math? Forget about it. But worst of all: he's almost 12 years old. "He's in grade six—but he's really at a grade two level. It's heartbreaking," says Savage, whose son has severe Attention Deficit and Hyperactivity Disorder (ADHD) and a number of other learning and behavioural problems. "He's very aggressive. He's been suspended more times than I can count."

Her son's problems have been "a huge financial burden," she says. Before she had a health plan, Savage was forking out $400 a month for his anti-psychotic medication. "But my biggest concern isn't what happens today; it's what happens when he's 18," says Savage, who works at a correctional facility. "I work with men who were diagnosed with childhood ADHD. Young Offenders have all the things Jarret has."

Sadly, Jarret's problems are not unique. About 10 per cent of Canadian children have some kind of learning disability, and another 20 per cent have some kind of behavioural problem. This is more than just a headache for their parents. Children who fall behind in school are at risk for unemployment and crime later on. Mental health problems are estimated to cost the Canadian economy around $50 billion a year; even a one-point drop in our average IQ costs us $6 billion a year. Mental disabilities can be inherited. But there is little doubt that environmental factors—namely, dangerous chemicals in industrial pollution and in consumer products, which Canadians are exposed to every single day—can damage the fragile, developing brains of children.

Between the 1920s and 1980s, lead was required to be added to gasoline—leaving Canada blanketed in millions of tons of the metal, which will never break down. It was also widely used in food cans, plumbing, and children's toys. Lead was also added to paint for many years. Based on Statistics Canada estimates, about one in five children in Canada live in pre-1960s homes and are at risk of exposure to old paint. And smelters are still a big source: Canadian industry released more than 3.5 million kilograms of lead in 2003 alone.

Today we know that for every increase of four micrograms of lead per decilitre of blood, children suffer a one-point drop in IQ. The "safe" limit for lead has been set at 10 micrograms per decilitre. But in the 1970s, almost 90 per cent of American children had blood lead levels above this level. Dr. Herbert Needleman, a Pittsburgh physician, made history in 1979 when he reported that children with higher blood lead levels have lower IQs. Then in 1996, Dr. Needleman reported in the *Journal of the American Medical Association* that 12-year-old boys with higher lead levels were more likely to have behavioural problems, like bullying, vandalism, shoplifting, and arson.

Thanks to the ban on leaded gasoline, blood lead levels have fallen by about 80 per cent since the 1970s. But lead is still a massive problem. A 2002 study in the journal *Environmental Health Perspectives* (EHP) estimated that lead poisoning costs the American economy $43.4 billion a year—compared to $2 billion for asthma, a problem we hear much more about. More than a million American children still have blood lead levels that exceed the "safe" limit [good lead statistics are not available for Canada].

And that "safe" limit should be revised. A 2003 paper in the *New England Journal of Medicine* showed that even below 10 micrograms per decilitre, children still suffered IQ deficits, leading most experts to conclude that there is no safe level for lead. "I believe that we don't know how smart our kids can be," says Dr. Needleman. "I am angry that we are so stupid about this."

Lead is just one of many "heavy" metals that we release into our environment that are harmful to our brains: cadmium, manganese, arsenic, copper, nickel, zinc, and mercury are all routinely detected in Canadian produce. In high doses, children exposed to mercury in the womb reap cerebral palsy, seizures, deafness, blindness, and retardation. Low doses result in brain damage and IQ loss. Mercury is mainly used in electronics, but it leaches from landfills when old computers are thrown out. Metal smelters and waste incinerators release it into the air. By far, however, the largest source of mercury in North America is coal-fired power stations. Altogether, Canadian smokestacks released more than 112,000 kilograms of mercury in 2003.

In the US, it is estimated that one in six babies are born with mercury levels exceeding the "safe" limit [as with lead, Canadian population estimates are not available]. Children most at risk for mercury poisoning eat sport-caught fish, because the metal can "magnify" up the food chain. Mercury is not the only brain-damaging chemical that concentrates in meat eaters. Polybrominated diphenylethers (PBDEs), a type of flame retardant chemicals, have made headlines in recent years as scientists have found astounding concentrations in fish, birds, grizzlies, seals, orca and beluga whales, polar bears, and (of course) humans. PBDEs are used to stop fire-prone products from igniting, like electronics, airplanes, carpets, curtains, and furniture. Some products contain as much as 30 per cent PBDEs by weight. PBDEs have never been made in Canada, but about 1.3 million kilograms of the chemicals were imported from the US in 2000 to be added to consumer products here (and that doesn't include imports laced with PBDEs).

Safety concerns prompted Germany, the Netherlands, and Sweden to restrict these chemicals in the 1980s. But Canada and the US did not, and a 20-year love affair with them has left Canadian women with 10 times more PBDEs in their breast milk than European women. Although good research on the impacts of PBDEs on humans is lacking,

Written by Zoe Cormier. From *Corporate Knights*, Volume 6, Issue 2 (2007). Reprinted with permission of the publisher.

results from animal studies are disconcerting. Mice exposed in the womb to even just a few parts per billion PBDEs suffer brain damage—hampering their attention, learning, memory, motor skills, and behaviour (dubbed by many scientists as "ADHD-like"). Pesticides—often linked to cancer—can also damage the mind, and the research is disturbing.

Dr. Elizabeth Guillette, an anthropologist at the University of Florida, travelled to the Yaqui Valley in Mexico in the late 1990s. One agricultural town in the valley had used pesticides intensely since the 1950s, while another town in the foothills had shunned them. What she discovered shocked her and everyone who read her 1998 paper in EHP. When she asked the valley children to draw a person for her, they drew bizarre figures of sticks and circles that didn't look like anything—and especially not like a person. "This blew my mind," she says. "At first I thought the drawings might have been some kind of a tribal symbol, but they weren't. The kids actually saw this as reality."

The biggest sources of heavy metals in the country, aside from coal-fired power plants, are the large metal smelters in Ontario and Quebec, like Alcan, Stelco, and Alcoa. Alcan ranks as the top producer of developmental toxicants in the entire country. It owns the bulk of the top 10 producers as ranked by Pollution Watch, using government data. It is, however, possible for a metal smelter to lessen its impact. Dofasco cut its releases of developmental toxicants by more than 234,000 kilograms between 1998 and 2002 at its Hamilton plant. According to Bill Gair, a spokesman for Dofasco, the company was able to cut its releases of heavy metals by sending its hazardous waste to a US recycling facility instead of a landfill.

The top releasers of lead and mercury in Canada are both recyclers: Stablex Canada's facility in Blainville, PQ, released more than 32,000 kilograms of mercury in 2004; and Zalev Brothers Co., a recycler outside of Windsor, ON, pumped out more than 3.8 million kilograms of lead that year. It is, of course, hard to point the finger at them. They're only disposing of what we throw away. Some recyclers, however, do go the extra mile. Noranda Recycling in Brampton, ON, is considered to be the only one of its kind in Canada. The facility processes more than a million pounds a month of old electronics. Before shredding, employees first remove parts containing heavy metals. Then, during shredding, the dust itself gets sucked up and recycled, instead of being vented outside. "We are imposing more costs on ourselves, but we want to exceed government standards," says Kelly McCaig for Noranda. "We are zero landfill and we participate in no export to developing countries, unlike most recyclers."

Although old electronics are still full of heavy metals and PBDEs, many of the big names are now eliminating hazardous materials from their products. Around the world, lead-tin solder is being phased out. Giants like Apple, Philips, Sony, Samsung, Panasonic, Hewlett-Packard, and Dell have all eliminated all PBDEs from their products, often using phosphorus-based flame inhibitors instead. Ikea

[due in part that the company is based in Sweden, which banned all PBDEs many years ago] has also banned PBDEs. None of its children's mattresses have contained any PBDEs for 15 years.

Although the environmental records of both the Liberals and Conservatives are by no means impressive, the government has taken some important steps towards protecting the health of Canadians recently. In December 2006, Prime Minister Stephen Harper and then-Environment Minister Rona Ambrose announced that Health and Environment Canada scientists had completed a review of 23,000 chemicals in use in Canada, and a new plan had been drafted to regulate them. This announcement was made with much fanfare and backslapping. Of course, none of our politicians mentioned that the review began seven years ago because the law required improvements to the Canadian Environmental Protection Act.

Then Ambrose announced that carmakers and steel mills will now be required to remove mercury switches from all vehicles before they are recycled. This is good—but a long time coming. Then the government announced the creation of a StatsCan biomonitoring program: a sampling of the chemicals and metals in the blood of 5,000 Canadians, to be completed by 2009. This will finally give us good estimates on things like lead and mercury levels. Experts have been asking for this program for years [the U.S. has done large-scale biomonitoring at the Centers for Disease Control and Prevention since the 1990s, and has had a comprehensive testing program since 2001].

Nevertheless, provincial and federal governments still have a lot to work on. The government needs to curb heavy-metal pollution. According to a 2005 analysis from the Commission for Environmental Cooperation, Canadian facilities emit 13 times more lead than their American counterparts. Coal-fired plants, and the mercury pollution they spawn, are still chugging away, especially in eastern Canada. The Ontario government broke its promise to close the province's coal-fired plants by 2007. Moreover, the federal government recently decided not to regulate lead in cheap costume jewelry. "It's a situation of trade trumping health—costume jewellery is all imported junk," says Kathy Cooper, senior researcher with the Canadian Environmental Law Association.

And, contrary to what the government claims, they are doing nothing to prevent the flow of PBDEs into Canadians. The government proudly announced in the fall of 2006 that they had classified PBDEs as toxic, and would ban them. Despite its claims that it is protecting Canadians, the government has actually done nothing, and is deliberately misleading the public. Here's why: PBDEs come in three forms: penta-, octa-, and deca-. Penta- and octa-, which are considered far more dangerous than deca-, have already been phased out almost everywhere in the world; the vast majority of PBDEs used in Canada are deca. Industry contends that deca- is safe, and that it does not break down into the more dangerous octa- and penta-. But recent studies show that deca- is itself toxic and that it does break down. The proposed regulations ban penta- and octa-, but not deca-. So the government is prohibiting the two kinds of PBDEs that aren't used anymore, and they aren't regulating the one that is. "Under law the government is obliged to ban this chemical," says Lisa Gue, environmental health policy analyst for the David Suzuki Foundation, which has legally challenged the new PBDE regulations.

One of the most important and overlooked problems of children's exposure to brain-damaging chemicals is the fact that children who are already disadvantaged are the most exposed. Children who live in poverty, who already suffer from poor nutrition, and are more at risk of dropping out of school tend to live in older homes with lead paint; they tend to eat sport-caught fish, live with old, crumbling foam furniture, and be exposed to insecticides in derelict urban housing (to control rats and roaches). "This isn't just a health issue; this is a social justice issue," says Cooper.

Discussion Questions

1. Do you think that industries polluting (now or in the past) the environment with heavy metals and/or governments should compensate individuals like Jarret for the handicaps they have? Whatever your view, explain and elaborate on your answer.

2. What difference, if any, does it make that, as the author of the article claims, the children most exposed to brain-damaging chemicals are children who are already disadvantaged? Whatever your answer, explain and elaborate.

3. If you were an (ethical) Minister of the Environment, what general plan of action would you propose, consistently with the normal ethical values of competitive markets, for curbing (perhaps even eliminating) heavy-metal pollution? Make sure you justify every aspect of your plan.

Notes to Chapter 10

1. See "The Case for Change" at www.chronicdiseaseprevention.ca/contents/case_for_change/case_for_change.asp.

2. Smoking rates have dropped from 35 percent in 1985 to 19 percent in 2006. See "Canadian Tobacco Use Monitoring Survey" by Health Canada at www.hc-sc,gc.ca/hi-vs/tobac-tabac/research-recherche/stat/ctums-esutc/index_e.html (under the various years).

3. Both issues went all the way to the Supreme Court, which found against the tobacco companies on the constitutional grounds (in *Imperial Tobacco Canada Ltd. v. Her Majesty the Queen in Right of British Columbia* [2005] 2 S.C.R. 473, 2005 SCC 49), while it rejected, a few months ago (April of 2007), the companies' leave to appeal on the jurisdictional grounds.

4. See www.cbc.ca/money/story/2005/02/21/tobacco-0502221.html.

5. *Ontario Sale of Goods Act*, section 15(1).

6. *Ontario Sale of Goods Act*, section 15(2).

7. See Ira Sager, "Upfront," *Business Week*, September 15, 2003, 12.

8. Richard T. George, "Ethical Responsibilities of Engineers in Large Organizations," *Business and Professional Ethics Journal* 1 (Fall 1981).

9. Dan Oldenburg, "Chrysler's Reversal in Airbag Debate," *San Francisco Chronicle*, August 23, 1983, in "Business Briefing," 9.

10. "Witness Says Police-Vest Maker Ignored Safety Concerns," *Wall Street Journal*, November 15, 2004, C1.

11. Marisa Manley, "Products Liability: You're More Exposed Than You Think," *Harvard Business Review* 65 (September/October 1987): 28–29.

12. "As ATVs Take Off in Sales, Deaths and Injuries Mount," *Wall Street Journal*, February 10, 2004, A1.

13. Melvyn A. J. Menezes, "Ethical Issues in Product Policy," in N. Craig Smith and John A. Quelch, eds., *Ethics in Marketing* (Homewood, IL: Irwin, 1993), 286.

14. "Child Contracts Reye's Syndrome," *ACLU News* (San Francisco), July/August 1993, 1.

15. N. Craig Smith and John A. Quelch, eds., *Ethics in Marketing* (Homewood, IL: Irwin, 1993), 337–339.

16. Jeffrey H. Birnbaum, "Pricing of Product Is Still an Art, Often Having Little Link to Costs," *Wall Street Journal*, November 25, 1981, sec. 2, 29.

17. Ibid.

18. Ibid. See also Matthew Miller, "Absolute Chaos," *Forbes*, December 13, 2004.

19. "U.S. Will Not Pursue Price-Fixing Case Against Mercedes Dealers," *New York Times*, December 25, 2003 (online).

20. *San Francisco Chronicle*, October 1, 1997, A3.

21. Constance L. Hays, "Panasonic to Return $16 Million to Consumers," *New York Times*, January 19, 1989, A1.

22. For a thorough look at this case, see M. David Ermann and Richard J. Lundman, *Corporate Deviance* (New York: Holt, Rinehart & Winston, 1982), ch. 5.

23. "Price-Fixing Probe Nets Dairy Giants," *San Jose Mercury News*, May 23, 1993, 8A.

24. "Why Do We Pay More?," *Business Week*, August 11, 2003, 26–27. See also Donald L. Barlett and James B. Steele, "Why We Pay So Much for Drugs," *Time*, February 2, 2004.

25. See Canadian Food Inspection Agency, under "Prosecution Bulletins" at www.inspection.gc.ca/english/corpaffr/projud/projude.shtml.

26. Michael J. McCarthy, "Taking the Value Out of Value-Sized," *Wall Street Journal*, August 14, 2002, D1. See also Omprakash K. Gupta and Anna S. Rominger, "Blind Man's Bluff: The Ethics of Quantity Surcharges," *Journal of Business Ethics* 15 (1996): 1299–1312.

27. Gupta and Rominger, "Blind Man's Bluff."

28. Roger Draper, "The Faithless Shepherd," *New York Review of Books*, June 26, 1986, 17.

29. Paul Stevens, "Weasel Words: God's Little Helpers," in Paul A. Eschhol, Alfred A. Rosa, and Virginia P. Clark, eds., *Language Awareness* (New York: St. Martin's Press, 1974), 156.

30. Samm Sinclair Baker, *The Permissible Lie* (New York: World Publishing, 1968), 16.

31. "FDA's Crackdown Adds a Wrinkle to Marketing of Antiaging Skin Treatments," *Wall Street Journal*, March 14, 2004, B1.

32. Ivan L. Preston, *The Great American Blow-Up: Puffery in Advertising and Selling*, rev. ed. (Madison: University of Wisconsin Press, 1996), 181.

33. Ibid., 24.

34. Wilson Bryan Key, *Subliminal Seduction* (New York: New American Library, 1973), 11.

35. "Hey Kid, Buy This," *Business Week*, June 30, 1997, 63.

36. Lisa J. Moore, "The Littlest Consumers," *This World*, *San Francisco Chronicle*, January 13, 1991, 8.

37. Wallace S. Snyder, "Ethics in Advertising: The Players, the Rules, the Scorecard," *Business and Professional Ethics Journal* 22 (Spring 2003): 41.

38. Randall Rothenberg, "Executives Defending Their Craft," *New York Times*, May 22, 1989, C7.

39. Theodore Levitt, "The Morality (?) of Advertising," *Harvard Business Review* 48 (July/August 1970): 84–92.

40. John Kenneth Galbraith, *The Affluent Society*, 3rd ed. (New York: Houghton Mifflin, 1976), 131.

41. John Kenneth Galbraith, *The New Industrial State* (New York: Signet, 1967), 219.

42. John Kenneth Galbraith, *The Economics of Innocent Fraud* (Boston: Houghton Mifflin, 2004), 12.

43. Draper, "The Faithless Shepherd," 16.

44. See Al Gini, "Work, Identity, and Self: How We Are Formed by the Work We Do," *Journal of Business Ethics* 17 (May 1998), 711.

45. This case study was written by Laurie Panagiotou; it is based on the findings of the Krever Inquiry published as Horace Krever, *Commission of Inquiry on the Blood System in Canada*, vol. 1–3 (Ottawa: Minister of Public Works and Government Services, 1997).

46. This case study is based on Diana B. Henriques, "Black Mark for a Good Citizen," *N.Y. Times*, November 26, 1995, sec. 3.1.

47. The case study is a reprint of Zoe Cormier's article "Brain Damage" in *Corporate Knights* (The Canadian Magazine for Responsible Business), vol. 6.2 (2007): 31–33.

THE ETHICS OF SALES

THOMAS L. CARSON

In this essay, Thomas L. Carson, professor of philosophy at Loyola University of Chicago, examines the moral obligations of salespeople. After explaining and criticizing David Holley's well-known account of the ethics of sales, Carson puts forward his own theory, which identifies four moral duties of salespeople. Carson contends that his theory provides intuitively plausible results in concrete cases, that it avoids the weaknesses of Holley's approach, and that it explains why different kinds of salespeople have different kinds of duties to their customers. He goes on to argue that the most plausible version of the Golden Rule supports his theory. He concludes by discussing several examples that illustrate and clarify his theory.

SALES

The ethics of sales is an important, but neglected, topic in business ethics. Approximately 10 percent of the U.S. work force is involved in sales. In addition, most of us occasionally sell major holdings such as used cars and real estate. Because sales were long governed by the principle of *caveat emptor*, discussions of the ethics of sales usually focus on the ethics of withholding information and the question "What sort of information is a salesperson obligated to reveal to customers?" One of the best treatments of this topic is David Holley's paper "A Moral Evaluation of Sales Practices." In this essay, I explain Holley's theory, propose several criticisms, and formulate what I take to be a more plausible theory about the duties of salespeople. My theory avoids the objections I raise against Holley and yields intuitively plausible results when applied to cases. I also defend my theory by appeal to the golden rule and offer a defense of the version of the golden rule to which I appeal.

PRELIMINARIES: A CONCEPTUAL ROADMAP

We need to distinguish between lying, deception, withholding information, and concealing information. Roughly, deception is intentionally causing someone to have false beliefs. Standard dictionary definitions of lying say that a lie is a false statement intended to deceive others. The *Oxford English Dictionary* (1989) defines a lie as: "a false statement made with the intent to deceive." *Webster's* (1963) gives the following definition of the verb *lie*: "to make an untrue statement with intent to deceive." . . . Lies that don't succeed in causing others to have false beliefs are not instances of deception. The word *deception* implies success in causing others to have false beliefs, but lying is often unsuccessful in causing deception. A further difference between lying and deception is that, while a lie must be a false statement, deception needn't involve false statements; true statements can be deceptive and many forms of deception do not involve making statements of any sort. Thus, many instances of deception do not constitute lying. Withholding information does not constitute deception. It is not a case of *causing* someone to have false beliefs; it is merely a case of failing to correct false beliefs or incomplete information. On the other hand, actively concealing information usually constitutes deception.

THE COMMON LAW PRINCIPLE OF *CAVEAT EMPTOR*

According to the common law principle of *caveat emptor*, sellers are not required to inform prospective buyers about the properties of the goods they sell. Under *caveat emptor*, sales and contracts to sell are legally enforceable even if the seller fails to inform the buyer of serious defects in the goods that are sold. Buyers themselves are responsible for determining the quality of the goods they purchase. In addition, English common law sometimes called for the enforcement of sales in cases in which sellers made false or misleading statements about the goods they sold (Atiyah 464–65).

Currently, all U.S. states operate under the Uniform Commercial Code of 1968. Section 2-313 of the code defines the notion of sellers' warranties (Preston 52). The code provides that all factual affirmations or statements about the goods being sold are warranties. This means that sales are not valid or legally enforceable if the seller makes false statements about the goods s/he is selling. The American legal system has developed the concept of an "implied" (as opposed to an express or explicit) warranty. Implied warranties are a significant limitation on the principle of *caveat emptor*. According to the Uniform Commercial Code, any transaction carries with it the following implied warranties: 1) that the seller owns the goods he is selling and 2) that the goods are "merchantable," i.e., suitable for the purposes for which they are sold (Preston 56–57). Many local ordinances require that people who sell real estate inform buyers about all known serious defects of the property they sell. These ordinances are also a significant limitation on the traditional principle of *caveat emptor*.

Deceptive sales practices also fall under the purview of the Federal Trade Commission (FTC). The FTC prohibits deceptive sales practices—practices likely to materially mislead reasonable consumers (FTC Statement 1983).

Many salespeople take complying with the law to be an acceptable moral standard for their conduct and claim that they have no moral duty to provide buyers with information about the goods they sell, except for that information which the law requires for an enforceable sale.

HOLLEY'S THEORY

Holley's theory is based on his concept of a "voluntary" or "mutually beneficial" market exchange (Holley uses the terms *voluntary exchange* and *mutually beneficial exchange* interchangeably). He says that a voluntary exchange occurs "only if" the following conditions are met (Holley takes his conditions to be *necessary* conditions for an acceptable exchange):

1. Both buyer and seller understand what they are giving up and what they are receiving in return.
2. Neither buyer nor seller is compelled to enter into the exchange as a result of coercion, severely restricted alternatives, or other constraints on the ability to choose.
3. Both buyer and seller are able at the time of the exchange to make rational judgments about its costs and benefits. (Holley 463)

These three conditions admit of degrees of satisfaction. An ideal exchange is an exchange involving people who are fully informed, fully rational, and "enter into the exchange entirely of their own volition" (Holley 464). The conditions for an ideal exchange are seldom, if ever, met in practice. However, Holley claims that it is still possible to have an "acceptable exchange" if the parties are "adequately informed, rational, and free from compulsion."

According to Holley, "the primary duty of salespeople to customers is to avoid undermining the conditions of an acceptable exchange." He makes it clear that, on his view, acts of omission (as well as acts of commission) can undermine the conditions of an acceptable exchange (Holley 464).

Because of the complexity of many goods and services, customers often lack information necessary for an acceptable exchange. Careful examination of products will not necessarily reveal problems or defects. According to Holley, *caveat emptor* is not acceptable as a moral principle, because customers often lack information necessary for an acceptable exchange. In such cases, salespeople are morally obligated to give information to the buyer. The question then is: *What kind of information* do salespeople need to provide buyers in order to ensure that the buyer is adequately informed? Holley attempts to answer this question in the following passage in which he appeals to the golden rule:

> Determining exactly how much information needs to be provided is not always clear-cut. We must in general rely on our assessments of what a reasonable person would want to know. As a practical guide, a salesperson might consider, "What would I want to know, if I were considering buying this product?" (Holley 467)

This principle is very demanding, perhaps more demanding than Holley realizes. Presumably, most reasonable people would *want* to know *a great deal* about the things they are thinking of buying. They might want to know *everything* relevant to the decision whether or not to buy something (more on this point shortly).

CRITICISMS OF HOLLEY

First, when time does not permit it, a salesperson cannot be morally obligated to provide all information necessary to ensure that the customer is adequately informed (all the information that a reasonable person would *want* to know if she were in the buyer's position). In many cases, reasonable customers would *want* to know a great deal of information. Often salespeople simply don't have the time to give all customers all the information Holley deems necessary for an acceptable exchange. Salespeople don't always know all the information that the buyer needs for an acceptable exchange. It cannot be a person's duty to do what is impossible—the statement that someone *ought* to do a certain act implies that she *can* do that act. Further, in many cases, salespeople don't know enough about the buyer's state of knowledge to know what information the buyer needs in order to be adequately informed. A salesperson might know that the buyer needs certain information in order to be adequately informed but not know whether or not the buyer possesses that information. One might reply that salespeople *should* know all the information necessary for an adequate exchange. However, on examination, this is not a plausible view. A salesperson in a large retail store cannot be expected to be knowledgeable about every product he sells. Often, it is impossible for realtors and used car salesmen to know much about the condition of the houses and cars they sell or the likelihood that they will need expensive repairs.

Second, Holley's theory implies that a salesperson in a store would be obligated to inform customers that a particular piece of merchandise in her store sells for less at a competing store if she knows this to be the case. (Presumably, she would *want* to know where she can get it for the lowest price, were she herself considering buying the product.) Not only do salespeople have no duty to provide this kind of information, (ordinarily) it would be wrong for them to do so.

Third, Holley's theory seems to yield unacceptable consequences in cases in which the buyer's alternatives are severely constrained. Suppose that a person with a very modest income attempts to buy a house in a small town. Her options are severely constrained, since there is only one house for sale in her price range. According to Holley, there can't be an acceptable exchange in such cases, because condition number 2 is not satisfied. However, it's not clear what he thinks sellers ought to do in such cases. The seller can't be expected to remove these constraints by giving the buyer money or building more homes in town. Holley's view seems to imply that it would be wrong for anyone to sell or rent housing to such a person. This result is unacceptable.

TOWARD A MORE PLAUSIBLE THEORY ABOUT THE ETHICS OF SALES

I believe that salespeople have the following moral duties regarding the disclosure of information when dealing with *rational adult consumers* (cases involving children or adults who are not fully rational raise special problems that I will not try to deal with here):

1. Salespeople should provide buyers with safety warnings and precautions about the goods they sell. (Sometimes it is enough for salespeople to call attention to written warnings and precautions that come with the goods and services in question. These warnings are unnecessary if the buyers already understand the dangers or precautions in question.)

2. Salespeople should refrain from lying and deception in their dealings with customers.

3. As much as their knowledge and time constraints permit, salespeople should fully answer questions about the products and services they sell. They should answer questions forthrightly and not evade questions or withhold information that has been asked for (even if this makes it less likely that they will make a successful sale). Salespeople are obligated to answer questions about the goods and services they sell. However, they are justified in refusing to answer questions that would require them to reveal information about what their competitors are selling. They are not obligated to answer questions about competing goods and services or give information about other sellers.

4. Salespeople should not try to "steer" customers toward purchases that they have reason to think will prove to be harmful to customers (financial harm counts) or that customers will come to regret.

These are *prima facie* duties that can conflict with other duties and are sometimes overridden by other duties. A *prima facie* duty is one's actual duty, other things being equal; it is an actual duty in the absence of conflicting duties of greater or equal importance. For example, my *prima facie* duty to keep promises is my actual duty in the absence of conflicting duties of equal or greater importance. The above is a *minimal list* of the duties of salespeople concerning the disclosure of information. I believe that the following are also *prima facie* duties of salespeople, but I am much less certain that these principles can be justified:

5. Salespeople should not sell customers goods or services they have reason to think will prove to be harmful to customers or that the customers will come to regret later, without giving the customers their reasons for thinking that this is the case. (This duty does not hold if the seller has good reasons to think that the customer already possesses the information in question.)

6. Salespeople should not sell items they know to be defective or of poor quality without alerting customers to this. (This duty does not hold if the buyer can be reasonably expected to know about the poor quality of what he is buying.)

I have what I take to be strong arguments for 1–4, but I'm not so sure that I can justify 5 and 6. I believe that reasonable people can disagree about 5 and 6. (I have very little to say about 5 and 6 in the present essay. See Carson [2001] for a discussion of arguments for 5 and 6.)

There are some important connections between duties 2, 4, and 6. Lying and deception in sales are not confined to lying to or deceiving customers about the goods one sells. Many salespeople misrepresent their own motives to customers/clients. Almost all salespeople invite the trust of customers/ clients and claim, implicitly or explicitly, to be acting in the interests of customers/clients. Salespeople often ask customers to defer to their judgment about what is best for them. For most salespeople, gaining the trust of customers or clients is essential for success. Many salespeople are *not* interested in helping customers in the way they represent themselves as being. A salesperson who misrepresents her motives, and intentions to customers violates rule 2. This simultaneous inviting and betrayal of trust is a kind of treachery. In ordinary cases, rules against lying and deception alone prohibit salespeople from steering customers toward goods or services they have reason to think will be bad for them. It is difficult to steer someone in this way without lying or deception, e.g., saying that you believe that a certain product is best for someone when you don't believe this to be the case. Similar remarks apply to selling defective goods. Often, it is impossible to do this without lying to or deceiving customers. In practice, most or many violations of rules 4 and 6 are also violations of rule 2.

A JUSTIFICATION FOR MY THEORY

Rules 1–4 yield intuitively plausible results in concrete cases and avoid all of the objections I raised against Holley. They can also be justified by appeal to the golden rule.

Taken together, rules 1–4 give us an intuitively plausible theory about the duties of salespeople regarding the disclosure of information; they give more acceptable results in actual cases than Holley's theory. They can account for cases in which the conduct of salespeople seems clearly wrong, e.g., cases of lying, deception, and steering customers into harmful decisions. Unlike Holley's theory, rules 1–4 do not make unreasonable demands on salespeople. They don't require that salespeople provide information that they don't have or spend more time with customers than they can spend. Nor do they require salespeople to divulge information about the virtues of what their competitors are selling.

In addition, my theory explains why different kinds of salespeople have different kinds of duties to their customers. For example, ordinarily, realtors have a duty to provide much more information to customers than sales clerks who sell inexpensive items in gift stores. My theory explains this difference in terms of the following:

1. the realtor's greater knowledge and expertise;

2. the much greater amount of time the realtor can devote to the customer;

3. the greater importance of the purchase of a home than the purchase of a small gift and the greater potential for harm or benefit to the buyer; and (in some cases)

4. implicit or explicit claims by the realtor to be acting on behalf of prospective home buyers (clerks in stores rarely make such claims).

The Golden Rule

I think that the golden rule is most plausibly construed as a consistency principle (those who violate the golden rule are guilty of inconsistency). The following version of the golden rule can be justified.

> **GR:** Consistency requires that if you think that it would be morally permissible for someone to do a certain act to another person, then you must consent to someone else doing the same act to you in relevantly similar circumstances.

How the Golden Rule Supports My Theory

Given this version of the golden rule, any rational and consistent moral judge who makes judgments about the moral obligations of salespeople will have to accept rules 1–4 as *prima facie* duties. Consider each duty in turn:

1. All of us have reason to fear the hazards about us in the world; we depend on others to warn us of those hazards. Few people would survive to adulthood were it not for the warnings of others about such things as oncoming cars, live electric wires, and approaching tornadoes. No one who values her own life can honestly say that she is willing to have others fail to warn her of dangers.

2. Like everyone else, a salesperson needs correct information in order to act effectively to achieve her goals and advance her interests. She is not willing to act on the basis of false beliefs. Consequently, she is not willing to have others deceive her or lie to her about matters relevant to her decisions in the marketplace. She is not willing to have members of other professions (such as law and medicine) make it a policy to deceive her or lie to her whenever they can gain financially from doing so.

3. Salespeople have questions about the goods and services they themselves buy. They can't say that they are willing to have others evade or refuse to answer those questions. We want our questions to be answered by salespeople or else we wouldn't ask them. We are not willing to have salespeople evade or refrain from answering our questions. (Digression. Rule 3 permits salespeople to refuse to answer questions that would force them to provide information about their competitors. Why should we say this? Why not say instead that salespeople are obligated to answer all questions that customers ask? The answer is as follows: A salesperson's actions affect both her customers and her employer. In applying the golden rule to this issue she can't simply ask what kind of information she would want were she in the customer's position [Holley poses the question in just this way]. Rule 3 can probably be improved upon, but it is a decent first approximation. A disinterested person who was not trying to give preference to the interests of salespeople, employers, or customers could endorse 3 as a policy for salespeople to follow. We can and must recognize the legitimacy of employers' demands for loyalty. The role of being an advocate or agent for someone who is selling things is legitimate within certain bounds—almost all of us are willing to have real estate agents work for us. A rational person could consent to the idea that everyone follow principles such as rule 3.)

4. All of us are capable of being manipulated by others into doing things that harm us, especially in cases in which others are more knowledgeable than we are. No one can consent to the idea that other people (or salespeople) should manipulate us into doing things that harm us whenever doing so is to their own advantage. Salespeople who claim that it would be permissible for them to make it a policy to deceive customers, fail to warn them about dangers, evade their questions, or manipulate them into doing things that are harmful to them whenever doing so is advantageous to them are inconsistent because they are not willing to have others do the same to them. They must allow that 1–4 are *prima facie* moral duties.

Rules 1–4 are only *prima facie* duties. The golden rule can account for the cases in which 1–4 are overridden by other more important duties. For example, we would be willing to have other people violate rules 1–4 if doing so were necessary in order to save the life of an innocent person. In practice, violating 1, 2, 3, or 4 is permissible only in very rare cases. The financial interests of salespeople seldom justify violations of 1, 2, 3, or 4. The fact that a salesperson can make more money by violating 1, 2, 3, or 4 would not justify her in violating any of these unless she has very pressing financial obligations that she cannot meet otherwise. Often, salespeople need to meet certain minimum sales quotas to avoid being fired. Suppose that a salesperson needs to make it a policy to violate 1–4 in order to met her sales quotas and keep her job. Would this justify her in violating 1–4? *Possibly*. But, in order for this to be the case, the following conditions would have to be met: (a) she has important moral obligations such as feeding and housing her family that require her to be employed (needing money to keep one's family in an expensive house or take them to Disney World wouldn't justify violating 1–4); and (b) she can't find another job that would enable her to meet her obligations without violating 1–4 (or other equally important duties). Those salespeople who can't keep their jobs or make an adequate income without violating 1–4 should seek other lines of employment.

A DEFENSE OF THE VERSION OF THE GOLDEN RULE EMPLOYED EARLIER

My argument is as follows:

1. Consistency requires that if you think that it would be morally permissible for someone to do a certain act to another person, then you must grant that it would be morally permissible for someone to do that same act to you in relevantly similar circumstances.

2. Consistency requires that if you think that it would be morally permissible for someone to do a certain act to you in certain circumstances, then you must consent to him/her doing that act to you in those circumstances.

Therefore,

> **GR:** Consistency requires that if you think that it would be morally permissible for someone to do a certain act to another person, then you must consent (not object to) someone doing the same act to you in relevantly similar circumstances. (You are inconsistent if you think that it would be morally permissible for someone to do a certain act to another person, but do not consent to someone doing the same act to you in relevantly similar circumstances.)

This argument is valid, i.e., the conclusion follows from the premises, and both its premises are true. Both premises are consistency requirements. Premise 1 addresses questions about the consistency of a person's different moral beliefs. Premise 2 addresses questions about whether a person's moral beliefs are consistent with her attitudes and actions. Our attitudes and actions can be either consistent or inconsistent with the moral judgments we accept.

Premise 1

Premise 1 follows from, or is a narrower version of, the universalizability principle (UP). The UP can be stated as follows:

> Consistency requires that, if one makes a moral judgment about a particular case, then one must make the same moral judgment about any similar case, unless there is a morally relevant difference between the cases.

Premise 1 is a principle of consistency for judgments about the moral permissibility of actions. The UP, by contrast, is a principle of consistency for *any kind of moral judgment*, including judgments about what things are good and bad.

Premise 2

How shall we understand what is meant by "consenting to" something? For our present purposes, we should not take consenting to something to be the same as desiring it or trying to bring it about. My thinking that it is morally permissible for you to beat me at chess does not commit me to desiring that you beat me, nor does it commit me to playing so as to allow you to beat me. Consenting to an action is more like not objecting to it, not criticizing, or not resenting the other person for doing it. If I think that it is permissible for you to beat me at chess then I cannot object to your beating me. I am inconsistent if I object to your doing something that I take to be morally permissible. If I claim that it is permissible for someone to do something to another person, then, on pain of inconsistency, I cannot object if someone else does the same thing to me in relevantly similar circumstances. The gist of my application of the golden rule to sales is that since we *do object* to salespeople doing such things as lying to us, deceiving us, and failing to answer our questions, we cannot consistently say that it is morally permissible for them to *do* these things.

EXAMPLES

I will discuss several cases to illustrate and clarify my theory.

Example A

I am selling a used car that I know has bad brakes; this is one of the reasons I am selling the car. You don't ask me any questions about the car, and I sell it to you without informing you of the problem with the brakes.

Example B

I am selling a used car that starts poorly in cold weather. You arrange to look at the car early in the morning on a very cold day. I don't own a garage so the car is out in the cold. With difficulty, I start it up and drive it for thirty minutes shortly before you look at it and then cover the car with snow to make it seem as if it hasn't been driven. The engine is still hot when you come and the car starts up immediately. You then purchase the car, remarking that you need a car that starts well in the cold to get to work, since you don't have a garage.

Example C

While working as a salesperson, I feign a friendly concern for a customer's interests. I say, "I will try to help you find the product that is best suited for your needs. I don't want you to spend any more money than you need to. Take as much time as you need." The customer believes me, but she is deceived. In fact, I couldn't care less about her welfare. I only want to sell her the highest priced item I can as quickly as I can. I don't like the customer; indeed, I am contemptuous of her.

In example A, I violate rule 1 and put the buyer and other motorists, passengers, and pedestrians at risk. In example B, I violate rules 2 and 5. In example C, I violate rule 2. In the absence of conflicting obligations that are at least as important as the rules I violate, my actions in cases A–C are morally wrong.

Example D: A Longer Case (an Actual Case)

In 1980, I received a one-year fellowship from The National Endowment for the Humanities. The fellowship paid for my salary, but not my fringe benefits. Someone in the benefits office of my university told me that I had the option of continuing my health insurance through the university if I paid for the premiums out of my own pocket. I told the benefits person that this was a lousy deal and that I could do better by going to a private insurance company. I went to the office of Prudential Insurance agent Mr. A. O. "Ed" Mokarem. I told him that I was looking for a one-year medical insurance policy to cover me during the period of the fellowship and that I planned to resume my university policy when I returned to teaching. (The university provided this policy free of charge to all faculty who were teaching.) He showed me a comparable Prudential policy that cost about half as much as the university's policy. He explained the policy to me. I asked him to fill out the forms so that I could purchase the policy. He then told me that there was a potential problem I should consider. He said roughly the following:

> You will want to return to your free university policy next year when you return to teaching. The Prudential policy is a one-year terminal policy. If you develop any serious medical problems during the next year, Prudential will probably consider you "uninsurable" and will not be willing to sell you health insurance in the future. If you buy the Prudential policy, you may encounter the same problems with your university policy. Since you will be dropping this policy *voluntarily*, they will have the right to underwrite your application for re-enrollment. If you develop a serious health problem during the next year, their underwriting decision could be "Total Rejection," imposing some waivers and/or exclusions, or (at best) subjecting your coverage to the "pre-existing conditions clause," which would not cover any pre-existing conditions until you have been covered under the new policy for at least a year.

If I left my current health insurance for a year, I risked developing a costly medical condition for which no one would be willing to insure me. That would have been a very foolish risk to take. So, I thanked him very much and, swallowing my pride, went back to renew my health insurance coverage through the university. I never bought any insurance from Mr. Mokarem and never had occasion to send him any business.

I have discussed this case with numerous classes through the years. It usually generates a lively discussion. Most of my students do not think that Mr. Mokarem was morally obligated to do what he did, but they don't think that what he did was wrong either—they regard his actions as supererogatory or above and beyond the call of duty.

My View About Example D On my theory, this is a difficult case to assess. If rules 1–4 are a salesperson's only duties concerning the disclosure of information, then Mr. Mokarem was not obligated to inform me as he did. (In this case, the information in question was information about a competing product—the university's health insurance policy.) If rule 5 is a prima facie duty of salespeople, then (assuming that he had no conflicting moral duties of greater or equal importance) it was his duty, all things considered, to inform me as he did. Since I am uncertain that 5 can be justified, I'm not sure whether or not Mr. Mokarem was obligated to do what he did or whether his actions were supererogatory. This case illustrates part of what is at stake in the question of whether rule 5 is a prima facie duty of salespeople.

Acknowledgments

This essay is a revised and abridged version of material from two earlier essays, "Deception and Withholding Information in Sales," *Business Ethics Quarterly* 11 (2001): 275–306, and "Ethical Issues in Selling and Advertising," *The Blackwell Guide to Business Ethics*, ed. Norman Bowie (Oxford: Blackwell, 2002), 186–205. Many thanks to Ivan Preston for his very generous and helpful advice and criticisms. Everyone interested in these topics should read his work.

References

Atiyah, P. S. (1979) *The Rise and Fall of Freedom of Contract*. Oxford: The Clarendon Press.

Carson, Thomas. (1988) "On the definition of lying: a reply to Jones and revisions." *Journal of Business Ethics*, 7: 509–14.

Carson, Thomas. (2001) "Deception and withholding information in sales." *Business Ethics Quarterly* 11: 275–306.

FTC policy statement on deception. (1983—still current) Available on the Web at: http://www.ftc.gov/bcp/guides/guides.htm.

Gensler, Harry. (1986) "A Kantian argument against abortion." *Philosophical Studies* 49: 83–98.

Holley, David. (1993) "A moral evaluation of sales practices." In Tom Beauchamp and Norman Bowie, eds., *Ethical Theory and Business*, fourth edition, 462–72. Englewood Cliffs, NJ: Prentice Hall.

Preston, Ivan. (1975) The Great American Blow-Up: Puffery in Advertising and *Selling*. Madison: University of Wisconsin Press, 1975.

Review and Discussion Questions

1. What's the difference between lying and deception? According to Carson, does withholding information constitute deception? What about concealing information?

2. What is the principle of caveat emptor? What is *merchantability*?

3. Holley writes that salespeople are required to avoid undermining the conditions of an acceptable exchange. What three conditions are necessary for an "acceptable exchange"?

4. Assess the three criticisms that Carson makes of Holley's theory. Do you find them persuasive?

5. According to Carson, what four duties do salespeople have? Explain how the Golden Rule supports these duties. Is Carson's interpretation of the Golden Rule the best way of understanding it? In your view, is the Golden Rule a basic principle of ethics? Explain why or why not. What implications does the Golden Rule have for salespeople?

6. Do Carson's duties 1 through 4 provide a more plausible account of the ethics of sales than Holley's theory does? Explain why or why not. Do you agree that the actions in examples A, B, and C are morally wrong?

7. Carson believes that he makes a strong case for duties 1 through 4, but that reasonable people can disagree about duties 5 and 6. In your view, do salespeople have duties 5 and 6? In example D, was Mr. Mokarem morally obligated to do what he did?

8. Do salespeople ever face ethical issues that Carson's theory doesn't answer? If so, give an example.

9. Have you encountered unethical conduct by a salesperson? Is such conduct widespread, or do most salespeople try to behave ethically? When salespeople do act unethically, what explains this, and what can be done about it?

THE INCONCLUSIVE ETHICAL CASE AGAINST MANIPULATIVE ADVERTISING

MICHAEL J. PHILLIPS

Critics of advertising maintain that it manipulates our needs and fears, increasing our propensity to consume and swaying our individual purchasing decisions. Granting for the sake of argument that the critics of advertising are correct about its effectiveness, Michael J. Phillips, professor emeritus of business administration at Indiana University, assesses four possible attacks on manipulative advertising, each from a different ethical perspective: (1) that manipulative advertising has negative consequences for utility, (2) that it undermines personal autonomy, (3) that it violates Kant's categorical imperative, and (4) that it weakens the personal virtue of its practitioners and victims. After considering one final, partial defense of manipulative advertising, he concludes that although the practice is morally problematic, there is room for doubt about its badness and no completely definite basis for condemning it.

This essay explores the ethical implications of [the] perception that advertisers successfully "exploit and manipulate the vast range of human fears and needs." It begins by defining its sense of the term *manipulative advertising*. Then the essay asserts for purposes of argument that manipulative advertising actually works. Specifically, I make two controversial assumptions about such advertising: (1) that it plays a major role in increasing the general propensity to consume, and (2) that it powerfully influences individual consumer purchase decisions. With the deck thus stacked against manipulative advertising, the essay goes on to inquire whether either assumption justifies its condemnation, by considering four ethical criticisms of manipulative advertising. Ethically, I conclude, manipulative advertising is a most problematic practice. If probabilistic assertions are valid in ethics, then the odds strongly favor the conclusion that manipulative advertising is wrong. Nevertheless, there still is room for doubt about its badness. Like the apparently easy kill that continually slips out of the hunter's sights, manipulative advertising evades the clean strike that would justify its condemnation for once and all.

WHAT IS MANIPULATIVE ADVERTISING?

. . . What, then, is manipulative advertising? . . . I define "manipulative advertising" as advertising that tries to favorably alter consumers' perceptions of the advertised product by appeals to factors other than the product's physical attributes and functional performance. There is no sharp line between such advertising and advertising that is non-manipulative; even purely informative ads are unlikely to feature unattractive people and depressing surroundings. Nor is it clear what proportion of American advertising can fairly be classed as manipulative. Suffice it to say that that proportion almost certainly is significant. As we will see, advertising's critics sometimes seem to think that all of it is manipulative.

Perhaps the most common example of manipulative advertising is a technique John Waide (1987, 73–74) calls

From *Business and Professional Ethics Journal* 13 (Winter 1994). Reprinted by permission of the author.

"associative advertising." Advertisers using this technique try to favorably influence consumer perceptions of a product by associating it with a nonmarket good (e.g., contentment, sex, vigor, power, status, friendship, or family) that the product ordinarily cannot supply on its own. By purchasing the product, their ads suggest, the consumer somehow will get the nonmarket good. Michael Schudson describes this familiar form of advertising as follows: "The ads say, typically, 'buy me and you will overcome the anxieties I have just reminded you about' or 'buy me and you will enjoy life' or 'buy me and be recognized as a successful person' or 'buy me and everything will be easier for you' or 'come spend a few dollars and share in this society of freedom, choice, novelty, and abundance'" (1986, 6). Through such linkages between product and non-market good, associative advertising seeks to increase the product's perceived value and thus to induce its purchase. Because these linkages (e.g., the connection between beer and attractive women) generally make little sense, such advertising is far removed from rational persuasion.

THE EFFECTS OF MANIPULATIVE ADVERTISING: WHAT THE CRITICS THINK

In the previous section, I tried to describe manipulative advertising in terms of sellers' *efforts*, rather than their actual accomplishments. But does manipulative advertising successfully influence consumers? As might be expected, advertising's critics generally answer this question in the affirmative. Perhaps the best-known example is chapter XI of John Kenneth Galbraith's *The Affluent Society*, where he described his well-known dependence effect.

Galbraith's dependence effect might be described as the way the process of consumer goods production creates and satisfies consumer wants (1958, 158). "That wants are, in fact, the fruit of production," he intoned, "will now be denied by few serious scholars" (154). In part, these wants result from emulation, as increased production means increased consumption for some, followed by even more consumption as others follow suit (154–55). But advertising and salesmanship provide an even more direct link between production and consumer wants. Those practices, Galbraith says:

[C]annot be reconciled with the notion of independently determined desires, for their central function is to create desires . . . . This is accomplished by the producer of goods or at his behest. A broad empirical relationship exists between what is spent on production of consumers' goods and what is spent in synthesizing the desires for that production. A new consumer product must be introduced with a suitable advertising campaign to arouse an interest in it. The path for an expansion of output must be paved by a suitable expansion in the advertising budget. Outlays for the manufacturing of a product are not more important in the strategy of modern business enterprise than outlays for the manufacturing of demand for the product. (155–56)

. . . To Galbraith, therefore, advertising in general is manipulative. In *The Affluent Society*, it apparently worked mainly to promote aggregate demand, rather than to shift demand from one brand to another. Many of advertising's critics follow Galbraith's lead by stressing how it socializes people to embrace consumerist values . . . .

From all this, it is a short step to the notion that advertising plays a major role in shaping and sustaining the modern society of material abundance. Implicitly, at least, some accounts of this kind liken society to a huge machine whose aim is the conversion of natural resources into consumer products. For the machine to work properly, its human components must be motivated to play their role in producing those products. This can be accomplished by: (1) implanting in people an intense desire for consumer goods, and (2) requiring that they do productive work to get the money to buy those goods . . . . Galbraith suggested that these social imperatives of production and consumption make the worker/ consumer resemble a squirrel who races full-tilt to keep abreast of a wheel propelled by his own efforts (1958, 154, 159).

Although they naturally evaluate the matter differently, business leaders often second the argument that advertising is essential to prosperity. In . . . an exchange on advertising expenditures by the fast-food industry, William H. Genge, the chairman of Ketchum Communications' board, wrote:

I regard the many millions of dollars spent by fast-food companies (and other retailers as well) as healthy and necessary stimulation of the consumption that makes our economy the most dynamic and productive in the world.

Some people talk as though large advertising budgets are wasteful and nonproductive. It just takes one simple question to put that down. The question is: Where does the money go? The answer is: It provides jobs and livelihoods for hundreds of thousands of people—not only in the advertising and communications sector but for all the people employed by fast-food companies and, indeed, all marketing organizations. (1985, 58–59)

"So," Genge concluded, "large advertising expenditures are not a misallocation of economic resources. They are, in fact, an essential allocation and the driving force behind consumption, job creation, and prosperity" (59).

Advertising that is sufficiently manipulative to create a consumer society also might be able to determine consumers' individual purchase decisions. Most often, I suppose, these would be brand choices within a particular product category, although advertising might also steer people toward certain products and away from others . . . .

ASSUMPTIONS AND PLAN OF ATTACK

As we have just seen, many critics of advertising say that it socializes people to a life of consumption. And some regard it as a strong influence on individual brand or product decisions. However, these beliefs are not universally shared. Some students of advertising doubt that ads do much to dictate individual brand choices. And even if advertising strongly influences consumer decisions, it does not follow that any specific ad invariably compels the purchase of the product it touts. The reason is that a particular product advertisement is only one of many factors—especially competing advertisements—influencing consumers (Hayek 1961, 347). For the same general reason, it is difficult to assess advertising's role in making people lifetime consumers . . . .

Despite such difficulties, this essay assumes for the sake of argument that manipulative advertising really works. Thus, I assume that such advertising strongly influences individual purchase decisions, and that it plays a major role in producing consumerist attitudes among the populace. In neither case, however, do I wish to specify all the links in the causal chain through which manipulative advertising does its work. In particular, I make no assumptions about the personal traits that render consumers responsive to manipulative advertising. Later in the essay, for example, I consider the possibility that manipulative advertising succeeds because consumers want and need it.

Operating under the assumptions just stated, I now consider four possible ethical attacks on manipulative advertising. These are the claims that such advertising: (1) has negative consequences for utility, (2) undermines personal autonomy, (3) violates Kant's categorical imperative, and (4) weakens the personal virtue of its practitioners and its victims. I also consider one qualified defense of manipulative advertising: that even though no moral person would choose it were he writing on a clean slate, by now its elimination would be worse than its continuance.

For each attack on manipulative advertising, I assume the validity of the relevant moral value or ethical theory, thus precluding defenses of manipulative advertising that attack the value or theory itself . . . .

UTILITARIANISM

As just stated, this essay assumes that advertising can manipulate people in two distinct ways: (1) by socializing them to embrace consumerist values, and (2) by dictating individual purchase decisions. One important utilitarian criticism of manipulative advertising seems mainly to involve the first of these effects. Another implicates the second effect . . . . I now discuss each of these utilitarian attacks in turn. Throughout, I explicitly or implicitly compare my assumed world in which manipulative advertising exists and is effective with a world in which all advertising is merely informative.

The Implications of the Dependence Effect

The Affluent Society marked Galbraith's arrival as a critic of consumer society and its works. For his critique to be persuasive, he had to counter the argument that America's enormous production of consumer goods is justified because people want, enjoy, and demand them. This required that he undermine at least two widespread beliefs: (1) that consumer desires are genuinely autonomous, and (2) that they produce significant satisfactions. As we saw earlier, he attacked the first assumption by maintaining that consumer wants are created by the productive process through which they are satisfied, with advertising serving as the main generator of those wants. This argument would have enabled Galbraith to contend that advertising is bad because it denies autonomy, but he seemed not to emphasize that point. Instead, he maintained that the satisfaction of advertising-induced desires generates little additional utility. His argument was that if advertising is needed to arouse consumer wants, they cannot be too strong. "The fact that wants can be synthesized by advertising, catalyzed by salesmanship, and shaped by the discreet manipulations of the persuaders shows that they are not very urgent. A man who is hungry need never be told of his need for food" (1958, 158).

As a result, Galbraith continued, one cannot assume that the increased production characterizing the modern affluent society generates corresponding increases in utility. Instead, as he summarizes the matter:

> [O]ur concern for goods . . . does not arise in spontaneous consumer need. Rather, the dependence effect means that it grows out of the process of production itself. If production is to increase, the wants must be effectively contrived. In the absence of the contrivance the increase would not occur. This is not true of all goods, but that it is true of a substantial part is sufficient. It means that since the demand for this part would not exist, were it not contrived, its utility or urgency, ex contrivance, is zero. If we regard this production as marginal, we may say that the marginal utility of present aggregate output, ex advertising and salesmanship, is zero. (160)

Because wants must be contrived for production to increase, on Galbraith's assumptions production would be lower were advertising completely informative. Since on those assumptions that contrived production generates little additional utility, however, the loss would not be much felt. Indeed, with resources shifted away from advertising and consumption and toward activities that improve the quality of our lives, overall utility might well grow in manipulative advertising's absence.

Galbraith's basic argument was that because consumer wants are contrived, they are not urgent; and that because they are not urgent, their satisfaction does not generate much utility. One way to attack his argument is to maintain that consumer desires really do arise from within the individual, but my two assumptions foreclose that possibility here. Another is to follow the lead established by Friedrich Hayek's 1961 critique of Galbraith's dependence effect. To Hayek, Galbraith's argument involves a massive non sequitur: the attempt to reason from a desire's origin outside the individual to its unimportance (1961, 346–47). If that assertion were valid, he thought, it would follow that "the whole cultural achievement of man is not important" (346).

Surely an individual's want for literature is not original with himself in the sense that he would experience it if literature were not produced. Does this mean that the production of literature cannot be defended as satisfying a want because it is only the production which provokes the demand? In this, as in the case of all cultural needs, it is unquestionably, in Professor Galbraith's words, "the process of satisfying the wants that creates the wants" (347).

Presumably, the same general point applies to utility-maximization. Just because product desire A originated within Cal Consumer while product desire B came his way through manipulative advertising, it does not follow that satisfying desire A would give him more utility than satisfying desire B. Indeed, as we will see presently, the opposite may be true.

The Frustration of Rational Interbrand Choices

The second major utilitarian objection to manipulative advertising concerns its power to distort consumer choices among brands and products. As R. M. Hare once observed:

> [T]he market economy is only defensible if it really does . . . lead to the maximum satisfaction of the preferences of the public. And it will not do this if it is distorted by various well-known undesirable practices . . . . By bringing it about that people decide on their purchases . . . after being deceived or in other ways manipulated, fraudulent advertisers impair the wisdom of the choices that the public makes and so distort the market in such a way that it does not function to maximize preference-satisfactions. (Hare 1984, 27–28)

For example, now suppose that Cal Consumer's preferences would find their optimum satisfaction in Product A. Intoxicated by Product B's manipulative advertising, Cal instead buys that product, which satisfies his original preferences less well than Product A. If Cal would have bought Product A in a regime where advertising is purely informative, presumably B's manipulative advertising cost him some utility.

The previous argument, however, might fail if manipulative advertising gives consumers satisfactions that they would not otherwise obtain from their purchases. In that event, the utility lost when manipulative advertising causes consumers to choose the wrong product for their needs must be weighed against the utility consumers gain from such advertising. Due to the inherent uncertainty of utility calculations, it may be unclear which effect would predominate. Sometimes, though, the gains could outweigh the losses: that is, manipulative advertising could generate more utility than purely informative advertising.

But how can "manipulated" desires and purchases generate more utility than their "rational" counterparts? One answer emerges from the dark masterpiece of the literature on manipulative advertising—Theodore Levitt's 1970 contribution to the *Harvard Business Review*. Levitt's main thesis is that "embellishment and distortion are among advertising's legitimate and socially desirable purposes" (Levitt 1970, 85). His determinedly nonlinear argument for that conclusion may be regarded as proceeding through several steps. The first is his assertion that when seen without illusions, human life is a poor thing. Natural reality, Levitt insists, is "crudely fashioned"; "crude, drab, and generally oppressive"; and "drab, dull, [and] anguished"

(86, 90). For this reason, people try to transcend it whenever they can. "Everyone everywhere wants to modify, transform, embellish, enrich, and reconstruct the world around him—to introduce into an otherwise harsh or bland existence some sort of purposeful and distorting alleviation" (87). People do so mainly through artistic endeavor, but also through advertising. "[W]e use art, architecture, literature, and the rest, and advertising as well, to shield ourselves, in advance of experience, from the stark and plain reality in which we are fated to live" (90). Thus, "[m]any of the so-called distortions of advertising, product design, and packaging may be viewed as a paradigm of the many responses that man makes to the conditions of survival in the environment" (90).

From all this, it follows that consumers demand more than "pure operating functionality" from the products they buy (89). As Charles Revson of Revlon, Inc. once said: "In the factory we make cosmetics; in the store we sell hope" (85). Thus, "[i]t is not cosmetic chemicals women want, but the seductive charm promised by the alluring symbols with which these chemicals have been surrounded—hence the rich and exotic packages in which they are sold, and the suggestive advertising with which they are promoted" (85). In other words, consumers demand an expanded notion of functionality which includes "'non-mechanical' utilities," and do so to "help . . . solve a problem of life" (89). Therefore, "the product" they buy includes not only narrowly functional attributes, but also the emotional or affective content produced by its packaging and advertising. "The promises and images which imaginative ads and sculptured packages induce in us are as much the product as the physical materials themselves . . . . [T]hese ads and packagings describe the product's fullness for us; in our minds, the product becomes a complex abstraction which is . . . the conception of a perfection which has not yet been experienced" (89–90) . . . .

To Levitt, therefore, we do not merely buy a physical product, but also a set of positive feelings connected with it by advertising. If his argument is sound, those feelings give us extra utility above and beyond the utility we get from the product's performance of its functions. This extra utility might well outweigh the utility we lose because manipulative advertising has made us buy a product that is suboptimum in purely functional terms and that we would not have bought were advertising only informative.

Is Levitt's argument sound? Although his description may not apply to all people, or even to most, it hardly seems ridiculous. People who object to Levitt's contention that human life is crude, drab, and dull should recall that he is speaking of a human life we infrequently experience—human life absent the embellishments all civilizations try to give it. If his contention is correct, the need to transcend our natural condition is an obvious motive for those embellishments. John Waide, however, insists that our need for embellishment can be satisfied without manipulative advertising—through, for example, ideals, fantasies, heroes, and dreams (Waide 1987, 76). But why assume this? If the need for comforting illusions is strong and pervasive, why should embellishment not extend to the products people buy?

Bigger problems, however, arise from Levitt's assumption that consumers are aware of advertising's illusions. If people know that advertising lies, how can they derive much psychic benefit—i.e., much utility—from its embellishments? Worse yet, products tend not to deliver on manipulative advertising's promises of sex, status, security, and the like. When this is so, how can such advertising deliver much utility to the consumers it controls (cf. Waide 1987, 75)? Indeed, the gap between manipulative advertising's implicit promises and its actual performance may lead to frustrated expectations and significant *disutility*.

Recall, however, that for Levitt consumers want and need to be manipulated because life without advertising's illusions is too much to bear. If so, it is unlikely that everyone would be *continuously* aware of advertising's illusions and the low chance of their realization. Only intermittently, in other words, would people assume a tough-minded, rational-actor mentality toward advertising. On other occasions, some would effectively suspend disbelief in advertising's embellishments. Although they might retain latent knowledge of those illusions, that knowledge would not be constantly present to their consciousness. And when the illusions rule, they could generate real satisfactions.

Are these assumptions about consumers realistic ones? To me, they are plausible as applied to some people some of the time . . . . There . . . is nothing ridiculous in assuming that people gain utility by accepting advertising's illusions, while retaining some latent and/or intermittent knowledge of their condition . . . .

AUTONOMY

All things considered, the utilitarian arguments against manipulative advertising are unimpressive. Indeed, utilitarianism might even support that practice. Galbraith claimed that little utility is generated when we satisfy contrived wants. But the connection between a desire's origin outside the individual and the low utility resulting from its satisfaction is unclear. At first glance, it appears that manipulative advertising robs consumers of utility by inducing them to buy functionally suboptimal products. But while this may be true, the resulting utility losses arguably are counterbalanced by the utility people gain from manipulative advertising . . . .

The Autonomy-Related Objection to Manipulative Advertising

To some people, however, the preceding points may say more about utilitarianism's deficiencies than about manipulative advertising's worth. One standard criticism of utilitarianism emphasizes its indifference to the moral quality of the means by which utility is maximized. Thus, even if manipulative advertising increases consumers' utility, it is bad because it does so by suppressing their ability to make intelligent, self-directed product choices on the basis of

their own values and interests. In a word, manipulative advertising now seems objectionable because it denies personal *autonomy*.

Among the many strands within the notion of autonomy, one of the most common equates it with self-government or self-determination. According to Steven Lukes, for example, autonomy is "self-direction"; the autonomous person's "thought and action are his own, and [are] not determined by agencies or causes outside his control" (Lukes 1973, 52). At the social level, Lukes adds, an individual is autonomous "to the degree to which he subjects the pressures and norms with which he is confronted to conscious and critical evaluation, and forms intentions and reaches practical decisions as the result of independent and rational reflection" (52).

If manipulative advertising has the effects this essay assumes, it apparently denies autonomy to the individuals it successfully controls. On this essay's assumptions, people become consumers and make product choices precisely through "agencies and causes outside [their] control," and not through "conscious and critical evaluation" or "independent and rational reflection." To Lippke [1990], moreover, advertising also has an "implicit content" that further suppresses autonomy. Among other things, this implicit content causes people to accept emotionalized, superficial, and oversimplified claims; desire ease and gratification rather than austerity and self-restraint; let advertisers dictate the meaning of the good life; defer to their peers; and think that consumer products are a means for acquiring life's nonmaterial goods (44–47). People so constituted are unlikely to be independent, self-governing agents who subject all social pressures to an internal critique. Nor is it likely that they would have much resistance to manipulative appeals to buy particular products.

Are Consumers Autonomous on Levitt's Assumptions?

On Levitt's assumptions, however, perhaps consumers do act autonomously when they submit to manipulative advertising. If Levitt is correct: (1) manipulative advertising works much as its critics say that it works; because (2) consumers suspend disbelief in its claims and embrace its illusions; because (3) they want, need, and demand those illusions to cope with human existence; while (4) nonetheless knowing on some level that those illusions indeed are illusions. In sum, one might say, advertising manipulates consumers because they knowingly and rationally want to be manipulated. That is, they half-consciously sacrifice their autonomy for reasons that make some sense on Levitt's assumptions about human life. In still other words, they more or less autonomously relinquish their autonomy . . . .

Levitt's argument, however, appears to concern only individual purchase decisions, and not advertising's assumed ability to socialize people to accept consumerism and reject autonomy. But his argument is broad enough to explain this second process. On Levitt's assumptions, people would more or less knowingly embrace consumerism because unfiltered reality is too much to bear, and would reject autonomy in favor of Lippke's "implicit content" because autonomy offers too little payoff at too much cost. If those assumptions are accurate, moreover, people arguably have sound reasons for behaving in these ways . . . .

THE CATEGORICAL IMPERATIVE

One problem with some of the claims discussed thus far is that they present difficult empirical issues. This is plainly true of Levitt's claims. It also is true of Galbraith's assertion that because advertising-induced wants originate outside the individual, they have low urgency and therefore generate little utility when they are satisfied. The same can be said of Hayek's response to Galbraith. Given these problems, maybe manipulative advertising is best addressed by ethical theories whose conclusions do not depend on empirical matters such as consumer psychology, or on manipulation's consequences for utility. Kant's categorical imperative is an obvious candidate.

R. M. Hare made two Kantian arguments against manipulative advertising. "Kantians will say . . . that to manipulate people is not to treat them as ends—certainly not as autonomous legislating members of a kingdom of ends . . . . But even apart from that it is something that we prefer not to happen to us and therefore shall not will it as a universal maxim" (Hare 1984, 28). His reference, of course, was to the two major formulations of Kant's categorical imperative. The first, which comes in several versions, underlies Hare's second argument. The version employed here goes as follows: "Act only on that maxim through which you can at the same time will that it should become a universal law" (Kant 1964, 88). According to the second major formulation of the imperative, one must "[a]ct in such a way that you always treat humanity, whether in your own person or in the person of any other, never simply as a means, but always at the same time as an end" (96).

Under either formulation of the imperative, it seems, manipulative advertising stands condemned. Under the first formulation, it seems difficult to identify a maxim that would: (1) clearly justify manipulative advertising, and (2) be universalized by any advertiser. Consider, for example, the following possibility: "In order to induce purchases and make money, business people can use advertising tactics that undermine the rational evaluation and choice of products by associating them with desired states to which they have little or no real relation." Presumably, no one would will the maxim's universalization, because to do so is to waive any moral objection to manipulative advertising aimed at oneself. Manipulative advertising apparently fares even worse under the second statement of the categorical imperative. As James Rachels has noted, under this formulation "we may never *manipulate* people, or *use* people, to achieve our purposes" (Rachels 1993, 129). Instead, we should respect their rational nature by giving them the information that will enable them to make informed, autonomous decisions (Rachels 1993, 129–30). As the term *manipulative advertising* suggests, businesses that employ it to generate sales obviously try to use people as means to their own ends, and do so precisely by undermining their rationality and their ability to make informed, autonomous decisions.

Even in the Kantian realm, however, empirical concerns intrude. Suppose again that Levitt is right in claiming that people want and need manipulative advertising. Given this assumption, the relevant maxim becomes something like the following: "In order to induce purchases and make money, people can use manipulative advertising tactics that undermine the rational evaluation and choice of products and services, but only when such advertising tactics liberate consumers from their dark, stark, and depressing natural existence." Although I cannot speak for everyone (or for Kant), I might will this maxim's universalization if I found Levitt's conception of the human condition at all plausible. This illustrates a common criticism of the first formulation of the categorical imperative: that one can manipulate the imperative to get the results one wishes by framing the maxim appropriately.

Even if Levitt's account is perfectly accurate, however, the second major statement of the imperative still creates problems for manipulative advertising. Here, the question seems to boil down to the following: are firms that employ manipulative advertising using a consumer merely as a means to their own ends and therefore violating the imperative if the consumer, in effect, needs and wants to be manipulated? If, as I suggested earlier, the suspension of disbelief required for one to accept manipulative advertising may be more or less reasonable, then advertisers conceivably *are* respecting consumers' rationality by providing them with product-related illusions . . . .

VIRTUE ETHICS

Earlier I depicted Galbraith as a utilitarian, but other moral aspirations probably were at work within *The Affluent Society*. The book opened with the following quotation from Alfred Marshall: "The economist, like everyone else, must concern himself with the ultimate aims of man." Galbraith's conviction that consumerism does not rank high among those aims pervades much of his writing, and almost certainly informed his critique of advertising. However, the ethical values and theories previously considered in this essay do not state and enjoin the desirable substantive conditions of human life . . . .

Waide's alternative to such approaches is to examine "the virtues and vices at stake" in manipulative advertising (1987, 73), and to see "what kind of lives are sustained" by it (77). Stanley Benn sounds the same note when he suggests that the key question about advertising is whether it promotes "a valuable kind of life," with this determination depending on "some objective assessment of what constitutes excellence in human beings" (1967, 273). Because manipulative advertising encourages advertisers to ignore the well-being of their targets and encourages those targets to neglect the cultivation of nonmarket goods, Waide concludes that it makes us less virtuous persons and therefore is morally objectionable (1987, 74–75). Many other critics of advertising make the same general point . . . . Heilbroner called advertising "perhaps the single most value-destroying activity of a business civilization," due to the "subversive influence of the relentless effort to persuade people to change their lifeways, not out of any knowledge of, or deeply held convictions about, the 'good life,' but merely to sell whatever article or service is being pandered" (1976, 113–14). His main specific complaint is that by offering a constant stream of half-truths and deceptions, advertising makes "cynics of us all" (114). Virginia Held makes a related point when she criticizes advertising for undermining intellectual and artistic integrity (1984, 64–66).

To Christopher Lasch, on the other hand, advertising's greatest evil may be its tendency to leave consumers "perpetually unsatisfied, restless, anxious, and bored" (1978, 72) . . . . One suspects that Lasch might reject advertising's consequences as inherently bad even if they did mark an increase in utility. The same probably holds for most of advertising's cultural critics. As a group, Michael Schudson remarks, they see "the emergence of a consumer culture as a devolution of manners, morals and even manhood, from a work-oriented production ethic of the past to the consumption, 'lifestyle'-obsessed, ethic-less pursuits of the present" (1986, 6–7).

Uniting all these varied criticisms of advertising is the notion that it promotes substantive behaviors, experiences, and states of character which are inherently undesirable, and that it is morally objectionable for this reason . . . . This essay assumes that manipulative advertising both creates a consumer culture and strongly influences individual purchase decisions. Its main means for accomplishing the second aim (and perhaps the first) is to associate the product with such nonmarket goods as sex, status, and power. On those assumptions, manipulative advertising almost certainly undermines such standard virtues as honesty and benevolence in its practitioners, and arguably dilutes its targets' moderation, reasonableness, self-control, self-discipline, and self-reliance (Rachels 1993, 163 [listing these virtues]) . . . .

MANIPULATIVE ADVERTISING'S LAST DEFENSE

All things considered, virtue ethics appears to be the best basis for attacking manipulative advertising. In particular, it seems to dispose of a defense that has plagued our other three attacks on such advertising: Levitt's claim that people want and need advertising's illusions and therefore more or less knowingly and willingly embrace it. Like our other bases for attacking manipulative advertising, however, virtue ethics is not assumed to be an absolute. This might mean that the claims of virtue would have to give way if human beings simply could not endure without advertising's illusions or if its psychic satisfactions give people enormous amounts of utility.

In any event, there is yet another possible defense of manipulative advertising. This defense is mainly utilitarian, but it also implicates my other three ethical criteria to some degree. It arises because by hypothesis all my criteria must be weighed against competing moral claims. The defense does not so much challenge the assertion that manipulative advertising is bad, as argue that it is the lesser of two evils.

Throughout this essay, I have assumed for the sake of argument that manipulative advertising's critics are correct in their assessment of its effects. As we have seen, these people usually maintain that manipulative advertising plays an important role in socializing people to consume. This means that on the critics' view of things, manipulative advertising is central to the functioning of modern consumer society. But if manipulative advertising is central to the system's operation, how safely can it be condemned? Assuming that the condemnation is effective, manipulative advertising disappears, and all advertising becomes informative, people gradually would be weaned from their consumerist ways. This is likely to create social instability, with a more authoritarian form of government the likely end result. That, in turn, could well mean an environment in which aggregate utility is lower than it is today, human autonomy and rational nature are less respected, and/or the virtues less recognized.

One set of reasons for these conclusions is largely economic. If people become less consumerist as manipulative advertising leaves the scene, aggregate demand and economic output should decline. At first glance, this would seem to be of little consequence because by hypothesis people would value material things less. The problem is that the economic losses probably will be unevenly distributed: for example, some businesses will fail and some will not, and some people will lose their jobs while others stay employed. These inequalities are a potential source of social instability. Both to redress them and to preserve order, government is likely to intervene. This may involve a significant increase in outright governmental coercion . . . .

To my knowledge, Waide is the only business ethicist to raise these kinds of problems, and he finds himself without a solution to them. Because "[i]t seems unlikely that [manipulative] advertising will end suddenly," however, Waide is "confident that we will have the time and the imagination to adapt our economy to do without it" (1987, 77). Although I suspect that Waide is too optimistic, I have no solution to the dilemma either. Thus, I am left with the unsatisfactory conclusion that while various moral arguments may provide sound bases for attacking manipulative advertising, prudential considerations dictate that none of them be pressed too vigorously. Manipulative advertising's ultimate justification, in other words, may be its status as a necessary evil.

CONCLUDING REMARKS

For all the preceding reasons, it seems that there is no completely definitive basis for condemning manipulative advertising. But this obviously is not to say that the practice is morally unproblematic. Of my four suggested attacks on the practice, virtue ethics seems the strongest, with Kantianism a close second, autonomy third, and utilitarianism last. Indeed, utilitarianism may even support manipulative advertising. The main reason is that the practice's three most important defenses—Levitt's argument, the assertion that there is little connection between a want's origin outside the individual and the benefit resulting from its satisfaction, and manipulative advertising's centrality to our economic system—are more or less utilitarian in nature.

Except perhaps for hard-core utilitarians, therefore, manipulative advertising actually works. Specifically, I assumed that such advertising is a morally dubious practice. However, this conclusion may depend heavily on a critical assumption made earlier: that manipulative advertising: (1) socializes people to adopt a consumerist lifestyle, and (2) strongly influences individual purchase decisions. But what happens if, by and large, each assumption is untrue?

On first impressions, at least, it appears that if manipulative advertising is inefficacious, utilitarianism, autonomy, and virtue ethics largely cease to be bases for criticizing it . . . .

However, Kantian objections to manipulative advertising might well remain even if it is inefficacious. On that assumption, admittedly, perhaps one would will the universalization of a maxim permitting such advertising. If manipulative advertising simply fails to work, moreover, maybe it does not treat consumers merely as means to advertisers' ends. But such arguments ignore the strong anticonsequentialism of Kant's ethics, which arguably renders advertising's ineffectiveness irrelevant. More importantly, those arguments ignore Kant's stress on the motives with which people should act. The only thing that is unqualifiedly good, Kant says, is a good will; and the good will is good not because of what it accomplishes, but simply because it wills the good (Kant 1964, 61–62). Even if manipulative advertising is unsuccessful, advertisers presumably try to make it work. Unless they believe that their efforts would benefit consumers in the end, it is unlikely that they are acting with a good will when they devise and employ their stratagems.

At a first cut, therefore, it seems that if manipulative advertising is ineffective, the only significant ethical objections to it are Kantian. (To these we might add the money wasted on the practice, as well as its effect on the virtue of its practitioners.) For those inclined to ignore Kantian objections, therefore, it seems that manipulative advertising's rightness or wrongness depends less on ethical theory than on empirical questions within the purview of the social sciences . . . . As the preceding discussion suggests, the most important such question is the extent to which manipulative advertising actually affects purchase decisions and socializes people to consume. Even if manipulative advertising actually has those effects, other more or less empirical issues would remain. These include the validity of Levitt's arguments, Galbraith's asserted connection between a desire's origin outside the individual and the low utility resulting from its satisfaction, and manipulative advertising's contribution to gross domestic product. All these questions, I submit, are unlikely to be answered any time soon.

References

Benn, S. (1967) "Freedom and persuasion." *The Australasian Journal of Philosophy* 45: 259–75.

Galbraith, J. K. (1958) *The Affluent Society* (Boston: Houghton Mifflin).

Genge, W. (1985) "Ads stimulate the economy." *Business and Society Review* 1, no. 55: 58–59.

Hare, R. M. (1984) "Commentary." *Business and Professional Ethics Journal* 3, nos. 3 & 4: 23–28.

Hayek, F. A. (1961) "The *non sequitur* of the 'dependence effect.'" *Southern Economic Journal* 27: 346–48.

Heilbroner, R. (1976) *Business Civilization in Decline* (New York: W. W. Norton).

Held, V. (1984) "Advertising and program content." *Business and Professional Ethics Journal* 3, nos. 3 & 4: 61–76.

Kant, I. (1964) *Groundwork of the Metaphysic of Morals* (New York: Harper Torchbook, H. J. Paton tr.).

Lasch, C. (1978) *The Culture of Narcissism: American Life in An Age of Diminishing Expectations* (New York: W. W. Norton).

Levitt, T. (1970). "The morality (!) of advertising." *Harvard Business Review* (July–August): 84–92.

Lippke, R. (1990) "Advertising and the social conditions of autonomy." *Business and Professional Ethics Journal* 8, no. 4: 35–58.

Lukes, S. (1973) *Individualism* (Oxford: Basil Blackwell).

Rachels, J. (1993) *The Elements of Moral Philosophy* (New York: McGraw-Hill, 2nd ed.).

Schudson, M. (1986). *Advertising, the Uneasy Persuasion: Its Dubious Impact on American Society* (New York: Basic Books, 2nd ed.).

Waide, J. (1987) "The making of self and world in advertising." *Journal of Business Ethics* 6, no. 2: 73–79.

Review and Discussion Questions

1. What is "manipulative advertising"? What is "associative advertising"? Give examples of advertisements that you consider manipulative. Does advertising socialize people to a life of consumption? To what extent does it influence or even dictate our individual brand and product choices?

2. Assess Galbraith's contention that because advertising induces or creates consumer wants, those wants are not urgent and their satisfaction does not generate much utility.

3. Is Levitt correct that consumers need and want the illusions of advertising? Is it true that as consumers we are buying not only a physical product, but also a set of positive feelings connected with it by advertising? Do you agree with Levitt that "embellishment and distortion are among advertising's legitimate and socially desirable purposes"? Do the promises and images of advertising bring us genuine satisfaction?

4. Hare advances two Kantian arguments against manipulative advertising (based on different ways of formulating Kant's categorical imperative). What are they?

5. Assuming that manipulative advertising is effective, does it undermine one's autonomy? Does it promote undesirable behaviours and character traits, as the virtue-ethics critique alleges?

6. Assess the argument that manipulative advertising is a necessary evil because it is central to the continued functioning of our socioeconomic system. In your view, does advertising play a positive or negative role in our society?

7. Is manipulative advertising wrong? What do you see as the strongest ethical argument against it? Suppose manipulative advertising doesn't work. Would it still be wrong?

WHY DO WE CONSUME SO MUCH?

JULIET B. SCHOR

The "we" in the title of Schor's essay is intended to refer broadly to the affluent 'global North' and particularly to affluent Americans. But one would be naive indeed if he or she thought that the "we" does not take into its purview also affluent Canadians. Both Americans and Canadians enjoy a level of material consumption far beyond the dreams of earlier generations. Our culture celebrates consumption, and consumerism and materialistic values dominate many people's lives. Why do we consume so much? In answering that question, economist Juliet B. Schor identifies three structural features of our economic system that have led us down a path of excessive consumerism. First, we are locked into a "cycle of work and spend." Second, we have failed to value the earth's capital, and, third, consuming has become a means to social esteem and belonging. Her provocative essay harks back to themes in Chapter 3 (on equality and injustice), Chapter 4 (on the nature and values of capitalism), and Chapter 7 (on today's workplace), and anticipates the environmental issues discussed in the next chapter.

"Why do we consume so much?" Observers of consumption have answered this question in many ways. Because it's our human nature. Because ads tell us to. Because we can't help ourselves. Because our economic system needs us to. Because we are trapped in a fruitless dynamic of desire, acquisition, and disappointment. Because he who dies with the most toys wins. Just because we can.

These answers are inadequate. But I believe we can find more satisfying ones by a critical application of both economic and sociological theory, which will not only help to explain why we consume the way we do, but also how we might start to live differently. But before proceeding I need to clarify two points. Whom do I mean by "we"? And what do I mean by "so much"?

The "we" is straightforward. I do not mean the "global" we. Indeed, the "global" we hardly consumes so much. Rather economic globalization, militarization, corruption, the monopolization of environmental resources, and the legacies of colonialism have meant that the global "South" doesn't consume enough—at least not in terms of basics such as food, clothing, shelter. In 1999, per capita GDP in

the Less Developed Countries (or "global South") was $3,410 (measured as purchasing power parity). By contrast the Developed Countries ("global North") enjoyed average per capita GDP of $24,430, a gap of about eight times. One third of the population in the global South (1.2 billion) lives on less than $1 per day; 2.8 billion live on less than $2 per day. Together, this 4 billion comprises two-thirds of the world's population.

The "we" also does not cover everyone in the U.S. As you are all aware, despite this nation's enormous wealth, there continue to be significant numbers of people whose incomes are below poverty, and who lack access to basic consumption needs, such as adequate and nutritious food, decent shelter, reasonable transportation, health care, education, and other basic needs. Although poverty rates have declined, more than 30 million Americans have incomes below the poverty line, and probably twice that number do not have what most of would consider an adequate standard of living . . . . Thus, my "we" . . . stands for the majority of Americans—those whose basic needs are met, who have discretionary income, the large middle classes whose standard of living has risen so dramatically over this century.

And what about "so much?" By this phrase I intend to signal the material abundance of contemporary U.S. consumption. Abundance in historical terms. In comparative terms. In ecological terms. And in absolute terms. Our lives are suffused with consuming—of material objects, experiences, services, media. There is increasingly little that we do which is not a consumption experience. Material abundance has only intensified in recent years, with the booming economy of the 1990s and early 21st century. Indeed, it is hard to describe our current consumer patterns in terms other than excess. For example, the average U.S. home has increased by more than 50% since the 1970s, rising more than 400 square feet, from 1,905 in 1987 to 2,322 in 1999 alone. (At the same time, there are an estimated 2 million homeless Americans, about 40% of whom are family groups.)

The number of vehicles per person has increased, as has the size and luxuriousness of those vehicles. The culture of excess has yielded $20,000 outdoor grills; $17,000 birthday parties for teen girls at FAO Schwarz; diamond studded bras from Victoria's Secret; a proliferation of Jaguars, Porsches and other luxury cars; status competitions in stone walls; professional quality appliances for people who are never home to cook; designer clothes for six year olds; and bed sheets costing a thousand dollars apiece. If these examples seem extreme, consider the more mundane example of clothes. Even ordinary ones. Clothing used to be costly, both because of materials and labor. Now, because of the combination of foreign sweatshops that don't even pay workers enough to eat, and artificially cheap materials, clothes are so plentiful that you can find them sold like beans or rice—by the pound. Charities are inundated with enormous amounts of superfluous clothing, for which there are no takers in our country. It's sent abroad in enormous quantities—sometimes to the detriment of local economies.

Americans spend more on cosmetics every year (in excess of $8 billion) than the extra expenditure needed to bring universal access to basic education for all children in the developing world. The U.S. and Europe together spend $17 billion a year on pet foods, more than the $13 billion increment it would cost to ensure basic health and nutrition around the world. And so on.

. . . I believe that the culture of consumption excess which now pervades this country is wreaking havoc in many important ways. It is ecologically unsustainable, and those impacts are reaching crisis levels, with global warming, species depletion, deforestation, depletion of water supplies, and a variety of other pressing ecological effects. It has become socially unsustainable, as Americans work ever longer hours to support the dizzying rise in consumer norms which has characterized the last decade. It is financially unsustainable for many households, as consumption patterns are maintained by depleting savings and taking on debt. And finally, I believe that the culture of excess is partly responsible for a rising culture of social exclusion—two decades of increasing income and wealth inequality have yielded a society in which Americans are more likely to join gated communities, to tolerate poverty in their midst, to disavow responsibility for others and to abdicate a sense of community responsibility or common purpose . . . .

These are strong claims. And they go very much against the conventional wisdom, both in economics, and throughout the culture more generally. What is that conventional wisdom? First, that consumption is good. That new and "improved" products really are improvements. That we consume because we love to. And that consuming has made our lives richer, fuller, more enjoyable, and better, in meaningful and important ways. Second, that more is always better. (After all, economics argues, if it weren't one could always ignore the extra consumption and be at least as well off as one was without it.) This superiority of more implies that sufficiency . . . is never attained in toto. (We may easily reach satiation with particular commodities, but not for consumption as a whole.) And third, the conventional wisdom argues that the consumer market is best left relatively unattended by public policy, with the exception of some special cases (e.g., dangerous products). The consumer is sovereign and knows what he or she likes far better than the "government." Attempts to improve social welfare by steering consumption in particular directions will only backfire.

Now these are not conclusions that follow *logically* from economic theory. Rather, they represent the consensus view from the discipline, consumer economics and history as it has been practiced. As I shall argue shortly, I believe that much of this consensus is based on faulty assumptions about how and why we consume. Assumptions that, if altered, can lead to some very different conclusions.

On the other side, there is also a conventional wisdom among the critics of consumer culture. They begin with the view that while consumption may at one time have contributed significantly to human welfare, once basic needs have been satisfied, it is far less capable of doing so. New Coke is no better than Old Coke . . . . Besides, the critics say, we drink too much Coke anyway, and it's not good for us. Far better to drink water. So why are we paying scarce dollars for a can of sugar water that rots our teeth? Answers range from the observation that it's addictive, to the fact that it's everywhere (through monopolistic practices, such as exclusive contracts in schools.) And most importantly, in the critics' accounts, we're seduced into consuming by powerful advertising images, which equate the product with being cool, young, vital, sexy, or becoming an object of desire. The theme of many critiques of contemporary consumption is that consuming is a false god—our new religion—and that it takes us away from the true and durable satisfactions life has to offer. Consuming provides only temporary pleasures, is excessively hedonistic and seductive, and speaks not to the best in us, but often the worst. Most of these critiques center on the role of advertising, marketing, and the media, to account for how we get trapped into unsatisfying consumerist lifestyles.

I have sketched the two ends of the spectrum of belief about consumer society. While each contains important truths, I believe both are flawed. I accept the proposition that consuming is generally a "good" to the individual—the idea that people persistently act in ways which are so detrimental to their well-being is hard for an economist to swallow. (I say "generally" because there is plenty of empirical validation for cases in which consumption is out of control at the individual level.) But I agree with the critics that, as a society, we have too much of it. Instead of focusing on advertising and marketing, I argue that there are structural features in the operation of the economic system that have led us down a path of excessive consumerism.

What are those structural features and how do they operate?

THE CYCLE OF WORK AND SPEND

The first is what I have called "the cycle of work and spend." In the standard economic story, the level of consumption is set mainly by people's choices about how much to work, and therefore how much income to earn . . . . The individual chooses between hours at work (which yield income) and leisure (a "good" in itself, but a costly one because it entails foregoing income). The income earned then determines the level of consumption . . . .

Thus, individual workers/consumers choose the level of working hours and the quantity of consumption. In this story, there is no possibility of "too much" or "too little" consumption. Those terms make no sense. Here, it is individuals' preferences that determine the quantity of consuming and free time. And whatever quantity is chosen must be optimal.

Now consider a situation in which individuals are not free to choose their hours of work, because employers set work norms and schedules, and those are tied to jobs. The individual has the ability to choose whether to work or not. But having taken a job, the hours are relatively inflexible. Furthermore, imagine that employers have a bias against allowing part-time or what I have called "short hour" jobs. Why is this? Because benefits are paid per person, not per hour; because employers prefer to hire fewer people; and because employees who work longer hours are more financially dependent on the firm. So the option of working less and earning less is not fully available. To see the point, consider that where employees do have the option to work short hours, they must pay large penalties—in the form of fewer or no benefits, and a significant reduction in upward career mobility.

There is also a dynamic aspect to this configuration: when productivity growth occurs, employers do not offer their employees the option of using it to reduce hours of work, but pass it on as income. And that turns into consumption . . . .

If there is not a freely functioning market in hours, and employers inhibit hours' reductions, then there is no sense in which one can describe the quantity of consumption as optimal. Rather, we get too much income and not enough leisure. It is not advertising, or marketing, or addictive commodities which create this "too much." It is the fact that more leisured, less consumerist lifestyles are structurally blocked—in the labor market. Having been offered only the long hours, high-income choice, it's hardly surprising that people choose to do lots of consuming. After working so hard, they feel deserving of their consumer comforts and luxuries. Indeed, consumption is the major form of reward for long hours and a harried pace of work. And consumer expenditures have become one means by which people with frenetic lives keep it all going—whether it's stress-busters like vacations, massages, or restaurant meals; the contracting out of household services; or the purchase of time-saving commodities . . . .

The too much work, not enough leisure story is more than theoretically possible. Average annual hours per capita have risen by 178 since 1973. Although some of the rise in hours of paid work has been accounted for by a shift from women's unpaid household production into employment, the picture from a household basis is unambiguous. The average household is devoting hundreds of additional hours to paid work in order to maintain its standard of living. According to the Council of Economic Advisers, between 1969 and 1999, annual hours of work for married couple households rose 18% (497 hours) and 28% in single-parent households (297 hours).

This has led to a widespread sense of time-squeeze. The fraction of Americans reporting that they "almost never" have time on their hands rose from 41% in 1982 to 56% in 1995.

In the National Survey of the Changing Workforce done by the Families and Work Institute, between a quarter and a third of all employees reported fairly serious and frequent problems of inadequate time for family, being in a bad mood or being too tired. A third of parents and a quarter of non-parents reported that "often or very often" "they do not have the energy to do things with their families or other important people in their lives."

The growth of work effort and time stress has resulted in increased desires for more time off the job. The National Survey of the Changing Workforce found that 63% of all employees said they worked more hours than they wished to, with median overwork at 11 hours per week. This represents a large increase to support my contention of a "cycle of work and spend."

THE ECOLOGICAL BIAS

The second structural feature that creates too much consumption is the overuse of "natural capital" (i.e., the ecological resources of the earth). This is a well-known argument within economics about particular kinds of pollution. If "air" is a free resource, corporations will pollute it "too much" because they do not have to pay for their pollution.

In practice, ecological resources are treated as externalities or free goods—after-thoughts in a world where production is created by capital and labor. The discipline of economics, and society more generally, has failed to consider the overall effects of treating natural capital so cavalierly. One result is that we consume too much, *in toto*. If we correctly accounted for the costs of ecological resources, or committed to using them sustainably (so that they would renew, rather than degrade over time), we would likely be producing less overall (and taking more leisure). Why? Because consumption would become more costly relative to free time.

What we consume would also shift, toward less ecologically damaging (and costly) products and services. Fewer SUVs and airplane trips. More organic farming. Fewer plastics and chemicals. Smaller but more durable wardrobes, cotton grown with fewer or no pesticides. (10% of the world's pesticide use is for cotton.) Less meat, more grain. Shade grown coffee. Solar and wind power. Instead of rising, as it has in the last decade, residential energy use would fall, as people economized on space and shifted toward energy–efficient practice. Ditto paper use, which incredibly enough given the introduction of computers, is rising in the United States.

IS THE ECOLOGICAL BIAS A SERIOUS ONE?

Ecological models suggest yes, that the rates at which resource use, pollution and ecological degradation are occurring far exceed the earth's absorption capacity . . . . One reason is that we have already undermined a significant amount of the earth's absorption capacity, so that some regenerative mechanisms are no longer able to reverse the overshoot. Downward spirals begin to dominate positive feedback loops. The model's effects can be seen in the concrete problems of:

Global warming. Warmer climate is associated with toxic algal blooms, increased flooding and droughts, thawing of the permafrost, increased weather uncertainty, deforestation through insect damage, and increased transmission of vector-borne infections. The United States, with 5% of the world's population, is responsible for 24% of global carbon dioxide emissions.

Species extinction. Among birds and mammals, species are now going extinct at rates that are estimated to be 100 to 1,000 times the natural rate of extinction. One in eight known plant species is threatened with extinction.

Ecosystem depletion. Since 1970, freshwater ecosystems have declined by 50%, marine ecosystems have declined by 30%, and world forests have declined by 10%. This rate of depletion is unprecedented in human history. Indeed, current rates of environmental resource use dwarf human usage in all of human history . . . .

Water shortages. Approximately 1/3 of the world's population now lives in areas with moderate to heavy stress on water supplies, and if current trends continue, that number is expected to be 2/3 in 30 years. Already, 28% of the world's population lacks access to safe drinking water, and 5 million people die each year from inadequate access to water.

Deforestation and soil erosion. Some researchers believe that humans have now reduced the earth's original forest cover by up to 50%. The World Resources Institute estimates that we are losing 9 million hectares a year and rates of deforestation in tropical forests have accelerated, not declined in the 1990s, compared to the 1980s. It is now estimated that two-thirds of agricultural land has been degraded in the past 50 years, and 40% has been strongly or very strongly degraded.

The disequilibrium between pollution sources and sinks has been caused by the rapid increases in economic output over the last fifty years, made possible by advances in production technology. World industrial production has been accelerating at an exponential rate. Global consumption has tripled between 1980 and 1997. At the current rate of growth of the world economy, output doubles every 21 years. A mere one percent increase, to 4%, leads to doubling every 15 years. Yet, we are already well beyond a sustainable relationship with the earth. And when we consider the ongoing worldwide replication of US lifestyles, the prognosis is even grimmer. Ecological footprint analysis (which looks at the global impact of any given consumer lifestyle) suggests that for the rest of the world to live as Americans do, we will need four additional planets . . . .

CONSUMPTION COMPETITIONS

I come now to my third argument, which is that we consume too much in part because consumption has become a social competition, something we engage in for the esteem, recognition, status, and even envy it confers. We consume conspicuously, and excessively, because consumer lifestyle have become such an important part of how we are defined and how we fit into socially differentiated communities. Veblen made this point most famously a hundred years ago. His analysis was based mainly on the wealthy and the would-be wealthy, for whom attaining and displaying visible wealth had become the *sine qua non* of social standing. But the phenomenon is far broader today, with the large majority of the population participating. Today it is less insidious in some ways, because it's not only offensive (I get the big diamond because my best friend doesn't have one), but has become defensive (I get the big diamond because my best friend does have one).

In *The Overspent American*, I discussed the ways in which this process has changed. Fifty years ago it was a comparison among peers. "Keeping up with the Joneses"—the colloquial description of consumption competitions, occurred mainly within a neighborhood setting. Because neighborhoods are relatively homogeneous in terms of the social status and economic resources of their members, the folks keeping up with the Joneses tended to be their equals. They did aspire, but rarely more than to increase their consumer expenditures by 10–20%. Smiths wanted the Joneses' Chevy and nifty fridge, not the Rockefellers' mansions and art collections.

That has changed. The "reference groups" (to use the sociological term) that Americans now use to calibrate their consumer aspirations have become more vertical and less horizontal (vertical in terms of economic and social standing). Now Rockefeller (or rather Bill Gates) has become an important aspirational target for millions of Americans, especially young ones. And even more importantly, the upper twenty percent of the population (roughly those making $100,000 a year or more) have become an aspirational target throughout society. A decent or comfortable standard of living—once a widespread goal—is no longer enough. Now the dominant goal is for status products, and luxury. There is plenty of survey evidence . . . which shows the increasing importance of earning a lot of money, earning more than others, getting rich, and acquiring the trappings of upper middle class or truly wealthy lifestyles—second homes, swimming pools, foreign travel, expensive wardrobes, etc. Perhaps most telling is the fact that getting rich is now the number one aspiration of American youth, more important than being a famous athlete or celebrity, or being really smart.

How this happened is an interesting story, but I believe one of the major factors has been the decline of community and sociability, especially on a neighborhood level, and the growing importance of media, and especially television, in purveying "information" about consumption

. . . . We find out about new consumer "trends" from movies and TV, print media both newspapers and magazines, and also the Internet. Our new "friends" are the ones we find on TV.

One consequence of this "up scaling of desire" is that consumer norms have risen faster and higher than in a world with more moderate consumer aspirations. This is partly because the target that everyone is chasing has become so prosperous—in addition to large increases in the *level* of income and wealth garnered by the top 2000, they have also increased their *share* dramatically. Between 1983 and 1998, the top 20% increased their share of income from 51.9% to 56.2%; their share of financial wealth rose from 81.3% to 83.4%. (So much for people's capitalism. The share of total financial wealth held by the top 1% stands at a stunning 47.3%, up from 42.9% in 1983. The bottom 60% holds no financial wealth at all, on average.) Unlike previous economic booms, this one did not yield a more equitable distribution of income and wealth.

The problem with consumption competition, such as the one we find ourselves in, is that they are difficult for individuals to resist. If everyone else is buying that SUV, we tend to want one too. And if we hold out for a while, avoiding the seductive message that the SUV will get us back to nature, and the simpler, slower, more meaningful life we crave, . . . then practical considerations start to weigh in. Everyone else has one, I'm no longer safe in a small vehicle. I can't see past all those behemoths; better elevate myself as well. Similarly with the up scaling to cell phones, or computers, or the kinds of lessons and cultural enhancements our children need to achieve in today's competitive world, or the kind of kitchen we have, and so on. We might all be happier driving slightly older cars, having fewer gizmos and gadgets, with a fashion style that didn't change quite so frequently, and maybe even with slightly smaller homes. In return we'd get with less debt and more financial security, more time outside of work, less anxiety about keeping up, and a healthier environment.

But in a consumption competition none of us can do it alone. Without a coordinating influence (be it the government, the church, the community . . . any social institution will do) each of us is trapped in what I once called the upward creep of desire. (Except that in recent years it has turned into a gallop.) So collectively we are in what game theorists call a Prisoner's Dilemma, where we could all benefit from a slowing down. It's like a ballgame when people start standing to get a better view. The first, few do succeed. (Those are the "early adopters" of new consumer trends, the Joneses we're all following.) But as everyone starts to stand, the quality of the view goes back to what it was, and everyone's legs get tired. Those who sit down on their own are drastically worse off. And the collective good can only be reached through the announcer's call: "Baseball fans, please sit down." I think that's where we've been in the last half-decade or so.

CONCLUSION

These then are my three arguments about why we consume too much: we are locked into a "cycle of work and spend," we have failed to value the earth's capital, and consuming has become a means to social esteem and belonging. In the process, we are undermining our quality of life. We fail to take enough leisure, and live excessively busy and stressful lives. We are poisoning the planet. And we find ourselves needing to earn too much money or going into debt, or getting stressed out by the rapid rise in consumer norms. Community, security, and the peace of mind that comes from having reached a state of sufficiency are increasingly elusive.

The standard economic analysis sees precious little of this. More is always better. Individuals will act in their interest to avoid these traps. Collective action failures or externalities are rarely more than small problems. Similarly, the consumer critics have failed to understand the structural dynamics that make consuming a rational choice for the individual, even if it is an irrational one for society as a whole. They take an excessively dim view of people's abilities to act well for themselves. And they underestimate how important consumption can be in a society organized around it. But they are certainly right, that excessive consumption has become a serious problem—from the standpoint of our daily lives, our ethical obligations to others around the world, from the standpoint of the earth and its sacred bounty.

In recent years, increasing numbers of Americans have come to these and similar conclusions. They are individually escaping "the cycle of work and spend," by downshifting (working less and spending less). They are joining the emerging voluntary simplicity movement, living modestly, volunteering their time, spending their days doing the things they are passionate about. They are joining study groups in their workplace and churches. Some are even organizing an anti-consumerist movement, participating in Buy-Nothing Day (the Friday after Thanksgiving) or designing sub-vertising (anti-ads which turn the tools of advertising and marketing against itself). They are protesting corporate globalization of the economy. They are joining organic farms and drinking shade grown coffee. They are riding bicycles. And they are opposing the corporate co-optation of their lifestyle, as the Gap, Honda, Starbucks and Time-Warner try to make money selling "simplicity" as the latest hip consumer trend.

But they (we) need more Americans to join. The domination of the consumer culture remains impressive, and as patriotic appeals to consume have become common . . . since Sept. 11, we should resist the temptation to run to the mall. Instead, let us take this very painful but special time to step back and ask some fundamental questions. Why do we consume so much? What are the effects of that consumption? And how can we create a community that respects the earth, respects each and every human being upon it, and truly meets human needs?

Review and Discussion Questions

1. Who is the "we" in the question "Why do we consume so much?" Do you think that the "we" can also properly apply to Canadians? Is Schor correct that "there is increasingly little that we do which is not a consumption experience"? And that we have become a culture of excessive consumption? Explain your answer.

2. Schor identifies three assumptions about consumption that constitute "conventional wisdom" today. What are they? By contrast, what do the critics of consumer culture say? Schor says that each position "contains important truths" but "both are flawed" (a point she returns to at the end of the essay). Explain how her position differs from both the defenders of consumer culture and its critics.

3. Explain why Schor believes that "more leisured, less consumerist lifestyles are structurally blocked." Why can't people simply choose to work less and enjoy more free time? Do you agree that working long hours encourages people to consume more?

4. Schor refers to the second structural feature that creates too much consumption as "the ecological bias." What does she mean by this? Do you agree with her that it is serious?

5. Explain why you agree or disagree with Schor's contention that consumption has become a social competition. How has the old concept of "keeping up with the Joneses" changed? Do you agree that it is difficult for individuals to resist or drop out of the consumption competition? Explain why or why not.

6. Would it be good for us as individuals and for society as a whole to escape from the culture of excessive consumption? Is this goal possible? If so, how? If not, why not?

Further Reading for Chapter 10

Robert L. Arrington, "Advertising and Behavior Control," *Journal of Business Ethics* 1 (February 1982); **John Waide**, "The Making of Self and World in Advertising," *Journal of Business Ethics* 6 (February 1987); **Roger Crisp**, "Persuasive Advertising, Autonomy, and the Creation of Desire," *Journal of Business Ethics* 6 (July 1987); **Richard L. Lippke**, "Advertising and the Social Conditions of Autonomy," *Business and Professional Ethics Journal* 8 (Winter 1989); and **Andrew Gustafson**, "Advertising's Impact on Morality in Society: Influencing Habits and Desires of Consumers," *Business and Society Review* 106 (Fall 2001) are valuable, philosophical discussions of advertising.

David M. Holley, "A Moral Evaluation of Sales Practices," *Business and Professional Ethics Journal* 5 (Fall 1987) is a seminal discussion of the ethics of sales. Holley revisits the subject in "Information Disclosure in Sales," *Journal of Business Ethics* 17 (April 1998) and replies to Thomas L. Carson in "Alternative Approaches to Applied Ethics: A Response to Carson's Critique," *Business Ethics Quarterly* 12 (January 2002).

Patrick E. Murphy, Gene R. Laczniak, Norman E. Bowie, and **Thomas A. Klein**, *Ethical Marketing* (Upper Saddle River, NJ: Prentice Hall, 2005) surveys a wide range of issues in marketing ethics, including researching and segmenting markets, product management, distribution and pricing, and sales.

Juliet Schor, *Born to Buy: The Commercialized Child and the New Consumer Culture* (New York: Simon & Schuster, 2005) is a well-researched critique of the ruthless targeting of children by advertisers and of their induction into consumerism.

N. Craig Smith and **John A. Quelch**, eds., *Ethics in Marketing* (Homewood, IL: Irwin, 1993) contains informative essays and case studies on all aspects of marketing ethics.

Edward Spence and **Brett Van Heekeren**, *Advertising Ethics* (Upper Saddle River, NJ: Prentice Hall, 2005) is a succinct and stimulating discussion of, among other issues, truth in advertising, endorsements and testimonials, target advertising, and stereotyping.

The Environment

In feeding, clothing, and sheltering ourselves and in manufacturing and consuming countless kinds of products, human beings have scarred the globe, contaminated the natural environment, and gobbled up the earth's resources. The effects of this environmental recklessness are now coming home to roost. Our rivers and lakes are dirty, and our air is unclean. The planet is warming, its protective ozone fraying. Lush forests are disappearing, and with them countless species of plants and animals. As our numbers have multiplied, half the world's wetlands have disappeared. Eighty percent of its grasslands now suffer from soil degradation; 20 percent of its drylands are in danger of turning into deserts, and groundwater is seriously depleted. As a result, the earth is losing its capacity to continue to provide the goods we need, threatening our economic well-being and ultimately our survival—so concludes a mammoth U.N.-sponsored assessment of global ecosystems.[1]

The environment is a huge topic, but as one expert remarks, "the concerns of environmental ethics might begin with the food on our plate."[2] With fertilizers, herbicides, and pesticides, agriculture uses hundreds of chemicals in crop production. Although chemically intensive agriculture has yielded many benefits, it is hard on the environment—both in terms of what it consumes and in its impact on the surrounding ecosystem. In addition to the ecological price we pay for what we eat, there is the risk of chemical residues left in food.

The last three decades have seen a dramatic increase in the application of pesticides in Canada and the United States. It has doubled in the U.S. and quadrupled in Canada. The danger posed by their application to human and animal health and well-being is grave indeed.[3] Because of exposure to pesticides, many fish and birds in the Great Lakes region have lost their ability to reproduce. After a pesticide spilled into Florida's Lake Apopka, alligators were born with half-sized penises. When laboratory rats were fed DDT, they developed genital abnormalities. Now researchers believe that by mimicking estrogen and testosterone, the chemicals in pesticides may threaten

human reproduction by disrupting the endocrine system that regulates it.[4] The pesticide problem is even more alarming when we consider children. Because they have smaller bodies and different eating patterns than adults, children's exposure to carcinogens and neurotoxins can be hundreds of times what is safe for them.[5]

Pesticides, of course, are not the only problem. Thanks to environmentally insensitive industrial, agricultural, and waste management practices, our bodies now contain measurable quantities of a wide range of unnatural metals and potentially hazardous chemicals, including PCBs, furans, dioxin, mercury, lead, benzene, and other toxic items.[6] One way they enter our bodies is through our water as various contaminants used in farming, manufacturing, and transportation run off into rivers, lakes, and underground reservoirs. A dramatic illustration of the varied and unsuspected ways in which such noxious substances eventually enter our bodies is provided by the findings of a group of scientists working in Devon Island in Nunavut. They found that the droppings of northern fulmars, coming back to the island to feed their young, are spreading high concentrations of pollutants (including mercury, PCBs, and DDT) over the land and lakes of the High Arctic. The pollutants were in the fish the seabirds ate (and bio-accumulated) in more southern latitudes.[7] Despite different pieces of environmental legislation in Canada and the United States, progress in combating water pollution has been slow and insufficient.

Pollutants also contaminate the air we breathe, despoiling vegetation and crops, corroding construction materials, and threatening our lives and health. In addition to that is the emission of nontoxic substances such as sulfur and nitrogen oxide, which are a major source of acid rain and of the smog that blankets so many cities, and of the dust, soot, smoke, and tiny drops of acid that create the fine-particle pollution known to be so dangerous to human health. Every year, over two billion pounds of hazardous materials, including tonnes of toxic chemicals, are emitted by U.S. companies into the air.[8]

On the whole, however, Canada's record on air pollution is very poor compared to that of other industrialized nations. A comprehensive Canadian study conducted in 2001, comparing Canada to the other members of the Organization for Economic Co-operation and Development (OECD)[9] with respect to twenty-five environmental indicators, found that "despite making progress, Canada is one of the worst air polluters among industrialized nations."[10] Although precise figures are impossible to obtain, there is little doubt that air pollution is responsible for thousands of deaths and millions of sick days every year because of air-related ailments (for example, asthma, emphysema, and lung cancer).[11] Air pollution is especially harmful to young people, whose lungs are still developing.[12] It also contributes to heart disease,[13] and pregnant women residing in regions with significant air pollution are up to three times more likely to give birth to children with serious birth defects.[14] Unfortunately, most Canadians live in large metropolitan areas or major urban corridors, where air pollution poses a year-round health risk.[15]

Related to the problem of atmospheric pollution is the issue of global warming. After years of study and debate, there is now a scientific consensus that human activity is indeed heating up the planet.[16] As we burn coal, oil, and gasoline for heat, electricity, and transportation, carbon dioxide (CO_2) is released into the atmosphere, trapping excess energy from the sun and warming the globe—the so-called greenhouse effect. The evidence of global warming is all around us. The past decade has been the hottest on record; in the Northern Hemisphere, spring now comes, on average, a week earlier than it used to. Storms have become more intense and weather patterns more erratic. The Arctic ice sheet is melting, and the world's glaciers are shrinking fast. Global warming also threatens countless plant and animal species with extinction.[17] Only by drastically reducing the consumption of fossil fuels can we hope to slow down this trend and stabilize the climate at current levels of disruption.

Surprisingly, one of the largest sources of pollution is not at all exotic—namely, the animals we raise for food. In fact, the ecological costs of producing beef, poultry, and pork are second only to the manufacture and use of cars and light trucks. In addition to the electrical energy, fuel, fertilizer, and pesticides consumed by the meat industry, there is the manure problem. The United States alone generates 1.4 billion tons (about 1.3 billion tonnes) of animal manure every year—130 times more than its annual production of human waste—while Canada's 16.7 million cattle, 14.7 million swine, and 154.8 million poultry contribute 320 million tons of "residual biomass." Someone has figured out that the manure from all Canada's hogs would fill the Rogers Centre in Toronto every 22 days.[18] This waste wasn't a problem when farms were small, and farmers used the manure as fertilizer. But giant farms with 100,000 hogs or a million chickens, all defecating in the same place, may seriously damage the environment.[19] Runoff and water pollution have been and are major concerns,[20] but now scientists are also worried about air pollution and the emission of noxious fumes from the disposal of animal waste.[21] Nuclear wastes, of course, are in a class by themselves. Significant danger arises from even the small amounts that are released into the atmosphere during normal operation of a nuclear power plant or in mining, processing, or transporting nuclear fuels. A nuclear-plant accident would, of course, have frightening consequences, as the 1986 disaster at Chernobyl, Ukraine, brought vividly home to the entire world. Illnesses caused by the fallout from Chernobyl are still emerging, twenty years later.[22] The province of Ontario has recently re-committed the province to greater use of nuclear energy for the production of electricity.[23] The disposal of nuclear wastes has to worry anyone who is sensitive not only to the health and safety his or her generation but also to the legacy we leave future generations. Will the nuclear wastes we bury today return to haunt our children or us tomorrow?

Small wonder, then, that considerable attention has focused on business and industry's responsibility for preserving the integrity of our natural environment. This chapter explores some of the moral dilemmas posed for business by our environmental relationships—not just the problem of pollution but also the ethical issues posed by the depletion of natural resources and by our treatment of animals. The chapter's purpose is not to argue that the environmental problems facing us are serious and that industry has greatly contributed to them. Few people today doubt this. Rather, this chapter is largely concerned with a more practical question: given the problems of environmental degradation, of resource depletion, and of the abuse of animals for commercial purposes, what are business's responsibilities? Specifically, this chapter examines the following topics:

1. The meaning and significance of *ecology*

2. The traditional business attitudes toward the environment that have encouraged environmental degradation and resource depletion

3. The moral problems underlying business's abuse of the environment—in particular, the question of externalities, the problem of free riders, and the right to a liveable environment

4. The costs of environmental protection and the question of who should pay them

5. Three methods—regulations, incentives, and pricing mechanisms—for pursuing our environmental goals

6. Some of the deeper and not fully resolved questions of environmental ethics: What obligations do we have to future generations? Does nature have value in itself? Is our commercial exploitation of animals immoral?

BUSINESS AND ECOLOGY

To deal intelligently with the question of business's responsibilities for the environment, one must realize that as business uses energy and materials, discharges waste, and produces products and services, it is functioning within an ecological system. *Ecology* refers to the science of the interrelationships among organisms and their environments. The operative term is "interrelationships," implying that an interdependence exists among all entities in the environment. In particular, we must not forget that human beings are part of nature and thus intricately connected with and interrelated to the natural environment.

In speaking about ecological matters, ecologists frequently use the term *ecosystem*, which refers to a total ecological community, both living and nonliving. Webs of interdependency structure ecosystems. Predators and prey, producers and consumers, hosts and parasites are linked, creating interlocking mechanisms—checks and balances—that stabilize the system.

An ordinary example of an ecosystem is a pond. It consists of a complex web of animal and vegetable life. Suppose that the area where the pond is located experiences a prolonged period of drought, or that someone begins to fish in the pond regularly, or that during a period of excessive rainfall, plant pesticides begin to spill into it. Under any of these circumstances, changes will occur in the relationships among the pond's constituent components. Damage to a particular form of plant life may mean that fewer fish can live in the pond; a particular species might even disappear. A change in the pond's ecosystem may also affect other ecosystems. Because of water contamination, for example, a herd of deer that live nearby may have to go elsewhere for water; their presence there may reduce the berry crop that had previously supported other animals. Thus, in considering any ecosystem, one must remember its complex and interrelated nature and the intricate network of interdependencies that bind it to other ecosystems.

Every living organism affects its environment, yet *Homo sapiens* possesses the power to upset dramatically the stability of natural ecosystems. In particular, many human commercial activities (for example, using pesticides and establishing oil fields) have unpredictable and disruptive consequences for ecosystems. For example, farmers in Manitoba may use nitrogen fertilizer. Excess nitrogen runs off their fields and finds its way into the Mississippi River and eventually into the Gulf of Mexico. There, in what has historically been America's best shrimping grounds, it has created what is known as the "dead zone," where the water is devoid of life to about 3 metres below the surface. This dead zone has now grown to about 22,015 square kilometres, an area the size of New Jersey.[24] On the other hand, tampering with ecosystems does not always have injurious effects. Sometimes unforeseen benefits result, as was true years ago when oil and gas drilling expanded into the Gulf of Mexico. Much to everyone's surprise, the operational docks, pipes, and platforms provided

a better place for lower forms of life to attach themselves to than the silt-laden sea ever did. This in turn increased the fish catch in the area. But even in fortuitous instances like this, environmental intrusions affect the integrity of ecosystems. And that's the point. Because an ecosystem represents a delicate balance of interrelated entities and because ecosystems are interlocked, an intrusion into one will affect its integrity and the integrity of others. And we are not usually so lucky in the results. Dr. Paul Ehrlich, one of the best-known exponents of ecological awareness, has put the matter succinctly. "There are a number of ecological rules it would be wise for people to remember," Ehrlich has written. "One of them is that there is no such thing as a free lunch. Another is that when we change something into something else, the new thing is usually more dangerous than what we had originally."[25]

In its role as the major instrument of production in our society, business cannot help but intrude into ecosystems. Yet not all intrusions or all kinds of intrusions are justifiable. In fact, precisely because of the interrelated nature of ecosystems and because intrusions generally produce serious unfavourable effects, business must scrupulously avoid actions, practices, and policies that have an undue impact on the environment. There's ample documentation to show that business has traditionally been remiss in both recognizing and adequately discharging its obligations in this regard. We needn't spend time retelling the sorry tale, but it does seem worthwhile to isolate some business attitudes that have been responsible for this indifference.

Business's Traditional Attitudes Toward the Environment

Several related attitudes, prevalent in our society in general and in business in particular, have led to or increased our environmental problems. One of these is the tendency to view the natural world as a "free and unlimited good"—that is, as something we can exploit, even squander, without regard to the future. Writer John Steinbeck once reflected on this attitude:

I have often wondered at the savagery and thoughtlessness with which our early settlers approached this rich continent. They came at it as though it were an enemy, which of course it was. They burned the forests and changed the rainfall; they swept the buffalo from the plains, blasted the streams, set fire to the grass, and ran a reckless scythe through the virgin and noble timber. Perhaps they felt that it was limitless and could never be exhausted and that a man could move on to new wonders endlessly. Certainly there are many examples to the contrary, but to a large extent the early people pillaged the country as though they hated it, as though they held it temporarily and might be driven off at any time.

This tendency toward irresponsibility persists in very many of us today; our rivers are poisoned by reckless dumping of sewage and toxic industrial wastes, the air of our cities is filthy and dangerous to breathe from the belching of uncontrolled products from combustion of coal, coke, oil, and gasoline. Our towns are girdled with wreckage and debris of our toys—our automobiles and our packaged pleasures. Through uninhibited spraying against one enemy we have destroyed the natural balances our survival depends on. All these evils can and must be overcome if America and Americans are to survive; but many of us conduct ourselves as our ancestors did, stealing from the future for our clear and present profit.[26]

Of course, the target of Steinbeck's criticism was the early American settlers and his own compatriots in the mid-1960s. But his shots would have also found a target in the attitudes and behaviour of Canadians toward the environment. Traditionally, business has considered the environment to be a free, virtually limitless good. In other words, air, water, land, and other natural resources from coal to beavers (trapped almost to extinction for their pelts in the nineteenth century) were seen as available for business to use as it saw fit. In this context, pollution and the depletion of natural resources are two aspects of the same problem: both involve using up natural resources that are limited. Pollution uses up clean air and water, just as extraction uses up the minerals or oil in the ground. The belief that both sorts of resources are unlimited and free promotes wasteful consumption of them.

Garrett Hardin describes the consequences of this attitude in his modern parable, "The Tragedy of the Commons." Hardin asks us to imagine villagers who allow their animals to graze in the commons, the collectively shared village pasture. Even though it is in the interest of each to permit his or her animals to graze without limit on the public land, the result of doing so is that the commons is soon overgrazed, making it of no further grazing value to anyone.[27]

Today the international fishing industry exemplifies Hardin's point: over-fishing by ships armed with advanced technology is dramatically reducing the world's stock of fish, threatening to undermine the whole industry.[28] No one knows this better than the fishermen of our Maritime provinces. But the moral of Hardin's story is perfectly general: when it comes to the "commons"—that is, to public or communal goods like air, water, and wilderness—problems arise as the result of individuals' and companies' following their own self-interest. Each believes that his or her own use of the commons has only a negligible effect, but the cumulative result can be the gradual destruction of the public domain, which makes everyone worse off. In the tragedy of the commons we have the reverse of Adam Smith's invisible hand: each person's pursuit of self-interest makes everyone worse off.

The tragedy of the commons also illustrates the more general point that there may well be a difference between the private costs and the social costs of a business activity. Chapter 5 discussed this issue when it described what

economists call "externalities," but it is worth reviewing the point in the present context.

Suppose a paper mill only partially treats the chemical wastes it releases into a lake that's used for fishing and recreational activities, thus saving on production costs. If the amount of effluent is great enough to reduce the fishing productivity of the lake, then while the mill's customers pay a lower price for its paper than they otherwise would, other people end up paying a higher price for fish. Moreover, the pollution may make the lake unfit for recreational activities such as swimming or for use as a source of potable water. The result is that other people and the public generally pay the cost of the mill's inadequate water-treatment system. Economists term this disparity between private industrial costs and public social costs a *spillover* or *externality*. In viewing things strictly in terms of private industrial costs, business overlooks spillover. This is an economic problem because the price of the paper does not reflect the true cost of producing it. Paper is underpriced and overproduced, thus leading to a misallocation of resources. This is also a moral problem because the purchasers of paper are not paying its full cost. Instead, part of the cost of producing paper is being unfairly imposed on other people.

The same sort of disparity between the private costs and the social costs of business activity also arises in the context of resource depletion, rather than pollution. For example, it takes about 379 kilolitres of water to make one automobile, but no manufacturer considers, let alone pays for, the damage done to the water table. Yet some countries find themselves in the environmentally unsustainable position of using more water than nature can replenish. For example, the United States uses up 284 litres of groundwater for every 227 that nature puts back in.[29]

In sum, then, externalities or spillover effects, pursuit of private interest at the expense of the commons, and a view of the environment as a free good that can be consumed without limit have combined with an ignorance of ecology and of the often-fragile interconnections and interdependencies of the natural world to create the serious environmental problems facing us today.

THE ETHICS OF ENVIRONMENTAL PROTECTION

Much of what we do in order to reduce, eliminate, or avoid pollution or the depletion of scarce natural resources is in our collective self-interest. Many measures that we take—for example, recycling our cans or installing catalytic converters in our cars—are steps that benefit all of us, collectively and individually: our air is more breathable and our landscapes less cluttered with garbage. But even if such measures benefit each and every one of us, there will still be a temptation to shirk individual responsibilities and be a "free rider." The individual person or company may rationalize that the little bit it adds to the total pollution problem doesn't make any difference. The firm benefits from the efforts of others to prevent pollution but "rides for free" by not making the same effort itself.

The unfairness here is obvious. Likewise, as explained in the previous section, the failure of companies to "internalize" their environmental "externalities" spells unfairness. Others are forced to pick up the tab when companies do not pay all the environmental costs involved in producing their own products. As mentioned in Chapter 5, those who adopt the broader view of corporate social responsibility emphasize that business and the rest of society have an implicit social contract. This contract reflects what society hopes to achieve by allowing business to operate; it sets the "rules of the game" that govern business activity. Companies that try to be free riders in environmental matters or who refuse to address the spillover or external costs of their business activity violate this contract.

So far this chapter has emphasized that we need to view the environment differently if we are to improve our quality of life and even to continue to exist. And it has just stressed how the failure of an individual or business to play its part is unfair. Some moral theorists, like William T. Blackstone, have gone further to argue that each of us has a human right to a liveable environment. "Each person," Blackstone argues, "has this right *qua* being human and because a livable environment is essential for one to fulfill his human capacities."[30] This right has emerged, he contends, as a result of changing environmental conditions, which affect the very possibility of human life as well as the possibility of realizing other human rights.

Recognition of a right to a liveable environment would strengthen further the ethical reasons for business to respect the integrity of the natural world. In addition, recognition of this moral right could, Blackstone suggests, form a sound basis for establishing a legal right to a liveable environment through legislation and even, perhaps, through constitutional provisions. An official recognition of such rights would enhance our ability to go after polluters and other abusers of the natural environment.

Acknowledging a human right to a liveable environment, however, does not solve many of the difficult problems facing us. In the effort to conserve irreplaceable resources, to protect the environment from further degradation, and to restore it to its former quality, we are still faced with difficult choices, each with its economic and moral costs. The next section focuses on pollution control, but most of the points apply equally to other problems of environmental protection, as well as to the conservation of scarce resources.

The Costs of Pollution Control

It is easy to say that we should do whatever it takes to improve the environment. Before this answer has any operational worth, however, we must consider a number of things. One is the quality of environment that we want. This can vary from an environment restored to its pristine state to one minimally improved over its current condition. Then there's the question of precisely what is necessary to bring about the kind of environment we want.

In some cases we may lack the technological capacity to restore the environment. Finally, an important concern in any determination of what should be done to improve the environment is a calculation of what it will cost.

To draw out this point, we must consider a major technique for determining the total costs of environmental improvement. *Cost–benefit analysis* is a device used to determine whether it's worthwhile to incur a particular cost—for instance, the cost of employing a particular pollution-control device. The general approach is to evaluate a project's direct and indirect costs and benefits, the difference being the net result for society. Suppose that the estimated environmental damage of operating a particular plant is $1 million per year, that closing the plant would have dire economic consequences for the community, and that the only technique that would permit the plant to operate in an environmentally non-damaging way would cost $6 million per year. In this case, cost–benefit analysis would rule against requiring the plant to introduce the new technique.* If the cost of the technique had been only $800,000, however, cost–benefit analysis would have favoured it.

Cost–benefit analysis can quickly get very complicated. For example, in determining whether it would be worthwhile to initiate more stringent air-pollution standards for a particular industry, a multitude of factors must be considered. Possible costs might include lower corporate profits, higher prices for consumers, unfavourable effects on employment, or adverse consequences for the nation's balance of payments. On the side of anticipated benefits, a reduction in airborne particulates over urban areas would reduce illness and premature death from bronchitis, lung cancer, and other respiratory diseases by some determinate percentage. The increase in life expectancy would have to be estimated along with projected savings in medical costs and increases in productivity. In addition, diminished industrial discharges would mean reduced property and crop damage from air pollution, and that would save more money.

This example suggests the extreme difficulty of making reliable estimates of actual costs and benefits, of putting price tags on the different effects of the policy being considered. Any empirical prediction in a case like this is bound to be controversial. This problem is compounded by the fact that decision makers are unlikely to know for certain all future results of the policy being studied. Not only is estimating the likelihood of its various possible effects difficult, but also some future effects may be entirely unanticipated.

The new discipline of ecological economics is attempting to expand further the boundaries of environmental cost–benefit analysis by calculating the value of an ecosystem in terms of what it would cost to provide the benefits and services it now furnishes us—for example, the

---

*Cost–benefit analysis would not, however, prevent other strategies for getting the plant to internalize this externality. It could be taxed $1 million or be required to reimburse those who suffer the $1 million loss.

worth of a wetland in terms of the cost of constructing structures that provide the same flood control and storm protection that natural wetlands do.[31] Although conventional economists dismiss the idea of equating the value of something with its replacement cost rather than with what people are willing to pay for it, ecological economists respond that traditional market pricing fails to capture the non-marketed externalities that nature provides, such as the nutrients that a forest recycles. In one study, for example, ecological economists established that a mangrove swamp in Thailand was worth 72 percent more when left intact to provide timber, charcoal, fish, and storm protection than when converted to a fish farm. "In every case we looked at," states Cambridge University biologist Andrew Balmford, "the loss of nature's services outweighed the benefits of development, often by large amounts."[32] Even putting aside the debate over ecological economics, cost–benefit analyses of rival environmental policies will frequently prove controversial because they inevitably involve making value judgments about non-monetary costs and benefits. Costs relative to time, effort, and discomfort can and must be introduced. Benefits can take even more numerous forms: health, convenience, comfort, enjoyment, leisure, self-fulfillment, freedom from odour, enhanced beauty, and so on. Benefits are especially difficult to calculate in environmental matters because they often take an aesthetic form. Some environmentalists, for example, may campaign for the preservation of a remote forest visited annually by only a handful of stalwart backpackers, whereas developers wish to convert it into a more accessible and frequented ski resort. Should the forest be preserved or should it be converted into a ski resort? Conflicting value judgments are at stake.

With the assistance of an economics-consulting firm, the U.S. Department of the Interior asked Americans how much they were willing to shell out for environmental restoration. For instance, what would each consent to pay to restore the ecological balance of the Grand Canyon, even if few of them will actually see or truly understand the improvements: Ten cents a month? A dollar a month? Ten dollars a month? The Department used this technique to justify reintroducing wolves into parts of Montana, Wyoming, and Idaho—a controversial move opposed by some taxpayers, ranchers, and consumers of beef. Some environmentalists applaud such attempts to calculate what economists call "non-use value," but others fear that the attempt to put a monetary price tag on ecosystems belittles the values they champion.[33] An evaluation of costs and benefits is unavoidably wed to value judgments—to assessments of worth and the ranking of values. Although a cost-effectiveness analysis may be necessary for determining the soundness of an environmental-preservation measure or a pollution-control project, it seems inevitable that any assessment of costs and benefits will be subject to various factual uncertainties and significantly influenced by the values one holds. This is especially true in situations where environmental concerns clash. Windmills, for example, offer a clean, endlessly renewable source of energy, but they blemish the natural landscape and can chop up migratory birds. Technology that replaces wood fibre with calcium carbonate in the production of paper saves trees, but mining it sometimes despoils bucolic areas.

Who Should Pay the Costs?

Studies of air pollution rules has shown that the costs of compliance are outweighed five to seven times by the economic benefits from reductions in hospitalization, emergency room visits, premature deaths, and lost workdays.[34] In addition, of course, money spent to minimize pollution benefits those paid to clean up or prevent the pollution. Indeed, restoring the environment could itself become a huge economic enterprise, a great source of jobs, profits, and poverty alleviation. Still, environmental protection and restoration do not come cheap, and determining who should pay the necessary costs raises a tough question of social justice. Two popular answers to this question currently circulate: that those responsible for causing the pollution ought to pay, and that those who stand to benefit from protection and restoration should pick up the tab.

Those Responsible The claim that those responsible for causing the pollution ought to pay the costs of pollution control and environmental restoration seems eminently fair until one asks a simple question. Just who is responsible for the pollution? Who are the polluters? Many people argue that big business is the chief polluter and therefore ought to bear the lion's share of the costs of environmental protection and restoration. Moreover, a policy of making polluters pick up the tab would probably have the desirable social effect of shifting income from the richer to the poorer and thus providing for a more equitable distribution of wealth. In the minds of some persons, the question of who should pay the bill is connected with the fair and just distribution of wealth.

Although business probably has benefited financially more than any other group from treating the environment as a free good, not all corporate wealth or even most of it has resulted directly from doing so. Moreover, consumers themselves have benefited enormously by not having to pay higher costs for products. In fact, some would argue that consumers are primarily to blame for pollution because they create the demand for the products whose production impairs the environment. Therefore, it is the consumer, not business, who should pay to protect and restore the environment. In this way, the argument goes, social costs are not unfairly passed on to those who have not incurred them.

However, both versions of the polluter-should-pay-the-bill thesis—one blaming big business, the other blaming consumers—largely ignore the manifold, deep-rooted causes of environmental degradation.

Two important causes of pollution in Canada have been the growing population in Canada and the United States and the increasing concentration of the population in both Canada and the States in large urban areas. In this connection, one must not forget that Canada and the United States share just over 8,000 kilometres of contiguous border and that about 75 percent of Canada's population lives within 150 kilometres of the American border. In 1900, the United States had a population of 76 million, while now, at the beginning of the twenty-first century, their population has nearly quadrupled to 300 million. Canada's population has more than quadrupled in the same period (from just over 5 million in 1901 to just over 30 million in 2001),[35] though in absolute numbers the Canadian population is ten times smaller than the American. But Canada, just like the United States, is increasingly an urbanized nation, and we are a long way from the rural, agriculturally oriented society we once were. According to the 2001 Census, 79.7 percent of the population lived in urban areas, concentrated in the Windsor–Quebec City Corridor, the Calgary–Edmonton Corridor, and the B.C. lower mainland. In fact, in Ontario and Quebec, the most populous and industrialized provinces, the urban population constituted 84 and 81 percent of the total population respectively.[36] This tremendous population growth and the consequent staggering level of urbanization—since the population growth has been almost exclusively within the confines of the large urban corridors—have brought with them an ever-increasing demand for goods and services, natural resources, energy, and industrial production. And these in turn have increased air, water, space, and noise pollution.

Another root cause of environmental problems is rising affluence. As people get more money to spend, they buy and consume more tangible goods, discard them more quickly, and produce more waste, all of which hasten degradation of the environment. In 2003 Canadians produce 383 kilograms of household waste per capita and the trend is upwards. Again in 2003 there were 20 million registered motor vehicles on the road and on farms and construction sites.[37] Our neighbours to the south produce almost twice as much garbage per person as we do,[38] while they own more than 221 million motor vehicles.[39] To make matters worse, there is a growing preference for big, gas-guzzling pickups, minivans, and sport-utility vehicles, which emit significantly more carbon dioxide (a principal cause of global warming) and nitrogen oxides (the main source of smog) than ordinary passenger cars do.

Thus, the enemy in the war against environmental abuse turns out to be all of us. No solution to the question of who should pay the costs of pollution control can ignore this fact.

Those Who Would Benefit A second popular reply to the payment problem is that those who will benefit from environmental improvement should pay the costs.

It's true that workers in certain industries and people living in certain neighbourhoods or regions benefit more than other people from environmental controls. The residents of the Windsor–Quebec City corridor, for instance, gain more from stringently enforced auto-emission standards than do those living in a remote corner of Manitoba. The trouble with this argument, though, is that every individual, rich or poor, and every institution, large or small, stands to profit in some way from environmental improvement, albeit not necessarily to the same degree. As a result, the claim that those who will benefit should pay the costs is not satisfactory, because everyone is touched by pollution. If, on the other hand, this position means that individuals and groups should pay to the degree that they will benefit, then one must wonder how this could possibly be determined. For example, changing the operation of the Glen Canyon Dam in the United States has raised electricity bills in the West, but it has reduced ecological damage to the Grand Canyon. Who benefits the most—local residents, visitors to the Grand Canyon, all who value this national resource—and how much should they pay? But perhaps the most serious objection to this thesis is that it seems to leave out responsibility as a legitimate criterion.

Any equitable solution to the problem of who should pay the bill of environmental cleanup should take into account responsibility as well as benefit. The preceding analysis suggests that we all share the blame for pollution and collectively stand to benefit from environmental improvement. This doesn't mean, however, that we can't pinpoint certain areas of industry as chronic polluters. Electric-power plants, for example, are one of the major sources of greenhouse gases, but not all plants are equally dirty. Rather, old coal-burning plants that have resisted modernization produce a disproportionate share of the pollution. Likewise, some companies can be singled out as having particularly distressing environmental records. Still, the point is that a fair and just program for assigning costs begins with a recognition that we all bear responsibility for environmental problems and that we all stand to benefit from correcting them. But even if we agree that it is only fair that everyone share the cost of environmental improvement, we can still wonder about how the bill ought to be paid. What would be the fairest and most effective way of handling those costs?

ACHIEVING OUR ENVIRONMENTAL GOALS

Without an environmentally informed citizenry making conscientious political, business, and consumer choices, it will prove impossible to reverse the degradation of our environment by halting pollution, stemming global warming, and reducing the utilization of natural resources to sustainable levels. Just as obviously, business and government must work together if we are to achieve our shared environmental goals. Government, in particular, has a crucial role to play by initiating programs that prod business into behaving in more environmentally responsible ways. That's easy to see. The more challenging moral and economic task is to determine fair and effective methods for doing so.

Three distinct approaches to environmental protection are the use of regulations, the use of incentives, and the use of pricing mechanisms. Although similar in some respects, they carry different assumptions about the roles of government and business, as well as about what's fair and just. Each approach has distinct advantages and weaknesses; each raises some questions of social justice.

Regulations

The regulatory approach makes use of direct public regulation and control in determining how the pollution bill is paid. Provincial and federal legislation and regulations formulated by agencies such as the Environmental Assessment and Approvals Branch (Ontario Ministry of the Environment) set environmental standards, which are then applied and enforced by those agencies, other regulatory bodies, and the courts. An emissions standard that, for example, prohibits industrial smokestacks from releasing more than a certain percentage of particulate matter would require plants exceeding that standard to comply with it by installing an appropriate pollution-control device.

A clear advantage to such a regulatory approach is that standards would be legally enforceable. Firms not meeting them could be fined or even shut down. Also, from the view of morality, such standards are fair in that they apply to all industries in the same way. There are, however, distinct disadvantages in this approach.

First, pollution statutes and regulations generally require polluters to use the strongest feasible means of pollution control. But that requires regulatory bodies to investigate pollution-control technologies and economic conditions in each industry to find the best technology that companies can afford. Such studies may require tens of thousands of pages of documentation, and legal proceedings may be necessary before the courts give final approval to the regulation. Moreover, expecting regulatory and monitoring agencies to master the economics and technology of dozens of industries, from petrochemicals to steel to electric utilities, may be unreasonable. They are bound to make mistakes, asking more from some companies than they can ultimately achieve while letting others off too lightly. Second, there's the question of both the equity and the economic sense of requiring compliance with universal standards, without regard for the idiosyncratic nature of each industry or the particular circumstances of individual firms. Is it reasonable to force two companies that cause very different amounts of environmental damage to spend the same amount on pollution abatement? In one U.S. case, the courts required two paper mills on the west coast to install expensive pollution-control equipment, even though their emissions were diluted effectively by the Pacific Ocean. It took a special act of the U.S. Congress to rescue the mills. Although universal environmental standards are fair in the sense that they apply to all equally, this very fact raises questions about their effectiveness. In attempting to legislate realistic and reliable standards for all, will government so dilute the standards that they become ineffectual? Regulation can also take away an industry's incentive to do more than the minimum required by law. No polluter has any incentive to discharge less muck than regulations allow. No entrepreneur has an incentive to devise technology that will bring pollution levels below the registered maximum. Moreover, firms have an incentive not to let regulatory agencies know that they are capable of polluting less. Under the regulatory approach, a government agency may have the desire to regulate pollution but lack the information to do it efficiently. The position of industry is reversed: it may have the information and the technology but not the desire to use it. Finally, there's the problem of displacement costs resulting from industrial relocation or shutdown due to environmental regulations. For example, in order to avoid meeting municipal or provincial environmental standards and regulations, companies may opt to relocate to another town or province or country where environmental requirements are less stringent. Consider also the marginal firms that would fail while attempting to meet the costs of such standards. One may well believe that marginal firms are already dying or that, in any case, they should get on with doing this, that and the other. Fine, but what about the economy of the small towns that depend on the operations of such firms?

On the other hand, if regulations are tougher for new entrants to an industry than for existing firms, as they often are, then new investment may be discouraged—even if newer plants would be cleaner than older ones. For example, a clause in the U.S. *Clean Air Act* exempts old coal-fired plants from complying with current emissions rules. As a result, much of America's electricity is produced by plants that are well over thirty years old and far dirtier than newer plants would be.[40] Perhaps at the time it was fair not to force existing plants into compliance with new rules. But is it still fair decades later? Clearly, then, a regulatory approach to environmental improvement, while having advantages, also raises serious questions.

Incentives

A widely supported approach to the problem of cost allocation for environmental improvement is government investment, subsidy, and general economic incentive. For instance, government might give firms a tax break for purchasing (and using) pollution-control equipment, or it might offer matching grants to companies that install such devices or it might even underwrite the costs of private corporations' developing or implementing environment-friendly technologies.[41] The U.S. Environmental Protection Agency (EPA) tried a novel approach in its "33/50 Program." It asked six hundred industrial facilities to reduce voluntarily their discharges of seventeen toxic contaminants, first by 33 percent, then by 50 percent. The incentive for firms to commit to the reductions was simply the public relations opportunities afforded by EPA press releases and outstanding performance awards—along with, perhaps, the firms' desire to stave off future regulatory action. By the time it ended, the Program had achieved its targets well in advance of the deadline.[42] The advantage of an incentive approach is that it minimizes government interference in business and encourages voluntary action rather than coercing compliance, as in the case of regulation. By allowing firms to move at their own pace, it avoids the evident unfairness to firms that cannot meet regulatory standards and must either relocate or fail. In addition, whereas regulated standards can encourage minimum legal compliance, an incentive approach provides an economic reason for going beyond minimal compliance. Firms have a financial inducement to do more than just meet the standards of regulatory agencies.

However, incentives are not without disadvantages which import moral issues. First, as an essentially voluntary device, an incentive program is likely to be slow. Environmental problems that cry out for a solution may continue to fester. Incentive programs may allow urgently needed action to be postponed. In addition, government incentive programs often amount to a subsidy for polluters, with polluting firms being paid not to pollute. Although this approach may sometimes address the economics of pollution more effectively than the regulatory approach, it nonetheless raises questions about the justice of benefiting not the victims of pollution but some of the egregious polluters. In addition, incentive programs are open to abuse, and determining their cost-effectiveness can be problematic. In particular, when it comes to tax incentives, unscrupulous firms may be able to distort the true costs of their anti-pollution expenditures when filing their tax returns.

Pricing Mechanisms

A third approach to the cost-allocation problem involves programs designed to charge firms for the amount of pollution they produce. This could take the form of pricing mechanisms, or effluent charges, which spell out the cost for a specific kind of pollution in a specific area at a specific time. The prices would vary from place to place and from time to time and would be tied to the amount of damage caused. For example, a firm or plant in the Golden Horseshoe region of Ontario, might pay much higher charges for discharging polluting emissions into the environment during the summer months than it would during the winter months. Whatever the set of prices, they would apply equally to every producer of a given type of pollution at the same time and place. The more a firm pollutes, the more it pays.

One advantage in this approach is that it places the cost of pollution control on the polluters. Pricing mechanisms or effluent charges would penalize, not compensate, industrial polluters. For many persons this is inherently fairer than a program that compensates polluters.

Also, because costs are internalized, firms would be encouraged to do more than meet the minimal requirements established under a strict regulatory policy. Under this approach a firm, in theory, could be charged for any amount of pollution and not just incur legal penalties whenever it exceeded a regulatory standard. In effect, pollution costs become production costs.

Pollution Permits Instead of imposing a tax or a fee on the pollutants released into the environment, the government could charge companies for pollution permits. Or it could auction off a limited number of permits. An even more market-oriented strategy is to give companies permits to discharge a limited amount of pollution and then to allow them to buy and sell the right to emit pollutants. With pollution permits, companies with low pollution levels can make money by selling their pollution rights to companies with poorer controls. Thus, each firm can estimate the relative costs of continuing to pollute as opposed to investing in cleaner procedures. The government can also set the precise amount of pollution it is prepared to allow and, by lowering the amount permitted over time, can reduce or even eliminate it.[43] Spurred by the Kyoto treaty on greenhouse gases a global market has emerged for trading carbon-emissions credits.[44] For both economic and scientific reasons, however, pricing mechanisms and pollution permits do not work well in all situations and for all environmental problems; dealing with mercury pollution is one example.[45] Still, economists generally favour using them wherever possible. However, they trouble many environmentalists. For one thing, the price tag for polluting seems arbitrary. How will effluent charges or permit prices be set? What is a fair price? Any decision seems bound to reflect debatable economic and value judgments. Moreover, environmentalists dislike the underlying principle of pricing mechanisms and pollution permits, viewing with suspicion anything that sounds like a "licence to pollute." They resent the implication that companies have a right to pollute and reject the notion that companies should be able to make money by selling that right to other firms. In fact, Michael J. Sandel, professor of government at Harvard, argues that it's immoral to buy the right to pollute. "Turning pollution into a commodity to be bought and sold removes the moral stigma that is properly associated with it," he says.[46] In sum, although each of these techniques—regulations, incentives, pricing mechanisms—has its advantages, none is without its weak points. Because there appears to be no single, ideal approach to all our environmental problems, a combination of regulation, incentive, effluent charges, and permits is probably called for. Any such combination must take into account not only effectiveness but also fairness to those who will have to foot the bill. Fairness in turn calls for input from all sectors of society, a deliberate commitment on the part of all parties to work in concert, a sizeable measure of good faith, and perhaps above all else a heightened sense of social justice. This is no mean challenge.

Still, environmental protection is not always a static tradeoff, with a fixed economic price to be paid for the gains we want. One reason is that higher environmental standards and properly designed regulatory programs can pressure corporations to invest capital in newer, state-of-the-art manufacturing technology; this both reduces pollution and enhances productive efficiency. In addition, international data in a range of industrial sectors show that innovation can minimize or even eliminate the costs of conforming to tougher environmental standards by increasing productivity, lowering total costs, and improving product quality.[47] The reason is that pollution is evidence of economic waste. The discharge of scrap, chemical wastes, toxic substances, or energy in the form of pollution is a sign that resources have been used inefficiently. For example, environmental regulations in the U.S. forced Dow Chemical to redesign the production process at its complex in California to avoid storing chemical waste in evaporation ponds. Not only did the new process reduce waste, but the company also found that it could reuse part of it as raw material in other parts of the plant. For a cost of $250,000 Dow is now saving $2.4 million each year.[48]

A broad array of economists, led by Nobel laureates Kenneth J. Arrow and Robert M. Solow, have urged that with regard to global warming, measures to reduce greenhouse gas emissions need not harm the economy and may in fact improve productivity in the long run. This is because many innovative, energy-efficient technologies are just waiting for the right financial incentives to enter the market.[49]

DELVING DEEPER INTO ENVIRONMENTAL ETHICS

So far, the discussion of environmental ethics has focused on business's obligation to understand its environmental responsibilities, to acknowledge and internalize its externalities (or spillovers), and to avoid free riding. It has stressed the extent to which environmental protection is in our collective self-interest, and it has looked at the operational and moral dilemmas involved in dealing with the costs of pollution.

The subject of environmental ethics can be pursued more deeply than this, and many moral theorists would advocate doing so. In particular, they would insist that we also consider our obligations to those who live outside our society. In proportion to their populations, many countries use an inordinately disproportionate amount of the globe's non-renewable resources. For example, the United States represents only 4.6 percent of the world's population but uses 30 percent of the world's refined oil. Tropical rain forests are of special concern. They are the earth's richest, oldest, and most complex ecosystems. Tropical forests are major reservoirs of biodiversity, home to 40 to 50 percent of all types of living things—as many as five million species of plants, animals, and insects. At least 20,200,000 hectares of tropical rain forest are destroyed each year, or 40.5 hectares every minute. And already half the globe's original rain forest has disappeared. Tropical forests are often cleared in an attempt to provide farms for growing Third World populations, but the affluence of people in

rich nations is responsible for much forest destruction. Central American forests are cleared in part for pasture land to make pet food and convenience food slightly cheaper in the United States. In Papua, New Guinea, forests are destroyed to supply cardboard packaging for Japanese electronic products. Thus, affluent persons in affluent nations thousands of miles away can cause more tropical forest destruction than a poor person living within the forest itself. The extravagant lifestyles of the more affluent nations, their dependence on foreign resources to satisfy their needs, and the impact of both on the resources and economies of other nations raise a variety of moral and political issues. This section mentions briefly just two of those problems.

First, there is the question of how the continued availability of foreign resources is to be secured. Will one nation's need for resources outside its territory lead it to dominate other lands, politically and economically, particularly in the Middle East, Asia, and Latin America? Leaving aside other problems with them, such projects of dominance are morally risky, because political and economic domination almost always involves violations of the rights and interests of the dominated population, as well as of the dominator's own moral ideals and values.

Second, there is the question of whether any nation has a right to consume the world's irreplaceable resources at a rate that is well out of proportion to the size of its population. Of course, nation A pays for its consumption of resources, like oil or wood or water, that other nations own, but in the view of many the fact that other nations acquiesce in nation A's disproportionate consumption of resources does not resolve the moral problem in A's doing so. Is A respecting the needs and interests of both its present co-inhabitants on this planet and the future generations who will live on Earth? This question is particularly burning now that scientists believe that human demand for natural resources has outstripped the biosphere's regenerative capacity.[50]

Obligations to Future Generations

Almost everybody feels intuitively that it would be wrong to empty the globe of resources and to irreparably contaminate the environment that we pass on to future generations. Certainly there is a danger that we will do both of these things. But the question of what moral obligations we have to future generations is surprisingly difficult, and discussion among philosophers has not resolved all the important theoretical issues.

Even though most of us agree that it would be immoral to make the world uninhabitable for future people, can we talk meaningfully of those future generations having a right that we not do this? After all, our remote descendants are not yet alive and thus cannot claim a right to a liveable environment. In fact, since these generations do not yet exist, they cannot be said, at present at any rate, to have any interests at all. How, then, can they have rights?

Professor of philosophy Joel Feinberg argues, however, that whatever future human beings turn out to be like, they will have interests that we can affect, for better or worse, right now. Even though we do not know who the future people will be, we do know that they will have interests and what the general nature of those interests will be. This is enough, he contends, both to talk coherently about their having rights and to impose a duty on us not to leave ecological time bombs for them.

Feinberg concedes that it doesn't make sense to talk about future people having a right to be born. The child that you could conceive tonight, if you felt like it, cannot intelligibly be said to have a right to be born. Thus, the rights of future generations are "contingent," says Feinberg, on those future people coming into existence. But this qualification does not affect his main contention: "The interests that [future people] are sure to have when they come into being . . . cry out for protection from invasions that can take place now."[51] Even if we are persuaded that future generations have rights, we still do not know exactly what those rights are or how they are to be balanced against the interests and rights of present people. If we substantially injure future generations to gain some small benefit for ourselves, we are being as selfish and short-sighted as we would be by hurting other people today for some slight advantage for ourselves. Normally, however, if the benefits of some environmental policy outweigh the costs, then a strong case can be made for adopting the policy. But what if it is the present generation that receives the benefits and future generations that pay the costs? Would it be unfair of us to adopt such a policy? Would doing so violate the rights of future people?

An additional puzzle is raised by the fact that policies we adopt will affect who is born in the future. Imagine that we must choose between two environmental policies, one of which would cause a slightly higher standard of living over the next century. Given the effects of those policies on the details of our lives, over time it would increasingly be true that people would marry different people under one policy than they would under the other. And even within the same marriages, children would increasingly be conceived at different times:

> Some of the people who are later born would owe their existence to our choice of one of the two policies. If we had chosen the other policy, these particular people would never have existed. And the proportion of those later born who owe their existence to our choice would, like ripples in a pool, steadily grow. We can plausibly assume that, after three centuries, there would be no one living in our community who would have been born whichever policy we chose.*

---

*Derek Parfit, *Reasons and Persons* (New York: Oxford University Press, 1986), 361. Parfit adds: "It may help to think about this question: How many of us could truly claim, 'Even if railways and motor cars had never been invented, I would still have been born'?"

This reasoning suggests that subsequent generations cannot complain about an environmental policy choice we make today that causes them to have fewer opportunities and a lower standard of living. If we had made a different choice, then those people would not have existed at all. On the other hand, it can be claimed that we act immorally in causing people to exist whose rights to equal opportunity and an equally high standard of living cannot be fulfilled. But if those future people knew the facts, would they regret that we acted as we did?[52] Perhaps it is mistaken to focus on the rights and interests of future people as individuals. Annette Baier argues that the important thing is to "recognize our obligations to consider the good of the continuing human community."[53] This stance suggests adopting a utilitarian perspective and seeking to maximize total human happiness through time. But a utilitarian approach is also not without problems. If our concern is with total happiness, we may be required to increase greatly the earth's population. Even if individuals on an overcrowded Earth do not have much happiness, there may still be more total happiness than there would be if we followed a population-control policy that resulted in fewer but better-off people. This distasteful conclusion has led some utilitarians to modify their theory and maintain that with regard to population policy we should aim for the highest average happiness rather than the highest total happiness. But this, too, is problematic because in theory one could, it seems, increase average happiness by eliminating unhappy people.

John Rawls has suggested another approach to the question of our obligations to future generations, an approach that reflects his general theory of justice (discussed in Chapter 3). He suggests that the members of each generation put themselves in the "original position." Then, without knowing what generation they belong to, they could decide what would be a just way of distributing resources between consecutive generations. They would have to balance how much they are willing to sacrifice for their descendants against how much they wish to inherit from their predecessors. In other words, the device of the original position and veil of ignorance might be used to determine our obligations to future generations—in particular, how much each generation should save for use by those who inherit the earth from it.[54]

The Value of Nature

A more radical approach to environmental ethics goes beyond the question of our obligations to future generations. It challenges the human-centred approach adopted so far. Implicit in the discussion has been the assumption that preservation of the environment is good solely because it is good for human beings. This reflects a characteristic human attitude that nature has no intrinsic value, that it has value only because people value it. If human nature was different and none of us cared about the beauty of, say, the Cape Breton coastline, then it would be without value.

Many writers on environmental issues do not recognize their anthropocentric, or human-oriented, bias. William F. Baxter is one who does. In discussing his approach to the pollution problem, Baxter mentions the fact that the use of DDT in food production is causing damage to the penguin population. He writes:

My criteria are oriented to people, not penguins. Damage to penguins, or sugar pines, or geological marvels is, without more, simply irrelevant . . . . Penguins are important because people enjoy seeing them walk about rocks . . . . In short, my observations about environmental problems will be people-oriented . . . . I have no interest in preserving penguins for their own sake . . . . I reject the proposition that we *ought* to respect the "balance of nature" or to "preserve the environment" unless the reason for doing so, express or implied, is the benefit of man.[55]

Contrast Baxter's position with what Holmes Rolston III calls the "naturalistic ethic." Advocates of a naturalistic ethic contend, contrary to Baxter's view, "that some natural objects, such as whooping cranes, are morally considerable in their own right, apart from human interests, or that some ecosystems, perhaps the Great Smokies, have intrinsic values, such as aesthetic beauty, from which we derive a duty to respect these landscapes."[56] Human beings may value a mountain for a variety of reasons—because they can hike it, build ski lifts on it, mine the ore deep inside it, or simply because they like looking at it. According to a naturalistic ethic, however, the value of the mountain is not simply a function of these human interests. Nature can have value in and of itself, apart from human beings.

Proponents of a naturalistic ethic contend that we have a particularly strong obligation to preserve species from extinction. Many environmentalists share this moral conviction, and it's easy to see why. Every year, three thousand animal and plant species disappear, and the rate of extinction is accelerating so rapidly that over the next hundred years or so the earth could lose half its species.[57] But do species really have value above and beyond the individuals that make them up? Scientists have formally identified 1.8 million species (including, for example, 6,700 kinds of starfish, 12,000 species of earthworm, and 400,000 types of beetle), and recent studies suggest that the number of species inhabiting the planet may be much, much higher—with perhaps as many as 30 million kinds of insects alone. Species are always coming into and going out of existence.[58] How valuable is this diversity of species, and how far are we morally required to go in maintaining it?

Adopting a naturalistic ethic would definitely alter our way of looking at nature and our understanding of our moral obligations to preserve and respect the natural environment. Many philosophers doubt, however, that nature has intrinsic value or that we can be said to have moral duties to nature. Having interests is a precondition, they would contend, of something's having rights or of our having moral duties to that thing. Natural objects, however, have no interests. Can a rock meaningfully be said to have an interest in not being eroded or in not being smashed into smaller pieces?

Plants and trees are different from rocks and streams. They are alive, and we can talk intelligibly about what is good or bad for a tree, plant, or vegetable. They can flourish or do poorly. Nonetheless, philosophers who discuss moral rights generally hold that this is not enough for plants to be said to have rights. To have rights, a thing must have genuine interests, and to have interests, most theorists contend, a thing must have beliefs and desires. Vegetative life, however, lacks any cognitive awareness. Claims to the contrary are biologically unsupportable.

Even if the plant world lacks rights, can it still have intrinsic value? Can we still have a moral obligation to respect that world and not abuse it? Or are the only morally relevant values the various interests of human beings and other sentient creatures? These are difficult questions. And there is no consensus among philosophers on how to answer them.

Our Treatment of Animals

Above a certain level of complexity, animals do have at least rudimentary cognitive awareness. No owner of a cat or dog doubts that his pet has beliefs and desires. Accordingly, a number of philosophers have recently defended the claim that animals can have rights. Because they have genuine interests, animals can have genuine moral rights—despite the fact that they cannot claim their rights, that they cannot speak, that we cannot reason with them, and that they themselves lack a moral sense. Animals, it is more and more widely contended, do not have to be equal to human beings to have certain moral rights that we must respect.

Rather than talking about animals' rights, utilitarians would stress that higher animals are sentient—that is, that they are capable of feeling pain. Accordingly, there can be no justifiable reason for excluding their pleasures and pains from the overall utilitarian calculus. As Jeremy Bentham, one of the founders of utilitarianism, put it: "The question is not, Can they *reason*? nor, Can they *talk*? but, Can they *suffer*?"[59] Our actions have effects on animals, and these consequences cannot be ignored. When one is deciding, then, what the morally right course of action is, the pleasures and pains of animals must also be taken into account.

Business affects the welfare of animals very substantially. One way is through experimentation and the testing of products on animals. Critics such as Peter Singer contend that the vast majority of experimentation and testing cannot be justified on moral grounds. Consider the "LD 50" test, which until recently was the standard method of testing new foodstuffs. The object of the test is to find the dosage level at which 50 percent of the test animals die. Nearly all test animals become very sick before finally succumbing or surviving. When the substance is harmless, huge doses must be forced down the animals, until in some cases the sheer volume kills them.[60] Utilitarians are in principle willing to permit testing and experimentation on animals, provided the overall results justify their pain and suffering. Not only is this proviso frequently ignored, but human beings typically disregard altogether the price the animals must pay. Consider the actions of the U.S. pharmaceutical firm Merck Sharp and Dohme, which sought to import chimpanzees to test a vaccine for hepatitis B. Chimps are an endangered species and highly intelligent. Capturing juvenile chimps requires shooting the mother. One analyst assessed the situation this way:

> The world has a growing population of 4 billion people and a dwindling population of some 50,000 chimpanzees. Since the vaccine seems unusually innocuous, and since the disease is only rarely fatal, it would perhaps be more just if the larger population could find some way of solving its problem that was not to the detriment of the smaller.[61]

Business's largest and most devastating impact on animals, however, is through the production of animal-related products—in particular, meat. Many of us still think of our chicken and beef as coming from something like the idyllic farms pictured in storybooks, where the animals roam contentedly and play with the farmer's children. But meat and egg production is big business, and a cruel business. In 2005 Canadian farmers produced 1.6 billion kilograms of beef, 1.2 billion kilograms of poultry meat, 588 million dozen eggs, and marketed approximately 31 million hogs. A third of the beef production is exported (mostly to the U.S.), a third of the hog production is exported to the United States, while 50 percent of our pork production is exported to over 80 countries. A swine barn in Saskatchewan costs $350–$370 per pig place.[62] In 2004–05 the beef, poultry and egg, and swine industries contributed about $25, $4, and $3 billion respectively to the Canadian economy. However impressive, these figures are small potatoes in comparison to the figures applicable to the American market. Every year in the United States ten billion birds and mammals are raised and killed for food.[63] There are 440 million laying hens. The sheer numbers and demand for efficiency in production have led producers to maintain animals in conditions that have often brought tears to the eyes of visitors.

The overwhelming majority (80 percent) of laying hens in the United States is housed in 3 percent of the known chicken farms (some farms house up to 2.5 million birds each). But the same conditions one finds in these mega-farms one will also find in the smaller Canadian concerns.[64] These birds live in small multi-tiered wire cages.[65] In these cages, hens are unable to satisfy such fundamental behavioural needs as stretching their wings, perching, walking, scratching, and nest building. Unsuited for wire cages, they suffer foot damage, feather loss, and other injuries. Birds are "debeaked" to prevent pecking injuries and cannibalism that occur typically due to overcrowding.[66]

Most of the hogs born each year in the United States or in Canada[67] spend their brief lives in intensive confinement where all aspects of their lives are strictly controlled. Piglets are weaned after only three weeks and placed in bare wire cages or tiny cement pens. Once they reach 50 pounds (about 23 kilograms), they are moved into bare six-foot (1.8 metre) stalls with concrete-slatted floors. Veal calves have even worse lives. To produce gourmet "milk-fed" veal, newborn calves are taken from their mothers and chained in crates measuring only 22 inches by 54 inches. Here they spend their entire lives. To prevent muscle development and speed weight gain, the calves are allowed absolutely no exercise; they are unable even to turn around or lie down. Their special diet of growth stimulators and antibiotics causes chronic diarrhea, and the withholding of iron to make their meat light-coloured makes them anemic. The calves are kept in total darkness to reduce restlessness.[68] The individuals involved in the meat and animal-products industries are not brutal, but the desire to cut business costs and to economize routinely leads to treatment of animals that can only be described as cruel. Philosopher and animal rights advocate Tom Regan describes their treatment this way:

> In increasing numbers, animals are being brought in off the land and raised indoors, in unnatural, crowded conditions—raised "intensively," to use the jargon of the animal industry . . . . The inhabitants of these "farms" are kept in cages, or stalls, or pens . . . living out their abbreviated lives in a technologically created and sustained environment: automated feeding, automated watering, automated light cycles, automated waste removal, automated what-not. And the crowding: as many as 9 hens in cages that measure 18 by 24 inches; veal calves confined to 22 inch wide stalls; hogs similarly confined, sometimes in tiers of cages, two, three, four rows high. Could any impartial, morally sensitive person view what goes on in a factory farm with benign approval?[69]

Moral vegetarians are people who reject the eating of meat on moral grounds. Their argument is simple and powerful: the raising of animals for meat, especially with modern factory farming, sacrifices the most important and basic interests of animals simply to satisfy human tastes. Would it be wrong to eat animals that were raised humanely, like those that run around freely and happily in children's picture books of farms? Unlike the lives of animals that we do in fact eat, the lives of such humanely raised animals, before being abruptly terminated, are not painful ones. Some philosophers would contend that it is permissible to raise animals for food if their lives are, on balance, positive. Other moral theorists challenge this view, contending that at least higher animals have a right to life and should not be killed.

This debate raises important philosophical issues; but it is also rather hypothetical. Given economic reality, mass production of meat at affordable prices dictates factory farming. The important moral issue, then, is the real suffering and unhappy lives that billions of creatures experience on the way to our dinner tables. This aspect of environmental ethics is often overlooked, but it raises profound and challenging questions for business and consumers alike.

There are hopeful signs that human attitudes toward animal suffering, in general, and factory farming, in particular, are changing. In Florida, for example, voters recently amended their state constitution so as to ban the confining of sows to cages so narrow that they cannot turn around. And McDonald's now requires its egg suppliers to provide each hen with a minimum of 72 square inches (464.5 square centimetres) of living space.[70] Other fast-food chains are following suit. For most American hens this is a 50 percent increase, but it falls well short of the European requirement that by 2012 all hens have at least 120 square inches as well as access to a perch and a nesting box to lay their eggs. In general, other countries are ahead of the United States with respect to their treatment of animals. In Britain now (and in the rest of Europe by 2007) it is illegal to treat pregnant sows or veal calves the way American companies do.[71] In New Zealand, one cannot experiment on great apes unless the research actually benefits the apes and this benefit outweighs their discomfort or suffering. And in 2002 the German constitution was changed to include the right of animals to be treated decently.[72]

SUMMARY

1. Business functions within a global ecological system. Because of the interrelated nature of ecosystems, and because intrusion into ecosystems frequently creates unfavourable effects, business must be sensitive to its impacts on the physical environment.

2. Traditionally, business has regarded the natural world as a free and unlimited good. Pollution and resource depletion are examples of situations in which each person's pursuit of self-interest can make everyone worse off (the "tragedy of the commons"). Business must be sensitive to possible disparities between its private economic costs and the social costs of its activities (the problem of externalities or spillovers).

3. Companies that attempt to be free riders in environmental matters or that refuse to address the external costs of their business activities behave unfairly. Some philosophers maintain, further, that each person has a human right to a liveable environment.

4. Pollution control has a price, and tradeoffs must be made. But weighing costs and benefits involves controversial factual assessments and value judgments. Any equitable solution to the problem of who should pay must recognize that all of us in some way contribute to the problem and benefit from correcting it.

5. Three methods for protecting the environment are regulations, incentives, and charges or permits for pollution. Each has advantages and disadvantages, but holding business to high environmental standards can push it to be more efficient and productive.

6. A broader view of environmental ethics considers our obligations to those in other societies and to future generations. Some philosophers argue that we must respect the right of future generations to inherit an environment that is not seriously damaged, but talk of the rights of future people raises puzzles.

7. Philosophers disagree about whether nature has intrinsic value. Some, adopting a human-oriented point of view, contend that the environment is valuable only because human beings value it. Those adopting a naturalistic ethic believe that the value of nature is not simply a function of human interests.

8. Through experimentation, testing, and the production of animal products, business has a very substantial impact on the welfare of animals. The meat and animal-products industries rely on factory-farming techniques, which many describe as cruel and horrible. Because of these conditions, moral vegetarians argue that meat eating is wrong.

CASE 11.1

Poverty and Pollution

It is called Brazil's "valley of death," and it may be the most polluted place on Earth. It lies about an hour's drive south of São Paulo, where the land suddenly drops 2,000 feet to a coastal plain. More than 100,000 people live in the valley, along with a variety of industrial plants that discharge thousands of tons of pollutants into the air every day. A reporter for *National Geographic* recalls that within an hour of his arrival in the valley, his chest began aching as the polluted air inflamed his bronchial tubes and restricted his breathing.[73] The air in the valley is loaded with toxins—among them benzene, a known carcinogen. One in ten of the area's factory workers has a low white-blood-cell count, a possible precursor to leukemia. Infant mortality is 10 percent higher here than in the region as a whole. Out of 40,000 urban residents in the valley municipality of Cubatão, nearly 13,000 cases of respiratory disease were reported in a recent year.

Few of the local inhabitants complain, however. For them, the fumes smell of jobs. They also distrust bids to buy their property by local industry, which wants to expand, as well as government efforts to relocate them to free home-sites on a landfill. One young mother says, "Yes, the children are often ill and sometimes can barely breathe. We want to live in another place, but we cannot afford to."

A university professor of public health, Dr. Oswaldo Campos, views the dirty air in Cubatão simply as the result of economic priorities. "Some say it is the price of progress," Campos comments, "but is it? Look who pays the price—the poor."[74] Maybe the poor do pay the price of pollution, but there are those who believe that they should have more of it. One of them is Lawrence Summers, who was chief economist of the World Bank and subsequently Secretary of the U.S. Treasury. He has argued that the bank should encourage the migration of dirty, polluting industries to the poorer, less-developed countries.[75] Why? First, Summers reasons, the costs of health-impairing pollution depend on the earnings forgone from increased injury and death. So polluting should be done in the countries with the lowest costs—that is, with the lowest wages. "The economic logic behind dumping a load of toxic waste in the lowest-wage country," he writes, "is impeccable."

Second, because pollution costs rise disproportionately as pollution increases, it makes sense to shift pollution from already dirty places such as Los Angeles to clean ones like the relatively underpopulated countries in Africa, whose air Summers describes as "vastly *under*-polluted." Third, people value a clean environment more as their incomes rise. If other things are equal, costs fall if pollution moves from affluent places to less affluent places.

Critics charge that Summers views the world through "the distorting prism of market economics" and that his ideas are "a recipe for ruin." Not only do the critics want

"greener" development in the Third World, but also they are outraged by Summers' assumption that the value of a life—or of increases or decreases in life expectancy—can be measured in terms of per capita income. This premise implies that an American's life is worth that of a hundred Kenyans and that society should value an extra year of life for a middle-level manager more than it values an extra year for a blue-collar, production-line worker.

Some economists, however, believe that Summers' ideas are basically on the right track. They emphasize that environmental policy always involves tradeoffs and that therefore we should seek a balance between costs and bene-fits. As a matter of fact, the greatest cause of misery in the Third World is poverty. If environmental controls slow growth, then fewer people will be lifted out of poverty by economic development. For this reason, they argue, the richer countries should not impose their standards of environmental protection on poorer nations.

But even if economic growth is the cure for poverty, other economists now believe that sound environmental policy is necessary for durable growth, or at least that growth and environmental protection may not be incompatible. First, environmental damage can undermine economic pro-ductivity, and the health effects of pollution on a country's workforce reduce output. Second, poverty itself is an important cause of environmental damage because people living at subsistence levels are unable to invest in environ-mental protection. Finally, if economic growth and develop-ment are defined broadly enough, then enhanced environmental quality is part and parcel of the improve-ment in welfare that development must bring. For example, 1 billion people in developing countries lack access to clean water while 1.7 billion suffer from inadequate sanitation. Economic development for them means improving their environment. Still, rich and poor countries tend to have different environmental concerns: Environmentalists in affluent nations worry about protecting endangered species, preserving biological diversity, saving the ozone, and pre-venting climate change, whereas their counterparts in poorer countries are more concerned with dirty air, dirty water, soil erosion, and deforestation.

UPDATE

According to a World Bank report, environmental condi-tions have improved in Cubatão, where, thanks to state action and an aroused population, pollution is no worse today than in other medium-sized industrial cities in Brazil. True, it's no paradise, but some days you can see the sun, children are healthier, and fish are returning to the river (though their tissues are laced with toxic metals).[76]

Discussion Questions

1. What attitudes and values on the part of business and others lead to the creation of areas like the "valley of death"?

2. Should the Third World have more pollution, as Lawrence Summers argues? Assess his argument that dirty industries should move to poorer and less-polluted areas.

3. Some say, "Pollution is the price of progress." Is this assertion correct? What is meant by "progress"? Who in fact pays the price? Explain both the moral and economic issues raised by the assertion. What are the connections between economic progress and development, on one hand, and pollution controls and environmental protection, on the other?

4. Do human beings have a moral right to a liveable environment? To a non-polluted environment? It might be argued that if people in the "valley of death" don't complain and don't wish to move, then they accept the risks of living there and the polluters are not violating their rights. Assess this argument.

5. Assess the argument that people in the Third World should learn from the errors of the West and seek development without pollution. Should there be uniform, global environmental standards, or should pollution-control standards be lower for less-developed countries?

CASE 11.2

Hamilton's Plastimet Fire[77]

On July 9, 1997 at 7:42 p.m. a call came through to the Hamilton Fire Department that a fire had broken out at the Plastimet Inc. recycling plant on Wellington St. North. When the firefighters arrived at the site two minutes later, the whole building was engulfed in flames which were giving off a huge plume of black, acrid smoke (visible even from the city of Guelph, 40 kilometres away) and depositing a black, gummy soot on the surrounding area. After pumping 22 million gallons of water on it, the firefighters finally put the fire out three days later (on July 12).

Hamilton, Ontario, is an industrialized city in the southwest corner of Lake Ontario with just over half-a-million inhabitants who are highly stratified in terms of class and occupation. The area of the city where the Plastimet plant was located is part of the North End, a large tract of land adjacent to the Hamilton harbour, which has remained as Hamilton's industrial zone ever since it was first developed in the mid-nineteenth century. Despite the presence in it of steel mills and associated industries, shipping yards, warehouses and recycling facilities, the North End is home (and was at the time of the fire) to about 3,000 people who are, by and large, socially and economically disadvantaged.

The Plastimet warehouse contained 400 tonnes of polyvinyl chloride (PVC) and other recyclable plastics. Under normal circumstances, these plastics present no danger to animal or vegetative life. When they burn, however, they release (at least) such substances as hydrogen chloride, carbon monoxide, oxides of nitrogen, heavy metals, vinyl chloride, benzene, polycyclic aromatic hydrocarbons, dioxin, and furans, all of which are highly toxic. For example, hydrogen chloride is transformed into hydrochloric acid once it comes into contact with water moisture

(for example, air, moisture on the skin and in the lungs, the water used to put out the fire). Dioxins and vinyl chloride are known to cause cancer, while furans are suspected of being carcinogenic.

Soon after the fire started, officials became concerned about the heavy smoke and prepared to evacuate the nearby Hamilton General Hospital and the Hamilton-Wentworth Detention Centre (or Barton Street jail). However, no evacuation took place.

While the fire was still going strong after nearly 48 hours (on July 11), officials started voluntary evacuation of the neighbourhood. Only 650 people were evacuated. On July 12, the fire was finally extinguished and the 650 people evacuated the day before were allowed to return to their homes. However, fearful of the presence of dioxins, official told people in the neighbourhood not to eat produce from their gardens. Six days later (July 18), officials warned *all* Hamiltonians not to eat produce from their gardens if there was evidence of soot on it. This ban was lifted a week later.

The Ontario Ministry of the Environment and Energy (MOEE) issued a report (available at www.ene.gov.on.ca/envision/techdocs/3598e.pdf) on the fire in October 1997. The report shows that higher than normal levels of almost all toxic chemicals mentioned were found, during the fire, in air, soil, and water samples taken from various places around the plant. Independent tests also showed very high levels of toxic substances in the air during the fire. Various tests also showed that once the fire was put out, the levels of these contaminants dropped to normal urban levels. The MOEE report indicates that there was widespread experience (especially by firefighters and police officers) of short-term ill effects such as headaches, eye and throat irritation, nausea, and sleep disorders, but concluded that long-term, serious effects (for example, chronic respiratory illness, reproductive anomalies or cancer) were unlikely to occur because of the shortness of exposure to high levels of toxins. This conclusion may or may not be right, but it certainly has done nothing to alleviate peoples' fears, especially since, six and a half years after the event, Captain Bob Shaw of the Hamilton Fire Department, who spent two days in the thick of the fire, died following a short battle with esophageal cancer.

At the time of the fire, the Plastimet facility had four fire code violations (apparently including lack of a sprinkler system) still outstanding since they had been identified (along with seven others) in October 1996. The site itself had a known history of metal contamination as a result of the past operations of a scrap metal company called Usarco that had gone into receivership in 1990. The owner of Usarco (and owner of the site Plastimet was renting for its operations) had a long history of environmental violations. Plastimet Inc. had set up operations in the abandoned building in 1995 without bothering to get a business licence from the City of Hamilton. Further, Plastimet did not need an MOEE certificate of approval for the plastics recycling operation. The Ontario Premier at the time, Mike Harris, suggested initially that a public inquiry into the fire might be necessary, but he changed his mind a few days later, and the province of Ontario has rejected a probe ever since, claiming that there is no evidence of wrongdoing on the part of the government.

UPDATE

The recent (August 10, 2008) explosion of propane containers at the Sunrise Propane depot in Downsview (in northwest Toronto), which resulted in two deaths and the evacuation of 12,500 nearby residents, raises dramatically the question of whether we (business, citizens, and especially government) have learned any lessons at all in the decade since the tragedy of the Plastimet fire.

Discussion Questions

1. Do you agree with the government of Ontario's position that there was no need to have a public inquiry into the Plastimet fire? In your view, does evidence for or against government wrongdoing make any difference to appointing a commission of public inquiry?

2. Look into the Province of Ontario's (or your own province's) legislation and regulations regarding public safety standards (as regards recycling operations) before and after the Plastimet fire, and assess whether they adequately protect public safety. Suggest ways of revising existing statues and regulation to improve safety. Beware that one should try to balance concerns over safety with concerns about freedom.

3. Do you think that self-regulation by the recycling industry itself (as opposed to government legislation) might best protect public safety? Explain fully your position.

CASE 11.3

Protecting Ontario's Boreal Forest

The Canadian boreal forest occupies 35 percent of Canada's total land area and represents 77 percent of Canada's total forested land, stretching from the Yukon to Newfoundland and Labrador in a wide band of hundreds of kilometres between the northern tundra and the southern grassland and mixed hardwood forests. It is part of the great chain of boreal forests one finds below the Arctic Circle also in Alaska, Russia, and the Scandinavian countries.

The Ontario boreal forest makes up about 43 percent of the province's landmass of 1.1 million square kilometres. There are two types of boreal forest in Ontario. The *southern boreal* forest ranges from north of the Great Lakes up to just below the 51st parallel. This part of the forest is already developed with extensive road networks, cities and towns, and industrial infrastructure, including lumber mills, mines and hydroelectric dams. Just north of the 51st parallel starts the great expanse of Ontario's *northern boreal* forest, one of

the last undeveloped spaces on the planet and a vital contributor to global and Canadian environmental health. It stores 97 billion tonnes of carbon dioxide, while it absorbs 12.5 million tonnes of carbon dioxide a year, contributing thus to the control of warming trends in the global climate. The extensive peat and wetlands of the boreal region act like a giant system of sponges, absorbing and filtering water and releasing it slowly into the surrounding landscape. This results in protection from flooding, cleaner water and higher water tables. It is also one of the world's largest intact ecosystems. The northern boreal region contains more than 200 sensitive species of animals—including polar bears, wolverines and caribou—as well as many species of migratory birds (250 million birds breed here annually). The region is home to about 24,000 people living in 36 communities. Most of these people are First Nations, living in remote communities far beyond the end of Ontario's road and infrastructure network. The northern boreal forest has been either officially or practically off limits to most industrial development—until recently.

Development is quickly shifting north, as the resources of the southern forest become depleted and greater demand puts pressure on companies to find new supplies. Such development could bring with it extinction for species at risk and massive destruction of songbird habitat. There are already 4,400 mineral claims staked in the north and plans for roads, hydro transmission lines, logging, and open pit mines.

Anticipating the inevitable development and exploitation of Ontario's northern forests and under pressure from various conservation groups, Ontario Premier Dalton McGuinty announced, on July 14, 2008, the biggest natural conservation project in Canadian history (see *The Globe and Mail*, July 15, 2008, A4): the government of Ontario will extend permanent protection to at least 225,000 square kilometres of the Far North Boreal region (that is, north of the 51st parallel) under its Far North Planning Initiative. Mining and logging will be permitted in the protected area, but only under stricter regulations and providing that local Aboriginal communities approve.

Ontario's Far North Planning Initiative and the promise to protect half of the northern boreal forest sounds great for the environment, the animals, plants, and First Nations inhabitants of the region. However, the proof of the pudding—especially when it is political—is in the eating. There are at least four sorts of considerations that might give pause to a committed conservationist.

First, the announcement is a promise to be fulfilled in the future. The Far North Planning Initiative is envisaged to be fully effected by 2015, while in the meantime the government will undertake land use planning exercises to decide what parts of the forest will be protected and how and where resource exploitation will take place. The timeframe of the implementation of the initiative seems rather long for an enterprise some parts of which are so time-sensitive (for example, species at risk of extinction).

Second, whether the protection is given by legislative act or by legal agreement among various interested parties, the forestry and mining industries will no doubt represent their interests forcefully. The forestry industry has already expressed its fears on how the initiative on the northern forest might affect existing arrangements—beneficial to the industry—in the southern forest!

Third, what will be eventually the extent and authority of the assent on the part of the First Nations communities which will presumably be required to approve resource development in the area?

Finally, a crucial element in any project to protect nature lies in the concepts and principles informing the protection and in the various regulations and procedures used to implement it in fact. The announcement has already suggested that the general principle informing the project is not one that subordinates human interests to the health and diversity of the natural environment, but one that will try to balance ecological concerns with human interests of various kinds. Under the circumstances, it is especially important to decide carefully which particular ecological variables (and the method used to select them) are to be "balanced" against which human needs or interests.

Discussion Questions (and a Project)

1. Do you think that Premier McGuinty's proposal is a good one? Explain fully your answer.

2. The Premier's proposal suggests that the general principle informing the conservation project is not one that subordinates human interests to the health and diversity of the natural environment, but one that will try to balance ecological concerns with human interests of various kinds. Do you think that this is a valid principle to proceed on? Explain fully your answer.

3. On the basis of what has happened to the southern portion of the boreal forest, explain what are the dangers to the northern portion? Explain why the "dangers" are indeed dangers. (That is, what are their adverse effects and on what aspect of the human and non-human environment?)

4. *Project.* Suppose that you are a committed environmentalist or conservationist who has been given the task of writing a report to the Ontario premier in which you outline your own plan of action for protecting the designated area of the boreal forest. In doing the research for your report, make sure that you consult: the government's own public/press releases and backgrounders to the announcement by Premier McGuinty; similar projects by other governments (for example, British Columbia's *Muskwa-Kechika Management Area Act* [1998]); publications or the websites of various conservation groups (Greenpeace, Ontario Nature); publications or the websites of the mining and forestry industries; studies on ecology-based conservation area management (see, for example, Robert P. Allen, *Coastal Information Team: Review Report*, 8–24, at www.citbc.org/c-citreview-jan05.pdf; or reports on the Muskwa-Kechika Management Area of British Columbia); publications or websites of Aboriginal groups, including the National Aboriginal Forestry Association.

Notes to Chapter 11

1. See *Millennium Ecosystem Assessment Synthesis Report* (March 2005), available at www.millenniumassessment.org. See also Eugene Linden, "Critical Condition," *Time* (Special Edition), April/May 2000, 19, 20.

2. Tom Regan, ed., *Earthbound: Introductory Essays in Environmental Ethics* (New York: Random House, 1984), 3.

3. See Statistics Canada, "Human Activity and the Environment, 2000," pp. 99, 202–203. Also John Wargo, *Our Children's Toxic Legacy: How Science and Law Fail to Protect Us from Pesticides* (New Haven, CT: Yale University Press, 1996); and "Group Names Most Contaminated Produce," *New York Times*, October 21, 2003, A18.

4. "From *Silent Spring* to Barren Spring?," *Business Week*, March 18, 1996, 42.

5. See Robin Walker and Gideon Forman, "Why Doctors Support Banning Pesticides," City Editorial in *Ottawa Citizen*, April 13, 2005; Anne Steinemann, "Human Exposure, Health Hazards, and Environmental Regulation," *Environmental Impact Assessment Review* 24 (2004): 695–710; also "Kids Need More Protection from Chemicals," *Los Angeles Times*, January 28, 1999, B9; and "Does It Pay to Buy Organic?," *Business Week*, September 6, 2004, 102.

6. For details, consult "Toxic America," *San Francisco Chronicle*, March 28, 2004, E1. See also Florence Williams, "Toxic Breast Milk?," *New York Times Magazine*, January 9, 2005, 21.

7. *Science*, July 15, 2005; see also Danielle Knight, "Canada: Arctic Pollution Linked to Industrial Plants and Incinerators" at www.corpwatch.org/article.php?id=510, October 3, 2000.

8. "Study Reveals How Much Industry Pollutes the Air," *San Francisco Chronicle*, March 23, 1989, A1; *New York Times 2005 Almanac* (New York: Penguin, 2005), 774; and "Toxic Release Increased in 2002, Study Says," *Wall Street Journal*, June 23, 2004.

9. A group of 30 industrialized countries, including most of the members of the European Union, Canada, the United States, Mexico, Japan, Korea, Australia, and New Zealand.

10. See David R. Boyd, "Canada vs. the OECD: An Environmental Comparison," 2001, a publication of the Eco-Research Chair of Environmental Law and Policy at the University of Victoria, 2, www.environmentalindicators.com/htdocs/PDF/Pgs1-10.pdf.

11. "Major Study Links Smoggy Days to More Deaths in 95 Urban Areas," *San Jose Mercury News*, November 17, 2004, 10A.

12. "Heavy Smog Cuts Teens' Lung Capacity," *San Francisco Chronicle*, September 9, 2004, A6.

13. "Study Links Soot to Heart Disease," *Wall Street Journal*, December 16, 2003, D7; and "Air Pollution a Risk in Heart Disease," *San Francisco Chronicle*, June 2, 2004, A4.

14. "Study Links Air Pollution, Heart Defects in Newborns," *San Jose Mercury News*, December 31, 2002, 17A.

15. Environment Canada, National Environmental Indicator Series 2003 at www.ec.gc.ca/soer-ree/English/Indicator_series/default.cfm under "Urban Air Quality." See also American Lung Association, "State of the Air 2005," available at www.lungusa.org.

16. For further discussion, see "Special Report: Global Warming," *Business Week*, August 16, 2004, 60–69, and "The Pentagon's Weather Nightmare," *Fortune*, February 9, 2004, 101–107.

17. J. Alan Pounds and Robert Puschendorf, "Ecology: Clouded Futures," *Nature* 427 (January 8, 2004): 107–109; and Chris D. Thomas et al., "Extinction Risk from Climate Change," *Nature* 427 (January 8, 2004): 145–148.

18. See www.statcan.ca/English/freepub/16F0025XIB/m/manure.htm.

19. Ken Silverstein, "Meat Factories," *Sierra*, January/February 1999. See also "Group's Surprising Beef with Meat Industry," *San Francisco Chronicle*, April 27, 1999, A1; "Big Farms Making a Mess of U.S. Waters, Cities Say," *New York Times*, February 10, 2002, sec. 1, 20; and "Hogging the Air," *Mother Jones*, July/August 2004, 20.

20. Canadians will not soon forget the Walkerton, Ontario, drinking water tragedy.

21. "U.S. Response to Air Pollution at Animal Farms Is Criticized," *Wall Street Journal*, December 18, 2002, B4; and "Huge Farm Cesspools Blamed for Noxious Clouds," *San Jose Mercury News*, May 11, 003, 9A.

22. See the report by the OECD's Nuclear Energy Agency, "Chernobyl: Assessment of Radiological and Health Impact 2002," 81–98, available at www.nea.fr.

23. See the Ontario Ministry of Energy website.

24. "The Dead Zone," *Economist*, August 24, 2002, 26.

25. "*Playboy* Interview: Dr. Paul Ehrlich," *Playboy*, August 1970, 56.

26. John Steinbeck, *America and Americans* (New York: Viking Press, 1966), 127.

27. Garrett Hardin, "The Tragedy of the Commons," *Science* 162 (December 13, 1968): 1243–1248.

28. "Heading for the Final Filet," *Economist*, October 2, 2004, 83. See also "Scientists Warn Fewer Kinds of Fish Are Swimming the Oceans," *New York Times*, July 29, 2005, A6.

29. Jonathan Rowe, "Accounting for the Commons," *Business Ethics*, Winter 2003, 4.

30. William T. Blackstone, "Ethics and Ecology," in William T. Blackstone, ed., *Philosophy and Environmental Crisis* (Athens: University of Georgia, 1974).

31. Sharon Begley, "Furry Math? Market Has Failed to Capture the True Value of Nature," *Wall Street Journal*, August 9, 2002, B1. See also "Are You Being Served?," *Economist*, April 23, 2005, 76–78.

32. Begley, "Furry Math?"

33. "Would You Pay More to Let Nature Thrive?," *San Jose Mercury News*, October 4, 1994, 1A. For the doubts of an economist, see Amartya Sen, "The Discipline of Cost–Benefit Analysis," *Journal of Legal Studies* 29 (June 2000): 946–950.

34. "Clean-Air Rules Worth It, Says White House Study," *San Jose Mercury News*, September 27, 2003, 7A.

35. See www.statcan.ca/english/freepub/16-201-XIE/0000516-201-XIE.pdf, Table B.1, p. 41.

36. See www.statcan.ca/english/freepub/16-201-XIE/0000516-201-XIE.pdf, Table B.6, p. 45.

37. See www.statcan.ca/english/freepub/16-201-XIE/0000516-201-XIE.pdf, Table 1.2, p. 2; Table B.14, p. 53.

38. *Business Horizons* 39 (January/February 1996): 67; *Time* (Special Edition), 87; and "Waste Not," *San Francisco Chronicle*, July 9, 2000, "Sunday," 1.

39. U.S. Census Bureau, *Statistical Abstract of the United States 2004–5* (Washington, DC: U.S. Government Printing Office, 2004), Table 1065.

40. Environmental Enemy No. 1," *Economist*, July 6, 2002, 11. See also "Dirty Secret: Coal Plants Could Be Much Cleaner," *New York Times*, May 22, 2005, sec. 3, 1.

41. See Western Economic Diversification Canada, "Implementing the Recommendations: Fiscal Incentives" at www.wd.gc.ca/innovation/etf/2005rpt/6a_e.asp; see also the U.S. "FutureGen" project at www.fossil.energy.gov/programs/powersystems/futuregen.

42. See www.epa.gov/oppt/3350.

43. The EPA in the United States successfully experimented with this strategy in the 1970s when it gave oil refineries two years to reduce lead content in gasoline. Refineries received quotas on lead, which they could then trade with one another. The same approach was adopted later in the *Clean Air Act* Amendments (1990) with respect to the sulfur dioxide (SO_2) emissions of electric utilities. See "How Many Planets? A Survey of the Global Environment," *Economist*, July 6, 2002, 16.

44. "A Green Future," *Economist*, September 11, 2004, 69; and "Welcome to Kyoto-Land," *Economist*, October 9, 2004, 57.

45. Paul Krugman, "The Mercury Scandal," *New York Times*, April 6, 2004 (online). See also "On the Air," *New Yorker*, May 3, 2004, 33.

46. Michael J. Sandel, "It's Immoral to Buy the Right to Pollute," *New York Times*, December 15, 1997, A19.

47. Michael E. Porter and Claas van der Linde, "Green and Competitive: Ending the Stalemate," *Harvard Business Review* 73 (September/October 1995): 120, 122, 125; and Mark Hertsgaard, "A Global Green Deal," *Time* (Special Edition), 82–83.

48. Porter and van der Linde, "Green and Competitive," 125–126, 128–129.

49. "Yes, Global Warming," *International Herald Tribune*, February 2, 1997, 8; and Hertsgaard, "A Global Green Deal," 82–83.

50. Mathis Wackernagel et al., "Tracking the Ecological Overshoot of the Human Economy," *Proceedings of the National Academy of Sciences* 99 (June 27, 2002): 9266.

51. Joel Feinberg, "The Rights of Animals and Unborn Generations," in Tom L. Beauchamp and Norman E. Bowie, eds., *Ethical Theory and Business*, 2nd ed. (Englewood Cliffs, NJ: Prentice Hall, 1983), 435.

52. Derek Parfit, *Reasons and Persons* (New York: Oxford University Press, 1986), 365.

53. Annette Baier, "The Rights of Past and Future Persons," in Joseph R. DesJardins and John J. McCall, eds., *Contemporary Issues in Business Ethics* (Belmont, CA: Wadsworth, 1985), 501; and Robert Elliot, "The Rights of Future People," *Journal of Applied Philosophy* 6 (1989).

54. See John Rawls, *A Theory of Justice*, rev. ed. (Cambridge, MA: Harvard University Press, 1999), 251–258.

55. William F. Baxter, *People or Penguins: The Case for Optimal Pollution* (New York: Columbia University Press, 1974), ch. 1.

56. Holmes Rolston III, "Just Environmental Business," in Tom Regan, ed., *Just Business: New Introductory Essays in Business Ethics* (New York: Random House, 1984), 325.

57. Steven M. Meyer, "End of the Wild," *Boston Review*, April/May 2004, 20.

58. See W. Wayt Gibbs, "On the Termination of Species," *Scientific American*, November 2001.

59. Jeremy Bentham, *An Introduction to the Principles of Morals and Legislation* (1789), ch. 17, sec. 2.

60. Peter Singer, "Animal Liberation," *New York Review of Books*, April 5, 1973.

61. Quoted by Rolston, "Just Environmental Business," 340.

62. See www.cattle.ca/factsheets/beefindustry.pdf, www.statcan.ca/english/freepub/23-015-XIE/23-015-XIE2006004.pdf (poultry), and www.statcan.ca/english/freepub/23-010-XIE/23-010-XIE2007002.pdf (hog).

63. Peter Singer, "Animal Liberation at 30," *New York Review of Books*, May 15, 2003, 25.

64. See Canadian Federation of Humane Societies at www.cfhs.ca/farm/battery_cages.

65. Tom L. Beauchamp, *Case Studies in Business, Society, and Ethics* (Englewood Cliffs, NJ: Prentice Hall, 1983), 118–119.

66. Bradley S. Miller, "The Dangers of Factory Farming," *Business and Society Review* 65 (Spring 1988): 44; and "What Humans Owe to Animals," *Economist*, August 19, 1995, 11.

67. See Canadian Federation of Humane Societies at www.cfhs.ca/farm/farming_in_canada.

68. Miller, "The Dangers of Factory Farming," 43, 44. For references, see n. 66 above.

69. Tom Regan, "Ethical Vegetarianism and Commercial Animal Farming," in Richard A. Wasserstrom, ed., *Today's Moral Problems*, 3rd ed. (New York: Macmillan, 1985), 463–464. See also "Also a Part of Creation," *Economist*, August 19, 1995, 19.

70. See Peter Singer, "Animal Liberation at 30," 26. For references, see n. 63 above.

71. Ibid.

72. "Animal Attraction," *Economist*, February 15, 2003, 75.

73. See Noel Grove, "Air: An Atmosphere of Uncertainty," *National Geographic*, April 1987.

74. Ibid.

75. The following paragraphs are based on "Let Them Eat Pollution," *Economist*, February 8, 1992, 66; "Pollution and the Poor," *Economist*, February 15, 1992, 18; "Economics Brief: A Greener Bank," *Economist*, May 23, 1992, 79; and "A Great Leap Forward," *Economist*, May 11, 2002.

76. David R. Wheeler, *Greening Industry* (New York: Oxford University Press, 1999), ch. 5.

77. Sources: *The Hamilton Spectator*, July 11–19, 1997; July 9, 2007; *Recycling Today Magazine* at www.recyclingtoday.com/news/news.asp?ID=7306&SubCatID=43&CatID=1; Cliff Holland and Charles Ross, "Plastimet Fire in Hamilton Left Toxic Residues and Unanswered Questions" at www.esemag.com/0997/fire.html; *McMaster Chemical Extracts*, 1, September 1998, at www.chemistry.mcmaster.ca/extracts/extracts98/plastimet_fire/plastimet_fire.htm; and Cheryl Lousley, "The Hamilton Plastimet Fire," *Journal of Social and Political Thought*, 1.1, at www.yorku.ca/jspot/1/lousley.htm.

The Place of Nonhumans in Environmental Issues

Peter Singer

Peter Singer's writings have catalyzed the debate over our treatment of animals. In the following essay, he argues that the effects of our environmental actions on nonhumans should figure directly in our deliberations about what we ought to do. Because animals can feel pleasure and pain and have the capacity for subjective experience, they can therefore be said to have interests, interests we must not ignore. Singer contends that we must extend the moral principle of "equal consideration of interests" to include the interests of non-humans, and he sketches the implications of our doing so—including the necessity of abandoning our present practice of rearing and killing other animals for food.

I. HUMANS AND NONHUMANS

When we humans change the environment in which we live, we often harm ourselves. If we discharge cadmium into a bay and eat shellfish from that bay, we become ill and may die. When our industries and automobiles pour noxious fumes into the atmosphere, we find a displeasing smell in the air, the long-term results of which may be every bit as deadly as cadmium poisoning. The harm that humans do the environment, however, does not rebound solely, or even chiefly, on humans. It is nonhumans who bear the most direct burden of human interference with nature.

By "nonhumans" I mean to refer to all living things other than human beings, though for reasons to be given later, it is with nonhuman animals, rather than plants, that I am chiefly concerned. It is also important, in the context of environmental issues, to note that living things may be regarded either collectively or as individuals. In debates about the environment the most important way of regarding living things collectively has been to regard them as species. Thus, when environmentalists worry about the future of the blue whale, they usually are thinking of the blue whale as a species, rather than of individual blue whales. But this is not, of course, the only way in which one can think of blue whales, or other animals, and one of the topics I shall discuss is whether we should be concerned about what we are doing to the environment primarily insofar as it

threatens entire species of nonhumans, or primarily insofar as it affects individual nonhuman animals.

The general question, then, is how the effects of our actions on the environment of nonhuman beings should figure in our deliberations about what we ought to do. There is an unlimited variety of contexts in which this issue could arise. To take just one: Suppose that it is considered necessary to build a new power station, and there are two sites, A and B, under consideration. In most respects the sites are equally suitable, but building the power station on site A would be more expensive because the greater depth of shifting soil at that site will require deeper foundations; on the other hand, to build on site B will destroy a favored breeding ground for thousands of wildfowl. Should the presence of the wildfowl enter into the decision as to where to build? And if so, in what manner should it enter, and how heavily should it weigh?

In a case like this the effects of our actions on nonhuman animals could be taken into account in two quite different ways: directly, giving the lives and welfare of nonhuman animals an intrinsic significance which must count in any moral calculation; or indirectly, so that the effects of our actions on nonhumans are morally significant only if they have consequences for humans . . . .

II. SPECIESISM

The view that the effects of our actions on other animals have no direct moral significance is not as likely to be openly advocated today as it was in the past; yet it is likely to be accepted implicitly and acted upon. When planners perform cost–benefit studies on new projects, the costs and benefits are costs and benefits for human beings only. This does not mean that the impact of [a] power station or highway on wildlife is ignored altogether, but it is included only indirectly. That a new reservoir would drown a valley teeming with wildlife is taken into account only under some such heading as the value of the facilities for recreation that the valley affords. In calculating this value, the cost–benefit study will be neutral between forms of recreation like hunting and shooting and those like bird watching and bush walking—in fact hunting and shooting are likely to contribute more to the benefit side of the calculations because larger sums of money are spent on them, and they therefore benefit manufacturers and retailers of firearms as well as the hunters and shooters themselves. The suffering experienced by the animals whose habitat is flooded is not reckoned into the costs of the operation; nor is the recreational value obtained by the hunters and shooters offset by the cost to the animals that their recreation involves.

Despite its venerable origin, the view that the effects of our actions on nonhuman animals have no intrinsic moral significance can be shown to be arbitrary and morally indefensible. If a being suffers, the fact that it is not a member of our own species cannot be a moral reason for failing to take its suffering into account. This becomes obvious if we consider the analogous attempt by white

The first five sections of this essay are reprinted from Peter Singer, "Not for Humans Only: The Place of Nonhumans in Environmental Ethics," in K. E. Goodpaster and K. M. Sayre, eds., *Ethics and Problems of the 21st Century* (Notre Dame, IN: University of Notre Dame Press, 1979). Reprinted by permission. The final section is reprinted by permission from Peter Singer, "All Animals Are Equal," *Philosophic Exchange* 1, no. 5 (Summer 1974). © 1974 The Center for Philosophic Exchange. (Section headings have been added.)

slaveowners to deny consideration to the interests of blacks. These white racists limited their moral concern to their own race, so the suffering of a black did not have the same moral significance as the suffering of a white. We now recognize that in doing so they were making an arbitrary distinction, and that the existence of suffering, rather than the race of the sufferer, is what is really morally significant. The point remains true if "species" is substituted for "race." The logic of racism and the logic of the position we have been discussing, which I have elsewhere referred to as "speciesism," are indistinguishable; and if we reject the former then consistency demands that we reject the latter too.

It should be clearly understood that the rejection of speciesism does not imply that the different species are in fact equal in respect of such characteristics as intelligence, physical strength, ability to communicate, capacity to suffer, ability to damage the environment, or anything else. After all, the moral principle of human equality cannot be taken as implying that all humans are equal in these respects either—if it did, we would have to give up the idea of human equality. That one being is more intelligent than another does not entitle him to enslave, exploit, or disregard the interests of the less intelligent being. The moral basis of equality among humans is not equality in fact, but the principle of equal consideration of interests, and it is this principle that, in consistency, must be extended to any nonhumans who have interests.

III. NONHUMANS HAVE INTERESTS

There may be some doubt about whether any nonhuman beings have interests. This doubt may arise because of uncertainty about what it is to have an interest, or because of uncertainty about the nature of some nonhuman beings. So far as the concept of "interest" is the cause of doubt, I take the view that only a being with subjective experiences, such as the experience of pleasure or the experience of pain, can have interests in the full sense of the term; and that any being with such experiences does have at least one interest, namely, the interest in experiencing pleasure and avoiding pain. Thus consciousness, or the capacity for subjective experience, is both a necessary and a sufficient condition for having an interest. While there may be a loose sense of the term in which we can say that it is in the interests of a tree to be watered, this attenuated sense of the term is not the sense covered by the principle of equal consideration of interests. All we mean when we say that it is in the interests of a tree to be watered is that the tree needs water if it is to continue to live and grow normally; if we regard this as evidence that the tree has interests, we might almost as well say that it is in the interests of a car to be lubricated regularly because the car needs lubrication if it is to run properly. In neither case can we really mean (unless we impute consciousness to trees or cars) that the tree or car has any preference about the matter.

The remaining doubt about whether nonhuman beings have interests is, then, a doubt about whether nonhuman beings have subjective experiences like the experience of pain. I have argued elsewhere that the commonsense view that birds and mammals feel pain is well founded, but more serious doubts arise as we move down the evolutionary scale. Vertebrate animals have nervous systems broadly similar to our own and behave in ways that resemble our own pain behavior when subjected to stimuli that we would find painful; so the inference that vertebrates are capable of feeling pain is a reasonable one, though not as strong as it is if limited to mammals and birds. When we go beyond vertebrates to insects, crustaceans, mollusks and so on, the existence of subjective states becomes more dubious, and with very simple organisms it is difficult to believe that they could be conscious. As for plants, though there have been sensational claims that plants are not only conscious, but even psychic, there is no hard evidence that supports even the more modest claim. The boundary of beings who may be taken as having interests is therefore not an abrupt boundary, but a broad range in which the assumption that the being has interests shifts from being so strong as to be virtually certain to being so weak as to be highly improbable. The principle of equal consideration of interests must be applied with this in mind, so that where there is a clash between a virtually certain interest and a highly doubtful one, it is the virtually certain interest that ought to prevail.

In this manner our moral concern ought to extend to all beings who have interests . . . .

IV. EQUAL CONSIDERATION OF INTERESTS

Giving equal consideration to the interests of two different beings does not mean treating them alike or holding their lives to be of equal value. We may recognize that the interests of one being are greater than those of another, and equal consideration will then lead us to sacrifice the being with lesser interests, if one or the other must be sacrificed. For instance, if for some reason a choice has to be made between saving the life of a normal human being and that of a dog, we might well decide to save the human because he, with his greater awareness of what is going to happen, will suffer more before he dies; we may also take into account the likelihood that it is the family and friends of the human who will suffer more; and finally, it would be the human who had the greater potential for future happiness. This decision would be in accordance with the principle of equal consideration of interests, for the interests of the dog get the same consideration as those of the human, and the loss to the dog is not discounted because the dog is not a member of our species. The outcome is as it is because the balance of interests favors the human. In a different situation—say, if the human were grossly mentally defective and without family or anyone else who would grieve for it—the balance of interests might favor the nonhuman. The more positive side of the principle of equal consideration is this: where interests are equal, they must be given equal weight. So where human and nonhuman animals share an interest—as in the case of the interest in avoiding physical pain—we must give as much weight to violations of the interest of the nonhumans as we do to similar violations of the human's interest. This does not mean, of course, that it is as bad to hit a horse with a stick as it is to hit a human being, for the same blow would cause less pain to the animal with the tougher skin. The principle holds between similar amounts of felt pain, and what this is will vary from case to case.

It may be objected that we cannot tell exactly how much pain another animal is suffering, and that therefore the principle is impossible to apply. While I do not deny the difficulty and even, so far as precise measurement is concerned, the impossibility of comparing the subjective experiences of members of different species, I do not think that the problem is different in kind from the problem of comparing the subjective experiences of two members of our own species. Yet this is something we do all the time, for instance when we judge that a wealthy person will suffer less by being taxed at a higher rate than a poor person will gain from the welfare benefits paid for by the tax; or when we decide to take our two children to the beach instead of to a fair, because although the older one would prefer the fair, the younger one has a stronger preference the other way. These comparisons may be very rough, but since there is nothing better, we must use them; it would be irrational to refuse to do so simply because they are rough. Moreover, rough as they are, there are many situations in which we can be reasonably sure which way the balance of interests lies. While a difference of species may make comparisons rougher still, the basic problem is the same, and the comparisons are still often good enough to use, in the absence of anything more precise . . . .

V. EXAMPLES

We can now draw at least one conclusion as to how the existence of nonhuman living things should enter into our deliberations about actions affecting the environment: Where our actions are likely to make animals suffer, that suffering must count in our deliberations, and it should count equally with a like amount of suffering by human beings, insofar as rough comparisons can be made.

The difficulty of making the required comparison will mean that the application of this conclusion is controversial in many cases, but there will be some situations in which it is clear enough. Take, for instance, the wholesale poisoning of animals that is euphemistically known as "pest control." The authorities who conduct these campaigns give no consideration to the suffering they inflict on the "pests," and invariably use the method of slaughter they believe to be cheapest and most effective. The result is that hundreds of millions of rabbits have died agonizing deaths from the artificially introduced disease, myxomatosis, or from poisons like "ten-eighty"; coyotes and other wild dogs have died painfully from cyanide poisoning; and all manner of wild animals have endured days of thirst, hunger, and fear with a mangled limb caught in a leg-hold trap. Granting, for the sake of argument, the necessity for pest control—though this has rightly been questioned—the fact remains that no serious attempts have been made to introduce alternative means of control and thereby reduce the incalculable amount of suffering caused by present methods. It would not, presumably, be beyond modern science to produce a substance which, when eaten by rabbits or coyotes, produced sterility instead of a drawn-out death. Such methods might be more expensive, but can anyone doubt that if a similar amount of human suffering were at stake, the expense would be borne?

Another clear instance in which the principle of equal consideration of interests would indicate methods different from those presently used is in the timber industry. There are two basic methods of obtaining timber from forests. One is to cut only selected mature or dead trees, leaving the forest substantially intact. The other, known as clear-cutting, involves chopping down everything that grows in a given area, and then reseeding. Obviously when a large area is clear-cut, wild animals find their whole living area destroyed in a few days, whereas selected felling makes a relatively minor disturbance. But clear-cutting is cheaper, and timber companies therefore use this method and will continue to do so unless forced to do otherwise. . . .

VI. THE MEAT INDUSTRY

For the great majority of human beings, especially in urban, industrialized societies, the most direct form of contact with members of other species is at meal-times: We eat them. In doing so we treat them purely as means to our ends. We regard their life and well-being as subordinate to our taste for a particular kind of dish. I say "taste" deliberately—this is purely a matter of pleasing our palate. There can be no defenses of eating flesh in terms of satisfying nutritional needs, since it has been established beyond doubt that we could satisfy our need for protein and other essential nutrients far more efficiently with a diet that replaced animal flesh by soy beans, or products derived from soy beans, and other high-protein vegetable products.

It is not merely the act of killing that indicates what we are ready to do to other species in order to gratify our tastes. The suffering we inflict on the animals while they are alive is perhaps an even clearer indication of our speciesism than the fact that we are prepared to kill them. In order to have meat on the table at a price that people can afford, our society tolerates methods of meat production that confine sentient animals in cramped, unsuitable conditions for the entire durations of their lives. Animals are treated like machines that convert fodder into flesh, and any innovation that results in a higher "conversion ratio" is liable to be adopted. As one authority on the subject has said, "cruelty is acknowledged only when profitability ceases." So hens are crowded four or five to a cage with a floor area of twenty inches by eighteen inches, or around the size of a single page of the *New York Times*. The cages have wire floors, since this reduces cleaning costs, though wire is unsuitable for the hens' feet; the floors slope, since this makes the eggs roll down for easy collection, although this makes it difficult for the hens to rest comfortably. In these conditions all the birds' natural instincts are thwarted: They cannot stretch their wings fully, walk freely, dust-bathe, scratch the ground, or build a nest. Although they have never known other conditions, observers have noticed that the birds vainly try to perform these actions. Frustrated at their inability to do so, they often develop what farmers call "vices," and peck each other to death. To prevent this, the beaks of young birds are often cut off.

This kind of treatment is not limited to poultry. Pigs are now also being reared in cages inside sheds. These animals are comparable to dogs in intelligence, and need a varied, stimulating environment if they are not to suffer from stress and boredom. Anyone who kept a dog in the way in which pigs are frequently kept would be liable to prosecution, in England at least, but because our interest in exploiting pigs is greater than our interest in exploiting dogs, we object to cruelty to dogs while consuming the produce of cruelty to pigs. Of the other animals, the condition of veal calves is perhaps worst of all, since these animals are so closely confined that they cannot even turn around or get up and lie down freely. In this way they do not develop unpalatable muscle. They are also made anemic and kept short of roughage, to keep their flesh pale, since white veal fetches a higher price; as a result they develop a craving for iron and roughage, and have been observed to gnaw wood off the sides of their stalls, and lick greedily at any rusty hinge that is within reach.

Since, as I have said, none of these practices cater to anything more than our pleasures of taste, our practice of rearing and killing other animals in order to eat them is a clear instance of the sacrifice of the most important interests of other beings in order to satisfy trivial interests of our own. To avoid speciesism we must stop this practice, and each of us has a moral obligation to cease supporting the practice. Our custom is all the support that the meat industry needs. The decision to cease giving it that support may be difficult, but it is no more difficult than it would have been for a white Southerner to go against the traditions of his society and free his slaves; if we do not change our dietary habits, how can we censure those slaveholders who would not change their own way of living?

Notes

1. For a fuller statement of this argument, see my *Animal Liberation* (New York: A New York Review Book, 1975), especially Ch. 1.

2. Ibid.

3. See, for instance, the comments by Arthur Galston in *Natural History*, 83, no. 3 (March 1974): 18, on the "evidence" cited in such books as *The Secret Life of Plants*.

4. Singer, *Animal Liberation*, pp. 20–23.

5. See J. Olsen, *Slaughter the Animals, Poison the Earth* (New York: Simon and Schuster, 1971), especially pp. 153–164.

6. See R. and V. Routley, *The Fight for the Forests* (Canberra: Australian National University Press, 1974); for a thoroughly documented indictment of clear-cutting in America, see *Time*, May 17, 1976.

7. Although one might think that killing a being is obviously the ultimate wrong one can do to it, I think that the infliction of suffering is a clearer indication of speciesism because it might be argued that at least part of what is wrong with killing a human is that most humans are conscious of their existence over time, and have desires and purposes that extend into the future—see, for instance, M. Tooley, "Abortion and Infanticide," *Philosophy and Public Affairs*, vol. 2, no. 1 (1972). Of course, if one took this view one would have to hold—as Tooley does—that killing a human infant or mental defective is not in itself wrong, and is less serious than killing certain higher mammals that probably do have a sense of their own existence over time.

8. Ruth Harrison, *Animal Machines* (Stuart, London, 1964). This book provides an eye-opening account of intensive farming methods for those unfamiliar with the subject.

Review and Discussion Questions

1. Describe the human practices that most clearly demonstrate speciesism.
2. Do you agree that animals have interests that human beings must take into account? If so, which animals and what interests? What about plants?
3. What does the principle of "equal consideration of interests" imply for our treatment of animals? What does it not imply?
4. Give examples of how adherence to the principle of equal consideration would change our conduct. What are the principle's implications for business?
5. Singer rejects "our practice of rearing and killing other animals in order to eat them." Explain why. How might a critic respond to his argument? Can meat eating be morally justified?

THE VALUE OF WILDERNESS

WILLIAM GREY

William Grey (who wrote this paper under his former name Godfrey-Smith) raises the issue of what sort of justification might be given in defending the preservation of wilderness. He reminds us that the Western ethical tradition typically ascribes value or goodness to the nonhuman world only insofar as it of some use or benefit to humans; that is, it values nonhumans only as a means to human ends. Accordingly, people by and large are apt to accept and be persuaded by instrumental justifications for the preservation of wilderness. Indeed, Grey believes that there are weighty arguments—he outlines four of them—in defense of wilderness on instrumental grounds. However, he also believes that such instrumental justifications are ultimately unsatisfying as we (at least some of us) do feel somehow that natural systems do possess intrinsic value. The next step would be to extend the boundaries of the "moral community" to include nonhuman items, including wilderness areas. But that step is not yet in sight. Grey is greatly influenced by the views of the great American naturalist and conservationist Aldo Leopold (1887–1948). Leopold's A Sand County Almanac—*to which Grey refers frequently—is an excellent starting point for anyone interested in ecological issues.*

This paper explores various grounds on which wilderness can be *valued*, and draws attention to problems of resolving conflict generated by these diverse grounds. I conclude that Western attitudes to nature are partially determined by background metaphysical assumptions which derive in particular from the philosophy of Descartes. These metaphysical preconceptions lead to the misconception that various alternative views about the natural environment are mystical or occult. Thus, an alternative non-Cartesian mode of conception involving holistic or systemic modes of thought is required to develop satisfactory attitudes to the natural world.

> Wilderness is the raw material out of which man has hammered the artifact called civilization.

—Aldo Leopold, A *Sand County Almanac*

The framework which I examine is the framework of *Western* attitudes toward our natural environment, and wilderness in particular. The philosophical task which I address is an exploration of attitudes toward wilderness, especially the sorts of justification to which we might legitimately appeal for the preservation of wilderness: what grounds can we advance to support the claim that wilderness is something which we should *value*?

There are two different ways of appraising something as valuable. It may be that the thing in question is good or valuable *for the sake* of something which we hold to be

valuable. In this case the thing is not considered to be good in itself; value in this sense is ascribed in virtue of the thing's being a *means* to some valued end, and not as an *end in itself*. Such values are standardly designated *instrumental* values. Not everything which we hold to be good or valuable can be good for the sake of something else: our values must ultimately be *grounded* in something which is held to be good or valuable in itself. Such things are said to be *intrinsically* valuable. As a matter of historical fact, those things which have been held to be intrinsically valuable, within our Western traditions of thought, have nearly always been taken to be states or conditions of *persons*, e.g., happiness, pleasure, knowledge, or self-realization, to name but a few.

It follows from this that a very central assumption of Western moral thought is that value can be ascribed to the nonhuman world only insofar as it is good for the sake of the well-being of human beings.[1] Our entire attitude toward the natural environment, therefore, has a decidedly anthropocentric bias, and this fact is reflected in the sorts of justification which are standardly provided for the preservation of the natural environment.

A number of thinkers, however, have become increasingly persuaded that our anthropocentric morality is in fact inadequate to provide a satisfactory basis for a moral philosophy of ecological obligation. It is for this reason that we hear not infrequently the claim that we need a "new morality." A new moral framework—that is, a network of recognized obligations and duties—is not, however, something that can be casually conjured up in order to satisfy some vaguely felt need. The task of developing a sound biologically based moral philosophy, a philosophy which is not anthropocentrically based, and which provides a satisfactory justification for ecological obligation and concern, is, I think, one of the most urgent tasks confronting moral philosophers at the present. It will entail a radical reworking of accepted attitudes—attitudes which we currently accept as "self-evident"—and this is not something which can emerge suddenly. Indeed, I think the seminal work remains largely to be done, though I suggest below the broad outline which an environmentally sound moral philosophy is likely to take.

In the absence of a comprehensive and convincing ecologically based morality we naturally fall back on *instrumental* justifications for concern for our natural surroundings, and for preserving wilderness areas and animal species. We can, I think, detect at least four main lines of instrumental justification for the preservation of wilderness. By *wilderness* I understand any reasonably large tract of the Earth, together with its plant and animal communities, which is substantially unmodified by humans and in particular by human technology. The natural contrast to *wilderness* and *nature* is an *artificial* or *domesticated* environment. The fact that there are borderline cases which are difficult to classify does not, of course, vitiate this distinction.

The first attitude toward wilderness espoused by conservationists to which I wish to draw attention is what I shall call the "cathedral" view. This is the view that wilderness areas provide a vital opportunity for spiritual revival, moral regeneration, and aesthetic delight. The enjoyment

From *Environmental Ethics* 1 (1979): 309–319. Reprinted with permission of the author.

of wilderness is often compared in this respect with religious or mystical experience. Preservation of magnificent wilderness areas for those who subscribe to this view is essential for human well-being, and its destruction is conceived as something akin to an act of vandalism, perhaps comparable to—some may regard it as more serious than[2]—the destruction of a magnificent and moving human edifice, such as the Parthenon, the Taj Mahal, or the Palace of Versailles.

Insofar as the "cathedral" view holds that value derives solely from human satisfactions gained from its contemplation it is clearly an instrumentalist attitude. It does, however, frequently approach an *intrinsic value* attitude, insofar as the feeling arises that there is importance in the fact that it is there to be contemplated, whether or not anyone actually takes advantage of this fact. Suppose for example, that some wilderness was so precariously balanced that *any* human intervention or contact would inevitably bring about its destruction. Those who maintained that the area should, nevertheless, be preserved, unexperienced and unenjoyed, would certainly be ascribing to it an intrinsic value.

The "cathedral" view with respect to wilderness in fact is a fairly recent innovation in Western thought. The predominant Graeco-Christian attitude, which generally speaking was the predominant Western attitude prior to eighteenth and nineteenth century romanticism, had been to view wilderness as threatening or alarming, an attitude still reflected in the figurative uses of the expression *wilderness*, clearly connoting a degenerate state to be avoided. Christianity, in general, has enjoined "the transformation of wilderness, those dreaded haunts of demons, the ancient nature-gods, into farm and pasture,"[3] that is, to a domesticated environment.

The second instrumental justification of the value of wilderness is what we might call the "laboratory" argument. This is the argument that wilderness areas provide vital subject matter for scientific inquiry which provides us with an understanding of the intricate interdependencies of biological systems, their modes of change and development, their energy cycles, and the source of their stabilities. If we are to understand our own biological dependencies, we require natural systems as a norm, to inform us of the biological laws which we transgress at our peril.

The third instrumentalist justification is the "silo" argument which points out that one excellent reason for preserving reasonable areas of the natural environment intact is that we thereby preserve a stockpile of genetic diversity, which it is certainly prudent to maintain as a backup in case something should suddenly go wrong with the simplified biological systems which, in general, constitute agriculture. Further, there is the related point that there is no way of anticipating our future needs, or the undiscovered applications of apparently useless plants, which might turn out to be, for example, the source of some pharmacologically valuable drug—a cure, say, for leukemia. This might be called, perhaps, the "rare herb" argument, and it provides another persuasive instrumental justification for the preservation of wilderness.

The final instrumental justification which I think should be mentioned is the "gymnasium" argument which regards the preservation of wilderness as important for athletic or recreational activities.

An obvious problem which arises from these instrumental arguments is that the various activities which they seek to justify are not always possible to reconcile with one another. The interests of the wilderness lover who subscribes to the "cathedral" view are not always reconcilable with those of the ordinary vacationist. Still more obvious is the conflict between the recreational use of wilderness and the interests of the miner, the farmer, and the timber merchant.

The conflict of interest which we encounter here is one which it is natural to try and settle through the economic calculus of cost-benefit considerations. So long as the worth of natural systems is believed to depend entirely on instrumental values, it is natural to suppose that we can sort out the conflict of interests within an objective frame of reference, by estimating the human satisfactions to be gained from the preservation of wilderness, and by weighing these against the satisfactions which are to be gained from those activities which may lead to its substantial modification, domestication, and possibly even, destruction.

Many thinkers are liable to encounter here a feeling of resistance to the suggestion that we can apply purely economic considerations to settle such conflicts of interest. The assumption behind economic patterns of thought, which underlie policy formulation and planning, is that the values which we attach to natural systems and to productive activities are commensurable; and this is an assumption which may be called into question. It is not simply a question of the difficulty of quantifying what value should be attached to the preservation of the natural environment. The feeling is more that economic considerations are simply out of place. This feeling is one which is often too lightly dismissed by tough-minded economists as being obscurely mystical or superstitious; but it is a view worth examining. What it amounts to, I suggest, is the belief that there is something *morally* objectionable in the destruction of natural systems, or at least in their wholesale elimination, and this is precisely the belief that natural systems, or economically "useless" species do possess an *intrinsic* value. That is, it is an attempt to articulate the rejection of the anthropocentric view that all value, ultimately, resides in *human* interests and concerns. But it is a difficult matter to try and provide justification for such attitudes, and this is, for reasons which are deeply bound up with the problems of resolving basic value conflict, a problem which I have discussed elsewhere.[4]

The belief that all values are commensurable, so that there is no problem *in principle* in providing a satisfactory resolution of value conflict, involves the assumption that the quantitative social sciences, in particular economics, can provide an *objective* frame of reference within which all conflicts of interest can be satisfactorily resolved. We should, however, note that in the application of cost-benefit analyses there is an inevitable bias in the sorts of values that figure in the calculation, viz., a bias toward those considerations which are readily quantifiable, and toward those interests which will be staunchly defended. This is a fairly trivial point, but it is one which has substantial consequences, for there are at least three categories of values and interests which are liable to be inadequately considered, or discounted altogether.[5] First, there are the interests of those who are too widely distributed spatially, or too incrementally affected over time, to be strongly supported by any single advocate. Second, there are the interests of persons not yet existing, viz., future generations, who are clearly liable to be affected by present policy, but who are clearly not in a position to press any claims. Third, there are interests not associated with humans at all, such as the "rights" of wild animals.[6]

This last consideration, in particular, is apt to impress many as ludicrous, as quite simply "unthinkable." It is an unquestioned axiom of our present code of ethics that the class of individuals to which we have obligations is the class of humans. The whole apparatus of rights and duties is in fact based on an ideal of reciprocal contractual obligations, and in terms of this model the class of individuals to whom we may stand in moral relations—i.e., those with whom we recognize a network of rights, duties, and obligations—is the class of humans. A major aspect of a satisfactory ethic of ecological obligation and concern will be to challenge this central anthropocentric assumption. I return to this point below.

Even restricting our attention to the class of human preference havers, however, we should be wary of dismissing as simply inadmissible the interests of future generations. The claims of posterity tend to be excluded from our policy deliberations not, I suspect, because we believe that future generations will be unaffected by our policies, but because we lack any clear idea as to how to set about attaching weight to their interests. This is an instance of the familiar problem of "the dwarfing of soft variables." In settling conflicts of interest, any consideration which cannot be precisely quantified tends to be given little weight, or more likely, left out of the equation altogether: "If you can't measure it, it doesn't exist."[7] The result of ignoring soft variables is a spurious appearance of completeness and precision, but in eliminating all soft variables from our cost-benefit calculations, the conclusion is decidedly biased. If, as seems plausible, it is *in principle* impossible to do justice to soft variables such as the interests of posterity, it may be that we have to abandon the idea that the economic models employed in cost-benefit calculations are universally applicable for sorting out all conflicts of interest. It may be necessary to abandon the economic calculus as the universal model for rational deliberation.[8]

Another category of soft variable which tends to be discounted from policy deliberations is that which concerns economically unimportant species of animals or plants. A familiar subterfuge which we frequently encounter is the attempt to invest such species with spurious economic value, as illustrated in the rare herb argument. A typical example of this, cited by Leopold, is the reaction of ornithologists to the threatened disappearance of certain species of songbirds: they at once came forward with some distinctly shaky evidence that they played an essential role in the control of insects.[9] The dominance of economic modes of thinking is again obvious: the evidence has to be economic in order to be acceptable. This exemplifies the way in which we turn to instrumentalist justifications for the maintenance of biotic diversity.

The alternative to such instrumentalist justifications, the alternative which Leopold advocated with great insight and eloquence, is to widen the boundary of the moral community to include animals, plants, the soil, or collectively *the land*.[10] This involves a radical shift in our conception of nature, so that land is recognized not simply as property, to be dealt with or disposed of as a matter of expediency: land in Leopold's view is not a commodity which belongs to us, but a community to which we belong. This change in conception is far-reaching and profound. It involves a shift in our metaphysical conception of nature—that is, a change in what sort of thing we take our natural surroundings to *be*. This is a point which I would like to elaborate, albeit sketchily.

The predominant Western conception of nature is exemplified in—and to no small extent is a consequence of—the philosophy of Descartes, in which nature is viewed as something separate and apart, to be transformed and controlled at will. Descartes divided the world into conscious thinking substances—minds—and extended, mechanically arranged substances—the rest of nature. It is true that we find in Western thought alternatives to the Cartesian metaphysical conception of nature—the views of Spinoza and Hegel might be mentioned in particular[11]—but the predominant spirit, especially among scientists, has been Cartesian. These metaphysical views have become deeply embedded in Western thought, which has induced us to view the world through Cartesian spectacles. One of the triumphs of Descartes' mechanistic view of nature has been the elimination of occult qualities and forces from the explanation of natural events. The natural world is to be understood, in the Cartesian model, in purely mechanistic terms. An unfortunate consequence of the triumph, nevertheless, has been a persistent fear among some thinkers that the rejection of Cartesian metaphysics may lead to the reinstatement of occult and mystical views of nature.

An important result of Descartes' sharp ontological division of the world into active mental substances and inert material substances, has been the alienation of man from the natural world. Although protests have been raised against Cartesian metaphysics ever since its inception, it has exercised a deep influence on our attitudes toward nature. Descartes' mechanistic conception of nature naturally leads to the view that it is possible in principle to obtain complete mastery and technical control over the natural world. It is significant to recall that for Descartes the paradigm instance of a natural object was a lump of wax, the perfect exemplification of malleability. This conception of natural objects as wholly pliable and passive is clearly one which leaves no room for anything like a network of obligations.

A natural corollary of the mechanistic conception of nature, and integral to the Cartesian method of inquiry, is the role played by reductive thinking. In order to understand a complex system one should, on this view, break it into its component parts and examine them. The Cartesian method of inquiry is a natural correlate of Cartesian metaphysics, and is a *leitmotif* of our science-based technology.

It should be stressed that a rejection of the Cartesian attitude and its method of inquiry need *not* involve a regression to occult and mystical views about the "sacredness" of the natural world, and the abandoning of systematic rational inquiry. It must be conceded, however, that the rejection of the view that nature is an exploitable commodity has, unfortunately, frequently taken this form. This sort of romantic nature mysticism *does* provide a powerful exhortation for exercising restraint in our behavior to the natural world, but it carries with it a very clear danger. This is that while prohibiting destructive acts toward the natural world, it equally prohibits constructive acts: we surely cannot rationally adopt a complete "hands off" policy with respect to nature, on the basis of what looks like the extremely implausible—and highly cynical—*a priori* assumption that *any* attempt to modify our surroundings is bound to be for the worse.

It may, however, be that advocates of the "sacredness" of nature are attempting to do no more than articulate the idea that natural systems have their own intrinsic value, and adopt this manner of speaking as a convenient way of rejecting the dominant anthropocentric morality. If *this* is all that is being claimed, then I have no quarrel with it. And it may be inevitable that this mode of expression is adopted in the absence of a developed ecologically sound alternative morality. But I think we should be wary of this style of justification; what is needed, as Passmore has nicely expressed it, is not the spiritualizing of nature, but the naturalizing of man.[12] This involves a shift from the piecemeal reductive conception of natural items to a *holistic* or systemic view in which we come to appreciate the symbiotic interdependencies of the natural world. On the holistic or total-field view, organisms—including man—are conceived as nodes in a biotic web of intrinsically related parts.[13] That is, our understanding of biological organisms require more than just an understanding of their structure and properties; we also have to attend seriously to their interrelations. Holistic or systemic thinking does not deny that organisms are complex physicochemical systems, but it affirms that the methods employed in establishing the high-level functional relationships expressed by physical laws are often of very limited importance in understanding the nature of biological systems. We may now be facing, in the terminology of Thomas Kuhn,[14] a shift from a physical to a biological paradigm in our understanding of nature. This seems to me to be an important aspect of the rejection of Cartesian metaphysics.

The limitations of the physical paradigm have long been accepted in the study of human society, but the tendency has been to treat social behavior and human action as quite distinct from the operations of our natural surrounding. The inappropriateness of the physical paradigm for understanding *human* society seems to me to be quite correct; what is comparatively new is the post-Cartesian realization that the physical paradigm is of more limited application for our understanding of *nature* than was previously supposed.

The holistic conception of the natural world contains, in my view, the possibility of extending the idea of community beyond human society. And in this way biological wisdom does, I think, carry implications for ethics. Just as Copernicus showed us that man does not occupy the physical center of the universe, Darwin and his successors have shown us that man occupies no *biologically* privileged position. We still have to assimilate the implications which this biological knowledge has for morality.

Can we regard man and the natural environment as constituting a community in any morally significant sense? Passmore, in particular, has claimed that this extended sense of community is entirely spurious.[15] Leopold, on the other hand, found the biological extension of community entirely natural.[16] If we regard a community as a collection of individuals who engage in cooperative behavior, Leopold's extension seems to me entirely legitimate. An ethic is no more than a code of conduct designed to ensure cooperative behavior among the members of a community. Such cooperative behavior is required to underpin the health of the community, in this biologically extended sense, *health* being understood as the biological capacity for self-renewal,[17] and *ill-health* as the degeneration or loss of this capacity.

Man, of course, cannot be placed on "all fours" with his biologically fellow creatures in all respects. In particular, man is the only creature who can act as a full-fledged moral agent, i.e., an individual capable of exercising reflective rational choice on the basis of principles. What distinguishes man from his fellow creatures is not the capacity to *act*, but the fact that his actions are, to a great extent, free from programming. This capacity to modify our own behavior is closely bound up with the capacity to acquire knowledge of the natural world, a capacity which has enabled us, to an unprecedented extent, to manipulate the environment, and—especially in the recent past—to alter it rapidly, violently, and globally. Our hope must be that the capacity for knowledge, which has made ecologically hazardous activities possible, will lead to a more profound understanding of the delicate biological interdependencies which some of these actions now threaten, and thereby generate the wisdom for restraint.

To those who are skeptical of the possibility of extending moral principles, in the manner of Leopold, to include items treated heretofore as matters of expediency, it can be pointed out that extensions have, to a limited extent, already taken place. One clear—if partial—instance, is in the treatment of animals. It is now generally accepted, and this is a comparatively recent innovation,[18] that we have at least a *prima facie* obligation not to treat animals cruelly or sadistically. And this certainly constitutes a shift in moral attitudes. If—as seems to be the case—cruelty to animals is accepted as intrinsically wrong, then there *is* at least one instance in which it is *not* a matter of moral indifference how we behave toward the nonhuman world.

More familiar perhaps are the moral revolutions which have occurred within the specific domain of human society—witness the progressive elimination of the "right" to racial, class, and sex exploitation. Each of these shifts involves the acceptance, on the part of some individuals, of new obligations, rights, and values which, to a previous generation, would have been considered unthinkable.[19] The essential step in recognizing an enlarged community involves coming to see, feel, and understand what was previously perceived as alien and apart: it is the evolution of the capacity of *empathy*.

I have digressed a little into the history of ideas, stressing in particular the importance of the influence of Descartes.[20] My justification for this excursion is that our present attitudes toward nature, and toward wilderness, are very largely the result of Descartes' metaphysical conception of what nature is, and the concomitant conception which man has of himself. Our metaphysical assumptions are frequently extremely influential invisible persuaders: they determine the boundaries of what is thinkable. In rejecting the Cartesian conception the following related shifts in attitudes can, I think, be discerned.

(1) A change from reductive convergent patterns of thought to divergent holistic patterns.

(2) A shift from man's conception of himself as the center of the biological world, to one in which he is conceived of as a component in a network of biological relations, a shift comparable to the Copernican discovery that man does not occupy the physical center of the universe.

(3) An appreciation of the fact that in modifying biological systems we do not simply modify the properties of a substance, but alter a network of relations. This rejection of the Cartesian conception of nature as a collection of independent physical parts is summed up in the popular ecological maxim "it is impossible to do only one thing."

(4) A recognition that the processes of nature are independent and indifferent to human interests and concerns.

(5) A recognition that biological systems are items which possess intrinsic value, in Kant's terminology, that they are "ends in themselves."

We can, however, provide—and it is important that we can provide—an answer to the question: "What is the *use* of wilderness?" We certainly ought to preserve and protect wilderness areas as gymnasiums, as laboratories, as stockpiles of genetic diversity, and as cathedrals. Each of these reasons provides a powerful and sufficient instrumental justification for their preservation. But note how the very posing of this question about the *utility* of wilderness reflects an anthropocentric system of values. From a genuinely ecocentric point of view the question "What is the *use* of happiness?"

The philosophical task is to try to provide adequate justification, or at least clear the way for a scheme of values according to which concern and sympathy for our environment is immediate and natural, and the desirability of protecting and preserving wilderness self-evident. When once controversial propositions become platitudes, the philosophical task will have been successful.

I will conclude, nevertheless, on a deflationary note. It seems to me (at least much of the time) that the shift in attitudes which I think is required for promoting genuinely harmonious relations with nature is too drastic, too "unthinkable," to be very persuasive for most people. If this is so, then it will be more expedient to justify the preservation of wilderness in terms of instrumentalist considerations; and I have argued that there *are* powerful arguments for preservation which can be derived from the purely anthropocentric considerations of human self-interest. I hope, however, that there will be some who feel that such anthropocentric considerations are not wholly satisfying, i.e., that they do not really do justice to our intuitions. But at a time when *human* rights are being treated in some quarters with a great deal of skepticism it is perhaps unrealistic to expect the rights of nonhumans to receive sympathetic attention. Perhaps, though, we should not be too abashed by this: extensions in ethics have seldom followed the path of political expediency.

Notes

1. Other cultures have certainly included the idea that nature should be valued for its own sake in their moral codes: see J. Baird Callicott and R. Ames, eds. *Nature in Asian Traditions of Thought: Essays in Environmental Philosophy* (Albany, NY: SUNY Press, 1989), Joseph Needham, "History and Human Values," in H. and S. Rose, eds. *The Radicalisation of Science* (London: Macmillan, 1976), pp. 90-117), and W.E.H. Stanner, *Aboriginal Man in Australia* (Sydney: Angus and Robertson, 1965), pp. 207–237.

2. We can after all *replace* human artefacts such as buildings with something closely similar, but the destruction of a wilderness or a biological species is irreversible.

3. John Passmore, *Man's Responsibility for Nature* (London: Duckworth, 1974; New York: Charles Scribner's Sons, 1974), p. 17; cf. chap. 5.

4. In "The Rights of Non-humans and Intrinsic Values," in J. Baird Callicott and Clare Palmer, eds. *Environmental Philosophy: Critical Concepts in the Environment* (London: Routledge, 2004), Vol. 1, pp. 311–326.

5. Cf. Laurence H. Tribe, "Policy Science: Analysis or Ideology?" *Philosophy and Public Affairs* 2 (1972–3): 66–110.

6. I should mention that I am a skeptic about "rights": it seems to me that talk about rights is always eliminable in favor of talk about legitimate claims for considerations, and obligations to respect those claims. Rights-talk does, however, have useful rhetorical effect in exhorting people to recognize claims. The reason for this is that claims pressed in these terms perform the crucial trick of shifting the onus of proof. This is accomplished by the fact that a *denial* of a right appears to be a more positive and deliberate act than merely refusing to acknowledge an obligation.

7. Laurence H. Tribe, "Trial by Mathematics: Precision and Ritual in Legal Process," *Harvard Law Review* 84 (1971): 1361.

8. Of course, in practice cost–benefit considerations *do* operate within deontic constraints, and we do *not* accept economics unrestrictedly as providing the model for rational deliberation. We would not accept exploitative child labor, for example, as a legitimate mode of production, no matter how favorable the economics. This is not just because we attach too high a cost to this form of labor: it is just unthinkable.

9. Aldo Leopold, "The Land Ethic" in *Sand County Almanac*, p. 210.

10. Cf. Aldo Leopold, "The Conservation Ethic," *Journal of Forestry* 31 (1933): 634–43, and "The Land Ethic," *Sand County Almanac*.

11. Cf. John Passmore, "Attitudes to Nature," in R. S. Peters, ed. *Nature and Conduct* (London: Macmillan, 1975), pp. 251–64.

12. *Ibid.*, p. 260.

13. Cf. Arne Naess, "The Shallow and the Deep, Long-Range Ecology Movement," *Inquiry* 16 (1973): 95–100.

14. T. S. Kuhn, *The Structure of Scientific Revolutions* (Chicago: University of Chicago Press, 1962).

15. Passmore, *Man's Responsibility for Nature*, chap. 6; "Attitudes to Nature," p. 262.

16. Leopold, "The Land Ethic."

17. *Ibid.*, p. 221.

18. Cf. Passmore, "The Treatment of Animals," *Journal of the History of Ideas* 36 (1975): 195–218.

19. Cf. Christopher D. Stone, "Should Trees Have Standing? Toward Legal Rights for Natural Objects," *Southern California Law Review* 45 (1972): 450–501.

20. Here I differ from the well-known claim of Lynn White that the Judeo-Christian tradition is predominantly responsible for the development of Western attitudes toward nature. See Lynn White, "The Historical Roots of Our Ecological Crisis," *Science* 155 (1967): 1203–7.

Review and Discussion Questions

1. Grey outlines four different arguments or positions that defend the preservation of wilderness on instrumental grounds. But he also believes that, in their defence of wilderness areas, these arguments appeal to human activities that "are not always possible to reconcile with one another." (a) Explain the four instrumental arguments alluded to by Grey. Are there any other instrumental arguments you can think of? (b) Does it really matter whether the various human activities, for the sake of which we wish to preserve wilderness areas, might not be reconciled with one another? Explain your answer.

2. Does wilderness, in your own view, have only instrumental value? Whatever your answer, elaborate and defend.

3. Grey ends his article on what he calls a "deflationary note." Do you think that nowadays, nearly thirty years after Grey wrote it, we are any nearer to including nonhumans, especially natural systems (for example, wilderness areas), into the moral community? Explain your answer with documented evidence.

Further Reading for Chapter 11

Robin Attfield, *Environmental Ethics* (Malden, MA: Blackwell, 2003), **Joseph R. DesJardins**, *Environmental Ethics*, 3rd ed. (Belmont, CA: Wadsworth, 2001), and **Holmes Rolston III**, *Philosophy Gone Wild: Environmental Ethics* (Buffalo, NY: Prometheus, 1990) are good introductions to environmental ethics.

W. Michael Hoffman, "Business and Environmental Ethics," *Business Ethics Quarterly* 1 (1991).

Dale Jamieson, ed., *A Companion to Environmental Ethics* (Malden, MA: Blackwell, 2001) and **Andrew Light** and **Holmes Rolston III**, eds., *Environmental Ethics: An Anthology* (Oxford: Blackwell, 2003) are valuable, although philosophically advanced, reference works.

Ronald Jeurissen and **Gerard Keijers**, "Future Generations and Business Ethics," *Business Ethics Quarterly* 14 (January 2004) takes a close look at this often neglected issue.

Lisa H. Newton, Catherine K. Dillingham, and **Joanne Cody**, *Watersheds: Classic Cases in Environmental Ethics*, 4th ed. (Belmont, CA: Wadsworth, 2006) offers ten detailed and insightful environmental case studies.

Joel Reichart and **Patricia H. Werhane**, eds., *Environmental Challenges to Business* (Bowling Green, OH: Philosophy Documentation Center, 2000) collects new essays on business and the environment by prominent business ethicists.

Mark Sagoff, *The Economy of Earth* (New York: Cambridge University Press, 1990) is an informed discussion of environmental policy.

Peter Singer, *Animal Liberation*, 2nd ed. (New York: Random House, 1990) is a seminal work advocating a radical change in our treatment of animals. **Gary L. Francione**, *Introduction to Animal Rights: Your Child or the Dog?* (Philadelphia: Temple University Press, 2000) offers a provocative but very readable critique of our treatment of animals.

James Sterba, ed., *Earth Ethics: Introductory Readings in Animal Rights and Environmental Ethics*, 2nd ed. (Upper Saddle River, NJ: Prentice Hall, 2000) is an excellent, wide-ranging collection of essays, representing different environmental and philosophical approaches.

Timothy S. Yoder, "Corporate Responsibility and the Environment," *Business and Society Review* 106 (Fall 2001) takes up the topic of corporate responsibility for environmental malfeasance.

Index